International Directory of

COMPANY HISTORIES

International Directory of

COMPANY HISTORIES

VOLUME 22

Editor

Jay P. Pederson

ST. JAMES PRESS

AN IMPRINT OF GALE

DETROIT • NEW YORK • LONDON

STAFF

Jay P. Pederson, *Editor*

Miranda H. Ferrara, *Project Manager*

Joann Cerrito, David J. Collins, Nicolet V. Elert, Kristin Hart,
Margaret Mazurkiewicz, Michael J. Tyrkus, *Contributing Editors*

Peter M. Gareffa, *Managing Editor, St. James Press*

Library of Congress Catalog Number: 89-190943

British Library Cataloguing in Publication Data

International directory of company histories. Vol. 22
I. Jay P. Pederson
338.7409

ISBN 1-55862-363-9

Printed in the United States of America

St. James Press is an imprint of Gale

Cover photograph: Montreal Stock Exchange Building
(courtesy Montreal Stock Exchange)

10 9 8 7 6 5 4 3 2 1

CONTENTS

Company Histories

PREFACE

The St. James Press series *The International Directory of Company Histories (IDCH)* is intended for reference use by students, business people, librarians, historians, economists, investors, job candidates, and others who seek to learn more about the historical development of the world's most important companies. To date, *IDCH* has covered over 3,200 companies in 22 volumes.

Inclusion Criteria

Most companies chosen for inclusion in *IDCH* have achieved a minimum of US$100 million in annual sales and are leading influences in their industries or geographical locations. Companies may be publicly held, private, or non-profit. State-owned companies that are important in their industries and that may operate much like public or private companies also are included. Wholly owned subsidiaries and divisions are profiled if they meet the requirements for inclusion. Entries on companies that have had major changes since they were last profiled may be selected for updating.

The *IDCH* series highlights 10% private and non-profit companies, and features updated entries on approximately 35 companies per volume.

Entry Format

Each entry begins with the company's legal name, the address of its headquarters, its telephone and fax numbers, and its web site. A statement of public, private, state, or parent ownership follows. A company with a legal name in both English and the language of its headquarters country is listed by the English name, with the native-language name in parentheses.

The company's founding or earliest incorporation date, the number of employees, and the most recent sales figures available follow. Sales figures are given in local currencies with equivalents in U.S. dollars. For some private companies, sales figures are estimates. The entry lists the exchanges on which a company's stock is traded, as well as the company's principal Standard Industrial Classification codes.

Entries generally contain a *Company Perspectives* box which provides a short summary of the company's mission, goals, and ideals, a list of *Principal Subsidiaries*, *Principal Divisions*, *Principal Operating Units*, and articles for *Further Reading*.

American spelling is used throughout *IDCH*, and the word "billion" is used in its U.S. sense of one thousand million.

Sources

Entries have been compiled from publicly accessible sources both in print and on the Internet such as general and academic periodicals, books, annual reports, and material supplied by the companies themselves.

Cumulative Indexes

IDCH contains two indexes: the **Index to Companies**, which provides an alphabetical index to companies discussed in the text as well as companies profiled, and the **Index to Industries**, which allows researchers to locate companies by their principal industry. Both indexes are cumulative and specific instructions for using them are found immediately preceding each index.

Suggestions Welcome

Comments and suggestions from users of *IDCH* on any aspect of the product as well as suggestions for companies to be included or updated are cordially invited. Please write:

The Editor
International Directory of Company Histories
St. James Press
835 Penobscot Building
Detroit, Michigan 48226-4094

ABBREVIATIONS FOR FORMS OF COMPANY INCORPORATION

A.B.	Aktiebolaget (Sweden)
A.G.	Aktiengesellschaft (Germany, Switzerland)
A.S.	Atieselskab (Denmark)
A.S.	Aksjeselskap (Denmark, Norway)
A.Ş.	Anomin Şirket (Turkey)
B.V.	Besloten Vennootschap met beperkte, Aansprakelijkheid (The Netherlands)
Co.	Company (United Kingdom, United States)
Corp.	Corporation (United States)
G.I.E.	Groupement d'Intérêt Economique (France)
GmbH	Gesellschaft mit beschränkter Haftung (Germany)
H.B.	Handelsbolaget (Sweden)
Inc.	Incorporated (United States)
KGaA	Kommanditgesellschaft auf Aktien (Germany)
K.K.	Kabushiki Kaisha (Japan)
LLC	Limited Liability Company (Middle East)
Ltd.	Limited (Canada, Japan, United Kingdom, United States)
N.V.	Naamloze Vennootschap (The Netherlands)
OY	Osakeyhtiöt (Finland)
PLC	Public Limited Company (United Kingdom)
PTY.	Proprietary (Australia, Hong Kong, South Africa)
S.A.	Société Anonyme (Belgium, France, Switzerland)
SpA	Società per Azioni (Italy)

ABBREVIATIONS FOR CURRENCY

DA	Algerian dinar
A$	Australian dollar
Sch	Austrian schilling
BFr	Belgian franc
Cr	Brazilian cruzado
C$	Canadian dollar
RMB	Chinese renminbi
DKr	Danish krone
E£	Egyptian pound
Fmk	Finnish markka
FFr	French franc
DM	German mark
HK$	Hong Kong dollar
Rs	Indian rupee
Rp	Indonesian rupiah
IR£	Irish pound
L	Italian lira
¥	Japanese yen
W	Korean won
KD	Kuwaiti dinar
LuxFr	Luxembourgian franc
M$	Malaysian ringgit
Dfl	Netherlands florin
NZ$	New Zealand dollar
N	Nigerian naira
NKr	Norwegian krone
RO	Omani rial
P	Philippine peso
Esc	Portuguese escudo
SRls	Saudi Arabian riyal
S$	Singapore dollar
R	South African rand
W	South Korean won
Pta	Spanish peseta
SKr	Swedish krona
SFr	Swiss franc
NT$	Taiwanese dollar
B	Thai baht
£	United Kingdom pound
$	United States dollar
B	Venezuelan bolivar
K	Zambian kwacha

International Directory of

COMPANY HISTORIES

AAON, Inc.

AAON, Inc.

2425 South Yukon Avenue
Tulsa, Oklahoma 74107
U.S.A.
(918) 583-2266
Fax: (918) 583-6094
Web site: http://www.aaon.com

Public Company
Incorporated: 1987 as Diamond Head Resources, Inc.
Employees: 556
Sales: $62.8 million (1996)
Stock Exchanges: NASDAQ
SICs: 3585 Refrigeration & Heating Equipment

AAON, Inc. designs, manufactures, sells, and services heating and air conditioning equipment for commercial rooftop use. It targets a niche market for those who want a semicustomized unit that costs less than a totally customized unit but meets the needs of each individual customer. Typically, AAON's units cost about five to ten percent more than standard mass produced units, but they offer lower cost of operation and maintenance. Its CP/AAON subsidiary manufactures a variety of heating/cooling coils used in the heating, ventilation, and air conditioning (HVAC) industry and provides coils to AAON as well as to other manufacturers. AAON's customers include national chains such as Target, Wal-Mart, Kmart, and Home Depot, and various school districts, shopping malls, and other local institutions and facilities. Buildings serviced by AAON's rooftop equipment usually have ten or fewer stories. AAON has about eight percent of the rooftop market and two percent of the coil market.

Origins and Founders

AAON's roots can be traced to 1928 when the John Zink Company (JZC) was started in Tulsa, Oklahoma to produce equipment for the oil industry. John Zink decided to diversify his firm's operations by making, installing, and servicing heating and, especially, air conditioning equipment for the mansions of Tulsa's wealthy oil men. Then in 1968 JZC's HVAC division began producing rooftop heating and air conditioning equipment for commercial customers. In 1970 McDonald's Restaurants became the first main customer for the rooftop units. Wal-Mart followed in 1971.

After founder John Zink died, his son negotiated the acquisition of JZC in 1972 by the Sunbeam Corporation. In 1981 the Sunbeam Corporation in turn was purchased by Allegheny International, Inc. Then in June 1987 Lone Star Technologies, Inc. purchased JZC, but its leaders decided to get out of the HVAC industry, for that division was doing only about $16 million in annual sales, while the rest of JZC was running about $100 million in annual sales. With Wal-Mart and McDonald's its only customers, HVAC was just a sidelight for JZC.

Corporate Changes During the 1980s

Two months later, on August 18, 1987, a shell company called Diamond Head Resources, Inc. was incorporated in Nevada by its founders, Jack M. Gertino of Salt Lake City, Wayne M. Rogers, Tod W. Anderson, and Jonathan A. Lewis. These individuals and other investors raised money through Diamond Head stock offerings during 1987 and early 1988. This money was raised for a potential business opportunity to be selected later; thus it was described as a blind pool or blank check offering.

In August 1988 AAON, Inc. was incorporated in Oklahoma for the purpose of acquiring the heating and air conditioning division of the John Zink Company, which took place the following month. AAON paid $9,219,000 for that acquisition, including $7,035,000 cash and the assumption of liabilities worth $2,184,000. Tulsa residents were willing to invest in the new company in part because the oil industry in Oklahoma was hurting. The rest of the John Zink Company was purchased by Koch Industries.

The corporate name AAON had no particular meaning; it was chosen so the company would be listed at the beginning of phone directories. It was pronounced ''aye-on.''

In June 1989 Diamond Head Resources acquired AAON, Inc. of Oklahoma, which became a wholly owned subsidiary. This deal was described as a ''reverse acquisition,'' as if AAON had acquired Diamond Head. The ownership of Diamond Head's stockholders was reduced in this transaction to 20 percent, and AAON's stockholders became the owners of 80 percent of Diamond Head, which changed its name to AAON, Inc., a Nevada corporation. AAON became a publicly traded company at this time.

AAON's first officers and directors included the following men, who retained their corporate positions in 1997. Norman H. Asbjornson, a professional engineer educated at Montana State University and the University of Nebraska, was the firm's president, treasurer, and director. He had worked for American Standard's Commercial Air-Conditioning Division from 1960 to 1972, Singer Corporation's Climate Control Division from 1972 to 1977, Nortek (a heating/air conditioner maker) from 1977 to 1987, and then the John Zink Company's HVAC Division until it was acquired by AAON. He was the key person who alerted others that the HVAC division was up for sale.

Another JZC manager who moved to AAON was Robert G. Fergus. A professional engineer who worked for JZC from 1980 to 1988, he joined AAON as its vice-president when it was first organized.

A third key person was William A. Bowen, who had worked for a North Carolina bank from 1955 to 1979, and then became the president, CEO, and board chairman of Tulsa's First National Bank and Trust Company. While serving as the president of the Tulsa Economic Development Foundation in 1987 and 1988, Bowen was instrumental in organizing investors to start AAON. He became the new firm's vice-president of finance and a director.

AAON's other founders included Secretary/Director John B. Johnson, Jr., a Tulsa attorney since 1961; Director Richard E. Minshall, president of Tulsa's Capital Advisors, Inc. since 1978; and Anthony Pantaleoni, a partner in the law firm of Fulbright Jaworski & Reavis McGrath in New York City.

AAON bought its Tulsa manufacturing plant and offices in late 1988 for $650,000. After extensive changes costing almost $1.9 million, the company began using the refurbished facilities in early 1989. The heavy industrial manufacturing and warehouse spaces totaled 172,000 square feet, and the offices were situated in an additional 12,000 square feet. The plant, located on 12 acres at 2425 South Yukon, featured two main assembly lines. From February to August 1989 the company built a new paint booth facility.

The firm in the late 1980s made two main lines of products. In late 1988 it began manufacturing its RE Series of air conditioners. The new machines were available in 19 different cooling sizes, ranging from two to 63 tons. A ton in the air conditioning industry was defined as the ability to reduce the temperature of one ton of water by 1°F in one hour.

AAON began building in late 1989 its RF Series with six cooling capacities, ranging from 60 to 140 tons. It was approved by the Electrical Testing Laboratories of Cortland, New York, a step that was not required by law but helped to increase product credibility and sales.

In its early years AAON manufactured rooftop units for two main customers, both retained from the John Zink Company era. In 1989 sales to Wal-Mart were $16 million, up from $5 million in both 1987 and 1988. McDonald's bought $12 million worth of products in 1989 as well as in 1988. About 89 percent of AAON's 1989 annual sales of $31.3 million were made to McDonald's and Wal-Mart.

In its first year of operations, AAON faced a major challenge. The firm that supplied its coils failed, leaving many machines half finished at the Tulsa plant. AAON was able to survive with the help of the Bank of Oklahoma, which increased its loan to the struggling new company from $5 million to $9 million. Because the Bank of Oklahoma believed in AAON during this crisis, AAON remained a loyal customer of the bank.

Developments in the 1990s

In 1991 AAON lost one of its main customers. McDonald's canceled orders for any new rooftop units but continued to buy replacement parts. The loss of such a major customer reduced sales by about $10 million per year.

In December 1991 AAON, Inc. of Nevada created a new subsidiary called CP/AAON, a Texas corporation, to acquire most of the assets of Coils Plus, Inc. of Longview, Texas. Coils Plus had been founded in 1984 to design and make new and replacement coils for the HVAC industry. AAON acquired this Texas company to make coils instead of upgrading its Tulsa plant because of inadequate sewage services in Tulsa.

Some of the company's directors, officers, and employees received the opportunity on March 11, 1992 to take advantage of AAON's new stock option plan. By March 5, 1997 AAON had granted options to 29 individuals, including eight officers or directors and 21 employees.

AAON expanded significantly in 1993. First, in January, its subsidiary CP/AAON purchased a 110,000-square-foot facility near its former plant in Longview, Texas, and moved into the newly renovated plant a couple months later. AAON was producing four types of rooftop units in 1993. Production of models in its RE Series continued, but they were replaced gradually by the more efficient models of the RH Series. The RF Series was still manufactured. Fourth, the company was starting to make the RG Series, a heat pump version of the RH Series.

In 1993 AAON's American customers included Wal-Mart, Kmart, Target, Mervyn's, Shopko, Discovery Zone, Meijer, Home Depot, Boston Chicken, Braum's, QuikTrip, Mazzio's, and Leaps and Bounds. The company also initiated overseas sales in 1993. It began delivering equipment to Cifra, Mexico's largest retailer. AAON also began shipping specially designed cooling units to the Middle East in 1993. These units were designed so that several could fit in one freight container, thus reducing shipping costs, a major expense for customers in the Middle East.

Other 1993 developments included 1) starting a cross-training program to increase worker flexibility, 2) spending about $1 million for replacement coils for units under warranty, and 3) completing a one-for-four reverse stock split, which retired almost $2 million of the firm's subordinated debt.

AAON had been listed on the NASDAQ Small Cap with the symbol AAON in December 1990. The company announced in November 1993 that its common stock would be traded on the NASDAQ National Market under the symbol AAON. NASDAQ's system of several competing dealers or market makers for the same stocks helped AAON stock become more visible and liquid. Fourteen market makers, including Salt Lake City's Alpine Securities Corporation, dealt with AAON stock when it first was sold on the NASDAQ National Market.

The First Analysis Securities Corporation (FASC) of Chicago in February 1994 gave AAON's stock a "strong buy" rating for several reasons. First, AAON had a large backlog of orders at the end of 1993 and had recently added a third assembly line. FASC also pointed out: "No other HVAC manufacturer is using AAON's semicustom approach . . . the energy efficiency of AAON's complete product line is the highest in the industry, according to data certified by the American Refrigeration Institute . . . the company has enjoyed a reputation among its customers for manufacturing a quality product and providing attentive customer service."

In January 1995 AAON introduced a new product, a desiccant heat recovery wheel called AAONAIRE. Designed for the company's RH, RF, and RG units, this technology increased the capacity of AAON's rooftop units by as much as 50 percent without any additional energy costs. The AAONAIRE patent was pending in 1997. AAONAIRE was created to meet the requirements of the 1990 U.S. Clean Air Act for better air quality in commercial buildings. That legislation resulted from so-called "sick-building syndrome," characterized by a cluster of symptoms such as headaches, colds, and eye and respiratory tract problems first reported in the 1970s.

In March 1995 CP/AAON expanded with the purchase of property and a 26,000-square-foot building next to its plant in Texas. The Tulsa plant also was enlarged to 332,000 square feet in 1995.

The firm's 1995 financial performance slipped from 1994. Revenues declined 16 percent from 1994 to $67.3 million, while net earnings decreased 61 percent to $2.1 million. In its 1995 Annual Report the company cited three reasons for this downturn. First, raw materials, such as aluminum and copper, cost more than in 1994. Second, price increases on coils made by CP/AAON resulted in seven percent fewer orders. Third, there was a major reduction in sales to AAON's two large national customers. AAON in 1995, as it had done previously, compensated to some extent by strengthening its sales force, which had success with an increasingly diverse group of customers, such as shopping malls, schools, and individual office buildings. From 1994 to 1995, orders from these company representatives increased from 49 percent of AAON's business to 65 percent. Thus the company shifted away from relying on the big national contracts.

That trend continued in 1996, when the company's biggest customer, Target Stores, accounted for just 14 percent of total sales, down from 17 percent in 1995. Also in 1996 AAON developed some new tools and methods to help its sales representatives. Product displays featuring actual units were sent around the nation. For the first time, sales personnel had access to display software that included the firm's many coil options, so they could sell coils as well as AAON's rooftop units. To keep Target Stores and other customers satisfied, AAON provided repair parts through six independent parts distributors and through its Tulsa manufacturing plant.

In 1996 AAON sold four lines of products, including the previously mentioned RH, RF, and RG Series. It also marketed its new HA Series, which was produced in nine sizes from four to 50 tons and featured horizontal discharge units for either ground or rooftop use. It began in 1997 replacing the RH Series with the RK units, which had rotary scroll compressors instead of the old piston compressors found in the RH products. AAON also had a patent pending on a new high efficiency blower developed for the RK Series.

The firm in 1996 emphasized adding equipment to improve productivity. For example, it found a way to make gas furnace components more efficiently. CP/AAON installed automatic equipment to process sheet metal at its Texas plant. The Tulsa plant added new production lines in 1996 to handle the increasing demand for AAON's larger capacity units. It should be noted that the company's assembly lines for nonstandardized equipment did not move, unlike the moving lines for mass produced units. That set form of production was one reason AAON's units were somewhat more expensive than standard equipment. Mass produced equipment sold for about $350 per ton of cooling capacity. Totally customized units sold for around $2,000 per ton. AAON's semicustomized products sold for about $400 per ton.

One of AAON's challenges in the 1990s was to deal with the federal government's ban on chlorofluorocarbons (CFCs) in air conditioners. CFCs originated in the 1930s and for many years were considered safe. But by the 1990s many scientists concluded that such man-made chemicals were at least partially responsible for reducing the protective ozone layer in the atmosphere. Like some other companies, AAON began using R-22, a hydrochlorofluorocarbon, instead of CFCs. According to AAON Engineering Manager Hank Bierwirth, in 1997 AAON was cooperating with Allied Chemical to test R-410A, a blend of two refrigerants favored to some degree by the Environmental Protection Agency. He said the new chemical probably would be phased in to replace R-22 after the turn of the century.

To aid customers seeking just the right cooling/heating coils, CP/AAON designed a Windows-based software program. Customers entered the specifications they needed, such as physical size and thermal capacity, and the program helped them decide what they required. Customers using this "Performance Program" software were able to receive updated versions. CP/AAON and AAON personnel used computer-aided design and manufacturing software to ensure that customers got what they needed.

AAON employed more individuals as the decade continued. On March 1, 1994 the firm had 369 employees and 120 temporary workers. That grew to 480 employees and 94 temporaries by March 1, 1996 and then to 556 employees and 157 temporaries by March 1, 1997. No AAON employees were represented by unions.

Although AAON knew of no particular hostile takeover attempt aimed at its assets, the firm's board of directors decided in 1997 to prepare for such a possibility. It unanimously approved an amendment to its Articles of Incorporation that required holders of two-thirds of outstanding shares to approve of any major changes, if the majority of the board did not agree to such changes. Nevada law required a majority vote of shares to make substantial changes in a company, so this proposal made it more difficult for someone to attempt a merger or other major changes.

Another change in the company's structure was designed to prevent a hostile takeover. In 1997 AAON's board voted to elect seven members on a staggered schedule. Two of those directors would be on the board until 1998; two would serve until 1999; and three directors would continue until 2000.

AAON made these changes realizing that their competitors in the HVAC industry were much larger companies. For example, Carrier Corporation, a subsidiary of United Technologies Corporation, in 1991 had sales of $3.8 billion, 37 percent of the HVAC industry, and employed almost 30,000 persons. Other major players in this industry included the Trane Company, a subsidiary of American Standard, Inc.; Lennox Industries, Inc.; and York International Corporation.

In April 1997 Jerry Levine in his report on AAON for BlueStone Capital Investment & Merchant Banking gave several reasons for his "buy" rating of AAON stock. Although AAON's growth in 1995 and 1996 was hurt by higher costs of raw materials, loss of business from two national accounts, and other factors, Levine concluded those "problems have finally been resolved and it would appear that AAON is now poised to again embark on a period of excellent revenue and earnings growth." He mentioned that more of AAON's sales were coming from its representatives and that national accounts even showed some positive signs. For example, Dillards Department Stores was a new national account.

AAON's Tulsa plant in 1996 was operating at only 27 percent of its estimated capacity. That was good evidence that the company could handle increased demands, which did occur in the first quarter of 1997. Revenues from January to March 1997 increased 25.6 percent and net income increased 70.9 percent over 1996 figures. If such short-term gains were maintained or increased in the long term, AAON's future looked positive.

In a telephone interview on September 18, 1997, CFO William Bowen reported that the firm was doing quite well. In fact, he said AAON had a "wonderful problem," a large backlog of orders, especially for larger capacity units. One way AAON responded in 1997 was to purchase for about $2 million a new machine from the Salvagnini Company in northern Italy. AAON looked all over the world to find this equipment. Bowen said this sheet metal assembly device could be programmed to take plain sheets of metal automatically and fold them into boxes and cut holes for input and output pipes and other accessories. AAON planned to purchase a second Salvagnini device after the first one was completely operational in late 1997. AAON used such investments in cutting-edge technology to meet its current demands and also prepare for long-term success in the future.

Principal Subsidiaries

CP/AAON (Texas); AAON, Inc. (Oklahoma).

Further Reading

Diamond Head Resources, Inc., Stock Prospectus, June 1, 1990.

"Report on AAON," *First Analysis Securities Corporation,* February 17, 1994.

"Research Report on AAON," *Southwest Securities,* September 14, 1994.

"Securities Report on AAON," *BlueStone Capital Investment & Merchant Banking,* April 16, 1997.

—David M. Walden

ABB Asea Brown Boveri Ltd.

P. O. Box 8131
CH-8050 Zurich
Switzerland
(01) 317 7111
Fax: (01) 311 9817
Web site: http://www.abb.com

Wholly Owned Subsidiary of ABB AB and ABB AG
Incorporated: 1988
Employees: 214,894
Sales: US$34.57 billion (1996)
SICs: 3511 Steam, Gas & Hydraulic Turbines; 3559 Special Industry Machinery, Not Elsewhere Classified; 3569 General Industrial Machinery & Equipment, Not Elsewhere Classified; 3612 Power, Distribution & Specialty Transformers; 3743 Railroad Equipment; 3823 Industrial Instruments for Measurement, Display & Control of Process Variables & Related Products; 3824 Totalizing Fluid Meters & Counting Devices

Formerly fierce competitors in the heavy-electrical and power-generation fields, Sweden's ASEA AB (which changed its name to ABB AB in February 1996) and Switzerland's BBC Brown Boveri Ltd. (which changed its name to ABB AG in February 1996) announced in August 1987 that the two companies would combine their assets to form a new company, called ABB Asea Brown Boveri Ltd. (ABB). The merger took effect on January 5, 1988. ABB is headquartered in Switzerland and owned equally by the two parent companies, which maintain separate stock listings in their own countries and act as holding companies for ABB. The merger, which created Europe's largest heavy-electrical combine, was designed to take advantage of ASEA's management strengths and Brown Boveri's technological and marketing expertise.

ABB's operations include three main business segments: power generation systems for utilities, industries, and independent power producers; electrical power transmission and distribution systems and products; and products, systems, and services for industrial processes and building systems. A fourth segment, rail transportation, is now part of ABB Daimler-Benz Transportation GmbH (ADtranz). A 50–50 joint venture with Germany's Daimler-Benz AG, ADtranz is the world's largest provider of total rail systems. Increasingly global in its operations, ABB transacts 57 percent of its total sales in Europe, 18 percent in the Americas, and 25 percent in Asia, Australasia, and Africa; Southeast Asia and China are ABB's main growth areas in the late 1990s. The Wallenberg family dynasty of Sweden holds a 25.5 percent indirect voting stake in ABB.

Early History of ASEA

Elektriska Aktiebolaget in Stockholm was established in 1883 by Ludwig Fredholm to manufacture dynamos based on the designs of a young engineer named Jonas Wenstrom. Wenstrom's innovative designs quickly led to financial success, and Fredholm soon wanted to expand the scope of his firm's operations. He arranged a merger with Wenstroms & Granstroms Elektriska Kraftbolag, a company founded by Jonas Wenstrom's brother Goran.

Allmanna Svenska Elektriska Aktiebolaget (ASEA) was created on November 18, 1890, to provide electrical equipment for Swedish industry. Goran Wenstrom shared presidential responsibilities with Fredholm, who also served as chairman of the board. After Fredholm's death in 1891, Wenstrom become sole president and Oscar F. Wijkman was appointed chairman.

The dawning of the electrical age provided ASEA with large new markets as the industrial and residential use of electricity became commonplace in Sweden. The company quickly established itself as a pioneer in the industrial field. ASEA's installation of electricity at a rolling mill in the town of Hofors is believed to be the first of its kind in the world, and in 1893, ASEA built Sweden's first three-phase electrical transmission, between Hellsjon and Crangesberg.

ASEA's early success was short-lived. In 1896 one of Sweden's leading inventors and industrialists, Gustaf de Laval, acquired a 50 percent interest in the company and both Wenstrom and Wijkman were ousted in a management reorga-

Company Perspectives:

The ABB Asea Brown Boveri Group is a federation of national companies. It finds efficient solutions for specific customers' problems and exports worldwide in specialized fields.

ABB uses a matrix structure for its organization: The ABB Group is made up of some 1,000 companies and more than 5,000 profit centers. Worldwide business activities are grouped into 4 Business Segments comprising 37 Business Areas. Each Business Area is responsible for global strategies, business plans, allocation of manufacturing, and product development. Local company managers, in turn, are responsible for operations in each country in line with the global strategy of the Business Area.

The Group is also managed in three global regions—Europe (including the former Soviet Union) Middle East and Africa—the Americas—Asia Pacific—to promote cross-border cooperation and support the development of ABB's composite plant business.

nization. But Laval's mismanagement of ASEA soon led the company into severe financial difficulties. With the help of the Stockholms Enskilda Bank, management opposed to Laval eventually extricated the company from his control. Disorganized and deeply in debt, the firm lost a significant share of the electrical equipment market in Sweden.

Stockholms Enskilda Bank played a major role in ASEA's financial recovery. In fact, it was only after the bank agreed to guarantee his salary that J. Sigfrid Edstrom, the former manager of the Gothenburg Tramways Company, agreed to become president of ASEA in 1903. Under Edstrom's direction, the company began to show a substantial profit by 1907. In addition, he expanded the firm's markets in Europe: subsidiaries were established in Great Britain, Spain, Denmark, Finland, and Russia between 1910 and 1914.

Although Sweden remained neutral during World War I, the company was adversely affected by the conflict. ASEA prospered during the early years of the war since the scarcity of coal stimulated the development of electricity, including the company's first major railway electrification project. Eventually, however, the firm lost many of its European markets due to the success of German submarine warfare. In Russia, all of ASEA's operations were interrupted by the revolution beginning in 1917.

The postwar years brought a deep recession to Sweden that lasted from 1920 to 1923. Yet Edstrom's cautious spending policies enabled the company to survive. By the late 1920s, ASEA was once again on the road to profitability and growth. In 1926 the company provided the electric locomotives and converter equipment for the first electric trains on the Stockholm-Gothenburg line, and in 1932 ASEA built the world's largest naturally cooled three-phase transformer.

During the 1930s, company management decided to concentrate on expanding and improving its domestic operations. After several years of negotiations, ASEA and LM Ericsson Telephone Company signed a pact in 1933 stipulating that the two companies would not compete with each other in certain sectors of the electrical market. As part of the agreement, ASEA purchased Elektromekano from Ericsson, giving ASEA undisputed control over a large portion of the electrical equipment market in Sweden.

In addition to its production of electric locomotives and rail equipment for Sweden's national railway electrification program, the firm expanded into new markets. ASEA purchased A.B. Svenska Flaktfabriken, a firm specializing in air-freight handling technology, and a large electric-motor manufacturer in Poland to augment its domestic production. In 1934 Edstrom was named chairman of the board and Arthur Linden, executive vice-president and a close Edstrom associate for many years, was named president. These two men directed the company's successful growth and expansion strategy until World War II.

Although Sweden remained neutral during World War II, once again war severely affected the country's economy. The Nazi occupation effectively curtailed ASEA's operations throughout Europe, and even to a significant extent in Sweden. A new president, Thorsten Ericson, was appointed in 1943, but this management change had little impact on the company's fortunes for the remainder of the war.

During the immediate postwar years, domestic power demands skyrocketed forcing utility companies to expand rapidly. ASEA was unable to meet this demand for electrical equipment due to shortages of material. To make matters worse, a five-month strike by metal workers played havoc with the company's delivery schedule, leaving ASEA unable to meet the demand from the Soviet Union for electric equipment based on a 1946 trade agreement between Sweden and the U.S.S.R.

In 1947 ASEA broke into the American market by signing a licensing agreement with the Ohio Brass Company for the local production of surge arrestors. During this time, ASEA also received substantial orders for the first stage of the massive Aswan Dam project in Egypt.

In 1949 Ake T. Vrethem, formerly with the Swedish State Power Board, was named president of ASEA and Ericson became chairman of the board. Under their direction, the company continued its pioneering efforts in several areas: ASEA supplied electrical equipment and technical expertise to the world's first 400 kilovolt AC transmission, between Harspranget and Hallsberg in 1952; the company claims to have produced the world's first synthetic diamonds using high-pressure technology in 1953, two years before General Electric announced a similar achievement in the United States; and ASEA supplied the first permanent high-voltage, direct current (HVDC) transmission, linking the Swedish mainland with the island of Gotland in 1954.

The company continued to play a critical role in Sweden's rail transit system. ASEA's locomotives accounted for virtually all the traffic on the country's rail network. In the mid-1950s, the firm introduced its "Ra" light-class electric locomotive, which was an immediate success and gave a boost to ASEA's efforts to market competitive locomotive models internationally.

Curt Nicolin Era at ASEA, 1961–80

In 1961 Curt Nicolin was appointed president. Nicolin restructured the parent company, introduced a new divisional organization, and relocated some of ASEA's manufacturing facilities. The company formed an electronics division, signaling the start of ASEA's transition from a traditional heavy electrical equipment manufacturer to an electronics company in which high-technology played an increasingly important role.

In the mid-1960s, ASEA's American market expanded considerably and became more important to the company's overall sales strategy. After serving customers such as the Tennessee Valley Authority, the company firmly established itself in the United States when it was chosen to supply HVDC equipment for the Pacific Internie Project on the West Coast.

ASEA also received an order to build Sweden's first full-scale nuclear power station during this period. The company then merged its nuclear division with the state-owned Atom-Energi to form ASEA Atom in 1968. ASEA acquired the remaining 50 percent state interest in Atom-Energi in 1982.

In 1963 ASEA achieved a major technological breakthrough with the introduction of an improved thyristor able to handle substantially more electrical current than existing devices. As a result, the company began manufacturing thyristor locomotives for Swedish and European rail systems. In the mid-1970s, ASEA worked with its American licensee, the electro-motive division of General Motors, to secure an order for 47 thyristor locomotives for use on Amtrak lines in the Boston-New York-Washington, D.C. corridor.

Nuclear power became an increasingly controversial issue in Sweden during the late 1970s. ASEA continued to manufacture nuclear reactors and received its first foreign order, from Finland. But in a 1980 national referendum Sweden voted to phase out nuclear power programs over a period of 25 years. The company was still allowed to complete orders for foreign reactors, but ASEA Atom's future looked bleak.

Curt Nicolin was also appointed chairman of the board in 1976. During the 1970s, however, Nicolin's management style was overwhelmed by the fast pace of changing technology. A large number of utility and electrical equipment manufacturing companies, including ASEA, experienced falling profits and lackluster growth.

Percy Barnevik Era at ASEA, 1980–88

ASEA began to revive in 1980, when 39-year-old Percy Barnevik was named managing director and, eventually, CEO. Barnevik immediately began a reorganization of the company's management strategy. ASEA had previously bid on projects with low profit margins for the sake of maintaining a minimum sales level and a certain number of employees, but under Barnevik's direction the company would emphasize high profit margin projects. Barnevik's strategy began to pay off quickly.

ASEA initiated a major expansion into high-tech areas, investing heavily in robotics and other state-of-the-art electronics. The development costs of robotics at first held profits down in that sector, but Barnevik viewed robotics as a long-term, high-growth area.

Barnevik also considered ASEA's industrial controls business, with products such as large automation controls, a high-growth sector. ASEA already had a major share of the rapidly expanding market for industrial energy controls, such as those that recycle waste heat. In addition, the company positioned itself to take advantage of a growing demand for pollution controls, spurred in part by the acid-rain controversy in Europe and North America.

In 1985 the company was accused of an illegal diversion of proprietary U.S. technology to the Soviet Union. A former ASEA vice-president was charged by Swedish authorities with tax evasion and violation of foreign exchange regulations in connection with the sale of six sophisticated computers with possible military applications. Barnevik insisted that the diversions occurred without management's approval.

Early History of BBC Brown Boveri

BBC Brown Boveri was established in 1891. The company's development is interesting because it was one of only a few multinational corporations to operate subsidiaries that were larger than the parent company. Because of the limitations of the Swiss domestic market, Brown Boveri established subsidiaries throughout Europe relatively early in its history, and at times had difficulty maintaining managerial control over some of its larger operating units. The merger with ASEA, a company which was praised for its strong management, was expected to help Brown Boveri reorganize and reassert control over its vast international network.

Brown Boveri's early activities included manufacturing electrical components such as electrical motors for locomotives and power-generating equipment for Europe's railway systems. In 1919 the company entered into a licensing agreement with the British manufacturing firm Vickers which gave the British firm the right to manufacture and sell Brown Boveri products throughout the British Empire and in some parts of Europe. The agreement gave Brown Boveri a significant amount of money and the promise of substantial annual revenue, and also helped the company expand into foreign markets at a time when protectionist policies inhibited international expansion.

In the early 1920s, Brown Boveri, already a geographically diversified company with successful operating subsidiaries in Italy, Germany, Norway, Austria, and the Balkans, suffered losses due to the devaluation of the French franc and the German mark. At the same time, in the Swiss domestic market, production costs increased while sales remained static, causing the company further losses. In 1924 Brown Boveri devalued its capital by 30 percent to cover the losses it had incurred. In 1927 the agreement with Vickers ran out and was not renewed.

During the same time, Brown Boveri's various subsidiaries grew rapidly. Industrialization throughout Europe created strong demand for the company's heavy electrical equipment. Italy's burgeoning railroad industry provided a particularly strong boost to Brown Boveri's Italian subsidiary, and the company's German facility actually did considerably more business than the Swiss parent. For the next few decades Brown Boveri grew as fast as technological developments in electrical engineering. Each of the company's subsidiaries tended to develop individually, as if it were a domestic company in the country in which it operated, and broad geographic coverage helped insulate the parent from severe crises when a certain region experienced economic difficulties.

This sort of segmented development had its drawbacks, however. After World War II, the cold war presented a variety of business opportunities for defense-related electrical contractors, but Brown Boveri's subsidiaries were seen as foreign companies in many of the countries in which they operated, sometimes making it difficult for the company to win lucrative contracts involving sensitive technology and other government contracts. The company, nevertheless, excelled at power generation, including nuclear power generators, and prospered in this field. Electrification efforts in the Third World also provided Brown Boveri with substantial profits.

Reorganization of Brown Boveri in 1970

In 1970 Brown Boveri began an extensive reorganization. The company's subsidiaries were divided into five groups: German, French, Swiss, "medium-sized" (seven manufacturing bases in Europe and Latin America), and Brown Boveri International (the remaining facilities). Each of these groups was further broken down into five product divisions: power generation, electronics, power distribution, traction equipment, and industrial equipment.

Throughout the 1970s, Brown Boveri struggled to expand into the U.S. market. The company negotiated a joint venture with Rockwell, the American manufacturer of high-tech military and aerospace applications, but the deal fell through when the two companies could not agree on financial terms. While Brown Boveri counted a handful of major U.S. customers as its clients, among them large utilities such as the Tennessee Valley Authority and American Electric, Brown Boveri's American market share was dismal considering the company's international standing (North American sales accounted for only 3.5 percent of total sales in 1974 and 1975), and the company continued to search for a means of effectively entering U.S. markets.

In 1974 Brown Boveri acquired the British controls and instrument manufacturer, George Kent. The deal at first raised concern in Britain over foreign ownership of such highly sensitive technology, but Brown Boveri prevailed with the encouragement of George Kent's rank-and-file employees, who feared the alternative of being bought by Britain's General Electric Company (GEC). The newly acquired company was renamed Brown Boveri Kent and made an excellent addition to the parent company's already diverse product line.

In the mid-1970s growing demand in the Middle East for large power-generating facilities distracted the company from its push into North America. Oil-rich African nations, like Nigeria, attempting to diversify their manufacturing capabilities also created new markets for Brown Boveri's heavy electrical engineering expertise.

In the early 1980s Brown Boveri's sales flattened out and the company's earnings declined. In 1983 Brown Boveri's German subsidiary in Mannheim, West Germany, which accounted for nearly half of the entire parent company's sales, rebounded. In spite of an increase in orders, however, the company's cost structure kept earnings down. In 1985 the subsidiary's performance improved as a result of cost-cutting measures but price decreases in the international market and unfavorable shifts in currency exchanges rates largely offset these gains. In 1986 the parent company acquired a significant block of shares in the Mannheim subsidiary, bringing its total stake to 75 percent.

In the later 1980s Brown Boveri took steps to reduce duplication of research and development among its various groups. While each subsidiary continued to do some product-development research for its individual market, theoretical research was unified under the parent company, making more efficient use of research funding. In 1987 the company introduced a supercharging system for diesel engines called Comprex. This system was capable of increasing an engine's horsepower by 35 percent and delivering up to 50 percent more torque at lower speeds. The Japanese automaker Mazda planned to use the new supercharger in its new diesel passenger models.

Formation of ABB in 1988

In August 1987 ASEA and Brown Boveri announced their intent to merge their assets for shares in a new company, ABB Asea Brown Boveri Ltd., to be owned equally by each parent company and to be headquartered in Zurich. When the merger took effect on January 5, 1988, ASEA's Curt Nicolin and Brown Boveri's Fritz Leutwiler became joint chairmen. ASEA's CEO, Percy Barnevik, became the new operating company's CEO, while his Brown Boveri counterpart became deputy CEO.

The joint venture between these two former competitors allowed them to combine expensive research-and-development efforts in superconductors, high-voltage chips, and control systems used in power plants. In addition, ASEA's strength in Scandinavia and northern Europe balanced Brown Boveri's strong presence in Austria, Italy, Switzerland, and West Germany.

The integration of the giant was the new management's first task. CEO Barnevik had been applauded for his excellent job of rationalization at ASEA. When he took the helm of that company in 1980 it was struggling but by 1986 it was earning 5.5 percent of total sales, compared to Brown Boveri's 1.5 percent. The companies hoped Barnevik would have similar success with Brown Boveri's operations. For his part, Barnevik aimed for ABB to achieve an overall operating margin of 10 percent.

In 1988 and 1989, ABB reorganized its existing operations by decentralizing and ruthlessly slashing bureaucracy. The combined corporate headquarters alone went from 2,000 to 176 employees. During the same period, ABB also went on an acquisition spree in Western Europe and the United States, purchasing a total of 55 companies. Perhaps most importantly, ABB was able to gain a foothold in North America, something both halves of ABB had struggled to achieve for the previous two decades. In early 1989 ABB formed a joint venture with the American electrical firm Westinghouse. ABB owned 45 percent of the new subsidiary, a manufacturer of electricity distribution systems for international markets. Then, in December 1989, ABB exercised its option to buy Westinghouse out of the venture, leaving ABB the sole owner of the company. That same month, the company agreed to buy Stamford, Connecticut-based Combustion Engineering Group, an unprofitable manufacturer of power generators and related equipment, for $1.56 billion. These U.S. investments, however, were not immediately successful for ABB, and the company, over the next few years, had to reorganize the acquired businesses, divesting $700 million in assets and trimming their payroll from 40,000 to 25,000.

Expansion in Asia and Eastern Europe and Major Restructurings in the 1990s

With recession plaguing the markets of Western Europe and North America in the early 1990s and with the continuing maturation of those markets, ABB decided that its future lay in the emerging markets of Eastern Europe and Asia, where opportunities for growth were plentiful and where it could set up lower-cost manufacturing operations. Although the company had virtually no operations in Eastern Europe at the beginning of the decade, through a series of acquisitions and joint ventures in eastern Germany, Poland, and Czechoslovakia, ABB had established a considerable presence in the region by 1992, employing 20,000 people in 30 companies. By the end of 1995, ABB had a network of 60 companies in Eastern Europe and the former Soviet Union, giving it the largest manufacturing operation of any western firm in the region. Operations in Poland and the Czech Republic continued to lead the way, but significant operations had also been established in Russia (3,000 employees), Romania (2,000 employees), and the Ukraine (1,500 employees).

At the same time, ABB began to expand more cautiously in Asia, laying the groundwork for $1 billion in investments there by the mid-1990s. In 1992 an operating structure was created for the Asia-Pacific region and more than 20 new manufacturing and service operations were established in the region through acquisitions, joint ventures, and other investments. Investments in Asia continued in 1993, the year that ABB carried out another major restructuring. This one involved the reorganizing of the company's global operations into three geographic regions: Europe (including the Middle East and Africa), the Americas, and Asia; the folding of six industrial business segments into the following four: power generation, power transmission and distribution, industrial and building systems, and rail transportation; and the streamlining of the executive committee to eight members (Barnevik, the heads of the three geographic regions, and the heads of the four business segments).

In 1994, in addition to making additional investments in Asia, ABB entered into a contract to build a $1 billion combined-cycle power plant in Malaysia. On January 1, 1996, ABB merged its rail transportation unit with that of Germany's Daimler-Benz AG to form ABB Daimler-Benz Transportation GmbH (ADtranz), a 50–50 joint venture which immediately became the largest provider of rail systems in the world. As part of the agreement, Daimler-Benz paid ABB $900 million in cash for its half share of the new venture since its rail operations were only about half the size of those of ABB.

In February 1996, the parent companies of ABB changed their names, with ASEA becoming ABB AB and Brown Boveri becoming ABB AG. At the same time, changes were made to ABB's board of directors. These changes were intended to reflect the company's increasingly global nature and to improve the relationship between the subsidiary and its parent companies. Further management changes came in October 1996 when Barnevik relinquished his position as chief executive of ABB in order to take over the chairmanship of Investor, the Wallenberg family holding company. Assuming the position of president and chief executive was Göran Lindahl, a 25-year company veteran who had been executive vice-president for power transmission and the Middle East and North Africa region. Barnevik remained ABB chairman. In June 1997 the Wallenberg group, in need of cash for a takeover, reduced its indirect voting stake in ABB from 32.7 percent to 25.5 percent.

In June 1996 ABB was awarded a contract by the government of Malaysia to play the lead role in the building of a $5 billion-plus hydroelectric power generation plant and transmission system at Bakun on the Balui River but this project ran into problems in the following year. As a result of the Asian economic crisis which hit Malaysia particularly hard, the Malaysian government was forced to announce an indefinite delay in the project in September 1997. Despite this setback, and the continuing uncertainty surrounding Asian economies, ABB did not pull back from its expansion in that region. In October 1997 the company announced yet another major restructuring in which it planned to shift thousands of jobs from Europe and the United States to Asia, cutting 10,000 jobs over an 18-month period. This was in addition to a 3,600-job cut announced just a few days earlier at ADtranz. ABB's executives were betting that the Asian economic crisis would be of relatively short duration and reasoned that, although they might lose business in the region in the short term, they could recoup some of these losses by taking advantage of the countries' weakened currencies which brought manufacturing costs down even further. To cover the costs of the reorganization, ABB took a charge of $850 million in the fourth quarter of 1997.

From its first year of operation in 1988 through its ninth year in 1996, ABB Asea Brown Boveri Ltd. had nearly doubled in size, increasing revenues from $17.83 billion to $34.57 billion. Although it failed to reach Barnevik's goal of a 10 percent operating margin for even a single year, the merged company was much more profitable than its predecessors, ASEA AB and BBC Brown Boveri Ltd., achieving a peak operating margin of 9.7 percent in 1995 before falling back to 8.8 percent in 1996. ABB was certainly much stronger, better managed, and more global in nature than its parent companies had been when operating independently. The question for this engineering giant at the turn of the millennium was whether the company's huge bet on Asia would pay off in the long run or lead to further financial difficulties.

Principal Subsidiaries

ABB Asia Pacific Ltd. (Hong Kong); ABB Asea Brown Boveri Pty. Ltd. (Australia); Asea Brown Boveri AG (Austria); Asea Brown Boveri S.A.-N.V. (Belgium); Asea Brown Boveri Ltda. (Brazil); Asea Brown Boveri Inc. (Canada); ABB China Ltd.; Asea Brown Boveri s.r.o. (Czech Republic); Asea Brown

Boveri A/S (Denmark); Asea Brown Boveri Europe Ltd. (Belgium); ABB Oy (Finland); Asea Brown Boveri S.A. (France); Asea Brown Boveri AG (Germany); Asea Brown Boveri S.A. (Greece); Asea Brown Boveri Ltd. (India); Asea Brown Boveri Ltd. (Ireland); Asea Brown Boveri S.p.A. (Italy); ABB K.K. (Japan); Asea Brown Boveri B.V. (Netherlands); Asea Brown Boveri AS (Norway); Asea Brown Boveri Ltd. (Poland); Asea Brown Boveri SGPS, S.A. (Portugal); Asea Brown Boveri Ltd. (Russia); Asea Brown Boveri Pte. Ltd. (Singapore); Asea Brown Boveri S.A. (Spain); Asea Brown Boveri AB (Sweden); ABB Management AG (Switzerland); Asea Brown Boveri Ltd. (Taiwan); Asea Brown Boveri Ltd. (U.K.); Asea Brown Boveri Inc. (U.S.A.); ABB Daimler-Benz Transportation GmbH (Germany; 50%).

Further Reading

''The ABB of Management,'' *Economist,* January 6, 1996, p. 56.

Andrews, Edmund L., ''ABB Will Cut 10,000 Jobs and Switch Focus to Asia,'' *New York Times,* October 22, 1997, p. 2D.

Ehrenkrona, Olof, *Nicolin: En svensk historia,* Stockholm: Timbro, 1991.

Fink, Ronald, ''The Tortoise Doesn't Always Win,'' *Financial World,* September 27, 1994, pp. 22, 24.

Gumbel, Peter, ''Daimler to Pay $900 Million to ABB As They Merge Railroad Operations,'' *Wall Street Journal,* March 17, 1995, p. 6A.

Guyon, Janet, ''ABB Fuses Units with One Set of Values: Managers Get Global Strategies to Work Locally,'' *Wall Street Journal,* October 2, 1996, p. 15A.

Hofheinz, Paul, ''Yes, You Can Win in Eastern Europe,'' *Fortune,* May 16, 1994, pp. 110–12.

''Is It a Bird? Is It a Manager?'' *Economist,* May 3, 1997, pp. 53–54.

Kapstein, Jonathan, and Dean Foust, ''An Insider Caper in Liechtenstein,'' *Business Week,* December 11, 1989, pp. 58–59.

Karlgaard, Rich, ''Percy Barnevik,'' *Forbes ASAP,* December 5, 1994, pp. 65–68.

Michaels, Daniel, ''ABB Showcases Growing Share of Poland's Market,'' *Wall Street Journal,* March 1, 1996, p. 5A.

'' 'Mr. Barnevik, Aren't You Happy Now?,' '' *Business Week,* September 27, 1993, p. 128L.

Rapoport, Carla, ''A Tough Swede Invades the U.S.,'' *Fortune,* June 29, 1992, pp. 76–79.

Reed, Stanley, ''The Wallenbergs' New Blood,'' *Business Week,* October 20, 1997, pp. 98, 102.

Smart, Tim, and Gail Edmondon, ''Slow Boil for ABB in the U.S.,'' *Business Week,* September 12, 1994, pp. 72–73.

Taylor, William, ''The Logic of Global Business: An Interview with ABB's Percy Barnevik,'' *Harvard Business Review,* March/April 1991.

Wagstyl, Stefan, ''Woven into the Fabric,'' *Financial Times,* January 10, 1996, p. 15.

—updated by David E. Salamie

ABC Supply Co., Inc.

One ABC Parkway
Beloit, Wisconsin 53511
U.S.A.
(608) 362-7777
Fax: 608-362-6529
Web site: http://www.abc-supply.com

Private Company
Incorporated: 1982
Employees: 2,300
Sales: $789 million (1996)
SICs: 5033, Roofing, Siding & Other Construction Products, Wholesale; 5039, Prefabricated Nonwood Structural Assemblies, Wholesale

ABC Supply Co., Inc., the largest roofing and siding wholesaler in the United States, is the brainchild of Ken Hendricks, a building industry veteran and son of a Janesville, Wisconsin roofing contractor. While Hendricks was still a boy, his father Joe had channeled hard work and a devotion to his trade into a reputation as a do-it-all roofer. Despite his father's prosperity, Ken Hendricks was initially unenthusiastic about following in his footsteps. Hendricks Senior's working life had been marked by 12-hour days and six-day weeks and a business that, while profitable, never grew because Joe Hendricks did not believe anyone could be trained to do the job as well as he did. Ken Hendricks wanted something different for himself.

International Roofing Company: 1963–79

Hendricks dropped out of high school in his junior year, working briefly at a General Motors auto plant and then at Wisconsin Power and Light. To fulfill his dream of becoming an architect, he also worked another 40 hours a week in the drafting department of a Janesville conveyor company and, to earn extra money, started roofing houses on the weekend. Only the roofing work survived, however, and, using the money he had saved from his 80-hour work weeks, in 1963 the 22-year-old Hendricks founded International Roofing Company. Within four years International Roofing had 500 employees and sales of $45 million a year. It had become the roofer of choice for many of the K-Marts and Arby's and McDonald's restaurants rising up in the midwest, and it had won contracts to roof a number of military bases around the country. By 1968 International had become the eighth largest roofing company in the United States.

Hendricks's success came at a steep price. He later admitted that in his early years, "I was not an ethical person. . . . Back then I was out there to get more money. If that meant cheating a little bit, I didn't feel there was anything wrong [with that]." To maximize profits he cut corners wherever possible and permitted his employees to do the same. If International Roofing could save money by fastening shingles with only three nails instead of four it did. Hendricks paid his employees the lowest wages he could get away with and, like his father before him, refused to delegate authority or expertise to any but the four or five superintendents he regarded as friends. Because he trusted no one but himself to oversee International's projects, he had to travel constantly. The hours and cut corners began to take their toll. "Eventually," he later told *Inc.* magazine, "I just got sick of what I was doing, so I phased the business down."

After about a decade at International's helm Hendricks reduced his involvement to spend more time with his family. International remained in business but focused only on projects in the Libertyville, Illinois and Beloit/Janesville and Madison, Wisconsin areas. In 1968 Hendricks had met his future second wife Diane, the daughter of a northern Wisconsin farmer and the recent recipient of a real estate license earned in night school. After dating for several years, they married in the 1970s and began buying up rundown or condemned homes. While Ken renovated them, Diane managed their rental. The couple soon had 200 renovated homes on the Janesville area market. They quickly learned, however, that property management could be a frustrating business, and tenant problems forced them to let several properties fall into disrepair.

They decided to branch out into the purchase and leasing of commercial and industrial properties and formed Hendricks Realty to formalize this new business. Hendricks also began buying asphalt shingles, which he then sold back to Interna-

Company Perspectives:

At ABC, we are committed to helping you stay profitable. We believe in individual "entrepreneurship." That is why we use all of our buying power with suppliers to bring you a quality selection of materials at the right place and time, at a competitive price. I have learned over the years that the best way to keep our customers is to keep our promises. That is why we are America's leading full-service roofing, siding, and window supplier. We look forward to being your dependable supplier!

tional Roofing, his back-burnered business. Soon other roofers were coming to Hendricks for supplies, and Hendricks began devoting more time to his young supply distributorship than to International Roofing.

ABC Supply Company: 1979–86

Although by the early 1980s Hendricks's real estate business had been his primary focus for more than ten years, his burgeoning roofing supply business was taking center stage. In June 1982 he purchased three supply centers owned by Bird & Sons, a century-old roofing manufacturer based in Walpole, Massachusetts. These first three ABC centers, based in Muskegon, Michigan and in Belleville and Springfield, Illinois, had been losing money for Bird & Sons but offered Hendricks the same "renovation" opportunity he had learned to exploit in the real estate industry. The makings of an entrepreneurial niche began to crystallize: if the customer service and product knowledge of the small independent roofing supplier could be combined with the buying power of a national chain, Hendricks's new business—American Builders & Contractors Supply Co.—could grab a serious slice of the national building supply market.

With his wife Diane heading ABC's finances and bank loan efforts, Hendricks acquired a headquarters location in Beloit, and by the end of its first full year of operations, ABC's sales had reached $4.5 million. In 1983 ABC purchased a building supplier in Green Bay, Wisconsin, and in the first five months of 1984 added five former Aluma building supply stores, 13 former GAF stores, and two former AA Distributors stores. Only two years in existence, ABC Supply earned a number three spot on *Inc.* magazine's "Inc. 500" listing of the fastest growing U.S. small companies, with Hendricks's other company, International Roofing, placing 30th. Because International Roofing was now competing with ABC's customers, Hendricks decided, essentially, to give it away to his largest customer to ensure that company's continued business. The liquidation was not only an unusually generous demonstration of the philosophy of "pleasing the customer," it also marked Hendricks's final comment on the destructive profits-*über-alles* philosophy by which he had built International Roofing.

Hendricks's acquisition spree continued in 1985 with the purchase of seven independent building centers and another seven former Genstar stores in November. By the end of the year ABC had made its first acquisition in Texas and had moved up to second place on the Inc. 500. In 1986 ABC acquired six former Nichols-Homeshield building supply centers and opened another eight new stores through purchases or internal store launches. In the space of less than 34 months, Hendricks had opened or acquired 48 stores (or roughly one new center every three weeks). By the end of 1986, ABC's empire stood at 600 employees and revenues of $183 million, earning it first place on the *Inc.'s* prestigious list.

"The Biggest Small Company in America": 1987–89

In the three years that followed, the general health of the U.S. economy offered Hendricks fewer opportunities to buy new stores at bargain-basement prices and ABC's torrid growth pace slowed. It acquired two new stores in all of 1987, five in 1988, and then seven in 1989 to expand its network to 70 centers. In 1987 Hendricks and his wife Diane were named Ernst & Young's "Entrepreneurs of the Year" and stepped back to consolidate their gains. They began developing wholly owned subsidiaries to manage crucial aspects of the operation such as trucking and construction and created 13 new "satellite" centers near existing ABC stores to absorb the high demand of large urban markets.

ABC's success was in large part due to the lessons Hendricks had learned while "winning ugly" at International Roofing. Instead of cutting expenses by cutting corners, he instituted a rigorous cost control structure based on the notion that the difference between successful and failed businesses was only three percent of sales. To recover that three percent, Hendricks adopted a simple three-pronged approach: use economies of scale to purchase products from national vendors at a discount; use benchmarking standards to reduce operations costs such as real estate and corporate overhead to industry-leading levels; and motivate employees through bonuses and open book management techniques.

The first strategy, economies of scale, could be achieved simply by aggressively acquiring failing but potentially salvageable building suppliers. By adding new stores to ABC's network every year, Hendricks strengthened his leverage to negotiate better deals with vendors. To find these target stores, he relied on his contacts in the industry. Calls to vendors, competitors, and credit managers told him which suppliers were late on their bills, facing bankruptcy, or looking to sell their businesses and retire. Partnerships that were splitting up, widowed wives trying to sell off their husband's assets, companies crippled by weak local economies—all gave Hendricks the opportunity to buy potentially healthy businesses at an affordable price.

Hendricks also reduced the waste companies traditionally accumulate in everyday business expenses. He bought used trucks and office furniture and refurbished them, for example, and found dilapidated but still sound commercial properties in inner cities where he knew most of his business would be found. Rather than build expensive new stores in outlying suburbs, where the relative newness of the surrounding properties mitigated against the need for his products, he focused on the remodeling markets in older sections of town where aging properties were being bought up and restored (three-quarters of ABC's roofing and siding was being sold to repair houses that were at least 50 years old). Hendricks also made sure that ABC's inventory costs were low by keeping only enough stock on hand to meet existing orders. Because of these cost-cutting measures, by 1991 ABC's annual inventory turnover rate was a healthy six times per year, its rent as a percentage of sales was 1.8 percent (versus 3.5 percent for the industry), and its truck expense was less than two percent of sales (versus 4.75 to 5.5 percent nationally).

Finally, Hendricks made sure all of his employees were enthusiastic, informed participants in the company's program by rewarding them for reducing expenses and pleasing customers. When adding a distressed supplier to the ABC chain, Hendricks gave the store's manager a chance to adapt to his system, preserving the fellow's job while saving himself the cost of hiring a new manager. He also gave the store's existing workers the choice of taking on more responsibility in exchange for a slight pay increase but also the promise of outsized bonuses when the store's bottom line improved. Each month the employees of every store were given a two-page report that detailed ABC's and the individual store's current profit-and-loss and expenses (sales, cost of goods sold, rent, vehicle repair costs, etc.) compared with the previous year as well as its ranking for each cost category vis-à-vis the other stores in the ABC network.

This ''open book'' management approach enabled even the lowliest ABC delivery driver to see that because ABC's profit margin on an order of shingles was slim a simple two-hour delay delivering the shingles wiped out the store's profit from the order. A crucial component of Hendricks's monthly report was the estimate of how much of a bonus (if any) the store had earned for the year. At the end of the year, each store manager received 40 percent of the store's bonus (sometimes amounting to $80,000), with the remainder divvied up among the store's employees at the manager's discretion. For employees making $18,000 to $20,000 a year this bonus could run an additional $3,000 to $10,000 a year. With such incentives dangling before them, by 1991 ABC's employees were generating a prodigious $450,000 a year in sales, more than twice the industry average.

''A Huge Market Share'': 1990–97

By early 1990 ABC's work force had grown to 850, its sales had climbed to $280 million, and it had yet to experience a year in which sales grew less than 25 percent. The recession in the northeast presented Hendricks with new buying opportunities in that region, and by the end of 1991 ABC had expanded to 92 stores in a network that now reached coast to coast. By September 1992 sales had vaulted to $750 million and Hendricks announced that, in keeping with the reclamation impulse that fueled ABC's sales, its new corporate office building would be erected in an abandoned manufacturing plant in downtown Beloit. Meanwhile, Hendricks's wife Diane had built an insurance company, American Patriot Insurance, that though initially designed only to handle the workers' compensation cases of ABC and its customers was on its way to outpacing even ABC in sales. By 1993 ABC was the twelfth largest private company in Wisconsin and by 1995 had climbed to 295 on *Forbes* magazine's ''Private 500'' ranking of American businesses.

In 1995 Hendricks began to strengthen ABC's position as the largest roofing and siding supplier in the United States by moving into manufacturing. Hendricks's purchase of Mule-Hide Products Co., a maker of commercial roofing (founded in 1906), and Amcraft Building Products Co., Inc., a manufacturer of vinyl siding and windows, symbolized his desire to increase ABC Supply's market share by ''vertically integrating'' it. For most companies, vertical integration meant entering each stage of their products' life cycle—from raw materials to distribution—by branching out from the products' manufacture backward into raw materials production, for example, or forward into marketing and distribution. But in what Hendricks joked was ''a reverse philosophy of integrating,'' ABC had grown in the opposite direction: it had made sure it had its customers first by amassing a huge network of local stores and only then created the sophisticated distribution network to tie them together. Finally, by moving into manufacture by acquiring roofing accessory manufacturers ABC also could begin stocking its stores with its own merchandise.

In April 1996, ABC acquired R. and W. Hawaii Wholesale, Inc., a large roofing and waterproofing material supplier, and by the end of the year could boast a work force of 2,100 employees and sales of $762 million. ABC now owned 25 percent of the building products industry and had the infrastructure to prove it: it had a fleet of 2,500 delivery vehicles alone in 1997 and in 1996 supplied enough materials to shingle 500,000 U.S. homes; side another two million; cover eight million square feet of flat roofs; and install 60 million square feet of soffit, gutter, downspout, and fascia. Moreover, it had nearly doubled in size since 1990. In 1996, Hendricks spoke optimistically of breaking the $100 billion sales mark in 1997 and then reaching $2 billion by the end of the century. ''If you think about it,'' Hendricks told the *Beloit Daily News,* ''every roof, every house and business and wall in the country, we'll have been involved with 26 or 27 percent of those at that point [1997]. That's a huge market share.''

In 1995 Hendricks hired Jeff Stentz to head ABC's acquisitions program. Stentz convinced Hendricks to change his focus from buying up troubled suppliers at a discount to paying more for healthier businesses that could offer ABC immediate returns. In 1996 ABC acquired some 15 companies, adding $100 million to its sales. Roughly seven more acquisitions—adding another $150 million—were planned for 1997. In June, ABC acquired Viking Building Products, a Connecticut-based distributor of home building supplies with sales of $85 million. As the second largest building supply chain in the northeast, Viking's 12 stores brought ABC's network to 210 locations in 41 states, comprising some 3.5 million square feet of inventory.

By the fall Hendricks had announced an aggressive new expansion program that would grow ABC at the rate of one new store a week. In October it purchased five building supply companies from Champ Industries, Inc. that added 31 stores in Texas, California, Oklahoma, Kansas, and Missouri and $198 million in sales to the ABC network.

Although ABC remained a staunchly family-run affair (five of Hendricks's children worked for the company in addition to his wife), it committed itself to adopting the new technologies and product lines that promised to protect its industry leadership. The computer technology that Hendricks had once decried as too expensive now managed not only ABC's administrative, bookkeeping, and inventory functions but in 1997 grew to include a home page on the World Wide Web and a database that integrated the inventories of all the stores in a particular region. Moreover, Hendricks began monitoring possible applications for satellite technology at ABC and began introducing videoconferencing in each of his stores so managers could help solve each other's problems.

The residential roofing products that had once dominated ABC's sales were now giving way to a new emphasis on increasing revenues from siding, windows, and commercial roofing as well as new product lines like insulation, building tools, and accessories. ''Our goal,'' ABC's director of purchasing told *Construction News* in 1996, ''is to be able to frame the entire exterior portion of the house.'' The inner city building remodeler who had once been ABC's bread and butter would now be joined by architects, plant engineers, building maintenance technicians—whoever needed roofing and siding for a structure, regardless of type.

By 1997 ABC was also offering customers new value-added services like free next morning deliveries, on-site product training seminars, customized catalogs, electronic ordering, and usage and trend analysis reports. Now in his late 50s, founder Ken Hendricks was still fighting the impulse to manage every aspect of the firm's operations and began looking for a chief operating officer to free him to plan for the company's long-term future. ''Somebody in the company has to think about what this industry is going to look like in five years and get ahead of that,'' he told an interviewer. ''I like to say we're the biggest small company in America. . . . We still pay attention to the details, and we know what it takes to do the job.''

Principal Subsidiaries

ABC Express; American Patriot Insurance; Hendricks Real Estate; Amcraft Building Products; Corporate Contractors Inc.; Mulehide Products Company.

Further Reading

''ABC Supply Co. Plans New Headquarters in Beloit,'' *Milwaukee Sentinel,* September 25, 1992.

''ABC Supply Sets Forth Aggressive Acquisition Strategy,'' *National Home Center News,* October 6, 1997, p. 9.

''Entrepreneur Preaches the Gospel of Reclamation,'' *Milwaukee Journal,* April 28, 1991.

Fenn, Donna, ''Higher Ground,'' *Inc.* (Inc. 500 issue), 1996, p. 93.

Gendron, George, ''Waste Not, Want Not,'' *Inc.,* March 1991, p. 33.

''Going for Broke,'' *Inc.,* September 1990, p. 35.

Stapleton, Shawn, ''ABC Owner Carries Big Goals for Future'' (ABC Supply Open House special section), *Beloit Daily News,* September 15, 1995.

——, ''ABC Success a Family Affair'' (ABC Supply Open House special section), *Beloit Daily News,* September 15, 1995.

——, ''Firm Scored Amazing Growth,'' (ABC Supply Open House special section), *Beloit Daily News,* September 15, 1995.

——, ''Room with a View'' (ABC Supply Open House special section), *Beloit Daily News,* September 15, 1995.

—Paul S. Bodine

Adtran Inc.

901 Explorer Boulevard
Huntsville, Alabama 35806-2807
U.S.A.
(205) 971-8000
Fax: (205) 971-8699
Web site: http://www.adtran.com

Public Company
Incorporated: 1985
Employees: 896
Sales: $250.1 million (1996)
Stock Exchanges: NASDAQ
SICs: 3661 Telephone & Telegraph Apparatus; 3825 Electric Measuring Instruments & Meters

In 1970, a 29-year-old electronics entrepreneur named Mark Smith founded Universal Data Systems (UDS) in Huntsville, Alabama, to make moderately priced data communications equipment for the growing U.S. computer industry. UDS's principal product was an early incarnation of today's commonplace computer modem, a device for connecting computers over phone lines so they can transmit data to each other. The first modems connected mainframe computers over dedicated phone lines using a standard called "serial synchronous data transmission," which required that the sending computer be perfectly synchronized with the receiving computer.

When the minicomputer began to introduce diversity into the computer industry in the 1970s, however, AT&T's Bell Laboratories created a new standard, "asynchronous serial data transmission" (ASDT), that enabled computer transmitters and receivers operating at different speeds to successfully transmit data to each other. Because ASDT would make possible the connection of different connector designs, electrical requirements, and transmission conditions, AT&T also developed a series of ASDT specifications that forced order on the world of minicomputer data communications. Moreover, because AT&T created the specs, industry users were forced to rent AT&T's ASDT data set, giving it effective control of the fledgling modem industry.

Of Modems and Monopoly: 1978–84

Then in the late 1970s the acoustic coupler was invented, suddenly making it possible for a computer modem to be connected to the phone line by simply inserting an ordinary telephone handset into the acoustic coupler's twin cups, which were shaped out of foam rubber to receive the handset and eliminate signal decay. The acoustic coupler converted the sound waves sent over the phone line into a stream of electrical signals the modem and computer could understand. More importantly, it opened the door for a modem industry that did not require the AT&T ASTD standard. Companies like Carterphone, Datec, Digicom, IBM, U.S. Robotics, and Universal Data Systems rose to create a new generation of initially expensive acoustic coupler modems, which transmitted data at 300 bits per second (bps)—at the time believed to be the fastest reliable data transmission speed possible over the phone network.

By 1978 UDS and its competitors began offering inexpensive acoustic coupler modems for the data communications market growing up around the mainframe computer centers of the nation's universities and scientific organizations (the focal points of the Internet's forerunner, ARPANET). That same year, however, electronics giant Motorola acquired UDS, and Smith became a Motorola vice-president. AT&T was meanwhile defending its ASTD modem turf, suing acoustic-coupler maker Carterphone for daring to ignore its modem specifications. The case went all the way to Supreme Court, where in 1984 the nine Justices ruled that AT&T had been running a monopoly in the U.S. local and long distance service and equipment markets.

As a consequence of the Court's trust-busting decision, the Federal Communications Commission (FCC) was granted regulatory control over the standards for telephone and computer communications AT&T once ruled, and Ma Bell herself was forced to spin off her local phone service businesses into seven regional bell operating companies (RBOCs), which were in turn prohibited from offering long distance phone service or manu-

Company Perspectives:

Mission: To design, develop and manufacture advanced transmission products for high-speed digital communications. Through a commitment to total customer satisfaction, ADTRAN continually develops and improves its products to meet changing needs while maintaining the highest level of quality and customer support.

facturing telecommunications equipment. With this landmark decision to inject competition into the telecommunications equipment industry, Smith saw an opportunity to step in and supply the telecommunications network equipment that the seven RBOCs—and over 1,300 independent U.S. phone companies—would now have buy on the open market.

Enter Adtran: 1985–91

With John Jurenko, Lonnie McMillian, and four other founders, Smith left Motorola for good in 1985 and formed Huntsville-based Adtran Inc. (for ''advanced transmission''), which opened for business in January 1986. Despite his roots in the modem industry, Smith saw the historic AT&T divestiture as opening a wider window of opportunity to manufacture an entire range of high-speed digital infrastructure products to optimize the performance of the nation's copper-wire phone network. ''We founded this company,'' Smith later told *Investor's Business Daily,* ''to take advantage of the trend toward complete digital systems . . . the technology of the future.'' Specifically, Adtran would focus on the manufacture of digital transmission telecommunications equipment for phone companies' ''Central Offices'' (the local telephone switching and distribution facility) and their ''Local Loops'' (the portion of the phone network connecting the Central Office to individual homes and offices).

In the mid-1990s, there were roughly 30,000 such Central Offices in North America, which provided their subscribers with access to a specific portion of the phone network's bandwidth either on a switched basis (known as ''switched access'') or on an exclusive basis (''private line''). From the central switching office, phone lines ran to the Local (or home) Loop, which numbered some 160 million in the United States alone in the mid-1990s. Local Loops consist of a circuit assembly housing a channel unit and U-Basic Rate Transmission Extender that plugs into a channel bank or shelf of the Central Office. Each Central Office contained several hundred to several thousand circuit assemblies, one for each telco subscriber. Seizing on this huge market, Adtran began designing and manufacturing speed-optimizing versions of these basic Central Office/Local Loop components, which would rely exclusively on digital rather than analog technology to wring the maximum performance out of conventional copper-wire phone lines. Adtran was soon developing a complete line of data transmission, repeater, extension, and termination products, from dataports and channel and data service units to digital repeaters and extenders (used to boost a phone signal in order to extend the distance of the transmission).

The heart of Adtran's first digital telco equipment line in the 1980s were its ''Digital Data Service'' (DDS) products, based on the pioneering DDS technology introduced by AT&T in the late 1970s and which were ideal for multiple-location data transmission operations such as linking automated teller machines to banks. Huge advances were being made in data transmission technology, and the unwieldy wire coils and unstable capacitors of early modems, for example, were being replaced by integrated circuits, quartz crystals, single-chip circuits, improved data compression methods, and cheaper manufacturing techniques. From its all-digital DDS technology, Adtran began developing ''digital signal zero'' data ports for interconnecting two channels in a telco's Central Office; OCU dataports (a kind of Central Office channel assembly) and related products for delivering DDS to telco subscribers; mid-span DDS repeaters for extending the Local Loop's service range; and Digital Data Station Termination equipment to monitor and detect problems in each individual circuit.

By 1991, Adtran had already gained leading market share in its target market, Central Office and Local Loop telecommunications equipment for U.S. telcos. To solidify its hold on these core telco customers—which five years later still accounted for 60 percent of its sales—Smith adopted a three-pronged strategy of new product development, customer service, and product excellence. But to reduce Adtran's vulnerability to the changes in the telcos' demand for equipment, he also sought out a new market: the corporate end-user served by the Local Loop, in a segment known as ''customer premises equipment'' (CPE). At the customer's premises, the phone signal transmitted by the Central Office is received by terminating equipment where it is converted for use in such products as LAN interconnection gear, video conferencing equipment, PBXs, and personal computers. Adtran's first CPE products were data service units, unveiled in 1991, and by 1996 it was manufacturing some 100 different types of these products alone. Within four years Adtran's corporate-user sales had grown to account for 20 percent of its sales.

OEMs and ISDN: 1992–94

With sales to corporate customers bolstering its telco revenues, Smith turned to a third target customer: original equipment manufacturers (OEMs). Adtran would now customize its standard Central Office equipment for manufacturers of telco and corporate-user equipment, producing ''private-label'' versions of its products under the nameplates of manufacturers of video delivery equipment and LAN interconnect equipment as well as information services providers. With its OEM customers underwriting the cost of modifying its products, Adtran collaboratively tested and refined the altered equipment with the OEMs, who often agreed to purchase a minimum number of products, which ranged from dataports, data service units, and other corporate-user products. By 1994, sales to OEMs accounted for 26 percent of sales and Smith took Adtran public in a $38 million offering.

With its three-tiered customer base—telcos, corporate end-users, and OEMs—now identified, Adtran began developing a nationwide sales force and network of equipment resellers and pumped prodigious sums into new product development. Smith's strategy was to assign his engineers the designing of new products with an eye toward their later redesign. When new technologies emerged or competitors' products shifted the playing field, Adtran would be able to enhance its next generation of products quickly and cheaply, allowing the savings to pass on to customers who in turn would reward the company with greater market share. The company's new-product life cycle was reduced to a brisk 18 months.

While AT&T's DDS technology was the backbone of Adtran's first digital products, as early as 1989 it had begun making devices for two new emerging data protocols—ISDN and HDSL. ISDN, short for Integrated Services Digital Network, used the telco's copper-wire phone lines to deliver up to 128,000 bps of text, video, audio, or fax data over a single phone line while simultaneously holding a phone conversation. Realizing the technology's potential, Adtran developed ISDN products for extending and terminating ISDN service from PBXs and Central Office switches to multiple locations. In 1993 it unveiled its ISDN Service Unit product family, the first of its kind on the market, which among other features allowed telco's to support ISDN calls without upgrading to ISDN-capable switches at all their Central Offices. By 1996 Adtran was the leading supplier of ISDN equipment to the RBOCs, with more than one million circuits established.

Although U.S. telcos could use their existing networks to provide roughly 80 percent of their customers with ISDN service, infrastructural limits prevented them from extending it to the remaining 20 percent without new technology. In the early 1990s the Midwestern RBOC, Ameritech, selected Adtran to develop a "Basic Rate ISDN dual loop extender" to push ISDN's range from the conventional limit of 18,000 feet to 29,000 without the use of expensive repeaters. In early 1996, Adtran demonstrated this technology to other U.S. telcos as Total Reach, and by the end of the year GTE, Pacific Bell, and BellSouth had signed on. Between 1995 and 1996 alone, Adtran's 50-odd ISDN products experienced a 41 percent increase in revenues. In 1996, Adtran introduced ISDN terminal adapters that automatically programmed ISDN modems with the correct phone line configuration information, greatly simplifying the ISDN installation process.

HDSL, T1, and POET: 1995–96

Adtran's 1989 introduction of ISDN devices was coupled with its first foray into another new speed-multiplying protocol named HDSL, for High bit-rate Digital Subscriber Line. HDSL emerged as a way of delivering a new data transmission service named T1 that was even faster than ISDN. Where ISDN lines could provide customers with two voice or data lines at up to 128,000 bps, T1 offered up to 24 individual voice or data channels capable of streaming a blistering 1,544,000 bps. HDSL permitted the telco's old-fashioned copper phone lines to carry this deluge of data for more than two miles without the use of expensive signal repeaters. Adtran's first HDSL product family was introduced in late 1993, well before widespread corporate use of the Internet necessitated the need for a reliable medium for quickly sending oceans of data. When the corporate world began to demand high-speed, high-volume data for its internal "intranets" in the mid-1990s, telcos turned to producers like Adtran to come up with a way to more efficiently carry T1 services over their copper phone lines, which had never been designed to transmit so much information.

The solution appeared to be HDSL2, a T1 delivery technology that could transport T1 data within a telco's Local Loop over a single pair of copper phone wires instead of the less efficient double pair required by HDSL. Adtran's HDSL2 solution was named POET, and it promised to reduce signal interference and extend T1's effective transmission distance—thus making T1 service cheaper for Corporate America. Adtran licensed the POET technology to Siemens and adapted it for other emerging network data services such as Frame Relay (an offshoot of Adtran's original data protocol, DDS), Fractional T1 (a T1 variant), and Primary Rate ISDN (an ISDN variant).

"The Right Place at the Right Time": 1997

By mid-1997, tests had revealed that Adtran's POET would not meet the performance specifications of all phone line regions, and such competitors as PairGain and Level One moved to establish another industry standard. Nevertheless, by early 1995 Adtran could claim roughly 15 percent of the $60 million HDSL-based product market in the United States. By 1996, hundreds of thousands of copper T1 lines were operating across the country, and HDSL's share of the installation of these T1 services had grown faster than anyone had expected. The company responded by sinking larger sums into HDSL engineering and technology (for example, developing its own custom HDSL integrated circuits) with the end strategy of controlling as much of the HDSL market as it enjoyed in DDS and ISDN products.

Adtran's runup since its 1994 initial public offering had been eruptive. By July 1996 its stock had peaked at $72 a share, up from some $15 in less than two years. A $50 million project to quadruple its Huntsville plant's production capacity had been announced, by the end of the year sales had broken past the $250 million mark, 125 new products had been launched in 1996 alone, and over a million Adtran-based Local Loops were operating worldwide. The company's investment in engineering and technology resulted in the release of 125 new products during the year. Moreover, only five percent of U.S. Local Loops were digital, suggesting that Adtran's engineers had plenty of room to run. "Our growth had been fueled by the convergence to digital even though the percentage is still small," Smith told *Investor's Business Daily*. "What we're doing now is taking advantage of those trends. It's nice to be lucky enough to be in the right place at the right time. In terms of whether [Adtran's success] is sustainable, that depends on how good of a job we do compared to everybody else in the business."

Unfortunately, perhaps for Adtran "everybody else" included such telecommunications powerhouses as Lucent Technologies, Motorola, and Paradyne. Adtran had enviable market share but its head start on the competition was not insurmountable. Moreover, in 1996 two of Adtran's customers—GTE and Sprint—accounted for 26 percent of its total sales. Worse yet, in 1996 the seven RBOCs claimed 36 percent of its sales, and the Telecommunications Act of 1996 once again allowed them to manufacture telecommunications equipment—Adtran's customers could now become its competitors. With telcos still accounting for 60 percent of its sales (corporate end-users and

OEMs claimed 28 and 12 percent, respectively), this posed no small threat. To stay ahead, Adtran had to keep rolling out the small, lightweight, sturdy products that had fueled its growth. In 1997, for example, it released its innovative Adtran Total Access System (Atlas) 800, a combination digital cross-connect system, ISDN access switch, T1 bandwidth manager, and remote access multiplexer rolled into one. It also had to penetrate the international market it had all but ignored until the mid-1990s. Although its international sales accounted for only 10 percent of total revenues in 1997 it was taking steps to corral overseas customers to the potential tune of 30 to 40 percent of total sales. Adtran had reached the corporate limelight by being the supplier of digital speed solutions to the copper analog telecom world; to stay there it would have to seize just such opportunities.

Further Reading

Breskin, Ira, "Speed Need," *Investor's Business Daily,* March 22, 1996, p. A4.

Elstrom, Peter, "Adtran Inc.," *Investor's Business Daily,* August 10, 1995, p. A5.

Finnerty, Brian, "Data Race," *Investor's Business Daily,* October 31, 1994, p. A6.

Fioravante, Janice, "Adtran Inc.," *Investor's Business Daily,* March 29, 1995, p. A6.

Robert, Don, et al, "No Longer Out of Reach," *Telephony,* October 30, 1995, p. 36.

Veit, Stan, "What Ever Happened to . . . 300-bps Modems?" *Computer Shopper,* July 1996.

—Paul S. Bodine

AirTran Holdings, Inc.

9955 AirTran Blvd.
Orlando, Florida 32827
U.S.A.
(407) 251-5600
Fax: (407) 251-5602
Web site: http://www.airtran.com

Public Company
Incorporated: 1993 as ValuJet, Inc.
Employees: 2,800
Sales: $219.64 million (1996)
Stock Exchanges: NASDAQ
SICs: 4512 Air Transportation, Scheduled

AirTran Holdings, Inc. is the product of the 1997 merger of ValuJet, Inc. with AirWays Corporation, the parent company of AirTran Airways, Inc. The merged operations served more than 40 cities, most in the eastern United States. Financially, ValuJet epitomized success among the budget start-ups of the earlier 1990s—small regional airlines that competed primarily on the basis of low fares. However, the crash of its Flight 592 threatened the credibility and very survival of this entire category of airlines.

The 1990s: The Age of the Start-Ups

Deregulation in the 1980s resulted in the demise of several significant American airlines, including Continental, Eastern, and Pan Am. With the industry dominated by a few surviving giants such as United and American Airlines, several entrants tried their hand at serving specific regional niches, trying either to compete on the basis of improved service and amenities (such as Kiwi International) or lower fares. Using this latter strategy, ValuJet, Inc. became the country's fastest-growing airline.

A group led by Lewis Jordan, a former executive at Continental Airlines, and Lawrence Priddy founded ValuJet, Inc. in 1993 as a no-frills airline. Jordan served as president; the more reserved Priddy, who had previously helped launch Atlantic Southeast Airlines, served as CEO (the two originally met while under the employ of the defunct Southern Airways, also based in Atlanta). Priddy had originally conceptualized ValuJet in 1992 with Maurice Gallagher and Timothy Flynn.

Paper tickets, assigned seats, in-flight meals, and frequent flyer miles were jettisoned. Customers, however, flocked to the carrier, seeking liberation from high ticket prices on the major airlines. Beginning with two planes, ValuJet grew to a fleet of 51 within three years. Its original eight routes (serving Atlanta and Jacksonville, Orlando, and Tampa, Florida) grew to 320.

Employees made do without frills, too. The pay structure was highly incentive-based; base salaries were rather modest: $42,000 for pilots-in-command, $14,000 for flight attendants. In fact, ValuJet only paid pilots when they completed flights. They paid for their own uniforms and even their own training. Executive perquisites were also limited; the corporate headquarters was furnished in an appropriately Spartan fashion: Jordan bragged the furniture came from bargain superstore Office Depot.

The company's critics contended maintenance and safety checks were thrown overboard as well. The least experienced pilots and mechanics were hired in order to save money. The pressure to produce consistently tempted pilots into flying in the face of equipment problems or inclement weather.

The company bought its planes second-hand from major carriers in the U.S. and as far away as Turkey. In order to further preserve capital, it owned no repair facilities or spare parts inventories and subcontracted all maintenance work.

AirTran Airways, a budget carrier like ValuJet, also began flying with a fleet of just two aircraft. Originally part of Mesaba, an affiliate of Northwest Airlines, it acquired tiny Conquest Sun in Fort Lauderdale and became known by the AirTran name in 1994. AirTran Airways found a new owner in September 1995—the holding company AirWays Corp. It would not expand nearly as quickly as ValuJet. It focused on the lower end of the market—leisure traffic to Orlando—and kept a low profile, running only a flight per day on most routes, in order to avoid prompting a fare war with a major airline.

Company Perspectives:

Everybody knew changes would have to be made at ValuJet. Changes in safety procedures, operations, customer service, how we handle reservations. Some big changes and lots of little ones. The changes are part of our commitment to provide a very enjoyable travel experience for a very affordable fare.

One dramatic change is that Atlanta-based ValuJet is merging with Orlando-based AirTran Airways. The new airline will have a fleet of 50 aircraft serving 45 cities and will enable us to better compete against larger airlines. That's important, because when we enter a market, bigger airlines lower their fares to compete with us. But these days, anybody can cut prices. We want to accomplish something more.

Our mission is to deliver affordable, convenient, safe, reliable air transportation to business and leisure travelers. To fulfill this mission, we needed to bring two airlines together to create a new one. More than 2,800 dedicated employees are working hard to make this new airline a success, and satisfy our customers. Our new airline includes product enhancements designed to make air travel a more enjoyable and convenient experience. Customers will soon be able to enjoy our new business class seating, pre-assigned seating and access to our affordable fares through travel agents.

A Too Rapid Ascent in the Mid-1990s

ValuJet accumulated $368 million in 1995 revenues. In spite of its popularity among civilian business travelers, the U.S. Department of Defense turned down the carrier for a contract ferrying military personnel, citing a lack of management competence and organization and substandard maintenance and training procedures. The number of forced landings had grown to 57 in 1995 from 15 the previous year.

On May 11, 1996, ValuJet Flight 592 crashed into the Everglades, killing all 110 people (including five crew members) on board. The FAA eventually determined that the DC-9, which had been bound for Atlanta, was downed by chemical oxygen generators that caught fire within its cargo hold.

The FAA grounded ValuJet on June 17, 1996, after weeks of newly intensified scrutiny. In the meantime, the flight attendants' union called for the ouster of Jordan and Priddy. They were not immediately successful, though in the fall, they moved to background roles as former Continental and TWA executive D. Joseph Corr was brought in as president. The airline's business community backers protested the groundings and urged the FAA to allow ValuJet back in the air.

ValuJet was cleared to resume limited operations—15 of 51 airplanes—in September. The carrier reorganized its maintenance and engineering management structure and revised the pay scale for pilots to be less dependent on performance incentives. It agreed to become recertified in maintenance-related areas, to provide permanent maintenance inspectors, to gain FAA approval before adding new aircraft, notify the FAA of major alterations or repairs, and provide the agency with computerized records. ValuJet also said it would use fewer subcontractors, whom it would be required to audit in the future. The airline also would commit to installing smoke detection systems on all its planes by 1998, two years ahead of an industry-wide federal mandate. In the next six months of operations, ValuJet would lose $39 million. Its sales for the year were $219.6 million. Intensified price competition from Delta Air Lines did not help the carrier.

The year 1996 was a bad one not just for ValuJet but for the entire flock of regional start-up airlines. Public confidence in this segment was shaken in particular; the explosion of TWA Flight 800 in July frightened passengers further. Eventually the major carriers cut fares as well to lure back customers. In its 1996 fiscal year, AirTran Airways, deemed the airline most seriously affected by the confidence crisis, lost $6.9 million. Other factors hurting the company's performance included a spare parts purchase of $2 million and engine replacements that were rendered more costly by the $1.1 million the airline spent to buy stranded passengers' tickets on alternate carriers. In addition, new competition from Delta Express and Southwest Airlines sent AirTran looking for additional hubs. (AirTran used Delta's ground handling service in Orlando and Cincinnati and five Delta gates at the Orlando International Airport.)

A New Name, New Attitude in 1997

The condition of AirTran Airways steadily improved in early 1997. It carried more passengers in May than it ever had before. The company added more than 200 jobs and saw its share price double. It opened new flights into the minor markets that were its focus, and applied for routes connecting some of these with New York City. In June, it teamed up with the commuter airline Comair (25 percent owned by Delta) in a code sharing agreement offering the AirTran Florida Connection to several Comair destinations in Florida and Nassau.

In July 1997, ValuJet Inc. and AirTran Airways announced the merger of their relative holding companies (which would produce fewer FAA complications than merging the operating companies right away). The merger, to become final in the fall of 1997, helped ValuJet sidestep the name's negative connotations resulting from intense media coverage of the Everglade crash. ValuJet's traditional popularity among business travelers also seemed to segue nicely with AirTran's tourist customers. At the time of the merger, ValuJet was operating 30 aircraft.

The AirTran Airways fleet consisted of 10 Boeing 737s. The company, one-third the size of ValuJet, also brought its Orlando maintenance facility to the deal. The airline, based in Orlando, Florida, served 28 cities. ValuJet supplied the funds to allow both carriers to fly more aircraft. ValuJet advanced AirTran $7 million in July 1997 and $5.7 million in September 1997. The company ordered 50 state-of-the-art MD-95 aircraft from McDonnell Douglas for $1 billion; they were scheduled to begin delivery in June 1999.

ValuJet president Joseph Corr became CEO of the new entity. While affordability remained the primary focus, among changes introduced were a new modestly-priced business class service, pre-assigned seating, and travel agent ticket sales.

As Orlando officials began vying to keep the new company's corporate headquarters, AirTran Airlines continued to utilize the ValuJet offices in Atlanta, while AirTran Airways remained at its site in Orlando. Atlanta and Washington, D.C., also wooed the company in hopes of landing planned maintenance and reservations centers as well.

In their new livery, the tail of AirTran jets sported the letter "a," said to mean "affordable." ValuJet achieved $219.64 million in revenues in 1996; AirWays, Inc.'s revenues were $102.62 million for the fiscal year ending in March 1997.

Principal Subsidiaries

AirTran Airlines, Inc.; AirTran Airways, Inc.

Further Reading

Burns, Matthew, "ValuJet Returns to Raleigh with a Smaller Fleet," *Atlanta Business Chronicle,* October 28, 1996.

Byrd, Alan, "AirTran Airlines Seeks Bite of the Big Apple," *Orlando Business Journal,* June 2, 1997.

——, "AirTran Airways Ups the Ante: Washington Is Newest Competitor," *Orlando Business Journal,* August 4, 1997.

——, "AirTran Flying Fuller Planes Than in Past Several Months," *Orlando Business Journal,* November 25, 1996.

——, "AirTran Pulling Out of Nose Dive?" *Orlando Business Journal,* April 28, 1997.

——, "City, County to Offer Incentives to AirTran," *Orlando Business Journal,* July 21, 1997.

——, "Delta Express Reroutes AirTran, Other Airlines," *Orlando Business Journal,* October 14, 1996.

Eckstrom, Kevin, "The ValuJet Merger: Three-Year-Old AirTran Is Small, No-Frills Airline," *Atlanta Journal and Constitution,* July 11, 1997.

Ho, Rodney, "ValuJet Hit with Long List of Demands," *Atlanta Constitution,* June 20, 1996, p. A1.

Newman, Heather, "Start-Up Airlines Face Scrutiny," *Gannett News Service,* July 15, 1996, p. S11.

Schiavo, Mary, and Sabra Chartrand, *Flying Blind, Flying Safe,* New York: Avon, 1997.

Thurston, Scott, "Management Team Taking a Back Seat in ValuJet Merger," *Atlanta Journal and Constitution,* July 13, 1997, p. D7.

——, "A Marriage of Convenience," *Atlanta Journal and Constitution,* July 11, 1997, p. H1.

——, "Top Men at ValuJet: One in the Spotlight, One Behind the Scenes," *Atlanta Journal and Constitution,* May 13, 1996, p. A13.

—Frederick C. Ingram

Electrolux

AKTIEBOLAGET ELECTROLUX

Aktiebolaget Electrolux

Lilla Essingen
S-105 45 Stockholm
Sweden
(08) 736 6000
Fax: (08) 656 4478
Web site: http://www.electrolux.se

Public Company
Incorporated: 1919 as Aktiebolaget Elektrolux
Employees: 112,140
Sales: SKr110 billion (US$16.15 billion) (1996)
Stock Exchanges: Stockholm London Geneva Paris Zurich Basel NASDAQ
SICs: 3524 Lawn & Garden Tractors, Home Lawn & Garden Equipment; 3559 Special Industry Machinery, Not Elsewhere Classified; 3589 Service Industry Machines, Not Elsewhere Classified; 3631 Household Cooking Equipment; 3632 Household Refrigerators and Home & Farm Freezers; 3635 Household Vacuum Cleaners; 3639 Household Appliances, Not Elsewhere Classified

To the average consumer, the name Electrolux says two things: vacuum cleaners and refrigerators. Through expansion, diversification, and a voracious appetite for acquisition, Aktiebolaget Electrolux became a major multinational by the 1980s. It still supplies its traditional products, claiming top position in the European household-appliance market and the number three position in household appliances in the United States (behind Whirlpool and General Electric). These products—which are marketed under such well-known brands as Electrolux, Frigidaire, Zanussi, Eureka, and AEG—accounted for about two-thirds of the company's 1996 turnover. About 10 percent of turnover came from such commercial appliances as food-service equipment for restaurants and institutions and commercial laundry equipment. Nearly 14 percent was derived from sales of outdoor products, including lawn mowers, garden tractors, chainsaws, and leaf blowers, under such brands as Husqvarna, Flymo, Poulan, and Weed Eater. The remaining 10 percent of turnover came from industrial products, whose operations were gradually divested in the 1990s in favor of a concentration on the other three core areas. The Wallenberg family of Sweden owns about half of Electrolux, with holdings dating back to 1956.

Beginnings in Vacuum Cleaners

The Electrolux empire originated in the perspicacity and marketing flair of Axel Wenner-Gren, who spotted the potential of the mobile vacuum cleaner only a few years after its invention by Englishman H. C. Booth in 1901. In 1910 the young Wenner-Gren bought a part share in the European agent of a U.S. company producing one of the early vacuum cleaners, the clumsy Santo Staubsauger. After a couple of years as a Santo salesman for the German-based agent, Wenner-Gren sold his share of the company and returned to Sweden, where the building blocks for the future Electrolux, Lux and Elektromekaniska AB, were already in place.

Sven Carlstedt had formed Elektromekaniska in 1910 to manufacture motors for a vacuum cleaner based on the Santo, which was produced by Swedish engineer Eberhardt Seger. Since its founding in 1901, Lux had manufactured kerosene lamps. Now confronted with a shrinking market owing to the introduction of electric lighting, Lux head, C. G. Lindblom, proposed to Sven Carlstedt that the two companies form a joint venture for the production and marketing of a new vacuum cleaner.

In 1912 Wenner-Gren became the agent for the Lux 1 vacuum cleaner in Germany, subsequently taking on the United Kingdom and France. Over the next few years Wenner-Gren's role in the company grew, and the machine gradually became lighter and more ergonomic. Wenner-Gren foresaw a potential sales bonanza in Europe after the end of World War I. Initially unable to persuade his colleagues to step up production capacity, he overcame their reluctance by guaranteeing a minimum sales figure through his own sales company, Svenska Elektron (later known as Finans AB Svetro).

Company Perspectives:

Electrolux is one of the world's leading manufacturers of indoor and outdoor household appliances, and of corresponding products for commercial users. These products make daily tasks easier and more convenient in millions of homes throughout the world. Every year, consumers in almost 100 countries buy more than 55 million Group products. More than 90% of Electrolux sales are outside Sweden, and the Group operates more than 500 companies in over 60 countries.

Lux and Elektromekaniska merged in 1919 as Aktiebolaget Elektrolux (the spelling was changed to Electrolux in 1957). Wenner-Gren became president and a major shareholder of the new company. In 1921 the Lux V was introduced. This new model resembled a modern cylindrical vacuum cleaner, but it glided along the floor on ski-like runners instead of wheels. The Lux V was to present serious competition to the upright Hoover machines in the 1920s.

The convenience and attractive styling of its product helped to get the new company off to a promising start, but the salesmanship of Electrolux's president probably played an even bigger part. Wenner-Gren was a great believer in the door-to-door sales techniques already espoused by competitors such as Hoover in the United States. Vacuum cleaners were demonstrated to potential customers in their own homes, and buyers were allowed to pay for their machines by installments. Wenner-Gren knew how to get the best out of his sales force.

To today's sales managers, sales training, competitions, and slogans like "Every home an Electrolux home" are familiar methods of boosting sales, but when Wenner-Gren introduced them they were revolutionary. He also believed in leading from the front. The story of how he sold a vacuum cleaner to the Vatican is part of company mythology. Four competitors demonstrated their machines first, each vacuuming their allocated area of carpet. When Wenner-Gren's turn came, instead of vacuuming the fifth area, he went over the first four again. The resultant bagful of dust persuaded the pope to add his palace to the growing number of Electrolux homes. Advertising, too, was imaginative. Not only did Electrolux make extensive use of the press, but in the late 1920s, citizens of Stockholm, Berlin, and London were liable to encounter bizarre vacuum cleaner-shaped cars in the streets.

Bizarre or not, the sales methods worked, and the company grew. Throughout the 1920s, new sales companies sprang up, not only all over Europe but also in the United States in 1924, Australia in 1925, and South America. Many of these were financed by Wenner-Gren himself rather than by Electrolux in Sweden. Vacuum cleaner-manufacturing plants also started to open overseas, first in Berlin in 1926 and a year later in Luton, England, and Courbevoie, France.

By 1928 Electrolux had sales of SKr70 million. It had five manufacturing plants, 350 worldwide offices, and 20 subsidiaries. In spite of this geographic expansion, the company was often short of funds, partly because of the system of payment by installments. It became clear that further growth would require increased capital, and it was decided to float the company on the London Stock Exchange and to issue more shares. Prior to flotation in 1928, Electrolux bought out many of the related companies owned by Wenner-Gren, though he retained his minority shareholding in the American Electrolux Corporation until 1949.

Flotation on the Stockholm stock exchange was postponed until 1930 owing to the stock market crash. When the shares did appear they were greeted with some mistrust, as it was thought that the company was overvalued and that sales would suffer during the anticipated recession. These doubts, however, were to prove unfounded.

Diversified into Refrigerators in the Mid-1920s

During the 1920s Electrolux introduced a number of new products, including floor-polishers, a natural progression from vacuum cleaners, which were brought out in 1927. However, the main diversification of the 1920s came through the acquisition in 1925 of Arctic, a company manufacturing a novel machine, the absorption refrigerator. This type of refrigerator has no moving parts, though early models required connection to a source of running water. Power can be provided by electricity, gas, or kerosene as opposed to the compression method of refrigeration, which relies on electric power. Early compressors were noisy and bulky, so the new Electrolux system had several advantages over its competitors' compression refrigerators.

A new air-cooled version of Electrolux's absorption refrigerators was introduced in 1931, and by 1936 more than one million had been sold. Demand for the machines grew as restrictions were placed on the use of food preservatives by legislation such as the United Kingdom Food Preservative Act of 1927. In the United States, Servel Inc. had acquired a license to manufacture Electrolux's refrigerators.

Electrolux's original vacuum cleaner factory on Lilla Essingen was devastated by fire in 1936. When it was rebuilt the following year, the opportunity was taken to fit it with the latest equipment and to install a central research laboratory.

In 1926 Wenner-Gren became chairman of the board, with Ernst Aurell taking over as president. During the 1930s Wenner-Gren remained chairman but reduced his involvement in the running of the company, prior to resigning from his post in 1939. Harry G. Faulkner, a British accountant who had been instrumental in the company's consolidation prior to the 1928 flotation, succeeded Aurell in 1930 and remained president throughout the 1930s.

With intensive marketing and continued investment in research and development, Electrolux rode out the Great Depression. By 1939 annual sales stood at SKr80 million. In 1939 Gustaf Sahlin, former president of the United States Electrolux Corporation, took over the presidency of the parent company from Faulkner. Throughout World War II, despite the loss of some manufacturing plants, Electrolux managed to maintain many of its usual activities, opening operations in Australia, Venezuela, and Colombia. At home in Sweden, it acquired companies in the fields of commercial laundry equipment and outboard motors. Much energy, however, was diverted into the war effort, including the manufacture of munitions and of air cleaners for the Swedish forces.

After the war Electrolux resumed its normal operations, initially under Elon V. Ekman, who became president in 1951, and from 1963 to 1967 under his successor Harry Wennberg. The period was not without setbacks, however. Many subsidiaries that had been opened in eastern European countries before the war disappeared from view behind the Iron Curtain. In addition, despite a British government contract to supply 50,000 built-in absorption refrigerators for prefabricated temporary houses, the company began to face problems in the refrigerator market. Compression technology had advanced and was proving more effective for the larger refrigerators that consumers were now demanding. Though at first the company concentrated on improving the design of the absorption refrigerator, Electrolux was eventually obliged to adopt compression technology.

Meanwhile, diversification continued. During the 1950s Electrolux started making household washing machines and dishwashers, and floor-cleaning-equipment production was extended to an increasing number of countries, including Brazil and Norway. When, in 1956, Axel Wenner-Gren sold his remaining shares in Electrolux to Wallenberg, a Swedish finance group, annual turnover exceeded SKr500 million. The association with Wallenberg has often stood Electrolux in good stead, helping, for example, to arrange overseas funding and to insulate the group from any hostile takeover bids.

In 1962, in an attempt to solve its refrigerator problems, Electrolux bought the Swedish firm of ElektroHelios. This firm, founded in 1919, had a major share of the Scandinavian market in compressor refrigerators and freezers, as well as making stoves. In the year following the acquisition, Electrolux launched a wide range of food-storage equipment, putting it in a strong position to benefit from the demands generated by the flourishing frozen-food industry.

Series of Major Acquisitions from Late 1960s Through Late 1980s

Until the 1960s Electrolux had continued to operate along the lines conceived by Wenner-Gren in the early years. A new phase began in 1967, when Hans Werthén was recruited from Ericsson, another member of the Wallenberg group of companies. Werthén remained with Electrolux for over 25 years, first as president, and from 1975 to 1991 as chairman, with Gösta Bystedt and then Anders Scharp succeeding him as president. Under this regime, a series of momentous acquisitions was to allow Electrolux to multiply its turnover by a factor of 60 in 20 years.

When Werthén took over management of the Electrolux group the company was in the doldrums; it had run into internal and external problems, and its technology was outmoded. Electrolux, an international company, had not been effectively integrated with its acquisition ElektroHelios, which still focused on the Scandinavian market. In many ways the merged companies had continued to behave as if they were still competitors, resulting in a net loss of market share in the refrigerator market. Only the vacuum cleaners were profitable: to use Werthén's own words, "they represented 125% of the profits."

Approaching the problem from a new perspective, Werthén managed to resolve the Electrolux-ElektroHelios conflict and get rid of the organizational overlap. His new head of production, Anders Scharp, set about updating production technology to challenge the much more advanced techniques he had seen in U.S. appliance factories. Werthén believed that Electrolux's problems could not be overcome simply by operational improvements. The company had a more fundamental problem: size.

As Werthén saw it, Electrolux was neither small enough to be a niche player, nor large enough to gain the economies of scale it needed to compete with such giants as Philips and AEG. Growth was the only way forward, and in the overcrowded market place for household goods, growth meant acquisitions.

The initial focus was on Scandinavia. One small competitor after another, many of them struggling for survival, was bought up by the growing company. The Norwegian stove manufacturer Elektra, the Danish white goods company Atlas, and the Finnish stove maker Slev were among the first acquisitions of the late 1960s. Soon Electrolux was shopping for competitors outside Scandinavia. The 1974 acquisition of Eureka, one of the longest-established vacuum cleaner companies in the United States, gave Electrolux a large slice of a valuable market overnight.

At around this time there were glimmerings of hope for the reemergence of the absorption refrigerator. The quiet-running units were ideally suited to installation in smaller living spaces, such as mobile homes and hotel rooms. Electrolux managers soon sensed these new opportunities. After taking over competitors Kreft (of Luxembourg) and Siegas (of Germany) in 1972, the group became world leader in this sector.

In addition to expanding its share of the company's existing markets, Electrolux soon started to see acquisitions as a way of entering new areas, particularly those related to existing product lines. Electrolux acquired the British lawnmower manufacturer Flymo in 1968 because Werthén saw lawnmowing as an activity allied to floor cleaning. The provision of cleaning services seemed a logical extension to the production of cleaning equipment, prompting the purchase of a half share in the Swedish cleaning company ASAB.

Buying up the venerable Swedish firm of Husqvarna in 1978 gave Electrolux not only a new pool of expertise in commercial refrigeration, but also a flourishing chainsaw-manufacturing concern, which complemented its interests in outdoor equipment. Taking over a clutch of other chainsaw manufacturers over the following decade—including the U.S. firm Poulan/Weed Eater in 1986—enabled Electrolux to claim leadership of the worldwide chainsaw market. The outdoor products sector was further strengthened and broadened through the acquisitions of American Yard Products in 1988 and of Allegretti & Co., a U.S. maker of battery-driven garden tools, in 1990.

This program of acquisitions brought some more radical departures from existing product lines. In 1973 Electrolux bought Facit, a Swedish office equipment company. The deal also brought to Electrolux the production of Ballingslöv kitchen and bathroom cabinets. Initial doubts about whether Electrolux had the know-how to manage a high-tech company proved unfounded.

The purchase of Swedish metal producer Gränges was greeted with equal skepticism, since again the connection between the new and existing businesses appeared to be rather tenuous. Gränges was seen as a troubled company, but when Electrolux bought it in 1980, Werthén had already been chairman of its board for three years and had overseen a marked upturn in its fortunes. Gränges became part of Electrolux in 1980, and by the late 1980s Gränges' aluminum products and car seat belts represented a major aspect of Electrolux's business, although other parts of Gränges were sold off.

Under the presidency of Anders Scharp, which began in 1981, Electrolux's program of acquisitions began to focus on the consolidation and expansion of existing lines. Takeovers became increasingly ambitious as Electrolux saw within its reach the chance to become one of the world leaders in household appliances. Major steps towards this goal were the acquisitions of Zanussi in Italy, White Consolidated in the United States (the third-largest white goods company in that country), and the white goods and catering equipment divisions of the United Kingdom's Thorn EMI, in 1984, 1986, and 1987, respectively.

Through the years, Electrolux gained a reputation for buying only when the price was right and for turning around sick companies, even at the cost of heavy staff cuts and management shake-ups. As the *Wall Street Journal* pointed out in 1986 in a piece about the acquisition of White Consolidated, the group balance sheet looked unhealthy immediately after some of the larger acquisitions, showing an equity-asset ratio as low as 21 percent.

Electrolux bounced back confidently, making divestments as well as acquisitions. One of Werthén's earliest acts as president had been the 1968 sale of AB Electrolux's minority shareholding in the United States Electrolux Corporation to Consolidated Foods, which raised SKr300 million, although the subsequent Eureka purchase had placed the company in the curious position of competing against its own brand name. Management continued this policy of judicious divestment following acquisitions, when it was considered that all or part of the new member did not fit in with the group's strategy. Facit, for instance, was sold to Ericsson in 1983, and shortly after the purchase of White Consolidated, its machine-tool division, White Machine Tools, was sold off.

Another method of raising cash was through the sale of assets, although Electrolux acquisitions were not primarily motivated by a desire to strip assets. In the case of Husqvarna, the purchase price of SKr120 million was more than covered within six months by the sale of its land and other property. A third way of recovering the costs of acquisition was the use of a troubled company's accumulated losses wherever possible to reduce the group's tax liability. This was a major incentive in the acquisition of Gränges.

Not every company was delighted to hear Electrolux knocking on its door. Many a takeover was resisted by the target company, although Electrolux was also sometimes called in to rescue a troubled company—as happened with Zanussi—or asked to act as a white knight—notably for the U.S. household appliance company Tappan in 1979.

Geographic Expansion and Restructurings Marked 1990s

The 1990s brought major changes to Electrolux, spearheaded by a new management team. Werthén resigned as chairman in early 1991, Scharp became chairman and CEO, and Leif Johansson was named president of the firm, taking over as CEO himself in 1994. During Werthén's long reign, Electrolux had grown tremendously through acquisitions but had failed to effectively consolidate the acquired operations into existing ones. The result was an unwieldy array of brands, which each had to be supported with separate production and marketing operations. Electrolux was further hurt in the early 1990s by an economic downturn in its core European and North American operations and by the maturing of the white goods sectors in those same markets, which intensified competition. All told, profits for Electrolux from 1990 through 1994 were much lower than the heights reached during the late 1980s. The new management team responded by seeking out new markets for its core products, by gradually divesting its noncore industrial products operations, and by streamlining its remaining business units.

Electrolux targeted Eastern Europe, Asia, South America, the Middle East, and southern Africa in its 1990s push for global growth. The company had already, in 1989, arranged for Sharp Corporation to distribute some of Electrolux's products in Japan. Subsequent moves in Asia included the setting up of joint ventures in China for the manufacture of compressors, vacuum cleaners, and water purifiers, and the acquisition of majority stakes in refrigerator and washing machine factories in India. In January 1996 another Chinese joint venture was established for the production of refrigerators and freezers for commercial users. The newly opened markets of Eastern Europe were first targeted with the 1991 purchase of the Hungarian white goods company Lehel. A 1995 joint venture with Poland's Myszkow FNE Swiatowit began making washing machines under the Zanussi brand. In Latin America, where Whirlpool was dominant, Electrolux acquired 99 percent of Refrigeração Paraná S.A. (Refripar) in 1996. Refripar (soon renamed Electrolux do Brazil) held the number two position among Brazilian white goods companies. Also in 1996, Electrolux purchased a 20 percent stake in Atlas Eléctrica S.A. of Costa Rica, the leading producer of refrigerators and stoves in Central America. By 1994, about 10 percent of Electrolux's sales came from outside the European Union and North America. This figure more than doubled by 1996 to 20.4 percent, with non-EU Europe accounting for seven percent, Latin America for 6.4 percent, Asia for 5.1 percent, Oceania for one percent, and Africa for 0.9 percent.

While undergoing this global expansion, Electrolux also moved gradually to concentrate solely on three core sectors: household appliances, commercial appliances, and outdoor products. Profits in the company's industrial products sector were falling and Scharp and Johansson determined that these noncore operations should be jettisoned. The culmination of this process came in 1996 and 1997, with the divestment of the Constructor group, producers of materials-handling equipment;

the sale of the Swedish electronics operations of Electrolux Electronics, and a sewing machines unit; and the spinoff of Gränges to the public. The final divestment came in August 1997 when Electrolux's goods protection operation, which sold tarpaulins and storage halls, was sold to MVI, a privately owned investment fund.

Electrolux greatly reduced its acquisitions activity in the European Union and North America in the 1990s, although there was one major addition. In 1992 the company bought a 10 percent stake in AEG Hausgeräte, the household appliance division of Germany's Daimler-Benz. This stake was increased to 20 percent in 1993 and the following year Electrolux purchased the remaining 80 percent for about US$437 million. The purchase brought the company another strong European brand, which fit well into a renewed brand strategy for Electrolux. The company sought to position the Electrolux brand as a global brand and Electrolux, Zanussi, and AEG as pan-European brands, while continuing to maintain strong local brands such as Faure in France and Tricity Bendix in the United Kingdom.

Along with the new brand strategy, Electrolux began in 1996 to reduce its fragmented operations and become more efficient. A pan-European logistics function was set up for white goods and floor-care products. In late 1996 the company's North American white goods operation, Frigidaire Company, was combined with the two North American outdoor products companies, Poulan/Weed Eater and American Yard Products, to form Frigidaire Home Products. Merging these operations made strategic sense since the trend in retailing was toward single retailers selling both indoor and outdoor appliances. Similar consolidations were planned for Electrolux's operations elsewhere in the world.

In April 1997 Johansson left Electrolux to become the chief executive at Volvo AB. Replacing him as Electrolux president and CEO was Michael Treschow, who had been president and CEO at Atlas Copco AB, a maker of industrial equipment and, like Electrolux, part of the Wallenberg dynasty. It was left to Treschow to announce, in June 1997, a major restructuring plan, which had already been agreed upon before he took over. Over a two-year period, Electrolux would lay off 12,000 of its workers (11 percent of its workforce) and close 25 plants and 50 warehouses (half of its global total), with the reductions coming mainly in Europe and North America. A charge of SKr2.5 billion (US$323 million) was incurred as the result of the restructuring in the second quarter of 1997.

The streamlining efforts of the 1990s were a clear outgrowth of the somewhat haphazard expansion of the preceding two decades. With its program of global expansion, a new emphasis on operating efficiency, and a collection of very strong brands, Electrolux appeared to have a formula for not just competing but thriving in the 21st century.

Principal Subsidiaries

Electrolux Contracting AB; Husqvarna AB; Electrolux Storkök AB; Electrolux Danmark A/S (Denmark); Oy Electrolux AB (Finland); Electrolux S.A. (France); Electrolux Associated Co. B.V. (The Netherlands); Electrolux Holding B.V. (The Netherlands); Electrolux Holding AG (Switzerland); Electrolux UK Ltd.; Electrolux Deutschland GmbH (Germany); FHP Motors GmbH (Germany; 71.4%); FHP Motors Beteiligungsverwaltungs-GmbH (Germany; 71.4%); Lehel Hütögepgyar Kft (Hungary; 42.8%); Electrolux Austria G.m.b.H. (Austria); Euro White Investment Corp. (Canada; 83.7%); White Consolidated Industries, Inc. (U.S.A.); Electrolux Ltda. (Brazil; 99.9%); Mexectro, S.A. de CV (Mexico); Maharaja International Ltd. (India; 51%); Electrolux (China) Co., Ltd., China; Electrolux Thailand Co. Ltd. (49%).

Further Reading

Brown-Humes, Christopher, "Electrolux to Plug into Households in Opening Markets," *Financial Times,* April 27, 1995, p. 25.

Burt, Tim, "Electrolux Set to Pull Out of Industrial Goods," *Financial Times,* October 30, 1996, p. 28.

Calian, Sara, "Electrolux to Cut Force by 11%, Mainly in North America, Europe," *Wall Street Journal,* June 13, 1997, p. A15.

Canedy, Dana, "Electrolux to Cut 12,000 Workers and Shut Plants," *New York Times,* June 13, 1997, p. D2.

"Electrolux Expects to Be No. 1 Appliance Maker," *Appliance Manufacturer,* February 1994, p. 20.

"Electrolux Plots a New Strategy," *Housewares,* January 1, 1990, p. 78.

Electrolux: Two Epochs That Shaped a Worldwide Group, Stockholm: Electrolux, 1989.

Gordon, Bob, *Early Electrical Appliances,* Princes Risborough, United Kingdom: Shire Publications Ltd., 1984.

Jancsurak, Joe, "Big Plans for Europe's Big Three," *Appliance Manufacturer,* April 1995, pp. 26–30.

Kapstein, Jonathan, and Zachary Schiller, "The Fast-Spinning Machine That Blew a Gasket," *Business Week,* September 10, 1990, pp. 50, 52.

Lorenz, Christopher, "The Birth of a 'Transnational,' " *Financial Times,* June 19, 1989.

McGrath, Neal, "New Broom Sweeps into Asia," *Asian Business,* March 1996, p. 22.

McIvor, Greg, "Electrolux Comes Under the Scalpel," *Financial Times,* October 29, 1997, p. 19.

Moss, Nicholas, and Hale Richards, "Mike the Knife Cuts Deep," *European,* June 19, 1997, p. 17.

"The Real Head of the Household," *Director,* November 1996, p. 17.

Reed, Stanley, "The Wallenbergs' New Blood," *Business Week,* October 20, 1997, pp. 98, 102.

Sparke, Penny, *Electrical Appliances: Twentieth-Century Design,* New York: E. P. Dutton, 1987.

"Sweden's Electrolux Plans for Expansion into Southeast Asia," *Wall Street Journal,* January 4, 1995, p. B7.

Tully, Shawn, "Electrolux Wants a Clean Sweep," *Fortune,* August 18, 1986, p. 60.

Zweig, Jason, "Cleaning Up," *Forbes,* December 11, 1989, p. 302.

—Alison Classe
—updated by David E. Salamie

AlliedSignal Inc.

101 Columbia Road
Morristown, New Jersey 07962-2497
U.S.A.
(973) 455-2000
Fax: (973) 455-4807
Web site: http://www.alliedsignal.com

Public Company
Incorporated: 1920 as the Allied Chemical & Dye Corporation
Employees: 76,600
Sales: $13.97 billion (1996)
Stock Exchanges: New York Pacific Midwest Amsterdam Basel Frankfurt Geneva London Paris Zurich
SICs: 2819 Industrial Inorganic Chemicals, Not Elsewhere Classified; 2821 Plastics Materials, Nonvulcanizable Elastomers & Synthetic Resins; 2823 Cellulosic Man-Made Fibers; 2824 Synthetic Organic Fibers Except Cellulosic; 2869 Industrial Organic Chemicals, Not Elsewhere Classified; 2899 Chemicals & Chemical Preparations, Not Elsewhere Classified; 3081 Unsupported Plastics Film & Sheet; 3083 Laminated Plastics, Plate, Sheet & Profile Shapes; 3089 Plastic Products, Not Elsewhere Classified; 3492 Fluid Power Valves & Hose Fittings; 3511 Steam, Gas & Hydraulic Turbines; 3593 Fluid Power Cylinders & Actuators; 3594 Fluid Power Pumps & Motors; 3672 Printed Circuit Boards; 3714 Motor Vehicle Parts & Accessories; 3724 Aircraft Engines & Engine Parts; 3728 Aircraft Parts & Auxiliary Equipment, Not Elsewhere Classified; 3812 Navigation, Guidance, Search & Detection Systems & Instruments; 5013 Motor Vehicle Supplies & New Parts; 5015 Motor Vehicle Parts, Used

AlliedSignal Inc., formed from the acquisition of Signal Companies, Inc. by Allied Corporation on August 6, 1985, is one of the largest industrial corporations in the world. The company provides a wide range of products for many industries, including aerospace and automotive parts, chemicals, fibers, plastics, and advanced materials. AlliedSignal has its roots in the chemical industry and has had experiences from its earliest days in acquiring and holding subsidiaries. It may be said that Allied-Signal, formerly Allied, was born large and has been gaining ground ever since.

Five Companies Merged to Form Allied in 1920

The outbreak of World War I convinced several executives in the fledgling American chemical industry that the United States should contest the German lead in this field. Among them were Dr. William H. Nichols, a respected chemist and president of General Chemical Company; Eugene Meyer, a publisher and financier; and Meyer's protégé, Orlando F. Weber. Meyer's efforts bore fruit on December 17, 1920, with the formation of the Allied Chemical & Dye Corporation, a merger of five companies which among them provided the new company with four basic ingredients of the chemical industry of the day: acids, alkalies, coal tar, and nitrogen. The acids were furnished by General Chemical, founded in 1899, whose president, Dr. Nichols, became Allied's first chairman. The alkalies were contributed by the Solvay Process Company, founded in 1881, and, like General Chemical, the leading American company in its field at the time of the creation of Allied. The Barrett Company, founded in 1858, was by 1920 the largest manufacturer of coal tar products in the United States, while Semet-Solvay, founded in 1895, was a builder and operator of coke ovens, a byproduct of which is coal tar. The National Aniline & Chemical Company, founded in 1917, at first merely supplied aniline oil, a substance used in making dyes, but its head, Orlando F. Weber, became Nichols's successor and moved the new company into the production of nitrogen.

Although it was Eugene Meyer's financial genius that had created Allied, it was Weber's personality and management style that influenced Allied's methods of doing business for generations to come, for good and for ill. Orlando Franklin Weber was born on October 6, 1878, in Grafton, Wisconsin. His father was a secretary of the Federated Trades Council in Mil-

Company Perspectives:

Our vision: We will be one of the world's premier companies, distinctive and successful in everything we do.

waukee and a socialist labor leader. The younger Weber, however, was drawn to private enterprise. He first opened a bicycle shop and then went into the automobile business, starting an agency in Chicago for the Pope-Toledo car in 1902. From Chicago he moved to Detroit and then to New York where he came to the attention of Meyer. Meyer put Weber in charge of the 1915 reorganization of Maxwell, an early automobile company whose name was to linger in the public mind long after the company folded, thanks to the jokes of Jack Benny. Weber followed Meyer into the War Finance Corporation during World War I and, as a result, became interested in the chemical industry. Since Weber's National Aniline had come through the war in the best financial shape of the five companies that formed Allied, it was only natural that Meyer should turn to his young associate to run the new chemical company.

Weber, first as president then as chairman, appropriated funds for a large plant to be built at Hopewell, Virginia, to fix nitrogen from the air for the production of synthetic ammonia. Ammonia could be turned into nitric acid which, when combined with the soda ash made by the Solvay component of Allied, produces sodium nitrate, a substance with an agricultural use as fertilizer and a military use as an ingredient in explosives. By the end of the 1920s Allied was doing a thriving business making and selling basic chemicals to the rest of American industry.

Important as this achievement was, it was on the financial aspect of running the company that Orlando Weber's personality left its most enduring mark. Weber was a mathematical genius who had a grasp of the most complicated and detailed economic theories and who could, when called upon, discuss them by the hour with no notes. He was also highly secretive, keeping vital information about the company locked up in his personal safe and sharing this information with as few people in company management as possible. He was regarded by many of those that knew him as an autocrat who refused to spend any more of his company's money than absolutely necessary.

The beneficial consequences of this unusual collection of personality traits was that, since Weber was a strong believer in a large reserve of liquid assets, Allied was able to survive the Great Depression relatively unscathed. From 1921 through 1939 Allied had no funded debt, never borrowed from banks, and paid a dividend every year, including 1932, the worst year of the Depression. The harmful consequences of Weber's eccentric personality were, first of all, a refusal by Allied to engage in basic research leading to new products. Weber justified this decision by maintaining that he did not want to compete with the companies that were Allied's customers. This policy, however, left Allied with a shrinking share of the market after World War II when new chemical products were introduced. Secondly, Weber's penchant for secrecy got him into trouble with his stockholders, to whom he refused to issue detailed reports, and eventually with the Securities and Exchange Commission which, in 1934, charged him with failing to provide enough information to allow government agencies to determine whether Allied was making or losing money. Weber justified his reticence by claiming that he needed to protect company secrets. Nevertheless, this secrecy, combined with his autocracy, resulted in the fact that the highest executives in the company were not conversant with the overall operation of the company when he retired in 1935. This gap in expertise was to plague Allied for the next 30 years.

Weber's autocracy took many forms, some petty and others significant. During his tenure, and for several years thereafter, Allied executives were forbidden to have their pictures taken for the media, forbidden to allow their biographies to appear in *Who's Who in America,* and forbidden to take part in meetings of trade associations. More significantly, lateral communication between executives within the company was made cumbersome. If, for example, the plant manager for ammonia wished to speak with the plant manager for soda ash, then each manager had to ask permission from their respective vice-presidents in order for the conversation to take place. The vice-presidents, in turn, would have to ask Weber. Weber himself could make this system work because he was the original guiding spirit of the company and consequently knew where each piece of the mosaic of company operations fit. When he left, however, Allied's corporate bureaucracy remained in place without anyone of Weber's talents to organize all the pieces.

Post-Weber Years Were Ones of Decline

Weber himself was the cause of this knowledge vacuum, as it were, at Allied. In order to keep Charles Nichols, son of the scholarly Dr. Nichols, and the Solvay family from taking control of the company, Weber put Allied in the hands of accountants. These accountants knew little of the chemical industry but were the next three chairmen of Allied: Henry Atherton, Fred Emmerich, and Glen B. Miller.

During their term of office, from 1935 to 1959, Allied made money—particularly during World War II—because basic chemicals were essential to the war effort, but its plants became obsolete. In 1935, under the chairmanship of Emmerich, Allied borrowed $200 million to modernize its plants. Emmerich found himself unable to update company policy, however, because division heads had acquired complete autonomy. No vice-president could make any decision without the concurrence of every other vice-president.

Glen B. Miller, Emmerich's successor, created the jobs of research vice-president and marketing vice-president, positions that had not existed at Allied previously. The company continued to drift without any coherent company policy or long-term strategy, however, because of the advanced age of its management. Kirby H. Fisk, who had experience in insurance and finance, was put in charge in 1959 and arranged a merger with Union Texas Natural Gas in 1962. Fisk then died of a heart attack, and Allied's board could not agree on a successor. A troika emerged: Chester M. Brown, who had a background in operations, became president and chief executive officer; Harry S. Ferguson, the accountants' champion, became chief administrative officer and chairman of the executive committee; and Howard Marshall, head of Union Texas before the merger, continued to run the petroleum concern but now with a strong voice in Allied's boardroom. Since there was no agreement as to who should be chairman of the board, the position was left vacant. Finally, Frederick Beebe, a member of Allied's board representing the interests of Eugene Meyer (Weber's mentor), set in motion the complicated legal machinery that reorganized the board of directors and brought in John T. Connor, a former Secretary of Commerce under Lyndon Johnson, to be president in 1967 and chairman of the board in 1969.

Recovery Began in Late 1960s

The accession of Connor marked the beginning of Allied's recovery. Connor found that Allied showed earnings on paper during the terms of his predecessors by means of unorthodox accounting methods, all perfectly legal but masking the fact that Allied had slipped from first to sixth place in the American chemical industry. In the 12 years of his involvement with Allied, Connor improved the corporate staff by hiring his own people, appropriated larger expenditures for the company's more profitable businesses, such as oil and gas, and moved the company away from its orientation on basic chemicals and toward intermediate and end products that utilize chemicals.

In May 1979 Edward L. Hennessy, Jr., arrived on the scene to further Allied's recovery and turn it into Allied-Signal, a more dynamic and promising company than its predecessors. Whether by accident or design, Allied's board chose as the new chairman of the board, president, and CEO a leader whose personality and abilities were similar to those traits of Orlando Weber's that proved beneficial to the company. Like Weber, Hennessy was an expert at mathematics, careful with corporate assets, and decisive. Unlike Weber, however, Hennessy was direct and explicit rather than secretive (though at times somewhat brusque) and, more importantly, devoted to the research and development that Weber shunned.

After taking charge, Hennessy directed Allied to the forefront of scientific and technological advances, sometimes at the expense of the chemical business conducted by Allied at the time of its formation. In September 1979, for instance, Allied discontinued its operations in coke, coal, and paving materials, selling its paving materials business, its Detroit, Michigan, and Ashland, Kentucky, coke plants, and two coal mines. Hennessy followed the lead of Connor in this policy, who had sold off the Barrett Company in 1967. These moves were prudent, since more money could be made in other areas, but they so changed the nature of the company's business that it became misleading to think of the modern Allied-Signal as primarily a chemical company.

Hennessy's positive contributions were largely in the area of acquiring high-tech businesses: Eltra in 1979, Bendix in 1983 (as a result of that company's ill-starred attempt to take over Martin Marietta), and Signal Companies, Inc., in 1985. Subsequently, Allied-Signal's business was conducted in three segments: aerospace/electronics (later known as just aerospace), automotive, and engineered materials. In 1985 the aerospace/electronics segment accounted for 39 percent of Allied-Signal's revenues, the automotive segment for 27 percent, and the engineered materials segment for 22 percent.

In 1985 Allied-Signal lost $279 million, the first loss in the company's history. This loss was attributed by Hennessy to the establishment of The Henley Group, Inc., a company formed from all of Allied-Signal's businesses outside the three business segments mentioned above, and to restructuring the bureaucracy of the company to a more modern configuration (all told, the company took $725 million in write-offs in 1985). In spite of this loss, sales in the aerospace/electronics segment rose 27 percent in 1985 and edged up one percent in the engineered materials segment. Sales in the automotive segment (components for brake systems, air and fuel filters, turbocharging equipment, and spark plugs) declined by four percent.

Hennessy remained Allied-Signal's CEO until July 1991 (and was chairman until year-end 1991). Although he had streamlined the company considerably through numerous divestments, including the 1986 spinoff of Henley and the sale of 7 more subsidiaries in 1987 for a total of $1.8 billion, and had increased revenues to a peak of $12.34 billion in 1990, Hennessy did not—according to many observers—pay enough attention to the company's profitability and allowed company debt to reach dangerously high levels. During the late 1980s and in 1990, Allied-Signal's after-tax return on sales were only in the 3.7 to 4.4 percent range; in 1991 the company was hurt further by the recession and it posted a net loss of $273 million. Meanwhile, long-term debt as a percent of total capital ranged from 30.8 to 34.9 percent.

Bossidy Era (1992–) Brought Host of Transformations

Larry Bossidy, the person brought in to succeed Hennessy, moved boldly and ruthlessly to transform AlliedSignal in a few short years (the hyphen in the company name was dropped in 1993). Bossidy had spent 34 years at General Electric Co., moving to AlliedSignal after having ascended to the position of vice-chairman—number two to GE's chairman, Jack F. Welch, Jr., a well-known slash-and-burn type manager.

Bossidy quickly initiated a housecleaning at AlliedSignal, most evident in the decline in the company workforce from 98,300 employees in 1991 to just 76,600 in 1996. Unprofitable business units were jettisoned; many of these were small, but a few were quite significant: the 1992 sale of the company's remaining 39 percent stake in Union Texas Petroleum for $940 million in net proceeds; the April 1996 sale of its braking business to Robert Bosch GmbH for $1.5 billion; and the November 1997 sale of its safety restraints business to BREED Technologies, Inc. for $710 million in cash. Capital spending was slashed, and Bossidy worked to change the corporate culture into a less bureaucratic, more team-oriented one, with resulting annual increases in productivity of almost six percent. These and other streamlining moves resulted in an AlliedSignal that was more profitable—after-tax return on sales was 7.3 percent in 1996—and less burdened by debt, as long-term debt as a percent of total capital was cut to 22.2 percent by 1996.

Under Bossidy's leadership, AlliedSignal also became much more selective with its acquisitions. Major acquisitions of note were limited to that of the $375 million purchase of the Lycoming Turbine Engine Division of Textron Inc. in 1994; the $245 million acquisition from Hoechst AG of a 95.8 percent interest in specialty chemicals manufacturer Riedel-de Haën AG in 1995; the estimated $400 million purchase of Prestone Products Corp., a maker of antifreeze and other auto-care products, in mid-1997; the June 1997 acquisition of Grimes Aerospace, a maker of aircraft lighting systems, from buyout firm Forstmann Little & Co.; and the October 1997 purchase of Astor Holdings Inc., a privately held maker of specialty waxes, adhesives, and sealants that fit well with AlliedSignal's burgeoning specialty chemicals division. The increased acquisitions activity of 1997 seemed to indicate an attempt to leverage the company's increasingly healthy state; in fact, the specialty chemical division alone set a goal in 1996 of doubling its $1 billion in annual revenue by 2000, with such acquisitions as Astor Holdings paving the way.

Continuous change continued to mark the Bossidy era as the company in October 1997 announced a restructuring whereby its three-sector structure was replaced by one consisting of the following 11 business units: Turbocharging Systems; Engines; Aerospace Equipment Systems; Electronics and Avionics Systems; Aerospace Marketing Sales & Service; Federal Manufacturing & Technologies; Automotive Products Group; Truck Brake Systems; Specialty Chemicals; Polymers; and Electronic Materials (the first six of these had comprised the Aerospace sector, the next two the Automotive sector, and the last three the Engineered Materials sector). This restructuring succeeded in eliminating a layer of management, and, in a press release, Bossidy said that each of the 11 business units "is a significant factor in its market and has global reach, world-class talent, and the critical mass to operate autonomously. Removing the sector layer will enable these businesses to make faster decisions and serve customers with greater speed, flexibility, and cost effectiveness."

By the late 1990s, AlliedSignal—thanks largely to its bold leader—was the envy of much of the industrial world. The company's great potential seemed to have finally been fulfilled. In the years to come, AlliedSignal was likely to continue to seek complementary acquisitions—increasingly outside the United States—as well as growing organically, in its quest to remain one of the top industrial corporations in the world.

Principal Subsidiaries

AlliedSignal International Finance Corporation; EM Sector Holdings Inc.; AlliedSignal Avionics Inc.; AlliedSignal Power Systems, Inc.; AlliedSignal Technologies Inc.; AlliedSignal Technical Services Corporation.

Principal Operating Units

Turbocharging Systems; Engines; Aerospace Equipment Systems; Electronics and Avionics Systems; Aerospace Marketing Sales & Service; Federal Manufacturing & Technologies; Automotive Products Group; Truck Brake Systems; Specialty Chemicals; Polymers; Electronic Materials.

Further Reading

Barr, Stephen, "Built for Speed," *Business Journal of New Jersey,* April 1993, pp. 50–53.

Best, James D., *The Digital Organization: AlliedSignal's Success with Business Technology,* New York: Wiley, 1997, 234 p.

Byrne, Harlan S., "Allied-Signal Inc.: The Shuffling Over, It Nurtures a Profitable Blend of Businesses," *Barron's,* June 18, 1990, pp. 49–50.

Cunningham, Mary, with Fran Schumer, *Powerplay: What Really Happened at Bendix,* New York: Linden Press/Simon and Schuster, 1984, 286 p.

Gilbert, Nick, "CEO of the Year: Larry Bossidy of AlliedSignal," *Financial World,* March 29, 1994, pp. 44, 48, 50, 52.

Hager, Bruce, "Taking an Ax to Allied," *Business Week,* November 4, 1991, p. 70.

Hennessy, Edward L., *Allied Corporation: Strength Through Diversification,* New York: Newcomen Society, 1984, 24 p.

Jackson, Tony, "Creating a Common Set of Values," *Financial Times,* June 5, 1997, p. 16.

"Larry Bossidy Won't Stop Pushing," *Fortune,* January 3, 1997, pp. 135–37.

McClenahen, John S., " '52 Fiefdoms' No More: How CEO Larry Bossidy Is Making AlliedSignal into a Premier Company," *Industry Week,* January 20, 1997, pp. 58–60, 62–63.

McCoy, Michael, "AlliedSignal Wants to Double Specialty Chemical Operations," *Chemical Market Reporter,* April 28, 1997, pp. 1, 37.

Mehta, Stephanie N., "Restructuring Is Announced by AlliedSignal," *Wall Street Journal,* October 2, 1997, p. A6.

Nulty, Peter, "Small Payoffs from Big Deals," *Fortune,* December 7, 1987, pp. 139, 142–43, 146.

Olcott, John W., "New Allied-Signal Chairman Stresses Customer Service," *Business & Commercial Aviation,* February 1992, p. 34.

Smith, Bruce A., "Leaner AlliedSignal Looks to Sustain Gains," *Aviation Week & Space Technology,* May 31, 1993, pp. 81–83.

Stewart, Thomas A., "Allied-Signal's Turnaround Blitz," *Fortune,* November 30, 1992, pp. 72–76.

Tully, Shawn, "So, Mr. Bossidy, We Know You Can Cut. Now Show Us How to Grow," *Fortune,* August 21, 1995, pp. 70–73, 76, 78, 80.

Willoughby, Jack, "The Cardinal Rule," *Forbes,* April 7, 1986, p. 34.

—updated by David E. Salamie

AMERICAN GREETINGS
...says it best

American Greetings Corporation

One American Road
Cleveland, Ohio 44144-2398
U.S.A.
(216) 252-7300
Fax: (216) 252-6777
Web site: http://www.amgreetings.com

Public Company
Incorporated: 1944 as American Greetings
Employees: 21,000
Sales: $2.16 billion (1997)
Stock Exchanges: NASDAQ
SICs: 2771 Greeting Card Publishing & Printing; 2671 Coated & Laminated Paper & Plastic Film; 2656 Sanitary Food Containers, Except Folding; 2679 Converted Paper & Paperboard Products, Not Elsewhere Classified; 5947 Gift, Novelty & Souvenir Shops

American Greetings Corporation, which advertises itself as ''the world's largest publicly owned manufacturer and distributor of greeting cards and related social expression products,'' is second only to Hallmark Cards, Inc. (a privately held corporation) in what has become an increasingly competitive and tight-margin industry. Since its founding in 1906 as a small Cleveland jobber's shop, American Greetings has enjoyed 91 consecutive years of increased revenue. Within recent decades growth has been driven especially by the company's creation, marketing, and licensing of such characters as Ziggy, the Care Bears, Holly Hobbie, and Strawberry Shortcake, as well as by a pronounced emphasis on ''anytime'' cards, a fast-growing niche area of the historically holiday- and occasional-oriented market. Strategies by which American plans to expand this niche area as well as appeal to a new card-buying public include its CreataCard vending machines, which allow shoppers to personally design and print their own cards, via touchscreen, both quickly and economically; its CreataCard Plus CD-ROM products, which allow users to print cards at home or have the company print them and mail them; and its various initiatives involving the marketing of its greeting cards through the Internet and online services. The company operates 31 plants in the United States, Canada, Mexico, the United Kingdom, France, South Africa, Australia, and New Zealand, and distributes its products through a network of more than 100,000 retail outlets in over 75 countries.

Early History

The birth of American Greetings roughly coincides with the birth of the U.S. greeting card industry, which was marked by the advent of occasional cards to complement the seasonal Christmas card trade. A Polish émigré named Jacob Sapirstein entered the fledgling industry in 1906 as an independent salesman. Sapirstein (known as ''J. S.'') had had some experience working with relatives in a hotel card shop. When the shop closed he established his own business, which consisted of buying picture postcards and reselling them to such local outlets as novelty shops, candy stores, and drugstores. Conducting his wholesaling enterprise from a horse-drawn wagon, J. S. enjoyed modest success and by 1918 welcomed his eldest son, nine-year-old Irving, as the first partner. In 1926 the Sapirstein Greeting Card Company solidified itself as a family business with the additional employment of Irving's brother Morris. Two years later, through the sales efforts of Morris and Irving, the company received its largest order since inception, a postcard contract worth $24,000. During 1929, a year after the Hall Brothers Company (Hallmark) had begun to advertise nationally, the Sapirsteins greatly furthered their eventual position as a mainstay of the market by becoming the first distributor to utilize display cabinets for its greeting cards. Three years later, the company began phasing out its dependency on suppliers, whose products were often inferior, by manufacturing its own line of greeting cards. Although Hallmark would retain until the 1980s a formidable industry lead due to its well-established name and high-quality image, the Sapirstein business was at least preparing itself to compete with the market leader.

The Great Depression had minimal negative impact on the company, as evinced by a continuing string of ''firsts'' during the 1930s. These included the hiring of the first sales representative in 1934; youngest son Harry's first year with the company in 1935; the opening of the first branch office and the first major

Company Perspectives:

American Greetings helps people everywhere express their innermost thoughts and feelings, enhance meaningful relationships, and celebrate life's milestones and special occasions. We also strive to: Be the industry's preferred greeting card supplier with superior retail sales performance. Provide the highest level of customer service at the lowest cost of doing business. Use technology to advance sales, operations, and retail partnerships. Deliver solid profitability and long-term shareholder value. Set the industry standard for a work environment that respects each associate and encourages creativity and innovation at all levels. Adhere to the highest standards of moral and ethical conduct in dealing with our customers, suppliers, shareholders, associates, and the community at large. Enrich the quality of life in all communities where we do business.

manufacturing facility in 1936; and the introduction of the first line of Forget Me Not cards in 1939. With the advent of the next decade the company, which had now renamed itself American Greetings Publishers, catapulted to national prominence with annual sales exceeding $1 million. In 1944 the family-owned and family-run business incorporated under its present name and in 1952, due to rapid population growth and subsequent plans for both acquisitions and expansion, the company went public.

Creation of Characters Began in 1967

A new era dawned in 1960 when J. S. became chairman of the board and Irving (who, like his brothers, had changed his last name to Stone) became president. This same year the company launched a cabinet manufacturing plant in Forest City, North Carolina, the first of many large capital expenditures necessary to keep pace with growth and fortify the company's large position in the industry. In 1967 the company introduced the Holly Hobbie character to wide public approval; this important creative move, which had huge potential for licensing spinoffs, eventually led to the formation of Those Characters From Cleveland, a subsidiary operation active since 1980 that became a valuable contributor to the company's financial health. The year following Holly Hobbie's debut, overall sales surpassed $100 million.

The 1970s were marked by a number of major events. The decade opened with the introduction of Soft Touch cards, so labeled for their combination of soft focus photography and touching sentiment. This new line became the most successful of any introduced in American Greetings' history. In 1972 the world was introduced to Ziggy, ''the world's most lovable loser.'' Even more so than Holly Hobbie (who by 1977 was the most popular female licensed character in the world), Ziggy became a perennial money-maker for the company, due especially to the royalty profits and publicity generated by his syndicated newspaper cartoon series, the creative rights for which were sold to Universal Press. In 1978 Irving Stone became chairman and CEO and Morry Weiss, Irving's son-in-law, was named president. During this changeover year, two new subsidiaries were established: Plus Mark, Inc., a manufacturer of Christmas gift wrap, boxed cards, and accessories, and A.G. Industries, Inc., the largest display fixture company in the country. By this time American Greetings possessed a view of itself as a leading mass-marketer to pharmacies, variety stores, discount stores, and supermarkets of lower-cost cards. Hallmark, which had ignored such venues until 1959, was now beginning to represent a serious threat to American's market share through its Ambassador card line. The most comforting news for American was that it, indisputably, dominated in terms of licensing revenue; the company reinforced this fact in 1980 with the unveiling of Strawberry Shortcake, whose array of products grossed $100 million in the first marketing year alone.

Industry Competition Increased in 1980s and 1990s

American celebrated its 75th anniversary in 1981 by recreating its 21-year-old emblem of the rose. This symbolic affirmation of quality and beauty dovetailed nicely with other key components of the new corporate identity program, including American's first foray into national television advertising as the Fresh Idea Company. Investors sensed a new surge in growth as they nearly doubled the stock price of American shares from October 1981 to May 1982. It was around this time that Weiss fueled investor fever by proclaiming, ''We want to be the dominant force in the industry.'' *Forbes* writer Jeff Blyskal noted that the company was ''actively upgrading its products and prices'' and opined: ''American Greetings is making a bold move. Weiss is pouring his licensing profits into an aggressive and well-timed campaign to challenge Hallmark.'' From 1981 to 1985 American grew from a half-billion to a billion-dollar company and thus attained one of the key corporate objectives it had set for itself. More important than this increase in total revenue, however, was American's astonishing net income increase of 613 percent in a 10-year period. What the company had failed to do, unfortunately, was enhance its market share with respect to Hallmark.

Gibson Greetings, the number three card-seller, shook the industry in 1986 with a vicious price war, which it commenced in an effort to increase its own 10 percent share. The price war ended the following year, but all three companies suffered profit losses from it, with virtually no change in their respective market positions (Hallmark still led with 45 percent and American followed with 35 percent; the bottom tier was still comprised of Gibson and several hundred much smaller manufacturers). American's recovery from this siege, as well as from downswings in noncard sales, was difficult. A 1988 *Forbes* article labeled the company ''Flounder,'' finding support for its dismal forecast in new earnings estimates ($1.05 per share versus $2.35 in 1985) and a 60 percent drop in stock price from its mid-1986 high of 42. Nevertheless, after hitting bottom in 1988 with a devastating drop in profits from $63 million to $33 million, American rebounded in 1989 to $44 million.

By 1991, American more than doubled its net income and once again became a feisty contender for the number one position. Although Hallmark's revenues were roughly double those of American, American showed 10 percent growth in sales for cards and related goods in 1991 while Hallmark reported only one percent. At least some of this renewed vigor was due to the appointment of longtime employee Ed Fruchtenbaum as the fourth and first non-family president and the elevation of Weiss to CEO. Under Weiss, American cut costs, streamlined its operations, and improved its idea-to-market development time (Desert Storm cards were shipped to retailers within a mere three-week period from initiation). With Fruchtenbaum, American further honed its day-to-day operations by placing special emphasis on its information systems (IS) technology. Through its IS department, the company created software to aid management, the sales force, and their retail customers in tracking inventories and reacting to buying trends. With the ability to supply sales managers and retailers with block-by-block demographic data, IS was an indispensable component of Fruchtenbaum's future plans, for pinpoint marketing represented the cutting edge of the industry. As Laurel Touby observed, "To keep his sales growing, Fruchtenbaum is [already] targeting narrow consumer segments, such as college students, while continuing to beef up service to retailers." Touby also speculated that "the company, whose assets include a picture-frame maker, a hair-accessory manufacturer, and a licensing arm, may also make more acquisitions in and out of cards."

The most important and promising acquisition by American during 1992 was the purchase of Custom Expressions, Inc., maker of the CreataCard units, which initially featured approximately 1,000 card options and were capable of producing cards for consumers, priced at $3.50 each, in less than four minutes. In October 1992 American installed a few thousand of the kiosks in mass-merchandise outlets nationwide, and had more than 7,000 of them installed by early 1994, by which time they were generating healthy revenue but only modest profits. Hallmark, owner of Touch Screen Greetings and the Personalize It! method, had filed suit against American in 1992 for patent infringement, but the suit was settled in 1995 with each company getting a worldwide, nonexclusive license to use the technology; no other details on the settlement were provided.

Also in 1992, Weiss became both chairman and CEO of American Greetings. Fruchtenbaum was promoted to president and chief operating officer, while Irving Stone assumed the title founder-chairman. Starting the following year, the company began to add to, subtract from, and reposition its mix of non-greeting-card operations. In 1993 American acquired Magnivision, the leading manufacturer and distributor of nonprescription reading glasses in the United States and 15 other countries. Three years later, American entered into talks with BEC Group Inc. to buy BEC's Foster Grant Group, a maker of sunglasses, but in the midst of the negotiations American decided it did not wish to pursue the purchase. Also in 1996, American began to reorganize portions of its consumer products group by converting product categories into strategic business units, a move designed to elevate these products from mere sidelines to semiautonomous units. Subsequently, the company's party goods line was relaunched in 1996 as DesignWare, while its candle line reemerged the following year as GuildHouse. Further such moves were planned for other lines. In March 1997, American announced that it had formed a new subsidiary, Learning Horizons, Inc., to manufacture and distribute supplemental educational products for preschool and elementary school students, including workbooks, science kits, flash cards, math kits, posters, audiocassettes, educational stickers, rubber stamps, and puzzles. The company in August 1997 sold two subsidiaries to Newell Co.: Acme Frame Products, Inc., maker and marketer of picture frames, and Wilhold Inc., producer and seller of hair accessory products. Further divestments were not immediately expected.

During this same period, American Greetings became more aggressive in pursuing markets outside the United States, whose maturing greeting card industry was seeing flat sales through most of the 1990s. In 1993 American launched the Forget-Me-Not brand in Canada, where it became that country's largest and broadest line of social expression cards. South Africa was the next target for company expansion, which came in the form of the 1995 purchase of an 80 percent stake in S.A. Greetings Corporation, one of the leading players in the $30 million South African greeting card market. The following year, American acquired John Sands, the number one greeting card company in both Australia and New Zealand.

By late 1995 the kiosk technology that showed such early promise was rapidly being rendered technologically obsolete by the increasing use of PCs and the Internet to make and deliver greeting cards. Lagging CreataCard sales led the company to take a charge of $52.1 million in November 1995 to reflect the decreased value of its kiosks. At the same time, however, American was moving quickly into the home PC and online arenas itself. By early 1996, the company had marketing tie-ins with three online services—Prodigy, CompuServe, and Microsoft Network. During fiscal 1997, American launched a web site, which allowed visitors to design cards and have them printed and mailed from the company fulfillment center in Cleveland. That year also saw the debut of two CD-ROM products, Personal CardShop for Home and Office and CreataCard Plus. The former enabled users to select from among 150 cards, personalize them, order them by modem, and have the card printed by the Cleveland fulfillment center. CreataCard Plus featured more than 3,000 predesigned greeting cards, invitations, stationery, and announcements, which could be printed at home on a color printer, sent by e-mail, or once again printed and delivered by the fulfillment center.

In the midst of all of this activity, of course, the greeting card war between American Greetings and Hallmark raged on. American gained ground in the 1990s, despite its market share remaining at the same level—35 percent—in 1996 as in 1990. During this same period, however, Hallmark's share fell from 50 percent to 42 percent. American nearly caught up with Hallmark in March 1996 when it tried to acquire the still-number-three Gibson, which claimed seven percent of the market. But that month, Gibson turned down American's $292 million takeover bid. In July 1997 American Greetings launched a massive revamping of its everyday card lines, aiming to replace, over the next 18 months, 80 percent of its everyday greeting cards as part of a new marketing strategy called "The All New American Way." The company hoped to gain market share by offering cards that met new marketplace needs arising from nine trends in American culture—for example, the increase in cultural diversity, changes in family dynamics, and longer and healthier lives.

Overall, the 1990s appeared a good period for American, as net sales grew from $1.29 billion in fiscal 1990 to $2.16 billion in fiscal 1997. During the same period, net income more than doubled, increasing from $72.2 million to $167.1 million. It also seemed clear that through such moves as the repositioning of its consumer products group, the targeting of additional overseas markets, the efforts to market cards electronically, and the introduction of a radical new marketing strategy that American Greetings would continue to reinvent itself in order to keep pressure on Hallmark in American's continuing quest to overtake its archrival.

Principal Subsidiaries

AGC Inc.; A.G. Industries, Inc.; Carlton Cards (France) SNC; Carlton Cards Limited (Canada); Carlton Cards Limited (U.K.); Carlton Cards Ltd. (Ireland); Carlton Cards Retail, Inc.; Carlton Mexico, S.A. de C.V.; CreataCard Interactive, Inc.; John Sands (Australia) Ltd. (U.S.A.); Learning Horizons, Inc.; Magnivision, Inc.; Plus Mark, Inc.; S.A. Greetings Corporation (PTY) Ltd. (South Africa; 80%); Those Characters From Cleveland, Inc.

Further Reading

''American Greetings Launches Custom Card System,'' *Greetings Magazine,* September 1992, p. 14.

Blyskal, Jeff, ''Greetings from the Competition,'' *Forbes,* March 29, 1982, pp. 36–37.

Bounds, Wendy, and Matt Murray, ''Card Makers Try New Ways to Greet a Paperless World,'' *Wall Street Journal,* March 19, 1996, pp. B1, B8.

Caminiti, Susan, ''The Fortune 500: America's Fastest-Growing Companies,'' *Fortune,* April 22, 1991, pp. 67–76.

Canedy, Dana, ''Wish You Weren't Here: It's Been Live and Let Live Until Today, But Now the Greeting Card Wars Are Under Way,'' *New York Times,* November 20, 1997, p. D1.

Chiu, Tony, and Joyce Wansley, ''Who's Red and Sweet and Filthy Rich? Strawberry Shortcake, Toyland's Newest Tyke-Coon,'' *People Weekly,* May 10, 1982, pp. 91–93.

''Corporate History,'' Cleveland: American Greetings Corporation, October 1997, 11 p.

Dorfman, John R., and Wendy Bounds, ''American Greetings Stock Gets Warm 'Hello' from Investment Pros Who Cite Mass Market,'' *Wall Street Journal,* June 11, 1994, p. C2.

Fitzgerald, Kate, '' 'Happy Birthday, (Name Here),' '' *Advertising Age,* February 21, 1994, p. 17.

''Hallmark, American at Odds Over Custom Card Patents,'' *Greetings Magazine,* November 1992, p. 13.

Jaffe, Thomas, ''Flounder,'' *Forbes,* April 25, 1988, p. 352.

Laurel, Touby, ''Congratulations on Your Big Earnings Increase!'' *Business Week,* August 17, 1992, p. 58.

Maturi, Richard J., ''High Tech Makes for High Touch: Managerial Know-How Keeps American Greetings Close to Customers,'' *Industry Week,* August 17, 1992, pp. 50–51.

McCune, Jenny C., ''Street Smart Selling,'' *Success,* May 1991, p. 22.

McMurray, Scott, ''Dealing a Whole New Deck of Cards: American Greetings Gets the High-Tech Message,'' *U.S. News & World Report,* December 4, 1995, pp. 68–69.

Mendelson, Seth, ''Above the Crowd,'' *Supermarket Business,* June 1996, p. 41.

Nelson, Emily, ''American Greetings Says It May Sell Certain Noncore Consumer Businesses,'' *Wall Street Journal,* January 14, 1997, p. B9.

——, ''Dearest Mom, Greetings from My CD-ROM,'' *Wall Street Journal,* September 4, 1996, pp. B1, B4.

Oliver, Suzanne, ''Christmas Card Blues,'' *Forbes,* December 24, 1990, p. 100.

Rifkin, Glenn, ''A Sentimental Journey to Success,'' *Computerworld,* August 28, 1989, pp. 55, 59.

Sanger, Elizabeth, ''Salutes for American Greetings,'' *Barron's,* October 27, 1986, p. 83.

Schwartz, Ela, ''The Next Cycle in Greeting Cards,'' *Discount Merchandiser,* July 1990, pp. 68–69.

Sparks, Debra, ''The Card Game,'' *Financial World,* July 5, 1994, pp. 28–29.

Weiss, Morry, *American Greetings Corporation,* New York: Newcomen Society in North America, 1982, 20 p.

—Jay P. Pederson
—updated by David E. Salamie

AMERICAN STORES COMPANY

American Stores Company

709 East South Temple
Salt Lake City, Utah 84102-1205
U.S.A.
(801) 539-0112
Fax: (801) 961-5574
Web site: http://www.americandrugstores.com

Public Company
Incorporated: 1965 as Skaggs Drug Centers, Inc.
Employees: 127,000
Sales: $18.68 billion (1996)
Stock Exchanges: New York Philadelphia Midwest Pacific
SICs: 5411 Grocery Stores; 5912 Drug Stores & Proprietary Stores; 6719 Offices of Holding Companies, Not Elsewhere Classified; 8099 Health & Allied Services, Not Elsewhere Classified

Built largely through the drive and ambition of one family, American Stores Company has developed into one of the leading food and drug retailers in the United States and is the third-largest grocery store chain (following Kroger Company and Safeway Stores). Among the company's grocery operations are more than 180 Acme Markets in Pennsylvania, New Jersey, Delaware, and Maryland; more than 185 Jewel food stores and Jewel Osco combination food and drugstores in Illinois, Iowa, Indiana, Wisconsin, New Mexico, and Utah; and more than 430 Lucky Stores in California and Nevada. Company drugstores include more than 430 Osco Drug stores in 20 states, mainly in the Midwest, and more than 300 Sav-on and Sav-on Express units in California and Nevada. American Stores also operates 20 home health care superstores under the Health 'n' Home name in four states and RxAmerica, a pharmacy benefits management company operated through a joint venture with Geneva Pharmaceuticals.

Beginnings As a Drugstore Chain

The history of American Stores is inextricably linked to that of the Skaggs family. Samuel Skaggs, the patriarch, opened a drugstore in Utah in 1915. In 1926 his six sons, including Leonard S., Sr., helped build Safeway Stores, which have since developed into the nation's second-largest supermarket chain. In 1932 L. J. Skaggs split with his brothers and opened his first Pay Less drugstore in Tacoma, Washington. In 1939 Leonard S., Sr., founded the Skaggs Drug Center chain and bought the California operations of Pay Less. And at about the same time, L. L. Skaggs founded the Osco Drug chain.

The combined operations of Skaggs Drug Centers and Skaggs Pay Less was known as Skaggs Companies, and it remained a modest enterprise through the 1940s. In 1950 Leonard S., Sr., died and his 26-year-old son, Leonard S., Jr., inherited the business. At the time, Skaggs Companies had posted sales of $9.6 million, .05 percent of what American Stores would report nearly five decades later.

Leonard S. Skaggs, Jr., more familiarly known as Sam, had ambitious plans for the family business. But those plans waited during the 1950s and early 1960s. Skaggs Companies made little news during this time, except in 1956 and 1957 when General Electric sued a group of Western retailers over their practice of selling GE products at less than the recommended price. Skaggs filed a countersuit, and as a result of the controversy, courts in Utah and other Western states overturned so-called ''fair trade'' laws that prohibited the discounting of merchandise.

In 1965 the company was incorporated as Skaggs Drug Centers, Inc. That same year, Skaggs bought 30 Super-S general merchandise stores from Safeway. By 1969, it had expanded its retail drug operations to 80 stores in 13 Western states and in that year earned $4.7 million on sales of $172.2 million. At that point, Sam Skaggs contemplated a merger that would enlarge his company even further. Skaggs Drug Centers negotiated with People's Drug Store, a retailer that would have expanded Skaggs's geographical base with 245 stores in eight Eastern states, but talks broke down when the companies could not reach mutually acceptable financial terms. In 1970, however, Skaggs did merge with Katz Drug, a move noteworthy not only because it allowed Skaggs to expand into the Midwest, but also because Katz owned the non-California operations of L. J. Skaggs's old Pay Less chain.

Company Perspectives:

The mission of American Stores Company is to be the premier, national, food and drug retailer, that understands and surpasses our customers' expectations for service, value, and convenience. Our success is directly dependent on our people who must work together as associates to fulfill this mission.

Combo Stores Debuted in 1970

Also in 1970, Skaggs entered into a joint venture with Albertson's, one of the largest supermarket chains in the western United States, which resulted in the first successful combined drug and food superstores. Traditionally, it had been difficult for drugstores and supermarkets to cross over into each other's territory because their goods were marketed differently. Skaggs had experimented with "combo" stores by opening one in Las Vegas, Nevada, in 1969, but needed more managerial expertise in grocery retailing to make them succeed on a large scale. A connection between Albertson's chairman, Joe Albertson, and the Skaggs family was not unprecedented; Albertson had worked for Safeway when the Skaggs brothers were running the chain.

The joint venture proved to be a considerable success. Over the next seven years, Skaggs-Albertson's Properties opened 58 combo stores in Oklahoma and the southeast, and in 1976, the last full year of the partnership, it generated $624 million in sales. But in 1977, both Skaggs and Albertson's realized that the venture had grown so large as to become nearly unmanageable. A merger between the two partners would have been an elegant solution, but both feared that it would result in antitrust litigation. Neither had enough money to acquire the other outright, and neither wanted to take on the capital-gains tax obligations of selling out. Irreconcilable differences in management philosophies were also rumored to have played a part in the split. So Skaggs-Albertson's Properties was dissolved, with each partner receiving half of its assets.

Overall, Skaggs Drug Centers prospered during the 1970s. In 1978 it posted earnings of $25 million on sales of $1.1 billion and operated 202 drugstores, most of them in the West and Southwest. And amid widespread concern over the state of the American economy, Sam Skaggs remained confident in the future of his company. "We're more or less recession-proof," he told *Business Week* in 1977. "People are going to brush their teeth and cure their headaches all the time."

Even so, the expansion of Skaggs's combo store operations slowed without the help of Albertson's muscle. In 1978 the company worked out an agreement to merge with Jewel Companies, a major Chicago-based food retailer. Sam Skaggs had tried to merge with Jewel 12 years earlier, and this time around he believed that integrating its decentralized management structure into his own essentially one-person operation would facilitate further expansion. Jewel chairman Donald Perkins, for his part, saw combo stores as the wave of the future, as supermarkets began to stock more nongrocery items, and sought Skaggs's expertise. The merger seemed mutually advantageous, but was torpedoed at the last moment when some of Skaggs's directors, concerned that they would lose their autonomy under the deal, failed to approve it.

Major Mergers in 1979 and 1984

Momentarily set back but undaunted, Sam Skaggs soon resumed his quest for a merger that would further his goal of building a food-and-drug retail juggernaut. He found one in 1979, when American Stores Company agreed to merge with Skaggs Companies. American Stores was by far the larger organization, with 758 supermarkets, 139 drugstores, 53 restaurants, and nine general-merchandise stores in nine states, but Skaggs was the one that survived the merger. The resulting entity bore the American Stores name, but was controlled by Skaggs management.

Thanks to the merger, American Stores posted $83 million in earnings on sales of nearly $8 billion in 1983. But its presence was still weak in the Midwest, New England, and Florida. To help overcome these remaining geographical shortcomings, Sam Skaggs made yet another attempt to merge with Jewel in 1984. But Weston Christopherson, who had succeeded Donald Perkins as chairman of Jewel, was opposed to a merger and Skaggs was forced to engineer a hostile takeover. On June 1, 1984, American Stores tendered an offer worth $1.1 billion for 67 percent of Jewel's outstanding shares at $70 per share.

For two weeks, Jewel management refused all comment on the offer, maintaining its silence even at a stormy shareholder's meeting before which Jewel shareholder groups controlling 20 percent of the company's stock had come out in favor of negotiating with American Stores. Finally, on June 14, Sam Skaggs and Jewel president Richard Kline reached an agreement after an all-night bargaining session. American Stores raised its bid for Jewel's preferred stock, increasing the total bid to $1.15 billion in cash and securities. In return, Jewel dropped plans for a defensive acquisition of Household International and accepted American Stores' offer. To help raise cash for the deal, American Stores sold its Rea & Derick drug chain in December 1984 to People's Drug, a subsidiary of Imasco Limited.

The acquisition of Jewel also returned L. L. Skaggs's Osco Drug chain to the Skaggs family ownership. And Sav-on Drug, another Jewel subsidiary, had been founded by C. J. Call, who had once been a business partner of another of Sam Skaggs's uncles, O. P. Skaggs.

Jewel added 193 supermarkets, 358 drugstores, 140 combo stores, 301 convenience stores, and 132 discount stores to the American Stores empire. But in 1985, American Stores found itself in legal trouble through its new subsidiary. A salmonella food-poisoning outbreak affecting some 20,000 people in the Midwest was traced to a Melrose, Illinois, dairy that had supplied tainted milk to Jewel stores. Two years later, Jewel was found not liable for punitive damages in Cook County Circuit Court, but agreed to pay compensatory damages estimated at $35 to $40 million.

Late 1980s Acquisition of Lucky Stores Ran into Snags

After two decades of intense merger-and-acquisition activity, American Stores was the largest drug retailer in the United

States, but only the third-largest grocery retailer. Furthermore, its 210-store Alpha Beta chain in California was struggling, plagued by high prices and a reputation for poor service. On March 22, 1988, American Stores made an unsolicited tender offer for Lucky Stores, an Alpha Beta competitor noted for high efficiency and low prices.

Lucky refused American Stores' first offer, worth $1.7 billion, or $45 per share of Lucky stock. By the end of the month, American Stores proposed to up its bid to $50 per share if Lucky would agree to a friendly takeover. Again Lucky rejected the offer as inadequate and was said to be contemplating defensive strategies. In May, Lucky agreed to a $2.4 billion, $61-per-share buyout by a company set up by Lucky management and the investment-banking firm Gibbons Green van Amerongen. On the one hand, this move seemed very much like a bid by Lucky managers to retain control of their company. But on the other, it could also have been a ploy to milk American Stores for a higher bid, since later that month Lucky allowed American Stores to examine confidential financial information that it had been withholding for several weeks and gave its suitor one week to respond with a better offer. On May 17 American Stores upped its bid to $2.5 billion, or $65 per share.

Five days later, Lucky accepted. American Stores was about to become the largest supermarket chain in the nation, leapfrogging over Kroger and Safeway Stores. Interest payments alone on its acquisition debt cut the company's earnings in 1988 by 36 percent from the previous year, but analysts called the deal worthwhile.

California Attorney General John Van de Kamp took to the warpath against the acquisition. In August, Van de Kamp asked the Federal Trade Commission to void it, claiming that a Lucky-Alpha Beta juggernaut would cost California consumers $400 million by reducing competition. The FTC refused (although it did force the divestiture of 37 Alpha Beta stores, which were sold in December 1988, the same month 38 Lucky stores in Arizona were also sold). Van de Kamp then took his case to court, and on September 29, a federal judge in Los Angeles issued a preliminary injunction against the merger. American Stores appealed, and in April 1989, an appeals court judge in San Francisco overturned the injunction. Van de Kamp appealed this reversal to the U.S. Supreme Court; meanwhile, American Stores continued to plan its assimilation of Lucky.

In 1988 Sam Skaggs reached the mandatory retirement age of 65, and in December of that year the company named vice-chairman Jonathan L. Scott to succeed him as CEO. It marked the end of an era for American Stores in more ways than one; not only would it be without a member of the Skaggs clan to handle day-to-day operations for the first time, but it would experience a profound change in management style as well. "Mr. Skaggs is a builder," Scott told the *Wall Street Journal.* "He's always been aggressive in acquisitions. My forte is more in how we operate those companies and how we grow them." So American Stores finished out the 1980s in a mood to consolidate.

1990s Retrenchment and Organizational Overhaul

The 1990s unfortunately got off to a rough start when the Supreme Court in April 1990 ruled in favor of the California attorney general. Subsequently, and wishing to avoid additional, lengthy litigation, American Stores the following month reached an agreement with Van de Kamp whereby the company was allowed to convert 14 Alpha Beta stores to the Lucky name but also had to sell—within five years—161 southern California stores, 152 Alpha Betas, and nine Luckys.

By this time, American Stores was burdened—primarily because of its purchase of Lucky Stores—with a long-term debt of $3.4 billion, an indication that it had perhaps overreached in its ambitious acquisitions strategy. Reducing this debt load became the prime challenge for the company; doing so was mainly accomplished through asset sales. In addition to the June 1991 sale of the Alpha Beta stores to Yucaipa Cos. for $251 million, American Stores also divested: 44 Buttrey Food & Drug stores located in Montana, Wyoming, Washington, Idaho, and North Dakota, through an October 1990 management-led $184 million leveraged buyout; 51 Osco Drug stores in Colorado, Utah, and Wyoming, which were sold in June 1991 to Pay Less Drug Stores, a division of Kmart Corp., for $60 million; and 74 Jewel Osco stores in Arkansas, Florida, Oklahoma, and Texas, sold to Albertson's for about $455 million. The company also put its 275-unit Acme Markets chain on the block in early 1991, but shortly thereafter decided not to sell Acme, apparently because the bids it received were not deemed sufficient. Despite this nonsale, by the end of fiscal 1992 long-term debt was down to $2.1 billion. In August 1992 Scott resigned as CEO and was replaced by Victor L. Lund, an American Stores executive with a financial background who had joined the company in 1977.

At the same time that it was making its major divestments of the early 1990s, American Stores also looked for opportunities to make strategic minor acquisitions, ones that would enhance its position in the main markets that it wished to serve. The company's California drugstore operations were enhanced through the early 1992 $60 million purchase of 85 CVS units, which were soon converted to the Sav-on banner. The following year the Midwest region received a boost when 55 Reliable Drug stores in Indiana, Illinois, Iowa, Kansas, and Missouri were bought. These were soon rebannered as Osco Drug stores.

American Stores continued to tinker with its holdings during the mid-1990s. In August 1994 its 33-store Star Market chain, fifth in market share in the Greater Boston area, was sold to an investment group for $285 million in cash and the assumption of debt. Star, which had come to American Stores as part of the 1984 acquisition of Jewel, was deemed expendable because the company wanted to focus on markets where it held first or second place in market share. In January 1995 the company sold 45 Acme Markets located in New York and northern Pennsylvania to Penn Traffic Co. for $94 million. The following month, American Stores spent about $37 million for 17 Clark Drug stores in southern California, which were then converted to the Sav-on name.

In an extension of its core drugstore business, American Stores in November 1995 launched a new category-killer format called Health 'n' Home, which was a 28,000-square-foot, 18,000-item home health care superstore. The first Health 'n' Home opened in Phoenix, Arizona, and by late 1997 there were 20 of them in four states. American Stores was also involved in the growing managed health care market through its joint ownership—with Geneva Pharmaceuticals, a subsidiary of Novartis Pharmaceuticals Corporation—of RxAmerica, a pharmacy benefits management company which existed to manage the prescription drug benefits provided to individuals through health care plans. RxAmerica also operated mail-order facilities offering prescriptions, vitamins, and other health care products at significant discounts.

Also in 1995, Sam Skaggs relinquished the chairmanship of American Stores to Lund. Skaggs still held an 18.3 percent stake in the company and a seat on the company board, and when he announced in July 1996 that he was exploring options for his stake, speculation about a possible takeover ran wild. But in February 1997 an agreement was reached between American Stores and Skaggs whereby the company would repurchase about 12.2 million of Skaggs's shares for $550 million, with the remaining shares subsequently being sold to the public through a secondary offering. Skaggs would lose his seat on the board when his stake was reduced to five percent.

For much of the 1990s, American Stores was focused on debt reduction and cleaning up its portfolio of holdings. By 1996 the company was ready for more radical changes. American Stores had long been run as a decentralized holding company, but in order to compete in the fierce environment of the late 1990s the company decided to transform itself into an integrated operating company. As part of this transition, the company also began to centralize companywide its procurement, warehousing, inventory control, distribution, and marketing operations. Another aspect of the plan involved the consolidating of the central support organizations of the drugstore and grocery store operations. At the same time, American Stores sought to initiate faster growth, this time primarily through the opening of new stores—not through acquisitions. A three-year plan was launched in 1996 which aimed to open 300 new stores, with an average of $1 billion spent each year on capital investments. For 1996 American Stores opened 111 new stores and acquired another 11; it also, however, closed 77 underperforming stores.

Because of its various divestments and store closings, American Stores had fewer stores in its empire in 1996 (1,695) than it did in 1990 (1,848). Consequently, net sales had fallen from $22.16 billion to $18.68 billion. The company, however, was already more profitable, as net earnings increased from $190.1 million in 1990 to $287 million in 1996. These trends, combined with its organizational transformation and aggressive organic expansion plan, added up to a promising—and perhaps less volatile—future.

Principal Subsidiaries

Jewel Companies, Inc.; Acme Markets, Inc.; Jewel Food Stores, Inc.; American Drug Stores, Inc.; RxAmerica, Inc.; Health 'n' Home Corporation; The Open Pharmacy Network, Inc.; American Food and Drug, Inc.; Jewel Osco Southwest, Inc.; Lucky Stores, Inc.; American Stores Properties, Inc.; American Stores Realty Corp.; Skaggs Telecommunications Service, Inc.; American Procurement and Logistics Company; ASC Services, Inc.; Kap's Kitchen and Pantry, Inc.

Further Reading

Coleman, Calmetta Y., "Biggest Holder to Sell Stake in American Stores," *Wall Street Journal,* February 24, 1997, p. C19.

Foust, Dean, and Tim Smart, "The Merger Parade Runs into a Brick Wall," *Business Week,* May 14, 1990, p. 38.

Gradt, Cathy, "Quick Meals Featured in New Format by American," *Supermarket News,* July 15, 1996, p. 23.

Grover, Ronald, "How Two Big Grocers Are Bringing Home the Bacon," *Business Week,* April 24, 1989, p. 141.

Marcial, Gene G., "American Stores May Wind Up in a Shopping Bag," *Business Week,* May 2, 1988, p. 117.

Nelson, Emily, "Kodak Has Pact to Be Exclusive Supplier of Photofinishing to American Stores Co.," *Wall Street Journal,* September 30, 1996, p. B9.

Ross, Julie Ritzer, "American Stores Revives Troubled Pharmacy Network," *Stores,* October 1995, pp. 28–29.

Smart, Tim, and Ronald Grover, "Pumping Up a State's Power to Bust Trusts," *Business Week,* January 15, 1990, p. 25.

Steinhauer, Jennifer, "It's a Clashing of the Guard (Old vs. New) at American Stores," *New York Times,* August 28, 1996, pp. D1, D6.

Tosh, Mark, "Pressure Points at American Stores," *Supermarket News,* June 20, 1994, pp. 1, 9, 53.

Zwiebach, Elliot, "American Accord Eases Operations," *Supermarket News,* January 8, 1990, p. 1.

——, "American Turns Attention Toward Reducing Its Debt," *Supermarket News,* June 18, 1990, p. 1.

——, "American's Council Pursues Change," *Supermarket News,* July 10, 1995, p. 1.

——, "American's Three-Year Plan: $3 Billion, 300 New Stores," *Supermarket News,* June 3, 1996, p. 7.

——, "Centralized Procurement Program Set by American," *Supermarket News,* April 29, 1996, p. 1.

—Douglas Sun
—updated by David E. Salamie

ARBED S.A.

Avenue de la Liberté 19
L-2930
Luxembourg
+352 47 92 23 60
Fax: +352 47 92 26 58
Web site: http://www.arbed.com

Public Company
Incorporated: 1882 as Société Anonyme des Hauts Fourneaux et Forges de Dudelange
Employees: 30,000
Sales: LuxFr232.2 billion (1996)
Stock Exchanges: Luxembourg Brussels Paris Frankfurt Amsterdam London
SICs: 3312 Blast Furnaces & Steel Mills; 3313 Electrometallurgical Products; 3316 Cold Finishing of Steel Shapes; 3317 Steel Pipe & Tubes; 5051 Metals Service Centers & Offices; 3315 Steel Wire & Related Products; 1622 Bridge, Tunnel, & Elevated Highway; 3351 Copper Rolling & Drawing

ARBED S.A., based in the Grand Duchy of Luxembourg, heads an international group of 189 companies engaged in every aspect of iron and steel production from the mining process to the production of highly sophisticated finished goods. It can be seen as both product and agent of the economic revolution that over the last century has transformed Luxembourg from a small agricultural nation into a major industrial power with its activities centered on the great iron- and steel-producing complexes in the southwest of the country.

The company is comprised of eight business sectors: flat products, wire drawing, long products, engineering, stainless steel, copper foil, sales and trading, and its Brazilian operations. Three-quarters of the group's turnover is accounted for by steel production and related activities. Though it has undergone extensive personnel reductions in the 1980s and 1990s, ARBED remains the Grand Duchy's largest industrial employer. It ranks among Europe's largest iron- and steel-producing groups, with an annual output of more than 11.75 million metric tons.

Early 19th-Century Origins

Iron has a long history in the area that now constitutes the Grand Duchy of Luxembourg. It was mined by the Celts, then later by the Romans, not only from alluvial deposits in the valleys of the rivers Eisch and Alzette but also from *minette*, found in the southwest of the region, which was low in iron content and high in phosphorus and whose rediscovery in the mid-19th century gave an impetus to the modern industry and decided its location. Traces have been found in the canton of Esch of underground mining by the Romans, who made charcoal from the wood of local forests to smelt the ore in primitive furnaces, obtaining the metal they then fashioned into arms and armor. After the Germanic invasions the recovery of *minette*, for which underground mining skills were needed, died out. Iron production based on alluvial ore persisted in the region as a domestic craft, providing household and farm implements during the succeeding centuries as the region slowly and intermittently evolved, despite periods of anarchy, civil war, plague, misrule, and invasion, toward a sense of identity. Smelting plants and forges were set up near sources of charcoal and water power, the first very small-scale blast furnace making its appearance in the region in 1564.

Iron- and steel-making emerged on an industrial scale in the middle of the 19th century, in the region that had been the Grand Duchy since 1815. It is there that the origins of ARBED lie, although the company itself did not come into being until 1911. When the years of adversity came to an end, there were Luxembourgers ready to seize the country's chance at prosperity—businessmen with the drive and confidence to adapt Luxembourg's natural, human, and technological resources to the huge but inconstant market for iron and steel opening up at home and especially abroad, as industrialization gathered pace.

Several circumstances converged to favor an upswing in iron and, increasingly, in steel production: the expanding use of the steam engine which allowed greater freedom in siting and a larger scale of operations; the rediscovery in south Luxembourg

Company Perspectives:

From an ethical point of view, the Group aims at: providing its customers with always better and more reliable products and services; improving the well-being of all its employees sharing common values within the ARBED Group and fostering personal relations within the Group; guaranteeing equitable treatment to all its shareholders; respecting the customs of each country without any national bias and adopting as an international Group a responsible and respectful attitude towards its environment.

of *minette* deposits that would not be exhausted until 1981; the construction of railway lines linking Luxembourg with the European systems; Luxembourg's entry in 1842 into the German customs union, the *Zollverein*; and the invention in 1878 by S.G. Thomas and P. Gilchrist of the Thomas-Gilchrist—or Thomas, or basic Bessemer—process, an improvement of the Bessemer converter, permitting elimination of the phosphorus that had hitherto presented problems in the smelting of the phosphoric *minette* ores of Luxembourg and Lorraine. When, following lengthy initiatives by Émile Mayrisch and Gaston Barbanson, Aciéries Réunies de Burbach-Eich-Dudelange was formed in 1911, it was on foundations laid earlier by a number of iron and steel manufacturers. The latter were mainly Luxembourgers, linked by several family connections as well as by business interests. They had built up three companies, whose resources were now to be combined and directed to modern large-scale production of steel and steel products centered on Esch-Schifflange.

Merger of Three Companies to Form ARBED in 1911

The first of the three companies, already operating and cooperating in close proximity to each other in the southwest of the Grand Duchy and in nearby Germany and Lorraine, was the Forges d'Eich—Le Gallais, Metz et Cie, founded in 1838. It had originated in 1838 when three brothers, Charles, Norbert, and Auguste Metz, who played major roles in Luxembourg industry, politics, and journalism, set up a limited partnership, Auguste Metz et Cie, known since 1865 as the Société des Forges d'Eich—Metz et Cie. In 1879 this company had acquired a license to use the Thomas-Gilchrist dephosphorization process. Its main works were at Dommeldange and Esch-Schifflange, the latter a joint venture started in 1871 by Norbert Metz and Victor Tesch, his cousin by marriage.

The second company, Société Anonyme des Mines du Luxembourg et des Forges de Sarrebruck, had been created in 1856 by Victor Tesch and other Belgians of Luxembourg origin. Its coke ovens and blast furnaces were at Burbach in Germany, northeast of Saarbrücken. The third company, the Société Anonyme des Hauts Fourneaux et Forges de Dudelange, had been established in 1882 by the first two companies in order to exploit the Thomas-Gilchrist process in a steel plant at Dudelange, where the first charge of Thomas steel was blown in 1886. In 1911 the first two companies were dissolved and their assets transferred to the third, whose title was changed to Aciéries Réunies de Burbach-Eich-Dudelange S.A. (ARBED).

By 1911 the first company's original Eich works were of minor importance. At Esch-Schifflange it had four blast furnaces, two of them belonging to the Société des Mines du Luxembourg et de Sarrebruck, and its works at Dommeldange had three blast furnaces and four electric furnaces. The second company's Burbach plant had eight blast furnaces, a steel works, and rolling mills. The third company's property at Dudelange comprised six blast furnaces, a steel works, and rolling mills. All three constituent companies also brought with them the iron ore mining concessions they held in Luxembourg and Lorraine. Between them the companies produced cast iron and Thomas steel; laminated items—semi-finished goods; and sections, girders, rails, and flat bars. With Émile Mayrisch, managing director from 1897 of the Société des Mines du Luxembourg et des Forges de Sarrebruck, as overall technical director of ARBED, the new company proceeded rapidly with its plans for modernization, vertical integration, and expansion.

In 1912 ARBED's annual output of crude steel was around 824,000 tons. Old furnaces, blowers, and other installations were being refurbished or replaced, and new, more efficient equipment was being brought in, notably equipment which utilized waste gases from smelting to power other processes further down the line. In 1913 new installations, including three blast furnaces, started up at the company's Esch-Schifflange and Esch-Belval works.

In April of the same year ARBED protected its coke supplies by forming a contractual association with the Eschweiler collieries—Eschweiler Bergwerks-Verein AG (EBV)—near Aachen, Germany. This move was in keeping with a policy of cooperation with other European firms, designed to ensure ARBED's supplies of raw materials—ore, coal, and coke—as well as to find customers for its crude, semi-finished, and finished products and to extend its product range. In 1913 ARBED joined with a Belgian cement-making firm to start a new company, later to become the Société Anonyme des Ciments Luxembourgeois, for their mutual advantage; in exchange for a site near the Esch-Schifflange works, together with a supply of slag and electric current, ARBED would receive cement for its own use at a reduced price.

In 1919, together with the French company Schneider et Cie, ARBED took over all the Luxembourgian and Lorraine iron mines, iron and steel works, including Belval, and wiredrawing works that had belonged before the war to the German company Rhein-Elbe Gelsenkirchener Bergwerks A.G., and set up two linked companies, the Société Métallurgique and the Société Minière des Terres Rouges, of which the first, the Société Métallurgique des Terres Rouges—at Esch-Belval—was to be absorbed in 1937 by ARBED, who acquired a majority holding in the second, the Société Minière des Terres Rouges, in 1954.

World War I Difficulties Persist into 1920s

ARBED was recovering from the setback to its ambitions suffered during World War I. As so often over the centuries, Luxembourg's geographical location had placed it between the hammer and the anvil of contending foreign powers. In spite of its neutral status, guaranteed since 1867, it was invaded by German troops as soon as war broke out, and occupied for the duration. The Grand Duchy has historic, linguistic, and commercial affinities with Belgium and France and with Germany, but the German invasion settled the question of where loyalties should lie in 1914. ARBED's situation was made particularly painful by its ownership of works—Burbach and Hostenbach—in enemy territory. Company policy was to lend as little comfort as possible to the occupying power, while safeguarding as far as possible the survival and future prospects of ARBED and its employees. In the Grand Duchy, after a brief initial shutdown, which the company had offered to prolong if the Luxembourgian government wished, production was resumed by the blast furnaces—four at Dudelange, one at Esch-Schifflange, and one at Dommeldange. Production followed in the steelworks and rolling mills of Dudelange and Esch-Schifflange and in the electric steelworks at Dommeldange. There were shortages of raw materials—fuel, manganese, and lubricants—and of staff, as well as of food. At one point, in 1917, the Germans occupied the factories in an effort to put down a protest strike by hungry workers. The Saar works, Burbach and Hostenbach, were also kept in operation while hostilities lasted, in spite of reduced supplies and the progressive call-up of staff to the German army. Over the war period, in spite of the new installations, ARBED's total monthly steel output dropped from nearly 87,000 tons in July 1914 to just under 50,000 tons in October 1918.

Undercapacity persisted after the war, with continuing fuel and transport problems, plus commercial difficulties arising from Luxembourg's economic isolation, which ended in 1922 with the treaty of economic union with Belgium. Long-term plans proceeded, including the linkage of all the plants located at Esch-sur-Alzette into one huge complex served by its own railway, completed in 1927; by gas-pipes; and by electric cables.

In 1920 ARBED set up a company, the Comptoir Métallurgique Luxembourgeois (COLUMETA), to deal with the sales of its wide range of products. This branch of the group's activities was to flourish and multiply worldwide, with most of the company's sales directed abroad. In 1976 the name COLUMETA was changed to TradeARBED; this company has foreign subsidiaries in 50 foreign countries and in every continent.

Also in 1920, ARBED acquired holdings in the German firm of Felten & Guilleaume, makers of wires, cables, and electrical apparatus; TAMET (Argentina), which produced metal tubes, frames, and bolts; Paul Wurth (Luxembourg) metal constructions; and the Helchteren-Zolder collieries in Belgium. In 1922 it bought a holding in the Belgian nail-making and wire-drawing Clouterie et Tréfilerie des Flandres.

After the death in a motor accident of Émile Mayrisch in 1928, the inter-war technical development of the group's mines and factories was led by Aloyse Meyer. The iron mines in Luxembourg and Lorraine were mechanized and modernized. At the steel works, major additions and improvements were made to installations and processes, with constant adjustments to methods of reducing impurities that were present in the ores or were introduced at the manufacturing stage. Production rose steeply, with peaks in 1929 and 1937. Meanwhile the company continued to provide for the welfare of its employees as it had from the beginning, through its own social services—including training, insurance, pensions, bonuses, and help with housing. Responsibility for some of these services has, of course, been taken over gradually by the state, pensions, for example, in 1931, and family allowances in 1947.

German Occupation Hampers Operations During World War II

In World War II, the Grand Duchy was occupied again, first by German troops, then from August 1940 to September 1944 by Nazi officials. Based on its World War I experience, ARBED had earlier moved out key officials and documents to places of safety, and had obtained legal powers to arrange for its operations to be directed from abroad. Once more production was prudently maintained, at a reduced level, by those who had to stay, working in the face of prolonged hardships and shortages. Output, diminished drastically during the war, ceased entirely for 11 months after the occupation and recovered only slowly from the fuel shortage and transport difficulties that were part of the aftermath of conflict. It was not until 1951 that ARBED reached full capacity once more and achieved production figures—nearly two million tons—that were higher than those of the previous peak years 1929 and 1937.

In the 1950s and 1960s ARBED continued its policy of development and integration within the group. The group expanded through acquisitions and participations at home and abroad—in Europe and South America—aimed at securing its supplies and diversifying its steel production. It continued moving downstream in advance of some of its larger and better-known European competitors.

In 1953 it absorbed the Clouterie et Tréfilerie des Flandres and in the following year acquired a majority holding in the Société Minière des Terres Rouges. In 1962 it was a major participant in the setting-up of the Sidérurgie Maritime company (SIDMAR) to construct an important complex, with integrated steelworks and marine terminal, on the Belgian coast.

Geographic and Product Diversification in 1960s and 1970s

In 1965 ARBED acquired a major holding in the Société Anonyme des Hauts Fourneaux et Aciéries de Differdange-St. Ingbert-Rumelange (HADIR), a consortium of Luxembourgian, French, and Belgian companies that had been developing since 1896. The consortium was absorbed completely by ARBED in 1967. HADIR's Differdange works augmented ARBED's Esch complex. In 1911 Differdange had begun to roll Grey beams. In 1959 ARBED's Dudelange works had started producing steel using the LD-AC (Linz-Donavitz-ARBED-Centre) process. ARBED's wire-works were grouped in 1968 to form a new company, ARBED-Felten & Guilleaume Tréfileries Réunies, which, with other later wire making acquisitions, was to become TrefilARBED in 1974. The 1970s saw the extension of ARBED's activities in several other directions: refractory products; reinforcing wires for car tires; mining operations in Brazil, the United States, and Korea; and mechanical engineering and steel construction. At the end of the 1970s ARBED accounted for a quarter of the Grand Duchy's gross national product. Two important structural measures taken in advance of the world steel crisis of the mid-1970s and 1980s were the establishment of the ARBED Research Centre in 1971 and of ARBED Finance S.A. in 1972, a holding company designed to provide finance for the group. The acronym ARBED S.A. was adopted in 1978 as the company's official name.

In 1975 the Luxembourgian economy went into a long recession caused by many factors: the continuing effects of the 1973 world oil crisis; strengthening foreign competition; inflation; rising wages; fluctuating foreign currencies; and depletion of the country's iron ore. ARBED's crisis lasted until 1984, and ever since then ARBED, like all other European steelmakers, has had to take account of falling demand for steel, increasing use of plastics, growing competition from the developing world, uncertainties about the new eastern European markets, and currency fluctuations.

Rationalization in 1980s

In the 1970s and 1980s overcapacity and financial losses called for vigorous adaptation—organizational, financial, and technological. Competitiveness had to be improved. Over the crisis period ARBED economized by reducing its debts, increasing its share capital, and shedding, without sackings, more than half of its work force, some being redeployed in new industries, others taking the early retirement, at 57 years of age, imposed on steelworkers by the government in 1980.

The company pursued a policy of rationalization. In 1984 the blast furnaces, the steelmaking facilities, and the hot rolling mill at Dudelange closed down. At the same time ARBED needed to invest in new equipment and implement the results of technological research. In 1980 the first continuous caster was commissioned at Esch-Schifflange, and in 1981 the first continuous annealing line went into service at SIDMAR's plant in Ghent.

For a time ARBED was helped by the European Economic Community steel quota system. The Luxembourg government provided some financial support on the restricted scale possible for a small country. When by 1983 ARBED could see the tide beginning to turn again, it was largely the result of the group's own efforts under the chairmanship of Emmanuel Tesch—a descendant of Victor Tesch, one of ARBED's founders. By the end of its boom year, 1989, helped by the peak in the post-crisis upturn of the European steel market, ARBED was able to pay its shareholders their first dividend since 1975.

In the first years of the 1980s the Luxembourgian steel industry had moved back to closer cooperation with Belgium. In 1987 ARBED acquired a three percent share in the Société Générale de Belgique. This holding company holds 25 percent of ARBED's shares while the government of Luxembourg holds 32 percent.

In 1983 ARBED began to detach itself from its group holdings in German steel companies. In 1988 it ended a 75-year association with its traditional supplier of metallurgical coke when Eschweiler Bergwerks-Verein (EBV) joined Ruhrkohle AG. Ruhrkohle, however, is contracted to provide the same service until the beginning of the next century.

In the boom year 1989, ARBED decided to double the capacities of the steel processing works at Galvalange, which produces goods for the construction industry—roofing, flashing, fencing—and for the car and goods vehicle industry—exhaust parts, cabs, and trailers—as well as garden tools and parts for domestic appliances such as microwave ovens, refrigerators, and air-conditioners.

The 1990s and Beyond

Along with the European steel industry in general, ARBED faced a number of pitfalls in the early 1990s. A recession combined with sluggish demand and heavy competition from low-priced imports to force prices steadily downward throughout the first half of the decade. Industrywide overcapacity and low productivity only exacerbated these problems. ARBED met these challenges with economical new production methods, alliance-building, and large reductions in employment levels.

Negotiations began in the summer of 1990 between ARBED and the large Belgian steel producer Cockerill Sambre for a partial merger that would pool most of the flat steel-making capacity of Cockerill Sambre's two plants in Wallonia and of ARBED's Sidmar subsidiary in Flanders. The plan fell through at the end of the year, partly because of regional differences between Flanders and Wallonia over possible closures. The failure of this deal did not discourage ARBED from pursuing several international affiliations in the 1990s. In 1990, acting with the Japanese firm Furukawa Electric, ARBED acquired Yates Circuit Foil (USA), which specialized in copper foil and electronic circuits. And in 1991, ARBED forged a distribution pact with Europe's largest steel producer, France's Usinor Sacilor SA.

With domestic coal and iron sources nearing depletion, ARBED began to wean itself from old-fashioned production methods. By mid-1997, the company had converted all its long products capacity from the traditional integrated process using pig iron to electric arc furnaces—known in the trade as minimills—using scrap steel. Since minimills required fewer personnel to produce as much steel, they also helped ARBED increase productivity. The company slashed employment levels in the early 1990s, cutting 2,700 positions in Luxembourg alone from 1996 through 1998. As was its custom, the company utilized government-funded attrition programs like early retirement, retraining, and job placement to achieve the reductions.

In July 1997 ARBED became the primary shareholder in the privatization of Spain's previously government-owned Corporacion Siderurgica Integral (CSI). The Luxembourgian company offered Pta 109 billion (US$832.1 million) worth of its stock (a 9.5 percent stake) in exchange for a 35 percent share of the Spanish steelmaker. It also pledged to invest an additional Pta 156 billion (US$1 billion) in CSI's operations. The affiliation increased ARBED's annual steel output by more than one-third, to over 16 million tons per year.

Although ARBED suffered a LuxFr1.2 billion (US$35 million) loss on sales of LuxFr232.2 billion (US$8.2 billion) in 1996, CEO Joseph Kinsch was optimistic about the company's future, noting growing demand, rising production, and price increases in a review of the first half of 1997.

Principal Subsidiaries

ARES SA (76.29%); Armasteel Belgium SA; Armasteel SA (Belgium); Ets Durieux SA (Belgium; 80%); Ecosider SA; Europrofil Deutschland GmbH (Germany); Europrofil France SA;

Europrofil SA; Flamm-Stahl GmbH (Germany); ISPC SA (85.17%); Newco Sarl & Cie Secs; Newco Sarl; ProfilARBED SA (99.99%); ProfilARBED Staalhandel BV (The Netherlands); ABC BV (The Netherlands); Anviroma NV (Belgium); Betonijzer Buigcentrale Limburg BV (The Netherlands); Borotrans Born BV (The Netherlands); Calimco BV (The Netherlands); Kielco Belgie NV (Belgium); Cogeaf BV (Belgium; 95.93%); Demanet-Cassart Aciers SA (Belgium); Ijzerhandel H. Houtappel BV (The Netherlands); ISSCO BV (The Netherlands); Kielco Belgie NV (Belgium); Kielco Nederland BV (The Netherlands); Lamot Tank-Transport NV (Belgium); Lamot Transport NV (Belgium); Leduc Trading NV (Belgium); Limbustaal BV (Belgium); Lommaert Algemene Handelsmij NV (Belgium); Lommaert Walserijprodukten BV (The Netherlands); M Soft NV (Belgium); Metalim NV (Belgium); Montan Staal BV (The Netherlands); Probat Profiel NV; Straalco Overpelt NV (Belgium); ProfilARBED Staalhandel Nederland BV (The Netherlands); STUL-Ste du Train Universel de Longwy Sa (France; 75%); Socadi; Socam Sarl; Stahlwerk Thruingen GmbH (Germany); VALPA-Valenciennes Parachevements SA (France); Brefin Verwaltungs-und Beteiligungs (Germany); Bregal-Bremer Galvanisierungs-GmbH (Germany; 50.1%); Cofrafer SA (France); Decosteel NV (Belgium); Europese Staal Prefabricatie NV Belgium); Laminoir de Dudelange SA; Sidmar NV (Belgium; 71.74%); STAHLwerke BREMEN GmbH (Germany; 67.68%); Sidcenter NV (Belgium); Sidstahl Deutschland Stahlhandels-GmbH (Germany); Sidstahl France SA (France); Sidstahl Luxembourg SA; Sidstahl NV (Belgium); Sikel NV; Al-Center NV (Belgium); Al-Fin NV (Belgium; 88.51%); ALZ Nederland BV; Albufin NV (Belgium); Arbed Americas Inc. (U.S.A.); Arkansas Steel Processing Inc. (U.S.A.); Coil-Tec Inc. (U.S.A.); Considar Inc. (U.S.A.); Excel Trading Corp. (U.S.A.); J & F Steel Corp. (U.S.A.); JBF Commercial Corp. (U.S.A.); JBF Financial Corp. (U.S.A.); MP Pipe Inc. (U.S.A.); PA Pipe (U.S.A.); Skyline Steel Corp. (U.S.A.); TradeARBED Canada Inc. (Canada); TradeARBED New York Inc. (U.S.A.); TrefilARBED Canada Inc. (Canada); TrefilARBED Inc. (U.S.A.); Ultra Metals Inc. (U.S.A.); Arbed International Trading SA; Almetal Beheer NV (Belgium); Almetal Holding NV (Belgium); Brasilux SA; Considar Europe SA (99.23%); TradeARBED Participations Sarl; TradeARBED Schweiz AG (Switzerland); Van Heyghen Recycling NV (Belgium); Circuit Foil Luxembourg SA (75%); Hein Lehmann AG (Germany; 96.31%); Hydrolux Sarl; (99.98%); MecanARBED Dommeldange Sarl; Soberi International NV (Belgium; 72.86%); Arbed Finanz Deutschland GmbH (Germany; 99%); Arbed Information Systems SA; Alinvest NV (Belgium); Allard Gieterij NV (Belgium); Arfilux Sarl; Brussimo NV; Egemin NV (Belgium; 94.33%); Finindus NV (Belgium; 50%); Immobiliere Schlassgoart Senc; Informabel Holding SA (Belgium); KIV-Kempense Investeringsvennootschap NV (Belgium); Luxengrais Sarl (75%); Plastigran NV (Belgium); SA Luxembourgeoise d'Exploitations Minieres; Sidarfin NV (Belgium); Sidfin International NV (Belgium; 50%); Sidinvest NV (Belgium; 76.57%); Sotel STe Cooperative Esch-sur-Alzette (77%); Sibral Participacoes Ltda (Brazil); Flachform Stahl AG & Co KG; Howard E. Perry; Hughes and Spencer.

Further Reading

"Arbed to Shut Electric Furnace for a Month," *American Metal Market,* January 12, 1996, p. 1.

Burgert, Philip, "Arbed Looks to Cut 2,700 Steel Jobs," *American Metal Market,* April 26, 1996, p. 1.

——, "Arbed Reports Loss for 1996," *American Metal Market,* April 7, 1997, p. 4.

——, "Arbed to Pay Spain $832.1M to Get CSI," *American Metal Market,* July 31, 1997, p. 12.

Chomé, Félix, ed., *Un Demi-Siécle d'Histoire Industrielle 1911–1964,* Luxembourg: ARBED Archives, [n.d.].

"Compact Plants Ahead for Europe," *American Metal Market,* July 19, 1996, p. 14.

LaRue, Gloria T., "British Group Moves to Kill Arbed Subsidy," *American Metal Market,* July 26, 1995, p. 1.

Munford, Christopher, "Arbed, Usinor Pursue Tightening Distribution," *American Metal Market,* December 7, 1993, p. 5.

Newcomer, James, *The Grand Duchy of Luxembourg,* Lanham, Md.: University Press of America, 1984.

Penson, Stuart, "Arbed Returns to Profitability," *American Metal Market,* May 12, 1995, p. 3.

Regan, James G., "Arbed's Steel Outlook Bright," *American Metal Market,* May 8, 1991, p. 3.

——, "Continent Reflects Arbed, Ilva Woes," *American Metal Market,* October 7, 1991, pp. 2–3.

—Olive Classe
—updated by April Dougal Gasbarre

Armstrong

Armstrong World Industries, Inc.

313 West Liberty Street
Lancaster, Pennsylvania 17603
U.S.A.
(717) 397-0611
Fax: (717) 396-4477
Web site: http://www.armstrong.com

Public Company
Incorporated: 1891 as Armstrong, Brother & Company, Inc.
Employees: 10,572
Sales: $2.16 billion (1996)
Stock Exchanges: New York Philadelphia Pacific
SICs: 2891 Adhesives & Sealants; 2952 Asphalt Felts & Coatings; 3253 Ceramic Wall & Floor Tile; 3996 Linoleum, Asphalt-Feltbase & Other and Surface Floor Coverings, Not Elsewhere Classified

Armstrong World Industries, Inc. is a leading international manufacturer and marketer of products used to finish interiors of homes and other buildings. Its products include floor coverings, ceilings, and adhesives. To a lesser extent the company also produces specialty products such as gaskets and insulation materials for the building, automotive, textile, and other industries. Armstrong also holds a 33 percent stake in Dal-Tile International Inc., a leading producer of ceramic tile in North America. About one-third of the company's overall sales are derived outside the United States.

Originated as Cork-Cutting Shop

In 1860 Thomas Morton Armstrong, a 24-year-old son of Scottish-Irish immigrants from Londonderry, Ireland, used $300 of savings from his job as a shipping clerk to buy a small cork-cutting shop in Pittsburgh. The firm was originally named for his partner in the venture, John O. Glass, but Glass's interest was purchased by Armstrong's brother in 1864 and the company's name was changed to Armstrong, Brother & Company.

Armstrong's original business was cutting cork stoppers, first by hand then after 1862 by machine, from the bark of cork trees which grow in Portugal, Spain, and northern Africa. During the Civil War, 1861 to 1865, the company made bottle stoppers for the Union Army and was singled out for official praise for fulfilling its contracts at the agreed prices with top-grade corks. This good publicity enabled Armstrong to land a large contract with a New York drug firm after the war, beginning the move toward national distribution of its products. In 1864 Thomas Armstrong pioneered the concept of brand-name recognition in his industry by stamping ''Armstrong'' on each cork and offering a written guarantee of quality with each sale.

Originally cork was purchased from American importers, but in 1878 Armstrong made arrangements to purchase, process, and ship corkwood and corks direct from Spain, thus beginning the foreign operations that eventually would make the company the largest cork processor in Spain. By the 1890s Armstrong was the world's largest cork company, employing more than 750 people, most of whom Thomas Armstrong knew by name. In 1891 the company incorporated as Armstrong, Brother & Company, Inc. and, in 1893, purchased the Lancaster Cork Works, beginning its long involvement with the Pennsylvania Dutch area. During the 1890s Armstrong expanded its cork product line to include insulation, cork-board, gaskets, and flexible coverings for machinery. In addition, foreign markets were expanded with sales offices opening in Montreal and Toronto in 1895. In that year the corporate name was changed to Armstrong Cork Company. Thomas Armstrong died in 1908 and was succeeded as president by his son, Charles Dickey Armstrong.

Expanded into Linoleum Floor Covering in Early 20th Century

Searching for new cork-based products, the company decided to add linoleum floor covering to its line and, in 1908, the first Armstrong linoleum was produced in a new plant in Lancaster. Invented in England in 1863 by Frederick Walton, linoleum was basically a mixture of cork flour, mineral fillers, and linseed oil, which was pressed under high temperature onto burlap backing and colored with pigments. The linoleum line was the beginning of the company's involvement with floor

Company Perspectives:

We will be a fast and flexible learning organization committed to ever-improving the value of Armstrong for our employees, customers, and shareholders.

We will be a world leader in all our businesses by excelling in customer satisfaction, innovation, marketing, and manufacturing.

These capabilities, our people, and our commitment to quality will be our global platform for growth.

products, which by thc 1990s, in a variety of modern forms, provided about half of its sales volume.

Under Charles Armstrong's leadership the firm expanded its product lines with cork insulating board and other insulating materials, packaging closures, and gaskets, as well as linoleum and related flooring materials, becoming in the process a much more consumer-oriented company than before. He also continued his father's policy of responsibility towards his employees by initiating benefits that were rare, if not unprecedented, early in this century. In 1909 he established free dental service for employees. Other pioneering examples of corporate responsibility followed: extra pay for overtime in 1913, shop committees to communicate with management in 1919, paid vacations in 1924, and group life insurance in 1931. Armstrong was one of the first U.S. companies to provide such fringe benefits as pensions and group medical insurance. Thus Charles Armstrong's presidency expressed the company's philosophy that employees should be provided for voluntarily by industry rather than by means of government compulsion.

Charles Armstrong became chairman of the board in 1928 and the next ycar John J. Evans succeeded him as president. In 1934, the vice-president, Henning Webb Prentis, Jr., who was to have a great impact on the company's development, became the next president of Armstrong.

Marketing Innovations Boosted Sales in the 1910s and 1920s

Prentis had joined the firm in 1907 when, as a 23-year-old with an M.A. in economics, he took a job with Armstrong's insulation division in Pittsburgh in order to gain some practical experience before beginning a teaching career. It was a significant hiring decision. Prentis became interested in the possibilities of advertising and public relations. He wrote the first promotional literature on cork products to be published by Armstrong, including selling aids for retailers and booklets on home decoration for consumers. In 1911 he became head of the tiny advertising department and persuaded management to support a three-year, $50,000 advertising campaign. In 1917 he arranged for the company's first national advertisement in the mass media, to appear in the September 1917 issue of the *Saturday Evening Post.* He pioneered his industry's recruitment of college graduates as salesmen and, with Charles Armstrong's support, helped develop the strenuous training programs that enormously strengthened company management. He improved distribution practices by initiating price lists with discounts based on quantities purchased, and insisted on the establishment of close, friendly relations with wholesalers and retailers.

Thanks largely to Prentis's marketing innovations, Armstrong grew substantially during the 1920s, reaching nearly $48 million in sales by 1929, when the company moved its headquarters from Pittsburgh to Lancaster, Pennsylvania. When the Great Depression cut sales in half and produced large losses by 1934, Prentis was appointed president to improve the company's situation. He diversified by purchasing rubber- and asphalt-tile factories, and in 1938 acquired two glass companies, Whitall Tatum and Hart Glass Manufacturing.

The company's personnel policies helped to maintain morale and loyalty during those hard times. One example was the research employee who was laid off because of the Great Depression but continued to come to work without pay and, eventually rehired, made significant contributions to the development of a new flooring process. With Armstrong's debt-free balance sheet, Prentis's efforts were successful. By 1935 dividends on the common stock were restored and in 1936 Armstrong had its most profitable year to that point, a stunning achievement at a time when the country was still in the grip of the Great Depression. By 1937 the common stock had climbed from a low of $3.25 in 1932 to a price of approximately $65.

In addition to improving Armstrong's profitability, Prentis became much more of a public figure than his predecessors. He spoke frequently on behalf of conservative business philosophies in opposition to the New Deal policies of the Roosevelt administration. He served as director of the United States Chamber of Commerce and as president of the National Association of Manufacturers. When World War II began, Prentis organized Armstrong's conversion to war production, including the establishment of a munitions division. In 1942 and 1943 he served as deputy director of the War Production Board for the Philadelphia region, becoming an employee of the government administration he had so frequently criticized.

Postwar Emphasis on Product Innovation

After the war, Armstrong prepared to meet the tremendous demand for building materials for new houses. Two more asphalt-tile plants, a fiberboard plant, and a bottle-closure plant were built. In addition the company expanded its industrial-adhesives business and added the production of glass bottles to its packaging division. By 1950 annual sales had climbed to $163 million, and earnings were at record levels. In that year Prentis became chairman of the board and was succeeded as president by Clifford J. Backstrand.

Backstrand's goal was to use the growth to date to increase profits. He emphasized not only marketing but also research, realizing that product innovation was essential for successful competition in the postwar period. He completed the building industry's biggest research-and-development center. To help sell products in the home-remodeling market, in 1953 Armstrong built in Lancaster an "idea house" filled with Armstrong products, to be used as a showcase for dealers and customers. Creativity within the company was encouraged by giving special recognition and awards to employees who came up with ideas for new products and new processes. During the 1950s cork was largely replaced by chemicals and synthetics as the basis of the company's products. By 1960 building materials accounted for 60 percent of sales, and industrial specialties and packaging were each 20 percent of sales. Backstrand improved the company's accounting methods for measuring the profitability of various operations, establishing the concept of return on capital employed as a gauge of achievement. In 1962 Backstrand became chairman and Maurice J. Warnock was appointed president.

By the early 1960s Armstrong had extensive foreign operations, manufacturing textile-mill supplies in India and flooring in plants in Canada, Britain, and West Germany, as well as continuing to process cork in Spain. Warnock attempted to reduce the company's strong dependency on the housing and construction markets by entering the consumer products field with a liquid wax plus detergent that cleaned and polished floors at once. Successful at first, this move to enter the supermarket-oriented consumer market eventually failed to justify its invested capital and was discontinued. Otherwise, Warnock's tenure as president was successful with new efficiencies in organization, improvement in flooring products, and continued growth in sales to $460 million in 1967. In 1966 and 1967 Armstrong entered the carpet business with the purchase of Brinton Carpets and E. & B. Carpet Mills. By the end of the 1960s, over one-third of Armstrong's sales came from products developed by the company within the previous decade. Armstrong invariably promoted from within and, in accordance with this policy, Warnock was succeeded in 1968 by a flooring executive who had spent his entire adult life with the company, James H. Binns.

Furniture Added in the Late 1960s

Binns's tenure as president from 1968 to 1978 brought significant changes in the makeup and direction of the company, based on his belief that Armstrong's future lay mainly in the interior-furnishings market, which was entering a boom period. In 1968 Armstrong acquired the furniture manufacturer Thomasville Furniture Industries and the furniture wholesaler Knapp & Tubbs, although the latter company was sold in 1972. In 1969 Binns sold the line of cleansers, waxes, and polishes to Chemway Corporation and the extensive packaging operations to Kerr Glass Manufacturing Company. The insulation-contracting business was sold to its former employees. Altogether Binns sold off businesses with about $125 million in annual sales, about one-fourth of sales volume. By the early 1970s about 90 percent of sales were concentrated in building products and home furnishings, and about 10 percent in industrial products such as gaskets and textile-mill supplies. This ratio continued into the 1990s.

In 1978 Binns became chairman of the board, and Harry A. Jensen served as president and CEO until his retirement in 1983. Through the 1970s and much of the 1980s Armstrong continued to grow in the same directions. The production of linoleum was discontinued in 1974, but the company continued to develop new types of resilient flooring, among which Solarian no-wax flooring became a well-known brand name. In 1980 the corporate name was changed to Armstrong World Industries, Inc. to reflect its growing international operations and the fact that it was no longer based on the cork business. Sales generally trended upward with some annual fluctuations due to changes in the building cycle, reaching $1 billion in 1977 and $2 billion in 1987. Earnings followed the same pattern with net income increasing from $66 million in 1979 to $187 million in 1989.

Ceramic Tile Added and Carpet Divested in the Late 1980s

Between 1983 and 1988, Joseph L. Jones served as president and chairman. His successor, William W. Adams, oversaw a series of significant events in the late 1980s. In 1988 Armstrong entered the ceramic-tile business by acquiring American Olean Tile Company from National Gypsum for $330 million, adding about $200 million to 1989 sales. In December 1989 Armstrong completed the sale of its carpet division, abandoning that business which was not producing an adequate return on investment, thus reducing annual sales by about $300 million. In addition, in 1989 the company sold Applied Color Systems, a small digital color-processing-control business.

In July 1989 Armstrong learned that the Belzberg family of Canada had acquired 9.85 percent of its stock and had announced the intention of gaining control of the company and selling its furniture and industrial products divisions. The Belzberg's stock ownership increased in 1990 to 11.7 percent. In April 1990, Senate Bill 1310 of the Pennsylvania legislature, the strongest antitakeover bill passed by any state, with support from Armstrong, became law. The bill provided for seizure of short-term profits in a failed takeover, limited voting rights of hostile shareholders, and guaranteed severance pay to employees who lost jobs because of a corporate takeover. A few days after passage of the law, the Belzbergs lost a proxy attempt at the company's annual meeting, seating only one of four candidates for directors on the board. At the end of the next month, the Belzbergs sold their Armstrong stock at a loss of about $18 million. In June 1990, Armstrong and the Belzberg affiliates resolved the remaining issues between them by withdrawing lawsuits and countersuits against each other.

Rocky Times in the 1990s

The early and mid-1990s saw the company continue to be involved in litigation relating to personal-injury suits and other claims based on asbestos-containing insulation products, a business that was sold by Armstrong in 1969. The claims were being paid by insurance income under the Wellington Agreement on asbestos-related claims. In 1988 Armstrong and 20 other companies replaced the Wellington Asbestos Claims Facility with the Center for Claims Resolution, which continued in operation through the mid-1990s. Other cases were brought by public school districts, private property owners, and others, including a lawsuit filed with the U.S. Supreme Court by 29 states. By 1994 Armstrong had recorded $198 million in liability and defense costs on its balance sheet, and estimated that it might be responsible for $245 million in additional liability by 2004.

Overall, this period was a fairly rocky one for Armstrong, punctuated with restructuring charges and divestments on the one hand and awards for quality and record sales on the other. In 1992 the company posted $165.5 million in restructuring charges, mainly to close four major manufacturing plants—two in the United States, one each in Canada and Belgium. Another $89.3 million restructuring charge was incurred the following year in relation to the elimination of hundreds of jobs. In fact, Armstrong's workforce became increasingly streamlined as the 1990s went on, with more than 6,300 fewer people employed in 1996 as in 1990. In the midst of these changes came a change in management as well, as George A. Lorch took over Adams's duties as president and CEO in September 1993 and then became chairman as well in April 1994 when Adams retired.

Momentous events proved to transform Armstrong during 1995. Although of only small financial consequence, the company's sale of its champagne cork business in Spain was important symbolically as it marked Armstrong's exit from its original business. More important was the divestment of the company's furniture business, which was struggling as a result of a long recession in the furniture market. In December Armstrong sold Thomasville Furniture to the maker of Broyhill and Lane furniture, INTERCO International Inc., for $331.2 million. Another struggling Armstrong business—its ceramic tile operations, which was beset with low-cost competitors in Spain and Italy—was also divested later that same month. In a deal with Dal-Tile International Inc., Armstrong traded $27.6 million and American Olean Tile for about a one-third stake in Dal-Tile. Also in 1995, Armstrong entered the European metal ceilings business through the acquisition of the U.K.-based Cape PLC. Finally, in October the company's Building Products Operations, after twice being named a finalist earlier in the decade, was awarded the prestigious Malcolm Baldrige National Quality Award, an honor that highlighted Armstrong's continued commitment to making quality products.

By 1996, then, Armstrong World Industries was involved in fewer core businesses than it had been for decades but held a leading position in nearly all of them. In the building area, the company specialized in floor coverings, ceilings, and adhesives, while its industrial products were led by insulation and gasketing materials. When its numbers were adjusted to reflect only these ongoing businesses, Armstrong posted record net sales of $2.16 billion in 1996, while net earnings hit $155.9 million, an increase of 26 percent over the previous year.

Following its 1995 divestments, Armstrong concentrated on bolstering its core operations, through joint ventures, alliances, and acquisitions. It also increasingly looked outside its home country for growth opportunities. In 1996 the company completed a joint venture ceiling plant in Shanghai and entered into joint ventures in Europe for the manufacture of soft-fiber and metal ceilings. Armstrong that same year formed an alliance with the Austria-based F. Egger Co. for the manufacture of laminate flooring, a new product category for the Armstrong flooring line. In 1997 the company entered into a battle with Sommer Allibert S.A. over which company would take over Domco Inc., a Quebec-based maker of flooring products. By October, with a lawsuit between Armstrong and Sommer Allibert pending, Armstrong's proposed $354 million acquisition of Domco was approved by the U.S. Federal Trade Commission.

Armstrong had come a long way from a one-room cork shop to its position in the late 1990s as a leader in the international home-furnishings industry with an outstanding brand-name reputation. The company was likely to continue to aggressively seek out opportunities to bolster its core businesses, both at home and abroad.

Principal Subsidiaries

Armstrong Cork Finance Corporation; Armstrong Enterprises, Inc.; Armstrong Industrial Specialties, Inc.; Armstrong Industrial Specialties International, Inc.; Armstrong Realty Group, Inc.; Armstrong Ventures, Inc.; Armstrong World Industries Asia, Inc.; Armstrong World Industries (Delaware) Inc.; Armstrong World Industries (India) Inc.; Armstrong World Industries Latin America, Inc.; A W I (Nevada), Inc.; Charleswater Products, Inc.; Chemline Industries, Inc.; IWF, Inc.; I.W. Insurance Company; The W.W. Henry Company; Alphacoustic (UK) Ltd.; Armstrong-ABC Co., Ltd. (Japan); Armstrong Architectural Products S.L. (Spain); Armstrong Building Products (U.K.); Armstrong Building Products B.V. (Netherlands); Armstrong Building Products Company (Shanghai) Ltd. (China); Armstrong Building Products G.m.b.H. (Germany); Armstrong Building Products S.A. (France); Armstrong Europa G.m.b.H. (Germany); Armstrong Europe Services (U.K.); Armstrong Floor Products Europe G.m.b.H. (Germany); Armstrong Floor Products Europe Ltd. (U.K.); Armstrong Floor Products Europe Sarl. (France); Armstrong FSC, Ltd. (Bermuda); Armstrong Industrial Specialties G.m.b.H. (Germany); Armstrong Industrial Specialties International, SARL (France); Armstrong Industrial Specialties Ltd. (U.K.); Armstrong Insulation (Panyu) Co, Ltd. (China); Armstrong Insulation Products (U.K.); Armstrong Insulation Products A.G. (Switzerland); Armstrong Insulation Products Benelux, S.A. (Belgium); Armstrong Insulation Products G.m.b.H. (Germany); Armstrong Insulation Products S.A. (Spain); Armstrong Insulation Products S.A. (France); Armstrong Insulation Products Sp. zo.o. (Poland); Armstrong Insulation Rus. (Russia); Armstrong (Japan) K.K.; Armstrong Metal Ceilings Ltd. (U.K.); Armstrong-Nyles Pty. Ltd. (Australia); Armstrong (Singapore) Pte. Ltd.; Armstrong Textile Products G.m.b.H. (Germany); Armstrong (U.K.) Investments; Armstrong World Industries-A.C.I. B.V. (Netherlands); Armstrong World Industries Canada Ltd.; Armstrong World Industries (China) Ltd.; Armstrong World Industries de Mexico, S.A. de C.V.; Armstrong World Industries do Brasil Ltda. (Brazil); Armstrong World Industries, G.m.b.H. (Germany); Armstrong World Industries (H.K.) Limited (Hong Kong); Armstrong World Industries Italia S.r.l. (Italy); Armstrong World Industries Korea, Ltd.; Armstrong World Industries Ltd. (U.K.); Armstrong World Industries Pty. Ltd. (Australia); Armstrong World Industries (Thailand) Ltd.; Inarco Limited (India; 40%); ISA Co., Ltd. (Japan; 25%); Liberty Commercial Services Ltd. (Bermuda).

Further Reading

Armstrong: A Historical Summary, Lancaster, Pa.: Armstrong World Industries, Inc., 1997.

Carlino, Maria, "Armstrong World Industries Inc.," *Journal of Commerce & Commercial,* March 1, 1996, p. 5A.

Coleman, Lisa, "All Dressed Up," *Forbes,* February 3, 1992, p. 108.

Coletti, Richard J., "Armstrong: Calling the Belzberg Bluff," *Financial World,* September 19, 1989, p. 16.

Franklin, Barbara Hackman, "Caught in a Sea Change: Armstrong World Industries Vs. the Belzbergs; An Anatomy of an End-of-an-Era Takeover Battle," *Directors & Boards,* Fall 1990, p. 39.

Henkoff, Ronald, "Floored? You *Can* Come Back," *Fortune,* February 21, 1994, pp. 95–96.

Jaffe, Thomas, "The Belzbergs, Again," *Forbes,* September 4, 1989, p. 316.

Mehler, William A., Jr., *Let the Buyer Have Faith: The Story of Armstrong,* Lancaster, Pa.: Armstrong World Industries, Inc., 1987, 228 p.

Sparks, Debra, "Armstrong: Weak Legs," *Financial World,* October 25, 1994, p. 20.

Sraeel, Holly A., "Product Testing Begins at Home: Armstrong World Industries, Inc. Uses Its Own Interior Products to Define Space," *Buildings,* July 1988, p. 42.

Weston, Rusty, "Painful Re-engineering Leads to Baldrige Award for Quality," *PC Week,* November 6, 1995, pp. 1, 143.

Wickens, Barbara, "A Fight for Control," *Maclean's,* May 14, 1990, p. 48.

Zweig, Phillip, "Armstrong: Not Just a Takeover Play," *Financial World,* April 5, 1988, p. 21.

—Bernard A. Block
—updated by David E. Salamie

Aspect Telecommunications Corporation

1170 Fox Drive
San Jose, California 95131-2312
U.S.A.
(408) 325-2200
Fax: (408) 325-2260
Web site: http://www.aspect.com

Public Company
Incorporated: 1985
Employees: 1,400
Sales: $309 million (1996)
Stock Exchanges: NASDAQ
SICs: 3661 Telephone & Telegraph Apparatus

Aspect Telecommunications Corporation is a global provider of telephone call distribution and information management systems. Aspect's products serve companies with mission-critical call centers that exist to generate revenue, service customers, and handle inquiries. It is the largest manufacturer of big dedicated ACDs (automatic call distributor software). Its products include call distributors, interactive response systems, management information and reporting tools, computer-telephony integration technology, and call center planning and forecasting packages. The company also provides services vital to call center environments, including business applications consulting, systems integration, and training. Aspect customers are service-oriented companies that require the capabilities of a multisystem, multisite, multivendor call center environment. More than 700 companies are served by Aspect products worldwide, including companies in health care, travel and hospitality, retail and catalogue, insurance, utilities, banking and finance, communications, and technologies industries. The *Wall Street Journal* reported a 1996 rating issued by the brokerage house Drexel Burnham Lambert, ranking Aspect Telecommunications first among large American corporations as the most shareholder-friendly company. Included among Aspect's competitors are AT&T, Northern Telecom, Inc., ROLM, Rockwell International Corporation, and Teknekron Infoswitch Corporation.

Pre-1980s: Callers on "Hold"

Based in the computer technology hub of Silicon Valley, in San Jose, California, Aspect Telecommunications was founded in 1985 by Jim Carreker, a Georgia Tech BSEE and Stanford University MS graduate in electronic engineering whose phone systems expertise grew from his days as a market researcher for Dataquest. His job required that he track the PBX (private branch exchange, or private telephone switchboard) business. After quitting Dataquest he started Aspect Telecommunications to develop software that could handle multiple automatic call-routing features previously unavailable. He adapted an open, programmable switch (Summa Four's SDS-1000), wrote some automatic call distributor software (ACD), and within months the company's flagship product, the Aspect CallCenter, was launched.

The earliest automatic call distributors had been developed in the early 1970s and were used by big airline reservation systems. The automated "receptionists" would simply hold calls in the order in which they were received, while playing music for the waiting caller. Carreker imagined a more efficient system that would allow the intended destination of a call made from a touch-tone telephone to be quickly determined automatically and rerouted to an operator. Since the advent of toll-free 800 numbers, phone lines had been increasingly inundated with calls. Business managers became concerned about keeping customers on hold for long periods of time, fearing that they would tire of waiting and hang up to call a competitor. Carreker's system could handle the traffic by interacting with the caller, distinguishing between types of calls, and then speedily routing each call to its proper destination. Aspect began replacing hundreds of their competitors' systems, and the company grew faster than the market. Aspect systems had the capability of handling more than a million call transactions each day. By handling calls efficiently, companies saved on labor expense: A site taking 10,000 calls per day could reduce its agent expense by as much as $100,000 per year for every ten seconds it saved per call.

1990: Initial Public Offering and Expanding Growth

Aspect made its initial public offering in May of 1990, raising $4 million by selling at 15 cents per share. The company soon was selling at 81 times its 1989 earnings. By 1993,

Company Perspectives:

In addition to adhering to core values, including satisfying customers, providing quality professional products and service, emphasis on employee integrity on every level, placing value on teamwork, and embracing flexibility in order to expand the scope of product offerings, Aspect Telecommunications Corporation seeks to achieve balance between the interests of all its stakeholders, including the communities in which they live and work. The company supports its communities through the Aspect Community Commitment Fund, which focuses on children and youth-at-risk, in the belief that healthy profitable companies have a stake in the quality of life in the communities where their employees live and work.

revenues grew to $106 million, up 50 percent over the previous year, and representing a 40 percent growth in installed base systems. Aspect expanded product offerings and introduced Aspect Enterprise Access, an architecture that allows the Aspect CallCenter System to function as a vital information server on a company's local or wide area enterprise-wide data network. The company reported that growth occurred in every channel of distribution and across a broad array of industries, system sizes, and applications.

Company strategy involved the provision of quality products distributed across a broad range of industries, rather than marketing to a narrow concentration in one or a few industry segments. Aspect executives also decided to focus on internal development programs that improved on the company's core products. New to the industry was the introduction of hand-held devices for initiating remote transactions. Cellular and wireless telephones, notebook computers with modems and faxes, and interactive television remote controls contributed further to caller flexibility. The company reports explained that their ''system architecture made use of industry-standard building blocks from the outset, including UNIX operating systems, SQL relational databases, TCP/IP networking, and the Microsoft Windows graphical user interface.'' The Aspect system allows a straightforward physical connection to public and private networks for voice, data, imaging, and other formats. The CallCenter System offers management information features including summary and detailed views of calling volumes, call handling efficiencies, trends, and other important information about each business application. Customers can manipulate detailed CallCenter data in a spreadsheet environment through its graphical capability. The company also introduced Aspect EnterpriseAccess, an open architecture that enables the Aspect CallCenter to be an information server on a corporate network. Each Aspect customer selects a basic system from one of ten standard models, then adds the appropriate interface cards and related equipment to meet their needs. Options may be added, such as the hardware and software to receive calling number Automatic Number Identification (ANI) from the public telephone network or software packages to forecast staffing needs or customize reports.

Increasingly, companies recognized that superior customer service would provide an advantage over competitors, giving customer satisfaction a prominent value in the manufacturing and service industries. The company soon began placing their systems in the banking and credit card industries. They added new technology, health care, and insurance customers. In the cable television and online services industries, Aspect installed systems for TimeWarner, Delphi, and America Online. In 1993 an agreement with the U.S. Government Internal Revenue Service resulted in the placement of a dozen new systems. Repeat customers in the commercial sector included Fidelity Investments, British Airways, DirectLine Insurance, Charles Schwab & Co., and NatWest Bank, all of which added to their initial Aspect CallCenter Systems. The customer base for 1993 grew to include First Union Bank, Mercedes Benz of North America, Chrysler Corporation, and SynOptics Communications. Increasingly, public utilities began using the company's systems in their customer service departments. Aspect adapted to the period of rapid growth by hiring more full-time employees in the areas of sales, support, marketing, finance, development (with approximately 12 percent of revenues set aside for product development), manufacturing, and administration. As part of its development program, the company implemented a strategy of holding application workshops to obtain customer feedback. It borrowed information from successful customers concerning how their businesses worked and how they innovated, and it studied areas that made those companies successful.

In an effort to remain abreast of leading edge technology, the company began a program for investing in promising start-up enterprises in fields related to call transaction processing, which allowed for a venture-style investment in Latitude Communications, a teleconferencing product company. It also decided to expand its focus on federal government sales opportunities. A new wholly owned subsidiary, Aspect Teleservices, was formed in Tucson, Arizona for the purpose of providing technical support services for companies in need of third-party assistance to their end-users—in particular, the company supports infrastructure software such as relational databases, networked operating systems, and other applications software.

Persian Gulf War Signaled Tentative Global Expansion

After intensive industry market studies conducted during the late 1980s and the introduction of toll-free service in England, Scotland, and Wales, Aspect established Aspect Telecommunications Ltd., a London-based subsidiary, formed to distribute and offer support to operations in the United Kingdom. In 1990 the company expanded into Canada and the Netherlands. Despite its success record to date, company officials carefully considered the possible effects of political and economic unrest following the Iraqi invasion of Kuwait. They decided to concentrate on building the business through existing channels rather than risking a too rapid international presence during this period of uncertainty. Instead, they focused on preparations for policies, development, and infrastructure that would accompany a later international expansion phase. By 1994 the company was ready to implement a decentralized, multicultural capacity.

Dirk Speas, a six-year veteran as an Aspect vice-president, moved to Amsterdam to lead in the next phase of European expansion. Aspect Telecommunications GmbH, a Frankfurt-based sales and support subsidiary, was formulated after the parent company's determination that Germany was the next most promising market. The German government approved the connection of the Aspect CallCenter System to their public exchange lines. In an effort to provide its system to customers throughout Germany, the company also entered into a partnership agreement with Controlware GmbH, a 15-year-old German company specializing in data networks and systems integration. In 1995 the geographical market was expanded to include system sales and installations in Belgium, Ireland, and Australia, and the company then began investigating possible marketing channels in the Asia/Pacific region.

By this time Aspect eclipsed Rockwell, the long-time leader in huge automatic call distributors, according to Newton of *Computer Telephony.* Holding $108 million in cash, Aspect sales for 1995 grew to $199 million, largely reflecting new orders for the company's core system, the Aspect CallCenter, and from its EnterpriseAccess and Agility Product offerings, which had been introduced in 1993 and 1994, respectively. Nearly 40 software applications partners continued to provide complementary products for Aspect customers, allowing the company to maintain a leadership position in the computer-telephony integration market. Aspect continued to focus on manufacturing software integral to the switch. It made improvements in its reliability and capacity, while allowing its partners to write the rest of the applicable software. Aspect assists in testing its parts, and it co-markets with its partners, often recommending customers to one another.

In the area of organizational leadership, James Carreker shifted from his position of company president. Dennis Haar assumed the role of president in conjunction with that of chief operating officer. Carreker stated in a company report that he would serve henceforth as company chairman and chief executive officer, which he said would allow more "time to focus on the longer-term strategic opportunities for Aspect." He added, "That we accomplished this transition during the quarter in which we were able to report our largest sequential revenue growth says a great deal about the wide internal acceptance of this appointment."

The company continued to grow. Revenues in 1996 increased by 55 percent from those in 1995. Aspect's operational base expanded into Austria, Belgium, Switzerland, Denmark, France, Luxembourg, South Africa, and Singapore. Its acquisition of TCS Management Group, Inc., a leading supplier of call center planning and forecasting software, provided the best-in-class tools to managers of mission-critical call centers. All of the senior management from TCS remained with the company after the acquisition. Overall, the company increased its employee count by 40 percent in a single year, while averaging one new CallCenter system installation each business day of the year. Aspect received a significant order from the United States Postal Service for a $20 million multisystem, including products and services—one of the largest single orders for call centers in many years. The company forecast an increase in competition and responded by accelerating efforts toward new technological insight by increasing spending in research and development by 37 percent to $35 million.

Virtual Solutions in the Late 1990s

When asked about subsequent trends, Carreker told reporter Harry Newton that the industry would experience a blending of call centers, blending inbound and outbound calling. He said that companies "will follow the sun," networking call centers around the globe, and would increasingly rely on media other than the telephone to bring in sales, including "video kiosks in shopping malls, CD-ROMs, PC modem entry, PDA sales entry, fax entry, the Internet, interactive cable TV." Recognizing that customers have come to expect rapid service, detailed information, and round-the-clock transaction handling, Aspect continued to develop its virtual call centers to accommodate every aspect of customer contact.

While denying that the company takes a textbook approach to managing growth, Carreker recommended that anyone seeking to understand more about the company should read the mainstream management literature of James C. Collins and Jerry I. Porras, who wrote the book *Built to Last,* which Carreker feels validates Aspect's corporate philosophy.

Principal Subsidiaries

Aspect Teleservices; Commerce Soft, Inc.; Aspect Telecommunications Ltd. (United Kingdom); Aspect Telecommunications B.V. (The Netherlands); Aspect Telecommunications Gmbh (Germany).

Further Reading

Dorfman, John, "Drexel's Spoil's Help Fund Rating of 'Friendly' Firms," *The Wall Street Journal,* April 18, 1996.

Lipp, Jane F., "Aspect Shows New Agility," *Business Communications Review,* November 1994, p. 66 (2).

Newton, Harry, "The Biggest CT Success Story Ever: Jim Carreker," *Computer Telephony,* October 1995.

Wiegner, Kathleen K., "Telephone Telepathy," *Forbes,* September 3, 1990, pp. 99–101.

—Terri Mozzone

Avis Rent A Car, Inc.

900 Old Country Road
Garden City, New York 11530
U.S.A.
(516) 222-3000
Fax: (516) 222-6677
Web site: http://www.avis.com

Public Company
Incorporated: 1946 as Avis Airlines Rent-A-Car System
Employees: 16,000
Sales: $1.87 billion (1996)
Stock Exchanges: New York
SICs: 7514 Passenger Car Rental

Avis Rent A Car, Inc. is the largest Avis system franchisee in the world, with more than 600 rental locations in the United States, Canada, Puerto Rico, the U.S. Virgin Islands, Argentina, Australia, and New Zealand (the Avis system as a whole consists of about 4,200 rental locations in approximately 160 countries, and comprises the second-largest general use car-rental business in the world, trailing Hertz Corporation). Known throughout its history for quality service, Avis Rent A Car caters primarily to business travelers (who account for about 60 percent of the company's domestic revenue), with a resulting concentration on airport rental locations (from which about 85 percent of domestic revenue is derived). Avis, Inc.—the predecessor company to Avis Rent A Car—was purchased by hotel and real estate franchiser HFS Inc. in 1996. The following year, HFS created Avis Rent A Car, Inc. and sold about 75 percent of the new company to the public. In the process, HFS retained the Avis brand name and the Wizard reservation system, so Avis Rent A Car now licenses the use of the Avis name from HFS and uses the Wizard System through a long-term service agreement.

Early History

Avis Airlines Rent-A-Car System was founded in 1946 by Warren E. Avis, a former Army Air Corps flyer. The owner of an automobile dealership in Detroit, Avis had the idea of providing car-rental services at airports, surmising that air travel would quickly become more popular than travel by rail. Using savings, dealership profits, and a $75,000 loan, he opened Avis Airlines Rent-A-Car System in two locations, at Willow Run Airport near Detroit and at Miami Airport in Florida. Avis's idea proved successful and his business grew quickly. Airports in New York, Chicago, Dallas, Washington, Los Angeles, and Houston were soon serviced by car-rental franchises licensed to use the Avis name.

By 1948, Avis was nationally known. In that year, the company dropped the "airlines" designation from its name, expanding operations beyond airports to serve hotels and businesses in urban areas. During the next six years, Avis also expanded internationally. In addition to its 185 locations in the United States, Avis acquired 10 in Canada and one in Mexico, and established ties with car-rental agencies throughout Europe and the United Kingdom. Warren E. Avis sold the company in 1954 to Richard S. Robie, a car-rental system owner operating in New England. Robie encouraged continued expansion, introducing a one-way car-rental system and a company charge card. Although Avis had revenues of $4 million in 1956, Robie was plagued by problems of cash flow incurred during his expansion efforts, and was forced to sell the company. Avis's new owners, the Amoskeag Company and other investors, continued to foster its growth, creating a new entity, Avis, Inc. Business operations were consolidated through the formation of a wholly owned subsidiary, Avis Rent A Car System, Inc.; electronic data processing was introduced to facilitate the company's innovative corporate charge card billing system; car leasing was established; and the licensee system was extended to include markets in Austria, Belgium, Norway, and Spain.

By 1962, Avis owned a fleet of 7,500 vehicles generating annual revenue of $25 million. The company was purchased that year by Lazard Freres and Company, an investment banking firm in New York City, and its corporate headquarters was moved to Garden City, New York. Under the direction of newly appointed president Robert Townsend, Avis launched a highly successful advertising campaign emphasizing its status as number two contender for car-rental market share. The slogan "We're only No. 2. We try harder" appealed to the public and contributed greatly to Avis's subsequent growth. In 1965, having attained annual revenues exceeding $74 million, Avis was acquired by International Telephone and Telegraph Corporation (IT&T); Winston V. Morrow, Jr., was appointed chief executive officer. During this time, international expansion again assumed paramount importance, and Avis increased its operations throughout Europe and Africa, becoming the leading car-rental company in Europe within eight years.

Enjoyed Strong Growth in the 1970s

Keeping pace with technological advances, in 1972 Avis introduced the first and largest computerized information system to be used in a U.S. car-rental business. The Wizard System, renovated in 1979, 1984, and the early 1990s, made reservations and processed rentals, maintained preventive maintenance schedules for Avis's vehicles, and generated for auto manufacturers lists of customers who purchased Avis's used cars. The system also provided electronically transmitted billing reports for use with corporate accounts.

During the same year, Avis became a public company when IT&T was ordered to sell several of its businesses. Forty-eight percent of Avis's shares were sold to the public; the balance was held in trust by a court official. During this time, Avis, along with other car-rental companies, began to sell their used cars directly to the consumer rather than to wholesalers. This became a lucrative source of income; by 1987, Avis was marketing approximately 50,000 used cars each year. In 1976 Colin M. Marshall became chief executive officer of Avis, and in the following year the company was purchased by Norton Simon, Incorporated for $174 million. James F. Calvano succeeded Marshall as chief executive officer in 1979; that same year, Avis concluded an advertising and marketing agreement with General Motors, agreeing to feature GM cars in its worldwide fleet. The 1970s was a decade of enormous growth for Avis both domestically and internationally. Several factors, including greater airline use, airline deregulation, and the increasing strength of Avis's European, African, and Middle Eastern operations, contributed to its jump in revenues from $162 million in 1970 to $673 million in 1979.

Difficult 1980s Led to Several Ownership Changes

The strong growth of the 1970s slowed in the early 1980s as high oil prices, soaring interest rates, and inflation plagued the global economy, reducing the volume of air travel and weakening the closely connected car-rental market. Price competition among the leading car-rental companies contributed to a $50 million loss for Avis in 1982; 2,400 jobs were cut as a result. J. Patrick Barrett, who became chief executive officer of the company in 1981, along with Joseph V. Vittoria, who became president and chief operating officer in 1983, and Alun Cathcart, who became group managing director and chief executive of the Europe/Africa/Middle East Division in the same year, provided new direction for the company. They reorganized management, reemphasized the company's "We try Harder" image, and introduced new technology, such as Avis Express service. Designed to facilitate fast passage through airline terminals, Avis Express processed rental agreements before customers deplaned, allowing the consumer a speedy departure from the airport. Earlier, Avis had introduced a computerized checkout system to its operations in Europe; by 1983, after further enhancements, only a few seconds were required for this system to produce a completed rental agreement. In 1984, Avis introduced Rapid Return, an automated self-service check-in device, to its U.S. franchises. A similar innovation called Rapid Rental, a credit-card prompted, computer-assisted transaction, followed shortly thereafter at testing locations in the United Kingdom and France. By 1987, all Avis's domestic and international operations were connected to its main computer in Garden City, New York.

Avis also changed owners a number of times in the 1980s. After being acquired by Esmark, Inc. in 1983, Avis was purchased along with Esmark by Beatrice Companies in 1984. Kohlberg, Kravis, Roberts & Company, a New York investment firm, acquired Beatrice Companies and Avis the following year in a leveraged buyout. In another leveraged buyout in 1986, Kohlberg sold Avis to Wesray Corporation, a New Jersey-based investment company, and its partner Avis management for $265 million and the assumption of $1.34 billion in debt. Avis's revenues for that year were $1 billion, a 26.2 percent share of the car-rental market. Wesray next sold Avis's domestic car leasing fleet to PHH Group, Incorporated of Hunt Valley, Maryland, the industry leader in corporate car leasing, for approximately $134 million. During 1986, Avis sold 65 percent of its European operations, known as Avis Europe PLC, to the public for approximately $290 million. Alun Cathcart remained as group managing director and chief executive of what was now a public company, becoming chairman in 1988. Under his direction, Avis Europe grew tremendously, diversifying and updating its services by purchasing such related companies as car leasing businesses and distributorships. In the United States, Avis introduced another technological advance in 1987 with Roving Rapid Return, a portable computer with a printer that allowed Avis employees to move around a rental lot and assist customers at their cars in easy, one-step checkout procedures. Also at this time, Avis's Wizard computer system developed the capacity to allow travel agents direct access to Avis rental vehicles for their customers through computerized communications with airline reservation centers.

Began Operating Under an ESOP in 1987

Avis was sold once again in 1987, this time to an employee stock ownership plan (ESOP) for $750 million and the assumption of $1 billion in debt. Under the plan, both buyers and lenders received tax breaks, and employees of the company became its owners, with Wesray retaining a 29 percent stake. Financing for the ESOP was provided by General Motors Acceptance Corporation, Chrysler Credit Corporation, and Pittsburgh National Bank, who loaned a combined $395 million; Irving Trust Company and a group of banks, who loaned $1 billion; Drexel, Burnham, Lambert, Incorporated, and Kleinwort, Benson Limited, who advanced a $255 million bridge loan; and stockholders, who purchased preferred stock for $135 million. A trustee, Citizens & Southern Trust Company of Atlanta, now known as NationsBank, held employees' shares.

The ESOP proved highly successful, boosting employee morale and prompting better service to consumers. When the plan went into effect, Avis's management introduced employee participation groups whose members included workers from all levels of the company. These groups met periodically, generating ideas that were frequently implemented to improve Avis's operations. For example, Avis employees suggested that the company provide managers with Avis charge cards for their expenses, which would save the cost of fees normally paid to charge card creditors. They also suggested such innovations as rental cars to be used specifically for nonsmokers and compilations of traffic law tips for each rental area. Joseph V. Vittoria, who became chairman and chief executive officer of Avis in 1987, commented enthusiastically about the ESOP in *Fortune:* "Believe me, the ESOP works, and it works very well." In another *Fortune* article Charles Finnie, an analyst at the Baltimore brokerage firm of Alex, Brown & Sons and an expert on the car-rental business, concurred: "Right now Avis is on a roll. The ESOP has really improved their morale and productivity and service." Robert W. Anderson, a director of corporate travel for Unisys, said in the same publication: "Employee ownership has got to be a winner. Avis is absolutely superior in customer service, though they were pretty good to begin with." Official figures underscored the success of the ESOP. Profits for the first half of 1988 were 35 percent higher than those of the same period a year earlier, market share increased to 27 percent, and customer complaints were down 35 percent from 1,918 in 1987 to 1,238 in 1988.

As the 1980s drew to a close, Avis, which had been exhibiting greater profit-sales ratios than Hertz Corporation since 1984, challenged Hertz's position as the number one car-rental agency in the United States. Internationally, relations between Avis, Inc. and Avis Europe PLC remained strong, as the companies' shared resources contributed to growth and prosperity for both. In addition, such programs as Avis Europe's "Avis in Touch," which provided travelers with travel planning guides, an answering service, and toll-free information numbers, and Avis, Inc.'s Preferred Express, which expedited rental procedures for frequent renters, enhanced customer service throughout the world. In 1987, Avis began to market its computer technology to the hotel industry through a newly formed subsidiary, WizCom International, Limited. The following year, Avis purchased its licensee in New Zealand, broadening the company's influence in the Pacific. Avis Europe became private in 1989, when it was purchased by Cilva Holdings PLC, comprised of Avis, Inc., which owned 8.8 percent of the shares; General Motors, 26.5 percent; and Lease International SA, 64.7 percent. Also in 1989, General Motors bought out Wesray's 29 percent stake in Avis, Inc.

1990s Brought Further Ownership Changes

Avis continued to emphasize innovation as it entered the 1990s. Company training programs in customer service, as well as comprehensive vehicle safety checks, were implemented. In 1992 the company tested a computer directional finder in several of its Orlando, Florida vehicles. This device, consisting of a dashboard monitor and computerized voice, helped drivers find their destinations by producing a series of beeps and dots to indicate direction. In 1992 Avis also introduced to its Sacramento, California, market 20 Chevrolet Luminas that would operate on either M85—a combination fuel made up of 85 percent methanol and 15 percent unleaded gasoline—unleaded gasoline, or a mixture of both. It was maintained that M85, an environmentally responsible product, would release 30 percent to 50 percent fewer pollutants into the atmosphere.

Meanwhile, the recession of the early 1990s initially provided benefits to the rental-car industry in North America as automakers, saddled with large inventories of cars they could not unload, sold the vehicles to Avis and other car renters at steep discounts. This in turn, however, brought numerous new competitors into the industry, which drove down rental prices. When the economy recovered in 1993 and 1994, the automakers were able to increase the prices they charged rental-car companies for the cars the companies needed. Rental-car companies in turn raised their rental rates, which dampened demand, leading to heavy losses by Avis and other companies and to an industry shakeout.

It was in this environment that after nine years under employee ownership Avis changed hands yet again. HFS Inc., the largest hotel franchiser in the United States and a franchiser of real-estate companies as well, paid $800 million for Avis in October 1996, purchasing both the ESOP interest and that of General Motors to gain full control. The buyout provoked controversy among some Avis employees who felt that their shares were being undervalued, but the deal went through nonetheless.

As a franchiser, HFS from the start planned to spin off the company-owned car-rental operations gained from the purchase of Avis, while retaining the rights to the Avis name and control of WizCom and the Wizard System. Along these lines, a new stripped-down company called Avis Rent A Car, Inc. (ARAC) was soon created, which comprised the company-owned car-rental operations. At the same time, HFS set up a subsidiary—HFS Car Rental, Inc.—to which it assigned the rights to the Avis name and which thus became the franchiser of the worldwide Avis rental system. Avis Rent A Car then entered into a 50-year franchise agreement with HFS Car Rental, thereby becoming an Avis system franchisee—the largest in the world. In return for the right to use the Avis name, ARAC agreed to pay HFS a royalty fee of between four and 4.5 percent of its revenues. WizCom International and Wizard Co., Inc. became subsidiaries of HFS; Avis Rent A Car thereby entered into a 50-year computer services agreement with WizCom for use of the Wizard System.

As HFS was laying plans for an initial public offering (IPO) of Avis Rent A Car stock, Vittoria retired as head of the company in February 1997. The following month R. Craig Hoenshell, a former American Express executive, was named chairman and chief executive of ARAC. In August 1997 ARAC acquired First Gray Line Corporation for about $195 million in cash. First Gray Line was the second-largest Avis franchisee in North America, having 70 locations in southern California, Arizona, and Nevada.

In September 1997 Avis Rent A Car went public through the long-planned IPO, with about 75 percent of the company sold to the public and the remaining 25 percent staying in HFS's hands. The resulting $330 million proceeds were mainly to be used to pay down ARAC's large long-term debt of nearly $3 billion.

Avis Rent A Car began its new era as a public company with public relations problems and investigations hanging over it.

From November 1996 to October 1997, accusations that Avis franchisees racially discriminated against minorities who sought rental cars were raised in North Carolina, Florida, and Pennsylvania. In October 1997, the U.S. Justice Department launched an investigation into these allegations, as well as into Avis management knowledge of the accusations—the latter being an issue that had the potential to raise uncomfortable questions about the IPO. It thus seemed likely that Avis Rent A Car's roller-coaster history would continue on course.

Principal Subsidiaries

Avis Rent A Car System, Inc.

Further Reading

Abelson, Reed, ''Avis Vs. Hertz: Investors, Start Your Calculators,'' *New York Times*, September 14, 1997, p. BU4.

''Acquisition of Avis, Inc. Completed by IT&T,'' *New York Times*, July 23, 1965.

''Avis Is Now Offering Autos That Use Variable Fuels,'' *Wall Street Journal*, May 6, 1992.

Avis: The Avis Story, Garden City, N.Y.: Avis, Inc., 1991.

''Beatrice Sheds Fat,'' *Fortune*, October 28, 1985.

Bernstein, Aaron, ''Should Avis Try Harder—For Its Employees?,'' *Business Week*, August 12, 1996, pp. 68–69.

Bigness, Jon, ''HFS Plans to Offer Avis to Public, Investigates Purchase of Alamo,'' *Wall Street Journal*, August 26, 1996, p. B4.

Brecher, John, ''Avis: An Orphan in a Merger War,'' *Newsweek*, July 11, 1983, p. 67.

Collingwood, Harris, ''With Its ESOP, Avis Tries Even Harder,'' *Business Week*, May 15, 1989.

Dahl, Jonathan, ''Tracking Travel,'' *Wall Street Journal*, March 13, 1992.

Dahl, Jonathan, and John D. Williams, ''Beatrice to Sell Avis to Group Led by Wesray,'' *Wall Street Journal*, April 30, 1986.

Employees Take the Wheel: A Study of Employee Ownership at Avis, Inc., New York: New York State Industrial Cooperation Council, 1989, 17 p.

Franz, Julie, ''Beatrice Sells Avis, Cuts Staff,'' *Advertising Age*, May 5, 1986.

Hawkins, Chuck, ''Is Avis Moving into the Passing Lane?,'' *Business Week*, May 9, 1988, p. 100.

Kirkpatrick, David, ''How the Workers Run Avis Better,'' *Fortune*, December 5, 1988, p. 103.

''Meanwhile, Back at the Airport,'' *Fortune*, October 28, 1996, p. 126.

Miller, Gay Sands, and Laurie P. Cohen, ''Avis Inc. Is Sold for Fifth Time in Four Years,'' *Wall Street Journal*, September 29, 1987.

Miller, Lisa, and Martha Brannigan, ''Car-Rental Mergers Leave Consumers in the Back Seat,'' *Wall Street Journal*, January 7, 1997, p. B4.

Reeves, Scott, ''Kick the Tires and Drive It Out: Avis to Benefit from Cross-Marketing,'' *Barron's*, September 15, 1997, p. 40.

Rogers, Michael, ''Beatrice Sheds Fat,'' *Fortune*, October 28, 1985, p. 10.

Spragins, Ellyn E., with Chuck Hawkins, and James E. Ellis, ''When You Own the Company, You Try Harder,'' *Business Week*, September 28, 1987.

Tannenbaum, Jeffrey A., and Stephanie N. Mehta, ''Bias at Single Store Can Taint Franchise Chain's Image: HFS's Avis Rental Unit Faces Allegations, But It Says Results Remain Strong,'' *Wall Street Journal*, March 6, 1997, p. B2.

—Grace Jeromski
—updated by David E. Salamie

Bachman's Inc.

6010 Lyndale Avenue South
Minneapolis, Minnesota 55419
U.S.A.
(612) 861-7600
Fax: (612) 861-7745

Private Company
Founded: 1885
Employees: 1,000
Sales: $65 million (1997 est.)
SICs: 5261 Retail Nurseries & Lawn & Garden Supply Stores

Bachman's Inc., family owned and operated for over a century, provides homes and businesses with a variety of horticultural-related products and services. The company's distinctive purple delivery trucks are a fixture of the Twin Cities floral market. In addition to marketing flowers and plants, Bachman's operates nursery and landscaping services and floral, gift, and garden centers.

Vegetable Farm Roots: 1880s-1920s

Henry Frederick William Bachman moved to the Minneapolis area in 1882, at the height of German immigration to Minnesota. Bachman worked in his uncle's vegetable and garden business and at a large fruit and produce company before striking out on his own. With his wife, Hattie, Bachman established a vegetable farm in 1885 on four acres of land. Their first harvest included potatoes, lettuce, onions, and squash.

Over the next decade the couple's family and holdings grew. By 1895, Bachman had 150 hotbeds and 11 greenhouses on his 44 acres of land. The Bachman children helped sustain the growing business. The boys worked in the fields and the greenhouses, while the girls helped their mother with meals for the hired hands.

In 1911, Bachman convinced a railroad company to build a spur line to his property, and he began transporting his produce to New York and Boston. In the winter months he manned the coal stove in the boxcars to keep the squash and potatoes from freezing during the long haul. He returned with a load of Eastern coal to heat the greenhouses. But in the 1920s, capitalizing on improvements in transportation, Southern farmers began pricing Northern greenhouse growers out of the market. Bachman's began shifting the balance of production from vegetables to flowers.

Appeal of Flowers Transcends Tough Times: 1930s–40s

Floral production began with Albert Bachman, who had inherited his mother's passion for flowers. Despite teasing from his brothers, he began raising carnations on his greenhouse bench—each of the brothers had an allotment of space. ''Before long he was tying bunches of carnations together and selling them outside the gates of Oak Hill Cemetery. His modest income did not challenge his brothers' belief that there was anything but folly in the growing of flowers,'' according to *Purple Packages: Bachman's 100 Years.*

Two years later, in 1916, Henry, seeking relief from his asthma symptoms, moved to California with Hattie and their three daughters. The homestead was divided among their sons. Albert and his wife, Olga, expanded the flower production. ''By the end of the 1920s an armful of carnations was earning more than a truckload of Minnesota-grown vegetables and everybody had stopped laughing at Albert,'' wrote Dick Youngblood. On April 9, 1929, the family business was incorporated as Henry Bachman's Sons.

In the early 1930s Albert established a nursery and landscape division which was operated by his son Larry. As their parents before them, the third generation of Bachmans had begun working in the family business at an early age. The boys worked in the fields and made deliveries. The girls helped with meals and laundry for the hired hands and worked in the retail store, which had been established in the mid-1920s.

Situated between a greenhouse and a tropical conservatory, the retail store offered flowers for 35 to 50 cents a bunch during the Depression years. Bachman's also filled floral arrangement orders, such as funeral wreaths, and began carrying some gift items.

World War II intervened in the lives of every American including the Bachmans. With the young men in military service, the women moved into accounting and production areas. Additional employees joined the ranks of the family business—some of whom later became family members as well. Albert and Olga lost a son to the war.

Bachman's began expanding in the postwar days. The Edina retail outlet, which had opened in 1941, was replaced by a larger store in 1947. The next year, the company established a vehicle service operation and purchased additional land and greenhouses next to Lake Minnetonka. The company also began to establish a reputation as an industry innovator by marketing techniques such as displaying premade floral arrangements in large coolers in the retail stores.

A Third Generation Makes Its Mark: 1950s–70s

In 1949, seven cousins formed the new leadership of the company, renamed Bachman's Inc. The business structure was formalized with Ralph Bachman heading the company as president. The goal of the third generation, according to the Bachman's company history, was "to sell more flowers to more people more often."

A flower shop opened in Dayton's downtown Minneapolis store early in the 1950s and in Southdale mall, also owned by Dayton's, in 1957. The Lyndale Avenue store—part of the original Bachman family homestead—was converted to a "supermarket" operation in 1958. Cart-pushing customers picked up plants from display tables and paid for their purchases at checkout counters. Sales skyrocketed.

With 1959 sales of $2.2 million, Bachman's ranked among the top five retail florists in the United States. Retail florist business accounted for 78 percent of sales, and the garden store and nursery operations brought in the remaining 22 percent. Sales had more than tripled in the decade since the passing of the torch to the third generation of Bachmans, who held all the company stock.

"More than two-thirds of Bachman's products are home-grown, progressing from seed to sale in its 34 greenhouses and three growing areas," wrote Bob Ylvisaker. But with expansion of air transportation during the 1950s Bachman's, like others in the florist industry, began bringing in more flowers from around the U.S. and the world. Some plants were more economical to purchase than produce. Bachman's reached out to the world in another aspect of its business as well, by telegraphing flowers internationally.

Bachman's moved into the mass marketing of flowers in the late 1960s. The first European Flower Market opened at Byerly's Foods in 1968. The small kiosks carried cut flowers and plants priced below regular florist shops. Ralph Bachman, then president, extended the concept to other supermarkets, as well as airports and department and discount stores. By 1970, the company operated 22 European Flower Markets in Minnesota. An additional 35 were operated by local florists in 15 states, Canada, and Norway.

The Pillsbury Company purchased the division in 1971, and Ralph Bachman ran the operation for the Minneapolis food giant. Stanley Bachman succeeded his brother as president of Bachman's. When expansion plans failed to meet expectations, Pillsbury sold the Minnesota segment of the operation back to Bachman's in 1976.

Bachman's upgraded its production facilities early in the 1970s. A $1 million greenhouse complex was added at Lakeville, Minnesota—a 438-acre site purchased in the mid-1960s for nursery production. The modern facility was equipped with artificial lighting and an automated watering system.

Although marked economic inflation during the 1970s hit the florist industry, causing fertilizer, transportation, and energy prices to escalate, Bachman innovation and persistence continued to drive the company forward. In the late 1970s, Bachman's spent over $2 million to transform its Lyndale Avenue store into a shopping center-greenhouse offering customers a broad range of products and services.

According to a February 1980 *Corporate Report Minnesota* article, average annual sales for retail florists—typically family-owned businesses—were about $100,000. Bachman's ended the 1970s with sales of $25 million. And after-tax profits had been averaging two to three percent of sales from 1975 to 1980. According to John Lundquist, the company invested about a half million a year on advertising.

Decades of Change: 1980s–90s

In an effort to keep the company vital, Bachman's shifted from a general manager to executive committee system in 1979. Merchandising Vice-President Ed Bazinet was one of the non-family members moved into a leadership role. Three years earlier, Bazinet had convinced the Bachman family to invest $50,000 in a gift wholesale division, eventually called Department 56. "Department 56's gift lines—virtually all developed by Bazinet—include ceramics, porcelain, bone china, toys, brass, ornaments, and music boxes. The most popular line is Snow Village, a collection of picturesque miniature buildings," reported *Corporate Report Minnesota* in December 1983.

Southeast Asian and European companies manufactured the giftware, and Bloomingdale's, Macy's, Neiman-Marcus, and Dayton's, were among the department stores carrying Department 56 items. The operation, which became known by its original accounting number, also sold to thousands of gift shops and national catalog companies. In 1984, the $15 million department was spun off as a subsidiary, and Ed Bazinet was appointed president. By then less than 10 percent of Department 56's products were sold by Bachman's retail stores.

The European Flower Market outlets, which had produced sales of $7.5 million in 1984, were eliminated in October 1989. The majority of the kiosks were closed and the names of the remaining outlets were changed to Bachman's. The company had shifted its retail focus to the other end of the spectrum.

"Bachman's opened a new store this month, but it isn't another of the firm's small gift shops that sell flowers in the company's signature purple wrap," wrote Barbara Pokela in a November 1989 *Star Tribune* article. The floral and garden center, their third store in the 75,000-square-foot range, carried everything from gardening supplies and gifts to patio furniture. Pokela reported the company wanted to alter the perception that Bachman's was only a flower and plant retailer, while remaining committed to its 30 smaller shops.

According to Bachman's company history, the company was an early promoter of foliage plants for home and business and began leasing plants in the 1960s. The interior landscaping division had sales of $3 million in the early 1980s. A decade later the Twin Cities plant leasing market, estimated to be about $10 million, began leveling off. Bachman's held about 1,000 accounts—ranging from $50 to several thousand dollars a month—in the increasingly competitive field.

Fourth generation family member Dale Bachman was named president early in 1992; his cousin Todd Bachman, who had headed the company since 1986, became CEO of Department 56. Forstmann Little & Co., a New York investment firm, purchased the Bachman's wholesale gift subsidiary late in 1992 for $284 million in stock and subordinated debt. Department 56, which had been growing by nearly 20 percent a year, had sales of $122 million in 1991.

The Twin Cities lawn and garden market, in spite of a series of setbacks in the late 1980s and early 1990s—drought, economic recession, and flooding—was expanding. In addition to the local garden store chains, Bachman's competed with discounters, home warehouse stores, and the Mall of America for the garden-related merchandise dollar. Bachman's closed three of its smaller stores and opened a fourth "superstore" in the Twin Cities in 1993.

Todd Bachman departed Department 56 and succeeded Stanley Bachman as chairman in 1994: the tradition of family leadership endured. Other traditions went forth as well. The annual Dayton's-Bachman's Flower show, held for over 30 years, continued to draw large numbers of Minnesotans eager for a taste of spring. And Bachman's persisted in its effort to creatively serve a changing marketplace.

The *Corporate Report Fact Book 1997* estimated Bachman's sales to be $65 million. At year-end the company operated 21 retail floral stores, six of them the large floral and garden centers; the indoor and outdoor landscaping divisions; and the wholesale nursery division. Bachman's continued to grow many of its products in its seven acres of greenhouses and on its 513-acre growing range. A seventh floral and garden center opening was planned for 1998.

Further Reading

Apgar, Sally, "Ceramics Dynamics," *Star Tribune* (Minneapolis), December 22, 1995, p. 1D.

"Bachman's Bullish Bear Market," *Corporate Report Minnesota,* December 1983, p. 22.

"Bachman's Inc.," *Corporate Report Fact Book 1997,* p. 533.

"Bachman's to Add Garden Centers," *Star Tribune* (Minneapolis), January 8, 1993, p. 3D.

Carideo, Tony, "Major Players Destined to Make a Killing from Department 56 Buyout," *Star Tribune* (Minneapolis), May 11, 1993, p. 2D.

Carol, Susan, "Services Plant, Prune and Pot Their Way to Profits," *Minneapolis/St. Paul CityBusiness,* July 22, 1991, pp. 12–13.

Feyder, Susan, "New Bachman's President Has Roots in the Business," *Star Tribune* (Minneapolis), February 17, 1992, p. 2D.

Howatt, Glenn, "Department 56 Is Sold to New York Investment Firm," *Star Tribune* (Minneapolis), October 8, 1992, p. 1D.

Lee, Betsy, "Bachman's: The Family That Prunes Together . . . ," *Corporate Report Minnesota,* February 1980, pp. 58–61, 106.

Lundquist, John, "Bachman's: From Family Florist to Nation's Largest," *Minneapolis Tribune,* February 9, 1981, p. 11A.

Maler, Kevin, "Plant Sellers Grow Like Weeds," *Minneapolis/St. Paul CityBusiness,* July 30–August 5, 1993, pp. 1, 30.

"Marketplace Pulse," *Star Tribune* (Minneapolis), August 11, 1989, p. 1D.

Pokela, Barbara, "Bachman's Opens 3rd Center in Maplewood," *Star Tribune* (Minneapolis), November 27, 1989, p. 7D.

"Todd Bachman New Chairman, CEO," *Star Tribune* (Minneapolis), September 9, 1994, p. 3D.

Wilkinson, Mike, "Bachman's in Bloom," *Corporate Report Minnesota,* July 1974, pp. 28–30.

Ylvisaker, Bob, "Bachman's Blooming Sales Put It Among U.S. Busiest," *Minneapolis Tribune,* March 20, 1960, pp. 9–10.

Youngblood, Dick, "A Fertile Field," *Star Tribune* (Minneapolis), September 4, 1988, p. 1D.

—Kathleen Peippo

Badger Meter, Inc.

Badger Meter, Inc.

4545 West Brown Deer Road
P. O. Box 23099
Milwaukee, Wisconsin 53223-0099
U.S.A.
(414) 355-0400
Fax: (414) 371-5956
Web site: http://www.badgermeter.com

Public Company
Incorporated: 1905
Employees: 940
Sales: $116 million (1996)
Stock Exchanges: American
SICs: 3824 Water & Gas Meters; 3823 Industrial Process Control Flow Meters & Instruments; 7389 Remote Meter Readers; 3491 Industrial Valves; 3492 Control Valves

Badger Meter, Inc. was born on the afternoon of March 8, 1905, when four Milwaukee businessmen incorporated the Badger Meter Manufacturing Company to fabricate frost-proof water meters for measuring water consumption in Midwestern homes. Badger's innovation was a meter with a soft, replaceable cast-iron bottom plate that ruptured when the water in the meter froze, thus relieving pressure on the meter and safeguarding its mechanical parts. Since frozen water pipes were an all too common occurrence in Wisconsin's bitter winters, Badger found a ready market and by 1910 was selling close to 3,700 eight-dollar meters a year. Under cofounder and now president John Leach, Badger initially operated out of a two-story machine shop in Milwaukee's downtown under the motto "Accuracy Durability Simplicity Capacity."

"Measuring the Water of the World": 1905–38

Within 13 years of its founding, Badger's annual production had climbed to 10,000 meters and it had expanded into bronze as well as cast iron and had added disc, turbine, and compound water meters to its line. With only 12 employees, Badger was forced to stay flexible to meet surges in demand. When an order for 200 or more meters came in, the entire company pulled weekend shifts, stopping only for a lunchtime "pail" of beer and a free dinner on Leach's tab at the end of the day. In 1919 Badger moved to a new facility that included the company's first foundry. Now able to fabricate its own metal components, Badger was soon taking on job shop work for other Milwaukee manufacturers, including bronze castings for A. O. Smith Corporation and auto hubs and fingers for Milwaukee Automotive Supply. A year later it transformed itself into a national company by appointing sales agents for Chicago, Kansas City, Brooklyn, Denver, and Portland.

In 1924 Leach was replaced as president by Charles Wright, who would guide the company for the next three decades. In the Roaring Twenties, Badger's business boomed as U.S. municipalities made expensive upgrades of their water department equipment. In 1925, for example, the City of Chicago signed a mammoth deal with Badger to produce 400 meters a *day*. Buoyed by such orders, Badger's earnings averaged almost $100,000 a year between 1924 and 1929, and before the Great Stock Market Crash of 1929, it declared a 300 percent stock dividend on its ample $365,000 surplus. Like many American companies, the Great Depression devastated Badger's business, forcing it to lower prices to maintain sales levels. Meters that sold for $7.75 in 1922 were discounted to $5 in 1932, and the average hourly wages of Badger's workers were almost halved, from 64 cents to 33 cents an hour. Badger extended long-term credit to its customers, slashed its workforce, and by 1937 was forced to ask its stockholders to relinquish the $165,000 in unpaid dividends still owed them.

On the brink of insolvency, the company was saved only by an order for 30,000 water meters from the government of Mexico City in 1933. In 1937, Franklin Roosevelt's New Deal gave a further boost to Badger's recovery by granting U.S. municipalities funds to install new water works. With steady sales to customers in Central and South America, by 1937 Badger's workforce, which had unionized the year before, had climbed to more than 200. Badger's worst days were behind it.

Company Perspectives:

Badger Meter, Inc., an independent company, will grow as a leading worldwide marketer and manufacturer of flow measurement and control products. Through the use of new technologies and product development, dedication to our customers and employees, commitment to improvement and innovation, we will continuously pursue superior performance in customer service, quality, and financial results.

Bomb Fuses for the War Effort: 1939–51

In 1939 Badger moved to solidify its business by expanding from water meters to grease and oil gun meters, which were used to measure the amount of motor oil and lubrication consumed in U.S. service stations. With America's entry into World War II, Badger Meter was conscripted by the federal government to apply its skills in manufacturing the clocklike mechanisms inside its water meters to the fabrication of bomb fuses. Fuse production—seven million in all were made—soon accounted for 95 percent of its total output, and in the space of a few months in 1942 Badger's employment more than doubled to 550. Like many U.S. companies during the war years, women came to comprise an ever larger portion of Badger's workforce, and the blue, all-cotton dresses they wore to prevent the buildup of static around the electrically sensitive fuses soon earned them the nickname Badger's "blue belles."

Despite the incredible growth brought on by the war, Badger's physical manufacturing plant entered the postwar period uncomfortably ill-equipped. When President Wright's sons returned from the war to learn their father's trade they found a company with no research function, no tool shop, and an antiquated machine room that relied on a single motor to power all the plant's machines. What is more, Badger was spending its money inefficiently. Rather than make the registers for its meters in house, it paid an outside firm to produce them, and by the late 1940s was also paying out $120,000 a year to an outside machine shop to make its tools and dies.

While Badger had been churning out bomb fuses, the American residential market's need for new water meters had been put on hold. Because of that pent-up demand and the housing boom unleashed by the demobilization of America's armed forces, Badger's sales vaulted forward in the late 1940s and 1950s. In 1946 it further diversified its product line by introducing the GMOP meter, a grease and oil-measuring meter that soon became the standard for U.S. makers of lubricating equipment. The outbreak of the Korean War in 1950 returned Badger to the bomb fuse-making business, which it continued to participate in until—21 million fuses later—it abandoned the munitions business for good in 1960.

Diversification Under James Wright: 1952–59

When Charles Wright died in 1952, his son James became Badger's third president and promptly began stepping up Badger's product diversification. He created the company's first new product R&D and testing department in 1953 and added new products through the acquisition of other companies throughout the 1950s. In 1954, for example, Badger acquired Precision Products of Oklahoma, a manufacturer of detonating mechanisms for the oil industry and timing components for parking meters and other instruments. Three years later it bought Counter and Control Corporation (CCC) of Milwaukee, a producer of electromechanical devices for counting shaft revolutions, lever strokes, and electrical impulses. In 1961, Wright merged Precision and CCC to form a Tulsa-based subsidiary named Precon. Finally, in 1958 Badger acquired Measure-Rite Inc. of California, a maker of propeller-driven flow and irrigation meters, which became a new Badger division.

In 1954 Wright had built a new state-of-the-art nonferrous foundry in Fall River, Wisconsin, 70 miles west of Milwaukee, that he hoped would further diversify Badger's business by enabling it to take on other manufacturers' machining jobs. Badger's wartime experience mass producing bomb fuses for the government did not translate to the commercial market, however. Rather than the large-run orders of a few parts that Wright had expected, Fall River was inundated with short-run orders for an enormous variety of products, which it was unable to juggle profitably. Moreover, to grow Fall River had to sell to Badger's competitors, who were unexcited by the prospect of enriching the subsidiary of an archrival. In 1959, Wright therefore sold Fall River to a group led by his brother William, enabling the facility to pursue new business while continuing to supply Badger with most of the castings it would use for the next four decades.

The South and Central American marketplace that had rescued Badger in the Depression years had virtually vanished in the years that followed as European meter companies gobbled up Badger's customers. In 1953 Badger countered by establishing a wholly owned subsidiary in Mexico City named Medidores Azteca, which in 1956 began to manufacture multi-jet water meters for the Mexican market. In 1966 Badger expanded into South America with a velocity meter manufacturing plant in Peru and then later established a subsidiary in Ecuador. Currency fluctuations and general South American economic uncertainty, however, convinced the company to sell off its interest in these firms in 1978. But Badger's 25-year-old Mexican connection remained strong, and in 1980 it opened a manufacturing plant for a new line of water meters in the Mexican border town of Nogales.

In 1961 Badger had formed an international division to manage all foreign sales, which by 1970 were accounting for one third of Badger's total residential sales. In 1967 it acquired W. Gottlob Volz, a Stuttgart-based meter maker that unfortunately ranked at the bottom of Germany's water meter industry. It stubbornly remained there, and in 1978 Badger was forced to sell it off. In 1973 Badger used Stuttgart as the base for a new European sales arm, Badger Meter Europe, which in 1983 became a full-fledged business unit that performed order processing, administrative functions, and valve and lube meter assembly and testing. By the mid-1990s fully 20 percent of Badger's annual sales went to overseas customers, and the opening of a new Singapore office in 1997 announced its intention to lift its international sales even higher.

The Easy-Read Meter and New Markets: 1960–69

Fifty-five years after its founding, residential water meters remained Badger's bread and butter. By the 1960s, however, the long housing boom of the postwar years was beginning to peter out, and new rivals like Rockwell and Neptune were threatening Badger's preeminence in its core business. Jim Wright's multi-pronged diversification efforts had been aimed at relieving Badger of its dependence on the home water meter market, and throughout the 1960s Badger's product line was extended by new stainless steel meters for measuring highly corrosive liquids such as fertilizers and acids, turbine-type meters for water softening equipment manufacturers, and a variety of other technologically sophisticated industrial meters. Moreover, early in the decade Badger engineers received development contracts from federal agencies to apply the noninvasive measuring technology known as nuclear magnetic resonance to the measurement of fluid flow. By 1968 this had culminated in the unveiling of a magnetic resonance flowmeter (MRF) that could measure the flow of chemicals inside a pipe without coming into contact with the fluid, thus improving the accuracy of the measurement.

The introduction of the Easy-Read water meter in 1960 signaled that Badger was not prepared to surrender the residential niche it had created in 1905. The Easy-Read used a magnetic coupling rather than the traditional mechanical coupling to make possible the creation of a sealed gear train and register unit. This improved measurement accuracy to 98 percent, eliminated water leakage into the meter, and solved the problem of fogging, which made the meter's register all but impossible to read. Because more than half of all water meters were situated outside in poorly lit areas, the Easy-Read's more legible register dial and rotating-digit counter also made it easier for meter readers to record water consumption data. Badger improved the Easy-Read still further in 1963 when it introduced the Read-O-Matic, a register that could be used with Easy-Read to read the meter's data remotely. Since the Read-O-Matic could be installed outside, it now became possible for meter readers to collect consumption data when homeowners were away.

Fueled by Easy-Read's success, Badger embarked on a new cycle of acquisition in the 1960s, extending its reach into increasingly high-tech applications of fluid-measuring technology. In 1963 it bought Technicon Instruments of California, a maker of chart recorders for water and sewage plants (folded into Badger's Precon operation); in 1964 it acquired Research Controls of Tulsa, a producer of small control valves for research, pilot plant, and commercial process applications; and in the same year it absorbed Noller Control Systems, a California manufacturer of telemetering and supervisory control systems.

The Noller purchase was Badger's first acquisition outside the meter industry and reflected Wright's desire to penetrate the water and sewage plant market by offering not only meters but the electronic equipment that managed them. Badger's purchase of Everson Manufacturing of Chicago, a maker of the chlorinators used in water treatment plants, sewage systems, and swimming pools, further solidified its presence in the water treatment and sewage market (it was eventually sold in 1982). Finally, in 1969 Badger founded a new subsidiary named Grafton Plastics (based in the Milwaukee suburb of Grafton) to supply the meter chambers, gears, number wheels, and other plastic components Badger had traditionally purchased from outside vendors.

Retrenching and Restructuring: 1969–74

Badger's transformation into a high-tech fluid-measurement firm came to a head in 1966 when it formed the Systems Division out of the supervisory control and communications management systems it had gained in the purchase of Noller Control Systems two years before. Badger was soon supplying computerized pollution control and water control and telemetering systems to water utilities and sanitary districts and then ventured even further afield with contracts to provide data terminals for such customers as stock exchanges and universities. Before the term *core competency* had become a corporate synonym for staying true to one's roots, Badger had realized as early as 1969 that it could no longer follow where its recent speculative high-tech ventures were leading it without jeopardizing the company's very profitability. In 1960 it therefore merged the Systems Division into Noller's Control System Division and pulled back from projects that would have led it into large computer systems and medical data collection systems.

In 1971, Wright listed Badger (now known simply as Badger Meter) on the American Stock Exchange and reorganized it into four semi-independent business groups: Flow Products, comprising the company's Milwaukee and Grafton operations; Environmental and Electronic Products, encompassing its Oklahoma Precision Products and California Electronics divisions; International, which consolidated all its foreign operations; and Corporate Administration, containing its corporate administrative functions. Then, after 22 years at Badger's helm, Wright relinquished the presidency to company veteran Robert Pfeffer in 1974. The pell-mell expansion of the 1960s had left Badger a profitable but financially leaky enterprise, and Pfeffer sought to complete the reorganization Wright had begun by trying to determine, as he later recalled, "where all the money was going." The U.S. economy refused to cooperate, however, and the recession of the mid-1970s brought skyrocketing copper prices, high interest rates and inflation, and intensified competition in the meter industry. Badger's sales kept growing but earnings swung wildly, and the company was forced to forego dividend payments to shareholders.

"Recordall" and Success in Industrial Products: 1975–82

James Wright's diversification efforts two decades before had expanded the potential sources of Badger's revenues, and in 1975, for the first time in its history, more than half of the company's profits came from products other than residential water heaters. When housing starts began to pick up in the late 1970s, Badger was ready with a new generation of home meters, christened Recordall. Like the Easy-Read before it, the Recordall promised to revolutionize the home water meter. It offered improved measuring accuracy for water consumption at any flow rate (a selling point to utilities supporting water conservation programs), a broader range of sizes for utilities to choose from, and an all-thermoplastic external design—which enabled Badger to sidestep high copper prices and give utilities a noncorroding meter to market to customers. But consumers never overcame their instinctive feeling that to be durable and reliable water meters had to be heavy and metal, and Badger eventually began to replace its plastic Recordall meters with traditional copper versions.

Badger's efforts to establish itself in the industrial flow measurement industry in the 1960s began bearing fruit in the 1970s when sales of industrial flowmeters took off, doubling between 1973 and 1978 alone. It established a separate division for its industrial products in 1979 and enjoyed increased sales to chemical and food processors, concrete batching plants, and suppliers of auto lubrication systems. Its waste and water treatment flow and control products were also making inroads, fueled by the development of ultrasonic flowmeter (UF) technology by Badger's Envirolab unit. UF technology was uniquely capable of giving accurate measurements of fluid flow in sewage, and in 1972 Badger scored a major coup when its UF meter was chosen to measure the surging water flow in California's earthquake-damaged Van Norman dam. When President Nixon cut funding for the Environmental Protection Agency in 1973, however, Badger had to refocus its precision flowmeter marketing efforts from the wastewater control industry to the petrochemical and chemical industries. With company sales at $58.5 million, in 1979 Pfeffer stepped down as Badger's president after less than seven years at the helm.

The Forbes Era: 1982–93

The recession of 1981–82 struck Midwestern manufacturing firms especially hard, and Badger Meter was no exception. Faced with flagging demand, in 1982 new CEO James Forbes was forced to implement a wage freeze, a reduction in benefits, forced early retirements, and an employee downsizing program that reduced the company's workforce from 1,300 to 960. Forbes also developed a new corporate mission that emphasized improved financial strength and market share, a new commitment to customer satisfaction and state-of-the-art technology, and a high-tech flow measurement technology image to replace Badger's historical reputation as a mere water meter maker. He also implemented an employee ownership program that placed almost a quarter of the firm's stock in the hands of its employees, with the rest held by its management, public shareholders, and the Wright family.

Because Badger was strapped for cash and had already incorporated the telemetering technology of its California-based Electronics Division into its knowledge base, Forbes also felt he could afford to cut loose that division, selling it in 1983 to General Signal. The same year, he divided Badger's products into two divisions organized by the markets they sold to rather than the products they manufactured, thus eliminating redundant sales efforts. The new Utility Division would encompass Badger's waste and wastewater and natural gas utilities customers, and the Industrial Division would comprise Badger's industrial and commercial customers, including the energy, petroleum, food and beverage, pharmaceutical, chemical, process waters, and concrete meter markets. Moreover, a new Operations Division would contain all Badger's Milwaukee- and Tulsa-based machined and engineering products, and the company's International Division would be broken up and integrated in the new Utility and Industrial divisions.

Between 1984 and 1994, Badger had spent more than $60 million on product development, plant and equipment, and systems and quality programs. One byproduct of this was the coming of age of automatic meter reading (AMR) technology, which Badger had first experimented with in the late 1960s. Advances in computer technology were finally making AMR cost-effective, and in 1986 Badger unveiled an inbound phone-based AMR system called ACCESSplus that used phone lines to call in meter readings at preset times and software to download them into utilities' billing systems. Four years later Badger signed an agreement to license ACCESSplus to American Meter in exchange for the right to incorporate American's radio-based TRACE meter reading technology into its own meter products. In 1993 Badger won a $15 million contract to supply TRACE-equipped Recordall meters to Mexico City, the world's largest residential water meter project at that time. In 1996, Badger was also retained by the City of Milwaukee to install AMR technology in all the city's water meters, and Badger closed a contract to become a leading supplier to the largest AMR project in the United States, under construction in Philadelphia.

Throughout the 1980s and 1990s Badger continued its pursuit of the cutting-edge flow measurement technology it had begun in the 1960s, unveiling a microprocessor-based ultrasonic flowmeter called the Compu-Sonic in 1985, a concrete admixture dispensing system the same year, an advanced flow meter for the natural gas industry (christened Tru-Therm) in 1993, and the Q-Tracker, a portable monitor for measuring infiltration and inflow in sewer systems. Not all its high-tech ventures bore fruit, however. Its purchase of Precision Measurement Inc. of Dallas in 1985 came to little when its leading technology, a calorimeter for measuring the heat-producing capability of natural gas in gas pipelines, proved impractical.

Positioning for a New Century: 1994–97

Forbes also led Badger aggressively into the increasingly popular quality management and manufacturing reengineering movements that swept through American corporations in the 1980s. Badger embraced continuous flow manufacturing, a technique that promised to improve productivity and manufacturing efficiency by seamlessly linking the previously isolated steps of the manufacturing process; purchased computer-aided design, flexible manufacturing, and computer-controlled machining systems; implemented a team-based approach throughout its corporate management structure; and installed a multimillion-dollar enterprise management software system that combined all its business operations into an integrated data network. By the mid-1990s, two hundred Badger workers could produce twice the number of meters that 600 workers produced only 12 years earlier.

By 1995, Badger had broken the $100 million level in sales and set the goal of reaching $200 million in sales by the turn of the century. Competing against mammoth instrument firms like Rockwell, Schlumberger, Asea Brown Boveri, and Emerson Electric, however, Badger had to remain a nimble, cutting-edge technology producer to preserve its market share. Producing superior measurement products was no longer enough; Forbes had therefore positioned Badger as a provider of interfaces between other firms' meter-reading technologies and its own meter products and opened the door to connectivity partnerships with such firms as Cellnet Data Systems and Instromet International, whose AMR and instrumentation products promised to expand the market for Badger's line. With the measurement technology needs of the industrial process industries continually expanding and the enormous growth potential of the AMR market, Badger's future appeared brighter than at any time in its 90-year history.

Principal Subsidiaries

Badger Meter Europe, GmbH (Germany); Badger Meter International Sales, Inc.; Badger Meter de Mexico, S.A. de C.V.; Badger Meter Limited (U.K.); Badger Meter de Las Americas, S.A. de C.V. (Mexico); Badger Meter Export, Inc. (Virgin Islands); Badger/Instromet LLC (50%); Badger Meter, Canada.

Further Reading

Badger Meter, "Metering Solutions, Digital Connectivity" (corporate brochure), Milwaukee, Wis.: Badger Meter, Inc., 1996.

Forbes, James L., "Focusing on Industry Leading Products" (interview), *Wall Street Corporate Reporter,* August 11–17, 1997.

Raasch, Janet Ellen, "A History of Badger Meter, Inc.," Milwaukee, Wis.: Badger Meter, Inc., 1995.

—Paul S. Bodine

Baker Hughes Incorporated

3900 Essex Lane, Suite 1200
Post Office Box 4740
Houston, Texas 77210-4740
U.S.A.
(713) 439-8600
Fax: (713) 439-8261
Web site: http://www.bakerhughes.com

Public Company
Incorporated: 1987
Employees: 16,800
Sales: $3.69 billion (1997)
Stock Exchanges: New York Pacific Zürich
SICs: 1389 Oil & Gas Field Services, Not Elsewhere Classified; 2899 Chemicals & Chemical Preparations, Not Elsewhere Classified; 3533 Oil & Gas Field Machinery & Equipment; 6719 Offices of Holding Companies, Not Elsewhere Classified

Baker Hughes Incorporated is the product of the 1987 merger of two oil-field-services companies with surprisingly similar histories. As the early Baker Oil Tools and Hughes Tool Company surged and retreated with their inventiveness and the vicissitudes of the global oil market, so will their offspring, a leading provider of products and services to the world petroleum and continuous process industries, including production and completion equipment, electrical submersible pumps, drill bits, drilling systems, specialty chemicals, systems integration solutions, and process systems for mining and other industries.

Baker and Hughes followed such similar paths that, despite their difficult combination in the late 1980s, it is not surprising that the two firms make for such a cozy modern fit. Both were founded shortly before World War I by aggressive entrepreneurs who won valuable patents and earned gushing royalties on early oil-extraction devices. Both continued as domestic powerhouses well past the turn of the century, when, at slightly different cues, they embarked on massive worldwide expansion and diversification projects. Baker and Hughes became public companies within 10 years of each other as the influence of their founding families diminished. The two rivals experienced the fluctuations of an unpredictable world oil market jarred by political and economic events. Finally, the companies suffered financial slumps in the lean years of the 1980s, leading to their turbulent but successful consolidation.

There were differences, however, between Baker Oil Tools—later Baker International—and Hughes Tool. Hughes became the neglected plaything of Howard Hughes, Jr., the founder's famous billionaire son, who used the oil company's constant wellspring of cash to finance financially successful ventures in airplanes, real estate, and motion pictures. Baker, on the other hand, built a reputation, through careful yet ambitious expansion, as one of the industry's best-run firms, largely on the efforts of E. H. Clark, an executive whose tenure spanned 40 years.

History of Hughes Tool Company

The invention of the first rotary drill bit, used to drill oil wells through rock, led to the creation of Sharp-Hughes Tool Company in 1909. Howard Hughes, Sr., and Sharp developed and manufactured the rotary drill bit, an invention so important to the fledgling oil industry of 1909 that variations of the same bit are used today. When Sharp died in 1912, Hughes bought Sharp's share of the business. Hughes incorporated the business the following year, and in 1915 dropped Sharp's name from the company. Armed with the exclusive patent to an essential product, Hughes brought his Houston-based company unrivaled market dominance for decades. Even after many key patents expired, during the 1930s and 1940s Hughes Tool was able to dominate the drill-bit business. During World War I Hughes developed a boring machine that could drill into enemy trenches. Explosives then could be dropped into the trenches. Although the secretary of war personally thanked Hughes for his contribution, the machine was never used because of the sudden shift, toward the end of the war, from trench warfare to active warfare.

If the market dominance of Hughes Tool was secured by the elder Howard Hughes before World War I, its tenor as an undiversified, closely held giant was set by the founder's son and namesake. The 19-year-old Howard Hughes, Jr., inherited the company in 1924 following the death of his father. Under Hughes, Jr., the oil-field-product company became a massive enterprise that he used largely to fund his various avocations. During World War II Hughes operated a gun plant and a strut-making facility for aircraft, in Dickinson, Texas.

Howard Hughes, who himself founded Hughes Aircraft Company, purchased over 78 percent of TransWorld Airlines' stock, and held a substantial investment in RKO Pictures, remained the sole owner of Hughes Tool until 1972, when he put the company on the market. Hughes Tool became a publicly owned company, in a transaction reportedly valued at $150 million. Although successful, despite a general slump in the drilling industry from 1958 to 1972, Hughes Tool had remained undiversified, primarily because Howard Hughes wanted it that way. ''Mr. Hughes, of course, felt he was personally diversified, so he never really considered diversifying the tool company,'' Raymond Holliday, a former Hughes chairman, told *Business Week,* October 13, 1980. With public stockholders and a booming oil economy, especially after the Organization of Petroleum Exportation Countries (OPEC) oil embargo of the early 1970s, Hughes Tool made up for lost time, bringing on worldwide acquisitions and start-up projects.

Under the leadership of chairman James Lesch the firm purchased the Byron Jackson oil-field-equipment division of Borg-Warner in 1974, for $46 million. In 1978 Hughes bought Brown Oil Tools, another family-owned business, whose founder had underutilized his 377 lucrative patents. With its massive expansion and the favorable oil-industry climate, Hughes Tool surged. By 1981—a peak year in the industry—new business activities, which largely meant non-drill-bit products and services, accounted for 55 percent of the company's sales.

When the bottom fell out of the market in 1982, Hughes found itself a bloated, overextended, and debt-ridden concern. Under the guidance of president William Kistler, an engineer who came up through the core drill-bit division, the company retrenched to its roots, concentrating on bits and shying away from services. For example, the company shut down 30 foreign offices and streamlined 11 divisions into one. In 1983 Hughes hired outside consultants Bain & Company to trim fat, laying off 36 percent of its workforce. The company still had one weapon neither world markets nor competitors could take away: a patented O-ring rock-bit seal. In 1986 Hughes won a $227 million patent-infringement judgment from Smith International, a California concern that had copied Hughes's drill seal too closely. In 1985 Hughes had been awarded $122 million from Dresser Industries for patent violation. One rival that had innovated around Hughes's patent rather than copying it was Baker International.

Hughes Tool floundered through the mid-1980s. For the three years beginning in 1983, Hughes lost $200 million. Often cited as a potential takeover target, the company was faced with an offer it could not refuse when approached for a merger with Baker.

History of Baker International Corporation

Like Hughes Tool, Baker grew out of a single invention—the Baker Casing Shoe—a device to ensure the uninterrupted flow of oil through a well, developed in 1907 by Californian Reuben C. ''Carl'' Baker. Baker licensed his patents and incorporated the Baker Casing Shoe Company in 1913, mainly to protect his numerous patents on products that would soon become the industry standard. During World War I Baker was a member of the local draft board, although his company did not devote any of its production to goods to support the war effort. Baker lived off his royalties until the 1920s when he began manufacturing his own tools. In 1928, after successfully manufacturing tools in Huntington Park, California, for several years, Baker called the company Baker Oil Tools, a name it would carry for 40 years.

The Great Depression hit Baker hard, causing it to lay off numerous workers, but the late 1930s and 1940s were years of solid growth. During this period the company started offices in many states including Texas, Wyoming, Illinois, Missouri, and Louisiana. During World War II Baker retooled to produce gun-recoil mechanisms. Following the war Baker prospered. In the 10 years after 1948 it opened 50 new offices in 16 states. In 1956 Carl Baker retired at age 85, leaving the company in the hands of Theodore Sutter, an executive who had joined the company in the early 1920s. Carl Baker died shortly after his retirement. Under Sutter the company began to expand globally, and it went public in 1961.

When E. H. ''Hubie'' Clark, Jr., assumed control of Baker in 1965, the company developed into a global powerhouse. Clark, who had joined the company as a recent mechanical-engineering graduate from the California Institute of Technology in 1947, led Baker, now based in Orange, California, to new heights. Although Baker remained based in California, in 1965 the company's Houston operation was as large as the California operation. Clark acquired some 20 companies, the largest of which was Reed Tool Company, a drill-bit manufacturer acquired in 1975. Clark worked hard to predict trends in oil supply and demand. Baker operations were begun in Peru, Nigeria, Libya, Iran, and Australia, among other countries, and in 1976 the company changed its name to Baker International Corporation.

The company's reputation for quality and Clark's renown as a manager put Baker into the 1980s in solid shape. Even Baker could not avoid the downturn of petroleum-related business after 1981. Clark and Baker president James D. Woods sought to improve efficiency in the slow-growing industry. The eventual answer was to merge with its Houston-based competitor, Hughes Tool. Both companies had been losing money and they hoped to eliminate overproduction by merging.

Merger of Baker and Hughes in 1987

''This industry is plagued with overcapacity,'' said one Baker official, as he announced on October 22, 1986, that the two oil-services firms would merge. Wall Street immediately applauded the move, a complex stock swap that favored Baker stockholders by giving them one share of the new company for each share they owned, compared with an eight-tenths-of-a-share deal for Hughes shareholders. Reflecting the greater general strength of Baker, its executives were to be given the top posts: Clark was to be the new chairman and Woods the new president and chief executive officer, while William A. Kistler, Hughes's chairman, would be named the merged company's vice-chairman. The new company's home would be Houston, where Hughes was based, and where Baker already had extensive operations. Baker's Orange, California, headquarters housed relatively few employees.

Wall Street showed its excitement over the merger by trading up the stock prices of both companies following the merger announcement, but the federal government frowned on the potential antitrust ramifications of combining two such powerful outfits. Indeed, the U.S. Justice Department announced on January 25, 1987, that it would attempt to block the merger, citing reduced competition in markets for some oil-exploration machinery. As top executives worked out a consent agreement with the Justice Department, Hughes executives attempted to pull out of the merger. Baker responded in strong terms: it would sue Hughes for $1 billion if it failed to carry through with the agreement. After several delays Hughes capitulated. On April 3, 1987, Hughes agreed to the terms of the consent decree—which included the divestiture of the domestic operations of Reed Tool Company and some other units—and the merger was completed, creating an oil-services company second in size only to Schlumberger.

Post-Merger Years Marked by Restructuring, Divestments, and Acquisitions

The consolidated company did not stop charging forward since its merger. Baker Hughes outpaced its competition in the late 1980s. Part of its success was in realignment: Woods slashed 6,000 jobs, closed several plants, and took a $1 billion write-off for restructuring expenses. The result was $90 million less in annual costs and impressive sales. The company was already profitable by fiscal 1988. Woods added the chairmanship of Baker Hughes to his title in 1989.

Throughout the late 1980s and early 1990s, Baker Hughes did not hesitate to divest itself of unprofitable and/or noncore operations and to bolster the company through acquisition. In May 1989 its long-time money-losing mining equipment operation was sold to Tampella Ltd. of Finland for $155 million. In April 1990 Baker Hughes added the world's leading maker of directional and horizontal drilling equipment, Eastman Christensen Company, in a $550 million deal with Norton Co. The U.S. Department of Justice approved the deal, but only after Baker Hughes agreed to divest its own diamond drill business. In 1992 Eastman Christensen was merged with Hughes Tool Company to form a new division called Hughes Christensen Company.

In 1991 Baker Hughes divested Baker Hughes Tubular Services and also spun off to the public its profitable but lawsuit-plagued BJ Services Inc. pumping service unit. Parker & Parsley Petroleum Co. had filed suit against Baker Hughes and Dresser Industries Inc.—the two of which had originally jointly owned the predecessor of BJ Services—alleging that BJ Services had shortchanged Parker & Parsley on materials used to stimulate wells. A 1990 jury verdict awarding Parker & Parsley $185 million was later overturned, but in 1993 the three parties settled out of court for $115 million, with both Baker Hughes and Dresser each responsible for half, or $57.5 million.

In 1992 Baker Hughes spent $350 million to buy Teleco Oilfield Services Inc. from Sonat Inc. Teleco was a pioneer in services for both directional and horizontal drilling. Later that year, Teleco and four other Baker Hughes companies specializing in drilling systems—Milpark Drilling Fluids, Baker Sand Control, Develco, and EXLOG—were combined into a new Baker Hughes INTEQ division, which enabled the company to offer comprehensive solutions for all phases of drilling projects.

Divestments continued in 1994 with the sales of EnviroTech Pumpsystems to the Weir Group of Scotland for $210 million and of EnviroTech Measurements & Controls to Thermo Electron Corp. for $134 million. In October 1995 Max L. Lukens, who had been with the company since 1981, was named president and chief operating officer, with Woods remaining chairman and CEO.

After enjoying its best post-merger year to date in fiscal 1996 (with $3.03 billion in revenues and profits of $176.4 million), Baker Hughes was busy in 1997 making acquisitions. In June, Baker Hughes acquired Drilex International Inc., a company that provides directional drilling services, for $108.8 million. Drilex was folded into Baker Hughes INTEQ. In July the company completed its $689 million purchase of Petrolite Corporation, thus augmenting its specialty chemical division which was soon renamed Baker Petrolite and which became the leading provider to the oil-field chemical market. Also in July, the Environmental Technology Division of German machinery maker Deutz AG was bought for $54.4 million; the division specialized in centrifuges and dryers and added to the existing centrifuge and filter product lines of the Baker Hughes Process Equipment Company. Finally, in October a $31.5 million deal to purchase Oil Dynamics, Inc. from Franklin Electric Co., Inc. was completed. Oil Dynamics was a manufacturer of electric submersible pumps used to lift crude oil and it was added to the company's Centrilift division.

The year 1997 was also noteworthy for the retirement of Woods, who had not only made the Baker Hughes merger happen but had also focused and bolstered the company's product and service lines through more than 30 separate divestments and acquisitions. Woods was succeeded by Lukens. Although rumors surfaced late in 1997 of a possible takeover of Baker Hughes by Schlumberger (rumors fueled in part by a strategic alliance between the two companies initiated in September 1996), such a combination would almost surely run into antitrust complications. Assuming it remained independent, Baker Hughes was well-positioned to continue to build on its strong variety of oil-field products and services.

Principal Divisions

Baker Hughes INTEQ; Baker Oil Tools; Hughes Christensen Company; Centrilift; Baker Petrolite; Baker Hughes Solutions; Baker Hughes Process Equipment Company.

Further Reading

The Baker Story, Houston: Baker International Inc., 1979.

Byrne, Harlan S., "Baker Hughes: It Shifts Operations to Exploit Overseas Drilling Activity," *Barron's,* April 6, 1992, pp. 47–48.

Grabarek, Brooke H., "Baker Hughes: Oil and Gas, or Hot Air?," *Financial World,* October 25, 1994, pp. 18, 20.

Ivey, Mark, "Baker Hughes: It Pays to Be a Big Spender," *Business Week,* March 12, 1990, p. 81.
Miller, William H., "A Merger That's Worked: Jim Woods Is Piloting Baker Hughes Inc. to Profit," *Industry Week,* April 15, 1991, pp. 21–23.
Norman, James R., "Black Gold or Black Hole?," *Forbes,* November 26, 1990, p. 10.
——, "Cloud over Baker," *Forbes,* May 11, 1992, p. 220.
——, "Hot Potato?," *Forbes,* July 9, 1990, pp. 38–39.
Tejada, Carlos, "Baker Hughes Inc. to Buy Petrolite in a Stock Deal," *Wall Street Journal,* February 27, 1997, p. C6.
Vogel, Todd, "Baker Hughes Lops Off a Weak Limb," *Business Week,* May 29, 1989, p. 34.

—Adam Lashinsky
—updated by David E. Salamie

B.A.T. Industries PLC

Windsor House
50 Victoria Street
London SW1H 0NL
England
+44 (171) 222-7979
Fax: +44 (171) 222-0122
Web site: http://www.batindustries.com

Public Company
Incorporated: 1902 as British American Tobacco Company Ltd.
Employees: 164,000
Sales:£24.4 billion (1996)
Stock Exchanges: London Montreal Amsterdam Frankfurt Hamburg Antwerp Düsseldorf Basle Zurich Paris Brussels Geneva
SICs: 2111 Cigarettes; 6311 Life Insurance; 6321 Accident & Health Insurance; 6331 Fire, Marine, & Casualty Insurance

B.A.T. Industries PLC is best known as a manufacturer of cigarettes, and for good reason; it sold 670 billion smokes in 1996, accounting for nearly 13 percent of the world's tobacco sales. B.A.T.'s stable of brands includes State Express 555, Benson & Hedges, Kent, Lucky Strike, Pall Mall, John Player, and Kool. In addition to its tobacco interests, the company owns U.S.-based Farmers insurance group as well as two British insurers, Allied Dunbar and Eagle Star. Insurance premium income totaled £10 billion in 1996, or 40 percent of overall revenues. Though its sliding stock price in 1996 and 1997 reflected the U.S. tobacco industry's woes, growing international tobacco operations compensated enough to give B.A.T. record pre-tax profits of £2.64 billion in 1996.

Early 20th-Century Foundations

B.A.T. was formed through an early 20th-century agreement between two competing tobacco companies: American Tobacco Company and the Imperial Tobacco Company. The rivalry was sparked by James Buchanan (''Buck'') Duke, founder and head of the highly successful American Tobacco Company, which had by the turn of the century captured 90 percent of the U.S. cigarette market. Armed with state-of-the-art cigarette manufacturing methods, Duke mounted an assault on the British tobacco market in 1901. In response to this competitive threat, several smaller independent British tobacco companies banded together to form the Imperial Tobacco Company Ltd.

Imperial Tobacco was able to resist American Tobacco's attempt to capture its native market but only after a prolonged trade war that proved very costly for both participants. American Tobacco having withdrawn from the English marketplace, Imperial was in a stronger position and decided to press its advantage.

It was when Imperial started to make moves toward the American market that chairman Duke saw the need for a compromise. A truce was called, and the two rival merchants agreed not to conduct business in each other's domestic markets. Each company also assigned brand rights to the other so that consumers who had grown used to a given brand would not be lost. This deal also initiated the creation of a new company, British American Tobacco, of which American owned a two-thirds share and Duke was the first chairman.

This new company, registered in London in 1902, acquired the recipes and trademarks of both originating companies. It also acquired all the export business and overseas production operations of each company. The new company's sales and growth potential seemed limited compared to the successes of Imperial and American. In time, however, British American Tobacco would grow, not only to outsell its parent companies, but to become the world's largest private-sector tobacco concern.

Steady but slow growth occurred during the first decade of the 20th century. Then in 1911 the United States Supreme Court ruled that American Tobacco was a monopoly and therefore illegal. The court, though requiring that Duke break up his successful American operation, did not want to deprive the American public of its tobacco or the American economy of a healthy business. Unable to come up with a viable solution, the

Company Perspectives:

Our twin goals are to improve the long term growth prospects of our businesses and to increase shareholder value.

court turned to Duke for help. The chairman of B.A.T. and of American Tobacco then devised his own, less damaging dismantling strategy, which the court accepted fully. American Tobacco canceled most of its covenants with B.A.T. and Imperial and sold all of its shares in B.A.T. Most of the shares sold went to British investors, and B.A.T. became listed on the London Stock Exchange.

This left British American Tobacco, still chaired by Duke, able to sell its product independently all over the world, except in the United Kingdom where it was still bound by its covenant with Imperial. Imperial at this time also retained a one-third share of B.A.T., but this did little to impair B.A.T.'s success. Duke's operation began rapid expansion of British exports and overseas operations. Many new subsidiaries were established around the world during the brief period between the disentanglement from American Tobacco and World War I. Local sources of raw materials were discovered and developed, and international sales grew steadily.

The war brought large numbers of women into the company for the first time. They were primarily employed in the distribution of cigarettes to the troops abroad, most of whom had switched to cigarettes from the less convenient pipe. Although brought on by the war, the switch to cigarettes caught on and became permanent. Many people never returned to the pipe, and B.A.T. began selling cigarettes in increasing numbers.

The end of the war brought even greater fortunes for B.A.T. Until Duke did so, no commercial enterprise was able to penetrate the Chinese market farther than the government coastal trading stations. B.A.T., now able to exploit the untapped interior market, achieved record growth in the years immediately following and maintained impressive sales levels throughout the rest of Duke's chairmanship. While chairman, Duke was B.A.T.'s pioneer in growth; the company's next chairman, Sir Hugo Cunliffe-Owen, was a pioneer of decentralization.

Decentralization in 1920s

Sir Hugo had been involved with B.A.T. since its inception. Early involvement in the negotiations between American Tobacco and Imperial endeared him to Duke, who appointed him director and secretary. He held those positions until Duke retired in 1923 (he died two years later) and then succeeded the founder as chairman. When Sir Hugo inherited the chair, B.A.T.'s capitalization had quadrupled since 1902 and its sales had grown by nearly a factor of 40. In 1923 B.A.T.'s world sales had grown to 50 billion cigarettes per year.

Sir Hugo visited China in 1923 to decentralize one of B.A.T.'s biggest operations. Chinese cigarette consumption had grown from 0.3 trillion in 1902 to 25 trillion in 1920, and to nearly 40 trillion by the time of his visit. Sir Hugo's plan was to restructure B.A.T. China Ltd. into independent regional units which could operate when local conditions deteriorated. As China was a major concern, Sir Hugo also spent a great deal of time and energy over the next two decades lobbying the Chinese government to minimize the taxation of tobacco.

Sir Hugo's decentralizing efforts spread from China to many of B.A.T.'s other international operations. The Chairman felt that increased local autonomy would lead to better decisions and improved group performance. This proved true despite skepticism that too much decentralization could produce an unwieldy corporate structure. In 1927 B.A.T. had the resources to enter the U.S. market, monopolized at one time by American Tobacco. Sir Hugo acquired Brown and Williamson, a small tobacco producer in North Carolina. With B.A.T.'s help, this modest company grew to become the third-largest cigarette manufacturer in the United States. This pattern of rapid growth from modest beginnings was maintained through the Depression era and steadily through World War II. At the end of the war, in 1945, Sir Hugo stepped down from the chairmanship and became simply titular president of B.A.T.

Without Sir Hugo's active participation, the management of B.A.T. did little other than maintain the company's steady growth through the late 1940s and 1950s. Profitability remained undiminished and the company was able successfully to weather the storm of communist revolution in China, at which time all of B.A.T. China Ltd.'s assets were nationalized. By 1962, B.A.T.'s capitalization was such that it was able to begin major moves toward diversification.

Diversification in 1960s and 1970s

During that year, B.A.T. acquired minority interest in two companies, neither of which was involved in tobacco production or sales. Mardon Packaging International handled cigarette packaging and was thus a logical choice for B.A.T. Wiggins Teape Ltd., on the other hand, was a large specialty paper manufacturer. Mardon was not highly successful at first. It was formed from five smaller packaging companies in cooperation with Imperial Tobacco and its first-year turnover was modest. It grew steadily, however, as most of B.A.T.'s investments have, and by the end of the 1970s was advancing turnover at a rate of 15 percent per annum.

The success of these two enterprises, which later became wholly owned subsidiaries of B.A.T., paved the way for further and greater B.A.T. acquisitions. The groundwork was now laid for B.A.T.'s transformation from a large tobacco company to an even larger conglomerate. While other major tobacco companies were attempting to diversify into other packaged goods, B.A.T. wasted little time in moving into unrelated but profitable fields. During the 1960s and early 1970s several major international fragrance and perfume houses were brought in to create a third leg in B.A.T.'s group. These included such internationally known concerns as Lentheric, Yardley, and Germaine Monteil.

Once these companies were thoroughly absorbed into B.A.T.'s operations, B.A.T. turned its eye toward a West German department store chain called Horten. At first a minority share was held and then, as before, the company was acquired as a whole. This led almost immediately to further department store chain acquisitions. Gimbels and Saks Fifth Avenue were acquired in the U.S., Kohl's and Department Stores International in the U.K., and Argos, the British catalogue store, joined in 1979. Patrick Sheehy, before becoming B.A.T.'s present chairman, was involved in one more such acquisition. Marshall Field department stores were the unwilling subject of a takeover bid conducted by the controversial team of Carl Icahn and Alan Clone. Sheehy was able to convince B.A.T. to make a "white knight" bid for the chain and managed to thwart Icahn's raid.

Many of these investments gave B.A.T. a good deal of trouble at first, just as Mardon had before. While Saks Fifth Avenue, which appealed to the upper middle-class consumer, maintained high profitability, Gimbels, despite efforts to bring in wealthier clientele, has had a consistently poor showing. With the exception of Gimbels, B.A.T. has been able to absorb and make a real success of its retailing leg as well as its earlier extension into paper.

In 1972 the treaty of Rome brought the United Kingdom into the EEC and with it an end to the agreements between B.A.T. and Imperial Tobacco. New restraint of trade laws prohibited their arrangement. The companies exchanged brand rights once again, each retaining full ownership of its original brands in the U.K. and Western Europe only. B.A.T. was able to keep its brand and trademark ownership in the rest of the world and in the duty free trade outside Western Europe. Ties with Imperial Tobacco were finally severed in 1980 when that company sold its remaining few shares in B.A.T. after having made major reductions over the preceding decade.

Due to the increasingly diversified nature of British American's interests, the name of the company was officially changed to B.A.T. Industries in 1976 and management was restructured for tighter control. B.A.T. Industries became a holding company for several smaller operating companies organized according to industry. These operating companies in turn controlled the individual manufacturing and retailing enterprises.

Appleton Papers was added to the B.A.T. operation in 1978. This American company established B.A.T. as the world leader in the manufacture of carbonless paper. That year B.A.T. also acquired Pegulan, a large home-improvements company in West Germany, as well as two fruit juice companies in Brazil. Other purchases followed in pulp production in Brazil and Portugal.

Acquisition of Financial Services Companies in 1980s

Within two years of his 1982 accession to B.A.T.'s chairmanship, Patrick Sheehy decided to add a fourth leg to B.A.T.'s existing three supports. Eagle Star, a British insurance group, was involved in an unfriendly takeover struggle with the West German firm Allianz when Sheehy contacted its chairman, Sir Denis Mountain, with a friendly proposal. Eagle Star, which had rejected a low bid from Allianz as "grossly inadequate," accepted a similar bid from B.A.T. since Sir Denis felt the two companies could work together well. In fact B.A.T. Industries saw a 26 percent rise in pre-tax profit during the first half of 1987, 45 percent of which was due to Eagle Star. Hambro Life Assurance, another large British firm, rounded out B.A.T.'s new fourth leg in financial services and became Allied Dunbar when it was acquired by B.A.T. in 1985.

After adding financial services to B.A.T.'s portfolio, Sheehy implemented a policy of "focusing and reshaping the business" rather than continuing to move into new areas. Sheehy felt that B.A.T. should only be involved in companies able to maintain a leadership position in their markets. This meant some significant divestitures for B.A.T. In 1984 British American Cosmetics, International Stores, and Kohl's Food Stores were all sold. Mardon Packaging was spun off to its own management in 1985 and in 1986 Gimbels and Kohl's (U.S.) department stores were put up for sale. That year 88 B.A.T. U.S. retail stores were also divested in the U.S. along with the West German Pegulan. Despite the trimming, or perhaps because of it, B.A.T.'s sales continued to rise; 1986 sales were up 12 percent over 1985.

Sheehy continued to decrease B.A.T.'s dependence on the tobacco industry such that by 1986 only 50 percent of B.A.T.'s pre-tax profit came from its tobacco group, down from 57 percent in 1985 and 71 percent in 1982. This change was not due to a reduction in tobacco sales, however, but to overall growth in the other groups, most notably Eagle Star, which increased its contribution to B.A.T.'s profits from 11 percent in 1985 to 19 percent in 1986. Furthermore, the company added the Farmers Group, America's fifth-largest insurer, to its roster of companies in 1988.

B.A.T.'s diversification efforts ended in 1989, when the company came under threat of a hostile takeover by British financier Sir James Goldsmith, who offered £13 billion (US$21 billion) for the conglomerate. The raid induced B.A.T. to divest several major retail and manufacturing properties, assets that investors like Goldsmith thought were undervalued as part of the conglomerate. In 1990 alone B.A.T. reaped more than £1.5 billion (US$2.5 billion) through the sale of the Saks and Marshall Field department store chains. That year also saw the spinoff of the conglomerate's Wiggins Teape Appleton papermaking interests. The company used part of the proceeds from its asset sales to repurchase about 10 percent of its own stock, thereby fortifying the share price and thwarting Goldsmith's raid in 1990. The asset sale continued into 1992, when B.A.T. divested some Australian insurance interests.

B.A.T. declared its intent to reclaim its world tobacco dominance with the 1994 acquisition of former parent company American Tobacco for US$1 billion in 1994. The acquisition gave B.A.T. the U.S. rights to the Lucky Strike and Pall Mall labels, thereby increasing its share of the American cigarette market to 18 percent and granting it worldwide control of these brands. While these venerable cigarette trademarks had long ago lost their leading positions in the American tobacco market, they were highly viable international brands. By 1994 B.A.T. appeared poised to reassert itself as a global tobacco juggernaut by parlaying these distinctly American labels into worldwide power brands. The company pushed especially hard in Eastern Europe and Asia.

Litigation Dominates Mid-1990s

B.A.T.'s Brown & Williamson subsidiary came under heavy fire in the mid-to-late 1990s. In 1995, former Brown & Williamson executive Dr. Jeffrey Wigand blew the whistle on what he claimed were decades of tobacco industry obfuscation of the harmful effects of smoking. After shelling out tens of millions of dollars each year on smoking litigation over the previous four decades, Brown & Williamson lost its first case in 1996, when Mrs. Grady Carter of Jacksonville, Florida, won a US$750,000 judgment against the company over the death of her husband. The decision—which in 1997 was still under appeal—triggered a flurry of similar lawsuits.

During this same time, the U.S. tobacco industry in general was feeling the pressure of dozens of lawsuits brought by state attorneys general who among other things charged that cigarette makers should reimburse state health care systems for the cost of treating ill smokers. In June 1997, the U.S. industry's Big Four—Philip Morris Companies, RJR Nabisco Holdings Corp., Brown & Williamson, and Loews Corp.'s Lorillard—agreed to a broad settlement that would pay out upwards of US$365 billion in damages over the next 25 years. The money would go toward health care expenses, antismoking campaigns, tobacco research, and stricter federal regulation of the industry and its products. By the fall of 1997, the agreement had yet to be crafted into law, and was expected to undergo some alteration during the ratification process.

B.A.T.'s mounting legal woes sent its stock price tumbling in 1996. The company lost more than 25 percent of its market value—£5.1 billion (US$8.5 billion)—from February 1996 to January 1997. Those who held on to B.A.T.'s stock began to clamor for the divestment of its tobacco interests, but CEO Martin Broughton and his executive team eschewed that strategy. In fact, Broughton's annual review of 1996 asserted the company's intent "to regain our position as the world's number one tobacco business and thereby deliver strong profit growth." In line with that goal, the conglomerate announced the US$1 billion acquisition of Mexican cigarette manufacturer Cigarrera La Moderna that June, providing further indication of its intent to buttress its international tobacco interests.

Principal Subsidiaries

British-American Tobacco (Holdings) Limited; BAT Capital Corporation (U.S.A.); British American Financial Services (UK and International) Ltd.; BAT International Finance plc; Tobacco Insurance Co. Ltd.; IMASCO Ltd. (Canada; 42%); Skandinavisk Tobakskompagni AS (Denmark; 32%); The West Indian Tobacco Co. Ltd. (Trinidad & Tobago; 47%); ITC Ltd. (India; 31%); VST Industries Ltd. (India; 30%). The company also lists subsidiaries in the following countries: Argentina, Australia, Bahamas, Bangladesh, Barbados, Belgium, Brazil, Bulgaria, Cambodia, Cameroon, Canada, Chile, China, Costa Rica, Cyprus, The Czech Republic, El Salvador, Finland, France, Germany, Ghana, Guyana, Honduras, Hong Kong, Hungary, Indonesia, Isle of Man, Kenya, La Reunion, Malawi, Malaysia, Mauritius, The Netherlands, New Zealand, Nicaragua, Nigeria Pakistan, Panama, Papua New Guinea, Poland, Portugal, Republic of Ireland, Romania, Russia, Sierra Leone, Singapore, Slovakia, South Africa, Spain, Sri Lanka, Surinam, Switzerland, Uganda, Ukraine, Uzbekistan, Venezuela, Vietnam, Zaire, and Zimbabwe.

Principal Divisions

Allied Dunbar; Eagle Star; Threadneedle Asset Management; Farmers Group; British American Tobacco.

Further Reading

"B.A.T. to Pay $1 Billion in Mexico Cigarette Deal," *New York Times*, July 23, 1997, p. C20.

"British Company Opposes Changes in Tobacco Deal," *New York Times*, July 31, 1997, p. A13.

"Chewing Up Tobacco," *Economist*, September 20, 1997, p. 70.

Dunham, Richard S., "Alright, Everybody, Back to the Table," *Business Week*, September 29, 1997, p. 34.

Fallon, James, "Hoylake Plans New Bid for B.A.T.," *WWD*, November 17, 1989, p. 2.

Gleick, Elizabeth, "Tobacco Blues," *Time*, March 11, 1996, pp. 54–59.

Kimelman, John, "Defensive Maneuver," *Financial World*, June 21, 1994, pp. 32–33.

"The Last Drag?" *Economist*, April 30, 1994, p. 75.

"Learning the Hard Way," *Economist*, September 30, 1989, pp. 70–71.

Noah, Timothy, "Clinton Refuses to Inhale," *U.S. News & World Report*, September 29, 1997, p. 66.

"No B.A.T. Man," *U.S. News & World Report*, May 7, 1990, p. 14.

Rublin, Lauren R., "Wall Street Keeps a Stiff Upper Lip, But Tobacco Has Taken a Body Blow," *Barron's*, August 19, 1996, pp. MW3–MW5.

Smolowe, Jill, "Sorry, Pardner," *Time*, June 30, 1997, pp. 24–29.

Valdmanis, Thor, "Where There's Smoke There's Ire," *Financial World*, January 21, 1997, pp. 38–40.

—updated by April Dougal Gasbarre

Beckman Coulter, Inc.

2500 Harbor Boulevard
P.O. Box 3100
Fullerton, California 92634-3100
U.S.A.
(714) 871-4848
Fax: (714) 773-8543
Web site: http://www.beckman.com

Public Company
Incorporated: 1958 as Coulter Electronics, Inc.
Employees: 5,000
Sales: $1.2 billion (1997)
Stock Exchanges: New York
SICs: 3841 Surgical & Medical Instruments

Beckman Coulter, Inc. is the world leader in the design and production of devices to automatically count and analyze blood cells, a key function of the modern clinical laboratory. Many hospitals and clinics rely on Coulter Counters. In fact, company literature declares that ''about 95% of all blood cell counters in use are either manufactured by Coulter or are clones. . . .'' Beckman Coulter also produces various reagents needed to run and maintain its machines. To assist its customers, Beckman Coulter provides a 24-hour hotline for technical assistance. These two sources give the firm significant portions of its annual revenues. With over 2,400 patents, the firm and its two founders, brothers Wallace and Joseph Coulter, Jr., are well-known for innovative technology. For example, this family firm provides monoclonal antibodies to help fight cancer cells and also an HIV test as part of its recent diversification. With subsidiaries in Canada, Asia, Europe, Africa, the Middle East, Latin America, Australia, and New Zealand, Beckman Coulter is a major international firm in the biomedical industry.

Getting Started

Wallace Coulter was the key person in the early history of Coulter Corporation (the name under which the company operated until early 1998). Born in 1913 in Little Rock, Arkansas, Coulter as a boy began experimenting with electricity. He pursued that interest through his high school years at Monroe, Louisiana, and as a student at Fulton, Missouri's Westminster College and at the Georgia Institute of Technology. He sold X-ray equipment for General Electric in Southeast Asia in the early 1930s, and then in 1937 he went to several nations after being forced out of China by the Japanese invasion.

In 1946 Wallace Coulter was working in Chicago, where he spent much of his spare time tinkering with electronics with his younger brother Joseph R. Coulter, Jr., who had graduated from Chicago's Illinois Institute of Technology and was working as a Motorola engineer. Working in his basement, Wallace in the late 1940s invented what became known as the Coulter Principle, a way of counting small particles in fluid. A test tube with a small pinhole was placed in a conductive solution, such as salt water, which contained the dissolved particles. A negative electrode was inserted into the tube, while a positive electrode was placed in the solution, creating an electric current. A vacuum pump drew the fluid through the pinhole, but each small particle interrupted the current and thus created a pulse. The size of the pulse indicated the size of the particle; the frequency of the pulses indicated how many particles were in the solution.

This basic discovery started automated hematology. Before Coulter Counters were developed, lab technicians had used time-consuming and somewhat unreliable manual methods to count red and white blood cells.

The Coulter brothers made and patented the first Coulter Counter Model A in 1953, with help from a federal grant. It automatically counted red blood cells in about 10 minutes. They continued to make Coulter Counters one-by-one and gradually hospitals requested more of these time-saving and accurate devices. In 1958 the Coulter brothers formed Coulter Electronics, Inc., and three years later they moved their growing business to Hialeah, Florida, next to Miami. Joseph Coulter focused on management, while Wallace worked to improve the Coulter Counter.

The Middle Years (1960–89)

Wallace Coulter's invention was recognized in 1960 when he received the John Scott Award for Scientific Achievement

Company Perspectives:

Beckman Coulter is . . . Science Serving Humanity. We exist to advance medical science. We apply the infinite promise of biotechnology to serve the world's healthcare needs. Our mission is to be recognized as the world leader in blood cell analysis systems. Our strategy for achieving this is: We will lead in the application of emerging technologies to meet the present and future needs of worldwide customers for blood cell analysis.

We will provide the best worldwide sales and customer support services.

We will foster a work environment characterized by open communications, quality practices, teamwork, pride, self-development, and respect for each individual.

We will remain private and independent.

for discovering a concept which revolutionized not only hematology, but also other industries. With this honor, patented technology, and little competition, the firm grew rapidly in the 1960s. By 1962 it had expanded to 15 nations on five continents. In the U.S., the company benefited from general healthcare expansion after Congress passed Medicare and Medicaid during the Lyndon Johnson administration.

As part of a post-World War II trend, Coulter employees in 1970 founded the Coulter Financial Federal Credit Union. This was part of a general family atmosphere at the firm, where employees often worked for many years.

Coulter's competitors finally began to challenge Coulter's domination of hematology in the 1980s, partly due to the expiration of some Coulter patents. For example, Technicon Instruments Corporation in the mid-1980s came out with the first automatic device to differentiate and count five different kinds of white blood cells (WBCs). Coulter already had a machine which analyzed three WBCs, but it waited at least three years before it introduced its five-cell analyzer. Because Technicon's machines were somewhat unreliable, Coulter eventually gained the advantage in this particular market.

Other rivals were Toa Medical Electronics Ltd., a Japanese firm which by the early 1990s had replaced Coulter as the main hematology company in Japan and was also progressing in Europe. Two other competitors, Ortho Diagnostic Systems Inc. and Instrumentation Laboratory, eventually dropped out of this competitive industry. Ortho in fact sold immunohematology technology to Abbott Laboratories in the late 1980s. Abbott had made minor attempts to enter the hematology market in the late 1970s but then expanded its efforts in the late 1980s and early 1990s. Coulter representatives, however, reported that its sales were not significantly hurt by Abbott. Nonetheless, by the 1980s Coulter did have competitors, unlike its earlier years.

In the mid-1980s Coulter began a major reorganization plan to respond to its growing competitors. For example, Coulter's market share in Spain dropped 30 percent, so it had to do something. Starting in 1987, Coulter replaced most of its overseas managers and began integrating and consolidating various international operations. To serve all its European customers, Coulter built a new reagent production plant in Germany and centralized its repair and spare parts warehousing at one location in France, instead of the five sites used previously. Such steps increased production and reduced labor requirements for Coulter's European subsidiaries.

In 1987 Coulter Corporation began implementing a manufacturing concept pioneered by the Japanese. This "just-in-time" (JIT) concept emphasized receiving parts and supplies just as they were needed on the production line, thus decreasing inventories and floor space requirements. That led to the company in 1990 embracing the total quality management (TQM) concept. These developments involved retraining managers, cross training workers, and a major shift in corporate culture to emphasize a team approach. According to Roger Lopez, Coulter's director of manufacturing operations, "It's become a way of life for us. We now use data. Instead of everybody's opinion, we let data do the talking. The managers' role changes. They become teachers, coaches, facilitators, champions of the process."

In the 1980s Wallace Coulter received numerous honors, including honorary doctorates in science, law, and engineering. In 1988 he received the Florida Industrialist of the Year Award. The following year he was honored by both the Association of Clinical Scientists and the American Society of Hematology. Wallace and Joseph Coulter, Jr., were two of America's wealthiest individuals and key players in promoting general business development in the Miami area.

Developments in the 1990s

After several years of operating in 37 separate buildings in Hialeah and Miami Lakes, Coulter Corporation by the early 1990s was ready for new facilities. So in 1992 it purchased from the Resolution Trust Corporation the 102 acres formerly owned by AmeriFirst, including five two-story buildings and plenty of space for expansion. It was located in the Miami suburb of Kendall.

By the early 1990s the Coulter Corporation had significant overseas exports, including about $3.5 million worth of products to Mexico. The firm thus benefited from the November 1993 passage of the North American Free Trade Agreement (NAFTA), which lowered trade restrictions with Mexico. In fact, President Clinton's Transportation Secretary Federico Pea in September 1993 visited the Coulter plant as part of a NAFTA promotional tour.

Coulter Corporation's main competitor, Toa Medical Electronics, began marketing the first automated device to count immature red blood cells called reticulocytes. Coulter responded by using that technology, in which lasers differentiate cell density and type, to add a new standard feature in its newest model.

In the 1990s Coulter Corporation offered a wide range of products. Its smaller semiautomated blood cell counters used in clinics and doctors' offices cost less than $10,000, while the larger STKS units were priced at over $100,000. It also manufactured flow cytometry devices for various industrial and biomedical customers.

By the 1990s the blood diagnostic market was growing only a few percent annually. That fact, coupled with Wallace Coulter's bout with cancer, led the firm to diversify into cancer research. In cooperation with Boston's Dana-Farber Institute, Coulter Corporation developed monoclonal antibodies to specifically target certain forms of cells. Coulter was aided up front by $3 million in venture capital funds from InterWest Partners of Menlo Park, California.

In August 1993 Coulter and the University of Michigan announced they had produced a monoclonal antibody to fight B-cells, white blood cells that proliferate and become malignant in non-Hodgkin's Lymphoma. Two years later Coulter Corporation and InterWest Partners of Menlo Park, California, created a subsidiary called Coulter Pharmaceuticals Inc., a Palo Alto, California, firm which conducted successful trials of this B-1 antibody system. Then in May 1996 InterWest Partners raised $22 million in a private stock sale to fund the clinical trials necessary to win FDA approval of this new product.

Coulter Pharmaceuticals on January 28, 1997, became a public firm, offering 2.5 million shares for $12 each. Two months later the subsidiary announced it had received a method-of-use patent for its B-1 Therapy, thus helping pioneer the new field of radioimmunotherapy. Meanwhile, Coulter Corporation in 1995 acquired a French biotechnology firm called Immunotech because of its product line of about 800 antibodies.

In the 1990s Coulter Corporation also developed a successful diagnostic test for the HIV virus, which causes AIDS. The Coulter HIV-1 p24 Antigen Assay was able to detect HIV only 19 days after initial exposure, six days earlier than other tests. Following FDA approval, in 1996 Coulter Corporation granted the California firm of Ortho Clinical Diagnostic, Inc., a subsidiary of Johnson & Johnson, the rights to sell its HIV diagnostic test worldwide. By the summer of 1997 Ortho Clinical had received permission from the Japanese government to market this diagnostic product. Abbott Laboratories received FDA approval for its HIV antigen test just six months after Coulter's test was approved in 1996.

In the 1990s Coulter put significant resources into laboratory automated systems. In 1992, for example, it created a partnership with IDS Ltd. of Japan, a manufacturer of robotic blood testing equipment. Coulter marketed and installed these devices and modified some of its products to work with this Japanese technology. Costing from $500,000 to $3 million apiece, these devices processed over 1,000 blood samples per hour and automatically logged the results in lab, nursing station, and hospital records.

Another Coulter joint venture in automated lab technology began in August 1995 when it became the sole worldwide distributor for the MICRO21 automatic microscope system developed by Intelligent Medical Imaging Inc. (IMI), a Palm Beach Gardens, Florida, firm started in 1989. This system was designed to accurately and quickly diagnose AIDS, anemia, most cancers, and other diseases.

In March 1997 Coulter settled a dispute with IMI. The arbitration agreement was that Coulter no longer would have exclusive rights to sell and distribute IMI's MICRO21 System. Coulter was paid $4.2 million to return 26 MICRO21 systems to IMI, which was developing its own sales force. IMI noted that Coulter in 1996 and 1997 had sold nine MICRO21 systems in Japan, so it looked forward to selling directly in such overseas markets. This agreement also stipulated that Coulter could continue on a nonexclusive basis to buy IMI products for worldwide distribution on the same terms as other distributors.

Coulter Corporation in July 1996 teamed up with two other firms to develop and promote automated laboratory systems. Lab-Interlink Inc. of Omaha, Nebraska, agreed to provide software for the automated systems, while Johnson & Johnson was responsible for sales, support, and service in this three-company alliance.

A New Owner

In the fall of 1997 Beckman Instruments, Inc., a firm with stock sold on the New York Exchange under the symbol BEC, announced that it was acquiring Coulter Corporation. Effective April 1998, the new firm was renamed Beckman Coulter, Inc. Based in Fullerton, California, Beckman paid $875 million cash for Coulter's outstanding shares and also about $275 million to retire Coulter's debts. To finance this transaction, Beckman negotiated a credit agreement with Citibank, Merrill Lynch, Bank of America, First Chicago, Industrial Bank of Japan, and several other banks in the U.S., Japan, Europe, and Latin America. Because almost 70 percent of the combined company's total revenues came from repeat sales of reagents and service, it expected to have strong cash flows in the future.

''The formation of this new company, Beckman Coulter, from two of the industry's most recognized and respected names not only creates a powerful presence in diagnostics, but also strengthens our life sciences business,'' said Louis T. Rosso, Beckman's chairman and CEO.

One major advantage of this merger was that the two firms sold different products to the same customers. Coulter was the major supplier of hematology analyzers, while Beckman provided a well-known line of automated devices for clinical chemistry and related diagnostic tests. Their combined product offerings would allow hospital laboratories to purchase more than 75 percent of their supplies and equipment from one firm, thus making one-stop shopping in this field more of a reality.

This acquisition saddled Beckman with massive debt. In fact, its debt-to-capital percentage approached 90 percent. And Beckman expected to lose almost $300 million in the fourth quarter of 1997 due to the costs of this acquisition. In spite of these negative factors, the combined firm considered it a wise move because consolidation could be expected to bring lower operating costs and expanded markets. Beckman's leaders said they would sell some real estate and use its increased cash flow to reduce its high debt, but some observers suspected that debt reduction would remain a major difficulty for the new firm.

Not surprisingly, various credit rating firms decreased Beckman's rating to speculative levels because of its acquisition of Coulter. For example, Standard & Poor's gave Beckman a BB+ rating.

Coulter and Beckman each brought relative strengths to this merger. Beckman expected that Coulter would help increase its usually weak sales among managed care firms and purchasing groups. On the other hand, Beckman's expertise in fiscal restraint and being accountable to stockholders were hoped to increase Coulter's profitability.

Beckman's 1997 purchase of Coulter surprised some analysts, who knew Coulter had sought a buyer for some time, partly because of the question of succession in this family-owned and -managed firm. Cofounder Joseph Coulter, Jr., had died in 1995. His daughter, Laura Coulter-Jones, replaced him as president of Coulter Corporation. Wallace Coulter, who never married and had no children, remained board chairman. Some observers speculated that either Roche or Johnson & Johnson would buy Coulter as it made the transition to the second generation of family leadership. The normally conservative Beckman had purchased several small firms, but this major acquisition broke new ground.

Beckman's Chairman Rosso explained that, "There were certain attractions to Beckman in our cultural and historical base. In that sense, we may have been emotionally well-positioned." Rosso was referring to Beckman Instruments being founded by Dr. Arnold Beckman in 1935 with the invention of the acidimeter, reminiscent of Wallace Coulter and Joseph Coulter developing the first Coulter Counter in the late 1940s and early 1950s. Both firms thus started with the invention of a single device.

The bottom line was that only time would tell if this merger proved successful. Although the merger had several positives, the trend to cut healthcare costs and the fact that medical diagnostics was not a growth industry indicated turbulent times ahead for the newly created Beckman Coulter, Inc.

Principal Subsidiaries

Coulter Electronics, Pty. Ltd. (Australia and New Zealand); Instrumentation Laboratory, Ges.m.b.H. (Austria); Coulter Electronics Ind. & Com. Ltda. (Brazil); Counter Electronics of Canada, Ltd.; Coultronics France, S.A.; Coulter Electronics, GmbH (Germany); Coulter Electronics (Hong Kong) Ltd.; Coulter K.K. (Japan); Coulter de Mexico S.A., DE C.V.; Coulter Electronics, Ltd. (Netherlands, U.K., and Turkey); Coulter Electronics Sales of Puerto Rico, Inc.; Coulter Electronics S.A. Pty. Ltd. (South Africa); Coulter Electronics S.A. (Venezuela); Coulter/Immunotech, Inc.; Izasa, S.A. (Spain); Instrumentation Laboratory AG (Switzerland); Instrumentation Laboratory, SpA (Italy); Coulter Pharmaceutical Inc.

Further Reading

Barciela, Susana, "Investing in People Pays Big Dividends; Survey Says Companies Reap Rewards When Employees Treated as Assets, not Debits," *Fresno Bee*, June 19, 1995, p. E1.

Bussey, Jane, "Trade Pact Called Boon for Florida by Transportation Chief Pena," *Knight-Ridder/Tribune Business News*, September 15, 1993.

Chandler, Michele, "FDA Approves Coulter Blood Test," *Knight-Ridder/Tribune News Service*, March 14, 1996.

Fields, Gregg, "A Life of Discovery," *Miami Herald*, April 27, 1992, pp. 23–24.

Kane, Cheryl, "Coulter Wins with White Elephant," *South Florida Business Journal*, October 26, 1992.

Miller, Susan, *South Florida Business Journal*, February 16, 1996.

Miracle, Barbara, "Innovation Is the Key," *Florida Trend*, March 1992, p. 42.

Nesse, Leslie K., "Coulter Changing Products Line," *South Florida Business Journal*, August 19, 1994, p. A4.

Norris, Melinda, "Automated Medical Lab Firm Starts to Get Global Exposure," *Omaha World Herald*, August 9, 1996.

"Plucking up Courage, Beckman Buys Coulter," *In Vivo: The Business and Medicine Report*, September 1997.

Upbin, Bruce, "What Have You Invented for Me Lately?" *Forbes*, December 16, 1996, pp. 330, 332.

—David M. Walden

BERINGER WINE ESTATES

Beringer Wine Estates Holdings, Inc.

1000 Pratt Avenue
St. Helena, California 94574
U.S.A.
(707) 963-7115
Fax: (707) 963-5430
Web site: http://www.beringer.com

Public Company
Incorporated: 1996 as Beringer Wine Estates Holdings, Inc.
Employees: 610
Sales: $269.4 (1997)
Stock Exchanges: NASDAQ
SICs: 2084 Wines, Brandy & Brandy Spirits

Owner of the oldest continuously operating winery in Napa Valley, California, Beringer Wine Estates Holdings, Inc. is a leading producer of premium California varietal table wines, marketing its wines under the Beringer, Meridian Vineyards, Chateau St. Jean, Napa Ridge, Chateau Souverain, and Stags' Leap brand names. Beringer Wine Estates was formed in 1996 to acquire the Chateau Souverain, Meridian Vineyards, Napa Ridge, and Beringer brands from Wine World, Inc., a subsidiary of Nestlé S.A., the global food, beverage, and candy conglomerate. Of these four brands, Beringer by far was the oldest, first appearing in the late 19th century when Jacob and Frederick Beringer opened their first winery. Subsequent generations of the Beringer family retained control over the Beringer brand for nearly a century before selling it to Nestlé in 1971. Under Nestlé's stewardship, the Chateau Souverain and Napa Ridge brands were acquired in 1986 and the Meridian Vineyards brand was introduced in 1990. Beringer Wine Estates subsequently added to the portfolio of brands, acquiring the Chateau St. Jean brand in 1996 and the Stags' Leap brand in 1997. With these wineries under its control during the late 1990s, Beringer Wine Estates ranked as the top seller of premium wines in the United States, controlling more than 14 percent of the domestic market and deriving the bulk of its sales from its Beringer White Zinfandel brand. In addition to its domestically produced wines, Beringer also distributed wines imported from Chile, France, and Italy, which were sold in the United States under the Tarapaca, Rivefort of France, and Gabbiano brand names, respectively. In 1997, when the company converted to public ownership, Beringer Wine Estates owned or controlled 9,400 acres of vineyards in California's Lake, Napa, San Luis Obispo, Santa Barbara, and Sonoma counties.

19th-Century Origins

The roots of Beringer Wine Estates stretched back to the mid-19th century, back to the hometown of the company's founders in Mainz, Germany. There, where the Rhine and Main rivers met, Jacob and Frederick Beringer spent their childhood and early adulthood growing up in the fertile, winemaking region known as the Rhine Valley. The two brothers developed an early interest in winemaking, particularly Jacob, but neither would express this passion in any meaningful way in their native Germany. Although the Rhine Valley was renowned for its prized vineyards, the lure of greater opportunities in the burgeoning United States drew each of them away from their homeland. Frederick was the first to go. Frederick left Mainz in 1863 and settled in New York, where the rumors of great promise lived up to their billing. Frederick wrote to Jacob in Mainz, urging his brother to come west and join him in New York. Intrigued, Jacob packed his bags and set sail for New York in 1868.

For Jacob Beringer, New York was not the mecca of opportunity his brother had described. Frederick's interests were in business, ideally suited to the vibrant and chaotic bustle of New York, but Jacob pined for the more sedate wine business and its rural setting. He had spent his years in Mainz studying winemaking and barrelmaking and had worked as a cellarmaster for a local wine company, becoming more comfortable in a wine cellar than on the streets of New York. Accordingly, Jacob left New York in 1870 and boarded a train for California, where rumor had it that the warm and sunny climate was ideal for growing wine grapes. Jacob took a train to San Francisco—dreaming of grapes while others dreamed of gold—and then traveled north to Napa Valley where he was pleased to find rocky, well-drained soil similar to the soil in his native Rhine Valley.

Company Perspectives:

Beringer Vineyards is the oldest continuously operating winery in the Napa Valley. Jacob Beringer's foresight in recognizing the quality and potential of grape growing in the Napa Valley is part of the living heritage of Beringer Vineyards. With the present use of state-of-the-art technology applied to age-old traditions Beringer Vineyard's wines continue to reflect a single-minded dedication to the making of memorable wines from great Napa Valley vineyards.

The conditions in Napa Valley were ideal for winemaking, and Jacob settled in, taking a job as a cellar foreman for another expatriated German winemaker, Charles Krug. By 1875 Jacob Beringer was ready to go it alone and, with financial assistance from his brother Frederick, he purchased his first property: the cornerstone of what would develop into the oldest continuously operating winery in Napa Valley. The first project on Jacob's agenda was to build the wine cellars required to store and age wine. To complete the job, Jacob hired Chinese laborers who were returning to the San Francisco area following the completion of the Trans-Continental Railroad and directed them to hand-chisel tunnels into the hillside of rock on his property. The tunnels took years to complete, but once they were completed they served as ideal wine cellars, where deep within the tunnel system temperatures remained 58°F regardless of the temperatures in Napa Valley.

Work began on the tunnels in 1876, the year Beringer Winery was formally established. While this epic, time-consuming project was being completed inch by inch, Jacob planted grapes and began building his winery. His first crush took place in 1877, and from there the methodical process of developing a fine wine ensued. It took until the early 1880s before the winery reached full-production capacity, but as soon as there were bottles of wine available Jacob began shipping them to his brother in New York. Frederick, in turn, opened a store and wine cellar in New York in 1880 to make room for the growing number of shipments. Three years after opening the store, Frederick moved to St. Helena to be closer to the family business and began building his home, which was modeled after the Beringer home in Mainz. Dubbed the "Rhine House," the 17-room mansion served as the home for the generations of Beringers. To make room for the sprawling mansion, Jacob's house was put on logs and rolled several hundred feet away.

The Beringer brothers began to distinguish themselves as competent vintners by the end of their first decade of business. In 1887 Beringer wines earned their first domestic awards, followed by international recognition two years later when Beringer's Riesling captured the coveted Silver Medal at the Paris Exhibition. Once given the seal of approval from the European wine community, the Beringer winery began to flourish, as Napa Valley vintners gradually earned the respect of connoisseurs overseas. Beringer's sales and profits swelled accordingly, giving Jacob and Frederick the financial resources to expand their winery and add vineyards. The company's stature increased, and as the century drew to a close, future growth appeared assured. The 1890s proved to be a lucrative decade for the Beringer winery, but as it would turn out, the last decade of the 19th century marked the end of an era at Beringer and the beginning of troubled times.

From the wine company's outset, Frederick Beringer had lent valuable talents to the enterprise. His penchant for business, his wealth, and his financial knowledge had contributed significantly to the company's success during its crucial development from a start-up winery to a recognized producer of premium wines. His death in 1901 delivered decisive repercussions, stripping the winery of its chief financial wizard. Jacob Beringer's contributions were not to be overlooked—the winery was his inspiration and without his gift for producing wines the Beringer winery could never have existed—but Frederick's death was a loss sorely felt by the Beringer winery. Without the aid of his brother, Jacob Beringer persevered and managed to keep the enterprise running, but another serious blow was delivered five years after Frederick's death. The 1906 San Francisco earthquake reduced the city to rubble and caused widespread damage throughout northern California, devastating the region and severely damaging the Beringer winery. Jacob mended the winery and vineyards, but by the decade's conclusion the combined effect of Frederick's death and the 1906 earthquake had conspired to make the first decade of the 20th century a disaster compared with the prodigious strides achieved during the 1890s.

Prohibition

At the turn of the century the Beringer winery lost its brains, and in the 1910s the company lost its heart. Jacob Beringer, the creator of the award-winning, internationally praised Beringer wines, died in 1915, paving the way for successive generations of Beringers to steward the fortunes of the Napa Valley winery. The first members of the family to take command were Jacob's children, who began their tenure of control just prior to perhaps the most anxiety-ridden years vintners could imagine. Prohibition, enacted in 1920, was five years away when Jacob died, but his children ensured the winery would continue to operate by securing a license to produce altar wines. Winery operators without such permission, of course, were forced to exit the business, which went a long way toward giving Beringer the distinction as the oldest continuously operating winery in Napa Valley during the 1990s.

Permission to keep producing wines during Prohibition also enabled Beringer to increase its production output in anticipation of the repeal of the 18th Amendment. The company produced 15,000 cases in 1932, one year before the production and consumption of alcohol was permitted again, giving the company an early lead over its domestic competitors. From 1933 forward it was business as usual at Beringer, as the company resumed production of its full line of varietal wines. Beringer family members, ensconced in the Rhine House, watched over the operation of the business in the decades following the repeal of Prohibition, adding vineyards occasionally as the company matured into an established veteran of winemaking. Beringer's progress during World War II, the 1950s, and into the 1960s occurred at a leisurely pace, remarkable only for the placid manner in which the company eased its way through the decades. By the 1960s, however, it became clear that the serenity exuded by the company was masking pervasive internal problems. This realization engendered sweeping changes and signaled the end of Beringer family ownership and management after nearly a century of control.

Acquired by Nestlé in 1971

For outsiders, the problems were hard to identify individually, but as a whole industry experts agreed that Beringer's difficulties were caused by decades of ineffective management. Nepotism had led to stagnation. Beringer was not the only wine company suffering from the ills of stagnation during the 1960s. Many of its domestic competitors were family-run businesses that, like Beringer, had failed to maintain their vineyards. Unsatisfactory wines were the result, and the ramification of inferior quality was declining business. By the end of the 1960s Beringer's difficulties had become grave enough for the family to divest their interests in the company. In 1971, after 95 years of control, the Beringer family sold the Beringer brand name, its wineries, and 700 acres of vineyards.

The new owner was Nestlé USA, Inc., a subsidiary of Nestlé S.A., the global food, beverage, and confection conglomerate based in Switzerland. After acquiring Beringer, Nestlé USA formed a subsidiary company named Wine World, Inc. to superintend the revitalization of the Beringer brand name and the Beringer vineyards. Beringer represented Nestlé's first foray into the wine business, but despite its inexperience the corporation demonstrated shrewd patience in resurrecting the Beringer business. The company took a long-term approach to rebuilding its new acquisition, anticipating it would take between ten and 15 years to orchestrate a complete turnaround. Nestlé, through Wine World, Inc., used this time to bring in new management, new technology, and sophisticated expertise in the art of producing wines. As Nestlé put its revitalization program into effect, the company's efforts were aided by a growing trend among U.S. consumers that would benefit it handsomely for its years of investment. Shortly after Nestlé acquired Beringer, U.S. consumers began to demonstrate a growing interest in high-quality, premium varietal wines. Previously, consumer preferences had favored generic, or ''jug'' wines, but during the 1970s and 1980s the American palate was becoming more discerning and, consequently, the demand for ''European-style'' wine was increasing. This general trend worked in Nestlé's favor as the slow process of rekindling the popularity of the Beringer brand in the United States was under way.

Vineyards that had been purchased during the Beringer family era of control received much greater attention under the auspices of Nestlé, such as Beringer's Knight Valley Vineyard located north of Calistoga, California, which was developed into an integral facet of Beringer's operations. Knight Valley and other Beringer vineyards were beneficiaries of sizable cash infusions from the deep coffers of Nestlé, and over time they either recovered their former luster or were substantially improved. The improvements raised the quality of Beringer wines and gradually the brand name was re-established in the eyes of consumers and wine critics. Although Beringer continued to rank behind such brands as Gallo, Carlo Rossi, Almaden, and Inglenook during the early 1980s, the brand was gaining ground on its competitors by consistently increasing its market share.

At roughly the same time Nestlé management could point to a full recovery of Beringer, the U.S. wine industry was expanding exponentially. Between the late 1970s and the late 1990s, the number of wineries in the country increased from 350 to 950, with much of that growth occurring during the 1980s, a decade when Nestlé was ready to expand as well. By the mid-1980s Nestlé management felt it had completed its number one priority of reviving the Beringer brand name and was ready to move on to secondary goals. In 1986 the company began expanding, acquiring Sonoma County-based Chateau Souverain, a winery founded in 1943 that specialized in producing red wines, particularly cabernet sauvignon, merlot, and zinfandel. Also in 1986 the company introduced a new brand named Napa Ridge, which used grapes from the coastal regions of California. Expansive vineyards in Santa Barbara were also purchased in 1986 and were used to produce wine for a brand named Meridian Vineyards, which was introduced in 1990.

1990s Brings New Ownership

By the early 1990s the Beringer enterprise was as healthy as it had been a century earlier when Jacob and Frederick Beringer enjoyed their greatest success. Nestlé management had transformed the venerable company into a leading wine producer that represented a prize for any interested suitor. In the mid-1990s an interested suitor came forward and set the stage for the second transfer of ownership in Beringer's history.

Eyeing the company with interest was Silverado Partners Acquisition Corp., which was controlled by an investment group that included Napa-based Silverado Partners and a buyout firm named Texas Pacific Group, controller of Continental Airlines. The two investment groups reached an agreement with Nestlé for the acquisition of the Beringer enterprise for $350 million. Once the deal was completed, Silverado Partners and Texas Pacific Group formed Beringer Wine Estates Holdings, Inc. to formally acquire Beringer, which took effect January 1, 1996. Beringer Wine Estates, as the new enterprise in charge of a 120-year-old business, immediately jumped on the acquisition trail to begin expanding its portfolio of properties. Shortly after its formation, Beringer Wine Estates purchased the Sonoma County-based Chateau St. Jean winery, a market leader in the production of premium chardonnay wines. The next acquisition target was the Stags' Leap Winery located in Napa Valley. Acquired in early 1997, the Stags' Leap Winery was an accomplished producer of red wines, with particular emphasis on cabernet sauvignon, merlot, and petite syrah.

With the additions made in 1996 and 1997 giving the company a total of 9,400 acres of vineyards, Beringer Wine Estates spent the months following the Stags' Leap Winery acquisition planning for an initial public offering (IPO) of stock, hoping the company's stock offering would coincide with a fall harvest expected to be the California wine industry's best ever. Beringer Wine Estates filed with the Securities and Exchange Commission in August 1997 and made its public debut at the end of October 1997, attracting $26 per share. Confident that the years ahead would witness the continued steady rise in annual sales, Beringer Wine Estates' management looked ahead to the remainder of the 1990s and the beginning of the 21st century with considerable optimism. At the time of its IPO, the company ranked as the top seller of premium wines in the United

States, and the directors of Beringer Wine Estates were intent on not relinquishing their position.

Principal Subsidiaries

Beringer Vineyards; Meridian Vineyards; Chateau St. Jean; Napa Ridge; Chateau Souverain; Stags' Leap Winery.

Further Reading

Beringer Wine Estates Holdings, Inc., ''Beringer History,'' http://www.beringer.com.

''Beringer Wine Estates Holdings, Inc.,'' http://www.ipocentral.com/ml_ipo/54453ml.html.

Bilas, Wendy Johnson, ''Beringer,'' *Encyclopedia of Consumer Brands,* Detroit: Gale Research Company, 1995.

Ferguson, Tim W., ''Uncorking Beringer,'' *Forbes,* November 3, 1997, p. 42.

Heald, Eleanor, and Heald, Ray, ''Beringer's Burgeoning Empire,'' *The Quarterly Review of Wines,* Autumn 1997, p. 32.

—Jeffrey L. Covell

Bestfoods

International Plaza
Post Office Box 8000
Englewood Cliffs, New Jersey 07632-9976
U.S.A.
(201) 894-4000
Fax: (201) 894-2186
Web site: http://www.cpcinternational.com

Public Company
Incorporated: 1906 as Corn Products Refining Company
Employees: 51,000
Sales: $9.84 billion (1996)
Stock Exchanges: New York Midwest Pacific Cincinnati Basel Frankfurt Geneva London Paris Zurich Lausanne
SICs: 2033 Canned Fruits, Vegetables, Preserves, Jams & Jellies; 2034 Dried & Dehydrated Fruits, Vegetables & Soup Mixes; 2035 Pickled Fruits & Vegetables, Salad Dressings, Vegetable Sauces & Seasonings; 2041 Flour & Other Grain Mill Products; 2051 Bread & Bakery Products, Except Cookies & Crackers; 2052 Cookies & Crackers; 2079 Shortening, Margarine, Fats & Oils, Not Elsewhere Classified; 2087 Flavoring Extracts & Flavoring Syrups, Not Elsewhere Classified; 2098 Macaroni, Spaghetti, Vermicelli & Noodles; 2099 Food Preparations, Not Elsewhere Classified

Bestfoods is one of the largest food companies in the United States, with two main businesses: consumer foods and baking. It is also one of the most international of U.S. food companies, with 75 percent of its consumer foods revenues coming from outside the U.S. The consumer foods business generated $6.91 billion in revenues in 1996, 45 percent of which came from Knorr soups, sauces, bouillons, and related products (including Mueller's pasta); 28 percent from dressings (Hellman's, Best Foods) and corn oil (Mazola); nine percent from corn starches (Argo, Maizena) and corn syrups (Karo); five percent from bread spreads (Skippy peanut butter); 4.5 percent from desserts (Alsa, Ambrosia); and 8.5 percent from other products. Also included within the consumer foods sector is the company's worldwide food-service business, which is known as Caterplan in most areas outside the United States, and which services restaurants, cafeterias, and other customers in 57 countries. Bestfoods' baking business—a predominantly North American operation—generated $1.57 billion in revenues in 1996 and is the largest fresh premium baker in the United States, with such brands as Entenmann's sweet baked goods; Thomas' English muffins; Oroweat, Arnold, Freihofer's, and Brownberry breads; Boboli Italian pizza crusts; and Sahara pita breads.

The company traces its roots to two main predecessors: Corn Products Refining Company (corn refining) and The Best Foods, Inc. (consumer food products), which merged in 1959 to become the Corn Products Company. This successor company changed its name to CPC International Inc. in 1969 in a move aiming at deemphasizing its corn-refining operations, which became increasingly less important over the decades—culminating in its December 31, 1997, spinoff to the public as Corn Products International, Inc. On January 1, 1998, CPC International changed its name to Bestfoods. The company's baking division was formed in October 1995 following the acquisition of the baking business of Kraft Foods, Inc.

History of Corn Products Refining Company

Bestfoods traces its corn-refining ancestry to the development in 1842 of the first workable method for extracting starch from corn. By the turn of the century, a number of corn refineries were processing corn to obtain its starch and sugar, including the Corn Products Company, a predecessor of Corn Products Refining and the producer of Karo corn syrup.

In 1900 the National Starch Manufacturing Company reached an agreement to cooperate with the United States Glucose Company, which was also a major stockholder in the United States Sugar Refining Company. By 1902, when the three companies officially merged to form the Corn Products

Company Perspectives:

CPC International is an international company comprising locally-managed operations in 62 countries. Each business has significant freedom to make decisions and act independently to further local and corporate business objectives.

All of our local businesses are also integral to a corporate organization that provides strategic guidelines and oversight, as well as constant reinforcement of CPC's shared values. These values call for the highest standards of moral and ethical behavior in all business dealings regardless of situation or geographic location. They express commitment to CPC's people and their career and personal development; to providing high-quality products that deliver value to our consumers and customers; to being good citizens in our communities; to ensuring safe workplaces and a clean environment; and to encouraging and rewarding qualities in our people that help achieve our business objectives, such as courage, candor, and conviction.

Company with C. H. Matthiessen as president, they produced about 84 percent of all American corn starch.

In 1901 Thomas Edward Bedford, an executive of Standard Oil of New Jersey, organized the New York Glucose Company to compete with the Corn Products Company. In January 1906, the two companies, together with Warner Sugar Refining Company, merged to form the Corn Products Refining Company (CP) and Bedford became president of the new group.

The new company, headquartered in New York City, continued to manufacture such products as corn starch, corn syrup, and corn oil. It acquired several other major corn wet milling businesses in subsequent years and soon became the undisputed giant of the industry. In 1906 CP opened sales offices in Germany and the United Kingdom.

By 1916 Corn Products manufactured more than 75 percent of all American-made glucose, selling roughly 30 percent of this to the confectionery industry. For some refined corn products it was said to have 90 percent of the U.S. market.

In the early 1900s the company responded to mounting competition by eliminating obsolete refining plants and replacing them with modern facilities to lower manufacturing costs. One of these plants, the world's largest corn-products manufacturing plant, was begun in 1908 near Summit, Illinois, and, when it was completed, processed about one-third of CP's total output at that time.

Corn Products continued to broaden its product line during its early years. Although by 1912 Karo corn syrup accounted for 80 percent of its sales, the company introduced Mazola corn oil in 1911, and at that time was also packaging syrups, jams, and both edible and laundry starches. Much of this production was sold to wholesalers for sale under private labels.

In 1913 the federal government brought suit against Corn Products and its related companies for violations of the Sherman Antitrust Act. The government charged CP with conspiracy to restrain trade in the corn-refining business by attempting to regulate the production and sale of many corn products, and asked the court to declare CP a combination in restraint of free trade, and therefore, to dissolve it. In 1919, following protracted litigation, the Supreme Court ordered CP to divest itself of several properties, but did not require that the company be dissolved.

The company continued to grow, purchasing its first overseas plant, in Germany, in 1919. In January 1921 the company purchased several more German production facilities. By the beginning of the 1930s Corn Products owned or licensed operations in Canada, Mexico, Czechoslovakia, England, France, Italy, the Netherlands, Switzerland, Yugoslavia, Argentina, Brazil, the Dominican Republic, and Japan. In 1930 CP's assets were about $80 million.

During the Great Depression the food industry was a relatively stable one. In 1931 Edward T. Bedford died. His successor at CP was George M. Moffett.

Amid continuing prosperity in the 1940s, Corn Products shut down its most visible public symbol: its large Edgewater, New Jersey, corn refinery, which could be seen from Manhattan across the Hudson River. The plant's mounting obsolescence, together with rising tariffs on Argentine corn, forced CP to ship Midwestern corn overland to the plant; the natural solution was to transfer its work to the Midwest.

During World War II the United States mounted an enormous lend-lease assistance program to aid the Allies while struggling to keep its own troops supplied. These wartime demands were felt nowhere more than in the agricultural-products industry. Corn supplies were restricted because of heavy demand and pricing structure. By April 1944, CP's Kansas City, Missouri, and Pekin, Illinois, refineries had been closed for lack of corn and the same kind of stoppage threatened its big Argo, Illinois, plant. It was not just a simple problem of shortage, however. The government-mandated price for corn was so low that farmers, with a limited amount of the grain, found it more profitable to feed the corn to their hogs than to sell it to refiners. Nonetheless, CP survived the war and soon was expanding again.

In April 1958 CP president William Brady announced that the company would acquire C. H. Knorr Company of West Germany, a maker of bouillon, dehydrated soups, and other convenience foods. This acquisition was the last in a long string of postwar acquisitions for the company. By 1958 CP was involved in the producing and processing of feed and grain, corn and chemical refining, banking, construction, and the running of a railroad and a shipping line.

History of The Best Foods, Inc.

The Best Foods, Inc. traced its beginnings to a number of 19th-century flaxseed, cottonseed, and flour-milling businesses. In December 1898 the company's oldest component, the American Linseed Company, was incorporated in New Jersey. American Linseed began to diversify in 1917, acquiring the Nucoa Butter Company, whose largest subsidiary, The Best Foods, Inc., produced margarine, mayonnaise, and other edible-oil products.

A second antecedent of Best Foods, American Cotton Oil Company, also moved from a basic commodity business to packaged-good marketing around 1920. In June 1922 American Cotton Oil sold its cottonseed-crushing mills in the South and began to concentrate on its soap-making subsidiary, the N.K. Fairbank Company. Among the subsidiary's products was Gold Dust, a popular brand of soap. The Gold Dust name was applied to the surviving consumer-products company, and the Gold Dust Corporation was incorporated in September 1923 in New Jersey. Gold Dust then acquired the F.F. Dalley Company's shoe polish lines, including the popular Shinola brand.

The union of American Linseed and Gold Dust occurred in 1928, when Gold Dust bought blocks of American Linseed stock, acquired American Linseed's packaged-goods division, and, in July 1928, finally bought the rest of the business, selling its flaxseed operations. In January 1929 the enlarged Gold Dust Corporation bought the Standard Milling Company, the oldest and second-largest American milling company. In 1930 Gold Dust's assets totaled about $41 million.

Less than two years after Gold Dust outbid the Postum Company for American Linseed, Gold Dust and Postum (which later became General Foods) entered a joint venture. The Best Foods division of Gold Dust and Postum's Richard Hellmann Company linked up to distribute the margarine, dressings, and spreads they both manufactured.

In November 1936 Gold Dust combined its three operating subsidiaries, 2-in-1 Shinola Bixby Corporation, Preserves and Honey, Inc., and Hecker-H-O Company, Inc. into a single corporation, taking the Hecker name for the whole. And in 1939 Hecker President George Morrow sold the Gold Dust soap business to Lever Brothers Company for $2.5 million.

In November 1942 Hecker paid General Foods $5.5 million for General Foods' 29 percent interest in the Best Foods-Hellmann shipping operation. The following month Hecker changed its name to The Best Foods, Inc.

In 1955 Best Foods made several important acquisitions. It first bought the Rit Dye Company after a series of transactions begun a decade earlier. Best Foods then acquired the Rosefield Packing Company, of Alameda, California, and Good Foods, Inc., of Minneapolis, Minnesota. The purchase of these two companies gave Best Foods ownership of the Skippy peanut butter brand. Best Foods also sold Standard Milling Company that year.

1959 Merger of CP and Best Foods

Following complicated preparations begun in September 1958, Corn Products Refining Company and The Best Foods, Inc. formally merged in May 1959 as Corn Products Company. The merger was the result of the recognition that CP's future relied on its ability to develop a successful grocery products business in order to maintain growth.

In 1959 and 1960 Corn Products Company established new businesses in the Philippines, France, Sweden, and Venezuela. The company continued growing throughout the decade, introducing Mazola margarine in the United States in 1961. In 1963 the company established a Knorr plant in Japan and began manufacturing starch in Pakistan. This growth enabled the company to surpass $1 billion in sales for the first time in 1966.

In April 1969 the company changed its name to CPC International Inc. Although it continued to add units in its chemicals and packaging divisions and also made a foray into restaurants with the purchase of the Dutch Pantry chain in 1969, CPC had clearly decided to emphasize packaged foods—the name change was intended to play down the company's corn refining operation. In 1969 sales of the company's consumer grocery products surpassed those of its wet-milled corn products for the first time.

S. B. Thomas, a baker of English muffins and other specialty breads, was bought in 1970. Ten years later the S. B. Thomas subsidiary bought Sahara brand pita bread. And, in 1983, CPC acquired the C. F. Mueller Company, one of the largest U.S. pasta makers, for $122 million.

During the 1970s Best Foods, as the consumer-foods division was then known, also started its first facility outside the United States, a vegetable oil manufacturing and packaging facility in Puerto Rico. In 1974 CPC's sales topped $2.5 billion, only four years later they surpassed $3 billion, and in 1980 sales were over $4 billion.

In 1981 and 1982 the company opened five new U.S. corn wet milling plants as CPC began a program to reduce costs and improve the productivity and capacity of its corn wet milling operations. Between 1983 and 1985 the company spent more than $400 million in ''Investment for Growth'' projects. The largest of these was the rebuilding of the company's huge Argo, Illinois, factory.

In 1986 CPC successfully fought off a takeover attempt by Ronald O. Perelman, chairman of the Revlon Group. The CPC board authorized a repurchase of over 20 percent of the company's stock, to be financed by borrowing and then repaying the debt by asset sale. CPC eventually bought back Perelman's 3.68 million shares for $88.5 million.

Restructuring and Acquisitions During Late 1980s and Early 1990s

Freed of Perelman, the company moved ahead with its takeover-prompted restructuring plans, completing the buyback of 20 percent of its stock in 1988 at a total cost of $836.9 million. Under this restructuring plan the company acquired several new companies and stripped away some of its poor performers. CPC also reduced its workforce by some 17 percent. In 1988 CPC consolidated its worldwide food operations into one group, a move away from the company's longtime practice of granting autonomy to its international operations.

The first of the company's new acquisitions was Arnold Foods Company, in November 1986. CPC paid $145 million for the bread company, whose sales were $230 million. Also in 1986 CPC bought the Old London melba toast baking business from Borden, Inc. for about $25 million and combined Old London, Arnold, and S. B. Thomas to form the Best Foods Baking Group. Several other smaller acquisitions brought the total cost of 1986 acquisitions to nearly $193 million. In 1987 and 1988 CPC spent about $200 million on packaged-food companies in Latin America, Brazil, Italy, France, Germany, and Great Britain.

During the same period CPC sold many holdings, including its $600 million European corn-milling operations and its South African unit. The company also sold its 50 percent interest in a Japanese food business and 50 percent of its food companies in Hong Kong, Malaysia, the Philippines, Singapore, Taiwan, and Thailand to Ajinomoto, its partner in a Japanese joint venture.

CPC also strengthened its successful food-service operation, which serves institutional customers. This fast-growth business, known as CPC Foodservice in the United States and Caterplan in Europe, Latin America, and Asia, generated about 10 percent of the company's grocery-product sales by the early 1990s.

After steering CPC through the takeover attempt and restructuring, CEO James R. Eiszner was named chairman in 1987, succeeding chairman James W. McKee, Jr. Eiszner continued to maximize CPC's international exposure, brand-name products, and healthy financial picture to allow the company to continue to grow worldwide. Overall, from 1986 through early 1990, CPC acquired 17 consumer food businesses—seven in Europe, four in Latin America, and three each in Canada and the United States. Most of these were small to medium companies and product lines. Another example of this measured growth strategy came in April 1990 when CPC paid SmithKline Beecham PLC $255 million for three food lines: Ambrosia desserts, Bovril beef extracts, and Marmite spread. In August of that same year Charles R. Shoemate became company CEO; the following month, following Eiszner's death, he became chairman as well. Shoemate had joined the company in 1962, working his way up to the presidency in October 1988.

Shoemate continued to expand CPC's operations into new countries in the early 1990s, including Hungary, the Czech Republic, Poland, Israel, and Indonesia. The overseas focus remained on growing through the acquisition of local brands; but once a local brand was purchased in a new market, CPC then leveraged its newfound distribution channel by introducing overseas brands in that market. By 1994, nearly two-thirds of sales and profits were generated outside the United States. That year, CPC recorded a pretax restructuring charge of $227 million to consolidate its food plants in Europe and the United States. During the following year, another plant-related restructuring led to a $75 million charge.

Mid-1990s: Baking In, Corn Refining Out

In the mid-1990s CPC continued to build its food products operations through acquisitions. In July 1995 the company paid U.K.-based Dalgety PLC about $280 million for its Golden Wonder Pot Noodle instant hot snacks business. Also in 1995 CPC purchased the France-based Lesieur mayonnaise and salad dressings business for about $50 million. The company's largest purchase that year—in fact the largest acquisition in company history—came through the October purchase of the baking business of Kraft Foods, Inc. for $865 million in cash. The purchase added to CPC's existing baking operations—Thomas' English muffins, Arnold and Brownberry bread, and Sahara pita bread—some of the top brands in the baking sector: Entenmann's and Freihofer's sweet baked products, Oroweat and Freihofer's breads, and Boboli Italian pizza crusts. Upon completion of the acquisition, all of these products were grouped within a newly formed CPC Baking Business unit, which by 1996 already surpassed CPC's corn refining business in size, generating $1.57 billion in revenues to the $1.37 billion for corn refining.

In 1996 the company agreed to pay a fine of $7 million to settle a civil antitrust lawsuit brought against CPC, Archer-Daniels-Midland Co., Cargill Inc., and other corn-refining companies alleging collusion and price-fixing. In February 1997 CPC announced that it planned to spin off its corn-refining business so that it could concentrate on building its packaged food and baking businesses. The spinoff to CPC shareholders was subsequently completed on December 31, 1997, thereby creating a new public company called Corn Products International, Inc. Since CPC had now divested itself of its corn refining roots, the company's management decided a new name was needed and settled on Bestfoods, in homage to the predecessor company known as The Best Foods, Inc.; to the company's North American business known as Best Foods; and to the Best Foods brand name used on the company's dressings sold in the western United States and in parts of Asia.

CPC took $83.2 million in after-tax charges relating to the spinoff in the second and third quarters of 1997. Meanwhile, yet another restructuring in its food operations led to a $155 million after-tax charge during the second quarter. In June 1997 CPC acquired the Spain-based Starlux food products business from Groupe Danone and Findim Investments S.A. The $160 million in revenues Starlux portfolio featured two leading Spanish brands: Starlux bouillons and Nocilla chocolate hazelnut spreads.

Freed to concentrate on its impressive and growing collection of packaged foods and baked goods brands, Bestfoods was likely to seek other strategic acquisitions similar to that of Starlux. But new product development efforts had been bolstered in the mid-1990s and were likely to play an equal—if not more important—role. For example, the company had in 1996 launched Hellmann's and Best Foods pourable salad dressings in the United States and in Latin America. Bestfoods' continued—and successful—overseas expansion also boded well for the future, as operations in eastern and central Europe and in China were already paying off handsomely.

Principal Subsidiaries

Arnold Foods Company, Inc.; Best Foods-Caribbean, Inc.; CPC Europe (Group) Ltd.; CPC Baking Co., Inc.; Entenmann's Inc.; Henri's Food Products Co. Inc.; S.B. Thomas, Inc.; Canada Starch Company Inc.; C.H. Knorr Nahrungsmittelfabrik Ges.mbH (Austria); CPC Monda N.V./S.A. (Belgium; 99.9%); CPC Foods A.S. (Czech Republic; 95.4%); CPC Foods A/S (Denmark); CPC Foods OY (Finland); CPC France S.A. (99.85%); CPC Maizena GmbH (Germany); CPC (Hellas) A.B.E.E. (Greece); CPC Benelux B.V. (the Netherlands); CPC Hungary RT; CPC Foods (Ireland) Ltd.; CPC Italia S.P.A. (99.98%); CPC Foods A/S (Norway); CPC Amino S.A. (Poland; 99.98%); Knorr Portuguesa-Productos Alimentares S.A. (Portugal); CPC Espana, S.A. (Spain); CPC Foods AB (Sweden); CPC Knorr Holdings AG (Switzerland); CPC

(United Kingdom) Ltd.; Israel Edible Products Ltd. ''TAMI'' (51%); CPC Kenya Ltd.; CPC Maghreb, S.A. (Morocco); CPC Tongaat Foods (Pty) Ltd. (South Africa; 50%); Refinerias de Maiz S.A.I.C. (Argentina); Refinacoes de Milho, Brasil Ltda. (Brazil); Industrias de Maiz y Alimentos S.A. (Chile); Industrias del Maiz S.A. (Colombia); Maizena de Costa Rica S.A.; Productos de Maiz y Alimentos S.A. (Guatemala); Productos de Maiz, S.A. de C.V. (Mexico); Alimentos y Productos de Maiz, S.A. (Peru; 99.9%); Industrializadora de Maiz, S.A. (Uruguay); Aliven S.A. (Venezuela); CPC (Guangzhou) Foods Ltd. (China; 80%); CPC/AJI (Hong Kong) Ltd. (Hong Kong); P.T. Knorr Indonesia; CPC/AJI (Malaysia) Sdn. Berhad (50%); CPC Rafham Limited (Pakistan; 51%); California Manufacturing Co., Inc. (Philippines; 50%); CPC/AJI (Singapore) Pte. Ltd. (50%); CPC/AJI (Taiwan) Ltd. (50%); CPC/AJI (Thailand) Ltd. (50%).

Further Reading

Bruner, Richard W., ''Hungary for Skippy,'' *Advertising Age,* September 2, 1991, p. 36.

Cook, James, ''Back to Business,'' *Forbes,* October 5, 1987, p. 40.

——, ''Handsome Is As Handsome Does,'' *Forbes,* March 3, 1980, p. 43.

——, ''How to Get More from Less,'' *Forbes,* May 7, 1984, p. 58.

''CPC International Name Will Change to Bestfoods,'' *Wall Street Journal,* October 17, 1997, p. B8.

Feldman, Amy, ''Have Distribution, Will Travel,'' *Forbes,* June 20, 1994, pp. 44–45.

Hwang, Suein L., ''CPC International Sets $227 Million Revamping Charge,'' *Wall Street Journal,* June 24, 1994, p. A12.

Jensen, Elizabeth, ''CPC Covets the Respect Accorded Its Food Brands,'' *Wall Street Journal,* October 23, 1997, p. B4.

——, ''CPC Plans to Spin Off Corn Refining,'' *Wall Street Journal,* February 27, 1997, pp. A3, A4.

Messenger, Bob, ''The World, According to CPC, '' *Food Processing,* August 1995, p. 36.

Ono, Yumiko, ''CPC Will Buy Kraft's Bakeries for $865 Million,'' *Wall Street Journal,* August 8, 1995, pp. A2, A5.

Roman, Monica, and Lois Therrien, ''How CPC Is Getting Fat on Muffins and Mayonnaise,'' *Business Week,* April 16, 1990, pp. 46–47.

Simon, Howard, ''US Food Company Finds Recipe for Global Growth,'' *Journal of Commerce & Commercial,* June 10, 1996, p. 7B.

Smith, Rod, ''CPC Reports Advancing to Fifth in List of Companies,'' *Feedstuffs,* May 1, 1995, p. 6.

Sparks, Debra, ''Dough Wars,'' *Financial World,* January 30, 1996, pp. 56–57.

Swientek, Bob, ''Bullish on Bouillon,'' *Prepared Foods,* September 1996, pp. 28–29, 32, 34, 36, 38.

Teitelbaum, Richard S., ''CPC's Global Spread,'' *Fortune,* October 22, 1990, p. 106.

Tomkins, Richard, ''Shake-Up Pushes CPC into Loss,'' *Financial Times,* July 13, 1994, p. 30.

—Diane Wylie
—updated by David E. Salamie

Black & Veatch LLP

8400 Ward Parkway
Kansas City, Missouri 64114
U.S.A.
(913) 339-2000
Fax: (913) 458-6030
Web site: http://www.bv.com

Private Company
Incorporated: 1915
Employees: 7,000
Sales: $1.4 billion (1996 est.)
SICs: 8711 Engineering Services; 8712 Architectural Services; 1629 Heavy Construction, Not Elsewhere Classified

Black & Veatch LLP is a leading global engineering and construction firm. With more than 3,000 current projects underway in 1997, the company projected 1997 revenues to be $2 billion for the year, up from $1.4 billion in 1996. Following a reorganization in 1996, Black & Veatch defined its major businesses as power, infrastructure, process, and buildings. The company also offered a number of related services. The Power Group, with five divisions, enjoyed a dominant position in the worldwide power generation industry. It was known for building reliable, cost-effective power plants on time and within budget, while also providing expertise in the field of power delivery. The Infrastructure Group, with eight divisions, provided a complete range of planning, design, construction management, and related services for environmental and civil engineering projects in areas such as water supply, treatment, and distribution; wastewater collection, treatment, and reuse; solid waste recycling and disposal; and hazardous and toxic waste management, among others. The Process Group consisted of the newly named Black & Veatch Pritchard, Inc. (formerly the Pritchard Corporation). With more than 70 years of experience in natural gas processing, petroleum refining, chemical synthesis, cryogenics, and energy-related services, Black & Veatch Pritchard offered a full range of services from feasibility studies to plant start-up and operator training. The Buildings Group provided a complete range of project delivery services for many different markets as well as architecture, planning, interior and graphic design, engineering, and program management services. In addition to the four above mentioned groups, Black & Veatch offered such related services as management consulting, procurement and construction for all types of telecommunications infrastructures, engineering and design services for various transportation industries, and airport services including airport planning, facilities design, engineering, and management services.

Company Origin As a Partnership Between E.B. Black and N.T. Veatch in 1915

The multi-billion-dollar construction and engineering firm that is Black & Veatch was formed as a partnership in 1915 in Kansas City, Missouri, between two men, Ernest Bateman Black and Nathan Thomas Veatch, Jr. According to the company's 75th anniversary annual report, the company's founders were "astute, careful businessmen who established and demanded exacting professional standards."

Veatch and Black were engineers who worked for the J.S. Worley Company, founded in 1908 by John Worley from Toledo, Ohio. When he started the company, Worley had invited Black, a former associate, to join him. Working out of a one-room office in Kansas City, which was then a bustling town full of opportunities, the two began designing and building water works, road paving, sewer systems, and electric lighting projects. The firm expanded in 1911 to a three-room office. It numbered some 32 communities among its clients. During the expansion N.T. Veatch]was hired as a resident engineer to work on the construction of electric light and water plants. In 1912 the firm changed its named to Worley & Black, with Worley as president and Black as vice-president. Two years later the firm expanded into a nine-room office, with Veatch listed as the principal engineer. By the end of 1914 the firm had completed projects for more than 100 communities and private companies.

After Worley left the firm in 1915 to pursue other interests, the partnership was reorganized in August 1915 under the name of Black & Veatch. The two men shared similar backgrounds:

Company Perspectives:

From St. Louis to Singapore, Black & Veatch is there. As an expert in engineering, procurement, and construction, we provide quality work on a fast track schedule for utilities, commerce, industry, and government agencies in more than 65 countries. And, we ensure that our clients receive the best possible value for their investment.

Black & Veatch has a staff of more than 6,000 in offices worldwide. Our professionals apply leading edge technology to study, design, construction, procurement, and management services for projects in the power, environmental, process, and buildings markets throughout the globe. We have the scope of capabilities and worldwide presence to perform any project, anywhere.

both were from Illinois but had grown up in Kansas and both were graduates of the University of Kansas. Shortly after the partnership was formed, the United States became involved in World War I. The newly formed partnership's struggle to survive was helped by obtaining its first federal contract from the War Department, to design and supervise the construction of Camp Pike in Little Rock, Arkansas.

Sustained Moderate Growth Throughout the 1920s and 1930s

Several factors helped Black & Veatch survive the tough times of the Great Depression that followed the stock market crash of 1929. One was the company's association with the Jackson County road project. Veatch, a Republican, was appointed by Harry S. Truman, then a county judge and later President of the United States, to a bipartisan team charged with designing and supervising the road system's construction. After Truman became President, Veatch was often invited to the White House.

Another factor that brought business to Black & Veatch was the passage of the Public Utilities Holding Company Act in 1935, which forced the breakup of large utility companies. With ownership in the companies being transferred, there was an increased need for appraisals and rate studies, many of which were conducted by Black & Veatch during the 1930s. In 1935 the firm was able to move to a larger office in Kansas City's Country Club Plaza, considered to be the first suburban shopping center in the country.

Federal Contracts During World War II

With the United States' involvement in World War II, Black & Veatch obtained federal contracts to manage the construction and engineering of numerous Army camps as well as several Army and Navy air bases. Toward the end of the war, Black & Veatch was hired by the Atomic Energy Commission to provide design work and engineering services for highly secret activities at Los Alamos, New Mexico, where the atomic bomb was being developed. In 1946 Black & Veatch created its Federal Division to handle these projects.

Following the end of World War II in 1945, Black & Veatch expanded into other new fields, including that of electric power. From early design projects for small systems, the firm soon began to be selected to work on major design assignments for large power companies.

Reorganization in the 1950s

Following Black's death in 1949, Veatch kept the firm's name and carried on as sole owner. The firm was later reorganized into a new partnership effective January 1, 1956, with Veatch as managing partner. In addition, the new organization included six executive partners and 23 general partners. By giving away these first partnerships, with the stipulation that retiring partners take nothing away from the firm, Veatch provided for the perpetuation of the organization and guaranteed orderly management transitions for the future.

In 1956 the growing firm designed and managed the construction of its new headquarters in Kansas City. The new two-story building was featured on the cover of *Engineering News-Record,* in part because it was unusual for a consulting engineering firm to design its own office building at that time. With 37,500 square feet, there was enough room for 350 employees and a 200-car parking lot. In 1963 the firm expanded the building to 53,000 square feet by adding a third floor.

After exploring the possibility of taking on overseas projects, Black & Veatch International was established as a subsidiary corporation in 1962 under the direction of Thomas B. Robinson, who would become Black & Veatch's managing partner upon Veatch's retirement in 1973. The first international project undertaken by Black & Veatch International was to design electric distribution system improvements for Dacca and Chittagong in East Pakistan (now Bangladesh).

Rapid Growth in the 1970s

With the company doubling in size between 1971 and 1975, Black & Veatch completed construction of a new six-story building for its offices in Overland Park, Kansas, in 1976. Located near College Boulevard and Lamar, the Power Building, as it was named, had more than 276,000 square feet. The area was primarily pasture land at the time, but the College Boulevard site would later become the center of a major commercial district for the greater Kansas City metropolitan area.

In the late 1970s Black & Veatch continued to grow and diversify through acquisitions. In 1977 it acquired Trotter-Yoder & Associates, a consulting engineering firm located in San Francisco, California, that would become the basis for Black & Veatch's West Coast division. That same year it also acquired Southern Science Applications, Inc., of Dunedin, Florida, which specialized in nuclear engineering consulting.

Two major acquisitions were made in the 1980s. The first, in 1982, was Moore Gardner & Associates, which became Black & Veatch's Asheboro, North Carolina, office. The second, in 1985, was the Pritchard Corporation, a petrochemical engineering company. Pritchard would become a key element of Black & Veatch's Process Group, which specialized in petroleum refining, natural gas processing, chemical synthesis, and other energy-related services to the process industry. In 1996, The Pritchard Corporation announced plans to change its name to Black & Veatch, and for 1997 adopted the transitional name of Black & Veatch Pritchard, Inc.

At a time when new development in the power field slumped as utilities relied on surplus generating capacity, Black & Veatch took a chance and allocated $30 million for the development of POWRTRAK, an automated power plant design and project management system. As POWRTRAK proved it could reduce costs while ensuring high levels of performance and operation, it became a key factor in Black & Veatch's leadership in the power plant design industry. By 1996 Black & Veatch had applied the POWRTRAK concepts to its own business systems and appointed John Voeller, the chief architect of POWRTRAK, to the new position of chief technology officer.

The passage of the Safe Drinking Water Act also brought a substantial amount of new business to Black & Veatch in the 1980s. The firm became heavily involved in the modification, upgrading, and expansion of municipal water plants to bring them into compliance with the new guidelines. Black & Veatch opened approximately thirty new offices during the decade to serve the growing municipal market.

International Growth in the 1990s

Black & Veatch began the 1990s with a new organization and new headquarters. At the beginning of 1989 the firm's executive partners, under the leadership of managing partner John H. Robinson, who had succeeded Thomas B. Robinson in 1983, reorganized the company into four operating groups: Energy, Environmental, Facilities, and Resources. The Energy Group was focused on power generation, transmission, and distribution. The Environmental Group covered a variety of environmental, infrastructure, and civil engineering projects, from water and wastewater treatment and distribution to dams and tunnels. The Facilities Group provided a range of architectural services to clients in different industries. The Resources Group offered a variety of support services in an expanding number of fields.

Black & Veatch also moved into new corporate headquarters at 8400 Ward Parkway in 1989. The company designed the 120,000-square-foot building to accommodate 500 employees in executive administration and other business units. In 1996 the company completed construction and began moving into a seven-story, 300,000-square-foot addition to the building. By the end of the 1980s, Black & Veatch had some 4,000 employees in offices worldwide and had completed more than 16,000 projects.

During the 1990s Black & Veatch saw more of its major projects coming from overseas than from the United States. As a result, the company took about a year longer than previous to complete approvals and obtain financing. Overall, revenues grew to $985 million in 1994. In May 1995 Black & Veatch merged with the British firm Binnie & Partners to form what the *New York Times* called "the biggest company in the world that engages in improving waste-water treatment and the supply of drinking water in developing countries." Binnie & Partners, "one of the longest established and most respected consulting partnerships in the United Kingdom," according to *Water Briefing,* added about 1,200 employees to Black & Veatch and approximately $65 million in annual revenues. The British firm became a separate division within Black & Veatch's Environmental Group.

Black & Veatch continued to grow its international business, with the stated goal of having at least half of its business come from overseas by the year 2000, with the acquisition in 1996 from Thames Water, Plc, of its Paterson Candy Ltd. (formerly, PWT Projects Ltd.), a British-based water treatment process contractor, and PROWA, a German engineering firm specializing in wastewater treatment, river engineering and hydraulics, water treatment, and hazardous waste management. In addition to acquiring those design and construction units from Thames Water, Black & Veatch entered into a strategic alliance with the firm to pursue large water and wastewater concessions in Eastern Europe, Asia, Africa, and South America. Thames Water was known as one of the world's leading water companies serving the city of London, England, and surrounding areas.

In 1996 Black & Veatch also completed a further reorganization and named new leaders to several business units. The four operating groups were realigned under power, infrastructure, process, and buildings. In addition, managing partner John H. Robinson, Jr., was named to the new position of chief development officer. At this time Black & Veatch was run by a management committee consisting of five managing partners, under the leadership of Chairman and Chief Executive Officer P.J. Adam. With the help of an outside consulting firm, Black & Veatch also streamlined the processes by which it delivered support services to its projects and business units.

Black & Veatch also aggressively diversified into new fields, such as telecommunications, in the mid-1990s, building more than 1,100 Personal Communications Services (PCS) antenna sites in the United States in 1996. The company expected its telecommunications division to contribute approximately 20 percent of overall revenues in 1996.

The theme of Black & Veatch's 1996 annual report was "Expect Success." With more than 3,000 projects underway in 1997 and a long list of awards to its credit, the company's clients could count on Black & Veatch for the engineering services they needed for successful projects. The company's plans for global expansion were given a boost in mid-1996 when the General Electric-led consortium that included Black & Veatch won a highly competitive $1.8 billion contract to build two nuclear reactors for the Taiwan Power Company. Together with the 1995 merger with Binnie & Partners and the 1996 acquisitions of PWT Projects Ltd. and PROWA Consulting, Black & Veatch appeared to have the resources and organizational skills to become an international leader in its field.

Principal Operating Units

Power Group; Infrastructure Group; Process Group; Buildings Group; Development Group.

Further Reading

''Black & Veatch Buys into Europe,'' *Process Engineering,* June 1997, p. 10.

''Black & Veatch Merges with Top British Consulting Firm,'' *Water Briefing,* May 17, 1995, p. 5.

''Black & Veatch Prepares to Build Out PCS Market,'' *RCR: Radio Communications Report,* November 11, 1996, p. 13.

''British Firm Merges with Black & Veatch,'' *New York Times,* May 9, 1995, p. 9C.

''G.E. Wins Hotly-Contested $1.8bn Nuclear Contract,'' *Power in Asia,* June 10, 1996, p. 25.

''General Electric Is Leading a Consortium That Won a $1.8 Bil Pact to Build 2 Nuclear Reactors at Taiwan's 'No. 4' Plant,'' *Business Week,* June 10, 1996, p. 56.

''Thames Water in Disposal,'' *Financial Times,* October 3, 1996, p. 22.

—David Bianco

Borden, Inc.

180 East Broad Street
Columbus, Ohio 43215-3799
U.S.A.
(614) 225-4000
Fax: (614) 225-3410

Wholly Owned Subsidiary of Kohlberg Kravis Roberts & Co.
Incorporated: 1899 as Borden Condensed Milk Company
Employees: 20,000
Sales: $5.77 billion (1996)
SICs: 2034 Dried & Dehydrated Fruits, Vegetables & Soup Mixes; 2096 Potato Chips, Corn Chips & Similar Snacks; 2098 Macaroni, Spaghetti, Vermicelli & Noodles; 2099 Food Preparations, Not Elsewhere Classified; 2821 Plastics Materials, Nonvulcanizable Elastomers & Synthetic Resins; 2891 Adhesives & Sealants; 3089 Plastic Products, Not Elsewhere Classified

The Borden, Inc. of the late 1990s is a diversified producer of pasta (including Catelli, Classico, Creamette, and other brands), snacks (Wise, Moore's, Quinlan), and bouillon and dry soup (Wyler's); consumer adhesives (Elmer's, Krazy Glue); and formaldehyde, resins, coatings, and other industrial chemicals. Following an overly aggressive consumer products acquisition drive from 1986 to 1991, the company ran up huge losses in 1992 and 1993 primarily because it had accumulated a scattered collection of unintegrated brands—many of them of the minor variety. Borden was consequently taken private in March 1995 when investment firm Kohlberg Kravis Roberts & Co. (KKR) paid $2 billion for the company. Under KKR's guidance, Borden subsequently underwent a major restructuring, shedding numerous brands—including Cracker Jack, Eagle Brand, Cremora, and ReaLemon—and entire businesses, including the dairy business upon which the company was founded, its global packaging unit, its consumer wallcoverings business, and the Borden Foods cheese business. As one of the oldest and most widely known companies in the United States—a company best known through most of its history as a dairy company—Borden has undergone a 1990s transformation that has been particularly dramatic.

Earliest Roots in Condensed Milk

Gail Borden, Jr., the company's founder, was born in 1801 in Norwich, New York. When his family migrated west, they stopped in Kentucky and Indiana Territory. Borden then moved to Mississippi before settling in Galveston, Texas. Along the way he worked as a surveyor, school teacher, farmer, and government official. He edited the first permanent newspaper in Texas, the *Telegraph & Texas Register,* and is said to have written the famous headline "Remember the Alamo."

Borden made a hobby of inventing things. Among his creations was the prairie schooner, an awkward, sail-powered wagon. Another Borden device, the lazy Susan, can now be found in households everywhere. He also concocted the unsavory, yet serviceable, "meat biscuit," a lightweight, nonperishable food suited to travelers. Although the meat biscuit was a commercial failure, it was hailed as a scientific breakthrough and in 1851 Borden was invited to London to receive the Great Council Medal from Queen Victoria.

During his passage back from London, Borden saw several children on board ship die after drinking contaminated milk. Because no one yet understood how to keep milk fresh, spoiled and even poisonous milk was not uncommon. Borden knew that the Shakers used vacuum pans to preserve fruit, and he began experimenting with a similar apparatus in search of a way to preserve milk. After much tinkering, he discovered he could prevent milk from souring by evaporating it over a slow heat in the vacuum. Believing that it resisted spoilage because its water content had been removed, he called his revolutionary product "condensed milk." As Louis Pasteur later demonstrated, however, it was the heat Borden used in his evaporation process that kept the milk from spoiling because it killed the bacteria in fresh milk.

Despite the apparent usefulness of condensed milk, the U.S. Patent office rejected Borden's patent application three

Company Perspectives:

We are dedicated to building consumer focused food brands serving people around the world, enriching their eating experience every day with great tasting, wholesome, grain-based meal solutions.

We accomplish this because we are a uniquely capable organization energized by common purpose and shared values.

Our growth and shared success will be driven by our singular focus on meeting consumer needs through innovation.

Through the pursuit of this mission and realization of our Vision, we will benefit our consumers, customers, suppliers, and communities as well as our associates and owners.

We will become the "World's Most Admired Food Company."

times. It was finally accepted on August 19, 1856, after Robert McFarlane, the editor of *Scientific American,* and John H. Currie, head of a research laboratory, convinced the commissioner of patents of the value of condensed milk. Soon afterward, Borden started a small processing operation near a dairy farm in Wolcottville, Connecticut, and opened a sales office in New York City. Consumers, however, took little notice of canned milk, and, after only a few months in business, sluggish sales forced Borden to return to Texas in need of more capital. Undaunted, he resumed production in 1857 in Burrville, Connecticut, under the name Gail Borden, Jr., and Company.

The second enterprise also struggled financially until Borden met Jeremiah Milbank, a wholesale grocer, banker, and railroad financier. With Milbank's funding they formed a partnership in 1858 known as the New York Condensed Milk Company. Another stroke of fortune came when Borden decided to advertise in an issue of *Leslie's Illustrated Weekly,* which coincidentally contained an article condemning the unsanitary conditions at city dairies and the practice by many unscrupulous dairymen of adding chalk and eggs to enhance their "swill milk," as it was called. Soon after the magazine appeared, the New York Condensed Milk Company was delivering condensed milk throughout lower Manhattan and in Jersey City, New Jersey.

In 1861 the U.S. government ordered 500 pounds of condensed milk for troops fighting in the Civil War. As the conflict grew, government orders increased, until Borden had to license other manufacturers to keep up with demand. After the war, the New York Condensed Milk Company had a ready-made customer base in both Union and Confederate veterans. To distinguish this product from its new competitors, Borden adopted the American bald eagle as his trademark.

Incorporated in 1899

Gail Borden, Jr., died in 1874, leaving management of the thriving company to his sons, John Gail and Henry Lee, who presided from 1874 to 1884 and 1884 to 1902, respectively. In 1875 the company diversified by offering delivery of fluid milk in New York and New Jersey. Ten years later, it pioneered the use of glass bottles for milk distribution. In 1892 Borden's fluid-milk business was expanded to Chicago and the company began to manufacture evaporated milk. Seven years later, Henry Lee Borden opened the first foreign branch, in Ontario, Canada, bringing to 18 the number of towns in which the company had facilities. In 1899, as fresh and condensed milk sales generated profits of $2 million, the company was incorporated as the Borden Condensed Milk Company.

William J. Rogers, the company's first president from outside the Borden family, took over in 1902. He was succeeded in 1910 by S. Frederick Taylor. Concentrating on its strongholds in New York, New Jersey, and Illinois, Borden built new evaporation facilities and tin can factories, as well as pasteurizing and bottling stations. Local dairy farmers often helped finance the construction, and in return Borden brought stability to milk markets, which at that time were subject to sudden fluctuations, by setting prices for six-month periods. Relations with milk suppliers remained generally friendly until the 1930s, when the market was glutted and farmers charged Borden and other distributors with conspiring to depress prices.

Toward the close of World War I, Borden strengthened its board of directors. Albert G. Milbank, a descendant of Jeremiah Milbank and a founding partner in the New York law firm of Milbank, Tweed, Hope & Webb, was named Borden's first chairman of the board in 1917. The following year, directors from outside the dairy industry were appointed for the first time. These changes reflected Borden's expanded business and helped to make possible its explosive growth in the next decade.

Late 1920s Buying Spree

Under Arthur W. Milburn, the Borden Company, as it was renamed in 1919, embarked on a buying spree that transformed it into a multinational conglomerate. Between 1927 and 1930, it bought more than 200 companies around the country and became the nation's largest distributor of fluid milk. In the process, it entered five new fields: ice cream, cheese, powdered milk, mincemeat, and adhesives. The J.M. Horton Ice Cream Company and the Reid Ice Cream Corporation, which Borden bought in 1928, were both well established on the East Coast. Ice cream fit logically into Borden's fluid-milk operations, as did cheese, which was added in 1929 when Borden acquired the Monroe Cheese Company, Chateau Cheese Company, Ltd., and several other leading producers. Two slightly more adventurous acquisitions proved instrumental in Borden's subsequent development. In 1927, it acquired the Merrell-Soule Company, whose None Such mincemeat and Klim powdered milk were sold throughout the world. Borden relied on the technology behind Klim when it developed instant coffee, coffee creamer, and other powdered foods during World War II.

In 1929 Borden acquired the Casein Company of America in Bainbridge, New York. This small company, which manufactured a cold-water-soluble, water-resistant adhesive from casein, a byproduct of skim milk, became the foundation of Borden's vast chemical operations.

In 1929 Borden became the holding company for four separate companies: Borden's Food Products Company, Inc.; Borden's Dairy Products Company, Inc.; Borden's Ice Cream and

Milk Company, Inc.; and Borden's Cheese & Produce Company, Inc. This structure was discontinued in 1936 and the subsidiaries became divisions.

Earnings plunged when the national economy stalled in the 1930s, but, more significantly, new price regulations on fluid milk irreversibly eroded profit margins. With the approval of the U.S. Department of Agriculture, many dairy farmers formed cooperatives to establish prices. Some states established milk-control boards to administer price supports to ensure adequate supplies and low cost to the consumer. Distributors such as Borden were forced to pay more for milk, but were prevented from passing the increased cost on to the consumer. When distributors tried to compensate for thinning margins by manipulating prices in unregulated regions, vehement, sometimes violent protests from farmers and consumers alike followed. In 1938 a federal grand jury in Chicago indicted Borden and several other competitors for antitrust violations. Although the charges were dropped two years later in a consent decree, price regulations continued and profit margins did not improve. Tax hikes and escalating wages in unionized cities such as Chicago also hurt profits.

Also in the 1930s, a line of ''prescription products'' was introduced. This line, marketed primarily to doctors, included products like Biolac, an evaporated infant food, and a modified milk sugar called Beta Lactose. Eventually these products led to the establishment of a special products division.

Theodore G. Montague, a former dairy owner and operator from Wisconsin, succeeded Milburn as head of Borden in 1937. In an effort to deal with regulatory policies and employee relations, which varied from one state to the next, Montague decentralized management under a system of checks and balances. He promoted low-volume, high-margin manufactured goods like cheese, mincemeat, condensed milk, and especially ice cream—Borden's most popular product and a leading source of income from the late 1930s through World War II.

Chemical Business Expanded in 1930s through 1950s

As it turned out, Montague's most important decision was to cultivate Borden's small adhesives business. By far the largest buyer of the company's glues was the forest products industry, where casein adhesives were used to coat paper and strengthen plywood. This swelling market prompted Borden to build its second glue plant in Seattle in the 1930s. But no sooner had the Seattle factory come on line than stronger, less expensive synthetics threatened to make casein compounds obsolete. Although adhesives accounted for less than one percent of its gross revenues, Montague embraced this new technology, and Borden developed its own urea and formaldehyde glues. These were followed in the early 1940s by even stronger phenol formaldehyde resins. By the 1950s, Borden had become a leading supplier of bonding agents to the lumber industry.

Borden's entry into the raw-chemical business followed naturally from its success in synthetic glues. It built a formaldehyde plant in Springfield, Oregon, to satisfy its own growing demand for this primary ingredient, but soon found that selling formaldehyde to competitors was very profitable. Four additional units were constructed, three in the United States and one in Curitiba, Brazil, in collaboration with Incola, S.A. By the late 1980s, Borden was one of the largest formaldehyde producers in the country.

The man responsible for the expansion of Borden's chemical business was Augustine R. Marusi. Marusi, whose background was in chemical engineering, joined Borden in the early 1950s as a salesman. He was sent to Brazil to oversee the completion of the Curitiba facility, but brought back in 1954 to be made head of the chemical division. He quickly overcame the resistance of the dairymen on the board of directors and steered Borden into printing inks, fertilizers, and the burgeoning new field of polyvinyl chloride (PVC), which became a mainstay of the chemical division along with adhesives. In 1954 Borden acquired three small thermoplastics firms that produced PVC resins for use in paper packaging and paint. Then, in 1957, the company began making raw PVC at plants in Illinois and Massachusetts for sale mainly to the phonograph-record and floor-covering industries. Within four years, Borden was manufacturing seven percent of all domestically produced PVC. Borden also developed acetate packaging films commonly used in supermarkets and acquired companies that made vinyl-coated fabrics and wall coverings.

In 1961 Borden and Uniroyal joined forces to build a huge petrochemical complex in Geismar, Louisiana, known as Monochem. Three-quarters of Monochem's output went to other Borden operations; it supplied methanol for Borden's formaldehyde production, vinyl-chloride monomer for its PVC production, and acetylene for its vinyl-acetate production. Over the years, as Borden enlarged Monochem's capacities and added new processes, the company became one of the largest and most integrated chemical companies in the world.

Harold W. Comfort, who became president in 1955 when Montague was made chairman of the board, supported Marusi's activities as a way of freeing the company from dependence on its increasingly less profitable dairy business. Comfort took other measures, too. He made many food acquisitions abroad and promoted foreign sales, especially in South and Central America, where the company faced fewer regulations and competitors than in Europe. While the national supermarket chains that emerged in the 1950s squeezed profits on fluid milk, they created market openings for processed, specialty groceries. Borden developed unique dairy products such as protein-enriched milk, premium-quality ice cream, and, later, diet cheeses, in order to establish supermarket niches. It also began a program of acquiring food manufacturers with well-known or one-of-a-kind items that were successful in the intense competition for supermarket shelf space. Among the companies it took over between 1959 and 1965 were the makers of Snow's seafood chowders (1959); Wyler's bouillon and powdered soft drinks (1961); ReaLemon lemon juice (1962); Cracker Jack candied popcorn and Campfire marshmallows (1964); Wise potato chips (1964); and Bama preserves (1965). In chemicals, too, Borden put new emphasis on its consumer products such as Elmer's Glue-All and Krylon spray paints.

Late 1960s Austerity Program

Marusi's success with the chemical division earned him a promotion to president in 1967 and the distinction of being

Borden's first non-dairy CEO. But disappointing performances in Borden's three major divisions—dairy, food, and chemicals—marked the early years of his reign. In response, Marusi announced a number of painful austerity measures. Borden sold its office building in Manhattan, moved its headquarters to Columbus, Ohio, and closed scores of unprofitable dairy facilities. In 1969 alone it took writeoffs totalling $70 million. Marusi also tightened the corporate office's control and greatly improved financial planning. He also doubled the budget for marketing, which had not kept pace with Borden's diversification—although Elsie the Cow had become one of the most widely recognized trademarks in the world since her introduction in 1936, she was of little use in selling PVC. Marusi further enhanced Borden's public relations with a program to contract with minority-owned businesses, an initiative that inspired the National Minority Purchasing Council, which Marusi helped establish.

Throughout this period, Borden's international operations also continued to grow apace. By 1968, the company had acquired or organized chemical interests in Argentina, Mexico, Canada, the Philippines, Colombia, France, Norway, and Nicaragua. Its food interests included companies in Canada, Puerto Rico, Bermuda, Mexico, Venezuela, Ireland, Spain, West Germany, and Sweden. In 1968 Borden organized Borden Inc. International, a division that was responsible for all international manufacturing and export operations.

The 1970s were a period of slow growth and cost reductions at Borden. In accordance with company policy, Marusi retired at age 65 in 1979. His impatience with product development had evolved into a management philosophy that Borden maintained into the early 1990s. Unlike other food companies that acquired smaller regional brands, Borden kept its regional brands regional, offering its new subsidiaries steady, cheaper supplies while the subsidiaries provided expertise in penetrating their particular markets. As a result, Borden spent little on national advertising and distribution and had a reduced vulnerability to product failure. Because of this low-profile yet aggressive approach, Marusi's successor, Eugene J. Sullivan, inherited a more efficient company.

Restructured in Early 1980s

Nonetheless, in 1980 Sullivan began a five-year, $1.5 billion restructuring. Intent on increasing shareholders' return on investment, Sullivan consolidated operations by cutting 5,000 employees and selling 48 companies in his six-year tenure.

Yet Borden grew during this period too. Sullivan purchased 33 companies—mostly in the packaged consumer products and specialty chemicals areas, two growth fields for Borden—and redirected the company toward consumer foods. Most of Sullivan's purchases were food businesses, and he built for Borden the second-largest market share for pasta and snack foods, two areas Borden emphasized heavily because of their potential for growth.

As the second in a line of three CEOs who ascended through the chemical industry, Sullivan still found it difficult to abandon the chemical market altogether. Marusi had kept Borden's chemical businesses but had found it increasingly difficult to keep a giant food company on top of dramatic changes in the chemical industry. Chemical manufacturing has significantly higher margins than food, but a depressed petrochemical market in the mid-1980s forced Sullivan to reevaluate Borden's ability to maintain long-term growth in the industry. As a result, Sullivan strengthened Borden's specialty chemicals and integrated international operations with domestic (both in food and chemicals), hoping to make production and marketing more efficient.

Acquisitions Spree, 1986–91

Compared to its competitors, Borden was considered a conservative, even unimaginative, company by analysts when R. J. Ventres took over as CEO in 1986. Its success in managing regional food companies was overlooked because it did not create national brands. Ventres soon changed Borden's image with a feverish spate of acquisitions, purchasing 91 companies, for a total $1.9 billion, between 1986 and 1991. These were mostly companies like Meadow Gold Dairies, Inc., that dovetailed nicely with existing operations. In 1987 Borden's 23 purchases—for a total of $442.6 million—made it the nation's most active acquirer according to *Mergers & Acquisitions*. Its $180 million purchase of the Prince Company that year made Borden the undisputed leader in U.S. pasta sales, as the owner of nine companies nationwide, representing nearly a third of the market. In 1988 Borden acquired 24 more operations for a total of $379.9 million, while in 1989 the company spent $264.3 million to make an additional 15 acquisitions.

Ventres also rediscovered the value of the company's dairy operations, which generate high-volume cash flow with little inventory expense because of rapid turnover. And Borden succeeded in doubling its snack food sales by 1989 through its growing national network of regional brands and its penetration of international markets in snack foods through acquisition.

At the same time, Ventres continued to consolidate. In 1987 the company's stock buy-back program left only 73.7 million shares outstanding, a 22 percent reduction since Marusi's retirement eight years earlier, while the company's basic chemicals and PVC resins operations were sold to the public as Borden Chemicals and Plastics Limited Partnership, further distancing the company from raw-chemical manufacturing. The company retained an initial 25 percent interest in this partnership, then reduced it to a two percent general partnership interest.

Huge 1992 and 1993 Losses Led to 1995 KKR Takeover

When A. S. D'Amato, a chemical engineer who had spent 30 years in Borden's chemical unit, took over—for the retiring Ventres—as CEO in October 1991 and as chairman in February 1992, he inherited a company that his predecessor had transformed from a chemical company with a significant dairy business as a sideline to a widely diversified packaged foods company with its chemical unit as a significant sideline and an increasingly less important dairy business. In doing so, Ventres had increased Borden's revenues from $5 billion in 1986 to $7.2 billion in 1991. The down side of this acquisitions-fueled growth was that Borden was an increasingly less profitable company, in large part due to management's failure to integrate its disparate brands, which were largely left to fend for themselves. For example, the company sold both pasta and pasta sauce, but did so through separate sales forces without any coordination. Already in 1991, net income fell to $294.9 million from the $363.6 million of 1990. Furthermore, Borden was much less profitable than other food companies.

D'Amato attempted to right the company ship through a sweeping reorganization launched in late 1992. The effort aimed to turn Borden into a more integrated company, which focused more on building national brands than on supporting numerous small regional ones. Unfortunately, this strategy backfired in a number of ways in a number of areas. For example, Borden put most of its marketing effort in the pasta area behind the Creamette brand, but this program only increased that brand's sales marginally while Borden's unsupported regional pasta brands suffered declining sales. Meanwhile, the dairy business was hurt badly by an unwise decision not to lower its milk prices after the price of raw milk fell; because of Borden's premium prices, many consumers switched to the brands of competitors, who had lowered their prices.

After posting a net loss of $364.4 million in 1992, in part as a result of a $377.2 million restructuring charge, 1993 was even worse. In December 1993 Borden announced yet another restructuring program, this one aiming to trim its operations so that it could concentrate on a smaller number of core areas: dairy, specialty foods, pasta, and industrial products. That month the company posted a pretax charge of $752.3 million, leading to a full-year net loss of $630.7 million. Much of the charge was incurred for the proposed divestiture of several businesses, including North American snacks, seafood, jams, and jellies. Under pressure for his ouster from institutional investors, D'Amato resigned that same month, and was replaced as CEO by Ervin R. Shames, who had once headed General Foods USA and Kraft USA and whom D'Amato had hired as president and chief operating officer in June 1993. Frank J. Tasco, a member of the board of directors since 1988, took over as chairman.

In the first several months of 1994, several operations were divested—a foodservice unit, an ice cream business in Japan, Bennett's sauces, clam products, and Bama jams and jellies—but a buyer for the large snack foods unit could not be found. In need of capital to invest in the brands it wished to retain, Borden accepted a $2 billion takeover offer from KKR that was announced in September 1994. On March 14, 1995, the takeover was complete and Borden had become a private company after 68 years of public trading, in an unusual transaction whereby shareholders of Borden were given shares of stock in RJR Nabisco Holdings Corp.—which KKR had acquired in a 1989 leveraged buyout—in exchange for their Borden shares. KKR's C. Robert Kidder became chairman and CEO of Borden.

Mid-1990s, KKR-Led Restructuring

In May 1995, Kidder began a dramatic restructuring of Borden. The company was reorganized into eleven business units, several of which were subsequently divested: Borden Foods Corporation, the largest unit; Borden/Meadow Gold Dairies, Inc., the dairy business, which was sold in September 1997 for $435 million to Mid-American Dairymen Inc. (Borden licensed to Mid-American the use of Elsie the Cow, but retained ownership of the trademark); Wise Foods, Inc., the North American snacks business; Wilhelm Weber GmbH, the German bakery operation, sold in December 1996; Elmer's Products, Inc., owner of the strong Elmer's and Krazy Glue brands; Borden Decorative Products, Inc., maker of consumer wallcoverings, sold for $320 million in late 1997; Borden Chemical, Inc., maker of industrial adhesives, resins, and coatings; Borden Global Packaging, divested to AEP Industries, Inc. in October 1996, with Borden receiving $255 million in cash plus a 34 percent equity stake in AEP; Borden Chemicals and Plastics L.P., of which Borden continued to maintain its two percent interest; Borden Services Company, which in 1997 became reSOURCE PARTNER, INC., a provider of infrastructure management services, both within and outside of Borden; and Borden Coatings and Graphics, which in 1996 was merged into Borden Chemical. Each unit was freestanding, sharply focused on its own line of business, had its own CEO and board of directors, and was supported with its own operating resources and capital base. This structure provided degrees of both decentralized (within Borden as a whole) and centralized management (within the separate units). In 1996 and 1997, the six remaining units of the initial eleven—Borden Foods, Wise Foods, Elmer's, Borden Chemical, Borden Chemicals and Plastics, and reSOURCE PARTNER—were joined by two more units, bringing the total to eight. In 1996 Borden Decor was formed out of existing operations in commercial wallcoverings and vinyl films and vinyls for various industrial uses. The following year, the corporate staff of Borden were included within a new unit called Borden Capital Management Partners.

In early 1997, Borden Foods announced a new strategy whereby it would focus on ''great tasting, wholesome, grain-based meal solutions''—in other words, pasta, pasta sauces, and bouillon and dry soup. This focus led to the late 1997 divestment of a host of longstanding Borden brands, which collectively accounted for about half of the $2 billion in 1996 Borden Foods sales: Cracker Jack, sold to PepsiCo, Inc.'s Frito Lay Company; Borden cheese, bought by Mid-American Dairymen Inc.; and Eagle Brand sweetened condensed milk, Cremora nondairy creamer, ReaLemon and ReaLime reconstituted juices, Kava acid-neutralized instant coffee, None Such mincemeat, and Borden canned eggnog, acquired as a group by a new entity called Eagle Family Foods, Inc. Much of the proceeds from these and other divestments were used to pay down company debt.

As of late 1997, the transformation of Borden had progressed considerably, but was not yet complete. Additional divestments were likely, but more importantly, the company was already beginning to grow again through strategic, measured acquisitions. In November 1997 Borden Chemical announced that it would acquire Melamine Chemicals, Inc., a Donaldsonville, Louisiana-based producer and marketer of melamine crystal, a substance used to make materials for adhesive, laminate, and coatings applications—a perfect fit with the unit's existing operations. It thus appeared that Borden, Inc. was well on the way to recovery.

Principal Operating Units

Borden Foods Corporation; Wise Foods, Inc.; Elmer's Products, Inc.; Borden Chemical, Inc.; Borden Decor; reSOURCE

PARTNER, INC.; Borden Chemicals and Plastics L.P. (2%); Borden Capital Management Partners.

Further Reading

Alster, Norm, ''Remaking Elsie,'' *Forbes,* December 25, 1989, pp. 106, 108, 110.

Brown, Paul B., ''Sprucing Up Elsie,'' *Forbes,* September 14, 1981, p. 235.

Buss, Dale D., ''Carving Up Borden,'' *Food Processing,* November 1994, pp. 30–31.

Carey, David, ''Boredom to Stardom,'' *Financial World,* February 9, 1988, p. 22.

Dagnoli, Judann, ''Borden Pumps Up Consumer Products,'' *Advertising Age,* November 10, 1986, p. 4.

Deveny, Kathleen, and Suein L. Hwang, ''Elsie's Bosses: A Defective Strategy of Heated Acquisitions Spoils Borden Name,'' *Wall Street Journal,* January 18, 1994, pp. A1, A10.

Finn, Edwin A., Jr., ''Off Brand: After a Steep Slide, the Worst May Be Over for Borden,'' *Barron's,* May 17, 1993, pp. 28–29.

Hwang, Suein, ''KKR's Appetite for Borden May Come Down to Pasta,'' *Wall Street Journal,* September 14, 1994, p. B4.

Jensen, Elizabeth, ''Crackerjack Plan? Borden to Sell Some Food Brands,'' *Wall Street Journal,* March 21, 1997, p. B5.

Lesly, Elizabeth, ''Borden Faces Facts: It's Time to Shed the Flab,'' *Business Week,* November 9, 1992, p. 44.

——, ''The Carving of Elsie, Slice by Slice,'' *Business Week,* January 17, 1994, p. 29.

——, ''Why Things Are So Sour at Borden,'' *Business Week,* November 22, 1993, pp. 78, 82, 84–85.

Lubove, Seth, ''Pulling It All Together,'' *Forbes,* March 2, 1992, pp. 94–96.

Nathans, Leah, ''Borden's Local Heroes,'' *Business Month,* December 1988, p. 33.

Saporito, Bill, ''How Borden Milks Packaged Goods,'' *Fortune,* December 21, 1987, p. 139.

Schifrin, Matthew, ''Greater Fool?,'' *Forbes,* December 19, 1994, pp. 48, 50.

——, ''Last Legs?,'' *Forbes,* September 12, 1994, pp. 150–54, 158.

Serwer, Andrew Evan, ''An Old Cow That Learned New Tricks,'' *Fortune,* December 22, 1986, p. 150.

Zinn, Laura, and Greg Burns, ''The RJR-Borden Deal: Is the Investor the Odd Man Out?,'' *Business Week,* October 10, 1994, pp. 110–11.

Zinn, Laura, Greg Burns, and Keith L. Alexander, ''Elsie May Be Ailing, But KKR Is Thinking Whipped Cream,'' *Business Week,* September 26, 1994, p. 55.

—updated by David E. Salamie

Boston Acoustics, Inc.

300 Jubilee Dr.
Peabody, Massachusetts 01961-6015
U.S.A.
(978) 538-5000
Fax: (978) 538-5100
Web site: http://www.bostonacoustics.com

Public Company
Incorporated: 1979
Employees: 295
Sales: $50.3 million (1997)
Stock Exchanges: NASDAQ
SICs: 3651 Household Audio & Video Equipment

Operating within the fiercely contested market for stereo speakers, Boston Acoustics, Inc. has managed to build a solid niche for itself alongside such competitors as Bose, JBL, and Infinity. It has done so through a strategy of careful growth and virtually debt-free operation, coupled with a strong product base and a network of independent dealers rather than large retailers. Little-known outside the world of audiophiles and stereo enthusiasts, Boston Acoustics had by the 1990s begun to attract some attention from Wall Street with its remarkably high profit margins.

The Cofounders Join Forces

In 1968, 28-year-old Andy Kotsatos was working as credit manager for the research and development division of KLH, a speaker manufacturer. There he met assistant sales manager Frank Reed, seven years his senior. The two men's personalities meshed both professionally and personally, and within a year both had left KLH to join Advent Corporation.

At Advent, Reed moved up to a position as vice-president of sales and marketing while Kotsatos moved laterally into a technical position, working on speaker design. In that capacity, he became closely involved with the creation of the Advent Loudspeaker, which at that time represented the cutting edge in stereo speaker equipment.

The two men worked at Advent for nearly a decade, and throughout much of that time they were developing the concepts that would form the foundation of Boston Acoustics. Their vision started with a product: high-quality speakers which they would market for a competitive price. But low prices would not be as important as quality, both in the speakers themselves and in the level of service customers received from the distributor who sold them. Even at this early stage, the distributor network—eventually to become a bedrock component of Boston Acoustics—was vital to Kotsatos and Reed's business plan.

In 1978, both men left Advent, and a year later, they established Boston Acoustics in Lynnfield, Massachusetts. Eventually their most high-end series of products, the Lynnfield speaker line, would carry the name of their company's hometown. Meanwhile Kotsatos and Reed began to imprint all aspects of their business—marketing, finances, distribution—with their own philosophies of growth and operations.

Developing "The Boston Sound"

Both Kotsatos and Reed believed in tight, conservative money management, and therefore they never had a hard time raising operating capital, even at the beginning. In fact, bankers were downright eager to lend them cash, but the two entrepreneurs refused to give in to the temptation to run up debt. All loans were short-term, paid off by the end of each fiscal year in March, so that they started again on April 1 with a clean slate.

With the company's bottom line relatively secure, Boston Acoustics began to establish itself as a maker of quality speaker equipment for both the home and auto markets. That required a focus on research and development.

The stereo speaker market has traditionally been a fragmented one, where no single company holds anything approaching a dominant position. Instead, a number of strong competitors battle each other fiercely, and this is especially true among the high-end audiophile makers, which manufacture products for stereo enthusiasts willing to spend thousands of dollars on a pair of speakers. Hence it is important for a competitor in such a market to maintain technological viability by constant improvements on its product line.

Company Perspectives:

The philosophy of Boston Acoustics is a simple one: Build the best sounding speaker possible at any given price.

This continues to be the case, and it certainly was so in 1979, when the world was on the cusp of explosive growth in the realm of electronics-based consumer products. The founders of Boston Acoustics, recognizing the value of putting money into research and development, began as a matter of course to spend about five cents of every sales dollar on design and engineering work.

The company used the term "the Boston Sound" to describe the special performance quality of its speakers, especially their tonal balance and the natural sound they delivered. To ensure that the Boston Sound was more than just hype, design and engineering teams continually tinkered with Boston Acoustics' products, working toward the ideal described in the company's own literature as "the precise reproduction of sound."

High-quality speakers are three-way components, consisting of a woofer, which delivers bass notes and very low tones; a tweeter, for high-pitched sounds; and the midrange, which covers the middle of the sound spectrum. At Boston Acoustics from the beginning, research and development were like the woofer—low not in importance, but in visibility—whereas the distribution force was like the tweeter: high-profile, out in front, the public's first line of contact with the company. The product could be the best available in its price range, but without the proper distribution network, sales would flag.

"It's like the catechism," Frank Reed, by then CEO and chairman, told *Barron's* in 1995. Referring to the Christian statement of faith, which maintains that humanity was created "in the image and likeness" of God, Reed said, "If you're a Boston Acoustics dealer, then no one else is going to a dealer who is not in the image and likeness of you." The company made a point of avoiding mass retailers, and instead distributed its product through a network of authorized distributors, most of whom ran small, privately owned stores.

This encouraged customer identification of the product with the dealer, emphasizing the idea of face-to-face contact and building the notion of a lifetime relationship with the company. It also gave Boston Acoustics greater control over the manner in which its products were presented and sold, and the company established guidelines for dealers' technical expertise regarding its product line. Thus the business which sold the speakers would most likely be the one to service them if necessary.

In line with its more person-to-person approach, Boston Acoustics did not put a significant proportion of its money into television or print advertising. Rather, much like a direct-marketing network, it concentrated its efforts on promoting itself to dealers, who would in turn promote it by word of mouth. Eighteen years after its founding, the company had developed $50 million in annual sales this way.

Between the product development end, virtually invisible to the public, and the high-profile distributor network was the company's midrange: its core of financial management principles developed by Kotsatos and Reed. These would guide its steady growth in the 1980s and its cautious expansion in the following decade.

Steady, Conservative Growth

Low-key in its marketing efforts, Boston Acoustics has seldom attracted much media attention outside of product ratings in magazines for audiophiles and other consumers. Hence the tone of a rare company profile, from *Barron's* in late 1995, resembled that of a reporter in search of the celebrated recluse played by Orson Welles in *Citizen Kane*: "Intrigued, we buzzed Boston Acoustics last week, keen on discovering how it earns money in a field littered with companies that don't."

Naturally the answers, as delivered by Kotsatos and Reed, were simple but far from easy. Kotsatos attributed their success to their high-quality line of speakers, but a number of companies make excellent products without generating the kinds of profits that draw attention from investors on Wall Street. Boston Acoustics, on the other hand, managed to grow steadily throughout the 1980s. And its profit margins were high, rising to some 14 cents on every dollar by the early 1990s.

What neither man said, though the fact is obvious from any close look at their company, is that they have consistently avoided the seductive appeal of growth for growth's sake. Reed, when asked if Boston Acoustics planned to acquire another company (which it did in 1996), indicated that they would not venture far from the realm of speakers: "I wouldn't take on a company I know nothing about."

Nor did he appear eager to heed the urging of some on Wall Street who would have had him take an aggressive sales strategy revolving around discounted pricing. In the speaker industry, he said, it would be a mistake to offer deep discounts, because consumers would then always expect such price reduction. Since one buys only a limited number of speakers in one's lifetime, an audiophile who had bought his or her old speakers on sale might wait a long time before purchasing new ones, hoping for the sale to come around again.

"If I grow the company at the expense of profits," Reed said, "I'll never get margins back again." And profit margins, rather than sales figures themselves, were always primary in Reed's interests.

Thus it must have come as a surprise to some in the financial industry when he and Kotsatos took the company public in 1986, after just seven years in business. Boston Acoustics began trading on the NASDAQ, and as *Barron's* noted, a $2 share purchased following the 1987 crash would have been worth $23 in 1991. This was impressive growth by any standard.

Meanwhile the company began to expand internationally. In March 1989 it formed an offshore subsidiary, Boston Acoustics Export Sales Corporation, located in the U.S. Virgin Islands. Within a few years, it had also established an Italian subsidiary, and it had authorized dealers in Canada, South America, Europe, and the Far East.

Growing Pains in the 1990s

Though cautious in the area of growth, the company continued to make strides in improving its products to keep pace with the ongoing technological revolution of the 1980s and the 1990s. Technology, Reed said, was one area ''where I allow myself to be a little excessive.'' By the mid-1990s, Boston Acoustics' Peabody, Massachusetts plant (the company moved in 1995) was ''as automated as any speaker company in North America.''

Using robotics technology in its manufacturing of woofers, Boston Acoustics produced speakers tested to −1 dB (decibel) tolerance, as compared to −3 dB for most of the industry. Whether built at the Peabody plant or outsourced to other manufacturers, all speaker systems were constructed according to designs created by the Boston Acoustics engineering department.

In 1997, the company had four basic product categories. At the high end were the Lynnfield series, a premium line which retailed for up to $5,000 per pair. The home series, on the other hand, ran the entire gamut from solid but inexpensive speakers for $150 to those verging on the premium range at $1,400. Likewise the automotive series had a wide spectrum of products, from basic $50 speakers to a $650 pair. Finally, there was the designer series, made to be flush-mounted into walls, ceilings, or floors, a line which priced anywhere from $130 to $500 a pair.

While Boston Acoustics speakers won awards at the International Consumer Electronics Show, and from magazines such as *Car Stereo Review*, the company received honors as well. In 1990, *Forbes* magazine named it one of the 200 best small companies in America, and later *Business Week* put Boston Acoustics on its own list of 100 such companies.

In the mid-1990s, the company had two minor setbacks in its bottom line, and both ironically were byproducts of growth—thus perhaps reinforcing the wisdom of its founders' cautious strategy. After moving from Lynnfield to Peabody in 1995, the company had 150,000 square feet on 11 acres of land, but in the process its usually impressive profit margins slipped just a bit. More serious, though hardly catastrophic, were the growing pains that came from Boston Acoustics' first major acquisition.

On June 21, 1996, Reed announced the completion of a deal to acquire Snell Acoustics, another manufacturer of high-end speaker systems in nearby Haverhill, Massachusetts. Reed appointed Ira Friedman, Boston Acoustics' vice-president of marketing, as president of the new subsidiary, which Kotsatos said would operate autonomously. (''We expect it to be a vigorous competitor to us, as well as others in the industry.'') By the end of its fiscal year on March 29, 1997, the parent company reported a decline in profits despite an increase in sales, which it attributed to losses at Snell.

In those nine months, something even more significant happened. Frank Reed, only 63 years old, died of a heart attack on November 19, 1996, in Lynnfield. Kotsatos, who at age 56 was already president and COO, became chairman, CEO, and treasurer on December 3. For the next four months he served in those capacities until board member Fred E. Faulkner became president and COO on March 25, 1997.

Reed's wife, Dorothy, passed away not long after he did, in January 1997. On June 13, the board bought back some 898,000 shares of its stock from the Reed family estate, for almost $24 million. Paul F. Reed, son of Frank and Dorothy, continued as the company's vice-president for administrative services.

Gateway to the Future

In November 1995, *Barron's* had written that Boston Acoustics' stock had never risen above an October 1991 high of $23. But starting in January 1997, the company's stocks began to climb, and they jumped after a February 17 announcement of a preliminary agreement to supply speakers to a distributor of multimedia computers.

On May 7, 1997, the company announced the finalization of that agreement, with South Dakota-based Gateway 2000. As Kotsatos stated, ''multimedia is now an integral part of computing,'' and therefore the agreement to supply its MicroMedia speakers with Gateway 2000's multimedia packages was a huge marketing boost.

In the late 1990s, an era when the electronics equipment industry as a whole was growing, the consumer electronics segment—which included stereo manufacturers—had fallen into a slump. This was due in part to consumers' uncertainties about their financial futures and thus the availability of disposable income, but also to the lack of new major products that would cause a splash in the way that compact discs, for instance, had in the late 1980s.

Yet Boston Acoustics defied the trend, and the backdrop of a slow-growing market only served to heighten its modest but steady success. Ironically, by pursuing carefully controlled growth, the company's founders ensured that their company would continue to expand while more overtly aggressive competitors stood still. Marveling at the company's profit margins of up to 15 cents on the dollar, stock analyst Tim Curro told *Barron's*, ''that's about as good as it gets.''

Principal Subsidiaries

Snell Acoustics; Boston Acoustics Foreign Sales Corporation (U.S. Virgin Islands); Boston Acoustics Securities Corp.; BA Acquisition Corp.; Boston Acoustics Italia, s.r.l. (Italy).

Further Reading

Brammer, Rhonda, ''Promising Picks,'' *Barron's*, June 3, 1996, pp. 17–18.

——, ''Sounds Good,'' *Barron's*, November 6, 1995, p. 19.

Meeks, Fleming, ''The 200 Best Small Companies in America: Bringing on the Flood,'' *Forbes*, November 12, 1990, pp. 212–18, 236–98.

Sheeline, William E., ''Regional Brokers Reveal Their Best Bets,'' *Fortune*, October 5, 1992, p. 28.

—Judson Knight

Boston Properties, Inc.

Boston Properties, Inc.

8 Arlington Street
Boston, Massachusetts 02116
U.S.A.
(617) 859-2600
Fax: (617) 536-3128

Public Company
Incorporated: 1970
Employees: 285
Sales: $269.9 million (1996)
Stock Exchanges: New York
SICs: 6512 Operators of Nonresidential Buildings; 6514 Operators of Dwellings Other Than Apartment Buildings; 6798 Real Estate Investment Trusts

The media empire of Mortimer B. Zuckerman, publisher of *U.S. News & World Report,* New York City's *Daily News*, and the *Atlantic Monthly,* was established from the fortune he amassed in commercial real-estate development. When Boston Properties, Inc. was reorganized in 1997 from a partnership of Zuckerman and Edward H. Linde to a publicly owned real-estate investment trust, it owned 63 office buildings, nine industrial properties, two hotels, and a parking garage. But it was a full-service real-estate company that also managed almost all its own properties, had put up buildings for other parties, and had substantial in-house expertise in acquisitions, development, financing, marketing, leasing, accounting, and legal services. The company's presence was chiefly in the Boston and Washington metropolitan areas.

Boston Properties, 1970–96

Born and raised in Montreal, Zuckerman earned a master's degree in business administration and two law degrees—one from Harvard Law School—before going to work for the Boston developer Cabot, Cabot & Forbes in 1962 at a starting salary of $8,750. Within three years he was chief financial officer and a partner in the firm, and by the time he was 30 he was worth $5 million. When Zuckerman left to open his own company at the beginning of 1970, he had a stake, along with Cabot, Cabot & Forbes, in 18 properties, including 12 California industrial and business parks. He and Linde, a colleague at the firm, also claimed about $4 million for their share of a Boston building. When the company offered only $2.2 million, they took the matter to court and eventually won their claim, plus $400,000 in interest.

Shortly after founding Boston Properties, Zuckerman took Linde as a quarter-share partner. Linde had the job of constructing buildings and managing properties, while Zuckerman made deals and arranged the financing. At first Boston Properties was most active on the West Coast. As the controlling general partner, it constructed the nine-building Hilltop Business Center in South San Francisco during the early 1970s and also built two industrial properties in this community.

By late 1985 Boston Properties owned and managed 53 buildings in Washington, Boston, and New York as well as California, with more than 9 million square feet of space. The market value of its portfolio was estimated at $1.3 billion, with 55 percent of the value borrowed, which was considered on the conservative side among developers. The company held its properties for the long term and had sold only two thus far. Boston Properties weathered the real estate recession of 1989–93 and claimed an average annual return of about 14.2 percent between 1992 and 1996. Between 1989 and 1996 it completed eight third-party development projects on a fee basis in the Baltimore, Boston, New York, and Washington metropolitan areas.

Greater Boston Development, 1970–97

Early in its career, Boston Properties was chosen by Boston Mayor Kevin White to build Park Plaza, a 10-acre, five-tower residential-retail-office complex overlooking the Public Gardens next to Boston Common, the city's downtown park. Opposition quickly arose from neighborhood groups objecting to the size and height of the development, especially because it would cast a shadow over the park. After seven years a scaled-down version was approved, but Boston Properties walked away from the project, "exhausted by the process," according to Zuckerman.

Boston Properties lost this battle but essentially won the war, because Zuckerman and Linde were so busy pushing Park Plaza that they had no time for other ventures that might have collapsed in the 1974–75 crash of the Boston real-estate market. With cash on hand the company bought sites cheap from financially troubled developers. Mayor White approved Boston Properties' plan to build a Marriott hotel (completed in 1982) on public waterfront land even though a committee he had appointed ranked it dead last among eight proposals. The company also won a competition to develop a Cambridge 24-acre urban-renewal site adjacent to the Massachusetts Institute of Technology, on which it constructed 10 buildings, including another Marriott hotel.

In the early 1970s Zuckerman and Linde identified the area of suburban Boston along Route 128 as ready for the development of modern office buildings, and they selected the quadrant west/northwest of Boston between the Massachusetts Turnpike and U.S. 93 as the most desirable area in which to concentrate their efforts. Between 1978 and 1988, Boston Properties acquired 13 key sites in that area and completed development of 17 office buildings on those sites, containing more than two million net rentable square feet.

Controversy developed over a plan by a limited partnership, with Zuckerman and Linde the largest investors, to build an office park on an 18-acre Concord site, which the partnership acquired already cleared in 1985, only 700 yards from Henry Thoreau's beloved Walden Pond. This plan conflicted with the intention by conservationists, led by musician Don Henley, to preserve 2,680-acre Walden Woods. In 1991 Zuckerman said he had sold his interest in the project for $4.2 million to an undisclosed buyer who would be co-owner of the site with Linde, with Boston Properties to continue as developer. Linde and his partner were said to be seeking more than $8 million for the site. According to the *Boston Globe,* when the tract was sold to the Walden Woods Project in 1993 for $3.5 million, the seller was Zuckerman himself.

Boston Properties began construction, in 1996, on its first speculative office project in seven years, starting work on a three-story, 102,000-square-foot building in Lexington, Massachusetts, a suburb of Boston. This structure was on the site of a 36-acre office park, purchased in 1985, that already held an existing office building. Boston Properties was investing about $5 million of its own money, with the remaining $14 million in development costs being financed with a bank loan. By mid-1997 it was fully leased to MediaOne of Delaware, Inc. Also in 1997, the company agreed to purchase, for $21.7 million, an existing office building in Quincy, another Boston suburb.

Greater Washington Development, 1979–97

Boston Properties opened a Washington office in 1979 and completed Capital Gallery, an office building south of the Mall and southwest of the Capitol, in 1981. Six years later it completed the U.S. International Trade Commission Building slightly to the east. After four years of negotiations, the company bought two full blocks to the southeast of these projects for Independence Square. A 360,000-square-foot building for the Office of the Comptroller of the Currency was completed on this site in 1991. Boston Properties led a partnership that in 1990 received a 20-year, $383-million lease for a new National Aeronautics and Space Administration headquarters to be built just east of One Independent Square. This structure, holding nearly 600,000 square feet of office space, was completed in 1992.

In 1981 Boston Properties formed a joint venture with *U.S. News & World Report* to construct a new headquarters for the magazine, a luxury hotel, an office building, and two condominium buildings. When Zuckerman purchased *U.S. News* in 1984 he acquired the other half of the real estate (although his publishing ventures were not integrated into Boston Properties). The magazine's headquarters building was sold in 1987 to Shuwa Corp., a Japanese firm, for about $80 million, reportedly a record price for office space in Washington. Boston Properties completed a 1-million-square-foot complex in the nation's capital near Rock Creek Park in 1986 that consisted of the 101-unit Edison House condominiums and mixed-use Whitman Place, in which the Association of American Medical Colleges rented five floors. The company also developed a 1-million-square-foot Federal Judiciary Building near Union Station but did not assume ownership of the structure.

Outside of Washington, Boston Properties was active in Montgomery and Prince George's County in Maryland and Fairfax County in Virginia. Between 1982 and the end of 1990 the company completed 14 office buildings on a 127-acre Springfield, Virginia, site off I-95, retaining 11 of them. (Two more were approaching completion in 1997.) Democracy Center, a three-building office complex in Bethesda, Maryland, was completed in 1988. By that time seven of nine planned buildings had been completed for the 66-acre Maryland 50 Industrial Park in Landover, of which the company retained three.

In 1995 Boston Properties made one of its rare sales, accepting $43.5 million from the Hyatt Corp. for the Park Hyatt Hotel in Washington. A Boston Properties executive said the company wanted to get out of the hotel business in order to focus strictly on commercial real estate. Hyatt, which wanted to continue operating the hotel, was concerned that a new owner might not retain its management contract.

The two Springfield office buildings nearing completion in 1997 were to be occupied by the U.S. Customs Service and Autometric, Inc. Boston Properties also was developing two office buildings in Reston, Virginia, with completion expected in 1999. One of the two was to be the headquarters of BDM International. The company also was redeveloping two Sugarland office buildings in Herndon, Virginia, which it acquired in 1996.

Manhattan Activities, 1983–97

Boston Properties entered New York City in 1983, when it bought for $84 million the land and architectural design for 599 Lexington Avenue, a 47-story office building planned to rise at 52nd Street and Lexington Avenue in midtown Manhattan, from a firm that had walked away from the project. Built without any rental commitments, this $300-million speculative venture was completed in 1986. The gamble paid off when more than half of the 1 million square feet of office space was leased before the end of the year without offering discounts. This building was Boston Properties' largest in 1997 and commanded higher rent per leased square foot than any other of its properties.

In 1985 Boston Properties made a winning bid of $455.1 million for one of the most valuable remaining parcels of prime Manhattan land, the New York Coliseum site at Columbus Circle on the southwestern periphery of Central Park. Its bid was a per-acre record and the largest sum of money ever offered for a piece of public land in New York. The company planned giant 58- and 68-story towers of office, hotel, retail, and condominium space flanking an enormous atrium, and it had lined up the investment-banking firm of Salomon Brothers as both co-owner and major tenant.

In a controversy eerily similar to that of Park Plaza, however, the proposal drew fierce opposition from community groups and such celebrities as Jacqueline Kennedy Onassis, Walter Cronkite, Henry Kissinger, and Bill Moyers. A prime objection was that the towers would throw long shadows over the southern part of the park in the afternoon. The opponents lost their case in federal court, but by then Salomon Brothers had backed out of the deal because of the 1987 Wall Street crash. The proposal was subsequently scaled down and did not officially die until 1994, when negotiations between Boston Properties and the site owner, the Metropolitan Transportation Authority, ended in acrimony.

Boston Properties announced in August 1997 that it had agreed to buy 280 Park Avenue, a complex of two large office towers in midtown Manhattan between East 48th and 49th streets, from the Bankers Trust Co. for $321 million. The company said Bankers Trust would remain as a tenant, as would most other corporate tenants. Linde said the company was seeking other investments in midtown Manhattan office buildings.

Boston Properties in 1997

Boston Properties owned 75 commercial properties with 11 million square feet of space in 1997, when Zuckerman and Linde filed to take the company public as a real-estate investment trust. Its properties consisted of 63 office buildings (including seven under development), nine industrial properties, two hotels, a Cambridge parking facility, and several tracts of undeveloped land. All these properties were in the Boston, New York, and Washington metropolitan areas except for the Hilltop Business Center and two industrial buildings in South San Francisco. All were being managed by the company except the two Marriott hotels and the parking garage. More than 10 percent of the company's space was being leased to federal agencies. In 1996 the company earned $7.3 million on revenues of $269.9 million. Its dividend represented an attractive 6.5 percent of the $25-a-share asking price.

On the debit side, the company's debt-to-market-capitalization ratio was a high 37 percent, and virtually all of the money raised by this offering would go to pay down the debt of 14 buildings. Boston Properties also lacked a large inventory of undeveloped land (only about 47.4 acres owned or under contract or option), meaning land purchases for new development would dilute earnings, at least in the near term. The company's $300 million credit line was considered modest by the standards of the late 1990s. And its federal-government tenants, although the ultimate in creditworthiness, were not paying top dollar. Some analysts said Boston Properties would need to make $500 million to $800 million in office deals each year to generate significant growth.

Investors, however, fully subscribed to the offering of Boston Properties' shares in June 1997 at $25 a share. After using most of the net proceeds of about $730 million to pay off mortgage debt, Boston Properties still retained $770 million in debts. Some 17.9 and 14 percent of the company remained in the hands of Zuckerman and Linde, respectively. Zuckerman continued to be chairman of the company, with Linde continuing as president and chief executive officer.

Principal Subsidiaries

Boston Properties Limited Partnership; Boston Properties Management, Inc.; ZL Hotel LLC.

Further Reading

Bagli, Charles V., ''A Stylish REIT Offering Could Stand a Little Trim,'' *New York Times,* June 15, 1997, Sec. 3, p. 4.

Canellos, Peter S., ''Walden Developer Says He Sold Interest in Site,'' *Boston Globe,* September 17, 1991, pp. 19, 23.

DePalma, Anthony, ''In a New Tower, a Waiting Rental Strategy Works,'' *New York Times,* December 7, 1986, Sec. 3, p. 7.

Diesenhouse, Susan, ''Near Boston, Developer Takes the Plunge: An Office Building on Speculation,'' *New York Times,* November 6, 1996, p. A20.

Finder, Alan, and Kennedy, Shawn G., ''Lessons in the Rubble of the Coliseum Deal,'' *New York Times,* July 23, 1994, pp. 1, 22.

Hilzenrath, David S., ''Zuckerman Wins NASA Lease,'' *Washington Post,* June 5, 1990, pp. D1, D6.

Kasindorf, Jeanie, ''Citizen Mort,'' *New York,* October 5, 1992, pp. 42, 45–47.

Kindleberger, Peter, ''At Walden Woods,'' *Boston Globe,* May 19, 1996, pp. A93, A96.

Kinkead, Gwen, ''Mort Zuckerman, Media's New Mogul,'' *Fortune,* October 14, 1985, pp. 191–192, 195–196.

Labate, John, ''Boston Properties Raises $800M,'' *Financial Times,* June 19, 1997, p. 36.

Lipmann, Joanne, ''Mort Zuckerman Seeks to Influence Opinion, Not Just Own Land,'' *Wall Street Journal,* September 27, 1985, pp. 1, 18.

Mishra, Upendra, ''Edward Linde: Developing a Following,'' *Boston Business Journal,* September 20, 1996, Sec. 3, p. 8.

Perlez, Jane, ''Mortimer Zuckerman: A Developer Who Thrives on High Stakes Dealing,'' *New York Times,* August 5, 1985, pp. B1, B3.

Vinocur, Barry, ''Boston Properties Wins Raves for Its Portfolio,'' *Barron's,* June 9, 1997, pp. 41–42.

—Robert Halasz

Broken Hill Proprietary Company Ltd.

48th Floor BHP Tower-Bourke Place
600 Bourke Street
Melbourne, Victoria 3000
Australia
+61 3 9609 3333
Fax: +61 3 9609-3015
Web site: http://www.bhp.com

Public Company
Incorporated: 1885
Employees: 50,887
Sales: A$19.8 billion (US$15.8 billion) (1996)
Stock Exchanges: Australia London Frankfurt Tokyo New Zealand Zürich New York
SICs: 1011 Iron Ores; 3312 Blast Furnaces & Steel Mills; 3310 Blast Furnace & Basic Steel Products; 1020 Copper Ores; 1220 Bituminous Coal & Lignite Mining; 1221 Bituminous Coal/Lignite-Surface; 1310 Crude Petroleum & Natural Gas; 1422 Crushed & Broken Limestone; 1311 Crude Petroleum & Natural Gas; 1061 Ferroalloy Ores, Except Vanadium; 4410 Deep Sea Foreign Transportation of Freight

Known throughout the world as ''the Big Australian,'' Broken Hill Proprietary Company Ltd. (BHP) is Australia's largest commercial organization, with operations in 70 nations worldwide. In 1997, it accounted for about eight percent of Australia's total exports. More than 95 percent of its annual revenues are derived from heavy industry, namely mining, steelmaking, and petroleum production. Though it got its start in mining, BHP's primary business since the early 20th century has been steel production. This segment accounted for nearly 40 percent of revenues in 1996. Mining operations, including copper, iron ore, coal, manganese, titanium, and platinum production, contributed more than one-third of BHP's sales in the mid-1990s. Inaugurated in the 1960s, BHP's petroleum business accounted for about one-fifth of revenues. The company also had a relatively small service sector, constituting less than five percent of annual sales.

Late 19th-Century Foundation

BHP owes its foundation to Charles Rasp, a boundary rider working in the early 1880s on the Mt. Gipps station near Silverton in New South Wales. As a boundary rider, Rasp patrolled the property, repairing fences and generally checking the property. The station was managed by George McCulloch. Rasp believed that a low broken-backed ridge on the property—the Broken Hill—contained argentiferous ores. He persuaded McCulloch and five others to form a syndicate for the purpose of testing the ridge. The first shaft sunk proved disappointing and some of the original syndicate members sold their shares, but the core members decided to raise the capital necessary for further investigation by floating a public company; they issued a prospectus in 1885 in the name of the Broken Hill Proprietary Company. Almost simultaneously, news arrived of a significant silver strike. BHP shares rose sharply in value once it was announced that the company's first consignment of 48 tons of ore had realized 35,605 ounces of silver, worth nearly £7,500.

None of the directors of the new company had been trained as mining engineers. BHP therefore imported the talents of two U.S. engineers, William Patton and Hermann Schlapp, whose technical work rescued the company's collapsing Big Mine at Broken Hill.

Easily accessible high grade ores, low labor and equipment costs, and high silver and lead prices made the 15-year period to the end of the 19th century extremely profitable for BHP. The establishment of a head office in Melbourne and a lead refinery at Port Pirie were evidence of the company's increasing contribution to and investment in the states of Victoria and South Australia but in New South Wales (NSW), around Broken Hill itself, the *laissez-faire* attitude of both BHP and the state government led to the growth of a primitive shanty town. The dangerous conditions in which the miners themselves had to work and the squalid circumstances in which their families had to live brought the Amalgamated Miners' Association (AMA) and other unions into conflict with BHP in 1889 and 1890. As a result of the 1892 slump in world silver and lead prices, BHP decided to scrap a work-practice agreement with the AMA and to prompt a showdown with a union movement it openly regarded with contempt. BHP led the other mining companies

Company Perspectives:

BHP seeks to be the world's best resources company.

In pursuit of this goal we bring together a unique combination of capabilities to link resources and technologies for the benefit of customers and communities worldwide.

We are committed to the development of our employees, consistently delivering benefit to our customers, contributing to the communities in which we live and work, and a high standard of care for the environment.

We value safety, honesty and excellence in all we do.

We will work together as one Company to fulfill these values and the growth to sustain them.

established at Broken Hill in the bitter and violent strike which ensued, declaring its intention of breaking free from union-imposed wage agreements by offering freedom of contract instead as the basis for future employment. After four months, with their leaders imprisoned, the unions capitulated and the work force returned to the mines, with the exception of known strike leaders whom BHP refused to re-employ. A legacy of bitterness had been created between labor and management, which was to surface repeatedly to poison BHP's relations both with its own employees and with the Australian labor movement in general. The ambivalent attitude towards their country's largest company that many Australians still retain arose from the 1892 strike and the many others which succeeded it.

Early 20th-Century Expansion into Steel

In the first decade of the 20th century, BHP faced a decline in silver prices coupled with the mining-out of the accessible top-side ores which had been cheap to mine. Henceforth it had to work the deeper-lying sulfide ores, a more costly operation compounded by the greater difficulty of extracting silver from this type of ore.

Guillaume Delprat, a Dutch engineer and chemist whom BHP had brought to Australia from Europe, provided the solution to the problem of treating sulfide ores with his invention in 1902 of the flotation process. This method and later variants enabled BHP and other Broken Hill companies to extract silver, lead, and especially zinc from sulfide tailings, which had until then been deemed almost worthless. Delprat had become BHP's general manager in 1899 and under his careful but imaginative stewardship BHP's productivity rose steadily.

Delprat and BHP's directors insisted that an important factor in the company's success was the flexibility that the free contract system of employment allowed amid fluctuating and uncertain world metals markets. They were staunch believers in loyalty to the company, hard work, and self-help, and held that these virtues rather than socialism or unionism were the real allies of the Australian worker. The union movement disagreed with this analysis and in 1905 militants urged the NSW government not to renew BHP's leases at the Big Mine. Two years later BHP announced that it could no longer honor the remainder of its existing wage agreements on the grounds that plunging metals prices made these unworkable.

Early in 1909 the AMA launched a new strike. This time BHP stood alone, its intransigence and stubborn refusal to deal with the union having alienated it from the other Broken Hill companies. The strike was marked throughout by exceptional violence and intimidation of scab labor brought in by BHP to work the mine. When Australia's Arbitration Court ruled against the company, the latter appealed to the High Court, unsuccessfully. BHP's response was to delay the opening of the mine and then reduce the number of workers employed.

Delprat and his fellow directors had already perceived that the Big Mine's days of economic productivity were numbered. Rather than buying new leases and opening new mines they decided that BHP's future lay in steel manufacture. At that time Australia possessed no steel industry and there was considerable skepticism both in Australia and abroad as to whether such an industry could be established successfully in a country far removed from the world's traditional steel markets and with no appreciable industrial base.

Delprat, however, was certain that a local steel producer could quickly capture a growing local market still dependent on costly imports from the United Kingdom and pointed to the advantages which Australia and BHP possessed—cheap energy in the form of large and accessible coal fields in NSW, and the company's own sizeable and high quality iron ore deposits at Iron Knob in South Australia. On the advice of a U.S. steel expert, David Baker, BHP chose Newcastle on the NSW coast as the site of its first steel works due to the proximity of the coalfields and the presence of both labor and manufacturing industry in the area. Newcastle was also connected by rail to Sydney, Australia's largest city and manufacturing center.

BHP acted swiftly to forestall the setting up of a proposed state-owned steel works. Baker designed the new plant along the latest U.S. lines, the whole project being financed out of an increase in share capital, two debenture issues, and the sale in 1915 of BHP's Port Pirie lead smelter to the Broken Hill Associated Smelters Company for £300,000. Steel production commenced in April 1915.

World War I Brings Increased Demand, Labor Unrest

Wartime demand for armaments and sheet steel ensured production at full capacity and guaranteed the steel mill's early years. At Broken Hill, however, inflation during World War I worsened conditions, producing strikes in 1915, 1917, and 1919, the last of which was settled in the unions' favor, resulting in a new 35-hour work week and a rise in wage rates. By this time, however, BHP's energies were focused on its expanding steel business and the Big Mine played a progressively smaller role in the company's calculations, closing altogether in 1939 and thereby ending BHP's association with Broken Hill.

In 1921 Delprat was succeeded by Essington Lewis, a mining engineer who had joined BHP in the first decade of the century and risen swiftly in the corporate hierarchy. Lewis continued the policy of supporting the establishment of secondary manufacturers who would use BHP steel in their products, thus creating new customers for the company and new industries for Australia.

The short-lived postwar steel boom was followed by a scramble for shrinking world markets. BHP suffered several handicaps in the race. The most serious of these was its having to serve a small home market with a diverse range of products, thereby failing to obtain the economies of scale achieved by its foreign competitors. In addition freight costs for export had soared due to the postwar shortage of shipping, and rises in the price of coal were reducing BHP's margins.

Lewis campaigned for protection, and the William M. Hughes government eventually imposed import duties on imported steel. The 1920 seamen's strike convinced BHP that it had to control its own shipping. This belief led to the foundation of BHP's fleet of dedicated ore carriers.

Despite import duties, foreign steel was still managing to undersell the local product. BHP announced it would have to shut down capacity unless the steel unions—chiefly the Federated Ironworkers Association (FIA)—were willing to accept wage reductions. This acceptance was not forthcoming and in May 1922 temporary closure of the Newcastle mill for a month was followed by a total shutdown lasting nine months until a ruling of the Arbitration Court compelled BHP to reopen it. Terrible hardship had been caused in the Newcastle area, and union leaders and elements in the Labour Party began to call for BHP's nationalization.

After this difficult start Lewis launched a program concentrating on improving the efficiency, safety, and cleanliness of the steel plant, all concepts closely linked in Lewis's mind and to which he attached the greatest importance. He placed particular emphasis on the replacement of old machinery, with the result that by the end of the 1920s BHP was operating one of the cleanest, safest, and most cost-effective steel plants in the world. Thus the Depression which began in 1929 and so devastated other Australian industries left the steel industry comparatively unscathed.

Just as control of shipping was essential to reduce freight costs, so Lewis reasoned that ownership of coal would make BHP independent of the demands of the mine owners. BHP therefore began to buy up coal mines, a foretaste of the great expansion of its coal interests in the 1970s and 1980s.

Challenges and Opportunities During the Great Depression

Although BHP entered the Depression with an unusually small debt burden—Lewis disliked paying for new machinery with borrowed money—and an efficient steel operation, it was not immune from the effects. A collapse of world prices in steel, silver, and lead forced BHP to reduce production levels and lay off large numbers of mill workers. The Big Mine was shut down until a rise in metals prices made reopening worthwhile, and from 1930 until 1932 BHP did not pay dividends to its shareholders. The company viewed with distrust the economic policies of Scullin's Labour government, which it regarded as populist and shortsighted. This attitude was mollified when the government sought to stimulate local industry by imposing a new round of duties on imports, and devalued the Australian currency to encourage Australian exporters. These measures, in tandem with BHP's underlying financial strength and Lewis's policy of low-cost selling, ensured the company's survival.

In 1935 BHP's only competitor in Australia, the struggling Australian Iron & Steel Company (AIS), sought a merger with its larger rival. BHP was quick to agree and at a stroke acquired AIS's valuable steelworks at Port Kembla, NSW, and its iron ore deposits at Yampi Sound in Western Australia. BHP's opponents attacked the merger as monopolistic and called for an official enquiry. The issue became intensely political with two future Australian prime ministers, John Curtin and Robert Menzies, respectively attacking and defending the merger.

Two years later the South Australian government asked BHP to construct a steel plant in the state. BHP, anxious to see its leases at Iron Knob extended, agreed to build a furnace and port at Whyalla on the Spencer Gulf. This and other investments in the years immediately prior to World War II were paid for by four major restructurings in the company's capital base.

In 1938 BHP became embroiled in another political battle when union labor refused to handle cargos of iron ore destined for Japan, at that time engaged in a brutal and aggressive war in China. BHP's insistence on carrying through its contractual obligations aroused strong emotions in Australia and Attorney General Robert Menzies's defense of BHP's action earned him the unflattering sobriquet of "pig-iron Bob."

In 1940 Menzies appointed Lewis Director General of Munitions with the responsibility of harnessing the nations' entire manufacturing industry to the war effort. Lewis applied to this demanding job all the energy and concentration which enabled BHP to achieve the new targets set by his wartime planning. New blast and open-hearth furnaces were built at Port Kembla and a shipyard established at Whyalla. Comparatively far removed from the area of battle, BHP's mills suffered no physical damage during the war, but were subjected to brief and ineffectual shelling of Newcastle by a Japanese submarine. However, the company lost two of its ore carriers to enemy torpedoes. Japan's frighteningly rapid advance into Southeast Asia up to Australia's not-so-distant neighbor, New Guinea, in 1942, served to quell union antagonism towards BHP. As this threat receded, the unions renewed their attacks, culminating in a protracted strike in late 1945, which began at Port Kembla and then drew in coal miners and seamen, rapidly assuming the proportions of a national crisis. Although the militant far Left in the unions failed to achieve its objective of BHP's nationalization and lost its influence during the strike, this episode had the effect of dampening BHP's plans for renewed investment in its steel business. Not until the end of the 1940s did this situation change, when a rising demand for steel encouraged increased production and investment.

In 1950 Lewis became chairman of BHP. Two years later he relinquished his position to Colin Syme, a lawyer who had joined BHP's board in 1937.

Return to Mining in Post-World War II Era

During the early 1950s Japan's resuscitated steel industry began to demonstrate its capacity for large-scale, low-cost production, which in the 1960s helped underwrite Japan's extraordinary economic growth. Once again the Japanese renewed their search abroad for low-cost iron ore reserves. The Australian government's lifting in 1960 of its prewar restrictions on the export of iron ore encouraged BHP to enter the field once again as a prospector. This entry led to the identification of large iron ore deposits, notably at Koolanyobbing, Western Australia, and Koolan Island, Western Australia. Quarries were commissioned at these two sites, but the centerpiece of BHP's iron ore business became the Mt. Newman ore body in the Pilbara region of Western Australia. In association with AMAX (American Metal Climax, Inc.) and CSR, the company established a joint venture operation to develop and operate the world's largest open-pit iron ore mine. BHP initially held a 30 percent interest but in 1985 bought out the remaining AMAX and CSR shareholdings.

During the early 1960s BHP transformed the nature of its business by deciding to enter the oil exploration and production industry. Australia's geology had tended to discourage oil prospecting but in 1960, true to its tradition of seeking expertise outside Australia, BHP asked the U.S. petroleum expert L. G. Weekes to examine some of its leases. Weekes advised BHP to drill offshore in the Bass Strait area. Despite the considerable technical difficulties involved, but encouraged by the subsidies of an Australian government keen to see the country's costly dependence on imported oil reduced, BHP went into a 50/50 partnership with Standard Oil's Australian subsidiary, Esso Standard. In 1964 the first well was commissioned in the Gippsland Basin area off the coast of Victoria. The extensive gas fields found as a corollary were developed for domestic use and export to Japan.

At about the same time, BHP began the development of a manganese mine at Groote Eylandte in the Gulf of Carpentaria. As at Mt. Newman this enterprise comprised not only the commissioning of the mine itself but also the building of a whole township, transport links, and a port area.

A booming minerals and steel market enabled BHP to double its net profit between 1960 and 1970. Such rapid growth began to outdistance a management structure that had remained essentially unaltered since Essington Lewis's day. On the advice of a firm of U.S. management consultants, BHP adopted the concept of independent profit centers, each responsible for its own performance.

Loss of Many Government Protections in 1970s

Such moves did not prevent BHP's critics from claiming that the company was still too large, too secretive, and above all too unaccountable to the Australian public for its decisions. Antimonopolists held that BHP's stranglehold on sales outlets prevented any rival steelmaker from setting up operations in Australia, while environmentalists questioned the company's record on industrial pollution. The unions attacked it for its strict adherence to the "minimum wage policy" laid down by the Arbitration Court, justified by BHP as a necessary measure in the light of competition from producers with lower labor costs, such as Japan and Taiwan.

The Labour Government elected in 1972 took several actions against BHP. Rex Connor, Minister for Minerals and Energy, attacked BHP for profiteering and proceeded to remove the subsidies BHP had been given for its oil exploration work. Tax concessions were canceled. Particularly irritating for the company were the decisions and comments of the Government's Prices Justification Tribunal before which BHP was required to defend its pricing policies.

In the middle of the decade BHP announced its decision to enter into a partnership with Shell to exploit the natural gas deposits found off the northern coast of Western Australia. Known as the North West Shelf Natural Gas Project, the justification for the huge investment needed lay in the interest shown by foreign energy consumers, especially the Japanese. Construction work began in 1981 and by 1984 the domestic gas phase of the project had been commissioned, followed by the launch of the export phase in 1989. Further offshore oil discoveries in the Timor Sea at Jabiru in the early 1980s launched another production program.

Besides Australia's vast iron ore deposits, foreign industries looked towards the country's coal fields as a source of energy not subject to the vagaries of Middle Eastern power politics and price instability. The sharp rises in oil prices in 1973 and 1979 began to renew BHP's interest in coal and coal mining for export purposes. In 1976–77, BHP acquired Peabody Coal's Australian assets, thereby gaining a 60 percent interest in the Moura and Kianga coal mines in Queensland. In 1979 the huge Gregory mine was opened, followed a year later by the Saxonvale mine in NSW. In 1985 BHP increased its holding in Thiess Dampier Mitsui, operator of the Moura and Kianga mines, to more than 80 percent.

External Events Foster Internal Change in 1980s

The early 1980s brought two separate threats that effected widescale change at BHP. In 1982, the conglomerate was subjected to an unwelcome takeover raid by Robert Holmes a Court, who would plague BHP throughout most of the decade. Having accumulated 30 percent of the corporation's stock, Holmes a Court proposed a drastic restructuring. At the same time, BHP's steel business was struggling with rising production costs and falling world steel prices as overcapacity in world production undercut world steel prices. In the wake of the 1987 stock market crash, Holmes a Court sold his stake back to BHP. The deal also gave BHP a one-third stake in International Brewing Investments (IBI), including a one-third share of Foster's Brewing. However, Holmes was successful in one regard, for his raid and the crisis of the global steel industry had forced BHP into a major rationalization. Under the direction of CEO Brian Loton and John Prescott, the head of the steel business, BHP invested A$22 billion in a decade-long restructuring.

The company reorganized into three main divisions: steel, minerals, and oil. In 1983 alone, nearly a third of the Steel Division's employees were made redundant. In an effort to safeguard the steel industry's future, the Labour Government of the day announced a five-year Steel Industry Plan under which the steel unions promised to refrain from industrial action in return for guarantees from BHP relating to security of employment for their members. Under the new dispensation BHP managed to transform itself from one of the world's most inefficient steelmakers into one of the few to achieve profitability in 1992.

Productivity increased from only 150 tons per worker per annum in 1982 to some 250 tons in 1984. The five-year plan was widely regarded as a milestone in Australian industrial relations. By the end of the decade, BHP had three integrated steelworks in Australia with total steelmaking capacity of almost seven million tons per year. It also operated a range of downstream processing facilities in Australia, and steel forming and building products facilities in Asia and the West Coast of the United States.

In 1984 BHP bought the U.S. mining and construction company Utah Mines Ltd. from General Electric. This move extended BHP's interests abroad into the United States, Canada, and South America; greatly enlarged BHP's interests in coal and iron ore; and helped make it one of the world's top copper miners. The acquisition also gave it a controlling interest in Chile's Escondida copper mine, the third largest in the world. This mine's low production costs and large reserves base meant it was also competitively positioned. Another significant acquisition for BHP was a 30 percent interest in the OK Tedi gold and copper mine in Papua New Guinea, which began producing in 1984. In Australia during the 1980s BHP commissioned gold mines at Ora Banda and Boddington and a new lead and zinc mine at Cadjebut. BHP added to its iron ore interests in the Pilbara region of Australia through the purchase in 1990 of the remaining 70 percent of Mt. Goldsworthy Mining Associates it did not already own. It has since sold a minority interest in Mt. Goldsworthy and a new iron ore mine named Yandi to its Japanese partners in the Mt. Newman joint venture. BHP Gold Mines Ltd. merged with Newmont Australia Ltd. in 1990. The merger created a major Australian gold company renamed Newcrest Mining Ltd. in which BHP had the largest single shareholding, 23 percent.

BHP invested A$5 billion in its oil division from 1987 to 1992. The major acquisitions of Monsanto Oil in 1986, Hamilton Oil in 1987, Gulf Energy Development in 1988, and of Pacific Resources Inc. in 1989 further increased BHP's strength in the fields of oil exploration and refining in the North Sea and Pacific Ocean. By 1992, it ranked 10th among the world's oil companies, and petroleum had become a significant contributor to overall profits, which totaled US$900 million on revenues of US$12 billion in 1992.

The 1990s and Beyond

Loton advanced to chairman in 1991, at which time John Prescott succeeded him as CEO. While remaining focused on BHP's core businesses, Prescott aimed to broaden the conglomerate's global reach. Acquisitions increased foreign properties from 28 percent of assets to over 40 percent from 1991 to 1996. By the latter year, international operations generated 70 percent of annual revenues. But not all of these purchases actually improved BHP's bottom line. In 1995, for example, BHP acquired Magma Copper Company, America's largest copper smelter, for A$3.2 billion (US$1.8 billion). At the time, copper prices were high and the deal was hailed as a major coup. But in 1996, an international trading scandal slashed copper prices by 30 percent. Other investments that tanked during this period included a Vietnamese oil field, the Foster's Brewing stake, and the Pacific Resources refinery in Hawaii. In fiscal 1997 (ended May 31), BHP was forced to write off A$1 billion on these and other investments, thereby reducing its net operating profits to A$410 million, down from a record A$1.6 billion in fiscal 1995. The company's stock dropped by over 20 percent in the middle of 1996.

Observers inside as well as outside the conglomerate began to suggest that BHP's parts were worth more than the whole. In August 1997, the heads of BHP's minerals and petroleum divisions resigned. An article in that month's *Economist* magazine noted that the petroleum executive John J. O'Connor had favored a spinoff of his division—BHP's most profitable operation at the time—and quit when a deal was not forthcoming. The *Economist* seemed to concur with O'Connor when it surmised that "the big Australian might be better off smaller."

However, BHP's diversity remained one of its strong points. In his 1997 message to shareholders, CEO and Managing Director Prescott reasserted the company's dedication to diversity, noting, "We have six groups of businesses that we are confident will continue to perform strongly against our criteria. These include the oil and gas activities in Bass Strait and the North West Shelf (Australia), Escondida (Chile) copper mine, our various iron ore businesses and most of our coal and flat products steel activities. These are the businesses we know best, where we see our major comparative advantages and were we achieve great results." At the same time, BHP appeared poised to become a major player in the global markets for precious metals and gems. In 1997, it received permission from the Canadian government to begin mining a major trove of diamonds in that country's Northwest Territories. BHP expected to begin production at the site in 1998, and forecast annual output at four million carats by 1999. The company also owned one of the world's most valuable gold mines, and was gleaning platinum from a site in Zimbabwe. Though the company was indeed becoming less "Australian" and more global, it seemed destined to remain "Big."

Principal Subsidiaries

Aquila Steel Company Pty. Ltd.; Associated Airlines Pty. Ltd. (55%); Australian Iron and Steel Pty. Ltd.; Australian Manganese Co. Ltd.; Australian Wire Industries Pty. Ltd.; AWI Holdings Pty. Ltd.; BHP Aerospace & Electronics Pty. Ltd.; BHP Capital No 20 Pty. Ltd.; BHP Development Finance Pty. Ltd.; BHP Engineering International Pte. Ltd. (Singapore); BHP Engineering Malaysia Sdn. Bdn.; BHP Engineering Pty. Ltd.; BHP Finance Ltd.; BHP Finance (U.S.A.) Ltd.; BHP Finance Services Pty. Ltd.; BHP Financial Services (U.K.); Ltd.; BHP Holdings (U.S.A.) Inc.; BHP Information Technology Sdn. Bhd. (Malaysia); BHP International Holdings Ltd. (Hong Kong); BHP Investment Holdings Ltd. (U.K.); BHP Iron Ore Ltd.; BHP Japan Pty. Ltd.; BHP Marine & General Insurances Pty. Ltd.; BHP Minerals Holdings Pty. Ltd.; BHP Minerals Norway Pty. Ltd.; BHP Minerals Zimbabwe Pty. Ltd.; BHP Nominees Pty. Ltd.; BHP Papua New Guinea Pty. Ltd.; BHP Petroleum International Pty. Ltd.; BHP Rail Products (Canada) Ltd.; BHP Rail Products Pty. Ltd.; BHP Refractories Ltd.; BHP Steel (AIS) Pty. Ltd.; BHP Steel Building Products (Guangzhou) Ltd. (China); BHP Steel Building Products (Shanghai) Ltd. (China); BHP Steel Building Products Vietnam Co. Ltd.; BHP Steel Canada Inc.; BHP Steel (JLA) Pty. Ltd.; BHP Stevedoring Pty. Ltd.; BHP Superannuation Investment Co. Pty. Ltd.;

BHP Trading New Zealand Ltd.; BHP Transport Pty. Ltd.; Groote Eylandt Mining Company Pty. Ltd.; John Lysaght (Australia) Pty. LTd.; Keithen Ltd.; NSW BHP Steel Ltd.; PT BHP Steel Indonesia (65%); Resources Insurances Pte. Ltd. (Singapore); Tasmanian Electro Metallurgical Company Pty. Ltd.; Tavela Ltd.; The World Marine & General Insurance PLC (U.K.); Bekaert-BHP Steel Cord Pty. Ltd. (50%); Elkem Mangan KS (Norway; 49%); Foster's Brewing Group Ltd. (36.6%); Koppers Australia Pty. Ltd. (50%); Orbital Engine Corporation Ltd. (25.1%); Samarco Mineracao SA (Brazil; 49%); Tubemakers of Australia Ltd. (49.4%).

Principal Divisions

BHP Copper; BHP Minerals; BHP Steel; BHP Petroleum; BHP Service Companies.

Further Reading

Aarons, Eric, *The Steel Octopus: The Story of BHP,* Sydney: Current Book Distributors, 1961.

Berman, Phyllis, "Magma-nificent Deal," *Forbes,* January 22, 1996, pp. 14–15.

BHP: 100 Years of Growing with Australia, Dubbo, N.S.W: Macquarie Publications, 1985.

"The Big Australian and the Tigers: Broken Hill Proprietary," *Economist,* July 8, 1995, pp. 60–61.

"The Big Australian Stumbles," *Economist,* September 28, 1996, p. 72.

Blainey, Geoffrey, *The Steel Master: A Life of Essington Lewis,* Carlton South, Victoria, Australia: Melbourne University Press, 1995.

Caney, Derek J., "BHP Deal with Magma Applauded by Industry," *American Metal Market,* December 4, 1995, p. 1.

"Corporate Carpentry: BHP," *Economist,* May 16, 1992, p. 88.

Dale, George, *The Industrial History of Broken Hill,* Melbourne: Fraser & Jenkinson, 1918.

The Fabulous Hill, Melbourne: Broken Hill Proprietary Company, 1961.

Haign, Gideon, *The Battle for BHP,* Melbourne: Information Australia With Allen & Unwin Australia, 1987.

Hoskins, Donald G., *The Ironmaster: The Life of Charles Hoskins, 1851–1926,* North Wollongong, N.S.W.: University of Wollongong Press, 1995.

How It All Began: BHP in Its 100th Year, Melbourne: BHP, 1985.

"Is There Life After Steel: Australia," *Economist,* June 21, 1997, p. 46.

Jacques, Bruce, "Minnows Swallowing Up the Whales," *Euromoney,* August 1986, pp. 132–136.

Jokiel, Lucy, "Striking It Big," *Hawaii Business,* April 1989, pp. 18–23.

Kriegler, Roy J., *Working for the Company,* Melbourne: Oxford University Press, 1980.

LaRue, Gloria T., "BHP Chief Executive Committed to Change," *American Metal Market,* October 14, 1996, p. 3.

Norman, James R. "Wake Up, Mate," *Forbes,* October 25, 1993, pp. 216–17.

Quinlan, Michael, *Monopoly Employer, The State and Industrial Conflict: Managerial Strategy in the Australian Steel Industry, 1945–1983,* Nathan, Qld.: Griffith University, School of Social and Industrial Administration, 1984.

Raggatt, H.G., *Mountains of Ore,* Melbourne: Lansdowne Press, 1968.

Sawer, Derek, *Australians in Company: BHP in Its 100th Year,* Melbourne: Broken Hill Proprietary Company Ltd., 1985.

"Sparkling: Diamond-Mining in Canada," *Economist,* January 25, 1997, pp. 59–60.

"Still Digging: BHP," *Economist,* August 16, 1997, p. 50.

Trengrove, A., *"What's Good for Australia . . . !": A History of BHP,* Stanmore, N.S.W.: Cassell Australia, 1975.

—D. H. O'Leary
—updated by April Dougal Gasbarre

Brooks Brothers Inc.

346 Madison Avenue
New York, New York 10017
U.S.A.
(212) 682-8800
Fax: (212) 885-6803

Wholly Owned Subsidiary of Marks & Spencer PLC
Incorporated: 1903
Employees: 2,150
Sales: £304.4 million (US$490.1 million) (1997)
SICs: 2321 Men's & Boys' Shirts, Except Work Shirts; 2323 Men's & Boys' Neckwear; 5699 Miscellaneous Apparel & Accessory Stores

Brooks Brothers Inc., a subsidiary of the British firm Marks & Spencer PLC, operates a chain of clothing stores in the United States. A traditional source of suits and accessories for conservative businessmen, Brooks Brothers is also a traditional choice for sportswear. Both for business and leisure, its classic styles derive from English models, often dating back to the 19th century. In the last years of the 20th century, however, its sportswear, in particular, took on a more casual, contemporary look. Brooks Brothers also carries merchandise for women and children. The chain included almost 100 retail stores in 1996 and at least 26 outlet units selling merchandise at a discount. Most of its goods were being supplied by outside sources.

Clothing the Elite, 1818–1945

Dating from 1818, Brooks Brothers was one of the first stores in the United States to offer ready-made clothing. Henry Sands Brooks bought a building and lot on the corner of Cherry and Catharine Streets in New York City for $15,250. After the founder died in 1833, his sons Henry and Daniel H. carried on the business, which they named H. and D.H. Brooks & Co. Henry subsequently died, and by 1850—when the name was changed to Brooks Brothers—control of the business had passed into the hands of Daniel and three younger sons of the founder. A new building replaced the original store in 1845.

Brooks Brothers opened a second store farther uptown, at the corner of Broadway and Grand Streets, in 1857. Both stores offered custom and ready-made clothing and a variety of piece goods, including cashmeres, velvet, silk, and satin. During the Civil War the company's patrons, for both uniforms and civilian wear, included Union generals Grant, Hooker, Sheridan, and Sherman. President Abraham Lincoln was a regular customer. He wore a frock coat bearing the Brooks Brothers label to his second inaugural, and it was said he was wearing this coat on the night of his assassination. Perhaps the identification of the firm with the Union cause accounted (if mere greed was not sufficient) for the looting and sacking of the Cherry Street store during the draft-protest riot of 1863 that ravaged the city for three days.

The Cherry Street store was rebuilt but was closed in 1874. The Grand Street store moved to the south end of Union Square in 1870, but this was only a temporary location, for it moved back downtown to Broadway and Bond Streets in 1874. Ten years later the store moved uptown, to Broadway and 22nd Streets. Daniel Brooks, the last survivor of the founder's sons, retired in 1879. Several former employees, as well as two of Daniel's nephews, then became partners in the firm. Two more nephews later became partners as well. The company was incorporated in 1903. A Newport, Rhode Island summer office was opened in 1909 and a Boston branch was opened in 1912. The flagship store made its last move uptown in 1915, when it opened in a new building constructed for it at Madison Avenue and 44th Street. Through it all, Brooks Brothers continued to clothe the nation's leaders, including Grant, Theodore Roosevelt, and Woodrow Wilson, all of whom took the presidential oath of office in the company's suits.

Brooks Brothers based its clothing on London styles and did most of its own manufacturing. Introduced about 1900, its standby ''Number One Sack Suit'' was loosely constructed, with straight-legged cuffed trousers and a three-button jacket that hung straight, without a tucked-in waist, and natural, unpadded shoulders. This suit style, imported from England, became popular among prep schoolers and Eastern college undergraduates, although the company also made a two-button model.

In 1900 Brooks Brothers introduced to the United States shirts with button-down collar tabs, adapted from the shirt worn by English polo players to keep the collar wings from flapping during play. The polo coat, originally designed to throw on over the riding habit following a match and white rather than camel, was introduced about 1910. The company also introduced from England the polo shirt, foulard tie, and deerstalker cap beloved of Sherlock Holmes. The Shetland sweater was brought over in the 1890s. Its pink shirt made its first appearance in 1900. India Madras for shirts and beachwear began to be displayed at this time. Brooks Brothers also may have introduced to America the seersucker suit, a staple in tropical parts of the British Empire.

Women began casting a hungry eye at Brooks Brothers furnishings about this time. The Shetland sweater was the first to fall into their hands, in 1912, and the polo coat followed in the early 1920s. Hollywood actors and actresses were among the company's best customers. Fred Astaire bought 50 foulard ties at a time; Maurice Chevalier bought its hats; Rudolf Valentino was a steady customer; Katharine Hepburn bought seersucker slacks; and Marlene Dietrich purchased silk dressing gowns. Tank-style bathing suits for women—daring in the 1920s—were borrowed from Brooks's swimwear, and many a pink shirt found its way into a woman's wardrobe. By the late 1940s a corner of the first floor had been set aside for women shoppers.

As a privately held company, Brooks Brothers did not disclose its financial condition, but it was reported to have earned more than $1 million before taxes in 1923. After that date earnings dropped steadily for ten years and by 1935, according to one account, it had an operating deficit of more than $1 million. (According to another account the company lost money only during 1938–40.) It was believed that the company needed to take in $3.6 million annually to break even at this point.

New Owners and New Styles, 1946–88

Brooks Brothers was sold in 1946 to Julius Garfinckel & Co., Inc., a Washington, D.C. department store operator that paid a little more than $3 million for 62 percent of the outstanding stock. (The minority shares were held by the department store John Wanamaker, which had bought them earlier from an old Brooks estate held in the custody of the Guaranty Trust Co.) With the sale, Winthrop H. Brooks, a great-grandson of the founder, stepped down as president, ending the family's guiding role in the business. Under Garfinckel's management, Brooks Brothers adopted more aggressive merchandising to boost sales and stabilized general operating expenses. The company's earnings rose steadily and reached $797,683 in fiscal 1955 (the year ending July 31, 1955).

Brooks Brothers also made a few concessions to changing times, such as adding synthetic fibers to some of its wool suits. These included a polyester-worsted blend (Brooks-Knit) and an all-worsted stretch suit (Brooks-Ease). The company also introduced wash-and-wear shirts in the form of Dacron and oxford cotton (Brooksweave). It began offering suit jackets with the suggestion of a waist and slight shoulder padding.

The 1950s were a very good decade for Brooks Brothers. After the wide, two-button, double-breasted suits and heavily padded shoulders of the previous decade, men seeking progress up the corporate ladder, especially on Wall Street and among Madison Avenue advertising agencies, turned in the early 1950s to the look dubbed "Ivy League." This style echoed Brooks Brothers by the adoption of natural shoulders and narrow lapels, with narrow ties the necessary accessory. (Brooks Brothers, however, refused to take this look to the "jivey Ivy" extreme popular at the time, keeping its lapels three inches wide and its ties 3½ inches wide.)

Also trendy during this decade were the Bermuda-length shorts the company brought to America, and shirts, jackets, and trousers of bleeding Madras. Women crowded the store to buy Bermuda shorts, pleated dress shirts, and sports shirts (with rhinestone buttons). In men's wear, by the late 1950s "Ivy League" was being challenged by the Continental Look, a chestier two-button style. After John F. Kennedy, wearing a two-button suit, outpointed three-buttoned Richard Nixon and won the presidency, Brooks Brothers, in 1961, unveiled a new two-button suit. It retained the company's natural shoulders, notched labels, and center vent, but was trimmer and more tailored, with a longer roll to the lapels and slightly more waist suppression.

The 1960s, of course, most emphatically was not Brooks Brothers' era. Even those young men who were following a conventional career path took to sporting longer hair and long sideburns and fostering what was called the "peacock revolution" by favoring European-styled or -influenced two-button suits. These were characterized by higher armholes, a more defined waist, wider lapels, and more shoulder padding. Brooks Brothers gave ground grudgingly, slowly widening the lapels until they reached 3⅞ inches on the two-button model and at least 3½ inches on the sack suit. The button-down shirt, a symbol of corporate uptightness, appeared to be dead.

"We knew we were losing our young people during the sixties," company President Frank T. Reilly told Stephen Birmingham in 1978, "and we wondered what would happen to that generation of young men when they entered the business community. Well, we found out what would happen. They came back to Brooks Brothers for their working clothes, and they stayed back. In the end, our customers always come back." Even button-down shirts made a comeback. Custom tailoring, however, came to an end in 1976; this long-standing service was accounting for only some half of one percent of company revenue.

The Brooks Brothers chain grew from 10 stores in 1970, stretching from coast to coast and including a second Manhattan outlet in the financial district, to 13 in 1973. Gross annual revenues were in the neighborhood of $70 million, and the firm made a record profit in 1975. More than 40 percent of its suits were being made in its Long Island City plant in New York City's borough of Queens, with the rest produced by other manufacturers to its specifications. The number of stores reached 24 in 1980. Three of these were in Tokyo, where the company first established a presence in 1979.

Marks & Spencer Subsidiary, 1988–97

Garfinckel's (now Garfinckel, Brooks Bros., Miller & Rhoads Inc.) sold Brooks Brothers to Allied Stores Corp. in 1980 for an estimated $228 million. The company passed in 1986, along with the other Allied holdings, to Campeau Corp., which sold it to the British clothier Marks & Spencer PLC in 1988 for $750 million. At this point the Brooks chain had grown to 47 stores in the United States and 21 more in Japan. (The Japanese stores belonged to a 51 percent Brooks-owned joint venture that was separate from the Marks & Spencer subsidiary Brooks Brothers Inc.) Observers regarded the purchase price as wildly inflated. The firm was said to be poorly managed, carrying many slow-moving items while letting others that were selling briskly fall out of stock.

To reduce expenses, Marks & Spencer installed computer systems to monitor inventory and ensure timely distribution. It also closed Brooks Brothers' Paterson, New Jersey shirt factory in 1989 and subcontracted most of the other clothing from the Long Island City plant to a Syracuse manufacturer. By mid-1993 all manufacturing was being done by outside contractors, except for three factories making shirts and ties.

The 1980s had not been kind to Brooks Brothers. The traders who thrived on Wall Street found the style wimpish and opted for a "power look" that included broadly striped shirts and strong shoulders. By 1990 this had given way to softer English-influenced clothing, but—unlike the sack—the suits had double vents (instead of a single center vent) and high lapels. Marks & Spencer introduced its own English-cut suits to Brooks Brothers, featuring a darted front with either two or three buttons, slightly padded shoulders, and pleated trousers (which Brooks Brothers had not carried since the early 1960s). The parent company was well aware that the standard three-button Brooks suit was accounting for only 38 percent of the chain's sales, compared with 55 percent in the past.

There were other significant changes: management installed escalators in the flagship store as part of a $7 million remodeling and put its shirts and sweaters out on the counter instead of locking them up in wood-framed glass cases. The second floor, traditionally given over to the sack suit, now presented an expanded sportswear selection. Women's wear, which was accounting for 12 percent of sales, moved to the third floor. For the growing number of men who spent spare hours in Manhattan's increasing number of health clubs, there were suits—including double-breasted ones—much wider in the chest than at the waist. There was a wide selection of leather and suede jackets and even sleeveless tank tops. Brooks Brothers also began opening factory outlet stores to market unsold merchandise, typically at 30 percent off. By the spring of 1994 there were 26, and they accounted for perhaps 25 percent of all U.S. sales.

To attract men not willing to pay $500 or more for a Brooks Brothers suit, the company developed what it called its Wardrobe Collection of "suit separates," consisting of jackets priced at $270 and trousers at $125. Separates also allowed a man whose waistline and shoulder proportions did not meet standard sizes to clothe themselves without major alterations on the jacket or pants. New dyeing techniques had allowed the company to match different bolts of fabric instead of having to use the same bolt to create a suit. And in 1993 Brooks Brothers introduced a wool-polyester suit that retailed for only $295 (compared with its top-of-the-line $895 Golden Fleece).

Brooks Brothers' sales grew from $277 million in fiscal 1989 (the year ended March 31, 1989) to $322 million in fiscal 1990, but operating income fell from $39 million to $23 million, in part because of frequent sales and promotions to eliminate slow-moving merchandise. In fiscal 1991 sales reached £163.2 million (US$300.3 million), but operating profit fell to £5.9 million (US$10.9 million). The company, according to analysts, was trapped by its image, caught between a new generation with whom the firm, because of its past, had no credibility, and long-time patrons who resented any change. A cost-cutting reduction in sales personnel, for example, inevitably meant less responsive service, and some customers maintained that the contracting out of manufacturing by the firm had resulted in a decline in quality.

But the company's management stuck to its strategy of keeping its core clientele while making its goods more appealing and affordable to a new generation. Sales rose to £180.7 million (US$314.4 million) in fiscal 1992 and £204.2 million (US$339 million) in 1993, while operating profits rose from £10.5 million (US$18.3 million) to £12.6 million (US$20.9 million). In fiscal 1994 sales came to £252.1 million (US$378.2 million) and operating profit to £14.8 million (US$22.2 million). Fiscal 1995, however, saw a sharp downturn in operating profit to £5.9 million (US$9.2 million) on sales of £258.4 million (US$403.1 million), leading to the resignation of company president William V. Roberti.

Under Joseph Gromek, the new chief executive, Brooks Brothers introduced its own eyewear frames and added such items as khaki pants and jeans to its clothing line, suitable for the "dress-down Fridays," adopted even on Wall Street. To deal with complaints that the firm was aloof and forbidding, it adopted a more open layout and better lighting for some stores and urged sales personnel to smile and greet visitors as they walked through the door. Musty window displays were updated. Above all there was a great deal more use of color, including royal blue sports coats, purple gingham shirts, yellow handkerchiefs, and ties in lime green, fuchsia, turquoise, and orange. Shirt color choices included burgundy, turquoise, and sea-foam green. In women's wear, Brooks Brothers introduced suede jackets and velour tops in pastel colors, Lycra knit tops, and even bright orange winter coats.

Long reluctant to market itself in any blatant way, Brooks Brothers introduced a $1.5 million in-house advertising campaign in 1997. It included the use of a 26-year-old model and Brooks Brothers clothing in fashion spreads. The Brooks Brothers credit card was reintroduced. The number of stores increased from 83 at the end of fiscal 1994 to nearly 100 at the end of fiscal 1996. Sales continued to rise and operating profits rebounded, from £286.1 million (US$446.3 million) and £10.7 million (US$16.7 million), respectively, in fiscal 1996 to £304.4 million (US$490.1 million) and £15.4 million (US$24.8 million) in fiscal 1997. (Sales and profit figures beginning in 1988 included the parent company's take from the Japanese Brooks Brothers joint venture.)

Further Reading

Bhargava, Sunita Wadekar, "What Next, Grunge Bathrobes?" *Business Week,* June 21, 1993, pp. 64, 68.

Birmingham, Stephen, "Well-Bred Clout," *Vogue,* April 1978, pp. 312, 318.

Brooks Brothers Centenary, 1818–1918, New York: Brooks Brothers, 1918.

Durant, John, and Mann, Lloyd, "Abe Lincoln Shopped Here," *Saturday Evening Post,* December 1, 1945, pp. 22–23, 121, 123, 125–126.

Elliott, Stuart, "Brooks Brothers Moves Beyond the Gray Flannel Suit," *New York Times,* September 19, 1997, p. D5.

"Garfinckel's Buy," *Fortune,* August 1946, p. 136.

Gavenas, Mary Lisa, "Ivy Covers New Ground," *New York Times Magazine* (Part II), March 18, 1990, pp. 62–63, 80.

Harris, Tim, "Brooks Brothers Dress with Style," *Marketing,* November 16, 1989, p. 16.

Levine, Joshua, "An Escalator? In Brooks Brothers?" *Forbes,* July 9, 1990, pp. 76–77.

Maremont, Mark, "Marks & Spencer Pays a Premium for Pinstripes," *Business Week,* April 18, 1988, p. 67.

Millstein, Gilbert, "The Suits on the Brooks Brothers Men," *New York Times Magazine,* August 5, 1976, pp. 28–29, 33, 35, 38–39.

Parker-Pope, Tara, "Brooks Brothers Gets a Boost from New Look," *Wall Street Journal,* May 22, 1996, pp. B1, B4.

Plimpton, George, "Fashion Is a Tradition at Brooks Brothers," *Gentlemen's Quarterly,* April 1959, pp. 74–75, 126–127.

Power, Gavin, "Brooks Bros. Opening Outlet Stores," *San Francisco Chronicle,* November 21, 1992, pp. B1–B2.

Ryan, Suzanne C., "A Part of Americana Loosens Up," *Boston Globe,* February 1, 1997, pp. A1, A7.

Strom, Stephanie, "A Quiet Alteration at Brooks Bros.," *New York Times,* November 21, 1992, pp. D1, D3.

—Robert Halasz

Brunswick Corporation

1 North Field Court
Lake Forest, Illinois 60045-4811
U.S.A.
(847) 735-4700
Fax: (847) 735-4765

Public Company
Incorporated: 1907 as Brunswick-Balke-Collender Company
Employees: 22,800
Sales: $3.16 billion (1996)
Stock Exchanges: New York Midwest Pacific London
SICs: 2821 Plastics Materials, Nonvulcanizable Elastomers & Synthetic Resins; 2891 Adhesives & Sealants; 3085 Plastic Bottles; 3086 Plastic Foam Products; 3089 Plastic Products, Not Elsewhere Classified; 3519 Internal Combustion Engines, Not Elsewhere Classified; 3585 Air Conditioning, Warm Air Heating Equipment & Commercial & Industrial Refrigeration Equipment; 3732 Boat Building & Repairing; 3751 Motorcycles, Bicycles & Parts; 3944 Games, Toys & Children's Vehicles, Except Dolls & Bicycles; 3949 Sporting & Athletic Goods, Not Elsewhere Classified; 5091 Sporting & Recreational Goods & Supplies; 7933 Bowling Alleys

Brunswick Corporation, the oldest and largest manufacturer of recreation and leisure-time products in the United States, has used its commercial successes in billiard and bowling products to become a large and diversified manufacturer of marine and recreational products. Brunswick began as a family firm, merged to become the Brunswick-Balke-Collender Company in 1884, and was renamed the Brunswick Corporation in 1960. During the 1980s the company, which once described itself as the ''General Motors of Sports,'' moved to dominate the marine and powerboat industry, while in the 1990s Brunswick expanded its recreational offerings to include bicycles, wagons, sleds, camping equipment, ice chests, and exercise equipment.

Early History

John Moses Brunswick was born in 1819 in Bremgarten, Switzerland. At 14, Brunswick immigrated to the United States. He landed in New York City and worked briefly as an errand boy for a German butcher but soon emigrated to Philadelphia, Pennsylvania, where he served a four-year apprenticeship in a carriage shop. In 1839 he moved to Harrisburg, Pennsylvania, where he worked as a journeyman carriage maker, and married Louisa Greiner. The Brunswicks moved to Cincinnati in 1840.

Brunswick found work as a journeyman carriage maker for several local firms until 1841, when a major economic downturn severely depressed the market for carriages. During the depression he worked as a steward on an Ohio River steamboat, then as a commercial trader. Though he prospered financially he became ill, and after spending several months in bed Brunswick used his accumulated commercial profits to open his own carriage shop in 1845.

Brunswick's Cincinnati, Ohio, woodworking shop began by making functional, high-quality carriages. Brunswick was willing to expand his product line and the shop soon began to produce cabinetwork, tables, and chairs. Brunswick boasted that ''if it is wood, we can make it, and we can make it better than anyone else.''

Brunswick's willingness to diversify was more than a manifestation of the pride that he took in his work; it was also an early attempt to diversify his product line to counteract fluctuations in the business cycle. For many years Brunswick's growth was internal, but in later years the firm acquired outside businesses to expand its product line.

Began Manufacturing Billiard Tables in the 1840s

By the mid-1840s the economy had begun to recover and with it came increased manufacturing activity. In this environment Brunswick began to prosper, and he became active in local political, religious, and social circles. Legend has it that in 1845, at a lavish dinner party, John Brunswick was led into another room where his host proudly displayed a fancy billiard table, which had been imported from England. Brunswick saw the

Company Perspectives:

Brunswick's growth strategy focuses on providing a wide range of high-quality consumer products that enrich the experiences of the active recreation enthusiast. The Company currently markets and manufactures leading brands to those who enjoy fishing, camping, biking, bowling, billiards, and pleasure boating. Clearly, Brunswick customers don't take their leisure sitting down. The active recreation market is where Brunswick wants to be, and where its commitment lies.

opportunity to expand his woodworking business. Thus began Brunswick's long association and ultimate domination of the sporting-goods market.

Billiards long had suffered from a poor reputation. Indeed, sports in general had very limited mass appeal in the United States prior to the 1850s. Sporting equipment was ornate and was designed for sale to men of wealth. Brunswick's first tables were elaborate luxury items, and as such found a limited market.

In 1848 Brunswick expanded his market by sending his half-brothers, David and Emanuel Brunswick, to Chicago to establish a sales office and factory. Other sales offices were opened in New Orleans, Louisiana, and St. Louis, Missouri, while half-brothers Joseph and Hyman Brunswick worked in the firm's Cincinnati offices. In 1858 the business was reorganized as J. M. Brunswick & Brother. In 1866, the company was renamed J. M. Brunswick & Brothers when Emanuel Brunswick joined Joseph and John Brunswick as a principal in the firm.

Mergers Created Brunswick-Balke-Collender Company in 1884

By the late 1860s the U.S. billiards market was dominated by three firms: Brunswick, Julius Balke's Cincinnati-based Great Western Billiard Manufactory, and a New York-based company named Phelan & Collender, run by Michael Phelan and his son-in-law, H. M. Collender. In 1873 Brunswick merged with Balke to form the J. M. Brunswick & Balke Company. In 1884, following the death of his father-in-law in 1879, Collender merged with Brunswick & Balke, to form the Brunswick-Balke-Collender Company.

During the 1870s Brunswick's half-brothers left the firm to start rival firms and billiard parlors in Chicago and San Francisco. It is not entirely clear under what circumstances each of them left but by 1872 Brunswick's son-in-law, Moses Bensinger, and two longtime employees were vice-presidents at Brunswick.

During this period of rapid growth John Brunswick remained in Cincinnati while Bensinger, who increasingly directed the company's day-to-day operations, greatly expanded the company's Chicago facilities. In July 1886 John Brunswick died. He was succeeded by H. M. Collender, who served as president until his own death in 1890. Julius Balke, too ill and old to take over as president, stepped aside, and—after buying out another vice-president—Bensinger was named president of Brunswick-Balke-Collender.

Bensinger aggressively expanded the firm's product line. Since many billiard tables were being sold to taverns, he expanded the company's line of carved wooden back bars. Back bars covered the wall behind a bar and served a functional and decorative purpose. They were intricate and elaborate status symbols and also greatly enhanced Brunswick's reputation for fine craftsmanship. Initially the bars were custom built, but their popularity soon had the company's Dubuque, Iowa, factory operating at full capacity. Before long Brunswick bars were installed across the United States and Canada.

Bowling Pins and Balls Added in the 1880s

In the 1880s Bensinger added another product line, bowling pins and bowling balls. Taverns had begun installing lanes, interest seemed to be growing, and Bensinger was determined to be ready for this new market. He actively promoted bowling as a participatory sport and helped to standardize the game. Bensinger also was instrumental in organizing the American Bowling Congress. Although the company continued to expand its markets and product lines, bowling was to become the financial backbone of the firm.

Throughout this growth and expansion, Brunswick remained a family firm. John Brunswick's surviving son, Benedict Brunswick, and Julius Balke, Jr., were Brunswick executives, and Bensinger's son, Benjamin Bensinger, worked first as a clerk, then as a salesman, and was rapidly moving his way up in the company. In 1904, upon the death of his father, Benjamin Bensinger became the president of Brunswick-Balke-Collender, at age 36. The firm had several sales offices, and manufacturing plants in Chicago, Cincinnati, Dubuque, and New York, and in 1906 Bensinger opened a large manufacturing plant in Muskegon, Michigan. The Muskegon plant, which grew to over one million square feet in the 1940s, became the cornerstone of the firm's manufacturing, producing such products as mineralite (hard rubber) bowling balls.

Prohibition Era (1920–33) Forced Diversification

In the 1910s the temperance movement threatened not only the fixtures and bar business but also billiards and bowling. In 1912, in anticipation of Prohibition—which started in 1920—Brunswick suspended its bar-fixtures operations, which accounted for one-fourth of annual sales, and sought to replace it with automobile tires and the world's first hard-rubber toilet seats. Rubber products best utilized the firm's existing facilities. By 1921 the Muskegon plant was producing 2,000 tires a day. Then the price of rubber tripled in 1922, Brunswick sold its tire line to B.F. Goodrich, who began to manufacture tires under the Brunswick name as the Brunswick Tire Company.

Brunswick also began to manufacture wood piano cases and phonograph cabinets. Edison Phonograph was the principal buyer of Brunswick's cabinets. The demand for phonographs was so strong that Bensinger decided that Brunswick should manufacture its own line of phonographs. By 1916 the Muskegon plant was producing Brunswick phonographs and putting them on the market for $150—40 percent less than comparable models. In 1922 it also began producing records under its own label. Jazz greats such as Duke Ellington, Cab Calloway, and Benny Goodman and classical artists such as Irene Pavlovska and Leopold Godowsky all recorded on the Brunswick label. In 1925 Brunswick teamed up with General Electric to manufacture an all-electric phonograph called the Panatrope, which came equipped with or without a radio. In 1930 Brunswick sold the Brunswick Panatrope & Radio Corporation to Warner Brothers for $10 million.

The company had gone public in 1924, and in 1930 Benjamin Bensinger was named chairman of the board and his oldest son, Bob Bensinger, became president. Bob Bensinger had worked for the firm since 1919 and with his brother, Ted, guided Brunswick through the Great Depression. Even with the repeal of Prohibition in 1933 and the popularity of pool halls, the Great Depression was hard on Brunswick. The company marketed a line of table-top refrigerators called the Blue Flash and a successful line of soda fountains to replace its once-thriving bar and fixture business.

During World War II Brunswick found new markets and new products and once again prospered. United Service Organizations (USO) centers and military bases eagerly purchased billiard and bowling equipment. Brunswick also made wartime products, including mortar shells, flares, assault boats, fuel cells, floating mines, aircraft instrument panels, and aluminum litters.

Postwar Era Brought Pinsetters and Outboard Motors

At the end of the war Brunswick became involved in a high-stakes battle with the American Machine and Foundry Company (AMF) over the automatic pinsetter for bowling alleys. AMF produced pinsetters in the late 1940s but these proved unreliable. In 1952 AMF installed an improved version of its machine and called it a pinspotter. Brunswick, which had toyed with the idea of an automatic pinsetter as early as 1911, had to develop a working pinsetter quickly or risk losing its domination of the bowling market. Telling customers that it would be ''worth waiting for,'' Brunswick scrambled to develop its own machine. In 1954 Brunswick formed the Pinsetter Corporation with Murray Corporation of America. By the time the pinsetters were in production in 1955, Brunswick had bought out Murray, and Brunswick aggressively sold its machine to a rapidly expanding market.

Brunswick's policy of selling pinsetters on credit, suburban expansion, and an aggressive advertising campaign all combined to make bowling centers enormously popular in the late 1950s. After the introduction of the pinsetter the company prospered as never before. Sales, which had been $33 million in 1954, jumped to $422 million in 1961. Although Brunswick's earnings did not leap correspondingly—sales were up almost 13-fold, but earnings increased just less than six times—Ted Bensinger, named CEO in 1954, received most of the credit for Brunswick gains. Brunswick acquired 18 new firms to further diversify its markets. Such companies as MacGregor Sports Products, Union Hardware, Zebco, and Owens Yacht Company made Brunswick a major force in equipment for golf, roller skating, fishing, and boating. Brunswick's most important purchase proved to be the 1961 acquisition of the Kiekhaefer Corporation, which built Mercury outboard motors.

Brunswick also sought firms outside recreational sports, and in 1959 it purchased A.S. Aloe and entered the medical-supply business. To complement the Aloe purchase Brunswick also acquired Sheridan Catheter & Instrument Corporation in 1960, Roehr Products Company in 1961, and Biological Research in 1961. Brunswick's medical-supply business became known as the Sherwood Medical Group. Brunswick also developed a popular line of school furniture in the 1950s and kept active in its defense-products division. The company, meanwhile, changed its name to Brunswick Corporation in 1960.

Further Diversification Moves Marked 1960s and 1970s

An unexpected decline in the bowling industry, which represented 60 percent of sales, in the early 1960s presented Brunswick with serious financial problems. Jack Hanigan was brought in as president in November 1963 to handle Brunswick's financial problems. Ted Bensinger became chairman and he and his brother both remained on the board of directors into the 1970s. Hanigan aggressively sought to reorganize Brunswick and to position the firm for future expansion. In 1965 he formed a technical and new-business division which developed, among other things, Brunsmet, a metal-fiber product. In 1967 Hanigan merged this division and the defense division into the technical-products division. These new divisions, along with further expansion of the company's medical lines, growth of the Kiekhaefer-Mercury products, and the recovery of bowling in the late 1960s, all helped Brunswick to reach record sales of $450 million in 1969.

The 1973–74 oil embargo caused problems at Brunswick, particularly in its profitable marine-engine division, but the company was able to further diversify its products and remained strong. The technical-products division continued to grow, producing, among other things, radomes and metal-fiber camouflage. Hanigan retired as chairman and CEO in 1976 and was replaced by K. Brooks Abernathy.

To promote stability Brunswick had been organized into four business groups: marine, medical, recreational, and technical. Jack Reichert, president of the Marine group, became president of Brunswick in 1977 as sales topped $1 billion for the first time. Not content, Brunswick moved into energy and transportation control systems by acquiring Vapor Corporation for $90 million in 1978, as well as actively expanding its international markets.

Marine and Recreation Products Achieved Predominance in the 1980s and 1990s

Brunswick successfully fought a hostile takeover bid by the Whittaker Corporation in 1982. Whittaker wanted Brunswick's Sherwood Medical Group medical-supply business. Whittaker was forced to withdraw its offer when American Home Products stepped in as a white knight, and Sherwood was sold to American Home Products in March 1982 for $425 million in Brunswick stock. In April 1982 Reichert took over as CEO of Brunswick. Reichert sought to decentralize Brunswick to improve efficiency and stress quality output. The firm's 11 sectors were reduced to 8, corporate staff was cut, and executive perquisites were trimmed, reducing bureaucratic costs. Reichert transferred division staff to production sites in an attempt to enhance product quality. He also moved to include hourly employees as shareholders and increased pension payments to former employees.

During the latter half of the 1980s, Brunswick made a series of significant moves aimed at not only reasserting itself in the field of recreation but also making recreation the company's main focus. In 1986 Brunswick acquired two pleasure-boat manufacturers, Bayliner Marine Corporation and Ray Industries (maker of Sea Ray boats), for $773 million. These purchases, along with the acquisitions of MonArk Boat, Marine Group, Fisher Marine, and Starcraft Power Boats in 1988, made Brunswick the world's largest manufacturer of pleasure boats and marine engines. These companies also made Brunswick vulnerable to fluctuations in marine sales.

Brunswick had enjoyed six consecutive years of record earnings from 1982 through 1988. That string of record years ended in 1989, when restructuring charges arising from a downturn in the marine market resulted in a net loss. In 1989 and 1990 Brunswick disposed of the business units that had theretofore comprised its technetics and industrial products divisions, leaving it with only its marine and recreation groups and a much smaller technical group of businesses.

Although the company returned to profitability in 1990, the economic downturn of the early 1990s severely depressed sales of pleasure boats and outboard motors, leading to net losses in 1991 and 1992 and net earnings of only $23.1 million in 1993. While weathering these rough seas, Brunswick put major acquisitions on hold and determined to concentrate solely on its marine and recreation segments. In February 1993 the company announced that it would divest its technical group. The sale to the newly formed Technical Products Group, Inc. was not culminated until April 1995, having been delayed by U.S. government investigations of its defense businesses. Also divested in 1995 was the company's Circus World Pizza operation, while 1996 saw the closure of a noncompetitive golf shaft business. Meanwhile, in April 1993 Brunswick moved into its new world headquarters building in Lake Forest, Illinois.

With Reichert planning to retire in 1995, Brunswick brought in John P. Reilly, formerly with Tenneco Inc., as president and heir apparent in the fall of 1994. He was forced out after only nine months, however, following reported conflicts among top executives. Subsequently, Reichert was succeeded in mid-1995 by Peter N. Larson, a former Johnson & Johnson executive.

In order to guard against future economic downturns—downturns that always hit the pleasure boat market particularly hard—Brunswick in the mid-1990s concentrated on expanding its recreational offerings to a wider variety of consumable goods, which tend to counterbalance such durable goods as boats. In anticipation of this expansion, Brunswick in the fall of 1995 created an Indoor Recreation Group to encompass the bowling and billiards operations, while an Outdoor Recreation Group featured the Zebco fishing equipment business. In early 1996 the company acquired Nelson/Weather-Rite, a unit of Roadmaster Industries Inc. that made camping equipment, for $120 million. Brunswick renamed this unit American Camper; it held the number-two position in the U.S. market and offered sleeping bags, tents, backpacks, and other products under the American Camper, Remington, and Weather-Rite brand names. American Camper became part of the Outdoor Recreation Group, as did Igloo Holdings Inc. after it was acquired in January 1997 for about $154 million in cash; Igloo was a market leader in ice chests, beverage coolers, and thermoelectric cooler/warmer products. Two months later, the Hoppe's line of hunting accessories was purchased from Penguin Industries, Inc.; Hoppe's, also added to Outdoor Recreation, was number one in gun cleaning and shooting accessories.

Brunswick next aimed to become a leader in the bicycle market. After spending $190 million in January 1997 to buy Roadmaster's bicycle division, which included the Flexible Flyer line of sleds and wagons, and the Roadmaster brand name, Brunswick in the spring of 1997 acquired Bell Sports Corp.'s Mongoose—a San Jose, California-based maker of higher-end mountain and BMX bikes—for $22 million. That same summer the company formed a Brunswick Bicycles division within the Outdoor Recreation Group to oversee the Roadmaster and Mongoose operations, and to launch a new brand that fall called Ride Hard aimed at the middle-tier of the market between the lower-end Roadmaster and higher-end Mongoose. The acquisition spree continued in July 1997 as Brunswick paid Mancuso & Co. $310 million for Life Fitness, maker of stationary bicycles, treadmills, stairclimbers, rowers, cross trainers, and strength training equipment for fitness centers worldwide.

After sales of $3.16 billion in 1996, Brunswick's sales for 1997 were up 15 percent during the first nine months of the year. Net earnings were down, but only because of a $98.5 million strategic charge for streamlining and consolidating various operations and for exiting from the manufacture of personal watercraft. As for the remainder of the decade, Brunswick was likely to continue to seek out acquisitions of market leaders in active recreation since it had set a goal of achieving $5 billion in sales by 2000. The company was also better positioned to weather the next economic downturn as it was increasingly less dependent on its marine operations.

Principal Subsidiaries

Marine Power Australia Pty. Limited; Appletree Ltd. (Bermuda); Centennial Assurance Company, Ltd. (Bermuda); Brunswick Bowling e Billiards Industria e Comercia Ltda. (Brazil); Brunswick Centres, Inc. (Canada); Brunswick International (Canada) Limited; Mercury Marine Limited (Canada); Zebco Sports France S.A. (France); Brunswick Bowling GmbH (Germany); Brunswick International GmbH (Germany); Marine Power Italia S.p.A. (Italy); Nippon Brunswick Kabushiki Kaisha (Japan; 50%); Mercury Marine Sdn Bhd (Malaysia); Brunswick Bowling & Billiards Mexico, S.A. de C.V. (Mexico); Productos Marine de Mexico, S.A. de C.V. (Mexico); Normalduns B.V. (Netherlands); Sea Ray Boats Europe B.V. (Netherlands); Brunswick AG (Switzerland); Brunswick Bowling & Billiards (U.K.) Limited; Brunswick International Sales Corporation (U.S. Virgin Islands).

Principal Operating Units

Mercury Marine Division; US Marine Division; Sea Ray Division; Brunswick Outdoor Recreation Group; Brunswick Indoor Recreation Group.

Further Reading

Baldo, Anthony, "Brunswick: Not Just a Takeover Play," *Financial World,* May 17, 1988, p. 11.

Bettner, Jill, "Bowling for Dollars," *Forbes,* September 12, 1983, p. 138.

Borden, Jeff, "Bowl Them Overseas: Brunswick Rolls in Asia, S. America," *Crain's Chicago Business,* October 16, 1995, pp. 17, 20–21.

"Brunswick's Dramatic Turnaround: An Interview with CEO Jack F. Reichert," *Journal of Business Strategy,* January/February 1988, p. 4.

Byrne, Harlan S., "Riding High Again," *Barron's,* May 23, 1994, p. 26.

David, Gregory E., "Sea Horses: Brunswick Powers Ahead of Outboard Marine in the Rebounding Boating Business," *Financial World,* November 8, 1994, pp. 34, 36.

Dubashi, Jagannath, "Bumbling Brunswick," *Financial World,* May 30, 1989, p. 30.

Fritz, Michael, "Brunswick Seeks Kingpin," *Crain's Chicago Business,* August 1, 1994, p. 1.

Gallagher, Leigh, "Brunswick Keeps Rolling with Newly-Formed Bike Division," *Sporting Goods Business,* July 21, 1997, p. 13.

Gibson, Richard, "Personality Rift, Reported U.S. Inquiries Dog Brunswick," *Wall Street Journal,* August 12, 1994, p. B4.

Kelly, Kevin, and Richard A. Melcher, "Men Overboard in Boatland," *Business Week,* August 22, 1994, pp. 30–31.

Kogan, Rick, *Brunswick: The Story of an American Company: The First 150 Years,* Lake Forest, Ill.: Brunswick Corporation, 1995, 153 p.

Melcher, Richard A., "Brunswick Wades into New Waters," *Business Week,* June 2, 1997, pp. 67, 70.

Murphy, H. Lee, "Amid Downturn at Brunswick, Its Billiard Unit on the Rebound," *Crain's Chicago Business,* August 27, 1990, p. 6.

Oneal, Michael, "Can Brunswick Weather Rougher Seas?," *Business Week,* September 5, 1988, p. 66.

Palmer, Jay, "Rough Seas: But Recovery Looms for Brunswick," *Barron's,* October 14, 1991, pp. 16–17.

"Revving Up Brunswick," *Financial World,* October 15, 1981, p. 31.

Rodengen, Jeffrey L., "A Great American Empire," *Boating,* September 1987, p. 71.

——, *Iron Fist: The Lives of Carl Kiekhaefer,* Fort Lauderdale, Fla.: Write Stuff Syndicate, 1991, 640 p.

Rudnitsky, Howard, "Any Offers?," *Forbes,* October 15, 1990, p. 48.

Siler, Julia Flynn, "Has Brunswick Gone Overboard in Powerboats?," *Business Week,* August 7, 1989, p. 27.

Slutsker, Gary, "Toes in the Water," *Forbes,* March 15, 1993, pp. 70, 72.

Weinschenk, Carl, "Brunswick Changes the Landscape," *Boating Industry,* January 1987, p. 13.

—Timothy E. Sullivan
—updated by David E. Salamie

Burton Snowboards Inc.

80 Industrial Parkway
Burlington, Vermont 05401
U.S.A.
(802) 862-4500
Fax: (802) 660-3250
Web site: http://www.burton.com

Private Company
Incorporated: 1977
Employees: 600
Sales: $120 million (1996 est.)
SICs: 3949 Sporting & Athletic Goods, Not Elsewhere Classified

One of the first snowboard companies in the world, Burton Snowboards Inc. designs, manufactures, and markets a full line of snowboarding equipment, clothing, and related accessories. Although snowboarding did not become a well-recognized sport until the early 1990s, Burton began manufacturing snowboards and bindings in 1977, when the company's founder started making his own boards in a borrowed woodworking shop in Stratton, Vermont. From these modest origins, Burton developed into a flourishing enterprise with offices in Europe and Japan that served customers in 27 countries. Recognized as an industry pioneer, Burton controlled roughly 40 percent of the U.S. snowboarding market during the late 1990s, more than any other company in the world.

Genesis of Snowboarding

Few individuals had a greater effect on the creation and the development of the snowboarding industry than Jake Burton Carpenter, the founder of Burton Snowboards. Carpenter's pioneering influence was irrefutable, but in the history of snowboarding there was one key individual whose contributions preceded Carpenter's. His name was Sherman Poppen. Although Carpenter was recognized as a pioneer—and deservedly so—Poppen's innovative work inspired Carpenter. Just as the hundreds of companies involved in the snowboarding industry during the 1990s were indebted to Carpenter, so too was Carpenter indebted to Poppen. Poppen never received the fanfare accorded to Carpenter, but in the history of Burton Snowboards, which framed the history of snowboarding itself, the origin of all that followed started in Poppen's garage in 1965.

A businessman residing in Muskegon, Michigan, Poppen was the inventor of the "Snurfer," the earliest version of the modern-day snowboard. Poppen assembled his first Snurfer on Christmas Day in 1965 when he nailed together two 36-inch skis with scraps of wood and gave the hastily created toy to his daughters. At first, Poppen was merely trying to create a diversion for his daughters to get them out of the house and away from his pregnant wife, but the toy proved to be an enormous hit among the neighborhood children, prompting Poppen to refine the design of the first Snurfer. Three months later, after tinkering with the design of the Snurfer and adding a rope to its front for the rider to grasp, Poppen had secured a patent for his invention and was ready to determine whether or not he had a marketable product. Poppen approached a friend of his who worked at Brunswick Bowling & Billiards Corp. and subsequently licensed the Snurfer to Brunswick. What followed was a renowned marketing disaster, but Poppen's misfortune proved to be the inspiration for Burton Snowboards.

Although the idea seemed logical, Brunswick never distributed Snurfers to sporting goods stores. Instead, the company distributed the snow toys to hardware stores, where they were sold for roughly $10. It was a major misstep, one that Harvard's business school used in later years as a case study to illustrate how not to market a new product. Although 500,000 Snurfers eventually were sold before Brunswick abandoned production, the results were dismal. Poppen later realized his error, remarking, "They [Brunswick] knew the bowling industry, but they sure as hell didn't know consumer products." Much of the finger-pointing at Brunswick stemmed from the fact that Snurfers had considerable market appeal, but the company had failed to exploit consumer interest.

1970s: Burton Snowboards Takes Shape

One of those who recognized Brunswick's errors was Jake Carpenter. When Carpenter was 14 years old he received one of the Brunswick-made Snurfers, and from that moment forward,

Company Perspectives:

Since 1977, Burton Snowboards has been driven to create the best snowboarding equipment in the world. Corporate headquarters are in Burlington, Vermont, with additional offices in Urawa, Japan, and Innsbruck, Austria. These three offices, employing just under 600 employees, are the main arteries that service the global snowboarding market. Burton Snowboards continues to be the industry leader, focusing its efforts on product development, R&D, and most importantly—riding. Everyone is out on the hill as much as possible. And with a free season pass and private lessons for Newbies, excuses for not riding are hard to find. Along with this dedication to the mountain, employees work in a casual but dedicated environment—jeans and T's with the option of bringing the family pooch. Burton believes in a strong work ethic and is committed to working as a team to achieve their goals. When they're not out snowboarding, they're back at the factory putting their experiences to work.

he had found his life's calling. Throughout high school and college, Carpenter labored to make improvements on the Snurfer, experimenting with one design after another during his hours away from classes. His devotion was tireless and his work was visionary. "I felt there was an opportunity for it [the Snurfer] to be better marketed," Carpenter later told *Sports Illustrated*. "For serious technology to be applied to it, so Snurfing could become a legitimate sport instead of a cheap toy. I knew there was an opportunity there. I couldn't believe Brunswick never took advantage of it." Carpenter's father, Tim, a writer and former Wall Street broker, was impressed with his son's diligence: "He wasn't the type of kid who set up lemonade stands, but once he had the idea for this board in his head, he put every bit of his energy into it."

After earning a degree in economics from New York University, Carpenter took a position at a small Manhattan investment bank. His tenure there, however, was brief. A small inheritance from his grandmother enabled Carpenter to quit his job at the bank and move, in 1977, to Stratton Mountain, Vermont. There, with $20,000 as a nest egg, Carpenter founded Burton Snowboards at age 23, taking the company's name from his middle name.

Jake Burton Carpenter worked nights as a bartender at Stratton's ski resort and spent his days honing his skills as a snowboard maker in the woodworking shop of a friend, Emo Henrich, who was director of the Stratton Mountain ski school. Carpenter constructed more than 100 models in Henrich's shop, trying different shapes, different types of wood, and experimenting with various laminating materials and binding designs before settling on what he deemed a marketable product. Although the improvements over the Snurfer design were vast, Carpenter's timing was off. "I was so naive," he later confided. "I thought I'd be selling boards and making money right away, but by the time I had a board ready, winter was over and nobody was interested." It was a frustrating start, but only the beginning in what would turn out to be an arduous undertaking. Carpenter was not only trying to develop a product and bring it to market, he also was trying to create the market in the first place. His perseverance, first displayed as a teenager in Cedarhurst, New York, would be tested for years to come.

After his disappointing first attempt at selling his boards, Carpenter went to Europe and spent the summer of 1978 testing his boards on the glaciers in Austria. When the winter season neared, Carpenter returned to the United States and steeled himself for another go at selling his boards. This time he was more prepared, and spent endless weeks traveling around the country attending trade shows. "I was afraid to go to the bathroom," Carpenter recalled. "I thought if I did, I might miss my only customer."

Compared to his first season of selling, Carpenter's 1978–79 season was a success, thanks in large part to more thorough market research and the establishment of a mail-order department, whose telephone rang in Carpenter's bedroom. Offices were set up in a former electrician's store in Londonderry, Vermont, where Carpenter, with a few friends lending a hand, produced his four-foot-long, eight-inch-wide snowboards. By the end of the season, Carpenter had sold 300 boards, but he was far short of his break-even point and was racking up debt with each passing day.

Snurfers at this point were more popular than ever, having transcended their ill-conceived marketing and distribution support to become a cult hit lionized at the National Snurfing Championships in Michigan. At the annual event in 1979, the Snurfer faithful gathered to compete in races on their boards, but their day of celebration was disrupted by the arrival of a newcomer: Jake Carpenter carrying one of his own snowboards. After convincing race officials to let him race by creating an open division, Carpenter strapped into his bindings and proceeded to win the race. Carpenter's victory sounded the death knell for Snurfers, ushering in a new era of snowboarding that focused on the continual improvement of technology. In this new era, Carpenter and Burton Snowboards would rise above all other rivals to reign supreme in a market that a decade later represented the fastest-growing sport in the United States.

1980s: Slow, Measured Growth

After his success at the Snurfing National Championships, Carpenter's problem was that the rampant growth of the snowboard market was still a decade away. Although there was palpable interest in the sport, there were not enough people willing to try snowboarding to support Carpenter and his business. By the end of the 1979–80 season, Carpenter had sold 700 boards, more than doubling his total during the previous season, but he still was well below his profitability point. Year by year, the financial loses mounted, leaving Carpenter $130,000 in debt by 1981. Carpenter managed to move forward, however, and with the financial support of his wife's family he developed better bindings, a high-technology plastic base, and added steel edges to his boards, which improved maneuverability exponentially. Slowly but steadily the changes made by Burton and the handful of other snowboarding pioneers increased the demand for snowboards, enabling Carpenter to break even for the first time in 1984, when sales reached the $1 million mark. Carpenter by this point had shed his last name to avoid confusion in business dealings and adopted Jake Burton as his full name.

The addition of steel edges to snowboards did much to persuade skiers to try snowboarding for the first time, but only a limited number of ski resorts allowed snowboards on their slopes. The battle to convince resort operators to allow snowboards on their slopes raged for years, with economics proving to be the decisive factor in resolving the war. The number of ski visits per year in the United States flattened out in 1979 and remained so for the ensuing two decades, forcing roughly half of the country's 1,000 ski resorts to close their operations by 1995. Accordingly, as business tapered off and snowboarding grew, resort operators were forced to embrace the new sport. In 1985, 93 percent of U.S. ski resorts banned snowboarding; by 1995, more than 90 percent of the resorts not only permitted snowboarding but also focused their marketing programs on attracting snowboarders. The chief benefactor of this development—of snowboarding's legitimacy—was Jake Burton and his promising company, Burton Snowboards.

On the heels of recording his first break-even year in 1984, Burton traveled to Europe and established a manufacturing plant in Innsbruck, Austria, in 1985. Previously, Burton had fulfilled orders from Europe for his boards on an individual basis. By the end of the following year, Burton could point to his first profit, as Burton Snowboards, nearly a decade after its creation, began operating in the black. For Burton and his company, it was the beginning of lucrative times after years of trying to succeed with meager financial resources. In the years ahead, snowboard manufacturers would find a vast and exuberant audience for their products, although the emergence of this iconoclastic crowd of consumers came as a surprise to many of snowboarding's early proponents. Originally, Burton and other manufacturers targeted their marketing efforts on experienced alpine skiers, hoping a considerable percentage of the veteran skiers would try snowboarding and stay with it. This market segment was referred to as the crossover market, but it never materialized in great numbers. Instead, snowboarding received a greater boost to its ranks from skateboarding and surfer enthusiasts, people who typically had never visited a ski resort. These converts to winter recreation were the source of snowboarding's explosive growth, fueling the growth of Burton Snowboards and all those companies that followed in its wake. The arrival of snowboarding's lifeblood—primarily teenagers—began with a trickle in 1985. By the early 1990s, the trickle had turned into a voluminous river.

Burton Snowboards in the 1990s

By the 1990s, snowboarding had moved into the mainstream, attracting headlines in newspapers, a perennially increasing number of participants, and a wave of start-up companies intent on grabbing a share of the lucrative, fast-growing market. Burton, who once operated in near isolation and generally was acknowledged only with bemused skepticism, found himself inundated with rivals on all flanks by the mid-1990s. More than 300 companies in the United States were competing for snowboard business in 1995, but all of the contenders took a backseat to Burton Snowboards. Operating in a highly fragmented industry, Burton Snowboards controlled an estimated 36 percent of the market, or twice as much as its nearest rival.

By 1997, Burton Snowboards was introducing its 1998 line of merchandise, the 20th year a new line of company-designed and -manufactured clothing, equipment, and accessories had debuted on the retail market. By this point, the company was selling more than 100,000 snowboards a year in North America, with sales in both Europe and Japan equal to the level registered in the United States. As the company charted its course past its 20th anniversary, the road ahead looked as promising as ever. Industry consolidation was expected to take place during the late 1990s and the early 21st century, as the smaller companies either exited the business or sold their operations to larger competitors. When this inevitable industry shake-up occurred, Burton Snowboards was expected to benefit significantly, as the big companies became bigger and the smaller companies were weeded out of the market. Viewed from this perspective, Burton Snowboard's position as the industry giant appeared guaranteed in the years ahead.

Principal Subsidiaries

Burton Sportartikel GmbH (Austria); Burton Snowboards (Japan).

Further Reading

Finkel, Michael, "Chairman of the Board," *Sports Illustrated,* January 13, 1997, p. 9.

Gallagher, Leigh, "Balance of Powder," *Sporting Goods Business,* February 24, 1997, p. 26.

Lane, Randall, "The Culture That Jake Built," *Forbes,* March 27, 1995, p. 45.

Olgeirson, Ian, "Snowboarding Craze Leaves Poppen Behind," *Denver Business Journal,* January 3, 1997, p. 19A.

—Jeffrey L. Covell

Calvin Klein

Calvin Klein, Inc.

205 West 39th Street
New York, New York 10018
U.S.A.
(212) 719-2600
Fax: (212) 292-7751

Private Company
Incorporated: 1967 as Calvin Klein Ltd.
Employees: 1,060
Sales: $260 million (1996 est.)
SICs: 2331 Women's, Misses' & Juniors' Blouses & Skirts; 2335 Women's, Misses' & Juniors' Dresses; 2337 Women's, Misses' & Juniors' Suits, Skirts & Coats; 2339 Men's & Boys' Clothing, Not Elsewhere Classified; 5137 Women's, Children's & Infants' Clothing & Accessories; 5611 Men's & Boys' Clothing & Accessory Stores; 5621 Women's Clothing Stores; 5632 Women's Accessory & Specialty Stores; 6719 Miscellaneous Homefurnishings Stores; 7319 Advertising, Not Elsewhere Classified; 7389 Business Services, Not Elsewhere Classified

Calvin Klein, Inc. designs, licenses, and, in some cases, produces clothing, accessories, fragrances, and home furnishings bearing the name of designer Calvin Klein. Since its inception, the company was a partnership between Klein and his childhood friend, Barry Schwartz. Named by *Time* in 1996 as one of the 25 most influential Americans, Klein made his impact not only by designing but also by marketing his wares through high-visibility advertisements created by the company's in-house agency, CRK Advertising. In 1996 worldwide retail sales of Calvin Klein products reached $4.4 billion. Most of these goods were manufactured and sold by other companies under license, but Calvin Klein, Inc. produced in-house high-fashion and midline collections of apparel and accessories and owned four retail stores.

Rocketing to Stardom in the 1970s

Born and reared in New York City's borough of the Bronx, Calvin Richard Klein decided he wanted to be a fashion designer at an early age. After graduating from the Fashion Institute of Technology in 1963 he worked for women's coat and suit manufacturers in Manhattan's garment district before opening his own business in 1968. A childhood friend, Barry Schwartz, loaned him $10,000 in start-up money and joined the firm a month later, after the family supermarket in Harlem that Schwartz had inherited was gutted in the riots that followed the assassination of Martin Luther King.

Klein rented a dingy showroom to exhibit a small line of samples. His big break came when a vice-president of Bonwit Teller stopped at the wrong floor of the building, liked what he saw, and invited Klein to bring his samples to the president's office. Klein wheeled the rack of clothes uptown personally and won an order of $50,000 (retail) on the spot. Bonwit's gave the merchandise impressive exposure, with window displays in its flagship Fifth Avenue store and full-page ads in the *New York Times*, and Calvin Klein was quickly besieged by orders. The fledgling company booked $1 million worth of business in its first year, reaching sales volume of $5 million by 1971.

Klein mainly designed women's coats and two-piece suits until 1972, when he began concentrating on sporty sweaters, skirts, dresses, shirts, and pants that could be mixed and matched for a complete wardrobe. The clothing featured the simplicity of line, muted earth tones, and classic fabrics that characterized his work and gave it an air of understated elegance. Klein won a Coty American Fashion Critics Award—fashion's Oscar—in 1973. He received an unprecedented third consecutive Coty Award for women's wear in 1975 and, at age 32, was elected to the group's Hall of Fame. That fiscal year (ending June 30, 1975) the firm shipped $12 million worth of merchandise, including swimsuits and dresses. It earned another $2 million to $6 million from licensing furs, umbrellas, sheets, shoes, scarves, belts, dresses, sunglasses, suedes, and patterns. Klein not only designed every item carrying his name but closely watched every step of the production process.

Company revenues rose to $40 million in fiscal 1976 and a startling $90 million in 1977. Because its prices were generally below those of its two major competitors, Ralph Lauren and Anne Klein, the firm won the loyalty of young working women as well as older, wealthier buyers. Calvin Klein merchandise was so hot that the company could pick and choose among stores that wanted to carry the company's products and blackball those that dared to try to return unsold goods. Seven hundred buyers and reporters were turned away from Klein's fall 1978 fashion show; the buyers who got in placed $28 million worth of orders within 48 hours.

Klein introduced his first menswear collection in 1978, telling the *New York Times Magazine* that he approached men's clothing "with the same philosophy as the women's. They're for Americans who like simple, comfortable but stylish clothes—but with nothing overscale or extreme." No less than 779 fabrics were used in the European-produced collection, which ranged from neckties to suits and overcoats. The production and sale of most of the men's clothing was licensed to Bidermann Industries. Also in 1978, Calvin Klein introduced his own line of fragrances and a complete makeup collection of 18 beauty and skin-care products that stressed neutral colors to give the face a natural effect. But the lightweight, rosy perfume (at $85 an ounce) needed to anchor the collection never caught on with the public. The fragrance and cosmetics business was sold to Minnetonka, Inc. in 1980.

Calvin Klein jeans, by contrast, were to become the company's biggest hit. Klein's first attempt, in 1976, to capitalize on the designer-jeans craze—at $50 a pair—was a failure. The following year, however, his company cut a deal to design the product for Puritan Fashions Corp., the largest dress manufacturer in the world. Klein raised the groin in his jeans to accentuate the crotch and pulled the seam up between the buttocks to give the rear more shape. A Times Square billboard of model Patti Hansen on her hands and knees, her derriere arched skyward and the Calvin Klein label on her right hip visible, caused a sensation and remained in place for four years. By 1979 Calvin Klein was second to Gloria Vanderbilt in designer-jeans sales, with one-fifth of the market. A company spokesman observed, "The tighter they are, the better they sell."

The biggest lift to Calvin Klein's jeans was the television campaign directed by Richard Avedon that featured 15-year-old model/actress Brooke Shields provocatively posed in a skin-tight pair of Calvin Klein jeans. In the best-remembered spot, she pronounced, "Do you know what comes between me and my Calvins? Nothing." In another she declared, "I've got seven Calvins in my closet, and if they could talk, I'd be *ruined.*" These suggestions of underage sexuality struck a public nerve and, following a flood of complaints, the New York flagship stations of all three networks banned the two ads from the air. Klein could shrug off the criticism, because sales of his jeans were then climbing to two million pairs a month. He added a jeans-inspired collection that included shirts, skirts, and jackets, also licensed to Puritan. These products accounted for about $100 million in sales in 1980.

Branching Out in the 1980s

In 1982 Calvin Klein entered the underwear business, once again exploiting the allure of youth in provocative poses to push the product. Photographer Bruce Weber's beefcake ads featured a brawny Olympic pole vaulter in various states of well-endowed undress. When the company rented space in 25 New York bus shelters to display advertising posters featuring the underwear, all 25 had their glass shattered and posters stolen overnight. The follow-up was predictable—a line of women's underwear featuring male-style briefs, and boxer shorts that retained the fly front. Both campaigns were hits. The men's line was part of the Bidermann license (which lapsed in 1987), while the women's skivvies so outstripped Calvin Klein's own manufacturing capabilities that in 1984 this division was sold to Kayser Roth Corp., a unit of Gulf & Western Industries, for about $11.2 million. Calvin Klein continued to design and create advertising for women's underwear, later adding hosiery and sleepwear lines.

In 1982 Puritan Fashions—nine percent owned by Klein and Schwartz—had sales of $245.6 million, of which licensed Calvin Klein products accounted for about 94 percent, earning $15.6 million in royalties for the firm. But Puritan's finances deteriorated as the designer-jeans boom ended and so, to protect their investment, in late 1983 Klein and Schwartz bought almost all the shares they did not already hold for $65.8 million in a leveraged buyout, with a Puritan subsidiary financing the purchase by taking out bank loans. The consolidated companies were renamed Calvin Klein Industries. After Puritan lost $11.3 million in 1984, Calvin Klein Industries placed $80 million in high-yield bonds (so-called junk bonds) through Michael Milken of Drexel Burnham Lambert Inc., mostly to keep Puritan afloat.

Registration statements filed with the Securities and Exchange Commission in connection with the junk bonds Calvin Klein issued afforded the public a rare look at the finances of the closely held enterprise. Calvin Klein Industries had 1984 revenue of $258.2 million and net income of $17.2 million, with Klein and Schwartz each collecting $12 million in salary, dividends, and other distributions. Puritan returned to profitability in 1985, earning $12.4 million. Nevertheless, Calvin Klein Industries had huge payments to make on its big junk-bond debt, and this financial problem seemed to be taking a toll on the designer. "Every color choice became life or death," he later told *Newsweek,* "because doing everything as well as possible meant survival." In 1988 he spent a month at the Hanley Hazelden Center in Minnesota to treat the cocaine addiction he had been combining with vodka and Valium.

When Minnetonka launched a new perfume called Obsession—at $170 an ounce—in 1985, Calvin Klein created a heavy-breathing print and TV campaign that cost more than $17 million in 10 months alone, followed by another $6 million campaign for Obsession for Men. One Weber print ad featured two nude men entwined around one female, another a naked couple with their groins pressed together, a third, three naked women, limbs entangled. A survey ranked the Obsession ads as the most memorable print advertisements of the year for four years in a row. TV commercials displayed a female model as the object of obsessive love by, in turn, a boy, a young man, an older man, and an older woman. Obsession quickly became the second-selling fragrance in the world. Combined with Obsession for Men and a line of body products, sales broke the $100 million mark by the end of 1987.

To complement Obsession, an oriental fragrance, in 1988 Calvin Klein introduced a floral scent, dubbed Eternity, which was marketed in perfume, cologne, cologne-spray, and body-cream forms. Newly married to his second wife, Klein devised a softer $18 million promotional campaign based on the themes of spirituality, love, marriage, and commitment. By the end of its first year on the market, Eternity had grossed $35 million. Minnetonka (14 percent owned by the Calvin Klein Sport division) was sold in 1989, with the Calvin Klein cosmetics/fragrance line fetching $376.2 million from Unilever Co.'s Chesebrough-Pond's subsidiary. Also in 1989, Calvin Klein opened its first full-line free-standing store, in a Dallas suburb. Products included Calvin Klein Sport lines for men and women, women's and men's underwear and sleepwear, hosiery, shoes, outerwear, accessories, cosmetics, and fragrances.

Rescue and Resurgence in the 1990s

In 1991 Calvin Klein introduced a new silk-scarf collection licensed to Ray Strauss Unlimited. Also that year, the company resumed menswear, licensing it to Gruppo GFT, an Italian manufacturer. Eyewear and sunglasses bearing the designer's name, previously made by Starline Optical Corp., were licensed to Marchon Eyewear. The big story that year, however, was the introduction of Escape, a $115-an-ounce "fruity, floral" scent. "After work you get away," Klein explained of the concept. "You escape, and you do it with style." Escape proved a hit and was followed in 1993 by Escape for Men.

Despite sizable royalty payments from these and other products, Calvin Klein was falling into financial trouble in the new decade. The company's revenue dropped 13 percent, to $197 million, in 1990 leading to a $4.3 million loss, the third time in five years the company had been in the red. The Puritan/Calvin Klein Sport division lost $14.2 million alone. Many younger women who could not afford the designer's flagship Collection line were not buying his clothes at all. A sexually suggestive, 116-page, insert for Calvin Klein Jeans in *Vanity Fair* in October 1991 failed to stimulate sales, prompting American retailers to contend that Klein had fallen out of touch with their customers.

Calvin Klein, Inc. was restored to financial health partly through the efforts of David Geffen, the entertainment tycoon who was a long-time friend of the designer. Geffen purchased $62 million of the company's debt securities in 1992 at a discount and was repaid in 1993, when the company took out a $58 million loan from Citibank. The firm then paid off the Citibank loan by licensing the underwear business to Warnaco Group Inc. for $64 million. Warnaco also won the license for a new venture, men's accessories.

Undeterred by suggestions that with the end of the "decadent" 1980s sex no longer sold, Klein introduced a new line of underwear, including $16 fly-button shorts, in 1992 with ads featuring Marky Mark (Mark Wahlberg), a muscular rap star. The campaign proved successful with both young men and women, grossing $85 million within 12 months. In 1994 a partnership later renamed Designer Holdings Ltd. bought Calvin Klein's fading jeans business for about $50 million. Calvin Klein introduced a khaki collection in 1996 and also licensed it to Designer Holdings, along with CK Calvin Klein Jeans Kids and CK Calvin Klein Kids Underwear, also introduced that year. Designer Holdings was acquired by Warnaco in 1997.

By 1995, when it opened a four-level, 22,000-square-foot minimalist-style emporium at Madison Avenue and East 60th Street in Manhattan, Calvin Klein had six stores in the United States. In addition, during 1993 and 1994, the company licensed Calvin Klein boutiques to operators in Barcelona, St. Moritz, Zurich, and Singapore and formed a partnership with four Japanese companies to create in-store shops there and to produce more licensed apparel. Four stores, in Manhattan, Dallas, Palm Beach and Costa Mesa, California, remained in 1997. The company also had an outlet store in Secaucus, New Jersey.

In 1994 Calvin Klein introduced cKone, a unisex fragrance that became another smash hit, grossing $60 million in its first three months. It was followed in 1996 by cKbe, promoted in a $20 million monochrome print and TV campaign directed by Richard Avedon that featured young models exposing lots of pierced and tattooed flesh. In a poll conducted by Louis Harris for *USA Today,* only four percent of the respondents expressed strong liking for the ads, while 57 percent said they disliked them. Advertising experts suggested that what was turning off the general public was precisely what was attracting the people who were buying the product, especially teenagers.

Advertisements for Calvin Klein jeans also continued to provoke controversy. Posters featuring the scrawny model Kate Moss were festooned with stickers reading "Feed this woman" by a Boston-area group called Boycott Anorexic Marketing. The company ignored the group but was unable to shrug off the reaction, especially from Christian groups, created by its summer 1995 campaign for CK Jeans, featuring models who appeared to be teenagers in states of undress that, according to one writer, "suggested auditions for low-budget porn movies." For the first time the company retreated, pulling the ads, which the designer maintained had been "misunderstood.... People didn't get that it's about modern young people who have an independent spirit and do the things they want to and can't be told or sold." A U.S. Justice Department investigation ended without charges after federal agents determined that no minors were used in the ads.

The controversial ads did not offend the market for whom the campaign was intended. CK Calvin Klein Jeans continued to be one of the strongest sellers among youths. "They want the Calvin Klein label," explained the executive editor of *Children's Business* in 1996. "Also at the point the children are over eight, they're pretty much deciding what they want to wear.... These lines ... have the cachet that comes from the adult market." Later that year a Calvin Klein underwear ad showing a 20-year-old male model in very tight gray briefs, posed with his legs wide apart, was dropped by the company's own licensee, Warnaco. Also in 1996, a group of parent-led anti-drug groups called for a boycott of Calvin Klein products to protest a new ad campaign that they said glamorized heroin addiction. The magazine and television advertisements in question featured gaunt, glassy-eyed models to promote cKbe.

In 1995 Calvin Klein launched, under license, a home collection composed of sheets, towels, and tableware. By 1997 only the designer's signature Calvin Klein women's collection of apparel and accessories and the CK Calvin Klein bridge collections of less-expensive women's and men's apparel (except in Europe, the Middle East, and Japan) were being manufactured by the company itself. Of the company's $260 million in sales in 1996, $141 million came from its in-house products and $119 million from royalties and designer income. Of worldwide retail sales of $4.4 billion, apparel accounted for $2.7 billion, fragrances for $1.5 billion, and other products for $200 million. Net profits were $41 million.

In 1997 Calvin Klein, Inc. was 43 percent owned by the designer and 43 percent owned by Schwartz, who was chairman and chief executive officer. The rest of the equity was held by family trusts. Gabriella Forte, a former Giorgio Armani executive, became the company's president in 1994 and was put in charge of day to day administration. In 1997 the company was divided into three parts: Collection, CK, and CK Jeans. In addition to apparel, each segment offered perfume, accessories, and items like housewares.

Further Reading

Agins, Teri, ''Shaken by a Series of Business Setbacks, Calvin Klein, Inc. Is Redesigning Itself,'' *Wall Street Journal,* March 21, 1994, pp. 1B, 4B.

Agins, Teri, and Jeffrey A. Trachtenberg, ''Calvin Klein Is Facing a Bid As Magic Touch Seems To Be Slipping,'' *Wall Street Journal,* November 22, 1991, pp. 1A, 9A.

Chambers, Andrea, ''Calvin Klein's Romantic Season,'' *New York Times Magazine,* January 30, 1977, pp. 46–48.

Cowley, Susan Cheever, ''Calvin Klein's Soft, Sexy Look,'' *Newsweek,* May 8, 1978, pp. 80–82, 84, 87.

Gaines, Steven, and Sharon Churcher, *Obsession: The Lives and Times of Calvin Klein.* New York: Birch Lane, 1994.

Gross, Michael, ''The Latest Calvin,'' *New York,* August 8, 1988, pp. 20–29.

Ingrassia, Michele, ''Calvin's World,'' *Newsweek,* September 11, 1995, pp. 60, 62–64, 66.

Kanner, Beatrice, ''The New Calvinism,'' *New York,* September 17, 1984, pp. 31, 35–36.

Kaplan, James, ''Triumph Calvinism,'' *New York,* September 18, 1995, pp. 46–52, 57, 101.

McQuade, Walter, ''The Bruising Businessman Behind Calvin Klein,'' *Fortune,* November 17, 1980, pp. 106–108, 112, 116, 118.

Ryan, Thomas J., ''Calvin Won't Follow Ralph onto the Big Board,'' *Daily News Record,* June 18, 1997, p. 17.

Steinhauer, Jennifer, ''Firm Grasp of Fashion: Tenacious President Transforms Calvin Klein,'' *New York Times,* November 7, 1997, pp. 1D, 6D.

—Robert Halasz

Carlson Companies, Inc.

Carlson Parkway
P.O. Box 59159
Minneapolis, Minnesota 55459
U.S.A.
(612) 540-5000
Fax: (612) 449-2219
Web site: http://www.carlson.com

Private Company
Incorporated: 1938 as the Gold Bond Stamp Company
Employees: 145,000
Sales: $15 billion (1996 est.)
SICs: 4724 Travel Agencies; 4725 Tour Operators; 5812 Eating Places; 6719 Offices of Holding Companies, Not Elsewhere Classified; 7011 Hotels & Motels; 7389 Business Services, Not Elsewhere Classified

Carlson Companies, Inc. comprises a rapidly growing Minneapolis-based worldwide corporation that encompasses three operating groups: Carlson Travel Group, concerned with worldwide travel management; Carlson Hospitality Worldwide, dealing in hotels and resorts (including Radisson, Regent, and Country Inns brands), restaurants (T.G.I. Friday's and Country Kitchen), and cruise ships (Radisson Seven Seas Cruises); and Carlson Marketing Group, the leading sales marketing agency in the United States. Carlson Travel Group includes the jointly owned (with Paris-based Wagonlit Travel, owned by Accor Group) Carlson Wagonlit Travel, the second-largest travel management network in the world, after American Express. These three groups operate in conjunction with one another to form one of the world's largest and most profitable private companies, which is poised to become a market leader in the travel, hospitality, and marketing services industry.

Founded on Trading Stamps

The story of Carlson Companies begins with founder, chairman, chief executive officer, and sole owner, Curtis L. Carlson. Carlson was born in Minneapolis, Minnesota, in 1914, the son of a Swedish immigrant and a first-generation American. Early on he showed entrepreneurial talent when he farmed out paper routes to his younger brothers, realizing a small profit on their labor. Upon graduation from the University of Minnesota, Carlson went to work for Procter & Gamble Company selling soap, but, after a year, he decided to go into business for himself.

With $55 of borrowed capital, the 23-year-old Carlson registered the Gold Bond Stamp Company with the Clerk of District Court in Minneapolis on June 8, 1938, in the midst of the Great Depression. Carlson had noticed that the Leader, a downtown Minneapolis department store, gave away coupons to its customers with each purchase that could be saved up and redeemed for cash or prizes. The point of the coupons was to encourage customer loyalty and spur sales. Carlson reasoned that what worked well for department stores would also work well for grocery stores. He was familiar with both forms of retailing from his work at Procter & Gamble and from his childhood, when his father had worked in the food business.

Carlson set up a mail drop, rented desk space in a downtown Minneapolis building, and paid a secretary in a nearby office $5 a month to answer the phone. Hanging onto his regular job for four additional months, he spent his evenings and weekends selling reluctant small grocers on his new trading stamp idea. Five months after he quit his steady job, Carlson made his first sale, in March 1939, to a small grocer in south Minneapolis. The store owner purchased $14.50 worth of Gold Bond stamps to dispense, which customers would then present to Carlson for redemption. Carlson guaranteed that his client would have the exclusive right within a 25-block area to give out Gold Bond trading stamps. To call attention to the sales incentive, Carlson plastered the store with posters and banners and distributed balloons and refreshments. The idea was a success and, by the end of the year, Carlson had added 39 more grocery stores to his list of clients.

With this progress, Carlson moved his growing firm to an office in south Minneapolis—in between a Chinese restaurant and a pinball machine repair shop—and took on an additional employee to handle the administrative side of things while he sold the Gold Bond program to grocers. In addition, he roped his wife into the business, dressing her up in a golden majorette's costume with a feathered hat and positioning her at a card table inside stores during their gala inaugurations of the Gold Bond program. Mrs. Carlson's job was to explain to homemakers how to save the stamps and redeem them for cash.

In 1940, strapped for cash, Carlson sold six $100 shares in his enterprise to friends but planned to buy them back when he became more solvent, since he was intent on retaining control of the company himself. By 1941, his client list had grown to include 200 merchants in the Minnesota area. With the entry of the United States into World War II at the end of that year, however, the fortunes of the Gold Bond Stamp Company went into a dive: wartime shortages eliminated the need for merchants to provide incentives to their customers. When ration books replaced trading stamp books in shoppers' hands, Carlson's company lost two-thirds of its business within three months. Carlson reduced the company to a skeleton operation when his two employees entered the military, and he began moonlighting as a manager in his father-in-law's children's clothing store in downtown Minneapolis to make ends meet for the duration of the war.

Rapid Expansion Followed World War II

In 1944, when Carlson was called up to join the war effort, he sold a half interest in the company to Truman Johnson, who had also been employed by Procter & Gamble, and left the business in his hands. At the war's end, the small firm was in dire need of rejuvenation. In 1946 Carlson vowed to expand the company into seven states within the next five years. Toward this end, he hired salesmen to work new territories, including next-door Wisconsin, and, farther afield, Texas, Indiana, and Oregon. In addition, the trading stamp concept was extended to outlets other than grocery stores. Accordingly, the Gold Bond stamp program was sold to gas stations, dry cleaners, and movie theaters. In a more imaginative vein, feed and grain millers, a turkey hatchery, and even undertakers signed on, as the men from Gold Bond urged merchants to invest two percent of their gross receipts in the incentive program, promising a 20 percent rise in sales.

By the early 1950s, Gold Bond stamps were offered in 11 Midwestern states. In 1953 Carlson scored a major coup, leaving behind forever the days of individual sales to "mom and pop"-type stores, when the largest grocery chain in the nation, Super Valu Stores, Inc., based in Minneapolis, began offering Gold Bond trading stamps. In a switch to accommodate the wishes of the chain store, the stamps were now redeemed for prizes, rather than cash, a much more complicated undertaking. Gold Bond was forced to open warehouses, maintain inventory, set up redemption centers, and hire people to staff them, a process by no means free of errors. Since Carlson had purchased stock in Super Valu when it implemented his program, he reaped a reward from the soaring value of the grocery store's stock, as well as from his own business, which notched $2.4 million in sales that year.

Through the connection with Super Valu, Gold Bond stamps gained a higher national public profile. When Kroger Company, a competing Midwest grocery store chain, approached the company about implementing a stamp program, Carlson inaugurated a second trading stamp, called Top Value Stamp Co., to avoid competition with the Super Valu line. Doubling the size of his company's workforce, Carlson expanded the Top Value line to grocery chains in other areas of the country, including the Northeast, Oklahoma, and Nebraska.

In 1957 Kroger, the company's original Top Value client, bought the Top Value portion of Carlson's business for $1 million. With this money, Carlson was able to buy out his more cautious partner, Truman Johnson, who had held a half-interest in Gold Bond since the war years. Carlson regained full control of the company in 1958.

Rapid expansion of the company continued throughout the late 1950s. Safeway Stores Incorporated, another large chain of grocery stores in the West and Southwest, was added to the fold, and the company also entered the international arena, inaugurating trading stamp operations in Canada, the Caribbean, Japan, and other countries. By the 1960s, the trading stamp business had become ubiquitous, and Gold Bond was one of the largest companies in the field. All but one of the top 20 American grocery store chains offered the trading stamps, and half of all gas stations provided them as well.

Began to Diversify in the 1960s

Nevertheless, the tide of consumer sentiment had begun to turn against the trading stamp industry. Trading stamps were blamed for inflated prices in stores: shoppers began to demand lower prices, not vouchers towards free prizes. Gold Bond lost Safeway's business, and it became clear that Gold Bond would have to diversify to other fields if it hoped to maintain its steady growth.

Carlson began diversification by purchasing real estate, buying large parcels of land in Minnetonka, a western suburb of Minneapolis, for future development. In addition, he purchased the Radisson Hotel, a high-profile property in downtown Minneapolis, in 1962, marking his company's entry into the hospitality industry. Both the hotel and the real estate transactions were intended to act as tax shelters for Gold Bond's earnings, enabling the company to retain as much of its profits as possible, so that it could use them to fuel further growth.

This growth took the company in a number of different directions. Throughout the 1960s, as the popularity of the trading stamp business continued to decline, Carlson's diversification and acquisition strategy took on more importance. As sole owner of Gold Bond, Carlson was able to manage his assets with virtually no outside surveillance or interference. Willing to take risks and amass debt, he sought to acquire businesses that were already in solid financial shape but had the potential to benefit from his company's proven sales savvy. The key elements of Carlson's philosophy of acquisition, then, were the capacity for growth and the possibility of replication. By 1973, the name of the Gold Bond Stamp Company had been changed to Carlson Companies, Inc., to better reflect the firm's expansion into new markets and businesses.

Companies purchased by Carlson included the Ardan Catalogue showrooms, a business related to the premium showrooms earlier opened by Gold Bond, and a number of properties that tied into the hotel business in some way, such as a wholesale food distributor called the May Company and the creation of a chain of restaurants and pubs known as the Haberdashery.

In addition, the company had extended its Radisson Hotel franchise, opening additional facilities, first in Minnesota, and then in other areas of the United States.

Farther afield, Carlson invested in a $7 million hardboard plant in northwestern Wisconsin. Failed projects included a chain of grocery stores called Piggly Wiggly, an investment in Caribbean shrimp boats, and a money-losing meatpacking plant. All were eventually shed by the growing company.

Although the Carlson Companies underwent a slight recession in 1975, one acquisition made during that year proved to be a consistent money-earner. T.G.I. Friday's (from the expression "Thank God It's Friday")—a chain of 11 restaurant-bars based in Dallas and featuring eclectic decor and an airy, multiple-floor arrangement—grew to encompass 73 branches within eight years. T.G.I. Friday's was soon joined by another restaurant chain, Country Kitchen International, which catered to the family market, with down-home decor and low-priced meals.

In 1978 Carlson began the acquisition of WaSko Gold Products, a New York City-based jewelry manufacturer, for about $18.2 million. This company fit in well with Carlson's Ardan company, which specialized in jewelry sales. By this time, Carlson had added several other retail businesses, including Naum Brothers, a catalog showroom based in Rochester, New York; the Indian Wells Oil Company, E. Weisman, dealing in tobacco and candy sales; Jason Empire, Inc., an importer of binoculars and telescopes; and the Premium Corporation, which provided sales incentive programs similar to those offered by the Gold Bond Stamp business.

After gaining experience in the hotel industry through the ownership of the Radisson Hotel chain, Carlson Companies ventured into the travel agency business in 1979. The addition of the well-known Ask Mr. Foster Agency (later known as Carlson Travel Network and still later as Carlson Leisure Group), founded in 1888 in St. Augustine, Florida, opened the door to the travel services industry, which Carlson would eventually grow to dominate.

In 1980 Carlson Companies announced plans for the real estate development west of Minneapolis that its founder had acquired in the late 1950s and 1960s as a tax shelter. The company proposed a 307-acre development, to be anchored by a new corporate headquarters building. The project would include businesses, restaurants, and a hotel, and was slated to cost $300 million and be called Carlson Center. Carlson Companies continued to manage its acquisitions, purchasing shares in a company called Modern Merchandising and selling off its groceries wholesaler, May Company, to another food company. The following year, Carlson added another company to its collection of marketing concerns, purchasing the E. F. MacDonald Company, a sales incentive and motivation business in Dayton, Ohio, and merging the company with its other holdings in this area.

By 1982 Carlson's holdings had grown to encompass 75 different companies with combined sales of $2.1 billion. Despite its move into a much broader arena of business, the conglomerate had managed to maintain a 33 percent compounded annual rate of growth for the 44th consecutive year. One of its holdings, Curtis Homes, offered a new approach to success in the housing construction market. Curtis Homes provided the basic outer shell of a house with the wiring and roof, leaving all inside finishing—floors, paneling, and so forth—to the buyer of the house. The end result was a low-priced home for the buyer and big business for the company. As a result, Curtis Homes was able to turn a profit even when housing sales overall were in a slump. Carlson later sold this operation to a competitor in this field in order to concentrate on businesses with which he was more familiar.

Along with the acquisition of new companies, Carlson grew by fostering development within the properties it already owned. In the restaurant business, that meant a proliferation of outlets within each franchise. The Country Kitchen restaurant chain, for instance, included 285 restaurants by the early 1980s, most of which were in small towns across North America. T.G.I. Friday's, with the highest sales per unit ($3.45 million average per store) of any American restaurant chain (and a favorite of founder Curt Carlson), opened 17 new locations in one year alone. By 1992 Friday's had over 200 restaurants throughout the world, many of which were franchised. The Radisson Hotel chain had increased to two dozen sites, including one near the pyramids in Egypt. Radisson Hotels International, as it became known (it was later called Radisson Hotels Worldwide), together with other Carlson Hospitality hotels, inns, and resorts, by the mid-1990s numbered over 345 properties throughout the world.

Despite this progress, Carlson found its empire suffering from a recession in the early 1980s. In June 1983, *Business Week* reported several problems for Carlson. Although Country Kitchens had opened a large number of restaurants, the chain was plagued by poor management and bad relations with its franchise owners; it failed to meet a four-year sales goal by a large margin, fulfilling just over one-quarter of its targeted growth. Ardan, the catalogue showroom, suffered from overexpansion, and its sales had not improved in several years. Radisson, the flagship hotel chain, seemed stalled in the doldrums of a highly competitive industry, apparently blocked from major advances. Business incentive programs and travel agency operations, too, had suffered in the recession.

Carlson Companies owed its historically steady and successful expansion over the course of decades to the tight control of its autocratic founder and sole owner, Curt Carlson. As Carlson neared the age of 80, however, it became clear that he would have to transfer some of his power to a capable successor. On January 1, 1983, Carlson appointed his son-in-law, Edwin C. (Skip) Gage III, to be executive vice-president. Gage had previously been the president of the Carlson Marketing Group, which ran the company's businesses associated with incentives and promotions; he had been groomed for many years to follow carefully in Carlson's footsteps. Gage told *Business Week* that he planned to "concentrate on doing very well the things we already do."

Began to Focus on Hospitality, Travel, and Marketing in the Mid-1980s

In the mid-1980s, Carlson Companies began to evolve from a conglomerate with somewhat disparate holdings to a more tightly organized company, focused on the hospitality, travel, and marketing businesses and the strengthening of the synergistic ties between the three groups. In addition, the company began to shift its emphasis from owning hotels and travel agencies to franchising them. This enabled Carlson to expand rapidly without large outlays of capital in a time when cash was scarce. It also enabled the company to realize millions in fees and royalties from its franchisees.

In 1986 Carlson moved to cash in on its relationship with nearly 500 different travel agencies and raise the number of bookings for its 22 hotels. Also in that year, the company announced the formation of a new chain of hotels, called Country Inns by Carlson, to serve a more middle-class segment of the market than the full-service, upscale Radisson line. Country Inns by Carlson were decorated with homey touches, including fireplaces in the lobbies and down-filled quilts on the beds.

By the following year, under the leadership of Juergen Bartels, a German-born former president of the Ramada Inn chain, Carlson's hotel holdings ranked near the top 10 in the nation in number of rooms. Through the careful selection of franchise holders and thorough staff training, the company sought to upgrade its properties and began to tailor its operations to fit the needs of the growing population of women business travelers. Building on these moves, Carlson set a new goal of becoming the preeminent travel company in the world. Towards this end, the company announced in the following year that it would nearly triple the number of hotels it owned, from 200 to 550, within the next few years.

In 1988 Carlson Companies underwent a corporate reorganization that resulted in the formation of Carlson Holdings, Inc., a parent company governance for all the properties of the Carlson family. This company consists of three divisions: one to manage the family's investments, one to handle commercial real estate scattered throughout North America, and the third made up of Carlson Companies. The Companies moved into a new corporate headquarters in 1989, two gleaming towers of glass on the Carlson land west of Minneapolis in the suburb of Minnetonka. Shortly thereafter, as if to symbolize that a new era had begun with the company's move into new quarters, Curt Carlson staged a ceremony in the rotunda of the new building, turning over the reins of the company to his son-in-law Skip Gage, who took over as chief executive officer. Although a thousand employees turned out to applaud their new leader, his tenure was brief.

Under Gage's command, the company announced more ambitious plans for expansion and proceeded to extend its international holdings, purchasing A. T. Mays, a British travel agency, and changing the name of Ask Mr. Foster to Carlson Travel Network to reflect a more global outlook. Amid talk of operations in eight new countries and a goal of 3,000 worldwide travel agencies, economic reality began to intrude. In late 1990, the Carlson Travel Network was forced to put some home office employees on a shortened work week to avoid layoffs, as its business was damaged by tension over the impending Persian Gulf War, which battered the travel industry.

In 1991 the recession continued, and profits for Carlson Companies dipped. Despite the fact that he had undergone quadruple bypass heart surgery early in the year, Curt Carlson dismissed Gage, still new in his job, in November 1991 and reassumed control of the company. At the same time, Carlson promoted his eldest daughter Marilyn to vice-chairman, apparently grooming her to follow him (Gage was married to Carlson's younger daughter Barbara). Despite the decline in profits, Carlson returned to oversee a company with a small debt load, growing in its targeted industries at a furious rate. By 1992 Carlson was adding a travel agency a day to the more than 2,000 it already owned, and a new hotel every 10 days. It planned to double the number of T.G.I. Friday's restaurants it ran to 400 within four years. The company had operations in 38 countries, and it took to the high seas as well in May 1992, when it inaugurated service on a futuristic-looking cruise ship, the *Radisson Diamond,* through its newly formed Radisson Seven Seas Cruises luxury cruise line.

Hospitality and Travel Groups Expanded in the Mid-1990s

By the mid-1990s, Carlson Marketing Group was struggling. At that time, the group specialized in direct marketing; performance improvement programs such as incentive programs that reward top salespeople; loyalty marketing such as frequent-flyer programs; and event and sports management. But this successor to the original trading stamp business generated only five percent of the revenue for Carlson Companies. The travel business generated 65 percent, while the hospitality operations contributed 30 percent. *Forbes* reported in October 1993 that the success of the travel and hospitality groups was at least partly attributable to Curtis Carlson allowing the heads of these groups considerable autonomy.

As head of the newly renamed Carlson Hospitality Worldwide, Bartels continued to achieve impressive, profitable growth with his consistent reliance on franchising; this trend continued under John A. Norlander, a 21-year veteran of Radisson and Carlson who took over for the departing Bartels in 1995. Friday's Hospitality Worldwide Inc., for example, had grown to more than 460 restaurants in 350 cities and 40 countries by mid-1997 and included not only the T.G.I. Friday's chain but also such spinoffs as Friday's Front Row Sports Grill and Friday's American Bar and such new concepts as Italianni's. By January 1998, Radisson Seven Seas Cruises boasted of six luxury liners with a total capacity of 1,202 berths, making it the fourth-largest luxury cruise line in the world. In late 1996, Carlson formed a partnership with Four Seasons Hotels Inc. to expand the Four Seasons' Regent luxury-hotel chain. Regent had nine hotels located primarily in Asian cities; through the partnership, Carlson would concentrate on building new Regent hotels in North America and Europe.

Carlson Travel Group, meanwhile, was headed by longtime Carlson executive Travis Tanner. The 1990s were difficult ones for travel agencies and mergers became commonplace as competition heated up. Tanner engineered a merger for Carlson as well, with Carlson Travel Network linking with Paris-based Wagonlit Travel to form Carlson Wagonlit Travel (CWT) in 1994. CWT was 50–50 owned by Carlson Companies and Accor Group, a France-based company with additional interests in hotels and car rental. CWT immediately became the second-largest travel agency in the world, trailing only American Express, with more than 4,000 offices in more than 141 countries and annual sales in excess of $9.5 billion. After essentially operating as one agency for a couple of years, Carlson Travel and Wagonlit were formerly merged in early 1997, with headquarters in Miami, Tanner acting as chairman, and Herve Gourio, who had headed Wagonlit, as cochairman. Carlson Companies, meanwhile, created Carlson Leisure Group (CLG) to act as the U.S. licensee of the Carlson Wagonlit Travel brand name for leisure travel, as well as to oversee non-Carlson Wagonlit travel operations—for example the 1997-launched Carlson Vacations, a leisure travel agency based in Russia. Also in 1997, CLG acquired Travel Agents International, a prominent U.S. leisure travel agency which made CLG the largest franchise travel agency company in North America, with more than 1,300 locations. And in mid-1997 CLG expanded in the United Kingdom with the purchase of Inspirations PLC and its 97-unit, Glasgow, Scotland-headquartered A.T. Mays travel agency, the fourth-largest such agency in the United Kingdom.

As the 21st century approached, Carlson Companies boasted an impressive and growing array of travel and hospitality operations, but the succession issue hung over the company like a dark cloud. Although it appeared Marilyn Carlson was slated to succeed the company founder, whether she would survive her father's rigorous scrutiny remained to be seen. Interestingly, Marilyn Carlson and Barbara Gage would each inherit half of the company in the event of their father's death, which could perhaps bring Skip Gage back into the leadership picture. And, oddly enough, in 1997 Curtis Carlson himself appeared to be thinking as much of the company's past as of its future, as he personally launched a new Carlson Companies group called Gold Points Group, which was touted as the Gold Bond trading stamp program for the electronic age, and which could perhaps be said to bring the company full circle.

Principal Operating Units

Carlson Hospitality Worldwide; Carlson Leisure Group; Carlson Marketing Group; Carlson Wagonlit Travel; Gold Points Group.

Further Reading

Bain, Laurie, "Carlson Plays to Win," *Restaurant Business*, June 10, 1987, p. 161.

Barnfather, Maurice, "Capital Formation," *Forbes*, March 29, 1982, p. 94.

Button, Graham, "Still Hungry at 75," *Forbes*, December 11, 1989, p. 302.

"Carlson Companies: Company Profile," *Nation's Restaurant News*, March 29, 1993.

Carlson, Curtis L., *Good as Gold: The Story of the Carlson Companies*, Minneapolis: Carlson Companies, Inc., 1994, 238 p.

"Curt Carlson: Will a One-Man Conglomerate Make Room at the Top?," *Business Week*, June 13, 1983.

Ellis, James E., "Curt Carlson Keeps It All in the Family," *Business Week*, September 30, 1991.

Ferguson, Tim W., "In Land of Lakes, He Cares Not if Economic Waters Are Rising," *Wall Street Journal*, October 23, 1990.

Fredericks, Alan, and Nadine Godwin, "Carlson Sets $4 Billion Sales Goal for Empire of Travel Companies," *Travel Weekly*, October 8, 1997, p. 1.

Kho, Nguyen, "Life with Father," *Town & Country*, August 1992.

"Looking at the World Through Gold Glasses," *Forbes*, March 15, 1975.

McDowell, Edwin, "Mellowed by Age, But Still a Tough Boss," *New York Times*, April 5, 1992.

Papa, Mary Bader, "A Son Named Marilyn," *Corporate Report-Minnesota*, March 1990, p. 27.

Pine, Carol, and Susan Mundale, *Self-Made: The Stories of 12 Minnesota Entrepreneurs*, Minneapolis: Dorn Books.

Quintanilla, Carl, "Carlson Pushes Growth Despite Woes in Travel Industry," *Wall Street Journal*, March 9, 1995, p. B4.

Rowe, Megan, "Carlson's Culture," *Lodging Hospitality*, October 1996, pp. 26–28.

Stern, William, "Hanging On," *Forbes*, October 25, 1993, pp. 194, 198.

Walker, Angela, "Global Goals Power Carlson Wagonlit," *Hotel & Motel Management*, April 25, 1994, p. 6.

White, Willmon L., *The Ultra Entrepreneur: Carl Carlson*, Phoenix: Gullers Pictorial, [1988], 139 p.

Wieffering, Eric J., "Carlson Companies: Smaller than You Thought, Revisited," *Corporate Report-Minnesota*, May 1993, p. 44.

—Elizabeth Rourke
—updated by David E. Salamie

Cedar Fair, L.P.

One Causeway Drive
Sandusky, Ohio 44870
U.S.A.
(419) 627-2233
Fax: (419)627-2260
Web site: http://www.cedarfair.com

Public Limited Partnership
Incorporated: 1987
Employees: 600
Sales: $250.5 million (1996)
Stock Exchanges: New York
SICs: 7996 Amusement Parks; 4785 Inspection & Fixed Facilities; 7011 Hotels & Motels; 4493 Marinas

Cedar Fair, L.P. is the parent company to a half-dozen of America's oldest and largest amusement parks. Cedar Point, the company's crown jewel, is the biggest seasonal amusement park in North America, attracting over three million visitors each summer. It's been acclaimed as both ''King of Amusement Parks'' and ''Queen of American Watering Places.'' In the fall of 1997, the parent company announced its plans to acquire its first year-round facility, California's Knott's Berry Farm. The company also operates Minnesota's Valleyfair, Pennsylvania's Wildwater Kingdom and Dorney Park, and twin attractions Oceans of Fun and Worlds of Fun in Missouri. With the addition of Knott's, the group expected to draw a combined total of nearly 10 million guests in 1998.

In contrast with such theme parks as Disney's Florida and California extravaganzas, Cedar Fair facilities focus on amusement. Flagship Cedar Point prides itself on having more thrill rides than any other park in the world. Its ''scream machine'' heritage stretches from 1892, when the 25-foot-high Switchback Railway thrilled riders with its 10 mph speeds, to the late 1990s, when a collection of a dozen roller coasters sent riders—in varying positions from sitting to standing—hurtling down 200-foot drops and through stomach-churning loops at over 70 mph. In 1996, Cedar Point earned its fifth consecutive designation as the world's ''Best Traditional Amusement Park'' from trade paper *Inside Track.*

19th-Century Origins

Cedar Fair's roots reach back to the late 1860s, when its founding park was just a sandy, cedar-bowered peninsula jutting out from the southern shore of Lake Erie. The impetus behind the endeavor has been traced to an 1867 editorial in the *Sandusky Register,* which suggested that ''Somebody should erect a bathing house on the lake side of Cedar Point, about a quarter of a mile from the lighthouse,'' noting that ''There is no finer place for bathing in the world.'' Though that last line may have been colored by a bit of provincial boosterism, there was enough truth in the statement to convince local businessman Louis Zistel to put up more than a dozen bath houses along the beach. He made money by renting bathing suits for 10 cents a day.

By 1870, Zistel had generated enough cash to finance the construction of a beer garden complete with a dance floor and a playground. The park's first ride, a water trapeze that swung thrill-seekers out over the lake, was launched in 1880. Over the course of the next decade, Cedar Point added water slides, a water toboggan, and a motorized ''sea swing.'' The park capped the 1880s with the construction of a Grand Pavilion, which featured a bar, dining rooms, an auditorium, and an opera house.

At some point during this period, ownership of the property transferred to a group of four local investors. In 1892 they built Cedar Point's first roller coaster, the Switchback Railway. Featuring a 25-foot drop, the lakeside ride reached top speeds of 10 miles per hour. Within five years, however, the group had exhausted its financial resources such that the park faced closure.

The Boeckling Era, 1897–1931

That's when wealthy Indianan George A. Boeckling came on the scene. Backed by a real estate fortune and a flair for showmanship, Boeckling ushered Cedar Point into an era of national prominence. Amenities and amusements were added rapidly after the turn of the century. The park's first modest overnight accommodation, the 20-room Bay Shore Hotel, was so successful that Boeckling built the sumptuously-appointed,

Company Perspectives:

Cedar Point's sole business is to entertain the public and cater to the comfort, health and happiness of the people.

600-room Hotel Breakers as well as a two-story "Coliseum" entertainment center in 1905. Three new roller coasters replaced the Switchback Railway during these hectic years: The Racer (1902), Dip the Dips (1908), and Leap the Dips (1912). Boeckling launched an electrified midway, featuring merry-go-round, skating rink, fun house, souvenir shops, live entertainment, and a circle swing—all illuminated by thousands of lights for nighttime fun—for the 1906 season.

The resort lured the rich and famous as well as the local yokels at the rate of 10,000 per day during the summer season. Boeckling's better-known guests included President William Taft, sharpshooter Annie Oakley, composer John Philip Sousa, and opera star Enrico Caruso. It was even said that Knute Rockne and Gus Dorais honed football's forward pass while working as lifeguards on the beaches of Cedar Point.

Fueled by this steady stream of nationally known celebrities and entertainment upgrades, the park continued to thrive under Boeckling's care, even after the Great Depression cast a pall over the national economy. The impresario slashed admission prices and booked big bands to keep his park afloat during the crisis, but when Boeckling died in 1931, Cedar Point—like many other amusement parks around the country—went into a long and deep decline. Without Boeckling's deep pockets and far-reaching imagination, the park was limited to hosting musical performances throughout the 1930s, 1940s, and into the 1950s.

Post-World War II Revival

By the mid-1950s, Cedar Point only had one working roller-coaster, and at least two investors thought it had more potential as a construction site than as an amusement park. The lakeside residential development envisioned by Toledo bond dealer George A. Roose and Cleveland investment banker Emile Legros stirred up statewide objections, including an alternative proposal to turn the 400-acre plot into a state park. The public backlash against this plan—not to mention a trip to Disneyland, which had just opened in 1955—convinced Roose and Legros to preserve the property as an amusement park and maintain the historic public beach. In 1957, they purchased a controlling interest in Cedar Point for $313,000.

Though the new owners had no experience in amusement park management, they quickly grasped one of the keys to success in their seasonal business: new attractions. Over the next eight years they invested $18 million in a parkwide overhaul. Improvements in access included the Cedar Point Causeway and a marina. The new owners built the Blue Streak roller coaster in 1964, inaugurated Frontiertown (the park's main themed area) and live stage shows in 1968, and added the Cedar Creek Mine Ride in 1969. The refurbishment increased admissions dramatically, crossing the 1 million mark in 1960 and exceeding 2 million five years later. Revenues grew from $3.5 million in 1961 to $4.4 million in 1965.

1970s Bring Increased Competition, Costs, and Profits

Cedar Point faced mounting competition for the amusement park dollar in the 1970s, when several major media companies (including Warner Communications, MCA, and Twentieth Century-Fox) entered the industry. The number of large-scale parks nationwide more than doubled from seven in 1970 to 18 by 1977. In order to raise the funds necessary to keep their park competitive, Roose and Legros reduced their combined stake in Cedar Point Inc. from about 85 percent to less than 10 percent through public and private stock placements. In 1975 Robert Munger, who had accumulated almost 10 percent of the company's equity over his 15-year tenure on its board of directors, assumed the role of president and CEO.

In order to attract new riders and retain its old ones, Cedar Point inaugurated what would become annual multimillion-dollar investment programs. A parkwide entrance fee was established in 1970, helping to finance a decade of new attractions. The company added a 15-story giant ferris wheel, the Jumbo Jet coaster, and the Frontier Carousel in 1972, and the IMAX large-scale cinema in 1975. But it was the latter years of the 1970s that would re-establish Cedar Point's reputation as the roller coaster capital of the world. The park launched the Corkscrew, the world's first triple-looping roller coaster, in 1976 and fired a salvo in the ongoing battle for "scream machine" dominance with the 1978 inauguration of the twin-tracked Gemini, the tallest, fastest coaster of its time. By the end of the decade, Cedar Point had the highest ride capacity of any amusement park in the country: 71,500 people per hour. Animal attractions like Jungle Larry's African Safari and the Oceana marine life complex were also brought on board.

Seasonal attendance crossed the 3 million mark in 1975 and rose another 15 percent on the launch of the Corkscrew the following year. Revenues multiplied from $4.4 million in 1965 to over $35 million in 1975. After several lean years of heavy reinvestments, Cedar Point began chalking up big profits, averaging a 28 percent return on equity from 1974 to 1979. The park's bulging coffers attracted takeover offers from Taft Broadcasting Co. (owner of Cincinnati's Kings Island amusement park), entertainment giant MCA Inc., Marriott Corp., and even Quaker Oats. But instead of being acquired, Cedar Point ended up taking over Valleyfair, a small Minnesota park, in 1978.

Limited Partnership Formed in 1980s

In 1982, management took the two parks private as Cedar Fair Partnership through a $142 million leveraged buyout financed in part by investment bank Lazard Freres and Britain's Pearson, plc. The company returned to public ownership as a master limited partnership in 1987, with units (shares) traded on the New York Stock Exchange under the symbol FUN. The new owners promoted Richard ("Dick") Kinzel, a 15-year veteran of the operation, from general manager of Valleyfair to president of Cedar Fair.

In the meantime, Cedar Point made good on its quest for new thrills, adding the Demon Drop, a ride that gave the sensation of free-falling 10 stories, in 1983; flume ride Thunder Canyon in 1986; the Iron Dragon suspended coaster in 1987; and the record-breaking Magnum SL-200, an $8 million coaster introduced in 1989 that dropped passengers more than 200 feet and reached a top speed of 72 mph. The facility reached back to its watery roots in 1988, when it launched Soak City water park. Though it was clearly second-fiddle to Cedar Point, Valleyfair was also growing during this period, adding a waterslide in 1982 and crossing the one million attendance mark in 1987.

By the end of the decade, Kinzel had boosted Cedar Fair's profit margins to 29 percent, more than double industry leader Disney's profitability.

Focus on Families in 1990s

Recalling its turn-of-the-century heyday as a nationally known family resort destination, Cedar Point started to beef up its overnight accommodations. The park opened the 96-unit Sandcastle Suites Hotel in 1990 and added a go-kart track, championship miniature golf course, and the family-oriented Berenstain Bear Country in 1992. A $4.3 million investment into Soak City more than doubled the waterpark, adding a 500,000 gallon wave pool, new water slides, and a special adults-only area featuring a swim-up bar.

But Cedar Point management did not forget its core clientele of thrill-seekers, adding the "tallest, steepest, fastest" rides of their kind throughout the 1990s. The park debuted the Mean Streak wooden coaster in 1991, the Snake River Falls flume ride in 1993, the Raptor inverted roller coaster in 1994, and the $12 million Mantis stand-up coaster in 1996. Guests at Cedar Fair's other parks found new thrills as well. The company introduced both Wild Thing, Valleyfair's first "megacoaster," and Worlds of Fun's Detonator, a ride that rocketed passengers 200 feet straight up, in 1996. That same year Cedar Fair installed RipCord rides, which mimicked bungee jumping and parachuting, at Cedar Point, Valleyfair, and Worlds of Fun.

Cedar Fair augmented its corporate holdings during this period as well, acquiring sister parks Wildwater Kingdom and Dorney Park, both of Pennsylvania, for an estimated $48 million in cash and Cedar Fair equity in 1992. Three years later, Cedar Fair added another pair of parks, Worlds of Fun and Oceans of Fun, both located near Kansas City, Missouri. The combination of organic growth and acquisitions more than doubled Cedar Fair's revenues from $119 million in 1990 to over $250 million by 1996, and pushed seasonal attendance over the 6 million mark. By this time, the parent company was netting a whopping $74.2 million on sales.

Cedar Fair announced its biggest acquisition to date, California's Knott's Berry Farm, in October 1997. Founded in the 1920s as a chicken restaurant, the heretofore family-owned Knott's is recognized as America's oldest theme (not amusement) park. It offered Cedar Fair a source of year-round income, since its locations in California and inside Minnesota's Mall of America were not limited to the three-month season of the company's other Midwestern properties, thereby mitigating the effect of bad weather on those parks. It also promised to add $120 million in annual revenues and 3.5 million guests to Cedar Fair's annual tally.

Principal Subsidiaries

Cedar Point Bridge Company; Cedar Point of Michigan, Inc.; Cedar Point Transportation Company.

Further Reading

Baumeister, Rita, *G.A. Boeckling,* Sandusky, Ohio: Acme Printing Co., [1982?].

Everett, Glenn D., *Fun at the Old Cedar Point,* Rutland, VT: Academy Books, 1989.

Francis, David W., *Cedar Point: The Queen of American Watering Places,* Fairview Park, Ohio: Amusement Park Books, 1995.

Gubernick, Lisa, " 'Terror with a Smile,' " *Forbes,* September 2, 1991, pp. 64–65.

Jaffee, Thomas, "Roller-Coaster Stock for a Roller-Coaster Market," *Forbes,* October 15, 1990, p. 236.

——, "Splash!" *Forbes,* August 31, 1992, p. 232.

"Midwest Resort Revives," *Business Week,* September 23, 1961, pp. 104–106.

O'Brien, Tim, " 'Biggest Break of Career' Shaped Management Philosophy of Cedar Point's Kinzel," *Amusement Business,* September 14, 1992, pp. 3–4.

——, "Cedar Fair Buys Worlds of Fun, Oceans of Fun," *Amusement Business,* June 26, 1995, pp. 1–2.

——, "Cedar Point Expanding Soak City to Boost Its Resort/Vacation Image," *Amusement Business,* August 19, 1996, pp. 25–26.

——, "Cedar Point, The Resort, Is World-Class Act," *Amusement Business,* August 7, 1995, p. 22.

——, "The King of the Coaster Parks Celebrates 125 Years of Thrills," *Amusement Business,* August 7, 1995, pp. 19–21.

——, "Local Market Has Long Reach," *Amusement Business,* August 7, 1995, p. 25.

Rohman, Laura, "The Waiting Game," *Forbes, June 21, 1982, pp. 78–79.*

Sloan, Allan, "A Visit to Munger World," *Forbes,* July 7, 1980, pp. 54, 56.

Slovak, Julianne, "Cedar Fair LP," *Fortune,* November 7, 1988, p. 64.

"Summer Resort Pays Off a Profit for All Seasons," *Business Week,* September 18, 1965, pp. 61–62, 67.

Uttal, Bro, "The Ride Is Getting Scarier for 'Theme Park' Owners," *Fortune,* December 1977, pp. 167–184.

Vanac, Mary, "Theme Park Owner Cedar Fair L.P. to Buy Knott's Berry Farm in California," *Akron Beacon Journal,* October 22, 1997, n.p.

"Why Taft Buys Amusement Parks," *Business Week,* November 25, 1972, p. 29.

—April Dougal Gasbarre

Celebrity, Inc.

4520 Old Troup Road
Tyler, Texas 75705
U.S.A.
(903) 561-3981
Fax: 800-581-2887

Public Company
Founded: 1968
Employees: 608
Sales: $115 million (1996)
Stock Exchanges: NASDAQ
SICs: 5193 Flowers & Florists' Supplies

Celebrity, Inc. is one of the leading suppliers of high-quality artificial flowers, foliage, flowering bushes and other decorative accessories to craft store chains and other specialty retailers and to wholesale florists throughout North America and Europe. Celebrity imports and/or produces over 9,000 home accent, decorative accessory and giftware items, including artificial floral arrangements, floor planters and trees, a wide range of decorative brass and textile products, and a broad line of seasonal items such as Christmas trees, wreaths, garlands and other ornamental products.

Initiating Changes and Growth

Celebrity, Inc. is somewhat of a giant among its competitors in the artificial flowers and decorative accessories arena, an estimated $5 billion annual market. In this industry which primarily consists of small, privately owned companies, Celebrity, based in Tyler, Texas, hopes to use its size and sophistication to capture more of this quickly expanding market through its growing manufacturing capabilities and high-quality products. Celebrity, founded in 1968, is a leading supplier of artificial flowers, foliage, flowering bushes, and other home decor items to both retailers and wholesalers across the U.S. and Europe. Through the acquisition of several manufacturing sites in the three years following its initial public offering in 1992 (Magicsilk, Inc.; The Cluett Corporation; and India Exotics, Inc.), Celebrity has expanded its presence through increased product lines, heightened standards for quality, and broadened its customer base. The company has expressed further possibilities for expanding their base of clientele, to potentially include department stores, specialized furniture stores, and import emporiums.

When Robert H. Patterson, Jr., assumed direction of Celebrity in 1984, several changes were implemented within the company. Looking to guide the company toward future growth, Patterson upgraded both its product line and its management information systems. The company sought to broaden its horizons by diversifying its clientele beyond discount retailers and instrumented the opening of a new distribution center in Charlotte, North Carolina. Finally in 1984, Patterson and Richard Yuen organized Celebrity Exports International (''Celebrity Hong Kong'').

Celebrity Hong Kong, which became a wholly owned subsidiary as of December 1992, was established to act as the company's exclusive purchasing agent. This facility contracts with over 60 factories in the Philippines, Thailand, Malaysia, Taiwan, and mainland China (where most silk flowers are made) for production of floral elements. The company also contracts with more than 20 factories in India for the production of decorative brass and textiles. The Celebrity Hong Kong site allows for better quality control and faster production than those of competitors who mostly deal with third party intermediaries, since shipments can be arranged to go directly to customers. The staff can also provide financing, customer documentation, and private labeling for its customers.

Through Celebrity Hong Kong the company works to develop original Celebrity designs with its overseas manufacturers. Because of its location, Celebrity Hong Kong is also better able to build relationships with manufacturers and be more aware of their capabilities. With a policy of paying full in cash within 10 days of manufacturer delivery to its Hong Kong site, the company believes it has strengthened its relationship with these facilities.

Because of the fragmented nature of this industry, Celebrity appreciated the opportunity to increase its strength and presence through acquisitions. In its beginnings Celebrity was mainly a distributor shortly after becoming public in 1992 when the company filed to sell just over two million shares of common stock for between $11 and $13 per share.

In an effort to create a greater range of products and raise sales, the company acquired certain assets of Magicsilk, Inc., including customer accounts and distribution capabilities. One of the best-known trade names in artificial flower production, Magicsilk helped increase the quality of Celebrity's artificial floral offerings and helped to diversify its customer base. It became apparent after its first full year of operations, however, that the financial goals set for Magicsilk were too lofty. Because of its affects on overall profitability (a net income of $2.9 million in fiscal 1993, down from $3.2 million in fiscal 1992), certain measures were taken to reduce costs. Included were the application of a more streamlined method of purchasing, more rigorous management, the placement of a new sales manager, and the downsizing of the Magicsilk workforce. These improvements sparked 1993 changes at Celebrity headquarters as well, with the addition of a financial controller, a vice-president of operations, and a new products manager.

Celebrity successfully acquired The Cluett Corporation of Winston-Salem, North Carolina, in 1993, to enter the company into the $280 million market of artificial trees, floor planters, and floral arrangements. Immediately exceeding financial expectations with fiscal 1993 revenues counting for 23 percent of Celebrity's total, Cluett earned an important place within the company with its well-recognized trademarks. This acquisition would prove to be a positive move for Celebrity, both financially and in terms of the expansion of its customer base, despite the hardship that fiscal year of the considerable nonrecurring expense that attaining the company caused. The Cluett unit broke its own sales record in third quarter 1997 when it accounted for 40 percent of the $26 million total sales for the company. The addition of the Cluett product line also expanded Celebrity's presence to parts of the country where it had not had a strong market share, in particular, the Northeast.

India Exotics, a St. Louis, Missouri-based importer of decorative brass and textile products, with revenues of approximately $10 million prior to purchase, was Celebrity's third acquisition. This 1995 addition to the company's expanding repertoire of merchandise helped establish Celebrity more deeply in the home decor market. As Chairman, CEO, and President Robert H. Patterson, Jr., stated in his 1995 president's letter, ''We've felt for sometime that a greater presence in the decorative accessories marketplace could add substantial leverage to our business by increasing our marketshare and accelerating and streamlining the flow of high quality decorative accessories from producers to retailers.'' Like Celebrity, India Exotics maintained a reputation for high quality and strong customer service. The subsidiary also kept a close relationship with a large manufacturer of decorative brass products in India. With Celebrity's acquisitions of Cluett and India Exotics, the company looked to become a major influence in the interior decoration market with these new pre-made and finished products. In a September 1997 press release, Patterson said, ''We believe our manufacturing operations, though significant in sales, remain largely untapped in terms of their potential to become predictable profit contributors to Celebrity.'' Thus the company expected significant additional financial growth from these 1990s additions.

Product Lines and Sales

Cashing in on sales related to consumers' increased spending on home-decor items in the retail craft industry, Celebrity saw 50 percent of 1995 sales going to craft stores. With approximately 3,000 customers, primarily in the South, Midwest, and East, in 1997 Celebrity had relationships with some of the largest craft store chains in the country, as well as with discount retailers, wholesale clubs, and wholesale florists. Twenty percent of 1995 sales went to customers only recently accessed by this market—the mass merchandisers—in addition to home centers and fabric stores; $9.4 million in fiscal 1996 sales, achieved mostly through Celebrity Hong Kong, were outside the U.S., primarily to European customers.

With three U.S. production facilities to assemble final products with overseas floral elements, three distribution centers, two wholesale supply houses, and two showrooms, Celebrity boasted a 9,000-plus item 1997 product line, up from a 5,000-item line in 1993. Merchandise included artificial flowers, flowering bushes and foliage, trees and floor planters, ready-made floral arrangements, decorative brass accessories, and decorative textile accessories. The growing Celebrity Christmas line was comprised of artificial Christmas trees, wreaths, garlands, and other ornamental products. In addition to craft stores, for whom artificial flowers are typically the largest single product sales category, Celebrity customers included pottery stores, commercial consumers such as hotels, stores and malls, and individual consumers—a growing 1990s market of those whose busy lifestyles do not afford time for the care of live plants. The depth of Celebrity's line allowed for the fulfillment of the needs of these markets in an industry Celebrity estimated was growing at a rate of 15 to 20 percent. The company also looked to expand into the boutique-retailing market, including Christmas stores, and to consumers who designed their own artificial flower arrangements, for themselves or resale through in-home businesses or craft shows.

Among its competitive advantages, Celebrity prided itself in its high-quality control, citing its Celebrity Hong Kong unit as a measure to maintain product component quality. Overseas contracted manufacturers were given periodic product inspections, both before and after shipment to the U.S.

Focus in the 1990s: Serving the Customer

The company's large size compared to its competition allowed for greater product range and service capabilities. Factory-direct shipping options and discounts offered to larger-volume clients are also important aspects of Celebrity. In fiscal 1993 Celebrity introduced electronic data interchange (EDI), allowing customers to place orders electronically to help speed the process. Fast, accurate order-filling was promoted; Celebrity was one of the first in the industry to use bar-coding for distribution, as most of its customers required this for inventory tracking and reordering. This method helped Celebrity achieve its 90 percent fill rate for bulk orders, compared to the industry average of 70 percent. An emphasis on in-store customer service was another notable feature the company maintained. By providing retailers with marketing strategies, merchandising concepts, and advice on advertising, Celebrity strove to accommodate its customers in a myriad of ways.

In response to the business atmosphere of the late 1990s, Celebrity looked to improve upon its historical successes in several ways. Included among these were to maintain the breadth of its product line. Through its three 1990s acquisitions, Celebrity increased its product line to include a greater variety of merchandise. Another effort was to decrease the inventory-to-sales ratio by carefully managing the inventory and removing slow performing items. Reducing sale to delivery time, cutting shipment time, and increasing direct shipments to consumers were also among the methods to maintain Celebrity's standards.

Record Gains; Learning from Losses Suffered

Following a record-setting fiscal 1995 with a net income of $3.8 million (or $0.60 per share), Celebrity increased both its operating margin and its market share. Then came a disappointing 1996. Carrying a net loss of $5.4 million ($0.86 per share), Celebrity felt the pain of adjusting to the 1990s market. With fewer, larger customers, Celebrity was greatly affected by retailers cutting back their purchasing due to the slow retail environment of late 1995. As many of their customers retained large inventories due to sluggish sales in late 1995 and early 1996, the restocking patterns the company expected did not occur. When two major customers then significantly cut back their ordering and subsequently filed for Chapter 11 bankruptcy protection, the company suffered its embarrassing net loss. In September 1997 came the resignation of Celebrity's CFO, James R. Thompson, as part of a "mutual agreement" with the board. Celebrity had a loss of $7 million ($1.11 a share) on sales of $32.2 million in its fiscal fourth quarter.

However, first quarter 1997 showed a rebound to profitability for the company, despite a rise in general and administrative expenses associated with the Dallas, Texas, Star Wholesale location, which opened in May 1997. Celebrity's adjustments to the 1990s, including such cost-cutting measures as the 1997 consolidation of the front office operations of Missouri-based India Exotics into Celebrity's Tyler, Texas, headquarters, were based on profitable operations with annual sales of $120 million, a figure lower than the company's sales plan. Through a new operating philosophy, Celebrity looked to the future in a positive manner, despite its recent setbacks.

Principal Subsidiaries

Star Wholesale Florist, Inc.; Magicsilk, Inc.; India Exotics, Inc.; Cluett Corporation; Celebrity Exports International Ltd. (Hong Kong).

Further Reading

"Business Brief—Celebrity Inc.: Loss of $4.3 Million Posted for Fiscal Fourth Quarter," *Wall Street Journal*, September 4, 1996.

Calian, Sara, "Celebrity Inc.: Letter of Intent Is Signed for Acquisition of Cluett," *Wall Street Journal*, October 8, 1993.

"Celebrity Inc.'s Chief of Finances Resigns After 4th-Quarter Loss," *Wall Street Journal*, September 9, 1997, p. B11.

"Celebrity Inc.'s Earnings Fall 89%," *Wall Street Journal*, February 1, 1996.

"New Securities Issues," *Wall Street Journal*, December 17, 1992, p. C22.

"OTC Focus: New-Stock Offerings Are Losing Luster, But Many Are Scheduled for Early 1993," *Wall Street Journal*, December 28, 1992, p. C1.

—Melissa West

CH2M Hill Ltd.

P.O. Box 22508
Denver, Colorado 80222
U.S.A.
(303) 771-0900
Fax: (303) 770-2616

Private Company
Founded: 1946
Employees: 7,030
Sales: $937 million (1996)
SICs: 8711 Engineering Services

CH2M Hill Ltd. is an engineering construction firm with several core services. It operates from offices across the U.S. and Canada, Europe, Asia and South America. The firm offers environmental services, including management of solid, water, and toxic wastes; pollution prevention; regulatory compliance, and risk and ecosystem management. CH2M Hill also specializes in nuclear services, including decontamination and decommissioning of nuclear sites, environmental restoration, toxic and radioactive waste containment, and other engineering services related to nuclear energy or weapons sites. The company is well-known for its water and wastewater operations. CH2M Hill worked on some innovative projects in this area, including early in its history an acclaimed wastewater treatment system that protected scenic Lake Tahoe from pollution and degradation. The company is also active in transportation services—planning, managing, and constructing transit systems, bridges, highways, ports, and airports. CH2M Hill also offers industrial engineering services, including designing facilities for the manufacture of microelectronics. The firm offers a variety of other miscellaneous services as well, such as management consulting and training of personnel, laboratory services, geotechnical engineering, and owning and operating infrastructure projects. Some examples include the company's consulting relationship with the highway bureau of Vietnam, managing various federal projects at Kelly Air Force Base in San Antonio, Texas, and environmental assessment and support to a U.S. firm operating the first Western style gas station in Kazakhstan. The firm is privately owned by its employees.

Beginnings

CH2M Hill began as the dream of three college students and their professor. Holly Cornell, Jim Howland, and Burke Hayes were all engineering students at Oregon State College in the 1930s. The three were inspired by their civil engineering professor, an Englishman named Fred Merryfield. While still undergraduates, the three discussed with Merryfield combining their abilities in an engineering firm. After graduation, Howland and Hayes did graduate work at MIT, and Cornell at Yale. Merryfield continued to teach at Oregon State. All four were in the military during World War II, but they corresponded and stayed in touch. In January 1946 they gathered in Corvallis, Oregon, and founded the engineering firm Cornell, Howland, Hayes & Merryfield. The four brought diverse but related skills to the new enterprise. Merryfield was an expert at planning for sanitary and hydraulics projects, and had personal and business connections up and down the West Coast. Hayes specialized in electrical engineering, and Howland and Cornell both had worked in hydraulics. Howland also had experience with soil mechanics, and Cornell with structural engineering. Before the year was out, the four original partners brought in two more engineers, Archie Rice and Ralph Roderick. Roderick and Rice both had strong backgrounds in sanitary engineering. Though they became partners on equal footing with the others, their names did not get added to the firm's. Cornell, Howland, Hayes & Merryfield was already too long. By the end of the 1940s the name was shortened to CH2M, shorthand for the first letters of the founders' last names.

CH2M's first projects centered around Oregon's Wilamette valley. Much of the work was related to water or wastewater. The firm had a competitive advantage in that it had an electrical engineer on staff, and its partners had advanced skills they had learned in graduate school, some unfamiliar to the West Coast. And with the war just over, many cities now had money to spend on engineering projects. CH2M grew quickly, and in just three years completed 200 projects. In 1949 CH2M built itself a new office in Corvallis, and in 1950 opened its first branch office, in Boise, Idaho.

The company's growth was also spurred by its technological advances. Partner Burke Hayes developed an innovative sewer pump in the 1950s, and this led to much new business. Hayes' FLOmatcher variable speed pump was designed for areas such

Company Perspectives:

CH2M HILL helps public and private clients worldwide realize a greater return on their investments in environmental technology and sustainable infrastructure. Our business involves project development, engineering and management of water, environmental and transportation infrastructure, as well as the design and construction of industrial facilities.

Because the firm is employee-owned, each of the 7,000 men and women of CH2M HILL has a personal stake in the organization's success. This means that each of our clients can expect quality service and personal attention from the CH2M HILL employees who serve them from nearby locations on six continents.

as the Pacific Northwest, where a great seasonal variation in rainfall makes a significant difference from summer to winter in the rate of flow a sewerage system must handle. This successful product brought attention to CH2M, and a separate company, General Service Corporation, was founded to market the FLO-matcher. The second innovative product spawned at CH2M was MicroFLOC, a water treatment process that was a significant advance over existing technology. Rice and Roderick, CH2M's two sanitary engineers, invented MicroFLOC in collaboration with others at the firm. MicroFLOC yielded cleaner water more quickly than other water treatment systems, and soon it was in demand not only in the Northwest but in the East as well.

In spite of its esteemed innovations and growing reputation, CH2M kept its growth relatively moderate during the 1950s and into the 1960s. The company opened a Seattle office in 1960, and another in Portland in 1962. The company took on six more partners around this time. CH2M incorporated in 1966, so that ownership could more easily be spread between the growing number of partners. Meanwhile, the company was taking on bigger profile projects. In 1965 CH2M began work on a wastewater treatment facility for Lake Tahoe, the scenic lake in the Sierra Nevada mountains between California and Nevada. CH2M took on this project in collaboration with a California engineering firm, Clair A. Hill & Associates. The two companies combined their efforts to construct one of the most advanced wastewater treatment systems of the time. It reduced wastewater discharge to near drinking water quality, and prevented water quality decline in the lake much beloved by tourists. This led to a similar project in Virginia, and a bigger national presence. The collaboration with Clair A. Hill & Associates proved fruitful too. The two companies had worked together on other projects in California, where Hill was a well-known company responsible for major projects, from irrigation, electrical, and sewerage projects to the construction of an entire town. Both firms were expanding, though CH2M, with 300 employees by 1969, was twice as big as Clair A. Hill & Associates. The two companies formally merged in 1971, and the new name became CH2M Hill Ltd.

National and International Expansion in the 1970s

CH2M Hill began to penetrate the East Coast in the 1970s, establishing an office in Reston, Virginia in 1971. The company took on work abroad as well, such as managing the expansion of Trinidad's water supply system. Though its projects were not all water-related, it was best known for its water and sewerage projects, and its reputation was strongest in the western U.S. It had gained work in California and Alaska after the acquisition of Clair A. Hill, and in the mid-1970s formed two subsidiaries, CH2M Hill Alaska and CH2M Hill Canada Ltd. To enhance its growth on the other side of the continent, CH2M Hill acquired Black Crow & Eidsness in 1977, an engineering firm based in Gainesville, Florida. Black Crow & Eidsness specialized in environmental engineering and water and wastewater projects. The firm had 200 employees, with seven offices throughout the Southeast, and branches in Philadelphia and Rochester, New York. It had constructed an award-winning zero discharge water treatment plant in St. Petersburg, Florida, and designed and constructed dozens of others across the Southeast.

By 1978, CH2M Hill had billings of over $50 million and had become the 10th-largest engineering firm in the country. The firm's original president, James Howland, had stepped down after 30 years, and another founding partner, Holly Cornell, ran the company as a "transitional president" until a replacement could be found. Though Cornell saw CH2M through its successful merger with Black Crow & Eidsness, he was not interested in running the company much longer. In 1978, CH2M Hill got its first president from outside the small group that had started the company. Harlan E. Moyer announced he would take the firm in a new direction, capitalizing on blossoming opportunities in the field of energy. The year Moyer took over, CH2M was awarded a Grand Conceptor award from the American Consulting Engineers Council for its design of a bio-gas plant in Colorado. The plant processed cattle manure into methane, replacing half the natural gas needs at the local power plant. The methane plant used many of CH2M's proven skills in water and waste treatment. Wastewater was recycled through algae ponds, and the algae itself could then be harvested as a protein source. Waste solids from the manure were recycled into fertilizer or feed supplement. Waste heat from the power plant fueled the algae ponds. CH2M also worked closely with the Environmental Protection Agency (EPA) in the late 1970s, managing wastewater projects in California, Idaho, Oregon, and elsewhere. Eventually, cleaning up waste ended up being more of a new direction for CH2M than the energy projects president Harlan Moyer had predicted.

Environmental Projects in the 1980s

CH2M Hill's reputation for expertise in wastewater treatment led to some very large projects in the 1980s. The company took on the role of prime consultant in 1980 for a $1.4 billion project to abate water pollution for the city of Milwaukee. Also in 1980 CH2M Hill won a contract with the EPA to identify hazardous waste sites. Two years later, the company became the manager of the so-called "Superfund" across the western United States. Superfund was created by Congress in 1980 to provide money for cleaning up the most pressing toxic and hazardous waste sites such as defunct weapons plants and abandoned industrial zones. CH2M Hill was in charge of $89 million in Superfund money, and was from the start one of a handful of engineering firms given primary Superfund contracts. As it took on more and more environmental clean-up work, CH2M saw its sales and profits rise. Between 1985 and 1987 alone, the company's sales were up 25 percent, and profits up a whopping 82 percent. By the late 1980s, CH2M Hill was the largest environmental engineering firm in the United States.

Responsibility for large projects and large budgets definitely had its drawbacks for the company, however. The water pollution project in Milwaukee the company had picked up in 1980 took most of the decade to complete. In 1988, three managers for one of CH2M's subcontractors on the project died in a gas explosion in a sewer tunnel. Workers for the subcontractor, S.A. Healy Co. of Chicago, found methane while boring a cross-town tunnel. The tunnel was evacuated, but not all the equipment was shut down, and three managers returned to check the site less than an hour after the evacuation. The three were killed, and both S.A. Healy Co. and CH2M Hill were charged with willful safety violations by the Occupational Safety and Health Administration (OSHA). Several months after the incident, Labor Secretary Elizabeth Dole publicly announced she was asking the Justice Department to bring criminal charges against CH2M Hill. The criminal charges were not ultimately brought, and OSHA's fine was overturned, but not until 1993. CH2M argued that it was responsible for the design of the sewer project, but was not in control of day-to-day construction work, and so won its appeal of the fine. Nevertheless, the company was saddled with the bad press for the accident.

In another case too, CH2M Hill found itself badgered and accused quite publicly, this time for cost overruns. The company had been in charge of Superfund money since the fund's inception, and ended up the largest single contractor in the Alternative Remedial Contracting Strategy (ARCS) program, with several contracts worth a total of $880 million. After an audit of the company's spending between 1987 and 1990, CH2M Hill was raked over the coals in a Congressional hearing. The public hearing brought to light questionable billing, such as for employee fishing licenses, for chocolates embossed with the company logo, and for a catered cruise. The congressman leading the hearings insisted that CH2M Hill had billed taxpayers for these items. In reality, billing was complicated, and regulation of expenses had not always been clear. Changes in billing regulations after the hearings were in some ways beneficial to CH2M Hill, but the media exposure was certainly a sour experience for the company.

The 1990s

At the beginning of the 1990s, CH2M Hill had grown to a company with 5,000 employees and annual revenue close to $500 million. The firm got a new president in 1991, Ralph R. Peterson. The company restructured in the early 1990s, after a long process of canvassing clients and employees for suggestions. Management was centralized from five district offices to just two. The company had operated five subsidiary companies, and its largest was streamlined to concentrate on only three lines of business. While consolidating its business at home, CH2M also expanded into more projects overseas. In 1991 it formed a joint venture with an Australian company, Gutteridge, Haskins & Davey, to handle the growing market in water and wastewater treatment in Australia. CH2M Hill took on a variety of other international projects in the 1990s. In another joint venture, it began a project to treat wastewater in the Chao Phraya River, which flows into Bangkok, Thailand. In a similar project, CH2M Hill worked with researchers at the University of Cincinnati to build a waste treatment plant at Lake Balaton, outside Budapest, Hungary. Also in Hungary, the company designed and built a wastewater treatment facility for a new Coca-Cola bottling plant. CH2M Hill, in addition, became a primary contractor for the Environmental Policy and Technology Project, an arm of the U.S. Agency for International Development. Through this project, CH2M researched environmentally sound ways to manage the forests of Russia's far east. In a similar project, CH2M also ran a demonstration plant in Tianjin, China, managing hazardous and toxic waste from new industries.

In 1996 the company grossed a record-breaking $937 million. A significant portion of its billings came from overseas projects. Large overseas projects in the late 1990s included construction in Malaysia in conjunction with a telecommunications improvement project run by U.S. West, and overseeing environmental cleanup in the New Independent States of the former Soviet Union. The company ventured in some new directions, too. Though many of its projects still centered around water treatment and environmental engineering, CH2M also worked in industrial design, helping a consortium of flat panel manufacturers reduce operating costs. The company continued to work on large environmental projects in the U.S. as well. Some included closing the U.S. Department of Energy's Rocky Flats, a former atomic bomb test site, and designing a plan to recycle the toxic glycol used to de-ice planes at Dayton International Airport.

Principal Subsidiaries

Industrial Design Corporation; Operations Management International; Capco.

Principal Operating Units

Water Business Group; Environmental Business Group; Transportation Business Group; Federal Systems Business Group.

Further Reading

Boyle, Bob, "CH2M Hill, Pipe Maker Liable in Defect Ruling," *ENR,* June 21, 1990, pp. 25–26.

"CH2M Hill: A Recruiter's Nightmare," *ENR,* September 9, 1991, p. 30.

"CH2M Hill Change Complete," *ENR,* February 22, 1993, p. 21.

"CH2M Hill Moves From Sewage into Energy," *ENR,* July 6, 1978, pp. 26–27.

"CH2M Hill's Fine Hinges on Definition of Its Role," *ENR,* May 11, 1989, pp. 9–10.

"Green Firms Cross Borders," *ENR,* January 14, 1991, p. 18.

Ichniowski, Tom, and Rubin, Debra, "Superfund Accounts Bring Dispute," *ENR,* March 30, 1992, p. 9.

Korman, Richard, "Dole Would Charge Designer," *ENR,* August 10, 1989, p. 14.

Krizan, William G.; Hazel Bradford; and Judy Schreiner, "CH2M Hill Cleared in Tunnel Explosion Case," *ENR,* September 6, 1993, pp. 6–7.

Rubin, Debra, and Steven W. Setzer, "Environmental Cleanup Firms Face Media Glare," *ENR,* October 19, 1992, p. 28.

Rubin, Debra, et al., "Cleanup Dollars Flow Like Water But Industry Is Awash in Problems," *ENR,* March 9, 1989, pp. 30–43.

Rubin, Debra K., "DOE and Contractors Begin Defusing Cold War Icon and Denver Eyesore," *ENR,* December 2, 1996, pp. 22–25.

Schreiner, Judy, "CH2M Hill 'Re-engineers' Self," *ENR,* August 30, 1993, p. 15.

—A. Woodward

CIGNA

CIGNA Corporation

One Liberty Place
Philadelphia, Pennsylvania 19192-1550
U.S.A.
(215) 761-1000
Fax: (215) 761-5515
Web site: http://www.cigna.com

Public Company
Incorporated: 1981
Employees: 42,800
Total Assets: $98.93 billion (1996)
Stock Exchanges: New York Pacific Philadelphia
SICs: 6311 Life Insurance; 6321 Accident & Health Insurance; 6331 Fire, Marine & Casualty Insurance; 6351 Surety Insurance; 6552 Land Subdividers & Developers, Except Cemeteries; 6719 Offices of Holding Companies, Not Elsewhere Classified; 6726 Unit Investment Trusts, Face-Amount Certificate Offices, Closed-End Management Investment Offices; 6798 Real Estate Investment Trusts; 8099 Health & Allied Services, Not Elsewhere Classified

CIGNA Corporation was formed in 1982, when INA Corporation, with its strong position in property and casualty insurance, and Connecticut General Corporation, with its strength in life insurance and employee benefits, merged. The resulting corporation immediately became one of the largest international, publicly owned insurance and financial-services companies based in the United States. During the initial decade and a half following the merger, CIGNA built its healthcare operations into the largest of its units, while at the same time moving out of personal property/casualty insurance as well as individual life insurance and annuities (in the United States). In addition to healthcare, CIGNA continued to offer the following products to its U.S. customers: group life, accident, and disability insurance; property and casualty insurance for businesses; pension and investment management; and reinsurance. Outside the United States, the company offered the following products through CIGNA International: individual life, accident, health, and disability insurance; group life and health insurance; and commercial property and casualty insurance.

CIGNA gained its preeminent position by combining some of the oldest and most important companies in the insurance marketplace. Its oldest subsidiary is Insurance Company of North America (INA), a company rich with tradition. INA was formed by a group of prominent Philadelphians in November 1792, in Pennsylvania's State House, where the Declaration of Independence had been signed just 16 years earlier. Connecticut General Life Insurance Company was incorporated in 1865. That company began to expand from its focus on life insurance and employee benefits almost a century later, when it acquired another company with a long history of its own, Aetna Insurance Company, in 1962. Another major component of CIGNA was put in place in 1984, when the company acquired the American Foreign Insurance Association (AFIA) to expand its international operations.

INA Founded in Philadelphia in 1792

Insurance Company of North America was organized in Philadelphia, then the financial center of the United States and its busiest port, when the country was just beginning to develop economically. With only 32 corporations and few native manufacturing concerns in the country, all marine insurance was written in London or in the United States by private individuals or partnerships that could afford to underwrite coverage.

In November and December 1792 a group of businessmen—including a carpenter, a cobbler, and a stationer, as well as bankers, lawyers, and merchants—met to set up a general insurance company. These businessmen had their own concerns at heart: they felt that their businesses could not grow unless reliable insurance was made available close to home. Only two small fire insurance companies had been formed in the new nation so far, and Philadelphia businessmen sought greater protection.

Insurance Company of North America wrote several policies on December 19, 1792, its first day in business. John M. Nesbitt, a Philadelphia merchant, was elected president of the company and Ebenezer Hazard, secretary. Hazard, a businessman, scholar, and historian, was responsible for the daily conduct of business. He kept the office open under sometimes less than

Company Perspectives:

At CIGNA, we intend to be the best at helping our customers enhance and extend their lives and protect their financial security. Satisfying customers is the key to meeting employee needs and shareholder expectations, and will enable CIGNA to build on our reputation as a financially strong and highly respected company.

We believe: Providing customers with products and services they value more than those of our competitors is critical to our success; talented, well-trained, committed, mutually supportive people—working to the highest standards of performance and integrity—are what make success possible; the profitable growth of our businesses makes career opportunities and personal growth possible; and profitability is the ultimate measure of our success.

ideal conditions, remaining in Philadelphia during the yellow fever epidemic of 1793. The Insurance Company of North America was incorporated by the Pennsylvania state legislature in 1794 and authorized to write marine, fire, and life insurance.

The company initially insured only ship hulls and cargoes in local and international commerce. In late 1794, however, INA's directors and officers agreed to insure buildings and their contents against fire, becoming the first U.S. company to offer insurance on personal possessions and on business inventories.

In the early 19th century, INA followed the pioneers west. In 1807 INA set up its first agency, in Lexington, Kentucky, establishing the American agency system. The company appointed independent agents as far as the frontiers of Pennsylvania, Kentucky, Ohio, and Tennessee. Banking on westward expansion, INA invested in toll bridges and toll roads and bought bonds of the just-purchased Louisiana Territory.

INA's westward expansion helped the company stay afloat when its marine insurance business lost money. Problems began in 1799 when Great Britain began to seize U.S. ships at sea. The maritime embargo of 1808, the War of 1812, and the depression of 1813 all had detrimental effects on the company's marine profits.

After the War of 1812 ended in 1815, the insurance environment became more competitive. As rates fell, INA faced a different kind of threat. John Inskeep, who became INA president in 1806, had the company invest profits instead of paying dividends. This conservative investment and reserve policy, coupled with its expanding fire insurance business, kept the company profitable.

In the mid-19th century, INA played a major role in forming the Philadelphia Board of Marine Underwriters, an organization which standardized premium rates and policy formats, gathered statistics, reported on insurance fraud, and kept up with commercial regulations and maritime law. A committee of the board reported on the seaworthiness of all vessels that entered the Port of Philadelphia. The board helped reduce operating expenses for the companies involved.

The formation of the Philadelphia Board of Marine Underwriters coincided with the high point for marine insurance in the 19th century. Between 1840 and 1861 U.S. foreign-trade tonnage quadrupled. The increase was due partially to the new clipper ships. Clipper ships were well built and had excellent safety records; in short, they were good insurance risks.

By 1859 INA had entered another lucrative area: the company insured gold shipments from the California gold fields, discovered a decade earlier. Its agent in California, Joshua P. Havens, sent premiums to INA's Philadelphia office in gold dust, which the secretary exchanged for currency.

From 1861 to 1865, when the Civil War disrupted many of INA's traditional markets, the company compensated by placing even more emphasis on the potential in the west. In 1861, as secession spread, the directors stopped accepting business or renewing policies in the south. In 1863 they organized offices in the west into a separate department. From 40 appointed local agents in the territory in 1860, the western-business department grew to 1,300 agents by 1876. In 1875, a decade after the Civil War, a southern department was also added.

INA Survived Series of Disasters, 1835–1906

Expansion in the west increased business but also posed a new risk. Rapidly growing cities were not well-built cities, and INA suffered losses in a series of major fires: 700 buildings burned in New York City in 1835; 1,000 buildings were lost in Pittsburgh, Pennsylvania, in 1845; most of St. Louis, Missouri, was lost in 1851; and Portland, Maine, was destroyed almost totally by fire in 1866.

The Great Chicago Fire, which started on October 8, 1871, burned about 17,450 buildings valued at $200 million. Claims for that fire left many insurance companies bankrupt. Eighty-three other companies could settle their claims only in part. INA was one of the 51 companies that did pay in full, settling legitimate claims totaling $650,000. Its reliability brought in new business.

INA, however, faced an even heavier loss a year later. The Boston Fire of November 9, 1872, gutted 600 buildings at a cost of $75 million, causing the collapse of 25 more insurance companies. INA faced the heaviest claim total—$988,530—but again paid in full.

On April 18, 1906, a 48-second earthquake shook San Francisco, California. Earthquake damage was slight, but the resulting fires were uncontrollable because water mains had ruptured. INA sent special agent Sheldon Catlin to the city to settle claims. Catlin found that most of the damage to property came from the fires, which had burned out of control for three days, not from the earthquake itself. Since INA was liable for fire damage but not earthquake damage, his determination was not a popular one within INA. Under pressure from other insurance companies, the home office decided to settle all claims at two-thirds value. On Catlin's recommendation, however, INA reversed its own decision, and agreed to pay all claims in full. That amounted to a liability of $3.7 million, plus $1.3 million in claims due from INA's affiliate, Alliance Insurance Company. INA was one of the 27 companies that paid claims from the San Francisco earthquake and fire in full.

As the company was expanding its fire insurance coverage, it also expanded its marine coverage inland. In 1890 INA established a lake-marine department in Chicago to cover risks during transit on rivers, lakes, and canals. The company originally refused to insure steamboats, an important part of the movement to settle the Mississippi River Valley, because steamboat captains were considered too reckless. At the end of the century George W. Neare & Company, a steamboat operator, persuaded INA president, Charles Platt, that insurance coverage was necessary to revitalize river transport. The company selected its risks carefully and eventually prospered in the field.

INA faced losses in its regular marine division in the last decade of the 19th century because such risks were hard to classify. During the mid-1890s Benjamin Rush, a conservative, old-line Philadelphian who came to work at INA as assistant to President Platt in 1894, worked nights and weekends with two young clerks to compile profit-and-loss statements for 198 route and cargo categories over a five-year period. His statistical analysis allowed the company to select risks more carefully. In 1900 INA posted the first profit in its marine line for many years, and the line remained profitable until World War I. Rush's work earned him the title ''father of modern marine underwriting.''

Expanding industry before World War I meant growth in the fire insurance business. John O. Platt, a nephew of Charles Platt and head of INA's fire branch, set up the improved-risk-engineering department to devise ways to make industry safer and thereby lower insurance risks. The department eventually offered three services: property valuation, fire prevention, and rate analysis.

Rush succeeded Eugene Ellison as president in 1916, in time to face claims due to attacks by German U-boats—INA paid $21,740 as its share of the coverage for the *Luisitania,* for example—and fires caused by sabotage in U.S. munitions plants. Nevertheless, World War I did not seriously threaten profits.

INA Added Automobile Insurance in Early 20th Century

Despite a generally conservative outlook, INA often insured unusual risks. Hence, in 1905, the company began to insure automobiles against fire and theft and added collision coverage in 1907. By the end of World War I, demand for this type of coverage had grown so much that INA organized a casualty affiliate, Indemnity Insurance Company, in 1920. The Great Depression hit Indemnity hard, but in 1932 INA brought in John A. Diemand, who had extensive experience in casualty insurance, to improve the company's performance.

With the approach of World War II, INA faced new problems. Male employees enlisted, and the company was not fully staffed. Cities were unable to replace outdated fire-fighting equipment, increasing risks. Auto insurance fell off due to gas rationing, and the lack of new-home construction affected property insurance lines. Ships unused to taking wartime security measures were lost to the Germans.

INA again found new and unusual risks to insure. The company wrote policies covering the accidental death of war correspondents and photographers, expanded its aviation coverage, covered test pilots, and insured 30 scientists working on the development of the atomic bomb at the Manhattan Project. ''We were pulling rates out of the air,'' Edwin H. Marshall, underwriter for these unusual coverages, told William H. A. Carr in *Perils, Named and Unnamed.*

INA Chief Promoted Multiple-Line Underwriting in Postwar Period

In the postwar years INA boomed along with the economy. During the 1940s, Diemand, by now president of the company, tackled a long-standing issue. INA had organized a casualty affiliate in 1920 because INA itself was forbidden by law to offer a full line of insurance. Diemand's advocacy of multiple-line underwriting authority, earlier promoted by Rush, now became a crusade. ''Every company should have the privilege of meeting the requirements of any policyholder at any time as long as there is no law or ruling of an insurance department to prevent it,'' Diemand said in his address on INA's 150th anniversary. Diemand felt that multiple-line underwriting would provide broader and more convenient coverage for policyholders, who would have access to insurance packages from one agent, and at the same time would enable companies to cut processing and marketing costs.

Diemand's major opposition came from insurance cartels and conservative insurance associations which regulated insurance sales. In 1945 Public Law 15 left regulation of the insurance industry to the states, and slowly states extended the right to sell multiple-line insurance. By 1955 the right had been granted in all states. This victory allowed Diemand to pioneer the company's comprehensive homeowners policy, offering fire, theft, personal liability, medical payment, and extended coverages.

In 1964 Bradford Smith, Jr., succeeded Diemand as chairman of the board and chief executive officer. Smith automated operations, reorganized the company along functional lines, and emphasized participative management, which he defined as taking individual responsibility and cooperating with all company branches.

Changes in the U.S. business environment as well as changes within the company prompted another reorganization in 1968. Insurance Company of North America became the major subsidiary of INA Corporation, which added diversified services through other subsidiaries and extended its regional and international network of offices. As part of its expansion, INA Corporation organized or acquired several life insurance subsidiaries, which remained relatively small compared to its major interests in property and casualty insurance. In the 1970s the company diversified into a related area when it began acquiring hospital management companies and health-maintenance organizations (HMO).

All of these moves reflected INA's desire to become a major financial organization offering a broad range of services. In 1981 the company saw a merger with Connecticut General Corporation (CG) as a way to achieve that goal. CG offered a major presence in employee benefits and life insurance to complement INA's activities in property and casualty insurance, and a combination was a way to operate more efficiently through economies of scale.

CG Founded in 1865 to Sell Life Insurance

Connecticut General dates back to 1865, when Guy R. Phelps, one of the founders of Connecticut Mutual Company, saw a need for ''substandard'' insurance, or life insurance for poor risks. Originally the new firm was to be called Connecticut

Invalid, but because of concern that the word "invalid" could be read in two ways, it became Connecticut General Life Insurance Company and began to insure healthy lives along with substandard risks. Two years later the company withdrew completely from insuring higher risks and, through conservative management, survived a period when many other life insurance companies failed.

Under President Thomas W. Russell, the company prospered from post-Civil War growth in life insurance sales. Within a few years, CG had agents in over 25 states, but increasing competition, rate cutting, and poor public perception of a company that had insured the disabled caused the sales force to shrink as quickly as it had grown. By the 1870s CG concentrated on New England and a few surrounding states.

The company's early policies, handwritten by clerks who had to demonstrate good penmanship to get the job, reflected the society they served. Death from drinking, hanging, or dueling canceled a policy. Travel was also restricted: a policyholder could not travel south of Virginia or Kentucky from June to November because of additional risk of illness due to heat. Late premium payments led to the automatic cancellation of a policy, with no grace period. Policies had no cash value, and benefits were paid in a lump sum, 90 days after proof of death, signed by five witnesses, was received.

Under Thomas Russell, CG weathered the depression following the panic of 1873 and a takeover attempt by Continental Life Insurance Company of Hartford, Connecticut. By 1880 the firm was again stable and began to grow.

Russell died in 1901 and was succeeded by Robert W. Huntington, who had joined the company as a clerk 11 years before. CG had only 12 home-office employees and was licensed to do business in four New England states, New York, Pennsylvania, and Ohio. Huntington emphasized good investments, especially in farm mortgages, railroads, and utilities. He also cut operating expenses and used the savings to enter new areas.

CG First Offered Group Insurance in 1910s

In 1912 CG created an accident department. The next year CG began to offer group insurance, insuring the 100 employees of the *Hartford Courant.* Group insurance developed slowly for CG until 1917, when changes in corporate taxes made it a deductible expense. CG established its group department in 1918 and got its first big contract—covering the 5,400 employees of Gulf Oil—that year. Business picked up again in 1919, when contributory plans were developed. Previously, employers had paid the total cost of coverage.

World War I meant a growing economy and more group insurance coverage, but when an influenza epidemic struck in the autumn of 1918, CG was hit particularly hard because it had a high proportion of very young policyholders. Although claims were high, the epidemic eventually encouraged more life insurance business.

During the 1920s Frazar Bullard Wilde, head of the company's Accident Division, brought CG into another new area, aviation insurance. Wilde had served in the field artillery in France during World War I, where the use of airplanes captured his imagination. In 1926, when other insurance companies were not yet convinced of the validity of insuring flight, Wilde began writing policies that covered aircraft passengers. In 1930 the company wrote a group life insurance policy for Western Air Express, which included 46 pilots, and in 1932 CG insured 1,000 employees of United Airlines as well.

When the stock market crashed in 1929, CG's diversified investments kept the company going, but within two years new business had decreased sharply and business cancellations mounted. In addition, the company's heavy investment in farm mortgages meant that, with increasing foreclosures and the inability to lease farms, CG became a farm owner. In most cases, the company retained the former owners as managers and encouraged them to save their pay to buy back the property.

Estate Planning and Employee Benefits in 1940s and 1950s

In 1936 Wilde succeeded Huntington as president. Wilde emphasized high-quality products and a good sales force. Ten years later he supported a new approach to marketing life insurance that would have a major impact on the company: estate planning. Stuart Smith, who had joined the company during the Great Depression, brought the estate-planning concept to CG. He emphasized the sale of life insurance as part of complete estate planning. When Smith was promoted to the home office in 1946, CG made estate planning the company's only approach to selling insurance. Smith taught the technique to Connecticut General agents, which enabled them to plan insurance coverage by taking into consideration a client's total assets, family circumstances, and plans for the future.

Another focal point after the war was the development of group hospital and surgical benefits to compete with the Blue Cross and Blue Shield plans which had just been created. Just as CG had supported emerging technology after World War I by insuring airline pilots and passengers, after World War II the company began insuring atomic energy workers, covering employees of the Brookhaven and Argonne laboratories.

CG had established a group pension service as early as 1929 to serve its group insurance policyholders. The introduction of a number of government policies encouraged growth in this arena. The Social Security Act, passed in 1935, stimulated private savings for pensions to supplement the government program; the Revenue Act of 1942 provided some tax incentives for employers to establish pension programs; and, after 1960, changes in Connecticut state law led to significant growth in CG's pension business.

Also in the postwar years, CG pioneered the financing of shopping centers, and company investment became a major factor in the development of the modern suburban shopping mall. In addition, CG financed commercial agricultural enterprises and provided loans on urban residential and business properties.

CG Acquired Aetna in 1962

In 1962 CG purchased Aetna Insurance Company (Aetna), a major firm in fire and casualty insurance, in order to broaden its position in insurance. Aetna brought a history even longer than its new parent's to the acquisition. The company was established in 1819 to sell casualty insurance, and two years later it became the first U.S. company to sell insurance in Canada. In 1851 the company began to sell life insurance too, but just two years later this part of its operations was spun off into a separate company, which became known as the Aetna Life and Casualty Company. The Aetna Insurance Company faced the same marine insurance risks as did INA, and it was also hit by massive claims due to urban fires in the late 19th century. Aetna's directors acted on a policy they voiced frequently after the Chicago Fire in 1871: "Every dollar must be paid." And pay they did. The company paid $3.78 million after the Chicago Fire, $1.6 million a year later in Boston, and almost $3 million following the San Francisco Earthquake and Fire. Aetna's ability to cover fully all of its losses enhanced its reputation as a major fire insurance company.

By the 1960s the acquisition of Aetna, with its sound fiscal management and preeminent position in fire and casualty insurance, was attractive to CG, which aimed to gain market position in property and casualty insurance, where it had virtually no operations at all. The acquisition was part of a trend in the industry toward larger companies that could offer full lines of insurance.

After acquiring Aetna as its property and casualty arm, CG began dramatic expansion of employee benefits programs, such as group health insurance and pensions. CG was most successful in life, health, and pensions, with its property and casualty operations remaining small. By 1981 group life and health benefits accounted for 33 percent of the company's operating income; individual life, health, and annuities for 28 percent; and property and casualty business for only 18 percent—down from almost 35 percent a decade earlier. In 1991, prior to the merger with INA, Connecticut General Insurance Corporation was renamed Connecticut General Corporation.

1982 Merger of INA and CG to Form CIGNA

As the trend toward larger multiline insurers accelerated, in 1981 INA and CG announced that they would bring their complementary interests together by forming CIGNA Corporation ("CIGNA" being a combination of the two company's initials). INA's strengths were the mirror image of CG's, with an extensive presence in the property and casualty fields, where it had operated the longest, and relatively small operations in group insurance. INA also had a strong international presence, while CG had focused primarily on U.S. markets. By March 31, 1982, all necessary approvals had been secured, and CIGNA was formed. Robert D. Kilpatrick of Connecticut General and Ralph Saul of INA became joint CEOs, and the board of directors was drawn equally from both predecessor organizations. In 1983 Philadelphia was selected as the headquarters for CIGNA.

The new company got off to a difficult start because of a declining economy in the early 1980s, but the anticipated economies of scale did materialize, and the company continued to expand. In 1984 CIGNA acquired AFIA, formerly the American Foreign Insurance Association, to strengthen its position abroad (and also to resolve the conflict between INA's independent international operations and Aetna's membership in AFIA).

AFIA had been formed in 1918 by a group of insurance executives to offer insurance written by its members overseas. After exploring conditions for insurance sales in Australia, New Zealand, Japan, Hong Kong, India, and Singapore, the board of AFIA established agencies in South America, Asia, and the Far East. AFIA weathered the Great Depression, but World War II, which engulfed many of the areas where the company was most profitable, slowed growth and cut profits. By 1949, however, AFIA was back on its feet and ready to expand along with the booming postwar economy. In 1984 the company had contacts in over 100 countries and offered CIGNA a good way to expand its international market. Merged into CIGNA's own substantial international operations, AFIA Worldwide became part of CIGNA International, which was renamed CIGNA WorldWide.

In 1987 the Aetna Insurance Company subsidiary was renamed CIGNA Property and Casualty Insurance Company. Two years later, CIGNA gave up the use of the Aetna name altogether when it transferred its rights to this trade name to Aetna Life and Casualty Company. In November 1989 William H. Taylor was named chairman of CIGNA, replacing the retiring Kilpatrick; Taylor had joined Connecticut General in 1964, was named chief financial officer upon the formation of CIGNA in 1982, and had become CEO in November 1988. Also in 1989, the company formed CIGNA International Financial Services to provide individual and group life and health insurance outside the United States. In 1993 CIGNA WorldWide and CIGNA International Financial Services were merged under the recycled name, CIGNA International.

Healthcare and Employee Benefits Emphasized in 1990s

By 1990 CIGNA was operating effectively in an insurance marketplace noteworthy for ever-larger competitors, and the company continued the trend when it acquired EQUICOR-Equitable HCA Corporation, a large group insurance and managed healthcare company and the nation's sixth-largest provider of employee benefits. The acquisition accelerated the growth of CIGNA's managed healthcare programs. From 1985 through 1993, the company invested a total of $1.5 billion to build a major managed-care business, just as the managed-care industry was beginning to explode. The newly renamed CIGNA HealthCare was by the early 1990s the company's largest and most profitable unit. By 1997 CIGNA HealthCare offered a full range of group medical, dental, disability, and life insurance products, with traditional fee-for-service plans marketed in all 50 states. The unit operated managed-care networks in 43 states, the District of Columbia, and Puerto Rico.

CIGNA HealthCare grew even larger in 1997 when it acquired Healthsource Inc.—a managed-care company with about 1.1 million members in HMOs operating in 15 states—for $1.4 billion, plus the assumption of $250 million in debt. Healthsource had been founded in 1985 by a group of doctors in Hooksett, New Hampshire, as an HMO serving rural areas and smaller cities. The company grew quickly through acquisitions but was experiencing some growing pains by the time of its acquisition by CIGNA. With the addition of Healthsource, CIGNA's medical HMOs had a total membership of 5.3 million, while the company's fee-for-service medical plans counted 7 million members.

CIGNA added to its employee benefits offerings in October 1997 with the formation of CIGNA IntegratedCare. This unit—a joint initiative of CIGNA HealthCare, CIGNA Group Insurance, and CIGNA Property & Casualty—was formed to offer employers fully integrated worker's compensation, disability, and medical-management services. This integrated approach was intended to lower employer's costs and improve care by eliminating gaps and redundancies.

At the same time that it was bolstering its employee life and health benefits operations, CIGNA was exiting from various noncore businesses and attempting to stem chronic losses incurred by CIGNA Property & Casualty. Generally, the company was looking to eliminate those business lines that were not strategically connected to other CIGNA businesses. For example, in the early 1990s the company's international operation dropped residential, auto, and travel insurance, while residential insurance was also dropped domestically. In July 1997 CIGNA announced that it would sell CIGNA Individual Insurance, which included individual life insurance and annuity operations in the United States, to Lincoln National Corporation for about $1.4 billion in cash.

CIGNA's property and casualty business, meanwhile, was continuing to lose money at an alarming rate because of weak underwriting standards and poor relations between the unit and its agents. Furthermore, a potential time bomb hung over it in the form of a large number of asbestos and environmental liabilities—potentially more than $4.5 billion worth—which was depressing the unit's financial-strength rating. These ratings are crucial to insurers in winning new business. CIGNA decided to create a "fire wall" between its problematic and standard liabilities by separating its domestic property and casualty operations into two units: one—called INA Holdings—to handle all ongoing business, and another—called Brandywine Holdings—to handle the asbestos and environmental liabilities. With this division in place, INA Holdings' ratings were expected to improve, and it was hoped that CIGNA's property and casualty business might return to the black. By early 1996, regulatory approval for the split had been received, despite opposition from industry competitors who were concerned that Brandywine might eventually run short of funds and have to be bailed out by a state guaranty fund—financed by the insurance companies themselves. In March 1997, however, a Pennsylvania appeals court vacated the plan's approval by the state of Pennsylvania and ordered new hearings.

In the intensely competitive environment of the turn of the millennium, it seems imperative that CIGNA turn around its struggling property and casualty business as quickly as possible, although the company may decide to divest itself of this troubled segment in order to concentrate further on its much more successful employee life and health benefits operations. Such a move would also provide funds for further acquisitions, and CIGNA will need to grow its healthcare operations to stay competitive in a rapidly consolidating industry.

Principal Subsidiaries

CIGNA Holdings, Inc.; Connecticut General Corporation; CG Trust Company; CIGNA Associates, Inc.; CIGNA Dental Health, Inc.; CIGNA Financial Advisors, Inc.; CIGNA Financial Partners, Inc.; CIGNA Financial Services, Inc.; CIGNA Health Corporation; CIGNA RE Corporation; Connecticut General Life Insurance Company; Disability Claim Services, Inc.; INA Life Insurance Company of New York; International Rehabilitation Associates, Inc.; Life Insurance Company of North America; MCC Behavorial Care, Inc.; TEL-DRUG, INC.; INA Corporation; CIGNA International Holdings, Ltd.; INA Financial Corporation; CIGNA Investment Group, Inc.; CIGNA International Finance Inc.; CIGNA Investment Advisory Company, Inc.; CIGNA Investments, Inc.

Further Reading

Burton, Thomas M., "Lincoln Agrees to Buy Units from Cigna," *Wall Street Journal,* July 29, 1997, pp. A3, A8.

Byrne, John A., and Richard Morais, "Cignoids Versus Afians," *Forbes,* September 24, 1984, p. 218.

Carr, William H. A., *Perils, Named and Unnamed: The Story of the Insurance Company of North America,* New York: McGraw-Hill, 1967.

Connecticut General Life Insurance Company, 1865–1965, Hartford, Conn.: Connecticut General Life Insurance Company, 1965.

"Could Cigna Be a Merger Casualty?" *Financial World,* September 19, 1984, p. 86.

David, Gregory E., "Beauty and the Beast," *Financial World,* November 9, 1993, pp. 79–81.

Hals, Tom, "The Cigna Split: What Will Be the Fallout?" *Philadelphia Business Journal,* February 16, 1996, p. 1.

James, Marquis, *Biography of a Business, 1792–1942: Insurance Company of North America,* Indianapolis, Ind.: Bobbs-Merrill, 1942, reprint, New York: Arno Press, 1976.

Jebsen, Per H., "Cigna Forms Unit to Offer New Services," *Wall Street Journal,* October 6, 1997, p. A11.

Lenckus, Dave, "CIGNA Reorganization Plan Unleashes Criticism," *Business Insurance,* December 23, 1996, p. 19.

Loomis, Carol J., and Margaret A. Elliott, "How Cigna Took a $1.2-Billion Bath," *Fortune,* March 17, 1986, p. 46.

Milligan, John W., "Robert Kilpatrick Hangs Tough," *Institutional Investor,* September 1987, p. 257.

O'Donnell, Thomas, and Laura Rohman, "The Honeymooners," *Forbes,* May 10, 1982, p. 124.

Ruwell, Mary Elizabeth, *Eighteenth Century Capitalism: The Formation of American Marine Insurance Companies,* New York: Garland, 1993.

Scism, Leslie, "Cigna Is Set Back on Restructuring; Hearing Ordered," *Wall Street Journal,* March 6, 1997, p. A4.

——, "Cigna's Pact to Buy Healthsource Inc. to Boost Firm's Managed-Care Business," *Wall Street Journal,* March 3, 1997, p. A4.

——, "For Cigna, Property-Casualty Line Still Proves Tricky," *Wall Street Journal,* August 21, 1995, p. B4.

Weber, Joseph, "Is CIGNA's Asbestos Plan Fireproof?" *Business Week,* December 16, 1996, p. 118.

Weber, Joseph, William Glasgall, and Richard A. Melcher, "Is Cigna Creating a Time Bomb?," *Business Week,* November 6, 1995, p. 158.

—Ginger G. Rodriguez
—updated by David E. Salamie

The Clorox Company

1221 Broadway Street
Oakland, California 94612
U.S.A.
(510) 271-7000
Fax: (510) 832-1463
Web site: http://www.clorox.com

Public Company
Incorporated: 1913 as the Electro-Alkaline Company
Employees: 5,500
Sales: $2.53 billion (1997)
Stock Exchanges: New York Pacific
SICs: 2035 Pickled Fruits & Vegetables, Salad Dressings, Vegetable Sauces & Seasonings; 2819 Industrial Inorganic Chemicals, Not Elsewhere Classified; 2841 Soap & Other Detergents, Except Specialty Cleaners; 2842 Specialty Cleaning, Polishing & Sanitation Preparations; 3999 Manufacturing Industries, Not Elsewhere Classified; 5141 Groceries, General Line; 8731 Commercial, Physical & Biological Research

Although best known for the household bleach that bears the firm's name, The Clorox Company is a diversified international manufacturer and marketer of a variety of consumer products ranging from household cleaners to salad dressings and from insecticides to cat litter. The company's professional products unit manufactures and markets cleaning and food products for institutional and professional markets and the food-service industry. About 16 percent of Clorox's sales are derived outside the United States through marketing channels in more than 70 countries. German conglomerate Henkel KGaA holds about a 28 percent stake in Clorox.

One-Product, Independent Company, 1913–57

Clorox was founded in 1913 as the Electro-Alkaline Company by five Oakland, California-area businessmen, only one of whom had any knowledge of chemistry. Their objective was to convert brine from ocean water into sodium hypochlorite bleach using an electrolytic process considered to be technologically advanced for its time. Each partner invested $100 in the new venture, and in August 1913 they purchased a plant site. The company's first product, Clorox liquid bleach, was packaged in five-gallon returnable containers and delivered by horse-drawn wagon to local breweries, dairies, and laundries for cleaning and disinfecting their facilities. Labels for the new product identified it as being ''made by electricity.''

An initial stock issue of 750 shares at $100 each provided $75,000 in start-up capital. The company struggled through its early years and often depended upon personal loans from its directors to pay expenses.

In 1916 a less concentrated liquid bleach product—5¼ percent sodium hypochlorite instead of 21 percent—for household use was developed and sold in amber glass pint bottles. William C. R. Murray, the company's general manager, came up with the idea of producing and promoting household bleach. Murray's wife, Annie, gave away samples of the formula to customers of the family's Oakland-based grocery store. Its value as a laundry aid, stain remover, deodorant, and disinfectant was also promoted by door-to-door salespeople who demonstrated how a solution of Clorox bleach and water could whiten an ink-stained piece of fabric. Orders were collected on the spot and then given to local grocers who purchased the necessary inventory from the company to fulfill them. Small and local at the time, Clorox was not affected by World War I.

In the 1920s Clorox's manufacturing plant could produce about 2,000 cases, or 48,000 bottles of bleach per day. Assembly line workers filled bottles by hand using hoses attached to overhead tanks. After being filled, the bottles were sealed with rubber stoppers and labeled, also by hand.

As demand for Clorox household bleach grew, the company expanded its manufacturing and distribution capabilities nationwide. By the early 1930s Clorox had become the best-selling liquid bleach in the country. The company was known by its amber glass bleach bottle, which continued to be used with minor adaptations in size and design until the early 1960s, when Clorox became the first bleach manufacturer to use plastic containers.

Company Perspectives:

We are a dynamic international organization whose principal business is building brand franchises in categories where we can best use our core strengths. Our products provide excellent value for consumers, and are sold primarily in grocery stores and other retail outlets in many parts of the world.

Our line of domestic retail products includes many of the country's best known brands of laundry additives, home cleaning and automotive appearance products, cat litters, insecticides, charcoal briquets, salad dressings, sauces, water filtration systems. The great majority of our products either lead or are a strong second in their categories.

In 1929 Murray became president of Clorox Chemical Company, a name that had replaced the company's original name in 1922. He served in that capacity until his sudden death in 1941, just prior to the United States's entry into World War II and was succeeded by William J. Roth. In contrast to Murray's relatively uneventful tenure, Roth immediately had to deal with the impact of the country's wartime involvement on the company. Due to the decreased availability of chlorine, the U.S. government permitted bleach manufacturers to reduce the concentration of sodium hypochlorite in their products. Roth, however, opted to decrease production rather than change the quality of Clorox bleach and jeopardize customer satisfaction. He also terminated a number of contracts for chlorine that had been negotiated before the war because those agreements paid suppliers too little for a substance now in such short supply. Although these decisions were costly at the time, the company retained the respect of the industry and customer loyalty once the war was over.

Subsidiary of Procter & Gamble, 1957–68

By the mid-1950s Clorox, still a one-product company, held the largest share of the domestic market for household bleach. The Procter & Gamble Company, a successful manufacturer of consumer products, viewed Clorox bleach as a compatible addition to its existing line of laundry products, and acquired the company in 1957.

Procter & Gamble changed the firm's name to The Clorox Company. However, within three months of the purchase, the Federal Trade Commission challenged the Clorox acquisition on the grounds that it might lessen competition or tend to create a monopoly in household liquid bleaches, a violation of the Clayton Act. Even though Procter & Gamble allowed Clorox to handle its own affairs, in 1967 the U.S. Supreme Court upheld the commission's order that Procter & Gamble divest itself of the Clorox operation. By 1969 Clorox had been spun off as a public company and was once again independent.

Diversified Following the Regaining of Independence in 1969

Clorox's new president, former Procter & Gamble executive Robert B. Shetterly, and his top management team faced a more competitive marketing environment in which enzyme laundry products were rapidly encroaching on Clorox's core business. Realizing that diversification beyond bleach was essential to the company's survival, Clorox management implemented a three-pronged strategic plan aimed at the acquisition and internal development of a line of nonfood grocery products, the acquisition of a food specialty business, and the development of a line of institutional food and cleaning products. They drew up a list of potential targets for acquisition, many of which were purchased within the year, including Jiffee Chemical Corporation, the manufacturer of Liquid-plumr drain opener; Shelco, which manufactured Jifoam aerosol oven cleaner; and the 409 division of Harrell International, which produced Formula 409 spray cleaners. One year later the company introduced Clorox 2, its first entry in the dry, nonchlorine segment of the bleach market.

In 1971 Clorox purchased McFadden Industries, makers of Litter Green cat litter. Clorox had first tested McFadden's product in the market with an option to acquire the entire company if the product proved successful. Clorox also acquired Grocery Store Products Company, which manufactured such specialty food products as B&B mushrooms, Kitchen Bouquet gravy thickener, and Cream of Rice cereal. A year later Clorox added a line of salad dressings and party dips to this operation by buying Hidden Valley Ranch Food Products. Sales of the company's chlorine bleach rebounded in the first years of the decade as concerns arose over the health and environmental effects of enzyme and phosphate detergents.

In 1972 Clorox met the third objective of its strategic plan with the acquisitions of Martin-Brower Corporation, a manufacturer and supplier of disposable packaging and paper goods for the food-service industry, and Nesbitt Food Products, a manufacturer and distributor of soft drink concentrates. Joining the fold the following year was Kingsford Corporation, a leading manufacturer of charcoal briquettes.

The company soon encountered a series of setbacks, however. Just after the Kingsford acquisition, a cool and wet summer depressed sales of charcoal and the recreational products manufactured by other parts of the Kingsford operation. Clorox's introduction of a new product, Mr. Mushroom, coincided unexpectedly with a nationwide botulism scare, which adversely affected Mr. Mushroom and the company's B&B brand. Mushroom production at its newly acquired Country Kitchen Foods subsidiary in England decreased significantly due to a virus in the fertilizer used. Sales of Clorox's cleaning products also fell because of consumers' fears of recession.

Although these problems led to a temporary halt in further acquisitions, the company successfully negotiated an agreement in 1974 with Henkel, a German producer of consumer and industrial food and cleaning products. Clorox gained access to Henkel's research-and-development capabilities and acquired manufacturing and marketing rights to Henkel-developed products in the United States, Canada, and Puerto Rico. Henkel in turn became a minority shareholder in Clorox. In 1975 a civil antitrust suit brought against both Clorox and Procter & Gamble by Purex Corporation, a competitor in the bleach market, came to trial. The suit sought over $520 million in damages, which Purex claimed had resulted from Procter & Gamble's acquisition of Clorox in the late 1950s. Purex admitted defeat in 1982, when the Supreme Court refused to hear the case. Both a federal court and federal appeals court had ruled that Purex had failed to prove that either company had caused it to suffer any loss of business.

Shetterly retired as chief executive officer in 1980 and was succeeded by Calvin Hatch, another former Procter & Gamble executive. Under Shetterly's leadership, the company had diversified beyond bleach into a number of other areas; however, most of these new ventures never became profitable. Conceding that Shetterly's growth plan had failed, Clorox sold its Martin-Brower subsidiary at a loss in 1979 to the U.K.-based Dalgety PLC, and Country Kitchen Foods—its British mushroom canning operation—to H.J. Heinz Company, Ltd., the U.K. subsidiary of the U.S. company. These divestitures gave Clorox plenty of capital to use in its search for niches in the consumer packaged-goods market in which the company could develop its own products and capture a dominant share.

Clorox devoted a significant amount of money and corporate support to research and development. Until the company was able to come up with a breakthrough product of its own, however, it continued to rely upon outside acquisitions to diversify its business and fill its new-product pipeline. Some of the acquisitions made under Hatch's leadership, such as the 1979 purchase of the Emil Villa chain of barbecue restaurants, paralleled Shetterly's mistakes in fueling growth but not profits, while other products gained through earlier acquisitions, such as Cream of Rice cereal, fell short of the company's goals and were eventually sold. Efforts to generate and rapidly build a base of international business were also stymied by solidly entrenched competition.

In 1981 the company acquired Comerco, a Tacoma, Washington-based producer of stains and wood preservatives marketed under the Olympic brand name to hardware and home-improvement stores. Two years later, the company purchased Lucite house paints from E.I. Du Pont de Nemours Company. Clorox attempted to model these acquisitions after its successful Kingsford charcoal operation, using marketing techniques and heavy advertising to produce premium-priced, brand-name products. The subsidiary formed to manage these businesses was never effectively able to integrate the operations of these two product lines nor to attain the company's sales expectations, however. It was sold to PPG Industries in 1989 at a loss of $20 million.

Over the years, Clorox had retained leadership of the laundry-bleach market despite numerous attempts by competitors to chip away at its share with other brand-name, private-label, and generic products. In 1982 Clorox faced its toughest challenge when Procter & Gamble decided to launch its own bleach product called Vibrant in a test market. Clorox quickly responded by introducing a new bleach with a similar formula called Wave. Although Vibrant never made it out of the test-market stage due to manufacturing problems, this competitive advance against Clorox set the stage for future attempts by each company to invade the markets for products long dominated by the other.

In 1986 Calvin Hatch retired as chairman, a post he had held since 1982, and was succeeded by president and CEO Charles R. Weaver. Jack W. Collins, the company's executive vice-president and chief operating officer, was promoted to Weaver's former positions. Beginning in 1987, the company diversified into another new business area by purchasing a number of bottled-water companies, including the Deer Park Spring Water Company and Deep Rock Water Company, followed by the Aqua Pure Water Company and Emerald Coast Water Company in 1988.

After several years of uneasy coexistence after the Vibrant incident, the battle between Clorox and Procter & Gamble for dominance of the consumer marketplace erupted. In 1988 the company introduced its Clorox Super Detergent brand of laundry soap powder in four western states and was quickly attacked by Procter & Gamble's new Tide With Bleach brand. Procter & Gamble also began the market test of a new brand of liquid bleach targeted at Clorox customers, a move intended to warn Clorox against entering the laundry detergent market. By mid-1989 Procter & Gamble had withdrawn its bleach product due to disappointing sales. Clorox kept its detergent on the market but continued to face an uphill battle against the entrenched brands. The fact that consumer preferences were slowly moving away from powders toward liquid detergents added to the company's marketing problems. In an attempt to inject new life into its consumer products business, the company acquired the Pine Sol cleaner and Combat insecticide lines of American Cyanamid Company in 1990 for $465 million, a price generally considered to be too high. That same year, Robert A. Bolingbroke became president, succeeding the retiring Collins.

After spending more than $225 million over three years developing and marketing its detergent, and having thereupon achieved only a three percent market share, Clorox in May 1991 abandoned this aggressive but misguided venture. The company took a $125 million pretax charge, largely to exit the detergent business, a charge that cut net earnings to $52.7 million for fiscal 1991, a 65.7 percent drop from the $153.6 million of the previous year. Clorox's entree into detergent was doubly damaging since Procter & Gamble's counterpunch—Tide With Bleach—also cut into sales of Clorox bleach, with Clorox 2 particularly hard hit, its sales falling 10 percent in fiscal 1991 alone. In addition to exiting the detergent business, Clorox around the same time pulled the plug on other ill-advised products it was testing, including a bar soap called Satine and Hidden Valley Ranch microwavable frozen entrees.

Sullivan Turned Company Around in the Mid-1990s

In the aftermath of the company's largely self-inflicted difficulties, Weaver retired in mid-1992. His selection for a successor, Bolingbroke, was rejected by the company board, who instead chose Craig Sullivan to be the new chairman and CEO. Bolingbroke soon resigned; Sullivan, a 21-year Clorox veteran who had been a group vice-president, eventually assumed the position of president as well; and the position of COO was eliminated in order to flatten the management structure.

Under Sullivan's leadership and with the help of a surging economy in the United States, Clorox achieved a remarkable turnaround during the mid-1990s. The largely single-digit year-on-year increases in net sales of the early 1990s gave way to 11.8 and 14.2 percent increases in fiscal 1996 and 1997, respectively, with net sales hitting a record $2.53 billion in 1997. Net earnings were on the rise as well, with another 1997 record of $249.4 million. Cleaning up and bolstering the company's product portfolio and expanding internationally fueled the resurgence.

Soon after becoming chairman, Sullivan ordered a comprehensive financial and strategic review of the company's entire line of products. The study identified three businesses—the Prince Castle restaurant equipment subsidiary, Deer Park bottled water, and the Moore's and Domani frozen food businesses—that accounted for 10 percent of company sales, 24 percent of its workforce, but none of its profits; these businesses also did not mesh well with the rest of Clorox's portfolio. All three were soon divested: Prince Castle was sold in June 1993; the following month, the bottled water business was sold; and in September 1993 Clorox sold Moore's and Domani to Ore-Ida Foods, a division of H.J. Heinz Co. The bottled water and frozen food businesses were sold for a combined $159.3 million.

The company's portfolio was subsequently shored up through a series of acquisitions and a renewed commitment to new product development. Clorox's strong balance sheet—with relatively low long-term debt and plenty of cash—placed it in perfect position to grow through acquisitions. In January 1994 the company acquired the S.O.S. brand of cleaning products from Miles Inc. for $116.5 million. Building on a joint venture it had been involved in since 1988, Clorox in fiscal 1995 purchased Canada-based Brita International Holdings, Inc., a manufacturer and marketer of Brita water filtration systems. In late 1995 the company extended its presence in the bug-killing business by purchasing the Black Flag line of insecticides from London's Reckitt & Colman Plc. Clorox then added Lestoil heavy-duty cleaner to its portfolio in mid-1996 in a deal with Procter & Gamble. And in December 1996 the company spent $360.1 million to acquire Armor All Products Corporation and its leading line of automotive cleaning products. Armor All became a wholly owned subsidiary of Clorox.

Meanwhile, notable new product successes included Floral Fresh Clorox, introduced in October 1995, and Lemon Fresh Pine-Sol, which debuted in February 1995 and was formulated after a survey discovered that many consumers did not like the smell of pine. During fiscal 1997 Formula 409 carpet cleaner was introduced, while the flagship Formula 409 all-purpose cleaner was reformulated to kill bacteria. The Clorox 2 color-safe bleach brand was revitalized in 1996 and 1997 through the relaunch of Clorox 2 liquid bleach as a concentrate and with the debut of Floral Fresh dry and liquid formulas.

In the long run, Sullivan's emphasis on international growth was perhaps the most important aspect of his multipronged revitalization program. During the early 1990s, Clorox derived only four percent of its net sales outside the United States. Sullivan created an international team to tackle overseas markets and set an ambitious goal of deriving a full 20 percent of sales from these markets by 2000. By 1997 Clorox was well on its way to meeting this goal as international sales reached 14 percent. Much of this growth was fueled through acquisitions, particularly in Latin America, where the company was able to quickly gain half of the bleach markets in Argentina and Colombia and 90 percent of the bleach market in Chile. Overall, Clorox spent $1 billion acquiring 26 companies from fiscal 1993 through fiscal 1997—23 of these were non-U.S. companies, primarily Latin American.

Of course, not everything has gone smoothly in the mid-1990s. In September 1997 the company recalled and stopped production of QuickSilver, an automotive wheel-cleaning product, after it was blamed for the death of a Canadian child. The company planned to eventually replace the product with a less-toxic alternative. Despite such setbacks, the future looked bright for Clorox. By continuing to make smart extensions of its product lines, aggressively seeking out strategic acquisitions, and taking continued advantage of overseas opportunities—with Asia the company's next major beachhead—Clorox's renaissance was likely to last well into the new millennium.

Principal Subsidiaries

Armor All Products Company; The Brita Products Company; The Clorox Company of Puerto Rico; The Clorox International Company; Clorox Products Manufacturing Company; Clorox Professional Products Company; The Clorox Sales Company; Clorox Services Company; The HV Food Products Company; HV Manufacturing Company; Kingsford Manufacturing Company; The Kingsford Products Company; Clorox Argentina S.A.; Clorox do Brazil Ltda.; Brita (Canada) Inc.; The Clorox Company of Canada, Ltd.; Clorox Chile S.A.; Tecnoclor S.A. (Colombia); Clorox (Guangzhou) Company Limited (China); Clorox Korea, Ltd.; Clorox de Mexico S.A. de C.V.

Further Reading

About the Company on its Diamond Anniversary, Oakland, Calif.: The Clorox Company, [1988].

Bagamery, Anne, ''Laundryman,'' *Forbes,* July 15, 1985, p. 120.

Barrett, Amy, ''Clorox: Washed Up?,'' *Financial World,* February 4, 1992, pp. 17–18.

Bole, Kristen, ''Southern Lights: South America Brightens Outlook for Clorox,'' *San Francisco Business Times,* June 14, 1996, p. 3.

Byrne, Harlan S., ''Clorox Co.,'' *Barron's,* December 3, 1990, p. 47.

Calandra, Thom, ''In the Hot Seat,'' *Forbes,* October 12, 1992, p. 126.

Carlsen, Clifford, ''Clorox Co. Positioned for Large Acquisition,'' *San Francisco Business Times,* November 20, 1992, p. 2A.

David, Gregory E., ''New, Improved . . .,'' *Financial World,* February 15, 1994, pp. 36–37.

Hamilton, Joan O'C., ''Brighter Days at Clorox,'' *Business Week,* June 16, 1997, pp. 62, 65.

Hof, Robert D., ''A Washout for Clorox?,'' *Business Week,* July 9, 1990, p. 32.

Jaffe, Thomas, ''No Soap,'' *Forbes,* August 13, 1984, p. 122.

Johnson, Bradley, ''Clorox's Identity Crisis,'' *Advertising Age,* May 6, 1991, pp. 1, 54.

——, ''What Sullivan Faces as New Clorox CEO,'' *Advertising Age,* June 1, 1992, p. 48.

Lappen, Alyssa A., ''Battling for a Bleachhead,'' *Forbes,* November 28, 1988, p. 138.

Levine, Jonathan B., ''Clorox Makes a Daring Move in the Laundry Room,'' *Business Week,* May 2, 1988, p. 36.

Neff, Jack, ''New Products Pump Clorox Growth,'' *Advertising Age,* June 16, 1997, p. 22.

Shao, Maria, ''A Bright Idea That Clorox Wishes It Never Had,'' *Business Week,* June 24, 1991, pp. 118–19.

Shetterly, Robert B., *Renaissance of the Clorox Company,* New York: Newcomen Society in North America, 1973, 16 p.

Shisgall, Oscar, *Eyes on Tomorrow: The Evolution of Procter & Gamble,* Chicago: J.G. Ferguson Publishing Company, 1981, 295 p.

—Sandy Schusteff
—updated by David E. Salamie

CompDent Corporation

100 Mansell Court East
Suite 400
Roswell, Georgia 30076-8228
U.S.A.
(770) 998-8936
Fax: (770) 998-6871
Web site: http://www.compdent.com

Public Company
Incorporated: 1978 as American Prepaid Professional Services, Inc.
Employees: 460
Sales: $141.1 million (1996)
Stock Exchanges: NASDAQ
SICs: 8099 Dentists Service Organizations; 6719 Holding Companies, Not Elsewhere Classified; 6324 Hospital & Medical Service Plans; 6411 Insurance; 8021 Offices & Clinics of Dentists

CompDent Corporation is a fully integrated dental management company that provides full-service dental benefits. A growing company in a fragmented industry, CompDent provides attractive options to both the consumers it serves and the dentists who participate in its plans. By building large networks of dental care facilities and providers, CompDent offers its members convenient locations and cost-saving programs. Dentists who work with CompDent may choose their preferred method of affiliation in the plans. Also among their efforts to provide quality services, the company carefully evaluates each potential participating dentist in its programs. Its Quality Management function, headed by the company's National Dental Director, includes a credential review, verification of license, DEA certification, and malpractice insurance verification.

A team of 40 direct sales people attend to CompDent's national group participants, and a group of over 8,000 independent agents work for the company focusing on smaller employers and individuals. In addition the company provides management services, MIS, member service, and billing and underwriting support to each state. Local offices are responsible for marketing and dental relations.

CompDent deals with both dental HMO programs and fee-for-service programs. In the dental HMO, dentists receive, along with the patient copayment, a capitation—a monthly flat fee for each patient rather than payment for specific treatments, whether or not the patient wants services that month. The patient benefits of dental HMOs include no deductibles and low copayments for visits, with payments of only 20 percent to 50 percent for special procedures. According to one analyst, "Under a capitated system, dentists don't want to see you (so) they have a lot of incentive to give high quality dental care." The fee-for-service arrangement allows dentists to sidestep the risks of managed care, but still get the volume of patients which are often missed by not joining an HMO. In such a program, dentists give patients discounts and then receive discounted fees for all services performed. Regarding its relatively new fee-for-service plans, CEO and Chairman David R. Klock told *Investor's Business Daily*, "[Dentists] know they will collect on all the services they perform. Some find this friendlier and are more likely to sign on." CompDent product offerings also include: CompSave, a discount fee-for-service product; CompNet, a PPO and network rental dental product; and ASO Services for self-insured dental plans.

Company Beginnings to 1990s Growth

CompDent was founded in 1978 as American Prepaid Professional Services, Inc. in Florida, and began *de novo* operations in seven other states in 1987. TA Associates arranged a buyout of APPS from its original investors for approximately $29.5 million in cash in June 1993. Business commenced under this new arrangement in July 1993.

Soon thereafter the company began its strides in growth through a series of acquisitions. December, 1994 was the date for acquiring both DentiCare, Inc. of Houston, Texas, and UniLife Insurance Co. DentiCare is a managed dental care company, and its acquisition increased the company's presence in this Texas market. UniLife, an indemnity insurer, was pur-

Company Perspectives:

Our mission is to remain, or become, the leading provider of managed dental care plans in each of our markets. Our business is really very simple. We offer our members affordable, convenient dental care—we make it easy for people to go to the dentist and we help build profitable dental practices, making it attractive for dentists to participate in our plans.

chased with plans to eventually phase out its dental indemnity business and/or to change its offerings to dual-choice, so that subscribers could choose their managed dental plans. The cost for this acquisition was $17 million, plus approximately $600,000 in transaction costs.

The company's initial public offering came in May 1995, as APPS Dental, Inc. (APPS ticker symbol on the NASDAQ exchange). Following this, in July 1995, CompDent Corp., located in Louisville, Kentucky, was acquired for $32.5 million, plus approximately $1.1 million in transaction fees. With operations in 13 states, together with DentiCare, this acquisition doubled the membership in the company managed dental care plan for a total of 1.4 million individuals in 16 states. After this large addition, the company's secondary offering of 3.4 million shares came in August 1995. This month also brought a name change, as APPS Dental, Inc. of Atlanta, Georgia, changed its name to CompDent Corporation. This change acknowledged the recent large acquisitions of DentiCare and CompDent, and was effective September 15, 1995. The company now traded under CPDN on the NASDAQ exchange.

A three-year contract with the State of North Carolina was won in November 1995, and began in January 1996. This was a big victory for CompDent, who had worked previously in the state for approximately two years. Because of the relatively few number of dentists in North Carolina, the company had difficulties recruiting new dentists to their program. With more customers to offer their professional clients, CompDent had more success in signing them on. In 1996 there were about 50 dentists working with the company, and about 9,000 of the 150,000 eligible state employees took part in CompDent's managed dental care plans. With the success of its recent acquisitions and contract awards, at year's end, 1995, the company's stock was up by a margin of 186 percent.

Texas Dental Plans, Inc. (Texas Dental) of San Antonio, Texas, and its subsidiary, National Dental Plans, Inc. were acquired in January 1996 for $23 million in cash. Texas Dental, a seller of referral fee-for-service plans, added roughly 400,000 plan members to CompDent's roster, and broadened their product lines. Texas membership then totaled over 500,000, which made CompDent a leader in the state's dental care program administrators. Texas Dental's network of over 5,000 dentists in 14 states bolstered the company's total coverage, adding on seven states for a total of 23 states and the District of Columbia.

The managed dental care industry, like CompDent, was growing through consolidation. To meet the increased demand, CompDent needed to continue to build a national network of facilities and clients by acquiring smaller managed dental care companies. As of February 1996, CompDent was the third largest managed dental care company in the country. Cigna and Prudential were the two largest.

In May 1996, Dental Care Plus Management Corp. (Dental Care) of Chicago, Illinois, and its wholly owned subsidiary, I.H.C.S., Inc. were acquired for $27 million in cash, and were scheduled to be fully integrated in 1997. With the addition of 450,000 members to its plans, CompDent was now one of the largest dental care administrators in Illinois, a state with the sixth largest concentration of managed dental care enrollment in 1996. These acquisitions helped the company earn a contract with the Illinois state government. Dental Care was a third party administrator and managed dental care provider, with approximately one-third of its members in managed care programs, the rest in employer-funded fee-for-service plans. I.H.C.S., Inc. processed claims for fee-for-service programs. Previously, CompDent did not have a claims processing unit. Claims for indemnity plans not sold in Illinois were processed by Shenandoah Life Insurance Co. of Roanoke, Virginia, which assumed all risks for the plans.

A new president of CompDent, Phyllis Klock, was elected in 1996. She began with the company in 1981 as a consultant, became vice-president of operations in 1986, then senior vice-president in 1993, and executive vice-president in 1996. Klock succeeded her husband, David, who remained as chairman and CEO. Dr. David Klock also began with the company as a consultant in 1981, was a board member since 1988, and then joined the company in 1991.

An additional 20,000 members were added to CompDent's plans with the March 1997 acquisition of American Dental Providers, Inc., and Diamond Dental for an undisclosed amount. These companies marked the expansion into CompDent's 24th covered state, Arkansas. The enlargement proved profitable to the company, as the six months ending June 30, 1997, reported record revenues of $76.04 million, up 15 percent from the same period in 1996.

1997 Expansion and Additions

In the first quarter of 1997, CompDent established Dental Health Management, Inc. (DHM), to provide management services to dental practices. The wholly owned subsidiary was expected to help expand CompDent dental networks in markets that were previously resistant to managed dental care programs. The unit was also planned to assist in the establishment of new dental offices where there was demand for CompDent products, but lack of participants. Philip Hertik, a CompDent board member since 1993, was elected president of DHM.

DHM entered into an agreement in June 1997 to acquire 21 dental facilities in Illinois for $14.3 million. It also entered into a 40-year management contract with the group practices, which consisted of 26 dentists that operated in these facilities. These offices were previously managed by the Effingham, Illinois-based Workman Management Group, Ltd. CompDent also optioned to acquire nine other dental centers managed by Workman Management Group, Ltd., over the next four years. As of

August 1997, DHM either owned or operated 27 offices in the South and Midwest, and planned to expand its operations even further. That same month DHM arranged an agreement with Quality Systems, Inc. to use Quality Systems' practice-management systems. The computer functions for this operation were centralized at CompDent's Roswell, Georgia, corporate headquarters. August 1997 also brought the resignation of CFO Sharon Graham. Graham's position was filled by Bruce Mitchell, an advisor to the company since 1981. At the time of his placement as interim CFO, he was also executive vice-president, corporate secretary, and general counsel to the company.

Together with a private equity firm, Golder Thoma Cressey Rauner, CompDent agreed to provide funding for Dental Health Development Corp. in September 1997. This corporation worked in the development of start-up dental facilities and was funded by a $15 million equity commitment from Golder Thomas Cressey Rauner and a $1.5 million investment by CompDent. Managed by DHM, Dental Health Development had its own independent board, and was to fund a total of 400 dental offices, and develop 35 to 50 *de novo* offices by 1999.

Room for Growth in the Future

In 1994, the National Association of Dental Plans in Dallas, Texas, approximated that 18.4 million people were enrolled in managed dental care plans, up from 7.8 million in 1990, showing growth of 25 percent per year. Still, CompDent estimated that one-half of Americans do not have dental insurance. An estimated 26,000 dentists were part of a dental HMO (15 percent of all general dentists), and an estimated 88 percent of dentists practiced either alone or with one partner. Facts such as these revealed how much potential room there was for expansion in this growing market. One health care fund manager noticed, ''From an investor perspective, it's a hot area because there aren't many of them yet. They're just beginning the transition from more indemnity-type practices to more managed-care plans.'' Industry, like CompDent, grew through consolidation. One way CompDent attracted new members was by building large groups of dentists in convenient locations. In 1997 the company operated approximately 4,500 dental facilities. With coverage of 24 states, CompDent boasted 2.2 million plan members, 65 percent of which were located in Florida, Illinois, and Texas. They served 19,000 group customers, including government groups, municipalities, school systems, and private industry. Regarding CompDent's growth and future capacities, then-president David R. Klock stated in his 1995 annual report, ''Our goal is to continue to build critical mass and to be not only an important regional managed dental plan, but . . . a strong national leader.'' CompDent seemed well on its way to achieving these goals.

Principal Subsidiaries

American Prepaid Professional Services, Inc.; American Dental Plan, Inc.; American Dental Plan of Georgia, Inc.; American Prepaid Dental Plan of Ohio, Inc.; American Dental Plan of Alabama, Inc.; American Dental Plan, Inc.; American Dental Plan of North Carolina, Inc.; DentiCare, Inc.; UniLife Insurance Co.; CompDent Corp.; Texas Dental Plans, Inc.; National Dental Plans, Inc.; Dental Plans International, Inc.; Dental Provider Resources, Inc.; Dental Care Plus Management Corp.; CompDent of Illinois, Inc. (formerly I.H.C.S.).

Further Reading

''CompDent Corp. and Dental Health Management Unit to Buy Assets of 21 Dental Facilities in Central and Southern Illinois for $14.3 Million,'' *Modern Healthcare*, July 14, 1997, p. 36.

''CompDent Will Acquire Dental Care Plus Management, a Third-Party Managed Dental Care Provider for $27 Million in Cash,'' *Chicago Tribune*, March 5, 1996, p. 3.

Epstein, Joseph, ''Dental Care Stocks: Open Wide,'' *Financial World*, December 16, 1996, p. 20.

Lau, Gloria, ''CompDent Thrives on Trend Toward Managed Dental Care,'' *Investor's Business Daily*,'' January 15, 1996, p. A4.

Purdy Levaux, Janet, ''New CompDent Plans Address Dentists' Managed-Care Angst,'' *Investor's Business Daily*, July 15, 1996, p. A4.

''Sell-Off in Atlanta-Based Dental Care Firm Seen As Buying Opportunity,'' *Tribune Business News*, February 16, 1996, p. 2160168.

—Melissa West

Corporate Express, Inc.

1 Environmental Way
Broomfield, Colorado 80021-3416
U.S.A.
(303) 664-2000
Fax: (303) 664-3981
Web site: http://www.corporate-express.com

Public Company
Incorporated: 1986
Employees: 27,000
Sales: $3.19 billion (1996)
Stock Exchanges: NASDAQ
SICs: 2677 Envelopes; 2761 Manifold Business Forms; 4215 Courier Services, Except by Air; 5021 Furniture; 5045 Computers & Computer Peripheral Equipment & Software; 5112 Stationery & Office Supplies; 5712 Furniture Stores; 5943 Stationery Stores; 7331 Direct Mail Advertising Services; 8741 Management Services

Corporate Express, Inc. is the world's largest provider of non-production goods and services and office products and services to large corporations and had a revenue of $3.196 billion for fiscal 1996.

From Czechoslovakia, with Love

The company was founded in Boulder, Colorado, by Jirka Rysavy, its chairman and CEO. Born in Czechoslovakia in 1954, the son of a civil engineer and an educational researcher, Rysavy became a hurdler for the Czech national team, competing in international track and field events. While attempting to reach the Olympics, Rysavy was forced out of competition due to injuries. In 1984, after earning a master's degree in engineering the previous year at the Technical University of Prague, he extended his travel visa and never returned to Czechoslovakia.

Barely speaking English, Rysavy spent a year in solitude in a remote part of Eastern Europe. After that, he traveled the world, sleeping on park benches and living on $3 a day, eventually finding himself in Boulder, Colorado, where he worked in a print shop for $3.35 an hour. After saving up $600, he started his own company, Transformational Economy, or Transecon, which sold recycled paper. Rysavy made $100,000 before taxes in his first year of business. Investing $30,000 of that money into a new venture following his strict vegetarian diet, Rysavy created Crystal Market, a natural foods retailer store, which made $2.5 million in sales in its first year. For a man with no business experience from a non-capitalist country, Rysavy was working wonders.

Planning to continue growing his foods business with additional health food markets, Rysavy got sidetracked when one of his neighbors in Boulder decided to sell an office supply store. Rysavy obtained the heavily indebted store for $100 and the assumption of $15,000 in overdue accounts payable. After renaming it Business Express and installing a computer system to track customers and sales, Rysavy realized that he would not be able to make the store successful by remaining a retail outlet. He noticed the successful accounts that a few local companies had with the store that bought supplies in large quantities. Moving quickly away from retail and towards corporate accounts, the company, renamed Corporate Express, within a year had made $2 million with a pretax margin of 14 percent.

In the fall of 1987, after seeing the success of his corporate strategy, Rysavy hired a researcher to collect material on the office supply industry. By December, Rysavy had a pile of research materials and spent two weeks on the beach in Hawaii wading through all of it. He discovered huge problems in the industry as a whole: thousands of office supply companies were sharing a $100 billion market, split up among local markets and not selling enough volume to get deep discounts from manufacturers. And with the number of office products being produced growing at an enormous rate most stores were overburdened with huge, slow-turning inventories.

Watching Staples and Office Depot begin to boom about the same time in the small business and home business retail market, Rysavy decided to try the same thing on a bigger scale by serving large corporations, companies with 100 or more employees, which accounted for $30 billion of the industry annu-

Company Perspectives:

Through procurement analysis and a close business partnership between the company and its clients, Corporate Express, Inc. is re-engineering the procurement process for providing office supplies, promotional products, desktop software, furniture, computer supplies, imaging supplies, cleaning supplies, same-day delivery and logistics management to its large corporate customers.

ally. Selling his health food store to Mike Gilliland for $300,000 (Gilliland went on to make Wild Oats into a natural grocery store chain worth $200 million), Rysavy invested it all and managed to leverage the $12.8 million pricetag on the office products division of NBI, a Denver-based company with a loss of $1 million on sales of $20 million. Desiring to repeat with NBI the strategy which had worked for his small Boulder store, Rysavy needed to install a computer system to analyze NBI's market and customers. Boyhood friend and computer software developer Pavel Bouska came from Munich to Colorado to help in 1988.

Clearing the Hurdles, 1992–96

In 1992, with Bouska's computer system up and running, Rysavy's company had attained 10 percent operating margins and would reach $65 million in sales by 1995. Striking out for the territories, Rysavy acquired his first companies outside of Colorado. The $31.6 million company acquired Trick & Murray, a $15 million office supply company, merging it with two other acquisitions in the Seattle area. In order to convince Trick & Murray to sell, Rysavy promised in three years to reach sales of $300 million. But at the end of 1992, the company posted revenues of $420 million. A year later, revenues rose to $520 million and the company continued its skyward climb. In 1994, the company completed six acquisitions in exchange for 1.7 million shares of stock swapped and revenues skyrocketed to $1.145 billion.

In 1995, the company moved forcefully into the international market with several foreign acquisitions. With over 14,000 employees in over 500 locations, the company's revenues reached an unprecedented $1.891 billion. Analysts estimated the company would reach $3 billion in the year 2000. They were wrong.

With two acquisitions in 1996, the company became a major player in the distribution of desktop software to corporations, both domestically and internationally. In February, the company acquired Young, a distributor of computer and imaging supplies and accessories, in a 4.4 million share stock swap. The company merged CEX Acquisition Corp., a wholly owned subsidiary of Corporate Express, into Young. In October, Corporate Express acquired France's leading supplier of computer software, the Paris-based company Nimsa, in a 1.1 million share stock swap and $2.3 million in cash. That month, the company also acquired a 51 percent interest in The Chisholm Group in the United Kingdom.

In order to deliver all of its product lines more efficiently, the company created its own delivery system. In March, the company acquired U.S. Delivery Systems, Inc. (USDS), the largest local same-day delivery service in the United States, in a 23.4 million share stock swap. The company merged DSU Acquisition Corp., a wholly owned subsidiary of Corporate Express, into USDS. Strengthening its domestic delivery infrastructure, the company acquired, in November, United TransNet, Inc. (UTI), the second-largest same-day delivery service provider in the United States, in a 6.3 million share stock swap. The company merged Bevo Acquisition Corp., a wholly owned subsidiary of Corporate Express, into UTI.

In 1996, the company acquired 104 firms, including 46 domestic office product distributors, 32 international office product distributors, and 11 delivery service companies for a total of $241.9 million in cash and approximately 3.6 million shares of stock swapped. Of the 32 international acquisitions, nine were in Canada, seven were in the United Kingdom, five were in Australia, and three were in New Zealand. With five acquisitions in Germany, two in Italy, and one (Nimsa) in France, Corporate Express entered the markets in those countries for the first time. In November, the company purchased the remaining 49 percent interest in The Chisholm Group in a stock swap and with options of up to $3.3 million, pushing the international operations of the company to account for approximately 18 percent of the company's total revenue.

From the company's inception, it has been uniquely focused on the development and deployment of innovative technology. In its early years, Corporate Express introduced inventory management systems far more sophisticated than those of many large corporations, systems which could electronically track sales and inventory by item and accurately predict future sales and inventory requirements. The company's belief in the competitive power of technology caused it to routinely reinvest much of its profits into the development of these proprietary information management systems. In 1996, approximately 300 systems architects and engineers were on the payroll of Corporate Express, showing the strength of the company's commitment to ongoing systems development and implementation.

In September, the company unveiled and began to implement a major upgrade to its proprietary global electronic commerce system. The company released ISIS 3.0, a new generation of hardware, software, and networking capabilities. When completed, it would be a dynamic program integrating all facets of the company's processes, organizational structure, systems, and customer service. The three-tier client/server computer architecture was the backbone of the company's Corporate Supplier model, seamlessly integrating three components, the customer's desktop with the company's distribution and service capabilities.

The back end of the system consisted of the actual Corporate Express company infrastructure, controlling product inventory, pricing, contracts, business practices, and delivery. Each customer account was customized by facility, price, supplier, and item. The centralized structure also allowed the consolidation of all customers' orders and invoicing, a capability especially valuable to corporations with multiple locations, as well as potentially providing a direct interface to their general ledger system. In addition, the back end system continually tracked and analyzed cost and demand patterns, allowing the company to forecast optimal reorder times and quantities, enabling the company to turn its inventory well in excess of the industry average and offering the customers a higher level of service.

At the front end, the customer's desktop, the system offered order entry featuring powerful search and display capabilities, rapid price look-up, customized order and payment approval, routing, and a secure connection for electronic commerce, allowing orders to be transmitted via a full range of traditional or electronic connections. The system was available to the customer without charge in a variety of formats, including a customized interface with customers' Intranet facilities. An Internet version of the system was being tested in late 1996 by certain key customers.

Within five years, the company's revenues had grown from $32 million to a staggering $3.196 billion, a 58 percent increase over 1995 revenues of $1.890 billion, blowing analysts' previous-year estimates away, and the company declared a 50 percent share dividend of its common stock, giving each shareholder an additional share of stock for every two shares held.

From Here to There, 1997 Onward

In 1997, the company continued its skyrocketing growth rate with more acquisitions. January saw the company acquiring Hermann Marketing, Inc. (HMI), the largest privately held supplier of promotional products to large corporations in the United States, Canada, the United Kingdom, and the Netherlands, in a 4.6 million share stock swap. The company merged Hermann Marketing Acquisition Corp., a wholly owned subsidiary of Corporate Express into HMI. Also in January, the company acquired Sofco-Mead, Inc. (SMI), one of the largest suppliers of janitorial and cleaning supplies in the U.S., in a 2.6 million share stock swap. The company merged IMS Acquisition Inc., a wholly owned subsidiary of Corporate Express into SMI.

By February, Corporate Express had acquired 15 additional companies, including St. Paul Book and Stationery, Inc. The St. Paul, Minnesota-based company was founded in 1851 and was one of the largest and oldest independent contract stationers in the United States. By June, the company had already acquired 13 additional companies for a total of $24.7 million. Two of the companies were contract stationers in Italy. Katro S.p.A. and Asite S.p.A. were purchased and consolidated into a new 120,000-square-foot distribution center located in Milan. Two other contract stationers were acquired in Cologne and Leipzig, Germany. The remaining nine acquisitions were in North America, including Everything for the Office, a $20 million-a-year contract stationer in Minneapolis, Minnesota.

September brought a definitive merger agreement with Data Documents Incorporated, a leading provider of forms management services and systems and custom business forms to large corporate customers, in a $195 million stock swap. The Omaha, Nebraska-based Data Documents added 85 new locations to the company. That month the company also finalized the expansion of its unsecured, multi-currency credit facility from $350 million to $500 million.

By mid-1997, the company employed some 27,000 people and operated from approximately 700 locations throughout the world, including 80 distribution centers located in the United States, Canada, Australia, New Zealand, Germany, France, Italy, and the United Kingdom. Customers select desired products and place orders by various means of electronic commerce, telephone, or fax, and receive next-business-day delivery via the company's fleet of over 10,000 delivery vehicles.

The company remained firmly committed to working toward preserving the Earth's environment through the creation of a nonprofit foundation. It also encouraged its employees, suppliers, and customers to adopt environmentally conservative practices such as disposing of trash properly, reusing old paper for notepads, and using electronic commerce to conserve paper and fossil fuels. Corporate Express also redesigned its shipping cartons to include more recycled materials; minimized the use of Styrofoam and plastic; initiated a toner cartridge collection, refill, and disposal system for numerous contract clients; increased the use of natural gas rather than unleaded gas in its fleet of trucks; and treated wet and dry waste items separately.

With such major customers as Oracle Corporation, Saturn Corporation, and Sun Microsystems, and heavy investors such as OfficeMax, the deep-discount office superstore chain, which owns 20.3 percent of the company (Rysavy owns 5.4 percent), the company could be expected to continue to significantly increase the scope of its operations throughout the United States, Canada, the United Kingdom, and Australia. In addition, with acquisitions in New Zealand, Germany, Italy, and France, the company aspired to enter new markets and attempt to capture more of the $300 billion-a-year global industry from Boise Cascade, Office Depot, Burhmann-Tetterode, and Staples, its largest competitors.

Principal Subsidiaries

ASAP Software Express, Inc.; Corporate Express Australia; Corporate Express, Inc. (Kansas City, Missouri); Corporate Express of Northern California, Inc.; Corporate Express of Texas, Inc.; Corporate Express of the East, Inc.; Corporate Express of the Mid-Atlantic, Inc.; Federal Sales Service, Inc.; Richard Young Journal, Inc.; Ross-Martin Co.; Siekert and Baum Corporate Express, Inc.; U.S. Delivery Systems, Inc.

Further Reading

Arreola, Sylvia Moya, "Largest Area Courier and Messenger Firms," *Houston Business Journal,* April 25, 1997, p. 22.

Aven, Paula, "Denver-Area Office Supply Companies," *Denver Business Journal,* February 24, 1995, p. 18A.

Avery, Susan, "Can Consolidated Continue?" *Purchasing,* October 17, 1996, p. 93.

Benjamin, Aubri, "Largest Courier and Messenger Service Firms," *South Florida Business Journal,* September 20, 1996, p. 18A.

Birkin, Danielle, "Busiest Area Messenger Services," *Business Journal—Portland,* July 4, 1997, p. 14.

Brown, Dionne, and Andrew Pratt, "Largest Office Furniture Companies," *South Florida Business Journal,* December 15, 1995, p. 4B.

"Corporate Express Acquisition," *Wall Street Journal,* November 7, 1996, p. B8(W).

"Corporate Express Agrees to Buy Data Documents," *New York Times,* September 12, 1997, p. C4(N)/D4(L).

"Corporate Express Cites $24.7 Million Expansion," *New York Times,* June 7, 1997, p. 23(N).

"Corporate Express Inc.," *Wall Street Journal,* January 9, 1997, p. B4(W)/A4(E).

"Corporate Express Stock Plummets on Earnings News," *New York Times,* March 6, 1997, p. C4(N)/D4(L).

"Corporate Express Stock Split," *Wall Street Journal,* January 23, 1997, p. C21(W).

"Data Documents Purchase Is Planned for $195 Million," *Wall Street Journal,* September 12, 1997, p. B4(W)/B4(E).

Edgerton, Jerry, "These Six Small Stocks Promise Big Gains," *Money,* Winter 1996, p. 66.

"The Hottest Entrepreneurs in America," *Inc.,* December 1995, p. 35.

"Jirka Rysavy: Chairman and CEO, Corporate Express," *Chain Store Age Executive with Shopping Center Age,* December 1995, p. 54.

"Jirka Rysavy, Corporate Express," *PI,* September 1996.

Ketelsen, James, "Learning the Hard Way," *Forbes,* December 18, 1995, p. 130.

Laderman, Jeffrey M., "Don't Worry, Be Bullish," *Business Week,* August 4, 1997, pp. 28–29.

——. "Three IPOs That'll Let You in On the Ground Floor," *Business Week,* June 6, 1994, p. 108.

Mullins, Robert, "Supply Firms Take New Owners, Battle with Chains," *Business Journal-Milwaukee,* April 15, 1995, p. 2A.

"Profit Fell 17% in Quarter on 40% Revenue Increase," *Wall Street Journal,* June 27, 1997, p. B5(W).

Rutledge, Tanya, "Office Products Giant to Build Mega-Project," *Houston Business Journal,* October 25, 1996, p. 1A.

Schine, Eric, "The Mountain Man of Office Gear," *Business Week,* May 5, 1997, p. 114.

Schonfeld, Erick, "Delivering Growth," *Fortune,* September 4, 1995, p. 137.

Svaldi, Aldo, "Corporate Express Shares Rebound from March Fall," *Denver Business Journal,* July 4, 1997, p. 4A.

Tejada, Carlos, "Corporate Express Says Earnings Trail Estimates, and Its Stock Almost Plummets 45%," *Wall Street Journal,* March 6, 1997, p. B2(W)/B10(E).

Vasquez, Beverly, "Corporate Express Turns 100: Dealmaking Flurry Makes Boulder Office Supplier Nation's Largest," *Denver Business Journal,* February 28, 1997, p. 6B.

—Daryl F. Mallett

The Cosmetic Center, Inc.

8839 Greenwood Place
Savage, Maryland 20763
U.S.A.
(301) 497-6800
Fax: (301) 497-6632
Web site: http://www.revlon.com

Public Subsidiary of Revlon Consumer Products Corporation
Incorporated: 1957 as Cosmetic & Fragrance Concepts, Inc.
Employees: 1,630
Sales: $133.8 million (1996)
Stock Exchanges: NASDAQ
SICs: 5912 Drugstores & Proprietary Stores; 5999 Miscellaneous Retail Stores, Not Elsewhere Classified; 7231 Beauty Shops

The Cosmetic Center, Inc. is a retail chain selling a wide range of brand-name cosmetics, fragrances, beauty aids, and related items. Company headquarters, a warehouse, and a distribution center all are located in Savage, Maryland. Cosmetic Center has expanded since its founding to metropolitan areas throughout the eastern United States, with 69 stores operating as of early 1997. Each store stocks more than 25,000 items and sells them at a substantial discount from manufacturers' suggested prices. The company fills a gap between high-end department stores and discount stores and drugstores. The Cosmetic Center also operates hair salons in most of its stores. Its wholesale division markets cosmetic products to independent drugstores and regional retail chains throughout the United States; and its distribution division markets the company's own product line.

Origin and Founders

Cosmetic Center was founded as a home-based business, Cosmetic & Fragrance Concepts, Inc., in 1957. Louis Weinstein and his wife, Anita, began operating a wholesale cosmetics distribution operation, dealing with independent drugstores from their Maryland apartment. The business soon required a warehouse, and eventually a retail store (Susan Kay Cosmetics, no relation to Mary Kay Cosmetics) was opened in 1973, at the urging of the founders' son, Mark Weinstein. During the early years the Weinstein company was privately owned and had limited operations in the Washington, D.C., area. By the mid-1980s, the business had grown to eight retail stores, and Louis Weinstein decided to begin offering stock to the public. Soon afterward he also replaced the company's management with a new team that concentrated on expanding the company, and in 1991 it was renamed The Cosmetic Center, Inc. Although Mark Weinstein became CEO, Louis Weinstein remained chairman of the company, and his death in 1995 was one of several events that threw the company into turmoil.

Rapid Expansion in the 1980s and Early 1990s

After its initial public stock offering in 1986, Cosmetic Center began to record a profit in every quarter. Company management, encouraged by the chain's success, began to focus on expanding both the number of retail stores and the geographic areas in which stores were located. Cosmetic Center targeted major Eastern metropolitan areas for expansion, and the number of stores operating increased every year through 1995. From the original ten stores operating in Washington, D.C., and Maryland in 1986, the company then opened several stores in the Chicago area, followed by stores in Richmond, Virginia; Charlotte/Raleigh/Durham, North Carolina; Philadelphia; and Atlanta. Cosmetic Center also developed its own cosmetic line, including a line of fragrance-free cosmetics added in 1994. The company began to report sales averaging $2.5 million per store.

The opening of eight stores in the Atlanta area in 1994 and early 1995 was viewed as part of a major expansion effort by Cosmetic Center's management. Senior Vice-President Allen D. Nehman explained that the company was hoping to draw professional working women who wanted one-stop shopping. ''The reason we've been successful,'' he told *Drug Store News,* ''is because we make the stores fun to shop. Everything we do, we do for the customer.'' While many products were still offered at a discount price, the approach was to offer more upscale products, as in major department stores, and to expand

Company Perspectives:

Historically, the primary retailers of cosmetic products have been department stores, drugstores and discount stores. Department stores offer primarily higher priced prestige items, usually at the manufacturers' suggested retail price. Traditional drugstores generally offer lower priced, mass-merchandised items and a limited selection of prestige items typically at the manufacturers' suggested retail price. Discount stores feature lower prices, but generally only offer mass-merchandised cosmetic products. The Company believes that the traditional industry marketing practices present an opportunity for a specialty retailer and that its distinctive combination of value pricing, breadth and depth of product selection, customer service, strategic store concentration and aggressive marketing creates a competitive advantage over other cosmetic product retailers.

the line of men's products. Plans were announced to make Cosmetic Center a national chain with 200 stores by the year 2000, with hopes of increasing sales from 1994's $124 million to $500 million within the same time period.

Death of the Founder and Takeover Attempts

Unfortunately, Cosmetic Center's plans for the remainder of the 1990s went awry when several unforeseen events converged in 1995. The first and perhaps the most devastating was the death of the company's founder, Louis Weinstein, on July 8, 1995. Only a month later, his widow, Anita (a major stockholder), and son, Mark (CEO of the company), were faced with a surprise hostile takeover attempt by Perfumania, Inc., a large Miami-based retail chain store selling fragrances. Perfumania initially offered stockholders more than 40 percent above the stock's value on the NASDAQ exchange. Cosmetic Center repeatedly rejected Perfumania's proposals, particularly concerned because Perfumania could not show any commitment from a financial institution that would give it funds to purchase Cosmetic Center.

Cosmetic Center's rejection of Perfumania did not end the takeover attempts. In November 1995, Regis Corporation (owner of a national chain of beauty salons) submitted its own proposal for buying Cosmetic Center. Although there were initial discussions about this possibility, Regis soon withdrew its proposal. In December 1995, Cosmetic Center once again was approached by a potential buyer, this time Phar-Mor, Inc., a national chain of drugstores. Under this proposal, Cosmetic Center would become a wholly owned subsidiary of Phar-Mor. However, Phar-Mor and Cosmetic Center could not come to an agreement on the purchase price or on the amount of Phar-Mor stock that would be given to Cosmetic Center stockholders, and so this proposal also fell through. This marked the end of takeover attempts, opening the way for a merger with a branch of Revlon Cosmetics that was finalized in 1997.

Atlanta Stores Closed

In 1996 Cosmetic Center received more bad news. Its Atlanta stores, a new market opened with such great hope just two years earlier, were financial disappointments. Costs were high, competition from department stores was unexpectedly strong, and sales were slow. After the stores rang up a $1 million loss during the 1996 fiscal year, Cosmetic Center decided to immediately close all eight Atlanta stores effective August 4, 1996. The closings resulted in an initial loss of over $4 million to the company, including payoffs of lease obligations (which would extend over the next several years), severance payments for almost 150 workers in the stores, and writeoffs of assets in the stores.

Financial Performance in the 1990s

The early 1990s were years of great growth and profit for Cosmetic Center. Net sales rose steadily, from $101.2 million in fiscal 1992 to $109.5 million in 1993 and $123.6 million in 1994. Net earnings soared during the same fiscal years, from $2.4 million in 1992 to almost $3.6 million in 1993 and $4.2 million in 1994. The number of stores also grew rapidly, from 39 in 1992 to 47 in 1993 and 61 in 1994 (with eight more stores opened in Atlanta during the fiscal 1995). Cosmetic Center began to market its own product line of cosmetics and opened hair salons in most of its stores, and all looked rosy.

Unfortunately, fiscal 1995 brought this trend to a crashing halt. With the Atlanta stores, Cosmetic Center now had 73 stores operating. The huge losses run up at the Atlanta stores and the death of founder Louis Weinstein (which involved a payroll expense of $0.8 million given to Weinstein's estate) were only part of the bad financial news. Retail sales in general were slow, attributed by some experts to the more casual approach taken by working women (with "casual Fridays" creeping into earlier parts of the week) and the increased competition from department stores. Cosmetic Center itself also noted the adverse effects of the shrinking independent drug store market on its wholesale division's sales. A further problem was the company's inability to reach a direct agreement with the manufacturers of major professional hair care products, allowing it to sell these products in its hair salons. Cosmetic Center had cancelled its agreements with secondary sources of hair care products in anticipation of reaching such an agreement, and so it found itself with extremely limited sources for these profitable products.

Consequently, Cosmetic Center had mediocre results in fiscal 1995 and gloomy results in fiscal 1996. Net sales in fiscal 1995 rose about seven percent, to $132.3 million. However, while retail sales rose about eight percent, wholesale sales fell almost 28 percent from the previous year, and net earnings plummeted to only $279,000. Fiscal 1996 brought no relief. Net sales overall rose only 1.1 percent, to $133.8 million. Retail sales rose almost two percent, but wholesale sales fell another 34.6 percent from the already-poor record of the previous year. With the closing of the Atlanta stores at the end of fiscal 1996, Cosmetic Center found itself facing a year of losses instead of its traditional earnings. The year brought a net loss of almost $4.8 million. Drops in sales and continued losses continued into the early part of the next fiscal year.

This crisis within the company led management to drastically reduce its plans for future expansion, given that an estimated $725,000 was required for each new store opening. It also helped Cosmetic Center reach the decision to merge with one of its major product sources, Revlon Consumer Products Corporation, in late 1996.

Revlon Merger

In October 1996, Cosmetic Center announced its plan to merge with a chain of discount cosmetic stores owned by the Revlon Consumer Products Corporation. The chain, a wholly owned subsidiary of Revlon operating under the name Prestige Fragrance & Cosmetics, Inc. (PFC), sold brand-name cosmetics, fragrances, and health and beauty products in almost 200 stores located in 41 states. Several of these stores were operated by Prestige under separate names: Colours & Scents, Visage, and The Cosmetic Warehouse. With this merger (formally termed a reverse acquisition), Revlon was initiating its own withdrawal from the retail cosmetics business, which it had been operating at a loss, in order to concentrate on its manufacturing operations. By the following month, Cosmetic Center and Revlon had already reached an agreement under which Cosmetic Center would remain as the surviving corporation.

According to materials submitted in early 1997 to its stockholders (who had to approve the merger in order for it to be completed), Cosmetic Center hoped that the merger would reverse its poor record of recent years. It believed that the combination of the two companies would "create an opportunity to achieve accelerated earnings growth through cost savings, synergies, and critical mass," according to an April 3, 1997 "Notice to Stockholders." Certainly the merger would give Cosmetic Center an entry into a wider national market, plus a solid link to a supplier of cosmetic products. In addition, it was hoped that this approach would avoid a repetition of the sort of dilemma caused by the company's loss of hair care product suppliers. PFC also brought along its office, warehouse, and distribution facilities in New Jersey, plus about 850 full-time employees.

It was anticipated that Cosmetic Center's current management would remain in place, but the board would be heavily occupied by persons with ties to PFC and Revlon, as well as notables such as former New York City mayor David N. Dinkins. The merger was officially approved by Cosmetic Center stockholders at the annual meeting of April 24, 1997. Although Cosmetic Center was the surviving corporation, for accounting purposes future financial reports would be made under the name of PFC.

Principal Subsidiaries

M. Steven Cosmetic Company, Inc.; Courtney Brooke, Inc.

Principal Divisions

Retail Division; Wholesale Division; Distribution Division.

Further Reading

"Chain Has Big Ambitions in Tough Market," *Baltimore Sun,* March 19, 1995, p. E1.

"Cosmetic Center Chairman Weinstein Takes Different Path to Higher Profits," *Warfield's Business Record,* May 21, 1993, p. 5.

"Cosmetic Center Covers Bases," *Shopping Center World,* May 1994, p. 64.

"Cosmetic Center Mounts Aggressive Expansion Program," *Drug Store News,* July 5, 1993, p. 5.

"Cosmetic Center Rejects Takeover Bid," *Baltimore Sun,* August 8, 1995, p. C11.

"Cosmetic Center to Pull Out of Atlanta," *Washington Post,* August 6, 1996, p. D3.

"Cosmetic Chain Adds Own Line," *Washington Business Journal,* March 25, 1994, p. 15.

Finkelstein, Anita J., "Cosmetic Center Storms Atlanta," *Women's Wear Daily,* October 7, 1994, p. 6.

"Maryland Firm, Revlon to Merge Stores," *Washington Post,* October 4, 1996, p. D1.

—Gerry Azzata

Cox Enterprises, Inc.

1400 Lake Hearn Drive
Atlanta, Georgia 30319
U.S.A.
(404) 843-5000
Fax: (404) 847-6299
Web site: http://www.cimedia.com/coxsites.html

Private Company
Incorporated: 1968
Employees: 43,000
Sales: $4.59 billion (1996)
SICs: 2711 Newspapers: Publishing, or Publishing & Printing; 2741 Miscellaneous Publishing; 4813 Telephone Communications, Except Radio Telephone; 4832 Radio Broadcasting Stations; 4833 Television Broadcasting Stations; 4841 Cable & Other Pay Television Services; 5012 Distribution of Automobiles & Other Motor Vehicles; 7313 Radio, Television & Publishers' Advertising Representatives; 7331 Direct Mail Advertising Services; 7812 Motion Picture & Video Tape Production

Cox Enterprises, Inc. is a diversified media company, with four core companies: Cox Communications, Inc., Cox Newspapers, Inc., Cox Broadcasting, Inc., and Manheim Auctions, Inc. Cox Communications is a publicly traded firm, majority owned by Cox Enterprises, which runs the fifth-largest cable television system in the country, with 3.3 million customers, and also provides digital personal communications services (PCS), high-speed Internet access, and local phone service. Cox Newspapers publishes 16 daily and 15 weekly newspapers in Colorado, Florida, Georgia, Ohio, North Carolina, and Texas. Cox Broadcasting operates 12 television stations; owns television and film production company Rysher Entertainment; runs TeleRep, the nation's largest television advertising sales representative firm; and holds a majority stake in the publicly traded Cox Radio, Inc., which is the ninth-largest radio group in the country with 49 stations. Manheim Auctions is the largest wholesale automobile auction company in the world, with 63 auction facilities in North America and additional operations in the United Kingdom and Puerto Rico. Among other operations is the 1996-formed Cox Interactive Media, Inc., which creates interactive entertainment and information services for the Internet. Cox Enterprises was not incorporated until 1968; before that it was an assortment of primarily newspaper businesses owned by the Cox family, with growing interests in radio and television broadcasting and in cable television. A dizzying series of acquisitions, mergers, divestments, public offerings, rearrangements of operations, and new ventures in the 1980s and 1990s have led Cox Enterprises to its late 20th-century position as a leading media conglomerate.

Cox Family Empire Began with Ohio Newspapers

In 1898 James M. Cox bought *The Dayton Evening News*—now the *Dayton Daily News*—in Dayton, Ohio, for $26,000 that he had raised from several friends. Cox, a native of rural Ohio, had been a schoolteacher; a reporter for *The Middletown Signal* in Middletown, Ohio, and for *The Cincinnati Enquirer*, in Cincinnati, Ohio; and a Washington, D.C.-based secretary to Ohio congressman Paul J. Sorg. Cox quickly became an influential newspaper publisher; in 1905 he bought the *Springfield Press-Republic,* also in Ohio, changed its name to the *Springfield Daily News,* and established a newspaper chain, which he called the News League of Ohio. He also entered politics; he represented Ohio's third district in Congress from 1909 to 1913 and was elected governor of Ohio in 1913. Cox was defeated when he ran for reelection in 1915, but won in 1917 and 1919, making him the state's first three-term governor. In 1920 he was the Democratic Party's presidential candidate, with future-president Franklin D. Roosevelt as his running mate. He lost the election to Warren G. Harding.

After the defeat and his completion of his gubernatorial term in 1921, Cox returned to public life only once, when Roosevelt, by then president, appointed him a delegate to the 1933 World Monetary and Economic Conference in London. Instead, Cox focused on his media business. In 1923 he acquired the *Miami Metropolis*, in Florida, changing its name to the *Miami Daily News,* and the *Canton News,* in Canton, Ohio. In 1930 he sold

Company Perspectives:

Cox Enterprises is positioned to meet the challenges of the future with an operating philosophy based on these principles: Our employees are the company's most important resource. We encourage individual initiative and entrepreneurship at every level. We value and reward achievement. Our customers are the company's lifeblood. We are dedicated to building lasting relationships with them, and to meeting their needs with high-quality service beyond their expectations. We embrace new technology to give our customers the variety and quality of services they demand. We invest in new business opportunities, with a mixture of caution and initiative, to enhance our growth. We believe it's good business to be good citizens of the communities we serve through volunteerism and financial support. We are committed to helping shape a better world. We do this by using our media to educate the public about important issues, such as the environment, and through responsible company and individual actions.

the Canton paper and bought the *Springfield Sun,* in Ohio. He entered broadcasting in 1934, establishing Dayton's first radio station, WHIO.

In 1939 Cox acquired *The Atlanta Journal,* in Georgia, and its AM radio station, WSB. The newspaper had been founded in 1883 and had gone through several owners; the radio station, which began broadcasting in 1922, was the South's first. As with other newspapers he had acquired, Cox wished for the Atlanta paper to maintain its own style and personality.

In 1948 Cox entered the new medium of television with WSB-[TV] in Atlanta; the company also set up WSB-[FM] as a companion to the original AM radio station. In 1949 the company acquired a second Dayton, Ohio, newspaper, *The Journal Herald,* and put WHIO-[TV] and WHIO-[FM] radio on the air in that city. In 1950 Cox acquired *The Atlanta Constitution. The Atlanta Journal* and *The Atlanta Constitution* began a combined Sunday edition while publishing separately during the week.

James Cox died in 1957 at age 87. His son, James M. Cox, Jr., succeeded him as the leader of the family businesses and oversaw continued expansion. The family acquired AM and FM radio stations and a television station, all operating under the call letters WSOC, in Charlotte, North Carolina, in 1959.

Entered Cable TV in Early 1960s

The Coxes were among the first major broadcasters to enter cable television, acquiring a cable system in Lewistown, Pennsylvania, in 1962. In 1963 they acquired KTVU-[TV] in the San Francisco-Oakland, California, area and radio stations WIOD-[AM] and WAIA-[FM] in Miami. In 1964 the Cox family established Cox Broadcasting Corporation to run the radio and television operations. The broadcasting concern had its shares publicly traded on the New York Stock Exchange, but the family retained substantial ownership. The same year, broadcasting and cable operations expanded with the purchase of WPXI-[TV] in Pittsburgh, Pennsylvania, and cable systems in Washington, Oregon, and California.

In 1966 Cox Broadcasting added a business- and technical-publishing division; in 1967 it went into motion-picture production. Its Bing Crosby Productions unit eventually made such movies as *Ben, Walking Tall,* and *The Reincarnation of Peter Proud.* In 1968 all the various Cox-owned newspapers were organized into Cox Enterprises, Inc., which remained a private company. The same year, Cox Broadcasting set up Cox Cable Communications, Inc. as a publicly traded, partially owned subsidiary.

Another 1968 event was the company's entry into the automobile-auction business, with the broadcasting group's purchase of auction facilities in Manheim, Pennsylvania; Bordentown, New Jersey; and Fredericksburg, Virginia. New and used car dealers traditionally have used auto auctions to buy and sell from each other. During the 1980s, banks with repossessed cars, car rental agencies, and fleet operators began to use auction facilities for sales.

In 1969 the newspaper group added three Florida daily papers: the *Palm Beach Daily News,* the *Palm Beach Evening Times,* and the *Palm Beach Post.* The broadcasting group's operations expanded that year with the purchase of Tele-Systems, a California cable operation, and of auto auctions in Kansas City, Missouri, and Lakeland, Florida. An auction facility in High Point, North Carolina, was added in 1970; a cable system in Santa Barbara, California, and an auto auction in Pittsburgh came on in 1971.

Acquired TeleRep in 1972

The following year brought the acquisition of TeleRep, a national television-advertising-sales representation firm, which sells time on client stations to national advertisers. The firm eventually added a programming arm, Television Program Enterprises, to produce and sell syndicated programming, including "Entertainment Tonight," "Star Search," and "Lifestyles of the Rich and Famous." An auto auction facility in Milwaukee, Wisconsin, also came into the company lineup in 1972.

The presidential election of 1972 brought a break in James Cox, Jr.'s association with the Democratic Party. Cox, who had attended the 1912 Democratic convention with his father, decided in 1972 to endorse President Richard M. Nixon for reelection over Senator George McGovern, and ordered all Cox Enterprises newspapers to do the same—the only time Cox ever became involved in the newspapers' editorial policies. Two editors resigned as a result. Eventually, the family allied itself with the Democrats again; Anne Cox Chambers, one of James Cox, Jr.'s two sisters, was an early supporter of Georgia governor Jimmy Carter and served as ambassador to Belgium when Carter became president. In the mid-1970s the Coxes' Atlanta newspapers switched from an anti-Carter to a pro-Carter stance, but management said the switch was not related to Chambers's support of Carter.

Also in 1972, Cox Cable announced plans to merge with American Television and Communications Corporation, but the Justice Department sued to block the deal. The suit led the companies to call off the transaction early in 1973; both contended the merger would not violate federal antitrust law, but noted the litigation could delay the deal by several months. Later in 1973, Cox Cable set a merger with LVO Cable Inc., but subsequently called it off because of market conditions. Another major event of 1973 was Cox Broadcasting's purchase of KFI-[AM], Los Angeles.

James Cox, Jr., died in 1974 at the age of 71. His sister Barbara Cox Anthony's husband, Garner Anthony, took over the primary direction of the family companies, and the expansion continued.

Cox Broadcasting added an auto auction in Orlando, Florida, in 1974, and one in Fresno, California, in 1975. Also in 1975, it bought a cable television system in Myrtle Beach, South Carolina. Cox Enterprises acquired four Texas newspapers in 1976—the *Austin American-Statesman,* the *Waco Tribune-Herald,* the *Port Arthur News,* and the *Lufkin Daily News.* The same year, Cox Broadcasting added KOST-[FM], Los Angeles, and acquired a cable system in Pensacola, Florida. It also acquired an auto-auction facility in Anaheim, California, and built one in Atlanta.

In 1977 the Cox Cable subsidiary was merged back into Cox Broadcasting; over the next three years, the broadcasting group added 26 cable television franchises, including one in Omaha, Nebraska, and another in New Orleans, Louisiana. Also in 1977, the broadcasting operation acquired WLIF-[FM], Baltimore, Maryland, and Cox Enterprises bought the *Mesa Tribune* in Arizona.

The broadcasting company acquired WZGO-[FM] in Philadelphia, Pennsylvania, in 1979; the newspaper group acquired Texas's *Longview Morning Journal* and the *Longview Daily News* in 1978 and the *Daily Sentinel,* of Grand Junction, Colorado, in 1979. Also in 1979, Cox Broadcasting discontinued motion-picture production, but continued to market its inventory, in favor of concentrating on its broadcasting and cable television businesses.

The major event of 1979, however, was the Cox family's negotiation of a sale of Cox Broadcasting to General Electric Company (GE), in what would have been the biggest broadcasting merger in history. The Coxes wanted to sell the broadcast concern apparently because they feared the Federal Communications Commission (FCC) eventually would force a breakup of their newspaper and broadcast operations in the cities where they had both—Atlanta, Dayton, and Miami. GE's extensive broadcast holdings, however, resulted in a barrage of complaints to the FCC about concentration of ownership; the delays resulting from these complaints delayed the sale and paved the way for price renegotiations, which led to the deal's collapse early in 1980. The Coxes were asking $637 million; GE's final offer was $570 million.

Both Cox companies went through more changes and expansion in the early 1980s. WSB-[TV] changed its network affiliation to ABC in 1980, after having been an NBC affiliate for more than 30 years. Cox Enterprises bought the *Tempe Daily News* in Arizona in 1980; Cox Broadcasting bought a Boston auto auction in 1981, and KDNL-[TV], St. Louis, Missouri, in 1982.

The broadcasting concern sold its business- and technical-publishing arm to Hearst Corporation in 1980; the aim, as with the end of film production, was to concentrate on the broadcasting and cable businesses. The auto auctions, although unrelated to these businesses, were retained because of their growth and profitability.

In 1982 Cox Broadcasting changed its name to Cox Communications, Inc. to better reflect its positions in both broadcasting and cable. The year 1983 was an acquisitive one. Cox Communications acquired auto auctions in Phoenix, Arizona, and in Toronto, Ontario, and a cable franchise in Staten Island, New York. The company also agreed to swap WLIF-[FM] in Baltimore for a Chicago FM station, WXFM, whose call letters subsequently were changed to WCKG; to buy a Detroit television station, WKBD, after divesting itself of a cable system in St. Clair Shores, Michigan; and to buy 90 percent of CyberTel, a radio common carrier system in St. Louis. These transactions were completed the following year. Also in 1983, Cox Enterprises bought the *Chandler Arizonan,* followed by the acquisition of another Arizona newspaper, the *Yuma Daily Sun,* in 1984. Cox Communications bought another auto auction, in Houston, Texas, in 1984.

1985 Merger of Cox Enterprises and Cox Communications

In 1985 Cox Enterprises purchased Cox Communications for $75 a share. Cox Enterprises had owned or controlled 40.2 percent of the communications company's 28.2 million outstanding shares. The combined corporation became the nation's 13th-largest media company; before the merger, Cox Communications ranked 19th and Cox Enterprises 21st.

Other 1985 events were the acquisition of a Texas newspaper, the *Orange Leader,* and an Orlando, Florida, TV station, WFTV; and a swap of a cable television system in Avon Park, Florida, for one owned by Storer Communications in Fortuna, California. In 1987 Cox Enterprises sold its Philadelphia radio station to Malrite Communications Group and sold its Datext unit to Lotus Development Corporation. It had established Datext, which packaged financial information on compact discs, in 1984. It also sold CyberTel to a St. Louis investor.

At the end of 1987 the company had another change in top leadership, as Garner Anthony stepped down from the post of chairman and chief executive officer of Cox Enterprises and was succeeded by his stepson, James C. Kennedy. Into the late 1990s, sisters Barbara Cox Anthony and Anne Cox Chambers remained active in the company, chairing the Dayton and Atlanta newspapers, respectively.

By 1988 Cox Enterprises' *Miami News,* like many afternoon newspapers, was suffering declining readership and advertising. Cox sought a buyer for the paper; there were discussions with a group of Chicago investors. A sale, however, could not be worked out, and Cox closed the paper at year-end. In 1989 Cox sold its St. Louis television station to Better Communications, but expanded in other areas. It acquired an equity stake in Blockbuster Entertainment Corporation and became a franchisee of Blockbuster Video stores. Other acquisitions were Trader Publications, a publisher of advertising-only magazines;

The Clipper, Inc., a publisher of coupon magazines; The Stuffit Company, a direct mailer of coupons and custom mailings; Main Street Advertising USA, a direct mail advertising company; Cox In-Store Advertising, formerly Buckler Broadcast Group, a point-of-purchase advertising business; and an interest in IP Services, Inc., a software company. It also entered into a joint venture with Picture Classified Network (PCN) to expand coverage and distribution of PCN's Gold Book automobile price guide. Also in 1989, Cox's cable group topped the 1.5 million customer mark.

By the early 1990s, Cox Enterprises consisted of four main operating companies: Cox Newspapers, Cox Cable Communications, Cox Broadcasting (television and radio stations, TeleRep, and Television Program Enterprises), and Manheim Auctions (the auto auctions business). In 1990 Cox sold two of its Texas newspapers, the *Port Arthur News* and *Orange Leader*, to American Publishing Company; Cox officials said they wanted to concentrate on the company's other Texas papers. The same year, Cox acquired two radio stations, WSUN-[AM] of Tampa, Florida, and KKWM-[FM], now KLRX-[FM] of Dallas. Revenues for Cox Enterprises topped the $2 billion mark for the first time that year.

In March 1991 the Justice Department sued Cox Enterprises for $3.67 million for failing, in 1986, to seek federal approval before buying a $101 million stake in Knight-Ridder, another communications company. The Justice Department asserted that Cox violated a law requiring individuals and groups to seek federal approval before buying large amounts of stock in another company. A lawyer for Cox Enterprises stated that Cox believed its purchase was not subject to the law because the shares were bought for investment purposes. Also in March, Manheim Auctions acquired GE auto auctions, adding 20 auctions to Manheim's 26, and making Manheim the world's largest auto auction company.

In April 1991 Trader Publications was merged with Landmark Target Media of Norfolk, Virginia, and Cox held 50 percent of the resulting company. In May the company announced it would sell its Blockbuster stores. In September, Cox added to its direct marketing operations—which were collectively known as Cox Target Media, Inc., part of Cox Newspapers—with the acquisition of Val-Pak Direct Marketing Systems, Inc. of Largo, Florida. Val-Pak was the leading U.S. cooperative direct mailer and specialized in sending several business ads in one envelope to targeted households.

PCS, Rysher, and Times Mirror Highlighted Mid-1990s

In 1991 Cox began testing cable-based personal communications services (PCS), leading to the first PCS call over cable lines in 1992. As a leader in the development of PCS—which functioned as a phone, pager, answering machine, and voice mail system, while also delivering crisper sound and more security than analog cellular phone technology—Cox was one of three companies awarded a pioneer's preference license from the FCC. Initially, this designation was to lead to free PCS licenses for Cox. But the federal government revised the rules surrounding PCS in 1994, and by early 1995 Cox had purchased two licenses, at only a 15 percent pioneer's discount, one covering southern California and the other for Omaha, Nebraska. In 1996 Cox launched PCS phone service in San Diego.

In 1994 Cox entered into an alliance that formed the Sprint Telecommunications Venture, renamed Sprint Spectrum LP in 1995. The alliance partners were Sprint Corp., with 40 percent of the venture; Tele-Communications Inc., 30 percent; and Cox and Comcast Corp., 15 percent each. In the early 1995 FCC auction of PCS licenses, Sprint Spectrum was the biggest winner, gaining the rights to wireless licenses in 31 major U.S. markets, covering a population of 156 million.

Cox Broadcasting, meanwhile, acquired Rysher Entertainment, a distributor of syndicated television shows, in March 1993, and later that year merged Television Program Enterprises into it. Rysher subsequently evolved into a network television and film production company, developing "Nash Bridges" for CBS, the television movie *Rasputin* for HBO, and the motion pictures *Primal Fear, Evening Star,* and *Big Night,* all in 1996 alone.

The heightened merger activity in the media industries in the 1990s led Cox to conclude that it had to grow to survive. Kennedy, in fact, set an ambitious goal for Cox Enterprises: to double its 1993 revenues of $2.68 billion within the next five years. The cable operations of Cox Cable Communications were the first major area targeted for expansion. In December 1993 Southwestern Bell Corp., one of the Baby Bells, announced it would invest $1.6 billion for a 40 percent stake in a joint venture with Cox that would own Cox Cable. Through this cash infusion, Cox Cable planned to quickly increase its base from 1.7 million subscribers, which made it the nation's sixth-largest cable system, to at least 4 million, which would vault it into the number three slot. The deal collapsed, however, when the FCC announced new cable regulations in early 1994 calling for a rollback in cable rates. The rollback altered the value that Southwestern Bell put on its investment in Cox Cable, and led to its backing out of the merger in April 1994.

A successful deal was consummated just months later, however, when Cox purchased the cable operations of Times Mirror Company for $2.3 billion in cash and stock. The deal closed in February 1995, increasing Cox Cable's base from 1.9 to 3.2 million customers and moving it into fifth place among cable operators. With the completion of the acquisition, Cox Cable became a publicly traded company under the name Cox Communications, Inc., with Cox Enterprises holding a 75 percent stake. Cox Communications then began selling and trading cable systems that were not strategically clustered in order to take advantage of economies of scale and achieve operational efficiencies.

By 1996, revenues for Cox Enterprises had reached an astonishing $4.59 billion, a 21 percent increase over 1995 and up 70 percent since 1993, when Kennedy set the goal of doubling revenue in five years. Various activities during 1996 set the stage for the company to meet this ambitious goal ahead of schedule. TeleRep, by this time the nation's leading television sales rep firm, jumped into the Internet field with the formation of Cox Interactive Sales to sell online advertising. Cox Communications launched the Cox@Home Network in Orange County, California, which provided high-speed Internet service via a cable modem. Cox Enterprises formed Cox Interactive Media, Inc. to produce and manage interactive Web products, targeting the local markets where the company already operated newspapers, television and radio stations, and cable systems. Manheim Auctions added an additional 11 auction locations, including 9 gained through the acquisition of Gateway Auto Auction of Granite City, Illinois. Manheim also entered the U.K. auto auction market through a joint venture called Independent Car Auctions Holdings Limited.

Perhaps the most significant event of 1996 came on the heels of the 1996 Telecommunications Act, which loosened federal regulations regarding ownership of radio and television stations. This act led to additional media mergers, and Cox Broadcasting positioned itself for growth by completing an initial public offering of its radio station group, which became known as Cox Radio Inc. Cox Broadcasting retained a 70 percent stake in the new company. With the $120 million generated through the offering, Cox Radio was able to more than double the number of stations it owned in a short span. By mid-1997, Cox Radio owned 49 stations, making it the ninth-largest radio group in the country.

Cox Enterprises had come a long way, from its Ohio newspaper roots to its place as one of the media giants of the late 20th century. Through the 1980s and 1990s, Cox had gained interests in nearly every sector of communications, media, and broadcasting. The company's consistent commitment to innovation and its quick adoption of new technologies will likely hold it in good stead in the rapidly changing high-tech world of the 21st century.

Principal Subsidiaries

Cox Communications, Inc. (75%); Cox Newspapers, Inc.; Cox Target Media, Inc.; Longstreet Press; Trader Publishing Co. (50%); Cox Broadcasting, Inc.; Cox Radio, Inc. (70%); Manheim Auctions, Inc.; Independent Car Auctions Holdings Limited (U.K.); Cox Interactive Media, Inc.; Lifestyle Marketing Group; Optical Data Corporation; Southeast Paper Manufacturing Co. (33%); Clarendon Farms, Inc.; Hualalai Land Corporation; Nine Bar Ranch Texas, Inc.

Further Reading

Cohen, Jodi B., "Cox Goes Digital," *Editor & Publisher,* August 3, 1996, p. 28.

Cox, James M., *Journey Through My Years,* New York: Simon & Schuster, 1946.

Criner, Kathleen, and Jane Wilson, "Watch Out for Cable, Easterly Says," *Editor & Publisher,* April 27, 1996, pp. 38, 105.

Greising, David, and Mark Landler, "This Time, Cox Reels in a Big Fish," *Business Week,* June 20, 1994, p. 39.

Gubernick, Lisa, "Big Decisions," *Forbes,* November 2, 1987, p. 222.

Harrigan, Susan, "Powerful Clan: The Coxes of Atlanta Rule a Media Empire with Quiet Authority," *Wall Street Journal,* September 26, 1980.

Jessell, Harry, "Cox's Jim Kennedy: Big Is Better," *Broadcasting & Cable,* June 20, 1994, pp. 23–27.

Keller, John J., "Sprint, Partners Map $4 Billion Phone Invasion," *Wall Street Journal,* March 29, 1995, p. B9.

Landler, Mark, and Bart Ziegler, "Southwestern Bell and Cox: A Deal with a Difference," *Business Week,* December 20, 1993, p. 39.

O'Shea, Dan, "Cable Deal Could Keep Cox Ticking," *Telephony,* June 13, 1994, p. 6.

Rose, Frederick, "Times Mirror Says Litigation Settlement Leaves Basic Agreement with Cox Intact," *Wall Street Journal,* October 13, 1994, p. B10.

——, "Times Mirror's Plan to Sell Cable TV Sparks Several Shareholder Lawsuits," *Wall Street Journal,* June 9, 1994, p. B6.

Rose, Frederick, and Anita Sharpe, "Cox Agrees to Buy Cable-TV Operations from Times Mirror in $2.3 Billion Deal," *Wall Street Journal,* June 6, 1994, pp. A3, A6.

Sharpe, Anita, and Mark Robichaux, "Cox Sees Times Mirror Cable System as Key to Survival," *Wall Street Journal,* July 7, 1994, p. B4.

——, "Southwestern Bell and Cox Cancel Venture," *Wall Street Journal,* April 6, 1994, pp. A3, A4.

—Trudy Ring
—updated by David E. Salamie

CSX Corporation

One James Center
901 East Cary Street
Richmond, Virginia 23219-4031
U.S.A.
(804) 782-1400
Fax: (804) 782-6747
Web site: http://www.csx.com

Public Company
Incorporated: 1978
Employees: 47,314
Sales: $10.54 billion (1996)
Stock Exchanges: New York London Zürich Midwest Boston Cincinnati Pacific Philadelphia
SICs: 4011 Railroads, Line-Haul Operating; 4412 Deep Sea Freight Transportation-Foreign; 4449 Freight Transportation-Water, Not Elsewhere Classified; 6531 Real Estate Agents & Managers; 6719 Offices of Holding Companies, Not Elsewhere Classified; 7011 Hotels & Motels

CSX Corporation is a leading transportation-based holding company that operates one of the United States's leading rail systems. The company's rail system is the largest in the eastern United States and the third-largest in the country as a whole, trailing only those of Union Pacific Corp. and Burlington Northern Santa Fe Corp. The system, run by the company's CSX Transportation Inc. unit, covers about 18,500 miles in 20 Southeastern, Eastern, and Midwest states and the Canadian province of Ontario. CSX also owns and operates the world's largest containership line, Sea-Land Service Inc.; the largest U.S. barge carrier, American Commercial Lines Inc.; the nation's only full-service intermodal transportation company, CSX Intermodal Inc.; and a leading provider of contract logistics services, including distribution, warehousing, assembly, and just-in-time delivery, Customized Transportation Inc. In addition, CSX manages extensive real estate development activities; operates several large resorts, including the Greenbrier Hotel at White Sulphur Springs, West Virginia; and holds a majority stake in Yukon Pacific Corporation, a promoter of a pipeline to transport natural gas from Alaska's North Slope to Valdez. CSX has remained at the center of the continuing consolidation of the railroad industry, most recently entering into a mid-1997 agreement to acquire 42 percent of Conrail's lines, mainly located in the northeastern states. In placing continued, though not exclusive, reliance on rail traffic, the company is looking back to its distant origins. CSX's railroad, the major part of its business over the years, is the end result of a long series of consolidations involving three historic railroad systems: the Seaboard Coast Line, the Chesapeake and Ohio Railway, and the Baltimore and Ohio Railroad, which together span nearly the entire history of railroading in the United States.

History of the Baltimore and Ohio Railroad

The Baltimore and Ohio Railroad (B&O) was chartered in February 1827 by a group of leading Baltimore businessmen with one of their number, Philip E. Thomas, as the first president. Its purpose was twofold: to challenge major canals, especially the Erie Canal, for trade to the west and to provide more efficient and cheaper freight and passenger service than was then available. In Baltimore's case this traffic passed over the National Road, which ran from Cumberland, Maryland, to Wheeling, West Virginia, on the Ohio River, with an eastward extension to Baltimore. The railroad's construction started on July 4, 1828, at a historic celebration presided over by Charles Carroll, the last surviving signer of the Declaration of Independence. The B&O's planners intended to use horses for motive power, but Peter Cooper's first locomotive used on the line, the diminutive *Tom Thumb*, made its first successful run in 1830, ending the railroad's need for horsepower.

Construction progress was slow, however, and the rail line from Baltimore to Wheeling wasn't completed until December 1852. A second western extension was completed to Parkersburg, West Virginia, in 1857, with connections to local railroads providing service to Columbus and Cincinnati, Ohio and to St. Louis, Missouri. The Ohio and West Virginia connections fostered a great increase in coal traffic from mid-western mines to the east. By 1860 revenues from coal were about one-third of

Company Perspectives:

CSX is a transportation company committed to being a leader in railroad, inland water, and containerized distribution networks.

To attract the human and financial resources necessary to achieve this leadership position, CSX will support our three major constituencies: For our customers, we will work as a partner to provide excellent service by meeting all agreed-upon commitments. For our employees, we will create a work environment that motivates and allows them to grow and develop and perform their jobs to the maximum of their capacity. For our shareholders, we will meet our goals to provide them with sustainable superior returns.

total rail freight revenue, a ratio that has changed little over the years. In 1990 coal provided 32 percent of CSX's rail revenue.

The B&O played a key role in the Civil War, as did many other railroads, and the line suffered accordingly with substantial damage to track and equipment. Growth continued after the war under the presidency of John W. Garrett, who served from 1858 to 1884, providing sound management in an era when railroad mismanagement was all too common. Track mileage increased from 521 in 1865 to nearly 1,700 by 1885. As the B&O continued to expand through construction and acquisition of smaller railroads, mileage increased to 3,200 by 1900, reaching 5,100 by 1920 and achieving a peak of about 6,350 in 1935.

After Garrett's presidency, increasing debt and an overgenerous dividend policy weakened the B&O financially while speculation in the company's stock hampered its fundraising ability. The financial panic of 1893 proved disastrous for the line, and in 1896 the B&O was placed in receivership. In the following decade and a half the reorganized railroad's mileage and revenues increased satisfactorily, but the B&O came under the control of the Pennsylvania Railroad, which had purchased a majority of its stock after the bankruptcy. The Pennsylvania involved itself briefly in the B&O's management, but sold its stock position in 1906 for fear of U.S. government antitrust action. Under the long presidency of Daniel Willard from 1910 to 1941, the B&O's physical plant and service were considerably improved, and the line, which now spread through western Pennsylvania, Ohio, West Virginia, Indiana, and Illinois, enjoyed increasing prosperity until the onset of the Great Depression in the 1930s.

The 1930s saw declining revenues, layoffs, and wage reductions. In 1932 dividends on the common stock were discontinued, not to be restored until 1952. Track mileage and locomotive and equipment rosters began a long decline that would continue until the B&O came under control of the Chesapeake and Ohio Railway (C&O) in 1963. Roy B. White, however, who served as president from 1941 to 1953, inherited from Willard a first-class railroad that offered excellent service. World War II provided renewed prosperity, but the B&O faced problems during the postwar years from inflation, debt for new equipment, declines in passenger traffic, and chronic labor disputes. U.S. President Harry Truman temporarily seized the nation's railroads in 1946 to offset a threatened nationwide strike, and similar crises occurred in 1948 and 1950.

During the B&O's last decade as an independent company, Howard E. Simpson served as president from 1953 to 1961, and Jervis Langdon Jr., served from 1961 to 1964. Operating revenues and net income generally declined during the 1950s as did track mileage and employment. Labor costs grew because of constant union pressure for higher wages. In the late 1950s as the B&O's traffic and revenue position worsened, the railroad began to consider the idea of a merger with a stronger partner. The C&O and the New York Central Railroad vied briefly for dominance, but in February 1961 the C&O announced that it controlled 61 percent of the B&O's stock. In 1962 the Interstate Commerce Commission (ICC) approved the C&O's request to take over the B&O, and on February 4, 1963, the C&O finally took control. The affiliation produced an 11,000-mile rail system, stretching from the Atlantic to the Mississippi River and from the Great Lakes to the southern edges of Virginia, West Virginia, and Kentucky, and brought to the B&O's rescue a smaller but significantly stronger railroad, not quite as old as the B&O, but with origins that also went back to the early years of railroading.

History of Chessie System

The C&O had its beginning in a short line railroad built to provide rail traffic to farmers and merchants in central Virginia. Chartered in 1836 as the Louisa Railroad, it originally covered 21 miles from Taylorsville to Frederick Hall, Virginia. In 1850 the line's name was changed to the Virginia Central Railroad, and by 1851 it extended eastward to Richmond, Virginia. A plan to extend westward to the Ohio River was delayed by the Civil War, during which the railroad served the Southern forces effectively but was heavily damaged. In 1867 the reorganized company changed its name to the Chesapeake and Ohio Railway Company and with financial backing from Collis P. Huntington, who subsequently became president from 1869 to 1888, the line was open from Richmond to Huntington, West Virginia, by 1873. The panic of 1873 ended in receivership for the C&O in 1875. In 1888 Huntington lost control to J. P. Morgan, who improved the railroad's performance such that, by 1900, the C&O was a solvent, well-managed 1,445-mile line connecting Newport News, Virginia, with Cincinnati, Ohio, and Louisville, Kentucky.

The C&O's history during the 20th century was characterized by conservative financial management supported by strong coal revenues. In 1947 the C&O made a major acquisition of the Pere Marquette Railroad with nearly 2,000 miles of track in the Midwest, New York, and Canada, and a sound base of merchandise traffic. The Pennsylvania and New York Central Railroads controlled C&O's stock from 1900 and 1909. During the 1920s and early 1930s control was exercised by Martis P. Van Sweringen and his brother, Oris P. Van Sweringen. From the mid-1930s, noted financier Robert R. Young owned a majority stock position, which he sold in 1954 to Cleveland investment banker Cyrus S. Eaton. By this time the C&O was a prosperous 5,000-mile line with $350 million in annual revenues and an exceptionally competent leader, Walter J. Tuohy, who had assumed the presidency in 1948. After completing the line's dieselization in the mid-1950s, Tuohy moved aggressively to expand the C&O by acquisition, leading to the 1963 merger with the B&O.

The unification of the two railroads proceeded slowly and deliberately with a common annual report appearing in 1964 and senior administrative positions being gradually combined during the 1960s and 1970s. The continued separate operations of the lines avoided the confusion and errors that led to the failure of the Penn Central combination during the same period. It also avoided a downgrading of C&O debt securities because of the weaker financial position of the B&O before the merger, and maximized the benefits of operating two railroads whose traffic was, for the most part, complementary.

Hays T. Watkins became chairman and chief executive officer of the combined C&O and B&O in 1971. He was a strong administrator, firing President John Hanifin in 1975 for spending $2 million on tennis courts at the railroad's resort, the Greenbrier Hotel. Watkins adopted the name Chessie System Inc. in 1972 for the combined railroads and formally became CEO of Chessie System in 1973. By the late 1970s only three percent of Chessie's $1.5 billion revenues were from non-rail sources, and Watkins was considering diversification and expansion. In 1978 Chessie proposed to the ICC a possible merger with the slightly larger southeastern railroad system, Seaboard Coast Line Industries Inc. Like the B&O and the Chessie, the Seaboard was a consolidation of several railroads whose history also reached back into the 19th century.

History of Seaboard Coast Line

The Seaboard's key component, the Atlantic Coast Line Railroad (ACL), began as a series of small railroads running along a northeast-southwest line parallel to the Atlantic coast and connecting communities along the "fall line," the imaginary line joining towns at the heads of navigation of the coastal rivers. The oldest part of the ACL was the Petersburg Railroad, chartered in 1830 to run from Petersburg, Virginia, south to the North Carolina border. The corporate parent of the ACL, however, was the Richmond and Petersburg Railroad, chartered in 1836. These and similar, small independent railroads running along the fall line through Virginia, North Carolina, South Carolina, Georgia, Alabama, and Florida were joined after the Civil War in a holding company at first called the American Improvement and Construction Company, formed in 1889. In 1893 the name was changed to the Atlantic Coast Line Company. In 1902 the ACL bought a controlling share of the Louisville and Nashville Railroad (L&N) and, following a 1914 reorganization, the name was changed again to the Atlantic Coast Line Railroad Company.

In 1958 the ACL, by then a 5,300-mile railroad with revenues of about $163 million, proposed a merger with one of its southeastern competitors, the Seaboard Air Line Railroad with 4,100 miles and roughly similar revenues. The ACL, with its affiliates, the 5,700-mile L&N and the smaller Clinchfield Railroad, tapping the coal and merchandise markets of the midwest, was the stronger of the two companies. The plan however, was to merge the ACL into the Seaboard to take advantage of the Seaboard's more modern corporate charter. The consolidation plan was filed with the ICC in 1960 but progress was slow, partly because of antitrust issues, with final approval not coming until 1967. The new company, eventually called Seaboard Coast Line Industries Inc., was the eighth-largest railroad in the United States, with revenues of about $1.2 billion.

Creation of CSX in 1980

The merger proposed in 1978 between the $1.5 billion Chessie and the $1.8 billion Seaboard offered benefits to both sides. It would give the Chessie a relatively inexpensive expansion into the booming southeast and would provide a useful capital infusion for the Seaboard, especially for its maintenance and equipment-starved L&N subsidiary. The ICC approved the merger in September 1980 and the two systems were consolidated into CSX Corporation on November 1, 1980. The Seaboard's Prime F. Osborn III became chairman and the Chessie's Hays T. Watkins became president. Watkins was clearly the dominant figure, becoming chairman in 1982 on Osborn's retirement.

As in the case of the B&O and C&O, the operational consolidation of the two railroad systems proceeded gradually, again to avoid the internal stresses that had marred the Penn Central merger. It was not for another decade that all of the railroad operations of Chessie and Seaboard were consolidated under the CSX Transportation Inc. subsidiary.

Diversification in the Later 1980s

Meanwhile, diversification was in the air in the 1980s. In 1983 CSX made a deal with Southern New England Telephone Company to place a fiber optics telecommunication system along the CSX rights-of-way. A more significant diversification move in 1983 was CSX's "white-knight" $1 billion purchase of Texas Gas Resources Corporation, with $2.9 billion in revenues, one of the United States's largest natural gas pipeline companies with substantial gas and petroleum reserves. For CSX, with revenues of $5 billion, this was a major expansion into natural resources, adding oil and gas to its already large coal holdings. Texas Gas had as a subsidiary the American Commercial Lines Inc. (ACL), a large barge operator. On July 24, 1984, the ICC voted to allow CSX to keep and operate this shipping firm, a reversal of longstanding government policy against letting railroads own steamship or barge lines.

Continuing this precedent, the ICC in 1987 voted to approve CSX's 1986 $800 million acquisition of Sea-Land Corporation, the largest U.S. ocean container-ship line (later known as Sea-Land Service Inc.). This purchase was a continuation of Watkins's somewhat controversial policy of structuring CSX as an intermodal transportation company capable of serving both national and international markets. CSX became heavily involved in resort operations following its 1986 purchase of Rockresorts, Inc., owner and manager of several luxury resorts, which CSX bought from Laurance Rockefeller. Also in 1986, CSX purchased a 30 percent interest (increased to a majority stake two years later) in Yukon Pacific Corporation, which aimed to construct the Trans-Alaska Gas System to transport natural gas via pipeline from Alaska's North Slope to Valdez. In 1987 CSX further extended its array of transportation services by forming CSX/Sea-Land Intermodal (later known as CSX

Intermodal Inc.), the nation's only transcontinental full-service intermodal company.

These acquisitions and initiatives were the last engineered by Watkins. The company's directors became disenchanted with CSX's low profits, declining return on investment, and stagnant stock price. Lagging rail profits, partially due to labor contracts and problems with the company's new acquisitions, resulted in major changes in management direction for CSX. A comprehensive restructuring program was announced by Watkins in 1988, but in April 1989 John W. Snow, a former federal highway official, was appointed president and chief executive officer of the company. Watkins continued as chairman until his retirement on January 31, 1991, when that position, too, was assumed by Snow.

CSX underwent a significant change in direction between 1988 and 1990. CSX's oil and gas businesses (with the exception of its Yukon Pacific stake) were sold in 1988 and 1989, resulting in a net gain of more than $200 million. Most of its resort properties and the telecommunications system were also sold, although CSX kept the Greenbrier Hotel and one smaller resort. A crew-reduction agreement was signed by the railroad with the United Transportation Union in 1989. This was a key step in Snow's plan to downsize the railroad, as well as other CSX operations, in order to increase profitability. CSX also improved its share earnings by using money from the gas and oil sale to buy back about 39 percent of its outstanding common stock. In his first years as chief executive, Snow installed a new management team determined to improve shipping and real estate profits and to focus on CSX's traditionally strong rail operations in order to earn a better return on the company's $12 billion asset base.

Strategic Acquisitions in the 1990s

With Snow's emphasis on improving both customer relations and profits, CSX's position grew ever stronger through the 1990s. Revenues increased steadily, from $8.21 billion in 1990 to $10.54 billion in 1996, while net earnings reached a peak of $855 million by 1996. Snow sought to leverage this strength by making selective, strategic acquisitions that would enhance and extend the company's core transportation operations.

In 1992 American Commercial Lines increased its barge capacity by more than one-third through the purchase of the Valley Line companies. Four years later, ACL acquired the marine assets of Conti-Carriers & Terminals Inc., adding 400 barges and eight towboats to a fleet that subsequently numbered 3,700 barges and 137 towboats. In early 1993 CSX acquired Customized Transportation Inc. (CTI), one of the leading logistics companies for the automotive industry, providing distribution, warehousing, and assembly on a contract basis for just-in-time delivery systems. CTI later added service in Europe and South America to its existing U.S. operations, and in 1996 began to service new industries, including electronics, retail, and chemicals. In 1996 Sea-Land entered into a global alliance with Danish shipping company Maersk Lines involving the sharing of vessels and terminals.

The company's acquisitions and initiatives of the early 1990s were largely overshadowed by CSX's attempted purchase of Conrail Inc., which began in October 1996. The 1990s had already seen the mega-mergers of Burlington Northern and Santa Fe to form Burlington Northern Santa Fe and of Union Pacific and Southern Pacific (whereby Union Pacific Corp. absorbed Southern Pacific). It appeared that Conrail and CSX would form the nation's largest railroad—including Conrail's lucrative routes to New York City—when Conrail agreed to CSX's $8.1 billion friendly takeover offer. But Norfolk Southern Corp.—CSX's archrival and a fellow eastern U.S. rail power that had twice before attempted to buy Conrail—stepped in with a $9.1 billion hostile takeover bid, prompting CSX in November to raise its offer to $8.4 billion. By March 1996, after Norfolk had raised its bid twice more, CSX, Norfolk, and Conrail reached a three-way agreement for a $10.2 billion takeover, with CSX paying $4.3 billion for 42 percent of Conrail's operations and Norfolk paying $5.9 billion for the other 58 percent. Although the outcome was less than the full merger originally sought, CSX would still gain about 4,500 miles of rail—including lines to New York, Boston, and Montreal—giving it a 23,000-mile system in 23 states and the provinces of Ontario and Quebec. Pending approval by the Surface Transportation Board which was expected sometime in 1998, CSX and Norfolk Southern would operate the two dominant railroads in the eastern United States, with CSX having a slight edge over the 21,000-mile Norfolk system and thus remaining the nation's third-largest railroad.

An increasing concern in the rapidly consolidating railroad industry of the mid-1990s was whether the mergers were compromising the system's safety. In the midst of CSX's seeking of regulatory approval of the Conrail takeover, a jury in New Orleans awarded damages of $3.37 billion, including $2.5 billion in punitive damages, against CSX in relation to a 1987 chemical-car fire. This September 1997 judgement was overturned two months later by the Louisiana Supreme Court, which sent it back to a lower court for reconsideration. CSX's safety record came under further fire when the Federal Railroad Administration issued a report in October 1997 criticizing CSX's safety procedures. The agency had started an investigation earlier in the year, following a collision between two CSX trains which killed one employee and injured another. The company paid $750,000 in fines for violations uncovered in the inquiry. More controversially, CSX Transportation hired the Federal Railroad Administration's safety chief shortly after release of the report, leading to criticism from safety advocates.

Assuming regulatory approval of the Conrail breakup, the consolidation of the company's newly acquired assets was likely to be CSX's number one priority into the 21st century. Just as the problems that resulted from the Penn Central merger led to the careful meshing of operations in previous CSX mergers, the kind of snafus encountered in the Union Pacific takeover of Southern Pacific would need to be avoided if CSX and Norfolk were to successfully divide Conrail. With the negotiation of the Conrail deal completed, the following question arose among industry observers—was railroad consolidation finally over? The next step, some felt, was the creation of two coast-to-coast giants, with CSX joining with either Southern Pacific or Burlington Northern Santa Fe and Norfolk Southern joining with the remaining partner. Whether or not further consolidation occurred, CSX was certain to remain at the center of the dynamic railroad industry.

Principal Subsidiaries

CSX Transportation Inc.; Sea-Land Service Inc.; CSX Intermodal Inc.; American Commercial Lines Inc.; Customized Transportation Inc.; CSX Technology, Inc.; The Greenbrier; Yukon Pacific Corporation; Grand Teton Lodge Company.

Further Reading

Dilts, James D., *The Great Road: The Building of the Baltimore and Ohio, the Nation's First Railroad, 1828–1853,* Stanford, Calif.: Stanford University Press, 1993.

Dorin, Patrick C., *The Chesapeake and Ohio Railway, George Washington's Railroad,* Seattle: Superior Publishing Co., 1981.

Dozier, Howard Douglas, *A History of the Atlantic Coast Line Railroad,* Boston: Houghton Mifflin, 1920, reprint, New York: A. M. Kelley, 1971.

Finn, Edwin A., Jr., "On the Right Track?," *Forbes,* May 16, 1988, p. 105.

Gold, Jackey, "CSX: Stoking Up the Largest U.S. Railroad," *Financial World,* February 4, 1992, p. 18.

Hungerford, Edward, *The Story of the Baltimore & Ohio Railroad, 1827–1927,* 1928, reprint, New York: Arno Press, 1972.

Kimelman, John, "It's the Customer, Stupid?," *Financial World,* January 3, 1995, pp. 31–32.

Kizzia, Tom, "Chessie-SCL Industries: A Merger of Equals," *Railway Age,* March 30, 1981, p. 26.

Lipin, Steven, and Daniel Machalaba, "CSX Agrees to Acquire Conrail for $8.1 Billion in Cash and Stock," *Wall Street Journal,* October 16, 1996, pp. 3A, 6A.

Machalaba, Daniel, and Anna Wilde Mathews, "How Norfolk's Chief Pulled Off Conrail Coup," *Wall Street Journal,* March 5, 1997, pp. 1B, 4B.

Machalaba, Daniel, and Steven Lipin, "CSX Raises Bid for Conrail to $8.4 Billion," *Wall Street Journal,* November 7, 1996, pp. 3A, 8A.

Martin, Justin, "The Great Train Game," *Fortune,* November 11, 1996, pp. 151–52, 154.

Mathews, Anna Wilde, "Jury Assesses CSX Punitive Damages of $2.5 Billion," *Wall Street Journal,* September 9, 1997, p. 6B.

Miller, Luther S., "The War Is Over. The Real Fight Begins," *Railway Age,* April 1997, pp. 31, 34, 36, 38.

Nomani, Asra Q., "CSX Unit Hires Safety Chief of Rail Agency," *Wall Street Journal,* October 21, 1997, p. 7B.

Norman, James R., "Full Steam Ahead," *Forbes,* June 7, 1993, pp. 14–15.

——, " 'We've Got a Clock on It,' " *Forbes,* June 25, 1990, p. 116.

Toothman, Fred Rees, *Working for the Chessie System: Olde King Coal's Prime Carrier,* Huntington, W.Va.: Vandalia Book Co., 1993.

Turner, Charles Wilson, *Chessie's Road,* Richmond, Va.: Garrett and Massie Incorporated, 1956.

Stover, John F., *History of the Baltimore and Ohio Railroad,* West Lafayette, Ind.: Purdue University Press, 1987.

Verespji, Michael A., "Rail Deregulation Gives CSX a Boost," *Industry Week,* October 13, 1980, p. 31.

Watkins, Hays T., "CSX: A Bold New Course," *Railway Age,* January 1986, p. 36.

Weber, Joseph, "Highballing Toward Two Big Railroads," *Business Week,* March 17, 1997, pp. 32–33.

——, "This Railroad Is Weary of Getting Sidetracked," *Business Week,* October 17, 1988, p. 60.

Welty, Gus, "CSX Puts It All Together," *Railway Age,* January 1987, p. 27.

—Bernard A. Block
—updated by David E. Salamie

Dal-Tile International Inc.

7834 Hawn Freeway
Dallas, Texas 75217
U.S.A.
(214) 398-1411
Fax: (214) 309-4300
Web site: http://www.daltile.com

Public Company
Incorporated: 1947 as Dallas Ceramic Co.
Employees: 7,600
Sales: $720.2 million (1996)
Stock Exchanges: New York
SICs: Ceramic Wall & Floor Tile; Offices of Holding Companies, Not Elsewhere Classified

Dal-Tile International Inc. was the largest manufacturer, distributor, and marketer of ceramic tile in North America in the mid-1990s. A vertically integrated holding company, Dal-Tile, through subsidiaries, offers a full range of wall, floor, and mosaic tiles as well as installation materials and tools and stone and quarry-related products purchased from other manufacturers. The company's products were being sold in the mid-1990s through a network of 222 company-operated sales centers to tile contractors, architects, design professionals, builders, developers, and individual consumers. Dal-Tile is also a significant supplier to home-center retailers such as The Home Depot and to flooring dealers.

Problem Acquisition, 1990–95

Dal-Tile began operations in 1947 as Dallas Ceramic Co., establishing its first wall-tile manufacturing facility and corporate headquarters in Dallas. A private company, it was owned by Juan (Jack) Brittingham and Robert Brittingham, Sr., who quietly built it into a world-class company. A Mexican plant was opened in 1955. The company was known as Dal-Tile Group, with manufacturing facilities in Texas, Pennsylvania, and Mexico, and 125 company-owned sales centers nationwide, when AEA Investors Inc. bought it in early 1990 for approximately $650 million, including $200 million in equity. Dal-Tile's 1989 revenue was reported to be $337 million. The Brittingham brothers netted at least $470 million after taxes from the sale and landed on *Forbes's* list of the 400 richest Americans. Robert's personal fortune was estimated at $350 million.

AEA Investors was just as publicity-shy as the Brittinghams, but its 90 or so investors were known to include former Secretary of State Henry Kissinger, former Secretary of Transportation Drew Lewis, former ambassador to Mexico Charles Pilliod, Jr., and retired corporate chief executive officers such as Walter Wriston of Citicorp and Roger Smith of General Motors. Its glittering client list notwithstanding, AEA paid approximately four times book value for a company about to fall into a slump because of a nationwide drop in commercial construction. After capital outlays, Dal-Tile's operating earnings of about $51 million in 1991 were barely adequate to cover the $43 million in interest AEA paid that year to service the debt it incurred to buy the company.

Also in 1991 the Texas Water Commission imposed a record $1 million fine against Dal-Tile for 12 years of illegally dumping hazardous, lead-contaminated waste into two gravel pits in southeastern Dallas County. It was the largest fine ever levied by a state agency for environmental violations. The company, which used glazing compounds containing lead to manufacture ceramic tiles, was required by law to send contaminated wastes from the manufacturing process to special landfills but, according to state investigators, dumped the material from 1975 to 1987 in pits that were not specially licensed. The commission also found that Dal-Tile used waste oils on farmland for dust control, failed to notify the state it had discharged industrial solid wastes into water, and failed to keep records of the waste and file annual reports.

This violation was uncovered by Lorrie Coterill, a housewife and mother of four who began worrying about odors coming from a gravel pit near her home—one of two in which Dal-Tile stored the contaminated wastes. She scaled the fence around the pit and found barrels leaking diesel fuel, evidence of illegal burning, and a sludge that was later found to contain lead, arsenic, cadmium, and other dangerous substances. The con-

Company Perspectives:

Our corporate vision: A team dedicated to grow our business by creating the best value for our customers through innovative products and exceptional customer service.

taminated pits were within 100 feet of some drinking wells and near swimming holes where children had played for years, although tests found no groundwater contamination, according to state officials.

In addition to the fine imposed on Dal-Tile, a federal grand jury indicted Robert Brittingham, Jr., and company president John Lomonaco on 17 criminal counts, including conspiracy to dump hazardous waste. Brittingham was found guilty in 1993, fined $4 million, and sentenced to five years' probation, which he began fulfilling with 15 hours a week in community service by financing and operating a $6 million lead-abatement program for Dallas. The total cost of the fines and dumpsite cleanup came to $16.5 million.

Despite these problems, Dal-Tile's new owner was bullish on its prospects because it saw a growing market at the expense of the 50 percent of tiles used in U.S. construction that were coming from abroad, mostly Italy. To compete with Italian firms, whose designs and product quality were far superior, Dal-Tile earmarked around $20 million to modernize its existing tile plants and build new ones. The company planned to open a new manufacturing plant in southeast Dallas in 1994 and a new, $18 million regional warehouse built adjacent to this plant. To bolster its residential business, Dal-Tile also was adding around 30 percent more sales outlets, at a cost of about $13 million. Between 1987 and the end of 1991 the company opened 76 showroom warehouses, which were serving as the primary outlets for its tile. Another 21 were opened in 1992, and 21 more were planned in 1993.

Overall sales in the tile industry fell 30 percent during 1990–91. Dal-Tile, however, was able to raise its revenues to $357.6 million in 1991 and $398 million in 1992. In 1993 the company sold $133 million worth of five-year notes to help pay down debt. According to the prospectus that accompanied the offering, Dal-Tile controlled 18 percent of the tile market in the United States. Moody's Investor Service gave the issue a poor rating, citing Dal-Tile's heavy debt and the cyclical nature of the construction industry. The company had warned in the prospectus that it did not expect to generate sufficient cash from operations to pay the notes at maturity.

Dal-Tile Chairman Billy Ray Cox retired in 1993 after 34 years with the company and was replaced by Pilliod. One of the new chief's first acts was to postpone the planned Dallas plant and warehouse project because of slower-than-expected sales. The creation of the North American Free Trade Association was good news for Dal-Tile, however, because the company was producing about one-fourth of its tiles in Mexico. The end of the 19 percent import duty on Mexican tiles meant a projected annual saving to the company of about $10 million.

Dal-Tile's revenues grew to $506.3 million in 1994, the year the company introduced high-end floor-tile products and significantly increased sales to home-center retailers. Even after paying $53.5 million in interest, it was able to record net income of $6.9 million. Net sales slumped to $478.8 million in 1995, but the company earned $2.1 million after taxes and after interest payments of $55.5 million.

Growth by Merger, 1995–96

In September 1995 American Olean Tile Co., a company with five ceramic-tile factories, agreed to merge with Dal-Tile. As a result of the transaction, which was completed in December, Armstrong World Industries Inc., American Olean Tile's parent company, became a significant shareholder in Dal-Tile. Armstrong also contributed $27.5 million in cash and received 37 percent of the common stock.

American Olean Tile's origins dated back to 1878, when American Encaustic Tiling Co., Ltd. was incorporated to acquire the business and assets of an even older company. An affiliate of this company started selling products of Olean Tile Co. in 1937. The American Olean Tile Co. was formed in 1948 as a joint venture of the two. National Gypsum Co. bought both American Encaustic and Olean Tile in 1958 and created American Olean Tile as a subsidiary. It was sold to Armstrong World Industries in 1988 for about $330 million.

American Olean differed from Dal-Tile in producing tiles for a network of independent ceramic-tile and floor-covering distributors as well as through more than 60 company outlets. Its glazed ceramic mosaics were being used primarily in schools, hospitals, malls, and office buildings. The company had manufacturing sites in Fayette, Alabama; Lewisport, Kentucky; Olean, New York; and Jackson, Tennessee. It also had a half-interest in a joint venture in Chihuahua, Mexico. American Olean had sales of about $250 million in 1995.

With the addition of American Olean Tile, Dal-Tile's revenues grew to $720.2 million in 1996. When allowing for the acquisition, however, sales were essentially flat, which the company attributed to problems in merging the computer systems of the two units, thereby leading to delays in delivering shipments to the company-owned sales centers. During the year Dal-Tile opened a state-of-the-art wall-tile facility in El Paso, Texas and acquired a floor-tile facility in Mt. Gilead, North Carolina. Dal-Tile became a publicly owned company in August 1996 with the completion of an initial public equity offering and began trading on the New York Stock Exchange.

In all, beginning in 1991 and extending through 1996, Dal-Tile invested about $130 million in capital expenditures, including about $85 million in new plants and state-of-the-art equipment to increase manufacturing capacity, improve efficiency, and develop new capabilities. Manufacturing capacity grew from 203 million to 343 million square feet over this period. By the fall of 1997, the number of manufacturing facilities had grown from 11 to 13, with total annual capacity of more than 425 million square feet of tile—enough to cover the state of Massachusetts.

Dal-Tile had interest expenses of $46.3 million during 1996 and took an extraordinary $29 million loss on early retirement of debt. Nevertheless, the company still had net income of $5.4 million during the year. Its long-term debt in April 1997 was $470.7 million. AEA Investors owned 53.5 percent of its stock and Armstrong World Industries owned 34.4 percent.

Dal-Tile in 1996

Dal-Tile's offerings in 1996 included different types of ceramic tile under the Dal-Tile and American Olean names and the new Homesource brand name, introduced in 1996. These company-manufactured product lines constituted one of the industry's broadest product offerings of colors, textures, and finishes, as well as the industry's largest offering of trim and angle pieces. Dal-Tile offered one of the broadest lines of glazed floor and wall tile, mosaic tile, porcelain tile, quarry tile, stone products, and allied products. In addition, it carried a selection of tile products from foreign manufacturers. Homesource was targeted for the do-it-yourself/buy-it-yourself market.

Dal-Tile had a network of 222 company-operated sales centers in 44 states at the end of 1996, up from 124 in 1990. About 72 percent of its net sales (excluding American Olean) in 1996 were made through these centers. Each one included a showroom, office space, and a warehouse in which inventory was stored, including a selection of products not manufactured by the company. The company was also supplying more than 1,000 home-center retail outlets nationwide.

Independent distributors at about 170 locations were distributing the American Olean brand to retail centers. In all, independent distributors accounted for about 52 percent of Dal-Tile's tile sales in 1996, compared with 33 percent for company-operated sales centers and 15 percent for home-center retailers. About 71 percent of Dal-Tile's net sales in 1996 were company-manufactured products, with the remainder being provided by other domestic manufacturers, as well as foreign manufacturers, located principally in Italy, Spain, Mexico, and Japan.

Dal-Tile's largest manufacturing facility at the end of 1996 was the one in Monterrey, Mexico, which accounted for about 45 percent of the company's annual manufacturing capacity. The others were in Fayette, Alabama; Lewisport, Kentucky; Mt. Gilead, North Carolina; Olean, New York; Gettysburg, Pennsylvania; Jackson, Tennessee; and Coleman, Conroe, Dallas, and El Paso, Texas. The company owned talc mining rights in Texas and clay mining rights in Kentucky.

Principal Subsidiaries

Dal-Tile of Canada Inc. (Canada); Dal-Tile Corporation; Dal-Tile Group Inc.; Dal-Tile Mexico, S.A. de C.V. (Mexico); Dal-Minerals Corporation; Materiales Ceramicos, S.A. de C.V. (Mexico); R&M Supplies, Inc.; Recumbrimientos Interceramic, S.A. de C.V. (Mexico; 49.99%).

Further Reading

"AEA Investors Inc. Confirms Purchase of Dal-Tile Group," *Wall Street Journal,* January 24, 1990, p. C21.

Berss, Marcia, "Buying at the Top," *Forbes,* May 11, 1992, p. 122.

——, "Slippery Tile," *Forbes,* December 6, 1993, pp. 14, 16.

Bowen, Bill, "Slow Sales Put Dal-Tile's Expansion on Back Burner," *Dallas Business Journal,* October 29, 1993, p. 4.

Carroll, Christine, "The Texas 100: The One Hundred Richest People in Texas," *Texas Monthly,* September 1993, p. 142 and continuation.

Countryman, Carol, "Worried Mom Cleans Up," *The Progressive,* February 1993, p. 14.

Files, Jennifer, "Dal-Tile Plans Merger," *Dallas Morning News,* December 23, 1995, p. F1.

"The Forbes 400; The Richest People in America," *Forbes,* October 22, 1990, p. 284.

Heidorn, Rich, Jr., "Lansdale Tile Maker in Merger," *Philadelphia Inquirer,* September 2, 1995, pp. D1, D8.

Marren, Joe, "Merger with Armstrong Paves Way for Tile Company," *Business First-Buffalo,* October 23, 1995, p. 16.

Nix, Mede, "Tile-Maker Hit with $1 Million Fine," *Dallas Times Herald,* March 14, 1991, p. A15.

Tanner, Lisa, "Dal-Tile Growth Fires $18M Project," *Dallas Business Journal,* October 2, 1992, p. 1.

——, "Dal-Tile Registers $75M Debt Offering," *Dallas Business Journal,* June 25, 1993, p. 5.

—Robert Halasz

Deckers Outdoor Corporation

495A S. Fairview
Goleta, California 93117
U.S.A.
(805) 967-7611
Fax: (805) 967-9722
Web site: http://www.teva.com

Public Company
Incorporated: 1975 as Deckers Corporation
Employees: 365
Sales: $102.3 million (1995)
Stock Exchanges: NASDAQ
SICs: 3021 Rubber & Plastics Footwear

Deckers Outdoor Corporation develops, manufactures, and markets high performance footwear and apparel that is used for outdoor sports and recreation activities, as well as for casual wear. The company's products are marketed under the brand names of Teva, Simple, Sensi, and Picante. Teva markets outdoor sports sandals that utilize a patented strapping system and is widely recognized as the founder and market leader of the sport sandal category. Simple Shoes are comfortable, fashionable closed-toe street shoes, and Sensi manufactures modestly priced casual sandals. Picante is a line of hand-woven cotton apparel that complements Deckers's footwear lines.

The Early Years

The beginnings of Deckers Outdoor Corporation can be traced to the mid-1970s, when the company was formed to produce and market sandals and other beachwear items. The company was marginally successful in the early years and was incorporated in California in 1975 under the name Deckers Corporation. The company's products never truly hit it big, however, until a river guide by the name of Mark Thatcher brought Deckers his Teva sandal concept in 1985.

Prior to the union between Thatcher and Deckers Corporation, Thatcher worked as a geophysicist at Cities Service Company in Houston, Texas until being laid off in 1982. At that time, he began guiding raft trips on the Colorado River through the Grand Canyon. It was then that he was introduced to a problem for which the solution would change his life. During the raft trips, Thatcher noticed that while traditional flip-flop shoes were light and quick drying, they tended to fall off his feet whenever he stepped into mud or water. Thus he decided to add another nylon strap around the back of his heel to hold the shoes in place.

Soon, other guides on the river were asking Thatcher to make them a pair of his newly created sport sandals. After that came requests for the shoes from his passengers. Thatcher realized that he had stumbled across an idea worth a gold mine, and he decided to go into business for himself. He named his sandals ''Teva'' (pronounced Teh' Vah), the Hebrew word for nature, and used the remainder of his $20,000 severance paycheck from Cities Service Company to make more sandals and get his back-strap idea patented.

For almost two years Thatcher traveled around in his car and sold sandals out of his trunk to retailers in the southwest. He inked a deal with California Pacific, a shoemaker, whereby the company produced his sandals and Thatcher acted as a salesman to distribute them into the retail arena. But beyond the production of the sandals, California Pacific offered Thatcher little or no support in his endeavor. In his first year on the road Thatcher sold only 200 pairs of his Teva sandals in rafting hot spots and resort towns.

By 1984, however, word of mouth had begun to help increase Thatcher's sales, and California Pacific began to realize Teva's potential. The company tried to stake a claim to both the Teva name and to Thatcher's invention, stating that Thatcher was merely an employee of their firm. The issue ended up in court, and after a long and ugly legal battle, Thatcher finally won his case against California Pacific in 1985. He severed ties with the company and began to search for a new entity to back his product. In less than a year Thatcher had set up an exclusive licensing agreement with Deckers Corporation to manufacture and distribute his Teva sandals to outdoor retail companies, department stores, and other smaller outdoor equipment retailers.

Company Perspectives:

Our goal is to achieve a level of operational excellence that will clearly distinguish Deckers from its competitors. Our customers can be confident in our ability to deliver a quality product when they need it, which offers the retailer a concrete advantage in doing business with Deckers.

Growth Through the Early 1990s

With Deckers Corporation acting as its new financial and managerial support, Teva was soon distributed into such nationwide channels as outdoor companies REI, EMS, and L.L. Bean, and department stores such as Nordstrom. The Teva sandal became wildly popular throughout a large portion of the western United States, based on its functional nature and the vast selection of outdoor activities in that region. The sandal also gained popularity on college campuses, where it became the latest trend in casual footwear. Teva soon became Deckers's most popular offering.

By 1991 outdoor sport sandals had become the latest footwear craze in the United States, with Teva strongly leading the pack in market share. The sandals were so popular, in fact, that people even began to wear them in cooler weather with socks, which helped to dramatically boost many retailers' sock sales for the year. At that point, Teva's sandal line had grown to include 30 different styles, all of which retailed at anywhere between $35 and $80.

Within a year Deckers had contracted for its first Teva advertisement account with Stein Robaire Helm of Los Angeles, to the tune of $1.3 million. Also that year, Deckers's president, Douglas B. Otto, became an equal partner in Sensi, Inc. Sensi was a manufacturer of casual-wear beach and spa sandals, and the company was brought in under the Deckers umbrella alongside Teva. Just as Teva sandals were recognized on the basis of their innovative qualities, Sensi sandals were as well; they utilized a special ventilated footbed that allowed for airflow around the foot.

Meanwhile, Teva had undergone some major changes since the first version was created by Thatcher almost a decade before. The sandals, which had started out merely as flat-soled thongs with a strap around the heel, had improved to the point that cushioning midsole materials were being used in the footbed and more effective rubber was being used for better outsole grip. The success brought about by Teva's innovations began to attract some other big names into the sport sandal industry. Soon Nike, Reebok, K-Swiss, Merrell, and Timberland all developed and offered their own versions of the sport sandal, which served to erode some of Teva's share of the market. The huge success of Nike's Air Deschutz sandal, for example, helped that company earn an almost 25 percent share of the then-$100 million sport sandal market by 1993.

Although the increased competition possessed the potential to steal away Teva's giant share of the sport sandal market, Deckers saw the entrances by other major companies as a positive. According to Teva's vice-president Peter Link in a February 1994 issue of *Sporting Goods Business,* "When a Nike comes in, it simply helps legitimize the category."

Nevertheless, to maintain its majority hold on the sport sandal market in the face of increased competition, Deckers began to diversify its offerings. First, the company added new models to its Teva line, including upscale casual-wear versions of the shoe that were made from leather materials and retailed at around $100 per pair. Then, in 1993, the company purchased a 50 percent share of Simple Shoes, Inc. for $10,000. Simple Shoes produced casual street shoes that were mainly marketed to the "twenty-something/Generation X" clientele. With the purchase, Deckers also began distributing the footwear line through its own existing channels.

The Mid-1990s and Beyond

In October of 1993 Deckers initiated a public offering of stock in its company at $15 per share and was incorporated as Deckers Outdoor Corporation. The company then finished the year on a high note, achieving $57.1 million in 1993 sales with net earnings of $6.3 million. Early in 1994 the company acquired the remaining 50 percent interest in Simple Shoes for $1.5 million, and the entire company was added to Deckers's holdings alongside Teva and Sensi.

The year 1994 also marked Deckers's entrance into the apparel market, as the company formed a joint venture agreement with Robert Eason, the owner of U.S. distribution rights for a line of hand-woven cotton apparel called Heirlooms. The Heirlooms line was the beginning of what later became the Picante division of Deckers Outdoor Corporation.

Meanwhile, just as Thatcher had begun to shoot his first Teva commercial, he was diagnosed with Type I diabetes. His body almost completely stopped producing its own insulin, which necessitated that he undergo daily injections. The disease forced Thatcher to alter his outgoing, adventurous lifestyle slightly, but he remained increasingly involved in the management of Deckers's Teva division. In fact, shortly thereafter he brought his father and sister aboard the company as Teva consultants in his hometown of Flagstaff, Arizona. By the close of fiscal 1994, Deckers's sales had jumped to $85.8 million.

In 1995 Deckers acquired Alp Sport Sandals and Ugg Holdings, Inc. Deckers's overall sales skyrocketed once again and for the first time broke the $100 million mark by topping off at $102.3 million. A total of 2.3 million pairs of Tevas alone were sold that year. Even so, the competition in the sport sandal market was steadily increasing. While Deckers's sales figures were jumping ahead dramatically each year, its share of the sandal market was actually slowly shrinking. There was an increasing number of new players entering the sport sandal arena all the time. As a means of maintaining its dominant position in the field, Deckers focused more readily on maintaining its high-quality image. The company avoided discount distribution channels and instead kept its products only in high-profile, quality retail stores.

As Deckers Outdoor Corporation neared the end of the century, it was continuing to position itself for future growth and profitability. The sport sandal market was showing no signs of declining sales any time in the near future, as overall industry sales actually continued to increase each year. Deckers still had yet to penetrate a great deal of the United States with its products, which actually worked in the company's favor because it meant that there was still an immense amount of room for growth. Furthermore, Deckers's commitment to innovation and to providing its customers with quality products and great customer service showed that the company had the potential to remain the industry leader far into the future.

Principal Subsidiaries

Sensi USA, Inc.; Simple Shoes, Inc.; Deckers Mexico, Inc.; Deckers Baja, S.A. de C.V. (Mexico); Holbrook Limited (Hong Kong); Heirlooms, Inc.; Decker Outdoor Corporation International; Phillipsburg Ltd. (Hong Kong); Deckers Trading, Inc. (U.S. Virgin Islands); Picante, S.A. (Guatemala); Trukke Winter Sports Products, Inc.; Ugg Holding, Inc.; Original American UHS Co.

Further Reading

Labate, John, ''Deckers Outdoor,'' *Fortune,* January 24, 1994, p. 91.

McEvoy, Christopher, ''Under Current,'' *Sporting Goods Business,* February 1994, p. 94.

Mitchell, Emily, and Otey, Anne-Martie, ''Flips That Won't Flop,'' *People,* September 9, 1996, p. 103.

Palmeri, Christopher, ''No More Chimp Toes,'' *Forbes,* July 5, 1993, p. 130.

''Tarsorial Splendor,'' *Time,* July 29, 1991, p. 61.

—Laura E. Whiteley

Defiance, Inc.

1111 Chester Ave., Suite 750
Cleveland, Ohio 44114
U.S.A.
(216) 861-6300
Fax: (216) 861-6006

Public Company
Founded: 1905 as Defiance Screw Machine Products
Employees: 729
Sales: $92.1 million (1997)
Stock Exchanges: NASDAQ
SICs: 3542 Machine Tools, Metal Forming Types; 3544 Special Dies & Tools; 3462 Iron & Steel Forgings; 8711 Engineering Services; 6719 Holding Companies, Not Elsewhere Classified

With approximately half of its annual sales to automakers General Motors Corporation, Ford Motor Company, and Chrysler Corporation (the ''Big Three''), Defiance, Inc. is carefully attuned to the latest trends in the automotive industry. In the 1990s the major domestic automakers began to insist that their suppliers have broad capabilities, thus allowing the automakers to source more work to fewer suppliers. In order to expand its capabilities and compete with other major automotive suppliers, Defiance transformed itself from being primarily a supplier of precision parts to one that could also offer engineering and testing services as well as prototype and production tooling.

Company Roots

In August 1985 the present Defiance, Inc. was incorporated in Delaware as a holding company for Defiance Precision Products, Inc. The company's primary business was manufacturing cam follower rollers (CFRs) for truck and automobile engines. It also produced other hardened and ground components for diesel engines. CFRs are miniature roller bearings that connect push rods to valve rocker arms. They were first used primarily in diesel engines to more efficiently move the rocker arms. As pressure grew on the automotive industry to improve fuel efficiency, CFRs became more widely used in gasoline engines as well.

Prior to incorporating in 1985, Defiance Precision Products was a private company that was established following a leveraged buyout of the CFR division of Spartech Corporation in 1981. That CFR division could trace its roots to Defiance Screw Machine Products, which was founded in Defiance, Ohio, in 1905. The company first became involved in the cam roller business in the early 1980s, when General Motors commissioned it to design a miniature roller bearing to reduce valve train friction in diesel car engines. The specialized bearings, known as cam follower rollers (CFRs), became the company's main product. Demand grew as General Motors began using them in gasoline engines as well as diesels.

Defiance Precision Products launched an initial public offering (IPO) of 750,000 shares on October 17, 1985, at $6 per share. The trading price of the stock rose quickly, and the company decided to make a secondary offering of $1.5 million shares on March 18, 1986, at $10.50 per share. Proceeds from the secondary offering were used for future acquisitions.

Embarked on Acquisitions Program, 1986–87

In December 1986 Defiance acquired SMTC Corporation with offices in Troy, Warren, and Westland, Michigan. It was conveniently located near the major automakers in southeastern Michigan, near Detroit. SMTC, later renamed Defiance Testing and Engineering Services, Inc., provided a full range of testing and simulation services of structural and mechanical systems, primarily for the U.S. transportation industry.

In January 1987 Defiance acquired four related companies: Hy-Form Products, Inc., Vaungarde, Inc., Binderline Development, Inc., and Draftline Engineering Co., in exchange for approximately 190,000 shares of common stock and $8,000 in cash. Hy-Form, Binderline, and Draftline were all located in the metropolitan Detroit area and provided prototype and production tooling systems to Detroit's Big Three automakers (Ford, General Motors, and Chrysler). They formed the core of what would become Defiance Tooling Systems in the 1990s. Vaun-

Company Perspectives:

Defiance, Inc. is recognized as a world-class supplier to the U.S. motor vehicle industry. We specialize in highly engineered products and services where we add value by developing imaginative solutions to our customers' challenges. Our three core businesses are: 1) Tooling Systems. Defiance Tooling Systems is a leading supplier of the full range of sheet metal product development services, including prototype and production tooling. We help U.S. auto manufacturers bring new models to market in shorter times with higher quality. 2) Testing Services. Defiance Testing & Engineering Services is a leading provider of sophisticated engineering, testing, simulation and validation services to U.S. automakers and their suppliers. We help bring quieter, safer, smoother-running vehicles to market in the shortest amount of time. 3) Precision Products. Defiance Precision Products is a major supplier of cam follower rollers, roller axles and other specialty anti-friction bearings and precision-machined components. Our products improve the efficiency and performance of gas and diesel engines.

garde, located in Owosso, Michigan, specialized in molding plastic parts using reaction injection molding (RIM) processes; it also was involved in painting plastic parts. Vaungarde served the automotive, heavy truck, agricultural, and recreational vehicle industries. Vaungarde was sold in 1996 when Defiance decided to refocus on its core capabilities.

Debt from Acquisitions Affects Bottom Line

Following that series of acquisitions, Defiance struggled financially for the next several years. In February 1987 it formed a short-lived subsidiary, Prime-Coat Technology, which was sold in April 1988. In fiscal year 1987 (ending June 30) the company reported a net loss of $3.0 million. The loss reflected a loss on operations, with the cost of goods sold, relocation charges, and general expenses exceeding net sales. On top of an operating loss of $1.8 million, the company also had to pay $1.7 million in interest expense.

While operations turned a profit of $603,000 in 1988, the company was saddled with $3.4 million in interest expense associated with its 1987 acquisitions. It reported a net loss of $4.7 million, the largest in its history. The company's losses in 1987 and 1988 were explained as due to the rapid expansion of the company through acquisitions.

Although the company showed a profit of $2.6 million in 1989, it struggled until 1992, when a new president and CEO was brought in. From 1986 through 1990, the company's stock price dropped from a high of $12.25 in 1986 to as low as $.37 in 1990.

On July 27, 1989, the company changed its name to Defiance, Inc. It began to separate services from products and include both as part of sales, reflecting the growing importance of its engineering testing and services subsidiary. Services had become a significant source of revenue. For 1990, Defiance reported overall net sales of $60.1 million, with $45.4 million in revenue from product sales and $14.7 million from services. Net earnings were only $176,000, with interest expense continuing to erode the company's operating earnings.

New CEO and President, 1992

After the company reported another net loss in 1991 of $940,000, Jerry A. Cooper was recruited to replace J. W. Gillis as president and CEO. Prior to joining Defiance, Cooper had been president and CEO of Bettcher Manufacturing Corporation, a metal forming company, since 1990. From 1977 to 1990 he was president and general manager of Mather Seal Company, a subsidiary of Federal-Mogul Corporation. Located in Milan, Michigan, Mather manufactured Teflon seals and other specialty products.

Perceiving that the trend among the Big Three was toward fewer and larger suppliers, Cooper reorganized five of Defiance's Detroit-area subsidiaries into the Defiance Group in 1992. These subsidiaries provided prototype and hard tooling systems to Detroit's automakers. The five subsidiaries forming the new Defiance Group were Defiance SMC (Troy-based), Binderline Development (St. Clair Shores), Draftline Engineering Co. (St. Clair Shores), Defiance STS (Westland), and Hy-Form Products (Livonia).

The new group was headed by Joel Bussell, who was recruited from Dana Corporation in September 1992. By grouping the five subsidiaries, which had been marketing their technical capabilities separately, Defiance hoped to position its Detroit-area-based engineering companies as a single source for designing vehicles, parts, and systems from concept to prototype. The individual companies could still separately pursue contracts that would only provide business to one company. Joint marketing capabilities, however, gave Defiance the ability to pursue contracts to engineer automotive systems and even whole vehicles. The five subsidiaries mainly engineered large structural components for automobiles, such as roofs, hoods, doors, and seats, as well as the tooling for those components.

Defiance Tooling Systems Organized in 1993

A further reorganization of the Defiance Group took place in 1993, when Hy-Form was combined with Binderline and Draftline to form Defiance Tooling Systems, Inc. In 1994 a fourth tooling operation was added when Defiance Tooling Systems leased the equipment of the former Distel Tool & Machine Co. in Warren, Michigan, and renamed it Hy-Form Products Plant Two. The equipment at the former Distel Tool & Machine Co. in Warren was leased to give Defiance Tooling Systems the capability to make hard production dies in addition to the softer prototype dies. As reported in *Crain's Detroit Business*, "Stephen Nash, president of Defiance Tooling Systems in Livonia, could see automotive tooling business gravitating to full-service suppliers."

After leasing the hard production equipment, Defiance won its biggest contract to date in August 1994: a $9.5 million assignment to produce prototype and production dies for parts on the 1997 replacement for the Chevrolet Corsica and Beretta.

With this contract, Defiance Tooling Systems became one of Detroit's newest full-service die suppliers. As Nash told *Crain's Detroit Business,* "The GM job definitely puts us in the same league with anybody else in Detroit."

Nash came to Defiance as head of Hy-Form Products in 1992. The operation had lost money in the previous two years and was facing an uncertain future. Nash was able to turn things around and motivate the company's 80-plus workers to improve profits and efficiency. One technique he used was to call weekly meetings where employees were given the latest financial figures and allowed to air their concerns. The meetings continued on a monthly basis after the division became profitable. In addition, an annual bonus plan was introduced that tied employee bonuses to companywide financial performance.

Nash also allowed the employees to form committees to look into possible improvements and make recommendations. In 1993 Hy-Form workers identified the need for an in-house computer-design facility to provide added customer convenience and eliminate the cost of subcontracting design work. An ad-hoc employee committee researched the available technology and estimated costs, then made a presentation to parent company Defiance, Inc.'s CEO Jerry Cooper, who gave tentative approval on the spot.

Nash was able to lease the equipment and building formerly occupied by Distel Tooling, one of Detroit's oldest and most recognized die-makers, after the shop closed in 1992. After hiring Distel Tool's former plant manager, Sanzio Piacentini, who had 42 years experience in tooling, Defiance Tooling reopened the shop as Hy-Form Plant Two in January 1994. Defiance planned to use the facility for the group's first major production-die job for a General Motors light truck to be manufactured in Indonesia. With the addition of the new Chevrolet work, employment at the plant was increased to 23 employees.

With approximately 200 employees in Defiance Tooling overall, it was well-positioned to take advantage of the Big Three's new policy of favoring full-service suppliers. For fiscal 1994 (ending June 30), tooling systems accounted for approximately 25 percent of Defiance, Inc.'s $81.6 million in sales. The company's remaining sales were divided among Defiance Testing and Engineering Services (approximately 25 percent), Defiance Precision Products (approximately 40 percent), and Vaungarde (10 percent).

New Banking Agreement Reflected Improved Financial Condition, 1994

After reporting net earnings of $909,000 on sales of $69.6 million in 1992, Defiance began to enjoy substantial profitability as the economy became more robust and the automotive industry thrived. In 1993 sales grew to $79.2 million, and net earnings were a respectable $3.4 million. The next year sales were up slightly to $81.6 million, but net earnings increased dramatically to $6 million. Between 1992 and 1994 the company had increased its operating profits from $3.6 million to $9.4 million. During that period services grew from 21 percent of total sales to 27 percent.

In July 1994 Defiance renegotiated its banking arrangements with Comerica Bank, its primary lender, reflecting the company's improved financial condition. Its term loan, revolving credit borrowings, and Industrial Revenue Bonds were no longer secured. The company was also no longer restricted from paying dividends, and it began to pay a quarterly dividend to shareholders. The bank's consent would still be required for the company to repurchase its stock or pledge any of its assets.

1995: Company's Most Profitable Year

The year 1995 got off to a great start, with Defiance reporting a 50 percent increase in net sales for the first quarter (ending September 30), excluding a gain from an accounting change. Net income for the first quarter was $1.5 million, up from $1 million for the same period of the prior year. For the year Defiance reported net sales of $92.5 million, up from $81.6 million in 1994, and net earnings of $6.6 million, up from $6.0 million in 1994. It was the best financial performance in the company's history. Between 1990 and 1994, the company's stock price rose from a range of $.37 to over $10 in 1994.

The year 1996 was a challenging one for the company, which opened a new roller plant but was hampered by customer delays on a major new CFR contract. Net sales were a record $104 million, but net earnings dropped to $1.6 million, their lowest level since Cooper joined Defiance in 1992. Higher costs associated with manufacturing precision products resulted in earnings from operations for 1996 of only $5.6 million, down from $11.2 million in 1995.

Net sales for 1997 declined by $11.9 million to $92.1 million. However, net earnings rose to a respectable $4.3 million. During the year Defiance stopped all hard tooling operations in May 1996, and the Vaungarde business was sold in August 1996. Management thought the sale of Vaungarde, which manufactured plastic moldings, would help Defiance better focus on its core operating capabilities. Vaungarde had reported an operating loss for the previous three years, losing $240,000 in 1995 and $834,000 in 1996. Defiance received a total of $3.8 million for its Vaungarde stock.

During 1997 the company's precision products division increased its sales as a percentage of the company's overall sales to 49 percent, up from 35 percent in 1996. Defiance Precision Products made specialty anti-friction bearings and precision-machined components. Its principal product was the cam follower roller (CFR). In 1997 Defiance claimed to hold a 40 percent market share of the domestic gasoline engine market for CFRs and was the dominant supplier of CFRs for the diesel engine market.

Management identified several growth opportunities for its precision products subsidiary. These included working with medium-duty truck makers in North America and car and truck makers in Europe to incorporate CFRs into their engines. The company was also actively working to supply CFRs for overhead cam engines at Chrysler, Ford, and General Motors. While CFRs work equally well on overhead cam engines, they were used primarily in push-rod engines, which are commonly found on vans, light trucks, sport-utility vehicles, and larger cars. Defiance Precision Products also had plans to move beyond its role as a component manufacturer and become a supplier of a preassembled valve-train subsystem that would include a roller, axle, and rocker arm. Management was also seeking to find new applications for its bearings and engine components to utilize its capabilities in precision machining, grinding, heat treating, assembly, and medium- to high-volume production.

Defiance Tooling Systems accounted for approximately 22 percent of the company's sales in 1997. During the year it handled its most complex program to date, a production tooling project for a new Ford van that involved delivering 35 different parts on the same date. During the year the company added to its production capacity by purchasing two new five-axis laser coordinate measurement machines (CMM) and another computer-numeric-controlled (CNC) milling machine.

Defiance Testing and Engineering accounted for approximately 28 percent of the company's sales in 1997, up from 23 percent in 1995. During the year it formed a joint venture with MIRA, one of the world's leading independent automotive research and development organizations. Based in England with additional operations in Asia and North America, MIRA could provide full-vehicle development and system integration to complement Defiance Testing and Engineering's expertise in noise, vibration, and harshness (NVH) testing and analysis. Management felt the need to expand its testing and engineering services capabilities, because automobile manufacturers were outsourcing more testing and requiring suppliers to engineer more of their own products and test them themselves. That is, while the original equipment manufacturers (OEMs) wanted more testing, they did not want to do it themselves, thus creating more business opportunities for Defiance.

Principal Subsidiaries

Defiance Precision Products, Inc.; Hy-Form Products, Inc.; Defiance Testing and Engineering Services, Inc.; Binderline Development, Inc.; Draftline Engineering Company.

Further Reading

Barkholz, David, "Tooling Firm Bucks Trend," *Crain's Detroit Business,* November 14, 1994, p. 3.

King, Angela, "Ohio Firm Pushes Local Companies," *Crain's Detroit Business,* October 26, 1992.

—David Bianco

DELUXE

Deluxe Corporation

3680 Victoria Street North
Shoreview, Minnesota 55126-2966
U.S.A.
(612) 483-7111
Fax: (612) 481-4163
Web site: http://www.deluxe.com

Public Company
Incorporated: 1920 as DeLuxe Check Printers, Inc.
Employees: 19,643
Sales: $1.90 billion (1996)
Stock Exchanges: New York
SICs: 2759 Commercial Printing, Not Elsewhere Classified; 2761 Manifold Business Forms; 2782 Blankbooks & Looseleaf Binders; 6099 Functions Related to Depository Banking, Not Elsewhere Classified; 7389 Business Services, Not Elsewhere Classified

A shining example of a company built upon the right idea at the right time, Deluxe Corporation is the largest supplier of checks, deposit slips, and other financial documents in the United States, holding a market share of over 50 percent. The company's long and enviable track record has in large part mirrored the evolution of American banking and financial services technology, from the relatively simple boom-and-bust 1920s through the complex decades of the 1950s and 1960s, when electronic automation revolutionized the industry, to the rise of the electronic funds transfer (EFT) in the latter decades of the 20th century. As recently as 1985, check printing accounted for 96 percent of Deluxe's sales. By 1996, however, this figure was lowered to 79 percent through an expanded focus on such products and services as processing software, account verification, ATM cards, sales development, business and health care forms, and direct marketing. For many analysts, the diversification was long overdue, particularly given repeated predictions that checks would soon be obsolete. And although the personal check continues to be viable and Deluxe has posted 58 consecutive years of sales increases, the company's profitability fell in the mid-1990s as a result of increased competition in the check printing business and less-than-stellar results from the company's non-check-printing operations.

Early History

The foundation for Deluxe was laid in 1905 when William Roy Hotchkiss purchased a small Wisconsin newspaper named *The Barron County Shield Well.* Acquainted with the printing business since boyhood, Hotchkiss thought he had found his niche, particularly after he became publisher and co-owner of the more prestigious *Dunn County News* of Menomonie in 1908. For the next five years Hotchkiss oversaw the development of this paper into the largest and most respected weekly in the state. A protracted illness, however, forced his early retirement from the newspaper business and his relocation to the more congenial climate of southern California. His entrepreneurial drive still intact, Hotchkiss decided to raise chickens but failed, despite conceiving the idea of selling precut chickens to grocery stores.

In 1915 Hotchkiss returned to the Midwest and settled in St. Paul, vowing, according to company annals, "to do one thing and one thing only, but do it better, faster and more economically than anyone else." Recalling his printing days and a special assignment of printing bank checks for a friend, Hotchkiss decided to claim the creation and marketing of personalized checks as his business. The distinctive feature of his checks would be quality imprinting of information unique to each customer. Hotchkiss borrowed $300 to secure the necessary equipment and a small office in the People's Bank Building in downtown St. Paul. In the two months of operations for 1915 the eager salesman attracted $23 in orders against $293 in expenses. Despite such unpromising numbers, the company would soon find success. As Terry Blake wrote in *A History of the Deluxe Corporation, 1915–1990,* several factors favored Hotchkiss's enterprise, particularly the printer's choice of location. The Minneapolis/St. Paul area, already densely populated with financial institutions, was destined to become a major national banking center—and therefore a major check clearinghouse—through Minneapolis's selection as the site of the Fed-

Company Perspectives:

Deluxe's vision is to partner for prosperity by pioneering information and payment solutions.

Deluxe's envisioned future is that we will transform our company from a confederation of businesses to an organization that acts as a single company and is the recognized leader in providing information and payment solutions to customers throughout the world.

Deluxe's mission is to provide integrated information, payment, and related services that create value for our customers throughout the world.

eral Reserve Bank of the Ninth District. Equally important was Hotchkiss's timing. In 1915 approximately five billion checks were issued by American businesses each year. This immense market was being served by various printing houses, none of which was more than regionally dominant, particularly noteworthy for its service, or even remotely prepared to foster new business in a virtually untapped domain: individual consumers.

Hotchkiss's early marketing of his company's services consisted of mail-order brochures sent to all regions of Minnesota. His first customers were healthy outstate banks, with less deposits than the Twin Cities banks but also far fewer check-printing competitors. In 1916 Hotchkiss succeeded in tapping the metropolitan market with contracts from both the People's Bank and the Western State Bank of St. Paul. Sales for his first full year of business reached $4,173. This same year Hotchkiss welcomed printer Einer Swanson as a business partner. Swanson replaced Hotchkiss as chief salesman and may also have been responsible for determining the company's name. The new arrangement allowed Hotchkiss, an instinctive inventor, the freedom to design and develop new machinery to enhance printing quality, speed delivery time, and save money. By 1918 the company's sales had soared to $18,961 and Hotchkiss issued his first catalog. The following year, as sales more than doubled, the company relocated to its first, full-sized plant. In 1920 Swanson and Hotchkiss incorporated as DeLuxe Check Printers, Inc. and became equal partners.

Growth during the 1920s was phenomenal because of both timing and the special imprint of Hotchkiss's vision. From the beginning he had decided that his business would emphasize quality and service. Service, for him, became synonymous with speed; he instituted the still standing company goal of 48-hour turnaround on any order, or "in one day, out the next." As the Federal Reserve established new banking districts, Deluxe, as soon as it was able, moved in to claim its share of the check business. First came Chicago, then Kansas City, then Cleveland, then New York. By the end of the decade, sales and net income had risen to $579,000 and $42,000, respectively.

Perhaps more indicative of the company's long-term prospects were Hotchkiss's unique advancements in check products and printing technology during the 1920s. In 1922 he developed one of the first small pocket checks—nicknamed the LH, or "Little Handy"—to complement the larger, end-register-style business check. The initial market for this new check was to be the wise and discerning consumer. As catalog copy from this era declared, "The Individualized Check today is considered almost as necessary in leading social and business circles as the calling or business card. It marks the user as a man of distinction and discrimination." Yet, as Blake pointed out, "Hotchkiss had no definite strategy for marketing the personalized Handy checks. Bankers, too, were skeptical of the horizontal register and deemed Hotchkiss's invention a fad. As a result, the LH, destined to become the most successful product in Deluxe's history, remained an obscure novelty for a number of years." Hotchkiss realized more immediate profits from a series of important, speed-enhancing inventions, which included the Hotchkiss Imprinting Press (HIP), patented in 1925; a two-way perforator, perfected the same year; and the Hotchkiss Lithograph Press (HLP), patented in 1928.

Revolutionary Sales Program Grew Revenues During the Great Depression

With the stock market crash in 1929 came an end to a free-spending era. From 1920 to 1929, Deluxe saw sales increase by an average of 32.3 percent annually. By comparison, from 1930 to 1939, sales increased only 55 percent for the entire 10-year span. After suffering its only full-year loss in 1932, the company began to rebound as newly elected President Franklin D. Roosevelt's sweeping reforms for the banking industry took hold. A potentially devastating period was transformed and, like F.D.R., Deluxe hastened the transformation with a revolutionary new sales program. The program was guided not by Hotchkiss but by George McSweeney, a former Deluxe paper supplier hired by the company in 1932 expressly for the task of building a sales force and boosting revenue. McSweeney emphasized personalized attention over catalog promotions and worked closely with bankers in developing personalized check programs. Viewing Deluxe as a service- (rather than product-) oriented business, he sought ways to aid financial institutions in boosting their own incomes. Promoting small checking accounts for individual customers, all of whom represented potential loan clients, became a mutual goal, and the LH, the mutually agreed upon tool to attract these customers. McSweeney also directed his sales force to refocus attention on serving rural banks; by 1939, this segment had grown to represent 58 percent of Deluxe's annual revenue. Finally, McSweeney instilled in his sales force a "guidance and counsel" approach. With the passing of the Social Security Act in 1935 came an opportunity for McSweeney and his representatives to thoroughly research the law and then educate their banking customers. "To McSweeney," writes Blake, "it was important for Deluxe to establish itself as a leader, and Deluxe's impressive anticipation of an industry-altering event like Social Security set a precedent the company has always followed."

In 1940 Deluxe saw sales surpass $1 million. A year later, McSweeney became company president at his own request. LH orders had multiplied from 1,000 in 1938 to 100,000 and would continue to grow exponentially. With World War II and the ration banking program which necessitated new ration checks, sales also jumped dramatically. A new service-monitoring system was instituted by production superintendent Joe Rose in 1948. Within a year, two-day delivery fulfillment advanced from 75 percent to nearly 90 percent. The advent of the teletypesetter and new plant construction in Chicago, Kansas City, and St. Paul capped the decade.

Steady Growth Continued from the 1950s Through the 1980s

During the 1950s, overall sales rose by 275 percent. Much of the company's growth could be attributed to the widespread popularity of the LH. Equally important was Deluxe's national coverage of the commercial banking industry. By 1960 it had contracted for a portion of sales with 99 percent of the country's commercial banks. Meanwhile, Deluxe's largest competitor, New York-based Todd Company, was struggling to hold market share after a corporate takeover. With 10 plants strategically spread across the United States to better serve its customers, Deluxe could boast sales of $24 million and anticipate a bright future, with steadily rising numbers for total domestic checks written, which now numbered nearly 13 billion. Furthermore, many bankers now accorded Deluxe special status as an industry leader. This was particularly true after Deluxe's fundamental involvement with the development of magnetic ink character recognition (MICR), which after years of back-and-forth negotiations between the American Bankers Association, leading high-tech companies, and check printers, was now becoming the industry norm.

With McSweeney's death in 1962 and the continuing maturation of MICR technology came numerous changes for the company. McSweeney's successor, Joe Rose, was faced with dire predictions that a checkless society would be a reality by 1970. Deluxe's recourse was to embrace MICR for all types of document processing and to launch a New Products Research Division. By 1967, sales for the three-year-old division from loan coupon books, process control documents, and deposit/withdrawal slips topped $1 million. Deluxe underwent another difficult, though ultimately beneficial, change in 1965 when it went public after pressure from various estates who complained of the artificially low trading prices for their stock. This same year, Rose satisfactorily settled another potential setback when the U.S. Post Office announced new coding and presorting regulations. A major user of the public mails, Deluxe could ill afford increased expenses or undue delays caused by the new regulations. Consequently, Rose met directly with the deputy postmaster general and obtained permission to establish his own in-plant post offices where mail could be easily sorted and sent to save the company and the local post offices both time and money. Rose closed the 1960s with more than $85 million in sales.

Despite serious inflation during the 1970s which caused production costs to rise, Deluxe performed well. By 1979 sales had risen to $366 million and net income to $39 million. This was especially impressive after considering the large capital expenditures involved in new plant openings, which arose at the pace of three per year. A considerable amount of new equipment, including minicomputers and the Deluxe Encoder Printer (DEP), also made their debut during this decade. Under Gene Olson, who became president in 1976 and CEO in 1978 (and stayed in these positions until 1986), Deluxe acceded to critics on Wall Street—long wary of the company's dependency on essentially one product—and cautiously diversified into pre-inked endorsement stamps.

Growth continued unabated during the 1980s; by 1988 sales had surpassed $1 billion. Among the new products that kept Deluxe firmly in place as a financial products market leader were three-on-a-page, computer-form business checks, pegboard checks, and money market related documents. Although the financial industry suffered repeatedly by failures of large-sized banks, such developments actually increased Deluxe's competitiveness, for as the institutions failed, numerous small check printers ceased business as well. By 1989, less than 10 full-service printers remained. In one sense, however, such events were singularly frightening, for few could anticipate the future of banking. Harold Haverty, elected president in 1983 and CEO in 1986, wrestled anew with the problem of diversification (analysts for *Forbes* had twice predicted the company's downfall, due to its traditionally cautious acquisition policy). In part to satisfy the analysts, but also to increase its presence as a provider of wide business services, Deluxe purchased Chex-Systems in April 1984, John A. Pratt and Associates in June 1985, and Colwell Systems in October 1985, consequently entering such new fields as account verification, marketing services, and direct-mail supply to the dental and medical industry. In December 1986 Deluxe purchased A. O. Smith Data Systems and instantly became a leader in the burgeoning EFT industry. In 1987 the company purchased Current, which soon became touted as "the nation's largest direct mail marketer of greeting cards and consumer specialty products." Meanwhile, Harold Haverty, a 32-year company veteran, became Deluxe's fifth CEO in 1986. And two years later, in a move symbolic of the company's diversification, Deluxe Check Printers, Inc. became simply Deluxe Corporation.

1990s Brought First Serious Difficulties

Under Haverty's direction, Deluxe stayed on the same course through the early 1990s, continuing to cautiously diversify. In 1990 ACH Systems was acquired to bolster the company's electronic funds transfer operation. Deluxe, the following year, acquired the Seattle-based Electronic Transaction Corp., which provided electronic check authorization services for retailers. The acquired firm managed the Shared Check Authorization Network (or SCAN), an association of retailers nationwide who exchange information on bad checks and closed customer accounts. In 1993 Deluxe bought PaperDirect, a mail-order supplier of specialty papers and other products, while 1994 brought National Revenue Corporation, a leading U.S. collections agency, into the company fold.

By 1993 it was becoming evident that not all was well at Deluxe. Although revenues continued their yearly rise, return on equity dropped below 25 percent for the first time in years to 17.4 percent. Net income fell substantially as well, from $202.8 million in 1992 to $141.9 million in 1993, due in part to a restructuring charge incurred as a result of the closure of about one-fourth of the company's check-printing plants, which were made redundant by other, higher tech plants. For the first time in company history, workers were laid off.

The company would continue to struggle for the next several years, buffeted by a variety of factors. The bank merger mania of the mid-1990s resulted in larger institutions which could demand lower check prices. Its check-printing business was also being pressured by new competition from more than two dozen marketers using direct mail to sell checks to consumers. At the same time, its efforts at diversification were not paying off; although the new businesses were generating more than 35 percent of overall company revenues, they were contributing less than 10 percent of the profits.

It was thus in this troubled environment that for the first time ever Deluxe looked outside for new leadership. In May 1995 John A. "Gus" Blanchard III was named the company's sixth CEO (and then became chairman as well the following year). Blanchard had gained plenty of experience helping companies deal with technology change through stints at AT&T and General Instruments Corp. Once on board at Deluxe, he moved quickly and decisively to restructure and streamline operations; to identify noncore, underperforming business that should be divested; and to reestablish growth through new products, alliances, and acquisitions.

In early 1996 Deluxe announced plans to trim operating costs by $150 million over a two-year period. Included herein was the planned closure of 26 of the company's 41 check-printing plants, a 30 percent reduction in capital spending, the implementation of a centralized purchasing function, and layoffs for 30 percent of the company's officers. Divested in 1996 were T/Maker Company (a maker of clipart and children's multimedia software, just acquired in 1994), Health Care Forms, Financial Alliance Processing Services, Inc. (a processor of credit and debit card transactions, just acquired in early 1995), Deluxe U.K. forms, and the internal bank forms business. Deluxe also placed PaperDirect and Current Social Expressions (i.e., the greeting cards, gift wrap, and related products—the Current Checks direct-mail operation was to remain with Deluxe) on the block, although it ran into initial trouble trying to find a buyer.

A restructuring of the remaining operations left Deluxe with four main business segments in 1997. Deluxe Paper Payment Systems consisted of the check printing services that remained the company's core, including Current Checks and Deluxe Canada Inc., which had been formed in 1994 to provide Canadian financial institutions with checks and financial forms. Deluxe Payment Protection Systems included account verification (ChexSystems), check authorization (SCAN), and collection agency (National Revenue) services, as well as the TheftNet employee screening service run by Deluxe Employment Screening Partners, Inc., a new subsidiary established in 1996. Deluxe Direct Response specialized in the development of targeted direct mail marketing campaigns for financial institutions, with four of its five units having been acquired or established in 1996 and 1997. Finally, Deluxe Electronic Payment Systems, Inc. grew out of the 1986-acquired A.O. Smith Data Systems and concentrated on electronic funds transfer services.

Blanchard's dramatic moves had quickly transformed Deluxe Corporation into a much more focused and strategically structured organization. These changes may have come just in the nick of time, as checks—though hardly dinosaurs—were beginning to show signs of decline. Checks had been growing at a rate of six percent a year in the early 1990s, but grew less than one percent in 1996—EFTs, telephone banking, and online banking were finally having a real impact. Still, Deluxe was likely to have several more years in which to establish enough non-check-printing business to offset the inevitable declining check revenues. To his credit, Blanchard seemed to already have Deluxe on the path toward doing just that.

Principal Subsidiaries

ChexSystems, Inc.; National Revenue Corporation; Deluxe Employment Screening Partners, Inc.; Current, Inc.; PaperDirect, Inc.; Nelco, Inc.; Fusion Marketing Group Inc.; Deluxe Canada Inc.

Principal Operating Units

Deluxe Paper Payment Systems; Deluxe Payment Protection Systems; Deluxe Direct Response; Deluxe Electronic Payment Systems, Inc.

Further Reading

Abelson, Reed, "The Check Is in the (Electronic) Mail," *Forbes,* January 6, 1992, p. 99.

Barthel, Matt, "To Bolster Checks, Deluxe Buys Authorization Service," *American Banker,* January 4, 1991, p. 3.

Blake, Terry, *A History of Deluxe Corporation, 1915–1990,* St. Paul: Deluxe Corporation, 1990, 48 p.

Byrne, Harlan S., "Deluxe Corp.: Diversifying Against Check-Free Banking," *Barron's,* April 26, 1993, pp. 39–40.

Chithelen, Ignatius, "Printing Money," *Forbes,* March 18, 1991, p. 116.

Kutler, Jeffrey, "3 ACH Operators Band Together," *American Banker,* April 20, 1992, p. 3.

Marjanovic, Steven, "Though Hedging, Deluxe Isn't Writing Off Checks," *American Banker,* March 26, 1997, p. 4.

Melcher, Richard A., "Deluxe Isn't Checking Out Yet," *Business Week,* February 26, 1996, pp. 94, 96.

Sawaya, Zina, "The Underpaid: Relative Pain (Harold Haverty)," *Forbes,* May 27, 1991, p. 222.

Zemke, Ron, and Dick Schaaf, "Deluxe Corporation," *The Service Edge: 101 Companies That Profit from Customer Care,* New York: New American Library, 1989.

—Jay P. Pederson
—updated by David E. Salamie

Diebold, Incorporated

5995 Mayfair Road
Post Office Box 3077
North Canton, Ohio 44720-8077
U.S.A.
(330) 489-4000
Fax: (330) 490-4549
Web site: http://www.diebold.com

Public Company
Incorporated: 1876 as Diebold Safe & Lock Co.
Employees: 5,980
Sales: $1.03 billion (1996)
Stock Exchanges: New York
SICs: 3499 Fabricated Metal Products, Except Machinery & Transportation Equipment; 3578 Calculating & Accounting Equipment; 3669 Electronic & Other Electrical Equipment & Components, Except Computer Equipment

In the wake of the 1871 Great Chicago Fire, natural disaster proved a boon for Diebold Bahmann & Co. when word spread that all 878 Diebold safes in the area, along with their contents, survived the flames. The Diebold safe's reputation as a haven from the elements came full circle more than a century later when Hurricane Andrew devastated much of South Florida in August 1992. A bank executive in Homestead, Florida, the city that bore the worst of the storm, reported weathering 160-mile-per-hour winds in a Diebold safe. Over the years, Diebold, Incorporated has diversified considerably, becoming the international leader in the production, sale, and servicing of automated teller machines (ATMs) and pioneering in such areas as campus card systems, smart card systems, and automated medication dispensing systems, while continuing to make safes, office equipment, and a variety of security and surveillance systems.

Early History

Charles Diebold first organized Diebold Bahmann in 1859, as a manufacturer of safes and vaults in Cincinnati, Ohio. In 1872 Diebold had outgrown its space in Cincinnati and transferred plant and headquarters to Canton, Ohio, where most of the post-fire orders were filled. In 1874 Wells Fargo of San Francisco chose Diebold to make what would be the world's largest vault. The following year, a special 47-car train transported the 32-foot-long, 27-foot-wide, 12-foot-high vault to San Francisco. In 1876 the company was incorporated under Ohio law as Diebold Safe & Lock Co. Following the Wells Fargo feat, Diebold continued to traffic in the colossal, selling the largest-ever commercial bank vault to Detroit National Bank in 1921. In 1968 the First National Bank of Chicago purchased the largest-ever double vault doors, with a combined weight of 87½ tons. Size aside, the company's abiding interest lay in developing equipment to stay one step ahead of bank robbers. In 1890 the company introduced manganese steel doors that were billed as TNT-proof. Through time, combination locks replaced keys, which could be copied. Safety hinges were introduced along with locks that jammed automatically after banking hours.

The company made a splash in 1954 by putting visually pleasing vault doors on the market. In the process of mechanically redesigning its bank vault equipment, the company canvassed bankers for suggested improvements to the standard. The overwhelming answer was that a plain slab of steel, particularly on the inside of the door—the side customers see—was an unworthy complement to a bank's carefully decorated public spaces. The company then hired Charles Deaton, a St. Louis industrial designer, to retool both the interior and exterior of the vaults. Despite the fact that the newly designed vaults cost around twice as much as the simpler models, they dominated new orders from customers.

Began to Diversify in the 1930s

While better and more secure vaults and safes continued to be key features in Diebold's product line, the market for safes and vaults has not always been dependable, relying as it does on the health of the banking industry. In the 1930s, Diebold began to diversify. In slightly over a decade, the company made seven major moves toward expansion. In 1936 the company acquired United Metal Products Co., also of Canton, a manufacturer of hollow metal doors and door frames. In 1938 Diebold made its first entrance into the office equipment business by introducing

Company Perspectives:

Diebold is a world leader in its core markets, with a unique combination of capabilities in card-based transaction systems, security, software, and customer service. It is expanding in a variety of markets as a leading-edge systems integrator and solutions provider. Drawing upon its technology expertise in each of these key areas, Diebold develops integrated, total solutions that enable customers to improve productivity, reduce costs, increase revenues, protect assets, and enhance consumer convenience.

the Cardineer Rotary File System. This was followed in 1944 with the acquisition of the Visible Records Equipment Company of Chicago, a former subsidiary and a manufacturer of vertical filing systems and other record-keeping equipment. That same year, Diebold bought the patents and manufacturing rights for Flofilm, a process that allowed companies to microfilm records in-house with a one-hour automatic developer. In 1945, buying rights to the Safe-T-Stak Steel Storage File further augmented Diebold's growing office equipment business. The following year, Diebold bought the safe and vault business of the York Safe & Lock Company. Finally, in January 1947, the bank equipment division of O.B. McClintock Co. of Minneapolis went over to Diebold. The products acquired from McClintock included burglar alarms, a bank vault ventilator (in case of lock-ins), and after-hour depositories. Amidst these acquisitions, in 1943 the company changed its name to Diebold, Incorporated to better reflect its diversified product line.

Several factors motivated Diebold's first expansion. World War II brought the safe and vault business as a whole out of rough years with a flurry of government armament contracts. Following the dismal economy of the 1930s, the war created a demand for manufacturers accustomed to high-precision work with hardened steels. For Diebold, as well as its main competitors York Safe and Mosler Safe Co., the war effort spelled a windfall. In 1942 Diebold, which had previously grossed around $3 million per year, brought in $40 million.

When the dust settled and the contracts disappeared with the end of the war, the company was fiscally sound but its executives were having trouble agreeing on Diebold's path of postwar reconversion. Amid the confusion, Eliot Ness joined the company's board in 1944. A former prohibition agent (of *The Untouchables* fame) and Cleveland director of safety, he represented the Rex family, who owned the largest single block of Diebold shares (38 percent). Ness, who became chairman of the board, engineered a spectacular takeover of York Safe. Located in York, Pennsylvania, York was the largest prewar producer of safes and vaults, with a strong sales base on the East Coast. However, the company had let its sales division deteriorate during the war, while Diebold's was intact. Seeing York's weakness, Diebold moved in. The deal came together with the help of Clint Murchison, Sr., a Texas oilman and a friend of future chairman Daniel Maggin. Murchison arranged for several insurance companies to make loans to Diebold for the purchase and personally guaranteed them. Diebold acquired all of York's patents, tools, service contracts, and orders as well as its sales branches. However, the York company had diversified to include plastics production and microfilm equipment and Diebold left the remaining business freestanding under the name York Industries, Inc.

Expansion Continued in the 1950s and 1960s

In the 1950s, Diebold cashed in on America's postwar migration to suburban areas, which created a demand for new bank branches and orders for safes as well as the full complement of office and security equipment. Thanks to its expansion during the 1940s, the company was able to meet the new demand for its products. The automobile-oriented suburban life brought buyers for the company's drive-in teller windows, which Diebold had started selling after the purchase of McClintock, along with the Diebold-McClintock burglar alarm and several models of after-hour depositories. In 1955 Diebold acquired K. F. Kline Co., a maker of steel lockers, shelving parts, storage bins, and storage and wardrobe cabinets. The Kline acquisition, combined with Diebold's previous business in record-handling and storage equipment, brought business equipment to account for approximately 50 percent of total volume in 1957.

In August 1958, Diebold acquired the entire stock of Herring-Hall-Marvin Safe Co. of Canada, Ltd., which became The Diebold Company of Canada Limited. In September 1959, Diebold acquired Herring-Hall-Marvin Safe Co. of Hamilton, Ohio. In addition to safes, Herring-Hall made teller counter equipment and the acquisition expanded Diebold's range of service to banks even further. The U.S. government subsequently took the merger to court on antitrust grounds, saying that Diebold and Herring-Hall were two of only three companies in the United States producing bank vault equipment. The Southern District Court of Ohio dismissed the case on the so-called "failing company doctrine," under which an acquisition in danger of antitrust challenges could be justified if it could be shown that the object of a takeover was in such poor shape that its continued existence would not substantially have altered the competitive environment. In 1961 the Justice Department asked the Supreme Court to review the case, saying that the defense should be less broadly defined. The high court recommended that the district court that dismissed the case should try it. In April 1963, before a trial could take place, Diebold and the Justice Department reached an agreement. Diebold would sell the safe and vault part of the Herring-Hall-Marvin operation within the year and agree not to buy any other vault or safe companies for another five years. That limitation would be stretched to 10 years if Herring-Hall was not sold within that time frame.

In the meantime, Diebold continued to expand. Along with the postwar growth in the number of banks in the country, the late 1950s and early 1960s saw an explosion in the per-person use of checks. This prompted Diebold to buy into the check-imprinting business. In 1963 the company acquired Consolidated Business Systems, Inc. and its subsidiary Young & Selden. That company was a maker of business forms and magnetic ink imprinting for checks. Diebold then sold off the business forms part of the business at a loss, but profitably ventured further into the check business with the purchase of the

ThriftiCheck Service Corporation later the same year. Diebold sold some assets of Young & Selden in 1970 and all of Thrifti-Check in 1974. Diebold was first listed on the New York Stock Exchange in April 1964, under the symbol DBD.

In 1965 the company added the products of the Lamson Corporation of Syracuse, New York, to its line of office equipment. A maker of materials-handling systems, Lamson became a division of Diebold. Among its products was a message-carrying system that used pneumatic tubes. When Diebold took over, it expanded the operations of the Syracuse plant and invested in research and development, resulting in the computer-regulated tube transport systems that were used to carry material between floors in large office buildings and continue to be used in drive-up remote teller stations. In 1970 Diebold acquired Florida Development Services, a Clearwater, Florida, company that made "modular" bank buildings. Those structures, used for small branch offices, could be transported to a site and assembled within 90 days. The following year the name was changed to Diebold Contracting Services, Inc. The concern was sold in 1979.

Quickly Became ATM Leader in 1970s

In the early 1970s, Diebold was faced with a slowdown in sales of security equipment. The company, led by longtime president and CEO Raymond Koontz, decided to respond by looking ahead and taking a chance on ATMs. Diebold invested heavily in electronic research, applied computer technology, ergonomic design, and software development and, in 1973, introduced the first ATM model. The ATM trade turned out to be a natural for the company that had been doing business with banks for over a century. While Diebold was a relative newcomer to this type of computer technology, its experience with cash-handling systems and security concerns made Diebold ATMs an attractive choice for banks. Within five years, up against competing products from IBM, NCR, Burroughs, TRW, and Honeywell, Diebold had captured 45 percent of the domestic market. In 1979 banks using Diebold ATMs included Bank of America, Citibank, Marine Midland, and the Shawmut Corp.

Through the early 1980s, the business press portrayed Diebold's ATM dominance over IBM and NCR as the pin-striped battle between David and a two-headed Goliath. "Those three letters I-B-M are the first thing we think of when we awake," *Forbes* quoted Earl Wearstler, then Diebold executive vice-president, as saying in 1980. But Diebold held its ground, working out a reciprocal sales agreement with Bunker Ramo, a maker of microcomputer-driven teller terminals with strong sales in Europe and the United States. To gain access to the Canadian ATM market, the company signed a sales and service agreement with Phillips, the international electronics company.

In 1985 and 1986, ATM orders from banks sagged in pace with a general slowdown in bank equipment sales. Diebold had to cut back on costs, but kept the research and development funds flowing toward finding additional applications for ATM technology and aggressively sought out nonbank ATM buyers. In 1985 National Transactions Systems ordered 1,000 cash-dispensing machines to be placed in West Coast 7-Eleven and Safeway stores. In 1986 Diebold announced 26 new products. These included self-serve video rental machines, credit card-activated gas station pumps, and interactive video systems to be used for dispensing tickets and information. For banks that wanted lower-cost cash networks, they also came out with automatic teller machines that were smaller and performed fewer operations, such as dispensing cash but not taking deposits.

1990s Saw Partnership Between Diebold and IBM and Several New Ventures

In July 1990, Diebold, the company that professed to having nightmares about IBM a decade earlier, announced a joint venture with its erstwhile competitor, which was dubbed InterBold. At the time, Diebold held a larger proportion of the domestic and world ATM markets than IBM, but the venture was designed to make the most of each parent company's expertise. Diebold owned the majority share of the partnership, at 70 percent. Through InterBold, Diebold benefited from IBM's strengths in software development and systems integration as well as from the company's strong position in Europe, Asia, and Latin America. Within a year of the venture, InterBold introduced the i Series ATM, the first ATM model to use "image-lift" technology. Image-lift allowed ATM users to see a picture of deposited checks on the ATM screen, and addressed customers' fears about trusting deposits to the machines. By 1992, InterBold had the only networked ATMs in Poland and held the leading position in Mexico, where the banking industry was in the process of privatization. The following year, Diebold formed a joint venture to manufacture and support ATMs in China. As the 1990s continued, Diebold made additional moves to enter or expand in such markets as Mexico, Venezuela, India, and Russia. These overseas moves helped to more than double Diebold's foreign sales during the first several years of the 1990s, with 22.3 percent of net sales coming from outside the United States by 1996.

Also during the 1990s, retail and other applications for card-activated transaction equipment continued to multiply; Diebold moved aggressively to leverage its ATM expertise into new applications which company CEO and chairman Robert Mahoney hoped would keep the company growing rapidly even as the market for ATMs began to mature. InterBold developed a "multi-media dispenser" capable of self-service distribution of postage stamps, airline tickets, travelers' checks, food stamps, and public transportation passes, among other items. In 1992 Diebold formed a joint venture with Nelson Vending Technology Limited of Toronto to distribute automated videocassette vending systems to convenience stores, drugstores, apartment complexes, business centers, hotels, hospitals, and other commercial centers.

In mid-1992 Diebold introduced an Integrated Campus Access Management (ICAM) system, which enabled students to use a single card to gain access to various campus buildings and to pay for meals, books, and vending machine items, as well as to get cash from an ATM. By the end of 1993, 20 colleges and universities had signed up for ICAM, including Texas A&M, Florida State, and the University of Illinois. This system was designed not only for college campuses but also for any other campus-like setting, such as hospitals, amusement parks, and prisons. By 1995 ICAM was making inroads into the primary and secondary school markets. In December of that year, Diebold bolstered its position through the $18.1 million acquisition of Griffin Technology Incorporated, a Farmington, New York-based company with revenue of $18 million that had installed its own card system on 250 college campuses (Diebold had installed about 40 systems by this time).

In yet another new venture, Diebold, through its nascent MedSelect Systems division, introduced an automated drug dispensing system in late 1995. The system allowed healthcare institutions to manage their supplies of pharmaceuticals and other supplies as well as to automatically bill patients as drugs and supplies are used.

In the mid-1990s Diebold also participated in leading-edge testing of so-called smart cards through its Advanced Card Systems division. In 1995 the company partnered with First Union Corporation to test a system whereby fans at Jacksonville Jaguars National Football League games purchased cards that they used to buy concessions and other stadium items. With each purchase, the transaction amount is automatically deducted from the current value of the card. The next year Diebold and First Union again teamed for the largest smart card test program yet—at the 1996 Summer Olympics in Atlanta. From a consumer standpoint, smart cards were touted as a convenient way for people to pay for small items, reducing the amount of cash they have to carry. Although the future of smart cards remained in doubt, Diebold's participation in their development showed the company's commitment to staying on the cutting edge.

With demand for ATMs continuing to grow, Diebold faced a lengthy production backlog in 1996, leading to its 1997 addition of three new U.S. manufacturing facilities in Staunton and Danville, Virginia, and in Lexington, North Carolina. The company also expanded and upgraded its existing U.S. plants in Canton and Sumter, South Carolina. Diebold continued to operate other manufacturing facilities in Germany, China, India, and the United States.

Although Diebold's share of the U.S. ATM market had fallen from about 55 percent in 1992 to about 40 percent in 1996—thanks in large part to new competitors, most notably Triton Systems Corp., based in Long Beach, Mississippi—the rapid growth in ATMs worldwide, 41 percent in 1996 alone, provided an environment for healthy growth and profitability. Diebold's net sales more than doubled from 1990 to 1996, from $476.1 million to $1.03 billion, while net income grew even faster, increasing from $27.1 million in 1990 to $97.4 million in 1996. The company was growing so fast that in late 1996 it was somewhat belatedly decided that the positions of president and COO—which Mahoney had assumed two years earlier while remaining CEO and chairman—should finally be given to someone else, namely Gregg A. Searle, who had been an executive vice-president.

Diebold's managers felt confident enough about the company's ability to sell ATMs overseas that in July 1997 they announced that the company intended to discontinue the InterBold joint venture with IBM, phasing it out over the following 18 months. Talks between Diebold and IBM were soon underway over Diebold buying IBM's 30 percent InterBold stake. This bold move was indicative of a company filled with confidence about its future. Still the world leader in the far-from-mature ATM market—and with numerous overseas markets still only starting to develop ATM networks—Diebold could count on many more years of revenues and profits from its bread-and-butter product line. And it also was aggressively seeking out the blockbusters of tomorrow through its involvement with ICAMs, medical dispensing systems, smart cards, and also transaction software for the Internet. Diebold could certainly face the new millennium feeling safe and secure.

Principal Subsidiaries

InterBold (70%); Diebold Holding Company, Inc.; The Diebold Company of Canada Limited; Diebold of Nevada, Inc.; Diebold Investment Company; DBD Investment Management Company; VDM Holding Company, Inc.; Diebold Foreign Sales Corporation (U.S. Virgin Islands); Diebold Credit Corporation; Diebold Finance Company, Inc.; Diebold International Limited (U.K.); Diebold Pacific, Limited (Hong Kong); ATM Finance, Inc.; Diebold Mexico Holding Company, Inc.; Diebold Latin America Holding Company, Inc.; Diebold HMA Private Limited (India; 50%); Diebold Mexico, S.A. de C.V.; DBD Resource Leasing, S.A. de C.V. (Mexico); Diebold OLTP Systems, C.A. (Venezuela; 50%); Diebold OLTP Systems, A.V.V. (Aruba; 50%); Starbuck Computer Empire, A.V.V. (Aruba; 50%); China Diebold Financial Equipment Company LTD. (65%); Central Security Systems, Incorporated; MedSelect Systems, Incorporated; Diebold Texas, Incorporated; Griffin Technology Incorporated; Mayfair Software Distribution, Inc.

Principal Operating Units

InterBold; Electronic Security Products; Physical Security Products; Service; MedSelect Systems; Advanced Card Systems.

Further Reading

Aeppel, Timothy, "Diebold May Open New Plants, Shift Tasks from Union," *Wall Street Journal,* October 23, 1996, p. B12.

Byrne, Harlan S., "Diebold," *Barron's,* January 13, 1992, p. 33.

——, "Diebold: ATM Maker's Future Looks As Solid As a Bank Vault," *Barron's,* November 15, 1993, pp. 47–48.

——, "Diebold Inc.: Belt-Tightening Reshapes Automated-Teller Leader," *Barron's,* December 4, 1989, p. 73.

——, "Looking Abroad," *Barron's,* May 1, 1995, p. 17.

"Diebold: A Future to Bank On—At Last," *Financial World,* July 15, 1979.

"Diebold Agrees to Sell Concern It Bought in 1959," *Wall Street Journal,* April 11, 1963.

"Diebold Annexes York's Line," *Business Week,* January 12, 1946.

"Diebold Cashes in on Bank Growth, Office Automation," *Barron's,* December 2, 1957.

"Earnings of Diebold Vault to Higher Level on Rapid U.S. Bank Expansion," *Barron's,* November 26, 1956.

Galuszka, Peter, David Lindorff, and Carol Marlack, "Are ATMs Still Money in the Bank?: Kingpins NCR and Diebold Scramble As Rivals Mushroom," *Business Week,* June 9, 1997, pp. 96, 98.

Guglielmo, Connie, "Here Come the Super-ATMs," *Fortune,* October 14, 1996, pp. 232, 234.

"High Court to Review Anti-Merger Suit Defense: Firm Was Failing," *Wall Street Journal,* November 7, 1961.

"IBM, Diebold Form Venture to Develop, Sell Bank Machines," *Wall Street Journal,* July 13, 1990.

Keenan, Charles, "A Bigger Diebold, Phasing Out IBM Alliance, Will Market ATMs Itself," *American Banker,* July 3, 1997, p. 8.

Mallory, Maria, "Will This ATM Team Be a Money Machine?," *Business Week,* September 17, 1990, p. 142F.
Marion, Larry, "The Early Risers," *Forbes,* October 27, 1980, p. 68.
Meagher, James P., Frank W. Campanella, and Pauline Yuelys, "Diebold Inc.: Banking on an Industry's Needs for Security, Automation," *Barron's,* February 8, 1988, p. 44.
"New Battle," *Forbes,* February 25, 1985, p. 163.
"The Safe Makers," *Financial World,* October 14, 1964.
"Selling Banks a High-Style Door for Vaults," *Business Week,* September 11, 1954.
"To Catch a Thief," *Forbes,* December 15, 1973.
Tracey, Brian, "Diebold Looking for New ATM Worlds to Conquer," *American Banker,* August 22, 1994, p. 15.
"Waiting for New Deals to Click," *Business Week,* June 6, 1964.

—Martha Schoolman
—updated by David E. Salamie

Donaldson, Lufkin & Jenrette, Inc.

277 Park Avenue
New York, New York 10172
U.S.A.
(212) 892-3000
Fax: (212) 892-4313
Web site: http://www.dlj.com

Public Company
Incorporated: 1959
Employees: 5,900
Operating Revenues: $2.76 billion (1996)
Stock Exchanges: New York
SICs: 6211 Security Brokers, Dealers & Flotation Companies; 6282 Investment Advice; 6289 Services Allied with the Exchange of Securities or Commodities, Not Elsewhere Classified; 6712 Offices of Bank Holding Companies, Not Elsewhere Classified; 6722 Management Investment Offices, Open-End; 6726 Unit Investment Trusts, Face-Amount Certificate Offices, and Closed-End Management Investment Offices

Donaldson, Lufkin & Jenrette, Inc. (DLJ) grew in a single generation from its founding to become one of the top ten U.S. investment-banking firms. DLJ also trades on its own account as a merchant banker. A holding company, DLJ also acts as a full-service securities broker, managing assets, clearing transactions, and providing financial research and advice as well as trust services to its clients. In 1995 one survey ranked DLJ second among 19 firms in the quality of its research. In 1996 it was rated as the leading underwriter of high-yield bonds and fourth as lead underwriter of domestic public issues. Although publicly traded, DLJ was 80 percent owned by The Equitable Cos. Inc. in 1997.

Fledgling Private Firm in the 1960s

William H. Donaldson and Dan W. Lufkin were former Yale and Harvard Business School classmates who were rooming together while working on Wall Street in 1959, when they decided to go into business for themselves as analysts researching stocks. They asked a colleague, Richard H. Jenrette—also a Harvard Business School classmate—to join them and raised $500,000 to $600,000 in start-up cash and collateral, buying a seat on the New York Stock Exchange and opening a small office with a staff of three. ''There wasn't much downside risk since we were all bachelors,'' Jenrette later recalled, ''and we weren't earning that much, no more than $7,000 or $8,000 a year.'' Each brought distinct skills to the partnership: the dynamic Lufkin excelled at recruiting clients, Donaldson was the ''deal'' man, and Jenrette gravitated toward administration while also heading a small investment-counseling unit. In 1962, however, Donaldson took over investment banking and administration while Jenrette became head of research.

The partners sought as clients institutional investors such as banks, mutual and pension funds, and insurance companies, rather than the general public. They made their early reputation with reports on small but promising growth companies for which they hoped to be repaid in brokerage commissions. A survey of DLJ's 51 basic recommendations during 1960–63 found it beating the Dow Jones industrial average by more than 50 percent, at least according to the firm's own reckoning. Most of its buy recommendations were companies with new products or services. By 1964 the firm had established a corporate pension-fund department and was targeting wealthy individual investors. It also entered investment banking by placing $10 million in debentures for companies and setting up a merger between W.R. Grace & Co. and DuBois Chemicals.

In 1967 DLJ made the largest single transaction ever in dollar value on the New York Stock Exchange—a $22.55-million trade of Harvey Aluminum Inc. common stock. Then, in 1970, DLJ shook up the financial establishment by becoming the first New York Stock Exchange member to offer its equity securities to the public, in contravention of the exchange's regulations. The firm, which raised about $11 million in this manner, established a holding company that was exempted from the stock exchange's restraints on member firms. Going public also allowed DLJ to acquire an assortment of firms unrelated to its core business, such as the pollster Louis Harris & Associates, Inc. and Meridian

Company Perspectives:

We have grown from a research boutique to a fully integrated investment and merchant bank, serving a diverse and demanding universe of domestic and international clients. The path we have followed has been illuminated by the same principles formulated during our early years: to keep clients' interests at the forefront of our business and to act as one firm in each client's behalf, marshaling our substantial financial and intellectual resources to help each client succeed.

Investment and Development Corp., a home builder. The three partners remained the firm's largest single stockholders.

Surviving the Difficult 1970s

DLJ's acquisition of the investment-counseling business formerly conducted by Moody's Investor Service, Inc. in 1970 placed it in the primary position as investment advisor to state and local retirement systems. When the long bull market of the 1960s suddenly came to an end, however, revenues fell from $32.4 million in 1969 to $21.9 million in 1970, and net income sank from $7.5 million to $2.5 million. Lufkin left DLJ in 1971 (although returning briefly in 1974–75), having amassed a fortune estimated at more than $35 million. Donaldson, who had been chairman and chief executive officer of the company, also left in 1973. Jenrette moved up from president and chief operating officer to succeed him.

DLJ earned $7.6 million on revenues of $46.3 million in 1972, a record it did not top until 1981. With the Arab oil embargo of 1973, the world economy fell into deep recession accompanied by double-digit inflation. This further depressed the stock market and ravaged the bond market which DLJ had entered in 1973. The firm was also hurt by the end of fixed commissions in 1973 and consequent competition from new discount brokers, and by its heavy investment in the unprofitable Meridian real estate investment trust. In 1974 DLJ lost $11.5 million on revenues of $60.3 million.

DLJ's stock, initially sold to the public at $15 a share, dropped to $1.75, and American Express, which owned 25 percent of the firm, was so disappointed that it spun off its holdings to its shareholders in the form of a stock dividend. "That was my lowest day," Jenrette later told a *New York Times* reporter. "American Express made us feel like the end of the world to me. But I had my pride on the line, and I didn't want it to be my epitaph that in the first year as chief executive, I broke the firm."

DLJ made its way back to profitability in 1975 by stressing cost controls. Sales from the company's own portfolio, including Louis Harris and Envirotech—a company DLJ put together itself—returned $75 million to the firm and its partners by the end of 1976. In hindsight, the firm's wisest decision during this period of restructuring was to back off from its announced sale of Alliance Capital Management Corp. for $7 million. This subsidiary subsequently grew into the largest pension fund manager on Wall Street and became the firm's chief source of income. DLJ also stepped up its underwriting activities. By 1976 the company could offer the institutional investor a full spectrum of investment vehicles, ranging from Treasury bills to venture capital funds.

In 1977 DLJ made two important purchases: Pershing & Co., one of the nation's largest trade clearing and cash-and-securities-settlements operations, and Wood, Struthers & Winthrop, Inc., an asset-management and brokerage firm. The company's venture capital operation could boast of having organized such successes as Geosource, a specialized oilfield-service company, and Shugart Associates, a manufacturer of floppy disks. By the end of the decade DLJ had offices in nine U.S. cities and in London, Paris, Zurich, and Hong Kong. Revenues reached $329.9 million in 1979, but net income was a disappointing $3.75 million, prompting the company to bring in John K. Castle, the head of its profit-oriented Sprout Capital Funds, as president and chief operating officer.

Junk-Bond and LBO Windfalls in the 1980s

Under Castle's administration, DLJ achieved 21 consecutive quarters of earnings increases. The firm's net income reached $24 million on revenues of $462.9 million in 1983. With offices in 16 U.S. cities besides New York and in 14 countries on four continents, DLJ was the 12th largest brokerage firm in the United States, with $338 million in capital. The Alliance subsidiary, which accounted for 40 percent of DLJ's profits, was managing $20 billion in pension fund assets. Nevertheless, the company's earnings on equity were only about 70 percent of the industry average.

About 22 percent of DLJ's shares were being held at this time by Competrol Ltd., an investment company controlled by Saudi Arabian investors who first bought shares in the firm in 1975. Another 22 percent of shares were controlled by officers and directors of the company. In November 1984 Jenrette agreed to sell the company to Equitable Life Assurance Society, the third largest U.S. insurer, for about $460 million in cash. He left the company, but his retirement proved short-lived as he became Equitable's chief investment officer in 1986 and its president and chief executive officer in 1990.

In 1985 DLJ sold its unprofitable futures trading businesses to Refco Inc. The Alliance unit was separated from DLJ by Equitable and taken public in 1988. Under Jenrette's watchful but encouraging eye, DLJ raised its commitment to the high-yield but risky securities known as junk bonds. During the 1980s the junk bond percentage of the firm's underwritings trailed only Drexel Burnham Lambert Inc. The October 1987 one day stock market crash did not shake DLJ's faith in this means of financing, even though Drexel Burnham Lambert foundered and its junk bond chief, Michael Milken, went to jail.

DLJ also staked about one-fifth of its equity capital of $900 million on leveraged buyouts, a lucrative but sometimes controversial means (often involving the issuing of junk bonds) of taking public companies private that was highly popular in the 1980s. Between 1985 and 1990 DLJ executed 23 buyouts, either alone or with partners, worth $13.5 billion. In 1989 alone the firm extended $2.5 billion in 11 bridge loans (temporary loans until permanent financing could be arranged) to troubled companies, nine of them in support of the leveraged buyouts it had helped to finance. Much of this money was provided by Equitable. The stakes that DLJ ventured in these deals, and the profits made from them, were immense: from the seven companies DLJ took private and then sold, the company reaped compounded yearly gains of 140 percent. In 1989 DLJ earned about $90 million before taxes on revenues of about $950 million.

Broad-Based Growth in the 1990s

In 1990 DLJ further enhanced its junk bond activities by hiring at least 20 former Drexel investment bankers. Pretax profits slumped but remained impressive at an estimated $50 million in 1990, the year that junk bonds crashed. Despite suffering an embarrassing setback when it paid $5.6 million plus interest to settle charges by the Securities and Exchange Commission that the company illegally used customers' stock in the care of its back offices, DLJ became one of the top 10 underwriters of stocks and bonds in 1990, up from 24th in 1982.

DLJ also set revenue and earnings records in 1991, according to estimates. The company's activities included many lucrative stock underwritings, trading in mortgage-backed securities and junk bonds, and a thriving restructuring business which helped companies that needed to issue or refinance junk bond debt. Among such companies were JPS Textile, MorningStar Foods, Saatchi & Saatchi PLC, and Southland Corp. Mortgage-backed bonds were the company's leading source of profit between 1990 and 1993.

DLJ's net revenues rose from $1.45 billion in 1992, when its pretax profit was an impressive $250 million, to $1.9 billion in 1993, when pretax profit passed $300 million. That year DLJ handled more initial public stock offerings than any other firm except Goldman Sachs and Merrill Lynch, and underwrote more than $8 billion worth of junk bonds, a field in which DLJ remained the acknowledged leader. Much of the firm's income also came from taxable fixed-income offerings and bond trading, activities in which its share had been minor only five or six years earlier. Much of DLJ's success was attributed to the 500-odd investment bankers the company had hired from other firms after the 1987 crash.

During 1994, a bad year for the securities industry, DLJ's net revenues slid to $1.5 billion, but the company achieved a coup when an investment fund it managed sold four television stations for $717 million that had been purchased the previous year for only $320 million. In 1995 The Equitable Cos., the parent company of Equitable Life, sold 20 percent of DLJ in a public offering for $27 a share, or $285.7 million. DLJ received $89.1 million in new capital from the sale, boosting the company's total capital to $2.2 billion. That year the company had net income of $179 million on record revenues of $2.08 billion. DLJ chairman, John Chalsty, earned $12.6 million in cash and stock, more than any other chief executive officer in the industry.

By 1996 DLJ's stock underwriting ranking had jumped from 15th to 4th in a decade, and the company was selling more than one-fifth of all new junk bonds, compared to five percent in 1989. The firm had record net revenues of $2.76 billion in 1996 and record net income of $291 million that year. Long-term debt was $1.6 billion in March 1997.

DLJ in 1996

In 1996 DLJ was conducting business through three principal operating groups. The Banking Group included: the Investment Banking Group, which managed and underwrote public offerings of securities, arranged private placements, and provided advisory and other services in connection with mergers, acquisitions, restructurings, and other financial transactions; the Merchant Banking Group which pursued direct investments in a variety of areas through a number of investment vehicles funded with capital provided primarily by institutional investors, the company, and its employees; and the Emerging Markets Group which specialized in client advisory services for mergers, acquisitions, and financial restructurings, as well as merchant banking and the underwriting, placement, and trading of equity, debt, and derivative securities in Latin America, Asia, and Eastern Europe.

The Capital Markets Group encompassed a broad range of activities, including trading, research, origination and distribution of equity and fixed-income securities, private equity investments, and venture capital. It consisted of the company's Fixed Income, Institutional Equities, and Equity Derivatives divisions; Antranet, a distributor of investment research products; and Sprout, its venture capital affiliate.

The Financial Services Group provided a broad array of services to individual investors and the financial intermediaries that represented them. One of these was the Pershing Division, which cleared transactions for more than 550 brokerage firms that collectively maintained over 1.4 million client accounts. The Investment Services Group provided high net worth individuals and medium- to smaller-sized institutions with access to the company's equity and fixed-income research, trading services, and underwriting. The Asset Management Group provided cash management, investment, and trust services primarily to high net worth individuals and institutional investors.

Among DLJ's operating groups, the Capital Markets Group accounted for 36.5 percent of its net revenues in 1996. The Banking Group accounted for 33.7 percent, and the Financial Services Group accounted for 29.8 percent. The company leased its headquarters in midtown Manhattan and 12 other U.S. cities as well as offices in 10 cities in Europe, Asia, and Latin America.

Principal Subsidiaries

Donaldson, Lufkin & Jenrette Securities Corp.

Principal Operating Units

Banking Group (consisting of the Investment Banking Group, Merchant Banking Group, and Emerging Market Group, and their subdivisions); Capital Markets Group (consisting of the Fixed Income, Institutional Equities, and Equity Derivative divisions, Antranet, and Sprout, and their subdivisions); Financial Services Group (consisting of the Pershing Division, Investment Services Group, and Asset Management Group, and their subdivisions).

Further Reading

Arenson, Karen W., "Restoration of Jenrette Firm," *New York Times,* August 21, 1980, pp. 1D, 4D.

Berss, Marcia, "It's Nice to Have a Sugar Daddy," *Forbes,* April 2, 1990, pp. 37–38.

Burck, Charles G., "Dan Lufkin Goes Public," *Fortune,* January 1972, pp. 108–12, 114.

Carey, David, "Junkyard Romp," *Financial World,* March 20, 1990, pp. 48–51.

"Courting the Big Stock Buyers," *Business Week,* February 22, 1964, pp. 96–98, 100, 102.

Elias, Christopher, "The Firm That Turned Its Research into Gold," *Insight on the News,* June 18, 1990, pp. 40–42.

Jensen, Michael C., "Wall Streeter, in Washington," *New York Times,* October 21, 1973, sec. 3, p. 7.

Morrison, Ann M., "The Venture Capitalist Who Tries to Win Them All," *Fortune,* January 28, 1980, pp. 96–99.

Nevans, Ronald, "Has Donaldson, Lufkin and Jenrette Lost Its Magic Touch?" *Financial World,* February 15, 1976, pp. 27–30.

O'Brian, Bridget, "Wall Street DLJ Keeps on Expanding, Says It's Ready for Major League Status," *Wall Street Journal,* September 26, 1996, pp. 1C, 21C.

Pratt, Tom, "The Very Private World of Donaldson, Lufkin & Jenrette," *Investment Dealers' Digest,* September 21, 1992, pp. 16–20.

Robards, Terry, "Big Board Defied by Member Firm," *New York Times,* May 23, 1969, pp. 1, 70.

Serwer, Andrew E., "Drexel's Heir," *Fortune,* April 14, 1997, pp. 104–06.

Siconolfi, Michael, and William Power, "Donaldson Lufkin's Recent Success Gives Bragging Rights to Parent Equitable Life," *Wall Street Journal,* November 27, 1991, pp. 1C, 15C.

Wayne, Leslie, "Forging the Equitable Connection," *New York Times,* November 18, 1984, Sec. 3, p. 5.

—Robert Halasz

The EMI Group

EMI Group plc

4 Tenterden Street
Hanover Square
London W1A 2AY
United Kingdom
(0171) 355-4848
Fax: (0171) 355-1308
Web site: http://www.emigroup.com

Public Company
Incorporated: 1996
Employees: 17,699
Sales: £3.39 billion (US$5.58 billion) (1997)
Stock Exchanges: London
SICs: 2741 Miscellaneous Publishing; 3652 Phonograph Records & Pre-Recorded Audio Tapes & Discs; 5735 Record & Prerecorded Tape Stores; 6719 Offices of Holding Companies, Not Elsewhere Classified

EMI Group plc is the fourth largest of the world's ''big six'' music giants. Demerged from Thorn EMI plc in 1996, after nearly 17 years of the EMI and Thorn ''duet,'' EMI Group now focuses almost exclusively on music—music recording, music publishing, and music retailing. In the recording arena, the company runs more than 60 labels in 46 countries, including noted pop/rock labels Capitol (Bonnie Raitt), Chrysalis (Billy Idol), and Virgin (Rolling Stones, Smashing Pumpkins, Spice Girls); rap's Priority Records (Ice Cube); Capitol Nashville (Garth Brooks) in country; the jazz of Blue Note (Cassandra Wilson); as well as classical labels EMI Classics and Virgin Classics, EMI Latin (Selena), and the labels of the EMI Christian Music Group. EMI Music Publishing is the world's largest music publisher, owning the rights to more than one million songs. Music retailing includes more than 330 HMV music stores and Dillons bookstores in nine countries (Australia, Canada, Germany, Hong Kong, Ireland, Japan, Singapore, the United Kingdom, and the United States), and HMV Direct, a comprehensive direct mail catalog business. EMI also holds investments in music television channels in Germany (VIVA and VIVA2) and in Asia (Channel V).

Earliest Roots in the Gramophone

Electric and Musical Industries (later known as EMI Ltd.) was formed in 1931 from the merger of The Gramophone Company and Colombia Graphophone Company. The gramophone was invented in 1887 by Emile Berliner. Ten years later, The Gramophone Company was founded in London as both a manufacturer of gramophones and as a recorder of records to play on the gramophone. In 1898 the company made its first recordings and opened branches in Germany, France, Italy, and central Europe. Additional offices were established in Russia in 1900, in India in 1901, in Japan in 1902, and in China in 1903. The Gramophone Company had its first major artist when opera singer Enrico Caruso recorded ten songs for the company in 1902.

The increasing popularity of recorded music was evidenced by the ownership of a gramophone by one-third of British households by 1913. As a result of World War I, The Gramophone Company lost its Russian and German operations. By 1930 the company's roster of artists included Italian conductor Arturo Toscanini, German opera conductor Wilhelm Furtwängler, English composer Sir Edward Elgar, and English conductor Sir Thomas Beecham. In 1931, the year EMI was formed, the recording studios at Abbey Road were opened and EMI demonstrated stereophonic recordings for the first time.

During the 1940s the company's artist lineup expanded to include Austrian conductor Herbert von Karajan and German conductor Otto Klemperer. The company in this decade also appointed its first A&R (artists and repertoire) managers to develop popular music talent in the United Kingdom; George Martin, who later signed the Beatles, was among these appointees. In 1952 EMI added Maria Callas to its artistic roster.

Over the years EMI organized a line of sophisticated electronic systems—an outgrowth of its gramophone manufacturing origins—which included early British radar equipment and the BBC's first television system. Meanwhile, the company enlarged its position in the music recording and publishing industries through the 1955 acquisition of Capitol Records, one of the leading record companies in the United States, with a roster that included Nat "King" Cole, Frank Sinatra, Peggy Lee, and Gene Vincent. Additional global moves were made when EMI entered the Mexican market in 1957 and with the establishment of joint venture Toshiba-EMI Ltd., a Japanese record company formed in partnership with Toshiba.

1960s Brought Beatles on Board

During the 1960s EMI's recording division experienced tremendous growth, largely on the strength of sales of records by the Beatles, who were signed by Martin in 1962, the same year their first single, "Love Me Do," was released. That same year Capitol Records released the first Beach Boys album, *Surfin' Safari.* The success of EMI in the 1960s was most evident in the British singles charts for 1964, which had EMI artists—eight different EMI artists—hold the number one position for 41 of the year's weeks. In 1966 the company released its first prerecorded cassettes. The following year EMI signed Pink Floyd. Queen was added to the roster in 1972.

By the late 1960s profits from the EMI recording division surpassed those of the electronics division and enabled EMI to purchase the entertainment organization of Sir Lew Grade and the cinema business of the Associated British Picture Corporation. As a result, EMI had become one of the largest motion picture entertainment concerns in the world by 1970.

The late 1960s and early 1970s saw EMI expand in the areas of music publishing and music retailing. In 1966 the company began to expand its HMV music store operation. The first HMV shop had been opened in 1921 on Oxford Street, London, by composer Sir Edward Elgar. By 1970 there were 15 HMVs; six years later there were 35 and HMV had become one of the leading music retailers in the United Kingdom. The music publishing operation was bolstered through a series of acquisitions. EMI purchased Keith Prowse Music Publishing and Central Songs in 1969, Affiliated Music Publishing in 1973, and the Screen Gems and Colgens music publishing companies in 1976, both of which were bought from Columbia Pictures Industries. In 1973 EMI had organized its music publishing operations within a newly formed EMI Music Publishing Ltd. subsidiary.

In the early 1970s, however, EMI was also burdened by heavy losses from its Capitol Records operation and a poorly planned investment in an Italian television manufacturer called Voxson. The most significant nonmusic development for EMI during this period was the introduction of a revolutionary new Computed Tomographic X-ray scanning device in 1972. The fact that EMI had developed this scanner, with no previous experience in X-ray equipment, caused many to seriously reconsider the company's prospects.

Profitable sales of the scanner in the United States were drastically reduced after the Carter administration restricted government aid to hospitals. In addition, EMI failed to anticipate a strong reaction from its competitors. General Electric subsequently introduced a similar but faster model that effectively removed EMI from the market.

By 1977 serious problems with the medical electronics division caused management to be broken up into three divisions, each responsible for its own profitability. At one point EMI even appeared willing to dispense with its recovering music operations. Instead, EMI's path led to its being taken over in 1979.

Thorn EMI Created in 1979

The financially ailing EMI became a takeover target for lighting and equipment rental giant Thorn Electrical Industries Ltd. Thorn had been established in 1928 as the Electrical Lamp Service Company by Jules Thorn, who remained at the helm until he retired in 1979, not coincidentally prior to the takeover of EMI (Thorn's domineering personality had squelched a proposed merger between the two firms a few years earlier).

Institutional investors, who held a three quarters voting majority in Thorn, expressed concern that a merger of the two companies would be problematic because Thorn and EMI were very different companies. In the event of a merger, Thorn would have to let EMI management run itself, at least for a few years, because it knew so little about EMI's businesses. Another cause for concern was that EMI's new management team, led by the very capable Lord Delfont, had to prove itself under difficult circumstances.

At the end of October 1979 EMI rejected a £145 million bid by Thorn. The offer was resubmitted the following week for £165 million and accepted. The new company's name was changed to Thorn EMI plc on March 3, 1980.

1980s Thorn EMI Restructuring

The various divisions within the old Thorn and EMI organizations continued to operate independently of each other and, to some extent, of the central management group. Management reimplemented a planning model developed by the Boston Consulting Group that provided for the development of new enterprises by channeling funds from profitable operations. This had the effect of starving the successful enterprises within the company of funds needed to maintain competitive product lines. Just as the model failed in the early 1970s, it was failing again a decade later. Thorn EMI was less like a successful operating company and more like a weak investment portfolio.

In an attempt to raise money and reduce losses during 1980 and 1981, the company sold its medical electronics business, its hotels and restaurant division, and parts of the leisure and entertainment division. Later in the 1980s, additional Thorn and EMI businesses were sold, including EMI's entertainment operations. By the late 1980s, under the leadership of CEO Colin Southgate, Thorn EMI had returned to the basic industries upon which Thorn and EMI had been separately built: music, lighting, rental and retail, and technology (including computer software and defense electronics). All told, during the 1980s Thorn EMI divested more than 50 noncore operations, bringing in more than US$700 million.

EMI Bolstered in the Late 1980s and Early 1990s

Although EMI's music operations had been neglected somewhat during the restructuring of Thorn EMI, they now became the beneficiary, as much of the cash generated by the asset sales was poured into acquisitions and expansions. In 1986 HMV became a separate division of Thorn EMI and an international expansion of the chain began. In 1990 alone, HMV outlets appeared for the first time in Australia, Japan, Hong Kong, and the United States. By 1996 there were more than 300 stores worldwide in eight countries, including Canada, Germany, and Ireland. In 1995 a U.K. bookstore chain called Dillons was acquired and was added to the HMV division.

EMI Music Publishing was bolstered through the 1989 acquisition of SBK Entertainment World, Inc. for £165 million (US$337 million). SBK was the onetime publishing unit of CBS Records, which consisted of a 250,000-song catalog, including "Singing in the Rain" and "You've Lost that Lovin' Feeling." This addition made EMI Music Publishing the top music publishing operation in the world; its catalog included more than 850,000 songs by late 1992. EMI's music recording unit, meanwhile, acquired several prominent labels. In 1990, 50 percent of Chrysalis Records was purchased, with the other half acquired two years later. Chrysalis brought such acts as Huey Lewis & The News, Billy Idol, and Sinead O'Connor to the EMI fold. The blockbuster acquisition, however, was that of Virgin Music Group Ltd., bought for £510 million (US$957 million) in 1992, a deal that included both record labels and publishing catalogs. The addition of Virgin, whose artists included the Rolling Stones, Phil Collins, and Janet Jackson, cemented EMI's position as one of the music industry's giants, alongside Time Warner, Sony, PolyGram, MCA (which later became Seagram's Universal Music Group), and Bertelsmann. Also acquired in 1992 was Sparrow Records, the largest Christian music label in the United States, which later became the centerpiece of the EMI Christian Music Group. Added in 1994 was Intercord, a leading independent record company in Germany. During the early 1990s EMI garnered blockbuster sales in the United States from the star of its Liberty label, country singer Garth Brooks (who later recorded for EMI's Capitol Nashville label). Virgin signed Janet Jackson to an exclusive, $60 million contract in 1996, the same year that the Beatles' *Anthology* albums posted large sales.

In 1994 EMI entered into the music television arena through joint ventures in Germany, where the VIVA and later the VIVA2 channels were launched, and in Asia, where Channel V was introduced. All of these stations devoted much of their airtime to domestic artists, whereas MTV, even in Germany, for example, tended to showcase English-language acts. The VIVA stations were co-owned by EMI, Bertelsmann, Time Warner, Philips (owner of PolyGram), and Sony. Channel V was 50 percent owned by News Corporation, with EMI, Time Warner, Sony, and Bertelsmann each holding a 12.5 percent stake.

1996 Demerger of Thorn EMI

Thorn EMI itself, meanwhile, was continuing to be transformed in the 1990s. Thorn's rental operations became the company's most important nonmusic unit and had been beefed up in 1987 through the £371 million acquisition of Rent-A-Center, a rent-to-own outfit based in the United States. In 1993 Thorn EMI sold its lighting division, the business upon which it had been founded. Over the course of several years and several transactions, the company's defense businesses had been divested by 1996. Thus Thorn EMI in mid-1996 had just two divisions—music and rental—both world leaders. They had little in common, however, leading to the long-anticipated August 29, 1996 demerger of Thorn and EMI, out of which emerged EMI Group plc and Thorn plc, both initially headed by Southgate as chairman. EMI Group included all of Thorn EMI's music-related operations: music recording, publishing, and retailing and the investments in the music channels. It also included the Dillons bookstores, which continued as part of the HMV Division. Several noncore businesses—Central Research Laboratories, Thorn Secure Science International, Thorn Transit Systems International, and a holding in Thorn Security—which EMI retained after the demerger, were divested less than a year later.

Rumors that the newly independent EMI would be taken over by one of the industry's other giants persisted for some time following the demerger, but had subsided some by late 1996. In October 1996 the debut album by the prefabricated Spice Girls posted huge sales; more than 17.5 million copies had been sold in the 12 months following its October 1996 release. EMI's immediate concern was the need to turn around its flagging North American music operations, which had managed to capture a mere eight percent of the US$12.5 billion U.S. market in 1996. In May 1997 North American management was shaken up, with Ken Berry, who was already president and chief executive of EMI Records Group International and chairman and chief executive of Virgin Music Group Worldwide, taking over. Berry became the worldwide president of the newly formed EMI Recorded Music unit, which comprised all three of these operations. At the same time, a restructuring of the U.S. operations—including the closing of the head offices of EMI-Capitol in New York—led EMI to record a charge of £117.2 million (US$192.8 million) in fiscal 1997. Later in 1997, EMI Music Publishing, already owner of the rights to more than one million songs, added a catalog of 15,000 songs from the Motown era—including "I Heard It through the Grapevine" and "My Girl"—in a deal with Berry Gordy, founder of Motown Records, worth up to £232 million (US$382 million).

EMI Group had come a long way over a 100-year history spanning the gramophone and the Spice Girls. Worldwide, EMI was the fourth largest music company in 1997. It could challenge the companies ahead of it with a turnaround of its North American operation, which held no better than fifth or sixth place in the United States, the largest and most profitable music market. EMI may look for additional acquisitions as one avenue to U.S. success, as evidenced by the fiscal 1997 purchases of 50 percent of rap label Priority Records (including the rapper Ice Cube), 49 percent of New York-based alternative label Matador Records, and all of Forefront Communications, the largest independent Christian music label in the United States, headlined by million-selling artist dc Talk. And as overall music sales in Europe and North America continued at a sluggish rate of growth in the late 1990s, EMI was also likely to continue to seek growth opportunities in the emerging markets of eastern Europe, Asia, the Middle East, and Latin America, where the company was achieving success marketing domestic talent.

Principal Subsidiaries

EMI Records Ltd.; EMI Music Publishing Ltd.; Capitol-EMI Music, Inc. (U.S.A.); EMI Entertainment World, Inc. (U.S.A.); EMI Music France S.A.; EMI Music Italy S.p.A.; EMI Electrola

GmbH (Germany); EMI Music Australia Pty. Ltd.; Chrysalis Records Ltd.; Capitol Records, Inc. (U.S.A.); Virgin Records Ltd.; Virgin Records America, Inc. (U.S.A.); Virgin Schallplatten GmbH (Germany); Groupe Virgin Disques S.A. (France); Toshiba-EMI Ltd. (Japan; 55%); EMI Group Home Electronics (UK) Ltd.; HMV Division; Dillons the Bookstore Division; EMI Group Finance plc; EMI Group North America Holdings, Inc. (U.S.A.); EMI Group North America, Inc. (U.S.A.); EMI Group International Holdings Ltd.

Further Reading

Boehm, Erich, "EMI Becoming Takeover That Never Was," *Variety*, December 23, 1996, pp. 29, 30.

Clark-Meads, Jeff, "EMI Upbeat on Global Biz," *Billboard*, March 8, 1997, p. 1.

Clark-Meads, Jeff, White, Adam, and Jeffrey, Don, "Thorn EMI Demerger Proceeding Smoothly," *Billboard*, August 31, 1996, pp. 1, 127.

"Duet for One: Thorn EMI," *Economist*, November 27, 1993, p. 71.

Foster, Anna, "Leading Light at Thorn," *Management Today*, August 1988, p. 46.

Foster, Geoffrey, "Three over Thirty," *Management Today*, May 1996, pp. 64–66.

Fuhrman, Peter, "Here Comes House Music," *Forbes*, December 21, 1992, pp. 44–46.

Gubernick, Lisa, "Don't Worry, He's Happy," *Forbes*, April 17, 1989, p. 154.

Iliot, Terry, "EMI Faces Thorny Dilemma," *Variety*, September 14, 1992, p. 32.

Martland, Peter, *Since Records Began: EMI, the First 100 Years*, Portland, Oreg.: Amadeus Press, 1997.

Midgley, Dominic, "Thorn EMI's Fissile Future," *Management Today*, August 1994, pp. 24–28.

Rawsthorn, Alice, "EMI Adds a Little Spice," *Financial Times*, November 23, 1996, p. WFT5.

——, "EMI Cuts Costs in N. America," *Financial Times*, May 28, 1997, p. 21.

——, "In Tune to a Little More Spicy Music," *Financial Times*, May 28, 1997, p. 23.

——, "Motown Founder Sells Hits for Up to $382M," *Financial Times*, July 2, 1997, p. 28.

——, "Thorn and EMI Prepare to Dance to Different Tunes," *Financial Times*, July 22, 1996, p. 23.

Rawsthorn, Alice, and Grant, Jeremy, "EMI Eyes Asian Market with Vietnam Tie-Up," *Financial Times*, May 29, 1997, p. 8.

Reilly, Patrick M., "EMI Has Chosen Ken Berry to Run Its North American Music Operations," *Wall Street Journal*, May 27, 1997, p. B11A.

——, "EMI, Hogtied, Finds Out You Don't Mess with Garth," *Wall Street Journal*, November 5, 1997, pp. B1, B12.

——, "Nancy Berry to Run Virgin Records, While Quartararo Is Expected to Leave," *Wall Street Journal*, September 22, 1997, p. B14.

Rifkin, Glenn, "EMI: Technology Brings the Music Giant a Whole New Spin," *Forbes ASAP*, February 27, 1995, pp. 32, 35–36, 38.

Rosenbluth, Jean, "Thorn-EMI Buys 50% of Chrysalis," *Variety*, March 29, 1989, pp. 57, 58.

"Spice Girl," *Forbes*, November 17, 1997, p. 14.

White, Adam, "EMI's U.S. Dealings Under the Microscope," *Billboard*, August 2, 1997, p. 59.

—updated by David E. Salamie

ESS Technology, Inc.

48401 Fremont Boulevard
Fremont, California 94538
U.S.A.
(510) 492-1088
Fax: (510) 492-1098

Public Company
Incorporated: 1984
Employees: 253
Sales: $226.5 million (1996)
Stock Exchanges: NASDAQ
SICs: 3661 Telephone & Telegraph Apparatus; 3672 Printed Circuit Boards; 3674 Semiconductors & Related Devices; 3679 Electronic Components, Not Elsewhere Classified

ESS Technology, Inc. manufactures highly integrated mixed signal semiconductor multimedia solutions, including software, for the personal computer and consumer electronics markets worldwide. The company is a world leader in single-chip audio solutions technology for sale to multimedia desktop and notebook computer manufacturers, a major supplier of digital video chips, and an emerging supplier of high-speed communications chipsets. The company was incorporated in California in 1984. President, CEO and Chairman Fred S. L. Chan was hired in November 1985 and elected a director in January 1986. Chan was founder and former president and CEO of AC Design Inc., a VLSI chip design center providing CAD, engineering, and design services, and cofounder, president, and CEO of CAD-CAM Technology Inc., a company in the business of CAE systems development.

Headquartered in Fremont, California, the company lists among its principal competitors C-Cube, Cirrus Logic, Creative Technology, Hyundai, LSI Logic, Lucent, Oak Technology, OPTi, Rockwell, SGS Thompson, Texas Instruments, Winbond, and Yamaha. Major customers have included PC manufacturers such as AST, AT&T, Acer, BTC, Compaq, Dell, Digital Equipment Corporation, Eastbase, ECS, FIC, Fujitsu, Gateway 2000, GVC, Hewlett-Packard, Hitachi, IBM, ICL, Inventec, JK Micro, Labway, Matsushita, Mitac, NEC, Quanta, Samsung, Seiko-Epson, Sony, Texas Instruments, Toshiba, Trigem, Universe Electron Corporation, Western Publishing, and Xirlink.

Leading the Way in PC Audio Technology, the 1990s

In 1992, the company realized net revenues of $23.7 million and net income of $4.8 million. October of that year saw Fred Chan appointed chairman of the board. The following year, the company posted sales and net income of $15.2 million and $283,000, respectively. In 1994 the company bounced back from its low revenue and income figures and became known as a pioneer in the industry of audio for personal computers when it introduced the first single-chip audio device under its product line AudioDrive, integrating all the elements for sound on the PC and eliminating the need for separate and expensive devices, such as add-in sound cards, for each function.

Since that time, the company has continued to lead the way in PC audio technology, enhancing sound quality and introducing superior low-power sound chips for notebook PCs. The company additionally developed its own approach to FM synthesis that improves the sound of game music, added three-dimensional audio spatialization to enrich the sound field, and has developed an array of software—from device drivers to applications—that enable its OEM (original equipment manufacturer) customers to offer rich sound functionality in their products.

In March 1995, the company was served with a patent infringement claim by Yamaha Corporation, in which the latter claimed the company's ESFM products infringed upon patents held by Yamaha. The U.S. District Court in Los Angeles denied the request for a preliminary injunction, which Yamaha promptly appealed. The decision was upheld in the U.S. Court of Appeals for the Federal Circuit in March of the following year. By May, the two companies had settled all legal proceedings with each other. The company completed its initial public offering in October 1995 with over eight million shares sold for approximately $61.8 million.

Company Perspectives:

Sound is one of the most critical elements of the multimedia experience. Progress in audio fidelity has been rapid, from the simple error beep of the earliest personal computers to the 16-bit, CD-quality stereo sound input and output of today's multimedia machines. The next stage of digital audio evolution has already begun with advanced music synthesis, multi-stream processing and realistic three-dimensional sound reproduction. ESS Technology, Inc. (ESS) is playing a major role in this transition by providing a range of tightly integrated, high-performance audio solutions. With its base of audio technology and market knowledge, ESS continues to add to the richness and intensity that sound adds to the multimedia experience.

With some of the company's competitors owning their own semiconductor manufacturing facilities, and with most of the company's semiconductor products being assembled by third-party vendors, including Amkor ANAM in Korea, ASAT in Hong Kong, Astra Microtronics in Indonesia, and Advanced Semiconductor Engineering and OSE in Taiwan, the company needed to do something to be able to more efficiently compete and keep its market share. Therefore, in November 1995, the company entered into agreements with two wafer foundries. In the first, with Taiwan Semiconductor Manufacturing Company Ltd., the company secured access to additional manufacturing capacity and certain proprietary technology. The second, with United Microelectronics Corporation, represented a joint venture in which the company would increase manufacturing capacity and engage in research and development. The company made similar agreements with Sharp Corporation in Japan and IC Works in California in 1996. The company purchased 16 acres of land in Fremont, California, upon which to build its new corporate facilities and ended the year with revenue reported at $105.7 million, a 216 percent jump over 1994 revenues, and net income of $29.9 million.

ESS began 1996 as a leader in providing audio solutions to the PC marketplace, with 35 percent of the market share. Able to manufacture a single-chip product that integrated all essential audio functions to enable PC manufacturers to deliver high-end sound capabilities, the company continued to show another year of dramatic growth. ESS also expanded into the digital video and fax/data modem marketplaces.

Successful Entry into the Video Market, 1996

The company made its entrance into the video market when, in January, it acquired VideoCore Technology Inc., a company that had been conducting research and development in integrated circuits which incorporate advanced digital video compression, for $5.7 million in cash and 525,000 shares of stock. After completing development of its first video product, the company introduced a new product line, called VideoDrive. The company's VideoDrive product family was built around a proprietary core engine, the programmable multimedia processor, which consisted of a digital signal processing architecture integrated with a RISC processor which offered the high performance needed to decompress and display video images. Because it was highly programmable, features, enhancements, and customized functionality through software could be easily added without redesigning the chip itself, significantly shortening time-to-market and reducing the overall system costs.

The first product in that line was a single-chip MPEG-1 video/audio system decoder that provided full-screen, full-motion video and selectable CD-quality audio for a variety of digital video playback applications such as karaoke players, VCD players, PC MPEG playback cards, and CD-XA video playback systems. An MPEG-2 fully-programmable video single-chip processor that incorporated the additional features needed for consumer electronics applications such as set-top boxes, multimedia PCs, and home entertainment units was announced as well. Shipments of these programmable chips began in the second quarter of the year to video CD player manufacturers worldwide, many in Asia, and, by year end, over 800,000 units had been shipped and the company had captured approximately 30 percent of the world market share.

The digital video marketplace was expanding rapidly. Driven by the continuing popularity of karaoke for home entertainment, especially in China; an increasing number of available movie titles for video CD players; and added system features and functions and lower video CD system costs, the acquisition of VideoCore and the subsequent development of VideoDrive enhanced the company's potential to acquire a large share of the marketplace.

Data and fax modem technology had revolutionized the speed and availability of information access. Use of the Internet and the World Wide Web alone had expanded beyond the academic and scientific communities to include most businesses and an increasing number of households. The modem itself was redefined to include not only high-speed data and fax communications capabilities, but also voice and audio features. Innovative applications, such as telephone answering machine and speakerphone functionality, continued to emerge. The company recognized the opportunity and the need for advanced communications products as a link for its multimedia solutions.

Expansion into Communications

Therefore, two months after the acquisition of VideoCore, the company expanded into the communications market with the acquisition of OSEE Corporation, an algorithm technology developer, for 217,000 shares of stock and $3.6 million in cash. Following the acquisition, the company combined OSEE's highly efficient and sophisticated modem algorithm technology with the company's existing audio technology, and introduced an integrated V.34bis fax/modem design, with significant advantages and support of speaker phone and Digital Simultaneous Voice and Data features. It was the company's first modem digital signal processor, which began production in early 1997 under the product line name of TeleDrive, and received favorable comments from Henderson Laboratories, an independent testing laboratory for modem products, being ranked "in the top 10 percent of modems" tested by that company and "easily #1 in the modems of its type."

New products released in 1996 included the ES1869 Audio-Drive product, a high-integration, single-chip audio solution with high-fidelity performance and 3D audio effects; an audio accelerator; and an AC'97-compatible codec solution, offering high-throughput streams processing and high-fidelity performance. On the video front, the company released an advanced single-chip MPEG-2 A/V and Transport decoder for set-top box and Digital Versatile Disk (DVD) applications. The company also developed a line of fax/modem solutions that helped link the individual PC to the outside world.

By the end of 1996, the company had shipped over 90 million sound chips to consumer and personal computer OEMs around the world and its single-chip PC audio business had grown over 100 percent per year since 1994. The company's new 93,000-square-foot corporate headquarters building in Fremont was completed; sales and technical support centers were added in Beijing, Tokyo, and Seoul; the company's new design center was opened in Austin, Texas; and plans for additional facilities were announced. The number of employees grew from 158 to 253 and revenues hit $226.5 million at the end of the year, a 114 percent increase over the 1995 numbers, with a net income of $21.6 million.

1997 and Beyond

In April 1997, the company's board of directors authorized the repurchase of up to two million shares of the company's stock and two additional buildings were constructed at the Fremont site to house additional engineering capacity. June saw the company acquire Platform Technologies Inc., a developer of multimedia subsystems in a $32.7 million stock swap. In July, the company received Dolby Digital (AC-3)/MPEG certification from Dolby Laboratories for its ES3308 dual-engine Programmable Multimedia Processor, a digital audio/video decoder, which would allow DVD players equipped with that chip to faithfully reproduce film soundtracks. August brought the company into a joint venture with InnovaCom Inc., a leading developer of MPEG-2 solutions for broadcast-quality video compression, located in Santa Clara, California, to develop MPEG-2 encoding and decoding solutions for DVD authoring systems and Digital Video Broadcast Set Top Boxes. In October, the company announced the industry's first video CD chip that enhanced video CD systems to include Graphical User Interface (GUI) and Internet hyperlink features.

Products under development near the end of 1997 included new audio accelerator chips optimized for a new class of high-performance, Windows-based multimedia applications, including advanced digital audio processing to enhance the sensation of fully-positional, three-dimensional sound.

As the Internet and the World Wide Web continued to generate tremendous demand for faster, more cost-effective modem technologies and the ever-increasing demand in digital video compression technology, the company's flexible programmable architecture and proven success in the video CD player market positioned it to be a continuing leader in the marketplace.

Further Reading

Brown, Peter, "ESS Debuts Final Member of DVD Trio," *Electronic News,* August 4, 1997, p. 27.

"Court Rejects Yamaha Motion Against ESS," *Electronic News,* May 8, 1995, p. 2.

"ESS Technology Inc.," *Electronics,* March 27, 1995, p. 16.

"ESS Technology Inc.," *Television Digest,* June 3, 1996, p. 15.

"ESS Unveils Series of Modem, Audio Sets," *Electronic News,* October 14, 1996, p. 14.

Hardie, Crista, "ESS Makes Multimedia Market Moves," *Electronic News,* February 26, 1996, p. 80.

——, "Legal Wrangling Over Audio Patents Settled," *Electronic News,* May 27, 1996, p. 45.

——, "Yamaha, ESS to Get Court Date," *Electronic News,* September 11, 1995, p. 78.

Krause, Reinhardt, "Audio Devices Making Noise in PC Markets," *Electronic News,* September 12, 1994, p. 1.

Maclellan, Andrew, "Philips, ESS Roll Multimedia Chips," *Electronic News,* November 20, 1995, p. 57.

"1-Chip MPEG-1 Contender Is Rolled Out by ESS Tech," *Electronic News,* January 6, 1997, p. 20.

Santoni, Andy, "Chip Makers Near Finish Line for PC98 Spec Compliance," *InfoWorld,* June 16, 1997, p. 34.

Schroeder, Erica, "ESS, Sierra Release Audio Chips: Sound Boards Using Them Due by Year's End," *PC Week,* October 5, 1992, p. 24.

Veverka, Mark, "Bright Picture: ESS Technology," *Wall Street Journal,* December 18, 1996, p. CA2(W).

—Daryl F. Mallett

Fallon McElligott Inc.

901 Marquette Ave.
Minneapolis, Minnesota 55402-3281
U.S.A.
(612) 321-2345
Fax: (612) 321-2601
Web site: http://www.fallon.com

Private Company
Founded: 1981
Employees: 350
Gross Billings: $500 million (1996 est.)
SICs: 7311 Advertising Agencies

With barely a decade and a half under its belt, Minneapolis-based Fallon McElligott Inc. (FM) emerged as America's hottest advertising agency in the mid-1990s. The firm's groaning trophy case holds two Agency of the Year awards from *Advertising Age* (1983 and 1996), *ADWEEK's* National Agency of the Year, and innumerable accolades from trade organizations and global advertising shows. Fallon McElligott's annual billings swelled from less than $150 million in 1990 to an estimated $500 million in 1997 on an influx of major new accounts, including United Airlines and Miller Brewing Company's Miller Lite. In the early 1990s, its roster of clients included some of the nation's biggest and most coveted accounts: Ameritech, BMW of North America, Lee Jeans, USA Network, Holiday Inn Worldwide, Brunswick Corporation's Mercury Marine division, The Coca-Cola Company, Ralston Purina Company, Jim Beam Brands, Weyerhaeuser, and Timex.

Having long limited its operations to creative, production, and media services, the agency expanded in the mid-1990s to incorporate a broad spectrum of advertising and public relations functions. With its domestic reputation firmly in place, FM set its sights on international growth as the turn of the 21st century approached. It established a New York arm in 1995 and was expected to launch a London operation in 1997.

Early 1980s Origins

The agency was established in 1981 as Fallon McElligott & Rice (FMR), and named for its three cofounders: Patrick Fallon, Tom McElligott, and Nancy Rice. Fallon and McElligott had first met in the late 1970s, when both were moonlighting with a freelance agency called Lunch Hour Ltd. After a year of planning, Fallon, McElligott, Rice, and Irv Fish formed a new, independent agency. Fallon was the agency ''suit'': the executive in charge of cultivating and coddling clients. Copywriter McElligott, once crowned ''King of Print,'' provided the creative genius that would become the agency's hallmark. Rice served as art director, and Fish was chief financial officer. The new partners crafted a mission statement that would remain essentially unchanged throughout its history: ''To be the premier creative agency in the nation that produces extraordinarily effective work for a short list of blue chip clients.''

In fact, FMR put the art of advertising above practically all else, even a client's comfort level. McElligott once told an *Inc.* magazine interviewer that his intention was to ''give clients the sort of advertising that makes the palms sweat a little, that makes you a bit nervous,'' adding, ''In my opinion, at least, these are the only ads worth running.'' The print medium was the agency's particular forte throughout the 1980s. FMR developed a recognizable style during this period, with ads featuring bold headlines. A piece for the Episcopal Church asked, ''Whose birthday is it anyway?'' above pictures of Jesus Christ and Santa Claus. A trade campaign for *Rolling Stone* titled ''Perception/Reality'' juxtaposed images of the magazine's perceived audience—hippies, earth shoes, and psychedelic-painted Volkswagen buses—against its actual readership—yuppies, Nikes, and Ford Mustangs—in order to convince high-end advertisers to place ads in the periodical.

FMR exhibited a talent for promoting not only its clients' brands and products, but also for getting itself noticed. The agency won numerous regional and national awards and used these credentials to draw media coverage as well as new clients to its Midwestern headquarters. Fallon reflected on the group's early success in a 1989 *ADWEEK* article, saying that ''Virtually everything we touched worked dramatically in the market-

Company Perspectives:

Mission: To be the premier creative agency in the world that produces extraordinarily effective work for a short list of blue chip clients.

place.'' FMR won accounts with Federal Express, Hush Puppies Shoes, Jack Daniels Distillery, the *Wall Street Journal*, Lee Jeans, and Porsche U.S.A. Critical acclaim came early, too. Just two years after its foundation, FMR was named ad agency of the year by *Advertising Age* magazine. The agency's style set the trend for cutting-edge advertising—especially print—throughout the 1980s. Annual billings mounted from about $24 million in 1984 to more than $110 million by 1987.

In 1985, Nancy Rice left the agency to form her own agency, Rice & Rice, with her husband, Nick. That same year, the remaining principles sold a majority interest in their agency to Scali, McCabe & Sloves—itself owned by international advertising powerhouse Ogilvy & Mather—for an estimated $6 million.

From its outset, FM cultivated a familial atmosphere that featured a flat organizational structure, few titles, and a very relaxed corporate culture. An April 1992 *ADWEEK* article called the agency ''obsessively egalitarian,'' so much so that clerical workers occupied the headquarters' coveted corner offices. Some competitors dubbed it ''Camp Fallon.'' As McElligott told *Madison Avenue* magazine in 1986, ''The unspoken contract [with employees] is to do the best work of their career, which means longer hours, really putting the screws to themselves. Our side is if they do their best work, we would not stop it; we'd have the courage to show it to the client.'' This covenant helped give employees, especially those of the creative department, an unusually high level of job satisfaction, which in turn resulted in low turnover. Though FM, like many other regional and national agencies, had now become part of a global family of ad agencies, it strove to maintain this aesthetic paradise.

''Dinka Incident'' Stunts Late 1980s Growth

Fallon McElligott suffered a self-inflicted black eye in 1987. That fall Dr. Neala Schleuning, director of the Mankato (Minnesota) State University Women's Center, attended a workshop on marketing given by Fallon McElligott employee Charles Anderson. Offended by what she perceived as sexist language—for example, the presentation featured several references to prostitution and the agency's ''BITCH BITCH BITCH'' campaign for the ''Dynasty'' television series—Schleuning wrote a critical letter to Anderson. Anderson responded by sending her a photo of a member of the East African Dinka tribe pressing his face to a cow's hindquarters. His accompanying letter suggested that Schleuning go to Africa and ''put a stop to [the Dinka's] horrible social practices.''

The astonishingly unprofessional behavior did not stop there. When Schleuning reported the incident to Fallon and McElligott, they responded by sending her a pith helmet and offering to pay her way to East Africa—but not back. Schleuning took the correspondence to the Minnesota Women's Consortium, which sent copies to FM's clients and the local news media a week before Christmas 1987. Not surprisingly, what came to be known as ''the Dinka incident'' launched a firestorm of controversy in the press and among FM's clients. Fallon apologized in writing to Schleuning on New Year's Eve, but the damage had already been done. In the year to come, the agency lost a total of $22 million worth of billings, including the U.S. WEST, Federal Express, and The *Wall Street Journal* accounts. Morale at ''Camp Fallon'' hit the skids.

FM's troubles continued in 1988, when Tom McElligott resigned over ''disagreements with management about the future creative direction.'' McElligott later admitted that he had struggled with alcoholism, though all involved stressed that the episode had nothing to do with his departure from the agency. He went into a month of treatment, and did not return to the advertising business until late 1989. Though the agency had dropped ''Rice'' from its name when Nancy Rice left in 1985, it retained the celebrated McElligott name into the 1990s.

Observers within and without the agency speculated that it would lose its cachet, having lost its most noted creative person. But as it turned out, Fallon McElligott's best trait has been its ability to read and adapt to the advertising industry's leading trends. And while its daring, funny, and sometimes shocking ads continued to garner attention and awards, it was ''the suit,'' Patrick Fallon, who would shepherd the company through this succession of near-disasters to unqualified success in the mid-1990s.

In 1990, Fallon was called to New York City, long the hub of the advertising world, to turn around FM's parent agency, Scali, McCabe & Sloves. That year SMS lost its flagship client, the $41 million Volvo account, over a television ad featuring a reinforced Volvo withstanding the weight of ''monster truck'' Bearfoot. Volvo's resignation from SMS ended a 23-year relationship. Fallon's presence helped inspire confidence among SMS's employees as well as its remaining clients. With the New York agency's future secure by early 1992, Fallon made a pivotal career move. Though he was reportedly tempted to stay on in New York, Fallon returned to Minneapolis with a slight revision to his agency's mission statement: to make it ''the premier creative agency in the *world*.''

Mid-1990s Ascent

Pat Burnham, who had served as associate creative director since 1985, succeeded McElligott as creative director in 1989. The first of many talented creative people hired by McElligott, Burnham inherited a team that was actually little diminished by the loss of its star. FM began to recover in 1989, winning accounts with Aveda Corporation, Amoco Oil Company, and an estimated $35 million worth of annual billings from Ralston Purina. In order to manage its growth, the agency limited its clientele to less than 25 accounts at any time.

Fallon thought he had found the stepping stone that would put his agency on the path to global eminence when FM was invited to pitch for the Compaq and MasterCard accounts in

1992. But after investing more than $250,000 and months of nights and weekends, the agency lost both clients to a competitor, so-called ''blue chip'' agency Ammirati and Puris. A major shakeup followed these missed opportunities. In 1993, Fallon and several other top executives borrowed $14 million to buy the agency back from Scali, McCabe & Sloves (by this time owned by WPP Group PLC). That same year, he asked for and received creative director Pat Burnham's resignation. Reflecting on the shakeup, Fallon told *ADWEEK's* Andrew Jaffe that, ''After MasterCard, I knew we needed a broader, more business-based product offering and new creative leadership.''

Fallon's new hires shed light on the agency's redirection. In Burnham's place came Bill Westbrook, a ''rainmaker'' adept at pitching potential clients, something that Burnham had been unwilling, if not unable, to do. To its creative core the agency added an integrated marketing department as well as design, editing, interactive, direct marketing, promotion research and planning, public relations, and account planning services. Westbrook further shook up FM's egalitarian culture by adopting the title president/creative director, and promoting or recruiting several group directors to report to him.

The shakeup worked. By the end of 1996, FM had won accounts with BMW, Prudential, Ameritech, United Airlines, Mercury Marine, Holiday Inn, the USA Network, and even McDonald's, which awarded it the Arch Deluxe campaign. Fallon McElligott capped off the year by winning the $150 million Miller Lite account. Total billings for the year reached an estimated $500 million, and FM won *Advertising Age's* Agency of the Year award.

Fallon McElligott's future in the mercurial world of advertising remained unclear. Client turnover continued to be a challenge for the agency in the mid-1990s. By 1997, for example, FM had resigned the McDonald's Arch Deluxe account and lost the Prudential campaign. The agency hoped to make up for the lost billings by winning the $75 million Domino's Pizza account then under review. Later that year, President/Creative Director Westbrook announced his intent to cut back on his day-to-day duties, raising speculation that the agency would be hiring yet another creative director in the near future. One element—perhaps the most important one—appeared constant, however: Pat Fallon. Having guided his agency through a number of difficulties to industrywide acclaim, Fallon still strove to maintain ''the premier creative agency in the world.''

Further Reading

''Adman Tom McElligott; Advertising's Hottest Creative Director Explains Why '95% of All Advertising Doesn't Work,' '' *Inc.*, July 1986, pp. 30–34.

Cohen, Warren, ''More Adventures in Advertising,'' *U.S. News & World Report,* January 20, 1997, p. 53.

Cooper, Ann, ''Coming into Fallon Country,'' *ADWEEK Eastern Edition,* January 17, 1994, pp. 34–37.

DeSalvo, Kathy, ''Fallon McElligott,'' *SHOOT,* December 13, 1996, pp. 33–38.

——, ''Future Fallon,'' *SHOOT,* June 14, 1996, pp. 21–23.

Froiland, Paul, ''Creativity Unlimited,'' *TC [Twin Cities],* June 1985, pp. 55–62, 64–65.

Geiger, Bob, ''Fallon Loses McElligott,'' *Advertising Age,* December 12, 1988, pp. 1, 67.

——, ''McElligott Confronts Alcoholism,'' *Advertising Age,* December 12, 1988, pp. 1, 67.

——, ''Rice Leaves FMR to Form Own Shop,'' *Advertising Age,* August 5, 1985, pp. 1–67.

Goldman, Debra, ''Camp Fallon,'' *ADWEEK Eastern Edition,* April 27, 1992, pp. 22–27.

——, ''Pat Fallon Plays Mr. Fix-It—And Helps Scali Around,'' *ADWEEK EASTERN EDITION,* March 16, 1992, p. 9.

——, ''Wild Pitch: MasterCard Was the Kind of High-Profile Account Agencies Wanted to Win at All Costs,'' *ADWEEK Eastern Edition,* September 28, 1992, pp. 24–30.

Harragan, Betty Lehan, ''The $10 Million Blunder,'' *Working Woman,* May 1988, pp. 94–98.

Heitzman, Beth, ''Fallon Buys Back Freedom from WPP,'' *ADWEEK Eastern Edition,* October 25, 1993, p. 5.

Heitzman, Beth, and David Kiley, ''Porsche Speeds Away from Fallon,'' *ADWEEK Eastern Edition,* January 18, 1993, pp. 1–2.

Jaffe, Andrew, ''Reach for the Skies,'' *ADWEEK Eastern Edition,* April 10, 1995, p. 25.

Jensen, Trevor, ''Fallon's Westbrook Wants 'Help,' '' *ADWEEK Eastern Edition,* August 18, 1997, p. 4.

Keller, Martin, ''Fallon McElligott Grows Up,'' *Corporate Report-Minnesota,* January 1991, pp. 61–64.

Kiley, David, and Beth Heitzman, ''Fallon McElligott: Creative Coming Attraction,'' *ADWEEK Eastern Edition,* May 10, 1993, pp. 1–2.

''Kiss That Job Goodbye,'' *Time,* January 25, 1988, p. 53.

Madison, Cathy, McCormack, Kevin, and Ellen Rooney Martin, ''National Agency Report Cards; The Year in Review,'' *ADWEEK Eastern Edition,* April 7, 1997, pp. 28–34.

——, ''Most Valuable Player; Pat Burnham,'' *ADWEEK Eastern Edition,* February 4, 1991, p. CR4.

——, ''Tom McElligott: The Demanding One Is Back,'' *ADWEEK Eastern Edition,* November 20, 1989, pp. 34–35.

Rich, Andrew, ''Adlife in Minneapolis,'' *Madison Avenue,* October 1986, pp. 52–53, 55–56.

Sellers, Patricia, ''Leo Burnett: Undone by an Upstart,'' *Fortune,* May 26, 1997, pp. 98–102.

Shahoda, Susan, ''Tom McElligott Exits from Fallon McElligott,'' *Back Stage,* December 16, 1988, pp. 1–2.

Sharkey, Betsy, ''Frozen Out: For Ten Years Pat Burnham Was the Creative Center of Arguably the Country's Most Creative Shop,'' *ADWEEK Eastern Edition,* March 22, 1993, pp. 28–33.

Spadoni, Marie, ''Fallon McElligott Rolls Stone into the '80s,'' *Advertising Age,* August 18, 1986, pp. S1, S9–S10.

—April Dougal Gasbarre

First Team Sports, Inc.

1201 Lund Boulevard
Anoka, Minnesota 55303
U.S.A.
(612) 576-3500
Fax: (612) 576-8000
Web site: http://www.ultrawheels.com

Public Company
Incorporated: 1986
Employees: 81
Sales: $76.44 million (1997)
Stock Exchanges: NASDAQ
SICs: 3949 Sporting & Athletic Goods, Not Elsewhere Classified

First Team Sports, Inc. is the world's second leading maker of in-line roller skates. In-line skates feature wheels mounted in a straight line, so that they function similar to the blade on an ice skate. The company's anchor product is a line of skates called UltraWheels. First Team Sports also markets skates under the brand name Skate Attack, and it provides in-line skates for sale under private labels. In addition to in-line skates, the company also produces ice skates, street hockey equipment, and other skate-related accessories. First Team Sports skates and other gear are sold at big sporting good chain stores, small independent sporting goods specialty stores, and through mass merchandise stores. In Europe, Japan, Australia, and Singapore, the company's products are marketed through independent sporting goods distributors.

Founded in 1986

First Team Sports was founded in 1986 by John Egart and David Soderquist. A year earlier, both men were toiling as Minneapolis-area sales representatives for foreign companies in the sporting goods business—Egart for German athletic shoe giant Adidas, Soderquist for Amer Sport, a Finnish hockey skate manufacturer. In the course of their travels among sporting goods stores, the pair began to notice the appearance of a new type of roller skate. The new skates were of the in-line variety and were being made by a young Minneapolis company called Rollerblade, Inc. Rollerblade was actually reintroducing a type of skate that had been popular briefly in the 1860s.

Jumped into In-Line Fray in 1986

From the buyers at sporting goods stores, Soderquist and Egart learned that demand was so strong for in-line skates that Rollerblade was having trouble keeping up with orders. Seizing the opportunity, the two men raised $380,000 in start-up money from friends, relatives, and new mortgages on their homes. They found a manufacturer in Taiwan to put the skates together and quickly began making sales calls to people they knew from Adidas and Amer Sport days, offering the new skates, dubbed UltraWheels, at prices about 15 percent lower than those of comparable models made by Rollerblade.

The going was rough at First Team Sports for the first couple of years. By 1987 the company was selling about $65,000 worth of skates a month, but losing $20,000 in the process. Founders Egart and Soderquist, who were not yet paying themselves anything for running the company, began to see the specter of bankruptcy looming over them. Just when things were beginning to look grim, the company found a savior in financier Wesley Hayne of the Minneapolis firm Hayne, Miller & Swearingen, Inc. Hayne agreed to help First Team Sports raise $2.6 million by selling 70 percent of the company to the public.

The bailout did not turn out to be entirely altruistic, however. Within two weeks of the much-needed cash infusion, Hayne and Carey Schumacher, another area businessman, started pressuring Egart and Soderquist to merge the company with a floundering fishing tackle and gun distribution firm. Egart and Soderquist saw this as the first stage of an assault on their control of First Team Sports and, therefore, resisted the merger. Rumors soon began to circulate that Egart and Soderquist were standing in the way of a move that would have benefited company stockholders.

Company Perspectives:

The mission of First Team Sports is to develop and market sporting goods products under specific brands through selected channels of distribution. First Team Sports continually develops its various products to meet the objectives of innovative design, exceptional price value, and high quality.

Founders Beat Back 1988 Proxy Challenge

The suspicions of Egart and Soderquist soon proved to be accurate. In January of 1988 former allies Hayne and Schumacher launched a proxy fight to bring about the proposed merger, a move that if successful would have most likely shoved Egart and Soderquist out of the picture. After five months of battle, Soderquist and Egart emerged victorious from the proxy war, enabling them to retain control of the company they had brought to life.

Although they managed to hang onto their company, one small problem remained—namely, how to get it to start making money. Part of the difficulty lay in the fact that the name Rollerblades had become virtually synonymous with ''in-line skates.'' Just getting the public to call the product by a name that was not associated with the competition was a challenge in itself. In early 1990 the company addressed the visibility problem by signing an endorsement contract with hockey superstar Wayne Gretzky, arguably the highest profile figure in the skating universe. The signing of Gretzky was a coup of major proportions. The company brought it about by making Gretzky an intriguing offer. Instead of paying his usual half million dollars per endorsement—out of the question for an upstart like First Team Sports—Egart and Soderquist persuaded Gretzky to take $100,000 a year in cash, plus options to buy 100,000 shares of stock at its current cheap rate. Gretzky would also get a percentage of the revenue from a signature line of skates.

Gretzky's involvement was fruitful. Company revenue for 1990 reached $3.5 million, more than double the previous year's total. More important, First Team Sports turned a profit of 12 cents a share, compared with a loss of 11 cents in 1989.

By 1991 UltraWheels were being distributed in the United States, Japan, Sweden, Mexico, and Germany. Sales continued to grow as in-line skates evolved from a specialty item for fitness buffs and hockey players trying to stay in shape through the summer, into a popular recreation item for the general public. Although Rollerblade remained well ahead of First Team Sports, the market for in-line skates was expanding quickly enough to keep both companies growing for the time being.

Continued Growth in Early 1990s

Following up on the success of Gretzky's endorsement, First Team Sports sought out additional skating celebrities to peddle its wares. By 1992 hockey star Brett Hull and figure skating champion Katerina Witt were also in the fold, with deals similar to the one the company had signed with Gretzky. Even with competition heating up to include dozens more in-line skate companies, First Team Sports continued to thrive in the number two spot behind industry leader Rollerblade. For fiscal 1993, the company recorded sales of $38 million, a 41 percent jump over the previous year, though still only about a third of Rollerblade's figure. Profits for the year reached $3 million. Those totals landed First Team Sports at number 15 on *Business Week*'s 1993 Hot Growth list.

Just when things seemed to be skating right along, however, First Team Sports encountered a couple of speed bumps. First, Rollerblade initiated an aggressive patent infringement campaign against First Team Sports and several other in-line skate companies. At about the same time, the company began experiencing the same kinds of growing pains that Rollerblade had gone through in the mid-1980s, opening the door for the creation of First Team Sports. The most obvious pain came in 1993, when a shift in manufacturing location from Taiwan to Minnesota—a change designed to speed delivery to U.S. customers—took longer than expected, leading to a huge backlog in skate orders. As a result, store owners were hesitant to place new orders while still waiting for old ones to be filled. Meanwhile, flooding of historic proportions soaked much of the Midwest, leaving few people in the region in much of a mood to skate that season. Sales and earnings both tumbled during the fiscal year that ended in February of 1994.

First Team Sports was able to bounce back strongly in 1995, which turned out to be a banner year. By this time, the company controlled about 15 percent of the in-line skate market with both its high-end UltraWheels line and another line called Skate Attack, aimed at the lower-priced market. In-line skating continued to grow as a hobby through the year, with the number of skate owners reaching 15 million. Across the United States, test youth roller-hockey leagues were springing up and plans for a professional league were in the works. First Team Sports also broke through with a new braking system for its skates in 1995. The DBS braking system utilized the kind of disk brake concept found on cars, a major improvement over the friction pad brakes found on most in-line skates. For fiscal 1995, the company earned $6.1 million on revenue of $86 million. Several national business journals, including *Forbes, Fortune,* and *Inc.,* cited First Team Sports for its achievements that year, and Egart and Soderquist received Entrepreneur of the Year Awards for Manufacturing. Future growth seemed secure as in-line skating started to catch on across Europe.

In 1996 First Team Sports recorded sales of $97.7 million, along with record earnings of $7.8 million. That year, the company introduced a new line of skates featuring a technology called Intec, which improved the durability and strength of the UltraWheels skates on which it was applied. First Team Sports also launched a program aimed at deepening its penetration into specialty sporting goods stores. Toward that end, the company developed a catalog of merchandise available only to independent stores and small chains of less than eight outlets.

A Tough Year in 1997

First Team Sports continued to broaden its presence in the public eye in 1997. The company launched an advertising campaign that included two 30-second television commercials, as well as advertising spots in movie theaters and on videos. Sponsorship of national and regional sporting events was also part of the mix, as was product placement of UltraWheels on the television shows ''Mad About You,'' ''Baywatch,'' and ''Clueless,'' and in a handful of feature films that included *Ransom* and *Jerry McGuire.* Hockey stars Gretzky and Hull continued to sponsor First Team Sports products both in advertisements and through personal appearances on behalf of the company.

In spite of the company's aggressive marketing efforts, First Team Sports saw its sales decline significantly in 1997, to $76.4 million. The drop was caused by a number of factors, including bad spring weather and increased competition, both of which affected the entire industry. Nevertheless, the company was able to gain market share with its flagship UltraWheels line. It also took steps to capture a healthy portion of sales to the growing market for ''extreme'' products, that is, skates specifically designed for rugged use by exceptionally aggressive skaters. The company introduced a new line called ''Sabotage'' specifically to meet the needs of those customers.

In addition to skates and accessories for aggressive skaters, First Team Sports also made overtures toward two other growing classes of skate consumers: fitness buffs and women. For the fitness market, 1997 brought the introduction of the Softec line of high-performance fitness skates, blending the best characteristics of the company's UltraWheels with the look and feel of a fitness shoe. For women, the company launched a line of protective gear designed to fit the contours of a woman's body. The line, called WSD, included ergonomically designed wrist guards, elbow pads, and knee pads. The company also offered six models of UltraWheels designed specifically for women.

In September of 1997 First Team Sports moved to make itself a force on ice as well as on wheels with the acquisition of the 89-year-old Hespeler Hockey Inc., a maker of professional-caliber ice skates for hockey. Just a couple of weeks after its purchase of Hespeler, the company announced that Gretzky had been made an executive officer and given a spot on the Hespeler board of directors in return for his expanded investment in First Team Sports.

The slump of fiscal 1997 did not stop the company from planning for expansion in other ways as well. Entering 1998, the company opened a European subsidiary based in Austria and launched several new skate lines. Its new Biofit series was described in company literature as ''the industry's first line of biomechanically designed skates.'' Two more new lines, Lite-Max and FlexTec, were introduced for recreational skaters. The company also redesigned its Sabotage line of aggressive skates.

Regardless of the obstacles that make it tough for any company to prosper in a competitive market, the fact remains that First Team Sports is a leading supplier of equipment for a sport that the Sporting Goods Manufacturers Association estimates to be one of the three fastest growing worldwide. If the company's attempts to win over customers by targeting its goods to specific markets proves successful, its prospects for continued growth appear solid.

Principal Subsidiaries

Hespeler Hockey Inc.; First Team Sports GmbH (Austria).

Further Reading

Adelson, Andrea, ''First Team Sports Is Skating Fast. Should Investors Ride Along?,'' *New York Times,* May 1, 1995, p. D4.
Comte, Elizabeth, ''Blade Runner,'' *Forbes,* October 12, 1992, p. 114.
Greising, David, ''First Team Sports: A Fleet No. 2 in the Rollerblade Derby,'' *Business Week,* March 24, 1993, p. 67.
Marcial, Gene G., ''Catching a Ride on UltraWheels,'' *Business Week,* March 18, 1991, p. 117.
Matzer, Marla, ''A Nice One for the Great One,'' *Forbes,* May 8, 1995, p. 88.
Phelps, David, ''Investor Community Wary of First Team for Moment,'' *Star Tribune* (Minneapolis), January 13, 1997, p. 1D.

—Robert R. Jacobson

Fleetwood Enterprises, Inc.

3125 Myers Street
Post Office Box 7638
Riverside, California 92513-7638
U.S.A.
(909) 351-3500
Fax: (909) 351-3373
Web site: http://www.fleetwood.com

Public Company
Incorporated: 1950 as Coach Specialties Company
Employees: 18,000
Sales: $2.87 billion (1997)
Stock Exchanges: New York Pacific
SICs: 2451 Mobile Homes; 2452 Prefabricated Wood Buildings & Components; 3716 Motor Homes; 3792 Travel Trailers & Campers

Fleetwood Enterprises, Inc. is the nation's largest maker of both manufactured housing and recreational vehicles (including motor homes, travel trailers, folding trailers, and truck campers). Manufactured housing is sold under the corporate name, Fleetwood. The company's line of motor homes are sold under various brands, including Jamboree, Bounder, Flair, Pace Arrow, Southwind, Tioga, Storm, and Discovery. Fleetwood's travel trailers are marketed under the names Avion, Prowler, Terry, Wilderness, Mallard, Savanna, and Westport. The company's folding trailer division, acquired in December 1989, manufactures products under the Coleman name. As a whole, Fleetwood recreational vehicles span the full range of the market, with their retail prices ranging from $3,000 to more than $200,000. Both housing and recreational vehicles are marketed through a network of more than 2,600 dealers in the United States and Canada. The company supplies its dealers from production facilities located in 18 states and in Canada. Fleetwood holds a 49 percent stake in Expression Homes, a joint venture with Pulte Corp. created in October 1997 that operates retail centers selling manufactured houses as well as offering home financing and insurance. Other company operations include two fiberglass manufacturing companies and a lumber milling unit.

From Window Blinds to Mobile Homes in the 1950s

Fleetwood was founded by the company's current chairman and CEO John C. Crean in a greenhouse in southern California in 1950. Under the name Coach Specialties Company, he and his wife manufactured and sold a new and improved line of window blinds for travel trailers. At the same time, Crean built a travel trailer for his own use. One of his window blind customers, a trailer dealer, was so impressed by the trailer's construction that a deal was struck for Crean to assemble trailer units with materials supplied to him by the dealer. Production was to be in quantities large enough to make sure the dealer could keep pace with his seasonal orders. As the summer travel trailer season came to a close, Crean continued his new enterprise but opted to build mobile homes instead of trailers. Mobile homes, currently referred to as manufactured housing, provided a more stable market for growth because of increasing demand for inexpensive housing in southern California. The name Fleetwood was chosen from a line of automobiles. By 1954 the company had outgrown its greenhouse to become a thriving enterprise with three production plants.

The growth of the manufactured home market was caused by the product's moderate price. The cost of a quality manufactured home runs about one-third that of an on-site constructed home, in each case excluding land. Off-site production eliminates the use of many different contractors, construction is not affected by weather, and less time is required for construction because every component arrives at the assembly point ready to use. Manufactured homes are trucked in sections to the homesite, where they are assembled in a matter of days, instead of the normal on-site construction times that can stretch into weeks and months.

Expanded into RVs in the 1960s and 1970s

In 1957 the company changed its name from Coach Specialties Company and reincorporated as Fleetwood Enterprises, Inc. During the 1950s the manufactured housing industry had split into two distinct markets. Fleetwood had its feet firmly planted in the mobile home market, and because of its healthy growth had accumulated a large cash surplus. The other market, the recreational vehicle (RV) market, Crean saw offered good opportunities. In 1964 Fleetwood acquired Terry Coach Indus-

Company Perspectives:

Fleetwood Enterprises, Inc., a Fortune 500 company listed on the New York Stock Exchange, is the nation's leading producer of manufactured housing and recreational vehicles. Headquartered in Riverside, California, the company employs over 18,000 people in plants located in 18 states and Canada.

The dream of home ownership is alive and well in America, and Fleetwood made that dream a reality for more than 65,000 families in fiscal 1997. Fleetwood builds quality, factory-built homes, enabling families to enjoy comfortable housing at affordable prices.

Fleetwood manufactures a wide array of recreational vehicles, including motor homes, travel trailers, folding camping trailers, and slide-in truck campers. Fleetwood RVs are designed to make leisure-time activities more enjoyable and enhance today's more active lifestyles.

tries, Inc. and Terry Coach Manufacturing, Inc. This was a time when an ever-increasing number of U.S. outdoor enthusiasts wanted to travel. The company's line of travel trailers included sleeping, eating, and bathroom facilities. As the size and weight of these units grew, Fleetwood designed and built a line of fifth-wheel travel trailers, a model that is exclusively built to be towed by larger pickup trucks. As sales grew and the market expanded, the company continued to open new production plants to meet increasing sales. In 1965 Fleetwood became a public company. By 1990 the company operated 12 travel trailer plants in the United States and Canada.

As the RV market boomed, Fleetwood continued to diversify with the acquisition of Pace-Arrow, Inc., a motor home manufacturer. The acquisition was a logical extension of the company's travel trailer business. Motor homes are similar to travel trailers in construction and use. The interior looks the same as a travel trailer except that the motor home provides an area for the driver. The entire unit is constructed on a purchased truck chassis. The product line offers two types, both of which are self-contained. Type A motor homes are full-size units, with sleeping room for four to eight people and typically equipped with air conditioning, on-board power generators, and stereo systems. Type C units are smaller, built on cut-away van chassis, and usually accommodate fewer people. At a time when inexpensive gasoline and the U.S. public's wanderlust fueled the RV market, Fleetwood was marketing a diverse product line, the prices of which accommodated a wide range of buyers' budgets. The company rounded out its product line with the acquisition, for cash, of Avion Coach Corporation in 1976. Avion augmented the company's line of trailers with its expensive, luxury class models. In 1977 the company incorporated in the state of Delaware, keeping the same name.

The 1970s was a period of rapid growth and expansion for Fleetwood. As the decade ended, the revolution in Iran, skyrocketing gasoline costs, and the buying public's fear of a recession, along with rising interest rates, created an across-the-board slump in sales. Two-thirds of Fleetwood's product line were vehicles that were intended for use on U.S. highways. Gasoline shortages, which in some states resulted in day-to-day rationing, along with the spiraling costs of fuel, shook the RV market to its foundations. Many manufacturers were forced out of business as RV retailers began closing their doors and defaulting on their bank-financed inventories. The ensuing recession brought with it escalating interest rates, making mortgages for all types of housing and for financing RVs prohibitive. The company, for the first time since the early 1950s, found itself in a situation calling for drastic cutbacks in production and staffing.

Encountered Various Troubles in the 1980s

The year 1980 was difficult for Fleetwood. It was forced to close nine of its production plants. The cutbacks closed three travel trailer plants, three motor home facilities, and three manufactured housing plants. Fleetwood had to consider massive worker layoffs.

Fleetwood was forced to take a hard look at its entire structure during these hard times. It developed a tightly focused management policy, employing regionalized management within its housing group, which permitted the company to react more quickly to market trends. Housing design and development was spread to five areas: West Coast, central, southeast, mid-Atlantic, and Florida. Each plant facility began operation as a separate profit center with day-to-day decisions made locally. Fleetwood slowly rode out the recession, and in 1982 Fleetwood's motor home division was projecting sales of 40,000 units in 1983.

The rapid growth and expansion Fleetwood had experienced in the 1980s had not been without legal and regulatory problems. The company is subject to provisions of the Housing and Community Development Act of 1974. These provisions, which are regulated by the U.S. Department of Housing and Urban Development (HUD), resulted in an action by the department against Fleetwood in 1985 claiming potential safety defects in 4,000 mobile homes made by the company during the years 1981 through 1984. Fleetwood was ordered to notify the owners of the mobile homes in question about possible defects in the units' walls, floors, and beams. The problems did prompt HUD to initiate an investigation into engineering techniques used by other mobile home manufacturers.

The four-year-old dispute came to a head in February 1988, resulting in a U.S. Justice Department complaint filed against Fleetwood in Wilmington, Delaware, seeking civil penalties in excess of $20 million. The complaint alleged the existence of certain standards violations in manufactured homes produced by several of Fleetwood's subsidiaries. On February 9, 1989, Fleetwood entered into a settlement agreement with HUD and the Justice Department. The settlement resulted in the dismissal of government charges against Fleetwood in exchange for a settlement payment.

Fleetwood, along with other companies in the manufactured housing industry, was the target of a class action suit filed in Delaware in 1985. The complaint alleged that veterans who had purchased mobile homes had paid excessive prices and finance charges as a result of illegal rebates that were falsely certified to the Veterans Administration by the manufacturers. In 1990 the court certified a class of plaintiffs consisting of certain veterans who purchased mobile homes from Fleetwood dating back as far as April 1981. Two of the company's subsidiaries pleaded guilty to six counts of filing false certifications in 1987, resulting in approximately $650,000 in fines and civil settlements.

Fleetwood Credit Corporation (FCC) was established in 1986. The finance company's objective was to become the major source of both wholesale and retail financing of Fleetwood's RV products on a nationwide basis. Using $25 million of its own funds, the company hired Robert B. Baker, former head of Nissan Motor Acceptance Corporation, to head the project. FCC began operations by servicing just 12 Orange County, California dealers. In the early 1990s the company had lending operations in southern and northern California, Oregon, Indiana, Massachusetts, Georgia, New Jersey, and Texas. Fleetwood Credit showed a net income of $2.9 million in 1990, a 56 percent increase over the previous year.

In 1989 Fleetwood acquired the Coleman Company's folding trailer business. The Coleman product line ranged in retail price from $2,000 to $10,000, and in 1989 it accounted for more than 30 percent of the folding trailer market. With the acquisition of this line, Fleetwood had products for most consumers' budgets. The company also introduced new lower-priced trailer models in response to changing market conditions.

Ups and Downs Marked the 1990s

The 1990s were an up-and-down period for Fleetwood as its results were affected by the economic downturn early in the decade, the mid-1990s recovery, and increasing competition in the later years of the decade. Following the difficult years of 1990 and 1991, revenues and operating income increased each year, although the growth rate for both slowed considerably by fiscal 1996 and 1997, as competitors began to eat away at Fleetwood's market share positions.

Fleetwood began the decade optimistic about the future, as evidenced by its 1990 $6.3 million purchase of a 75-acre parcel in southern California that it planned to develop as a site-built housing tract. This would have been the company's first foray into nonmanufactured housing, but after several years of preliminary work on the project, it decided in 1996 not to pursue the project. By that time the land was worth only $2.8 million, thanks to the collapse of the California real estate market.

Another attempt at expansion failed as well, when the company looked for growth outside the maturing U.S. motor home market. In September 1992 Fleetwood acquired an 80 percent interest in Niesmann & Bischoff, a Koblenz, Germany-based manufacturer of luxury-priced ($150,000 to $300,000) motor homes under the brands Clou Liner and Clou Trend. Continued weakness in the German economy, however, led to slow sales following the purchase, even after Fleetwood introduced lower-priced models. In May 1996 Fleetwood gave up on its European adventure, selling its stake in Niesmann & Bischoff and taking a $28 million charge for fiscal 1996 in the process.

May 1996 also saw another divestment, and a further focusing in on core operations, through the sale of Fleetwood Credit to Associates First Capital Corporation for $156.6 million, resulting in an after-tax gain of $33.9 million for fiscal 1997. In conjunction with the sale, Fleetwood and Associates First Capital signed a long-term operating agreement that assured financing continuity.

These divestments came at a time when Fleetwood needed to devote more attention to its domestic manufactured housing and RV units, both of which were losing ground to aggressive competitors. The company's share of the manufactured housing market reached a peak of 21.6 percent in 1994, then declined to 20.1 percent in 1995 and to 18.5 percent in 1996. On the rise was Auburn Hills, Michigan-based Champion Enterprises Inc., which had grown rapidly in the mid-1990s through acquisitions, was undercutting Fleetwood's prices, and had attained 16.5 percent of the market by 1996. In the RV sector, Fleetwood's share of the motor home market, the most lucrative RV niche, fell from 34 percent in 1992 to 27.5 percent in 1996. Winnebago remained a fairly distant second at 16.7 percent, but Winnebago and other competitors had gained edges over Fleetwood by introducing popular space-increasing slideouts to their motor homes well before Fleetwood added them in fiscal 1996.

Like many an industry leader, Fleetwood had seemed to take its longstanding top positions for granted. The company began in 1996 and 1997 to become more customer-focused, for example by realigning its manufactured housing operations into three autonomous regional units, which brought decision-making closer to the customer level. Fiscal 1997 saw the establishment of 49 Fleetwood Home Centers, which were retail centers selling only Fleetwood homes and designed to offer improved customer service. In October 1997 the company entered into a joint venture (49 percent owned by Fleetwood) with Bloomfield Hills, Michigan-based Pulte Corp. to form Expression Homes, a venture intended to establish a nationwide network of retail centers where manufactured homes would be sold and home financing and insurance would be offered. It intended to grow through acquisitions, including the purchase of some of Fleetwood's independent agents. Fleetwood saw Expression Homes as a way that its homes could be marketed in a more consistent and cohesive way. The question for Fleetwood was whether moves such as these would be enough for it to remain the number one maker of manufactured homes and RVs in the 21st century.

Principal Subsidiaries

Fleetwood Homes of Arizona, Inc.; Fleetwood Homes of California, Inc.; Fleetwood Homes of Florida, Inc.; Fleetwood Homes of Georgia, Inc.; Fleetwood Homes of Idaho, Inc.; Fleetwood Homes of Indiana, Inc.; Fleetwood Homes of Mississippi, Inc.; Fleetwood Homes of North Carolina, Inc.; Fleetwood Homes of Oregon, Inc.; Fleetwood Homes of Pennsylvania, Inc.; Fleetwood Homes of Tennessee, Inc.; Fleetwood Homes of Texas, Inc.; Fleetwood Homes of Virginia, Inc.; Fleetwood Homes of Washington, Inc.; Fleetwood Motor Homes of California, Inc.; Fleetwood Motor Homes of Indiana, Inc.; Fleetwood Motor Homes of Pennsylvania, Inc.; Fleetwood Travel Trailers of California, Inc.; Fleetwood Travel Trailers of Indiana, Inc.; Fleetwood Travel Trailers of Maryland, Inc.; Fleetwood Travel Trailers of Nebraska, Inc.; Fleetwood Travel Trailers of Ohio, Inc.; Fleetwood Travel Trailers of Oregon, Inc.; Fleetwood Travel Trailers of Texas, Inc.; Fleetwood Travel

Trailers of Virginia, Inc.; Fleetwood Folding Trailers, Inc.; Gold Shield, Inc.; Gold Shield of Indiana, Inc.; Hauser Lake Lumber Operation, Inc.; Buckingham Development Co.; Continental Lumber Products, Inc.; Fleetwood Foreign Sales Corp. (U.S. Virgin Islands); Fleetwood Holidays, Inc.; Fleetwood Insurance Services, Inc.; Fleetwood International, Inc.; Gibralter Insurance Company, Ltd. (Bermuda); Expression Homes (49%).

Further Reading

Clifford, Mark, "Business As Usual," *Forbes,* November 18, 1985, p. 62.

Flint, Jerry, "John Crean's Recipe for Success," *Forbes,* October 25, 1993, pp. 200, 204.

"A Glimpse of Fleetwood Enterprises, Inc.," Fleetwood Enterprises corporate typescript, 1987.

Goldenberg, Sherman, "Fleetwood Stresses '92 Economy, New Quality Program," *RV Business,* October 7, 1991, pp. 1, 11.

Granelli, James S., "Fleetwood, Pulte to Form Alliance," *Los Angeles Times,* October 9, 1997, pp. D2, D6.

——, "Fleetwood's Elden Smith: The View from the Top," *RV Business,* November 1993, pp. 32–33.

McCarthy, Tom, "Fleetwood Plans More European Acquisitions, Class C Production," *RV Business,* November 1992, pp. 11, 12.

Paris, Ellen, "Keeping Its Powder Dry," *Forbes,* October 11, 1982, p. 130.

Reingold, Jennifer, "Fleetwood Enterprises: Movin' on Up," *Financial World,* October 26, 1993, p. 22.

Rescigno, Richard, "Revved Up for Recovery: Recreational-Vehicle Makers Seem Ready to Roll Again," *Barron's,* June 17, 1991, pp. 14–15, 37–39.

Witherall, Graham, "Just a Speed Bump?," *Los Angeles Times,* August 24, 1997, p. D1.

—William R. Grossman
—updated by David E. Salamie

Fort James Corporation

120 Tredegar Street
Richmond, Virginia 23219
U.S.A.
(804) 644-5411
Fax: (804) 649-4428
Web site: http://www.jamesrivercorp.com

Public Company
Incorporated: 1997
Employees: 30,000
Sales: $7.0 billion (1996 est.)
Stock Exchanges: New York
SICs: 0811 Timber Tracts; 0831 Forest Nurseries & Forest Products; 2297 Nonwoven Fabrics; 2611 Pulp Mills; 2621 Paper Mills; 2656 Sanitary Food Containers, Except Folding; 2657 Folding Paperboard Boxes, Including Sanitary; 2671 Coated & Laminated Paper & Plastic Film; 2673 Plastics, Foil & Coated Paper Bags; 2676 Sanitary Paper Products; 2679 Converted Paper & Paperboard Products, Not Elsewhere Classified; 2861 Gum & Wood Chemicals; 3086 Plastic Foam Products; 3089 Plastic Products, Not Elsewhere Classified

Fort James Corporation is one of the largest makers of tissues, napkins, and other paper products in the world. It holds the number two position in tissues, trailing Kimberly-Clark Corp. Among the company's many consumer brands are Brawny paper towels, Quilted Northern bathroom tissue, Vanity Fair napkins, Zee towel and tissue products, Mardi Gras napkins and paper towels, Green Forest tissues, and Dixie plates, cups, and cutlery; commercial brands are sold under the Preference and Envision brands. The company maintains operations in the United States, Canada, and Europe. Fort James was created in August 1997 through the merger of James River Corporation of Virginia, which was based in Richmond, Virginia, and was founded in 1969, and Fort Howard Corporation, which operated out of Green Bay, Wisconsin, and traced its history back to 1919.

Founding of James River in 1969

When Ethyl Corporation of Richmond, Virginia, was selling the Abermarle mill, its original papermaking facilities, in 1969, Brenton S. Halsey and Robert C. Williams, then two Ethyl engineers, snapped it up. The river that flowed past the paper mill inherited a namesake in the newly formed James River Corporation of Virginia. Ethyl had decided to concentrate on chemicals. The mill's 25-ton-a-day paper machine and equipment left over from the 1850s could not produce enough of the commodity grades of paper that were the preferred profit-makers of much of the paper and pulp industry at the time. The operation was losing money badly. Halsey and Williams, independently interested in turning the mill around, ran into each other at a Richmond investment banker's office and decided to work together. The two, who would soon be known as ''Brent 'n' Bob,'' raised the capital, and bought the operation for $1.5 million. The two men then jointly designed the company's logo. Halsey served as president of the fledgling firm, while Williams served as CEO.

They then followed a pattern that soon would become familiar to them. They determined that the mill was best suited to the production of specialty papers. They recognized that specialty paper requires a more worker-intensive, decentralized operation, with an emphasis on a knowledgeable and well-trained marketing and sales force. Halsey and Williams felt that large corporations were overlooking opportunities in specialty papers. They used their engineering expertise to upgrade the mill's output to produce automotive air- and oil-filter papers, which had a high profit margin, and developed an in-house trucking system to provide immediate service to clients. By the end of a year they had coaxed earnings of $166,000 out of the aging mill.

Acquisitions Fueled Growth in the 1970s

In 1971 James River acquired the St. Regis Paper Company's specialty mill in Pepperell, Massachusetts. James River employed many of the practices in the acquisition that would be company hallmarks for the next decade: friendly takeovers of ailing businesses that assure the cooperation of the seller; a decentralized approach that provides each mill with its own general manager, sales manager, production manager, and re-

Company Perspectives:

Our mission is to exploit James River's excellent paper-based brands and existing value-added businesses, to propel the company into the ranks of first-tier companies—indicated by top quartile performance in our peer group in the aggregate of: total shareholder wealth creation; improvement in return on sales; improvement in return on assets; increase in unit sales volume per employee; new products as a percent of sales; change in aggregate market share.

search-and-development director; and the utilization of middle managers within the acquired company to run it. James River also emphasized employee involvement and good relations with labor unions; in addition, it implemented company-wide profit sharing years before such plans became fashionable. James River's takeovers also often involved the firing of most executives and the negotiation of wage concessions from workers.

On March 16, 1973, the company went public, selling 165,000 shares of common stock. Staying true to the nature of the company, Halsey and Williams began a company-subsidized employee stock-purchase plan.

In 1975 James River acquired J-Mass from Weyerhaeuser. In 1977 James River bought a failing mill in Jay, Maine, from International Paper. The output was changed from book paper to paper for airline tickets and copying machines. In its first year under James River ownership the Jay mill made $3 million. The same year James River took over Reigel Products Corporation from Southwest Forest Industries. By 1979 it had $96 million in sales. In 1978 Halsey and Williams purchased Scott Graphics from Scott Paper Company, renamed it James River Graphics, and started producing film coatings. By the end of the decade James River had made 10 acquisitions, had nearly 4,000 employees, and reached $297.9 million in annual sales.

Expanded into Consumer Paper in the 1980s

In 1980 Gulf + Western sold its 80 percent interest in Brown Company to James River in return for cash and James River stock. Gulf + Western Chairman Charlie Bluhdorn was confident that James River stock would be more profitable than Brown was for Gulf + Western. For James River, the acquisition was crucial. The deal included a Berlin, New Hampshire, pulp mill and its surrounding 170,000 acres of timberland. It was James River's first in-house source of pulp, providing 40 percent of the company's pulp needs. Along with the pulp, the deal included paper towels, folding cartons for food packaging, and a small cup operation. James River intended to divest these product lines; they were, however, unable to find a buyer. As a result, the deal doubled James River's size and, for the first time, put it in the consumer-paper business; the filter specialists were suddenly makers of tissues, cups, and cereal boxes as well. While this diversification came about almost by accident and broke with the successful pattern of the 1970s, it turned out to be fortuitous. The new decade brought with it a slump in the auto industry, traditionally a big buyer of coated paper and other James River products. James River adjusted. By the end of 1981 industrial products only accounted for one-quarter of James River sales; communication and packaging papers, now a more stable market, made up the remaining 75 percent.

Once in consumer paper, James River did not shrink from new acquisitions. In 1982, Halsey and Williams once again used a stock-and-cash deal to double the size of the company; they bought the Dixie/Northern division, makers of Dixie cups; Northern toilet paper; Bolt, Brawny, and Gala towels; and folding cartons. The former owner, American Can Company, did not take James River's offer to buy seriously at first; it could not see how little James River would finance the deal. Finance it James River did, and soon James River was applying its usual success formula to Dixie/Northern. American Can had been cutting corners on quality. James River cut costs by laying off 200 salaried and 120 hourly workers. It improved sales by redesigning products and emphasizing marketing. With American Can's Alabama pulp mill included in the deal, James River became 70 percent self-sufficient in pulp. James River's chief financial officer, David McKittrick, told *Financial World,* June 2, 1987, "When you peeled back the layers of complexity imposed on Dixie/Northern by American Can, you saw that the companies were in fact doing quite well and that business was actually sort of on a roll."

Many analysts thought that the debt created by all these acquisitions would slow the company down. In 1983, however, Halsey and Williams purchased the H.P. Smith Paper Company, a subsidiary of Phillips Petroleum; a Canadian pulp mill from American Can; and Diamond International's pulp and paper-making operations, including mills in New Hampshire, New York, and Massachusetts. The latter added the Vanity Fair brand of tissues and towels, giving James River a ready-made market in the Northeast.

The following year, James River moved its Northern bathroom paper and Brawny towels into the Northeast as well. In a campaign they called Operation Yankee, the company used a price-slashing policy and $20 million in advertising to take on Procter & Gamble and Scott Paper, the leaders in the field. Halsey said the new emphasis on expanding markets for its existing products reflected an industry slump, the lack of potential acquisitions, and the desire to direct capital toward internal improvements.

The acquisitions, however, did not cease. In April 1984 James River broke onto the international scene with the purchase of GB Papers in Scotland. In 1985 and 1986 the additions of the Arkon Corporation and the Cerex division of Monsanto were made, pushing James River further into the nonwovens market. These were relatively small purchases, however, leading up to the May 1986 acquisition of most of the interests of Crown Zellerbach Corporation, which once again doubled the size of James River. The company was now the number two tissue maker in the country, with a potential of $4.5 billion in total sales, and more than 35,000 employees. The new company, however, would take longer to consolidate than Halsey and Williams anticipated.

The deal had not been an easy one. Halsey had stepped into the middle of a hostile takeover bid by Sir James Goldsmith, who had been angling for control of Crown in a raid replete with poison pill defenses and greenmail. Because of James River's intervention, Crown shareholders saw their stock skyrocket, and had the option of buying into James River. James River got all the Crown papermaking operations. Goldsmith, however, might have gotten the best of the deal: property worth more than $1 billion, including Crown's 1.6 million acres of timber. Goldsmith sold the timberland to Hanson PLC for $1.3 billion in 1990.

Smaller acquisitions continued to make headlines, as well: Canada Cup, Specialty Papers Company, and Amarin Plastics were bought in 1987; and Dunn Paper Company; the U.K. photo and drawing papers business of Wiggins Teape Group; and Armstrong Rees Ederer Inc. were bought in 1988. Acquiring half of France's Kaysersberg, S.A., went a long way towards satisfying Halsey's desire to challenge Scott Paper's supremacy in the European tissue market. Overseas acquisitions were also made in Sweden, Spain, Turkey, and the United Kingdom. By 1988 the company was so big that the Federal Trade Commission blocked a proposed purchase of a South African-owned flexible packaging operation, with fears of reducing competition in that field.

The huge size of the company was affecting profits as well. From 1984 to 1988, the return on shareholders' equity fell from 26 percent to 10.7 percent. The high price of pulp, combined with James River's skyrocketing need for pulp, was the biggest culprit in this downturn. In fiscal 1989 James River was forced to buy 470,000 tons of market pulp domestically, with its new needs in Europe adding to the pulp deficit. This led to strategies to increase the internal supply of pulp: a Marathon, Ontario, pulp mill was tapped for a $280 million expansion in 1989. Williams also considered the use of recycled paper as a fiber source to be a major trend in the industry. James River was among the first producers to express interest in the use of recycled fiber for printing and writing paper production. The need for more fiber coincided with pending legislation that would require the use of some recycled fiber. By the end of 1989, there was some additional relief in sight for James River in the form of a major dip in pulp prices.

Restructuring Moves Highlighted Difficult 1990s

There were indications, however, that James River's woes went deeper than pulp supply; after 20 years of endless acquisitions, it seemed possible that Halsey and Williams had bitten off more than they could chew. Many plants needed upgrading, but the company did not have the capital to make all major overhauls that were necessary. In April 1990 the company announced a 13.1 percent decrease in income from the previous year. Capital expenditures were down 16 percent. In May James River sold its nonwovens group for a much-needed infusion of cash. In August Halsey announced a major restructuring: the company would sell or shut down operations with annual sales of $1.3 billion. James River was lopping off the arm that had started the company: specialty papers. Williams declared that the company's emphasis was now consumer products. James River would be made up of three businesses: consumer products, communications paper, and packaging. In the midst of this metamorphosis, in October 1990, Halsey, while retaining his mantle as chairman, stepped down as CEO in favor of Williams. The move was part of a long-considered management transition plan. The switch from the more acquisitionally minded Halsey to the managerially inclined Williams seemed appropriate to the newly retrenched company. In May 1991 the company sold its specialty papers business for $337 million in cash and preferred stock to AEA Investors, a management-led investor group, which then founded Specialty Coatings Group Inc.

By 1992, the year Halsey retired as chairman and Williams added that role to his duties, James River was continuing to struggle as the economic downturn highlighted the cyclicality of the company's mix of assets. Revenue from bathroom tissue was being severely reduced thanks to pricing wars initiated by such competitors as Kimberly-Clark and Procter & Gamble, while the company's communication papers operations were hurt by extremely depressed prices. Profits were reduced by the company's high operating costs, which were at least in part caused by James River's failure to reduce or eliminate redundancies that had crept into the operations as a result of the two decades of acquisitions. In response, James River in late 1992 launched another restructuring program, this one aimed at reducing labor and production costs in order for the company to be more competitive. A resulting charge of $305.3 million was recorded in 1992's fourth quarter. By 1994, the company was able to reduce expenses by $200 million a year.

As the U.S. economy began its mid-1990s recovery and James River began to return to profitability, the company continued to restructure, eventually deciding to focus almost exclusively on consumer products. In March 1994 James River sold its 50 percent interest in Coastal Paper Company, a producer of lightweight papers based in Mississippi. That same year, the company sold 47,000 acres of timberlands. In August 1995 the company spun off to shareholders Crown Vantage Inc., which included much of James River's communications papers unit and the specialty paper-based part of its packaging business. $480 million in proceeds from this spinoff were used in part to pay down the company's still heavy long-term debt. In October 1995 Miles L. Marsh was brought on board as CEO, and in the following January became chairman as well, replacing the retiring Williams. Marsh, who had most recently engineered the turnaround of Pet Inc., brought to James River much-needed experience in consumer products.

Meanwhile, James River was building up a significant presence in consumer paper products in Europe. The company was the driving force behind the 1990 establishment of a joint venture called Jamont and by 1996 had bought out all of its partners to take full control of the venture. By that time, Jamont had established itself as the number three maker of towel and tissue products in Europe, with a market share of about 15 percent. Based in Brussels, the firm had 23 plants in 10 European countries. Nearly 30 percent of James River's 1996 revenues were generated from its European operations. In early 1997 the company announced plans to open its first plant in Russia for the manufacture of bathroom tissue and napkins.

Divestments continued in 1996. In May the specialty operations business—which included specialty paper plate, napkin, and related tableware products—was sold to Fonda Group Inc. for about $30 million. In August the company's flexible packaging group went to Printpack for $372.7 million. And in October Progressive Ink Company, LLC spent $27 million to buy James

River's CZ Inks Division, which specialized in high quality inks for packaging applications. The divestments enabled James River to substantially reduce its long-term debt, which fell from $2.67 billion in 1994 to $1.85 billion in 1996. Improved operational efficiency and Marsh's bolstering of marketing efforts helped the company post healthy 1996 net income of $157.3 million.

1997 Merger with Fort Howard to Form Fort James

In late 1995 Kimberly-Clark had solidified its number one position in tissue products with its acquisition of Scott Paper Co. James River in turn moved to bolster its number two position by engineering the 1997 merger with Fort Howard Corporation, which created Fort James Corporation. Although called by the companies' executives a ''merger of equals,'' the transaction really amounted to a James River takeover of the much-smaller Fort Howard.

Based in Green Bay, Wisconsin, Fort Howard was founded in 1919 by Austin Edward Cofrin. Traditionally secretive about its low-cost production techniques and its balance sheets, Fort Howard became a public company for the first time only in 1971, at which time its sales were about $100 million. Ten years later, sales exceeded $500 million. In 1988 Fort Howard became a private company once again thanks to a management-led highly leveraged buyout which left the company saddled with about $3.7 billion in debt. The company struggled over the next several years, burdened by this debt load and buffeted by the economic downturn of the early 1990s. After several delays, Fort Howard finally went public again in early 1995 through an initial public offering. In 1996 the company posted sales of $1.6 billion (compared to James River's $5.69 billion).

Fort Howard brought to the merger not only a strong presence in tissue manufacturing but also a leading position in the commercial and industrial market—a perfect complement to James River's consumer market strength. Fort Howard was also considered a low-cost operator—heavily utilizing recycled paper in its manufacturing; this experience in efficiency was expected to be leveraged companywide in the newly formed Fort James. A potential source of difficulty for Fort James was the mixture of Fort Howard's nonunion plants with James River's unionized facilities. The merger itself was a transaction valued at about $3.4 billion in stock, with the new company also assuming about $2.4 billion of Fort Howard debt. Soon after completion of the merger in August 1997, Fort James took charges of $45.2 million for early extinguishment of debt and $53.9 million for merger-related costs. James River's Marsh became Fort James's chairman and CEO, while Michael T. Riordan, Fort Howard's chairman and CEO, became president and COO of Fort James. The initial board of directors included 11 people from James River and four from Fort Howard.

In addition to the potential conflict arising from the mix of union and nonunion operations, Fort James also had to deal with a bathroom tissue price-fixing lawsuit filed in May 1997 by the attorney general of Florida, which named both James River and Fort Howard, in addition to Kimberly-Clark, Georgia-Pacific, and others. The suit focused only on tissue sold in the commercial market, seeking damages as high as $600 million. This suit, the meshing of the various operations of the two predecessor companies, and an early 1998 establishment of Fort James headquarters in Deerfield, Illinois, guaranteed a hectic—if generally promising—beginning for a new American company.

Principal Subsidiaries

James River Corporation; Fort Howard Corporation; Jamont N.V. (Belgium); Canada Cup Business; James River-Marathon, Ltd. (Canada); Hygie France; Dixie Benders Limited (U.K.; 50%); GB Papers Limited (U.K.).

Principal Operating Units

North American Consumer & Commercial Products; European Consumer Products; Packaging; Communications Papers.

Further Reading

Berman, Phyllis, ''A Sweetheart of a Deal,'' *Forbes,* September 3, 1990, pp. 39–40.

Carpenter, Kimberley, and John P. Tarpey, ''A Southern Papermaker's Yankee Campaign,'' *Business Week,* October 14, 1985.

Cox, Jacqueline, ''James River Chief Cited for Paper Industry Efforts,'' *Paper Trade Journal,* December 15, 1981.

Ferguson, Kelly H., ''James River Corp.: Refocus, Redefine, Restructure,'' *Pulp & Paper,* November 1994, pp. 36–37.

Guyon, Janet, ''A Joint-Venture Papermaker Casts Net Across Europe: James River's Jamont Pins Ambitions on Its 13 Companies Across 10 Nations,'' *Wall Street Journal,* December 7, 1992, p. B4.

James River Corporation: Two Decades of Growth, Richmond, Va.: James River Corporation of Virginia, [1989].

Kimelman, John, ''River of No Returns,'' *Financial World,* June 8, 1993, pp. 49–50.

Lipin, Steven, ''James River, Fort Howard in Merger Pact,'' *Wall Street Journal,* May 5, 1997, pp. A3, A6.

Novack, Janet, '' 'We Make Dozens of Mistakes, But They're All Little,' '' *Forbes,* November 28, 1988, p. 186.

Smith, Kenneth E., ''*P&P* Interview: James River Leaders Plan for Continued Strong Growth,'' *Pulp & Paper,* January 1984.

Welsh, Jonathan, ''Florida Suit Accuses Several Companies of Conspiring to Fix Toilet-Paper Prices,'' *Wall Street Journal,* May 14, 1997, p. B11.

—David Isaacson
—updated by David E. Salamie

FRENCH FRAGRANCES, INC.

French Fragrances, Inc.

14100 Northwest 60th Avenue
Miami Lakes, Florida 33014
U.S.A.
(305) 818-8000
Fax: (305) 556-8392
Web site: http://www.frenchfragrances.com

Public Company
Incorporated: 1960 as Suave Shoe Corporation
Employees: 170
Sales: $140.5 million (1996)
Stock Exchanges: NASDAQ
SICs: 2844 Toilet Preparations

French Fragrances, Inc. manufactures and markets fragrances and other scented cosmetic products for men and women. The company's product offerings include the brand names Geoffrey Beene, Halston, Benetton, Elancyl, Faconnable, Ombre Rose, Lapidus, Balenciaga, Chevignon, and Talisman. Although the Halston and Geoffrey Beene fragrance products are sold mainly at high-quality department stores, the majority of French Fragrances' products are sold through mass marketing channels such as Wal-Mart, Kmart, T.J. Maxx, and Target. The company also owns nearly one-half of another fragrance distributor, Fine Fragrances.

The Early Years as Suave Shoe Corporation

Although French Fragrances, Inc. was founded as a manufacturer of fragrance and cosmetics products in 1992, the company can actually trace its beginnings back to 1960. At that time, two Cuban refugees began an unbranded shoe-making business called Suave Shoe Corporation. The enterprise was riddled with numerous problems in its early years, however, and labor strikes caused the shoe factories to close down and threatened to put Suave out of business. Also problematic was the rapid pace at which Suave's owners attempted to expand the company through acquisitions, which served to erode much of its early potential for profit.

Throughout the 1970s and early 1980s, Suave Shoe purchased Oriental Trading Corp., Shoe Supply, Inc., Allied Shoe Corp., Cabrera Vulcan Shoe Corp., Universal Shoes, Inc., Siboney Shoe Corp., Carol's Shoe Corp., American Knitting Mills of Miami, Inc., and Bari Shoes, Inc. The company soon found that it had overextended itself, however, and began selling off some of its holdings in 1984. The first to go was American Knitting Mills of Miami, Inc., which was the division having the least to do with Suave's operations. Next, Suave sold Bari Shoes, Inc. in 1986. Four years later the company decided to sell its entire Shoe Import Division, which consisted mainly of Oriental Trading Corp. The struggling division was sold to Oriental Acquisition Corp. for $7.5 million and the assumption of most of the liabilities involved in that division.

Even after the divestiture of the company's most problematic divisions, the remainder of Suave Shoe Corporation was still in financial trouble. The year 1989 had seen the company lose $4.3 million on sales of $21.3 million, and the future did not look much brighter. Increased competition from foreign shoe manufacturers was beginning to affect the company's sales adversely and, consequently, its potential to reap a profit. After a failed attempt at restructuring its operations, Suave Shoe decided to discontinue most of its manufacturing activity in late 1994.

Suave Shoe Teams Up with French Fragrances in 1995

Meanwhile, French Fragrances, Inc. had been formed in 1992 as a spinoff of National Trading Manufacturing, Inc. National Trading was founded in 1953 as a manufacturer of souvenirs, jewelry, and perfumes. The company came to be controlled by Rafael Kravec in 1981. In 1992 the perfume division was successful enough to function on its own as a privately held enterprise, and thus French Fragrances was formed to continue developing and manufacturing perfumes, colognes, and other scented cosmetic products. After its formation, Kravec became the company's first president and chief executive officer.

In early 1995 one of the members of French Fragrances' board of directors who had previously served on Suave Shoe's

Company Perspectives:

The Company's objective is to maintain and enhance its position as a leading distributor of prestige fragrance and related cosmetic products.

board of directors introduced the two entities. Suave Shoe Corporation, after discontinuing its shoe manufacturing operations, was actively searching for a buyer for its manufacturing facility. French Fragrances, on the other hand, was in the market to purchase a larger facility for its distribution operations. Furthermore, French Fragrances had been exploring the possibility of going public to fund further growth. The two companies met for negotiations and began to hammer out a deal that entailed merging the assets of French Fragrances into those of Suave Shoe. The deal, essentially, was to be a reverse takeover of Suave Shoe, to push French Fragrances into the public realm.

The merger was completed in November 1995, with the new company retaining the name French Fragrances, Inc. A total of 20 percent of the new company's equity went to Suave Shoe's shareholders, with the remaining 80 percent going to shareholders of French Fragrances. J.W. Nevil Thomas, who had served as French Fragrances' chairman of the board prior to the merger, remained in the same capacity following the merger. Similarly, E. Scott Beattie remained as French Fragrances' vice-chairman and assistant secretary, and Rafael Kravec continued to serve as the company's president and CEO.

After the completion of the merger agreement, French Fragrances engaged solely in the business of developing, manufacturing, marketing, and distributing perfume, cologne, and other scented cosmetics products. All shoe manufacturing operations were ceased prior to the merger and have never been reinstated.

French Fragrances' Product Offerings

Traditionally, the fragrance industry has been divided into prestige products that are distributed through department stores and specialty stores and mass market products that are distributed through drug store chains and discount retailers. Manufacturers of prestige fragrances typically restrict the distribution of their products, to ensure that their items are marketed in high-profile, quality retail settings. This practice helps maintain the reputation of and demand for such products. Mass market fragrance products, on the other hand, are distributed throughout the discount retail arena to stores such as Walgreen's, Target, Wal-Mart, Kmart, Eckerd, T.J. Maxx, and Marshall's.

French Fragrances deals in both realms of the fragrance market, offering a total of more than 1,700 individual brand name items to its retail customers in both settings. The company distributes its prestige products to more than 300 retail customer accounts, which equal a total of more than 3,000 store locations throughout the country. In addition, mass market products are also distributed to more than 900 mass merchant accounts, which equal a total of more than 20,000 store locations throughout the country.

French Fragrances either manufactures or has obtained distribution rights to the following fragrance lines: Halston, which includes the brands Halston, Catalyst, 1–12, and Z–14; Geoffrey Beene, which includes the brands Grey Flannel, Bowling Green, and Chance; Cofci, which includes the brands Salvador Dali, Laguna, Dalissime, Cafe, Taxi, and Watt; Benetton, which includes the brands Colors of Benetton and Tribu; and Versace, which includes the brands Gianni Versace, Signature, V'E, L'Homme, Versus, and Jeans. The company also distributes the Galenic Elancyl skin care products made by Pierre Fabre throughout the United States on an exclusive basis. Other products that French Fragrances deals with are Faconnable, Ombre Rose, Lapidus, Balenciaga, Chevignon, and Talisman.

The End of the Century and Beyond

With an impressive array of product offerings under its umbrella and a large scope of distribution channels to work with, French Fragrances posted 1995 sales of $88.0 million and achieved a net income of $3.0 million. The company then began to focus on methods for becoming more efficient in its operations. One major change was the company's heavy investment in updated technology. Implemented near the end of the 1990s was new electronic data interchange software from American Software. The software solution package included integrated accounting, order processing, and scheduling applications. One of the new system's greatest advantages was that it allowed French Fragrances' retailers to order products electronically and then custom-schedule delivery so as to avoid having excess inventory on hand.

In 1996 the company announced plans to initiate a secondary offering of its stock as a means of raising capital to continue its expansion efforts. The following three main business strategies were identified by the company: (1) to acquire and maintain control of additional fragrance brands, (2) to further expand direct distribution, and (3) to provide value-added services.

With respect to the first of the three objectives listed above, French Fragrances noted the benefits that it had gained as a result of either its brand ownership or exclusive distribution rights to different fragrances in the past. Although the company made clear its support of the practice of owning and/or controlling fragrance lines, by 1997 it had made no plans to acquire the rights to any more products and also was not actively searching for prospects.

The company had, however, announced plans to expand its distribution capabilities. It began attempting to increase the number and scope of retailers to which it shipped products, in addition to developing marketing programs that would better serve its retail customers' needs. To add value to the products it shipped to retailers, French Fragrances began to include in-store displays and planograms for the layout of each shipment of fragrance product to a store. The hope was that French Fragrances would make itself so easy to work with that more retailers would jump on the bandwagon and do business with the company.

In 1997 French Fragrances was ranked number 41 on *Business Week*'s list of ''100 Hot Growth Companies.'' The recognition helped increase awareness of French Fragrances for manufacturers looking for someone to distribute their product. According to French Fragrances' CFO William Mueller in the July 1997 issue of The *South Florida Business Journal,* ''Manufacturers who might want to break into the U.S. mass market now know who we are. And the more manufacturers we get, the more important we are to the mass market. It's a snowball effect.'' The accolades came to the company following its record sales in 1996 of $140.5 million.

As the end of the century drew near, French Fragrances was moving to position itself for continued growth and profitability. After just five years of operating on its own and after just a couple years as a public entity, French Fragrances had become a leading manufacturer and distributor of fragrance products in the United States. More than 95 percent of its business was occurring domestically, in a market that accounted for approximately half of the worldwide fragrance industry sales. To expand its distribution successfully, it appeared that French Fragrances would need to tackle the international market in the years ahead.

Principal Subsidiaries

Fine Fragrances (approx. 50%); Florida Coating Industries, Inc.; GB Parfums, Inc.; Suave Holding Corp.

Further Reading

''Company in a Hurry,'' *Financial World,* June 15, 1981, p. 57.

''French Expects to Raise $30M in 2nd Offering,'' *Women's Wear Daily,* July 1, 1996, p. 11.

Matas, Alina, ''Merger Will Put Shoe-maker in Perfume Business,'' *Miami Herald,* May 24, 1995.

Mirones, Pedro, ''Suave Shoe Announces Restructuring of Operations,'' *Business Wire,* September 9, 1994.

''Suave Shoe Getting a French Accent,'' *Women's Wear Daily,* May 26, 1995, p. 4.

Westlund, Richard, ''South Florida Firms Keep on Growing—Right on to *Business Week's* Hot 100 Explosive Growth for Three Very Different Companies Grabs Magazine's Attention,'' *South Florida Business Journal,* July 1997, p. 6.

—Laura E. Whiteley

Frigidaire Home Products

6000 Perimeter Drive
Dublin, Ohio 43107
U.S.A.
(614) 792-4100
Fax: (614) 792-4776
Web site: http://www.frigidaire.com

Wholly Owned Subsidiary of Aktiebolaget Electrolux
Incorporated: 1916 as Guardian Refrigerator Company
Employees: 1,428
Sales: $3.5 billion (1996 est.)
SICs: 3630 Household Appliances; 3524 Lawn & Garden Equipment

Celebrating its 80th anniversary in 1996, Frigidaire Home Products ranks third among America's manufacturers of "white goods" or major household appliances. In the 1990s, the company offered a complete line of branded appliances, including refrigerators, freezers, washers, dryers, microwaves, air conditioners, gas and electric stoves, and dishwashers. For many decades, Frigidaire was owned and operated as a division of automobile giant General Motors Corporation. Throughout its first half-century in business, Frigidaire earned renown as one of the appliance industry's most innovative companies. But by the late 1970s, cutthroat pricing had pushed the GM division into the red. Acquired by White Consolidated Industries (WCI) in 1979, Frigidaire was subsumed under the WCI Major Appliances Group and existed primarily as a brand in the parent's diverse lineup.

The Frigidaire corporate entity was revived after 1986, when WCI became a subsidiary of Sweden's AB Electrolux. A 1991 reorganization brought all of the brands in WCI's Major Appliance Group under the aegis of Frigidaire Co. Brands offered by the reborn subsidiary included White-Westinghouse, Kelvinator, and Gibson. Under Electrolux, Frigidaire was repositioned as an upscale brand. Its Gallery and Gallery Professional lines featured European styling and high-performance features.

Origins in the Early 20th Century

Frigidaire's history reaches back to the earliest days of the household refrigerator. The company was founded in 1916, when engineer Alfred Mellowes and a group of investors formed the Guardian Refrigerator Company in Fort Wayne, Indiana. Just a year earlier, Mellowes had constructed the first true refrigerator, as opposed to an ice box with a refrigeration unit, by attaching an electric refrigeration system to a wooden cabinet. Mellowes set up a small factory and started hand-assembling the appliances, but it was very slow going with workers taking over a week to make each refrigerator. Within less than two years, the company had lost over $30,000 and was headed for bankruptcy.

Recognizing the efficacy of Mellowes' concept, General Motors Corp. president, William C. Durant, personally acquired Guardian and renamed the company and its products "Frigidaire." In 1919 Durant sold the business to General Motors, moved the operation to Detroit and converted its manufacturing process to mass production. Though productivity increased dramatically, the $775, nine-cubic-foot refrigerators were still priced out of the reach of most consumers.

Frigidaire came into its own after 1921, when General Motors transferred the division to its Delco Light subsidiary in Dayton, Ohio. With guidance from electrical engineer and Delco president Charles F. Kettering, Frigidaire made rapid progress. Incremental innovations over the first half of the decade transformed the wooden food cabinet into a porcelain-coated, insulated, steel "fridge" with temperature controls. Frigidaire also diversified its product line with a number of cooling appliances, especially in the commercial arena. Over the course of the decade the company introduced ice-cream cabinets, refrigerated soda fountains, milk coolers, drinking fountains, room air conditioners, and display freezers for groceries.

The implementation of efficient manufacturing processes brought the price of a Frigidaire refrigerator down to $468 per unit by 1926. Having surpassed the sales revenues of Delco Light, the refrigerator division was made a subsidiary in its own right in 1926, with Elmer G. Biechler at the helm as general manager. Technological innovations and production efficien-

Company Perspectives:

At Frigidaire, we believe appliance design isn't just about the product; it's about you, the consumer. It's about solving your time and space problems. Helping you achieve the look you want. And eliminating some of the inconveniences you deal with on a daily basis.

The result is a family of appliances engineered to meet and exceed your expectations. Beautiful sculpted lines. Affordable stainless steel. Features so intuitive they'll surprise you.

cies allowed Frigidaire to sell more than one million refrigerators from 1919 to 1929.

Frigidaire's growth continued to accelerate in the 1930s in spite of the Great Depression. Total refrigerator production topped two and a half million by 1932 and climbed to over six million by 1941. Frigidaire also made its first diversifications outside of its core refrigeration niche during the late 1930s, introducing a range, oven, water heater, clothes washer, and clothes dryer before the decade was out. On the eve of World War II, Frigidaire boasted the world's largest refrigerator plant and over 20,000 employees in the United States and abroad.

Frigidaire Goes to War: The 1940s

Like so many other ''nonessential'' industries, appliance makers were drafted into military production during World War II. Though Frigidaire continued to produce refrigerators until April 1942, the company won its first military contract in September 1940, even before the United States was officially involved in the war. Frigidaire made a wide variety of aircraft parts and assemblies, including propellers, gas tanks, artillery, and bomb hangars. Over the course of the global conflict, the company produced more than 200,000 Browning Machine Guns. The company also put out tank assemblies and automotive engine parts.

Along with nine of its competitors, Frigidaire got a headstart on the postwar market in 1943, when it was granted permission to recommence refrigerator production. The company completed its first household refrigerator in July 1945, and by June 1949 had returned production to one million units per year.

Frigidaire continued to set the pace for appliance industry innovation in the 1950s, introducing automatic ice-makers and auto-defrost refrigerators in 1952 and a frost-free model in 1958. The company also helped make appliance design an important factor in the industry, launching color-matched groupings of appliances in 1954 and the ''Sheer Look,'' a streamlined design, in 1956.

Acquisition by WCI in 1979

All segments of the appliance industry came under assault from increasing imports in the decades following World War II, engendering heavy price cutting among domestic manufacturers. Led by Edward Reddig, White Consolidated Industries was forged in this competitive atmosphere, expanding from a tiny sewing machine manufacturer into one of America's leading appliance manufacturers. In 1960, Reddig began amassing a coterie of big name appliance manufacturers that had fallen on hard times, including Kelvinator, Westinghouse, and Philco. WCI targeted Frigidaire in the late 1970s. Having lost an estimated $40 million on sales of $450 million in 1978, GM sold Frigidaire to WCI for about $120 million in 1979.

Under its new owners, Frigidaire shifted from an emphasis on industry-leading innovation to the pursuit of manufacturing efficiency. WCI transformed its losing acquisitions into moneymakers by slashing both administrative and production ranks, trimming product lines to the biggest sellers, and implementing what *Business Week* called ''Scrooge-like'' cost controls. Perhaps most damaging to the long-term performance of Frigidaire and the other brands in WCI's stable was the eradication of research and development, a function that had fueled the company's many industry ''firsts.'' Furthermore, instead of emphasizing cutting-edge design, Frigidaire was promoted as a reliable brand with the slogan ''Here today, here tomorrow.''

WCI was itself acquired by Sweden's AB Electrolux in 1986 as part of a two decade, round-the-world acquisition spree that added more than 300 companies to the Electrolux family and made it one of the world's largest appliance manufacturers.

Upscale Positioning in the 1990s

After more than a decade in the shadow of WCI, Frigidaire regained the spotlight in 1991, when parent Electrolux supplanted the unimaginative WCI identity with Frigidaire, making the Ohio-based company the leader of a family of brands that included Tappan, Gibson, Kelvinator, White-Westinghouse, and Euroflair. Under the direction of longtime Electrolux executive Hans G. Backman Frigidaire got a brand makeover as well, including a new logo (a stylized crown with five peaks for the five lead brands), a new slogan (''Frigidaire Company . . . creating a better tomorrow!''), and an upscale positioning for the Frigidaire brand. Instead of competing with lowest-common-denominator imports on price, the new parent hoped to differentiate Frigidaire as a highly desirable brand.

With a target of doubling its U.S. market share by the turn of the 20th century, Frigidaire teamed with another Electrolux subsidiary, Italy's Zanussi, to adapt European design and performance features to its high-end offerings for the U.S. market. The 1993 launch of the UltraStyle line, featuring over 100 coordinated, energy-efficient appliances, was the culmination of a five-year, $.5 billion redesign effort. Just two years later, Frigidaire boosted its advertising budget to record levels to support the introduction of its Gallery and Gallery Professional lines of commercial-style appliances. Noise and CFC reduction were also important concerns. Electrolux didn't neglect operations, either, plowing over $650 million into manufacturing improvements from 1986 to 1996. The company also consolidated its office structure at Dublin, Ohio and laid off hundreds of workers in 1993.

Frigidaire's new designs won a number of awards in the mid-1990s. Its front-load Tumble Action Washer, which used 40 percent less water than conventional American top-load models, earned honors from *Home Magazine* and *Today's Homeowner*. The latter magazine also named Frigidaire's Gallery Precision Wash Dishwasher one of the Best New Products of 1997. This quiet new model used less water and detergent than its predecessors.

Electrolux merged Frigidaire with its two outdoor appliance businesses—Poulan/Weed Eater and American Yard Products—to form Frigidaire Home Products in 1997. This consolidation was seen as a way of increasing distribution efficiencies since all three businesses had retail outlets in common. Electrolux also hoped that it would be able to consolidate similar manufacturing functions among the company's subsidiaries.

Though some observers felt that there was a danger of cannibalization among the company's WCI-created family of brands, Frigidaire appeared to be devoted to its multi-brand strategy. Tappan, which became a part of the Frigidaire group after the Electrolux acquisition, was strong in cooking appliances, White-Westinghouse was positioned as a value line, Gibson was sold to independent retailers through distributors, and Kelvinator was targeted at first-time appliance buyers. All the brands were considered ''step-up'' models leading eventually to the flagship Frigidaire and its upscale lines. Frigidaire was the only brand to merit consumer advertising.

In spite of its efforts at repositioning the brand, Frigidaire remained something of a disappointment to Electrolux through the early 1990s. Even after several major reorganizations, the U.S. appliance-maker continued to exert a negative influence on the parent company's bottom line. Though it ranked third in its home market, Frigidaire was a distant competitor to industry leaders General Electric Co.'s Appliances division and Whirlpool Corp., each of which boasted double the volume of their Ohio-based rival. At the same time, fourth-ranking Maytag was gunning for Frigidaire's market share. The parent company continued to express confidence in Frigidaire's ability to effect a turnaround, but noted that the U.S. subsidiary's early 1990s performance was ''weak.''

Further Reading

''All Systems Go,'' *Appliance Manufacturer*, October 1991, pp. 6F–8F.

Beatty, Gerry, ''Frigidaire Gets Praise from Parent,'' *HFN The Weekly Newspaper for the Home Furnishing Network*, November 7, 1994, p. 62.

——, ''Frigidaire's System Makes Its Brands Work Together,'' *HFN The Weekly Newspaper for the Home Furnishing Network*, January 22, 1996, pp. 88–89.

——,''Major Move: Frigidaire Firms Up Programs to Challenge for Market Leadership,'' *HFN The Weekly Newspaper for the Home Furnishing Network*, February 15, 1993, pp. 82–84.

——, ''Stretching a Name; Electrolux Dubs Home Unit 'Frigidaire,' '' *HFN The Weekly Newspaper for the Home Furnishing Network*, February 3, 1997, pp. 67–68.

Cayer, Shirley, '' 'White Goods' Wars—Continued,'' *Purchasing*, May 7, 1992, pp. 69–72.

Fallon, James, ''AB Electrolux: Frigidaire Still Lags,'' *HFN The Weekly Newspaper for the Home Furnishing Network*, November 11, 1996, p. 84.

——, ''Electrolux: Merger Is a First Step,'' *HFN The Weekly Newspaper for the Home Furnishing Network*, December 30, 1996, p. 73.

''Frigidaire's Massive Gallery Ad Campaign,'' *HFN The Weekly Newspaper for the Home Furnishing Network*, February 6, 1995, pp. 66–67.

''Frigidaire Realignment a Wrap,'' *HFN The Weekly Newspaper for the Home Furnishing Network*, August 9, 1993, p. 80.

GM Frigidaire at War, Dayton, Ohio: Frigidaire Division, General Motors Corp., ca. 1944.

''Manufacturing Strategy Solidified,'' *Appliance Manufacturer*, October 1991, pp. 28F–33F.

''Now: Market Driven,'' *Appliance Manufacturer*, October 1991, pp. 14F–15F.

Remich, Norman C., Jr., ''Flair for Frigidaire,'' *Appliance Manufacturer*, August 1997, p. 94.

''Striving for Service Superiority,'' *Appliance Manufacturer*, October 1991, p. 18F.

''White Consolidated's New Appliance Punch,'' *Business Week*, May 7, 1979, pp. 94–98.

—April Dougal Gasbarre

Frontier Airlines, Inc.

12015 East 46th Ave.
Denver, Colorado 80239-3116
U.S.A.
(303) 371-7400
Fax: (303) 371-9669
Web site: http://www.flyfrontier.com

Public Company
Incorporated: 1946 as Monarch Air Lines
Employees: 800
Sales: $70.4 million (1996)
Stock Exchanges: NASDAQ
SICs: 4512 Air Transportation, Scheduled

Frontier Airlines, Inc. was reborn in 1993, borrowing the name of the carrier that had previously served the Rockies and Midwest for nearly 50 years. The name was not merely a superficial brand: several of the new Frontier's executives and 75 percent of its starting work force had been associated with the original carrier. Frontier operated about a dozen 737s, competing as a low-fare carrier on several high-volume routes.

A Flock of Postwar Start-Ups

A merger of three small postwar carriers created the original Frontier Airlines on June 1, 1950. All three flew war surplus Douglas DC-3s (known as C-47s in the U.S. military) in their struggle to eke a living carrying whatever mail and passengers they could across the western sky. Monarch Air Lines began flying out of Denver in 1947. Future partner Challenger Airlines began serving Denver from its Salt Lake City base the next year, when the last of the three, Arizona Airways, began its flights to the Mexican border. Frontier's territory spanned 40 cities along the Rocky Mountains from Montana to the Mexican border. Challenger Airlines, which would merge with Frontier in 1967, was of the same generation, beginning operations in 1949. Monarch supplied Frontier's first president, Hal S. Darr.

Rapid Growth in the 1960s

Mines, dams, and national parks, and other developments diverted increasing streams of passengers through Frontier Airlines. By 1960, more than 30 new cities had been added, extending its routes east into the Dakotas and Missouri.

New low-cost fare plans spurred still more passengers to fly Frontier in the 1960s, making it the country's fastest growing regional carrier. The Vacationland Fare effectively gave passengers a 30-day pass for $100. The Standby Plan offered last-minute available seats for half price.

The company began flying the Convair 340, a popular replacement for the smaller DC-3, in 1959. These were replaced by still larger, faster Convair 580 turbojet aircraft within a few years. As impressive as the Convair 580 was, the five Boeing 727-100 airliners Frontier bought in 1965 for $55 million propelled the company into the age of modern jet travel. General Tire and Rubber Company bought a controlling interest in the airline through its subsidiary RKO General, Inc. The company's 1966 revenues were $1.74 million, resulting in its highest ever profits. Frontier's fleet included 20 planes, two of them 727s.

The company proved continuously successful in winning new routes from the Civil Aeronautics Board. After its merger with Fort Worth's Central Airlines in October 1967, Frontier served 114 cities with 56 planes.

A Bit of Turbulence Entering the 1970s

The entry into Kansas City and St. Louis brought Frontier into direct competition—vigorous competition—with Trans World Airlines. In 1969, Frontier replaced its first five 727s with Boeing 737s. It also opened its combination headquarters and maintenance center in Denver. In spite of the optimistic additions, the airline failed to turn a profit in 1970. Al Feldman had assumed the company's leadership in 1971, and instituted a quick turnaround.

Frontier continued to offer new routes and set new records, serving its highest number of paying passengers in 1973 while

Company Perspectives:

Frontier Airlines, Inc. is a low-fare, full-service airline based in Denver, Colorado. Principally serving markets abandoned by Continental Airlines during that carrier's downsizing of its Denver hub in 1993 and 1994, the Company currently operates routes linking its Denver hub to 14 cities in 11 states covering the western two-thirds of the United States. The Company's current route system extends from Denver to Los Angeles, San Diego and San Francisco, California; Chicago and Bloomington/Normal, Illinois; Seattle/Tacoma, Washington; Las Vegas, Nevada; Phoenix, Arizona; St. Louis, Missouri; Minneapolis/St. Paul, Minnesota; Salt Lake City, Utah; Omaha, Nebraska; Albuquerque, New Mexico; and El Paso, Texas. At present, the Company utilizes four gates at Denver International Airport for approximately 54 daily flight departures and arrivals.

receiving fewer complaints than any other regional airline. Its first international flight landed in Winnipeg in 1974. Four years later, Frontier crossed the border into Mexico.

A Dip in the 1980s

Although fuel costs rose and traffic fell, 1980 gave Frontier its highest profit to date: $23.2 million. The company had grown to employ 5,800 people and operated 60 aircraft, serving 86 cities. In 1982, the company phased out its turboprops and added the state-of-the-art McDonnell-Douglas MD-80. Reflecting its enormous strides, the company was reorganized, becoming a subsidiary of Frontier Holdings, Inc. on May 6, 1982.

A blizzard closed the Denver airport for two days around Christmas 1982, helping to smother the company's profits. After a terrific decade, Frontier lost about $45 million the next two years, placing the company in its most serious crisis.

After proposals to sell the company's shares to its employees and a bid by corporate raider Frank Lorenzo, People Express Airlines bought it in 1985. However, Frontier continued to falter and filed for bankruptcy in 1986. Its assets were sold off and many of its routes were taken over by Lorenzo's Continental Airlines.

The 1990s: A New Frontier

A $7.6 million initial public offering in May plus other venture capital funded the launch of a new Denver-based carrier in 1993. Unlike another new airline which had purchased the venerable name of a bankrupt carrier, Pan Am, at an auction, the new Frontier bore real resemblance to its former self. Its first CEO, Hank Lund, had been an executive at the original airline, and seven other former executives would join him. Samuel D. Addoms would become Frontier's CEO in January 1995. In addition, after digesting 5,000 resumes, the company filled 150 of 200 available slots with former Frontier employees.

On July 5, 1994, the reborn airline began flying between Denver and a handful of cities in North Dakota. Soon airports in Montana, Nebraska, New Mexico, Nevada, and Texas again began receiving requests to land from jets with a name they had not heard in several years. Ironically, the carrier's old rival, Continental, helped provide space for Frontier when it scaled back its operations at the new $4 billion Denver International Airport. Frontier's rebirth had originally been conceived as a charter operation.

The company's early strategy paralleled that of the original: providing flights on underserved routes rather than striving for the low-prices of some of its contemporaries. However, just as with the original, price competition in major markets became part of Frontier's game plan.

United Airlines, which had more than a 70 percent market share at Denver International, refused to use the company for feeder flights. (United's employees had killed its bid for the old Frontier in the mid-1980s, protesting the absorption of Frontier employees.) Frontier's planes remained less than half full until late in 1995 when, like its predecessor, it began competing on a price basis in major markets. In fact, operations in its original eight markets were suspended so the planes could be deployed on higher volume routes. Eventually, Frontier would reach cooperative agreements with 65 airlines.

In September 1995, a secondary public offering brought in $7.3 million of needed capital. Additional stock worth $3 million had been sold in May.

Frontier's fleet was comprised of several used Boeing 737s, one of the industry's most reliable and most sought-after. The company's expansion plans were limited by the availability of these planes. Across the tail sections were plastered photographs of western wildlife, such as grazing bison, howling timberwolves, or fox kits. In 1996, Frontier opened a facility in Denver which allowed it to handle its own routine maintenance.

In 1997, Frontier accused ''monopolist'' United Airlines of dumping—intentionally operating a large number of flights in order to gain market share—and other antitrust violations. These were prompted, according to Frontier, by the company's second profitable quarter.

As a low-price Colorado airline, Western Pacific was often compared with the new Frontier. They both operated the Boeing 737; WestPac, based 100 miles south of Denver at Colorado Springs, operated 19, which would have made a combined fleet of 34 aircraft.

In June 1997, the two agreed to merge. However, the merger was called off at the end of September. Differences in culture and operating philosophy were cited as the prime factors. The next week, WestPac announced it was seeking Chapter 11 bankruptcy protection but planned to remain in the air. In spite of losses earlier in the year, Frontier seemed to be faring better, posting increases in summer traffic.

Besides meeting its ever-present needs for capital, future challenges for Frontier included retrofitting its fleet with hush kits (at $2 million per plane) to meet federal noise regulations; one runway at Denver International had already been closed to certain of its aircraft due to the airport's noise agreement with the city of Denver.

Although the reincarnated Frontier Airlines seemed to possess just a shadow of the original Frontier's might, Monarch Air Lines was small and struggling in its first few years as well. If the company could survive its confrontation with the world's largest airline, who knew what heights the new phoenix would reach?

Further Reading

''Airline Deregulation Poses Policy Puzzle,'' *Denver Business Journal,* February 3, 1997.

''Bandits at Nine O'Clock: Despite a Recent Upturn in the Fortunes of America's Big Airlines, the Country's Skies Still Favour the Small and Nimble,'' *Economist,* February 17, 1996.

Dempsey, Paul Stephen, ''Fighting Modern-Day Robber Barons,'' *Denver Business Journal,* January 27, 1997.

Dubroff, Henry, ''United and the Upstarts Begin Round Two,'' *Denver Business Journal,* November 18, 1996.

''Frontier Set to Double Fleet Size with 737s,'' *Airfinance Journal,* September 1996, p. 17.

''Give Frontier Execs Credit for Air Merger,'' *Denver Business Journal,* July 14, 1997.

''Justice Department Reviews Claims of Airlines' Price Squeeze,'' *Los Angeles Times,* February 12, 1997, p. D1.

Lieber, Ronald B., ''Dead Airline Names Take Off Again,'' *Fortune,* March 4, 1996.

Moorman, Robert W., ''The 'New' New Frontier,'' *Air Transport World,* August 1996, pp. 86–87.

Rosato, Donna, ''Western Pacific Dumps Frontier,'' *USA Today,* September 30, 1997, p. 12B.

Sanders, Michael J. ''Strategic Use of Technology: A Blueprint for Implementation,'' *Journal of Information Management,* Spring 1987, pp. 17–26.

Scott, William B., ''Western Pacific, Frontier Merger Raises Stakes at Denver Hub,'' *Aviation Week and Space Technology,* July 7, 1997, p. 52.

''Start-Ups Fly into Financial Head Wind,'' *USA Today,* February 11, 1996.

Svaldi, Aldo, ''Delta Stalls WestPac's Name Hunt,'' *Denver Business Journal,* July 21, 1997.

Tammerlin, Drummond, ''Losing Altitude: Discount Airlines Are Struggling, Even As the Major Carriers Raise Fares,'' *Time,* July 14, 1997.

Thurston, Scott, ''ValuJet, Frontier Cry Foul at Big Airlines' Pricing Tactics,'' *Atlanta Journal and Constitution,* February 2, 1997, p. F5.

Williamson, Richard, ''Western Pacific to Keep Flying,'' *Rocky Mountain News,* October 7, 1997.

—Frederick C. Ingram

G-III Apparel Group, Ltd.

345 West 37th Street
New York, New York 10018
U.S.A.
(212) 629-8830
Fax: (212) 967-1487

Public Company
Incorporated: 1974 as G-III Leather Fashions, Inc.
Employees: 239
Sales: $117.7 (1997)
Stock Exchanges: NASDAQ
SICs: 2386 Leather & Sheep-Lined Clothing; 5136 Men's & Boys' Clothing & Furnishings; 5137 Women's, Children's & Infants' Clothing & Accessories; 5699 Miscellaneous Apparel & Accessory Stores

G-III Apparel Group, Ltd. designs, manufactures, imports, and markets an extensive range of leather and non-leather apparel, including coats, jackets, pants, skirts, and other sportswear items for both men and women. Moderately priced women's leather apparel represented about one-third of its sales in 1996. The company had about 2,300 customers, including nationwide chains of department and specialty retail stores, price clubs, and individual specialty boutiques. Virtually all of its products were being manufactured by independent contractors in the Far East and India.

Private Company, 1956–89

Aron Goldfarb was running a leather apparel business, opened in 1956 in New York City's garment district, that specialized in men's bomber jackets when his 22-year-old son Morris joined the company in 1972. Morris Goldfarb augmented the business (which was reorganized in 1974 as G-III Leather Fashions, Inc.) with overseas production facilities, selling moderately priced women's leather coats and jackets under the G-III label. The company expanded its product lines and began selling higher priced, more fashion-oriented women's leather apparel under the Siena label in 1981. The Siena line remained a minor segment of the company's overall business, however.

By 1988 G-III was among the largest, if not the largest, independent importer and wholesaler of leather apparel in the United States. The company had net income of $727,000 on net sales of $30.3 million in fiscal 1987 (the year ended July 31, 1987) and net income of $2.7 million on net sales of $50 million in fiscal 1988. G-III was growing rapidly, but like most leatherwear companies, it was undercapitalized. The firm attracted the interest of Lyle Berman, a Minnesota-based entrepreneur who had organized Ante Corp. as a venture capital firm and knew the Goldfarbs personally. Like them, Berman had operated a family-owned leather apparel business, although on a retail level.

Berman was not shy about what he could offer the Goldfarbs, in addition to $1.5 million in capital. "The biggest thing is that they were getting Lyle Berman," he told a reporter in 1990. "In the retail leather industry, I'm considered to be a driving force. After all, my company became the biggest retailer of leather apparel in the United States. I ran it from one store to 200. . . . I can look at Morris and say, 'Morris, without Lyle Berman you could have gone public, but I know in my heart you wouldn't have. You would have procrastinated.' " Berman added that G-III's expertise was primarily in women's wear, while his was in men's wear, an area in which G-III wanted a larger presence.

An agreement was reached in August 1989 by which Ante acquired G-III in an exchange of stock. Ante shareholders received 15 percent of the outstanding common stock in the merged entity, which took the name G-III Apparel Group, Ltd. The Goldfarbs remained in charge of management, and Berman became a director. G-III earned an impressive $9.5 million on net sales of $98.8 million in fiscal 1989. In December 1989, G-III, now publicly held because of the merger, collected about $18 million, and Aron Goldfarb another $6 million, in a secondary offering that marketed nearly one-third of the outstanding common stock at $13 a share. Following the offering, some 39 percent of the stock was owned by Morris Goldfarb and 18 percent by Aron Goldfarb.

Broadening Its Base, 1990–94

G-III began marketing higher priced women's leather apparel under the Cayenne as well as Siena label in 1988 and introduced a line of men's leather apparel, primarily consisting of jackets and coats sold under the G-III label, in the same year. In 1990 it formed a textile division to design, import, and market a moderately priced line of women's textile outerwear and sportswear under the J.L. Colebrook label. The company replaced the Cayenne label with the Siena Studio label for its midpriced line of women's leather apparel during 1991 and introduced a men's textile apparel line in the fall of 1992. To a lesser extent it also sold leather apparel under private retail labels.

G-III's moderately priced apparel for women typically retailed in 1990 at from $40 for sportswear items to $300 for coats. The men's wear line consisted of coats and jackets in the $150-to-$500 range. Moderately priced apparel for women accounted for more than 85 percent of net sales in fiscal 1989, while men's wear accounted for only five percent. G-III's goods were being sold mainly to department and specialty stores in the United States, but sales were being made also to cable television shopping networks and direct mail catalogue companies. The number of customers to whom goods were shipped increased from about 1,000 in fiscal 1989 to about 2,000 in fiscal 1990, when revenues reached $161.9 million and net income was $9.6 million. Units of The Limited accounted for 32 percent of G-III's sales in that year.

G-III opened a 13-person branch office in Seoul, South Korea at this time to act as an intermediary between the company and various Korean and Hong Kong manufacturers. Its activities did not sit well with David Winn, president of Winlet Fashions, a competitor. Winn told *Crain's New York Business,* "Morris has literally walked into my factory in Korea and taken our designs. . . . I think he has illusions of grandeur. He really wants to take over the whole market, and he's so headstrong he just might do it, whatever the cost." G-III also opened a showroom in Los Angeles and a retail store in Secaucus, New Jersey in 1990.

Leather was being touted in this period as representing "sex and status for everyone from the punk rocker to the secretary to Ivana Trump," according to a trade newspaper executive. In the 1970s the industry had been turning out unwieldy, boxlike coats and jackets in dull colors, but the product offered in 1990 was being made from animal skins that had been treated to be more supple and colorful. It could be embossed and silk-screened to achieve many looks.

During fiscal 1991 G-III's revenues fell to $142 million and its net income fell to $1.3 million. Although revenues recovered in 1992, earnings, at $3.3 million, remained well below the 1990 peak. Of $175.5 million in sales during fiscal 1992, leather accounted for 90 percent. Analysts said the company controlled about 12 percent of the women's leather market and three percent of the men's market. The G-III label accounted for 70 percent of sales in that year, private-label merchandise for 20 percent, and the fast-growing Colebrook textile division, which featured coats and jackets in a variety of fabrics that included wools, cottons, and synthetic blends, for ten percent.

Global Apparel Sourcing Ltd. was established by G-III in 1993 to act as the sourcing arm for retailers who wanted production of any type of apparel merchandising. G-III had expanded its own sourcing efforts; when the company went public in 1989, almost all of its merchandise was being produced in South Korea, but by early 1993 Korea was accounting for only half, with the balance spread to other areas, including Hong Kong and Indonesia. About 20 percent of the company's goods were being produced in the United States by independent contractors.

G-III signed a licensing agreement with NFL Properties, Inc. in 1993 for a line of leather outerwear developed as a joint venture between G-III and Washington Redskins linebacker Carl Banks. The agreement provided for the production of Team NFL licensed leather and leather/fabric-combination outerwear for Big & Tall Men. In addition, the agreement provided for the production of Team NFL licensed leather outerwear for NFL Spirit for Women and NFL Kids sizes small to extra large. All jackets were emblazoned with NFL teams and colors. A 1995 licensing agreement with Kenneth Cole Production called for G-III to produce and market three outerwear labels bearing the Kenneth Cole name in leather, high-tech nylons, rubberized fabrics, and moss microfiber. This line debuted in 1996, the year G-III also entered into an agreement with the National Hockey League to market a line of outerwear apparel with the NHL team logos.

By early 1994 G-III had opened six retail factory-outlet stores to sell in-season merchandise and overstock. It opened a new 30,000-square-foot corporate showroom on Seventh Avenue in Manhattan's garment district that year and a new women's wool coat division called Billycoat. Men's outerwear was being offered in G-III leather and J.L. Colebrook fabric lines. Leather was accounting for about two-thirds of overall company sales volume.

Also in 1994, G-III signed an agreement with the Chinese government to jointly own a leather apparel factory in northern China and market the products in that country. G-III would own 39 percent of the factory, with the Chinese government holding the remainder. The pact was expected ultimately to lead to the opening of jointly owned retail stores in China, the company said.

Declining Revenues, 1995–97

During fiscal 1994 (the year ended January 31, 1994) G-III had net income of $1.3 million on peak sales of $208.9 million. The following year was a disastrous one, with the company losing $11.7 million on net sales of $171.4 million. A share of company stock fell as low as $1.25. With many retail outlets shutting down and heavy competition from big fashion designers, G-III was suffering from a lack of brand identity or resources to establish one. Sales fell still further in fiscal 1996, to $121.7 million, but the company lost only $397,000 by reducing costs through tighter control of inventory levels and improved product sourcing.

Revenues fell still further, to $117.7 million, in fiscal 1997, but the company had net income of $3.1 million, mainly because of further economy measures, such as consolidating merchandise divisions, reducing inventory, decreasing borrowing levels, and subleasing one of its warehouses. G-III also closed three of its seven retail stores. The company's long-term debt was only $919,000 in July 1996. Morris Goldfarb held 34 percent of the common stock, Aron Goldfarb held 19 percent, and Berman held 4.8 percent.

In 1996 the company merged its G-III leather and J.L. Colebrook cloth outerwear divisions. The merger appeared to be an economy measure allowing the company to close one of its Seventh Avenue showrooms and field a single customer service team for both labels, although Morris Goldfarb said he expected no layoffs as a result of the consolidation because of the addition of Kenneth Cole and Polar Bear, a European outerwear line G-III had agreed in 1995 to distribute.

G-III formed a joint venture in 1997 with BET Holdings to produce a BET line of outerwear, sportswear, and accessories aimed at African-American and urban shoppers. BET Holdings' core business was Black Entertainment Television, a cable network offering music video shows and syndicated programs to 47 million households. Also in 1997, Goldfarb rewarded Jeanette Nostra-Katz, a veteran company executive, by vacating the presidency and promoting her to the office, although he remained chief executive officer. An industry analyst said she was impressed by Nostra-Katz's efforts to enhance product development and reduce G-III's seasonal dependence on fall and winter apparel.

In fiscal 1997 G-III had about 2,300 customers, ranging from specialty retail and department stores to smaller specialty stores, price clubs, and individual specialty boutiques. The Sam's Club and Wal-Mart divisions of Wal-Mart Stores accounted for 12.8 percent of the company's sales. Sales of moderately priced women's leather apparel accounted for about 34 percent of G-III's net sales. The G-III line of this apparel typically was selling from $30 for sportswear to $400 for coats. The higher priced Siena collection typically retailed from $300 for sportswear items to $1,000 for coats. Siena Studios, the intermediate line, ranged in price between $100 for skirts and $600 for outerwear.

Men's leather outerwear, sold under the G-III label, typically retailed between $40 and $400. Moderately priced women's textile outerwear and sportswear, sold under the Colebrook & Co. label, was retailing for between $50 and $130. Men's textile apparel, consisted of moderately priced outerwear, was retailing from $25 to $175. Women's moderately priced woolen coats and raincoats sold under the Vision label were retailing in the range of $100 to $200. The company's private-label business was described in *Crain's New York Business* as its "bread and butter" and "stronger than ever."

Substantially all of G-III's products were being manufactured by foreign independent contractors, located principally in South Korea, China, Indonesia, and, to a lesser extent, India, the Philippines, and Hong Kong. Certain products were being manufactured at a company-owned factory in Indonesia and its partially owned factory in China. A select number of garments were being manufactured for the company by independent contractors in the metropolitan New York City area. G-III was leasing a five-story building and showrooms in New York City and a warehouse and distribution facility in Secaucus, New Jersey. It also was leasing a showroom in Los Angeles and four retail outlet stores. In addition, the company maintained branch offices in Hong Kong and Seoul, South Korea.

Principal Subsidiaries

G-III Apparel Manufacturing, Inc.; G-III Hong Kong Ltd. (Hong Kong); G-III Leather Fashions, Inc.; G-III Retail Outlets, Inc.; Global Apparel Sourcing, Ltd.; Global International Trading Company (South Korea); Indawa Holding Corp.; P.T. Balihides (Indonesia); P.T. Tatabuana Raya (Indonesia); Siena Leather, Ltd.; Wee-Beez International Trading Co. (Hong Kong).

Further Reading

"Coat Tales," *Women's Wear Daily,* July 30, 1996, p. 9.

Feller, Alan, "G-III Apparel Group Ltd. Signs Leather Outerwear Agreement with NFL Properties," *Business Wire,* September 21, 1993.

Fiedler, Terry, "Blind Faith: Investors Who Anted Up for Leather Expert Lyle Berman's Blind Pool Won Big," *Corporate Report Minnesota,* March 1990, p. 39 and continuation.

"Firm Signs Pact with China for Joint Venture There," *Wall Street Journal,* March 7, 1994, p. A6.

Friedman, Arthur, "G-III's United Front," *Women's Wear Daily,* February 15, 1994, p. 28.

Gault, Ylonda, "Stretching Leather," *Crain's New York Business,* January 29, 1990, p. 3.

——, "Surviving a Clothes Call," *Crain's New York Business,* April 28, 1997, p. 13.

"Kenneth Cole Licenses G-III for Leather, Cloth Outerwear," *Women's Wear Daily,* December 12, 1995, p. 11.

MacIntosh, Jeane, "G-III Branching Out with New Line and Stores," *Women's Wear Daily,* March 23, 1993, p. 17.

"Market Basket," *Women's Wear Daily,* February 11, 1997, p. 10.

—Robert Halasz

GAF MATERIALS
CORPORATION

GAF Corporation

1361 Alps Road
Wayne, New Jersey 07470
U.S.A.
(973) 628-3000
Fax: (973) 628-3311
Web site: http://www.gaf.com

Private Company
Incorporated: 1929 as American I.G. Chemical Corporation
Employees: 3,300
Sales: $850 million (1996 est.)
SICs: 2952 Asphalt Felts & Coatings; 3229 Pressed & Blown Glass & Glassware, Not Elsewhere Classified; 5039 Construction Materials, Not Elsewhere Classified; 6719 Offices of Holding Companies, Not Elsewhere Classified

The GAF Corporation of the late 1990s essentially consists of its GAF Materials Corporation subsidiary, the largest manufacturer of residential and commercial roofing products in the United States. GAF Chemicals Corporation, a maker of specialty chemicals, was the company's other major subsidiary, until it was taken public in 1991 as International Specialty Products, Inc. (ISP), with GAF retaining an 80 percent stake. ISP was subsequently distributed to GAF shareholders in 1997, leaving GAF with no interest in its former subsidiary. GAF's rich history covers more than 150 years and includes separate ownership by German chemical giants Frederick Bayer & Company and I.G. Farben; seizures of the company by the U.S. government during World War I and World War II; a 23-year period of control by the U.S. government starting in 1942; sale to the public in 1965 in one of the largest competitive auctions in Wall Street history; a 1983 proxy takeover led by Samuel J. Heyman; being taken private in 1989; and the 1990s spinoff of the specialty chemicals operations. Heyman still owns most of GAF Corporation and remains the company chairman.

Bayer and I.G. Farben Roots

GAF had auspicious beginnings. The company was founded in April 1929, as an American arm of the enormous German chemicals trust, I.G. Farben-industrie. Known throughout the world as I.G. Dyes, the German corporation was involved in most areas of the worldwide chemicals industry, pressing forward with massive investments in research. In 1929 I.G. Dyes was classed as the largest industrial corporation in Europe. Six executives from I.G. Dyes joined with a handful of prominent American businessmen—among them Edsel Ford, president of the Ford Motor Company; Walter Teagle, president of the Standard Oil Company of New Jersey; Charles Mitchell, chairman of the National City Bank; and Paul Warburg, chairman of the Industrial Acceptance Bank—to form the board of directors of the American I.G. Chemical Corporation.

For its plant facilities, the new corporation acquired substantial interests in Agfa-Ansco Corporation of upstate New York and General Aniline Works, Inc., which operated in New York and New Jersey. Agfa-Ansco's roots dated to a photographic supply business, the Edward Anthony Company, set up in New York City in 1842. During the Civil War, Matthew Brady used supplies from Edward Anthony to capture his famous photographs. In the early 20th century, Agfa-Ansco ranked second to Kodak in U.S. production of photographic materials and film.

General Aniline Works, formerly the Grasselli Chemical Company, had established itself as a major manufacturer of synthetic organic chemicals and dyestuffs since its founding in Rensselaer, New York, in 1882 as Hudson River Aniline Color Works Company. Hudson River was later acquired by the leading German chemical firm of the late 19th century, Frederick Bayer & Company, which renamed it the Bayer Company in 1913. This company made the first Bayer aspirin sold in the United States in 1905. The Bayer Company was seized by the U.S. government during World War I because of its German ownership and was sold at auction to Sterling Products in 1918. Sterling subsequently sold Bayer's chemical business to the Grasselli Chemical Company. After I.G. Farben acquired Grasselli in 1928, Farben changed Grasselli's name to General Aniline Works, Inc.

The plans for American I.G. were to provide competition to other American chemicals firms and to exploit the patents of I.G. Dyes in the new American market, which it did over the next decade. Initially, the company's trump card was its process for the hydrogenation of coal, which produced gasoline as a by-product; this largely accounted for the initial interest that the presidents of Ford and Standard Oil had in the new corporation. Other products that were developed and distributed by American I.G. included dyestuffs; pharmaceuticals; solvents; lacquers; photographic products and films; synthetic silk and other fabrics; a range of nitrogen products, including chemical fertilizers; and an array of other organic and inorganic chemicals.

In 1939 the company changed its name to the General Aniline and Film Corporation, after having acquired all of General Aniline Works and merged with Agfa-Ansco, of whose stock it owned 81 percent. By that time it had received approximately 3,900 patents for its vast stock of chemical formulations.

From the beginning, General Aniline was designed to be largely controlled by and dependent upon German direction and research. Almost all of its research took place in Germany, and chemical intermediates were manufactured in that country and sent to U.S. plants only for final preparation. The company's consistent success was earned through a steady performance in the fields of dyes, chemicals, and photographic products. In fact, General Aniline was the leading U.S. manufacturer of dyestuffs until du Pont caught up in the late 1930s. An acquisition that had an impact on the company's future was that of the Ozalid Corporation, a producer of copying equipment, in 1940.

Seizure During World War II

General Aniline and Film survived some early criticisms of its very existence by Americans who questioned the prudence of such a large German concern operating in the United States. The company's record was legitimate, but the direct participation in its management by German citizens had raised some cautious eyebrows on Wall Street and in Washington. Soon after it became apparent that the United States would be an active participant in World War II, General Aniline was seized by the U.S. government in February 1942, under the Trading with the Enemy Act. It was the largest asset taken over by the United States in World War II.

This move developed into a longstanding legal dispute between the U.S. government and I.G. Chemie, a Swiss holding company that was the majority stockholder of General Aniline. Prior to 1940 I.G. Chemie had been a branch of I.G. Dyes, but the company contended that it broke all relations with Germany during that year, becoming an independent corporation called Interhandel. The U.S. view was that I.G. Chemie remained a front for I.G. Dyes, despite its claims to the contrary. An out-of-court settlement between the Justice Department and Interhandel was finally reached over 20 years later—General Aniline would be sold to the public, and proceeds from the sale would be split 60 percent/40 percent, with the United States receiving the majority share.

Period of U.S. Government Control, 1942–65

Between 1942 and 1965, General Aniline was managed by government-appointed directors. It was a turbulent, minimally profitable time for the company. All told, during this period the company had seven different chief executives and over 80 directors. In several regards the government's hands were tied, preventing it from acting as freely and spontaneously as most managers could during this period. The rapid turnover of directors in itself created a barrier to long-term planning. The directors were excessively cautious, in most cases focusing on immediate rather than long-term results, never knowing when the company would be sold to the public. The pending lawsuit with Interhandel created an atmosphere resistant to risk-taking, as each potential move by General Aniline was accompanied by threats of further legal action by Interhandel. For instance, one injunction, obtained by Interhandel in 1957 in order to prevent dilution of General Aniline's equity, prohibited the company from issuing its shares for acquisitions or from entering the equity and capital markets for money with which to expand. As board president Jack Frye stated in 1953, "One of the problems of this company is that, due to its ownership situation, the management, the boards of directors, and all concerned are extremely cautious about making expenditures. In trying to avoid mistakes, they actually move more slowly than do their competitors."

Because of these restrictions, General Aniline's growth was stagnant compared to competitors in the same industries. In film and photographic equipment, the company competed chiefly with Kodak, in chemicals with du Pont, and in copying equipment with Xerox. All these firms, indeed each of the industries in question, experienced unprecedented growth and diversification through the postwar period and into the 1970s.

In spite of its cautious management and modest overall growth, General Aniline did achieve some significant successes in the 20 years after the government takeover. One bright spot was the work of the brilliant chemical engineer, Dr. Jesse Werner, who led the task of replicating the formulas of all the important compounds that were formerly produced at the parent company in Germany. A central research laboratory for the dyes and chemicals divisions was set up in Easton, Pennsylvania, in 1942, employing 400 chemists. Management was more venturesome in this area than in others and spent a good deal of money on product and market research and on the development of chemicals. These divisions produced an array of successful innovations including a chlorinecaustic plant set up in New Jersey in 1956, and the company's pioneering efforts in the field of synthetic detergents. The most important technical triumph was General Aniline's success with acetylene derivatives, a fledgling branch of chemistry in which the company's progress far surpassed its competitors'.

In the 1920s an I.G. Dyes chemist, Julius Walter Reppe, found a way of handling acetylene under pressure without explosion, something that was previously thought by chemists to be impossible. Reppe's patented processes were found in General Aniline's American vaults in 1940 and were used as a basis for research by the chemists in Easton. Some of the earliest marketable uses of acetylene-based chemicals were the PVP (polyvinylpyrrolidone) family of products, which use a white powder that is the product of the pressurized combination of acetylene and formaldehyde; some of its uses are as a blood volume expander, suspending agent, tablet binder, and a fungicide, as well as a component in cosmetics, photographic chemicals, ink, paints, adhesives, detergents, and glass.

As of 1962, General Aniline remained the sole producer of the immensely profitable acetylene derivatives in the United States. The commercial success of acetylene products can be largely attributed to Dr. Jesse Werner, who had risen through the technical ranks of the company in the 1940s, and who was named director of commercial development in 1952, charged with the responsibility of exploiting the chemists' discoveries. He implemented large-scale plans for the growing industrial uses of acetylene compounds and eventually became company president in 1962, the first chief executive of General Aniline to have worked his way up from the laboratory.

Although a large amount of money was poured into chemicals and dyestuffs research, the photography and copying equipment divisions were relatively neglected. Two discoveries by researchers in the Agfa-Ansco labs would have had a large impact on the industry, had they only received attention and funds for marketing. In the mid-1940s, a chemist named Vsevolod Tulagin invented a new dye system for color photography. His scientific peers believed it was better than what was on the market, but the business managers had little confidence that they could have a product that was of higher quality than Kodak's offerings. Then in 1951–52, Ansco developed a color movie film that was far more realistic than the super-real colors being viewed on movie screens at the time. In addition, the Ansco film could be developed within ten hours, on location, which was unheard of in the industry. Again, the circumspect General Aniline board refused to allocate the funds for an Anscofilm plant that would make production feasible.

The Ozalid division, which produced copying equipment, suffered from a similar lack of support. Its development of small office copiers and all-purpose copiers was sluggish in a booming industry, and its marketing organization was under-equipped with money and personnel. In addition, Ozalid's management was even more erratic than that of parent General Aniline; between 1957 and 1963 Ozalid had eight chief executives.

Despite all the shortcomings with Ansco and Ozalid, each maintained steady profit levels through the 1960s; the industries in which they competed were expanding rapidly, so even with decreased percentage market shares, Ozalid and Ansco could remain profitable. Ansco's concentration during this period shifted from the amateur photographic market to the commercial market, and the subsidiary handled substantial government contracts as well. As a point of interest, the camera used by the astronaut John Glenn was a modified Ansco Autoset. Ozalid's chief market share was in the engineering field; its process involving the use of diazo-sensitized paper to produce an image upon exposure to ammonia was one of the best and cheapest at the time and achieved great success in the reproduction of engineering drawings.

Sale to the Public in 1965

A benchmark in General Aniline's history came on March 9, 1965, when the 23-year control by the U.S. government ended with the biggest sale of stock by competitive bidding in Wall Street history. Dr. Werner, who had been appointed president and chief executive officer of General Aniline in 1962 and was voted chairman of the board on October 5, 1964, stood at the helm of the company as it entered this period of rebirth. He consolidated the company into two divisions: dyestuffs and chemicals, and photography and reproduction. In the 23 years since the U.S. seizure of General Aniline, its research program had earned almost 2,000 patents, and optimism for the company's future ran high.

Unfortunately, General Aniline was actually entering a new 20-year era of questionable management, during which Werner ran through a diverse roster of managers, products, and industries, which never quite panned out as his plans predicted. By the end of this period, in 1981, the firm's shares were selling for less than one-third of their 1965 offering price, and the company placed 1,004th out of 1,023 in the profitability rankings in *Forbes* magazine. Back in 1966, Werner planned to focus on growth in the company's four existing fields, because, as he said, "We have too many product lines, too much diversity for our size."

Expansion into Roofing in 1967 with Ruberoid

General Aniline's only significant acquisition during Werner's tenure was the 1967 purchase of Ruberoid Corporation, which added roofing and related products to the company's lines. This forerunner of the GAF Materials Corporation subsidiary was founded in 1886 in Bound Brook, New Jersey, as the Standard Paint Company. The year of its founding, Standard Paint introduced RUBEROID, the first ready-to-lay asphalt roofing material, which was developed by company chemist, William Griscom. This product, which achieved mass-market status over the next two decades, revolutionized the roofing industry because of its rubberlike quality and its distribution in convenient rolls. In 1898 the RUBEROID product was enhanced when Standard Paint began to embed artificially colored ceramic granules in it, improving the product's durability, fire resistance, and attractiveness.

In 1921 Standard Paint recognized the importance of its flagship product by adopting a new name, The Ruberoid Company. Ruberoid subsequently enhanced its position as a leader in the roofing industry when it introduced Tite-On Shingles in 1933. These were the first interlocking roofing shingles in the country and were much better able to withstand severe weather conditions than previously available shingles. In 1967, the year of its acquisition by General Aniline, the company introduced its Timberline Series laminated shingles, which improved the appearance of roofs and quickly became the top-selling laminated product on the market.

Struggling Through the Early 1980s

Meanwhile, the general trend between 1962 and 1982 was that research, development, and marketing outlays consistently fell short of what would have been necessary to forge market leaders for the newly named GAF Corporation (the acronym-derived name was officially adopted in April 1968). The photographic and copying business serves as a case study. This division offered a product line that was much narrower than its competitors', including no color film for its offset printers; its annual research and development expenditures averaged one percent of revenue from the division. A GAF customer observed in 1979 that "GAF's salesmen are very good, but there are just not enough of them."

Obviously, GAF must have experienced some positive feedback for its efforts or the company would not exist today. Werner's record also showed enough merit to withstand the pressures of a 1971 proxy fight, which was led by a family of stockholders who claimed he had "grossly mismanaged" the company during his career. Much of the company's profitability was the result of successes in the chemicals division, where there was consistent progress in production and sales of acetylene derivatives, surfactants (detergents), engineering thermoplastics, and mineral granules used for roofing shingles. Surfactants and acetylene products were sold worldwide to the pharmaceuticals, cosmetics, plastics, automotive, agricultural, textiles, oil and gas, paints, and paper production industries. GAF was one of only two worldwide producers of butanediol, itself an acetylene derivative, which was in turn used in the formulation of thermoplastic polyester compounds which had an enormous range of uses in the automotive, electrical/electronics, appliances, and other industries. The company also produced iron powders for the aerospace and electronics industries, products which were developed during the Werner years.

Heyman Takes Over in 1983 Proxy Fight

In 1978 Dr. Werner sold the consumer photo and processing operations, as well as the dyes and pigments interests, because of continued poor showings. This was the beginning of a massive five-year divestment program which, by the end of 1982, left GAF with only its two strongest lines, chemicals and building materials, as well as the New York City classical radio station WNCN, which the company had purchased for $22 million in June 1976 and which operated as a subsidiary, GAF Broadcasting Co. All in all, over half of GAF's assets were shed during this period. Werner had seemingly played all his cards, but just when the trimmed-down company's future again began to look bright, another proxy fight hit GAF, this one much more bitter and hard-fought than that of 1971. After a two-year battle, Werner lost out to an aggressive stockholder named Samuel J. Heyman, a real estate brokerage owner who had no previous corporate management experience.

Heyman assumed the directorship of GAF on December 14, 1983, with promises to trim all but the most profitable operations, including initial plans to liquidate the chemicals division. After thoroughly examining all of the company's records, however, he saw great potential for growth in building supplies and chemicals. He first eliminated some management positions, slashed operating expenses by 23 percent in his first nine months, and moved the company's headquarters from Manhattan to quiet Wayne, New Jersey. To instill a better sense of teamwork at the company, he decentralized management. Werner had called virtually all the shots himself, but Heyman wanted to spread decision-making responsibilities among regional and divisional managers.

The first 20 months of Heyman's leadership brought remarkable success to GAF, based primarily on cost-cutting and effective management rather than on the expansion of lines of business. Still, under Heyman capital expenditures and research and development outlays were far greater than they had been in the Werner years.

In September 1985 Heyman stated, "We have no plans to take over other companies, but we are looking at the possible acquisition of businesses that would complement our existing chemical lines." Over the following 18 months, however, GAF attempted hostile takeovers of engineering plastics and specialty chemicals concerns, Union-Carbide Corporation and Borg-Warner, and of a construction and industrial gas firm, CBI Industries. All three takeovers were ultimately thwarted, but the first two netted huge amounts of cash for GAF through the company's sale of its stock shares in the targeted firms. GAF's shares in Union-Carbide brought in close to $250 million, and the stock in Borg-Warner, purchased by eventual Borg-Warner buyer Merrill Lynch, earned $206 million for GAF. GAF's shares in CBI netted a smaller but still significant $7 million.

Typical of the new management's approach to business, Heyman steered much of these cash surpluses back into research for the building supplies and chemicals divisions. GAF sold its engineering plastics business in 1986 but remained one of only two producers of butanediol, which achieved steady increases in demand during this period. In 1988 GAF acquired Sutton Laboratories, a leading manufacturer of cosmetic preservatives.

The building materials division had been the market leader in residential roofing since the 1970s, and in the 1980s the division made major strides in the commercial roofing market. Even during the home-building lag of the early 1980s, GAF Materials Corporation was earning steady profits; then, business boomed in new home roofing, and grew even faster in premium re-roofing products designed to upgrade the appearance and value of homes. GAF led the trend toward fiberglass as well as simulated woodshake roofing products.

The 1980s culminated for GAF with the company being taken private in 1989 through a $1.4 billion highly leveraged buyout led by Heyman and 75 other members of management; only $43 million in cash was put up as part of the deal. At the time of the buyout GAF's operating subsidiaries were GAF Chemicals Corporation, GAF Materials Corporation (GAFMC), and GAF Broadcasting Co., Inc.

Transformation in the 1990s

GAF Corporation had been through innumerable changes in its long history, but the events of the 1990s altered the company like no others. By the late 1990s the company had spun off its specialty chemicals division, which had been the company's mainstay through most of its history, and was exclusively manufacturing roofing products. This transformation began in 1991 when Heyman engineered an initial public offering of GAF Chemicals, newly named International Specialty Products, Inc. (ISP). Heyman used the $285 million generated from the offering to pay down company debt, which was still high as the result of the 1989 leveraged buyout. Over the next few years, however, ISP fell on hard times, as competitors moved in to challenge the company's dominance of certain key sectors.

For example, Arco Chemical built a new plant to manufacture butanediol, ISP's mainstay raw material, and was able to offer prices lower than ISP's for products made from the chemical. Likewise, in 1992 BASF began operation of a new plant in Louisiana to make hair-care specialty chemicals; its modern machinery was more efficient than ISP's outmoded equipment, leading to competitive advantages in terms of time-to-market. ISP's operating income fell almost 47 percent from 1991 to 1993, while revenues decreased four percent during the same period. By late 1994 ISP's stock had fallen almost 50 percent since the IPO.

Meanwhile, the staid GAFMC was quietly and steadily growing through a series of strategic acquisitions that enabled the company to offer complete roofing systems in both the residential and commercial markets. GAFMC purchased Cobra Ventilation Products, a maker of premier attic ventilation products, in 1992; International Permalite, a manufacturer of low thermal roofing insulation products, in 1994; U.S. Intec, a producer of an extensive line of commercial roofing products, in 1995; and Leatherback Industries, a supplier of roofing felts and construction papers for the residential market, in 1997. Continuing to maintain its top position in the U.S. roofing materials industry, GAFMC's sales grew to more than $850 million by 1996, a more than 50 percent increase over the $559 million of 1993.

In March 1996 GAF sold the sole radio station owned by GAF Broadcasting—by that time known as WAXQ—to the Entercorn radio group for $90 million. The more significant divestment, however, came in January of the following year when GAF Corporation's remaining stake in ISP was distributed to GAF shareholders, severing the last direct connection between GAF and ISP, although Heyman remained ISP chairman. By this time, ISP had been turned around through a renewed commitment to research and development and through an aggressive program of overseas expansion, including the opening of new plants in Europe in 1993 and in the Far East in 1995. Revenues surpassed $700 million for the first time in 1996, while operating income increased 12 consecutive quarters on a year-to-year basis starting in 1994.

GAF Corporation neared the new millennium exclusively as a roofing supplies company but as the leader in its sole industry. Although representing only a fraction of the rich history of GAF Corporation, GAF Materials Corporation was the top company in its field, was growing rapidly, and continued to proudly carry the GAF name.

Principal Subsidiaries

G-I Holdings Inc.; G Industries Corporation; GAF Building Materials Corporation; Building Materials Corporation of America.

Further Reading

Briggs, Jean A., " 'I Like It Here,' " *Forbes,* March 15, 1982, p. 35.

Carey, David, "Sam's Math," *Financial World,* April 19, 1988, p. 26.

Drew, Christopher, "Ruling Could Jeopardize Class-Action Settlements," *New York Times,* June 27, 1997, pp. D1, D15.

"Duel's End: Heyman Finally Wins GAF," *Fortune,* January 9, 1984, p. 7.

Frank, Allan Dodds, "Shark Bait?" *Forbes,* November 18, 1985, p. 114.

Gannes, Stuart, "The Proxy Fighter Who's Turning Around GAF," *Fortune,* February 4, 1985, p. 84.

Hager, Bruce, "Now Comes Sam Heyman, Global Industrialist," *Business Week,* July 15, 1991, pp. 110–11.

Jaffe, Thomas, "Will Sam Play It Again?," *Forbes,* May 4, 1987, p. 182.

Kiesche, Elizabeth S., "GAF's Chemicals Go Public—As ISP," *Chemical Week,* September 18, 1991, pp. 22–23.

——, "ISP Redoubles Efforts and Rethinks Expectations," *Chemical Week,* November 10, 1993, p. 78.

"The Man Who Came to Stay," *Forbes,* February 14, 1983, p. 14.

Moukheiber, Zina, "The Rise and Fall of Sam Heyman," *Forbes,* October 24, 1994, pp. 42–43.

Ramirez, Anthony, "Restless GAF Is on the Prowl," *Fortune,* February 3, 1986, p. 32.

Teitelman, Robert, "Looks Who's Getting Rich on GAF," *Financial World,* January 12, 1988, p. 11.

—updated by David E. Salamie

THE GAINSCO COMPANIES

Gainsco, Inc.

500 Commerce Street
Fort Worth, Texas 76102
U.S.A.
(817) 336-2500
Fax: (817) 335-1230

Public Company
Incorporated: 1978
Employees: 120
Total Assets: $297 million (1996)
Stock Exchanges: New York
SICs: 6331 Fire, Marine & Casualty Insurance; 6719 Offices of Holding Companies, Not Elsewhere Classified; 7372 Prepackaged Software

Gainsco, Inc. is a holding company for subsidiaries that write property and casualty insurance, concentrating on specialty excess and surplus markets within the commercial auto, auto garage, and general liability markets. Its customers for general liability are small businesses such as car washes, janitorial services, and contractors. Those for commercial auto coverage include short-haul truckers, local haulers of specialized freight, artisans, and tradepersons. Auto garage liability insurance is sold primarily to car and recreational vehicle dealers, auto repair shops, and wrecker/towers. These clients are avoided by most insurance companies as too hazardous to qualify for coverage. Because of this, companies like Gainsco are allowed by state insurance authorities to charge higher premiums for their excess and surplus policies. All of the company's 203 agents in 1996 were independent.

Private Company, 1978–86

Gainsco was founded in 1978 by Joseph D. Macchia, the son of a New York City milkman. Macchia graduated from Fairfield University in 1957 and after serving in the Marines, became first a salesman, then an executive, for a series of insurance companies. In 1975 he became president of deficit-ridden Early American Insurance Co., a small insurer of automobiles. Macchia moved the company out of the highly competitive, regulated personal auto business and into serving small businesses, such as offering commercial auto policies to contractors, fire and theft policies to used car and mobile home dealers, and general liability to dry cleaners. Early American began turning a profit within 18 months.

Macchia left Early American to found Gainsco in 1978, borrowing $500,000 from a bank and setting up offices in Fort Worth, Texas. By then he had honed his strategy: to identify various types of risks where his company could price its coverages favorably and maximize the potential for profitable underwriting. At first, in order to minimize his risk, Macchia had to sell the policies he had written to reinsurers, keeping only a small commission. In order to accumulate enough capital so that he could accept more risk, and hence increase his profit, Macchia sold 70 percent of Gainsco to a Minneapolis-based company in 1979 for $2.5 million. Gainsco now was able to keep 30 cents of each premium dollar, selling the other 70 percent to a reinsurer and pocketing a commission of 25 to 30 percent on it. "You don't have to be a rocket scientist to do what we do," Gainsco's founder told *Forbes* in 1991. "All you have to do is exercise discipline, not get greedy, and be patient as hell."

In 1982, the first year for which figures were available to the public, Gainsco had net income of $670,000 on revenues of $12.1 million. In 1983 and 1984, however, the company lost $480,000 and $553,000, respectively. During 1984, which was Gainsco's last unprofitable year, the company sharply curtailed its writing of personal lines of insurance. In 1985 it had net income of $774,000 on income of $21 million. The following year Gainsco went public, taking in $8 million by offering about one-fourth of its shares of common stock at $7 per share.

Rising Profits, 1986–92

By the end of 1986 Gainsco was writing property and casualty insurance in 26 states, concentrating its efforts on certain specialty excess and surplus markets within the commercial auto, general liability and auto garage lines. Commercial auto coverage underwritten by the company included risks associ-

Company Perspectives:

Esprit: The dictionary defines it simply as spirit. But true meaning surpasses mere definition. At GAINSCO, Esprit de Corps is synergistic. A winning team is always much more than the sum of its parts.

Esprit anticipates and overcomes. Esprit is quick and eager to crest the hill and go another mile. Esprit is the joy of being part of something bigger than yourself. Something big enough to include everyone and yet small enough to hear a single voice.

Esprit soars on the wings of a dream and yet remains anchored on the firm ground of what is.

Esprit dedicates itself to the common goals of the group and yet speaks to the needs of individuals. It is the spontaneous choreography of achievement, finding joy in a challenge and pleasure in the work.

Esprit seeks alternatives and finds opportunity at every turn.

Esprit begins with an open door, an open mind and an open hand that reaches out. See for yourself—Esprit is its own reward.

ated with local haulers of specialized freight (such as sand and gravel), artisans' and tradespersons' vehicles, and trucking companies (other than long haulers). General liability insurance was underwritten to a liability limit of $500,000 for small businesses such as car washes, janitorial services, small contractors, apartment buildings, and grocery stores. The auto garage program included garage liability, garage keepers' legal liability, and dealer open-lot coverage. Other property and liability insurance coverages offered included commercial multiperil insurance, monoline fire insurance, and a small amount of personal motor home and recreational vehicle insurance.

Some of Gainsco's business was more exotic. By the end of 1991 it had insured an estimated 300 Christmas events, paying only one claim of any size: $5,000 to the parents of a child who took a fall running up a mall ramp to get a closer look at Santa Claus. The company also insured Thanksgiving Day turkey shoots, New Year's Eve festivities, Easter Egg contests, Independence Day parades, and Halloween haunted houses. Gainsco even had its only reference guide, which it called the Easy Rater Fun Pak, for calculating the risks of insuring such celebrations.

Gainsco owned a 3.38-acre tract of land in Fort Worth in 1986 and a 10,000-square-foot building on the lot, from which its operations were conducted, although the company later moved its headquarters to a larger building in another part of Fort Worth. The company had net income of $2.3 million during the year even though its revenues fell to $18.3 million. About 64 percent of its gross premiums of $32.6 million resulted from business done in Texas, Louisiana, and Mississippi. By the end of 1987 Gainsco was writing insurance in 37 states. Net income increased to $3.2 million on total revenue of $19.4 million. The company had no long-term debt. Gainsco gradually doubled the number of its outstanding shares through a series of stock dividends.

During 1988 Gainsco expanded its business to cover 43 states, and by the end of 1989 the company was writing insurance in 46 states. Commercial auto coverage showed the biggest increase, accounting for 48 percent of total premiums in 1989. That year the company completed a reinsurance arrangement that allowed its agents to double the general insurance liability limit to $1 million. Gainsco had net income of $3.8 million and $5.3 million on total revenues of $25.9 million and $36.6 million in 1988 and 1989, respectively. Macchia held 12.7 percent of the company's stock in 1988.

By 1990 Gainsco's record of rising profits was beginning to attract the interest of the business press. *Barron's* noted that by taking on clients whom other insurers avoided as too risky, Gainsco typically charged premiums anywhere from 25 percent to 75 percent higher than standard rates for more conventional types of coverage. Its loss ratio—the amount paid out in claims—was averaging only about 45 cents on the premium dollar, compared to more than 80 cents for the property and casualty industry as a whole. By this time Gainsco had enough capital to make it unnecessary to sell more than small pieces of its policies to reinsurers. Net income kept rising, to $6.6 million and $8.5 million on total revenues of $48.3 million and $60.5 million in 1990 and 1991, respectively. During 1991 commercial auto policies reached a peak 63 percent of the company's $68 million in premiums.

Gainsco enjoyed record results again in 1992, its net income rising to $13.2 million on total revenues of $85.7 million. Describing the business to a *Chief Executive* interviewer, Macchia said, "In the commercial auto area, we underwrite a lot of owner-operated truckers, pulp wood haulers, anything that rolls. The smaller the better. On the general liability side, we do a lot of small contractors—carpenters, plumbers, electricians, one-man grocery stores." Most of the company's considerable investment portfolio—$139.4 million at the end of 1993—was in high-quality, tax-exempt municipal bonds. Fearing hyperinflation as a result of the growing federal debt, Macchia had purchased several million dollars worth of gold and opened a Swiss bank account. Conservatism, he said, "runs in the family," citing his grandfather, who converted everything he had to gold at the beginning of World War II and buried it.

Continued Prosperity, 1993–96

After eight consecutive years of rising profits, Gainsco stumbled for the first time in 1993. The company's net income was down, although only slightly, to $13 million, and its total revenues dropped to $84.4 million. The following year saw renewed growth, to $15.2 million in net income and $93.5 million in total revenues, and the company now was writing policies in every state but Maine. The majority of gross premiums in 1994 came from California, Florida, Kentucky, Louisiana, Pennsylvania, and Texas. To prod the 150 agents selling its policies, Gainsco had a "Buddy Team" program requiring employees, from executives all the way down to receptionists and file clerks, to make calls. "I learned a long time ago that one of the main ways you get business is to ask for it," Macchia told a reporter.

Net income advanced to a record $17.6 million in 1995 on total revenues of $108 million. That year, for the fifth time, Gainsco was named one of the 200 best small companies in

America by *Forbes.* Interviewed for *National Underwriter,* Macchia credited his employees, whom he called ''a well oiled marketing machine, calling agents asking how they can help and what they can do to make doing business with Gainsco easier.'' He noted that they could earn up to 50 percent bonuses if they helped agents exceed their premium volume goals. The emphasis on working with agents resulted in an increase in average premium per agent/office, from $237,000 in 1987 to more than $600,000 in 1994. Macchia also noted that the company used a team approach in determining pricing.

During 1996 Gainsco's net income dipped to $16 million on record revenues of $119 million. Of its gross premiums of $110 million, commercial auto insurance accounted for 57 percent, auto garage for 24 percent, general liability for 18 percent, and other lines for one percent. The company had no debt and an investment portfolio of $204.6 million, of which 90 percent was in bonds. Gainsco was doing business through 203 nonaffiliated general agents. Of its total in premiums, about 73 percent came from California, Florida, Georgia, Illinois, Kentucky, Louisiana, Pennsylvania, Tennessee, Texas, and West Virginia. Macchia held 11.4 percent of the company's common stock in February 1997.

Commercial auto coverage was being written only for vehicles primarily operated within the state of garaging and one state beyond, or 1,000 miles, whichever was greater. Liability and physical damage coverages for these risks was limited to $1 million per accident and $100,000 per unit. The maximum liability for auto garage or general liability coverage also was $1 million. Gainsco also was issuing a variety of other policies, including monoline property insurance and restricted commercial property policies covering fire, extended coverage, vandalism, and malicious mischief for commercial establishments, with a limit of $200,000. A total of 35,903 policies were in force at the end of 1996. In order to reduce its liability on individual risks and to protect against catastrophe claims, Gainsco was purchasing reinsurance from three companies in 1997. Through a wholly owned subsidiary, Gainsco was also marketing a computer software package related to insurance agents.

Principal Subsidiaries

Agents Processing System, Inc.; Gainsco County Mutual Insurance Company; Gainsco Service Corp.; General Agents Insurance Company of America, Inc.; General Agents Premium Finance Company; MGA Agency, Inc.; MGA Insurance Company, Inc.; MGA Premium Finance Company; Risk Retention Administrators Inc.

Further Reading

Bowers, Brent, ''St. Nick's Shopping List Includes Holiday Protection,'' *Wall Street Journal,* December 20, 1991, p. B2.

Byrne, Harlan S., ''Gainsco Inc.,'' *Barron's,* April 16, 1990, p. 42.

——, ''Sound Policies,'' *Barron's,* February 27, 1995, p. 20.

Geer, Carolyn T., '' 'Be Patient and Don't Get Greedy,' '' *Forbes,* July 8, 1991, pp. 80–81.

Gilbert, Evelyn, ''*Forbes*: Gainsco Among 200 Best Small U.S. Firms,'' *National Underwriter,* November 20, 1995, p. 31.

Kimelman, John, ''The Lloyd's of Fort Worth,'' *Financial World,* April 27, 1993, p. 57.

Marcial, Gene G., ''Insuring Those the Others Ignore,'' *Business Week,* May 31, 1993, p. 79.

McCarthy, Joseph L., ''Joseph Macchia,'' *Chief Executive,* January/February 1993, p. 18.

Slovak, Julianne, ''Gainsco,'' *Fortune,* May 21, 1990, p. 104.

—Robert Halasz

Gencor Ltd.

6 Hollard Street
Johannesburg, 2001
P.O. Box 61820
2107 Marshalltown
South Africa
(11) 3769111
Fax: (11) 8384716

Public Company
Incorporated: 1895 as General Mining and Finance Corporation Ltd.
Employees: 1,361
Sales: R13.24 billion (1996)
Stock Exchanges: Johannesburg
SICs: 1000 Metal Mining

Gencor Ltd., formerly General Mining Union Corporation Ltd., is one of South Africa's top mining houses. After the company's Billiton unit became an independent company in 1997, the "new" Gencor was left to concentrate on precious metals.

Turn-of-the-Century Origins

Gencor is the product of a 1980 merger between General Mining and Finance Corporation and Union Corporation, both of which were founded in the 19th century. General Mining was founded on December 30, 1895, by two Germans, George and Leopold Albu, who controlled a number of gold mines. In the same year they changed the name of their firm from G&L Albu to General Mining and Finance Corporation.

In its early years the company's activities were focused primarily on gold; developing new mines and managing existing ones. In 1910, the company had seven mines under its management, including such well-known names as Meyer and Charlton, Van Ryn Gold Mines Estate, and West Rand Consolidated Mines, and was developing another two.

World War I was a difficult time for the industry; a flat gold price was accompanied by flagging productivity and rising costs on all fronts. The shortage of unskilled labor was a major issue, and its costs increased as contractors, who had to recruit and deliver the workers to the mines, became involved. The mines also had problems during this period with labor unrest, principally among white miners. The best-known example was the 1922 General Strike, during which two months of production were lost. In 1919, activities were diversified with the formation of Transvaal Silver and Base Metals to mine the lode outcrops and lead-bearing ore which the company owned. After six years, this venture was closed owing to its poor prospects. More successful was General Mining's acquisition of a large stake, during the 1920s, in Phoenix Oil and Transport Company, which had major interests in Romanian oil companies.

The mining houses were equally hard hit by World War II, which resulted in shortages of all forms of labor, lack of machinery, and delays in plant and machinery delivery. Good news came soon after, however, with the discovery of the Free State gold fields, which General Mining, together with other mining houses, had the right to develop. It also participated in the opening of gold mines on the Far West Rand. General Mining achieved some notable firsts: it was the first mining house to use the cyanide process for the extraction of gold; and, through West Rand Cons, it was the first mining house in the country to produce uranium.

Postwar Acquisitions

During the 1950s the company's activities were boosted when it gained control of the Consolidated Rand-Transvaal Mining Group. This control brought with it a substantial interest in the gold mine Geduld; platinum, through Lydenburg; pipe fabrication; and sugar.

In 1964 the company merged with Strathmore Consolidated Investments and came to control two mines on Klerksdorp gold field; Stilfontein, and Buffelsfontein. A major change took place during the 1960s when the Afrikaner-dominated mining house Federale Mynbou took control of General Mining. This was effected with the assistance of Anglo American, and its chairman Harry Oppenheimer in particular, who wished to assist the Afrikaans business community to get a better foothold in the mining industry. This aim had a political purpose: to

Company Perspectives:

The major strategic moves of the past few years, and those planned for the near future, have enabled Gencor to aspire to a place amongst the world's great mining companies in the early 21st century. The establishment in 1996 of a new group structure based on commodity units, onto which the Billiton assets have been integrated, marks an important step in achieving this strategic objective. ''Gencor has undergone a remarkable transformation,'' says Brian Gilbertson, the group's executive chairman, ''and the outcome is a US$5 billion company, focused sharply on its seven core commodity businesses. Each of these is dollar based; and each has attributes that merit the tag 'world class,' be it low operating costs, quality of ore reserves, efficiency of process and/or scale of operations. The group is soundly structured and prudently financed; our management structure is clearly defined, with an ambitious and motivated executive team; we are blessed with an excellent portfolio of world class businesses and there are many opportunities ahead of us. I believe that Gencor is well placed to take up the challenge of the future.''

counteract government policies which sought to separate Afrikaner from English, whites from black, by showing that these groups could cooperate in the same spheres of interest.

The outcome was that Federale made the takeover while Anglo took a substantial minority interest. Later, in 1965, it was decided to merge Federale and General Mining with Federale gaining effective control.

The merger resulted in the creation of the Federale Mynbou/ General Mining group, the country's largest producer of uranium, accounting for more than a third of output, and also producing approximately 7.25 percent of the country's gold. ''Federale Mynbou'' was dropped from the group's name in 1965. The group's 10 collieries produced 10 percent of the country's output and it had further mineral interests—asbestos fiber production, platinum, and copper. It was also involved in oil production, exploration, and marketing and managed the petroleum company Trek.

The late 1960s saw a program of diversification. It was the era of conglomerates and the prospects for gold were not exciting. However, many new projects pursued, particularly in the industrial field, were not compatible with the company's expertise, and failed. The turnaround came in 1970 with the arrival of Dr. Wim De Villiers as chief executive. He instituted a rationalization of activities which led to improved profitability. The major changes he implemented concerned decentralized management, strategic planning, and better utilization of labor. On the industrial side, De Villiers sold off the consumer interests of General Mining.

A Major Claim in the 1980s

The other company involved in the eventual 1980 merger, Union Corporation, was of a similar age to General Mining. It was founded in 1897 by a German, Adolf Goertz, the local representative of Deutsche Bank, and was initially known as A. Goertz and Co. Goertz became involved in the gold rush and staked 326 claims on the Modderfontein farm on the East Rand, from which emerged the Modder Deep Levels mine, ''the jewelbox of the Reef,'' in Goertz's words.

In 1902 Goertz and Co., with the assistance of U.K. and French investors, who took up shares, became the first Transvaal finance house to obtain a London listing. During World War I the company changed its name to Union Corporation.

There was much uncertainty in the early days, with financing for the Modderfontein mine being obtained literally hours before war broke out. After the declaration of war, all transactions with Germany were frozen.

From 1908, Union Corporation pioneered the Far East Rand, and in 1938 it discovered the Orange Free State gold fields. The first shaft was sunk at St. Helena in 1947, which became the first mine to produce gold in the Orange Free State. In 1951 came the discovery of the Evander gold field, over which Union Corporation had sole control. It established four mines there: Bracken, Kinross, Leslie, and Winkelhaak.

Later mining ventures included involvement in Impala Platinum, where mining began in 1969. Impala was the first platinum concern in the world to provide an integrated operation from the mining of the ore to the marketing of high purity platinum group metals. The gold mine Unisel was developed in 1974, and in 1978 Beisa, the first mine in the country to be established as a primary uranium producer, was opened.

Union Corporation also owned the original interest in Richards Bay and helped put together Richards Bay Minerals, which mines heavy mineral deposits from sand dunes north of the harbor, recovering ilmenite, rutile, zircon, and titanium. General Mining's rights in Richards Bay were later merged with these.

Union Corporation's diversification into the manufacturing industry started in earnest in 1936–37, with the formation of the paper company Sappi in the East Rand town of Springs. It was a long-term grassroots project which only really became profitable in the 1970s.

During the 1960s, investments were acquired in the packaging company Kohler Brothers; African Coasters, forerunner of Unicorn Shipping Lines; and engineering companies Darling and Hodgson and Evelyn Haddon. At the time of the 1980 merger, Union Corporation had a 58 percent stake in Sappi, 74 percent of Kohler Brothers, 55 percent of Darling and Hodgson, 17 percent of Haggie—a wire rope manufacturer—and 27 percent of Kanhym. It also held a stake in Capital and Counties, the U.K. property concern which later became the major investment of First International Trust, the overseas arm of the Liberty Life group, a major player in the South African insurance field.

In 1978, 56 percent of Union Corporation's assets were in minerals, including 33 percent in gold. It was operating seven gold mines—Marievale, Bracken, Kinross, St. Helena, Winkelhaak, Leslie, and Grootvlei—in addition to developing the

Unisel gold mine. Approximately 50 percent of net income came from industrial interests in the fiscal year 1977–78.

Although the General Mining/Union Corporation merger was only consummated in 1980, the courtship had begun in 1974 when General Mining acquired a 29.9 percent stake in Union Corporation after a tremendous battle with Gold Fields of South Africa. A further step was taken in 1976 when Union Corporation became a subsidiary of General Mining and the takeover, still spoken of as the country's most bitterly contested hostile bid, was completed four years later.

The decade under De Villiers had been a golden one for General Mining, whose earnings per share increased at an average rate of 26.2 percent per annum over the period. Prior to De Villiers's arrival, the company had paid a maintained dividend—unchanged for the ten years up to 1968, with the dividend only marginally higher in 1969. At the time of the merger, Union Corporation and General Mining were the fourth- and fifth-largest mining houses in South Africa, ranked by equity capitalization. More than a third of each company's income derived from manufacturing.

The major reason for the merger was General Mining's need to create an improved capital base from which to undertake new investments, such as the first phase of Sappi's Ngodwana mill, the Beatrix mine, which was initially funded from within, and the Beisa uranium mine. There were also the additional benefits of manpower rationalization and, with the exception of gold, the two groups' activities supplemented each other rather than overlapping. It was also felt that Union Corporation's growth prospects would be improved through closer links with the ruling Afrikaner power bloc.

Given the hostile nature of the bid, it was inevitable that merging the two corporations would take time. Initially they remained separate operating entities, merging their corresponding product divisions whenever conditions were favorable. The process was apparently more complex than anyone imagined, and the period 1980–86 was to prove difficult for the group. In 1982 the two major stakeholders, Sanlam and Rembrandt, clashed over Gencor. Sanlam, the second-largest South African life insurer, had been a major shareholder in the two companies which joined to form Federale Mynbou, and thus become involved in General Mining, and subsequently Gencor. The result of the clash was the replacement of De Villiers—later a member of the cabinet—as chief executive by former Union Corporation managing director Ted Pavitt, after a clash between De Villiers and Dr. Andries Wassenaar, head of Sanlam, about the management of Gencor.

In the early 1980s, Gencor started to expand its interests, particularly in manufacturing, thinking that the outlook for metals, especially base metals, was poor. However, the group was caught by recession, high inflation, and high interest rates, which pushed up costs of new investments and led to a R410 million rights issue in 1984 to reduce leverage.

The biggest project was a R1.6 billion expansion at Sappi, which was plagued by technical difficulties and cost overruns. Problems were also experienced at Tedelex and Kanhym, which likewise needed to resort to rights issues. Foreign exchange losses of R200 million in 1984, with Impala and Tedelex worst hit, were followed, in 1985, by appalling performances by the manufacturing interests: Sappi, Kohler, Tedelex, and Kanhym.

The group's industrial relations image within the industry also took a battering at this time following troubles at Impala and Marievale and, later, mining disasters involving multiple fatalities at Kinross and St. Helena. The Beisa uranium mine which opened in 1981 was closed in 1984, having constantly failed to produce profits. This was primarily the result of a soft world uranium market.

The perception that all was not well within the group was compounded in 1983 by the group's failure to find a new chief executive to succeed De Villiers. It settled instead for management by its five most senior executives: Johan Fritz, George Clark, Basil Landau, Tom de Beer, and Hugh Smith. Pavitt had relinquished executive responsibilities in August 1984.

Over the course of that year manufacturing interests were underperforming; there was massive foreign loan exposure, and Gencor appeared to be something of a rudderless ship. The executive committee was thought to be concerning itself too much with operational issues and not enough with strategy and planning. Investor confidence waned. To some extent, such perception was unfair. Steps were being taken to address problems, such as the 1984 reorganization of mining and industrial interests in line with a policy of greater divisional autonomy.

Major developments were also underway, including that of the Beatrix mine, perhaps the most successful new gold mine of the 1980s; the development by Sappi of the massive mill at Ngodwana; and the gaining of control of Samancor. Gencor raised its stake in Samancor from around 30 percent to 50 percent by swapping various interests with Iscor, the state steel producer which was the controlling shareholder in Samancor. Next to these, the problems at Tedelex and Kanhym were relatively minor. Still, they were symptoms of malaise.

The interest in Samancor dated back to the 1970s when General Mining took steps to become more involved in the production of ferrochrome. At the time, General Mining held 15 percent of Montrose Chrome. After building up a controlling stake in Montrose, it went on to buy Union Corporation's operations, but the quantum leap in the formation of what is today Samancor came with the Tubatse ferrochrome project, a 50-50 joint venture with Union Carbide, which was bought out in the 1980s.

Gencor had battled with Anglo American for control of Samancor. The government had stepped in at one stage to prevent a successful Anglo bid, on monopoly grounds. At that time, Samancor was not a chrome company but a manganese company controlled by Iscor. Anglo later put its manganese interests into Iscor and took a 25 percent stake in Samancor.

Another important event was the creation in November 1983 of Genbel, through the merger of Gencor's investment holding companies UCI and Sentrust. UCI, on the Union Corporation side, was formed in 1946 to explore the Evander gold field. It was listed in the 1960s as part of a pyramid exercise to raise funds for the development of Kinross. Through a pyramid exercise, a holding company could control a large number of companies with a combined capital very much greater than its own, since it needed to hold only half or even less of the shares of its subsidiaries.

General Mining had no less than seven similar companies, whose most valuable assets were interests in the Free State and Klerksdorp gold fields. They were combined in 1968 to form Sentrust, which eventually constituted about a third of the merged Genbel as against UCI's two-thirds.

Historically, Genbel grew by exploring mineral rights and then putting these into new mines in exchange for shares, thus becoming an investment company by default. It continued to grow from opportunities offered by the Gencor group, as well as through developing its own mineral rights.

While the 1984–85 period was a difficult one for the South African economy, Gencor's particular difficulties were compounded by an identity crisis. Staff had not outgrown their previous allegiances and still tended to see themselves as Union Corporation or General Mining employees. The two corporate cultures were very different. Union Corporation had a reputation for good engineering and exploration, and General Mining for financial engineering.

The Key to Surviving in the 1990s

Gencor's failings were analyzed in 1986 in a report commissioned by Federale, at that time controlling company of Gencor, and produced by Arthur D. Little, the U.S.-based management consultants. The report contained some strong criticisms, accusing the group of lack of focus and direction, weak leadership, and a lack of corporate loyalty amongst employees. The report served as a spur to change but the man to whom it fell to implement this, Derek Keys, appointed executive chairman in April 1986, had no background in mining, having come from the industrial group Malbak. The appointment was not universally popular, and caused Johan Fritz to resign and Basil Landau to take early retirement.

Keys made a number of important moves, one of which was to separate the manufacturing interests. He brought Malbak into the group and then sold into it all the manufacturing interests—bar Sappi, which was much too large, and Trek, which later found a home in Engen. Thus at one stroke the manufacturing interests were separated from the mining interests, and Malbak was given the task of managing them. Previously, the manufacturing interests had been managed in true mining house style—from the center. Keys and Grant Thomas, managing director at Malbak, introduced a new decentralized structure.

This was part of Keys's strategy of increasing the powers of divisional managers within the group. Head office staff was cut from 1,700 to 54 by 1989. In many ways, Keys was responsible for putting into practice the decentralized management philosophy first articulated 15 years earlier by De Villiers.

The period from Keys's arrival was one of considerable expansion and growth, both organic and through acquisitions. On the mining side, the Oryx gold mine was developed as well as the smaller Weltevreden mine near Klerksdorp, and Impala Platinum developed the Karee mine. In 1989, Gencor bought a 30.7 percent controlling interest in Alusaf, the Richards Bay aluminum smelter, from the Industrial Development Corporation for R270 million. A R1.47 billion rights issue in 1989 helped fund these developments and acquisitions. Other acquisitions included Sappi's purchase of Saiccor, which specializes in the productions of chemical cellulose pulp, and of a 49 percent interest in the Usuthu pulp mill in Swaziland. In mid-1990 Sappi also bought five paper mills in the U.K. subsidiary Malbak, while Abercom Holdings bid £42million for the U.K.-quoted packaging group MY Holdings.

Another important event was the publication in 1988 of the Gencor mission, a brief statement of the group's fundamental corporate goals, which went a long way toward clarifying to the public and to its employees what Gencor stood for. In Keys's words, ''Now they know that Gencor has only two businesses—to start or to acquire major businesses and to accelerate the development of those businesses which it already has.''

Two major developments took place within Gencor in 1989. The first was the formation of General Mining Metals and Minerals Limited (Genmin) in March 1989. Genmin was made responsible for managing the group's mining, metals, and minerals interests, which comprise some 60 operations. These included 14 gold mines, the base metals group Samancor, the platinum producer Impala, the coal group Trans-Natal, and the minerals division.

The second major development was the formation of Engen, the company responsible for the group's energy interests, which included exploration and refining of crude oil and marketing of the final products. General Mining had first become involved in the petroleum sector back in 1968 when it participated in a joint venture launching the country's first petrol marketing company, Trek Beleggings (Trek Investment). The key event in the formation of Engen took place in July 1989 with Gencor's purchase, for US$150 million, of Mobil Southern Africa from its disinvesting parent company. Its major assets were a refinery in Durban, the Mobil management team, and a country-wide network of approximately 1,150 service station sites.

Engen's other major interests included: the Trek network of petroleum outlets; 20 percent interest in the oil and gas exploration outfit, Soekor; and a 30 percent stake in, as well as the management contract for, Mossgas, a synthetic fuels venture.

In 1991 Gencor was an investment holding company with a mining house as its major interest. It has been left, in Keys's words, as ''a pool of risk capital with connected businesses that are in our sphere of control but which in no sense can be regarded as one large business.''

Control rested with the Sanlam insurance group, still a major shareholder in Federale Mynbou. The other major shareholder, Rembrandt, the tobacco and luxury goods empire built up by South African entrepreneur Anton Rupert, controlled such companies as Rothmans, Dunhill, and Cartier Monde. Rembrandt had been willing to put up money for Gencor acquisitions.

The decade since Gencor's formation was a time of upheaval for the group. In the first half of the 1980s there was a lack of direction at Gencor but this had changed with the advent of Derek Keys.

A New Gencor for a New Century

Keys was succeeded by Brian Gilbertson, who presided over Gencor at a time when politicians viewed the pyramid structure of such conglomerates with suspicion. Unbundling these complicated structures would also tend to increase share prices, which were traditionally undervalued in this system. Subsequently, Gencor divested itself of Engen, Genbel, Malbak, and Sappi.

Gencor bought Billiton International from Royal Dutch Shell in 1994 for £780 million, giving Gencor the opportunity to operate as an aluminum trader as well as producer. However, Billiton was not to remain very long under Gencor's umbrella.

In 1995, Alusaf began operating the mammoth Hillside Aluminum Smelter, which, when combined with the upgrade of a smaller Alusaf facility, nearly doubled Africa's production of the metal. The company planned an even larger smelter in Mozambique. Rangold bought some of Gengold's less profitable mines in 1995, while Gengold acquired some new mines of its own.

The European Commission scuttled Gencor's plans to merge Implats with Lonrho's platinum interests (LPD) on anti-competition grounds. The only other competitor in South Africa, the EC reasoned, would have been Amplats (the platinum interests of Anglo American Corp.), and Russia was the only other external supplier. Gencor already owned a 27 percent share in the Lonrho operations Western Platinum and Eastern Platinum.

Steel and ferroalloys contributed most (31.7 percent) to revenues in 1996; aluminum accounted for the next largest share (27 percent). Other operations each contributed less than a tenth of total revenues. Approximately half the company's revenues came from abroad.

In 1997, Gencor's base metals and non-gold interests were split off as a separate company, Billiton, to be based in London. Alusaf, titanium producer Richards Bay Minerals, and the steel and ferroalloys division remained part of Billiton after the transition. The company had a market capitalization of £4.6 billion (US$7.7 billion). The new Gencor would henceforth specialize in precious metals.

A US$194 million sale of mines and exploration rights to Eldorado Gold Corporation, based in Canada, was canceled in the summer of 1997. An unstable gold market was cited as the cause. The company continued to stake out investments in Australia, Indonesia, and Vietnam.

Principal Subsidiaries

Gencor (UK) Ltd.; Impala Platinum Holdings Limited (46%); Western Platinum Limited (27%); Eastern Platinum Limited (27%).

Principal Operating Units

Gold; Platinum; New Business and Trading.

Further Reading

"All That Glitters: Gencor," *Economist,* March 9, 1996.

Benjamin, Paul, "Mining Stands on the Brink of New Era," *Business Day,* September 20, 1996.

Beresford, Belinda, "Gencor to Separate Gold, Other Interests," *Business Day,* June 2, 1997.

Dhliwayo, Dominic, "Mega Aluminum Smelter for Maputo?" *African Business,* January 1997, pp. 27–28.

Freimond, Chris, "Rob Angel—Driving Engen," *Executive,* May 1990.

"Gencor to Shed Base Metals and Buy Australian Nickel," *New York Times,* June 19, 1997.

Green, Timothy, *The New World of Gold,* New York: Walker and Co., 1981.

Jones, J. D. F., *Through Fortress and Rock: The Story of Gencor 1895–1995,* Johannesburg: J. Ball, 1996.

Kilalea, Des, "Gencor Looks Ahead," *Finance Week,* April 27-May 3, 1989.

McKay, David, "Gencor, Australian Firm in Indonesian Deal," *Business Day,* October 23, 1996.

——, "Gencor to Revise Mozambique Plan," *Business Day,* February 26, 1997.

McNulty, Andrew, "Man of the Year—Gencor's Derek Keys," *Financial Mail,* December 25, 1987.

"Meet Genmin," Johannesburg, Gencor, March 1990.

"Mining Survey," Supplement to *Financial Mail,* July 28, 1978.

Ross, Priscilla, "Implats' Impasse," *African Business,* June 1996, p. 22.

Scudder, Brian, "Tiny Shouts, But Nobody Listens," *African Business,* January 1996, p. 23.

"South African Conglomerates: The Unbundling Begins," *Economist,* May 15, 1993.

"South African Gold: A New Vein," *Economist,* September 27, 1997.

"Unbundling: Restructuring the Corporate Scene," *Barron's,* October 11, 1993, p. 72.

—Philip Gawith
—updated by Frederick C. Ingram

Gianni Versace SpA

Via Della Spiga 25
I-20121 Milan
Italy
+39 2 760 931
Fax: +39 2 760 004 122
Web site: http://www.moda.iol.it/stilisti/versace

Private Company
Founded: 1977
Employees: 1,200
Sales: L845 billion (US$557 million) (1996)
SICs: 2329 Men's & Boy's Clothing; 2335 Women's Dresses; 3911 Jewelry; 3961 Costume Jewelry

Headquartered in a Milanese palazzo, Gianni Versace SpA is second only to rival house Giorgio Armani among Italy's fashion designers. The Versace name is estimated to generate US$2 billion at retail and US$1 billion wholesale. the company's diverse offerings enable people to swathe themselves in Versace from head to toe, including lingerie, umbrellas, makeup, hosiery, shoes, watches, jewelry, and fragrances. Clients can even surround themselves with furnishings from the Home Signature line of decor. Lines within the Versace group include Istante, Versus, Versace Jeans Couture, Versace Sport, Versatile, Versace Classic 2, Young Versace, and Home Signature. By the late 1990s, the fashion empire stretched from the design table to manufacturing sites to the sales counter. Its wares are distributed through more than 300 boutiques and 2,000 affiliated stores.

The privately held business was within months of going public when, on July 15, 1997, its founder and namesake, award-winning Italian fashion designer Gianni Versace, was gunned down in front of his Miami Beach mansion. The 50-year-old's untimely death threatened to unravel his company. But for virtually all of its 20 years in business, the apparel house has been a family affair. Gianni's older brother, Santo, managed the finances, while younger sister Donatella oversaw advertising, accessories, and her own line within the group. In the wake of the family tragedy, Donatella assumed the role of chief designer. Both were committed to taking the company public in 1998.

Late 1970s Foundation

Born in southern Italy in 1946, Gianni Versace was the son of an appliance salesman and a seamstress. His mother, Francesca, fashioned gowns for the region's elite. Gianni is said to have started down the road to high fashion when, as a boy, he made little dolls and puppets from the snippets of fabric that littered the floor of her studio. After studying architecture, Gianni stayed in his hometown of Reggio Calabria through the 1960s, first apprenticing with his mother and later running two separate boutiques showcasing his men's and women's fashions.

In 1972 Ezio Nicosia, owner of Florentine Flowers of Lucca, invited Gianni to move to Milan and design a knitwear collection for fall and winter. The 25-year-old's designs were so successful that he earned a Volkswagen convertible as a bonus to his regular fee. In the years to come, Versace contracted with De Parisini of Santa Margherita, Callaghan, Alma, and Genny Group's ready-to-wear lines. Versace created the Complice collection for Genny before striking out on his own in 1977 and presenting his first signature collection the following spring. His brightly colored, sexy styles for women generated sales of L20 billion (US$11 million) that first year. Versace opened his first Milanese boutique and brought out his first menswear collection in 1978.

Older brother Santo was with him from the beginning, having moved to Milan in 1976. An accountant, Santo put his business administration degree to good use as managing director and chairman of Gianni Versace SpA. Younger sister Donatella started out coordinating accessories with Gianni's designs, and quickly moved into advertising and promotion. Perhaps most importantly, she served as what Gianni called his "inspiring muse." The three siblings shared ownership of the apparel firm, albeit not evenly; Gianni held 45 percent, Santo 35 percent, and Donatella 20 percent.

Showmanship Drives Design House in 1980s

Versace cultivated symbiotic relationships with arts and artists, especially in the areas of theater, popular music, and dance. These ties would prove mutually beneficial; Versace fashioned

Company Perspectives:

"I've always said that I would like to mix rock and simplicity because this is fashion, they're the extremes, chic and shock. That's why Lady Diana and Madonna—two of the most important women of the moment—wear Versace and I think I'm satisfied by this. Even if it took me twenty years, I've got to where I wanted to go." —Gianni Versace

the costumes and clothing that kept the famous looking chic, and his clients served as walking billboards for the designer's wares. Versace forged especially close ties to the Teatro alla Scala. This "sideline" was reflected in his fashion collections, which took on a theatricality of their own. His circle of celebrity friends/clients widened in step with his design prowess. Richard Avedon photographed his collections. Andy Warhol painted his portrait. Later, Sylvester Stallone and Madonna modeled for his advertisements.

Versace's own paradoxical tastes were reflected in his designs. As he told the *New York Times*'s Amy M. Spindler in an interview just before his death, "contrasts [are] the key to all my creations." He designed costumes for Elton John's rock concerts as well as ballets produced by Maurice Bejart. His famous female fans ranged from punky, slutty Courtney Love to impeccably chic Diana, Princess of Wales. He was called a "rock 'n' rolling exhibitionist," "vividly committed to the hedonism of late 20th-century culture," but he was also known as a devoted brother and uncle. These disparities found expression in designs that always featured some element of "intentional imperfection": draped gowns of metal mesh, leopard-print babydoll dresses, asymmetrical necklines and hemlines, and lace/metal combinations. Other Versace trademarks would emerge over the course of the 1980s; colorful silk prints, high heels, baroque themes, leather, and overt sexuality.

The designer's Fall/Winter women's collection earned Versace his first major award, the first of four career L'Occhio d'Oros, in 1982. With his creative reputation firmly in place, Versace moved quickly to capitalize on his brand equity. Like fashion icons before him, Versace realized that while most women could not afford a $15,000 signature dress, many more could afford a distinctively printed silk scarf or a watch with his Medusa-head logo. The designer started his diversification with fragrances. Accessories—most produced from Versace designs by licensees—ran the gamut from socks to umbrellas, sunglasses, jewelry, and watches. Versace was also quick to make international forays, establishing company-owned and franchised boutiques in Europe and Asia in the early 1980s. By the mid-1990s, 25 percent of sales would come from Asia.

March 1985 saw the introduction of Versace's first Istante collection, a ready-to-wear line of "conservative-chic" clothing designed by Gianni with help from longtime companion Antonio D'Amico and sister Donatella. Istante was organized not only as a separate brand, but also a distinct subsidiary of the Versace group, Istante Vesa s.r.l. In 1989, Versace introduced Atelier Versace, a haute couture line featuring custom-made fashions costing tens of thousands of dollars. Also launched in 1989, the Versus line was Donatella's venue. Its ready-to-wear garments were targeted at a younger, trendier audience. By the mid-1990s, Versus would generate 10 percent of corporate sales.

By 1989, Gianni Versace SpA's annual revenues totaled L158 billion, with net income of L7.6 billion. At this time, the Versace brand was generating L520 billion at wholesale.

Rapid Diversification Paces 1990s Expansion

The family business stepped up the pace of growth through brand extension—known in fashion parlance as "product pyramiding"—in the 1990s. In 1991, the company introduced Versatile, a line of designer clothes for full-figured women that included leopard catsuits, pleated miniskirts, and bejeweled bustiers in bright colors. That same year, Versace brought out Versace Jeans Couture, a casual line of clothing headlined by $200 jeans. A line of Home Signature tableware, bath and bed linens, lamps, carpets, and more, was launched in 1993. The company diversified into the highly competitive realm of color cosmetics with the European introduction of Versace Make-up in 1997. It was a rapid, but well-considered expansion that was careful not to oversaturate and possibly diminish the brand's aura of exclusivity and cachet.

Analysts praised the company's managerial and manufacturing agility. John Roussant of *Business Week* noted that "The Versaces typically made decisions with lightning speed—a key competitive advantage in an industry where styles and fads change overnight." Over the years, Versace also accumulated controlling interests in 10 of its manufacturing licensees, a factor that enabled the company to seize the initiative when a product proved particularly popular. Weekly sales reports kept the family troika up-to-date on their company's hottest items.

Geographic as well as product diversification proved vital to Versace's expansion. In 1994, Europe was still the company's largest market, accounting for half of annual revenues. Though the company had established its initial U.S. boutique in Coconut Grove, Florida, in 1981, North America generated less than 20 percent of sales in 1994. That year, Gianni and Santo announced their intent to make the U.S. Versace's primary export market and a generator of at least 30 percent of annual sales. Santo told *WWD's* Sara Gay Forden that "The U.S. is our leading priority right now. It has to become our biggest export market." The strategy for achieving this goal included the establishment of an American distribution subsidiary and the launch of a nine-story boutique in a landmark New York City building on Fifth Avenue.

Sales more than doubled, from L221 billion in 1990 to L510 billion in 1994, while net income mushroomed from L14.2 billion to L39.7 billion. In 1994, the Versace brand generated nearly L1.2 trillion at wholesale.

Versace planned a mid-decade initial public offering to finance continued growth. In fact, preparations for this eventuality can be traced to 1986, when Versace opened his books to the public and hired an accounting firm to audit the records. In the spring of 1997 Gianni told *Business Week*'s Rome bureau chief John Roussant, "I'd like people to be as crazy for my shares as they are for my clothes." Finance man Santo concurred, telling Sara Gay Forden of *WWD* that the siblings sought to "give this group a life that is autonomous from that of its founders. A company that goes public is like a company that automatically acquires a second and third generation. It is a commitment to carry Versace beyond its founders.'' Versace bypassed the Milan stock market, instead seeking a listing on the New York Stock Exchange. In May 1997, Gianni Versace SpA spun off L150 billion (US$86.9 million) worth of family property—including lavish homes and artwork—to a private company known as Ordersystem.

However, the company had some troubling issues to overcome before winning the confidence of the investment community. In May 1997 Santo Versace was found guilty of bribing tax officials, a conviction that the Versace chairman predictably appealed. Then there were the persistent—and steadfastly renounced—rumors that the company had links to organized crime. Versace's European boutiques suffered six burglaries in just four months in 1996, losing L500 million (US$320,000) worth of merchandise. Though none of these issues—perceived or real—were devastating, the Versaces sought to remove any encumbrances to its initial stock valuation.

Founder's Murder Brings Unexpected Transition

All involved with Versace realized a public stock offering had the potential to serve as a turning point for the company, one that could shift its already-impressive growth into high gear. But no one could have predicted the transition forced by spree killer Andrew Cunanan, who shot Gianni Versace twice in the head at point blank range on the morning of July 15, 1997.

More than one critic noted that Versace ''was killed at his peak, a time when his continual retooling of his inventions had produced his best work ever.'' Trade magazine *Daily News Record* asserted that ''fashion has lost one of its brightest superstars at the height of his career.'' *Time* magazine's John Greenwald concurred that ''at his death, the designer was at the height of his powers.'' Barely a month before he had introduced what the *Daily News Record* called ''one of the strongest collections in years.'' News of Versace's death spurred a run on the more than 2,000 boutiques and department stores worldwide that carried his branded goods. But clients new and old soon found that the designer's demise would not necessarily doom his company.

Though many design houses have died along with their founders, fashion analysts cited several attributes that would help the Versace group outlive its namesake. Foremost were the well-known brand and Medusa-head logo, embodying a core identity from which new product lines could continue to evolve. And while Gianni Versace had been personally responsible for the creation of the signature lines that generated 45 percent of his company's profits, he had already assembled an international team of design assistants headed by sister Donatella. Furthermore, Donatella had taken on increased responsibilities for several years in the mid-1990s, when Gianni was diagnosed with cancer of the lymph nodes. His 1996 recovery made the murder all the more ironic. A statement released by the family shortly after Versace's death asserted that ''the indomitable spirit, the amazing vitality and the faith in creativity that makes Gianni Versace so important to everyone is something that we are completely committed to and most capable of continuing.''

Preparations for the 1998 initial public offering continued. Within days of his murder, Gianni had hired investment banking house Morgan Stanley to underwrite the $350 million stock offering. That September, his surviving siblings moved to consolidate three directly controlled subsidiaries—Istante Vesa SRL, manufacturing arm Alias SpA, and boutique chain Modifin SA—into Gianni Versace SpA.

Gianni Versace left *de facto* control of his global enterprise in the hands of sister Donatella by bequeathing his stake in the company to her 11-year-old daughter, Allegra Beck. Donatella presented her first emotion-charged signature collection in October 1997 to a crowd of very supportive designers, Hollywood celebrities, and rock stars. Trade magazine *WWD* cheered her designs of rubber, leather, silk, and beads with the headline, ''Bravo, Donatella!''

Further Reading

Bellafante, Ginia, ''La Dolce Vita: Gianni Versace Sold the World a Fantasy of Unrestrained Opulence,'' *Time,* July 28, 1997, pp. 36–42.

Bounds, Wendy, and Beth Burkstrand, ''Shoppers Pay Respects to Versace at Cash Registers Across Country,'' *Wall Street Journal,* July 17, 1997, p. B1.

Boyd, Suzanne, *Maclean's,* July 28, 1997, p. 25.

''Bravo Donatella!,'' *WWD,* October 10, 1997, pp. 1–3.

Carloni, Maria Vittoria, ''Stylists at Work: The Secrets of the Versace Team,'' *Panorama,* May 10, 1995, http://www.moda.iol.it/stilisti/versace/articol.htm.

Conti, Samantha, ''Versace Wills His Stake to Niece,'' *WWD,* September 18, 1997, p. 8.

Costin, Glynis, ''Remembering Gianni,'' *Los Angeles Magazine,* September 1997, pp. 78–83.

Daspin, Eileen, ''Breaking the Rules,'' *WWD,* March 11, 1992, p. S30.

DeCarlo, Frank, ''Legacy of a Celebrity Designer,'' *Newsweek,* July 28, 1997, p. 40.

Foley, Bridget, ''Donatella's First Collection,'' *WWD,* October 1, 1997, pp. 1–2.

Forden, Sara Gay, ''Versace Going Forward with IPO Preparations,'' *WWD,* August 14, 1997, p. 13.

——, ''Versace Sets Sights on Wall Street,'' *WWD,* February 23, 1994, p. 18.

——, ''Very Versace: Making America No. 1,'' *WWD,* November 1, 1994, p. 15.

Greenwald, John, ''Will His Fashion Empire Survive?'' *Time,* July 28, 1997, p. 42.

Kaplan, Don, ''Versace's Flagship Boutique Opens Today,'' *Daily News Record,* August 26, 1996, p. 6.

Luscombe, Belinda, ''Little Sister, Big Success,'' *Time,* October 20, 1997, p. 119.

Martin, Richard, *Versace,* New York: Vendome Press, 1997.

Pener, Degen, ''Murder in Miami,'' *Entertainment Weekly,* July 25, 1997, pp. 6–7.

Socha, Miles, ''Carrying on After the Death of a Designer,'' *Daily News Record,* September 19, 1997, p. 6.

——, ''The Versace Legacy: Bold and Baroque,'' *Daily News Record,* July 16, 1997, p. 1.

Spindler, Amy M., ''Versace's Errors Showed Him a Way,'' *New York Times,* August 5, 1997, p. B9.

Steinhauer, Jennifer, ''His Good Label Lives After Him,'' *New York Times,* July 19, 1997, pp. 31, 33.

Versace, Gianni, *South Beach Stories,* Milano: Leonardo Arte, 1993.

''The Versace Story,'' http://www.moda.iol.it/stilisti/versace/story.htm.

Walsh, Sharon, ''Versace Empire's Fate Up to Family,'' *Washington Post,* July 17, 1997, p. C3.

—April Dougal Gasbarre

THE QUALITY FOOD PEOPLE

Giant Food Inc.

6400 Sheriff Road
Landover, Maryland 20785
U.S.A.
(301) 341-4100
Fax: (301) 618-4970

Public Company
Incorporated: 1935 as Giant Food Shopping Center Inc.
Employees: 27,000
Sales: $3.88 billion (1997)
Stock Exchanges: American Pacific Philadelphia
SICs: 4225 General Warehousing & Storage; 5411 Grocery Stores; 5912 Drug Stores & Proprietary Stores; 6531 Real Estate Agents & Managers

From its Depression-era beginnings as Giant Food Shopping Center Inc., Giant Food Inc. has become a large, vertically integrated regional supermarket and pharmacy chain. Giant operates 173 supermarkets (133 of which are combination food and drug stores); 110 are in the Washington, D.C., metropolitan area; 42 are in the Baltimore, Maryland, metropolitan area; with the remainder elsewhere in Virginia and Maryland and in Delaware, New Jersey, and Pennsylvania (they operate under the name ''Super G'' in these last three states; under ''Giant'' everywhere else). Its stores are large (average size is 45,000 square feet; 61 stores are larger than 50,000 square feet), and focus on providing their customers with quality, value, and service. Giant dominates its main market areas with 45 percent of the Washington market and a large share of the Baltimore market. The company also runs three freestanding pharmacies in Virginia, Maryland, and Washington, D.C. In addition, Giant's GFS Realty, Inc. subsidiary owns or controls 18 shopping centers and five freestanding combination food and drug stores. Distribution centers are located in Landover, Maryland, and Jessup, Maryland. Half of Giant Food's voting stock is owned by U.K. food retailer J. Sainsbury PLC, which also owns Shaw's Supermarkets, a New England grocery chain.

Great Depression Beginnings

Starting a new business during the Great Depression was a risk for Giant's founder, Nehemiah Myer (N. M.) Cohen, but he had been watching the progress of the ''supermarkets'' that had begun to open in the early 1930s and felt that they were the business of the future. Cohen, a rabbi, had emigrated from Palestine after World War I and settled in Carnegie, Pennsylvania, where he soon opened a kosher meat market. He later moved to Lancaster, Pennsylvania, and eventually opened three butcher shops there. To open his first supermarket Cohen sought the help of food distributor Samuel Lehrman, who provided the financial backing. Lehrman's son Jacob was also a partner in the venture. They chose Washington, D.C., as their location, figuring that government employment would keep the economy there stable. Giant Food Shopping Center opened its doors in early 1936 as Washington's first mass-merchandised supermarket. Amid the unemployment and breadlines that followed the 1929 stock market crash, Giant Food made its impact on the community by introducing both self-service and one-stop shopping to the consumer. Coupled with its lower prices, these features kept the store busy and crowded from its opening days.

By 1939 Giant had expanded to three stores. Giant's fourth store had a brick-and-glass facade that spelled out its name and was lighted at night, an innovation at the time. Just as the United States entered World War II, Giant opened its sixth store, in Arlington, Virginia, the first outside of the District of Columbia.

The war had a detrimental effect on the supermarket industry as personnel shortages, product shortages, and rationing became prevalent. Giant, like many other businesses, began employing women to counter the manpower shortage, and female checkers soon became a permanent part of the American grocery store.

Moved to Vertically Integrate in Postwar Years

Giant stopped expanding during the war, but in 1945 it opened two new stores in Washington and one in Virginia. In the late 1940s, Giant began to move toward vertical integration, leasing a slaughterhouse to ship meat to all its stores. In 1948 Giant bought the Sheridan Bakery, which had been supplying baked goods to the chain. Renamed for Jacob Lehrman's daughter, Heidi Bakery continuously provided bread and baked goods for all Giant stores both from the original bakery location in Silver Spring, Maryland, and from the in-store bakeries developed in later years. (In 1965 the bakery baked a 700-pound cake for President Lyndon Johnson's Inaugural Ball.) In 1952 Giant opened the Giant Retail Bakery in downtown Washington to sell only bakery goods, but this venture was not successful and was closed within a few years. By 1949 Giant had 19 stores, including three in Maryland and three in Virginia.

Between 1950 and 1952, Giant added five new stores, joining in the general expansion of the American economy. At this time, the shopping center concept was taking hold in America and Giant put a new store in the Congressional Plaza Shopping Center in Rockville, Maryland. In 1955 Giant Construction Company was incorporated to build Giant stores. Giant Food Properties—an independent company which eventually came under the control of Giant and was later known as GFS Realty, Inc.—was established to handle the sale and lease of real estate for the company.

In 1955 the chain opened its first store in Baltimore and in 1956, its first in the Richmond, Virginia, market. By this time 48 percent of all its stores were located in shopping centers. In 1958, riding a new merchandising trend of combination supermarket/department/discount stores, Giant opened its first Super Giant store and within a year had opened eight more. Also in 1958 the company opened its new headquarters and distribution center on a 40-acre site in Landover, Maryland. At the same time, an addition to the Heidi Bakery doubled its production capacity.

In 1957 Giant Food Shopping Center Inc. became Giant Food Inc., and fiscal 1958 saw sales of more than $100 million dollars. In 1959 the company, with 53 stores (including nine Super Giants) went public.

During this time Giant computerized its inventory data, customer information, and payroll and bookkeeping operations. Customer service features added in the 1950s included self-opening doors, mechanized checkouts, and open display cases to make meats and frozen food directly accessible to the customer.

In the 1950s, Giant initiated a scholarship program to encourage students to pursue food management careers. Two of the first five recipients later became senior vice-presidents at Giant. This scholarship program is only one of the ways in which Giant has contributed to the community over the years. In the aftermath of the racial unrest of the 1960s, Giant took a leading role in providing food for those made homeless by riots. Giant's then-president Joseph B. Danzansky also directed a food drive, in which local and national businesses supplied food for demonstrators camped in "Resurrection City" in Washington during a two-week protest to call attention to the poor in America.

In 1961 Giant's stock began trading on the American Stock Exchange as well as the Washington branch of the Philadelphia-Baltimore Stock Exchange. In its stores, Giant began developing its private-label products and offering plastic housewares and specialty food items in response to customer demands. Giant built its first combination food store and pharmacy in 1962.

Although the company had been criticized for bypassing predominantly black neighborhoods, by the mid-1960s Giant did begin to open stores in the inner city. In the rioting that followed the assassination of Martin Luther King, Jr., in 1968, store managers and black employees faced down angry mobs at Giant stores, and the chain escaped much of the looting and damage of the period.

Giant's management implemented three policies during this time which were designed to decrease employee turnover. It began recognizing talented young workers (age 25 and under) and giving them increased management responsibility—the company dedicated itself to promoting from within—and an employee tuition-assistance program was started.

In 1964 founder N. M. Cohen stepped down as president and became chairman of the board, a newly created position. Joseph Danzansky, longtime legal counsel, became president. This election touched off a legal battle for control of Giant between the Cohen family and Jacob Lehrman. The Cohens gained operating control of the company, through their control of four of the seven seats on the board of directors, but Lehrman remained on the board (the Cohen and Lehrman families continued to each hold 50 percent of Giant's voting stock). In 1977 N. M. Cohen was made honorary chairman of the board, Danzansky became chairman, and N. M.'s son Israel became president and CEO—becoming chairman as well upon Danzansky's death in 1979. Izzy, as he was known, had been in the business since he was a delivery boy in his father's butcher shops before the days of Giant Food. He continued his father's informal and friendly, but strict, management style.

The 1970s were the "decade of the consumer"; Giant responded to this movement by hiring its own consumer advocate, Esther Peterson, formerly a consumer adviser to the Kennedy and Johnson administrations. The company began a program of providing information to consumers about the food they were buying, and also worked with the Food and Drug Administration to develop and test nutrition labeling. Educational and informational brochures were distributed for free, and unit pricing and open dating were implemented. In 1972 Giant opened its Quality Assurance Laboratory to monitor the quality and safety of the food it sold, and in 1974 the company implemented a toy-safety program by pledging to sell only those toys certified safe by the manufacturer.

In another move toward vertical integration, Giant built a warehouse and grocery-distribution center in Jessup, Maryland. The Jessup center opened in 1973 and was a model of automated operations. Danzansky described it in 1974 to *Nation's Business* as "a Buck Rogers kind of thing. Push a button and the stuff almost jumps on the truck."

In the early 1970s Giant sold its four freestanding Super Giant stores to Woolco and rededicated itself to food retailing. In the inflationary period of the middle 1970s, Giant began discounting its prices, gambling that increased volume would counterbalance lower prices. In fiscal 1979 the company had its first billion-dollar year.

In 1975 Giant began using computer-assisted checkout and in 1979 it installed price-scanning equipment in all of its stores. While Giant was making supermarket history by implementing scanners, consumer activists and legislators in Washington accused the company of using the scanning system to trick unwary customers into paying higher prices since prices were posted only on shelves, not each item. Giant weathered the storm of protests and proved with its data that the system reduced operating costs.

Continued to Expand and Vertically Integrate in the 1980s

Giant Food in the 1980s continued both expansion and vertical integration to hold and build its place in its market. In 1982 it opened Someplace Special in McLean, Virginia, a gourmet food store that sold specialty items and offered services such as menu planning, flower arranging, delivery service, and catering for its affluent customers. While not its most profitable store, Giant used Someplace Special to test consumer demand for gourmet food and other specialty items. The chain also experimented with warehouse-type stores, opening three under the name Save Right; these were eventually converted to the Giant name. In 1982 Giant closed its Richmond, Virginia, stores after 25 years of operating in that city. By the mid-1980s about half of Giant's stores were food and pharmacy combinations. In the 1970s Giant had created Pants Corral stores in its Super Giants as part of a deal to sell Levi's jeans. The Pants Corral division, which also included 30 freestanding stores, was sold in 1985.

Expansion at Giant in the 1980s included increasing store size; in 1983 it opened a 60,000-square-foot store in a former Super Giant. This flagship store stocked some 40,000 items and combined such features as gourmet food, cosmetics, bulk food items, an in-store bakery, and a salad bar. Vertical integration continued with the opening of an ice cream plant and a soda-bottling plant in 1985, both in Jessup, Maryland. Giant also focused on remodeling and redesigning existing stores in the late 1980s.

Giant attributed much of its success over the years to the principles on which it was founded, the personal philosophy of founder N. M. Cohen. Cohen not only closely monitored his business to spot trends, but was the force behind the company's continuous emphasis on quality, value, and service. Active in the company until he was 90, the elder Cohen died in 1984 at age 93.

Consumer-oriented programs continued to be a part of Giant's service. Giant initiated a point-of-purchase ''special diet alert'' shelf label to increase customer awareness of low-fat, low-calorie, and low-sodium foods. Sales of these items were monitored for two years and data supplied to the U.S. Food and Drug Administration for use in measuring the effectiveness of such shelf-labeling programs. Giant also participated in an ''Eat for Health'' campaign with the National Cancer Institute. Bulk food bins, which allow customers to buy the amount they want, and increased availability of specialty food items were offered in response to consumer input, and Giant launched a corporate customer service center to handle questions, concerns, and compliments from both customers and employees.

Expanded into New Territories in 1990s

Giant's growth slowed some in the early 1990s as the company found that it had little room to expand within the existing markets it served. Competition was becoming more heated; discounters and warehousers—including Leedmark, Shopper's Food Warehouse, Price Club, and BJ's Wholesale Club—were cutting into Giant's market share in Washington and Baltimore. Giant began the decade with 149 stores and had added just 6 stores to the total by the end of 1993. The company did, however, enter the discount drugstore market in 1991 with the opening of its first Super G Deep Discount Drug Store in Maryland. Two other freestanding pharmacies were soon opened in Virginia and Washington. In September 1992, Israel Cohen, then 79, named Pete L. Manos president of Giant, while Cohen remained chairman and CEO. Manos, who was now Cohen's heir apparent, had joined Giant as an accounting clerk in 1960 and worked his way up to the position of vice-president of food operations by 1985.

The years 1994 and 1995 were particularly momentous ones for Giant Food. In early 1994, the company opened its first store outside of Washington, D.C., Maryland, and Virginia with the debut of a store in Bear, Delaware, a suburb of Wilmington. Eastern Pennsylvania and southern New Jersey were soon added to the mix as well, with the company counting on these new northern markets as its base for future growth. Barred from using the Giant name in Pennsylvania, the company decided on the name ''Super G'' for its supermarkets in the new territories. By mid-1997, there were two Super Gs in Delaware, six in New Jersey, and two in Pennsylvania.

In November 1994, the heirs of Jacob Lehrman (who had died in 1974) sold their 50 percent voting stake and their 16 percent in nonvoting equity to J. Sainsbury, a U.K. supermarket firm, for $325 million. Cohen still held the other 50 percent in voting equity and control of four of the board seats, while Sainsbury now controlled three board seats. Sainsbury, unable for regulatory reasons to expand further in its home country, had turned to the United States for growth. It had purchased an initial stake in Shaw's Supermarkets, a New England chain, in 1983 then gained full control over Shaw's four years later. Analysts speculated that Sainsbury would eventually take control of Giant as well, and use its two U.S. chains as a base for a nationwide chain.

When Cohen died in November 1995 at the age of 83, speculation about the control of Giant was once again rife. Cohen's will, however, passed his 50 percent voting stake and control of Giant to a holding company controlled by a five-person management team consisting of Manos, who succeeded Cohen as chairman and CEO; Alvin Dobbin, executive vice-president and COO; David W. Rutstein, senior vice-president and general counsel; David B. Sykes, senior vice-president of finance; and Lillian Cohen Solomon, Cohen's sister. Although Sainsbury continued to deny that it wanted to take over Giant, the U.K. firm did increase its nonvoting stake in Giant to 20 percent in 1996.

Despite tough competition in its new Delaware, New Jersey, and Pennsylvania markets, Giant stepped up its expansion plans in 1996 when it announced it would open between 35 and 45 new stores in these states over the next decade. In June 1997 the company announced that it planned to open a new discount drugstore chain called Giant Discount Drug, with an initial 10 to 20 freestanding units slated for the Baltimore and Washington, D.C., areas. Meanwhile, a five-week truck driver strike that ended in January 1997 hurt Giant's financial performance in fiscal 1997; sales increased only marginally, from $3.86 billion in 1996 to $3.88 billion, while net income fell from $102.2 million in 1996 to $85.5 million.

Despite the small setback of 1997, Giant Food was still one of the most admired regional supermarket chains in the country. Throughout its history, its emphasis on quality, value, and service had held it in good stead. By continuing to expand geographically and increasing its freestanding drugstore operations in the late 1990s, Giant seemed to have a solid plan for growth within its highly competitive, low-margin fields.

Principal Subsidiaries

Giant of Maryland, Inc.; Giant of Salisbury, Inc.; Giant Construction Company, Inc.; GF McLean Shopping Center, Inc.; GFS Realty, Inc.; Warex-Jessup, Inc.; Bursil, Inc.; Cole Engineering, Inc.; LECO, Inc.; Giant Automatic Money Systems, Inc.; Shaw Community Supermarket, Inc. (85%); Bayside Traffic Services of Maryland, Inc.; Super G, Inc.; Montrose Crossing, Inc.; Friendship Macomb SC, Inc.; Giant of Talbot Co., Inc.; Giant of Cherry Hill, Inc.

Further Reading

Chisholm, Rupert, ''Giant Food to Speed Store Growth,'' *Supermarket News,* August 15, 1994, p. 7.

D'Innocenzio, Anne, ''Giant Unveils Plan to Spur Growth,'' *Supermarket News,* September 20, 1993, p. 10.

——, ''Naming of President at Giant Signals Change and Continuity,'' *Supermarket News,* September 21, 1992, p. 6.

Fallon, James, ''Sainsbury Plans to Boost Stake in Giant,'' *Supermarket News,* November 28, 1994, p. 4.

Farhi, Paul, ''Cohen, Lehrman Feuded for Years over Strategy,'' *Washington Post,* October 4, 1994, p. A10.

Fix, Janet L., '' 'My Dad Was Active Until He Was 90,' '' *Forbes,* November 4, 1985, p. 110.

Flood, Ramona G., ''Giant to Start Nonfood Category Management,'' *Supermarket News,* September 18, 1995, pp. 39, 59.

Marcial, Gene G., ''Giant Food: Good Enough to Eat?,'' *Business Week,* September 16, 1996, p. 96.

Orgel, David, ''Giant Charts Its Course for 21st Century,'' *Supermarket News,* June 17, 1996, p. 4.

——, ''Giant's Flexibility Continues Success,'' *Supermarket News,* December 16, 1996, pp. 66–67, 69.

——, ''Giant Steps,'' *Supermarket News,* December 16, 1996, pp. 1, 64–65, 69.

Owens, Jennifer, ''Giant Food CEO Sees Tough Road Ahead,'' *Supermarket News,* September 15, 1997, p. 6.

——, ''Giant Seeks Sites for New Drug Store Chain,'' *Supermarket News,* June 16, 1997, p. 48.

Pressler, Margaret Webb, ''Giant Food Speeds Up Northward Expansion,'' *Washington Post,* June 5, 1996, p. F1.

——, ''Israel Cohen, Chairman of Giant Food, Dies at 83,'' *Washington Post,* November 24, 1995, p. A1.

——, ''Who's Going to Mind the Store?,'' *Washington Post,* November 27, 1995, p. F12.

Saporito, Bill, ''The Giant of the Regional Food Chains,'' *Fortune,* November 25, 1985, p. 27.

Swisher, Kara, ''A Corporate Gentle Giant: New Partner Seems Unlikely to Change Israel Cohen's Leadership of Grocery Empire,'' *Washington Post,* October 24, 1994, p. F1.

Turcsik, Richard, ''Giant Sees Slide as Reversible,'' *Supermarket News,* September 16, 1991, p. 4.

Weinstein, Steve, ''Giant Steps,'' *Progressive Grocer,* November 1994, pp. 28–30, 34, 36.

Zwiebach, Elliot, ''Manos Leads Giant After Cohen's Death,'' *Supermarket News,* December 4, 1995, pp. 1, 62.

——, ''Sainsbury to Buy 50% of Giant's Voting Stock,'' *Supermarket News,* October 10, 1994, p. 1.

—updated by David E. Salamie

Goya Foods Inc.

100 Severn Drive
Secaucus, New Jersey 07094-1800
U.S.A.
(201) 348-4900
Fax: (201) 348-6609
Web site: http://www.wkbk.com/goya

Private Company
Founded: 1936
Employees: 2,000
Sales: $540 million (1995 est.)
SICs: 2099 Food Preparations, Not Elsewhere Classified; 5149 Groceries, General Line

With almost 1,000 items on sale, Goya Foods Inc. is the second largest Hispanic-owned company in the United States in the late 1990s. Its products include a full range of grocery, dairy, and frozen goods aimed at the general public as well as people of Latin American or Iberian birth or ancestry. The family-owned company maintains manufacturing and/or distribution facilities in the mainland United States, the Caribbean, and Spain.

Goya Foods to 1980

Goya Foods was founded in 1936 by Prudencio Unanue. He had left Spain as a youth in 1903 for Puerto Rico, where he established a small food business. He later moved to the metropolitan New York area and became a food broker for products imported from Spain. When the Spanish Civil War broke out in 1936, food supplies were cut off, and Unanue found himself out of work. He obtained a shipment of Moroccan sardines from a Spanish company and, with his wife, packaged them in a small Manhattan warehouse, selling to grocery stores. Unanue kept the Goya brand name of the sardines and also gave the Goya name to the olives and olive oil that he imported and sold.

Business picked up dramatically with the heavy influx of Puerto Ricans to New York City in the years immediately after World War II. Unanue established two canneries in Bayamon, Puerto Rico to produce the foods the newcomers could not buy in supermarkets, such as beef-tripe stew, tropical juices, *pasteles* (meat-filled pasties), *gandules* (pigeon peas), and some 25 varieties of beans. Goya salesmen went to the small Puerto Rican-owned grocery stores called *bodegas* to take orders for these goods. According to one of the founder's grandsons, other companies were selling foods to New York's Hispanics, but "the one thing that we did that was different was advertise, something unheard of in the '50s." Because management could not find an advertising agency that it felt was suitable to the company's needs, Goya formed its own: Inter-Americas Advertising Agency.

By 1969 Goya Foods was selling to food stores in the Midwest as well as along the East Coast from Boston to Miami, servicing 7,000 accounts through 67 Spanish-speaking salesmen. The company's packaging facilities were in Brooklyn. (Goya de Puerto Rico, the separate family-run corporation formed in 1949, was responsible for operations on the island.) The nation's largest distributor of Latin foods, Goya estimated that 80 percent of its customers were ethnic Puerto Ricans or Cubans. Revenues, which had increased 35 percent annually for the last four years, came to more than $20 million in 1968 for the company's 650 items. Prudencio's son Joseph became president and chief executive officer of the company in the early 1970s.

By 1979 Goya Foods had almost 1,000 employees and estimated annual sales of $90 million. The cooking, seasoning, and quality control for all 700 items was being done in Puerto Rico, which accounted for about a quarter of the sales total. A plant in Seville, Spain processed all the olive oil, olives, and capers, and another in the Dominican Republic handled pigeon peas and the fruit pulp for Goya's tropical juices. The company also owned a Chicago warehouse for distribution in the Midwest and other areas of expanding Hispanic population growth and a Florida fresh produce facility that made Goya one of the largest grocery wholesalers in the Miami area. The main facility had moved from Brooklyn to Secaucus, New Jersey, where the company had a 275,000-square-foot distribution and packaging plant.

Vertically integrated Goya had its own fleet of trucks, offering retailers direct, next day delivery from the warehouses.

Its salesmen dealt directly with the retailers (rather than through wholesalers or brokers), making weekly visits to all its accounts and selling Goya's goods to the smallest *bodega* at the same prices it did to supermarkets, which were now accounting for half of revenues. According to the company's sales chief, this was a comparatively recent change, because ''Fifteen years ago we had a hard time appealing to supermarkets. People told us they didn't want to offend their white customers.''

Steady Growth in the 1980s

By the end of 1981, when Goya's estimated revenues of $150 million made it the largest Hispanic-run firm in the country, it had 9,300 clients and 120 salesmen. Rice and beans each were accounting for about 15 to 20 percent of Goya's sales in 1982. Seasonings, including sauces as well as herbs, spices, and condiments, made up another 15 to 20 percent, and olives and olive oils accounted for 10 to 15 percent. Goya's 700-odd items (counting different product sizes) also included preserves, stews, canned vegetables and meats, soups, cheeses, and crackers, along with such exotic items as African red-palm oil, Cuban mango paste, Jamaican ginger beer, and malta—a nonalcoholic, noncarbonated licorice-tasting beverage composed of grain, malt, and hops. The company had enjoyed only limited success, however, reaching the highly competitive Cuban market in Florida. And Caribbean-oriented Goya had completely failed to crack the rapidly growing Mexican food market with the product line it introduced about 1977.

Around this time Goya also began an English-language television campaign intended to raise its market share by titillating the palates of mainstream Americans. In one ad Hispanics touted kidney beans and black-eyed peas to Anglo friends; in another the actress Hermione Gingold recommended Coco Goya, a cream-of-coconut mix for pina coladas. A new push in 1984, emphasizing foods that were both healthy and expensive, was aimed partly at the children and grandchildren of Hispanic immigrants. By praising the virtues of Caribbean foods, these ads were intended, said Goya's president, to ''remind them of their heritage, though you can't push that too far.'' One corporate insider joked that if all else failed ''we can always start another revolution in a Latin American country,'' thereby increasing immigration to the United States.

In fact, even discounting the civil wars in Nicaragua and El Salvador that were driving many refugees to the United States, Latin American migration northward was on the rise, swelling Goya's potential customer base. In 1985 the company opened a distribution center in Tampa and raised its estimated annual revenue to $250 million, with Hispanics accounting for close to 90 percent and the East Coast for 80 percent of mainland U.S. sales. For the rapidly growing Colombian community, Goya had added soda crackers and a block chocolate used in making hot beverages. Frozen products included *empanadillas* (beef-filled turnovers), *rellenos de papas* (potato balls stuffed with spices and meat), tamales, squid, codfish croquettes, paella, and tropical vegetables such as pigeon peas, *yautia,* and *yuca.* Nectar drinks and a line of frozen cocktail mixes were considered crossover items aimed at Anglos as well as Hispanics.

Mexican food, based on corn and chili peppers, continued to be a loser for the company, unfamiliar with a cuisine so different from that of the Caribbean, which used milder seasonings and rice as the staple grain. In 1981 Goya made another bid for the market, offering its own jalapeno peppers, chili sauce, refried beans, and taco shells. After this line failed, too, the company, in 1986, imported some foods from Mexico to sell in the Houston area, where it opened a warehouse. Many of the goods turned out to be shoddy, and others were delivered only erratically. In 1991 Goya tried again, buying a Houston distributor of Mexican food that it hoped would teach it how to reach the market. Although only five percent of the company's revenue was coming from Mexican foods, to become truly national Goya needed to establish a presence on the West Coast, where 70 percent of the Hispanic population was Mexican.

To retain its existing customer base, Goya's 200 salesmen—always clad in suits and ties—carried pocket-sized computers to feed orders into the company's data processing system. This sales force was expected to update information constantly on a community's ethnic composition, so that the company could regularly update its product offerings to match immigrant tastes. Supermarkets generally displayed all of Goya's products together. Spanish-language advertising was being handled by four in-house agencies based in New York, Chicago, Miami, and Puerto Rico, each one making its own media decisions. This posed special problems, since, as the company's marketing director pointed out in 1993, ''The language has to be neutral. You have to take a little bit of each country and put in the ad to get balanced for all nationalities.''

Aimed at non-Hispanic women, the English-language advertisements and commercials were being farmed to two outside agencies in the 1980s. One of them promoted Sazon, a spice package; the other promoted Adobo, a flavor enhancer for meat and poultry. A series of ''Elegant Goyas'' ads in the *New York Times* plugged the company's beans, olives, seasonings, and *tapas* (Spanish appetizers). Goya also was maintaining its long-standing high profile in Hispanic communities, contributing to charities and sponsoring sports teams and dance and theater troupes. A Goya float could be found in almost every one of the Puerto Rican Day parades held each June. In 1995 the company was represented at 18 parades and festivals in the New York area alone. The company sponsored a Metropolitan Museum of Art exhibition of the works of Francisco Goya that year; in return the museum served Goya Foods in the museum restaurant for the run of the show.

Reaching Out Further in the 1990s

Goya's revenues reached $410 million in 1991 and $453 million in 1992. It was continuing to introduce new products, including frozen bread pudding and corn bread, several Caribbean-style rice mixes, and salsas and guacamole for the Mexican market. The company also had added distribution facilities in Webster, Massachusetts and West Deptford, New Jersey, to better serve its northeast corridor market, and a new production facility for seasonings in Miami. The Secaucus warehouse was buying all of its more-than 80 frozen foods and half of the other products it sold from outside sources.

In 1994 Goya's product mix was even more varied and exotic, including *tostones* (fried green plantains) from Honduras, *nopalitos* (sliced cactus) from Mexico, and *harina pan,* a

Venezuelan corn flour used to make *arepas,* somewhat similar to English muffins. By 1995 sales had topped the $500 million mark and the company had 85 inventory control numbers for its bean products alone. Beans, indeed, well reflected the company's multinational product mix. Cubans, Mexicans, and Nicaraguans called them *frijoles,* but in Puerto Rico and the Dominican Republic they were *habichuelas,* and in Argentina, Paraguay, and Uruguay they were called *porotos.* Cubans in Miami wanted black beans, dry in 14-ounce packages. Puerto Ricans in New York preferred pink beans in water-packed cans. Nicaraguans looked for red beans. Mexicans, who wanted their beans refried, bought dry beans in sacks of four or 10 pounds.

Goya's line of soft drink flavors also was being chosen on the basis of their popularity in the homelands of the company's immigrant base. Strawberry, for example, was the top flavor in Mexico, while pineapple was a Caribbean favorite. These flavors were introduced in 1997, along with mandarin orange, fruit punch, tamarind, and lemon-lime. Other sodas being marketed by Goya were coconut water (water with creamy pulp from young, green coconuts), champagne cola, pina, mango, guava, and ginger beer. The carbonated line was being distributed in 38 states. Goya also offered a wide selection of tropical nectars, teas, and juices, plus Goya Malta and Malta Light.

In an effort to reach out to non-Hispanic customers, Goya recast its labels in 1997 to include the English as well as Spanish name of each product on the front, instead of the back, as previously. Joseph F. Unanue, son of the company president, said the change also was an acknowledgment that Hispanics in the United States were becoming more assimilated, citing a recent survey that showed 35 percent considered themselves primarily English speakers. Accordingly, Goya's English-language advertising was being refocused to target these acculturalized Hispanics by adding a more Latin feel and including rice and beans when prepared foods were featured. The U.S. Hispanic population was nearing 30 million in 1997, with buying power estimated at $228 billion annually.

Goya remained a private, entirely family-owned company in the 1990s. Two of the founder's four sons and at least six of his 18 grandchildren were working for the firm. The Unanues had a combined net worth estimated at $400 million in 1993.

Further Reading

Briceno, Carlos, "Goya Says Its Soft Drinks Speak the Language of New Immigrants," *Beverage World (Perspectives),* August 31, 1997, p. 22.

Brown, Christie, "Goya O'Boya," *Forbes,* February 26, 1996, p. 102.

Deutsch, Claudia H., "Goya Braces for a Challenge from the Food Giants," *New York Times,* February 24, 1991, Sec. 3, p. 5.

Giges, Nancy, "Hispanic Marketer Goya Plans Mass-Market Bid," *Advertising Age,* October 11, 1982, pp. 4, 61.

"Goya Foods: A New Conquistador?" *Sales Marketing,* March 15, 1969, pp. 37–38.

"Goya Sales Target: Not Just Hispanic," *New York Times,* March 26, 1984, pp. D1, D8.

Lowenstein, Roger, "Goya Foods Inc. No. 1 in Hispanic Market, Aims To Broaden Base," *Wall Street Journal,* March 23, 1982, pp. 1, 24.

McAlevey, Peter, "Selling to the Anglos," *Newsweek,* May 17, 1982, p. 84.

McCoy, Frank, "Goya: A Lot More Than Black Beans and *Sofrito,*" *Business Week,* December 7, 1987, pp. 137–138.

Richards, Rhonda, "Goya Foods Born of a Job Lost," *USA Today,* May 10, 1993, pp. 1E–2E.

Schultz, Ellen, "Goya Crosses All the Borders," *Marketing & Media Decisions,* September 1986, pp. 78–80, 82, 84.

Trachtenberg, Jeffrey A., "Latin Beat," *Forbes,* October 1, 1984, pp. 234, 236.

Trager, Cara S., "Goya Foods Tests Mainstream Market's Waters," *Advertising Age,* February 9, 1987, pp. S20–S21.

Vidal, David, "Goya: Spanish Flavor in U.S.," *New York Times,* April 23, 1979, pp. D1, D5.

Walters, David C., "Goya Grows, Seeks New Market," *Christian Science Monitor,* May 27, 1993, p. 8.

Wheelan, Carol, "Goya Gains as Hispanic Market Grows," *Food & Beverage Marketing,* November 1986, pp. 27–28.

Whitfield, Mimi, "How Four Companies Reach the Hispanic Market," *Knight-Ridder/Tribune Business News,* October 29, 1995, p. 10290327.

——, "New Jersey-Based Goya Foods Targets 'New Hispanics,'" *Knight-Ridder/Tribune Business News,* September 26, 1997, p. 926B0961.

Zinn, Laura, "Run to the Supermarket and Pick Me Up Some Cactus," *Business Week,* June 20, 1994, pp. 70–71.

—Robert Halasz

Harold's Stores, Inc.

765 Asp
Norman, Oklahoma 73069
U.S.A.
(405) 329-4045
Fax: (405) 366-2588
Web site: http://www.harolds.com

Public Company
Incorporated: 1948
Employees: 1,345
Sales: $108.23 million (1997)
Stock Exchanges: American
SICs: 5611 Men's & Boys' Clothing & Accessory Stores; 5621 Women's Clothing Stores; 5632 Women's Accessory & Specialty Stores

Harold's Stores, Inc. is a merchant and manufacturer of updated but classically styled men's and women's apparel. Each store in the chain features upscale specialty clothes for men and women ages 20 through 50, although typically the "updated traditional" styles appeal mostly to young executives and college students. Harold's designs many items exclusively for sales in its stores. The company markets its private label items through retail stores and through a direct-response catalog. Harold's maintains four distinct styles of stores. The first type of store offers full lines of original exclusive and semi-exclusive apparel for men and women. Secondly, some stores sell women's apparel and Old School Clothing brand men's sportswear. Other Harold's stores sell only women's clothing. Finally, Harold's outlet stores feature items with discounted prices or products with slow sales. The company's trademarks include Harold's, Harold Powell, Old School Clothing Company, and OSCC Bespoke.

The First Harold's

Harold's began in 1948 when Harold Powell founded a men's apparel business in a 900-square-foot store on Campus Corner across from the University of Oklahoma. Other stores followed, many in notable locations; for example, Powell opened a store in Utica Square, the oldest regional shopping center in Tulsa, Oklahoma, established in 1952. The company decorated this outlet—like each of its stores—with antiques, special fixtures, and visual props.

Product Development at Harold's

Harold's traditionally imported much of its merchandise from the United Kingdom, Italy, and the Far East. The company's merchandisers visited Europe regularly throughout the years for fashion ideas. Harold's historically worked with only a few vendors to ensure control of the design and manufacturing processes involved in manufacturing its private-label items.

Powell's product development philosophy set the stage for Harold's stores to offer new styles before its competitors. Stores featured clothing designed for Harold's or selected by the company's buyers from the merchandise of U.S., European, and Asian manufacturers. Harold's stores carried coordinated sportswear, dresses, coats, outerwear, shoes, and accessories for women. In 1997, women's apparel accounted for 78 percent of all sales, with 95 percent of sales attributed to Harold's product development and proprietary labels. Twenty-two percent of total sales in 1997 were men's apparel, 90 percent attributed to Harold's proprietary labels—Old School Clothing, in particular. Harold's tailored clothing for men included suits, sport coats, sportswear, shoes, and furnishings.

The 1970s

During the 1970s, Harold's continued to expand in store numbers and in customer services. In 1973 The Farm, a freestanding store in a 20-acre shopping center in Tulsa, Oklahoma, opened. A year later, Harold's first offered a proprietary credit card to its customers. "The company believes that providing its own credit card enhances customer loyalty while providing customers with additional credit," explained a Harold's 10-K report. By the end of the decade, Harold's established its first store beyond the borders of Oklahoma. "As the first Harold's store opened outside of Oklahoma, the company's Highland

Company Perspectives:

Every individual, hand-built store expresses our passion for going one step beyond that which is normal in modern retailing. Each location defines our all-consuming goal in creating for our customers a total shopping experience. And most importantly, every store proves that our success is based not only on the bottom line, but on a promise that our foremost consideration is and always will be helping people look and feel their very best.

Park Village location in Dallas, Texas, was a big gamble,'' recalled an annual report. ''After all, what right-minded Texan would be interested in anything from Oklahoma? Well, as it turns out, a lot of Texans were interested.'' Opened in 1977, the Highland Park Village store eventually became known for selling the highest volume of women's apparel in the chain.

The 1980s

In the next decade, Harold's established more and more retail outlets. In 1980, a store opened in Jackson, Mississippi, in the Rogue Compound. Harold's launched another store in 1986 in Fort Worth, Texas. Harold's became a public company in 1987 and added still more retail outlets throughout the remainder of the decade. In 1989, for example, a store with a full line of women's apparel and Old School Clothing Company sportswear for men debuted near Memphis, Tennessee, in Saddle Creek South in Germantown. That same year also saw the market testing of Harold's first direct-response catalog.

Stores—Plus Catalog Marketing—in the 1990s

In March 1990 Harold's issued its first catalog. The company mailed its catalog to 100,000 addresses from its in-house database. Harold's viewed the catalog as a sales tool, a vehicle for market research, and a promotion device for announcing new stores. In fiscal 1992 the catalog earned $620,000 in sales. By 1997, the single catalog grew to six issues of nearly 100 pages each annually. With 72 million copies in circulation, the catalog sold more than $8.88 million of merchandise.

Despite initiating the catalog, Harold's remained energetic in establishing new and enhancing existing retail outlets. The company moved its Fort Worth, Texas, store to the University Park Village shopping center, regularly frequented by Texas Christian University students—in 1990. In 1994, Harold's added a full line of men's clothing to the Highland Village Park store in Dallas, Texas. In July of that year, a women's apparel and Old School Clothing Company store opened in Charlotte, North Carolina. Austin, Texas, received a new women's apparel store in September. In October, a full-line of women's and men's clothing store debuted in Plano, Texas, and a women's and Old School Clothing store opened in Phoenix, Arizona, in November.

More Harold's stores began operations in 1995. A third outlet facility opened in Norman, adjacent to the original store. This store offered consumers discounts—from 30 to 70 percent off regular prices—on prior years' styles. In the spring, Harold's established a store in the Plaza Frontenac, a regional shopping mall in St. Louis, Missouri. Stores also opened in Louisville, Kentucky, and in Baton Rouge, Louisiana, and an outlet center began operations in Hillsboro, Texas, in 1995. ''Nothing about our Hillsboro outlet facility says outlet,'' revealed the 1996 annual report. ''From the extravagant wooden barn-like store front to the cold drinks offered to customers by sales associates, you'd never know this is a store where closeout bargains are to be found. And that's one reason Harold's Outlet is so different from the other national outlet stores that make up the Hillsboro Outlet Center in Hillsboro, Texas.''

Vendor Negotiations in 1995

Harold's negotiated a new arrangement with its largest apparel vendor—CMT Enterprises, Inc.—in 1995. In the past, Harold's paid CMT Enterprises for producing and manufacturing items; however, Harold's retained control of the design process. Under the new arrangement, CMT, acting as an agent of Harold's, purchased raw materials and oversaw the manufacturing of Harold's products by contractors. CMT Enterprises received a commission on the cost of finished items, resulting in financial savings for Harold's and an increased inventory of piece goods and work in process. Harold's ''believes its new relationship with CMT permits the company to control the quality and cost of the company's inventory purchases,'' reported a company 10-K.

Harold's also launched its first restaurant in 1995. The company established Cafe Plaid next to the original Harold's store in Norman, Oklahoma, near one of the company's outlet facilities. ''The idea was to create synergism between the cafe and the store,'' the 1996 annual report explained. ''Diners might be interested in checking out Harold's seasonal styles. Likewise, shoppers might want to take a break in Cafe Plaid. . . . Together, Cafe Plaid, Harold's Outlet, and the original Harold's store offer shoppers a variety of attractive incentives to visit the Campus Corner area. Management expects that the long-term effect will be advantageous to all three entities, not to mention other unrelated Campus Corner merchants.''

In 1996, Harold's offered 460,000 shares of newly issued common stock, raising more than $6 million in the sale. With the additional capital, the company continued updating and building new stores aggressively in 1996. The original store in Norman underwent a two-phase expansion project, including a significant enlargement of its women's apparel section. Harold's opened full-line men's and women's apparel stores in Leawood, Kansas; Raleigh, North Carolina; McLean, Virginia; and Littleton, Colorado. A women's clothing and men's Old School Clothes sportswear store also opened in Greenville, South Carolina, and Norman, Oklahoma, became home to yet another Harold's outlet facility in 1996.

In November 1996, Harold's initiated a store under the name Harold Powell in Houston, Texas. (An existing, unrelated men's clothing retailer in Houston called Harold's necessitated the name change.) Centrally located to the city's affluent areas, the store carried full lines of men's and women's clothing and accessories under a Harold Powell label. The company's 1996 annual report revealed that "despite the inconvenience of having to modify our store name to Harold Powell. . . , our presence in Houston has flourished amid all the legal controversies over the name."

The number of Harold's stores grew throughout 1997, as well. The company opened another store in Memphis, Tennessee, in the "Mall of the Twenty-first Century"—Wolfchase Galleria. In addition, full-line men's and women's apparel stores were launched in Wichita, Kansas; Columbus, Ohio; Richmond, Virginia; and Birmingham, Alabama. Outlet stores debuted at the Sealy Outlet Center in Houston, Texas, and in Norman, Oklahoma. In addition, Harold's relocated its Fort Worth store to a new area of University Park Village, and the original Harold's store—still in operation—stretched to 26,000 square feet through a location expansion program.

As of February 1997, Harold's operated 42 stores in 18 states. In each instance, these retail outlets were located in shopping centers and malls near other top-of-the-line retailers—often in the vicinity of colleges. Harold's expansion over the years resulted in sales as well as physical growth. According to a William E. Read and Company report, "Harold's historical sales growth has been dramatic the past five years as the company has expanded its retail men's and women's upscale apparel operations. . . . Sales for fiscal February 1, 1997, totaled $108.2 million compared to $49.3 million in 1993, an increase of 120 percent for the five-year period, or a sales growth rate of 21.8 percent annually."

In 1997, Harold's maintained its headquarters in Norman, Oklahoma, in the Boomer Building, a former theater just one block from the very first Harold's store. Harold's also operated a distribution center in Norman, as well as merchandising and production offices in Dallas, Texas.

Plans for the Future

Harold's witnessed a decline in catalog sales in 1997. Owing to this, the company shifted its focus to reducing catalog expenses in upcoming years. Nevertheless, investment and securities firm William E. Read and Company noted that "catalog sales continue to be a bright spot for Harold's." Hence, the retailer's plans for the future included increasing the circulation of the direct-response catalog while maintaining sales momentum at its stores. Harold's believed its success in the future depended most on increasing the number of its men's and women's apparel stores. "Our expansion efforts are continuing," wrote Harold G. Powell, founder and chairman of the board, in a letter to stockholders, "and we look forward to welcoming several new stores to the Harold's family in the year to come." The company expected to open at least three stores in 1998, to relocate one store, and to expand one existing store.

Further Reading

"Harold's Stores, Inc. Announces the Opening of an Outlet in Sealy, Texas" (press release), Norman, Okla.: Harold's Stores, Inc., November 20, 1997.

"Harold's Stores, Inc., Releases Sales Results for the Third Quarter and Thirty-Nine Weeks Ended November 1, 1997" (press release), Norman, Okla.: Harold's Stores, Inc., November 6, 1997.

Southwest Securities, "Harold's Stores, Inc.," Dallas, Tex.: Southwest Securities, December 4, 1997.

William E. Read & Co., "Harold's Stores, Inc.," Dallas, Tex.: William E. Read & Co., December 4, 1997.

—Charity Anne Dorgan

Hawaiian Airlines, Inc.

3375 Koapaka Street, Suite G-350
Honolulu, Hawaii 96819
U.S.A.
(808) 835-3700
Fax: (808) 835-3690
Web site: http://www.hawaiianair.com

Public Company
Incorporated: 1929 as Inter-Island Airways, Ltd.
Employees: 2,500
Sales: $384.47 million (1996)
Stock Exchanges: American
SICs: 4512 Air Transportation, Scheduled

Hawaiian Airlines, Inc. flies between the Hawaiian Islands, several cities in the western U.S. mainland and South Pacific destinations. Billing itself as Hawaii's "flagship" carrier, it seeks to outpace even the Concorde (which does visit Hawaii rarely on world tours) by infusing five million passengers per year with Hawaiian sights, sounds, and smells as soon as they step into the plane. In spite of high ratings from customers, Hawaiian often finds itself navigating over financially dire straits.

Lifting Off in the 1930s

Hawaiian Airlines, Inc. began as Inter-Island Airways, Ltd., the brainchild of naval aviator Stanley Kennedy. In 1929, Kennedy was employed as general manager of Inter-Island Steam Navigation Company, whose directors he persuaded to establish a passenger airline linking the major Hawaiian Islands. The company was incorporated on January 30 and its first flights departed John Rogers Airport in Honolulu on November 11, bound for Maui and Hawaii (the Big Island), the beginning of thrice-weekly service. The company's fleet consisted of two amphibious Sikorsky S-38s, which carried eight passengers each. At that time, statehood was several decades away, although Hawaii had already become a coveted, if remote, tourist destination. Inter-Island introduced airmail service between Oahu (site of Honolulu), Hawaii, and Kauai in 1934. The next year the fleet expanded to include 16-passenger Sikorsky S-43s to accommodate the mail and increased passenger traffic.

The company became known as Hawaiian Airlines in 1941. The ubiquitous twin-engine Douglas DC-3 gave Hawaiian still more capacity and began its long-term relationship with the manufacturer. During WWII, all inter-island flights were placed under military jurisdiction. Its planes were also used in wartime to carry cargo and service nearby Pacific islands. Between 1944 and 1948, TWA was a one-fifth owner of the company.

Cold War Competition

Competition had landed in the islands with the 1946 creation of Trans-Pacific Airlines, forerunner of Aloha Airlines. The Convair 340s Hawaiian added in 1952 gave it the advantage of modern, air conditioned and pressurized cabins. A single four-engine DC-6 purchased in 1958 allowed the carrier to operate long-distance military charters. In 1966, booming residential and tourist traffic prompted Hawaiian to begin operating the McDonnell Douglas DC-9, the first jet turbine aircraft to be used on inter-island flights. The islands were now no more than 30 minutes from each other. This type would be used for at least 30 more years.

Although Hawaiian typically was able to bring the newest, most advanced aircraft to the market, competition with Aloha reduced both carriers' margins so severely that the two agreed to merge in 1970—a plan which was abandoned the next year.

The Deregulated 1980s

In the late 1970s, deregulation brought still more cutthroat competition. Although deregulation allowed the company to add service to the South Pacific (Pago Pago, American Samoa, and Nuku'alofa, Tonga), and was able to fill its planes more than any other airline, the amount the company made per passenger was not similarly impressive. In 1982, Hawaiian adopted the corporate name HAL.

Along with the new South Pacific scheduled routes, overseas charter services were offered in 1984 with the company's three DC-8s. Five of the popular Lockheed L-1011 widebody aircraft

Company Perspectives:

Hawaii's largest airline since its founding 67 years ago, Hawaiian Airlines today serves 14 domestic and international destinations in the Pacific region. It specializes in air transportation among the Hawaiian Islands and bringing visitors to Hawaii from points in the Western U.S. and the South Pacific.

Carrying approximately 5 million passengers a year, Hawaiian Airlines provides high-frequency jet service daily to seven destinations on six Hawaiian Islands and weekly service to the South Pacific destinations of Tahiti and American Samoa. In North America it provides daily service to Hawaii from Los Angeles, San Francisco, Seattle, Las Vegas, and Portland, Oregon.

were added the next year to fulfill these roles as well. In addition, HAL began serving the West Coast via Los Angeles. Routes to San Francisco and Seattle were added in 1986. A fare war ensued between United and Continental, which also served Hawaii from the West Coast. The year would show the company's last profit for at least another decade.

The company built the West Maui Airport in 1987. HAL also stepped up its offering to Polynesia. By 1987, Western Samoa, Tahiti, and Rarotonga were linked with Hawaii, not by outrigger canoe, but DC-8 jetliner.

Losing Altitude in the 1990s

A group of investors led by Jet America founder J. Thomas Talbot bought a 46.5 percent stake in HAL for $37 million in 1989. Talbot assumed the positions of CEO and chairman. Former baseball commissioner Peter Ueberroth was also an investor in the Talbot group.

Although there were some minor incidents, HAL had built an impressive safety record while transporting more than 100 million passengers. In 1990, *Condé Nast Traveler* pronounced the airline one of the world's safest after a 20-year survey. The magazine's readers also consistently ranked it one of their favorites in the U.S. The carrier was recognized by the trade magazine *Onboard Services* and the World Airline Entertainment Association for its superior in-flight cuisine and audio programs.

Challenges against the airline mounted in 1991. After 45 years, Aloha Airlines finally succeeded in capturing the dominant share (61 percent) of inter-island traffic. HAL also lost three South Pacific routes to Northwest Airlines in a deal which gave Northwest a minority share (25 percent) in exchange for $20 million. Peter Ueberroth's younger brother John, who had previously led the Carlson Travel Group, succeeded Talbot as HAL chairman. Losses for 1991 amounted to $99 million (including a one-time accounting charge of $36.7 million).

As if ferocious competition and high fuel costs were not enough to deflate the company's tentative comeback, Hurricane Iniki chased away an estimated $7 million of HAL's business in 1992. The next year, it opted for Chapter 11 bankruptcy protection and John Ueberroth stepped down as chairman.

In 1993, the company sold the DC-8s that it had used on South Pacific flights, resulting in more modest Polynesian coverage. The next year, it ceased flights to West Maui Airport, which could not service jets, as it sold its fleet of propeller-driven aircraft. (Jets could operate from Maui's Kahului Airport; eventually HAL would fly between Maui and the Mainland in direct competition with a United Airlines route.) Further competition landed in the fall of 1994 in the form of budget carrier Mahalo Air.

A New Lease on Life in the Mid-1990s

The company resumed its old name of Hawaiian Airlines as it emerged from bankruptcy protection in 1994, still able to fly but also susceptible to chronic cash shortages. AMR Corp., parent of American Airlines, began providing technical expertise to Hawaiian, which enrolled in American's frequent flyer program and replaced its L-1011s with DC-10s leased from AMR, which also assumed maintenance duties.

New York's Smith Management Co. provided $20 million of desperately needed cash in 1996. The Airline Investors Partnership it assembled bought two-thirds of the company, and Smith president John Adams assumed the role of chairman of the Hawaiian board. The group nevertheless displayed such confidence in Nobles that he retained the duties of CEO and president. The airline needed a $3 million loan from Smith to keep running until the deal could be approved. Later in the year, a Hawaiian stock offering raised $39 million.

Various players made concessions to keep Hawaiian in the sky. AMR Corp. extended the carrier credit and reduced its rates on Hawaiian's leased DC-10 jets by nearly 30 percent. Hawaiian's four unions approved less remunerative contracts.

Hawaiian was a very busy airline, operating over 150 flights per day, and its volume increased steadily into the late 1990s. Its new route to Las Vegas, the favorite holiday destination of Hawaii residents, proved highly popular. However, higher fuel costs for its longer flights gutted profits. The company lost $2.4 million in the first quarter of 1997 and $4.1 million for the previous year, thanks to a 20 percent increase in fuel prices.

Hawaiian Airlines served 14 destinations. Its 50 percent market share in inter-island flights (to the six major Hawaiian Islands) accounted for about 40 percent of revenues. Daily West Coast flights (to Los Angeles, San Francisco, Seattle, Las Vegas, and Portland) brought in another 50 percent, with about six percent coming from the company's air service to weekly flights to the South Pacific (American Samoa and Tahiti, where the company had a monopoly on air service to and from Honolulu). The company maintained limited cargo and mail operations. In the late-1990s, its fleet was comprised of about 13 DC-9s (all but two leased) for inter-island flights and 8 DC-10s (all leased) for long-range flights.

Flying into a New Century

In February 1997, Bruce Nobles stepped down as CEO to be replaced by travel executive Paul Casey. In spite of a slack tourist market in Hawaii (which prompted the state to suspend airport landing fees), a number of initiatives seemed likely to pay off for the airline. It began using the new AIRMAX computerized routing system, supplied by AMR subsidiary SABRE Decision Technologies, which promised more efficient scheduling of flights. The airline took part in the trials of a new satellite-based system designed to allow pilots greater control in selecting routes. And code-sharing agreements with American, Continental, Northwest, and Reno Air should ensure a steady flow of customers from the Mainland. These factors, and the backing of enthusiastic supporters, suggested a positive outlook for Hawaiian Airlines.

Further Reading

Altonn, Helen, and Debra Barayuga, ''Ailing Jetliner Returns Safely,'' *Honolulu Star-Bulletin,* August 8, 1996.

Altonn, Helen, and Russ Lynch, ''Tough New International Rules Imposed on Flights to and from Hawaii,'' *Honolulu Star-Bulletin,* July 26, 1997.

Bartlett, Tony, ''Broker on Maui Sues Hawaiian Over Undelivered Airline Coupons,'' *Travel Weekly,* November 30, 1995, p. 1.

——, ''Code Sharing with Hawaiian Gives Mahalo Link to Mainland,'' *Travel Weekly,* July 25, 1996, p. 20.

Daysog, Rick, ''Hawaiian Connects with Northwest Air,'' *Honolulu Star-Bulletin,* May 21, 1996.

Dornheim, Michael A., ''Investment Company Takes Over Hawaiian Airlines,'' *Aviation Week and Space Technology,* February 19, 1996, pp. 34–35.

Gomes, Andrew, ''Hawaiian Asks to Shift Overseas Flights into Interisland Territory,'' *Pacific Business News,* February 10, 1997.

''Hawaiian Deal Will Pay Debts,'' *Airfinance Journal,* March 1996, p. 8.

Ige, Ken, ''Hawaiian Air Reconfigures Gates,'' *Honolulu Star-Bulletin,* February 7, 1997.

Lynch, Russ, ''Casey's Salary Flies High at Hawaiian,'' *Honolulu Star-Bulletin,* April 4, 1997.

——, ''Discount Stock Offering to Boost Hawaiian Air Capital,'' *Honolulu Star-Bulletin,* June 3, 1996.

——, ''Hawaiian Air Exec: We Didn't React Fast Enough,'' *Honolulu Star-Bulletin,* May 23, 1997.

——, ''Hawaiian Air's New Owners Like Turnarounds,'' *Honolulu Star-Bulletin,* October 11, 1996.

——, ''United and Hawaiian Step in During a Usually Slow Time,'' *Honolulu Star-Bulletin,* September 5, 1996.

Oda, Dennis, ''Nobles Piloted Hawaiian Out of Turbulence,'' *Honolulu Star-Bulletin,* February 2, 1997.

Sensui, Dean, ''Hawaiian Air to Fly Direct S.F.-Maui Route,'' *Honolulu Star-Bulletin,* April 18, 1997.

Yuen, Mike, ''To Boost Tourism, Cayetano Puts a Moratorium on the Landing Fees Air Carriers Have to Pay,'' *Honolulu Star-Bulletin,* September 9, 1997.

—Frederick C. Ingram

Health Care & Retirement Corporation

One SeaGate
Toledo, Ohio 43604-2616
U.S.A.
(419) 252-5500
Fax: (419) 252-5510

Public Company
Founded: 1944 as Lima Lumber Company
Employees: 20,000
Sales: $782 million (1996)
Stock Exchanges: New York
SICs: 8051 Skilled Nursing Care Facilities; 8361 Residential Care

With operations in 16 states, Health Care & Retirement Corporation (HCR) ranks among America's top five providers of long-term care and skilled nursing services through a network of more than 300 facilities with about 16,500 beds. At the core of the company is a network of 128 retirement and nursing homes, known in the industry as long-term care facilities. In the late 1980s and early 1990s, HCR expanded into subacute care, including rehabilitation clinics, home healthcare, and pharmacy services. By the end of 1996, it had 66 outpatient therapy clinics and 33 home healthcare offices. Many of these adjunct facilities were connected to its nursing and retirement homes. These more recent developments are considered a key to future growth.

HCR's history stretches back more than 50 years, but the company has only been involved in the operation of nursing homes since 1974. Its stock has been publicly traded since late 1991, when HCR was spun off from parent Owens-Illinois Inc., which had owned the nursing home group since 1984. Fueled by a combination of organic growth, diversification, and acquisitions, the company's sales and profits recorded double-digit annual percentage increases in the early and mid-1990s. Revenues increased from $497.1 million in 1992 to $782 million in 1996, and net income more than doubled from $26.5 million to $59.4 million during the period.

Origins in 1940s

This company has undergone a half-century metamorphosis from a lumberyard to a diversified construction concern, to a nursing home company. Health Care & Retirement Corporation's roots stretch back to a family-owned lumber business headquartered in northwest Ohio. In 1944, C. V. Wolfe and two partners acquired the Lima Lumber Company. Though the lumber business was then a sideline to his regular employment, Wolfe had by the end of the decade bought out his partners and added lumberyards in the nearby towns of Wapakoneta and St. Marys. Perceiving an opportunity for growth in the post-World War II housing boom, Wolfe finally quit his day job in 1952 and diversified into construction with the creation of C.V. Wolfe & Co. C.V.'s son F. D. Wolfe, an alumnus of Harvard Business School, joined the growing family business soon after his graduation in 1955.

Together they created the Lima Mortgage Co. in 1957 to offer mortgage services to their construction clients. Just three years later, the Wolfes boosted their loan servicing operations to over $10 million via the acquisition of a controlling interest in First Toledo Corporation, an FHA mortgage lender. In 1962, the family changed the name of this company to Western Ohio Corp. and divested the mortgage business to concentrate on real estate development, most notably the development of nursing homes. The family built its first long-term care facility in 1963, and it leased that first property to an outside operator.

The Wolfes continued to develop their construction interests throughout the 1960s as well, adding several quarries, concrete and asphalt plants, and even trucking operations.

F. D. Wolfe succeeded his father as chairman of the family business upon his father's death in 1967. This change in leadership presaged a 1970 reorganization that transformed the wide-ranging conglomeration still known as Lima Lumber into Wolfe Industries, Inc., a business with four primary subsidiaries: Lima Lumber, Inc., in charge of building materials; Wolfe Industries Construction Company, builder of nursing homes; Western Ohio Corporation, with trucking, investment, and other operations; and Western Ohio Transportation Company, a stone hauler.

Company Perspectives:

Health Care & Retirement Corporation is a company that puts genuine caring into health care. We create a caring environment in our nursing centers that is a way of life for our residents, as well as our employees.

We have the foresight to adapt to a constantly changing industry, and the insight to offer compassionate care to each individual resident.

Our Vision is focused on the single purpose of providing the best care for each resident. And with that goal never out of sight, Our Vision is never out of mind.

Nursing Homes Come to the Fore in 1970s

In the early 1970s, F. D. Wolfe created a publicly-owned real estate investment trust (REIT), the Health Care Fund (later renamed Health Care REIT, Inc.) to finance nursing home construction projects. According to SEC documents, the fund was ''the first real estate investment trust to invest exclusively in health care facilities.'' Within two years, Wolfe Industries was busy building eight nursing homes, most under contract to be operated by outside interests. The company undertook management of its first facility in 1974, when it acquired Indian Lake Manor, a 62-bed nursing home. In 1975 the company created Heartland Health Care Company to acquire Heartland of Perrysburg (Ohio), an upscale 136-bed nursing home. In 1977, the company expanded its reach into the neighboring state of West Virginia through the acquisition of two more nursing homes, thereby adding over 400 beds to its total capacity.

This new business proved quite profitable. Sales more than doubled, from $25 million in 1975 to $59 million by 1979, while net increased from $1 million to $2 million.

The company finally abandoned all its non-healthcare operations in 1981, when it spun off these businesses as Wolfe Industries, Inc. and retained the nursing home business as Health Care and Retirement Corporation of America. The company went public that same year, raising $4.7 million via the sale of an 18 percent stake (525,000 shares) at $9 per share. A second offering of 825,000 shares at about $14.50 per share raised $12 million in 1983.

HCR continued to grow through acquisition in the early 1980s, purchasing two dozen relatively small facilities in Ohio, Indiana, West Virginia, and Kentucky in 1982 and six more in 1983. During this period, HCR's construction arm also built more than three dozen nursing home facilities for lease and purchase by other companies. By the end of 1984, the company owned a total of 46 facilities with over 5,000 beds, and had broken into the nursing home industry's top 10. Net income had grown to $7.3 million on revenues of $96 million. That December, HCR was acquired by Owens-Illinois, Inc. (O-I), a Toledo, Ohio-based industrial firm. F. D. Wolfe resigned at that time, ending 40 years under the direction of a member of the Wolfe family.

HCR prospered under O-I. Acquisitions and new construction quadrupled the business from less than $100 million revenues in 1984 to $418.3 million in 1990. The number of facilities owned increased from 46 to 135 during this period, and the number of beds grew from about 5,000 to over 17,500. Oddly enough, only HCR's profitability suffered under O-I. Net profit rose to a high of $12.8 million in 1987 before sliding to $6.5 million in 1990.

The 1990s and Beyond

Owens-Illinois, which had itself been taken private through a leveraged buyout in 1987, spun off HCR to the public in October 1991, netting O-I nearly $250 million. The following year, HCR concentrated its operations in the states of Ohio, Michigan, and Florida by divesting all its Connecticut and Massachusetts centers and acquiring an Ohio-based rehabilitation therapy company, Heartland Rehabilitation Services, Inc. Growth through acquisition continued in 1994, when HCR purchased two privately held businesses in the Mid-Atlantic region.

Under the direction of Paul Ormond, who served as president from 1986 and CEO after the spinoff, the company distinguished itself not only by its size, but also by its strategies for profitable expansion. For example, HCR sought to maintain a ''quality mix'' of patients. This industry terminology refers to the percentage of Medicare and private-paying (i.e., non-Medicaid) residents in its long-term facilities. Since Medicare reimbursements were higher than those made by Medicaid—and private individuals paid even more—more ''quality'' clients meant higher profits. HCR's well-designed and -furnished, upscale facilities attracted residents who could afford such niceties. At about 68 percent, HCR's ranked among the industry's highest quality mix ratios.

HCR also broadened its areas of specialization to include home and hospice care, vision care, pharmacy service, rehabilitation therapy, and other subacute services. This diversification promised several benefits. Many of these services commanded higher fees and reaped higher profit margins than routine long-term care. They also expanded HCR's potential client base to include people of all ages who required short-term rehabilitation to recover from orthopedic or cardiac surgery as well as wound care and intravenous therapy. And while HCR made more money on these services, its facilities were 30 percent to 60 percent cheaper than care at a hospital, making it an attractive alternative for third-party payers seeking to cut costs in the increasingly competitive healthcare industry.

HCR's revenue and net income rose dramatically in the early 1990s. Sales expanded from $418.3 million in 1990 to $782 million in 1996. At the same time, HCR became more efficient at what it did, reducing basic operating expenses from 84.1 percent of sales in 1990 to just under 80 percent in 1996, helping to push net income from $6.5 million to $59.4 million.

HCR's savvy strategizing positioned it well for the late 1990s and early 21st century. Aging baby boomers with rising life expectancies promised a growing pool of potential retirement and nursing home residents. Demographic experts forecast that the number of Americans aged 85 and over would double from 3.3 million to 6.6 million by 2010. Furthermore, cost-cutting pressures on the healthcare industry overall fueled a shift from long, expensive hospital stays to subacute facilities like those being developed by HCR. Any seniors who managed to avoid the nursing home were still potential candidates for HCR's specialized outpatient and rehabilitation services. Even the company's Heartland service mark, which graces almost half of these long-term care centers, has the potential to become an important brand in the elder-oriented market to come.

Principal Subsidiaries

HCRC Inc.; Ancillary Services Management, Inc.; RVA Management Services, Inc.; Vision Management Services, Inc.; HCR Acquisition Corp.; Heartland CarePartners, Inc.; HCR Home Health Care and Hospice, Inc.; Heartland Home Health Care Services, Inc.; Heartland Hospice Services, Inc.; Heartland Services Corp.; HCR Rehabilitation Corp.; Heartland Rehabilitation Services, Inc.; Health Care and Retirement Corp. Of America; Care Corp.; Georgian Bloomfield, Inc.; Georgian Court Nursing Home of Tulsa, Inc.; Heartland of Indian Lake Rehab. Center, Inc.; Heartland of Martinsburg, Inc.; HGCC of Allentown, Inc.; Lincoln Health Care, Inc.; River Hills Nursing Home, Inc.; Washtenaw Hills Manor, Inc.; HCRA of Texas, Inc.; Care Corporation Holdings, Inc.; Care Real Estate, Inc.; Canterbury Village, Inc.; Care Manors, Inc.; Birchwood Manor, Inc.; Donahoe Manor, Inc.; East Michigan Care Corporation; Greenview Manor, Inc.; Ionia Manor, Inc.; Knollview Manor, Inc.; Marina View Manor, Inc.; Ridgeview Manor, Inc.; Springhill Manor, Inc.; Sun Valley Manor, Inc.; Three Rivers Manor, Inc.; Washington Manor Nursing Home, Inc.; Whitehall Manor, Inc.; Care Manors of New England, Inc.; Birch Manor Nursing Home, Inc.; Crescent Hill Manor, Inc.; Elms Manor Nursing Home, Inc.; Kensington Manor, Inc.; Mapleview Nursing Home, Inc.; Meadows Manor, Inc.; Oak Manor Nursing Home, Inc.; Pine Manor Nursing Home, Inc.; Spruce Manor Nursing Home, Inc.; Union Square Nursing Center, Inc.; Valley View Manor, Inc.; Waterbury Manor, Inc.

Further Reading

ABN AMRO Chicago Corporation, ''Health Care & Retirement Corp.,'' The Investext Group, May 15, 1997.

Donaldson, Lufkin & Jenrette Securities, ''Health Care and Retirement—Company Report,'' The Investext Group, December 3, 1993.

''Going for the Geezers,'' *Fortune,* December 25, 1995, p. 86.

Goodwin, William, ''Continental Wins Lead Bank Role for Owens Unit,'' *American Banker,* September 9, 1991, pp. 16–17.

Health Care and Retirement Corporation of America Chronological History, Toledo, OH: Health Care & Retirement Corporation, 1994.

McDonald & Company Securities, Inc., ''Health Care & Retirement Corporation—Company Report,'' The Investext Group, January 31, 1996.

Merrill Lynch Capital Markets, ''Healthcare Retirement Corporation—Company Report,'' The Investext Group, July 18, 1997.

Meyer, Richard S., ''Total Quality Management and The National Labor Relations Act,'' *Labor Law Journal,* November 1994, pp. 718–721.

''Update and Stay Tuned,'' *Monthly Labor Review,* July 1995, p. 79.

Weiss, Gary, ''Excellent Prognosis: The Outlook for Nursing Home Chains Is Glowing,'' *Barron's,* May 28, 1984, pp. 6–7.

Yarborough, Mary Helen, ''LPNs As Supervisors: Far-Reaching Impact?'' *HR Focus,* August 1994, p. 3.

—April Dougal Gasbarre

Henkel Manco Inc.

31250 Just Imagine Dr.
Avon, Ohio 44011
U.S.A.
(440) 937-7000
Fax: (440) 937-7077
Web site: http://www.manco.com

Wholly Owned Subsidiary of Henkel KGaA
Founded: 1950 as Melvin A. Anderson Co.
Employees: 350
Sales: $167 million (1997)
SICs: 5113 Packing Materials For Shipping; 2671 Paper Coated & Laminated—Packaging; 2672 Coated & Laminated Paper, Not Elsewhere Classified; 3089 Plastics Products, Not Elsewhere Classified; 2891 Adhesives & Sealants

Headquartered in a suburb of Cleveland, Ohio, Henkel Manco Inc. sells more duct tape than any other company in America—enough to circle the Earth 15 times. In addition to its duct tape dominance, the company designs and markets a growing variety of branded products including mailing and shipping supplies, weather-stripping, craft products, and housewares. Manco was founded in 1950 and was privately owned from 1971, when Chairman and CEO John J. "Jack" Kahl bought the company, to late 1997. Kahl is the widely praised engineer of Manco's transformation from an $80,000 distributor into a multimillion-dollar entrepreneurial phenomenon. In 1997, the company announced that it would be acquired by Germany's Henkel KGaA, a diversified manufacturer with $10 billion in annual sales. Renamed Henkel Manco Inc., the Ohio company was expected to be merged into the German firm's $2.5 billion consumer adhesives business, encompassing products under the Loctite and LePage brands.

World War II Origins of Duct Tape and Manco

The company traces its roots to 1950, when it was founded by Melvin A. Anderson in Cleveland, Ohio. Anderson named the company after himself and set out to supply duct and electrical tape to area factories.

According to Manco and other sources, duct tape was among the many breakthrough products developed during World War II. Created by a subsidiary of Johnson & Johnson, the material featured a cloth base coated with rubberized adhesive on one side and an army green polymer coating on the other. The resulting tape was strong, but its cloth base made it easy to tear to size. Soldiers found the material indispensable, and used it to seal ammunition boxes and repair everything from jeeps to battleships. The duct tape moniker developed after the war, when the reinforced, waterproof adhesive was widely used to repair and connect duct work.

Kahl made his rendezvous with duct tape destiny in the early 1960s, when he made a sales call at Anderson's office. Whether or not he sold the founder a life insurance policy has become extraneous to the company folklore; what is important is that Anderson invited Kahl to join the duct tape firm as its only sales rep. When Kahl came on board, Anderson was generating just $80,000 in sales. By the advent of the 1970s, Kahl had been instrumental in increasing the company's sales tenfold and expanding its reach to five states. His reward? A meager bonus. Kahl resigned over inadequate compensation in 1971. Without his sales whiz, Anderson was forced to sell the company to none other than Kahl, who borrowed $192,000 and effected a mini-leveraged buyout. The new owner abbreviated the company name from Melvin A. Anderson Co. to Manco.

Turning from industrial sales to the retail market, Kahl more than tripled sales to $3 million by 1976, thereby enabling him to pay off his LBO debt. But it was an after-hours meeting with a buyer from Wal-Mart Stores, Inc. that would herald a period of fantastic growth for the duct tape marketer. Noting that the energy crisis and an especially cold winter could combine to boost demand for weather-stripping, Kahl decided to make his first product diversification in 1977. He launched the new product at a Dallas trade show that fall, and received an $88,000 order—Manco's largest to that point—from what would become America's biggest mass merchandiser, Wal-Mart. (Kahl would later count Wal-Mart founder Sam Walton among his many mentors.) Along the way, Kahl and company also picked up contracts with

Company Perspectives:

Manco's mission is to build a consumer products company that offers products and services to our customers that will bring quality and care to their lives. Our backyard, the United States, is our foundation for growth, and we will strive always to build new buying and selling partnerships globally. Quality products and caring personal relationships will always be the formula used for delivering extraordinary value to our only boss, the Customer.

retail behemoths Kmart Corp. and Ace Hardware. Sales soared from about $4 million in 1977 to $11 million in 1980.

Harnessing the Power of the Brand in the 1980s

In 1984, Kahl decided to differentiate his product through packaging and brand identity. For more than 30 years, duct tape had been sold in large, sticky, anonymous stacks; the stuff was so strong, it was often hard to pry a single roll lose from its mates. Tiny Manco beat such tape industry giants as 3M, Scotch, and Mystic, becoming first to shrink-wrap individual rolls of lowly duct tape and plaster its green corporate logo on the package. The company also gathered up many of the different types of tape scattered throughout the store into a single ''tape center'' that took one-stop-shopping down to the product level.

Instead of trying to correct the many consumers who mispronounced and misspelled the name of his product, Kahl embraced ''duck tape'' and registered it as a trademark. An endearing, bright yellow cartoon duck—Manco T. Duck—soon personified the helpful nature of the company's products. Powered by the ''webbed warrior,'' Manco's sales jumped from $25 million in 1982 to $32 million in 1985. This rapid growth spurred a move from Cleveland proper to a new, campus-like headquarters on 22 acres in the suburb of Westlake.

Kahl often said that his long-term goal for Manco was to make it a $1 billion company with a customer base of 100,000. Realizing that he would be very hard-pressed to sell a billion dollars' worth of duct tape—even given the apparently universal appeal of the product—Kahl embarked on a wide-ranging product diversification. Consultation with Wal-Mart resulted in the development of the CareMail line of about two dozen shipping and mailing products launched in 1986. Manco T. Duck donned a blue hat and mail pouch to promote the products. By the early 1990s, CareMail would encompass over 200 different items, including bubble wrap, labels, padded envelopes, and specially sized boxes.

Corporate Culture Considered a Key Element of Success

Jack Kahl's formative years were steeped in religion. He was educated in parochial schools and at John Carroll University, a Catholic institution, and was even said to have considered the priestly vocation. Kahl's business attitudes reflected his personal experiences. In 1995, he told *Forbes*'s Dyan Machan that ''There isn't much difference between religion and what we practice here. Religion is a set of beliefs. A company can have, or be, a religion.'' In fact, Manco's headquarters have had some church-like attributes, including bell-ringing to herald happy announcements, weekly meetings, and a ''Temple of Quotes'' featuring inspirational messages of employees' choosing. Even the company's promotional material took on an evangelical tone. Though (hopefully) tongue-in-cheek, Manco's web site extols ''the Duck'' as ''a champion for those in need, and a shining example of a friendly and trusting spirit that can make a real difference in people's lives.'' Mindful of his own shoddy treatment at the hand of his previous boss, Kahl was generous with company perks. He created an employee stock option plan with 30 percent of Manco's equity; built on-site fitness facilities; and offered education reimbursement programs.

But while Kahl was devoted to his business, he did not take it or himself too seriously. Take for example ''Duck Challenge Day.'' Corporate legend has it that this annual end-of-the-fiscal-year event got its start in 1990, when Kahl told sons John and Bill (both sales managers) that if they could boost sales from a projected $56 million to over $60 million, he would jump in the lake in front of Manco's suburban headquarters. It was no frivolous wager; Manco's fiscal year winds up at the end of September, meaning that Kahl would be taking his dip during the chill of October in Cleveland. Revenues ended up at $60.09 million that year—just enough for Kahl to take the plunge. The event expanded into a company-wide challenge as well as a media event, culminating in 1997's ''Global Duck Tape Summit.'' That year, Kahl displayed ''the World's Largest Roll of Duck Tape'' (500 lbs.), had his headquarters city named ''Duck Tape Capital of the World,'' and entertained such luminaries of the duct tape establishment as Jim Berg and Tim Nyberg, authors of two books on the wonder adhesive; PBS's Red Green, fictional antihero of the *Red Green Show*; and musician Terry Anderson, who has written and performed odes to duct tape.

The 1990s and Beyond

Manco continued to broaden its consumer products offerings in the new decade, adding 150 new items in 1990 alone. Kid'sCRAFT, a line of proprietary paints, glues, and stickers designed for children, was launched in 1993. In 1995, the company launched Easy Liner non-adhesive shelf and drawer liners. In 1997, the company debuted Softex, a new line of bath, shower, and sink mats that promised the non-skid and cushioning qualities of traditional rubber mats while offering enhanced mildew-resistance. That same year, Manco launched its Draft Busters brand window insulation kit with the company's first large-scale radio campaign.

New product launches helped push Manco's annual sales over the $100 million mark in September 1994, and revenues rose more than 50 percent in the ensuing two years to $167 million. As it had in the past, rapid growth propelled another corporate move, this time to a 200-acre site in Avon, Ohio, and an $8 million headquarters building. The new home base must not have featured a pond, because when Manco exceeded its profit goal in 1997, Jack Kahl had his head shaved instead of taking a ducky dip. That fall Jack Kahl's oldest son, John Kahl,

Jr., was promoted to president, replacing Tom Corbo, who had served in that capacity since 1992.

In 1992, Jack Kahl told Chris Thompson of *Crain's Cleveland Business* that ''People say, 'Everything is for sale.' No. This [Manco] is not for sale.'' That certainty evaporated five years later, when Kahl found a way to become the head of a multi-billion adhesive business: he sold Manco to Germany's Henkel Group for an undisclosed amount. Renamed Henkel Manco Inc., the Ohio company was expected to be merged into the German firm's $2.5 billion consumer adhesives business, encompassing products under the Loctite and LePage brands. Kahl, his sons, and the rest of Manco's management team were expected to keep their positions at the merged company.

Further Reading

Ashyk, Loretta, ''Great Business Weather for 'Ducks' Boosts Manco,'' *Crain's Cleveland Business,* June 1, 1987, pp. 2–3.

''At Manco Inc., The Makers of Duct Tape, All the Employees Are Partners,'' *Cleveland Magazine,* February 1, 1992, p. 33.

Canedy, Dana, ''Coming in on a Wing and Duct Tape,'' *Plain Dealer,* 16 June 1993, p. 1A.

Collins, James, *Built to Last: Successful Habits of Visionary Companies,* New York: HarperBusiness, 1994.

Davis, Patricia, ''It Could Be Worse—They Could Just Duct Tape His Hair and Yank,'' *Wall Street Journal,* October 24, 1997, p. B1.

Garfield, Charles A., *Second to None: How Our Smartest Companies Put People First,* Homewood, Ill.: Business One Irwin, 1992.

Gendron, George, ''Follow the Leaders,'' *Inc.,* February 1991, p. 12.

Gleisser, Marcus, ''Manco Sold to Germany Company,'' *Plain Dealer,* November 8, 1997, pp. 1C, 3C.

Greco, Susan, ''The Art of Selling,'' *Inc.,* June 1993, pp. 72–77.

Hyatt, Joshua, ''Steal This Strategy,'' *Inc.,* February 1991, pp. 48–55.

Machan, Dyan, ''Religion? Business? What's the Difference?'' *Forbes,* November 6, 1995, pp. 78–80.

Sabath, Donald, ''Duck Tape Firm Sticks to Its $1 Billion Plan,'' *Plain Dealer,* October 8, 1994, p. 1C.

——, ''Manco Duct Tape Firm Develops Plan to Sell Products Worldwide,'' *Plain Dealer,* January 7, 1992, p. 4F.

——, ''Navy's Seagoing Tape Just Ducky for Homes, *Plain Dealer,* September 4, 1984, pp. 1C, 5C.

Talbott, Stephen, ''Manco Inc. Makes Tapes, Products That 'Care' Alot,'' *Plain Dealer,* December 1, 1987, pp. 1C, 6C.

Thompson, Chris, ''Manco Crafts Charge into Children's Market,'' *Crain's Cleveland Business,* October 25, 1993, pp. 1–2.

——, ''Manco's Chief Always Learning,'' *Crain's Cleveland Business,* November 11, 1991, pp. 1–2.

Verspej, Michael A. ''Where Ducks and Fun Mean Success,'' *Industry Week,* March 18, 1991, pp. 28–30.

Yerak, Becky, ''Consumers Stick with Manco Duct Tape,'' *Plain Dealer,* October 24, 1997, pp. 1C, 2-C.

—April Dougal Gasbarre

Hercules Inc.

Hercules Plaza
1313 N. Market Street
Wilmington, Delaware 19894-0001
U.S.A.
(302) 594-5000
Fax: (302) 594-5400
Web site: http://www.herc.com

Public Company
Incorporated: 1912 as Hercules Powder Company
Employees: 8,000
Sales: $2.06 billion (1996)
Stock Exchanges: New York
SICs: 2890 Miscellaneous Chemical Products

Over its lifetime, Hercules Inc. has served as both a model of chemical industry management and a slow-moving corporate behemoth. With its downturns inspiring leadership changes and restructuring, Hercules usually has landed not just on its feet but ahead of the pack.

The Hercules Powder Company was one of the several small explosives companies acquired by the Du Pont Company in the 1880s. By the beginning of the 20th century Du Pont had absorbed so many of its competitors that it was producing two-thirds of the dynamite and gunpowder sold in the United States. In 1912 a federal court, citing the Sherman Anti-Trust Act, ordered Du Pont broken up. It was through this court-ordered action that the Hercules Powder Company was reborn, a manufacturer of explosives ostensibly separate from Du Pont.

The division of the Du Pont Company into Du Pont, Atlas Powder Company, and Hercules Powder Company, was intended to foster competition in the explosives industry, but in reality the antitrust agreement allowed the connection between Hercules and the parent company to remain intact. The new company was staffed by executives who had been transplanted from the Du Pont headquarters across the street into the main offices of Hercules in Wilmington, Delaware. As *Fortune* magazine remarked in 1935, ''The Hercules headquarters is in Wilmington and breathes heavily Dupontizied air.'' Not only did the Du Pont family retain a substantial financial interest in Hercules, but as late as 1970 the president of Hercules was related to the Du Pont family.

The Hercules Powder Company was set up as a fully developed business entity, complete with several explosives factories, a healthy segment of the explosives market, and a $5 million ''loan'' in its treasury. It operated successfully and made a profit from its very first year. Given its early advantage it is not surprising that Hercules developed into one of the larger chemical companies in the United States.

Hercules began as an explosives company serving the mining industry, gun owners, and the military. In the first month of operation its facility in Hazardville, New Jersey, exploded. Hercules had plants up and down the East Coast, however, and the loss of the Hazardville plant was not financially disastrous. Like other manufacturers of explosives, Hercules preferred many small plants to a few large ones. Due to the company's risks involved in product transportation, these plants were located in proximity to customers, rather than near the source of raw materials.

The company's first big break came in 1916 when Hercules signed a lucrative contract to supply Britain with acetone, a contract that stipulated, however, that no known sources of acetone be used. Hercules sent ships out to the Pacific to harvest giant kelp, which was used to produce the solvent Britain needed. That same year Hercules paid large dividends on its stock shares. The company also benefited from its sale of gunpowder to the army.

In 1920 Hercules began to manufacture cotton cellulose from the lint left over from cotton seeds once the high-quality cotton has been extracted. Cotton cellulose is a fiber that has hundreds of industrial uses. When treated with nitroglycerine it becomes nitrocellulose, important in the production of lacquers and plastics. Hercules quickly became the world's leading maker of cotton cellulose. This early effort at diversification in no way threatened Du Pont, which also manufactured nitrocellulose, but only for its own uses.

Company Perspectives:

Hercules Incorporated is a global manufacturer of chemical specialty products used in a variety of home, office, and industrial products. Core businesses and their key products are: Aqualon, for water-soluble polymers that thicken latex paints; Paper Technology, for strength and sizing aids used in manufacturing paper; Resins, for hydrocarbon and rosin resins used in adhesives; and Food Gums, for natural gum ingredients in food and beverages. Major equity companies are Alliant Techsystems, a technology leader in aerospace and defense, and a joint venture that combines the Hercules Fiber business with the Danaklon Group. With expert technical and sales service, innovative product development, and the number one or two positions in their major markets, Hercules' businesses generate excellent returns on capital, stable and strong operating margins, and good free cash flow. Hercules' unique technology base centers on the conversion of natural raw materials—pine stumps, wood pulp, cotton linters, citrus peels, and seaweed—into value-added chemical specialties. The corporation's focus is on sustainable, long-term growth in shareholder value, driven by new product growth and continuous improvement in manufacturing costs.

Throughout its history Hercules has been successful at transforming a previously worthless substance into something useful. But for every time Hercules has succeeded in this kind of endeavor, it has also failed. The company's foray into naval stores is an example of this. Naval stores is a term that refers to products derived from tree sap, and recalls the early use of pitch to caulk boats. Gums, turpentine, and various adhesives are all referred to as naval stores. In 1920 a Senate committee predicted that the virgin pine forests from which high-quality naval stores were derived would soon be exhausted and that there would be no naval stores industry left in the U.S. The management at Hercules saw, or thought it saw, a chance to corner the naval stores market.

Hercules joined forces with Yaryan, one of the few companies that distilled rosin from tree stumps rather than pitch. After buying rights to pull stumps and building a new rosin distilling plant, Hercules quickly became the world's largest producer of naval stores. But a problem soon arose: the expected shortage of naval stores never materialized. Hercules, the Senate Committee, and the naval stores industry overlooked the fact that pine trees grow back rather quickly, and that with proper management there would be plenty of pitch. Hercules was stuck with fields full of stumps, facilities to process the stumps, and a large amount of inferior turpentine. Turpentine derived from stumps is dark in color and hence unsuitable for some uses in finishing and painting furniture.

Endowed with sufficient capital (a legacy from Du Pont), Hercules was able to salvage its naval stores division by developing a paler turpentine and convincing its customers that wood (as opposed to pitch) naval stores were a bargain. In 1935 naval stores, the second largest of the company's investments, provided the smallest percentage of company sales. Naval stores and products derived from them eventually became a mainstay of the company, albeit one with slow growth. Not until the mid-1970s did the naval stores division emerge as a profitable endeavor. It was the explosives division which ensured the company's financial stability throughout the Depression.

By 1935 Hercules had five divisions: explosives, naval stores, nitrocellulose, chemical cotton, and paper products. Chemical cotton is made from the short fibers of cotton unsuitable for weaving, which are pressed into sheets and sold to industries as a source of cellulose. The paper products division began in 1931 with the purchase of Paper Makers Chemical Corporation, which provided 70 percent of U.S. demand for the rosin "sizing" used to stiffen paper.

At the time of America's entrance into World War II Hercules was the country's largest producer of naval stores and the third-largest producer of explosives. Business was good during the war and company coffers were stuffed with legitimate and illegitimate gains. Hercules, Atlas, and Du Pont were convicted of a joint price-fixing scheme, and Du Pont was assessed a $40,000 dollar fine. Hercules' annual reports during this period concentrate on plans for reducing the company's size once the war ended because the demands of the war had swelled the company's workforce to twice its previous size.

Three years after the war ended Hercules emerged from what a later industry analyst called "a big sleep." The demand for nitrocellulose, paper chemicals, and naval stores, products Hercules was depending on in peacetime, was growing at a snail's pace. Sales were averaging an unremarkable $200 million a year. However, in the 1950s the company entered two markets it would later dominate: DMT and polypropylene.

Consistent with its "waste not, want not" approach to new chemicals, Hercules began to use waste gases from refineries to manufacture polypropylene, an increasingly important type of plastic. Polypropylene was used for food packaging, among other things. DMT is the chemical base for polyester fiber and was sold as a commodity to both chemical and polyester makers, including Du Pont. Besides these new products Hercules continued to look for new uses for naval stores from which it already derived chemicals used in insecticides, textiles, paints, and rubber.

Between 1955 and 1963 Hercules saw its sales double, due in large part to government contracts. In 1959 Hercules diversified into rocket fuels and propulsion systems for the Polaris, Minuteman, and Honest John missiles. Sales of aerospace equipment and fuels accounted for almost 10 percent of sales in 1961, 15 percent in 1962, and 25 percent in 1963. Throughout the Vietnam War Hercules continued to derive approximately 25 percent of its profits from rocket fuels, anti-personnel weapons, and specialty chemicals such as Agent Orange and napalm.

The man who presided over Hercules in the 1960s was George Thouron, a relative of the Du Ponts. He described Hercules' policy towards expansion as "sticking close to profit-producing fields." A profile in *Fortune* magazine describes Thouron as a quiet man. As the article noted, "his main interest is in his prize Guernsey cattle."

Thouron knew that the war in Indochina would not last forever, and undertook an ambitious reorientation of the company toward the production of plastics, polyester, and other petrochemicals. A contemporary observer remarked that "few companies have expanded further or faster than Hercules Inc." Herculon, the company's synthetic fabric, had garnered almost 11 percent of the market for upholstery material. A water soluble gum called CMC also made money for the company. CMC was as versatile as Herculon was stain-resistant: it made its way into products as diverse as ice cream, embalming fluid, diet products, and vaginal jelly. "From womb to tomb," one company pundit quipped.

In 1968, the company changed its name from Hercules Powder Company to Hercules Inc. The 1960s and early 1970s were an auspicious time for Hercules. Although the foray into plastics had required large capital and research expenditures that depressed earnings, Hercules remained a profitable and steadily growing company. High inflation actually helped the synthetics industry since the prices of natural fibers outpaced the cost of synthetics.

In 1973, however, Hercules learned that oil can be economically as volatile as nitroglycerin. The Arab Oil Embargo was a disaster for the petrochemical industry. And if the embargo were not enough, two years later the demand for naval stores crashed just months after a rosin shortage had been predicted. Hercules, anticipating a shortage, had ordered millions of pounds of rosin at twice the usual price. Around the time that the first rosin-laden ships arrived it became clear that Hercules' customers, also fearful of a shortage, were overstocked with the material. The rosin problem, combined with a drop in the fibers market, caused sales to drop 90 percent. Hercules stock went down 17 percent. The year 1975 was not a good one for most chemical companies, but the difficulties that Hercules experienced were more than its share.

Werner Brown was the company's president during these years. In 1977 he was promoted, and chose Alexander Giacco to be the next president. Hercules had become an inordinately large company; its overheads and the size of its workforce were both excessive. In his first year as president Giacco fired or forced into retirement 700 middle managers and three executive vice-presidents. Giacco had a managerial style that differed from that of the mild-mannered Brown, and Giacco's restructuring of the company reflected that. Giacco streamlined Hercules to make it more of a monarchy. "He runs the company like an extension of himself," said one analyst. In order to stay in touch with the various divisions, Giacco invested in advanced communications equipment and computers. He also reduced the managerial levels between himself and the foremen from 12 to six. His position in the company is suggested by his description of a new product. "I heard Gene Shalit say that candy wrapping paper made too much crinkling noise in movie houses. So we developed a candy wrapper that has no crinkle."

In many ways Giacco's plan for Hercules resembles the strategy his mentor, Werner Brown, mapped out in the early 1970s: shift from commodity to value-added (specialty) chemicals, get rid of unprofitable divisions, and derive more profits from existing product lines. Giacco also led the company away from its longstanding tradition of basic chemical research into more immediately profitable, application-based inquiry. After the fiasco in 1975 when two unrelated markets crashed at the same time, Hercules has experimented with the proper combination of products taking to heart the teachings of economist Charles Reeder: "There's a simple two word answer to why chemical company earnings vary all over the lot. The words are 'product mix.' "

This product mix had eluded Hercules. One thing was certain, however; Hercules' mix would not include petrochemicals. In 1975, 43 percent of its fixable assets were in petrochemicals, but within a decade these assets were liquidated. Naval stores, responsible in 1985 for a decline in operating profits, also fell out of favor. Demand for CMC, the binding agent, declined because the oil industry was not using it for drilling. Propylene fibers and film, food flavors and fragrances (relatively new ventures) paper chemicals, aerospace, and graphite fibers were included in the future recipe for success. The company's plants for manufacturing DMT and explosives were among two dozen sold between 1975 and 1985.

One shining success during this period was the growth of the stagnant polypropylene market. Hercules entered into a joint venture with the Italian firm Montedison, with whom it had previously teamed up in the pharmaceutical company Adria Labs, in order to take advantage of Montedison's newly developed, extremely efficient process for manufacturing polypropylene. Because the material cost so little, Giacco promoted the use of it to replace other materials in all types of products, including cigarette filters. It was mixed with polyethylene to produce a synthetic wood pulp replacement.

The company's herbicide business, maintained during the 1960s, was not profitable and its liabilities continued to haunt Hercules well after it closed the Reasor-Hill plant in Jacksonville, Arkansas. After five years of class action litigation on behalf of U.S. veterans exposed to Agent Orange, the company paid $18 million in 1983 to settle claims in the case. Its product's extremely low levels of the impurity dioxin, which was perceived to be the primary pathogen in Agent Orange, mitigated the portion Hercules paid of the total $180 million settlement with several other manufacturers.

The overall success in its aerospace business segued nicely with its line of graphite composites, which had steadily gained acceptance during the 1970s to become a mainstay in high performance aircraft. In 1986, Dick Rutan and Jeana Yeager flew the company's Magnamite carbon composites into the history book when their experimental craft the Voyager circled the globe.

David Hollingsworth succeeded Giacco as chairman and CEO in 1987. After Hollingsworth sold the company's share of the HIMONT polypropylene venture to Montedison, Giacco resigned from the board, offended at the loss of a sure growth center. As in the last period after the top office changed hands, several poorly performing, mature businesses were sold off. Advanced materials and flavors and food ingredients—particularly natural additives based on pectin and carrageenan—were the focus of intended growth. The company bought out Henkel KgaA's share of the Aqualon Group, formed in 1986 to make cellulose derivatives and water-soluble polymers.

The 1990s were another period of readjustment. Hercules impressed investors with its 1991 introduction of Slendid, a fat substitute made from citrus pectin (it would first be used in a commercial product five years later, in J.R. Simplot frozen French fries). However, its aerospace unit, which surged forward in the late 1970s, suffered serious setbacks in its program to develop engines for the Titan IV program. Overall, the year was a disappointing start for a new CEO, Tom Gossage. He would devote the next five years to enhancing the company's value to shareholders, and succeeded in building Hercules' market value to nearly three times what it was when his tenure began (from \$1.6 billion to \$4.4 billion).

In 1996 another CEO, R. Keith Elliott, took the reigns at Hercules. The company's successful composites business was sold to Hexcel Corporation that year. A new, lower cost carrageenan plant was being built in the Philippines. Hercules entered a joint venture of its polypropylene fiber business with Jacob Holm & Sons A/S (Denmark) in 1997. Earlier it had signed agreements to co-produce hydrogenated hydrocarbon resins in China with the Beijing Yanshan Petrochemical Company. One of the smaller CMC subsidiaries, Aqualon do Brasil, was sold to Grupo Gusmao dos Santos. In 1997, Hercules and its partner Mallinckrodt Inc. sold their Tastemaker venture to Roche for \$1.1 billion.

Hercules has been able to shed product lines that had once been crucial to its success once they lost their luster. With periodic management shakeups a part of the company's business cycle, the company seemed a giant limber enough to thrive in the unpredictable conditions of the next century.

Principal Subsidiaries

Hercules Fibers Argentina S.A.; Patex Chemie GmbH (Austria); Hercules International Trade Corporation Limited (HINTCO) (Bahamas); Hercules Belgium N.V.; S.A. Hercules Europe N.V. (Belgium); Curtis Bay Insurance Co., Ltd. (Bermuda); Hercules do Brasil Produtos Quimicos Ltda.; Genu Products Canada Ltd.; Hercules Canada Inc.; Quimica Hercules de Colombia S.A.; Hercules CZ s.r.o. (Czech Republic); Copenhagen Pectin A/S (Denmark); Hercules Limited (U.K.); Oy Hercofinn Ab (Finland); Aqualon France B.V.; Hercules S.A. (France); Hercules GmbH (Germany); Pomosin GmbH (Germany); Hercules China Limited (Hong Kong); Hercules Italia S.p.A.; Hercules Japan Ltd.; Hercules Fibras de Mexico, S.A. de C.V.; Quimica Hercules, S.A. de C.V. (Mexico); Hercules B.V. (Netherlands); Hercules Singapore Pte Ltd.; Hercules Quimica, S.A. (Spain); Hercules AB (Sweden); Hercules Overseas Corporation (Virgin Islands); Alga Marinas S.A. (Chile; 70%); Shanghai Hercules Chemicals Company, Ltd. (China; 60%); Abieta Chemie GmbH (Germany; 50%); P.T. Hercules Mas Indonesia (49%); Rika-Hercules Incorporated (Japan; 50%); Hercules Korea Chemical Co. Ltd. (99%); Taloquimia, S.A. (Mexico; 49%); Pakistan Gum Industries Limited (49%); Taiwan Hercules Chemicals Inc. (97%); Alliant Techsystems Inc. (30%); BHC Laboratories, Inc. (50%); Hercules-Sanyo, Inc. (50%).

Principal Divisions

Aqualon; Food Gums; Paper Technology; Resins; Fibers.

Further Reading

Brown, Werner C., and Alexander F. Goacco, *Hercules Incorporated: A Study in Creative Chemistry*, New York: Newcomen Society in North America, 1977.

''Building Successful Global Partnerships,'' *Journal of Business Strategy*, September/October 1988, pp. 12–15.

Corbo, Vincent J., ''Five Great Myths About Hercules,'' Merrill Lynch Chemical Conference, March 12, 1997, http://www.herc.com/abouthercules/news/speeches/031297vc.htm.

Dyer, Davis, and David B. Sicilia, *Labors of a Modern Hercules: The Evolution of a Chemical Company,* Boston: Harvard Business School Press, 1990.

Plishner, Emily S., and William Freedman, ''The Labors of Hercules,'' *Chemical Week,* August 23, 1995, pp. 29–31.

Rotman, David, ''Hercules Looks to Regain R&D Strength,'' *Chemical Week,* May 1, 1996, pp. 56–57.

—updated by Frederick C. Ingram

Hooper Holmes, Inc.

170 Mount Airy Road
Basking Ridge, New Jersey 07920
U.S.A.
(908) 766-5000
Fax: (908) 766-5729

Public Company
Incorporated: 1899
Employees: 1700
Sales: $156.3 million (1996)
Stock Exchanges: American
SICs: 8099 Health & Allied Services

Hooper Holmes, Inc. is the nation's leading provider of alternate-site health information, primarily for life and health insurance companies. With 200 offices in 50 states, the company's network of medical professionals conducts physical examinations, testing, and personal health interviews. The information gathered is used by insurance underwriters to assess risks and make informed decisions before selling a policy to any particular customer. Hooper Holmes performed approximately 2.7 million tests in 1997 on insurance applicants under its trade name Portamedic.

A Turn-of-the-Century Alliance

A predecessor company to Hooper Holmes, The National Insurance Information Bureau was founded in 1899 by two partners, William DeMattos Hooper and Bayard P. Holmes. Hooper had been educated at Oxford University, England, and immigrated to the United States via Canada in 1870. For five years he worked as the city librarian of Indianapolis, Indiana, before taking a position as actuary of the Railroad Officials and Employees Accident Association of Indianapolis. He was recognized as a talented writer, and as someone of considerable organizational and statistical skills. His partner, Holmes, came from an influential New York family—his maternal grandfather, Joseph Reynolds, served as a commissioned Brigadier General following the War of 1812, and worked as a judge in the State of New York and as a member of the United States Congress. His grandson, Bayard, proved himself an entrepreneurially innovative heir. He graduated from Cornell University and received his law degree from New York University. While still at Cornell, Holmes became fascinated with the criminal mind after reading a book entitled, *Criminology,* written by an Italian psychologist. Instead of entering into the practice of law, Holmes became a New York book agent for the purpose of selling the book which had so intrigued him. That effort led to his acquaintance with Tom Lonergan, manager of Thiel's Service Company, one of the leading New York City detective organizations of the day. Lonergan eventually offered Holmes a job with his detective agency, telling him, ''If you really want to make a study of criminology from the inside, come in and see me.''

In the days prior to sufficient in-house investigative departments, insurance companies would hire a detective agency to investigate questionable claims, thus aligning the industries of insurance and investigation. After becoming manager of Thiel's New York Office, Holmes became assistant general manager of the company. By this time he had also established the Holmes Mercantile Agency, independently providing underwriting information for insurance companies—where his work soon brought him into contact with William Hooper, who had served as actuary to the International Association of Accident Underwriters.

The two men decided to form a partnership with the intention of providing nationwide information for accident, life, health, and disability insurance contracts, and to protect subscribers from fraudulent insurance practices, which might be attempted by present or prospective policyholders. Hooper was elected president after the 1906 incorporation of their newly named firm, The Hooper Holmes Information Bureau. In 1907 Hooper Holmes acquired the Holmes Mercantile Agency. Vital to the success of the claims clearinghouse was the expansion of membership and increasing claims reporting activity. Member companies would submit all claims paid by them to the Hooper Holmes central database, i.e. the Casualty Index, where they could then have access to information provided by other member companies' claims activity reports, enabling them to identify potentially risky insurees. Reports from that period indicate that 14.9 percent of accident claims were ''from persons who had previous claims,

Company Perspectives:

Hooper Holmes offers the industry's widest geographic coverage and up-to-date technology to ensure timely, accurate delivery of health information. Hooper Holmes' mission is to be recognized as a quality service provider that meets the needs of its customers, employees, and shareholders. We pride ourselves on anticipating new challenges that face our clients and finding solutions to help them adapt to change. The Company's ongoing strategy is to combine positive industry trends, increased market presence, entrance into related markets and our superior technology to become the leading health information services provider in the life and health insurance industry.

ranging up to three people on their tenth accident claim.'' In an effort to uncover fraudulent claims, the company organized a system for comparing ''sound alike'' surnames (and first-name variations), with other information such as date of birth and address.

Rapid Growth Through the 1920s

Membership grew rapidly with transportation subscribers accounting for nearly one-third of the accident claim reports. People riding on passenger trains and city streetcars filed a high number of casualty claims against those companies, and all of the major railroads and many regional lines held individual memberships. In many instances, preexisting injuries, or fraud—often a pattern of systematically filed claims—were revealed in the file search.

In 1912, following the death of William Hooper, Holmes assumed the presidency of the company. John J. King, a friend and former colleague from Thiel's (and former stagecoach driver and investigator), became the new assistant manager. Under King's direction, Hooper Holmes developed a network of branch offices extending throughout the United States and Canada. By 1917, according to company reports, 4.5 million records were on file, ''representing fully eighty percent of the accident and health business written in the United States.'' (When former U.S. President Calvin Coolidge was a young lawyer he occasionally made investigations for the company, charging a fee of 50 cents per case).

Throughout the 1920s and 1930s Hooper Holmes expanded very rapidly, especially as the automobile gained in popularity and accident claims increased. After 1920, following the passage of The Volstead Act—prohibiting the manufacture and sale of liquor—widespread bootlegging by organized gangs and others, often involving intoxication, high-speed chases, and general lawlessness, posed a major challenge to the insurance industry. An Hooper Holmes article from the period stated that ''The effect is seen in life insurance, in automobile insurance, in health and accident insurance, in the prolongation of malingering and complication of claims arising under workmen's compensation, in robbery and burglary epidemics, homicides and other phases familiar to every insurance man.'' One insurance company reported receiving an average of 10 applications per day which investigators attributed to persons involved in the bootlegging trade.

1930: New Ownership

By 1917 King had been elected vice-president, and by 1930 he became president and general manager, while Holmes served as chairman and assumed semi-retirement until his death in 1931. During the Great Depression King managed to maintain full employment for his entire staff, although the company imposed a 10 percent salary cut during their most difficult months. Management began to consider a diversification plan to offset the general decline in the insurance business, which the company lamented in its bulletin: ''The dollars which should have gone for various kinds of insurance; the dollars which might have gone into new homes, new automobiles, new business enterprises . . . were dropped into the bottomless maw of stock speculation . . .''. King invested heavily in the company. Over the next decade he and his children bought all of the outstanding Hooper Holmes stock.

As part of their diversification program, the company began providing credit reporting services to financial institutions, utilizing the previously unemployed to investigate property and asset information. This enabled lenders to extend repayment terms when feasible. In 1934, with almost 60 branch offices in operation, the company experienced a 25.8 percent gain in revenues, largely attributable to this new service. They also entered into the field of Market Research, conducting audience surveys for radio and for private industry. Total revenues increased from approximately $1.5 million in 1935 to $2.1 million by 1940.

Investigative Services Provided During World War II

During World War II insurance sales began a decline largely due to the drain of manpower and resources expended toward the war effort. King responded by obtaining contracts from the federal government, offering security investigative services. Government work represented 46 percent of Hooper Holmes's revenues for the year 1943, primarily related to investigations into defense industry employment.

John King died in 1948, leaving leadership responsibility for the company to his two sons, Edward and Charles, serving as president and executive vice-president, respectively. Improvements in communications systems marked the era of their leadership. Teletype machines, electric files, office copiers, and eventually computers were among the technological innovations which streamlined office procedures. Around 1959, Hooper Holmes helped to pioneer experiments involving photographically recording insured dwellings as an aid to evaluating underwriting risks through the purchase of Polaroid cameras for all of their inspectors.

The introduction of computers made it possible to incorporate high-volume credit information services. In 1963, Hooper Holmes established The Credit Index, a clearinghouse for the Credit Industry offering subscribers credit information about individuals who are delinquent on payments for merchandise or services. Subscribers to the Index included major companies in the book and record club business, mail order and catalogue mail order, petroleum credit card, and general credit card industries.

1980s: Public Offering and Restructuring

The King family continued to own the company until it went public in 1984, and James M. McNamee, who had started at Hooper Holmes in 1968 as a management trainee, became president. He immediately began selling off some of the divisions, choosing to concentrate on home healthcare services and health information. According to Dan Goldblatt of *Business News,* "Those choices would almost be the undoing of Hooper Holmes—and perhaps its salvation." McNamee made a score of acquisitions, building the company from approximately $50 million in 1984 to $252 million a decade later. In 1993 Hooper Holmes bought a large home healthcare firm, Norrell Health Care of Atlanta. McNamee told Goldblatt that Hooper Holmes could not integrate the larger business into their operation: their systems failed to work, the business itself, which involved sending nurses and health aides into people's homes, was too decentralized and became unmanageable. Also, competition with other larger healthcare networks and Medicaid and Medicare changes affecting home health dollars affected Hooper Holmes's profits. One division, Nurse's House Call, had plenty of business but the company was having a difficult time collecting receivables, forcing the company—a company with an historic aversion to debt—to borrow $50 million to cover lagging income. The profit margin could not compare to that of the firm's information products, resulting in the decision to reconsider their focus.

In 1995 Hooper Holmes negotiated an asset swap, trading its home health business for Olsten's (a New York temporary employment firm) ASB/Meditest division, which performed medical examinations on applicants for insurance policies, plus $34.5 million in cash. Profit margins soon increased from the 1.5 to 2 percent range before the swap to more than 6.5 percent by 1997.

Insurers worried about "buyer's remorse," meaning that the longer buyers wait, the more likely they are to change their mind about wanting a policy. In an effort to reduce the time between medical lab testing—sometimes taking several weeks—and the transfer of that data to insurers, Hooper Holmes signed a 1993 letter of intent with Home Office Reference Laboratory, Inc. of Kansas (providing marketing and technical support), to create an electronic data interchange (EDI) computer network. Hooper Holmes was also teaming with EDS, a Texas electronic data company that General Motors purchased from Ross Perot, to develop the nation's first centralized underwriting information clearinghouse, providing information to customers in the United States and Canada.

A New Company Limb: Artificial Intelligence in the 1990s

Blood and urine tests, physical examinations, and other procedures which are required before an insurer can decide whether to issue a policy were electronically sent to the network, which are then relayed to the carrier, saving on time and paperwork. The network allowed tests to be completed within 72 hours. The system featured an artificial intelligence-decision-support system that assisted companies in the underwriting process. The system evaluated test results from information providers, and determined whether more tests were required. The evaluation and test results were sent to the carrier simultaneously. The speedier process not only allowed insurance companies to provide better service to customers, but it also shortened the time it took for agents to receive their commission, resulting in more satisfied agents and providers.

With the 1996 Food and Drug Administration approval of at-home HIV tests, ushered into the marketplace by Johnson and Johnson Co., some people who tested positive did not tell their insurance providers. The enormous costs involved in treating AIDS patients prompted insurers to reevaluate their testing criteria. All of the major and most of the minor insurance companies began testing every applicant, greatly increasing the volume of information handled by Hooper Holmes.

Following Hooper Holmes's sale of its home nursing unit, revenues increased, and by the end of 1996, the company's bank debt was reduced from $28.8 million to $6.3 million. The company began providing specimen collection and related health information to a clinical research organization involved in managing clinical trials, expanding on market opportunities. By 1997, some of Hooper Holmes's biggest clients—among the 900 insurance companies it serves—included Prudential Insurance Co. of America, State Farm Life Insurance Co., and Metropolitan Life Insurance Co., with Prudential making up almost seven percent of Hooper Holmes's business. Testing approximately 250,000 applicants a month, the company controlled 25 to 35 percent of the U.S. market.

Hooper Holmes began a 1996 restructuring program to integrate the three key components of their information technology infrastructure: MIS, their centralized management information reporting system that tied together branches and the corporate offices; the Client Services group, which fulfilled the multiple information needs of customers; and Infolink, the channel that delivered financial and health information reports electronically to customers. Functioning as a single entity, the company hoped the integration of the divisions would allow more efficiency in service delivery and in adaptability to future change.

A more recent company venture involved contract work for a research organization utilizing Hooper Holmes's network of medical personnel to obtain specimens for tests. The data gathered was needed for studies the research company provided to pharmaceutical companies. Following the company tradition for quality and efficiency, management continued to streamline its operations. For the future, President, Chairman, and CEO McNamee envisioned changes in the way insurance would be marketed, according to Goldblatt of *Business News.* He predicted that more and more policies would be sold directly to consumers. "We expect to offer an alternative to the sales force," said McNamee. He envisioned a process by which information traveled back and forth, flowing through the growing files of Hooper Holmes.

Principal Subsidiaries

Policy Management Systems Corporation (PMSI).

Principal Divisions

Portamedic; ASB/Meditest.

Further Reading

Abelson, Reed, ''Companies to Watch,'' *Fortune,* July 3, 1989, p. 112.
''The AFGC 100,'' *Individual Investor,* September 1997.
Goldblatt, Dan, ''Hooper Holmes Goes Back to the Future,'' *Business News,* March 3–9, 1997.
Greenwald, Nathan, ''Hot Stocks,'' *Individual Investor,* July 1997.
''Hooper Holmes, Inc., A Commemorative Collection, 1899–1967,'' Basking Ridge, N.J.: Hooper Holmes, Inc., 1984.
Jones, David C., ''Network to Speed Transfer of Underwriting Data,'' *National Underwriter,* December 27, 1993, p. 28.
Marcial, Gene G., ''Open Wide and Say Hooper Holmes,'' *Business Week,* September 16, 1996, p. 96.
Pachuta, Michael J., ''Hooper Holmes Leads Market for Insurance Medical Exams,'' *Investor's Business Daily,* February 21, 1997.

—Terri Mozzone

Horace Mann®
Insuring America's Educational Community

Horace Mann Educators Corporation

1 Horace Mann Plaza
Springfield, Illinois 62715-0001
U.S.A.
(217) 789-2500
Fax: (217) 788-5157
Web site: http://www.horacemann.com

Public Company
Incorporated: 1945
Employees: 2,700
Total Assets: $3.86 billion (1996)
Stock Exchanges: New York
SICs: 6331 Fire, Marine, & Casualty Insurance; 6311 Life Insurance; 6719 Holding Companies, Not Elsewhere Classified

An insurance holding company, Horace Mann Educators Corporation is a leading insurer serving educators in the United States. The company carries a variety of lines of insurance. First, the company offers private passenger automobile insurance in the forms of personal liability, collision coverage, and comprehensive coverage. Horace Mann also sells homeowners insurance against fire and theft, as well as individual life insurance policies, including traditional term and whole life and flexible life insurance that combines term life with interest-sensitive whole life and interest-bearing accounts. In addition, the company deals in tax-qualified annuities and life insurance and provides group life and disability insurance to school employees.

Serving U.S. Educators

Horace Mann operates predominantly in North Carolina, Texas, Illinois, Minnesota, and California, although its overall market includes the 4.5 million employees in public school districts across the United States. This includes 2.8 million elementary and public school teachers, in addition to 1.7 million administrators, office workers, maintenance personnel, bus drivers, and support staff. According to a Standard & Poor's insurance rating analysis, ''Horace Mann gears its products primarily to teachers and other employees of public schools and their families. This tends to be a well-educated, conservative, and financially stable market that possesses favorable insurance-risk characteristics. Customers typically have moderate annual incomes; employment is not recession sensitive, and many educators belong to two-income households. Their financial planning tends to focus on security, primary insurance needs, and conservative savings.''

Approximately 10 percent of all U.S. school employees are insured by Horace Mann through a network of 1,000 agents (who also act as field underwriters) or through their membership in the National Education Association (NEA). The NEA is comprised of more than two million members, and in 1994 Horace Mann enjoyed NEA-sponsorship in 42 states. ''Horace Mann,'' a Standard & Poor's insurance rating analysis revealed, ''has flourished by offering a broad range of personal insurance products to primary and secondary educators. The niche marketing strategy, accompanied by prudent underwriting standards, has translated into impressive underwriting margins and strong operating income.''

Indeed, Horace Mann's agents have been successful for the company. They are, in fact, key to the company's operations. As Standard & Poor's indicated: ''A cornerstone of Horace Mann's marketing strategy is its exclusive agency force who are company employees. . . . These agents sell only the company's products and all agents are required to sell both life insurance and property/casualty products. Many of these agents previously were teachers and principals who utilize their contacts among, and knowledge of, the target market. Through personal contact and identification of customers' needs, the company's agents seek to build a strong client relationship and provide a complete package of insurance protection.''

Horace Mann Educators Corporation maintains four subsidiaries: Allegiance Life Insurance Company, Horace Mann Life Insurance Company, Horace Mann Service Corporation, and Teachers Insurance Company.

Founded by Educators

Horace Mann's dedication to the educator market is no surprise since it was founded by two teachers in Springfield, Illinois, in 1945. Wishing to provide automobile insurance for

Company Perspectives:

For more than 50 years, Horace Mann's greatest strength has been its commitment to meeting the insurance needs of America's educators and their families. This focus has made the company a leader in its field, a position it maintains by offering high-quality, competitively priced products and a superior level of customer service.

their association peers, the two teachers established the Illinois Education Association Mutual Assurance Company. Later they renamed the company Horace Mann, after the father of public education in the United States, to testify to the company's commitment to educators.

Expansion began shortly after the company was established. Within two years, Horace Mann offered automobile insurance to teachers in other states. By 1949, the company extended into the life insurance business, providing a full-range of life insurance services to educators and their families. In 1961, when the U.S. Congress created legislation for tax-deferred annuities, Horace Mann also ventured into the annuity market.

Changing Hands

In 1974, INA Corporation, an insurance and financial services company headquartered in Philadelphia, Pennsylvania, began to purchase more and more holdings of Horace Mann. Eventually, INA gained control of the company in 1975. In 1982, INA Corporation merged with Connecticut General Corporation to form CIGNA, a holding company. That year Paul J. Kardos assumed the presidency and position of chief executive officer at Horace Mann. As the company's leader he guided Horace Mann through a management-led buyout and, later, an initial public offering. (Kardos, a graduate of Grove City College in Pennsylvania, joined Horace Mann in 1977. Previously he worked at the Life Insurance Company of North America.)

In 1989, Kardos and other Horace Mann management purchased the company from CIGNA with the financial assistance of an investor group. GGvA, an investment banking firm specializing in management-led buyouts, controlled the LBO. That same year, Horace Mann began managing Allegiance Insurance Company, a property and casualty insurance firm located in California.

Kardos coordinated Horace Mann's initial public offering in 1991. Each share of common stock sold for $18. At that time, the company's focus also shifted away from exposure to collateralized mortgage obligations (CMOs) and towards investment in tax-exempt securities. as market conditions have been attractive.

Horace Mann acquired Allegiance Insurance, which by then served 400,000 educators, in 1994. The company also introduced a program that year, Pathways, to facilitate the sale of life insurance by its agents. Pathways trained agents to close sales. "The Pathways program is a highly effective training tool that provides agents with a step-by-step process for closing sales in all lines of business," revealed a Horace Mann annual report. "Its success is demonstrated by the many experienced Horace Mann agents who rely on the program." And close sales they did.

In 1995, Horace Mann was able to repurchase half of GGvA's interest in the company. In July, Horace Mann issued a secondary offering of stock to sell the remaining six million shares at $23.38 each in the United States and abroad. In addition, more than 900,000 over-allotment shares worth $20 million were sold, reducing borrowings under the company's bank credit line. At the time, Kardos reported that: "We are pleased by the positive market acceptance of our offering, as evidenced by several market barometers. We gained a large number of new institutional investors, enhanced the liquidity of our shares by increasing public float by some 40 percent, and witnessed a more than 20 percent share price gain since the stock repurchase and secondary offering were announced." The overall effect of the sales, though, was to close the disposition of a 44 percent control interest of common stock. "Removing this uncertainty," said Kardos in *Business Week,* "returns our total focus to business growth and further increases shareholder value."

The company also expanded the size of its board of directors in 1995. Directors grew from eight to nine in number. Horace Mann also introduced its AutoEase program in all 50 states. The program allowed the payment of monthly automobile insurance premiums through electronic funds transfers from bank accounts.

A Year of Milestones

In 1996, Ward's Financial included Horace Mann on its lists of the 50 top property/casualty and life/health insurers. This placed the company among the safest and best-performing insurers in the United States. To be included on the lists, an insurer had to withstand scrutiny of its performance over the past five years. Ward's Financial listed only the companies with the highest profits demonstrating the most security in each market segment.

At this time, the National Education Association selected Horace Mann to provide professional liability insurance for its 2.2 million members in a three-year contract. The company's plans offered NEA members protection from personal financial liability as the result of employment-related occurrences.

For the first time in the company's history, its sales force exceeded 1,000 agents in 1996. "Two primary factors drove this growth," noted the 1996 annual report. "First, our recruiting efforts have become more targeted and effective, so that not only are we hiring more agents, those we are hiring now are more likely to succeed. Second, we are seeing positive results from programs designed to improve agent retention. Most of these are geared to new agents—those with less than two years experience—since turnover drops off sharply once agents pass this milestone."

One existing program, the Pathways program, was revised and extended to include automobile and homeowners insurance as well as life insurance to assist agents in closing sales. The company also developed new programs to enhance the effectiveness of agents. For instance, Horace Mann instituted the Service on Call program to assist newer agents not yet able to secure office support or secretarial staff. The program allowed an agent to forward calls to a home office when he or she was on sales calls. This enabled home office service representatives to respond personally to callers. In addition Horace Mann issued new educational and promotional material about annuities for its agents, as well as distributed three videos about retirement planning for use at seminars.

Toward the end of the year, Horace Mann began to withdraw from the group medical insurance business. The company's group medical line lost $1.2 million in 1995 and more than $3 million in 1996. Though the group medical line accounted for close to seven percent of Horace Mann's total premiums written, the company intended to stop writing new group medical policies by January 1997 and to cease renewing group medical insurance policies by January 1998. According to Kardos, ''Horace Mann's strategic withdrawal from the group medical business will allow the company to focus on its core lines of business, including its group life and disability insurance.'' Ending its group medical line cost the company $8 million in net operating losses plus charges for severance and other expenses. In total, 40 positions were eliminated at Horace Mann by 1998.

A Year of Innovations

Innovations—focusing on core business lines—to assist agents continued throughout 1997. Horace Mann provided its leading 400 agents with a database on disk to assist with their monthly marketing programs. Updated monthly, the disk helped agents identify clients for cross-selling. The disk even contained information and programming to pre-fill paperwork for agents. Horace Mann planned to extend this service to others besides leading agents in the years ahead.

Horace Mann also introduced new products for agents to sell in 1997. The company launched five new term life products and three new variable annuity funds, notably small cap, international, and socially responsible funds.

In March 1997, Horace Mann accepted an Aon Group option program enabling the company to replace up to $100 million in equity in the event of a catastrophe. A risk management innovation, this multi-year, $100 million Catastrophe Equity Put was fully underwritten by Centre Reinsurance Ltd. and completed Horace Mann's plans to augment its reinsurance structure. When Horace Mann finalized the program, its rating by A. M. Best increase from ''excellent'' to ''superior.''

Priorities in the Future

Horace Mann hoped to strengthen its relationship with educators and their organizations in the future. By the year 2000, the total educator market should reach 10 million. Horace Mann expected a two percent growth in its target market by 2000, with an eight percent annual turnover in the teacher market. Moreover, the company anticipated an increase of five million non-teacher school employees to the year 2000.

To serve its growing market, Horace Mann planned to invest in its agents, products, and customer service. The company hoped to control expenses in the future and to anticipate and counter moves by its competitors, thereby enhancing value for Horace Mann shareholders. ''Our plan. . .,'' wrote chairman of the board Ralph S. Saul and Kardos in their 1996 letter to shareholders, ''is to build on our successes and further accelerate the company's forward momentum.''

Principal Subsidiaries

Allegiance Life Insurance Company; Horace Mann Life Insurance Company; Horace Mann Service Corporation; Teachers Insurance Company.

Further Reading

''Aon Announces Completion of $100 Million Catastrophe Equity Put for Horace Mann Educators Corporation,'' *Business Wire,* March 31, 1997, p. 3311339.

''Corporate Profile for Horace Mann Educators,'' *Business Wire,* September 1, 1995, p. 9011088.

''Corporate Profile for Horace Mann Educators,'' *Business Wire,* September 27, 1996, p. 9271013.

''Horace Mann Completes Secondary Offering; Over-allotment Proceeds of $20 Million Will Be Used to Reduce Bank Borrowings,'' *Business Wire,* July 31, 1995, p. 7311116.

''Horace Mann Educators Announces Public Offering,'' *Business Wire,* July 20, 1995, p. 7201028.

''Horace Mann Educators Expands Size of Board of Directors,'' *Business Wire,* June 15, 1995, p. 6151149.

''Horace Mann to Accelerate Withdrawal from Group Medical Business,'' *Business Wire,* October 16, 1997, p. 10161408.

''Horace Mann to Provide Liability Insurance for NEA Members,'' *Business Wire,* April 22, 1996, p. 4221161.

''Horace Mann to Withdraw from Group Medical Insurance Business,'' *Business Wire,* December 9, 1996, p. 12091247.

Lenckus, Dave, ''To Make Ward's List, Insurers Must Meet Tough Requirements,'' *Business Insurance,* August 26, 1996.

——, ''Ward's List Looks Beyond Numbers,'' *Business Insurance,* August 26, 1996.

''Standard & Poor's Insurance Rating Analysis, Life/Health: Horace Mann Life Insurance Company,'' New York: Standard & Poor's, January 17, 1996.

''Standard & Poor's Insurance Rating Analysis, Property/Casualty: Horace Mann Insurance Company,'' New York: Standard & Poor's, January 31, 1996.

—Charity Anne Dorgan

Hughes Markets, Inc.

14005 Live Oak Avenue
Irwindale, California 91706
U.S.A.
(818) 856-6060
Fax: (818) 856-6020

Wholly Owned Subsidiary of Quality Food Centers, Inc.
Incorporated: 1952
Employees: 5,100
Sales: $1.25 billion (1996)
Stock Exchanges: NASDAQ
SICs: 5411 Grocery Stores

A respected operator in the southern California supermarket industry, Hughes Markets, Inc. operates a chain of grocery stores in the greater Los Angeles area. For 45 years Hughes Markets was privately owned and family-operated, but in 1997 the company was acquired by Quality Food Centers, Inc., a Seattle, Washington-based supermarket chain. During the late 1990s, the company operated 56 stores and controlled 5.5 percent of the southern California market.

Origins

The key to Hughes Markets' success in the fiercely competitive southern California grocery store industry was its adherence to a simple and focused operating philosophy, the originator of which was the company's founder, Joseph Hughes. Hughes spent his adulthood working in grocery stores, starting in 1934 when he went to work for Thriftmart in New Jersey. He stayed with Thriftmart for nearly 20 years, then packed his bags in 1952 and made the transcontinental trip to southern California, where he would lay the foundation for one of the region's largest supermarket chains.

Although Hughes had spent nearly a lifetime's work at Thriftmart in New Jersey, he would spend another 30 years working as a grocery store operator in southern California. Hughes embarked on the second half of his lengthy career in 1952, when he opened a Thriftmart franchise in Studio City. From there he opened two more Thriftmart franchises during the next two years, one in Van Nuys and another in Hollywood. The opening of his next store, which was located in then-rural Granada Hills, marked a symbolic moment in Hughes's life. When he opened the doors to his fourth store, gone was the familiar Thriftmart sign marking the entrance. For the first time in 20 years, Hughes had no ties to Thriftmart. The sign above his store—the first store he could genuinely call his own—read: Hughes Market. Over the course of the next four decades, the sign that debuted in Granada Hills would become a fixture in the southern California supermarket industry, as Hughes and his family shaped the company into a powerful regional force.

Joe Hughes was brought up in an era when running a grocery store was a relatively uncomplicated task, a period when small, family-owned stores blanketed the country, dominated their industry, and rarely tried to be anything else than a grocery store. This would all change during Hughes Markets' development into an industry stalwart. During the latter half of the 20th century, grocery stores became shopping destinations aspiring to fulfill a broad spectrum of consumers' needs. As the size of stores swelled beyond 50,000 square feet, banks, pharmacies, lawn and garden departments, bakeries, on-site cooking establishments, and sundry other ''concepts'' made their debut, transforming the definition of the grocery store format. During this sweeping revolution within the grocery store industry, Hughes Markets rarely strayed from the original course charted by Joe Hughes, and when it did, success was generally the result.

This constancy of the Hughes Markets enterprise stemmed, in part, from its distinction as a privately owned, family-operated business. Two generations of the Hughes family bridged Hughes Markets' founding and its acquisition by Quality Food Centers, and it was clearly evident that the second generation learned much from the first. Roger Hughes, the son of Joe Hughes, began working at the family's grocery stores during the early years of the company. While his father slowly expanded the number of Hughes Markets operating in southern California, Roger Hughes divided his time between school and the grocery store business, attending Loyola High School during the day and managing the liquor department at the Studio City store during his off-hours. Roger Hughes did not initially commit himself to a career as a grocery store operator and the inheritor of the family business, but after a two-year stint in the U.S. Navy and after being graduated from the University of Southern California, Hughes resolved to devote himself to the perpetuation of the growing Hughes Markets enterprise. He would have a long wait.

Joe Hughes worked tirelessly at developing Hughes Markets into a success, working six days a week and spending the seventh driving around in his car to visit the stores in his fiefdom. Expansion, which many of his supermarket brethren financed by accumulating hefty bank debt or by relinquishing control to investors in exchange for cash, was pursued slowly and achieved debt-free. Joe Hughes expanded by acquiring small grocery store owners and parts belonging to larger operators. He stressed simplicity and a narrow focus, yet occasionally he emerged as an industry innovator. In the early 1960s, while Hughes was cementing his reputation as a traditionalist, he donned the hat of a pioneer by becoming the first supermarket chain operator in southern California to feature fresh fish markets in his stores.

Hughes's son Roger, meanwhile, had ample time to absorb all the nuances of his father's leadership style. After holding a variety of positions at the company's stores following his completion of studies at the University of Southern California, Roger Hughes was eventually promoted to manager of the company's Sherman Oaks store in 1962. Three years later, he was promoted to general manager of the store. It was at this point—in 1965—that he copied a page from his father's ascent in the grocery store business by arranging with Joe Hughes to operate the Sherman Oaks store much like a franchise. This arrangement, with Roger Hughes in charge of the Sherman Oaks store and his father in charge of all the rest, existed for the next two decades; its conclusion ushered in a new era of leadership at Hughes Markets.

Second Generation Takes Command in 1982

Joe Hughes died in 1982, 30 years after he had arrived in southern California to open a Thriftmart franchise. During his years in the Los Angeles area, Hughes had built his namesake company into a roughly $400 million in sales grocery concern that was known for its emphasis on fresh produce, meats, fish, and customer service. Hughes Markets was regarded as a quiet and conservative member of the southern California supermarket fraternity. Roger Hughes inherited this legacy, and did little to alter it. Having spent more than 20 years learning the grocery business under his father's tutelage, Roger Hughes was imbued with his father's business perspective and, consequently, carried out his executive duties much like his father would have done.

Although Roger Hughes stuck close to the course charted by his father and continued to direct and present Hughes Markets as a quiet, conservative enterprise, he was more growth-minded than his father. By the end of the 1980s, Roger Hughes's influence over the fortunes of the company was readily discernible. Revenues more than doubled during his first seven years of control, rising to $885 million, and the number of Hughes Markets increased to 45 stores. Although the pace of growth was decidedly more animated under the stewardship of Roger Hughes, the way in which the growth was achieved was done in much the same way as during Joe Hughes's tenure: debt-free and in small bursts, as opposed to one massive boost via a merger or acquisition.

1990s: Expansion and New Ownership

Hughes Markets stayed to its tried and true course as it entered the 1990s, conspicuous by its absence from the spate of megamergers that swept through the southern California supermarket industry during the late 1980s. Massive, sprawling chains such as Vons Stores, Lucky Stores, and Ralphs were made even larger after they swallowed up large competitors. Public stock offerings filed by these supermarket chains helped fill their war chests, giving them the cash to make large acquisitions and to finance expansion. When public stock offerings were not an option, banks were. Supermarket chains borrowed heavily to build a string of new stores and to tailor their stores to reflect the trend of the day. Inside, as the square footage increased dramatically, supermarkets were replete with specialty items and services to attract all tastes and fulfill nearly every desire. Nothing, it seemed, was outside the pale of the supermarket format.

Hughes Markets, the old-fashioned member of the supermarket constituency in the Los Angeles area, bucked nearly all the trends its competitors embraced during the 1980s and early 1990s. The company was privately owned (a rarity). It was family-operated (a further distinction). And its stores, which generally measured 25,000 square feet, focused on a single and simple format (another characteristic that set it apart from the other large supermarket chains). In these respects Hughes Markets appeared to be behind the times; a quaint and stodgy chain that had failed to adopt what were perceived as the successful attributes of a supermarket operator. The company's stature, however, belied this assessment. In 1990, Hughes Markets reached the billion dollar mark in sales, a figure that would have put it at the top of its industry in almost any other market except southern California. The spree of megamergers had transformed giants into behemoths, making Hughes Markets relatively small when compared to the upper echelon of its class, but few could argue with the company's success—least of all Roger Hughes.

Hughes was unlike his father in at least one respect. No chairman of Hughes Markets had ever talked to reporters from the business press until Roger Hughes broke the silence in 1989. In fact, the company operated without a public relations department. When Roger Hughes finally did share his thoughts with inquiring journalists, the succinct phrases that followed mirrored the traditional, unassuming nature of Hughes Markets and, perhaps, Joe Hughes himself. When questioned about his company's reliance on a single format and its refusal to delve into specialty markets, Hughes stated flatly, "We can't walk and chew gum at the same time." When pressed further on the same topic, Hughes answered, "The simple things are working. They've been working for 30 years." In reference to the money that could be raised by converting to public ownership like many of his competitors had done, Hughes explained, "I guess public capital would be nice, but I'm not comfortable with the trade off. Looking at quarter-to-quarter results for the benefit of someone back in New York—I'm not very good at that. I just don't see an IPO (initial public offering) in the picture for us, unless we get really desperate.'' When asked why his stores were smaller than the rest of the chains with at least $1 billion in sales, Hughes answered, ''We think that's [Hughes Markets' store size] big enough for our locations, and for who we are. We're not big in general merchandise, we don't have pharmacies, and we're not trying to draw from all over town. We like it that way . . . and the rent's a lot cheaper.'' In defense of his refusal to ape the expansion pace set by his competitors, Hughes responded, ''If we wanted to go out and build 20 stores next week, we'd have no problem. We just don't feel like we can grow any faster and hire the kind of quality personnel that we know it takes to run these stores. We want to grow as fast as we can grow realistically and still be Hughes Markets.''

The company entered the 1990s as the largest privately owned Los Angeles-based supermarket chain and was in the process of ensuring that no rival usurped its reigning position. Although Roger Hughes was opposed to rapid growth, he had initiated a slightly accelerated expansion program while his competitors celebrated monthly store openings. Hughes Markets opened four stores in 1989, five more in 1990, and slated five additional stores for their debut in 1991. When the company announced it had eclipsed the $1 billion mark in revenues in February 1990, there were 52 stores composing the chain. That milestone achievement was reached the same month the company presented itself as an industry pioneer by becoming the first regional chain to implement a storewide recycling program.

As this program was being put into place and the celebratory mood springing from the achievement of collecting $1 billion in sales was in full swing, the telltale signs of economically bleak times were already appearing. A nationwide recession began to stifle economic growth during the early 1990s, and Hughes Markets responded by shelving its strategy of opening between three to five stores per year. Instead, the company concentrated on renovating more stores than usual, and bided its time until the stormy economic climate cleared.

Although the pace of store renovations picked up, the company did not abandon its expansion strategy entirely during the early 1990s. Between 1992 and early 1994, five new stores were opened, and in 1993 construction of a new office and warehouse complex in Irwindale was completed. The distribution complex, comprising three buildings, consisted of a 36,000-square-foot office building, a 137,000-square-foot facility for produce, delicatessen, and meat, and a 443,000-square-foot warehouse for dry groceries, general merchandise, and liquor. The size of the complex suggested there were high expectations for future growth, despite the less-than-ideal economic conditions. The warehouse, projected to meet the company's needs for the ensuing 10 years, had sufficient capacity to handle three times the number of Hughes Markets in existence in 1993, which pointed to the anticipation of aggressive growth in the decade ahead.

Hughes Markets' rate of expansion resumed its pre-recession pace by the mid-1990s, when four new stores were opened in 1995. Two more stores debuted in 1996, helping push sales up to $1.25 billion and lifting the company's store count to 56, but by November 1996 the focus on expansion took a back seat to momentous news from company headquarters. After nearly a half-century of operating as a privately owned, family-run company, Hughes Markets was preparing to join ranks with a publicly owned supermarket chain and bring an end to its distinction as the quiet independent competing against publicly traded chains.

In November 1996, Quality Food Centers, Inc. (QFC), a 64-store supermarket chain based in Seattle, Washington, announced it had signed a merger agreement to acquire Hughes Markets for $360 million in cash. Under the terms of the agreement, Roger Hughes would relinquish his title as chairman, retain his chief executive officer title, and his management staff and all Hughes Markets employees would remain in place, with Hughes Markets and QFC slated to operate as separate business units under a holding company formed by QFC. For QFC, the deal represented the first move out of its home state and a significant step toward the realization of its ambitious expansion strategy. For Hughes Markets, the merger allowed it to keep its personnel in place and provided funds for future expansion. Said Hughes, ''One of the family's concerns with any sale was that we didn't want to disturb the employees, and we were able to consummate this and have all our people remain in place. Once the merger is completed, we'll have more financial clout and we'll be in a better position to grow.''

The acquisition was completed in March 1997 for $358.8 million. With Hughes serving as president and chief executive officer, Hughes Markets, under the auspices of QFC's holding company, planned to open three or four stores a year into the late 1990s. Acquisitions of smaller grocery store chains were in the offing as well, thanks to the added financial reserves gained from the deal with QFC. With its 45-year history as a privately owned company behind it, Hughes Markets embarked on a new future in the public spotlight. The essence of the company, however, remained the same.

Further Reading

Cook, Dan, ''A Quiet Giant: Hughes Markets Has Grown Steadily, Without Debt or Public Fanfare,'' *California Business,* June 1991, p. 50.

Frook, John Evan, ''Hughes Markets Bags Distinction of Being First to Have Storewide Recycling Program,'' *Los Angeles Business Journal,* February 12, 1990, p. 6.

Partch, Ken, ''Hughes Makes the Conventional Exceptional . . . and It Works,'' *Supermarket Business,* September 1990, p. 26.

Tobenkin, David, ''Hughes Markets: Supermarket Chain Keeps Things Simple,'' *Los Angeles Business Journal,* February 5, 1990, p. S18.

Zwiebach, Elliot, ''QFC to Buy Hughes for $360 Million in Cash,'' *Supermarket News,* November 25, 1996, p. 1.

——, ''QFC Wraps Hughes Deal; Multiregional Role Planned,'' *Supermarket News,* March 24, 1997, p. 1.

—Jeffrey L. Covell

Hvide Marine Incorporated

P.O. Box 13038
2200 Eller Drive
Fort Lauderdale, Florida 33316
U.S.A.
(954) 523-2200
Fax: (954) 527-1772

Public Company
Incorporated: 1958
Employees: 1,035
Sales: $109.35 million (1996)
Stock Exchanges: NASDAQ
SICs: 4492 Towing & Tugboat Services; 4412 Deep Sea Foreign Transport of Freight; 4424 Deep Sea Domestic Transport of Freight

Hvide Marine Incorporated is among the leading domestic and international marine support and transportation services companies. Dominant in the domestic chemical transportation trade, the company also holds a significant position in petroleum product transportation. Based in Port Everglades, Florida, the company operates a fleet of 217 vessels in two core businesses, marine support services and marine transportation services. It primarily serves the offshore energy industry, in which Hvide's Seabulk Offshore Ltd. subsidiary is the third largest operator of supply and crew boats in the Gulf of Mexico. Its marine support services include 186 vessels. In addition, its Seabulk Offshore International subsidiary is the largest independent operator in the Arabian Gulf. The company's offshore and harbor towing includes the divisions Tampa Bay Towing, Port Everglades Towing, Mobile Bay Towing, and Port Canaveral Towing. Its marine transportation services business comprises 31 vessels that carry petroleum products to power plants in northern Florida and southern Georgia, in addition to specialty and industrial chemicals from Gulf Coast refineries to destinations along the East and West Coasts.

Company Origins

Hvide Marine Incorporated began in 1958 as a Port Everglades harbor tugboat operator and almost immediately expanded to Port Canaveral, just as America's space program was getting under way. NASA and the U.S. Navy used tugboats from Hvide's Port Canaveral Towing business in downrange rescue and recovery missions. Port Everglades and Port Canaveral Towing are the sole suppliers of ship docking and undocking services in their respective ports. Revenue derived from tugboat operations is primarily a function of the number of tugs available to provide services, the rates charged for their services, and the volume of vessel traffic requiring docking and other ship-assist services. The company shifts tugboats among ports depending upon demand.

Building a Fleet in the 1970s

In 1975 the company acquired its first petroleum product carrier. Hvide's fuel transport vessel worked solely for Shell Oil Company—under a long-term contract that extends until January 2000—hauling gasoline and crude oil from refineries in Texas and Louisiana to tank farms in Port Everglades, Tampa, and Jacksonville, Florida. Since entering service Hvide's *Seabulk Challenger* derived all of its revenue from successive voyage and time charters to Shell, a lucrative charter arrangement that provided Hvide Marine with 22 percent of its total revenues in 1993. The *Challenger* is a catamaran tugboat and barge combination conceived and patented by J. Erik Hvide, son of Hans Hvide, the company's founder.

Hvide's Sun State Marine Services, Inc. subsidiary is based in Green Cove Springs, Florida and transports fuel oil and other petroleum products to destinations along the Gulf Coast. It also operates a shipyard that maintains Hvide's vessels as well as making repairs to other commercial and military vessels.

The company began transporting specialty chemicals in 1977 with the launching of the *Seabulk Magnachem,* followed by the launching of the *Seabulk America,* the newest chemical tanker to enter the domestic trade. Hvide's two chemical carriers generally worked out of Houston and Corpus Christi, Texas. Specialty and industrial chemicals were transported from Gulf Coast refineries to destinations along the East and West Coasts. The chemical transportation business soon constituted a second place position in terms of company earnings, following Hvide's marine support services. With a single ex-

Company Perspectives:

Hvide Marine Incorporated provides benchmark quality performance to our customers based on innovative solutions, safety, environmental responsibility, dedicated professional employees and modern efficient equipment, guided by Godly principles. Our growth strategy is clear: We will continue to grow through accretive acquisitions in our four niche businesses—Offshore Energy Support, Offshore & Harbor Towing, Chemical Transportation and Petroleum Product Transportation. Specifically, our goals include the desire to be one of the dominant companies and a quality leader for our customers in each of our market segments; and to generate annual revenues greater than $500 million by December 31, 2000; to have net income equal to or greater than ten percent of revenues, and to give a total return to shareholders of at least 20 percent annually. Hvide Marine Incorporated will continue to create added value for our shareholders, our customers and our employees.

ception, all of Hvide's chemical carriers have full double bottoms as stipulated in the Oil Pollution Act of 1990, which mandates the use of double-hull vessels in the domestic trade by the year 2015. The vessels have specially coated or stainless steel cargo tanks and up to 25 cargo compartments. The cargoes may include caustic soda, alcohols, phosphoric acid, and lubricating oils. Revenue derived from chemical transportation operations was entirely attributable to the operations of Ocean Specialty Tankers Corporation (OSTC), a company equally owned by OMI Corporation and Hvide Marine. Hvide's revenues from chemical transportation consisted of distributions from OSTC attributed to the company's two chemical carriers marketed by OSTC and based on a formula that took into account individual vessel performance characteristics applied to OSTC's revenue (net of fuel costs, port charges, and overhead).

Technology and Expansion in the 1980s

Hvide Marine expanded into offshore energy support vessels with the acquisition of eight supply boats in 1989. Supply boats are typically 180 feet in length and are used to ferry equipment and material to offshore drilling and production rigs. Increased demand for the company's offshore energy support services has been related to fundamental changes in the U.S. Gulf of Mexico energy industry, including improvements in exploration technologies, such as computer-aided exploration and 3!D seismic (which increase drilling success rates), improvements in subsea completion and production technologies that have led to increased deepwater drilling and development, and expansion of the region's infrastructure that has improved the economics of developing smaller oil and gas fields. In addition, to replace reserves and maintain production, continuous drilling has become necessary, because of short reserve-life characteristics of U.S. Gulf of Mexico gas production.

Hvide Marine reported that revenues had increased from more than $33 million in 1989 to $45 million in 1991, but dropped to $36.6 million in 1992, with slight gains in the following year. In 1994 the 36-year-old Hvide Marine, which was one of Florida's largest privately held companies, filed for its initial public offering (IPO). In its filing application, the company stated that it intended to remain focused on developing its U.S. markets and that it intended to build a new 5,000-horsepower tugboat that uses the latest technological advances. The intention was to offer three and a half million shares at about $17 each. The company was hoping to land more than $50 million to finance six proposed acquisitions (the company had signed contracts for the purchase of nine additional tugboats, six fuel barges, and 28 offshore vessels). Hvide also hoped to repay debt, to redeem preferred stock held by Hans J. Hvide, to buy out a partnership that owned about 20 percent interest in some of the vessels, and to finance general corporate expenses. Approximately $5 million from the IPO was to be earmarked for the repayment of debt, leaving a balance of $51.3 million due to California Federal Bank and Den Norske Bank. The company had about $2.60 in debt for each $1 in equity, according to the filing. At that time Hvide held the exclusive franchise to operate tugs at Port Everglades and at Port Canaveral and owned or operated ten tugboats, two chemical carriers, and 18 other vessels. Outsiders were apparently confident in Hvide's abilities to perform. Alison Turner reported in the *South Florida Business Journal* that Hvide Marine was a well respected business in south Florida. She was supported in her appraisal by a maritime lawyer, who remarked, "They [Hvide Marine] are creative in their development of business," then added, "Their intellectual creativity has created a value business."

As it happened, the revenues needed were financed instead by proceeds from the issuance of Senior Notes, Junior Notes, and certain equity securities to members of a group of investors, according to the company reports. In 1996 the company did finally complete the IPO, which resulted in proceeds of approximately $76.7 million. Of the net proceeds almost half was used to fund the cash portion ($35.5 million out of $97.5 million total) of the purchase price of three chemical carriers, ten supply boats, and one crew boat.

An industry controversy erupted in early 1996 when the Transportation Department's Maritime Administration (Marad) agreed to provide $215 in loan guarantees in support of an expensive joint venture to construct five double-hulled tankers for Hvide Marine and Koninklijke Van Ommeren. The companies were lured by the Marad loans, which covered 87.5 percent of the construction costs. The tankers, intended for the U.S. coastal oil trade, would be built by the Newport News Shipbuilding and Dry Dock Company division of Tenneco Inc. The order represented a first domestic construction contract for Jones Act tankers since 1984. (The Jones Act requires that all cargo ships traveling between domestic ports be built in U.S. shipyards.) The ships were slated for a 1998 delivery, despite assessments by Marad analysts that determined that the new ships would not turn a profit for several years beyond their delivery date. Kirby Corporation, one of the larger independent shipping companies, sued to block the loan guarantees, fearing that the new tankers would keep shipping rates down. Others argued that there was not a need for replacement tonnage at this point in time, reasoning that tonnage additions would be built when needed, without artificial stimulus. Some predicted that the venture was a great risk to the companies involved. According to the trade paper *Oil Daily* at least one observer asked, "Does it really make sense to build tankers, when you're competing against barges?" Writer Alan Kovski added, "For short hauls, barges easily win the competition with ships, leaving ships to compete primarily for movements from Gulf Coast refineries to Florida and farther up the East Coast—not a booming business. And integrated tug-and-barge vessels extend the competitive range of barges.''

The $240 million Double Eagle tankers were built for half of what they would have cost in 1991, according to company officials, who noted that the Oil Pollution Act of 1990, which established a mandatory replacement schedule of all single-skin ships entering U.S. waters, also influenced their decision. The Marad loan, reduced construction costs, and the impending need of upcoming ship replacements convinced Erik Hvide, chairman and CEO, that the plan would be profitable.

Marad Title XI loan guarantees require economic viability in a project, which is judged by a ten percent return on equity over the life of the vessels. Erik Hvide remained optimistic. He told Kovski, ''If the five ships were added to the coastal trade today, they would help prevent rate spikes during periods of high demand, as occurred in December, 1995.'' He added, ''But mandatory ship retirements will leave even greater potential for rate spikes unless even more new vessels are built.''

Full Steam Ahead in 1997

Hvide Marine wasted little time in implementing its strategy for international expansion, in anticipation of strong growth opportunities. In May of 1997 the company reported that it agreed to purchase a fleet of 37 vessels for $61 million from Gulf Marine & Maintenance Offshore Service Company of Dubai, United Arab emirates. The new fleet allows offshore energy support in the Arabian Gulf, with operations lapping around the Indian subcontinent to Brunei in Southeast Asia. To head the new base, Jim McDowell, a former director for Seabulk Offshore in Lafayette, was positioned. Further expansion from the subsidiary-base is planned for the growing markets of the Middle and Far East. Tugboats, specialized construction and maintenance vessels, and crewboats were among the newly acquired assets, bringing Hvide's fleet to number 160 vessels that service the offshore energy industry and the domestic chemical transportation trade.

In a major expansion of its international operations, the company signed agreements in December of 1997 to acquire, for approximately $284 million, the 36-vessel offshore energy support fleet of the Isle of Jersey-based Care Group. Erik Hvide described the purchase as ''a first-class fleet and our single biggest expansion to date, giving us access to new markets in West Africa, South Africa, Argentina and the North Sea.'' He announced that the move ''added critical mass to our operations in Southeast Asia and represents a further consolidation of the worldwide oil field services business.'' Acquisitions from Gulf Maintenance, International Marine Services, Selat Marine Services, and the Care transaction brought 116 new vessels acquired by Hvide for the international support market in seven months of 1997. The company expected that the Care Group acquisition alone would add $90 million in revenues in the first full year of operation.

Long-term debt stood at $108 million at the end of 1996, of which approximately $33 million was repaid in February of 1997. A second public offering in January of 1997 resulted in net proceeds to the company of approximately $94 million, of which $10.2 million was used to repay remaining principal of and interest on the Senior Notes and other indebtedness. The remaining $58.1 million was used to fund vessel acquisitions and vessel refurbishments as well as to fund portions of future vessel acquisitions; the remainder was intended for general corporate expenses.

In 1994 Erik Hvide made a sketch in a yellow legal pad and came up with the design for a revolutionary new ship docking module (SDM). The design was refined by Hvide engineers and consultants at a Seattle, Washington design studio, Elliott Bay Design Group. The end result was a 90-foot, 4,000-horsepower, flying-saucer-like vessel, sporting twin Caterpillar 3516B diesel engines, intended for ship docking and harbor-assist work. Extremely maneuverable, the vessel would be the first capable of generating 100 percent of its bollard pull in any direction, requiring a mere two-person crew. Inspiration for the design came from the design of the *Broward,* a tractor tug designed for tanker escort work. The SDM's drives are mounted fore and aft and offset from center, giving it equal propulsion in all directions, a feature that distinguishes the vessel from all others of its type. Halter Marine of Lockport, Louisiana would build the ship docking modules for a price of approximately $4.75 million each. Hvide Marine contracted for three SDMs scheduled for completion in early 1998 and has applied for patent protection of their design in the United States and in numerous foreign countries.

The company takes great pride in setting industry standards and offers intensive training/rescue programs in conjunction with the U.S. Coast Guard, to ensure that new employees are trained in fire fighting, water survival, and various skills necessary for work at sea. Hvide's preemptive mindset seems to flow through every aspect of its operation, including a strong religious avowal, an interesting focus for a globally expanding company.

Principal Subsidiaries

Seabulk Offshore, Ltd; Seabulk Offshore International; Sun State Marine Services, Inc.; Ocean Specialty Tankers Corporation; Hvide Marine Transport.

Principal Divisions

Port Everglades Towing; Mobile Bay Towing; Tampa Bay Towing; Port Canaveral Towing.

Further Reading

''Hvide Marine's Acquisition,'' *Wall Street Journal,* May 27, 1997, p. A13.

''Hvide to Buy Tug Fleet,'' *Oil Daily,* September 5, 1997, p. 7.

Kovski, Alan, ''Building of Jones Act Tankers to Resume with $20 Million Contract for Tenneco Unit,'' *Oil Daily,* February 15, 1996, p. 3.

——, ''Federal Loans Accelerate Choices Faced by Shipping Firms,'' *Oil Daily,* March 6, 1996, p. 2.

''Purchase of 37 Vessels Set with Gulf Marine of Dubai,'' *Wall Street Journal,* May 15, 1997, p. B4.

Turner, Alison, ''Hvide Marine Sets $50 Million IPO,'' *South Florida Business Journal,* May 13, 1994, p. 1A.

—Terri Mozzone

Hyperion Software Corporation

900 Long Ridge Rd.
Stamford, Connecticut 06902
U.S.A.
(203) 703-3000
Fax: (203) 595-8500
Web site: http://www.hysoft.com

Public Company
Incorporated: 1981 as Information Management Reporting Services
Employees: 1,226
Sales: $222.83 million (1997)
Stock Exchanges: NASDAQ
SICs: 7372 Prepackaged Software

Hyperion Software Corporation is one of the world's leading providers of financial software. It ranks first worldwide in budgeting software revenue and third worldwide in client/server accounting software revenue. Some 3,000 businesses and organizations, including 50 percent of the *Fortune* 500, use its high-tech products for analyzing their present finances, planning future earnings, and studying past growth as a means of predicting growth to come.

In the old days, a company might have hired a financial analyst, but in the frenetic business climate that evolved in the late 20th century, it became necessary for a number of people along the corporate ladder—not just a single analyst—to understand aspects of the company's financial picture. Packages and applications from Hyperion offer users the ability to consolidate the various parts of their financial database and work on solutions together, thus facilitating a much greater degree of responsiveness to changing business conditions. In the fast-moving world of global commerce, it was not surprising that Hyperion's growth was similarly meteoric: from $66 million in annual revenues during 1993 to almost four times that much in just four years.

Beginnings As IMRS

Robert Thomson formed the company that would become Hyperion in 1981. Thomson, a native of Scotland, had worked for Citicorp in London before coming to the U.S. While employed by the multinational bank, he had begun to see the need for improvement on the old methods of providing financial information via computers. Up to that time, such information had been delivered by a method called time-sharing, the use of a large mainframe server to provide data. Time-sharing was cumbersome, and required the extensive involvement of a company's information services (IS) or information technology (IT) departments.

Thomson realized that if he could develop a software product that would make it possible for a number of users to access financial data via their personal computers rather than a mainframe, companies would pay to access this type of technology. Out of this inspiration came a company, which Thomson named Information Management Reporting Services or IMRS. (By 1985 the acronym would become the name, and the company would drop the lengthier title for which it had originally stood.)

The first product produced by IMRS was Micro Control, which it began selling in 1983. Micro Control could be described as second-generation financial software, because it used the emerging computer technology of networks rather than mainframes. Whereas a mainframe was a single all-important server accessed by terminals that only allowed for limited input of data, networks offered users the opportunity to link autonomous personal computers or PCs. It was like the difference between requiring an operator to place a call, as the first telephone users had to do, and being able to dial a number directly.

Perakis Makes His Mark

In 1985, Thomson asked James A. Perakis to come on board. Forty-one years old at that time, Perakis had worked from 1979 to 1983 as chief financial officer of Interactive Data Corporation, a company that like IMRS supplied data and software to the financial world. After serving for two years as senior vice-president and general manager of Chase Decision Systems, an Interactive Data subsidiary, Perakis in September 1985 joined IMRS as a director and CEO.

As Perakis recalled in an interview with *Management Accounting* a decade later, some venture capitalists of their mutual acquaintance had introduced the two men because Perakis's

Company Perspectives:

Improving Customers' Financial Performance Through Analysis.

Analytic solutions from Hyperion Software enable companies to improve financial performance by maximizing the value of information. Hyperion's market-leading, Internet-enabled applications support and enhance enterprise-wide financial processes including planning, budgeting, forecasting, accounting, consolidation, and performance analysis. Hyperion is recognized for outstanding customer service and rapid, successful implementations.

skills offered Thomson an opportunity to make use of professional management in order to grow the company. And grow they did, though they agreed that they would do so "slowly and carefully," especially since "The business was generating cash, so there was no need to roll the dice."

In 1986, Perakis put a direct-sales force into operation marketing Micro Control. Under his direction, they sold the product as the solution to a number of needs, not just a means of reporting financial transactions. Like Thomson before him, Perakis had seen that their product could perform an important function for businesses, but he took it a step further, observing that the old mainframe system placed enormous demands on a company's IS department to analyze data and produce reports. Micro Control promised to take the burden off IS while delivering information more quickly and with greater efficiency.

A Critical Juncture

Perakis in 1987 took over as president from Thomson, who remained a member of the board of directors. Around this time, the company came to what would turn out to be a crucial turning point, though no one—Perakis included—realized it then.

In the area of hardware, Micro Control was made for PC-based systems linked in local area networks (LANs), and this was clearly the wave of the future in 1987 and 1988. But what about a software platform? DOS, long the standard operating system for IBM-compatible software, had seen its day, and makers of applications such as Micro Control were at a crossroads as to whether they would go with OS/2 technology or Windows-based systems.

IMRS chose Windows, and that made all the difference. Perakis, however, was quick to admit that the all-important decision was due more to the input of users rather than any sort of prophetic gift regarding the future of operating systems. Users of Micro Control had evaluated OS/2 as cumbersome and expensive, and they judged Windows more efficient.

Therefore in 1989, IMRS produced its first Windows-based product, OnTrack, and soon afterward began re-creating Micro Control as a Windows application. During the same year, the company purchased the FASTAR product line from competitor Hoechst Celanese, and in 1991 it went public on the NASDAQ. Clearly IMRS was poised for takeoff, and there was just one thing holding it down: its name.

Soaring with the Sun God

Perakis, who called the IMRS name "a handicap," believed that in conjunction with the move to Windows technology, the company could effectively relaunch its products with a newer, sexier brand name. Seeking to highlight the hypertext capability of OnTrack, which allowed a user to access information about a particular topic simply by clicking on the title of that topic, Perakis went looking in the dictionary for words which began with *hyper-*.

There he found the name of the titan Hyperion, a quasi-divine figure from Greek mythology who ruled over the sun, moon, and stars. Whereas "IMRS" was a liability because it was not memorable, the name Hyperion stuck in people's minds, and that was why, four years later, the entire company changed its name to Hyperion. After the February 1995 name change, Perakis observed, "I think we have more equity now in the name Hyperion than we did in the name IMRS over its 14 years."

Meanwhile, Hyperion grew rapidly, both in its annual sales and in its worldwide presence. In 1994, it acquired the Pillar Corporation and its product line, as well as a Scandinavian subsidiary, and established development offices in Beaverton, Oregon. Sales grew at the staggering rate of more than 40 percent a year: from $66 million in 1993 to $94 million in 1994 to $137 million in 1995. By 1996, the rate of increase dropped as sales grew to $172 million, but in 1997, the growth picked up again as it climbed to more than $222 million.

On June 4, 1996, Perakis turned over the role of president to Peter F. DiGiammarino, 42 years old. The latter also took on a newly formed chief operating officer position and became a director on the board, while Perakis maintained his dual role as chairman and CEO.

The company caused a big splash with the introduction of its online analytical processing (OLAP) software in 1996, and the stock market responded favorably to a May 1997 announcement of a strategy to integrate its programs with the Microsoft BackOffice suite. Two months later, in July, Hyperion scored an international distribution coup by entering into a sales agreement with the Baan Company, a Dutch software marketer, for the remarketing of its software solutions.

Strategic alliances have been, and continue to be, a key element in Hyperion's growth strategy. On October 29, 1997, for instance, the company entered into a partnership with Mincom, a Brisbane, Australia-based software maker. Also on that day, it formalized its Alliance Network into three categories: Software Alliances such as the one with Mincom; Technology Alliances with companies that assist it in being able to deliver a higher standard of solutions to its customers; and Service Alliances such as an agreement with the "Big 6" accounting firms, whereby all elements work to study customers' needs and develop integrated solutions.

Poised for Continued Growth

Over the years, Hyperion has built a number of product and service lines, among which are Hyperion Enterprise, Hyperion

Pillar, and Hyperion OLAP. Hyperion Enterprise is an application for consolidating business information and reports, bringing together numerous ledgers into a single unified whole. Development began in mid-1988, and the product debuted in July 1991. In the three years leading up to 1997, when Hyperion released its fifth edition of Hyperion Enterprise, the product accounted for some 60 percent of the company's worldwide revenues.

Hyperion Pillar is a flexible Windows-based solution that allows users to import and export materials to and from virtually any financial software system. As its name suggests, it is made for up-and-down integration and interaction within a corporate financial structure, enabling users to build their budgets from the ground up. Starting with a series of line items, the budget comes together in a method modeled on the way people actually think, using units, rates, and amounts piece-by-piece to arrive at a comprehensive whole.

Hyperion OLAP, released in April 1996, offers users the ability to implement multidimensional analysis for solving such complex problems as how to increase product line profitability by making incremental changes here and there. ''Multidimensional'' means just that: whereas most spreadsheets are two-dimensional, in the shape of a graph or at best a three-dimensional cube, Hyperion OLAP allows analysis in as many as 16 dimensions. Online access makes it possible for a number of users in various parts of the world to work with the data at the same time.

Perakis had promised in 1995 that accounting applications would be one of the company's primary areas for growth in the future, and in March of that year, Hyperion had already released the first of its accounting products. Made for ease of use, they allow users to ''drill down,'' going from the top-line figures by successive steps to the raw data from which those figures were derived. Accounting products include Hyperion Ledger, Hyperion Reporting, Hyperion Tools, Hyperion Admin, Hyperion Payables, Hyperion Receivables, and Hyperion Assets.

The company produces several modules made to be used with a variety of its products, and one of the most notable is ''Spider-Man,'' which debuted in August 1996. Like search engines on the World Wide Web, it is made to ''crawl,'' in this case through a company's financial reports to provide an intelligent view of the data contained in them. Hyperion Analyst, released in April 1996, and Hyperion Schedules, a product introduced in November 1995, also provide specialized cross-application capabilities.

Hyperion markets services, including design consulting and implementation support for its products. The company also offers training to improve proficiency with its applications. Some of these services are covered in the annual software license agreement, whereby a customer pays a fixed percentage of the list price for which they bought the software in the first place, and in return receives ongoing customer support. Other services are charged on a time and materials basis. In the 1990s, Hyperion made approximately half of its money from new software licenses, and the other half from renewals of existing licenses and services.

The company has an active user group composed of outside people who use their products. They help Hyperion identify areas for improvement in its products, and make suggestions about how to enhance the solutions it provides. In 1997 the company held its annual conference for the user group in Orlando, Florida, with 2,300 people in attendance from more than 850 companies.

As of 1997, Hyperion had licensed use of its software applications to more than 3,200 companies. Among Hyperion's customers have been Aetna Life & Casualty, American Express, Bayer, BellSouth, Campbell Soup, Chase Manhattan, Eastman Kodak, Ford Motor Credit, Glaxco Wellcome, Johnson & Johnson, Lotus Development, Pepsi, Rockwell International, and UPS.

James Perakis, in his 1995 interview with *Management Accounting*, said that the greatest challenge for his company was to maintain its momentum. Though Hyperion did not continue in the late 1990s to sustain the wild rate of growth that had characterized the early part of the decade, it was by any measure a healthy enterprise with great promise. The future continued to look bright for the company that bore the name of the sun god.

Principal Subsidiaries

Hyperion Software Operations Inc.; Hyperion Software Corporation of Canada, Ltd.; Hyperion Software Europe S.r.l. (Italy); Hyperion Software Italia s.r.l.; Hyperion Software Foreign Sales Corp. (Barbados); Hyperion Software (U.K.) plc.; Hyperion Software Deutschland GmbH (Germany); Hyperion Softwarevertribs-Gesellschaft MbH (Austria); Hyperion Software France S.A.; Hyperion Software BeLux S.A. (Belgium); Hyperion Software Nederland, B.V. (The Netherlands); Hyperion Software Asia Pte. Ltd. (Singapore); IMRS Hyperion Software Iberica, S.A. (Spain); Hyperion Software Nordic AB (Sweden); Hyperion KK (Japan).

Further Reading

Frye, Colleen, and Deborah Melewski, ''Top 100 Independent Software Dealers: . . . Hyperion Software Corp,'' *Software Magazine*, July 1995, p. 105.

Greenberg, Ilan, ''Hyperion Acquires OLAP Engine to Rev Up Enterprise Line of Financial Apps,'' *InfoWorld*, December 11, 1995, p. 46.

Krill, Paul, ''Solutions Arrive for Year-2000 Data Date Glitch,'' *InfoWorld*, January 6, 1997, p. 30.

Stein, Tom, ''Hyperion Adds OLAP,'' *Informationweek*, November 11, 1996, pp. 100–02.

Teach, Edward, ''View Masters,'' *CFO: The Magazine For Senior Financial Executives*, January 1997, pp. 47–52.

Williams, Kathy, and James Hart, ''Hyperion: Software Titan,'' *Management Accounting*, September 1995, pp. 75–78.

—Judson Knight

Illinois Tool Works Inc.

3600 West Lake Road
Glenview, Illinois 60025-5811
U.S.A.
(847) 724-7500
Fax: (847) 657-4392
Web site: http://www.itwinc.com

Public Company
Incorporated: 1915
Employees: 24,400
Sales: $4.99 billion (1996)
Stock Exchanges: New York Midwest
SICs: 2891 Adhesives & Sealants; 3089 Plastic Products, Not Elsewhere Classified; 3548 Electric & Gas Welding & Soldering Equipment; 3564 Industrial & Commercial Fans, Blowers & Air Purification Equipment; 3643 Current-Carrying Wiring Devices; 3953 Marking Devices; 3965 Fasteners, Buttons, Needles & Pins

In 1912, four Smith brothers advertised for experienced manufacturing workers to help them set up a new business producing metal-cutting tools to serve expanding midwestern industry. With the backing of their wealthy and influential father, Byron Laflin Smith, the brothers formed Illinois Tool Works Inc. in Chicago. The company prospered. Under Smith family management through much of its history—the family still owned about 28 percent of the company in the late 1990s—Illinois Tool Works became known as a company with conservative management and innovative products that made big profits on small items. By the 1990s the company was somewhat changed with management placing a greater emphasis on acquisitions, even if it meant going into debt. ITW, as the company is generally called, operates 365 decentralized businesses that are organized into two main business segments—Engineered Components, and Industrial Systems and Consumables.

Early History

In 1857, just 20 years after the city of Chicago was incorporated, Byron Laflin Smith's father set up Merchants' Loan & Trust to help fledgling businesses get off the ground, becoming the first Chicago resident to own a Chicago banking institution. The city's population was approximately trebling each decade as railroads and the Great Lakes made it a transportation and manufacturing center. As the city grew, the corresponding real estate boom made rich men richer. The elder Smith took advantage of all these opportunities to make his family one of the wealthiest and most influential in the Midwest.

After graduating from the University of Chicago, Byron Smith went to work for his father at Merchants' Loan & Trust. Working in the family business did not last long, however. When he was 25 years old, Smith struck out on his own, founding the Northern Trust Company in 1879, which was to become one of the city's premier banking institutions.

A successful man in his own right by the early years of the 20th century, Smith saw other opportunities in the growing city. Through his business connections, Smith realized that there was an increasing need for large-scale production of machine tools for the growing transportation and communication industries. These emerging industries needed more parts than small machine shops could provide, and Smith thought he and his sons Solomon, Harold C., Walter, and Bruce were just the men to fill the need.

In 1912 the Smiths placed an advertisement for experienced manufacturing workers. They chose Frank W. England, Paul B. Goddard, Oscar T. Hegg, and Carl G. Olson to help get Illinois Tool Works off the ground, and Harold and Walter Smith managed the new company. Solomon Smith continued to work at Northern Trust—he succeeded his father as president when Byron died two years later—and Bruce went to work in New York.

In 1915 Harold C. Smith became president of Illinois Tool Works, and Walter and Solomon Smith continued to serve on the board of directors. Harold built on the company's initial success in selling tools to manufacturers and soon expanded the company's product line into truck transmissions, pumps, com-

Company Perspectives:

ITW strives to improve our customers' competitive positions by increasing productivity and quality while reducing manufacturing and assembly costs. ITW achieves this goal through its decentralized operations in 34 countries. These units respond to customers' needs by establishing production facilities in proximity to the markets served and create close working relationships with our customers. ITW's many businesses around the world are focused on serving their customers' and industries' diverse requirements. Despite the variety of markets served, the underlying goals that drive all ITW businesses are common: to create value and improve operating efficiencies for every customer.

pressors, and automobile steering assemblies. While investing heavily in modern plants and equipment, Smith insisted on the conservative financial approach that ITW became known for, maintaining cash reserves and eschewing debt. Under Smith, ITW also became known for producing high-quality products. Smith's strategy served the growing company well when World War I broke out; the war years boosted company profits handsomely.

Expansion into Fasteners in the 1920s

In 1923 ITW engineered a new product that brought it into a different industry niche. The Shakeproof fastener, the first twisted-tooth lock washer, was to lead ITW into the profitable area of industrial fasteners. Shakeproof became a separate operating division offering a full line of related items, including preassembled washers and screws and thread-cutting screws. Each item in the Shakeproof division's product line sold for an average of less than one cent a piece, but ITW took the leadership position in the industry and its sales volume produced strong profits.

Harold C. Smith died in 1936. He had built ITW into an industry leader in metal-cutting tools, manufacturing components, and industrial fasteners. Smith had been an industry leader as well, serving as director of both the Illinois Manufacturers Association and the National Association of Manufacturers. After Smith's death, his son, Harold Byron Smith, became president of ITW. The oldest of four boys, Harold B. Smith had joined the company in 1931. Harold B. Smith followed his father's successful, conservative management practices, but he introduced some innovations as well. Smith emphasized research and development, encouraging engineers to develop new products, even outside of ITW's traditional product areas. He also decentralized the company, setting up separate divisions to pursue specific markets. This philosophy, followed by Smith's successors, meant forming individual operating units that concentrate only on their own product niche.

Under Harold B. Smith, ITW became known as a problem solver. Its salesforce developed new products to answer customers' specific needs—even when customers had not requested a solution—a practice that led to increased sales.

World War II, like World War I, produced a boom for the company, which by this time manufactured components for almost every type of equipment needed for the war effort. Even the wartime labor shortage could not prevent ITW from increasing its cash reserves.

Continued Expansion in the 1950s

Smith put some of the company's wartime profit into research and development, leading directly to expansion in the 1950s. One new and profitable area was plastic and combination metal-plastic fasteners. The company already had extensive expertise in the fastener industry with its Shakeproof division. Successful plastics manufacture and marketing led to the formation of another new operating unit, Fastex, in 1955.

Another area of expansion after the war, based in part on ITW's experience with plastics, was into the production of electrical controls and instruments. ITW's Licon division was formed in 1959 to produce electric switches and electromechanical products. ITW became a leader in miniaturizing these components. Its solid-state switches and preassembled switch panels brought the company into the computer and defense industries in addition to increasing sales in its traditional industrial base.

It was clear by this time that Illinois Tool Works was outgrowing its name; it no longer manufactured just tools. Smith set up a separate Illinois Tools division during the 1950s to concentrate on the original cutting-tool business and the company's initials, ITW, became the more frequently used, although unofficial, name for the business as a whole.

ITW's special expertise in gears led to two other developments during the 1950s. The company set up the Illinois Tools Division Gear School in 1958 to train engineers—especially those of customer firms—in the intricacies of gearing. ITW's development of the Spiroid right-angle gear led Smith to found the Spiroid operating unit in 1959 to produce specialty gearing for defense and general industries.

Introduction of Plastic Six-Pack Holders in the Early 1960s

A new opportunity emerged from ITW research and development in the early 1960s. Company engineers had been looking for less bulky, lower-cost packaging than the traditional cardboard boxing used for six-packs of beverages. Metal holders cut both the fingers of the customers and, occasionally, the cans they were meant to hold. ITW's increasing familiarity with plastics led to the invention of a flexible plastic collar to hold the cans. This simple patented invention generated substantial savings for beverage makers, from 40 percent to 60 percent according to ITW estimates. It led to the formation of another new operating unit, Hi-Cone, in 1962. In the decades since, plastic drink packaging has virtually replaced cardboard packaging for six-packs. The six-pack holder became one of ITW's most important moneymakers, and earnings from the Hi-Cone division offset fluctuations in profits from the company's products that served heavy industry.

In 1970 Harold B. Smith stepped down from the chairmanship of ITW. By this time ITW was an internationally recognized name. The Smith family's emphasis on decentralized operation meant that many of the company's production facilities were near large overseas customers, often under the control of local subsidiaries in the country where they were located. ITW components supplied heavy industries, the food and beverage industries, and the packaging industries in West Germany, Belgium, Australia, Spain, Italy, France, Great Britain, and New Zealand. The company's performance, however, suffered from the inflation that plagued the economy of the 1970s.

With Harold B. Smith's retirement, the first non-Smith, Silas S. Cathcart, became the chairman of ITW. Smith's son, Harold B. Smith, Jr., served as president and chief operating officer from 1972 through 1981, and Smith family members continued to serve on the board of directors. Under this leadership, the 1970s saw some new developments despite the sluggish economy. Most notable was ITW's entry into the adhesives industry with the purchase of Devcon Corporation. Devcon was a leader in specialty chemicals and manufactured adhesives and sealants.

Acquisitions at Center Stage in the 1980s and 1990s

When John D. Nichols took over as CEO in 1982, he was determined to keep ITW growing by investing more cash into the development of new product lines and in acquisitions, while cutting costs elsewhere to maintain profitability. He kept production costs low, for example, by developing what he termed "focus factories," where a single product was produced in a highly automated setting.

Nichols expanded ITW's industrial tools and systems businesses by purchasing Heartland Components, a maker of customized replacement industrial parts, in 1982; Southern Gage, a manufacturer of industrial gages, and N.A. Woodworth, a maker of tool-holding equipment, in 1984; and Magnaflux, a maker of nondestructive testing equipment and supplies, in 1985. Nichols formed a separate operating unit for automotive controls in 1983, and a division for producing equipment for offshore geophysical exploration, Linac, in 1984.

In 1986 Nichols made another significant acquisition when he purchased Signode Industries for $524 million. The Glenview, Illinois, manufacturer of plastic and steel strapping for bundling items, sketch film, and industrial tape fit in well with ITW's own plastics line. Nichols followed company tradition by breaking Signode down into smaller units, and within a year and a half over 20 new products had been developed as a result of the acquisition, which nearly doubled ITW's revenues. Also in 1986, Cathcart retired as chairman, with Nichols replacing him, while retaining the position of CEO.

Under Nichols, ITW acquired 27 companies in related product lines in the 1980s, while only 3 firms had been purchased before Nichols's tenure. These acquisitions meant that company debt reached higher levels than in the past, but these levels were not out of line with other industrial firms. More importantly, revenues surpassed the $2 billion mark for the first time in 1989 and earnings continued to increase steadily, reaching $182.4 million that year.

Acquisitions continued to fuel spectacular growth in the 1990s for ITW, growth that was only partially slowed down by the recession of the early years of the decade. The largest of 15 acquisitions in 1990 was that of the $200 million revenue DeVilbiss spray painting equipment business of Eagle Industries Inc. which built on the prior year's purchase of Ransburg Corporation, also a maker of spray painting equipment. In 1993 ITW added the Miller Group Ltd., a maker of arc welding equipment which had $250 million in revenues. As usual, Miller's operations were soon broken apart, with seven separate units emerging.

The years 1995 and 1996 were transitional ones for ITW, as Nichols handpicked a successor and then stepped aside. W. James Farrell, a 30-year ITW veteran who had served as president, moved into the CEO position in September 1995, replacing the retiring Nichols as chairman in May 1996. During his 14 years as CEO, Nichols oversaw an amazing period of growth—from $450 million in 1981 to $4.18 billion in 1995 when earnings reached $387.6 million. Through Nichols's aggressive acquisition program and his commitment to a decentralized organizational structure, ITW boasted of 365 separate operating units by 1996. During his tenure, Nichols also increased the company's presence outside the United States such that by 1996 about 35 percent of revenues were derived overseas, primarily from European operations.

The Farrell-led ITW essentially picked up where Nichols left off. The company made 19 acquisitions in 1996, including Hobart Brothers Company, a maker of welding products, and the Australian-based Azon Limited, a manufacturer of strapping and other industrial products. The possibility that Farrell would be even more aggressive than Nichols was raised in late 1995 when ITW made its first hostile takeover bid in the company's history, a $134 million offer for fastener maker Elco Industries Inc., a venture that failed after ITW was outbid for Elco by Textron.

Soon after taking over, Farrell hinted that some organizational changes might be needed at ITW as he raised doubts about the wisdom of a nearly $5 billion company being divided into 365 operating units. Nonetheless, with company revenue growing 20 percent per year and profits increasing even faster (40 percent in 1995 and 25 percent in 1996), it was hard to argue with the proven ITW formula. ITW was certainly likely, however, to look more to overseas markets for growth than it had in the past.

Principal Subsidiaries

Azon Limited (Australia); Buell Industries, Inc.; Burseryds Bruk AB (Sweden); Coding Products Inc.; Cumberland Leasing Co.; Elettro GiBi S.p.A. (Italy); Gema Volstatic AG (Switzerland); Gerrard Strapping Systems Ltd. (New Zealand); Gerrard Strapping Systems Pty Ltd. (Australia); Hobart Brothers Company; Hobart Brothers of Canada, Inc.; ITW Austria Vertriebs-Ges.m.b.H. (Austria); ITW Ateco GmbH (Germany); ITW Befestigungssyteme GmbH (Germany); ITW Canada Inc.; ITW de France S.A.; ITW (Deutschland) GmbH (Germany);

ITW Espana S.A. (Spain); ITW Fastex Italia S.p.A. (Italy); ITW Gunther (France); ITW Holding S.A. (France); ITW Holdings Proprietary (Australia); ITW Holdings U.K.; ITW International Finance S.A.S. (France); ITW International Holdings Inc.; ITW Ireland; ITW Leasing & Investments Inc.; ITW Limited (U.K.); ITW Meritex Sdn Bhd (Malaysia); ITW Mortgage Investments I, Inc.; ITW Mortgage Investments II, Inc.; ITW Mortgage Investments III, Inc.; ITW Oberflachentechnik GmbH (Germany); ITW Overseas Investments Corp.; ITW Real Estate L.L.C.; ITW Residuals Inc.; ITW Tech Co. Inc.; Illinois Tool Works FSC Inc. (Barbados); IspraControl s.r.l. (Italy); Liljendals Bruk Ab (Finland); The Loveshaw Corporation; Lys Fusion S.p.A. (Italy); Medalist Industries, Inc.; Miller Electric Mfg. Co.; Miller Europe, S.p.A. (Italy); Miller Thermal, Inc.; Mima, Inc.; Minigrip Inc.; N. A. Woodworth Company; Orgapack AG (Switzerland); Orgapack Holding AG (Switzerland); Paslode Corporation; Pro/Mark Corporation; Ransburg Corporation; Ransburg Industrial Finishing KK (Japan); Shippers Paper Products Company; Signode France; Signode Kabushiki Kaisha (Japan); Signode Systems GmbH (Germany); Societe de Prospection et d'Invention Techniques (France); W. A. Deutsher Pty. Ltd. (Australia).

Principal Operating Units

Engineered Components Segment; Industrial Systems and Consumables Segment; Leasing and Investments Segment.

Further Reading

Boorstin, Daniel J., *The Americans: The National Experience,* New York: Vintage Books, 1965.

Byrne, Harlan S., "Illinois Tool Works: Satisfying Customers . . . and Investors," *Barron's,* November 16, 1992, pp. 51–52.

——, "A New Chapter," *Barron's,* December 11, 1995, p. 18.

——, "A Patent Success," *Barron's,* May 23, 1994, p. 23.

Dubashi, Jagannath, "Illinois Tool: Buy This Global Niche Meister on Weakness?" *Financial World,* December 24, 1991, pp. 16–17.

——, "Illinois Tool Works, Really!" *Financial World,* July 26, 1988, pp. 12, 14.

Friedman, Dorian, and Paul Glastris, "Tougher than Nails: Illinois Tool Works Is a Profit Machine," *U.S. News & World Report,* June 10, 1991, pp. 49–51.

Henkoff, Ronald, "The Ultimate Nuts & Bolts Co.," *Fortune,* July 16, 1990, pp. 70–73.

Lashinsky, Adam, "Blue Bloods Go for Jugular: Why ITW Has Turned Hostile," *Crain's Chicago Business,* September 11, 1995, pp. 3, 54.

Loeffelholz, Suzanne, "Illinois Tool Works: Waiting for Godot," *Financial World,* April 18, 1989, p. 15.

—Ginger G. Rodriguez
—updated by David E. Salamie

Industrias Penoles, S.A. de C.V.

48 Rio de la Plata
06500 Mexico City, D.F.
Mexico
(525) 231-3131
Fax: (525) 231-3636

Public Company
Founded: 1887 as Compania Minera de Penoles
Employees: 8,333
Sales: 5.75 billion pesos (US$845.6 million) (1995)
Stock Exchanges: Mexico City
SICs: 1021 Copper Ores; 1031 Lead & Zinc Ores; 1041 Gold Ores; 1044 Silver Ores; 1099 Miscellaneous Metal Ores, Not Elsewhere Classified; 2819 Industrial Inorganic Chemicals, Not Elsewhere Classified; 2899 Chemicals & Chemical Preparations, Not Elsewhere Classified; 3339 Primary Smelting & Refining of Nonferrous Metals, Except Copper & Aluminum

Industrias Penoles, S.A. de C.V. is the world's leading refiner of primary silver. It was mining and refining almost two-thirds of the silver in Mexico, which ranked first among nations in primary silver output, in the mid-1990s. It also was extracting and refining more than 90 percent of Mexico's lead, about 40 percent of its gold, and about 25 percent of its zinc. Industrias Penoles operates the most important nonferrous metals complex in Latin America, including a lead smelter, electrolytic zinc plant, and lead-silver refinery. The company also produces both inorganic and organic chemicals, including fertilizers.

Founding and Growth to 1945

The Compania Minera de Penoles was founded in 1887 to exploit the silver-lead mines at Mapimi, in the state of Durango, that had been discovered by the Spanish in 1598. During the late 19th century the Durango-Mapimi Mining Co. of Council Bluffs, Iowa united the principal mines and smelted some 20 tons of ore a day but was unable to make a profit. Operating with capital provided by a Spanish investor, Charles Reidt made a major new strike. The Compania Minera de Penoles was organized in 1887 to exploit this deposit and by 1892 had opened a smelter to treat the ores. Large-scale operations began during 1893–94, when the company introduced electricity and built a railroad to connect the mines and smelter, a task that involved construction of a suspension bridge.

By 1903 Penoles was the largest independent base-metal enterprise in Mexico, producing lead, silver, and arsenic. Its revenues rose from 673,000 pesos (US$336,500) in 1893 to more than four million pesos (US$2 million) in 1899. The profits were immense for Penoles and its backers, Minerales y Metales, S.A. and the German-controlled American Metal Co., for the enterprise yielded dividends of 100,000 pesos (US$50,000) per month on a total capitalization of only 250,000 pesos (US$125,000). With its profits Penoles and its subsidiary, the Mexican Metal Co., bought mines in other areas of northern Mexico and was strong enough to survive the chaos of the 1910–1917 Mexican Revolution.

Minerales y Metales was merged in 1920 into Penoles, which in turn became a wholly owned subsidiary of American Metal in 1923. Using its cash reserves, American Metal had acquired additional properties during the revolution, including smelters in Torreon and Monterrey and their rail connections. Most of the ore treated at these facilities came from the Mapimi area, but these mines were being depleted, and the Mapimi smelter was eventually abandoned. With the end of this supply, the Torreon and Monterrey smelters turned to custom work for other clients. Penoles, however, had many other mining properties by this time, including a silver-lead deposit in Santa Eulalia and coal mines at Agujita, both purchased during the revolution.

Despite mixed results, Penoles retained its ranking in the 1920s as the second largest mining company in Mexico. Ore from Santa Eulalia and Santa Barbara in the state of Chihuahua was shipped to Torreon. The company took over a pyritic copper ore deposit in the state of Guerrero that was difficult to refine and solved the problem, building a 300 ton mill. But the Monterrey smelter had to cast around for business because Penoles's lead ores in the area were being depleted and ventures in the states of Durango, Guanajuato, Oaxaca, and Zacatecas were unsuccessful. The Torreon smelter was closed in 1932 because of falling lead and silver prices during the Great Depression.

Under Mexican Ownership, 1961–90

Compania Metalurgica de Penoles was formed after World War II to lease the smelting and refining plants of Compania Minera de Penoles. San Francisco Mines of Mexico Ltd. (37.5 percent owned by American Metal) received the contract to smelt and refine the lead and copper production of both Peñoles companies. The two were merged by 1961, when American Metal (now American Metal Climax, Inc.) sold a 51 percent interest in Metalurgica Mexicana Penoles, S.A. (Met-Mex Penoles) to the Mexican nationals Raul Bailleres and Jose A. Garcia. The sale was mandated by a law requiring all mining companies in Mexico to be majority owned by Mexicans. Bailleres was a founder of the first mining financial institution, Credito Minero y Mercantil, S.A., in 1934, and had 15 years' experience in managing the buying and selling of nearly all the gold, silver, and mercury in the country.

American Metal Climax sold the remaining 49 percent to Bailleres and Garcia in 1965 for about $10 million. Penoles thereby became the first major mining and smelting company in Mexico to be completely Mexican-owned, although Bernard Rohe, an American citizen, remained its chief executive officer until 1983. The company had diversified into industrial chemicals, organizing a subsidiary to produce sodium sulphate in 1963. Penoles became a public company in 1968, when it first offered shares on the Bolsa, Mexico's stock exchange. Beginning in 1969, it also began borrowing heavily from U.S. banks to finance a massive, eight-year, $500-million, exploration and development program.

By 1977 Industrias Penoles had raised its estimated mineral reserves more than tenfold and had opened enough new silver mines to enable Mexico to pass the Soviet Union as the world's leading producer of the metal. It was the twelfth largest company in Mexico that year, with sales of 6.89 billion pesos (about US$313 million), compared with only US$92 million in 1972, and income more than three times the US$5 million 1972 level. The company also expanded the scope of its activities by acquiring Refractarios Mexicanos, S.A. de C.V. in 1973.

By 1980 Industrias Penoles was producing gold, silver, lead, zinc, copper, cadmium, bismuth, sodium sulphate, sulphuric acid, magnesium oxide, fluorspar, granular refractories, and refractory bricks. Net sales came to 21.7 billion pesos (US$947.6 million) in 1980, when net income was 1.8 billion pesos (US$78.6 million). This was an exceptionally strong year, for silver prices reached a record $50.35 an ounce. By early 1982 silver had sunk to $4.50 an ounce, and that year an international payments crisis sent the peso into free fall. At first glance, this seemed a recipe for disaster for Penoles, but the company was selling most of its products abroad for dollars and incurring its costs in devalued pesos. Record profits enabled it to reduce its foreign debt of US$208 million in 1983 to US$141 million at the end of 1985. That year it had net sales of US$597.3 million and net profit of US$10.5 million, of which chemical production now accounted for about 40 percent. The company had added barite to its product mix during this period.

By 1986 Penoles's position was strong enough to consider new acquisitions. That year it bought out Bethlehem Steel's 40 percent share of its Met-Mex Penoles metals processing subsidiary. The company remained a majority partner in mining ventures with AMAX (the former American Metal Climax) and two other companies. Its other joint ventures included one with the Finnish firm Outokumpu in zinc mining and with A.P. Green Refractories to manufacture refractory materials with its magnesium oxide production. Outside of Mexico, Penoles had a sodium sulphate joint venture in Spain, a refractories plant in Argentina, an acquisition in France from Vielle Montaign, large acquisitions in Japan, and trading companies in New York City and Sao Paulo, Brazil. Alberto Bailleres, the company chairman, held 20 percent of its stock in 1987.

Penoles in the 1990s

Net sales reached two trillion pesos (US$663 million) in 1991, and net profit was 129.6 billion pesos (US$42.9 million). A joint venture with U.S. Cyprus Minerals Corp. and a venture capital affiliate of the giant financial services firm Banamex was established in 1990 for one of the richest ore deposits in Mexico—about 8.5 million metric tons of minable reserves, principally zinc, silver, and lead. During 1993 Penoles increased its stake in this joint venture, Minera Bismark, S.A., to 90 percent by acquiring Cyprus's 40 percent holding. It assumed full ownership of the enterprise in 1995. Penoles withdrew from the manufacture of refractories in 1994 by selling properties, including its share in the joint venture with Green, to subsidiaries of the U.S. company Indresco, Inc. for US$75 million. This sector of its business accounted for US$71 million in sales the previous year.

In 1994 Penoles started gold mining operations in Durango through a subsidiary, Minera Mexicana La Cienega, and opened a mine producing zinc and silver in the state of Mexico, in participation with a Japanese firm, through 51 percent owned Minera Tizapa. In 1995 it opened a lead and zinc mine named La Negra in the state of Queretaro through Minera Capela, a wholly owned subsidiary. Also in 1995, Penoles incorporated subsidiaries in Peru and Argentina to explore and exploit mining concessions.

Because it was selling a high percentage of its goods abroad, Penoles remained profitable despite the economic crisis that gripped Mexico following the devaluation of the peso in December 1994. Net sales dropped, in dollar terms, from 3.73 billion pesos in 1994 (US$1.07 billion) to 5.75 billion pesos (US$845.6 million). Net income, however, rose from 28.8 million pesos (US$8.2 million) to 1.01 billion pesos (US$148.5 million). Export sales represented 60 percent of the 1995 total, with the United States accounting for 62 percent of export sales and Japan for 16 percent. The long-term debt fell from 2.09 billion pesos (US$597 million) to 1.86 billion pesos (US$273.5 million). Alberto Bailleres remained chairman of the board. In addition to his holdings in Penoles, Bailleres controlled the insurer Grupo Nacional Provincial and had an estimated net worth of US$1.8 billion in mid-1996.

During 1996 Industrias Penoles announced it would invest $70 million in a new silver-rich mining project in the state of Zacatecas, with the start-up date scheduled sometime in 1998.

This mine had proven reserves of 23.2 million metric tons—mostly silver ore, with some zinc, lead, and copper. Also in 1996, Industrias Penoles agreed to pay $160 million to take full control of the Rosario companies, primarily producing silver, gold, lead, and zinc, from its joint venture partner Alumax Inc. This company had been spun off from AMAX in 1993, when AMAX was acquired by Cyprus Minerals, which then became Cyprus AMAX Minerals Co.

Penoles purchased a 51 percent share in Peru's largest metallurgical complex, state-owned La Oroya, in 1997 for $194 million. The complex, consisting of smelters and refineries to produce copper, lead, and zinc, plus some gold and silver, from ores, was expected to add nearly $500 million to the company's revenues and just under $50 million in operating income. Its chief liability was that La Oroya was one of the most environmentally damaged mining sites in Peru. Also in 1997, a consortium composed of Industrias Penoles and Grupo Acerero del Norte purchased, for $23 million, a 25-year operating concession on the previously government-owned, 442 mile Coahuila-Durango railway line.

Industrias Penoles in 1996

The heart of Industrias Penoles was Met-Mex Penoles, which operated the Torreon complex. This subsidiary of Metales Penoles accounted for 72 percent of its 1994 revenues. It was seven percent owned by U.S. interests. Also important was Compania Fresnillo, a 60 percent owned subsidiary of Minas Penoles producing lead, zinc, and other metal concentrates. The other 40 percent was U.S. owned. Fresnillo's revenues came to 20 percent of the parent company's total in 1994. Another subsidiary of Minas Penoles was Compania Minera Las Torres. Founded in 1966, it had 45 percent U.S.-Canadian participation in 1985, but this fell to 14 percent in 1995. Las Torres's revenues came to five percent of the parent company's in 1994. Silver accounted for some 35 percent of Industrias Penoles's revenues in the mid-1990s. Lead and zinc accounted for another 31 percent, and gold accounted for 13 percent.

In the mid-1990s Minas Penoles, the company's mining group, was producing, through six operating companies, gold, silver, lead, zinc, copper, and tungsten. Metales Penoles, the Metals Group, was operating, through Met-Mex Penoles, the Torreon complex, which consisted of a lead smelter, zinc plant, lead-silver refinery, two sulfuric acid plants, and cadmium, bismuth, ammonium sulphate, antimonium trioxide, cadmium oxide, and liquid sulphur dioxide plants. Through Quimicos Industriales Penoles, its Chemicals Division, the company operated four companies in the inorganic chemicals area, producing magnesium oxide and sodium sulphate from brines; magnesium oxide from sea water and chemical lime; and other chemical products, such as fertilizers, some of which were obtained using raw materials from Met-Mex.

Principal Subsidiaries

Corporativo Penoles, S.A. de C.V.; Metales Penoles, S.A. de C.V.; Minas Penoles, S.A. de C.V.; Quimica Magna, S.A. de C.V.; Quimicos Industriales Penoles, S.A. de C.V.; Servicios Industriales Penoles, S.A. de C.V.; Termimar S.A. de C.V.

Further Reading

"Alumax Selling Rosario Stake," *American Metal Market,* May 29, 1996, p. 2.

"American Metal Climax Sells Its 49% Interest in Penoles of Mexico," *Wall Street Journal,* July 22, 1965, p. 8.

Bernstein, Marvin D., *The Mexican Mining Industry, 1890–1950,* Albany: State University of New York, 1964, pp. 39, 67–68, 119–120, 141, 146, 173.

Dorfman, John R., "If Any Stock Can Be Said to Have Silver Lining, This Mexican Mining Concern Just Could Be It," *Wall Street Journal,* March 3, 1992, p. C2.

"Industrias Penoles Finds a Silver Lining in the Plight of the Peso," *Business Week,* November 28, 1983, p. 76.

"Industrias Penoles: Mining Mexican Silver with U.S. Money," *Business Week,* August 21, 1978, pp. 110–112.

"Mexican Comparison," *Mining Journal,* December 22, 1995, p. 487.

"Mexico's Industrial Groups," *Business Latin America,* April 27, 1987, p. 132.

"Penoles Gains a Foothold in Peru," *El Fianciero International Edition,* May 5–11, 1997, p. 17.

Scrutton, Alistair, "Penoles Wins Peruvian Mining Bid," *Financial Times,* April 22, 1997, p. 33.

Smith, Arthur, "Prospecting by Penoles Expected to Yield Rich Silver Find in Mexico," *American Metal Market,* April 13, 1976, pp. 1, 13.

—Robert Halasz

In Focus Systems, Inc.

27700B SW Parkway Avenue
Wilsonville, Oregon 97070-9812
U.S.A.
(503) 685-8888
Fax: (503) 685-8839
Web site: http://www.infs.com

Public Company
Incorporated: 1986
Employees: 504
Sales: $258.5 million (1996)
Stock Exchanges: NASDAQ
SICs: 3679 Electronic Components, Not Elsewhere Classified

In Focus Systems, Inc. was founded and incorporated in 1986 by Paul Gulick and Steven Hix as an information display system maker. Since that time, the two, who had previously worked together at Tektronix, Inc. and Planar Systems, Inc., have helped guide the company to become the world market leader in the development, manufacture, and marketing of innovative multimedia projection products using flat-panel liquid crystal display (LCD) technology.

The LCD Product Line and ESS Sales Network

LCD projection is much cheaper to produce and allows much more flexibility than slide presentations, enabling the user to present video, audio, graphics, and data output from personal computers, workstations, VCRs, laser disc players, and other electronic devices. LCD projection systems can be used in businesses, schools, and government agencies for training sessions, meetings, sales presentations, technical seminars, and other applications involving the sharing of computer-generated and/or video information with an audience. The products manufactured by In Focus are compatible with all major personal computers and most video sources used in business and education.

In Focus is headquartered in a 203,000-square-foot leased office and manufacturing space in Wilsonville, Oregon. The company's LitePro series makes up the projection system product line and its Smartview and PowerView series make up the color LCD projection panel product line. The company sells its brand name products through distributors, dealers, catalogs, governmental sales agencies, and over 165 audio/visual dealers, computer dealers, and presentation specialists. A two-tier distribution system has been set up with partners such as Ingram-Micro, Tech Data, Merisel, MicroAge, and Access Graphics to resell the company's products to value-added resellers throughout North America. Internationally, the company sells its products throughout the world via 70 international distributors in more than 60 countries. International sales managers in Miami, Singapore, and Amsterdam work with the international distributors to move the products. The company also has a private-label arrangement with Boxlight Corporation, which resells the company's color LCD projection panels and projectors under its own label. Major customers have included such companies as United Technologies, the U.S. Army, Tektronix, General Motors, IBM, and Hewlett-Packard.

Additional facilities are located in Atlanta, Georgia; Memphis, Tennessee; and the Netherlands, where, in addition to the headquarters, telephone support and technical training is provided. Hardware repair is conducted at the headquarters and through authorized agents in Singapore, Belgium, and throughout the world.

Powering Up, 1987–89

In 1987, a year after the startup, the company was shipping its first product, a CGA-compatible monochrome display panel which, when placed on an overhead projector, displayed the output of a personal computer onto the screen. In 1988, the company posted revenues of $8.5 million and a net income of $640,000. The following year the company created the industry's first true-color LCD projection panel and posted revenues of $11.5 million, but had a net loss of approximately $1 million. Since then, the company has expanded its product line to include an integrated unit that has its own light source, much like a slide projector, and can display prerecorded images from

Company Perspectives:

In Focus Systems, Inc. was founded and incorporated in 1986 to develop, manufacture and market innovative multimedia projection products using flat-panel liquid crystal display (LCD) technology to present video, audio, graphics and data output from personal computers (PCs), workstations, VCRs, laser disc players and other electronic devices for use in businesses, schools and government agencies for training sessions, meetings, sales presentations, technical seminars and other applications involving the sharing of computer-generated and/or video information with an audience. The products are compatible with all major personal computers and most video sources used in business and education.

a PC and active matrix displays capable of displaying full-motion video.

Rather than focusing on just the high-tech, high-priced segments of the market, In Focus concentrated on all areas of the market, attempting to introduce the industry's lowest-priced color LCD. In 1984, when still working for Brown Boveri in Switzerland, In Focus scientist Terry Scheffer invented Super Twist Nematic (STN) technology. Most people in the industry claimed that STN technology would not run fast enough to respond to video rates. In 1989, Scheffer invented and In Focus patented Triple Super Twist Nematic (TSTN) technology, which applied monochrome LCD technology to color LCDs and allowed the company to create a lower-priced LCD projection product. The TSTN technology utilized three panels rather than the standard one panel utilized by normal projection panel systems. The company also developed Subtractive Birefringement Effect (SaBRE) technology to remove one of those panels.

Growth During the 1990s

In February 1990, the company formed In Focus Systems FSC, Inc. to provide creative presentation services to *Fortune* 500 and other companies. After posting first quarter revenues of $5.5 million with a net income of $850,000, things were looking much better for the company than at the end of the previous year.

However, later in the year, Advanced Display Manufacturers of America asked the U.S. Department of Commerce and the International Trade Commission to instigate an investigation into Japanese manufacturers who, they claimed, were dumping their flat panel displays into the marketplace. A 2.3 percent across-the-board tariff was imposed on all Japanese display manufacturers, including Kyocera, which manufactured LCD cells for In Focus. Competition began heating up as a company called nView arrived on the scene with a thin film transistor (TFT), or active matrix, product manufactured by Sharp, for $5,900. Rumors also began circulating at that time that Toshiba, Hitachi, and Hoseidon would soon announce similar products. Although the company had its own TFT product sitting on the shelf ready to go, it did not want to get into the market until an inexpensive model could be produced, as Telex, in conjunction with Hitachi, had already tried to enter the market with a product selling for $4,300 and had failed.

In Focus did release a new low-cost, 16-color PC Viewer targeted toward the educational marketplace, and LightPro LS, a portable, self-contained presentation system designed to replace the old-fashioned three-gun CRT projectors manufactured by such companies as Sony, Barco, and ElectroHome, at a fraction of the cost.

The company went public in December 1990, posting revenues of $11.4 million in the fourth quarter, with $1.8 million in net income, and a total of $36.7 million on the year, with net income of $5.5 million, a huge improvement over 1989. In January 1991, the company released a new product called LiteShow II and, with first quarter revenue at $13 million and net income of $2.1 million, the company posted its best-ever quarter results.

After determining that panels employing TFT technology were being produced in volumes too small and at too high a price to make the product viable, the company planned to introduce its own TFT products to the marketplace which, at the time, was dominated by nView. In Focus's stock soared when it was announced that Compaq had obtained the exclusive rights to the company's TSTN technology for use in portable computer displays in its battery-operated notebook-type machines, as well as AC-power computers. However, when Compaq proved unable to adapt the company's color LCD technology into its product line, the agreement was terminated.

As competitors began to make their entrance, the marketplace for LCD display panels and projectors grew to approximately $200 million and an expected growth rate of 20 percent per year, with the fastest-growing segments of the marketplace being color display panels and self-contained projectors, while the monochrome panel market began shrinking. But the company continued growing, posting revenues of $49.5 million on the year, with net income of $4.69 million.

In April 1992, John V. Harker, formerly executive vice-president of Genicom Corp., succeeded Steven Hix as president and CEO, freeing Hix to focus his attention on technology and long-range corporate strategy, as well as his role as chairman of the board. By June of that same year, In Focus and Sharp had emerged as the two leading competitors in the color LCD display market. A company called Proxima came in a close third. In Focus had already had a run-in with Proxima in court when the latter attempted to market a product based on the In Focus-patented TSTN technology. In Focus sued and won. The rest of the marketplace was fairly fragmented, with a number of smaller companies manufacturing TFT display panels. Speculation was rife in the industry and among investment houses that large companies, such as Sony, Matsushita, and Hitachi, would enter the marketplace, increasing competition.

That same year, in October, the company created and entered into an equal-partnership venture with Motorola Inc. called Motif Inc. The reason Motif was created was to jointly establish and develop a plant in the United States to manufacture and market low-cost, video-speed LCDs and to market and distribute controlling application specific integrated circuits (ASICs) embodying In Focus' Active Addressing technology and design of integrated circuits. The LCDs would be developed by In Focus and the ASICs by Motorola. This would allow both companies to access the wider marketplace offered by handheld computer games, personal digital assistants, pagers, and laptop computers. Motorola took a minority shareholder position in In Focus Systems Inc. (20 percent) by purchasing 2.2 million shares at $10 per share.

The company ended 1992 with revenues of $59.8 million and net income of $3.9 million. In 1993, the company introduced the portable PanelBook series, project display devices no larger than notebook computers and ended that year with $73.5 million in revenues and $6 million in net income.

In 1994, with only a dozen or so companies in the industry, primarily young and entrepreneurial in nature, the company was well ahead of the game in its technological development. That would all change over the next few years as the industry exploded with growth. That year, the company formed the subsidiary In Focus Services, Inc. and, in August, acquired certain assets and liabilities of Genigraphics Corporation and Genigraphics Service Corporation for $1.5 million, an acquisition which helped lead to a 67 percent increase in sales for 1994. The company also formed a strategic research and development relationship with office furniture giant Steelcase. New products included the PowerView 950 and the PanelBook 750 projection panels. In addition, the company formed an alliance with Electrohome to begin producing a large-screen LCD projector called Showstar in early 1995.

Due to yield problems and resulting increased investment requirements, October saw the restructuring of Motif. The plan to produce LCD panels was scrapped and the venture began providing greater focus on the development of its core Active Addressing chip technology. That month, Steven Hix also relinquished to Harker his post as chairman to continue devoting more time to strategy and technology, as well as a new joint venture with In Focus called Sarif, of which he became chairman and CEO.

Early in 1995, the company and Motorola scrapped plans for Motif Inc. to jointly build computer displays and the company bought back one million shares of its stock from Motorola for $18 million; Motorola sold the remaining 1.2 million shares and began exploring the possibility of using certain Motif technology in the design of integrated circuits. The breakup of this alliance, however, did not deter the company from pushing forward relationships with other companies and soon In Focus teamed up with Adobe Systems to market multimedia products. Meanwhile, Proxima overtook Sharp as the number two company in the industry.

The board of directors was increased to four seats when Peter Behrendt, chairman of Exabyte Corporation, was added. Revenues for 1995 were $202.8 million, a 65 percent increase over revenues from 1994, helped by an increase in sales of the LitePro 560, 570, and 580 series products, which were manufactured for the company by an outside source with lower margins. Net income was $10.4 million.

Adjusting to the Boom, 1996 and Beyond

Two short years prior, the company was one of only a dozen in the industry, but in 1996 there was a boom, and suddenly there were more than 40 manufacturers and distributors all vying for part of the market, including such established companies as Sharp Corporation, Hitachi, NEC, Epson, Sanyo, Sony, General Electric, Matsushita, Mitsubishi, Seiko, Panasonic, IBM, JVC, 3M, Toshiba, Polaroid, Proxima Corporation, ASK, Davis Liquid Crystals, Eastman Kodak, and Liesengang, as well as newcomers The Alpine Group, nView Corporation, Cree Research Inc., Kopin Corporation, OIS Optical Imaging Systems, Planar Systems, Photonics Imaging, Sayett Group Inc., SI Diamond Technology, and Three-Five Systems.

Facing increasing price competition in the VGA projection systems market as new competitors continued to enter, the company made codevelopment relationships with such companies as Texas Instruments and Hughes Elcan Optical Technologies, developed hot links in Microsoft's PowerPoint 97, and strengthened the company's board of directors by naming Jack D. Kuehler, former president of IBM, to the board, bringing the total number of directors to five.

Despite a 33 percent drop in the company's stock in mid-1996 amidst increasing encroachment and new projection products released at the Infocomm trade show that year by Sony, Sanyo, Panasonic, and Sharp, revenues for the company in 1996 reached $258.5 million, a 27 percent increase over the previous year, helped by an increase in unit sales of the company's complete line of LitePro projection products and a reduction in the company's workforce as a cost containment effort.

The company believed its ability to compete in the projection display market depended on certain key product characteristics, such as resolution, brightness, range and quality of colors, portability, display speed, power requirements, and price. With added competition—and expecting additional competition as new technologies, applications, and products were introduced—the company believed that technological change in the industry, and within its own doors, would continue to move forward at an incredible pace. An already proven leader in the industry, In Focus Systems was poised to remain on top of what analysts predicted would become a $38 billion worldwide industry by the year 2000.

Principal Subsidiaries

In Focus Services, Inc.

Further Reading

Andrews, Walter, "Motif Funding Rise Eyes Consumer As First IC Slips," *Electronic News,* March 28, 1994, p. 8.

Bernard, Viki, "In Focus Unveils Color LCD Panels," *PC Week,* May 2, 1994, p. 33.

Chinnock, Chris B., "Au Revoir, Overheads," *Byte,* February 1996, p. 34.

"David Sarnoff Research Center in Princeton, N.J., and In Focus Systems Inc. of Wilsonville, Ore. . . ," *Electronics,* October 24, 1994, p. 16.

DeTar, Jim, "Motorola Sale of In Focus Stock Raises Questions on Display ICs," *Electronic News,* April 3, 1995, p. 1.

——, "Texas Instruments Inks Display Device Accords," *Electronic News,* April 24, 1995, p. 1.

DiCarlo, Lisa, "Projectors Let Users Take Show on the Road," *PC Week,* April 8, 1996, p. 34.

Dorsch, Jeff, and Carol Haber, ''In Focus Revamps LCD Operations,'' *Electronic News,* October 17, 1994, p. 1.
''Earnings for In Focus Expected to Fall Short of Analysts' Estimates,'' *Wall Street Journal,* September 17, 1996, p. A9A(W)/A13C(E).
''Earnings to Trail Estimates Due to Production Delays,'' *Wall Street Journal,* April 3, 1997, p. B8(W)/A8(E).
Hamm, Steve, ''A Sharper Image,'' *PC Week,* April 3, 1995, p. A9.
Hicks, Adam A., ''Project High-Resolution Presentations Across the Room,'' *PC Magazines,* July 1994, p. 66.
''In Focus Buys Genigraphics Service Bureau,'' *Business Journal-Portland,* August 12, 1994, p. 6.
''In Focus LCD Projector Fares Well in Screen Tests,'' *PC Week,* April 28, 1997, p. 55.
''In Focus Shows Lightweight Projector,'' *PC Week,* March 24, 1997, p. 54.
''In Focus Systems,'' *Television Digest,* April 3, 1995, p. 15.
''In Focus Systems Stock Off on Competition Worry,'' *New York Times,* June 15, 1996, p. 15(N)/33(L).
Marcial, Gene G., ''Small-Caps to Watch,'' *Business Week,* June 9, 1997, p. 102.
Poor, Alfred, ''LCD Projectors Take the Next Step,'' *PC Magazine,* November 18, 1997, p. 45.
Poor, Alfred, Winn L. Rosch, and Denis Tom, ''Lighter and Brighter: Portable Projectors,'' *PC Magazine,* August 1997, p. 258.
''Technology Brief—In Focus Systems Inc.: Firm Is to Buy One Million of Its Shares from Motorola,'' *Wall Street Journal,* March 28, 1995.
Yegyazarian, Anush, ''Focusing on Brilliant Projects,'' *PC Magazine,* March 15, 1994, p. 62.

—Daryl F. Mallett

Information Builders, Inc.

Two Penn Plaza
New York, New York 10001
U.S.A.
(212) 736-4433
Fax: (212) 967-6406
Web site: http://www.ibi.com

Private Company
Incorporated: 1975
Employees: 1,700
Sales: $263 million (1996 est.)
SICs: 6794 Patent Owners & Lessors; 7372 Prepackaged Software; 7373 Computer Integrated Systems Design

Information Builders, Inc. (IBI), a computer software firm, is one of the largest privately held companies in New York City. It ranked among the world's top 20 independent software vendors in the mid 1990s and was recognized as an industry leader in fourth-generation-language (4GL) technology, specializing in information access and analysis. A 4GL is designed to help users create complex data queries and build client/server applications around databases. IBI's Focus software was the most widely used 4GL product in the world by 1990. Focus and the company's other software all shared a common middleware architecture intended to eliminate the complexities and support headaches that could result from adding new vendors each time a new application systems was required. The company also offered technical support, training, and a complete range of professional consulting services from its 85 worldwide offices in 1997.

Focus-Driven Growth, 1975–87

Information Builders was founded in 1975 by Gerald C. Cohen, Peter Mittelman, and Martin Slagowitz. Cohen, a native New Yorker who in 1997 still lived on Manhattan's Upper West Side where he grew up, remained president and chief executive officer of the firm through the late 1990s. A graduate of St. John's College in New Mexico, Cohen began developing Ramis software—often cited as the world's first 4GL—with an engineering team at Mathematica, Inc., in 1965. ''We pioneered an industry,'' Cohen later told Mike Bucken of *Software Magazine* in a 1990 interview. ''Ramis was the first non-procedural language and the first to be sold outside [the] IBM [sales force].''

Once Ramis had been developed, Cohen took charge of selling the product. This experience gave him new ideas on selling software directly to large corporations and led him to leave Mathematica in order to found Information Builders with Peter Mittelman (also a Ramis developer) and Martin Slagowitz. ''Mathematica was really a consulting firm,'' Cohen explained to Bucken. ''Selling software by a strictly consulting company wasn't the way to go. . . .That was the reason I left.''

Information Builders quickly created Focus, a software product that allows computer users who want to manipulate a database—names and addresses on a mailing list, for example—with little training and using standard English. Originally intended as a mainframe-oriented product that could be accessed remotely through time-sharing systems, Focus was itself developed on leased IBM mainframe time, bartered from a software service company that also provided seed money and terminals. Additional funding in IBI's first year came from RCA, which also agreed to purchase a Focus license while it was still being developed, and Tymshare, a Silicon Valley-based service bureau that contracted to distribute the product for use over its network. ''When we started out, our clients did credit checks on us,'' Mittelman recalled. ''Now we do credit checks on our clients.''

Time sharing fell out of widespread use by 1980, but leasing the original Focus, designed to run on IBM 4300 machines, to time-sharing firms was vital to Information Builders during its early years. By contrast, turning to direct sales of the software, Cohen recalled, was ''a very big decision'' that required a significant investment. ''Time sharing had given us an unparalleled opportunity,'' he told Bucken, ''but we could see that people were going in-house [to develop applications]. So we began to build an infrastructure to sell the product.'' This infrastructure was completely funded internally from the company's steady stream of license fees.

Company Perspectives:

Information Builders develops and markets software and professional services for the creation of high-performance business information systems at large, data-intensive organizations. These products and services form an integrated yet open technology framework for Enterprise Data Access, Enterprise Decision Support Systems, Data Warehousing, On-Line Transaction Processing Applications, Internet Integration, and Packaged Application Integration and Productivity.

Information Builders secured its first international contract, from Datema Co. of Sweden, in 1977. The company's first subsidiary opened in London in 1980, followed by InfoBuild, a Canadian subsidiary, in 1982. FUSE, the first Focus user group (training center), was formed in 1979, with the first branch established in Palo Alto, California. Information Builders had 25 employees and about $3 million in annual revenues by 1980.

The firm made an early marketing decision to sell Focus not as a database management system (DBMS) but as an ''information builder.'' ''We knew that if we went in and said we were a DBMS vendor, they would say they already had one,'' Cohen explained. David Kemler, hired as the company's first salesperson in 1977 and later becoming its sales and marketing vice-president, said that, from the start, Focus was marketed as ''a 4GL front end. We were precluded from going into large shops and saying we had a database because they already had IMS [from IBM].'' Nevertheless, most users purchased the Focus DBMS as an option with the 4GL, and by 1990 it was being used in 99 percent of IBI's customer sites, according to Kemler.

The revenue stream from time-sharing licensees also enabled Information Builders to fund development of a version of Focus for the personal computer market. The company first attempted to enter the PC field in 1980 by porting Focus to the Apple II model but decided the computer was too slow. In 1982 IBI began work on a version for the IBM PC. Just as it was determining that this model also lacked adequate performance, IBM came out with its improved XT version. Focus was ready to serve this computer when the first shipments of the machine were made in 1983, thereby enabling Information Builders to become an early power in the microcomputer business.

In 1985 the PC version was expanded with a single-user release, the addition of a network version, and a host-language interface to enable programs written in traditional programming languages to create, build, and maintain PC/Focus databases. Upgrade kits were free for customers under IBI's extended maintenance and service contract, $550 for other current users, and $1,595 for new users.

Focus versions for the Digital Equipment Corp.'s VAX line and Wang's VS-based systems were released in 1986. They were followed by versions for the Macintosh PC, variations of the Unix operating system, the NCR Workstation 300, and the Convegent Technologies Ngen computers. Focus versions for the proprietary minicomputer offerings of Hewlett-Packard Co., Tandem Computers Inc., and IBM's AS/400 were released in 1988. Each version was in effect a different product requiring a separate development and marketing team.

By the end of 1987 Information Builders was among the three largest privately held software companies in the United States, with revenue expected to top $110 million in that year. Focus, the market leader in fourth-generation language, was still the company's only product, with an estimated 29 percent of the market at U.S. IBM and plug-compatible manufacturers' sites. IBI had added capabilities for graphics, spreadsheets, and report writing to core database-management systems such as IBM's IMS and DB2 and Digital's Rdb.

New Products, 1987–95

In 1987 Information Builders made its first acquisition, Level Five Research, Inc. Cohen believed that this Florida company would help IBI offer more decision-support products to its Focus lineup, such as problem analysis and intelligent documentation. Level 5 was an expert-system shell running on MS-DOS-based personal computers and Digital minicomputers running VAX/VMS. By 1990 work had been completed on a Level 5 module to include with Focus, and a team was working to develop versions for all Focus platforms. IBI was also marketing PRL3, an expert-system development tool for the VAX, and Insight 2+ for IBM PC's and compatibles.

Cohen told *Computerworld* in 1987 that Information Builders was ''not selling product but selling service.'' The firm was offering service that year at 20 offices around the United States and had 125 employees to help customers get their applications running. By 1990 IBI had 53 user groups in the United States. It also had opened a development center in Paris. A German subsidiary opened later in the year. IBI was ranked in 1991 as the 15th-largest independent software company in the United States, with 1990 revenues of $191 million, up from $130 million in 1988 and $155 million in 1989. The company claimed 600,000 Focus users in early 1990. It had sold 100,000 PC Focus licenses and installed 5,000 copies of mainframe and minicomputer Focus versions.

Information Builders introduced a new product line, EDA (Enterprise Data Access) in 1991. The purpose of this product was to gain entry into the fast growing client-server market, where networks of small computers communicated with each other or mainframes. The problem to be solved was access to data in the huge range of incompatible machines, operating systems, and databases in corporate networks. EDA/SQL used an ANSI (American National Standards Institution) version of SQL as a standard interchange format. Running on a PC or workstation, the client bit of EDA/SQL ''talked'' to the server bit, running on a file-server, minicomputer, or mainframe. The server then talked to a range of databases, which might not use SQL. In Europe, however, not many databases, and even fewer applications programs, were using ANSI SQL, so that other products were also needed to service this market.

By the end of 1997 the EDA family of middleware products extended the reach of virtually any application or tool that supported either SQL or RPC, for transparent access to more than 65 of the most widely used proprietary databases, files, and application programs in 35 interconnected operating environments.

By 1993 Focus was running on about one million computers, with 35 percent of sales derived from overseas, mainly Japan. PC-based versions of Focus were selling for $795, while those designed for mainframes cost $150,000. More than half of the Focus software was still running on mainframes, but this business was dwindling as a share of the total market. Focus still accounted for 80 percent of IBI's revenues whereas EDA/SQL, including several upgrades and new versions, brought in only about 10 percent. IBI was also doing design work for select clients including the U.S. Air Force.

Information Builders joined an alliance in 1994 led by Amdahl Corp., best known for mainframe computers compatible with IBM. Amdahl announced it would enter the market for massively parallel database machines to be built by nCube Corp. using software from IBI and Oracle Corp. Amdahl claimed that the alliance would develop electronic repositories that could store and retrieve vast amounts of data.

Also in 1994, IBI came out with its first version of Focus for Windows software. Interviewed by *InformationWeek*, Cohen acknowledged that the Focus business was slowing down but predicted a rebirth when the company came out with a graphical-user interface version. He also observed that the VAX market was declining and that the company had experienced a "disastrous time in Europe," but he added that its European subsidiaries had been rebuilt and that business overseas had rebounded. Acknowledging that IBI's EDA business had been slow to meet expectations, Cohen defended the product line, saying that it was "growing fast."

Information Builders' revenue came to $227 million in 1993 and $243 million in 1994, of which packaged software sales were $200 million and $204 million, respectively. During 1994 the company introduced Focus Reporter for Windows 1.5, as well as Focus Personal Service and EDA/Copy Manager for Lotus Notes for the IBM AS/400. The company signed agreements with Oracle and Informix to build new middleware gateways for their flagship environments and announced an expanded relationship with Microsoft to deliver an integrated family of EDA/SQL solutions for the company's Windows NT operating system. By 1995 the company had 28 sales offices in the United States, with 500 people in the field. It also had three offices in Canada and 13 international subsidiaries.

Information Builders in 1996–97

Information Builders introduced WebFocus in 1996, a tool designed to let database administrators display reports on the World Wide Web. Users could display charts and graphs using any standard Web browser. WebFocus worked with most common databases and was fully compatible with the IBI client/server reporting system. Another IBI introduction that year was Cactus, a software product for developing and partitioning three-tier applications spanning heterogeneous operating systems, mainframes, midrange servers, personal computers, and workstations. To work correctly, Cactus required programmer training in a proprietary language and EDA/SQL server products.

In 1997 Information Builders prepared to move its headquarters from 1250 Broadway to nearby Two Penn Plaza, leasing three floors for a total of 179,000 square feet of office space. It also added 30,000 square feet of space at nearby 330 West 34th Street for back-office operations. The 15-year leases were valued at more than $100 million. In order to keep the firm from moving its 800-plus employees to New Jersey, New York City contributed nearly $5 million in sales tax incentives and cheap energy. IBI retained about 27,000 square feet—two floors—at 1250 Broadway. The company had 10 foreign subsidiaries and representatives in 25 foreign countries, plus Hong Kong and the Gulf states. IBI regularly published technical journals, a quarterly newsletter, and a features magazine.

Principal Subsidiaries

Information Builders Belgium S.A.; Information Builders (Canada) Inc.; Information Builders (Deutschland) GmbH; Information Builders France S.A.; Information Builders Iberica S.A. (Portugal); Information Builders Iberica S.A. (Spain); Information Builders (Netherlands) B.V.; Information Builders Pty. Ltd. (Australia); Information Builders Switzerland A.G.; Information Builders (UK) Ltd.

Principal Divisions

Enterprise Data Access; Integrated Solutions; Micro Products; Open Systems; Specialized Systems.

Further Reading

Alper, Alan, "Focus Pulls Information Builders to Top," *Computerworld,* November 30, 1987, pp. 87, 92.

Bucken, Mike, "Timing the Industry and the Technology," *Software Magazine,* February 1990, pp. 78–81.

Cox, John, "IBI Cactus Tool Set Hooks Up to Web," *Network World,* June 10, 1996, p. 8.

Feldman, Amy, "Data Entry at 2 Penn Plaza: Software Firm Moves In," *Crain's New York Business,* May 5, 1997, p. 16.

"IBI's Refocus on the Future," *InformationWeek,* October 3, 1994, pp. 42, 44–45.

McNatt, Robert, "A Software Giant Starring on B'way," *Crain's New York Business,* March 22, 1993, pp. 1, 34.

Schofield, Jack, "Breathing New Life into Those Obsolete Databases," *Guardian,* September 19, 1991, p. 33.

Stoughton, Alan S., "Cactus Offers Solid Three-Tier Client/Server Solution," *Infoworld,* June 16, 1997, p. 150.

"Top 100 Independent Software Vendors," *Software Magazine,* July 1995, p. 91.

Wagner, Mitch, "IBI's Report-Writer Focuses on the Web," *Computerworld,* August 12, 1996, p. 67.

—Robert Halasz

The Interpublic Group of Companies, Inc.

1271 Avenue of the Americas
New York, New York 10020
U.S.A.
(212) 399-8000
Fax: (212) 399-8130

Public Company
Incorporated: 1961
Employees: 21,700
Gross Billings: $2.53 billion (1996)
Stock Exchanges: New York
SICs: 7311 Advertising Agencies; 8741 Management Services 6719 Holding Companies, Not Elsewhere Classified; 4841 Cable & Other Pay Television Services

The second-largest advertising company in the world, The Interpublic Group of Companies, Inc. operates as a holding company for a group of advertising agencies and media firms that include McCann-Erickson Worldwide, Ammirati Puris Lintas, the Lowe Group, and Western International Media. Through its subsidiaries, Interpublic serves more than 4,000 clients in more than 110 countries, providing advertising programs, direct marketing, market research, and other marketing services. Interpublic's advertising agencies compete against one another for clients, yet all benefit from the resources and connections of their parent company, Interpublic.

Origins

In 1956 Marion Harper, then chief executive officer and chairman of McCann-Erickson, began to implement his vision of fashioning an advertising company modeled after General Motors, a vigorous conglomerate consisting of equally vigorous but largely autonomous divisions. He arranged for McCann-Erickson to buy the Marshalk Company advertising firm of New York. The move was unprecedented because Harper declared that the two agencies (McCann-Erickson and Marshalk) would be operated as competing companies. Harper's intention was to avoid the conflict of interest problem that plagued all agencies attempting to procure accounts from competing clients. He felt that if Marshalk and McCann were separately run, a camera manufacturer looking to hire McCann would not care that Marshalk did the advertising for another camera manufacturer. Most people within the industry viewed the idea with skepticism, but Harper proved them wrong. Both agencies continued to grow while often servicing rival clients.

That was only the beginning. In January 1961 Interpublic was established as a holding company, and McCann-Erickson became its largest subsidiary. What followed was a rapid, occasionally reckless, six-year period of expansion and acquisition. Harper purchased majority interests in a variety of advertising firms all over the world. The network of affiliates was global; but it was also chaotic, mismanaged, and unprofitable. In 1967 Interpublic was billing at over $700 million, yet still insolvent. Unable to repay its loans, the company nearly went into receivership. Only through a radical restructuring of management practices and sales of subsidiaries was the agency saved. One of the casualties was Marion Harper himself. He was ousted from the chairmanship of the company by the governing board. Harper was therefore not able to personally direct his ''dream-agency'' to fruition. Doing so was left to others.

Although Interpublic was not officially incorporated until 1961, its history dates back 50 years earlier. In 1911 the U.S. Supreme Court dismantled the Rockefeller Standard Oil Trust and divided it into 37 different companies. The largest of these was Standard Oil of New Jersey (now Exxon). Harrison McCann, who had been advertising manager at the Rockefeller Trust for a number of years, opened up his own ad agency and took on Jersey Standard as his first client. The age of the automobile was soon to come and with it an increase in the demand for refined petroleum products. As the advertising man for the world's largest oil company, McCann was poised for success.

In 1930 McCann merged his agency with that of Alfred Erickson to form the McCann-Erickson Company. Despite the Depression and World War II, the newly conjoined firm managed to grow in billings and importance; by 1945 McCann-

Company Perspectives:

It is always useful to reflect on how our Company has succeeded in posting such strong and consistent gains over the past 20 years. Interpublic pioneered the concept of complementary but competing networks back in the '60s. Our mission is the same now as it was then: Our agencies concentrate on developing their unique positioning, philosophy and communication skills and then bring that fully to bear in working with their clients and growing their business, while we at the parent company develop overall strategy, provide management oversight and assume any and all functions that economically can best be performed centrally.

Erickson was doing close to $40 million in business, making it the fifth-largest advertising firm in the United States.

When Marion Harper began working at the McCann-Erickson agency in the 1930s, he was employed neither as a copywriter nor as an account executive; he was a clerk in the mailroom. After delivering the day's mail he would visit the research department and learn what he could. He proved a remarkable student; he was made manager of copy research at the age of 26 and then promoted to director of research at 30. Two years later, Harrison McCann promoted Harper again—this time to president of McCann-Erickson Advertising. In the short span of nine years Harper rose through the ranks of the agency to become president of the company.

During the period of Harper's mercurial ascendancy, McCann-Erickson was experiencing the most lucrative decade of its history. In 1954 the agency surpassed $100 million in billings for the first time. Then, between 1955 and 1956, the agency added over $45 million worth of new business to its balance sheet. Among the new clients were the Westinghouse appliance division, Chesterfield tobacco, and Mennen personal hygiene products. However, these accounts were overshadowed by the fourth new customer gained by McCann at this time, namely, Coca-Cola. Though Coke was a large $15 million account in 1956, it was the soft drink company's potential for future growth that made it such an attractive customer. For McCann-Erickson, Coca-Cola was an investment in the coming era of "recreation and refreshment." Today it remains the most coveted and guarded member of McCann-Erickson's client roster.

Also at this time McCann-Erickson moved to establish itself in a variety of less conventional foreign advertising markets. Long the leading agency in Latin America and Europe, the company purchased the third-largest ad firm in Australia and began to actively pursue business in the Orient. By 1960 McCann-Erickson had billings of $100 million outside the U.S., with a substantial portion coming from the Asia-Pacific area.

Interpublic Formed in 1961

When Marion Harper became president of McCann-Erickson the agency was considered a research-oriented firm that took a methodical approach to its advertising. It was the "organization man's" agency. Like Stanley Resor at the rival J. Walter Thompson company, Harper was a firm believer in the use of social science techniques in advertising. He was always looking for a way to accurately predict consumer response and had a bureaucrat's love for statistics. In fact, he had such reverence for facts and figures that he would occasionally sacrifice loyalty for the prospect of future earnings. In one instance he voluntarily resigned the large and longstanding Chrysler account to take on the smaller but potentially more lucrative business of General Motor's Buick division. A tireless worker, Harper would often labor at his desk for 48 hours at a stretch. He once confided in a friend, "I have been captured by what I chased." In 1960 he took his first vacation since being hired by McCann. A year later Interpublic was established, and Harper was forced to work more feverishly than ever.

Interpublic was envisioned by Harper as a family of rival sons. The various affiliates and subsidiaries would compete against each other for accounts and would operate separately. The one thing binding them together would be their mutual membership in the holding company and their ties to the parent agency's financial and informational resources. It was intended to be a "horizontal" system: the different Interpublic divisions could produce campaigns for competing products. The structure, though an ingenious way of getting around the conflict of interest problem that can make agency growth difficult, did not always work. For instance, Nestle's chocolate, a longtime McCann client, left Interpublic in 1963 after the purchase of the Erwin Wasey firm brought Carnation onto the Interpublic roster. In addition, the cost of buying so many small and medium-sized ad shops, not to mention the occasional acquisition of a large agency, was prohibitive. The overhead involved in keeping the entire business operational was staggering. The rapid expansion of Interpublic required the one thing that Marion Harper's intellect could not provide, namely, adequate management. In 1966 Harper's sprawling conglomerate included 24 divisions, 8,300 employees, a fleet of five airplanes, and billings of $711 million. Yet it rarely broke even. The following year Interpublic and Harper reached their collective nadir. The company incurred a $3 million deficit and defaulted on agreements with two New York banks. At one point in 1967 a group of investment bankers offered to buy Interpublic in its entirety for the small sum of $5 million, but the deal was never finalized.

With the danger of receivership imminent, Interpublic needed to take drastic measures to save itself. The man responsible for instituting the changes was Robert Healy. Healy had been an executive at the firm for a number of years but went into voluntary exile in Switzerland over managerial differences with Marion Harper. In the autumn of 1967 the board brought Healy back from Geneva to reverse the mismanaged expansion that was hurting Interpublic. After Marion Harper was ousted as the chief executive officer and chairman, Healy was put in charge. Given a short time allowance by Interpublic's creditors, Healy persuaded his employees to loan the company $3.5 million in return for convertible debentures. In addition, a number of clients agreed to pay in advance for future advertising services. These two factors permitted Interpublic to remain in business. Then, with the help of an additional $10 million in loans, the company went public in 1971.

When Marion Harper walked out of the Interpublic office he left behind the prototype of the "mega-agencies" which emerged in the late 1970s and 1980s. He also left behind a personal mystique. After being forced out of Interpublic he opened up his own small "boutique" agency, but this venture only lasted a year or two. He then kept himself out of public view for over a decade. In 1980 he was discovered living at his mother's house in Oklahoma City—penniless.

By selling public stock and reducing its comparatively high payroll costs (59 percent of gross income), Interpublic stabilized its finances. It began operating again at a profit. In 1973 Paul Foley succeeded Robert Healy as chief executive officer and chairman and ushered in a new era of growth at the company. Billings topped $1 billion for the first time in 1974 and plans were drawn up for renewed expansion. The Campbell-Ewald company, longtime ad agency for Chevrolet, was acquired in 1973. This move was followed five years later by the $32 million purchase of the SSC&B firm, the largest merger in advertising history at the time. These two acquisitions, along with Interpublic's strong overseas presence at a time when the American dollar was weak, led the company to record profits. At the end of 1978 Interpublic was billing in excess of $2 billion.

New Management for 1980s, 1990s

Throughout Interpublic's history its largest and most important clients have been Exxon and Coca-Cola. Then in the mid-1970s Lever Brothers came to Interpublic with SSC&B and Chevrolet with Campbell-Ewald. By 1979 Miller Beer would also come to rank near the top four. Miller came to McCann-Erickson as a struggling $20 million client in 1970. Bill Backer (who had coined the phrases "Things Go Better with Coke" and "It's the Real Thing") and Carl Spielvogel went to work on Miller's market share. They came up with the "Miller Time" slogan and were responsible for the Miller Lite commercials which feature famous athletes. Between 1970 and 1979 Miller Beer prospered. Spielvogel thought that his success, not only with Miller but also with Coca-Cola and various other accounts, would gain him the position of chairman at Interpublic when Foley retired. The job went to Spielvogel's rival Philip Geier. Both Backer and Spielvogel resigned and formed their own agency, taking the Miller business away from McCann-Erickson in the process. Miller was no longer a $20 million account; it was now worth over $100 million. News of the defection dropped Interpublic's stock price five points.

Coca-Cola, feeling pressure from Pepsi and upset with the departure of Backer and Spielvogel, issued an ultimatum to McCann-Erickson: "90 days to come up with a new campaign or we take our $750 million account somewhere else." Fortunately, the account was saved by the phrase "Have a Coke and a smile," and a commercial which featured Pittsburgh Steeler football player "Mean" Joe Green giving a young fan the uniform off his back.

After this initial scare Philip Geier became more comfortable as chief executive officer and chairman of Interpublic, but not too comfortable. In the 1980s Interpublic suffered a decline of business in Europe. The offices in Great Britain and France lost a variety of important clients (e.g., Bass Beer and Gillette), and Campbell-Ewald's European division operated at a loss. These difficulties were particularly troublesome to Interpublic since 65 percent of its billings were outside of the United States. Geier fought back, increasing Interpublic's expansion in Asia where Interpublic ranked as the number one American-based agency.

By the late 1980s, Interpublic had 166 offices in 50 countries. The four company divisions created advertising for such products as: Coca-Cola, Buick, Viceroy cigarettes, Inglenook wine, Exxon, Early Time bourbon, and Kentucky Fried Chicken (McCann-Erickson); Pall Mall and Lucky Strike cigarettes, Johnson & Johnson baby shampoo, Lipton tea, Noxzema, and Bayer aspirin (SSC&B); Chevrolet and Smirnoff vodka (Campbell-Ewald); Minute Maid, Sprite, A-1 Steak Sauce, and Grey Poupon mustard (Marshalk).

1990s Growth

Although the appointment of Geier to Interpublic's top post sparked some resentment, at least in Spielvogel's case, few were dismayed by the results Geier achieved, particularly the company's shareholders, who watched their investments swell under Geier's tenure. As the company entered the 1990s, Geier and his chief financial officer, Eugene Beard, could point to impressive financial gains after their first decade of control over the fortunes of Interpublic. Revenues more than tripled between the early 1980s and early 1990s, rising to $1.9 billion in 1992. Interpublic's stock demonstrated a more animated leap, increasing 15-fold between 1982 and 1992. Much of this growth was achieved during the 1980s, when the advertising industry was growing robustly, but when the advertising industry's years of vigorous growth came screeching to a halt in 1990, the full measure of Geier's influence could be gauged.

When the advertising industry fell on hard times along with other sectors of the nation's economy during the recessive early 1990s, other international agglomerations of advertising agencies suffered miserably. Companies such as WPP Group and Saatchi & Saatchi watched their business evaporate and their earnings erode, as an era of corporate cutbacks and wholesale downsizing began. In contrast to the 1980s, the early 1990s were years in which advertising agencies were forced to sell not only advertising ideas to corporate America, but the value of advertising itself. For many of Interpublic's ilk, the transition from the fertile 1980s to the sterile 1990s was not a smooth segue. Business was down on all fronts, and inured to the prosperous years of the 1980s, advertising agencies floundered financially. Interpublic, however, distinguished itself from the industry pack and continued to radiate remarkable financial health during the early 1990s.

The company's success during the transition from the 1980s to the 1990s was attributed to Geier, whose penchant for assiduous cost control maintained the momentum built up during the 1980s. Further, Geier was lauded for his practice of ceding creative authority to Interpublic's four agencies, which by this point served 4,000 clients in 91 countries. "It's tricky in any business to balance the need for creative independence in a far-flung enterprise with the need for accountability and controls," noted one industry observer. "Interpublic shows that it can be done even in a particularly volatile business."

As the recession intensified during the early 1990s, Interpublic continued to shine. In late 1993, the company registered one of the most prolific growth spurts in the history of the media business, landing $1 billion worth of business during a three-day period. On a Monday in early December 1993, McCann-Erickson was awarded a $200 million Johnson & Johnson account for national television advertising. Two days later, General Motors handed McCann-Erickson its $300 million national print advertising account and Lintas delivered its $500 million national television advertising account, giving all those at Interpublic, and particularly those at McCann-Erickson, ample cause for celebration.

In early 1994, Geier exercised his role as chief strategist for all Interpublic agencies by advising the company's subsidiaries to develop interactive media capabilities. Geier was intent on securing a leading position in a burgeoning area of advertising, and McCann-Erickson was the first to respond by forming a business unit called McCann Interactive. Other Interpublic agencies followed suit, until all of Interpublic's interactive activities were organized into one entity in early 1995, an Interpublic subsidiary christened Allied Communications Group.

On the heels of this development, Interpublic suffered its first meaningful setback during the first half of the decade. In mid-1995, McCann-Erickson lost Coca-Cola's advertising contract, an account it had held for 40 years. Although McCann-Erickson retained Coca-Cola's media account, the news was devastating, although not unexpected. In late 1992, Coca-Cola had transferred the work on its main brand to Creative Artists Agency, which marked the beginning of a painful, two-year period for McCann-Erickson executives as they awaited further word from Coca-Cola. The 1995 decision by Coca-Cola was expected to damage Interpublic's reputation as much as its financial status, but Geier was not about to let Coca-Cola's departure from Interpublic's portfolio derail his strategy of global expansion.

Following the worrisome news in 1995, Interpublic proved to be more resilient than some expected. Financially, the company did not miss a beat, registering strong gains in revenues in 1995 and 1996. Interpublic eclipsed the $2 billion in commissions and fees in 1995 and collected more than $2.5 billion in revenues the following year. These increases were primarily attributable to the continued worldwide expansion of the company's business through strategic acquisitions and investments, the main thrust of Geier's strategy. No acquisition was larger during the mid-1990s than the May 1996 purchase of DraftDirect Worldwide, the largest independent direct marketing firm in the world. As Geier plotted the future course of the Interpublic family of agencies, further acquisitions were expected, acquisitions that would enable Geier to create the best advertising and communications company in the world. With this lofty goal underpinning Interpublic's strategy for the future, the company headed into the late 1990s intent on developing the fullest possible range of communications capabilities.

Principal Subsidiaries

McCann-Erickson Worldwide; Ammirati Puris Lintas; Campbell-Ewald; The Lowe Group; DraftDirect Worldwide; Western International Media; Allied Communications Group.

Further Reading

Dougherty, Philip, "Backer and Spielvogel Set the Standard for Growth," *New York Times,* June 1, 1980.

Fox, Stephen, *The Mirror Makers,* New York: Morrow, 1984.

"Interpublic Group Reports Results for Second Quarter 1997," *PR Newswire,* July 24, 1997, p. 72.

Marshall, Caroline, "Quiet American Stays Mum As Coke Loosens Ties," *Campaign,* July 14, 1995, p. 10.

Morgenson, Gretchen, "Sibling Rivalry," *Forbes,* February 15, 1993, p. 119.

Wall, Kathleen, "At Interpublic, Family Feud Over Motorola," *ADWEEK Eastern Edition,* November 13, 1995, p. 5.

—updated by Jeffrey L. Covell

Kal Kan Foods, Inc.

3250 East 44th Street
Vernon, California 90058
U.S.A.
(213) 587-2727
Fax: (213) 586-8347

Wholly Owned Subsidiary of Mars, Inc.
Incorporated: 1936 as Stirling Packing Company
Employees: 1,200 (1993)
Sales: $220 million (1993)
SICs: 2047 Dog & Cat Food

Kal Kan Foods, Inc. is a noted manufacturer, exporter, and importer of pet foods in the United States. A market leader, the company produces a variety of pet food products, as well as sponsors animal-related charitable events.

At First a Horse-Kill Operation

Headquartered near Los Angeles, California, Kal Kan began manufacturing pet food in 1936. First known as the Stirling Packing Company, Kal Kan operated as a horse-kill enterprise owned by a Californian who bred thoroughbreds and promoted race horses.

In 1952, the company's Vernon, California, plant unionized as Butchers Local 563, which merged with Local 770 in 1986. Kal Kan eventually operated facilities throughout the United States; however, the Vernon plant remained the company's only unionized facility throughout 1997. Plant employees processed and packed Kal Kan, Pedigree, and Waltham brand pet foods.

The Early Pet Food Industry

In the 1960s, the pet food industry in the United States was but an outgrowth of the grain-based livestock feed business. Dry pet foods utilized vegetable and soy proteins in place of meat, and other pet foods were made of meat byproducts, which were high in fat and smelled badly. Yet, Kal Kan carved a niche for itself as an industry leader in the United States.

At this time, the Mars Candy Company, a large, multinational firm run by Forrest Mars, Sr., eagerly purchased Kal Kan. In addition to candy, the Mars Company excelled in the manufacture of pet food overseas. According to Bill Saporito, a writer for *Fortune,* Forrest Mars ''started a pet food industry long before people in those countries [Europe] would even consider feeding Fifi out of a can. His kind of pioneering required an organization that could take an expansion strategy and execute it without much help.'' Mars's Pedigree Petfoods, an English company, launched Whiskas cat food in Europe in 1959. A healthy, meat-based cat food, Whiskas was the first brand to offer varieties of pet food. It became the major cat food brand in Europe, as well as in Australia and Japan.

After Mars purchased Kal Kan, he renamed the company's brand dog foods as Pedigree, and the company's Mealtime brand became Pedigree Mealtime. ''The Pedigree change was brilliantly executed,'' noted Saporito. Kal Kan solidified its position as a leader in the U.S. dog food market.

Whiskas Comes to America

The popularity of cats as pets surpassed that of dogs in the 1980s. Since British Whiskas outsold its competitors three to one, parent company Mars saw an opportunity in the U.S. cat food market for Kal Kan. (Though Kal Kan controlled a leading share of the American cat food market, the company had long been associated with dog food by the general public.) In 1988, Mars renamed Kal Kan brand cat food as Whiskas, and the company's Crave brand became Whiskas Dry. Mars used the same recipe for U.S. and British versions of Whiskas; however, each used local ingredients. Kal Kan's cat food received new packaging—a label with a cat mask logo—and a new slogan: ''The cat food your cat prefers is now called Whiskas.'' Changing the names of Kal Kan's cat food brands gave parent company Mars international efficiency in marketing cat food. As one competitor told *Fortune* magazine, ''One thing Mars does better than any public company is understand the true importance of the international markets.''

Company Perspectives:

Manufacturing quality pet food since 1936.

After switching to Mars' global brand, though, Kal Kan's position in the cat food marketplace slid. As Saporito observed, ''Kal Kan's big cat food brand, Whiskas, has turned into, well, a dog.'' In fact, the company lost half of its market share in cat food during the change to the Whiskas name. So, late in the 1980s, Kal Kan worked to expand the cat food market in America. John Murray, vice-president of sales at Kal Kan, revealed in a 1991 ad in *Supermarket Business* that ''we felt that to take on existing leaders with similar products was unlikely to be successful. And from the retailer's standpoint, for us to go for a share without enlarging the market would be to swap pieces of the pie. As far as we were concerned, the name of the game was trying to enlarge that pie.'' Expecting about $300 million in Whiskas sales, the company upgraded its product's quality and palatability by utilizing meat-based formulations and less fat. In the process, Kal Kan created better-smelling cat food.

Kal Kan also increased its advertising budget to promote Whiskas to American cat owners. Cat owners offered testimonials for the cat food in television commercials and other advertisements. With the product innovations backed by these new marketing efforts, Whiskas became a national brand in the United States, too.

Pet Food in the 1990s

During the early 1990s, a broad recession eroded international pet food sales, yet Mars remained the leader in the international marketplace. Kal Kan's parent controlled 60 percent by value and 60 percent by volume of the industry. Mars sold products in 30 countries, including the bestselling brands in the world—Whiskas and Sheba—and in Europe—Kit-E-Kat. Pedigree's Whiskas, sold in six countries, was the number one brand. For its part, Kal Kan offered 29 textured varieties of Whiskas in the United States, including chunky, minced, and choice cuts. Kal Kan also offered three additional varieties of dried Whiskas.

To capitalize on its ability to offer variety in pet food products, Kal Kan began offering more specialized items. In 1990, for instance, Kal Kan launched Whiskas Select Entrees. Made of minced meat and priced higher than standard products, Whiskas Select Entrees were on par with Mars' Sheba brand, which was made with meat chunks.

Kal Kan instituted several ancillary services to pet food buyers beginning in 1991. Kal Kan first employed in-store nutritional centers that year, as well as sponsored the ''Help Keep Animals in Our Lives'' Campaign as a charitable activity. The company donated redeemed Kal Kan coupons to the World Wildlife Fund as a public service.

In 1992, Kal Kan changed advertising agencies to D'Arcy Macius Benton & Bowles. The pet food company also joined other major corporations—Kellogg's and Coca-Cola, for example—as a sponsor of the U.S. Olympic team. Kal Kan coordinated ''petathlons'' in which dogs in three weight classes and their owners competed in events such as 30-meter dashes, slaloms, hill climbs, tunnels, mazes, and hurdles in 20 U.S. cities. Gymnast Peter Vidmar, an Olympic gold medalist, chaired the events, which were judged by the U.S. Dog Agility Association. In addition, Kal Kan donated a percentage from its sales of Pedigree brands to the U.S. Olympic team, guaranteeing a donation of at least $1.5 million. Unlike other sponsors, however, Kal Kan presented one caveat. As Andrew Evan Serwer noted in *Fortune* magazine in 1992: ''Both Kal Kan and the U.S. Olympic Committee stress that Kal Kan is not the official dog food for members of the U.S. Olympic team.''

Such events complemented parent company Mars's plans for global expansion and marketing. Mars thought, explained Saporito, that ''because we live in a homogenizing universe, many products can be sold the same way everywhere. One world, one brand, one message. That's why Mars has heavily backed such global sporting events as the World Cup and the Olympics. This simplicity of sell generates savings in advertising, packaging, distribution, and staff.''

New Products During the 1990s

In 1993, Kal Kan's scientific brand dog food, Expert, debuted as a competitor to Hill's Science Diet and Iams brands for the specialty vet market. Marketed through supermarkets, Expert missed its target audience, since consumers typically purchase specialty dog foods at their vets' offices or in pet stores. Sales were disastrous. Nevertheless, the company persevered in introducing the new product to the marketplace, including launching a companion product—Whiskas Expert Diet for cats. Kal Kan is ''an enormously tough competitor,'' admitted one pet food industry representative. ''And they stick with it; but the downside is that they throw good money after bad. No publicly traded company would ever stay in a business that long and lose that much money.'' When all was totaled, Kal Kan lost $50 million introducing Expert to consumers.

Undeterred, the company continued developing and marketing new products. For example, Kal Kan first offered Whiskas Ultramilk, a lactose-free beverage for cats, in 1993. More digestible than regular milk and better tasting, Ultramilk was made from flavored malt, a favorite of cats. The cat drink was richer and creamier than milk, yet equal to it in nutrients. Shelf stable, Ultramilk sold in local grocery stores. Kal Kan introduced Ultramilk in the following markets: Boston, Baltimore, Hartford/New Haven, Philadelphia, New York, Washington, and Phoenix.

Kal Kan also introduced several snack foods for pets in 1993. First, it launched Whiskas Crunch, a low-fat snack for cats that acted as an appetite stimulant. This crunchy mixture sprinkled on canned cat food increased a pet's total food intake.

Then Kal Kan announced Pedigree Dentabone for dogs, which provided 20 percent of a dog's daily nutrition. In addition, Dentabone offered dogs full-range chewing for dental care, specifically reducing plaque and tartar. Pedigree Snackos also debuted in 1993. These air-dried beef strips served as a protein supplement for dogs, notable for increasing a pet's muscle tone. The company also began marketing tender beef-and-chicken dog treats called Pedigree Tandem.

By 1994, Kal Kan helped Mars to achieve the status of the largest pet food business in the world. Annual sales for Kal Kan's parent company neared $4 billion. So, despite some setbacks, Kal Kan continued to introduce new products. In 1996, for example, Kal Kan initiated special formulations of dog foods for different age dogs, notably Pedigree Lifestages Dry Dog Food and Dry Puppy Food.

Innovations to existing products continued as well. The company improved Whiskas Senior Dry Cat Food, a new formulation for older, inactive cats. As an incentive to purchase the pet food for older cats, Kal Kan offered coupons promoting the Whiskas line. In 1997, Kal Kan developed a soy-free formula for Pedigree Snackos. Kal Kan promoted Snackos with a buy one, get one free offer through Petsmart. Whiskas Dry Cat Food also gained a new flavor in 1997. Kal Kan introduced Whiskas Dry Cat Food with Salmon and Rice as a highly digestible food that facilitated skin and coat maintenance in pets. The product claimed to be manufactured with real salmon and no artificial flavors or colors. Endorsed by Waltham Centre for Pet Care and Nutrition, the new formula also included Vitalife, a combination of 40 vitamins, minerals, and nutrients especially for cats. Ads advised cat owners to ''Make friends for life with Whiskas.''

In the years beyond 1997, Kal Kan no doubt would work to maintain its position as a leader in the pet food industry. More new products and enhancements to existing formulas of dog and cat foods could be expected in the future.

Further Reading

Ackerman, Stephen J., and Judith Levine Willis, ''Pet Cuisine: Feeding Galloping Gourmets,'' *FDA Consumer,* March 1991, p. 28.

Dorman, Evelyn, ''Whiskas,'' *Encyclopedia of Consumer Brands,* Detroit: St. James Press, 1994, pp. 635–37.

Garry, Michael, ''Scratching out a Niche,'' *Progressive Grocer,* November 1992, p. 89.

''Kal Kan Introduces Whiskas, Pedigree Cat and Dog Snacks,'' *Supermarket News,* May 8, 1995, p. 110.

''Kal Kan Offers Lactose-free Milk for Cats,'' *Supermarket News,* January 18, 1993, p. 36.

''Kal Kan Pet Food Workers Enjoy Nation's Top Pay and Benefits,'' *The Voice* (Hollywood, California; UFCW Local 770 newsletter), December 1997.

Klepacki, Laura, ''Animal Magnetism: Supermarkets Are Using Specialty Products and Deals to Win Back Pet Food Sales from the Competition,'' *Supermarket News,* September 21, 1992, p. 17.

Larson, Melissa, ''New Packages Herald Year of the Cat,'' *Packaging,* April 1989, p. 8.

McKay, Betsy, ''How to Sell Pet Food in Russia,'' *Advertising Age,* May 17, 1993.

Michels, Antony J., Andrew Evan Serwer, and Allison McCormick, ''Animals Do Their Bit for Recycling, the Olympics, and Alternative Energy,'' *Fortune,* July 27, 1992, p. 14.

Otto, Allison, ''It's Raining Cat and Dog Food,'' *Prepared Foods,* April 1989, p. 40.

''Pedigree Lifestages Dry Dog Food, Dry Puppy Food,'' *Product Alert,* March 25, 1996.

''Pedigree Snackos Dog Snacks—with Beef,'' *Product Alert,* June 23, 1997.

Saporito, Bill, ''The Eclipse of Mars,'' *Fortune,* November 28, 1994, p. 82.

Schifrin, Matthew, ''Mom's Cooking Was Never Like This,'' *Forbes,* August 19, 1991, p. 50.

Toor, Mat, ''Pedigree Chums Bounds to the Top As Whiskas Fails to Land on Its Feet,'' *Marketing,* July 25, 1991, p. 15.

''Whiskas Dry Cat Food—Senior,'' *Product Alert,* May 13, 1996.

''Whiskas Dry Cat Food—with Salmon and Rice,'' *Product Alert,* July 14, 1997.

World's Greatest Brands, New York: John Wiley & Sons, 1992, p. 8.

—Charity Anne Dorgan

Kerr-McGee Corporation

Kerr-McGee Center
123 Robert S. Kerr Avenue
Oklahoma City, Oklahoma 73102
U.S.A.
(405) 270-1313
Fax: (405) 270-3123

Public Company
Incorporated: 1932 as A&K Petroleum Company
Employees: 3,851
Sales: $1.93 billion (1996)
Stock Exchanges: New York Boston Midwest Pacific Philadelphia
SICs: 1221 Surface Mining—Bituminous Coal & Lignite; 1222 Underground Mining—Bituminous Coal; 1311 Crude Petroleum & Natural Gas; 2816 Inorganic Pigments; 2819 Industrial Inorganic Chemicals, Not Elsewhere Classified

From its beginning as a small drilling company during the Great Depression, Kerr-McGee Corporation has grown to become one of the country's more successful medium-sized energy and chemical companies. Kerr-McGee's operations focus on three areas: oil and natural gas production, production and marketing of inorganic industrial chemicals, and coal mining and marketing.

Company Origins in Oil Drilling Contracting

The Great Depression was just around the corner when Anderson & Kerr Drilling Company was founded near Oklahoma City, Oklahoma, in July 1929. The company's assets amounted to three boilers and two steam rigs, and the company was one of many small oil-related firms vying for drilling contracts in a city that was booming. The local newspaper, the *Daily Oklahoman,* in October 1929, mentioned the October stock market crash briefly under the headline, "Business Men are Unnecessarily Troubled by Crash of Stocks." This town wasn't feeling the depression—there was oil here and plenty of it.

While James L. Anderson handled the equipment end, Robert S. Kerr sought drilling contracts, operating from a hotel room and going home only on weekends. Anderson was said to have "a nose for oil" and the ability to drill more economically than others, and Kerr was a talented capital raiser. Financing the young company was a constant challenge. It faced rising debt, strong competition, and the need to keep busy, when Kerr, still relatively unknown, met with Frank Phillips, founder of Phillips Petroleum Company. Kerr wanted to drill some of Phillips's leases in the area, and he eventually won a contract. As Kerr's longtime associate, Rex Hawks, told John Samuel Ezell, in *Innovations in Energy: The Story of Kerr-McGee,* "As Kerr was about to leave, he turned and said, 'By the way, Mr. Phillips, there's one little item I was about to forget.' When asked what that was Kerr replied that he would have to borrow $20,000 to sink the well. Phillips then 'cussed a little while and exclaimed, 'You spend all this time wanting the job and haven't the money to drill it with.' Kerr 'hemmed and hawed,' but in the end Phillips called [his office] . . . and said, 'Let this damn man have $20,000 to drill this lease with.' " Kerr's bold drive and inexhaustible belief in his company kept the company moving forward through times when the speculative nature of the business and the tough competition would have folded a less determined company.

In 1932 the company opened an office for its staff of 11 in Oklahoma City and was incorporated as A&K Petroleum Company. In 1935 its first public offering of 120,000 shares of common stock was made available at $5.00 per share. In 1936 when the company was negotiating a second stock offering, Anderson decided that the company was growing to a size he no longer felt comfortable managing, and he opted to sell his interest in the A&K.

The year 1937 was a critical time. The economy was in recession, oil prices were decreasing, and there was no money to finance drilling. The company's directors recognized a need for leadership at the executive level to move the company's exploration and production into the black. They were willing to bank a large part of their holdings on two men from Phillips Petroleum, offering them salaries that dwarfed their own by comparison. Robert Lynn became executive vice-president of the company which, in these formative years, restructured and renamed its operations several times. He played a prominent role in the company, then called Kerlyn Oil Company, for five years. Dean A. McGee, the second man from Phillips, was to direct the company on a new course almost immediately. His presence was felt until his death in 1989.

McGee, who had been Phillips's chief geologist, relied heavily on credit, faith, and hard labor. Within a year the company made its first major oil discovery—the Magnolia field in Columbia County, Arkansas. The revenues from the Magnolia discovery fueled further expansion.

Demand for oil was rising dramatically as a result of wartime needs, however the company struggled under debt, taxes, government restrictions, a shortage of capital and manpower, as well as continuing low prices for its products. Kerr and his workers continued making deals, leveraging assets, and using their talents to keep operating. Kerlyn was chronically short of capital in its early years and often had to stop drilling until money could be raised to continue. Much of its capital came from small contributions of $1,000 to $3,000. In 1943 a deal was struck in which Phillips Petroleum put up 75 percent of the cost for half a share in any Kerlyn venture in which it participated. That year, the company's exploratory drilling, or wildcatting, led to discovery of oil to the northwest of Oklahoma City, setting off the west Edmonton boom. The U.S. Bureau of Mines categorized this find as the year's "greatest addition of new oil."

In 1942, confident that the company was in capable hands and certain that his primary role was to be played out in public office, Bob Kerr made a long-desired move into politics. That year he was elected governor of Oklahoma, and throughout successive political roles, including U.S. senator, Kerr remained an active member of the company's board until his death in 1963.

When Kerr made his move into politics Robert Lynn decided to leave the company. From the time he joined the firm, McGee had acted as a key figure in the company. He was the logical choice to move into Lynn's leadership role, and in 1946 the company changed its name to Kerr-McGee Oil Industries, Inc. McGee became executive vice-president in 1942 and was made president of Kerr-McGee in 1957.

Expansion into Downstream Operations in 1945

Exploration activities continued to increase as Kerr-McGee expanded its drilling operations to the Gulf of Mexico. Seeking to capitalize on the increased need for refined oil products, the company also moved into "downstream" operations with the purchase of its first refinery in 1945. Downstream activities generally include transportation, refining, storage, marketing, distribution, and slop disposal—in short, all activities that follow the upstream activities of exploration and production.

In the postwar 1940s the energy needs of the United States were rising dramatically. The country was using as much oil in one year as did the entire world in 1938. Kerr-McGee responded to this trend with many firsts in oil exploration and production, including in 1947, the completion of the world's first commercial oil well that was out of sight and safety of land, 11 miles off Louisiana's shore. This marked the beginning of the nation's offshore drilling industry. The company added natural gas processing with the purchase of three plants in Oklahoma in 1951, and a fourth in Pampa, Texas, in 1952.

Diversification in the 1950s and 1960s

As the cold war escalated, the government's need for uranium to fuel the atomic bomb program also grew. Kerr-McGee was the first oil company to enter the uranium industry when it acquired mining properties on a Navaho reservation in Arizona in 1952. Mills were needed to process the materials, and Kerr-McGee soon moved into this area, completing its first mill in the fall of 1954. Soon thereafter the company began construction of the country's largest uranium-processing mill, which was brought onstream in 1958.

In 1955 the company moved into major retailing with its purchase of the Deep Rock Oil Corporation. Building upon an established base of service stations in the midwestern states, Kerr-McGee formed a subsidiary, Deep Rock Oil Company, to continue this aspect of expansion. During this period, Kerr-McGee also expanded its refining capabilities, with the purchase of Cato Oil and Grease Company, and Triangle Refineries, a major wholesaler of petroleum products. Transworld Drilling Company Limited was formed to handle Kerr-McGee's domestic and overseas contract drilling in 1958.

The company remained strong in a very competitive industry by making use of innovative methods in its oil production. In 1961 the company was making use of drilling devices that eventually were used to complete the largest vertical shaft successfully drilled by rotary methods in North America at the time. In 1962 the company commissioned the world's largest submersible offshore drilling unit, and in 1963 it built a new research center in Oklahoma City.

In its drive to become a total energy company, Kerr-McGee continued to push into other energy-related areas, entering the forestry business in 1963 with its purchase of two suppliers of railroad cross-ties, and acquiring several fertilizer-marketing companies in the early 1960s, which in 1965 were consolidated into Kerr-McGee Chemical Corporation.

In 1965 Kerr-McGee Oil Industries, Inc. became Kerr-McGee Corporation, a name that better represented the company's diversified holdings. Growth and expansion continued. Although Kerr-McGee had begun doing business in industrial chemicals, its 1967 merger with American Potash and Chemical Corporation marked the company's major entry into the market. This gave the company control of 13,000 acres of a dry lake bed in Searles Valley, California, from which it began extracting brine to produce soda ash, boron products, sodium sulfate, and potash. Two industrial chemical plants were also included in the acquisition, making Kerr-McGee a major processor of a number of industrial chemicals, including the company's most profitable chemical product, titanium dioxide, a white pigment used mainly in the manufacture of paint and plastics.

In 1970 Kerr-McGee was a major player in six of the eight parts of the nuclear fuel cycle, including exploration, mining, milling, conversion of uranium oxide into uranium hexafluoride at a new Sequoya facility in eastern Oklahoma, pelletizing of these materials, and fabrication of fuel elements at its Cimarron Facility in Oklahoma.

At this time the oil industry was undergoing major change. The Organization of Petroleum Exporting Countries's oil embargo in 1973 sent the price of gasoline and energy soaring, and the U.S. public was forced to begin conserving. It was a time of opportunity for energy companies; revenues were increasing and the government was bending over backwards to encourage exploration and production by deregulating and offering hefty tax credits. Despite these favorable conditions, however, Kerr-McGee's performance slipped in a number of areas, as the company lost its lead in offshore drilling and suffered from a lack of managerial direction. Chairman since 1963 and CEO since 1967, Dean McGee instigated an organizational restructuring that, among other changes, established two new subsidiaries, Kerr-McGee Coal Corporation led by Frank McPherson, and Kerr-McGee Nuclear Corporation led by R. T. Zitting. The restructuring was meant to give the company the strength needed to compete in the increasingly complex, turbulent world market.

Kerr-McGee's oil exploration and production operations grew substantially through the mid-1970s. In 1974 the company increased its refining capabilities significantly with the acquisition of the Southwestern Refining Company, Inc., in Corpus Christi, Texas. In 1976 the company expanded its production activities into the Arabian Gulf and the North Sea, and participated in the discovery of the Beatrice oil field, off Scotland's shore.

Coal operations began proving lucrative when the first commercial deliveries of steam coal—coal used to produce steam—were made from surface mining operations in Wyoming in 1978. In the same year, soda ash production began at the company's Argus, California, facility, significantly increasing the company's industrial chemical output.

The Silkwood Case and Other Controversies in the 1970s

The concerns of environmentalists began to loom large in the 1970s, and litigation took up more of the company's time and money. Although there had been previous charges made against Kerr-McGee involving worker safety and environmental contamination, the highly publicized case of Karen Silkwood, which began in 1974, highlighted the hazardous nature of nuclear energy and raised important questions regarding corporate accountability. The Oil, Chemical and Atomic Workers Union alleged that Kerr-McGee's Cimarron River plutonium plant near Oklahoma City, was manufacturing faulty fuel rods, falsifying product inspection records, and, in certain cases, risking the safety of its employees.

Silkwood, a 28 year-old lab technician at Cimarron and one of the union's most active members, was involved in substantiating the charges before the Atomic Energy Commission. Silkwood had suffered radiation exposure in a series of unexplained incidents and had then been killed in an automobile crash while on her way to meet with an Atomic Energy Commission official and a *New York Times* reporter. Although never confirmed, her untimely death led to speculation of foul play and prompted a federal investigation into safety and security at the plant. Following additional problems with worker contamination and a National Public Radio report alleging the misplacement of a significant quantity of plutonium, the company finally shut down the Cimarron plant. In 1986 Karen Silkwood's family settled an $11.5 million plutonium-contamination lawsuit against Kerr-McGee for $1.38 million with Kerr-McGee admitting no liability in the case.

Creating further negative publicity for the embattled company, Kerr-McGee's nuclear-fuel processing plant in Gore, Oklahoma, was cited by the Nuclear Regulatory Commission for 15 health and safety infractions between 1978 and 1986. In 1986 an overfilled cylinder of uranium hexafluoride exploded, releasing a toxic cloud of radioactive hydrofluoric acid. One employee died, and 110 people were hospitalized. This fueled public outcry and set in motion a number of legal proceedings. The controversy surrounding the incident was further exacerbated when the Nuclear Regulatory Commission accused Kerr-McGee of giving a false statement during the commission's investigation.

Kerr-McGee's uranium mining, milling, and processing operations accounted for two percent of its revenues, while costing $72 million in losses between 1982 and 1986. Aside from the environmental problems, demand had fallen off significantly. Kerr-McGee's leadership was still confident that the slump in demand would reverse itself and that its substantial uranium reserves would pay off in the 1990s.

Aside from the problems associated with uranium production, the company's oil operations were not expanding satisfactorily. Kerr-McGee's failure to pay scientists competitive salaries through the tumultuous, highly competitive 1970s proved especially harmful to the company's bread-and-butter oil exploration and production. A market-research firm estimated that between 1980 and 1984 Kerr-McGee's oil reserves fell 21 percent and gas reserves fell 10 percent. In 1986 an estimate by Morgan Stanley & Company put Kerr-McGee's average cost for finding a barrel of oil at $13.03; the average cost for 12 competitors was $7.35 per barrel.

After years of expanding to fulfill its goal of becoming ''the total energy company,'' Kerr-McGee was involved in a wide variety of resource enterprises, including uranium and plutonium mining, milling, and processing; chemicals and coal; contract drilling; refining; gasoline retailing; and timber. Many analysts felt that Kerr-McGee suffered from too much diversification. Earnings dropped from $211 million in 1981 to $118 million in 1983. In 1983 Dean McGee stepped aside as chairman and Frank A. McPherson was named his successor.

McPherson Era Marked by Lengthy Restructuring, 1983–97

Soon after taking over, McPherson embarked on a long-term slimming down of Kerr-McGee's operations. When the fertilizer market began to suffer in the 1980s, McPherson sold off the company's potash operations to Vertac Chemical in 1985 and divested its phosphate mines in the following year. In 1988 McPherson finally decided to sell the company's troublesome uranium interests, which were divested by the end of 1989. In late 1990 and early 1991, Kerr-McGee severed its remaining tie with the company's roots by selling off its contract drilling operations as well as divesting its soda products operations;

together, the contract drilling and soda products sales brought in $340 million after taxes.

By the end of 1991 Kerr-McGee was focused exclusively on oil and natural gas, chemicals, and coal, but McPherson was not finished cutting. The company's petroleum refining and marketing unit was losing money, leading to the mid-1992 decision to explore the sale, merger, or restructuring of this troubled operation. After failing in an effort to sell the unit as a package—which included four refineries, several terminals, a 1,300-mile pipeline, and 51 service stations in Oklahoma, Kansas, and Texas—Kerr-McGee succeeded in divesting them piecemeal in 1995. Of the approximately $400 million brought in through the sales, about $300 million was used to buy back company stock, with the remainder going to pay down debt, which had dropped to $632 million in 1995 compared to $886 million in 1991.

Meanwhile, Kerr-McGee was working to beef up its remaining core businesses. In 1991 production started at titanium dioxide plants in Western Australia and Saudi Arabia, helping to establish the company as a global producer and marketer of pigment. In the area of oil and gas exploration, three major North Sea fields came onstream in 1993, with one of them setting a record for fast-track development through the use of the first permanently moored floating production, storage, and offloading facility in the North Sea. Kerr-McGee was also achieving success through exploration ventures in Indonesia (onshore), the Gulf of Mexico (the deepwater Pompano project), the South China Sea (through a partnership with Amoco Corp.), and China's Bohai Bay. Overall, the company's proven crude-oil reserves in 1996 stood at 170 million barrels, 45 percent more than in 1989.

At the same time that the company was drilling around the globe, however, Kerr-McGee was pulling back from its North American onshore oil and natural gas exploration and production operations, in what the company called "part of the effort to further focus our operations." After divesting some of its North American onshore fields in late 1995 and 1996, Kerr-McGee merged what remained into Devon Energy Corporation in exchange for a 31 percent stake in Devon.

As a result of the McPherson-led cuts, Kerr-McGee was a much smaller company ($1.93 billion in 1996 sales, compared to $3.68 billion in 1990 and $3.15 billion in 1985) but also a much more profitable one (net income was a record $220 million in 1996, compared to $150 million in 1990 and $137 million in 1985). The restructuring behind it—and the nightmarish memories of its ill-fated venture into the nuclear industry finally beginning to recede—the company could now focus on growing its three core businesses. It would have to do so, however, under new leadership. McPherson retired in early 1997, and Luke R. Corbett, who had been named president and chief operating officer in 1995, became the company's fourth chairman and CEO.

Principal Subsidiaries

Kerr-McGee Chemical Corporation; Kerr-McGee China Petroleum Ltd. (Bahamas); Kerr-McGee Coal Corporation; Kerr-McGee Credit Corporation; Kerr-McGee Oil (U.K.) PLC.

Further Reading

Barrett, Amy, "Kerr-McGee: New Tricks for an Old Dog?" *Financial World,* October 15, 1991, p. 18.

Ezell, John Samuel, *Innovations in Energy: The Story of Kerr-McGee,* Norman: University of Oklahoma Press, 1979.

Fan, Aliza, "Kerr-McGee Focuses on Production After Losing Downstream Burden," *Oil Daily,* March 25, 1996, p. 3.

Kohn, Howard, *Who Killed Karen Silkwood?* New York: Summit Books, 1981.

Mack, Toni, "Playing with the Majors," *Forbes,* November 13, 1989, p. 92.

McGee, Dean A., *Evolution into Total Energy: The Story of Kerr-McGee Corporation,* New York: Newcomen Society in North America, 1971.

Rashke, Richard L., *The Killing of Karen Silkwood: The Story behind the Kerr-McGee Plutonium Case,* Boston: Houghton Mifflin, 1981.

Reifenberg, Anne, "Publicity-Shy Kerr-McGee Draws Unwelcome Spotlight," *Wall Street Journal,* September 8, 1995, p. B4.

—Carole Healy
—updated by David E. Salamie

KERRY PROPERTIES LIMITED
嘉里建設有限公司

Kerry Properties Limited

34th Floor, Bank of China Tower
1 Garden Road
Central
Hong Kong
(852) 296-72373

Public Company
Incorporated: 1996
Employees: 1,209
Sales: US$388.61 million (1996)
Stock Exchanges: Hong Kong
SICs: 6552 Subdividers & Developers, Not Elsewhere Classified; 6531 Real Estate Agents & Managers

Kerry Properties Limited is one of the most prominent companies in the enormous network of companies owned or controlled by Robert Kuok. Kerry Properties principally buys and develops real estate in Asia. It owns both residential and commercial property in Hong Kong as well as office buildings, car parks, and apartment buildings in China. It has a large stake in several major construction projects such as the Western Harbor Crossing Tunnel and a new airfreight terminal in Hong Kong, and the Shanghai expressway in China. It also owns millions of square feet of *godown* (warehouse) space in Hong Kong. Kerry Properties works closely with the Shangri-La chain of luxury hotels, which is also owned and operated by Robert Kuok companies. Kerry often buys the land that the hotels are later built on, and develops commercial and residential buildings in neighborhoods surrounding a Shangri-La hotel.

Robert Kuok is one of the most powerful businessmen in Asia, a figure comparable to Rupert Murdoch in the vastness of his holdings. Kuok's businesses include sugar plantations and refineries; shipping companies; edible oil refineries and distributorships; chemical plants; construction projects including prominent new office buildings in China, Malaysia, the Philippines, and elsewhere; the Shangri-La hotel chain; Coca-Cola bottling franchises in Australia and China; the largest English-language daily newspaper in Hong Kong; and a controlling stake in a Hong Kong television network, which is the world's largest producer of Chinese-language programming. These businesses are densely interconnected. Most are private companies. Some, like Kerry Properties, are publicly owned, and others, such as the Coca-Cola bottling franchise in China, are joint ventures. Many are operated by members of the Kuok family. Robert Kuok himself, aged 74 in 1997, is actively involved to varying degrees in the management of his many companies.

The 1960s—The Sugar King

Robert Kuok was born in Malaysia in 1923, the son of emigrants from Fujian, China. His father was a trader in various commodities, and was a successful and moderately wealthy man. The family lived in the city of Johore Bahru, which is immediately across the strait from the island of Singapore. Kuok's father understood the benefits of the English language to businessmen, and the three Kuok sons attended the finest English schools in Malaysia. Robert Kuok's classmates or contemporaries at college included Lee Kuan Yew, later prime minister of Singapore, Tun Hussein Onn, later prime minister of Malaysia, and many others who rose to political or entrepreneurial prominence. Kuok's close ties to the wealthy and powerful in several Asian countries were often a prime factor in his ability to do business, and many of these ties were cemented when he was in his teens.

When the Japanese invaded Singapore in 1942, Kuok found work with Mitsubishi, and became fluent in Japanese. Then Kuok's father died in 1949, leaving his fortune to his three sons, Robert, Phillip, and William. William Kuok became a guerilla working for Malaysian independence. He was ambushed and killed by British forces in 1952. Robert and Phillip used their inheritance to found a company they named Kuok Brothers, and they began buying and selling rice and sugar. The business expanded when Malaysia won its independence from Britain in 1957. Many British traders left, and the Kuoks were able to work on a much larger scale. The sugar business in particular was volatile, and Robert Kuok had a great knack for dangerous speculating. It was apparently Robert Kuok and not his brother who had the direct day-to-day control of sugar trading. Years

Company Perspectives:

Kerry Properties Limited has been formed to hold the Hong Kong and China property and infrastructure investments of the Kuok Group—an international, multi-faceted conglomerate with interests ranging from commodities trading and media to the renowned Shangri-La hotel chain. Kerry Properties builds its success on its commitment to quality and an entrepreneurial flair for selecting prime sites in quality locations. With the depth of management expertise of the Kuok Group behind it, Kerry Properties is poised for further growth following the reunification of Hong Kong and China.

later Kuok recalled his sugar speculating with a shudder, because as a young man he had taken such enormous risks. But the risks paid off. By the 1970s, Robert Kuok was known as the Sugar King. At times he controlled up to 10 percent of the world sugar market. During the build-up of the sugar business, Kuok diversified into several other areas. Kuok Brothers became a major sugar distributor in and around Malaysia, as well as the country's largest sugar refiner in the 1960s. The company chartered ships for moving its sugar, and soon bought shipping lines. The company diversified as well into banking, insurance, and real estate development. Kuok diversified geographically also. His first business was centered in Kuala Lampur, though he also operated for a time from London, after his brother William was killed. In the early 1970s, he shifted his base to Singapore, and in the late 1970s moved to Hong Kong. Kuok ran his Hong Kong sugar trading business principally through a private company he named Kerry Trading.

Expansion into Hotels in the 1970s

The Sugar King's profits can only be guessed at. Hong Kong law did not require disclosure of profits from private companies, so all Kerry Trading brought in was known only to Kuok and his trusted managers. But even before world sugar prices soared in 1973, Kuok clearly had money to spend. He began investing in a hotel in Singapore in 1971. At the time, there was a shortage of hotel space in the island nation. Kuok had stayed in some of Europe's most luxurious hotels, and he concluded that as Singapore attracted an ever larger international business and tourist population, a fine hotel would prosper. Kuok built a hotel in partnership with other local rice traders, on land he owned. The Shangri-La was open for business years before competitors set about building similar luxury hotels, and so Kuok's hotel was immensely profitable. Kuok moved to Hong Kong in 1979, and built a second Shangri-La there in 1981. The hotels were run at first by the prominent U.S. hotel company Westin. Then in 1983 Kuok formed his own company to manage his hotels, Shangri-La Hotels & Resorts. The ownership of the hotel chain was given to a separate Kuok company, Shangri-La Asia Ltd.

Next Kuok formed a joint venture with the state-owned Urban Development Authority in Malaysia, and built another Shangri-La hotel and an office complex on land Kuok owned in downtown Kuala Lampur. This project was planned at a time when Kuala Lampur badly needed office space as well as international hotels. In Singapore, Kuok had been ahead of the trend, and got his hotel operating well before the peak of the Singapore building boom. The Kuala Lampur Shangri-La unfortunately was not completed until 1985, just when the Kuala Lampur building boom was cooling down. So this hotel was not a money-maker right away. Nevertheless, Kuok seemed sure the hotel chain as a whole would be profitable in the future. He built a fourth Shangri-La in Bangkok, which opened in 1986, and began building another in Beijing.

Kuok also began building two hotels in the Philippines in 1986, even though that was the year longtime dictator Ferdinand Marcos fled the country, and the political stability of the country was in doubt. His expansion into the Philippines at such a time was a typical Kuok move. Where other business people might have stayed away, to wait and see what would happen, Kuok started building. No matter the crisis, he always proved himself capable of remaining in the good graces of governments. For instance, he had traded with China even during the Cultural Revolution, and had continued to work with the Malaysian government in the 1970s during a time when many ethnic Chinese were being forced to sell out in favor of Malaysians. Kuok had excellent relations with both the prime ministers of Singapore and Malaysia, and was in one case even an intermediary between them in a potentially explosive case of a Malaysian businessman jailed in Singapore. Kuok also cultivated a close relationship with President Suharto in Indonesia, and was a friend and business partner of Liem Sioe Liong, Indonesia's wealthiest man. Kuok's extensive personal ties smoothed his business dealings, and he was able to invest and build across Asia despite troubling shifts in regimes.

Investments in China in the 1980s

Kuok began investing in China well before it became fashionable to do so. He had traded there for a long time in sugar, rice, and edible oils. In the early 1980s he bought property and built hotels in Beijing and in Shanghai and Shenzhen. He made a huge investment in 1984, committing to build the World Trade Centre in Beijing. The project was initially estimated to cost US$300 million, and probably cost $530 million to complete. Kuok planned to build the hotel, office, and convention center complex in a joint venture between Kerry Trading and China Foreign Economic and Trade Consultants. Kerry had a 49 percent stake, the Chinese company, 51 percent. The World Trade Centre was still not completed at the time of the Tiananmen massacre in June 1989. The brutal squelching of the prodemocracy movement led to the decay of many joint ventures in China. Kuok's Shangri-La hotels in China went empty in the aftermath of the crackdown. In spite of his own monetary loss, Kuok shovelled more money into the World Trade Centre, and conveyed his loyalty to the Chinese government. Perhaps because of this, Kuok enjoyed almost unprecedented ease in getting large projects okayed in China. He had built six hotels by 1993, invested in an oil refinery, and was buying up choice downtown acreage in a dozen Chinese cities. Kuok's companies, mostly in partnership with local Chinese companies, built apartment buildings, offices, and car parks, often clustered around a Shangri-La hotel. In 1995 Kuok entered a joint venture with an Australian company, CSR, which had a growing business in building materials in China.

Other Investments in the 1990s

The number of companies owned or controlled by Robert Kuok was estimated at more than 250 in 1986, and 10 years later there were even more. Many were owned by Kuok family members, and there were many joint ventures between separate Kuok companies. There was not a clear structure or hierarchy within the network of companies. Even the hotel chain, Shangri-La, was not all under a single ownership. Therefore it is easiest to explain the Kuok group's growth geographically and by industry, rather than by company. The Kuok empire grew even more geographically diverse by the 1990s. There were two Shangri-La hotels in Fiji, several more in Indonesia, a total of six across Malaysia by 1997, and now two in Singapore. In addition there was a Shangri-La hotel in Seoul, South Korea, and in Bangkok, Thailand. Kuok also began building a more modest chain of hotels, called Traders, that catered to business travelers rather than tourists. Kuok built Traders hotels in the Philippines, Singapore, and in Myanmar (Burma). His Shangri-La Hotels & Resorts, the hotel management company, also ran a hotel in Vancouver, Canada. Kuok's sugar, rice, and edible oil trading and manufacturing ventures sprawled across Malaysia, Indonesia, Vietnam, China, Hong Kong, Singapore, and Thailand by the late 1990s. There were many other diverse, smaller lines of business, for example a chain of cinemas in Singapore and a cigar manufacturer in the Philippines.

Kuok also invested significantly in media in Hong Kong in the 1990s. In 1993 he bought 35 percent of the *South China Morning Post,* Hong Kong's largest English-language daily newspaper. The paper was highly profitable, though sources quoted in a 1997 *Euromoney* profile of Kuok suggested that there may have been a motive beyond money. Kuok had close ties to the mainland Chinese government, and the *Euromoney* article surmised that Kuok made his investment in the influential newspaper in part in order to put the paper "in safe hands" (i.e., favorable to China) as the turnover of Hong Kong to China approached. Whatever the reason, Kuok also went on to invest in Hong Kong film, music, magazines, and television by purchasing large stakes in two media companies, Television Broadcasts (TVB) and TVE Holdings. TVE, a media conglomerate, and TVB, the largest producer of Chinese-language television programming in the world, were both controlled by a renowned Hong Kong film director, Sir Run Run Shaw. Kuok wrested control of TVE from Shaw in 1996 in an unprecedented hostile takeover.

Kuok's Kerry Group, the private Hong Kong company that later became Kerry Properties, took a step in a new direction in 1993 by winning the Coca-Cola franchise for much of mainland China. The company seems to have been chosen in large part for Robert Kuok's extensive business contacts in China, and Kerry Group's known ability to get large projects approved and built. Kerry Group took 87.5 percent and Coke the remaining 12.5 percent in the joint venture that was estimated to be worth billions. Then Kerry Group made a striking acquisition in 1996. It paid US$518 million for a 9.275 percent stake in Coca-Cola Amatil, an Australian company that was one of Coca-Cola's anchor bottlers and its most important bottler serving Asia. The investment gave a Kuok executive a seat on the Coca-Cola Amatil board, and consolidated Kerry Group's position as a major Coke distributor.

Recent Developments

Kerry Group went public in July 1996, and was listed on the Hang Seng index in Hong Kong. It changed its name to Kerry Properties, and it is now the leading public company in the Kuok group. Kerry Properties owned much of the land under and around the Chinese Shangri-La hotels, as well as many warehouses in Hong Kong and commercial and residential buildings and property in both Hong Kong and China. Kerry Properties was also involved in large construction projects such as the Western Harbour tunnel, which links Hong Kong Island to the West Kowloon expressway on the mainland. Kerry Properties also won a contract estimated at HK$12 billion to develop housing, offices, and shops on the rail corridor leading to a new airport. The newly public company retained Robert Kuok's two eldest sons on the board, as well as top executives from other Asian and Western companies. By going public and seeking foreign investors, Kerry Properties seemed to be readying itself to carry on even without the direct management of its founder, Robert Kuok, who turned 74 in 1997.

Kerry Properties announced in its initial public offering that it was explicitly interested in attracting foreign investors, and the company seemed to be stepping away from the close family control of many of Robert Kuok's companies. It seemed a lucrative investment for people looking to get in on the expanding China market, as the company had bought property years earlier and was now selling or developing it at high prices. Kerry's first announced six-month results were double that of the same period a year earlier, before its reorganization, and the company cheerfully expected record profits. It had many ongoing construction projects by 1997, including a 70 percent stake in a hydroelectric dam it was building in Benxi, China. The company also had an enviable portfolio of property. In 1997 Kerry derived considerable income from the sale and rental of units in office towers in Hong Kong and in mainland China, and from the sale of luxury townhouses. The company built two new godowns (warehouses) in 1997, giving the company a total of 4.4 million square feet of godown space in Hong Kong. The company had many projects in the works as well, such as a scheme to build three 50-story apartment towers in the city of Sham Tseng, and the expansion of facilities Kerry had a 25 percent interest in at the Shenzhen Kaifeng Terminal in mainland China. In August 1997 the company listed its profits for the six-month period ending June 30: up 189 percent from the same period a year earlier. With its valuable real estate portfolio and proven ability to carry out ambitious construction plans, Kerry seemed ready to bring in ever greater profits as long as China was growing and building.

Further Reading

Clifford, Mark L., and Nicole Harris, "Coke Pours into Asia," *Business Week,* October 28, 1996, p. 72.

Cottrell, Robert, "The Silent Empire of the Kuok Family," *Far Eastern Economic Review,* October 30, 1986, pp. 59–65.

Davies, Simon, "Shangri-La Asia in HKDollars 735m Flotation," *Financial Times,* May 28, 1993, p. 27.

Davies, Simon, and Kieran Cooke, "Secret Life of the Rich and Well-Connected," *Financial Times,* September 13, 1993, p. 22.

Holberton, Simon, "Kuok Sells Part of TVB Holding for HKDollars 1bn," *Financial Times,* September 3, 1994, p. 9.

Keenan, Faith, ''Kuok Vs. Shaw,'' *Far Eastern Economic Review,* March 28, 1996, p. 66.

''Kerry, Kuok in 228m Yuan Dam Venture,'' *Singapore Business Times,* February 18, 1997, p. 17.

Lucas, Louise, ''Kerry Properties Doubles Net,'' *Financial Times,* August 21, 1996, p. 22.

''Malaysia,'' *Forbes,* December 19, 1983, p. 120.

''The Private Life of Robert Kuok,'' *Euromoney Magazine,* February 15, 1997, pp. 92–95.

Ridding, John, ''Shangri-La Asia in HK$1.2 Billion Acquisition,'' *Financial Times,* August 14, 1997, p. 25.

——, ''South China Morning Post Ahead,'' *Financial Times,* September 15, 1997, p. 27.

——, ''Trading Halted in HK Media Groups,'' *Financial Times,* February 13, 1996, p. 31.

''Robert Kuok,'' *Forbes,* July 18, 1994, pp. 144–45.

''Robert Kuok,'' *Fortune,* December 28, 1981, p. 24.

''Room Service,'' *Economist,* June 1, 1996, pp. 62–63.

Tait, Nikki, ''Kuok and CSR in Construction Materials Deal,'' *Financial Times,* September 29, 1995, p. 27.

—— ''Kuok Group Takes 9% Holding in CCA,'' *Financial Times,* August 9, 1996, p. 19.

Tanzer, Andrew, ''The Amazing Mr. Kuok,'' *Forbes,* July 28, 1997, pp. 90–96.

—A. Woodward

Kitty Hawk, Inc.

1515 West 20th Street
DFW International Airport, Texas 75261
U.S.A.
(800) 654-8966
Fax: (972) 456-2298
Web site: http://www.kha.com

Public Company
Incorporated: 1985
Employees: 281
Sales: $164 million (1996)
Stock Exchanges: NASDAQ
SICs: 4522 Air Transportation, Nonscheduled; 4731 Arrangement Transport, Freight and Cargo; 6729 Holding Companies, Not Elsewhere Classified

Kitty Hawk, Inc. is a holding company that provides air freight and logistics charter services throughout the world. The company is a leader in the United States among on-demand air charter services and scheduled air cargo shipping firms. The expedited air forwarder operates from auxiliary airports, ensuring less traffic and thereby achieving faster response times. In fact, faster service is Kitty Hawk's hallmark. The company offers next-flight-out or same-day deliveries. Its average delivery time is three and one-half hours from the time a customer first places an order until final delivery. Kitty Hawk operates Kitty Hawk Air Cargo, Inc.; Kitty Hawk Systems, Inc., which designs and markets data systems using proprietary software; and Kitty Hawk Financial, which offers financial services to the aviation industry.

Tom Christopher's Business Takes Flight in 1970s

M. Tom Christopher, in sales for Burlington Northern Air Freight, started a little sideline business for himself in 1976. When one of his clients missed Burlington's last flight, Christopher, also a pilot, volunteered to fly the shipment of hydraulic hoses in his Beechcraft Baron. He only asked that the client pay for the gas.

Christopher continued these special flights while working full-time at Burlington for about two years. When he refused to share a $35,000 commission for flying explosives to Italy in 1978, Burlington executives were irritated; the vice-president of marketing dismissed Christopher, his top sales executive in the Dallas area. By that time, however, Christopher's sideline business was strong enough to support him. The former sales associate had so much business that he established his sideline as Christopher Charters, Inc. With only one airplane, Christopher contacted the charter companies listed in the local Yellow Pages to fly freight for his clients. By 1985, Christopher earned enough to purchase one of these charter companies, Dallas-based Kitty Hawk Airways, also in business since 1978.

Air Freight and Air Logistics Services

Christopher merged his company with the charter service to form the current Kitty Hawk in 1985. He then split Kitty Hawk into two divisions that contributed equally to the company's revenues. One division—Kitty Hawk Air Cargo—acted as an air charter logistics service that offered on-demand shipping and same-day delivery to high-profile clients such as General Motors, IBM, the *Wall Street Journal,* and medical firms. Kitty Hawk Air Cargo provided a high level of service to clients willing to pay a high price to overcome time constraints. ''We're an emergency business,'' Christopher explained in *Air Cargo World.* ''You call with an emergency, and we run out and immediately jump in the airplane and move the freight.'' Kitty Hawk Air Cargo typically transported its cargo 650 miles in three and one-half hours at a cost of $5,800 per shipment. Kitty Hawk Air Cargo was comprised of a fleet of 25 company-owned aircraft, as well as three leased aircraft. By 1997, Kitty Hawk flew as much as 40 percent of all on-demand cargo flights in the United States.

Kitty Hawk's second division—Kitty Hawk Charters, Inc.—offered logistics services using proprietary computer software. Basically, Kitty Hawk Charters transported freight for other carriers, including Burlington Air Express, DHK Airways, and Emery Worldwide. Kitty Hawk moved the freight using its own aircraft and crews; its clients only paid for fuel and operating expenses.

Company Perspectives:

The Kitty Hawk commitment to growth and quality begins with the company's Mission Statement: To be the standard of excellence, pursuing happiness for our employees and families, our suppliers, stockholders, and customers; outperforming in everything we do.

Excellent Customer Service

Christopher made pleasing customers a priority for Kitty Hawk. Kitty Hawk achieved a 99 percent on-time/reliability ratio for many of its customers. When the company flew for the U.S. Air Force's Log Air program—until the program ceased operations in 1992—Kitty Hawk maintained a 100 percent reliability ratio. It was the only service in the program to attain a perfect record while serving this important customer. According to the Kitty Hawk company overview, ''Service means being responsive, creative, and cost conscious. Excellent service creates a repeat customer and turns one-time engagements into long-term relationships. Kitty Hawk is known for delivering fair pricing and extraordinary quality service. This on-demand service philosophy has become the standard for all facets of the Kitty Hawk services. . . . One of the best records for performance and customer satisfaction in the scheduled cargo airline and air charter business belongs to Kitty Hawk.''

Kitty Hawk instituted a Total Quality Management (TQM) program in 1993 as an extension of its customer service philosophy. As the company's overview revealed: ''Kitty Hawk's leadership and its employees are excited about the current and long-term benefits of the formalized TQM program. The effects of this program and leadership's commitment to quality and excellence in serving its customers will flow throughout the organization and Kitty Hawk's customers will experience it in even greater measure than in the past.''

Kitty Hawk's dedication to service began to be recognized formally. The CEO Institute and the Caruth Institute of the Business School at Southern Methodist University named Kitty Hawk Dallas's sixth fastest growing company in 1993. That same year, the Entrepreneur Institute honored Christopher with the Entrepreneur of the Year Award in the service businesses category.

Christopher Wins When He Loses in 1990s

In 1993 Kitty Hawk won then lost a major Express Mail contract, but in so doing the company further proved the mettle of its leadership. Although Kitty Hawk lost the billion-dollar contract in a court challenge, it nevertheless received an $18.5 million settlement. Donna Steph Hansard, a writer for *Air Cargo World,* commented about Christopher: ''Any businessman who can walk away with $18.5 million in losing a contract, obviously knows how to manage a deal.''

Christopher once again demonstrated his business acumen in 1994. Kitty Hawk first considered a public offering of its stock that year, but a falling market prompted Christopher to rethink going public. Kitty Hawk stock at that time would not yield Christopher's price, so he postponed the company's initial public offering until 1996.

International Presence in the Mid-1990s

In the meantime, the company began building its business in intracontinental traffic. In 1995 Kitty Hawk secured its first international contract. The company flew a load of fish from some islands in Micronesia to Japan. Other contracts in the Pacific Rim, Europe, and South America followed. Though the company's aircraft did not fly freight between the continents, Kitty Hawk flights were busy within each continent. ''We see ourselves as domestic operators—whether that is domestic in North America, South America, Europe, or Asia,'' Christopher explained to *Air Cargo World* in 1997. ''We're not flying over big bodies of water, but we can be domestic in each continent. That is our uniqueness.''

Kitty Hawk also established an office at an airport in Pontiac, Michigan, a suburb of Detroit, in 1995. Eventually, the company situated warehouses at airports throughout the world to support the distribution of critical parts for its major clients such as General Motors, IBM, and other clients with high volumes and low margins.

Kitty Hawk as a Public Company

In 1996, Christopher launched the initial public offering of Kitty Hawk stock in order to grow the company's cargo business. Capital acquired from the sale of company stock was slated for the acquisition of new aircraft, particularly for the purchase of additional 727s. Creating a public company was part of Christopher's overall growth strategy, however, not just a demand for more capital. As Christopher explained in *Air Cargo World,* ''To grow at the rate we want[ed] to grow, while the banks were eager to lend us money, it seemed a nice balance to have that public shareholder out there. While the logistics division grows through pure sales efforts; the charter division grows through the acquisition of aircraft.''

In October Kitty Hawk offered stock at $12 per share. The price of stock quickly rose to $14 a share, then dropped to $8 in December. By May 1997, however, Kitty Hawk stock once again sold at $14 a share. In total, the initial sale of stock raised $30 million for the company. Christopher retained 65 percent of Kitty Hawk's stock, company employees owned five percent, and the remaining 30 percent went to public stockholders.

Expanding and Diversifying the Customer Base

Kitty Hawk's work to diversify its client base proved especially fruitful in 1996 when a strike at General Motors, one of the charter service's largest customers, stopped operations at the automaker. In a letter to stockholders, Christopher explained why broadening the company's customer base was critical: ''I believe our commitment to reliable, quality service pays off. The thousands of flights that we handle for the automotive industry represent a considerable amount of our business, but for more than two months in the fall of 1996, we received virtually no revenue from a key automotive customer because of strike-related plant shutdowns. In past years, this loss of revenue would have dealt us a very heavy blow. However, business from other customers enabled us to maintain our positive financial performance during the automotive strike.''

The year 1996 also marked Kitty Hawk's first U.S. Postal Service Christmas Network mail delivery contract. ''We lost a lot of sleep and a lot of sweat waiting for this award,'' Christopher revealed in *Air Cargo Report.* Upon earning the contract, Kitty Hawk delivered the U.S. mail to 25 cities from December 11 through December 24. Valued at $21 million, the contract accounted for about 15 percent of the company's annual revenue.

Consolidation, Acquisition and Expansion

Kitty Hawk moved to a 42,000-square-foot facility at the Dallas-Fort Worth International Airport. The company consolidated many of its operations into the new space, including melding Kitty Hawk Air Cargo with Kitty Hawk Charters. Sales, executive and corporate offices, and Kitty Hawk Systems also occupied space in the new facility, which included a large hangar and a flight operations area.

In 1997 Kitty Hawk's fleet was comprised of 30 aircraft—727s, DC-9s, and turbo prop Convairs. The company's fleet grew substantially in August of that year when Kitty Hawk purchased 16 Boeing 727s from the Kalitta Group for more than $50 million. The sale was part of an overall agreement to merge the large, privately held Kalitta Group companies into the smaller, public Kitty Hawk.

According to the *Air Cargo Report,* the merger was ''designed to capitalize on the strengths of both of the all-cargo carriers.'' Traditionally, the Kalitta Group, operators of passenger charters and cargo freight services, earned a reputation for its maintenance and equipment. These assets nicely complemented Kitty Hawk's dominance in high-tech marketing. The *Air Cargo Report* commented that the deal ''will combine the strengths of both companies and give the new entity a larger market share and 'more clout.' ''

Kitty Hawk absorbed Kalitta's American International Airways, Inc., American International Freight, American International Cargo, Kalitta Flying Service, Inc., Flight One Logistics, Inc., and OK Turbines, Inc. With the merger, Kitty Hawk operated 32 727s, five DC-9s, and eight Convairs. In return, Connie Kalitta, chairman and owner of the Kalitta Group, received cash, stock, and a management position. Above all, the Kalitta Group became a public company through the merger.

FAA Regulations for 727s

Despite the fact that in 15 years no 727 freight carriers ever crashed, in 1997 the Federal Aviation Administration (FAA) considered safety modifications for the aircraft in order to repair structural flaws near the main cargo door. The approximate cost of the repairs totaled between $3,000 and $5,000 per plane. The FAA also sought to limit the amount of freight flown on 727s, an edict that worked to Kitty Hawk's advantage. Since freight loads remained constant, more flights would be needed to move the same amount of cargo. At the time, industry analyst Helane Becker of Smith Barney observed in *Air Cargo World:* ''If the FAA limits the pounds that can be put on the aircraft [727s], the freight won't go away. It will simply result in more turns in aircraft. For Kitty Hawk, this could turn into a huge potential revenue benefit.''

With Kitty Hawk in control of the 727 situation, its position in the industry seemed secure in late 1997. In the future, Kitty Hawk planned to expand its services abroad, particularly in Europe and the Far East. The company also intended to augment its network of strategically placed warehouses to facilitate the delivery of critical parts for its clients. Given the FAA's favorable regulatory environment and the company's well-defined direction, Smith Barney's Becker declared in *Air Cargo World* in 1997 that ''we are very enthusiastic about Kitty Hawk's outlook and continued prospects.''

Principal Subsidiaries

Kitty Hawk Air Cargo, Inc.; Kitty Hawk Charters; Kitty Hawk Systems, Inc.; Kitty Hawk Financial.

Further Reading

''Contracts—Christmas Came Early for Kitty Hawk Air Cargo,'' *Air Cargo Report,* September 12, 1996.

Hansard, Donna Steph, ''Chartering New Paths in Logistics,'' *Air Cargo World,* June 1997, p. 42.

''Kitty Hawk Opens Office Near Detroit,'' *Air Cargo Report,* October 12, 1995.

''Kitty Hawk Set to Join Forces with Kalitta Group,'' *Air Cargo Report,* August 14, 1997.

—Charity Anne Dorgan

The Liberty Corporation

Box 789
Greenville, South Carolina 29602-0789
U.S.A.
(864) 609-8111
Fax: (864) 609-3120

Public Company
Incorporated: 1905 as Southeastern Life Insurance Company
Employees: 3,000
Total Assets: $3.06 billion (1996)
Stock Exchanges: New York
SICs: 6311 Life Insurance; 4833 Television Broadcasting; 6719 Holding Companies, Not Elsewhere Classified

The Liberty Corporation provides several types of insurance services and owns Cosmos Broadcasting, which operates television stations in several states. The company has been an important financial presence in South Carolina for most of the century.

Turn-of-the-Century Origins

Liberty Corporation's story begins in Spartanburg, South Carolina, in 1905 with the creation of the Southeastern Life Insurance Company, formed by insurance agent Elliott Estes and textile tycoon A. H. Twitchell. The company was steeped in support from the "sound, safe, conservative business element" (as the *Spartanburg Weekly Herald* described it), which contributed its first board of directors. Estes's old offices initially housed the company. John A. Law, a former banker, textile executive and one of the founding directors, bought the first policy, worth $5,000.

In spite of strong community and government support, within a few years Southeastern ran into serious trouble due to lax financial practices on the part of management (reckless investing, giving cash advances on commissions) and agents (accepting promissory notes as down payments on policies). After two years of takeover rumors, Estes resigned as shareholders initiated a reorganization in 1910 and named Arch Calvert to the top office.

Soon afterward, though, a group led by lumber executive T. Oregon Lawton bought out the company and relocated it to nearby Greenville. Within 10 years the more stringent management performed by Lawton's team increased the company's policies in force from just over $3 million to $18 million, while assets increased in value over six times, to $1.5 million. In 1915, Southeastern erected a new headquarters in downtown Greenville, topped with a giant illuminated Roman warrior.

Industrial Insurance Catches on After World War I

Textile mills in South Carolina made the fabric of life for the thousands who worked 11-hour days, shopped in mill-owned shops, and slept in mill-owned housing. As Doyle Boggs would record in Liberty's official history, the mills also gave the lower caste just enough money to become potential life insurance customers.

In this environment, W. Frank Hipp founded The Liberty Life Insurance Company in Greenville in 1919. He had just finished a two-year convalescence from tuberculosis by starting a successful business trading textile securities. The stern, practical Hipp had begun selling insurance for Southeastern in 1912 and before that had worked for Pacific Mutual Life. Hipp's venture was designed with the mill worker in mind. Premiums of even two or three cents would be collected on a weekly basis—a concept known as "industrial insurance."

In spite of the company's immediate success—it issued $1.7 million worth of new insurance in 1920—a rift developed between Hipp and his board of directors, who were keen on diversification. They were ousted, although the company began to offer ordinary life insurance in 1922. The same year, The Liberty Life was able to gain a small toehold at the other end of the state, in Charleston, by acquiring Home Life and Accident Insurance Company of Charleston.

Company Perspectives:

We are a company that always has been committed to meeting basic human needs: offering the financial security that strengthens family ties; providing the means to help people communicate with each other; and serving as a source for the capital that is so critical to the American promise of economic freedom and progress. This heritage has made our company a leader in its field, and it will continue to inspire Liberty's growth as we look ahead to the next century.

Prevailing Throughout a Perilous Depression in the 1930s

At Southeastern, Lawton resigned in 1924 and also started a new business, the Pioneer Life Insurance Company. W. O. Milford, a musician by training, took over as CEO. The company merged with Associated Life in 1929, part of the unstable financial empire of Rogers Clark Caldwell.

In 1929, Liberty was tallying $1 million in annual premium income in spite of severe hard times and labor unrest in the textile industry. The Independence Insurance Company was created to service extremely low income accounts. Liberty absorbed two struggling companies the next year, the Great American Life Insurance Company and People's Life.

Liberty began broadcasting in 1930, when it purchased the newly formed Columbia, South Carolina radio station WIS, whose call letters—derived from the slogan ''wonderful iodine state''—celebrated the region's unique mineral attributes. Hipp believed maintaining the station would garner positive regard for the insurance company though not necessarily earn any income on its own. Hipp invested heavily in equipment, hired promising people (including Godfrey Richard Shafto, the station's first manager and later one of the founders of Broadcast Music International, Inc.), and the venture proved profitable within months. WCSC radio, a subsequent Charleston acquisition, did not perform nearly as well out of the gate.

In 1931, The Liberty bought a controlling interest in Southeastern. The Bank of Tennessee was, like Associated Life, controlled by Caldwell, and when it failed most of Associate Life's subsidiaries went bankrupt. W. Frank Hipp rescued his old employer from receivership. Ten years later the two operations would be entirely integrated, although this process occurred, like a military campaign, in steps. The Southeastern's more traditional product line suffered heavily as numerous savings and loans institutions failed in the Great Depression, and Hipp executed a corporate coup, ousting both officers and employees and instituting a stricter financial regimen. In 1933, a common management scheme was worked out for the two separately operating companies, which were merged in 1941, the resulting company dropping the article ''The'' to become known simply as Liberty Life Insurance Company. The old Liberty Life's operations were continued under the name Surety Life Insurance Company.

A New Role After World War II

W. Frank Hipp died in 1943. After an interim filled by H. L. Vogel, his son Francis assumed the role of president. Less authoritarian than his father, he empowered trusted associates and exerted influence through carefully maintained relationships. In spite of the potential for instability inherent in the change of leadership and wartime austerity, Liberty managed to survive fairly well.

Its ranks full with demobilized veterans, Liberty increased its expansion into North Carolina after World War II. It focused more on long-term sales due to newfound postwar prosperity and the erosion of the mill system. The new approach was reinforced through vigorous training.

Liberty also expanded its radio broadcasting presence in North and South Carolina as it jockeyed for upcoming FCC television licenses. The Broadcasting Company of the South was created in 1950 to manage these operations and took in $718,236 the next year. Three years later, Liberty's first television station, NBC affiliate WIS-TV, began broadcasting from Columbia. The station was part-owned by Marseco Corporation.

In 1955, the company moved into an impressive new $2.5 million headquarters building. By then, an office in Atlanta had opened and Liberty agents scoured most of the Southeast. By the end of the decade, Liberty was insuring $1 billion worth of people and property and had just become computerized. The company had also lobbied effectively to manage industry regulation, calls for public health insurance, and the threat of heavier taxation.

The Broadcasting Company of the South changed its name to Cosmos Broadcasting Corporation after acquiring Toledo's WTOL-TV in 1965. Its five-year foray into cable broadcasting in the Charlotte area withered under FCC scrutiny. Soon after, though, Cosmos acquired another broadcasting jewel: WDSU-TV in New Orleans.

Insuring a Good Life in the 1960s and 1970s

A highly successful initial public offering took place in 1964. The Hipp family retained the majority of shares. In 1967 The Liberty Corporation holding company was formed and Liberty Life came under control of the parent; the next year both Cosmos and Surety Investment Company followed suit. However, a conceived merger with the South Carolina National Bank was squelched by pending federal antitrust legislation. The Liberty Corporation became the fourth South Carolina company to trade on the New York Stock Exchange in 1969 and a new subsidiary, Liberty Properties, Inc., the successor to Surety Investments, was organized to manage the real estate portfolio. Liberty Properties did not fare well in the next few years of recession and increasing construction costs.

Herman Hipp, former president of the Liberty Life subsidiary, became president and CEO of The Liberty Corporation in 1977. The next year, he merged Liberty Properties into Liberty Life. A $1 million ''Have a Good Life'' health promotion campaign was launched to enhance the company's image and to combat growing public suspicion regarding the life insurance industry.

Cosmos began buying radio stations again in 1979 with the purchase of Sarasota's WQSR-FM. It also bought Orion Broadcasting, which owned several television and radio stations in the Midwest, for $73 million.

W. Hayne Hipp succeeded Herman Hipp as Liberty Corporation president and CEO only two years into the latter's tenure. The Liberty Corporation bought United Fidelity of Texas and then sold it in 1982 for $70 million, nearly twice its purchase price. The company gained new management perspectives during the acquisition. At the same time, it upgraded its computer and training technology.

A new headquarters was completed in 1982; it would also house Cosmos Broadcasting which had previously been located in Columbia. By the mid-1980s, Liberty Life had $10 billion in policies in force. Cosmos owned ten radio and TV stations scattered from Toledo to Sarasota. Liberty Properties Group had been able to divest itself of its poorly-performing vacation home developments and concentrate on more viable residential and commercial opportunities.

Anticipating the Needs of a New Century

Liberty entered the pre-need market via the acquisition of several companies beginning in 1992: Pierce National Life (which had Canadian operations), Estate Assurance Company, American Funeral Assurance Company, and North American National Corporation, which owned Pan-Western Life Insurance Company, Howard Life Insurance Company, and Brookings International Life Insurance Company. All of these operations were merged into Pierce National by 1995. Two other Louisiana-based providers of home service insurance were also acquired in the mid-1990s: Magnolia Financial Corporation and State National Capital Corporation.

CableVantage was formed in 1994 in order to promote cable television advertising. The company had sold all of its radio stations in the 1980s. Liberty Corporation focused on building its strengths in the mid-1990s under the leadership of Hayne Hipp, who assumed the position upon the death of his father in July 1995. Two years later, the company sold $70 million worth of office and industrial property to Liberty Property Trust, an unrelated company based in Malvern, Pennsylvania.

Liberty Corporation also proved successful in administering insurance policies for other companies. Liberty Insurance Services (LIS) was created in 1992 and became one of the top life TPAs (Third Party Administration firms) in the country, with over 700,000 policies under administration for external client companies. LIS also serviced over three million policies for Liberty Corporation subsidiaries.

After special charges, The Liberty Corporation earned $37 million on 1996 revenues of $619 million. The company had $20 billion worth of policies in force; insurance revenues were $482 million. Seventy-seven percent of Liberty Life's revenues were in life insurance. Total broadcasting revenues were $137 million in 1996.

Liberty Corporation has had sufficient capital and skills to meet various challenges throughout the century. Its brand of cautious innovation (a function of its ownership, according to Hayne Hipp) and concentration on key areas of expertise seemed likely to assure it an equally successful future.

Principal Subsidiaries

Liberty Life Insurance Co.; Pierce National Life Insurance Co.; Liberty Insurance Services Corp.; Cosmos Broadcasting Corp.

Principal Divisions

Insurance Marketing; Insurance Services; Television Broadcasting.

Further Reading

Boggs, Doyle, *The Liberty Spirit,* Greenville, S.C.: The Liberty Corporation, 1986.

Golden Anniversary History, Greenville, S.C.: Liberty Life Insurance Company, 1955.

Harney, Kenneth, "Fannie Mae Scuttles Mortgage Life Proposal," *Newsday,* August 1, 1997, p. D2.

Hendrix, Lee Corley, *Hipp Family History and Genealogy,* 1978.

Hipp, Francis M., "Liberty Corporation," Greenville, S.C.: Newcomen Society of North America, 1981.

"Liberty Sells 18 Properties for $17 Million," *Greenville News,* June 3, 1997, p. 6D.

Little, Loyd, "Liberty Continues to Stake New Ground," *Greenville News,* March 28, 1993, p. G1.

Roberts, John, "Liberty Corp. Venture to Create 75 Jobs," *Greenville News,* January 1, 1996, p. 6D.

——, "Things Are Looking Up at Liberty," *Greenville News,* February 25, 1996, p. G4.

Williamson, Miryam, "Brain Hunt," *Computerworld,* June 30, 1997, p. 77.

—Frederick C. Ingram

LLOYD'S

LLOYD'S OF LONDON

Lloyd's of London

1 Lime Street
London EC3M 7HA
United Kingdom
+44 (171) 623-7100
Fax: +44 (171) 626-2389
Web site: http://www.lloydsoflondon.co.uk

Wholly Owned Society of Corporation of Lloyd's
Incorporated: 1871 as Society of Lloyd's
Employees: 2,042
Total Assets:£27.3 billion (1995)
SICs: 6411 Insurance Agents, Brokers & Service

Perhaps the world's most famous insurance group, Lloyd's of London is a uniquely organized insurance market. It does not sell insurance per se, but regulates a market through which insurance contracts are transacted. The organization is a society of individuals—and, since 1994, corporations—that accept liability for claims under insurances accepted on their behalf. Business can be placed only by approved insurance brokers, known as Lloyd's brokers, which are in turn grouped in 164 underwriting syndicates. One person, the active underwriter, is empowered to accept insurances on behalf of the syndicate members. A syndicate is not a partnership: each member is liable only for a personal fraction of any insurance. Each syndicate has a managing agency which appoints the active underwriter. The membership of a syndicate varies from year to year. Each member's affairs at Lloyd's are managed by a member's agent. What began simply as a meeting place for persons interested in marine insurance has evolved into a regulated market for general insurance all over the world.

Over the course of its more than three centuries in business, this unique group has brokered policies for the routine—it is Great Britain's leading automotive insurer—as well as the weird. Unusual contracts written at Lloyd's have included: a food critic who insured his taste buds for £250,000; a comedy troupe that took out a policy to cover the risk that an audience might die laughing; and rock star Bruce Springsteen, who insured his voice for £3.5 million. Though the group's most famous claim is probably the sinking of the *Titanic* in 1912, numerous and massive claims in the late 1980s and early 1990s threatened to "sink" the venerable Lloyd's.

Prompted by aggregate losses of more than £7.9 billion (US$12.4 billion) from 1988 through 1992, Lloyd's was compelled to reform some long-held precepts. For over three hundred years, individual underwriting members, called Names, accepted unlimited personal liability for the policies they signed. Facing a lawsuit that eventually cost the group more than £3 billion, Lloyd's formally inaugurated limited individual liability in 1993. That year's creation of Equitas, a separate reinsurer to assume all of Lloyd's pre-1993 liabilities, appeared to set Lloyd's back on the trail to consistent profitability. The market achieved total net income of over £2 billion in 1993 and 1994.

Origins As 17th-Century Coffeehouse

In the 1680s Edward Lloyd opened a coffeehouse in Tower Street, London, near the docks. He sought to attract a clientele of persons connected with shipping and in particular marine underwriters, those willing to transact marine insurance. By 1689 he was well established. In 1691 his coffeehouse moved to Lombard Street. Lloyd provided shipping intelligence. After his death in 1713 the business was carried on by a succession of masters. From 1734 the business published *Lloyd's List,* a newspaper featuring shipping news. The paper still appears daily.

In the early 18th century Lloyd's became the main, though not the only, place where marine underwriters congregated. The Bubble Act of 1720 gave two newly formed corporations, The London Assurance and The Royal Exchange Assurance, the exclusive right to transact marine insurance as corporations, but expressly allowed individual private underwriters to continue operating. The two corporations exercised the utmost caution and took only a fraction of the growing market, leaving scope for private underwriters. Some of these were also willing to effect gambling insurances, where the policyholder did not stand to lose financially if the event insured against occurred, that is, he had no insurable interest. Such insurances on ships

Company Perspectives:

Lloyd's is one of the world's oldest and most established international insurance and reinsurance markets, transacting business worth billions of pounds in premiums every year. It is not an insurance company but a competitive market where individual underwriters accept risks on behalf of some 164 syndicates of individual and corporate members whose resources provide the security behind Lloyd's policies. Lloyd's is a broker market. Business comes into the market through Lloyd's brokers who bring business from clients and other brokers and intermediaries from all over the world.

and cargoes were forbidden by an Act of 1745 but persisted on lives and specific events.

In 1769 some underwriters who disapproved of gambling insurances broke away. They persuaded a Lloyd's waiter, Thomas Fielding, to open a New Lloyd's Coffee House which, in five years, drove the old one out of business. The new Lloyd's became cramped. In 1771 nine merchants, underwriters, and brokers formed a committee which took over the premises and appointed two masters to run them. Lloyd's moved into the Royal Exchange in 1773. By the Life Assurance Act, 1774, Parliament prohibited gambling insurance on lives, thus vindicating the stand of those who had reorganized Lloyd's.

In 1779 Lloyd's had only 179 subscribers. These enjoyed the sole right of entry to the underwriting room at Lloyd's. The wars with France from 1792 to 1815 brought great prosperity for marine insurers, among them John Julius Angerstein, an underwriter and broker who served as chairman in 1786, from 1790 to 1796, and again in 1806. At the height of the wars the number of subscribers rose to over 2,000.

Lloyd's Membership Declines in Early 19th Century

British entrepreneurs chafed at the law against new marine insurance companies. In 1824 the Bubble Act was at last repealed, but peace had signaled a decline in marine insurance. The number of subscribers fell from 2,150 in 1814 to 953 in 1843. In 1846, to raise money, a higher subscription was imposed on those subscribers who underwrote insurances and only 189 paid. In 1844, the committee of Lloyd's abolished the office of the masters and assumed full responsibility, through its secretary, for administering the market.

In 1848 Captain G.A. Halsted of the Royal Navy was appointed secretary, a post he held for 20 years. From 1850 Lloyd's began to appoint politically prestigious persons from outside its own community to the chairmanship. The most notable was G. J. Goschen, a young liberal member of Parliament who later became chancellor of the exchequer. He was chairman from 1869 to 1886 and again from 1893 to 1901. After 1901 Lloyd's reverted to having chairmen who worked in the market.

During the first half of the 19th century the committee was largely concerned with intelligence-gathering for the benefit of Lloyd's members. Beginning in 1811 it appointed firms and persons in ports throughout the world to provide shipping information. By 1829 there were over 350 Lloyd's Agents, as they were called. Lloyd's Agents receive no remuneration except for services rendered to underwriters such as surveying damaged property. They could, however, hope for some commercial advantage from their association with Lloyd's.

Marine underwriters have always felt the need for information about ship construction. As early as 1760 they formed a registration society which published a book of details of ships for the use of subscribers only. In 1798 shipowners began publishing a similar book. In 1834 the two publications were merged to form Lloyd's Register of Shipping, administered by a committee representing shipowners, merchants, and marine underwriters. The register operates as a corporation separate from Lloyd's.

The provision of intelligence loomed large in the work of Henry Hozier, who was secretary from 1874 to 1906. In addition to strengthening Lloyd's' central staff, he saw the desirability of getting information promptly, and set up coastal telegraph stations for that purpose. By 1884 Lloyd's had 17 stations at home and six abroad. They worked in cooperation with the Admiralty. Hozier was knighted. He was a pioneer of wireless telegraphy which Lloyd's used early in the 20th century.

Incorporation in 1871

For much of the 19th century the committee exercised little power over its underwriting members. Lloyd's remained a loosely run club. Not until 1851 did a general meeting resolve that any member becoming bankrupt should forfeit his membership. Legislation was sought to strengthen the committee's powers. The Lloyd's Act, 1871, made Lloyd's a corporation, the Society of Lloyd's. The objectives of the society were stated as the carrying on of marine insurance by members and the collection and publication of intelligence. At that time Lloyd's' participation in non-marine insurance was negligible and the Act made no reference to it or, indeed, to insurance brokers.

Between 1849 and 1870 the underwriting membership of Lloyd's had doubled. The committee became increasingly concerned to see that applicants for membership had the necessary means to support their underwriting. From 1856, in a few cases, guarantees or deposits were required, but it was not until 1882 that they became mandatory. Even then they related only to marine insurance.

After 1871 the volume of non-marine insurance became significant. Its growth was largely due to the efforts of C. E. Heath, an underwriter who began his own business in 1881. Besides transacting fire insurance he pioneered new forms such as all risks insurance on property on land, and on household burglary. C. E. Heath underwrote on behalf of a syndicate which in 1887 comprised 15 Names.

The years 1875 to 1900 saw the accelerating development of Lloyd's in two respects. Thanks to the activities of Lloyd's brokers, much business began to reach Lloyd's from the United States and other overseas sources. Reinsurance, that is, the acceptance of liabilities assumed by direct insurers under their own policies, came to be transacted at Lloyd's, which pioneered novel forms of reinsurance contracts.

Standards Set Under Heath in Early 20th Century

In 1908, at Heath's prompting, Lloyd's took steps towards tightening security under Lloyd's' policies. A general meeting agreed that all underwriters should provide certificates of solvency from approved auditors and that premiums be held in trust accounts for the payment of claims. This had beneficial effects in the following year. The Assurance Companies Act, passed in 1909, which for the first time imposed a measure of regulation on companies transacting the main classes of general insurance, left to the Corporation of Lloyd's the primary responsibility for regulating Lloyd's underwriters, as did subsequent regulatory Acts.

World War I affected Lloyd's favorably, creating a large demand for war-risk coverage at high premiums. The state took 80 percent of the war risk on ships, leaving 20 percent to private underwriters. The state also insured cargoes at sea at fixed rates, leaving underwriters free to offer lower rates for any business they wanted. They made large profits on the desirable cargo business while the state was losing money on the residue. Insurance of war risk on property on land was left to private enterprise for three years. Lloyd's took the lead in providing coverage where most insurance companies were unwilling to do so. The business proved profitable.

At Lloyd's, all policies were prepared by brokers who then had to take them to the underwriting room for signature on behalf of all the syndicates concerned, a tedious process. In 1916, to save clerical labor, the committee sanctioned an optional system whereby policies could be signed on behalf of all the underwriters concerned in a new bureau, Lloyd's Policy Signing Bureau. In 1924 use of the bureau, renamed Lloyd's Policy Signing Office, became mandatory.

The first quarter of the 20th century saw the development of three new classes of insurance—motor, aviation, and credit. Credit insurance involved a guarantee that monies due would be paid. In 1923, one syndicate transacting this business failed through reckless underwriting. The committee of Lloyd's banned future direct insurance by way of financial guarantees but allowed reinsurance of such business to continue.

The reputation of Lloyd's depends on claims being met by underwriters. Some underwriting syndicates may fail through dishonesty or poor underwriting. In 1927 Lloyd's set up a central fund, financed by a continuing small levy on premiums. This fund is held in trust for the benefit of policyholders whose claims are not met.

In World War II Lloyd's again prospered although war risks were undertaken by the government. Special arrangements had to be made to protect Lloyd's' U.S. business. Lloyd's established a U.S. trust fund into which all premiums in U.S. dollars had to be paid and held for the benefit of policyholders.

The first half of the 20th century was a profitable time for Lloyd's. Its underwriters proved themselves more flexible than insurance companies. They identified risks overcharged by company cartel rates and, by selective underwriting, skimmed the cream of the business. Large insurances had to be shared among many individual underwriters. The increasing size of insurances led to a growth in the size of syndicates. In 1890 a syndicate with ten Names was exceptional. By 1952 there were 16 syndicates with 100 Names or more. The largest had more than 300 Names. Large syndicates developed for motor insurance, of which Lloyd's had no more than five percent of the £100 million market in 1950.

The growth of Lloyd's had three consequences. Firstly, the need for further underwriting capacity started a hunt for new Names to provide the capital required. Brokers were well placed to find people. They also organized underwriting syndicates. A number called underwriting agents acted as both members' agents and managing agents. Secondly, the various interests at Lloyd's formed market associations to deal collectively with the problems they encountered. Marine underwriters formed their own association within Lloyd's in 1909. An association for fire and accident—non-marine—underwriters was formed in 1910 and Lloyd's Insurance Brokers' Association was founded. Though underwriters at Lloyd's wrote the group's first auto policy in 1901—it was a marine policy that purported the vehicle to be ''a ship navigating on dry land''—Lloyd's Motor Underwriters' Association was not formed until 1931. Lloyd's Aviation Underwriters' Association dates from 1935. Thirdly, pressure on space at the Royal Exchange became acute. In 1928 Lloyd's moved out to specially built premises in Leadenhall Street.

Rapid Growth in Postwar Era

The years since 1950 saw the most spectacular growth at Lloyd's. In 1957 a further building had to be opened on an adjoining site across Lime Street. In 1983 the old Leadenhall Street building was demolished and Lloyd's commissioned a new structure, designed by Richard Rogers, for the site. This was opened in 1986, the Lime Street building being retained. Meanwhile much work had been transferred to out-stations at Chatham and Colchester.

Between 1952 and 1968 the membership of Lloyd's nearly doubled, from 3,157 to 6,052. In considering how to increase underwriting capacity, Lloyd's appointed a working party under the chairmanship of the Earl of Cromer. Meanwhile, in 1969, membership, hitherto confined to the commonwealth, was opened to nationals of all countries. Eligibility was extended to British women in 1970. It was not until 1972 that women were admitted to the underwriting room.

The Cromer working party issued its report in 1970. It favored the admission of corporations as members, but this recommendation was not adopted. However, thanks to the profitability of Lloyd's, membership again rose steeply, reaching 20,145 in 1982 and 33,532 in 1988, although by 1990 it had fallen to 28,770.

One growth area since 1950 has been U.K. motor insurance. Lloyd's holds one-sixth of the market, thanks partly to a modification of Lloyd's' normal procedure which required all business to be transacted in the underwriting room. Since 1965, Lloyd's has allowed motor syndicates to deal directly with non-Lloyd's intermediaries if they are sponsored by a Lloyd's broker. Motor syndicates therefore can operate as if they were insurance companies.

About half of Lloyd's' business is derived from the United States. U.S. insurance brokers have cast envious eyes on Lloyd's brokers who alone have access to Lloyd's and therefore receive commissions on all business placed there. The big Lloyd's brokers found themselves exposed to takeover overtures from their U.S. counterparts. In 1979 Marsh & McLennan, the largest U.S. broker, acquired C.T. Bowring. In 1982 Alexander & Alexander acquired Alexander Howden. Since 1982 two Lloyd's brokers have acquired two large U.S. brokers: Sedgwick took over Fred S. James and Willis Faber merged with Corroon & Black.

In a market such as Lloyd's, where hundreds of enterprises competed from time to time, unsatisfactory situations arise. One such event was the affair of the Sasse syndicate in 1976. Its active underwriter authorized an underwriting firm in New York to write business on his syndicate's behalf. The firm transacted a large volume of bad business which led to heavy losses. The Sasse syndicate exceeded the premium income it was authorized to write. Some members of the syndicate, faced with heavy calls, sued Lloyd's, alleging that losses arose from a failure to supervise. It became apparent that the machinery of Lloyd's was not working properly. In 1979 the committee appointed a working party under the chairmanship of Sir Henry Fisher to examine self-regulation at Lloyd's. The working party reported in 1980. It made 79 recommendations for improvements. Apart from a general tightening up, the working party recommended a new governing body with wider powers. It drew attention to the growing influence of the big brokers. In 1978 the six largest brokerage groups had placed more than half of Lloyd's' business and the proportion was growing.

Record Profits in 1980s Give Way to Unprecedented Losses in 1990s

Lloyd's accepted the main recommendations and sought legislative powers to bring them into effect. The result was the Lloyd's Act of 1982. This act put a new body, the Council of Lloyd's, over the committee, which had consisted of 16 persons, mainly underwriters, active in the Lloyd's market. The council was to include, in addition to the 16 committee members, eight representatives of the Names not working in the market—external members—and three nominated persons not members of Lloyd's. At the prompting of the governor of the Bank of England, prominent accountant Ian Hay Davison was appointed chief executive and became a nominated person and one of three deputy chairmen of Lloyd's. The Act also provided for the separation of brokers and managing agents. They were to divest themselves of financial interests in each other. The separation was achieved by 1987.

At about the time of the Act, scandals erupted involving two leading broker groups. Large amounts of premiums had been siphoned off from some profitable syndicates by means of reinsurance with companies in which the chairmen and other directors of the groups had a financial interest. The reverberations of these events continued for some years with expulsions and suspensions, but none involved any loss to policyholders as distinct from Names. Lloyd's' premium income did not suffer. The council made determined efforts to stamp out internal abuses.

In 1986 the government appointed the Neill Committee to consider whether those who participated at Lloyd's as Names had protection comparable to that provided for investors under the Financial Services Act of 1986. The following year the committee reported a number of shortcomings and made 70 recommendations for remedy. They included an amendment to the constitution of the council by which it would consist of 12 working members of Lloyd's, eight representatives of external members, and eight nominated members from outside Lloyd's, including the chief executive, so that the working members would be in the minority. The council accepted the recommendations beginning with the change to its membership. In three years most of the other changes were implemented.

Lloyd's appeared to be on a roll in the 1980s, chalking up record net income in 1986 and attracting thousands of nouveau riche to swell the ranks of Names to a high of 32,433 in 1988. But that veneer of success was shattered in the late 1980s, when a string of large claims brought massive losses to bear on the 300-year-old institution. Claims stemming from marine disasters such as the 1988 explosion of the *Piper Alpha* oil rig and the 1989 Exxon *Valdez* oil spill combined with natural disasters including the San Francisco earthquake and Hurricane Hugo, both in 1989. Final accounting for 1988 (which was not reported until 1991 due to a three-year lag in Lloyd's financial reporting cycle) revealed a net loss of £509 million, Lloyd's first shortfall in more than two decades. At the same time, Lloyd's United States operations were hit with retrospective liability for disability caused by asbestosis and for pollution damage. Faced with personal financial ruin, thousands of Names refused to honor their debts, instead launching preemptive lawsuits against Lloyd's for recourse. Thousands more Names resigned, shrinking Lloyd's membership to less than 10,000 by 1997; three even committed suicide. With individual and syndicate failures mounting, Lloyd's racked up five consecutive losses totaling £7.9 billion (US$12.4 billion) from 1988 through 1992.

The crisis compelled extraordinary, heretofore unthinkable changes at Lloyd's. Guided by former broker Chairman David Rowland, several reforms were set in motion in 1993. For the first time in its history, Lloyd's permitted corporate and institutional investors to underwrite policies. The first corporate members joined the organization in 1994. In a revolutionary departure from the long-held principle of unlimited liability, Lloyd's restricted individual Names' financial obligations to 80 percent of premium income, with excess losses reverting to a reserve funded by annual membership dues. It created a reinsurer, dubbed Equitas in 1994, to assume all liabilities incurred by Lloyd's prior to 1993. The new entity was funded by £859 million levied on Lloyd's' remaining members. In 1996, Lloyd's adopted annual accounting and achieved a £3.1 billion settlement with litigants.

In spite of the obstacles it encountered in the late 1980s and early 1990s, Lloyd's remained the largest and most innovative insurance market in the world. In fact, its overall assets increased from £17.9 billion in 1990 to £27.3 billion in 1995. Lloyd's returned to profitability in 1993, recording net income of £1.1 billion that year and a preliminary profit of £1 billion in 1994 as well.

Principal Subsidiaries

Additional Securities Ltd.; Lloyd's of London Press Ltd.

Further Reading

Brown, Antony, *Hazard Unlimited,* Colchester: Lloyd's of London Press, 1987.
Cockerell, Hugh, *Lloyd's of London, a Portrait,* Cambridge: Woodhead-Faulkner, 1984.
Davison, Ian Hay, *A View of the Room: Lloyd's Change and Disclosure,* London: Weidenfeld and Nicolson, 1987.
England, Robert Stowe, "At the Brink: Facing Unpaid Debts Close to $1.7 Billion, Lloyd's of London Fights for Its Life," *Financial World,* November 21, 1995, pp. 70–72.
Flower, Raymond, and Michael Wynn Jones, *Lloyd's of London: An Illustrated History,* Colchester: Lloyd's of London Press, 1981.
The Future of Lloyd's and the London Insurance Market, New York: Practicing Law Institute, 1992.
Gibb, D. E. W., *Lloyd's of London: A Study in Individualism,* London: Macmillan, 1957.
Gunn, Cathy, *Nightmare on Lime Street: Whatever Happened to Lloyd's of London?* London: Smith Gryphon Publishers, 1993.
Hodgson, Godfrey, *Lloyd's of London: A Reputation at Risk,* London: Penguin Books, 1986.
"Leaking at the Seams," *Economist,* January 26, 1991, pp. 69–70.
Lloyd's of London: A New World of Capital—Is The Genie Out of the Bottle? Hartford, Conn.: Conning & Co., 1996.
Pitt, William, "An Outsider's Insider Tackles the Mess at Lloyd's," *Institutional Investor,* February 1993, pp. 143–145.
Proctor, Patrick, *For Whom the Bell Tolls,* Harlow: Matching Press, 1996.
Raphael, Adam, *Ultimate Risk,* London: Corgi Books, 1995.
Self Regulation at Lloyd's: Report of the Fisher Working Party, London: Lloyd's of London, 1980.
Regulatory Arrangements at Lloyd's: Report of the Committee of Enquiry (Neill Report), London: HMSO, 1987.
White, Patrick, *Lloyd's: Post Reconstruction and Renewal,* London: FT Financial Publishing, 1997.
Wright, Charles, and C. E. Fayle, *A History of Lloyd's from the Founding of Lloyd's Coffee House to the Present Day,* London: Macmillan, 1928.

—Hugh Cockerell
—updated by April Dougal Gasbarre

Lojas Arapuã S.A.

Rua Sergipe, 475
São Paulo SP 01243-912
Brazil
+55 (11) 256-1155
Fax: +55 (11) 258-8320
Web site: http://www.arapua.com.br

Public Company
Incorporated: 1957
Employees: 6,700
Sales: Cr2.2 billion (US$2.2 billion) (1996)
Stock Exchanges: São Paulo Rio de Janeiro
SICs: 5722 Household Appliance Stores; 5731 Radio, TV, & Electronic Stores

With an estimated 16 percent of the Brazilian market for durable consumer goods, Lojas Arapuã S.A. is that nation's largest retailer of household appliances and electronics. The company has more than 260 stores and six distribution centers throughout Brazil. Most are concentrated in the populous southeast, but the chain has units in all but four of Brazil's 26 states. Creative financing programs and heavy advertising helped Arapuã rise to its industry-leading status. In 1996, over two-thirds of the chain's sales revenues were made through consumer finance programs.

Though its stock is publicly traded, the chain is controlled by the Fenicia Group through its Simeira Comercio e Industria Ltda. subsidiary. Arapuã accounts for about two-thirds of Fenicia's revenues. Fenicia's other interests include food processing, financing, and civil construction. Arapuã markets a wide variety of household appliances and electronics. In its ongoing quest to keep pace with the demands of the Brazilian consumer, the company introduced personal computer equipment to the lineup in 1996. Lojas Arapuã also offered the Lotus line, an in-house brand of such small appliances as coffee makers, juicers, blenders and mixers, steam irons, and hair dryers. Longtime chairman Jorge Jacob took the company public on Brazilian stock exchanges in 1995. The company began selling American Depository Receipts, or ADRs, the following year.

Mid-20th-Century Origins

The Arapuã saga is a rags-to-riches tale that reflects the upward mobility of a nation as well as a family. It opens in the 1940s with the Jacobs, a family of second-generation immigrants who had moved from the Middle Eastern nation of Lebanon to South America's Brazil in the early 20th century. They ran a textiles shop in the small town of Lins, about 200 miles inland from the city of São Paulo. Tragedy befell the family when both parents died in 1950, leaving the business to 16-year-old Jorge Wilson Simeira Jacob. Although as a minor he was banned from many legal functions, Jacob continued to operate the shop.

At this time, Brazil was entering a period of democratization, modernization, and rapid industrial growth. The virtual dictatorship of Getzlio Vargas was supplanted by democratic elections after 1945. Under the presidency of Juscelino Kubitschek de Oliveira from 1956 to 1961, Brazil's gross national product mounted by over six percent each year as the government made large investments in infrastructure. The 23-year-old Jacob was not one to be left behind in this era of growth. In 1957, he diversified into household appliances, adding the types of modern conveniences that by this time were commonplace in American homes: clothes washers, refrigerators, stoves, and even toys, furniture, and clothing—virtually anything an upwardly mobile Brazilian might want. It was at this time that he changed the store's name to Lojas Arapuã, the "lively bird shop." That same year Jacobs established the company's second retail outlet in the city of Araçatuba, about 50 miles inland from Lins.

However, there was an important caveat to this period of rapid economic expansion; government spending was largely financed through borrowing. During the Kubitschek administration the nation's foreign debt doubled and the cost of living tripled, yet most people's standard of living worsened. Perhaps most importantly, the government's policies set off rampant inflation, ranging as high as 2,000 percent per year at its worst. Ironically, high inflation had an important effect on consumerism as it related to Arapuã. It discouraged saving and encouraged spending; instead of watching their money lose value on a daily basis in a savings account, Brazilians hurried to "invest" their earnings in affordable items that had intrinsic value. Appliances fit the bill perfectly.

Company Perspectives:

Lojas Arapuã S.A. is the only specialty retailer of household appliances and consumer electronics in Brazil and one of the largest in terms of sales. Arapuã's sales mix is divided into ten main lines: televisions, refrigerators, audio equipment, VCRs, stoves, freezers, washing machines, microwaves, portable appliances and home office products, including personal computers and printing machines.

Pioneering Consumer Credit in the 1960s

Jacobs's timing proved prescient when Brazil came under military rule in 1964, ushering in an era of economic planning dubbed ''the Brazilian miracle.'' Under the administration of Castelo Branco from 1964 to 1966, the country enjoyed rising standards of living, low inflation, and economic expansion. This economic trend endured a series of political crises into the early 1970s. With increased real incomes came demand for modern conveniences, and Lojas Arapuã was there to fulfill this need.

For the many whose expectations were higher than their incomes, Jacob pioneered consumer credit in 1967. That year, he acquired Fenícia S.A. and was authorized by the Central Bank of Brazil to finance purchases in his stores. The move heralded a new era for Arapuã and its customers. Jacob tailored his financing programs to fit the needs of Brazil's working poor, offering lengthy payoff periods of up to two-and-a-half years and correspondingly low monthly payments. He made it even easier in the mid-1990s, revising the credit policy so that the monthly payment did not amount to more than one-fifth of a client's monthly net earnings. At that time, most of Arapuã's customers made less than Cr500 per month. Of course, Jacob was not motivated entirely by magnanimity to his clients; interest on their debts averaged 72 percent annually in 1996, adding a second layer of profit to Arapuã's margin.

A majority of Arapuã's customers took advantage of the credit program, and the finance operation soon gained precedence over the appliance chain. Jacob eventually reorganized his company, with Fenicia as the parent company and Lojas Arapuã its key subsidiary. Over the years, Fenicia invested in food processing, construction, and other interests, but Lojas Arapuã continued to account for most of the group's sales and profits. The chain boasted more than 50 stores by 1974. An expansion into Brazil's northwest region brought the store count to nearly 140 by 1980. Acquisitions added stores in Rio de Janeiro and other southern states mid-decade.

Evolution into High-Tech Niche Marketer in 1990s

Jacob's success did not bring complacency, however. In the late 1980s, he made a pilgrimage to that holy land of consumerism, the United States. Seeking enlightenment he visited Circuit City and Best Buy. Within days Jacob had embraced the tenets of niche marketing, and hurried home to spread the gospel. With his nephew and heir apparent Ricardo Jacob, Arapuã's CEO, the chairman set a reorganization in motion in 1989, stripping his stores of about one-fourth of their product lines, leaving only appliances and electronics. The Jacobs also dumped over 85 percent of their suppliers, thereby streamlining procurement. Jorge Jacob told *Forbes* magazine's Kerry A. Dolan that his competitors thought his changes were ''crazy.''

In keeping with the Arapuã slogan, ''Tuned in on you,'' consumer electronics, including televisions, VCRs, and audio equipment, generated over 40 percent of Arapuã's sales volume in the mid-1990s. These were followed by white goods—refrigerators, stoves, and washing machines—which contributed about one-third of revenues. The company's own Lotus brand of such small appliances as hair dryers, blenders, and steam irons added 22 percent of sales. Launched in 200 stores by the end of 1996, personal computers and peripherals accounted for a less than five percent of sales that year. The chain hoped to market PCs in all its stores by the end of 1997.

The chain was privately held until 1995, when Jacob sold about Cr80 million worth of equity on the São Paulo and Rio de Janeiro stock markets. Arapuã invested some of the proceeds in a computer automation program dubbed the ''Paper Free Sales System'' which upgraded point-of-sale cashier stations with barcode scanners. In 1996 Arapuã joined forces with two key suppliers to develop an electronic data interchange (EDI) system to manage inventory and distribution. The company also embarked on a chainwide remodeling effort and opened dozens of new stores. Arapuã even had to recruit a new sales staff, supplanting computer-phobic older sales reps with better-educated, and often younger, workers.

Arapuã enjoyed rising sales volume in the early 1990s, with annual revenues increasing from about Cr750 million in 1990 to nearly Cr1.7 billion by the end of 1996. Net profits topped Cr116 million, giving the chain a net margin of almost seven percent of gross sales. (In order to provide a basis of comparison from year to year, the company uses the Full Monetary Correction Method to account for inflation. Previous years' financial results are therefore restated each year to reflect the inflationary climate.)

Arapuã faced several challenges during this period. Although Brazilian President Fernando Henrique Cardoso's currency stabilization strategies had succeeded in slashing annual inflation rates from nearly 1,800 percent in 1989 to less than 10 percent in 1997, a recession and high unemployment cut Arapuã's sales that year. According to the company's third quarter report, revenues for the first nine months of 1997 slid 16 percent from the previous year, and defaults on Arapuã's bread-and-butter consumer credit accounts rose to Cr84 million. The chain also faced competition from a fast-growing rival, Globex Group's Ponto Frio Bonzao, in the 1990s. Acquisitions boosted the Ponto Frio chain to over 200 stores with sales of Cr550 million by the end of 1992.

The changing economic and competitive landscape brought about changes at Lojas Arapuã as well. In January 1997, the company started setting aside 6.7 percent of each financed sale to allow for bad debts. As inflation fell, Arapuã's financing programs became less attractive to consumers, forcing the company to compete on cash prices and even offer interest-free ''same-as-cash'' credit programs. From 1996 to 1997 television prices dropped by about one-fourth, VCRs sold for nearly one-third less, and white goods dropped 10 percent. Not surprisingly, these adjustments cut the company's gross profit margin from 23 percent in the first nine months of 1996 to 16 percent in the comparable period of 1997. As of September 30, the company was running a Cr97.4 million deficit on the year.

Principal Subsidiaries

Arapuã Importacao e Comercio S.A. (69.5%).

Further Reading

''Arapuã : Revenues Could Reach R$850 Mil in 1991 Vs. R$750 Mil in 1990,'' *Jornal do Brasil,* October 8, 1991, p. 10.

''Arapuã Will Invest US$3 Mil to Informatize 350 Shops,'' *Gazeta Mercantil,* February 18, 1994, p. 8.

''Brazil's Maybe Miracle Man,'' *Economist,* February 12, 1994, p. 37.

''Casas Buri: Ponto Frio Bonzao Buys This Electronic Household Appliances Retailer,'' *Exame,* May 1992, p. 50.

Dolan, Kerry A., ''A Lively Bird That Gets the Worm,'' *Forbes,* November 3, 1997, pp. 338–339.

Stevens, James R. ''Appliance Market Grows in South America,'' *Appliance Manufacturer,* September 1994, p. 8.

Taylor, Robert, ''Cardoso's Next Battle,'' *Banker,* January 1997, pp. 59–60.

—April Dougal Gasbarre

Lost Arrow Inc.

259 W. Santa Clara Street
Ventura, California 93001-2545
U.S.A.
(805) 643-8616
Fax: (805) 653-6355
Web site: http://www.patagonia.com

Private Company
Incorporated: 1973 as Great Pacific Iron Works
Employees: 550
Sales: $130 million (1997 est.)
SICs: 5699 Miscellaneous Apparel & Accessory Stores

Lost Arrow Inc. is the holding company for the highly successful Patagonia brand of outdoor equipment and clothing. The company's founder, Yvon Chouinard, is a legendary rock climber and mountaineer. Chouinard designed or redesigned most of the standard equipment used by climbers today, including the ice axe, carabiners, and pitons. The company operates a small number of free-standing Patagonia stores in the U.S. and abroad, and sells its line through roughly 1,200 dealers in the U.S., Europe, and Japan. The company has been a design leader in several areas, pioneering specialized synthetic fabrics as well as bold, bright colors widely imitated by other outdoor apparel manufacturers. For many years Patagonia also ran a ballyhooed catalog business. The catalog defied every marketing rule, yet was notably profitable. The company is rare in its intense dedication to environmental preservation. One percent of all sales is given to environmental groups yearly. The company is privately held, with only three stockholders—founder Yvon Chouinard, his wife, Malinda, and former Patagonia general manager Kris McDivitt Tompkins.

Early History

The company began quite haphazardly, as a way for its founder to make enough money to back his passion for rock climbing. Chouinard, of French-Canadian descent, was born in Maine in 1938. At the age of eight he moved with his family from Maine to Burbank, California. He had formerly attended a school where only French was spoken, and he spoke no English. He was thrust into a regular English language public school, where he floundered. Chouinard credits his early school experience with shaping him into a loner. Though he excelled at athletics, he was uncomfortable with team sports and did not like to perform in front of people. In high school he became fascinated with falconry, and learned to climb or rapel down cliffs to reach falcon nests. After a scary rapelling accident, he decided to learn to climb *up* the cliffs instead. He had a great natural talent for climbing, and even as a teenager made daunting solo ascents of rock faces that had not been climbed before. After high school, Chouinard attended a junior college and studied geography, but climbing was his vocation. The equipment used then for climbing was mostly imported from Europe. A basic piece of equipment all climbers use are called pitons—metal spikes that can be wedged into the rock to hold the rope. Before Chouinard, pitons were made out of malleable iron. They were soft enough that they could be easily fitted into cracks of irregular shape. Chouinard met a Swiss blacksmith who was also a dedicated rock climber, and who had made his own pitons out of old car axles. The tough, unmalleable steel alloy the blacksmith used seemed to Chouinard to make the pitons much safer. They would not bend or come out of the rock if a climber fell. So Chouinard learned blacksmithing from a book, and began making his own pitons out of chrome-molybdenum steel. He made them on a portable coal forge, and sold them from his car at various favorite rock climbing sites. In 1957 Chouinard borrowed a little over $800 from his parents and bought a forging die. He set himself up in a shed behind his parents' house in Burbank and manufactured aluminum carabiners—D-ring shaped pieces of climbers' harness. This backyard venture became Chouinard Equipment.

Chouinard Equipment's first mail-order catalog came out in 1964. It was only a one-page list of equipment and prices, with advice not to expect speedy delivery during the climbing season. As demand for his climbing equipment grew, Chouinard moved his workshop to a shed near the beach in Ventura, California (because Chouinard was also fond of surfing), and he took on a partner, Thomas Frost. Frost was also an avid climber, and he had a degree in aeronautical engineering. Frost's expertise allowed the company to take on more complicated designs, and to make more pieces by machine. Sales in the first few years were only several thousand dollars, and Chouinard and his employees took off frequently to climb. But the company grew in spite of itself. The quality of Chouinard's products was clearly better than that made in Europe (European manufacturers subsequently changed their designs and materials to match Chouinard's), and even though the cost was substantially more, climbers were happy to pay. Sales doubled each year from 1966 to 1972, and the catalog became more impressive. The catalog was full of climbing instructions, discussions of the ethics of removing your pitons from the rock versus leaving them in, quotations from diverse sages, and in-depth descriptions of each piece of equipment. It resembled a book more than a commercial catalog, and the 1972 catalog was even reviewed in The *American Alpine Journal* book review section, because it was considered the finest literature available on climbing.

Expansion in the 1970s

Chouinard Equipment incorporated in 1973, changing its name to Great Pacific Iron Works. There were still only about a dozen employees, many of them climbers with little business background. Chouinard also enticed some fine craftsmen to join the company, bringing in artisans from Korea and Mexico. The catalog grew both in its distribution and complexity. The company printed 10,000 catalogs in 1972, and by 1976 it was distributing over 35,000. By 1977, sales stood at around $2 million. The company's market share was enviable. In the 1970s, Great Pacific Iron Works had an estimated 80 percent share of the U.S. climbing equipment market and was an unchallenged leader.

The company was run extremely informally. Chouinard's wife and nephew worked for the company, and many employees were attracted to Great Pacific Iron Works because of its location near a prime surfing beach. Chouinard himself was notorious for not being at his desk. He ran the company from afar while fly fishing in Idaho or climbing in Argentina. The ethos of the company was that it was selling equipment for outdoors enthusiasts, made by outdoors enthusiasts. Many of Chouinard's ideas for new equipment and designs came from his actual needs while on his adventures, and he seemed to have an uncanny ability to rethink items others only made do with. His innovations ranged from comfort to life-saving safety, and the Great Pacific Iron Works catalog listed items from the non-sagging, cool mesh fishing vest to the Chouinard-Frost ice axe, which had revolutionized ice climbing.

The company really began to grow when the catalog began offering clothing as well as equipment. Chouinard's focus had been on extremely durable clothing, such as shorts made from a heavy-duty corduroy imported from England. In the mid-1970s, Great Pacific began selling rugby shirts and shorts, also imported from England. They proved extremely popular, and other new clothing sold well, too. The catalog introduced jackets made from a synthetic fleece material. The synthetic, called pile, was offered as an improvement over wool, because it was lighter weight and quicker to dry. This was the first of the technologically advanced materials that became a hallmark of the company. In 1976 Chouinard consolidated the clothing part of his business into a separate company, named Patagonia after the remote region of Argentina. Clothing made from the new pile material soon accounted for more than half of all Patagonia's sales. The climbing equipment business continued under the original name, Chouinard Equipment. This was sold in 1989, after insurance costs drove it into Chapter 11.

Mass Popularity in the 1980s

By the end of the 1970s, sales were several million dollars annually, but the company was still run quite casually. Chouinard hired a financial manager, Steve Peterson, in 1978. Peterson attempted to analyze the company's finances by breaking it down into separate product lines, and trying to determine which items were responsible for how much profit. This kind of basic accounting had not been done before—money simply came and went. Peterson tried to bring other changes to the company, such as establishing a board of directors with people on it from larger companies. Chouinard, the founder, resisted these changes, and essentially was uninterested in the financial aspect of the business. Peterson was succeeded by another chief financial officer, Galliano Mondin, in 1986. Mondin struggled, like his predecessor, to bring order to the company's finances. It was a difficult job to begin with, given the company's uncorporate culture, and it was perhaps made more difficult since Patagonia was experiencing rocketing growth. Sales grew from the two or three million in the late 1970s to about $24 million in 1986. By 1988, sales had quadrupled, to $96 million. The bank that handled the company's accounts, Security Pacific, apparently made do with Patagonia's slapdash recordkeeping because the company was clearly growing and profitable. Even founder Chouinard, ever aloof from finances, apparently became personally interested in managing the company's growth a little more closely, on the theory that the more the company made, the more it could give away. Chouinard had instituted a tithing program, giving away one percent of sales to various environmental causes, and he was very interested in using his company to influence people's treatment of the earth. Consequently, Chouinard hired a former ski resort president, Pat O'Donnell, as CEO in 1988, and O'Donnell hired a new CFO with experience in apparel, as well as a former Marshall Field executive to take over the catalog operation.

But the hiring did not stop there. As these three attempted to rein in the company, Chouinard hired more designers, and let them hire more designers, or hire their friends, and the founder continued to bring in people he had met surfing or elsewhere. Payroll and other costs burgeoned at the end of the 1980s, despite the advice of the new executives from more traditional business backgrounds. Many of the employees had uncommon dedication to the company, calling themselves "Patagoniacs," and the company was clearly a great place for creative, individualistic people to work. Workers were encouraged to take off in the middle of the day to jog, surf, or play volleyball, and their input on the clothes and equipment was of utmost value.

The untraditional nature of Patagonia encouraged almost cultish admiration for the company and its products. The catalog was perhaps the best example of the mindset of the company, and the image the Patagonia brand projected. The catalog was full of text, written like a letter to a friend rather than descriptions of products. An essay on Flaubert was not out of place in the catalog. Photos of products were often supplied by customers, and in most cases it was not possible to see the clothing very clearly. The distinctive Patagonia label, with its mountain silhouette, would most certainly *not* be visible. The catalog advertised Patagonia's toll-free numbers for rock climbing or kayaking advice. The number to call to order clothes, however, was not toll-free, and notoriously hard to find. An interview with the catalog's marketing manager in a 1988 *Inc.* article has her huffing that the catalog's copy would *never* imply that customers should *buy* something. The title of the *Inc.* article is aptly "The Anti-Marketers." Almost every aspect of the catalog went against the grain of traditional marketing advice. And yet the Patagonia catalog was one of the most successful mail-order businesses in the country.

Patagonia's popularity boomed beyond its earliest customer core of outdoor enthusiasts. By the early 1990s, many dedicated Patagonia fans were people who only wanted to look like outdoor adventurers. The clothes had a high reputation for quality, which was matched by high price. By the early 1990s, many manufacturers had successfully imitated Patagonia style and materials, and were selling comparable garments for much less. As leaner economic times sagged retail markets by 1991, Patagonia found itself with a huge domestic backlog and a bloated payroll. Though its international business was still growing, the U.S. market was stagnant. The company's bank shortened its line of credit, and later required an immediate cash payment of $2.5 million on an earlier loan. In July 1991, the company had to resort to selling inventory below cost, and 20 percent of the work force was let go. The next catalog announced a new, pared-down stock. It was now not necessary to sell "volleyball shorts," just shorts would do. Instead of five ski pant styles, customers were given a choice between only two. Overall, the number of items for sale dropped by 40 percent. The catalog distribution was also curtailed. Chouinard at first announced that he wanted to halt the catalog altogether, but it was eventually cut back to two mailings a year instead of four. Chouinard also announced in various interviews that he wanted to halt the company's growth altogether. He was more interested in ecology than in business, and he did not want his company to get any bigger.

Readjustment in the Mid-1990s

Despite its founder's dire talk, Patagonia continued to prosper. After the drastic measures taken in 1991, the company seemed under better control. Hiring was no longer indiscriminate, though the workers who were retained were still given some of the most generous benefits in the country, with a subsidized child care center adjoining the company cafeteria, and of course surfing breaks. The company opened more retail stores in the U.S. and abroad. In 1995 a Patagonia store opened in a fashionable district in Manhattan, alongside some of the city's most trendy retailers. Sales in 1995 were actually the company's best ever, close to $154 million. Though other retailers copied its products and even the style of its catalog, a cachet still clung to the Patagonia brand. And the company still innovated successfully, marketing for example clothing made from a fleece fabric derived from recycled soda bottles. In 1996 President Clinton praised the company for its extensive benefits for workers and their families, and the *New York Times* ran a profile of Patagonia lauding it for its high percentage (nearly 60 percent) of women in top-paying managerial positions. The company continues to give generously to environmental funds, and is a standout in the garment industry for monitoring contractors for labor law violations. Patagonia seems to have negotiated a tricky boundary, becoming broadly popular but without losing its core mission, which is not primarily to make money.

Further Reading

Adelson, Andrea, "Casual, Worker-Friendly, and a Moneymaker, Too," *New York Times,* June 30, 1996, p. F8.

Bernstein, Jeremy, "Ascending," *New Yorker,* January 31, 1977, pp. 36–52.

Brown, Paul B., "The Anti-Marketers," *Inc.,* March 1988, pp. 62–72.

Gutner, Toddi, "Travails in Patagonia," *Forbes,* September 2, 1991, p. 14.

Kahn, Joseph P., "Lost Arrow," *Inc.,* December 1984, pp. 72–74.

Klinkenborg, Verlyn, "The Adventures of a Renaissance Fun Hog," *Esquire,* January 1988, pp. 92–98.

Meeks, Fleming, "The Man Is the Message," *Forbes,* April 17, 1989, pp. 148–52.

Randall, Glenn, "Riding Herd on the Charity Trail," *Backpacker,* July 1988, pp. 26–27.

Serwer, Andrew E., "Patagonia CEO Reels Company In," *Fortune,* December 14, 1992, p. 177.

Steinbreder, John, "He's in His Element in the Elements," *Sports Illustrated,* February 11, 1991, pp. 198–201.

Ward, Timothy Jack, "The Great Outdoors, Now in SoHo," *New York Times,* June 1, 1995, p. C3.

Welles, Edward O., "Lost in Patagonia," *Inc.,* August 1992, pp. 44–57.

—A. Woodward

Lund Food Holdings, Inc.

4100 W. 50th Street
Second Floor
Edina, Minnesota 55424
U.S.A.
(612) 927-3663
Fax: (612) 915-2600
Web site: http://www.byerlys.com

Private Company
Incorporated: 1964 as Lunds, Inc.
Employees: 4,300
Sales: $400 million (1997 est.)
SICs: 5411 Grocery Stores

Lund Food Holdings, Inc. is the parent company of Minnesota-based retail grocery stores Lunds, Inc. and Byerly's, Inc. The two high-quality grocers, which had been competitors in the Twin Cities for nearly 30 years, were merged in 1997 to form a 19-store chain with annual sales estimated at $400 million.

Lund's Roots: The 1920s Through the 1960s

Russell T. Lund moved to Minneapolis, Minnesota, from Amery, Wisconsin, in the 1920s with the intention of going to college, but a summer job changed his career plans. Lund's employer, Tom Cordalis, the operator of the cheese and cracker department of Hove's grocery store, offered him full-time employment and the opportunity to buy into the business.

In 1937, armed with retail grocery experience and plans to sell popped popcorn to Los Angeles grocers, Lund moved his family to California. His product was a hit. When Lund returned to Minneapolis and Hove's in 1939, he used profits from the venture for real estate. Lund leased his Lake Street and Hennepin Avenue building to Hove's and built a second store in the Minneapolis suburb of Edina, where Hove's opened a second store in 1942.

Lund had established himself in oil and gas exploration as well as real estate by the 1960s, but he continued to hold an interest in Hove's though his partnership in Cordalis and Lund, which operated the meat, dairy, and produce areas of the store. A dispute between Lund and Hove's regarding control of the business ended a 40-year business relationship. When Hove's' leases on the two stores expired, Lund chose not to renew them. In 1964, Lund established his own stores at the sites and opened a bakery to serve them.

Growing Reputation for Quality: 1970s and 1980s

Lunds, Inc. earned a reputation as a top quality grocer in the Twin Cities. Five Lunds stores held about four percent of the market and generated $48 million in annual revenues by 1978. In addition to setting standards for freshness and variety, Lund built a loyal clientele through exceptional customer service. Personal greetings by employees, complementary coffee, free use of the telephone, and pride in filling special orders contributed to an atmosphere that kept bringing customers back. Only about one-half of one percent of total revenues was spent on advertising which sold Lunds rather than specific products.

Russell Lund, Sr., was followed by nephew H. Ted Lund as head of the company beginning in 1973. Frank Gleeson, a longtime Lunds employee, became the first non-family president of the seven-store chain in 1986, when revenues were approaching the $100 million mark. Family leadership of Lunds was resumed in 1991 when Gleeson retired and was succeeded by Russell T. (Tres) Lund III.

While he was still in high school, Tres Lund was coached by his grandfather in the workings of the retail grocery business. The younger Lund had planned to gain some work experience on Wall Street after graduating with a degree in business in 1985, but with Ted Lund and Frank Gleeson nearing retirement, Tres Lund returned to Minnesota. He gained a working knowledge of Lunds before stepping in as vice-president of operations and later as president and CEO.

The 1990s: Times of Change for Lunds, Inc.

Founder Russell Lund, Sr., who had remained active in the store well into his 70s, died in 1992. The Lund family and Lunds, Inc. had to weather more death and intense media coverage later that year when Russell Lund, Jr.—father to Tres, son of Russell, Sr., and holder of 36 percent interest in Lunds, Inc.—was charged with a double homicide and later committed suicide. Tres Lund, 30 years old at the time, had been at the helm of the company for only about a year.

The company celebrated 55 years in the retail grocery business in 1994. Annual sales had climbed to about $118 million. Gillian Judge, in a March 1994 *Twin Cities Business Monthly* article, estimated earnings to be about $2.1 million. The eight-store chain continued to hold its own in an industry which had become dominated by huge no-frill food stores during the 1980s. Piper Jaffray analyst Brooks O'Neill said in the Judge article, "They have managed to tailor the stores to the needs and desires of the neighborhoods in which they operate, they have excellent locations, they knock you over with [personalized] service—these big stores clearly cannot come close to that."

In addition to breathing new life into Lunds, Inc. with plans for store renovation, expansion of the catering business, and the purchase of prepared dinner business name and concept, Tres Lund brought in a new leadership style. Judge wrote, "Lund revitalized the board of directors, sought more advice from senior managers, and gave greater autonomy and responsibility to the stores' department managers. Supermarket analysts—who admit to knowing little about this very privately held company—say that Lund seems to have surrounded himself with good people." Day-to-day operations were handled by Lunds Vice-President Frank Worrell while Lund split his time between Lunds, Inc., the real estate, and the oil and gas concerns, which each held about one third of the family's fortune.

Early in 1996, Lunds closed the doors of one of its stores. Mike Kaszuba wrote in January 1996, "This wasn't just any grocery store. This was Lunds, a marble-floored, gourmet coffee-selling symbol of every thing upscale in one of the Twin Cities' most affluent suburbs. Lunds, an institution of sorts in the Twin Cities, in fact had never before been forced to close a store." Lunds attributed the cause of the closing to the number of financially stretched consumers in the market, while Kaszuba noted Lunds' staple product prices were often higher than other area stores.

In March 1996, the company announced renovation plans for the oldest and smallest of the stores. The urban Minneapolis store was switched to a "marketplace" venue with a separate entrance for its expanded deli and convenience food section and the addition of a mezzanine-level seating area. In April 1997, Lunds merged with its primary Twin Cities competitor, Byerly's, Inc.

Byerly's Brightens the Twin Cities Food Market: 1960s–80s

Donald D. Byerly opened his first store in 1968 as Byerly Foods. His father, Russell Byerly, former chairman of the board of Minnesota-based grocery wholesaler Supervalu Inc., was a partner in the business until his death in 1977. The luxury supermarket did $5 million in business in 1969, its first full year of operation.

Beginning with a commitment to providing quality products and steering away from traditional advertising and pricing techniques, Byerly's offered customers a first class shopping environment. Carpeted floors, chandeliers, soft lighting, wall papering, and solid oak trim, plus gift shops, restaurants, postal service, and resident home economists complemented the full service meat, fish, and produce departments, in-store bakeries, and delicatessens. Byerly's four stores reached $50 million in sales by the end of its first decade.

The grocery business had been a lifelong passion for Byerly. He began with weekend inventories alongside his father, went on to earn a degree in food marketing, and worked in the retail end of the food industry for other operators. The opening of his $4 million, 92,000-square-foot flagship store in the Minneapolis suburb of St. Louis Park drew national interest, including a front page article in the *Wall Street Journal.*

In that article, Lawrence Ingrassia wrote, "The furnishings and specialty shops set Byerly's apart from its chief competitor for upper-class Twin Cities shoppers, Lunds, an independent chain of six supermarkets. Lunds also carries a wide selection—about 13,000 items—and is known for top quality food. But the comparisons end there." Ingrassia called Byerly's "the Bloomingdale's of the supermarket world."

Sales for the seven-store Byerly's chain were between $130 and $150 million in the mid-1980s. And the upscale supermarkets were well-known tourist attractions. Byerly's held about five percent of the Twin Cities market, compared with four percent for Lunds, and 20 percent for Supervalu-owned Cub Foods, a super-warehouse store. On a low note, Byerly's failed to turn around two Atlanta supermarkets purchased from the bankrupt independent owner.

Big Changes at Byerly's: 1990s

Founder and sole owner Don Byerly began to phase himself out of the daily operation of the stores in the late 1980s. Tom Harberts, who came on board in 1970 and guided the building and opening of several of the stores and the Byerly's frozen soup manufacturing plant, was named president in 1989. In mid-1990, Byerly sold controlling interest of the $200 million chain. Minneapolis-based Goldner Hawn Johnson & Morrison, and M.H. Equity Corp, an affiliate of Manufacturers Hanover Trust Company of New York, became equity partners. Harberts was named CEO and also shared in the ownership along with other senior managers.

When Harberts suddenly resigned in May 1994, Dale Riley, a Byerly's veteran and chief operating officer, and Jack Morrison, chairman of the board and partner at Goldner Hawn Johnson & Morrison, assumed leadership of the Byerly's stores. The company cited management philosophy differences as the reason for Harberts's departure. In a *Minneapolis/St. Paul CityBusiness* article by Jennifer Waters, Morrison said, "We had a tendency to be a little reactive to industry changes. We were very conscious of protecting what we had, but we weren't moving forward.'' Plans to expand outside Minnesota had been simmering since the late 1980s while in the meantime no-frills grocers began offering more services, and discounters such as Target, Wal-Mart, and Kmart were building grocery-carrying supercenters.

The new management introduced changes in the Byerly's style: traditional chandeliers were dropped from the newest (10th) store and replaced by a huge mural, and the company set its first image advertising campaign in motion. In 1995, restaurant service was cut back or eliminated from some stores, and the lineup of third party convenience foods vendors located within the stores was expanded.

Byerly's opened three stores in 1996 and thus gained a 30 percent increase in size in one year. The Chicago stores, located in the suburbs of Highland Park and Schaumburg, were the first of 10 stores the company planned for the area by the year 2000. The new Minnesota store dedicated about 30 percent of its space, or three times the industry average, to products in the convenience foods category. Ready-to-eat items ranging from Chinese take-out and chicken to Atlantic cod and sushi enticed shoppers to stay and eat in the 60-seat dining area with a fireplace and stuffed furniture. The company also developed a line of ready-to-cook food.

A New Partnership for the Future

The majority-owner investment firms, wishing to cash out of the company, began seeking a buyer in 1996: Lunds purchased the chain. According to Ann Merrill, ''By making the purchase, Lund eliminated the possibility of a new, deep-pocketed competitor arriving on the scene.'' The purchase price was estimated to be $90 million. Lunds stores switched to the longtime Byerly's wholesaler as part of the deal.

Lunds chose not to purchase the two Chicago stores. As Mary Ellen Podmolik reported, ''Despite its devout following in Minnesota, where it has 11 stores, Byerly's has had problems here, analysts say. The expensively decorated stores attracted customers for the strong selection of prepared foods, but shoppers bought basic items elsewhere.'' Chicago food retailer Dominick's Finer Foods purchased the two stores.

The Lunds and Byerly's stores were combined under Lund Food Holdings, Inc. in April 1997. Byerly's retained its name and continued to operate its two production plants in addition to the Minnesota stores. Former Byerly's president, Dale Riley, was named executive vice-president and chief operating officer, and an executive team with four members from each company was set in place. Tres Lund served as president and CEO of the new $400 million company. Crossovers of popular products, store remodeling, and expansion plans were on the table, as well as strategies to meet the increased competition from giant retailers on one side and convenience food outlets on the other.

Principal Subsidiaries

Lunds, Inc.; Byerly's, Inc.

Further Reading

''Byerly's 25: A Tradition of Style,'' *Byerly's Bag*, Edina, Minn.: Byerly's, Inc., 1993.

Christensen, Wayne, ''A Touch of Class at the Supermarket,'' *Corporate Report Minnesota*, February 1978, pp. 29–32, 72–77.

Feyder, Susan, ''Byerly's Prestige,'' *Minneapolis Star*, September 4, 1979.

Fredrickson, Tom, ''Lunds to Go Caters to Busy Consumers.'' *Minneapolis/St. Paul CityBusiness*, October 21, 1994, p. 2.

Gage, Amy, ''Uptown Lunds Grocery Store in Minneapolis, Minn., to Cater to Urban Lifestyle,'' *St. Paul Pioneer Press*, March 11, 1996.

Ingrassia, Lawrence, ''A Bag from Byerly's Is the Stylish Place to Stow the Garbage,'' *Wall Street Journal*, June 4, 1980, pp. 1, 34.

Jones, Jim, ''His Stores Have Changed Twin Cities Supermarkets,'' *Star Tribune* (Minneapolis), September 15, 1986, p. 1M.

Judge, Gillian, ''Fresh Grocer,'' *Twin Cities Business Monthly*, March 1994, pp. 27–30.

Kaszuba, Mike, ''Lunds Closing Has Eden Prairie Puzzled,'' *Star Tribune* (Minneapolis), January 15, 1996, p. 1B.

Kennedy, Tony, ''The Lund Legacy: The Fortune,'' *Star Tribune* (Minneapolis), November 8, 1992, p. 1A.

——, ''Paper, Plastic or Prospectus? Lunds and Byerly's May Merge,'' *Star Tribune* (Minneapolis), February 12, 1997, p. 1.

Marcotty, Josephine, ''Byerly to Share Chain Ownership,'' *Star Tribune* (Minneapolis), July 13, 1990, p. 1D.

——, ''Can-Do Leader to 'Export' Byerly's,'' *Star Tribune* (Minneapolis), January 22, 1990, p. 1D.

Merrill, Ann, ''In the Bag: Lund Food Holdings Completes Acquisition of Byerly's,'' *Star Tribune* (Minneapolis), April 30, 1997, p. 1.

''Is Byerly's on the Market?'' *Star Tribune* (Minneapolis), October 29, 1996, p. 1D.

——, ''Lunds to Buy Byerly's: All to Stay Open,'' *Star Tribune* (Minneapolis), March 5, 1997, p. 1.

——, ''New Menu for Grocers,'' *Star Tribune* (Minneapolis), November 3, 1996, p. 1D.

——, ''A Young and Steady Hand,'' *Star Tribune* (Minneapolis), July 27, 1997, pp. 1D, 5D.

Nissen, Todd, ''Lunds Inc. Carries on After Tragedy,'' *Minneapolis/St. Paul CityBusiness*, September 25, 1992.

Peterson, Susan E., ''New Lunds President Says Retail Is to His Taste,'' *Star Tribune* (Minneapolis), May 18, 1987, p. 2M.

Pheifer, Pat, ''Russell T. Lund Dies; Grocery Chain Founder Gave Much to Community,'' *Star Tribune* (Minneapolis), February 13, 1992, p. 1B.

Podmolik, Mary Ellen, ''Byerly's Closes Local Stores,'' *Chicago Sun-Times*, March 5, 1997, p. 59.

——, ''Byerly's Markets' Short Stint Here May Be Near End,'' *Chicago Sun-Times*, February 28, 1997, p. 43.

''Up from the Switchboard,'' *Corporate Report Minnesota*, May 1980, p. 96.

Waters, Jennifer, ''Dropping the Chandelier,'' *Minneapolis/St. Paul CityBusiness*, October 7, 1994, pp. 1, 34.

Youngblood, Dick, ''You Can Even Get 'Gator Aid at Lunds,'' *Star Tribune* (Minneapolis), August 18, 1991, p. 1D.

—Kathleen Peippo

Mack Trucks, Inc.

2100 Mack Blvd.
Allentown, Pennsylvania 18105
U.S.A.
(610) 709-3011
Fax: (610) 709-3308
Web site: http://www.macktrucks.com

Wholly Owned Subsidiary of Renault V.I.
Incorporated: 1901 as Mack Brothers Company
Employees: 5,231
Sales: US$2.14 billion (1995)
SICs: 3711 Motor Vehicles & Car Bodies

A prominent fixture in the U.S. truck industry, Mack Trucks, Inc. is one of North America's largest producers of heavy-duty trucks and major product components. In addition to its widely recognized line of heavy-duty trucks, Mack produced a line of medium-duty trucks throughout North America. During the late 1990s, Mack trucks were sold and serviced in more than 65 countries through a network of more than 860 sales, parts, and service centers.

Early 20th-Century Origins

It was by hauling heavy artillery pieces through the mud of World War I battlefields that Mack trucks first earned their famous nickname. Legend has it that a British officer, trying to free an artillery piece that was mired in mud, coined the name "bulldog" when he called out to a Mack driver, "Bring that bulldog over here." Management liked the term. In 1932 Mack began putting the bulldog emblem on the front of all trucks and in the 1960s, to raise company morale, Mack produced bulldog pins, carpets, flags, T-shirts, and other items. The square-shouldered grimly-determined bulldog is an appropriate symbol. Mack, a quality-conscious, pioneering truck manufacturer, has a history of cash flow problems and near collapses.

The youngest of five brothers, 14-year-old Jack Mack ran away from his Pennsylvania home in 1878 to join the Teamsters and work as a stationary mechanic. In 1893 Jack, with his brother Augustus, purchased a small carriage and wagon building firm in Brooklyn, New York. The firm was ruined by the financial panics of the 1890s, and the two brothers were forced to enter the business of maintaining and repairing engines, rather than manufacturing them.

During this time they began to experiment with new types of self-propelled vehicles. The Macks had exacting standards, and both an electric car and a steam-powered wagon were dumped into the East River for having too many mechanical flaws. But in 1900, after eight years of testing, the brothers finally produced a vehicle that satisfied them. "Old Number One," the first successful bus built in America, was a chain-driven vehicle that featured a Mack-built four-cylinder engine, a cone-type clutch and a three-speed transmission. It conveyed 20 sightseers at a time through Brooklyn's Prospect Park. The vehicle, which was converted into a truck in 1908 and finally retired in 1917, was the first Mack "million-miler."

Orders for more buses came rapidly, and Jack and Augustus, joined by their other brothers, incorporated Mack Brothers Company in New York with a capitalization of $35,000. In addition to manufacturing buses, the young company pioneered the design of custom-built, heavy-duty trucks. This ran against the prevailing wisdom on such matters. Automakers at that time considered trucks a poor relation to the automobile, and manufactured them from surplus or obsolete auto parts. They made trucks in order to keep their shops busy during periods of slow business. Jack Mack, however, anticipating that the days of the horse and wagon were numbered, decided to make trucks with a capacity of 1 to 7½ tons. He introduced the "seat-over-engine" truck, made a 7-ton, 5-cubic-yard dump truck for the construction of the New York City subway, and began manufacturing rail cars and engine-driven fire trucks. By 1911 the Mack Brothers Company, manufacturers of "The Leading Gasoline Truck in America," had 825 employees producing about 600 units a year.

Due to depressed market conditions the demand for trucks slowly diminished and the company, which had relocated to Allentown, Pennsylvania, merged first with the Saurer Motor Company and then the Hewitt Motor Company. The new man-

Company Perspectives:

A Mack truck is different from the rest. Where our competition joins components from various suppliers and calls it a truck, we build the powertrain as well as the vehicle. The result is what we call balanced design*—a truck in which each component is engineered to function perfectly with others. While balanced design is not new at Mack, our partnership with the worldwide Renault company has multiplied and diversified the resources behind the philosophy. It's given us more R&D. New quality assurance programs. And it's helped us implement a company-wide Total Quality Management philosophy that ensures that each Mack employee is committed to quality control, problem prevention and continuous improvement.*

agement did not meet the approval of Jack and three of his brothers, and they left the company. Although regrettable, their departure did not end Mack innovation. The new chief engineer, Edward R. Hewitt, designed a medium-duty Mack truck that was the mainstay of the market from 1914 until 1936. The AB Mack featured a four-cylinder engine with a three-speed transmission, a worm drive rear axle, and two large inspection ports that allowed a quick inspection of the crankshaft and rod bearings. Hewitt's successor, Alfred F. Masury, designed the Mack AC, a heavy-duty, chain-driven truck that featured clutch brakes to prevent its gears from clashing. This was the truck that hauled artillery pieces in Europe during World War I. Its performance there gave rise to the phrase "Built like a Mack truck."

With improved roads and an increased demand for point-to-point delivery, the truck industry prospered in the 1920s. For Mack, which was producing more than 7,000 units by 1927, sales rose from $22 million in 1919 to $55 million in 1927. The company added improved cooling systems, four-speed transmissions, dual-reduction drive, and the Mack Rubber Shock Insulator (the first major breakthrough in vibration dampening since automobiles were introduced) to the AB and AC models.

At the end of the decade Mack launched a line of high-speed, six-cylinder trucks. These models, designated the BJ, BM, BX, and BQ, marked the beginning of the transition from slow, four-cylinder trucks to high-speed transports. Mack also manufactured the country's first practical off-highway dumper designated the AP. It was used in the construction of the Hoover Dam.

The Depression had a devastating effect on Mack. In addition to the drop in demand, light-duty trucks introduced by other manufacturers created competition for Mack's large models. Mack sales dropped 75 percent between 1929 and 1932. But the company fought back. Instead of reducing production Mack offered a new line of small trucks, and introduced the CH and CJ cab-over-engine models. The cab-over-engine design, the best way of getting a ⅓–⅔ distribution by weight on the front and rear axles, was necessitated by laws restricting axle loading, gross vehicle weights, and overall lengths. Despite the depression, Mack's new line was successful. Those manufacturers in financial distress, needing more efficient ways of transporting goods, turned to the transportation that offered the lowest cost per ton per mile, namely, the truck. Furthermore, the urban demand for public transit ensured a strong bus market.

Mack's leadership of the industry continued in 1938 with the introduction of the Mack Diesel, the first diesel engine made by a truck manufacturer. In 1940 Mack sales hit $44 million on domestic deliveries of 7,754 units, with a net profit of $1.8 million. By making heavy-duty trucks, small delivery trucks, dump units, buses, and fire trucks, Mack offered the most comprehensive product line of any truck manufacturer.

World War II and Postwar Years

As early as 1940 Mack began producing the NR military six-wheeler, a tank transporter that would be used for British General Montgomery's North African campaign. After Pearl Harbor, Mack produced virtually nothing but military equipment, including power trains for tanks, military trucks, torpedo bombers, and the "MO" which pulled 150 mm field guns. Since it suspended civilian truck production for the duration of the war, Mack set up an extensive maintenance network which enabled those trucks to remain in running condition. Its contribution to the war effort won the company numerous government awards.

But that contribution meant little in the post-World War II environment. Strikes and new taxes resulted in a loss of profits for the company in 1946, while contract renegotiations and a soft market made the late 1940s a financially difficult period in general for Mack. In 1952 the manufacturer again reversed its fortunes by introducing the best-selling "B" series. These trucks featured a widened chassis frame in front for easier maintenance, a wider front axle for improved maneuverability, and rounded fenders with a sleek hood and cab. This appearance was a significant change from earlier long-nosed and box-shaped trucks. By the time the "B" series was discontinued in 1966 approximately 127,000 models had been sold.

Another major innovation was the END 673 "Thermodyne" diesel engine which was introduced in 1953 and featured direct fuel injection, allowing for greater power (170 horsepower) and reliability. Close to 80 percent of the heavy-duty "B" trucks were sold with Thermodyne engines.

These innovations notwithstanding, Mack's financial condition declined drastically in the 1950s and early 1960s. Finance-oriented executives, with no experience in truck manufacturing, deferred maintenance and allowed facilities to deteriorate in order to maintain a strong cash flow. Corporate offices were moved to Montvale, New Jersey, effectively isolating management from union employees. This management style, in conjunction with repeated work stoppages and strikes, left the company with reduced sales. From 1959 to 1964 earnings fell from $15.8 million to $3.4 million. A proposed merger with Chrysler Corporation, which might have saved the company, was not approved by the Justice Department.

In 1965 a dispirited management offered the presidency to career trucking executive Zenon C. R. Hansen. He eagerly accepted the challenge. "Many well-informed individuals advised me that I was taking over a sinking ship . . . that Mack was too far gone to save . . . that Mack would either go under or be absorbed by one of our competitors,'' Hansen said later. ''But I thought they were wrong. Mack still had a great name, a great product, and above all it had the people.''

Hansen assured employees that there would be internal promotions and a cessation to the firings, and he distributed bulldog flags, jewelry, rugs, and other items to boost morale. He set up an accelerated program to improve all the previously deferred maintenance. Corporate offices were moved back to Allentown, and a new assembly plant was built on the West Coast. He also approved manufacture of the ''Maxidyne'' diesel engine, which produced constant horsepower over a wide operating range. It featured a simple five-speed transmission, compared with earlier transmissions which had 10, 13, or 15 speeds.

These reforms helped Mack improve its financial situation by 1967. But the company remained plagued by a lack of capital. It was forced to stockpile millions of dollars of parts to ensure production of enough trucks during high demand periods, while at the same time advancing millions of dollars in loans to customers. In order to ease this crisis, Mack agreed to become an affiliate of Signal Oil & Gas Company in 1967 on the condition it was guaranteed complete autonomy.

However, Mack did not stay abreast with the industry innovations during the 1970s. Because profits went back to the parent company, Mack could not modernize its plants. It did introduce an air-to-air intercooled diesel engine in 1973, the ENDT 676 ''Maxidyne,'' which featured 285 horsepower, 1,080 pound/feet of torque. But industry deregulation and foreign competition drained Mack's profits, and those of other American truck manufacturers as well.

1980s Malaise

To cope with these problems the new president, John Curcio, persuaded the French auto manufacturer Renault to purchase 41 percent of Mack from Signal for $228 million in 1983. Renault not only contributed new capital, but also helped to distribute the Mack light trucks. In 1983 the company went public, although it was unable to pay dividends. Cost-cutting measures by Curcio, which reduced expenses $160 million in four years, returned the truck manufacturer to a sound financial condition in 1984 for the first time since 1980. Sales increased by 73 percent to $2.1 billion. But a write-off on the antiquated Allentown plant led to $58 million in losses during 1985.

Early in 1986 Mack announced it was moving its main production plant from Allentown to an $80 million computerized facility in Winsboro, South Carolina. The Allentown plant, built in 1926, was so old that trucks were still spray-painted by hand. Parts had to be moved by forklifts since there was no robotic technology. Furthermore, in Pennsylvania unionized labor cost close to $23 an hour including benefits, compared to labor costs of about $12 an hour in the South.

In 1986 Curcio told *Forbes* magazine that truck transportation had become more efficient, causing the demand for trucks to drop to 125,000 a year. The country's seven largest manufacturers had a combined production capacity of 230,000 trucks a year. ''In the next five years, we expect a major skirmish, if not a major war,'' he said.

Curcio's words were prophetic, for Mack did indeed find itself embattled as the 1980s progressed, but the company's fight for survival was an introspective one rather than a war raged against competitors. Mack was beset by myriad problems during the 1980s, problems that stemmed from its relationship with Renault and precluded the smooth operation of the trucking company's activities. Renault officials had mistakenly thought they could direct Mack's operation from Renault headquarters near Paris, and were slow to recognize their mistake. Quality control slipped, as a result. Under the stewardship of Renault, Mack failed to keep pace with its competitors in centralizing purchasing and trimming costs incurred from design and production processes. Renault also failed to expand Mack's distribution network, leaving the truck manufacturer with dealers and service centers situated primarily in the East, far removed from the majority of long-haul truckers who were Western-based. The impact on Mack was decisive and devastating. Executives in France may not have realized what was happening, but Mack's customers did, and they demonstrated their recognition by taking their business elsewhere. Mack's market share, which had stood as high as 20 percent in the late 1970s, was cut in half during the 1980s. By the end of the decade, the situation had become grave enough to set off alarms in Paris.

Mack entered the 1990s losing $20 million a month, part way through a five-year period when the truck manufacturer racked up a staggering $900 million loss. The company was teetering on the brink of bankruptcy. Its trucks broke down at an alarming rate and its distributors frequently were too far way to provide expedient assistance. Employee morale was depressingly low. To begin curing Mack's numerous problems, Renault officials made two important decisions in 1990. First, pressing financial concerns were given a reprieve when Renault V.I., the commercial vehicle division of the Renault Group, acquired the remaining 55 percent of Mack it did not already own. Second, and perhaps most importantly, Elios Pascual was dispatched from Renault's truck division to Mack's headquarters in Allentown. To Pascual, who assumed the title of chief executive officer of Mack, fell the task of arresting the truck manufacturer's deleterious financial slide and turning the venerable company around.

Turnaround Begins in 1990

Pascual immediately set about cutting costs, improving manufacturing quality and efficiency, and instilling a sense of pride among Mack employees. A plant was closed in Ontario, Canada, the number of Mack suppliers was sharply reduced, and the company's finance division was sold. Pascual ordered a redesign of Mack trucks, which greatly increased productivity. In 1991, 2.5 trucks were produced each year per employee; by 1994, four trucks were produced each year per employee. As these productivity figures rose, Mack's payroll shrank, making the turnaround more dramatic. From more than 13,000 employees during the mid-1980s, the number of workers was reduced to roughly 7,000 by the early 1990s, with the sharpest reductions coming from the salaried ranks.

Although Pascual orchestrated sweeping changes throughout Mack's operations, the impact of these changes did not materialize immediately. The company continued to languish throughout the early years of the 1990s, making little ground in the face of mounting competition. In 1993, when Mack lost $64 million on revenues of $1.7 billion, the U.S. heavy-duty truck industry recorded its greatest sales volume in the previous 15 years, engendering sizeable profit totals for many of the industry's largest players. Mack was excluded from the celebrations. Progress was being made, however, and the supporting evidence was readily discernible by the mid-1990s.

By the end of 1995, Mack had improved its market share for the third year in a row after four consecutive years of decline. The changes implemented in 1990 were showing their effect at last. After recording financial losses every year during the 1990s, Mack moved back into the black in 1995, returning to profitability after a long absence. The market for Class 8 trucks was in a slump in 1995, declining more than 15 percent, but Mack held its own and gained some ground. The company's market share rose during the year—up to 12.1 percent—making 1995 the fourth consecutive year in which Mack increased its share of the market. Further, Mack was one of only two manufacturers to increase its market share in a declining market. On this bright note, the company celebrated its 95th anniversary with renewed optimism and charted its course for the future, intent on bringing the unique Mack mystique into the 21st century.

Principal Subsidiaries

Mack Americus, Inc.; Mack Canada, Inc.; Mack Properties, Inc.; Mack Truck Worldwide Ltd.; Mack Truck Australia Pty., Ltd.

Further Reading

Berss, Marcia, "Mack Malaise," *Forbes,* April 11, 1994, p. 73.

Hannon, Kerry, "Missed Turn," *Forbes,* August 7, 1989, p. 10.

Hansen, Zenon C. R., *The Legend of the Bulldog,* New York: Newcomen Society, 1974.

Jocou, Pierre, "Beyond Buzzwords: TQM at Mack Trucks," *Chief Executive,* September 1996, p. 54.

Sawyer, Christopher A., "Mack Under Attack," *Automotive Industries,* February 1992, p. 111.

Simonian, Haig, "Recovering Its Faded Image As the Bulldog Breed," *Financial Times,* March 12, 1996, p. 32.

Sternberg, Ernest R., *A History of Motor Truck Development,* Warrendale, Pa.: Society of Automotive Engineers, 1981.

—updated by Jeffrey L. Covell

Makita Corporation

3-11-8, Sumiyoshi-Cho
Anjo City
Aichi Prefecture
Japan
+566 98-1711
Fax: +566 98-6021

Public Company
Incorporated: 1938 as Makita Electric Works, Ltd.
Employees: 7,444
Sales: ¥186.2 billion (US$1.5 billion) (1997)
Stock Exchanges: Tokyo Nagoya Osaka New York Amsterdam Luxembourg
SICs: 3546 Power-Driven Handtools; 3553 Woodworking Machinery; 7699 Repair Services, Not Elsewhere Classified; 3699 Electrical Equipment & Supplies, Not Elsewhere Classified; 3629 Electrical Industrial Apparatus, Not Elsewhere Classified

Makita Corporation is Japan's number-one manufacturer and exporter of electric power tools. The company develops, manufactures, and distributes tools in four areas. Makita's portable general purpose division, which accounted for nearly 50 percent of 1997 revenues, encompasses drills, jackhammers, sanders, screwdrivers, and other construction equipment. The portable woodworking segment includes saws, routers, nailers, and other carpentry tools. It generated about 20 percent of sales in 1997. Stationary woodworking machines, including table saws, planer-jointers, and band saws for installation, contributed less than 2.5 percent of sales. Though it had traditionally targeted the professional user, Makita's distinctive turquoise tools increasingly appealed to the do-it-yourself market. Consumer tools included heavy-duty and household vacuums, submersible pumps, lawn mowers, and garden tools. These made up around 10 percent of annual revenues. Makita's parts and repair services were another important business area, contributing nearly 20 percent of revenues in 1997.

Having launched multinational operations in 1970, Makita boasted more than 100 sales offices and 28 overseas subsidiaries in the mid-1990s. North America was its oldest and largest foreign market, constituting just under 30 percent of sales. Though it only made up 12 percent of revenues in 1997, Southeast Asia was Makita's fastest-growing market, with sales increasing 22 percent from 1995 to 1997.

20th-Century Foundation and Development

The company traces its history to 1915 and the establishment of a repair shop for electric tools and equipment in Nagoya, Japan, midway between Tokyo and Osaka. It was incorporated in 1938 as Makita Electric Works, Ltd.

But it was not until 1958 and the administration of president Juiro Goto that the company diversified into the manufacture of electric power tools. A 1962 public stock offering raised funds for the program. Within just over a decade, Makita had leapfrogged to the top of the Japanese power tool market. The company credited its success in the domestic power tool market to high quality construction, pioneering research and development, and a unique system of direct distribution. Instead of relying on wholesalers to market its tools to retailers, Makita employed its own direct sales force. The close relationships engendered by this system gave the company insights into the needs of retailers as well as the end user, thereby fueling innovation.

With their brushed metal casings, the company's earliest tools look bulky, heavy, and primitive by today's standards. Over the years, Makita traded metal casings for shock-resistant, turquoise plastic; added multi-speed motors and electronic controls; and developed a mind-numbing variety of accessories. Makita targeted professional tool users in the carpentry, construction, timber, and masonry trades with its powerful, durable equipment that often cost two to three times as much as a typical tool made for the consumer market. Focusing on the high end of the power tool industry mitigated price competition, thereby boosting profit margins substantially.

Company Perspectives:

As a truly global supplier of a comprehensive array of power tools and related products, Makita is working to meet the sophisticated and diverse needs of its customers through its international manufacturing, marketing, and after-sales networks. Backed by these extensive networks and supported by its strong product development capabilities, Makita is striving for further growth in markets worldwide by rapidly introducing innovative, reliable, and high-quality power and other tools. In addition, Makita is contributing to the betterment of the communities in which it conducts business and is promoting various environmental protection activities.

Overseas Expansion Begins in 1970s

Realizing the limitations of the domestic market, Goto sought global expansion in the 1970s. Stock offerings in 1968 and 1970 generated a ''war chest'' that financed Makita's overseas campaign. The company employed a multinationalist strategy, establishing a new subsidiary in each target market. Makita set up a foothold in the United States first, in 1970. Within just four years, the company had operations in France, the United Kingdom, Australia, Canada, the Netherlands, and Italy. The late 1970s and early 1980s witnessed the creation of subsidiaries in Germany, Belgium, Brazil, Austria, and Singapore.

Makita used its comparatively low-cost production base to advantage in Europe and America. By the end of the 1970s, the company had captured almost one-fifth of the global professional tool market nearly matching Black & Decker's market share. As an unidentified analyst told *Fortune's* Bill Sapirito in 1984, ''Basically, Makita had them by the you-know-whats and just said, 'Cough.' ''

By this time, competition between Makita and U.S. industry leader Black & Decker had saturated that country's market for power tools to the point that sales growth appeared limited to replacements, parts, and trade-ups. In fact, manufacturer's sales slid 16 percent from 1980 to 1983. Fortunately, the development of cordless rechargeable power tools established a whole new avenue of growth. After 10 years of research and development, Makita launched its first cordless tool, a drill, in 1978. Eliminating the cord freed the worker from the power source, but early cordless models had several limitations. They were often heavier and less powerful than their corded forebears, had very limited running time, and required long periods to recharge. Though these factors kept cordless tools out of many professionals' tool chests, they did appeal to the home handyman whose projects were less demanding. Improvements in battery technology throughout the late 20th century boosted power and running time while reducing recharging time. By the late 1980s, Makita's 9.6 volt family of cordless tools was beginning to find their way onto construction sites.

Overseas Factories Established in 1980s

A variety of factors encouraged Makita to begin to establish manufacturing operations outside Japan during this period. Rising labor and production costs at home combined with a desire to minimize the effect of currency fluctuations and circumvent many trade restrictions while simultaneously reducing shipping expenses. Makita set up production facilities—dubbed ''transplants'' in business jargon—in Canada in 1980, Brazil in 1981, the U.S. in 1985, and the U.K. in 1991. By the end of 1997, the company's Chinese factory was churning out over 100,000 power tools each month.

Makita also continued to expand its global presence throughout the late 1980s and 1990s, establishing sales, distribution, and service operations in Spain, Taiwan, Hong Kong, China, New Zealand, Mexico, Hungary, and Korea. The company augmented its manufacturing capabilities with the creation of plants in the United Kingdom (1991) and China (1993).

New Products Drive Power Tool Market in 1990s

Makita pursued new product development in the 1990s, focusing on ergonomics as well as dust, sound, and vibration control. In 1991, the company bought into the market for gasoline-powered tools like chainsaws via the acquisition of Germany's Sachs-Dolmer G.m.b.H. Research and development costs averaged 1.7 percent of sales mid-decade, and totaled ¥2.7 billion (US$21.4 million) in 1997. By that time, Makita held more than 150 patents worldwide and applications for hundreds more were pending. Some of the company's discoveries applied Makita's power tool know-how to home and garden appliances including cordless vacuum cleaners, rechargeable electric lawn mowers, remote-controlled drapery openers, and hedge trimmers. However, as Makita reached out to the consumer market, it had to take special care not to alienate its core constituency of professional tool buyers. The company launched two new lines of cordless tools powered by 12 volt and 14 volt battery systems in 1997 as well.

By the early 1990s, Makita had captured over 50 percent of the US$400 million U.S. market for professional tools, far surpassing American power tool maker Black & Decker (B&D). But B&D moved to reclaim the segment in 1992, when it relaunched the DeWalt brand as its pro-tool standard-bearer. The construction-yellow competitor to Makita soon took the segment by storm. Such industry observers *as Fortune's* Patricia Sellers characterized Makita as ''complacent'' in the face of this renewed competition.

And in fact, Makita's strategy remained unchanged as the turn of the 21st century approached. Masahiko Goto, who had succeeded Juiro Goto as president in 1984, continued to lead Makita into the late 1990s. In his annual message for fiscal 1997, Goto expressed Makita's ''aim to become a 'Strong Company' '' by ''developing products that accurately meet the needs of the market, increasing overseas production and further rationalizing production processes at its domestic production facilities, and strengthening its sales and distribution bases.'' This rather unimaginative plan did not serve Makita well in the 1990s.

Sales declined from ¥178.9 billion (US$1.4 billion) in 1993 to less than ¥160 billion (US$1.3 billion) in 1996 before recovering to ¥186.2 billion (US$1.5 billion) in 1997. Net income fared worse, falling by more than 30 percent from ¥9.8 billion (US$79 million) in 1993 to ¥6.7 billion (US$54.4 million) in

1995, then rebounding somewhat to ¥8.1 billion (US$65.4 million) by 1997. The company's stock price mirrored its less-than-stellar fiscal results; its NYSE-traded ADRs slid from a high of US$21.63 in 1994 to less than US$13 in 1997.

Principal Subsidiaries

Makita U.S.A. Inc.; Makita Corp. of America (U.S.A.); Makita Mexico, S.A. de C.V.; Makita Canada Inc. (Canada); Makita do Brasil Ltda. (Brazil; 90.4%); Makita (Australia) Pty. Ltd.; Makita (New Zealand) Ltd.; Makita International Europe Ltd. (U.K.); Makita (U.K.) Ltd.; Makita Manufacturing Europe Ltd. (U.K.); Makita France S.A. (France); Makita Benelux B.V. (Netherlands); Euro Makita Corp. B.V. (Netherlands); S.A. Makita N.V. (Belgium); Makita S.p.A. (Italy); Makita Werkzeug G.m.b.H. (Germany); Dolmar G.m.b.H. (Germany); Makita Werkzeug Gesellschaft m.b.H. (Austria); Makita S.R.O. (Czech Republic); Makita Sp. AO.o. (Poland); Makita kft. (Hungary); Makita S.A. (Spain); Makita Singapore Pte. Ltd.; Makita (Taiwan) Ltd.; Makita Power Tools (H.K.) Ltd. (Hong Kong); Makita (Korea) Ltd. (South Korea); Makita (China) Co., Ltd.; Shiroyama Development Co., Ltd.; Makita Ichigu Co., Ltd.; TMK Co., Ltd.

Further Reading

Cory, James M., "Power Tools; Products and Prospects," *Chilton's Hardware Age*, June 1985, pp. 45–47.

"Electric Tool Industry Nearing Judgment Day," *Business Japan*, May 1987, pp. 45–46.

"Japan's Power Tool Industry," *Japan 21st*, June 1995, pp. 28–29.

Kelly, Joseph M., "Cordless Tool Makers Power Up to Meet Market Demands," *Home Improvement Market*, September 1996, pp. 66–67.

——, "Power Tool Makers Battle in Court," *Home Improvement Market*, August 1996, p. 49.

Sapirito, Bill, "Black & Decker's Gamble on 'Globalization,' " *Fortune*, May 14, 1984, pp. 40–44.

Sellers, Patricia, "New Selling Tool: The Acura Concept," *Fortune*, February 24, 1992, pp. 88–89.

Smutko, Liz, "Building a Pro-Quality Niche," *Chilton's Hardware Age*, May 1994, pp. 59–61.

"Splinters," *Forbes*, June 6, 1983, p. 161.

—April Dougal Gasbarre

Malt-O-Meal Company

2600 IDS Tower
80 South 8th Street
Minneapolis, Minnesota 55402-2297
U.S.A.
(612) 338-8551
Fax: (612) 339-5710
Web site: http://www.malt-o-meal.com

Private Company
Incorporated: 1919 as Campbell Cereal Company
Employees: 800
Sales: $300 million (1997 est.)
SICs: 2043 Cereal Breakfast Foods

Malt-O-Meal Company, best known as a hot cereal manufacturer for the majority of its years in business, is the leader in the value-priced, bagged ready-to-eat U.S. cereal market. The low-profile company produces and markets cereals under its own and private-label names.

The Early Years: 1910s–50s

Malt-O-Meal Company founder John S. Campbell's first job was in his father's grain milling company. After serving in World War I, Campbell returned home to Owatonna, Minnesota and invested $800 (poker earnings, according to a 1969 *Minneapolis Tribune* article by Charles B. McFadden) in his own business venture. "My idea was to make a cereal that tasted better and cooked quicker than the top-selling wheat farina product, Cream of Wheat, which then took about 30 minutes to cook. Malt gave me the flavor I wanted and toasting reduced the cooking time of my finished product to two or three minutes."

In 1919 Campbell Cereal Company began operating out of an old creamery building rented for $11 per month. Initially a one-man venture, Campbell processed the malt and wheat in an iron cylinder with a gas burner, then packaged and sold the cereal he named Malt-O-Meal. He quickly found there was an art to selling a new product and hired a salesman, who offered free customer samples to retail grocers. Distribution was limited to southern Minnesota and northern Iowa during the first few years.

Campbell experimented with radio promotion in 1925 on WLS in Chicago. Kids were offered the chance to win a free toy by sending in a joke and Malt-O-Meal box top to the "Steamboat Bill" show. Grocers were flocked with requests for the cereal: Malt-O-Meal began gaining shelf space. The WLS promotion, which began as a two-week trial, ran for more than a year. Additional promotions were aired on stations in the midwest, southwest, and far west.

With business booming, Campbell moved the company into the Simpson Mill, which had once been operated by his father and an uncle. In 1927 the company relocated to Northfield, Minnesota, in the Ames Mill. The southwestern market opened up in the late 1920s thanks to a Texas businessman named C.C. Lindley. Campbell established a Minneapolis sales and marketing office in 1932 and began working with an advertising agency.

Campbell's Corn Flakes was introduced in 1939. Because of stiff competition from Kellogg, the ready-to-eat cereal was dropped in 1942. Meanwhile, Malt-O-Meal sales climbed steadily. Box sizes changed in the late 1940s, but the product itself remained the same. In 1953 the Campbell Cereal Company was renamed the Malt-O-Meal Company. Sales by the privately held business nearly doubled from 1948 to 1958.

Changing Marketplace: 1960s–70s

Competitor Cream of Wheat was purchased by the National Biscuit Company in 1961, the year Malt-O-Meal added a second flavor. Chocolate Flavored Malt-O-Meal kept the company's momentum going as industrywide sales began to drop off. In 1965 Malt-O-Meal expanded operating space with the purchase of the Carnation Creamery building, which was renamed the Campbell Mill. John Campbell was succeeded as president of Malt-O-Meal by his son-in-law Glenn S. Brooks in 1966; Brooks joined the company in 1956 and had been appointed vice-president and general manager in 1965.

Malt-O-Meal sales flattened out in the mid-1960s. U.S. consumers were buying more and more convenience and sweetened foods. Beginning in 1966, Malt-O-Meal began producing State Fair brand Puffed Wheat and Puffed Rice at its new plant site. The next year, Malt-O-Meal entered the snack food market with Soy Town roasted and salted soy beans. The purchase of Profile Extrusion Company marked the first major diversification for the 46-year-old company. The 20-employee, vinyl plastic subsidiary produced component parts for other manufacturers.

Malt-O-Meal employed a total of 55 people in its two Northfield plants and Minneapolis office by 1969. Malt-O-Meal 100 Plus, which the company touted as the first hot cereal with 100 percent of the established daily minimum requirements of vitamins and iron, was added to the hot cereal line in 1969 but discontinued four years later. Pophitt Cereals, Inc., purchased in 1970, bolstered Malt-O-Meal's ready-to-eat cereal segment with its Whiffs and Sunland Puffed Wheat and Puffed Rice line.

Chairman and CEO John Campbell died in 1971. The company he founded had extended its reach throughout the western two-thirds of the country. Yet Malt-O-Meal remained a relatively small independent company holding less than three percent of the hot cereal market versus the 64 percent held by Quaker Oats.

Malt-O-Meal took another bite into the ready-to-eat cereal market in the early 1970s, when the company began to box private-label cereals for grocery store chains such as Super Valu and Kroger. In 1976 Malt-O-Meal introduced Toasty O's, a lower-cost, bagged version of General Mill's Cheerios. A second major brand imitation, Sugar Puffs, hit the market in 1980. The push into the ready-to-eat market helped revenues double between 1975 and 1980.

Expansion Accelerates: 1980s

During the first half of the 1980s, the company introduced several more national brand knockoffs: Raisin Bran, Corn Flakes, Crispy Rice, Sugar Frosted Flakes, and Honey & Nut Toasty O's. In 1985 the ready-to-eat cereal segment of business contributed about two-thirds of the year's estimated $50 million in revenues. Malt-O-Meal's revenues had doubled again between 1980 and 1985. John W. Lettmann, who worked in the marketing department at General Mills before coming on board as Brooks's assistant in 1971, was named president in 1986.

Malt-O-Meal increased the size of its package in 1982. With the exception of instant products, the hot cereal market had continued to stagnate. Malt-O-Meal introduced an instant hot cereal in 1987, but the latecomer never gained significant market share and was discontinued in 1990. Malt-O-Meal Plus 40% Oat Bran was manufactured between 1988 to 1992. And the company divested itself of two other business ventures in the 1980s: the snack food business was sold, and Profile Extrusion became an independent company.

Chair and CEO Brooks died in 1988. During his tenure the company had grown from 20 to 300 employees and revenues reached an estimated $77 million. The company was producing approximately 150 cereal items, including its own brands, private-label brands, and bulk or single-serving cereals for the food service operations of major cereal companies.

Price increases by the top-of-the-line, ready-to-eat cereal makers had opened a window of opportunity for Malt-O-Meal in the 1980s. Budget-conscious consumers balked at paying upwards of $4 a box for national brands. By forgoing expensive advertising and packaging, Malt-O-Meal offered a comparable product for about half the price of the high-profile cereals: limited magazine, radio, and television ads emphasized that message. Selling through food brokers instead of staffing a large internal sales force also helped Malt-O-Meal keep prices down.

Malt-O-Meal's strategy paid off on the bottom line. In a September 1990 *Forbes* magazine article, John Harris estimated 1989 profits to be $4 million. Harris wrote, ''Only a handful of regional and independent cereal companies remain in a business in which a new product introduction can easily cost $15 million.'' Despite purchase offers, Malt-O-Meal continued to be held by members of the founding family.

Challenges of the 1990s and Beyond

Revenues reached an estimated $137 million in 1991. Malt-O-Meal sales had grown at a compound annual rate of just less than 17 percent since 1975, according to a May 1992 *Star Tribune* article by Dick Youngblood. The company added to its production facilities nine times during that same time period. The well-trained employees, numbering more than 450, were divided into production teams.

Malt-O-Meal had pumped in about $100 million on plant and equipment during the 1980s and first few years of the 1990s, according to Youngblood. But while its laboratories could copy the ingredients of big name cereals—only trademarks, names, and technologies could be patented—they still faced some marketing barriers. Time-crunched consumers tended to buy familiar brands, and many potential customers viewed Malt-O-Meal as only a hot cereal maker.

So with about a dozen different flavors in its bagged cereal lineup, Malt-O-Meal began experimenting with additional advertising. General Mills quickly complained that their TV ad comparison of Toasty O's to Cheerios was misleading in terms of taste and price. The National Advertising Division of the Better Business Bureau agreed, and Malt-O-Meal pulled the 1992 ad.

Sales topped the $200 million mark in 1993, two years ahead of Lettmann's target date, according to a March 1994 *St. Paul Pioneer Press* article by Dave Beal. Malt-O-Meal celebrated its 75th anniversary in 1994 with the ground-breaking for a three-year expansion estimated by Beal to cost about $80 million. The 70 percent increase in space would boost the facility to 860,000 square feet and make it one of the largest manufacturing plants in Minnesota.

While Malt-O-Meal bagged cereal sales were growing, the private-label boxed cereals continued to bring in about half the ready-to-eat cereal revenues. Malt-O-Meal held an estimated 25 percent share of the U.S. private-label market. Ralston Purina (later Ralcorp Holdings Inc.) held about 60 percent. But, according to the Beal article, market analysts believed Ralston's share was falling while Malt-O-Meal was on the rise.

The value end of the cereal business was growing at a faster pace than the overall industry and both small and large companies wanted to tap into the market. Minnesota-based Grist Mill Inc., which packaged granola cereal under its own name and private labels, began offering several more cereal varieties in 1993. Quaker Oats, which held 15 percent of the bagged cereal market through its Stokely Van Camp subsidiary's Popeye brand, began putting its own name on the lower-cost bags in 1994. Malt-O-Meal held about 75 percent of the bagged cereal market.

Malt-O-Meal moved to increase consumer awareness of bagged cereals through a new take on its advertising. Laurie Freeman wrote in a July 1995 *Advertising Age* article, ''The 'Walk This Way' spot shows regular folks doing a duck walk—squatting down and waddling by the lower shelves of the cereal aisle, where Malt-O-Meal cereals are usually found.'' The humorous television ad aired in 13 key markets, including Minneapolis, Seattle, and Phoenix, and on network cable. But Malt-O-Meal's ad budget remained minuscule compared with those of the national brands.

The production commenced on five more ready-to-eat cereals, Tootie Fruities, Apple Cinnamon Toasty O's, Coco Roos, Marshmallow Mateys, and Corn Bursts, between 1989 and 1995. Malt-O-Meal added Apple & Cinnamon to the hot cereal offerings in 1995. Original and chocolate-flavored cereals, and Maple & Brown Sugar Malt-O-Meal, which had been produced since 1992, completed the line that produced about 15 percent of total company sales of about $250 million.

In 1996 Malt-O-Meal was the first value-priced cereal maker to lower its prices in response to price cuts by Kellogg, General Mills, and Philip Morris, owner of Post and Nabisco brands. The companies were trying to halt market share erosion caused by the value-priced offerings. Although Malt-O-Meal had not raised its prices in five years, an average of 12 percent was knocked off ten of its cereals to maintain an 80 cents to $1.00 price differentiation.

Commodity price fluctuations affected both the small and large cereal makers in the 1990s and would continue to play a factor in Malt-O-Meal's earnings in the future. Corn, wheat, oats, and rice were the primary grains used by cereal producers. In the past Malt-O-Meal management and employees had responded by improving production efficiencies to keep costs in check without having to raise prices. Increased competition in the value end of the market and price wars among the giant cereal makers could also put pressure on the company.

Further Reading

Beal, Dave, ''Malt-O-Meal Heats Up,'' *St. Paul Pioneer Press,* March 28, 1994, pp. 1B, 3B.

Egerstrom, Lee, ''Malt-O-Meal of Minneapolis Cuts Prices on Its Breakfast Cereals,'' *St. Paul Pioneer Press,* July 9, 1996.

''Founder of Cereal Company Dies at 83,'' *Minneapolis Star,* November 2, 1971.

Fredrickson, Tom, ''Rivals Could Milk Gain from Kellogg Price Hike,'' *Minneapolis/St. Paul CityBusiness,* February 18, 1994.

Freeman, Laurie, ''Malt-O-Meal Stirring Up the Competition,'' *Advertising Age,* July 17, 1994, p. 4.

''Glenn Brooks Is Named President of Malt-O-Meal,'' *Minneapolis Tribune,* April 20, 1966.

''Good Ideas,'' *Twin Cities Business Monthly,* April 1997, p. 11.

Harris, John, ''Your Taste Buds Won't Know, Your Pocketbook Will,'' *Forbes,* September 3, 1990, pp. 88, 90.

Jones, Gwenyth, ''Firm Says Hot Cereal Sales Gain,'' *Minneapolis Star,* May 9, 1958.

Kennedy, Tony, ''Battle of the Cereals,'' *Star Tribune* (Minneapolis), October 28, 1992, p. 6D.

——, ''Grist Mill Is Expanding to Private-Label Cereals,'' *Star Tribune* (Minneapolis), December 18, 1992, p. 5D.

——, ''Quaker To Put Its Brand on Bagged Cereals in Bid for Larger Share of the Budget Market,'' *Star Tribune* (Minneapolis), January 24, 1995.

Kurschner, Dale, ''Cold Cereals Are Hot Sellers in Strategy by Malt-O-Meal,'' *Minneapolis/St. Paul CityBusiness,* July 23–29, 1990, pp. 1, 18.

''Malt-O-Meal,'' *Minneapolis Tribune,* January 17, 1971.

''Malt-O-Meal Co. Acquires Vinyl Plastics Firm,'' *Minneapolis Star,* November 17, 1967.

''Malt-O-Meal Company,'' *Corporate Report Fact Book 1997,* p. 583.

''Malt-O-Meal: 75 Years of Tradition and Progress,'' *Northfield News,* Special Section, 1994.

McFadden, Charles B., ''Malt-O-Meal Began As $800 Gamble,'' *Minneapolis Tribune,* September 21, 1969.

Peterson, Susan E., ''Malt-O-Meal's New Chief Takes Over in Era of Change,'' *Star Tribune* (Minneapolis), February 10, 1986, p. 2M.

Smith, M.L., ''Executive Glenn Brooks Dies at 61,'' *Star Tribune* (Minneapolis), June 14, 1988, p. 6B.

Youngblood, Dick, ''Malt-O-Meal Story a Series of Cereals,'' *Star Tribune* (Minneapolis), May 4, 1992, p. 2D.

—Kathleen Peippo

Manufactured Home Communities, Inc.

Two North Riverside Plaza
Suite #600
Chicago, Illinois 60606
U.S.A.
(312) 474-1122
Fax: (312) 474-0205

Public Company
Incorporated: 1993
Employees: 465
Sales: $105 million (1996)
Stock Exchanges: New York
SICs: 6798 Real Estate Investment Trusts

Manufactured Home Communities, Inc. is one of the most successful and fastest-growing real estate investment trusts (REIT) in the United States. The company owns or possesses a majority interest in 69 manufactured home communities (as opposed to site-built residences) in 19 states. Normally, an REIT is primarily engaged in closed-end investments in real estate or in related mortgage assets management and operations, so that the company could meet the requirements of the Real Estate Investment Trust Act of 1960, which exempts such trusts from corporate income and capital gains taxes, provided that the company invest primarily in specified assets, pay out most of its income to shareholders, and meet certain criteria regarding the dispersion of trust ownership. Manufactured Home Communities is not subject to federal income tax, therefore, to the extent its REIT taxable income is distributed to its stockholders. The company's total revenues amounted to $105 million in 1996, and its acquisitions during the same year brought the total number of its sites to 27,356, making the company one of the countries largest owners and operators of manufactured housing communities.

Early History

The driving force behind the growth and development of Manufactured Home Communities is Samuel Zell, a Chicago-based entrepreneur with a penchant for motorcycles, not unlike one of his billionaire contemporaries, the late Malcolm Forbes. Having been raised and educated in modest circumstances in the Midwest. Zell met his future partner while an undergraduate student at the University of Michigan. Robert Lurie, another ambitious product of a middle-class American family, struck up a friendship with Zell that was to last a lifetime. Roommates and fraternity brothers at the university during the late 1960s, Zell and Lurie decided to form a business partnership with the intention of acquiring and managing a corporate empire.

In what developed into an affectionate and symbiotic partnership, the first move made by the enterprising young men was the formation of Equity Group Investment, Inc., the company that would become the holding firm for their burgeoning empire. As Zell traveled back and forth across the United States doing what he does best, namely, making multimillion-dollar deals, Lurie remained the cornerstone of the firm and established a solid foundation for the company's day-to-day operations and financial management. Soon the two men were owners of real estate properties, and investors in major private and public operating companies throughout the U.S. By the mid-1970s, Zell and Lurie had become millionaires.

Zell and Lurie developed a reputation for free-wheeling, no-holds-barred business deals, specializing in the acquisition, reconfiguration, and turnaround of an extremely diverse range of companies. One of the more arcane financial arrangements made by Lurie and Zell during the late 1970s involved a $400 million tax-loss carry-forward which enabled Zell to transform his newly purchased Itel Corporation, an integrated network and cabling firm, into a vehicle that engaged in the acquisition of other companies. As their holdings increased, Zell and Lurie became owners of hundreds of millions of dollars of real estate, and such disparate companies as real estate investment trusts, integrated network and cabling firms, a fertilizer company, an international communications company, and a management fund that specialized in corporate turnarounds.

Change and Transition During the 1980s

Lurie and Zell continued their winning ways during the early part of the 1980s, accruing one acquisition after another in the

Company Perspectives:

Our mission is to operate high quality manufactured housing communities responsibly and ethically, to share an absolute passion for excellence and resident satisfaction at every level. To empower every employee to take initiative and be a creative agent of change. To set and meet aggressive goals that benefit our residents, employees and shareholders.

building of their corporate monolith. Yet Lurie began to feel listless and unwell, and after returning from a doctor's appointment told his lifelong partner that he had lung cancer. Zell was distraught by the news, but the two men continued their partnership while Lurie battled his disease. At the same time, however, Lurie was not unaware of the seriousness of his condition and decided to groom a possible successor in the event of his passing away. When Robert Lurie died in 1990, his hand-chosen protégé, Sheli Rosenberg, a lawyer who had been trained by Lurie and Zell since coming to work for Equity Group Investments in 1979 as its in-house lawyer, did not lose a step in taking over the day-to-day operations of what had developed into a corporate giant.

As Rosenberg assumed the chores and responsibilities of Lurie during the mid- and late 1980s, commercial banking capital had all but dried up, and the real estate market was hard hit by overcapacity. Consequently Zell, still affected by the death of his closest friend and loyal business partner, was entirely thwarted in his fervor for making business deals due to the lack of available cash. Rosenberg, well trained by Lurie, suggested to Zell that the next logical step was to take public many of the larger companies the two partners had purchased during the 1980s. Soon Zell and Rosenberg had raised over $600 million by selling shares in companies such as American Classic Voyages, a major cruise ship operator; Vigoro, a large fertilizer firm; and numerous apartment holdings. With his new head of operations, Zell was back in business and with Rosenberg's help successfully set up the Zell/Chilmark merchant banking fund capitalized at over one billion, and the two billion Zell/Merrill Lynch Real Estate Opportunity Partners Fund.

The Early 1990s

It was during the mid-1980s that Zell and Lurie had organized a manufactured housing community business named Mobile Home Communities, Inc., along with certain already established limited partnerships, that owned and operated 41 manufactured housing communities. Manufactured home communities had grown in popularity throughout the 1980s, and the two partners saw an investment opportunity that was hard to avoid. One of the most important reasons for the growth of such communities was the average cost of approximately $23 per square foot of living space, less than half of what it costs in site-built homes. For a growing number of people, especially the elderly living on fixed incomes, this was the only way to achieve home ownership. With centralized entrances, paved streets, club houses, exercise rooms, swimming pools, tennis courts, cable television and organized social activities, manufactured housing communities offered a highly attractive lifestyle to many retirees.

Renamed Manufactured Home Communities, Inc. and organized as a real estate investment trust (REIT), the company went public in 1993. From its inception, Manufactured Home Communities was the largest national manufactured housing community REIT in existence, with 50 company-owned communities in 17 states, and containing more than 16,000 homesites. In just a few short months after its initial public offering in March, the company acquired over 4,000 additional homesites and significantly increased its revenues and income. By the end of fiscal 1993, Manufactured Home Communities had increased its revenue by 22 percent over the previous year, from $34.5 to $42 million.

The year 1994 was a successful one for Manufactured Home Communities. Total revenues for the company increased 64 percent, impressive by any standard, to $68 million. The primary reason for this dramatic increase was the number of acquisitions made by Zell and his management team. During 1994 alone, Manufactured Home Communities grew from 50 communities with 20,000 homesites to 67 communities with over 25,000 homesites. In addition to completing an offering of 4 million shares of stock and raising approximately $76 million in four days, the company also announced a two-for-one stock split.

Since the average monthly rent in one of Zell's Manufactured Home Communities amounted to a total of only $294, not only retired people but younger residents began moving into manufactured housing rather than conventional homes. Due to the fact that manufactured homes are built at a factory, not onsite, and then shipped to the housing community location, the actual construction time for the unit is measured in days instead of months. This type of manufactured construction results in lower costs, usually between 20 percent and 50 percent less than the normal construction of an onsite home. In 1994, company statistics reveal that 80 percent of Manufactured Home Communities residents were retired people, while the remaining 20 percent were young adults.

Acquisitions during this period of time were numerous, including the six manufactured housing communities of Palm Shadows, Brentwood Manor, Del Rey, Oak Bend, Spanish Oaks and the Heritage, and the entire holdings of DeAnza Group Properties, which alone accounted for an additional 5,738 sites in 11 communities. Most of these acquisitions increased the company's presence in the sunbelt states of Arizona, New Mexico, and Nevada. Having acquired some of the finest manufactured home communities in the nation, one of the earlier properties purchased by the company, Pine Lakes in North Ft. Myers, Florida, was listed in 1994 in *The 50 Best Retirement Communities in America.*

Continued Growth During the Mid-1990s

Without interruption, revenues for the company continued to grow at an impressive rate. By the end of fiscal 1995, Manufactured Home Communities had increased its revenues by 41 percent over the previous year, from $68 million to $96 million. Much of this was due to the successful integration of the properties acquired in 1993 and 1994. The average occupancy rate at the company's housing communities increased slightly from 1994 to 1995, while the average monthly rent per site increased a modest eight percent. An aggressive internal cost control program significantly reduced the company's administrative expenses to under 10 percent of total revenues. Yet Zell and his management team continued to search for bargain acquisitions, and added a total of 225 sites to the company's portfolio for 1995.

As a real estate investment trust, Manufactured Home Communities used its capital and management skills to identify and acquire high-quality communities that enhanced its portfolio and, consequently, its earnings and stock price per share. In 1996, the company made $50 million in acquisitions, including Waterford Estates in Wilmington, Delaware, Candlelight Village in Columbus, Indiana, Casa del Sol I and Casa del Sol II in Phoenix, Arizona, and California Hawaiian Mobile Estates, a manufactured housing community located near San Jose, California. Most of these acquisitions were made near resort or vacation areas, and were highly attractive to retired persons looking for value in a housing site.

With a hefty supply of capital at his disposal, Zell continued his acquisition strategy even more aggressively by making an unsolicited offer of approximately $400 million for Chateau Properties, Inc., a REIT based in Clinton, Michigan, with 47 manufactured home communities and over 20,000 sites nationwide. Management at Chateau Properties, however, was not inclined to accept Zell's offer. Undeterred, Zell offered a surprising $26 per share for Chateau, at one time a 12 percent premium over its closing stock price. Still management at Chateau refused and, instead, accepted a merger with ROC Communities, Inc., an Engelwood, Colorado, manufactured home community firm for approximately $300 million.

Unfortunately, as Zell and his management team focused on a growth through acquisition strategy, revenues at Manufactured Home Communities slowed dramatically. From 1995 to 1996, the company's total revenues grew from $96 million to $105 million. The large number of acquisitions during the early and mid-1990s had left the company with a large unanticipated overhead and, in spite of administrative cost-cutting measures, earnings for the company and its stock price began to drop precipitously. Realizing his mistake, Zell shuffled some of the management team at Manufactured Home Communities to other positions within his corporate empire, with the result of a gradually improving earnings performance for the company.

With management now stable, Zell is confident that he can increase the holdings of Manufactured Home Communities, while at the same time continuing its aggressive expansion strategy. Since Zell is on the board of directors or runs 25 other companies within his empire, a good management team at Manufactured Home Communities is essential for its continued growth and success.

Principal Subsidiaries

DeAnza Group, Inc.; Realty Systems, Inc.

Further Reading

"Chateau Properties Inc.," *Wall Street Journal,* October 4, 1996, p. A4(E).

"Chateau Properties Inc.," *Wall Street Journal,* November 14, 1996, p. B4(E).

Lipin, Steve, "Manufactured Home Offers $400 Million for Chateau in Challenge to ROC Deal," *Wall Street Journal,* August 19, 1966, p. A3(E).

"Manufactured Home Buyback," *Wall Street Journal,* May 15, 1997, p. B6(E).

"Manufactured Home's Purchase," *Wall Street Journal,* March 17, 1997, p. B11(E).

Melcher, Richard A., "Has Sam Been Minding the Store? With Parts of His Empire Languishing, Zell Is Bolstering Management," *Business Week,* November 13, 1995, pp. 120–121.

Pacelle, Mitchell, "Zell Drops His Offer for Chateau, Sweetens Merger Proposal Terms," *Wall Street Journal,* November 8, 1996, p. B6(E).

Upbin, Bruce, "A Zelluva Partner," *Forbes,* June 2, 1997 pp. 122–123.

Vinocur, Barry, "Sam Zell's Offer for Chateau Properties Exposes a Flaw in a Common REIT Structure," *Barron's,* August 26, 1996, p. 34(1).

Wangensteen, Betsy, "Zell's Hidden Asset: Just One of the Boys," *Crain's Chicago Business,* November 4, 1996, p. 1.

—Thomas Derdak

Marie Brizard & Roger International S.A.

130-142, rue Fondaudège BP 557
33002 Bordeaux Cedex
France
(33) 5.56.01.85.85
Fax: (33) 5.56.01.85.99

Public Company
Incorporated: 1755
Employees: 938
Sales: FFr1.9 billion (1996)
Stock Exchanges: Paris
SICs: 2084 Wines, Brandy & Brandy Spirits; 2085 Distilled & Blended Liquors; 2086 Bottled & Canned Soft Drinks

While most companies are content to count their histories in years, Marie Brizard & Roger International S.A. count theirs in generations. With the tenth generation represented among the company's leadership and principal shareholders, the Bordeaux-based alcoholic beverage producer is one of France's oldest continuously operated, family-controlled enterprises. Famed for its anisette cordials—indeed, many credit the company with originating the *anisette de Bordeaux* category—Marie Brizard has developed an extensive portfolio of company-produced and licensed alcoholic and non-alcoholic beverages, as well as a worldwide distribution network, enabling the company to maintain its independence despite the intense consolidation of the industry during the 1980s and 1990s.

Part of Marie Brizard's longevity is credited to the company's early implementation of a diversified product line. Indeed, the company's flagship anise-flavored cordial, the renowned Marie Brizard anisette, accounted for just seven percent of the company's annual revenues in 1996. The Marie Brizard label also includes an extensive range of fruit-flavored liqueurs, and popular aperitifs and digestifs including Chocolat Royal, Charleston Follies, and Védrenne. The company's Old Lady's gin is one of France's top-selling gins, with sales of some 1.5 million bottles per year. The company-produced spirits line also include Berger Blanc and Berger Pastis anise-liqueurs, Gautier cognac, Lochmore Scotch whiskey, and Mohawk vodka . Marie Brizard also distributes a range of licensed labels, including Whyte & Mackay whiskeys in France, Cutty Sark in Australia, and the rums Le Mauny and Duquesne in France, and Gosling's in the United States. Together, the spirits category accounted for 34 percent of Marie Brizard's 1996 sales.

Marie Brizard has also diversified beyond alcoholic beverages, allowing the company to weather the declining consumption—spurred in part by heavy taxes imposed on purchases of alcoholic beverages—of the 1980s and 1990s. Marie Brizard and its subsidiaries hold leadership positions in the fruit juices, syrups, and concentrates segments. The company's Cidou brand is France's leading fruit juice label in the brick category. The company's Sport, Lieutard, Védrenne, and Altovisto syrups—popularly mixed with carbonated and non-carbonated water—capture strong sales in the bottled and premium categories. The company also leads the fruit juice concentrates category with its Pulco brand. In 1996, the non-alcoholic beverages category represented 43 percent of company sales.

Marie Brizard also produces and distributes a range of wines, champagnes, and sparkling wines, some of which originates from the company's own vineyards. Champagnes are represented by the company's house brands Philipponnat and Abel Lepitre, as well as agency brands including Mommessin in the United States and Australia, and Rothschild in the United States. Marie Brizard sparkling wine labels include Grandin des Caves de la Bouvraie, Paul Bur, and Veuve du Vernay, while the company's still wines include the labels Bodega Rioja Marques del Puerto in Spain and Hermit's Brook and Kindelwood, in Australia. Under the Duc de Birac label, Marie Brizard also produces its pineau des Charentes, a French regional favorite.

Despite the emergence of such global beverage distribution giants as Seagram, Grand Met, and France's own Pernod-Ricard, Marie Brizard has developed a strong international presence, with sales of its products in more than 150 countries. France remains the company's strongest source of revenues, accounting for 67 percent of 1996 sales. Spain, with 10 percent of sales, and the United States, with six percent of sales, represent the company's most important international markets. In conjunction with its distribution network, Marie Brizard, which operates more than 10 production and distribution facilities in

France, has also developed a global production presence, with plants in Spain and Portugal, and sales networks in the United States, Belgium, Netherlands, Australia, and Japan.

Marie Brizard is led by CEO Paul Glotin, representing the eighth generation of the founding family. Unlike many family-owned firms, however, Marie Brizard has long incorporated non-family members in key management and directorship positions, and the company celebrated its 10th anniversary as a public company—listed on the Paris secondary market—in 1994. Family members wishing to join the company must fulfill a number of criteria, and even then must wait for a position to open. In 1996, the company posted revenues of FFr1.9 billion, down slightly from the year before. The company's earnings have also been under pressure at the mid-point in the decade, posting net losses of FFr24 million and FFr37 million in 1995 and 1996, respectively.

A Taste for the 18th Century

Marie Brizard represented a rarity in 18th century French economic life. Where women were, for the most part, shut out of commerce, Marie Brizard not only led her own company, but founded the company herself. Unmarried at the age of 41, Marie Brizard—according to company legend—gave part of her time nursing the ill in Bordeaux's hospitals. One of her patients had come to France from one of the country's colonial islands. Grateful for her care, the patient gave Marie Brizard the recipe for an elixir popular in his home country, a beverage purported to possess all manner of properties conducive to good health. Marie Brizard's determination to perfect and produce this beverage, as the legend continued, came more from altruism than from commercialism.

In reality, anise-flavored drinks had already made their appearance earlier in the century. Marie Brizard's father, Pierre, owned a small distillery and produced anisette prior to his death in 1743. The distillery would eventually be transferred to Marie Brizard's name in 1755, coincidentally when Pierre's creditors won a judgment demanding that Pierre's debts be paid. In that year, Marie Brizard joined with Jean-Baptiste Roger, married to one of her nieces, who brought in a supply of capital, while Marie Brizard supplied the family-owned distillery equipment. The company's operations officially started in 1755, purchasing green anise from Spain and installing itself in a distillery in Bordeaux to produce its anisette. The beverage proved a quick success in the court of King Louis XV, and soon became a popular liqueur among France's privileged class.

The company soon added the ''international'' element to its name. At the time, Bordeaux was one of the most important ports in Europe, particularly through its position in the spice trade. As Marie Brizard's anisette recipe was dependent on imported spices, the company began trading bottles of its anisette for spices, bringing the Marie Brizard label to such French territories as Haiti and Louisiana by the early 1760s. By the end of the century, the company was firmly established and prosperous.

Jean-Baptiste Roger died in 1795, and his share of the company was transferred to his widow. Marie Brizard would die in 1801, at the age of 87. By then, however, Marie, with no children of her own, had transferred the company to Roger's widow and sons. While prosperous, the company entered the 19th century a relatively modest concern in a field crowded with anise-flavored drinks. Yet, by the end of the century, Marie Brizard had seen most of its competitors disappear. Marie Brizard itself had earned a reputation for its quality, top-shelf liqueur. Another factor in the company's success was its longstanding refusal to allow nepotism to play a part in its management. Family members wishing to enter the business were required to gain a strong degree of experience. At the same time, the company showed no reluctance in hiring talent from outside the family. The company had also begun diversifying beyond anisette, launching its own cognac in the 1860s, bitters in the 1870s, a creme de cocoa in 1880, a creme de menthe in 1890, while also producing cherry and apricot brandies and other fruit-flavored liqueurs. The diversification performed well for the company, which saw sales rise from 21 million ancient francs in the 1870s to 71 million ancient francs at the turn of the century.

Expanding in the 20th Century

While exports had continued to build during the 19th century, it was in the early decades of the 20th century that foreign sales began to take on a true importance for the company. Marie Brizard first looked toward Spain, a premier producer of anise and one of the largest markets for anise-flavored drinks. In 1904, Marie Brizard opened its first foreign sales branch and warehouse, in the Spanish Pyrenees region. In 1924, the company installed its first Spanish distillery. Over the next 60 years, the company would expand its Spanish production capacity to three plants, and capture more than 30 percent of Spain's anise-beverage market.

As Marie Brizard continued to build its sales of anisette to the foreign market, the company also recognized the need to diversify its offerings. At the turn of the century, the company had launched a new creme de cocoa label, Topaze, which proved a strong success. Following World War I, Marie Brizard began developing its product line, clinging to alcoholic beverages, starting with rum, with the Charleston label, and soon followed by gin, under the Old Lady's label, the latter building in sales to become the top-selling gin in France. The company also launched an intensive expansion program, modernizing and building new production facilities. Growth slowed during the Depression years and sales continued to remain slow through the years following World War II. Nonetheless, by the late 1950s, the company's sales were topping 100 million ancient francs. During the 1950s, the company also began making a strategy shift, adding the distribution of other brands to its own brand names. One of the first of these came in 1956, when Marie Brizard sought to add a new spirits category, Scotch whiskey. For this, the company teamed up with another family-run enterprise, the William Grant Company of Scotland, becoming the exclusive French distributor for that company's Grant's whiskey—which would become the largest-selling whiskey in France, and the eighth-largest worldwide—and later Glenfiddich and Clan MacGregor labels.

In the early 1970s, however, Marie Brizard was quick to recognize the clouds looming over the alcoholic beverages industry. A number of factors were beginning to place pressure on liquor sales: the rising health concerns, particularly the recognition of alcoholism as a disease, coupled with increasing dietary and weight consciousness, which saw digestif consumption—the primary market for anisette—decline in favor of continued aperitif consumption. The 1970s also saw the first in a long series of increasing tax burdens on alcohol sales. In 1973, Marie Brizard took the first step beyond the alcoholic beverage category, forming an association with the fruit juice specialist Ralli, of Aubagne, to create a line of citrus-flavored fruit juice drinks. In 1975, the company launched the first in its line of Pulco concentrated fruit juice drinks, Pulco Citron, which was followed by Pulco Orange. The Pulco launch was a success: in four years, sales of the fruit juices quadrupled, reaching FFr58 million, and Marie Brizard captured some 90 percent of the category it had invented. The Pulco brand also found success beyond the French border in Belgium, Germany, and Spain. In 1980, Marie Brizard acquired Ralli, marking the company's first acquisition.

The company remained a fairly modest operation, with sales of FFr360 million and 350 employees in the early 1980s. But Marie Brizard, by then led by Paul and Gérard Glotin, the eighth generation of the Roger line, was preparing to step up the company's expansion. The first step towards this end came in 1981, when the family-owned company opened its capital to outside investors, selling six percent of the company. This step was followed by a public offering in 1984, when the company was listed on the Paris secondary market. This move, however, would introduce waves in the longstanding relationship between Marie Brizard and William Grant. At the offering, the Grant family company—wary of this breach in the tradition of family ownership—bought up the majority of the shares introduced to the public. Yet, even with nearly nine percent of Marie Brizard's shares, the Grant family found itself excluded from Marie Brizard's board of directors and its decisions regarding the company's future.

Meanwhile, Marie Brizard was preparing to round out its beverages offerings. In 1987, the company moved into the champagne category, acquiring Champagne Philipponnat label and production operations. Two years later, Marie Brizard added the company Grand Champagnes de Reims and its Abel Lepitre label. While the move into champagne proved less than successful—and would eventually drag the company into the red in the 1990s—Marie Brizard found fortune through a number of other expansion moves. In 1988, the company acquired SLJFB Vedrenne, the leading producer of cassis de Bourgogne liqueurs.

Other acquisitions followed in the early 1990s. In 1991, the company expanded its non-alcoholic beverages sales with the purchases of the Abel Bresson line of syrups, popularly mixed with carbonated and non-carbonated water, and the Cidou brand of fruit juices. At the same time, Marie Brizard was also putting in place a distribution network that would enable it to survive as an independent despite massive consolidation in the distribution industry. Faced with competing against global goliaths such as Seagram and Guinness, Marie Brizard began developing what it dubbed its "spiderweb strategy," building, through joint-ventures and alliances, a European distribution network among other independent and family-owned beverage producers, including Codorniu of Spain, Peter Eckes of Germany, and O'Darby of Ireland. Meanwhile, Marie Brizard also set up a Netherlands-based holding company, Marie Brizard European Development, to oversee the company's future acquisition activities.

Between 1991 and 1995, the company stepped up its expansion, both in France and overseas. The company acquired Mohawk, a vodka producer and distribution network in the United States, renamed as Marie Brizard Wines and Spirits USA, and purchased a distributor, Pat Foods, for its products in Australia. The company also acquired Caves Altovisto, adding that company's wines, sparkling wines, and other liqueurs and spirits, as well as a distribution arm in Portugal. In Belgium, the company added the Cinoco distribution network. By 1993, the company's sales reached FFr1.8 billion, more than four times its revenues just ten years earlier.

The tensions building between Marie Brizard and William Grant, however, came to a head at the beginning of 1994. As of January 1994, the Grant family announced that it was ending its 35-year-old relationship with Marie Brizard, having secretly reached an agreement with another French distributor. The loss of the Grant distributorship caused a crisis at Marie Brizard, which saw its revenues plunge to FFr1.4 billion for the 1994 year.

Nonetheless, by the end of 1995, Marie Brizard was able to overcome the Grant loss, rebuilding revenues to more than FFr1.9 billion. In 1994, Marie Brizard found a new Scotch whiskey distribution partner in Whyte and Mackay, and also added several other labels, including Janneau amargnac, Ferrieira port, and La Mauny rum. These new distribution agreements helped to buffer some of the sales slump due to the Grant loss. Aiding the company's sales was its January 1995 purchase of Marseilles-based Berger, a producer of anise drinks, syrups, and sparkling wines founded in 1923.

Absorbing Berger, which posted FFr815 million in sales in 1994, would give Marie Brizard a slight case of indigestion—coupled with continued losses in its champagnes segment, the restructuring effort following the Berger merger would dip Marie Brizard into the red, with net losses of FFr24 million and FFr37 million for 1995 and 1996, respectively. In February 1995, however, Marie Brizard was buoyed somewhat when it was awarded damages of FFr130 million in its breach-of-contract lawsuit against Grant. And strengthened by the Berger merger, Marie Brizard & Roger International—and its tenth-generation family leadership—looked forward to maintaining its position as one of France's oldest family-owned, independent companies.

Principal Subsidiaries

Marie Brizard Berger Diffusion (France); Berger S.A.(France); Champagne Philipponnat S.A. (France); Sorevi S.A. (France); S.N. Caves de la Bouvraie S.A.R.L. (France); Danflou Vedrenne S.A. (France); Cognac Gautier S.A. Gemaco (France); Cidou S.A. (France); Marie Brizard Espana S.A. (Spain); Bodega Marques del Puerto (Spain); Caves Altoviso Vinicola do Passadouro LDA (Portugal); Caves Quinta da Corga LDA (Portugal); S.A. Cinoco N.V. (Belgium); Marie Brizard European Development N.V. (Netherlands); Marie Brizard Wines & Spirits USA; Pat Foods Pty Ltd. (Australia); M.B.R.I. Japan.

Further Reading

Durieux, Isabelle, "Guerre de familles," *L'Expansion,* October 24, 1994, pp. 78–80.

"Marie-Brizard: une recette de longevité," *L'Expansion,* October 1982, pp. 227–29.

—M. L. Cohen

Marvin Lumber & Cedar Company

Highway 11, P.O. Box 100
Warroad, Minnesota 56763
U.S.A.
(218) 386-1430
Fax: (218) 386-2925
Web site: http://www.marvin.com

Private Company
Founded: 1904 as Marvin Timber and Cedar Company
Employees: 4,000
Sales: $300 million (1996 est.)
SICs: 5031 Lumber, Plywood & Millwork

Marvin Lumber & Cedar Company, known as Marvin Windows & Doors, manufactures top-of-the-line wood-frame windows for custom luxury-home building and for the remodeling segment of the construction market. The company also builds patio door units and lower-cost windows at plants outside of Minnesota. In spite of location barriers—the Warroad-based company is headquartered in the northernmost region of the contiguous 48 states and is closer to Winnipeg, Canada, than to Minneapolis/St. Paul—the Marvin family business has extended its reach throughout the U.S. and into Canada, Japan, and Mexico.

A Small-Town Business: 1900s–50s

George Marvin moved to Warroad in 1904 to manage a grain elevator and lumber yard. The Canadian owners shut down the business and moved back across the border two years later when they discovered the region did not produce enough raw grain and lumber for their operations. Marvin bought the lumber yard, established his own business, Marvin Timber and Cedar Company, and began selling goods to the settlers in the area. The company changed its name to Marvin Lumber and Cedar in 1912.

Located in a remote region about six miles from the Canadian border, Marvin's business operation was small but diverse. In addition to the lumber, Marvin established feed, hardware, and grain mill ventures. George's oldest son, William (Bill), joined the company in 1939; he was the eighth employee of the 35-year-old business. The younger Marvin, a graduate of the University of Minnesota with degrees in agronomy and agricultural economics, briefly worked for General Mills before being called home to the family business when his uncle became ill.

The seeds of the window operation were sown about that time when Harry York, the lumber yard manager, persuaded the Marvins to allow him to build barn windows during the slow winter months. When window sales proved successful, barn sash and screens were added to the product line. The woodworking capability opened the door for government subcontracts for ammunition boxes and food containers during World War II, and the company's labor force jumped to 50 people. Anticipating the need for postwar rural jobs, Bill Marvin and his father turned their sight back to window manufacturing. The Warroad company began operating as Marvin Windows in 1951, and Bill Marvin succeed his father as head of the business in 1957.

Rising from the Ashes: 1960s–80s

In 1961, a fire destroyed the Marvin plant. The window operation was insured for only 57 percent of its total value. Loans from the Rural Electrification Administration (REA)—which provided power to the area—and the Small Business Administration (SBA) got the business back on its feet. Marvin employed 200 by 1970.

The company became airborne in 1976. Ellen Wojahn wrote in an April 1981 *Corporate Report Minnesota* article, ''All roads do *not* lead to Warroad. To interest his potential customers, Marvin often has to fly them in on the company plane. But the effort is worth it, because he has found that, when attempting to sell energy-efficient wood windows and patio doors, seeing—and shivering—is believing.'' According to Wojahn, Marvin would often reinforce the image of the north woods by taking his guests to visit the Christian Brothers hockey stick plant as well. ''You've got to build a sort of romance in a person's mind,'' he said.

Sales doubled from 1977 to 1979, but the housing industry was at the beginning of a dramatic downturn. Stung by an economic recession and mortgage interest rates as high as 17 percent, housing starts fell from 2.1 million units in late 1978 to 900,000 units in mid-1980. Marvin sales dropped 12 percent in 1980 to $40 million. The work week at the plant was temporarily shortened to four days while other manufacturers were laying off employees.

Marvin's ''made-to-order'' philosophy proved to be an asset to the company during the housing slump. The remodeling, renovation, and custom-home segments of the industry continued to generate business during the tight economic times, and since Marvin milled and stored and assembled component parts per order, the company had greater production flexibility than companies producing and stockpiling completed standard-sized windows. In addition, the company's trucking fleet, which had been established in the 1950s, allowed Marvin to ship its product quickly once the order had been made and filled. In turn, they trucked in Ponderosa pine from their own rough wood plant in Oregon, as well as, glass, screen, and hardware from other manufacturers located around the country.

The 11-acre Warroad plant operated with a peak work force of 1,150 in 1981: the population of its hometown was only 1,200. Marvin hired 16 percent of Roseau County's labor force and drew employees from a large geographic area, including the economically depressed Minnesota Iron Range. The non-union plant had instituted employee profit sharing in 1957. Nearly half the employees were women, and another small percentage were elderly—the company had no mandatory retirement age. Bill Marvin, in the Wojahn article, credited his employees for the success of the company. But faced with a limited labor market and wishing to capitalize on the housing growth in the South, Marvin built a patio door plant in Ripley, Tennessee, in 1981.

Housing starts rebounded in 1983 and remained steady into 1988. But during the same period the remodeling market jumped from $45 billion to $90 billion. Much of the U.S. housing stock had been built between the 1930s and 1950s and was ready for repair and remodeling. Hundreds of window manufacturers vied for a piece of the action. Marvin flourished.

In an April 30, 1990, *Forbes* article, John Harris called Marvin ''the nation's fastest-growing producer of custom-made wood windows and doors.'' Sales for the privately held company had increased from $40 to $265 million over the last decade, and profits for 1989 were up 19 percent to an estimated $26 million, according to Harris. But Bayport, Minnesota-based Andersen Corp. held fast to first place with an estimated $1 billion in sales, and Rolscreen Co.'s Iowa-based Pella Windows held the number two spot with estimated annual sales of $350 million. Both companies were also privately held.

Marvin's impressive array of products included curved glass windows, round-top windows, and window reproductions. Marvin offered more options for glass than Andersen. Ninety distributors, located throughout the U.S., and in Japan and Canada, sold windows and doors to 3,000 lumber yards and specialty stores. Since the company built its product to order, retailers and distributors carried catalogs and display windows but no inventory.

A Rough Start to the 1990s

Housing starts began to slip again in 1989, but other problems were on the horizon. In 1990 Marvin was hit with a $2 million civil penalty, the largest ever imposed by the state of Minnesota, for improper storage and disposal of about 400 barrels of toxic chemical waste—paint, solvents, and wood preservative. The company was also charged with a criminal gross misdemeanor under a new state environmental law. Marvin's former safety director faced criminal felony prosecution for directing illegal activity and falsifying records.

The legal action against Marvin generated a heated debate among the state's policy makers, the governor, the attorney general, newspaper columnists, and others over the application of the law. While admitting they had been out of compliance, Marvin said the company was treated unfairly and shifted a planned expansion of the window operation from Minnesota to its door factory in Tennessee. Public reaction was also intense in the northwestern part of the state where the Marvin family played a large role, not only in the economy, but in the community. The Marvin family members had donated money to projects as diverse as the high school pool, a library and historical center, and a hockey arena.

According to an August 1994 *Corporate Report Minnesota* article, the Marvin family still controlled all the company stock. Over the years, the family had turned down numerous buyout offers and refrained from taking the growing company public. A third generation of Marvins was ready to continue the work of Bill and his brothers. In 1995, Jake Marvin, who was in line to take over the helm from his father, was succeeded by his sister Susan as president of Marvin Windows & Doors. As chief operating officer Jake continued to oversee all 13 family businesses—the largest by far was the window and door operation.

Susan Marvin, like the other family members involved with the company, worked in the plant as a youth. After earning a journalism degree and gaining marketing experience, she joined the company in 1981 and convinced the board to open a one-person advertising office in the Twin Cities. ''Soon after that, a misunderstood advertising slogan began to fuel the company's 1980s growth spurt, propelling it from a one-of-the-pack regional window company to an industry leader,'' according to Susan E. Peterson.

''Marvin Windows Are Made to Order'' was interpreted as custom-made by the industry and drew orders for odd-sized and -shaped windows; the company capitalized on the mistake and tapped into the growing remodeling business. The one-person shop grew to 30, and Marvin advanced to senior vice-president of sales and marketing prior to being named president. Marvin had also been elected chair of the Minnesota Chamber of Commerce in 1994; Marvin became more involved with the state's business and political affairs, according to a December 1994 *Corporate Report Minnesota* article by Lee Schafer and Eric J. Wieffering, after the company's 1990 environmental law problems.

In 1995, the company began manufacturing a lower-cost line of windows. The Integrity windows, manufactured in Fargo, North Dakota, were earmarked for the builders market. The windows were insulated with a composite material—Ultrex—

manufactured by Fargo-based Tecton Products. Marvin established its partnership with Tecton in 1992. (Marvin owned 85 percent of Tecton, according to a May 1997 *Corporate Report Minnesota* article.)

In 1996, the company became engaged in a dispute over the direction of different partnership, Viratec Thin Films, Inc., a joint venture with Apogee Enterprises, Inc. of Bloomington, Minnesota. Viratec, a subsidiary of Marcon Coating, Inc., an architectural glass venture established by Marvin and Apogee in 1985, was developing an anti-glare coating for cathode ray tubes. Both Marvin and Apogee took legal action to dissolve the 50–50 partnership. Apogee was granted the right to buy Marvin's share in both companies for $41 million. Marvin had been purchasing 30 to 35 percent of Marcon's production, which included low-emissivity glass.

Marvin, a winner of the 1996 Governor's Award for Excellence in Pollution Prevention, was honored for its pollution control program six years after incurring huge environmental fines. The company brought on board a loss control expert from, a large insurance broker as the new director of risk management. Changes such as a move to less toxic products, improved employee training, and product redesign resulted in a dramatic reduction in the generation of toxic chemicals and a savings of $100,000 per year, according to an article by Dick Youngblood.

Future Changes

By 1997, the cornerstone Warroad manufacturing facility had grown to cover more than 40 acres and employ over 3,000 people. Marvin planned to open a new plant to build its fast-growing line of wood-clad windows in Grafton, North Dakota, by the first quarter of 1989. The company faced the challenge of a changing industry, one in which huge conglomerates had begun to buy up smaller window makers and pick up market share. According to Jane Brissett, Marvin's move toward decentralized operations may have been a response to those changes. In addition Marvin, like other wood-window makers, was exploring other new products and materials to bring them into the 21st century.

Further Reading

Beal, Dave, "Can Roseau County Keep It Up?" *St. Paul Pioneer Press,* March 4, 1991, p. 1.

——, "Close-Knit Family Members Set Style, Mood, Direction," *St. Paul Pioneer Press,* March 4, 1991.

Brissett, Jane, "Warroad's Window on the World," *Corporate Report Minnesota,* May 1997, pp. 46–48.

DeSilver, Drew, "Apogee Partnership Crumbles," *Minneapolis/ St. Paul City Business,* January 12–18, 1996, pp. 1, 29.

Harris, John, "The Window Frame As Fashion Item," *Forbes,* April 30, 1990, pp. 125, 128, 133.

Oakes, Larry, "Marvin Says It Won't Expand in State," *Star Tribune* (Minneapolis), February 22, 1991, p. 1B.

Peterson, Susan E., "Apogee Gets Custody in Marvin Divorce," *Star Tribune* (Minneapolis), March 5, 1996, p. 1D.

——, "Full Speed Ahead," *Star Tribune* (Minneapolis), November 20, 1995, p. 1D.

——, "Marvin Chooses Grafton, N.D. for New Window Plant," *Star Tribune* (Minneapolis), November 15, 1996, p. 1D.

——, "Marvin Parent Will Receive $41 Million in Settlement of Dispute with Apogee," *Star Tribune* (Minneapolis), January 14, 1997, p. 3D.

Rebuffoni, Dean, "Marvin Windows Gets $2 Million Waste Fine," *Star Tribune* (Minneapolis), November 29, 1990, p. 1A.

Schafer, Lee, and Eric J. Wieffering, "The End of Isolationism," *Corporate Report Minnesota,* December 1994, p. 76.

——, "The Wealthiest Minnesotans," *Corporate Report Minnesota,* August 1994, p. 34.

Sundstrom, Ingrid, "Marvin Windows Plans to Build 40,000-Square-Foot Fargo Plant, *Star Tribune* (Minneapolis), June 15, 1991, p. 1D.

——, "Windowmaking Newcomer Settles Near 'Big 3,' " *Star Tribune* (Minneapolis), April 10, 1988, p. 1D.

"Susan Marvin President of Window Firm," *Star Tribune* (Minneapolis), September 28, 1995, p. 3D.

Wojahn, Ellen, "Looking into Marvin Windows," *Corporate Report Minnesota,* April 1981, pp. 51–53, 142–46.

Youngblood, Dick, "Marvin Windows Pollution Justified Penalties," *Star Tribune* (Minneapolis), March 6, 1991, p. 1D.

——, "Six Years After Big Fine, Marvin Wins Award for Its Work to Reduce Pollution," *Star Tribune* (Minneapolis), June 19, 1996, p. 2D.

—Kathleen Peippo

Maytag Corporation

403 West Fourth Street North
Newton, Iowa 50208
U.S.A.
(515) 792-7000
Fax: (515) 791-8793
Web site: http://www.maytag.com

Public Company
Incorporated: 1925 as Maytag Company
Employees: 20,464
Sales: $3.00 billion (1996)
Stock Exchanges: New York
SICs: 3581 Automatic Vending Machines; 3582 Commercial Laundry, Dry Cleaning & Pressing Machines; 3631 Household Cooking Equipment; 3632 Household Refrigerators & Home & Farm Freezers; 3633 Household Laundry Equipment; 3635 Household Vacuum Cleaners; 3639 Household Appliances, Not Elsewhere Classified

Maytag Corporation is one of the leading appliance manufacturers in the United States. It sells washers, dryers, ovens, refrigerators, and dishwashers under both premium brands (Maytag and Jenn-Air) and mid-to-lower price value brands (Magic Chef and Admiral). The Maytag brand is also used on coin-operated and commercial laundry equipment. The company also sells Hoover vacuum cleaners and other floor-care products in North America; Dixie-Narco vending machines and glass-front coolers; and commercial ovens, fryers, and charbroilers for the food service industry under the Blodgett Ovens, Pitco Frialator, MagiKitch'n, and Blodgett-Combi Ovens brands. More than 90 percent of Maytag's revenues are derived in North America; Maytag International is the company's export arm, while a joint venture produces the RSD brand washing machine in China. Maytag's reputation rests on the dependability of its machines, and the Maytag "lonely repairman"—featured in company advertising since 1957—has become an American icon.

Dependability Became Company Watchword Early On

Maytag Company was started by Frederick Louis Maytag and three partners in 1893 to produce threshing-machine band cutters and self-feeder attachments. The company soon began to produce other pieces of farm machinery, not all of it top quality: its corn husker, called the Success, caused the partners many problems because of its poor quality, and farmers often called Maytag out to their fields to fix the Success. When Maytag bought out his partners in 1907, he had learned his lesson; a Maytag product would always be dependable.

Maytag built his first washer in 1907, to bring his agricultural-equipment company through the slow-selling season as well as to fill a need for home-use washing machines. Home washing machines were already on the market, but Maytag wanted to make them more efficient. His first washer, called the Pastime, revolutionized washing. It had a cypress tub with a hand crank that forced the clothes through the water and against corrugated sides. The washer was a hit, and Maytag continued to improve on it. In 1911 he brought out the first electric washing machine, and in 1914 he introduced the gas-engine Multi-Motor for customers without access to electricity. The first aluminum washer tub was brought out in 1919, and the Gyrofoam, the first washer to clean with only water action, rather than friction, entered the marketplace in 1922. This revolutionary washer was the first with an agitator at the bottom of the tub instead of the top. This change allowed for the elimination of friction. Sales of this machine pushed Maytag, previously the 38th-largest U.S. washing machine company, into first place.

At this juncture, the farm-implement portion of the business was discontinued. L. B. Maytag, son of the founder, became president of the company in 1920. Under his direction the company began to market nationally. In 1925 Maytag incorporated and was listed on the New York Stock Exchange. In 1926 another Maytag son, E. H. Maytag, assumed the presidency and held the position until his death in 1940. Over the next several years, a number of interesting attachments were offered on washers. A butter churn and a meat grinder were two options offered to buyers. By 1927 Maytag had produced one million washers.

Company Perspectives:

Maytag Corporation designs, builds, and markets products that make life easier, simpler, and more convenient. With a heritage of more than 100 years and a name synonymous with dependability, Maytag has evolved into a corporation built on great brands, great products, great distribution, and strong financial discipline. Maytag is a leading producer of premium brand major appliances, commercial and coin-operated laundry equipment, floor care products, and soft-drink vending machines. The corporation's businesses are linked through a strategy based on brand strength, product innovation, and dependability in meeting consumer needs.

During the Great Depression, Maytag held its own; the company even made money. At his father's death in 1940, Fred Maytag II, grandson of the founder, took over the presidency. During World War II, the company made only special components for military equipment. In 1946 production of washers started up again, and in 1949 the first automatic washers were produced in a new plant built for that purpose. In 1946 Maytag began marketing a line of ranges and refrigerators made by other companies under the Maytag name. During the Korean War the company again produced parts for military equipment, although washer production continued.

Reputation as Premium Brand Secured in Postwar Years

During the 1950s the appliance industry grew rapidly. Maytag first entered the commercial laundry field at this time, manufacturing washers and dryers for commercial self-service laundries and commercial operators. During these years full-line appliance producers began targeting Maytag's market. Full-line operators—such as General Electric, Whirlpool, and Frigidaire—provided washers and dryers, refrigerators, stoves, and other appliances. Maytag was much smaller than the full-line producers. It limited itself to the manufacture of washers and dryers, which it marketed with ranges and refrigerators built by other companies, and established its reputation as a premium brand.

The ranges and refrigerators Maytag had been marketing with its washers and dryers were dropped in 1955 and 1960, respectively, but the company soon reentered the field with its own portable dishwasher and a line of food-waste disposers in 1968. When Fred Maytag II, the last family member involved in the company's management, died in 1962, E. G. Higdon was named president and George M. Umbreit became chairman and CEO.

By the late 1970s over 70 percent of U.S. households were equipped with washers and dryers. Laundry-equipment sales had peaked in 1973 and the lifetime of such equipment was 10 to 12 years—often longer for Maytag. To help boost sales, prices became more competitive. Chairman Daniel J. Krumm, who had been elected president in 1972, set the company in a new direction in 1980 when he made the decision to make Maytag into a full-line producer, eventually selling a wide range of major appliances rather than just washers, dryers, and dishwashers.

Transformed into Full-Line Producer in the 1980s

The expansion was effected by acquisition. The first purchase was Hardwick Stove Company in 1981, followed in 1982 by Jenn-Air Corporation, the leading manufacturer of indoor electric grills with stove-top vent systems. These products added a full line of gas and electric cooking appliances to the Maytag line and were sold under the Maytag umbrella. Maytag Company intended this diversification to increase its sales in both the new-home market as well as the replacement market; companies make bids to developers based on kitchen packages, not individual components. The larger replacement market had also changed: large chains selling several brands side by side dominated the market. Chairman Krumm felt the diversification was necessary despite the cyclical nature of the building industry.

The new strategy paid off. Consumers began to buy again, and Maytag's sales increased in all areas in 1983. In May 1986 the move toward becoming a full-line producer continued with the purchase of the Magic Chef group of companies in a $737 million stock swap. Magic Chef's Admiral brand gave Maytag a presence in the refrigerator and freezer sector. Besides Admiral refrigerators, Magic Chef also produced other home appliances under the names Toastmaster, Magic Chef, and Norge. The merger gave Maytag the fourth-largest share of the U.S. appliance market. It also brought vending machine manufacturer Dixie-Narco Inc., with its number one position in soft-drink vending equipment, into the fold.

The Magic Chef purchase also helped protect Maytag from the threat of takeover. As the industry consolidated and other companies began to sell higher-priced appliances—Maytag's traditional forte—Krumm responded by moving into the medium-priced market. Magic Chef was Maytag's first step into that market.

The merger of Maytag and Magic Chef doubled Maytag's size and necessitated a restructuring. Maytag Company's name was changed to Maytag Corporation and three major appliance groups were formed: the Maytag appliance division, Magic Chef, and the Admiral appliance division (the Admiral division was consolidated into the other groups in 1988). Hardwick Stoves and Jenn-Air were included in the Maytag division. The president of Magic Chef remained as head of that division, which included Toastmaster—sold in 1987—Dixie-Narco, and Magic Chef air conditioning operations. The Admiral division included Norge and Warwick product lines, part of the old Magic Chef. Each division was given a great deal of autonomy. Other mergers within the industry during 1986 resulted in four companies—Whirlpool, General Electric, White Consolidated Industries, and Maytag—controlling 80 percent of the industry.

By the late 1980s Krumm was ready to move Maytag into foreign markets. With the aim of being a European competitor before the unification of the European Economic Community in 1992, Maytag bought Chicago Pacific Corp. in early 1989 for $961 million. The primary reason for this purchase was Chicago Pacific's Hoover division. Hoover produced and sold high-quality washers, dryers, refrigerators, dishwashers, and other products primarily in Great Britain and Australia, but also in continental Europe. It also sold vacuum cleaners in the United States, a new product for Maytag. (Chicago Pacific also owned furniture operations, which Maytag sold later in 1989 to Ladd Furniture for $213.4 million.) Another reason for the Chicago Pacific purchase was to further ward off takeover. The $500 million debt the company assumed with the acquisition helped make the company less attractive to raiders. Meanwhile, 1989 also saw the debut of the first refrigerators bearing the Maytag brand.

1990s Retrenchment

Maytag's acquisitions spree led directly to a troubled period in the early 1990s. Profits declined each year from 1990 to 1992 as the company was hit hard by the recession and the increased competition that it engendered, and was further weakened by a continuing high debt load. The acquisition of Hoover was turning into a near-disaster as the European operations were in the red year after year, a situation made even worse in 1992 when Hoover Europe made a serious miscalculation in offering two free transatlantic airline tickets to anyone buying a Hoover product in the United Kingdom for as little as $165. More than 220,000 people responded to this almost-too-good-to-be-true deal, leading not only to a financial folly but also to a near public relations disaster when the company delayed getting tickets to people claiming them, as well as to litigation that continued for years to come. The fiasco led to the firing of three top executives at Hoover Europe, as well as Maytag being forced to take a $30 million charge in 1993 to cover the costs of the ill-fated promotion.

In the midst of these troubles, Krumm—the architect of the 1980s expansion—retired in late 1992, and was succeeded as chairman and CEO by Leonard A. Hadley, who had been company president. It did not take Hadley long to determine that it would be best in the long run if Maytag pulled back from its overseas ambitions and concentrated on putting its North American house in order. Hoover Europe alone had lost a total of $163 million from the date of its purchase by Maytag through 1994. In late 1994 Maytag sold its Hoover Australia unit to Southcorp Holdings for $82.1 million in cash, resulting in an after-tax loss of $16.4 million. In the second quarter of the following year, Maytag sold Hoover Europe to Italian appliance maker Candy SpA for $164.3 million in cash, resulting in an after-tax loss of $135.4 million. Maytag retained the Hoover North America operation. Proceeds from these sales were largely used to pay down the company's long-term debt, which stood at just $488.5 million by 1996, compared to nearly $800 million in the early 1990s.

By 1996, Maytag was on the upswing. Although revenues of $3 billion were slightly lower than at the beginning of the decade in part due to the divestments of 1994 and 1995, the net income of $162.4 million represented a high point for the decade so far. That figure would have been even higher, if it were not for the $24.4 million restructuring charge the company took early that year in connection with the consolidation of its two separate major appliance operations into a single operation called Maytag Appliances, which was handed responsibility for all sales, marketing, manufacturing, logistics, and customer service functions for the Maytag, Jenn-Air, Admiral, and Magic Chef brands. Freed from its overseas headache, Maytag also began to revitalize its appliance lines through record 1996 capital spending of $220 million, much of which went toward new product development and improvements in existing lines. Among new products introduced were washers and dryers tagged with a new brand: Performa by Maytag; these were priced lower than Maytag brand products but carried some of the Maytag cachet. On the high end of the scale, the company jumped onto the front-loading washer bandwagon with the March 1997 debut of the Neptune high-efficiency model. In the refrigerator arena—Maytag's weakest product line—a three-year, $180 million redesign effort culminated with the April 1997 introduction of a new generation of Maytag, Jenn-Air, Magic Chef, and Admiral models that had increased capacity, were quieter, included several pull-out features, and boasted of faster temperature recovery following the opening of the freezer or refrigerator door. Some of the credit for these innovations went to Lloyd D. Ward, whom Hadley had recruited from PepsiCo's Frito-Lay unit in early 1996 to become executive vice-president of Maytag and president of Maytag Appliances—and perhaps heir apparent to Hadley.

Despite the heavy investments in North America, Maytag had not entirely given up on overseas growth. Like numerous other companies in the mid-1990s, Maytag decided to move into the burgeoning Chinese market. It did so in September 1996 with an initial $70 million investment to set up a series of joint ventures with the Hefei Rongshida Group Corporation, the leading washing machine firm in China, marketing its products under the well-known RSD brand. Maytag initially teamed with Hefei Rongshida in the production and marketing of washing machines, but planned to extend the venture into refrigerators during a second phase.

Further evidence of the stronger financial position of Maytag came with the $93.5 million purchase of G.S. Blodgett Corp. in late 1997. The privately held Blodgett—which traced its origins to the Blodgett Oven Co. founded in Burlington, Vermont, in 1848—was a manufacturer of commercial ovens, fryers, and charbroilers for the food service industry, thus representing a logical extension of Maytag's product lines and customers. Blodgett was the company's first acquisition since that of Chicago Pacific in 1989.

The Maytag Corporation of the late 1990s was stronger than it had been in years. Through heightened new product introductions; strategic, manageable acquisitions; and selective overseas ventures the company was positioning itself for steady, profitable growth, while at the same time maintaining its reputation for quality.

Principal Subsidiaries

G.S. Blodgett Corp.; D.N. Holdings, Inc.; Dixie-Narco Inc.; Maytag Foreign Sales Corporation (Virgin Islands); The Hoover Company; Maytag International Inc.; Maharashtra Investment, Inc.; Hoover Mexicana S.A. de C.V. (Mexico); Hoover Holdings Inc.; Juver Industrial S.A. de C.V. (Mexico); Maytag International Limited (U.K.); Maytag Ltd. (Canada); Maytag Worldwide N.V. (The Netherlands Antilles); AERA Limited (Hong Kong); Maytag International Investments, Inc.; Maytag International Investments B.V. (The Netherlands Antilles); Hefei Rongshida Co. Ltd. (China; 50.5%).

Further Reading

''At 80, Maytag Feels 'Terrific,' '' *Appliance Manufacturer,* November 1987, p. 28.

Bremner, Brian, and Mark Maremont, ''Maytag's Foreign Fling Isn't Much Fun After All,'' *Business Week,* September 4, 1989, pp. 32–33.

Bulkeley, William M., ''Wring in the New: Washers That Load from Front Are Hot,'' *Wall Street Journal,* April 29, 1997, pp. A1, A5.

Byrne, Harlan S., ''Maytag Corp.: Hope for Growth Lies in European Operations,'' *Barron's,* May 25, 1992, pp. 35–36.

——, ''The Predator or the Prey?,'' *Barron's,* March 3, 1997, pp. 22, 24.

——, ''Remaking Maytag,'' *Barron's,* August 21, 1989, pp. 12–13.

David, Gregory E., ''Breaking the Spell,'' *Financial World,* May 10, 1994, pp. 34, 36.

Dubashi, Jagannath, ''Taken to the Cleaners,'' *Financial World,* August 4, 1992, p. 28.

Geisi, Steve, ''Maytag Revs $35M in Product Noise,'' *Brandweek,* February 17, 1997, pp. 1, 6.

——, ''Spin-Cycle Doctor,'' *Brandweek,* March 10, 1997, pp. 38–40.

Gold, Howard, ''Maytag Steps Out: Boxed in for Years in Its Traditional Markets, Maytag Is Starting to Behave in an Uncharacteristically Venturesome Way,'' *Forbes,* December 17, 1984, p. 96.

Hannon, Kerry, ''Damned If You Do . . .,'' *Forbes,* March 20, 1989, p. 201.

Harris, John, ''Wake Up, Maytag Man!,'' *Forbes,* November 13, 1989, pp. 308, 310.

Hill, Andrew, and Michael Cassell, ''Candy Pulls Hoover Away from the Mangle,'' *Financial Times,* May 31, 1995, p. 21.

Hillinger, Charles, ''Washdays, Birthdays: Maytag Notes 80 Years,'' *Los Angeles Times,* May 8, 1987.

Hoover, Robert, and John Hoover, *An American Quality Legend: How Maytag Saved Our Moms, Vexed the Competition, and Presaged America's Quality Revolution,* New York: McGraw-Hill, 1993, 239 p.

''In Pursuit of Quality,'' *Appliance Manufacturer,* November 1987, p. 38.

Kelly, Kevin, Fred Guterl, and Roon Lewald, ''Can Maytag's Repairman Get Out of This Fix?,'' *Business Week,* October 26, 1992, pp. 54–55.

''Maytag: Wizard of White Goods,'' *Dun's Business Month,* December 1985, p. 34.

Quintanilla, Carl, ''Lloyd Ward Puts a New Spin on Maytag,'' *Wall Street Journal,* November 26, 1996, pp. B1, B8.

Remick, Norman C., Jr., ''Maytag: A China Connection,'' *Appliance Manufacturer,* February 1997, p. G16.

The Spirit of Maytag: 100 Years of Dependability: 1893–1993, Newton, Iowa: Maytag Corporation, [1993].

Upbin, Bruce, ''Global, Schmobal,'' *Forbes,* March 10, 1997, pp. 64, 66.

—Vera A. Emmons
—updated by David E. Salamie

THE MIDDLEBY CORPORATION
THE BRAND BEHIND THE BRANDS

The Middleby Corporation

1400 Toastmaster Drive
Elgin, Illinois 60120
U.S.A.
(847) 741-3300
Fax: (847) 741-0015
Web site: http://www.middleby.com

Public Company
Incorporated: 1985
Employees: 965
Sales: $124.8 million (1996)
Stock Exchanges: NASDAQ
SICs: 3556 Food Products Machinery; 6719 Holding Companies, Not Elsewhere Classified

The Middleby Corporation is a major designer, manufacturer, and marketer of a wide range of commercial and institutional foodservice equipment. Its products include conveyor and infrared ovens used in the quick-service pizza industry; heavy-duty cooking equipment such as ranges, convection ovens, broilers, and grills used in restaurants and other institutional kitchens; commercial toasters, mixers, griddles, and other cooking equipment used in quick-service and full-service restaurants; and other innovative foodservice products that Middleby either manufactures or distributes. According to its annual report, The Middleby Corporation is ''the brand behind America's best-loved, foodservice brands.''

Middleby sells to a diverse group of customers of all sizes, whose ''success depends on serving well-prepared menu items that keep diners coming back for more.'' The company claims that its customers lead the fast-growing segments of the foodservice industry: full-service restaurants, quick-service chains, supermarket and convenience stores, resorts, hotels, stadiums, schools, hospitals, long-term care and correctional facilities, and other institutions. It counts among its customers the top 100 quick-service chains.

Since its predecessor company acquired the Middleby Marshall Oven Co., Inc., in 1983, The Middleby Corporation has grown from a company that essentially sold conveyor ovens to customers in the United States to one that offers a broad line of cooking equipment to customers around the world. Middleby entered the rapidly growing international foodservice market around 1990, and by 1996 international sales accounted for 37 percent of the company's total sales. Fueling the international growth of the foodservice market has been the expansion of American restaurant chains, especially the quick-service chains, into other countries.

Incorporated in 1985

The Middleby Corporation was incorporated in Delaware on May 14, 1985, as a successor to TMC Industries Ltd. From 1978 to 1985, TMC Industries was the parent company of WWG Industries, Inc., a Georgia-based carpet manufacturer. TMC Industries had acquired WWG Industries in 1978 for $100 million from Champion International Corporation. High interest rates and a collapsing housing market forced WWG Industries into Chapter 11 bankruptcy protection in the early 1980s. When it emerged from Chapter 11 protection in 1983, largely under the guidance of William F. Whitman, Jr., a former PaineWebber executive, WWG Industries acquired the Middleby Marshall Oven Co., Inc., in a highly leveraged deal.

Middleby Marshall was a well-established manufacturer of conveyor ovens with a reputation for high quality products. It was founded in 1888 by Joseph Middleby, who owned a bakery supply firm, and John Marshall, a licensed engineer. The business was created to produce custom designed movable ovens. Up to the time it was acquired in 1983, the company specialized in developing and introducing new innovations in baking technology and equipment. In 1976 descendants of the founding families sold the company to Stewart Systems, Inc., a Dallas-based baking systems engineering firm.

The 1983 sale of Middleby Marshall was engineered by David P. Riley, who managed the unit for Stewart Systems, and William F. Whitman, Jr. Riley first saw the possibility of split-

Company Perspectives:

Our mission is to be a world class manufacturer, distributor and provider of premium equipment and services for the foodservice industry. Middleby is dedicated to being the leading brand behind the market's favorite foodservice brands. From concept to kitchen, our team is committed to providing the best solutions for our customers worldwide.

ting off Middleby Marshall from Stewart in 1982 and contacted an investment banker about a possible leveraged buyout. A year later Whitman emerged as a partner after steering WWG out of bankruptcy. Following the acquisition of Middleby Marshall by WWG, Whitman held 51 percent of the new company and became chairman of the board, and Riley was named president and, later, chief executive officer. Recalling the acquisition, Whitman told *Crain's Chicago Business,* "I liked the company because of its proprietary, patented oven, with its strong margins. The company also has a sterling, almost Rolls Royce, reputation."

The leading pizza chains, notably Domino's Pizza Inc. and the Pizza Hut subsidiary of PepsiCo Inc., recognized the superiority of Middleby Marshall's conveyor ovens, whose greater cooking speed and patented cooking methods enabled them to guarantee faster pizza deliveries. With WWG Industries as Middleby Marshall's parent company, Middleby Marshall benefited from WWG's net loss carry-forward tax benefits, which were valued at $50 million, and its status as a public company.

First Years Difficult for The Middleby Corporation

The first two years for Middleby were marked by flat sales and earnings, and the company reported a net loss of $1.1 million on net sales of $24.8 million in 1986. Cooking ovens were the company's core business, accounting for approximately 75 percent of net sales. Its recent acquisition of Reynolds Electric Co. for $1.4 million in cash gave Middleby a presence in the commercial mixer business, but it was facing stiff competition from Hobart Corporation, which held an 80 percent share of the $100 million commercial mixer market. Middleby looked to its core business for future growth and enjoyed 40 percent margins on the sales of its cooking ovens.

In November 1986 Middleby divested itself of its revolving-tray oven business, Culter Industries, Inc., for $200,000. The unit had been a significant drag on earnings, accounting for only 12 percent of sales while occupying some 35 percent of manufacturing space. Following the sale, earnings improved with the help of other cost-cutting measures, and in 1987 Middleby reported net income of $629,000 on net sales to $29.1 million, a 17 percent increase in net sales over the previous year.

Achieved Record Sales and Net Income in 1988

Middleby posted record sales in 1988, up 18 percent over the previous year to $34.2 million, and net income of $4.2 million, a peak it was unable to match in subsequent years (through 1996). Middleby was able to improve its balance sheet and eliminate much of its debt, significantly reducing interest expense and improving the bottom line of its income statement. At the end of 1986, debt had accounted for 97 percent of Middleby's capital structure. In November 1987 the company was able to refinance and reduce debt to 61 percent, with 25 percent preferred stock and 14 percent shareholders' equity accounting for the company's remaining capitalization. Middleby's strong performance in 1988 then allowed it to prepay all of its revolving bank debt more than four years ahead of schedule, so that by year-end 1988 debt represented only 34 percent of the company's capitalization.

On July 13, 1988, the company's stock, which had been trading on NASDAQ over-the-counter markets, was listed on the American Stock Exchange (AMEX). In December the company began a cash dividend program, starting with a $.02 quarterly dividend and a special year-end dividend of $.03 per share. To improve the liquidity and marketability of the company's stock, a five-for-four common stock split was effected June 1, 1988. The dividends would be suspended in 1991, however, and no further dividends have been paid.

At this time, the company's principal product was the Pacesetter oven, which was sold to what was then called "fastfood chain" markets and, especially, pizza makers. Middleby's strategy was to broaden the acceptance of Pacesetter ovens in other foodservice markets, while at the same time broadening its product base. Other products included conventional deck ovens (Middleby entered the market in 1988 with a South Korea-manufactured product), a proprietary oven ventilation system (introduced in 1987), and Titan brand commercial electric food mixers and related accessories.

Looking ahead, overall market conditions were promising. Foodservice sales were $213 billion in 1988, or about five percent of the gross national product (GNP). Fast-food chains were the fastest growing subgroup with $63 billion in sales projected for 1989. Pizza sales were greater than $20 billion annually, and the two largest chains, Pizza Hut and Domino's, were Middleby's two largest customers.

Major Acquisition in 1989

Full of confidence in the future growth of the foodservice market and not anticipating the recession of the early 1990s, Middleby acquired the Foodservice Equipment Group of Hussmann Corporation, a subsidiary of Whitman Corporation, for $62.5 million on July 14, 1989. The acquisition included four established businesses with well-known industry brand names: Southbend (heavy duty cooking equipment), Toastmaster (cooking and warming equipment), Victory (refrigeration), and Seco (holding and serving systems). It should be noted that an unaffiliated company, Toastmaster, Inc., owned the rights to the Toastmaster brand name for consumer products; Toastmaster products manufactured by Middleby were limited to commercial products for the foodservice industry.

To finance the acquisition, Middleby took on a significant amount of debt, again raising its annual interest expense. It entered into a $77.5 million credit agreement with a major lending institution. It reduced its debt somewhat by applying the proceeds from the sale of its Southern Equipment Company Division of St. Louis in February 1990 for $7.9 million in cash to a group of private investors that included managers of the company.

After the acquisition, the new businesses reported a $10 million loss for the first half of 1989, three times the amount originally forecast. In 1990 Middleby brought a lawsuit against Whitman, parent of Hussmann, over the Foodservice Equipment Group acquisition. The suit was settled in Middleby's favor in October 1992, when the jury awarded Middleby $27 million. The award was later set aside by a judge on a technicality, but Middleby and Hussmann reached a $19.5 million cash settlement out of court in 1993.

In the suit, Middleby claimed that Hussmann's overly optimistic financial projections led it to pay too much for the companies. The losses greatly affected Middleby's financial performance over the next several years. Even though 1989 sales more than doubled to $72.2 million from $34.2 million in 1988, net income dropped 86 percent to only $573,000. While the reduction of net income was due in part to the poor performance of the newly acquired subsidiaries, Middleby had also assumed a gigantic debt in the acquisition and was saddled with $3.6 million in interest expense in 1989, more than three times its 1988 level of about $1 million.

Middleby's growing interest expense continued to negatively impact the company's bottom line in 1990, a year in which the company also experienced flat sales volume in a highly competitive environment. Interest expense grew to $8.3 million in 1990. The company was forced to take drastic cost-cutting measures during the year, reducing the work force at continuing operations by 22 percent and slashing administrative and overhead costs by 25 percent. Still, Middleby reported a net loss of $978,000 on record sales of $113 million for the year.

International Growth in 1990s

In April 1990 Middleby acquired a majority interest in Asbury Associates Inc., a foodservice equipment manufacturer and distributor based in Manila, the Philippines. It was a key step in building an international organization. Middleby increased its interest in Asbury to 80 percent in 1991, and it was soon expanded from serving the Pacific basin to become Middleby's export distributor throughout the world, except Canada, where Middleby owned a distributor called Escan. In 1991 Asbury established a separate unit, Fab-Asia, Inc., in metropolitan Manila to fabricate kitchen equipment for the Asian market and to produce some components for Middleby's domestic factories. Asbury's new corporate headquarters were opened in Miramar, Florida, in October 1992.

The year 1991 was one of international growth that was offset by declining domestic sales. International business increased by 33 percent over 1990, accounting for 21 percent of Middleby's total sales in 1991. The next year Asbury's sales doubled as it expanded sales in Latin America, the Middle East, and Europe. Middleby reported higher net sales in 1992 of $110 million, up from $103 million in 1991, and reduced its net loss for the year to $1.9 million from $7.5 million in 1991.

On August 21, 1992, Middleby completed the sale of its Seco division, which was one of the units acquired from Hussmann in 1989, to a newly formed company called Seco Products Corporation. Net proceeds of $11 million were used to reduce debt. Middleby retained a minority interest in the new company, which it later sold in 1995 for $1.4 million net of expenses.

During the first half of 1992 Middleby consolidated its foodservice equipment divisions, closing plants in Niles and Morton Grove, Illinois, and consolidating production at an Elgin, Illinois facility to save nearly $2 million in annual overhead expenses. The previous year Middleby had consolidated the Middleby Marshall and Toastmaster divisions into a newly formed Cooking Systems Group. During 1991 Middleby had also closed its Montreal manufacturing operations and dissolved its U.K. distribution center.

Middleby Cooking Systems Group Established in 1993

In 1993 management was consolidated at the Elgin-based Middleby Cooking Systems Group, the company's largest operating unit. David P. Riley, parent company Middleby's president and CEO, also assumed presidency of the newly formed Middleby Cooking Systems Group. Middleby Marshall became part of Middleby Cooking Systems, with Middleby Marshall's General Manager John Hastings named corporate executive vice-president, chief financial officer, and vice-president of administration. Two other financial executives left the company as part of the consolidation. Hastings told *Crain's Chicago Business,* "The management changes have basically been driven by the desire to reduce overhead and streamline decision-making."

As part of its strategy to introduce new products into a relatively flat foodservice equipment market, Middleby formed a joint venture in 1993 with Rational GmbH, a German manufacturer of high-tech oven equipment that combined steam and convection cooking capabilities. The joint venture, called Rational Cooking Systems International, Inc., and headquartered in Schaumburg, Illinois, targeted the expanding U.S. market for high-tech ovens. Middleby would distribute the German company's product under the trade name Rational Combi-Steamer. Middleby marketed both compact floor and countertop units that were capable of multiple cooking processes, including cooking, baking, roasting, steaming, poaching, blanching, boiling, basting, grilling, and pressure cooking.

Returned to Profitability in 1994

Middleby did not return to profitability until 1994, reporting net income of $3.0 million on net sales of $130.0 million. It noted in its annual report that results from operations confirmed the expansion of margins and operating income increased fivefold. (Middleby had reported net income of $3.4 million in 1993, but that was helped by a one-time $7.7 million income item related to the settlement of its 1990 lawsuit with Hussmann and Whitman.) The balance sheet was restructured with an influx of new capital, and a new incentive system was put into place to link managers' compensation directly to shareholder return.

Middleby also noted in its annual report that it had repositioned itself to participate "in the rapid worldwide expansion of the hotel and fast food restaurant chains." Through its export management company, Asbury Associates, Middleby had the "unique capacity to offer turnkey, 'concept to kitchen floor' packages worldwide." In 1994 international sales accounted for one-quarter of total sales.

As part of a major expansion of the company's manufacturing capabilities in the Philippines, Middleby Philippines Corporation (MPC) was incorporated in 1995. Middleby owned 80 percent of MPC, with the remaining 20 percent in the hands of local management. MPC's predecessor, Fab-Asia, Inc., was formed in 1991, with Middleby owning a majority interest. Middleby increased its ownership to 80 percent in 1994, and the operating assets of Fab-Asia were transferred to MPC on January 1, 1996. In April 1996 it moved to a new facility. MPC primarily served the Asian operations of major foodservice chains and hotels.

On January 23, 1997, Middleby sold its Victory Refrigeration Company to an investor group led by local management at Victory for approximately $11.8 million. Middleby had acquired Victory as part of its Foodservice Equipment Group acquisition in 1990. When Middleby's previous years' earnings were restated to exclude Victory, international sales accounted for an even greater proportion of the company's earnings.

For fiscal 1996, international sales accounted for approximately 37 percent of total sales, up from 36 percent of the previous year's restated sales. With operations organized under two international business units and two domestic units, Middleby reported net earnings from continuing operations of $473,000 on net sales of $124.8 million in 1996. Earnings were adversely affected by one-time losses from discontinued operations (Victory) of approximately $1.1 million. Income from operations was $8.7 million, more than enough to offset the company's interest expense of $4.4 million.

Recognizing the need to improve its capital structure by reducing debt and increasing shareholder equity, Middleby announced a public offering of stock in September 1997 at a price of $10 per share. Management hoped to raise approximately $18.5 million, which would be used in part to reduce debt. The company's stock had been trading on the NASDAQ National Market since November 1995, when it switched from the American Stock Exchange. The reason for the switch was to "provide broader liquidity for our shareholders and offer greater coverage within the investment community," according to Chairman Whitman. Following Middleby's 1997 public offering, at least one investment firm began covering the stock, giving it an "outperform-significantly" rating.

Principal Operating Units

Middleby Marshall, Inc. (Elgin, Illinois); Middleby Cooking Systems Group (Elgin, Illinois); Southbend (Fuquay-Varina, North Carolina); Asbury Associates (Miramar, Florida); Middleby Philippines Corporation.

Further Reading

Bremner, Brian, "Oven Firm Reheats: Middleby Eyes Sizzling Growth," *Crain's Chicago Business,* August 10, 1988, p. 1.

Carroll, S. R., "Middleby Corp. Is Really Cookin'," *Chicago Tribune,* September 24, 1995.

Durgin, Hillary, "Middleby Turning Up Heat with Joint Venture," *Crain's Chicago Business,* September 20, 1993, p. 40.

Elstrom, Peter J. W., "Debt Restructuring Will Fuel Oven Maker's Market Growth," *Crain's Chicago Business,* May 9, 1988, p. 59.

——, "Disputed Buyout Cooks Oven-Maker," *Crain's Chicago Business,* June 18, 1990, p. 1.

"Middleby Adopts Management Stock Ownership Plan," *Business Wire,* March 4, 1994.

"The Middleby Corporation Reports Financing Package," *Business Wire,* January 10, 1995.

"The Middleby Corporation to Move to NASDAQ from AMEX," *Business Wire,* November 14, 1995.

Murphy, H. Lee, "Court Ruling Bolsters Ailing Middleby Corp.," *Crain's Chicago Business,* October 19, 1992, p. 33.

——, "Middleby's Managers to Take Its Performance Personally," *Crain's Chicago Business,* March 28, 1994, p. 40.

Ott, James F., "The Middleby Corporation Wins $27,000,000 Verdict Against Hussmann," *Business Wire,* September 28, 1992.

—David Bianco

The Miner Group International

3430 Winnetka Avenue
Minneapolis, Minnesota 55427-2021
U.S.A.
(612) 504-6200
Fax: (612) 542-8122
Web site: http://www.mellosmello.com/index.html

Private Company
Incorporated: 1980 as Mello Smello
Employees: 700
Sales: $136.5 million (1996)
SICs: 5199 Nondurable Goods, Not Elsewhere Classified; 2752 Commercial Printing, Lithographic; 7336 Commercial Art & Graphic Design

Calling The Miner Group International a printing business really fails to capture the essence of this company. It is true that most of the operations that make up The Miner Group are engaged primarily in printing, from the multicolor web heatset presses of its NorthPrint International subsidiary to the high-tech sheet-fed equipment at another subsidiary, Olympic, just to name a couple. Add to that, however, the company's ability to develop marketing strategies, produce state-of-the-art graphics, publish nationwide magazines, and make sophisticated plastic packages, and you have a much clearer picture of the Miner empire's scope, and the sophisticated way in which its various elements are integrated. The Miner Group is a collection of 15 separate companies, employing 700 workers at 28 locations, primarily in Minnesota. Through strategic acquisitions and startups, The Miner Group has positioned itself as a one-stop, fully integrated marketing/printing/graphics concern capable of seeing complex projects through from start to finish. All of the Miner companies are linked together by a sophisticated voice/data communications network, enabling each company to tap into the resources of the others as necessary.

The Miner Group was launched in 1980 by the husband and wife team of John and Leah Miner. After a brief banking career at First National Bank, where the Miners met, Jon Miner bought into a printing company called Impressions Inc. in 1968. Over the next dozen years, he became an expert in the printing industry, before a disagreement with his business partner led Miner to sell out his share. In the aftermath of that falling out, the Miners bought a small gift and novelty manufacturing company in 1980. Among the company's products at the time they acquired it—along with the inevitable candles and wind chimes—was a modest line of children's stickers that featured the "scratch-and-smell" concept developed by 3M Corporation. Scratch-and-smell involves coating a surface with an odor that is released when it is scratched.

Scratched (and Sniffed) Way to Rapid Growth

The line of scratch-and-smell stickers proved to be so popular that the Miners decided to buy the license for the scratch-and-smell technology, known as microencapsulation, from 3M and make it the cornerstone of their business. Dubbing their new company Mello Smello, they began applying a wide array of smells to a huge assortment of new products for kids. The Miners stoked demand for their aromatic products with a successful marketing strategy that turned wacky stickers into sought-after collectible items.

As Mello Smello's scratch-and-smell products grew in popularity, the company sought to expand the ways in which the technology could be applied. From simple stickers, the products began taking on more complex forms, such as puzzles, games, Holiday theme items, and the like. The early success of Mello Smello created a need for greater printing and marketing capabilities. The Miners met these needs both by building new facilities and by going on a shopping spree. The company began gobbling up smaller operations that supported its core business.

According to Jon Miner, there was no master plan to the way the company grew over the next several years. "One thing led to another . . . we're evolving, we move forward," he was quoted as saying in the Minnesota business journal *Format.* Most of that evolution was in the direction of printing, the industry of which The Miner Group is generally considered a part. As the company built up and acquired new printing capabilities, new business opportunities that relied on that capability

Company Perspectives:

The success of The Miner Group International is based on our commitment to building strategic partnerships with our customers, helping them to meet their objectives. We provide a seamless, one-stop production resource.

soon presented themselves. Soon Miner was printing children-oriented products for a number of large corporations. Among the company's first customers for this type of work were several national fast-food chains, for whom Miner began printing animated kid's meal boxes, bags, placemats, tray liners, and other related items.

Broadened Focus Through the 1980s

The next step in the evolution of The Miner Group again involved licensing agreements. The company began licensing such child-friendly images as Batman, Disney characters, and Teenage Mutant Ninja Turtles for use on its products. Some of them were scented with the company's licensed scratch-and-smell coating, while others were left to sell on their own merits. Meanwhile the list of big companies for whom Miner provided specialty products continued to grow, as the company added products such as cereal box prizes for Kellogg Company and General Mills to the work it was already doing for the likes of McDonald's and Taco Bell.

Once it was well established as a diverse force in the printing business, Miner went on to expand into fields that came into contact with printing on several different sides. Rather than merely print marketing materials that have been conceived by a second firm, to be used by yet another company, Miner saw an opportunity to cut out the extraneous middle man by providing its own marketing services. This notion led to the creation of InterNatural Designs Inc. (IDI), a marketing strategy subsidiary closely tied to the company's flagship Mello Smello operation. Now Miner was able to see many projects through from start to finish. For example, the company could help a fast-food chain develop a promotional project for a particular target market; conceive a set of products—game cards, bags, tray liners, etc.—to support the promotional effort; and print all of those products at one of its growing list of printing facilities.

At the other end of the spectrum, Miner added binding and sophisticated graphics and prepress support facilities, and soon the company was in the contract publishing business. From its modest beginnings putting out small puzzle and game magazines aimed at children, the company evolved into a full-blown publisher of all sorts of materials. In particular, Miner became heavily involved in sports magazines, churning out several national and regional hockey and golf journals. Among the successful magazines produced by Miner's publishing subsidiary, The Publishing Group (TPG), were *USA Hockey InLine, American Hockey Magazine, Minnesota Golfer,* and *Virginia Golfer.* So successful were the company's sports magazines, that in 1997 the division that produced them was spun off as TPG Sports, a new subsidiary specializing in sports publishing and marketing. Other Miner publications have included a national children's magazine and in-flight magazines for Delta Airlines.

Throughout, however, Mello Smello, the seed from which the Miner empire sprouted, remained the company's biggest money generator. By the middle of the 1990s, Mello Smello was operating through different divisions on several distinct fronts. The Retail division continued to churn out a wide range of children's products featuring licensed images from the most popular family movies of the day. The Schools division specialized in products for fundraising programs and special events at schools.

Late 1980s Bring New Plants

In 1989 Jon Miner was informed that NorthPrint Company, a nearly century-old printing firm in his home town of Grand Rapids, Minnesota, was filing for chapter 11 bankruptcy and was close to folding. Always active in community affairs around Grand Rapids—he already owned the nearby resort that his parents used to run—Miner bought the plant and saved the 25 jobs that it provided. Rather than make NorthPrint a charity case, however, Miner invested several million dollars in the facility, turning it into an important and productive part of the Miner system. Although the original intention was to use NorthPrint primarily for jobs within the Group, it soon began printing for outside clients as well, and within five years its employee roster had quadrupled to nearly 100 workers. NorthPrint's specialties included catalogs and direct-mail inserts, as well as such Miner standbys as food tray liners and printed bags. NorthPrint was not the only crumbling Grand Rapids institution bailed out by Jon Miner. He also restored and opened to the public the Grand Rapids home in which entertainer Judy Garland was born. An adjacent Judy Garland Children's Museum was planned for the site as well.

While most of the Miner operations remained based in the Twin Cities area, the company expanded its geographic scope by adding the Tempe, Arizona-based SouthPrint International as a sister printing company to NorthPrint. This southwestern presence enabled Miner to serve customers in that region with the same quick turnaround times it was able to offer its clients in the North. Other printing companies added along the way included Advanced Web Technologies, a flexographic printer; Print Technologies, Inc., specialists in one- and two-color demand printing; and Olympic, a high-tech prepress and sheet fed printer. As the printing industry continued to incorporate advances in computer graphics, Miner sought out ways to keep toward the front of the pack. Digital Marketing, Inc., a state-of-the-art company specializing in customized printing using the latest digital and electronic equipment, was added in the 1990s, allowing Miner to compete effectively in the market for short-run projects requiring frequent changes. Another subsidiary, the Photography Group, put Miner among the leaders in digital photographic processing.

With so many printing facilities doing work for each other, it eventually became apparent that having its own internal trucking company would save the company the expense and headaches associated with contracting transportation services from an outsider. With the creation of Miner Group Express, the company had the means for a smooth flow of materials between its various subsidiary printers and processors.

Although most of the building blocks that have gone into the building of The Miner Group have connected directly to the company's core printing business, there are exceptions. The most obvious was the company's 1988 investment in EZ Gard, developer of a line of athletic mouth guards. Created by 21-year-old wunderkind Jon Kittleson, the EZ Gard mouthpiece provided better mouth and jaw protection than older models. It was quickly embraced by many professional athletes, and became popular in both the National Football League and National Hockey League. EZ Gard later came up with the "Shock Doctor," a customized mouthpiece that keeps the jaw fixed in what the company calls the "power position," a slight separation between upper and lower jaws. Research suggests, according to company claims, that by keeping the jaw from clenching tightly shut the Shock Doctor can actually increase strength and improve sports performance dramatically. Major boosters of EZ Gard have included Olympic wrestler Dennis Koslowski and former Minnesota Viking star Chris Doleman. Always on the lookout for potential links between its subsidiaries, Miner has embarked on many sports safety programs for children, combining the resources of EZ Gard, Mello Smello, and other members of team Miner.

New Directions for the High-Tech 1990s

By 1994 The Miner Group had well in excess of $100 in revenue. In June 1996, Leah Miner, who had been serving as president of the company's Mello Smello division, died of cancer. Cofounder Jon Miner continued to run the Group as a solo act—albeit with a supporting cast of hundreds—after his wife's death. By that year, the company's annual revenue had grown to $136.5 million. During the summer of 1997, it appeared as if Miner would be purchased by the Minnesota-based Taylor Corp., one of the nation's largest printers of wedding cards. The transaction was never completed, however, and Miner forged ahead with its own plans.

The second half of the 1990s has seen Miner working to remain at the technological forefront of the printing industry. Toward that end, the company began to devote substantial energy to internet/intranet operations. In particular, its Epic Media, Digital Marketing, and Landscape subsidiaries worked to develop interactive, on-line programs that allowed businesses to create sales materials delivered over the internet, customized for each recipient. Epic Media also designed an image databasing system securable by employee passwords. With these sorts of products in hand, and more of them in various stages of development, The Miner Group prepared to enter the 21st century with a firm handle on the present and future printing—and marketing, and publishing, and graphics, and mouth protection—needs of the clients it serves.

Principal Subsidiaries

Advanced Web Technologies; Print Technologies, Inc.; Corporate Images Worldwide, Inc.; The Photography Group; Digital Marketing Inc.; NorthPrint International; Mello Smello; Pro Plastics; SouthPrint International; Olympic; Miner Group Express; Package Technology International; TPG Graphics International; Internatural Designs Strategy Group; EZ Gard; Epic Media.

Further Reading

Bremer, Karl D., *America's North Coast Gateway,* Minneapolis: Josten's Publishing Group, Inc., 1993.

Brissett, Jane E., and Jill P. Burcum, "Entrepreneur Sees Printing Investment As Giving Back to Grand Rapids," *Corporate Report Minnesota,* December 1994, p. 17.

Davis, Riccardo A., "Minnesota's Taylor Corp. to Purchase Miner Group of Minneapolis," *St. Paul Pioneer Press,* July 13, 1997.

Ehrlich, Jennifer, "Mergers and Acquisitions Talk Heats Up As Industry Competition Intensified," *Minneapolis/St. Paul CityBusiness,* September 8, 1997.

Miner Update, vols. 28–29, Minneapolis: Miner Group International, 1996, 1997.

O'Meara, Sheri, "The Miner Touch," *Format,* August 1996, p. 1.

Youngblood, Dick, "Entrepreneurs Sniff Out $100 Million Business Using 3M Technology," *Star Tribune* (Minneapolis).

—Robert R. Jacobson

Minntech Corporation

14605 28th Avenue North
Minneapolis, Minnesota 55447
U.S.A.
(612) 553-3300
Fax: (612) 553-3387

Public Company
Incorporated: 1974 as Renal Systems, Inc.
Employees: 350
Sales: $65.9 million (1997)
Stock Exchanges: NASDAQ
SICs: 3589 Service Industry Machinery, Not Elsewhere Classified; 3841 Surgical & Medical Instruments

Minntech Corporation, a leading producer and developer of dialysis solutions and sterilization systems, primarily markets to hospitals, clinics, and kidney treatment centers in the United States. Internally developed technologies generated an array of products used for open heart surgery and endoscopic procedures, as well as kidney dialysis. Minntech's small but growing water filtration division, which serves medical and industrial markets, is set to expand into food and beverage markets.

An Uncertain Start in the 1970s

Louis C. Cosentino, a Brooklyn, New York native with a doctorate in biomedical engineering, joined Minnesota-based Medtronic, Inc. in 1972 as director of advanced research and development. One of his assignments involved improving kidney dialysis fluids, and Cosentino suggested that Medtronic extend their business into building better kidney dialysis equipment as well. When the idea was rejected, Cosentino started his own business with $700,000 from private investors. Renal Systems, Inc. was established in 1974; in the first year the company produced 60,000 gallons of hemodialysis concentrates, which were used to prepare a dialysate, or salt solution, for kidney dialysis treatments.

According to Carol Pine and Susan Mundale's January 1989 *Corporate Report Minnesota* article, the company's early days were marked by uncertainty. The country was in an economic recession, and an oil embargo jeopardized Minntech's raw material supply. Demand for its products actually threatened the company's survival in 1976, when expenditures for raw materials exceeded cash on hand. Pine and Mundale wrote, ''Renal Systems survived thanks to a loan guaranteed by a friend and member of the company's board of directors, and because of Cosentino's persistence and ability to rally employees.''

Minntech developed electronic devices for hemodialysis, such as a blood pump and an air bubble detector, and added to its line of concentrates by 1978. An automatic dialyzer reprocessing system, which rinsed, cleaned, tested, and sterilized dialyzers for reuse, was introduced in 1982 and sold under the name Renatron. And in 1983 a cold sterilant, which replaced cleaners such as bleach and formaldehyde, joined the list of Minntech's kidney dialysis products.

Move to Public Ownership in the Early 1980s

The company brought in $6 million through a public stock offering in 1983, after which the company changed its name to Minntech. Sales for the fiscal year were nearly $12 million, with hemodialysis concentrates bringing in about 53 percent of revenues. The combination of new products and influx of capital seemed to bode well for the company, but the United States was in an era of health care cost containment.

Federal control of payments for Medicare patients was extended by the Medicare Prospective Payment System in 1983. With treatment reimbursements based on procedure classification rather than actual costs, hospitals had to cut back. Minntech sales fell to $8.1 million in 1985 and losses approached $1 million. The company cut personnel by 34 percent. Cosentino directed the company toward nondialysis and nonmedical product development to turn the tide.

In response to the cost-cutting trend, Minntech introduced a concentrate manufacturing system, the Renapak, which allowed dialysis facilities to prepare and store concentrates on-site. The company entered the cardiosurgery market via a hemoconcentrator, a devise that removed excess fluid from the blood during open heart surgery. Medical product giant C.R. Bard, Inc., which had already agreed to fund the development of a coronary angioplasty catheter reprocessor, agreed to contribute $1 million toward development of a blood oxygenator, a device that replaced lung function during open heart surgery. Bard, the world's largest supplier of both coronary angioplasty catheters and disposable oxygenators, agreed to market the Minntech oxygenator exclusively for five years.

Costs related to oxygenator manufacturing start-up and the development of an industrial water purification product resulted in fiscal year 1988 losses of about a half million on $13 million in revenues. But according to a July 1988 *Minneapolis/St. Paul CityBusiness* article by Diane Beulke, local analysts remained optimistic about the company's future, in part because of the number of products it had in the works. Beulke wrote, ''Minntech is somewhat unique among small medical device companies in its vertical integration. Everything from research and development to machine tooling to manufacturing, assembly, and quality control, and marketing is done by Minntech's 150 employees at its plant in Plymouth.''

Minntech's game plan paid off in fiscal 1989 with record revenues of $18.7 million, a 43 percent increase over fiscal 1988. Dialysis growth exceeded industry averages for the year, and the reprocessing and sterilant business grew by 40 percent for the third consecutive year. Blood oxygenators sales rebounded from a shaky start—Minntech had voluntarily recalled 2,500 units—and the company set record earnings of 48 cents per share. The core hemoconcentrate segment of the business continued to thrive as well; Minntech ranked second in the worldwide market. The company opened a European subsidiary in 1991 to increase sales and reduce manufacturing and transportation costs.

The Pleasures and Perils of the Early 1990s

Minntech earned a spot on *Forbes* magazine's 200 best small publicly traded companies list in 1992, 1993, and 1994 with a five-year return on equity of 19 percent. But internal and external forces slowed its growth. The medical technology sector, which had soared in 1990 and 1991, was on the decline and further depressed by President Clinton's health care reform proposals. In addition, Minntech found a number of its new products stalled in lengthy U.S. Food and Drug Administration (FDA) approval processes.

But Cosentino kept the company forging ahead. With its Bard blood oxygenator contract set to expire, Minntech moved to expand its cardiosurgery division. The sales force was bolstered and more than half the 1995 fiscal year research and development budget was targeted toward the $200–$300 million cardiosurgery market. Nearly 40 percent of Minntech's fiscal 1994 revenues of $47.5 million had been derived from the cardiosurgery unit. The minimum purchase deal with Bard had been bringing in more than $10 million in oxygenator sales per year.

Minntech had become one of the top three oxygenator makers in the world. A second generation oxygenator, which was about half the size of the original and required less of the patient's blood to prime for use, was in the works. Cardiosurgery competitors included Minnesota-based companies Medtronic and Avecor Cardiovascular Inc., Colorado-based Cobe Cardiovascular Inc., and California-based Bentley Laboratories.

New products, such as the Primus dialyzer, a second generation Minntech artificial kidney, and the Cathetron catheter reprocessor, which was sold only in Europe, helped drive up sales in fiscal 1995. By moving toward the creation of complete medical product systems—everything from machines to chemicals—Minntech was positioning itself to be competitive in a market that was cutting its number of vendors to cut costs.

Demand for the proprietary hollow fibers used in a number of products pushed Minntech to scale up production. The expansion took a bite out of the company's fiscal 1996 earnings and drove down its stock price. Minntech's woes were soon compounded when the company advised hospitals to stop using its Biocor oxygenator because of nine incidents of unexplained blood pressure drops during surgical procedures over a nine-month period. Although no injuries were reported, and competitors' products had reported similar incidents, Minntech's stock price took another beating.

The Biocor, Minntech's second generation oxygenator, had been used outside the United States since November of 1995, but FDA approval for domestic use was pending. Minntech canceled the advisory a month later, in July 1996, and reported that the pressure drop was user related and the problem would be addressed through retraining and modifications in instructions and product labeling.

Pressure on the company continued in October 1996, when the FDA moved to investigate charges by former Minntech employees regarding violations of federal regulations in the manufacture and distribution of kidney dialysis filters. The kidney dialysis filters—bundles of thousands of hollow fibers encased in clear plastic and surrounded by a salt solution—remove blood impurities in patients with kidney failure. Defective filters can further jeopardize the health of patients.

Minntech had only one competitor for the polysulfone filter, which worked more quickly than the standard polypropylene filters, but that competitor held 99 percent of the market. German-based filter maker Fresenius Ag merged with National Medical Care, a chain of 625 U.S. kidney dialysis centers, and created the world's largest kidney dialysis company in October 1996.

Judith Yates Borger wrote in an October 17, 1996 *St. Paul Pioneer Press* article, ''To be sure, the company is facing the toughest test of its 22-year history. Within the past year, about one-third of its management-level employees—including two chief financial officers and two vice-presidents—resigned or were fired.'' Although founder Cosentino had earned praise for his in-depth knowledge of engineering, he had been criticized for his management style as the company grew. Minntech's stock price, which had fallen by half within the past six months, was trading around the $11 mark when the FDA reported that it found only minor administrative deviations during its investigation.

A Change in Leadership and Future Direction

Chairman and CEO Cosentino stepped down from his operating duties in February 1997. Executive Vice-President Thomas J. McGoldrick stepped in as acting president and CEO and officially succeeded Cosentino in March. Cosentino remained on the board and later received a three-year scientific consulting contract. McGoldrick, a 12-year Minntech veteran, worked for Cardiac Pacemakers, Inc. and Medtronic prior to joining the company.

McGoldrick halted kidney dialysis filter production in March 1997 and shifted Minntech's focus back toward kidney dialysis reprocessing equipment and kidney dialysis solutions, which provided the majority of 1996 revenues. The Cathetron catheter reprocessing system, which had been marketed only outside the United States, was discontinued as well. Minntech cut its work force by 20 percent and restructured internal operations. Product discontinuation contributed to a net loss of $3.4 million or 51 cents per share for the year ending March 31.

During fiscal 1997 dialysis products contributed 32 percent and reprocessing products brought in 38 percent of sales. Cardiosurgery sales, which had declined with the phaseout of the second minimum purchase agreement with Bard, produced 26 percent of sales. Water filtration brought in the remaining four percent. International sales, with main markets in Western Europe and the Far East, accounted for about 18 percent of total revenues.

Fiscal 1997 marked the first full year of Minntech Japan Corporation, a joint venture with Japanese investors to move cardiosurgery products into the Asian Pacific market. The company had already established hemoconcentrator sales through a private label agreement with a major Japanese corporation. Minntech B.V., based in The Netherlands, was slated to begin manufacturing operations in fiscal 1998.

New markets emerged on the horizon when the U.S. Environmental Protection Agency (EPA) approved the Minncare cold sterilant as a sanitizer for nonporous food contact surfaces in fiscal 1997. The product could now be sold to beverage, food, dairy, wine, and beer manufacturers.

Minntech moved to improve hemofilter sales by tapping into an established distribution and marketing network in October 1997. Minntech announced a multiyear exclusive distribution agreement with Baxter Healthcare Corporation, the principal U.S. operating subsidiary of Baxter International, Inc., a world market leader in biotechnology, cardiovascular medicine, renal and intravenous systems/medical products.

The Biocor blood oxygenator, which received clearance for U.S. sales in fiscal 1997 but had been delayed for more than two years in the FDA approval process, entered a mature, highly competitive market. But Minntech's reprocessing products were well positioned to support health care cost-cutting methods.

Further Reading

Barrett, William P., "The Perils of Success," *Forbes,* November 3, 1997.

Barshay, Jill J., "CEO Steps Down at Minntech Corp.," *Star Tribune* (Minneapolis), February 1, 1997, p. 1D.

——, "Minntech Corp. Receives Approval from FDA for New Blood Oxygenator," *Star Tribune* (Minneapolis), March 8, 1997, p. 1D.

Beulke, Diane, "Minntech: Oxygenator to Breathe New Life into Profits," *Minneapolis/St. Paul CityBusiness,* July 25, 1988, p. 14.

Borger, Judith Yates, "Cosentino Quits As Chief Executive of Minntech," *St. Paul Pioneer Press,* February 1, 1997.

——, "FDA Investigates Claims About Minntech Filters," *St. Paul Pioneer Press,* October 17, 1996.

——, "Med-Tech Firm Has Troubled Atmosphere," *St. Paul Pioneer Press,* October 17, 1996.

——, "Minntech Cuts 30 Jobs; Income Drops Sharply," *St. Paul Pioneer Press,* January 25, 1997.

——, "Minntech Ends Advisory on Product," *St. Paul Pioneer Press,* July 19, 1996.

——, "Minntech: FDA Has Found No Support for Allegations," *St. Paul Pioneer Press,* October 29, 1996.

——, "Minntech Will Stop Making Filter, Faces Year-End Loss," *St. Paul Pioneer Press,* April 8, 1997.

"Corporate Capsule: Minntech Corp.," *Minneapolis/St. Paul CityBusiness,* January 29, 1990, p. 21; December 8, 1995; and October 31, 1997, p. 37.

Gross, Steve, and Slovut, Gordon, "Minntech Stock Drops 20 Percent on Report of Safety Advisory About Renalin," *Star Tribune* (Minneapolis), October 13, 1992, p. 1D.

Iverson, Doug, "Investors Avoiding Minnesota's Medical Technology Sector," *St. Paul Pioneer Press,* April 4, 1994.

——, "Minntech Pulls Medical Device from Hospitals," *St. Paul Pioneer Press,* June 27, 1996.

"Minntech Corporation," *Corporate Report Fact Book 1997,* p. 377.

"Minntech, Founder Reunite," *St. Paul Pioneer Press,* May 2, 1997.

Mundale, Susan, and Pine, Carol, "Seven Years Later," *Corporate Report Minnesota,* January 1989, pp. 65–67.

Mutsch, Edward L., "Periscope: Renal Systems Inc.," *Corporate Report Minnesota,* March 1984, p. 160.

Nissen, Todd, "Minntech Corp. Soon May Live Up to Its Word After All," *Minneapolis/St. Paul CityBusiness,* February 12, 1990, pp. 8–9.

——, "Minntech Plans U.K. Unit To Boost Sales and Cut Costs," *Minneapolis/St. Paul CityBusiness,* May 6, 1991, p. 3.

Peterson, Susan E., "Honored by Forbes," *Star Tribune* (Minneapolis), October 27, 1992, p. 5D.

Solberg, Carla, "Minntech Plans New Product Bundling," *Minneapolis/St. Paul CityBusiness,* April 19, 1996.

——, "Minntech Puts Heart into New Product Line," *Minneapolis/St. Paul CityBusiness,* October 14, 1994.

—Kathleen Peippo

Moulinex S.A.

11, rue Jules-Ferry
BP 45
93171 Bagnolet Cedex
France
(33): 01.41.99.41.99
Fax: (33) 01.43.34.32.10

Public Company
Incorporated: 1953 as Société d'Etudes Chimie et Mechanique Légumex
Employees: 8,400
Sales: FFr7.69 billion (1996)
Stock Exchanges: Paris
SICs: 3634 Electric Housewares & Fans; 3631 Household Cooking Equipment; 3635 Household Vacuum Cleaners; 3639 Household Appliances, Not Elsewhere Classified

Moulinex S.A., the once proud leader of the European small household appliance market, has seen troubled times for most of the 1990s. With sales slipping, and losses topping FFr700 million for its 1995 fiscal year, Moulinex has also seen longtime rival SEB overtake its home French market. Yet a revised shareholder structure, and an intensive restructuring program led by CEO Pierre Blayau, formerly of French retailing giant Pinault-Printemps-Redoute, appear to be pulling Moulinex out of a slump that began as early as the late 1970s. By June 1997, the company was able to announce its first net profit—of FFr29 million on sales of nearly FFr7.7 billion—in five years.

Under the Moulinex and Krups brand names, Moulinex continues its original focus on small appliances, principally for the kitchen. The three principal categories of the company's product lines—Breakfast, Food Preparation, and Cooking—are complemented by Moulinex's Floor Care (vacuum cleaners), Fabrics (irons), and Beauty/Health (hair dryers, electric toothbrushes) products. The Breakfast segment, including coffee makers, coffee grinders, espresso machines, and toasters, accounts for 29 percent of the company's annual sales, as does the Food Preparation segment's mixers, food processors, choppers, grinders, and centrifuges. Cooking equipment, including microwave, mini- and convection ovens, as well as deep fryers and grills, represent 26 percent of the company's revenues. Europe, at more than 75 percent of Moulinex's annual revenues, remains the company's primary market; in the U.S. and Asian markets, facing stiff local competition, Moulinex remains a somewhat small, but respected player.

A Stroke of Genius in the 1930s

For much of its history, Moulinex would remain the ''child'' of its founder Jean Mantelet. Born in 1900, Mantelet entered manufacturing in 1922, starting up a small business producing copper sulfate (also known as blue vitriol, used as an insecticide) sprayers for the agricultural market. By 1926, however, Mantelet gravitated towards the domestic appliance market that would become his fortune and in 1929, Mantelet founded the forerunner to Moulinex, Manufacture d'Emboutissage de Bagnolet, producing small, manual domestic appliances. Three years later, Mantelet had a stroke of genius that would prove the foundation of his first success.

Moulinex legend has it that Mantelet was inspired by his wife, or more accurately, the lumpy puree she served him one day for a meal. Mantelet saw a need for an improved device, one that would use a rotating motion to peel and prepare vegetables, while reducing the effort required by this chore. In 1932, Mantelet introduced his Moulinette ''moulin à légumes'' or vegetable mill at the Lyon Fair. Mantelet's experience in Lyon would prove equally provident for the future direction of his company. With a price of 36 francs, Mantelet found no takers for his vegetable mill Two months later, Mantelet brought the mill to the Paris Fair. This time, he priced the mill at 20 francs—and found immediate success. By the end of that year, Mantelet was producing some 2,000 mills per day and became convinced that his future and that of his company lay in low-end, mass-market products.

Even as Europe slipped into the Great Depression, Mantelet continued to believe in the viability of mass-market manufacturing. In 1937, inspired by Henry Ford's assembly line success,

Mantelet acquired a four-acre factory in Alençon, and moved production to that Normandy village, beginning the company's long—and somewhat fateful—association with that region. With the vegetable mill becoming a mainstay of any self-respecting French kitchen, Mantelet continued to devote his inventiveness to the household. Between 1929 and 1953, Mantelet's company would win more than 90 patents, for products such as the Mouli-Noix, a nutcracker; the Mouli-Râpe, a vegetable scraper; and the Mouli-Sel, a salt and spice mill. In 1953, Mantelet was awarded a patent for a new device, a manually operated, rotating vegetable peeler and scraper. In that year, Mantelet incorporated his company under the name Société d'Etudes Chimie et Méchanique (SECM). Two years later, after perfecting the new device, Mantelet adopted the more evocative "Legumex" (a combination of the French "légume" or vegetable, and "expansion") brand name.

The Légumex peeler was an instant hit. Within two months, the company had sold more than 36,500 units, and by the end of the year, more than 134,000 of the machines had been sold. Yet this success paled in comparison with Mantelet's next triumph. Only one year later, Mantelet brought the company into the era of the electric appliance. In 1956, SECM introduced its electric coffee mill, dubbed the Moulinex, at a price of 2,800 francs—less than half the price of any other coffee mill on the market. As Chantelet himself wrote, "A new price is a new market." By the end of that first year, the Moulinex had sold nearly 1.5 million units, capturing 50 percent of this "new" market. During this time, also, Moulinex adopted its famous slogan, "Moulinex Libère la Femme!" (Moulinex liberates women), capturing the imagination of housewives eager to escape the drudgery of household chores in the economic renaissance of postwar Europe.

Flush with this success, Mantelet changed the name of his company, in 1957, to capitalize on the fame of the Moulinex. The company also began rapidly enhancing its product lines, while remaining true to Mantelet's cherished mass-market, low-price category. By 1962, Moulinex had grown to become the premier French-based electric home appliance producer, dominating in particular the coffee mill market, with a 66 percent share, the hair dryer market, with a 62 percent share, and the mixers and blenders market, with a 75 percent share.

The economic boom of the 1960s continued to lift Moulinex's fortunes. The company was expanding, opening a series of factories centered exclusively in the Normandy region. Moulinex quickly became the region's premier private employer, growing from 800 employees in the late 1950s to more than 12,000 just 20 years later. In 1969, Moulinex went public, trading on the Paris stock exchange. By 1978, with annual sales of FFr1.67 billion, the company had risen to the rank of 92 among France's largest corporations, while nearly 65 percent of sales came from beyond France. Mantelet himself was listed among the top 25 wealthiest men in France. Yet trouble was brewing for the company: if Moulinex's first 20 years had seen phenomenal success, its next two decades would present near-constant struggles.

The Decline of a Giant in the 1980s

A variety of factors would contribute to Moulinex's difficulties, not the least of which was Mantelet himself. By the beginning of the 1980s, the company faced an increasingly saturated market. With 95 percent of French households already owning irons, 87 percent with a vacuum cleaner, and 70 percent with a pressure cooker, reflecting a similar situation throughout much of the key domestic appliance market, Moulinex found little room for maneuvering. A similar situation existed beyond France, in much of Moulinex's core European market. Meanwhile, Moulinex's belated implantation in the United States, begun in 1975 with the opening of a subsidiary production facility, was less than a sparkling success—the company had backed its U.S. entry on a single product, a food processor dubbed "La Machine," but this failed to capture the imagination of the U.S. household.

Moulinex's sales held steady, if stagnant, buoyed principally by the 1978 introduction of the first microwave ovens for the home market. But if the microwave proved a hit, the company would also produce a string of flops. Such was the case with its electric yogurt maker, its professional-style steam press, its electric pasta maker, among others. The company's total volume was slipping, as were its profits before the recession of the early 1980s had even got underway. Yet the company—that is, the 80-year-old Mantelet—refused to take the steps necessary to react to these changing market conditions. The company's employee list would remain swollen at 12,000 workers, and would even continue to grow. Mantelet—who, with no children of his own, often referred to Moulinex as his only child; in turn, Mantelet was known as "Papy" to his employees—refused to consider consolidating production and closing any of its many factories. Automating production, which had already become a necessity in the manufacturing world, also remained excluded from the Moulinex world. In the face of declining sales, the company reluctantly instituted a series of temporary layoffs, and would attempt other stopgap measures, such as four-day workweeks.

Indeed, the company would find itself in an embarrassing position. Despite the need to take more drastic measures to improve both productivity and profitability, Moulinex had firmly implanted itself in the Normandy region—to the exclusion of anywhere else. The company had long been the region's largest private employer, an honor that was quickly becoming a burden and placed Moulinex in a delicate position. Any move the company might make, in terms of eliminating payroll, would have severe repercussions for the region's economy. Only the recession of the early 1980s enabled the company to trim its payroll, scaling back to 8,500 employees. By the mid-1980s, however, Moulinex had once again rebuilt its workforce to nearly 10,000.

More ominously, however, the Moulinex image itself had begun to suffer. Once the pride of the French kitchen, the Moulinex name had become synonymous with low-end, technologically uninspired products. But the market was changing rapidly. Households no longer sought out simply a basic product, but instead demanded the more feature-rich packages offered by the increasing numbers of Moulinex's competitors. Here, too, Mantelet was seen as an impediment. Stubbornly focused on production on the one hand, and marketing on the other, Mantelet had long ignored a third crucial component of the home appliance market: distribution. Yet product distribution was undergoing a grand shift in France and elsewhere. The rise of mass distributors, including the hypermarket phenomenon, was rapidly drawing customers from the traditional small retail store. Mantelet's relationship with the company's distributors remained strained at best. With many of the new mass distribution arrivals proclaiming a policy of selling low-end, mass-market products "at cost," and with other distributors seeking higher profit margins on sales, Moulinex allowed a flood of competitors—especially the emerging Asian industrial giants—to push its products off the store shelves.

When the crisis of the early 1980s hit full force toward the middle of the decade, Moulinex was in no condition to react. Sales slipped, profits plunged, and by 1985 the company posted its first-ever net loss. The company's near-future prospects were bleak indeed, especially as the company's inventory continued to rise to alarming levels, reaching some 18 percent of its total revenues. Meanwhile, Moulinex's last new product success, the introduction of a mini-oven in 1982, would wait years for a successor. But finding an heir for the company's product line would prove simple in comparison to the issue of Moulinex's future leadership. Mantelet, turning 85 at the mid-decade mark, was finding it difficult to let go of his "child." With no children of his own, Mantelet had long refused to begin grooming a successor—a situation not uncommon among self-made business leaders of Mantelet's generation. Observers, particularly in the stock market, had long been clamoring for clarity on the issue. By the mid-1980s the issue of Mantelet's succession had become an affair of the state, with the unions representing the Moulinex workforce calling for government intervention to force Mantelet to pass on the reins of his company's leadership.

For his part, Mantelet had been making reluctant moves to find a new parent for his child. At the beginning of the decade, he had begun seeking a merger of Moulinex with another corporation. Philips, Electrolux, and others expressed interest in adopting the French small appliance flagship. In 1984, the company was nearly sold to Black & Decker; that agreement, however, was scuttled by Mantelet's refusal to give up his majority control. And rather than softening his position, Mantelet would make any acquisition of the company more difficult, particularly with his insistence that any new parent be a French-based concern, that the employee base be maintained at its current levels, and that any merger agreement would in fact remain a partnership agreement. Despite these requirements, Moulinex nonetheless appeared at last to have found a suitor in Scovill, the American industrial group, which purchased some 20 percent of Moulinex in a planned takeover. However, Moulinex's increasing losses ended the chances of a marriage, friendly or not, with Scovill.

The clouds that had been hanging over Moulinex would soon turn into a full-scale storm. In March 1986, Mantelet suffered a stroke, rendering him paralyzed on one side and partially aphasic. Suddenly, the company found itself with no leadership at all. Yet Mantelet, far from becoming more supple, actually hardened in his resistance at giving up his company. Refusing still to name a successor, Mantelet seemed simply unable to give up the firm to which he had devoted so much of his life. For much of the following year, Moulinex effectively remained without a leader. At last, in 1987, the crisis at the company forced Mantelet's hand. While still refusing to choose a successor, and continuing to cling to ultimate control of the company, Mantelet turned the company's reins over to three of his top managers: Gilbert Torelli, in charge of sales; Roland Darneau, in charge of production; and Michel Vannoorenberghe, in charge of finance.

The trio went to work attacking the problems of a company in full disarray, taking measures that included shutting the company's factories four days each month, and persuading Mantelet to reduce the company's workforce by 1,300 employees—primarily through early retirements and other voluntary incentives. Meanwhile, Moulinex began inching towards what was fast becoming its sole recourse in the issue of Mantelet's succession—an employee buyout of the company. At last, Mantelet allowed this move to occur in 1988. But an employee buyout was seen as a difficult maneuver in the best of situations. And Moulinex's precarious position—coupled with the sheer size of the proposition—made a successful buyout seem remote indeed. In fact, the buyout of Moulinex by its employees—with principal ownership falling to Torelli, Darneau, and Vannoorenbergh—introduced a new phase of crisis for the company.

Restructured Hopes for the 1990s

Yet the new management—although remaining under Mantelet's control—appeared to make a promising start. Moulinex relaunched its product line, updating its designs and features, to the extent that by the start of the 1990s, nearly all of the company's products were less than 18 months old. The company's marketing was revised as well, with a successful advertising campaign helping to improve Moutlinex's image among consumers. Meanwhile, the company began shifting into the higher-margin high-end market. At the same time, the company began, for the first time in history, to look outside its operations for growth. In 1988, the company acquired small appliance makers Swan and Girmi, and followed these acquisitions with that of the Krups brand in 1991. The result was a fresh growth spurt in the company's sales, which neared FFr3 billion by 1989. By the time the Krups acquisition was fully consolidated, Moulinex's revenues topped FFr8 billion.

Once again, however, Mantelet seemed to impede the progress of his company. This time, it was Mantelet's death in 1991 that sparked a new company crisis. To the end, Mantelet had refused to choose a protégé to lead the company. Upon his death, a power struggle erupted among the principal shareholders, Torelli, Darneau, and Vannoorenbergh. As the trio fought amongst themselves for ultimate control, the company itself once again slipped into disarray. Factories became more or less fiefdoms, with managers making independent decisions as central control all but disappeared. Abuses grew rampant: one executive reportedly ran up company credit charges of more than FFr5 million per year; another granted himself a FFr400,000 Mercedes—before quitting the company. Meanwhile, the payroll once again swelled to more than 14,500 owner-employees, including a large number of superfluous middle managers, just at a time when a fresh recession was brewing, plunging the European economies into a prolonged crisis.

The employee buyout had become a trap. As the recession took hold, sales collapsed and profits disappeared, reducing Moulinex to nearly five years of losses. Yet the company was paralyzed from taking the most necessary steps: drastic cuts in payroll, the closing of a number of its outdated factories, and the stepping up of the automation of the remaining production activities. With the tension among the top three managers and principal owners reaching its own crisis level—ranging from tapping telephones to reportedly coming to blows in the halls of the company's headquarters—Moulinex needed to free itself of its employee-ownership arrangement.

In 1993, a quartet of financiers rode in to the rescue. The holding giant Euris, the Suez Bank subsidiary Soffo, Francarep of Groupe Rothschild, and IDI orchestrated a buyout of the majority of Moulinex's shares, taking control of the company's operations. While the quartet might have expected to perform a quick turnaround—and in the process a fast return on their investment—the restructuring of Moulinex would require another four years before the company returned to even meager profitability. One source of this delay was, once again, the company's position in the Normandy region, and the awkward—if not politically suicidal—necessity of shutting down some of its facilities. Yet, in order to compete successfully, the company needed desperately to transfer much of its production, at least for its low-end products overseas, to the lower-cost Asian region, and also to the company's new facility in Mexico, the latter essential if Moulinex still hoped to make its presence felt in the important North American markets.

Moulinex would remain in more or less of a holding pattern until 1996, when Pierre Blayau was named as the company's CEO. Meanwhile, losses had reached alarming levels, climbing to more than FFr700 million in 1995. Blayau, however, came to the company with a reputation as a specialist in overcoming crisis conditions—and for having the temperament that was not shy about taking drastic measures. In June 1996, then, Blayau announced the closing of two of Moulinex's oldest factories and the reduction of the company's workforce by more than one-third by the turn of the century. Where such an announcement would have previously met with extreme resistance in the Normandy region, by 1996, there seemed no other choice if Moulinex was to survive. By 1997, Blayau's restructuring of the company seemed to be bearing fruit: in June 1997, the company announced its first—albeit somewhat symbolic—return to profitability in more than five years.

Further Reading

Beaufils, Vincent, "Moulinex Broie du Noir," *L'Expansion*, February 6, 1987, p. 78.

Dupuy, Georges, "Moulinex: la Grande Manoeuvre de Blayau," *L'Express*, June 27, 1996, p. 68.

Le Guilledoux, Dominique, "Moulinex, l'Amer Hiver des Sacrifices," *Le Monde*, January 28, 1997, p. 13.

Marseille, Jacques, "Grandeur et Déclin de Moulinex," *L'Expansion*, November 25, 1993, p. 120.

Tatu, Natacha, "Blayau Va Passer Moulinex à la Moulinette," *Nouvel Observateur*, June 13, 1996, p. 74.

—M. L. Cohen

Murphy Family Farms Inc.

P.O. Box 759
Rose Hill, North Carolina 28458
U.S.A.
(800) 311-9458
Fax: (919) 289-6400

Private Company
Incorporated: 1969
Employees: 800
Sales: $775 million (1997 est.)
SICs: 0213 Hogs; 2048 Prepared Feeds, Not Elsewhere Classified; 2041 Flour & Other Grain Mill Products

The largest swine production company in the United States, Murphy Family Farms Inc. supervises operations that raise piglets to hogs for slaughter in a six-state territory. Murphy Family Farms contracts with other farmers to use their land and their labor to fatten hogs for market, relying on 500 contract farmers in North Carolina, Oklahoma, Missouri, Iowa, Kansas, and Illinois to raise its swine. The company is considered an innovator in the breeding and fattening of swine, having developed a systematic, scientifically-based method for raising hogs. The investment has worked wonders, building the company into a market leader. In 1997, the company controlled 125 sow farms, housing a total of 275,000 sows, twice as many as its nearest competitor. All told, the company watched over six million hogs in 1997 during their maturation to market weight. A privately owned company, Murphy Family Farms is headed by Wendell Murphy, who built the business into a national leader. Murphy owns two-thirds of his company. The remaining one-third is jointly owned by three members of his immediate family.

Origins

No one in the history of U.S. agriculture had a greater influence on swine breeding than Wendell Murphy, a self-made billionaire in the business of raising hogs for slaughter. Murphy's dominance in the science of raising hogs was unquestioned in the 1990s, but when he began his ascent in the 1960s no one, including Murphy himself, could have imagined he would build a massive empire populated by hogs. Murphy did not set out to become a hog farmer, and neither did he hail from the hub of hog farming. Murphy was born and raised in North Carolina, where tobacco farming was the agricultural pursuit of choice. Hog farming, on the other hand, was most prevalent in the Midwest, where Iowans reigned as the nation's champion hog farmers.

After adolescence, Murphy left the sleepy confines of Rose Hill for Raleigh, where he studied agriculture at North Carolina State. He completed his studies in 1960, leaving with a degree in agriculture, and immediately took a job teaching agriculture for $4,080 a year at a high school near Rose Hill. While Murphy spent his days teaching, his wife worked as an office clerk. Together, after two years of work, the young couple saved $3,000, which they handed over for a $10,000 mill that ground corn. The balance came from Wendell's father, a tobacco farmer, who guaranteed a bank loan for the remaining $7,000. Wendell's father shouldered the financial risk somewhat begrudgingly, acquiescing only on condition that his son keep teaching school during the days. "I had to nag Daddy for months for that money," Wendell Murphy remembered, but once he had it he was in business as a grain miller.

Murphy sold his feed to neighboring farmers and used whatever he could not sell to add another activity to his already busy days and nights as a school teacher and grain miller. Murphy started raising pigs. He sprinkled his leftover grain in a mud pit, and waited until his hogs fattened to their market weight of 250 pounds. The number of boars and sows quickly proliferated. By 1968, their numbers had increased to such an extent that Murphy stopped selling feed to other farmers and used all of his yield to feed his hogs. Although not the only hog farmer in North Carolina, Murphy was an oddity of sorts, but despite his ill-suited geographic setting he had committed himself to a life of hog rearing. The severity of his commitment was demonstrated as soon as disaster struck.

1969: A Defining Crucible

In 1969, one year after Murphy had exchanged his hopes as a grain supplier for hopes as a hog farmer, a cholera epidemic swept through his farm. At the time Murphy watched over a drift of 3,000 swine. Their continued existence was not permissible. Each one of Murphy's hogs was destroyed by officials from the U.S. Department of Agriculture (USDA) shortly after the disease manifested itself. It was a summary end to Murphy's fledgling occupation as a hog farmer, exacerbated by the quarantine enforced by the USDA once all Murphy's hogs were slaughtered. Although the devastation could not have been more complete, Murphy was determined to find a way back into the hog farming business.

Making another go at hog farming was a difficult task considering Murphy's farm had been quarantined, leaving him without any swine or land, but Murphy used this glaring deficiency to his advantage. He introduced contract farming to the hog business, borrowing a practice that had been used nearly exclusively by poultry farmers. Murphy approached his tobacco farming neighbors, offered them the necessary fences, food, and piglets, and had others raise his hogs for him. In exchange for providing labor and land, Murphy's contractors received $1 for every hog taken in at eight weeks old and returned 15 weeks later, at which time Murphy could cart his fattened hogs to the packinghouse. It was a perfect arrangement for a farm-less hog farmer strapped for cash, and a welcomed opportunity for anyone taking on the duties of one of Murphy's contract farmers. Raising hogs for Murphy provided a guaranteed source of income, a luxury not often enjoyed in farming.

Contract hog farming solved Murphy's post-cholera dilemma, providing a quick solution to a short-term problem. However, contract hog farming, realized its greatest strength for Murphy as a long-term approach, allowing him to expand his operation without having to purchase land. With plenty of farmers ready to jump at the chance of securing a steady stream of income, Murphy's only obstacle was the intensity of his own ambition, which was not found lacking. During the 1970s and 1980s, Murphy expanded throughout North Carolina, building his hog farming business into a statewide enterprise. The only major problem Murphy had to contend with as he spread his operation across his home state was the chief reason why Iowans were renowned as hog farmers and North Carolinans were not. Grain, particularly corn, was abundant and inexpensive in the Midwest, providing hog farmers from Iowa and neighboring states with ample, cheap feed for their hogs. Considering that roughly 65 percent of a hog farm's costs were incurred from feeding the hogs, cheap grain represented a significant advantage for Midwestern hog farms and an elusive treat for Murphy. For help with this inherent problem for North Carolina hog farmers, Murphy turned to agriculture experts. The answers he received made Murphy a billionaire.

In retrospect, the 1969 cholera epidemic proved to be a valuable lesson for Murphy. It served as the impetus for two pioneering moves that made Murphy Family Farms the unrivaled giant in U.S. hog farming. First, the epidemic barred Murphy from using his land to raise hogs, forcing him to turn to contract hog farming. Second, it taught him first-hand the devastation delivered by disease, the biggest risk for pig farmers. Never wishing to endure the catastrophic losses resulting from disease again, Murphy had to find a better way to raise hogs. He had to find a better way not only to protect his hogs from disease, but also to somehow loosen the tight grip Midwestern farmers had on the hog market. To do so, Murphy realized the only way he could compete was to embrace the latest technology and discover a more efficient method to raise hogs, an approach that would increase his sows' yield and better manage his costs and time. Murphy's experts developed such an approach, and Murphy Family Farms benefitted mightily.

At the time, there was not much science in the centuries-old business of raising hogs for slaughter. Typically, there were between 2,000 and 3,000 hogs on one farm, penned together from birth until they reached the magic weight of 250 pounds. Murphy's experts found this method self-defeating. They divided the life cycle of a hog destined for slaughter into three stages, with the parameters of each stage dictated by the overwhelming need of every hog farmer—and particularly Murphy—to avoid exposure to disease.

Murphy's technicians discovered that during the first two weeks of nursing, a sow passed on vital antibodies to her young. After that juncture, the sow starts passing on diseases. The agriculture experts also pointed out that older hogs pass on disease to younger hogs, making the scenario of 3,000 hogs, young and old, penned together into the same enclosure a recipe for disease. This knowledge prompted sweeping changes in the manner in which Murphy Family Farms' hogs were raised. After piglets turned 15 days old, Murphy took them away from the sows, herded them into sanitized former school buses and shuttled them to the next contract farm. The growing piglets stayed at their second home until they reached 50 pounds, which generally required approximately 50 days. Next, to avoid the diseases passed on by older hogs, that same group of hogs, now 10 weeks old, was sent to a finishing farm for the remaining 21 weeks it took to reach the market weight of 250 pounds. By raising his hogs in this manner, Murphy gained the advantage he needed to shrug many Midwestern hog farmers aside and fuel his rise toward becoming the largest hog farmer in the United States.

Dominance in the 1990s

By the 1990s, Murphy's contributions to the science of raising hogs could be measured on a national scale. Between 1989 and 1994, the number of hogs per farm in North Carolina ballooned five-fold, compared to a 60 percent increase nationwide. In 1989, North Carolina produced 5.4 percent of the country's pork. By the late 1990s, North Carolina produced 11 percent of the nation's pork, second only to Iowa. Murphy's new, science-driven approach to hog fattening was responsible for a discernible shift in the nation's geographic orientation of hog farming.

Underpinned by a proven formula for success, Murphy Family Farms did not restrict its business activities to the boundaries defining North Carolina. The company had done much to tilt the pork production scale in North Carolina's favor, but the Murphy Family Farms' program of hog raising was too successful to remain in one state. Further, the company's system of contract farms made the Murphy Family Farms formula ideal for export into other regions. The company expanded into Iowa in 1986 and a decade later was moving into Kansas, with neighboring states brought under the company's purview during the interim. In each state, the same procedure developed in North Carolina was followed strictly, with the emphasis on creating a disease-free environment as severe as ever. Particular attention was paid to the company's all-important sow farms. Any contract farmers hoping to do business with Murphy Family Farms were forbidden to operate hog farms within one mile of a company sow farm. To enter one of the company's sow farms, visitors and workers were required to shed their clothes, shower, and wear company-provided coveralls and rubber boots. Inside the sow farms, the largest of which housed 3,600 sows constantly mating, gestating, and delivering, workers wore earplugs as a defense against the deafening squeals of a Murphy Family Farms sow farm operating at full efficiency. Inside the nursing rooms, the sound was more soothing, as the songs of Garth Brooks and other singers were piped 24 hours a day into the areas housing piglets. Intended to calm the piglets and accustom them to the sound of human voices, the musical recordings were one aspect of the science employed by Murphy Family Farms to raise as many hogs as possible. Although the methods used by Murphy Family Farms would have struck past generations of hog farmers as eccentric, few could argue with the company's success.

By the late 1990s, Murphy Family Farms was averaging an annual output of an estimated 22 piglets per sow. The national average was less than 15 piglets per sow. In terms of the costly necessity of feeding hogs, Murphy Family Farms again far exceeded the national average. Typically, hog farmers used four pounds of feed to realize one pound of weight gain on a hog. Murphy Family Farms only used three pounds to put on the same weight. Clearly, Murphy's desire to increase efficiency in the 1970s and 1980s had materialized by the 1990s, and his dominance in the industry supported this conclusion. In 1997, after expansion had carried the company outside of North Carolina into Oklahoma, Missouri, Iowa, Kansas, and Illinois, Murphy Family Farms owned 275,000 sows, twice as many as its closest rival, Carroll's Foods, and six million hogs. With this remarkable lead over its competitors, Murphy Family Farms looked to the next century and the continued success of its groundbreaking procedures for raising hogs.

Principal Subsidiaries

Murphy of Oklahoma; Murphy of Missouri; Murphy of Iowa; Murphy of Kansas; Murphy of Illinois.

Further Reading

Guebert, Alan, "Lawsuit Mars Indianapolis Pork Industry Conference," *Knight-Ridder/Tribune Business News,* June 2, 1997, p. 6.

Hays, Jean, "World's Largest Hog Producer Applies to Open Hog Farm in Kansas," *Knight-Ridder/Tribune Business News,* July 2, 1997, p. 7.

House, Charles, "Murphy Farms Launches New Feed Mill in North Carolina," *Feedstuffs,* January 3, 1994, p. 18.

Roth, Daniel, "The Ray Kroc of Pigsties," *Forbes,* October 13, 1997, p. 42.

—Jeffrey L. Covell

Nantucket Allserve, Inc.

45 Dunster Street
Cambridge, Massachusetts 02138
U.S.A.
(617) 868-3600
Fax: (617) 868-5490
Web site: http://www.juiceguys.com

Private Company
Incorporated: 1990
Employees: 100
Sales: $30 million (1996 est.)
SICs: 2086 Bottled and Canned Soft Drinks & Carbonated Waters

A start-up company of the 1990s, Nantucket Allserve, Inc. was one of the fastest-growing entries among the ''new age'' fruit-flavored alternatives to traditional soft drinks. This hotly competitive market was led by Snapple, which sold an estimated 23.6 million cases in 1996, compared to an estimated 2.3 million for Nantucket Allserve. Fruit beverages accounted in 1995 for $12.5 billion of the $169.5 billion beverage industry, which was selling an average of 2.5 bottled drinks to each American each day.

Struggling for a Toehold, 1989–92

The ''real world'' held no allure for Tom Scott and Tom First when they were attending Brown University. ''In our senior year all our friends were interviewing for jobs at big New York firms,'' First told Judy Temes in the *Boston Globe.* Instead, after graduation in 1989, the two headed for Nantucket, the island off Cape Cod where they had both vacationed as children. First and Scott had spent the previous summer on the island operating ''Allserve,'' a motorboat that became a floating convenience store after Scott swapped it with his father in exchange for his car. The two Toms delivered food, beer, ice, cigarettes, newspapers, and laundry to yachts in the harbor—and even performed services like pumping out bilge tanks. They also converted an icehouse in the harbor into a general store.

Reality set in during the bleak winter months on the island. First and Scott worked odd jobs and cast around for some other way to stay solvent. For a cooking contest, First tried to recreate a peach drink he had sampled in Spain. After his potion of peaches, sugar, and water, mixed in a blender, won a prize, the two decided to make the drink the nucleus of a new business. ''I remember thinking it could be a big thing,'' Scott said, ''but to us, big might mean $50,000.''

At first, First and Scott sold peach nectar by the glass off the deck of Allserve. The response was so enthusiastic that within weeks they began pouring it into recycled wine bottles they ordered from a catalogue at 20 cents each, capping the bottles with a hand press they bought for $170. They sold 2,000 bottles at $1 each all over the island. Business was so good the two invested their combined savings of $17,000 to have 1,700 cases of the nectar professionally pasteurized and bottled in New York. Before the summer was out they were selling the drink on the neighboring island of Martha's Vineyard and parts of Cape Cod as well as Nantucket. During the last months of 1990 First and Scott introduced three flavors: peach-orange (their best seller), lemonade, and cranberry-grapefruit. The young entrepreneurs took in an impressive $52,000 in their first year of business.

At this point in their enterprise, First and Scott began receiving an education in hardball economics. A Philadelphia juice man, who had helped them develop new blends and arrange for bottling, cut them loose, charging them with trying to muscle in on his own territory. Without this contact, the only bottler they could interest in the juice was not equipped to handle the heated liquid needed for pasteurization. ''We had bottles exploding on us, we had caps blowing off. We had bottles freezing in the winter,'' Scott recalled. Moreover, some of Nantucket Nectars' distributors proved treacherous, stashing the bottles in nooks and crannies where they could not threaten the competition.

All the money the partners had grossed, as well as their own savings and family loans, had been sunk into production and distribution. Scott was so strapped for money that he spent the summer of 1991 sleeping in his car. ''And even when we lived in homes, we never turned on the electricity,'' said First. ''We burned our pallets in a wood stove to keep warm.'' In the course of their struggles, the two Toms took odd jobs like waiting on tables, shucking scallops, and shampooing dogs. "We were naive, and we didn't know it," Scott recalled. "We just refused to quit. And refusing to quit can get you through a lot."

Nantucket Nectars' fortunes began to turn around when an Ohio bottler agreed to spend $10,000 to equip his plant to handle a 12-ounce bottle for the drinks. During 1992 Scott and First began distributing their product in Washington, D.C., landing accounts in museums and colleges, and even in Congress. Revenues climbed from about $200,000 in 1991 to about $300,000 in 1992. Even so, the two were having trouble keeping their heads above water. A few of their employees, who had gone unpaid all year, stole more than $100,000 in merchandise from a Boston-area warehouse before the two noticed that something was amiss. "We often wondered if we could go on at all," Scott told Temes. "We lived like vagabonds."

Going Big Time, 1993–94

To keep the business running, Scott and First needed a backer, whom they found, while cleaning his yacht, in the person of Michael Egan. The owner of Alamo Rent A Car, Egan received about 100 unsolicited proposals per year and had never made an investment outside his industry, but he put down $500,000 for a half-interest in the fledgling juice company, now dubbed "Nantucket Allserve." "I was more fascinated by them than the product," Egan told Temes in 1994. "I've never seen two young guys who've sacrificed more to get a business going. Even today they live on peanuts." Interviewed in 1997 by Julia Flaherty for the *New York Times,* Egan confirmed that he had invested in the entrepreneurs rather than in their business. "The juice wasn't actually too good," he said. "They had some flavors that were horrible. They had this bayberry tea that had to be about the worst-tasting, snake-oil elixir you could find and put in a bottle."

With the cash from Egan, Nantucket Allserve was ready to go big time. Scott and First added new flavors and improved the taste of their offerings by using more-expensive cane sugar, instead of the industry-standard corn syrup, as a sweetener for the company's fruit cocktails. By the end of 1993 there were 16 different Nantucket Nectars, most of them all-juice drinks. After bottling, the product was shipped to the company's leased warehouses in Boston and Washington. Ten thousand cases were sent to about 120 stores in 15 states each month. In the Boston area, Nantucket Allserve was delivering and selling 1,000 cases a week. Revenues reached about $1.3 million that year.

A Boston upscale cafe said the company's juices were "selling themselves," but Scott and First found that to move more product they had to hire salespeople to convince more retailers to stock the Nantucket Nectars. The two also sought to raise consumer demand by formulating and airing radio spots. One slogan, also printed on the bottle labels (along with a Nantucket seascape), declared, "We're Juice Guys. We don't wear ties to work." This slogan was more successful than the follow-up "We knew you'd be back," which turned off listeners by its arrogance.

In an ongoing publicity campaign, Scott and First sent purple Winnebagos around the country—seven were in operation in 1997—to distribute free samples of the purple-capped product. The company also set up purple tents at football games and street fairs near the many college campuses of the Boston area and sold T-shirts sporting the Nantucket Nectars logo. Community activities became another form of promotion. Nantucket Nectars co-sponsored "Hoops for the Hungry," a D.C. basketball tournament. The company also sponsored the 1996 AIDS Walk in San Francisco, took part in the annual Earth Day observance in Boston and New York City, and organized an annual party in Boston to provide warm clothing for the homeless.

During 1994 Nantucket Allserve's revenues surged to $6 million, but its founders failed to turn a profit. Adding more than 100 new employees to the base staff of seven was one reason, but more important was the discovery that forging a distribution system amounted to an unacceptably expensive form of on-the-job training. Scott and First had expanded their network to five warehouses and 18 trucks, hired a sales force, and begun distributing other beverages, including Arizona Iced Teas and Clearly Canadian sparkling water. But the system's volume still was too small, and after the company sustained a $1 million loss in 1994, Nantucket Allserve dropped the distribution operation and turned to outside services. This reduced the average cost for delivering a case to retailers from $3 to $2.

Double-Digit Revenues, 1995–97

Nantucket Allserve earned its first profit in 1995: an estimated $225,000 on revenues of some $15 million. Then, in 1996, sales doubled to an estimated $30 million, and profit before taxes rose to $600,000. That year Nantucket Allserve was ranked by *Inc.* as the 13th-fastest-growing private company in the United States. Revenue was projected to double once again in 1997, to $60 million. In September 1997 the company made its first Nantucket Nectars shipment to the coffee-bar chain Starbucks, which was planning to sell the drinks in about 200 of its East Coast outlets. The product was available at this point in more than 30 states (mainly on the East and West Coasts) and Canada, France, Great Britain, South Korea, and Central and South America.

Nantucket Nectars products in 1997 ranged from 100 percent fruit juice, iced tea, and lemonade, to "juice cocktails" with only about 20 percent juice at a time when some competitors were marketing drinks with as little as one percent juice. Among Nantucket's offerings were Pineapple Orange Banana 100% Juice, which was sweetened with white grape juice, and Kiwi Berry Juice Cocktail, which was 21 percent juice and contained water and cane sugar as well as pear, kiwi, and passion fruit juices. Mixed flavors included Apple Raspberry, Pineapple Orange Banana, Pineapple Orange Guava, Watermelon Strawberry, and Half & Half (iced tea and lemonade). Container sizes ranged from 12 to 36 ounces, but the midsized 17.5-ounce bottle was the best seller of the three.

The company introduced a new line called Nantucket Super Nectars in July 1997. These six concoctions were meant to appeal to health-conscious consumers by mixing herbs like ginseng and wheat grass with fruit juices. "Green Angel" combined herbs like echinacea with white grapes, bananas, and juices. "Chi'i Green Tea" was a tea-and-ginseng mix, "Protein Smoothie," a soy-protein drink, and "Gingko Mango" a blend of ginkgo herb and orange and mango juices. ''Vital-C'' was a fruit juice made from the vitamin-C-rich acerola berry. ''Red Guaranta Tea'' was an herbal tea made with white clover honey, cranberry juice, and guarana nut berry—a plant native to the Amazon with properties similar to caffeine. These specialty juices retailed at a recommended price of $1.79 compared to $1.09 for the standard drinks and were initially marketed only in New England.

Prior to the Nantucket Super Nectars, the company line consisted of eight 12-ounce juices and juice cocktails, six 17.5-ounce juices, eight 17.5-ounce juice cocktails, nine 17.5-ounce lemonades and ice teas, and eight 36-ounce juices and juice cocktails. Pressed Apple Juice and Cranberry (a juice cocktail) were the only ones being marketed in all three sizes. Nineteen were in kosher form. The apples came from New York, the lemons from Florida, the oranges from California, and the cranberries from Nantucket. No preservatives or additives were used in any of the drinks.

In 1997 Nantucket Allserve was using bottling plants in Warwick, Rhode Island; Reading, Pennsylvania; Lakeland, Florida; and Benicia, California. Company offices were relocated from Nantucket in 1992—first to Brighton, Massachusetts, then to Boston, finally to a former Harvard University fraternity house in Cambridge where the tieless Toms allowed their dogs to roam the purple-colored premises. The company was also running a Juice Guys juice bar on Nantucket as a prototype for others planned to open around the country.

Further Reading

Burger, Katrina, ''A Drink with an Attitude,'' *Forbes,* February 10, 1997, pp. 112–113.

Flaherty, Julia, ''Sailing on a Rising Tide of Juice,'' *New York Times,* September 17, 1997, pp. 1D, 5D.

Flynn, Sean, ''Beverage Isle,'' *Boston Magazine,* March 1997, pp. 23–25.

Marriott, Anne, ''Nantucket Nectars Partners Drink in Success,'' *Washington Times,* June 5, 1997, p. 8B.

McCloy, Andrew P., ''Nantucket Nectars Pours Out New Health-Conscious Product Line,'' *Boston Business Journal,* July 18, 1997, p. 9.

Muller, Joann, ''Fostering Corporate Culture,'' *Boston Globe,* pp. 73, 76.

O'Shea, John, ''A Couple of Juice Guys,'' *Cape Cod Life,* September 1995.

Temes, Judy, ''Island Entrepreneurs: To Live on Nantucket, Tom and Tom Shucked Clams, Pumped Sewage, and Started Bottling Juice,'' *Boston Globe,* January 30, 1994, pp. 52–53.

Weinstein, Bob, ''Drinking Buddies,'' *Business Start-Ups,* February 1995, pp. 52–53.

—Robert Halasz

National Instruments Corporation

6504 Bridge Point Parkway
Austin, Texas 78730-5039
U.S.A.
(512) 794-0100
Fax: (512) 794-8411
Web site: http://www.natinst.com

Public Company
Incorporated: 1976
Employees: 1,289
Sales: $200.7 million (1996)
Stock Exchanges: NASDAQ
SICs: 3826 Laboratory Analytical Instruments; 7372 Prepackaged Software

National Instruments Corporation is a leading developer of computer-based instrumentation hardware and software products used in a wide range of industries, spread across two large markets: test and measurement and industrial automation. This includes specialty interface cards for general commercial, industrial, and scientific applications.

Billing itself as "The Virtual Instrumentation Company," National Instruments offers hundreds of products that serve primarily scientists and engineers involved in test and measurement applications and industrial automation systems. The company creates flexible application software and modular, multifunctional hardware that combines with industry-standard personal computers and workstations to create user-defined "virtual instruments," providing productivity tools for scientists and engineers to do their experimentation, research and development, and manufacture of products. Some industries using virtual instrumentation systems include the automotive, biomedical, telecommunications, electronics, and aerospace industries. The company's products are also used in the pharmaceutical, chemical, and food industries and the tools are used to aid in tracking factory operations and control equipment.

How It All Started, 1976–89

The company was founded in 1976 by President and Chairman Dr. James J. Truchard, a former managing director of the Applied Research Laboratories' Acoustical Measurements Division at the University of Texas at Austin, and fellow engineers Jeffrey L. Kodosky and William Nowlin, and was incorporated in Texas in May of that year. The three were involved in dozens of projects ranging from basic research to applied products and developing systems for testing military equipment, primarily for the U.S. Navy. By the time they left the university, Truchard had worked on or been involved in systems on virtually every ship and submarine in the Navy.

The company was founded with the goal of creating "a company that could grow by doing very innovative work that could be widely used." Citing frustrations at the research lab of "having projects that would be developed just to sit on the shelf," Truchard "wanted products that could go out into the marketplace and leverage standard technology to be very effective in what they do." Applying for a $10,000 loan from a local bank, the founders pooled their savings from their state teacher retirement funds and started the company in a room behind Truchard's garage and sometimes adjourned to Kodosky's kitchen. A 300-square-foot office space was eventually rented and Truchard hired a neighbor part-time as the company's first non-founder employee.

The company's first product was an interface that connected stand-alone test equipment to PDP-11 UNIBUS computers. Nowlin, serving as a director and secretary, and Truchard designed the hardware and Kodosky, serving as a director, wrote the software. Truchard doubled as the marketing director, writing the company's press releases. The first product was shipped in 1977 and, by the early 1980s, the company was doing both custom instrumentation work and manufacturing off-the-shelf products. From 1977 to 1997, the company's revenues grew steadily.

Kodosky was appointed vice-president of the company in 1978 and was promoted to vice-president of research and development in 1980. In 1983, the fledgling company dropped its custom work and focused on building off-the-shelf GPIB prod-

Company Perspectives:

National Instruments manufactures software and hardware products for personal computers (PCs) and workstations that scientists and engineers use to build their own specific instruments, known as "virtual instruments." These user-defined systems are for test and measurement and industrial automation applications such as automated testing, laboratory automation, factory automation, physiological monitoring, numerical analysis and data visualization.

ucts (inter-tool communication devices, similar to printer ports). The same year, the company introduced its first GPIB interface for the IBM personal computer (PC) and IBM selected the company as its supplier for the same. Realizing that an application software environment would be needed which engineers and scientists could utilize with GPIB interface products in instrumentation control applications, Truchard charged Kodosky with creating an intuitive software product for that purpose. After spending three years armed with 10 Macintosh computers, tons of junk food, no windows or clocks, and the occasional foraging trips to a local Middle Eastern restaurant, the development team created Laboratory Virtual Instrument Engineering Workbench, also known as LabVIEW, which was released in 1986 for use with Macintosh computers. In an article in the July 12, 1996 issue of *Investor's Business Daily,* Truchard said, "with LabVIEW," the company's flagship application software, the company's "goal was to do for scientists and engineers what the spreadsheet had done for financial analysis."

The following year, National Instruments released LabWindows, which allowed scientists and engineers a set of tools which simplified the development of instrumentation applications using C and BASIC on DOS-based PCs. LabWindows provided programmers who preferred text-based languages a set of interactive code generation development tools, but let them continue programming with the methodology they had become familiar with.

In 1987, the company expanded its hardware line to include Macintosh NuBus data acquisition boards, coinciding with Apple Computer's launch of the Macintosh II PC. Current Vice-President of Marketing Timothy R. Dehne joined the company in 1987 as an applications engineer. Also that year, the company opened its first international office in Tokyo. In 1989, the company began issuing a quarterly newsletter, *Instrumentation Newsletter,* with feature articles, new product information, user-solution case studies, and new instrumentation technology to educate current and prospective customers about the company's products and technologies.

Impressive Growth During the 1990s

As the company entered the 1990s, it was growing by leaps and bounds. In 1990, NASA utilized a computer software program developed by the company to help trace fuel system leaks affecting space shuttle launches. Total revenues reached $44.7 million, with net income of $6 million. In 1991, the company achieved revenues of $59.5 million, with net income of $3 million. By 1992, the company had exhibited approximately 40 percent growth per year for the previous 10 years and revenues jumped to nearly $83 million.

By January 1993, the company's products were being utilized in a wide range of industries. Major customers included such giant corporations as 3M, Apple Computer, AT&T, Boeing, Chrysler, Daimler Benz, E.I. DuPont, Eastman Kodak, Ford, General Electric, General Motors, IBM, Intel Corp., McDonnell Douglas, Motorola, and Proctor & Gamble; such research facilities as Lawrence Livermore National Labs, Los Alamos National Labs, and Sandia National Labs; Purdue University, the University of California, and the University of Texas; NASA; and a number of foreign companies.

That same year, the company purchased the rights to HiQ, a Macintosh-based, integrated graphical environment, numerical analysis, and data visualization software package which allowed the company to deliver all the software components needed for the scientific method. The company's revenues that year ended up at $105.5 million, a 27 percent increase over the previous year, with a net income of $10.1 million.

In 1994 the company was reincorporated in Delaware. The company went public in March 1995 with an initial offering of three million shares of common stock that brought in $39.6 million. That year, the company added a 140,000-square-foot manufacturing and engineering facility to the existing 153,000 square feet of office space on 69 acres it owned in north Austin. The company also became ISO 9002 compliant. Revenues that year hit $164.9 million.

In 1996, the company introduced a total of 96 new products, bringing its total of new products released to more than 600, for testing in such diverse applications automotive cruise control, emissions and air bags; satellites; Patriot missiles; professionals' golf swings; the U.S. rowing team's form; space shuttle experiments; and a number of consumer and medical programs. The company's products were also used to manufacture paper, Ben & Jerry's ice cream, and to sort kiwi fruit.

One product released in 1996 was in the Fieldbus hardware market. A group called Foundation Fieldbus was created with the mission of inventing standards which would allow different brands of industrial automation products to work with each other. Some of the companies involved in the group included Allen-Bradley Co., Fuji Electric Co., Honeywell Inc., Siemens Industrial Automation Inc., and Toshiba Group. The company released one of the first Fieldbus hardware technologies, which companies in the Foundation planned to incorporate into their products, allowing them to connect with other similarly equipped products. A second product unveiled in 1996 was called "image acquisition." Designed for a potentially lucrative market, the hardware studied a picture of a product on an assembly line and automatically compared it to what the product should look like. The company's largest competitor in this market was Natick, Massachusetts-based Cognex Corp. A third product released in 1996 was ComponentWorks, a software product designed to work in tandem with Microsoft's Virtual

Basic application development tools to compete with the company's own LabVIEW software.

September saw the launch of the company's industrial automation software, called BridgeVIEW, which would help companies control heating and cooling systems, programmable logic controllers, pumps, valves, and other hardware used in manufacturing. BridgeVIEW, which competed against software from Irvine, California-based Wonderware Corp. and Germany-based Siemens AG, drew on technology already used in the company's well-established LabVIEW "virtual instruments" software. The overall industrial automation market was believed to be worth about $20 billion in 1997. The man-machine interface part, in which BridgeVIEW competed, was worth $215 million. But it was considered one of the most promising segments of the market and analysts believed it could grow to $1 billion by the end of the 20th century.

Also in 1996, National Instruments acquired a number of new companies and/or products. Early in the year, the company purchased technology from France-based Graftek for image analysis and acquisition, which complemented the company's already strong base of data acquisition products. In April, National Instruments purchased Georgetown Systems, Inc., a start-up company which was creating software to compete with National Instruments' LabVIEW flagship software product and Irvine, California-based Wonderware Corp.'s software, for approximately $2 million. The company integrated Georgetown's Windows-based Lookout software into its own. And late in the year, the company acquired the SQL Toolkit software from Boston, Massachusetts-based Ellipsis Products Inc., which would be used to integrate the company's software tools into the corporate environment.

Poised for the Future

By July 1996, the company had expanded to 28 sales offices worldwide, adding facilities in Hong Kong, Japan, Singapore, and Taiwan. *Forbes* ranked National at number 53 on the magazine's list of the Top 200 Small Companies in America. At the year's end, the company had 2,057 employees, revenues for the year hit $200.7 million, and net income came in at $25.5 million. From 1992 to 1997, the company enjoyed an average annual growth rate of 29 percent. By mid-1997, the company was distributing its software and hardware products through a direct sales organization, OEMs, independent distributors, and systems integrators and had 46 sales offices in North America and 29 locations in 22 countries throughout the world.

That year, the company released version 4.1 of LabVIEW, which NASA used to monitor the Mars Pathfinder Rover and Motorola used on the world's first satellite-based phone network, the Iridium Satellite Project. The company also released a new line of computer-based multimeters, oscilloscopes, and other instruments, a new line of PCI-based data acquisition boards for Windows NT/95/3.1, and Ver. 3.1 of the HiQ data visualization and report generation software for Windows NT/95. The company was also again named to *Forbes* magazine's Top Small Companies list. With offices around the globe, and with new strategic alliances being forged regularly, National Instruments appeared in good position to continue growing by leaps and bounds.

Further Reading

Burrows, Peter, "National Instruments Profits by Balancing Hardware with Software: The Company Grows 40% Per Year by Tying Its Application Development Software to a Quiet but Steady Stream of Equipment Sales," *Electronic Business*, April 27, 1992, p. 47.

Cunningham, Cara A., "National Instruments Brings LabVIEW to Windows, Unix: Graphical Tool Eases Creation of Test Software," *PC Week*, September 21, 1992, p. 76.

Franklin, Richard, "An Emphasis on Innovation," *Wall Street Corporate Reporter*, February 17–23, 1997.

——, "Texas' National Instruments Celebrates 20 Years," *Knight-Ridder/Tribune Business News*, May 15, 1996, p. 5150324.

Kimball, James G., "NI Has Right Chemistry in Software Solutions," *Business Marketing*, April 1994, p. 26.

Krause, Reinhardt, "Defending Prime Niche in Software Market," *Investor's Business Daily*, July 12, 1996.

Ladendorf, Kirk, "Austin, Texas-Based National Instruments Sets Records for Sales, Profit," *Knight-Ridder/Tribune Business News*, January 29, 1997, p. 129B1268.

——, "View from the Lab Is Quite Nice for Austin's National Instruments Inc.," *Austin American-Statesman*, December 1, 1991.

Murphy, Shelby L., "Revolutionary Ideas Propel National Instruments' Growth," *Austin Business Journal*, November 1996, pp. B4, B19.

"National Instruments Corp.," *Wall Street Journal*, June 6, 1997, p. B5.

Palmeri, Christopher, "The Virtual Oscilloscope," *Forbes*, October 20, 1997, p. 200.

——, "Wizards Create Easier Setups," *R&D*, May 1997, p. 73.

Tarsala, Michael, "Branching into Lucrative Industrial Markets," *Investor's Business Daily*, March 4, 1997.

—Daryl F. Mallett

National Railroad Passenger Corporation

80 Massachusetts Ave., NE
Washington, D.C. 20002
U.S.A.
(202) 906-3860
Fax: (202) 906-3864
Web site: http://www.amtrak.com

Private Company
Founded: 1971
Employees: 23,000
Sales: $1.6 billion (1996)
SICs: 7999 Railroads, Line-Haul Operating

The National Railroad Passenger Corporation, better known as Amtrak, is the United States' national rail passenger service, providing train transportation between major cities as well as commuter service and delivery of mail and express freight. A private corporation, Amtrak is almost wholly owned by the U.S. Department of Transportation.

The Creation

On May 1, 1971, the first passenger trains operated by the National Railroad Passenger Corporation (NRPC) pulled out of stations around the country, beginning what was depicted as a two-year federal undertaking to revive (and save) long-distance, intercity rail passenger service in the United States.

Congress had created the NRPC the previous year with the passage of the Railroad Passenger Service Act. The act established a private company, incorporated in the District of Columbia. Most of the new company's stock was owned by the Department of Transportation, and it was governed by a board of directors made up of the Secretary of Transportation, the head of the NRPC, and 11 other members, the majority appointed by the president. During its first year of existence, the corporation was known as Railpax. After it began operations, the nickname was changed to Amtrak, a contraction of the words America and track.

NPRC was charged with accomplishing three goals, described in the Amtrak Source Book as: ''To operate rail passenger service on a for-profit basis; to use innovative operating and marketing concepts to fully develop the potential of modern railway passenger service to meet intercity transportation needs; and to provide a modern, efficient intercity rail passenger service.'' Congress authorized grants of $40 million for operations and loan guarantees of $100 million for new equipment. Direct funding was to last only two years, by which time the corporation was to be completely self-supporting.

Background

By the time Congress created NRPC, intercity rail passenger service in the United States had been in a 20-year decline. Until the 1950s, railroads were the only way to travel long distances. But during that decade, the federal government began financing the interstate highway system, a $41 billion, 16-year project, and, as jet airplanes were introduced, significantly increased its support for the construction and improvement of airports.

Airplanes, personal automobiles, and buses began competing with the country's railroads for long-distance travel. The railroads responded to the competition with new equipment on their prestige long-distance routes, replacing steam locomotives with diesel engines, and introducing lightweight stainless steel passenger cars with air-conditioning and double glazed windows. But as the number of passengers continued to drop, the rail companies had little incentive to make major capital investments to upgrade their tracks, signaling, stations, and maintenance facilities. Why, they thought, should their profitable freight business subsidize a means of intercity transportation that was competing with systems receiving federal and state tax dollars. By 1958, rail service accounted for just four percent of intercity travel.

The decline in rail passenger service and the deterioration of passenger facilities continued during the 1960s. By the end of the decade, the number of passenger trains had dropped to 500, down from more than 20,000 some 40 years earlier, and only 12,000 passenger cars remained in service. Losses from passenger service operations in 1970 came to more than $1.8 billion dollars in 1997 dollars. Most of the loss was on long-distance, intercity travel. Commuter and suburban lines obviously were less affected by airlines and, at least during the 1960s, lost little ridership to buses and private cars. Many of the railroad compa-

Company Perspectives:

We are America's passenger railroad. Our mission is to consistently deliver a high-quality, safe, on-time rail passenger service that exceeds customer expectations.

nies filed applications to get out of the intercity service on most or all of their routes. Among the most critical was the proposal by Penn Central (the merged Pennsylvania Railroad and New York Central Railroad) to eliminate all its passenger service in the Northeast and Midwest.

Federal Action

The Railroad Passenger Service Act allowed the railroad companies to transfer their money-losing passenger operations to NPRC in exchange for either a tax write-off or Amtrak stock. Only three lines, the Denver & Rio Grande Western, the Rock Island, and the Southern, did not join Amtrak, opting to continue their own passenger service.

The basic network of routes for the new corporation was developed by the Transportation Department with assistance from the Interstate Commerce Commission, the railroad unions, 15 railroad companies, 43 states, some 3,000 members of the public, and numerous U.S. Senators and Representatives. Factors considered in selecting the routes included existing routes, cost, ridership potential, size of the terminal cities (had to have a population of at least 1 million), and the condition of the tracks and facilities (no funds were allocated for improving these).

Between January and May 1971, as the new corporation got itself organized, a major argument developed regarding the company's objective: was it to reintroduce the traditional, and well-known, long-distance routes of the past, such as the ''Empire Builder,'' ''San Francisco Zephyr,'' and ''Super Chief,'' or should it concentrate on introducing high speed (150 mph) rail corridors? Those two visions of passenger service in the United States would haunt the NPRC for decades.

The 1970s—Amtrak's First Decade

Although it operated in 43 states over 24,000 miles of track, the enterprise Amtrak began managing on May 1, 1971, was hardly a national transportation system. Essentially, Amtrak was a travel broker. It operated 119 passenger trains, a multicolored assortment of some 1,200 cars—coaches, diners, sleepers, and observation cars—with an average age of 20 years. The individual railroads donated some cars to Amtrak but continued to own the stations, terminals, yards, locomotives, and maintenance facilities, and employed all the people who worked on the passenger trains and in the stations and yards. In its first year, Amtrak leased the crews and equipment, along with the seat reservation, booking, communication, and dispatching systems from the various freight lines. In 1972, Amtrak began buying the diesel locomotives from the railroads and initiated a program of rebuilding and refurbishing the engines to improve on-time performance.

The tracks Amtrak's ''rainbow'' trains ran on also were owned by the freight companies. For access to the rights of way, which was guaranteed by the legislation, Amtrak paid the freight companies a rental charge. That charge was determined by a formula established in the federal statute. The legislation also gave Amtrak trains priority dispatching over freight trains, but did not address the issue of liability in cases of injuries. Despite the logistical problems and uncomfortable rolling stock, Amtrak was able to keep the passengers it inherited in 1971, and during its first two years even increased ridership.

The creation of Amtrak seemed to generate three conclusions. Some people believed the new entity was really expected to revive intercity rail traffic. The more skeptical seemed to think that this was a last gasp effort and that once the equipment finally gave out, that would be the end of it. Others within the industry and among the passengers saw it as a ruse to eliminate routes in sparsely populated areas while keeping rail service along corridors between major cities in the Northeast and on the West Coast.

None of these occurred after Amtrak's first two years because OPEC, the cartel of oil-producing countries, cut back the production of oil. The resulting energy crunch in 1973 and 1974 caused the price of gasoline (and airline tickets) to increase and lines at gas stations to grow long. Many Americans (and politicians) increased their support of alternative means of transportation, including rail passenger service. Congress approved funding for fiscal years 1972–73 totaling $179.1 million in grants and $100 million in guaranteed loans. In 1973, Amtrak began ordering new equipment.

The new silver trains with the red and blue Amtrak logo attracted more riders and marketing became easier. A centralized and computerized reservations system also helped improve service. During the decade, the company purchased 600 Amfleet and Amfleet II cars and 284 Superliners, including locomotives, coaches, lounges, sleepers, and dining facilities.

Amtrak also began to take control of yard and station facilities, reservation offices, and all personnel except for train and engine crews. In 1972, Amtrak employed about 1,500 administrative and clerical workers. Within two years, as the company assumed responsibility for more of the passenger service operations, employment climbed to 8,500.

The Northeast Corridor (NEC)

As Amtrak was placing its equipment orders, the major freight lines in the Northeast were going bankrupt. As creditors, shareholders, railroad unions, and other railroads (who shipped to and from the East) cried for some action, the federal government took a step that would have a huge impact on Amtrak. The Regional Rail Reorganization Act of 1973 created Conrail (Consolidated Rail Corporation), a federally supported freight company made up of seven bankrupt railroads operating in the Northeast. The legislation also supported funding for preliminary engineering work to improve the Northeast Corridor in order to cut passenger travel times between Boston, New York, and Washington, D.C.

Three years later, following the passage of the Railroad Revitalization and Regulatory Reform Act in 1976, Amtrak acquired 621 miles of right-of way from Conrail. Most of the routes, about 450 miles, were in the Northeast Corridor, from

Washington, D.C. to Boston. The acquisition also included lines from Philadelphia to Harrisburg, Pennsylvania; from New Haven, Connecticut, to Springfield, Massachusetts; and from Porter, Indiana, to Kalamazoo, Michigan. For a switch, now freight trains would have to pay Amtrak to use these rails. As part of the legislation, Congress authorized $1.9 billion over five years to rebuild and improve the tracks and facilities in the NEC.

Along with the tracks, Amtrak also came into possession of rail yards, maintenance facilities, and all the stations along their new routes. The real estate included Pennsylvania Station in New York City and 30th Street Station in Philadelphia, along with some 100 smaller station properties, and half interests in Chicago's Union Station and in Washington, D.C.'s Union Station. With these acquisitions, Amtrak employment nearly doubled, to 16,500, as the company assumed new operations and maintenance responsibilities.

The capital investments made to reduce travel time in the Northeast Corridor by rebuilding tracks and introducing new equipment received most of the attention during the late 1970s. But development was begun on another high-speed corridor, between Los Angeles and San Diego, and other corridors were being studied for high-speed potential.

During the last half of the 1970s, Congress changed the way it financed Amtrak's capital improvements. Instead of loan guarantees, which had amounted to $900 million between 1971 and 1975, or a designated source of income as was provided for highways and airports, Amtrak began receiving direct capital grants, which had to be requested and approved annually, making it difficult to plan and finance capital investments. Amtrak continued to receive separate annual operating grants.

The company's annual revenue during the decade averaged $252 million, and represented less than 40 percent of its operating expenditures. The growing deficits led the Carter Administration to push for more efficient operations and cuts in costs. Proposals to eliminate routes as a means of reducing costs generally went nowhere as Senators and Representatives fought to keep trains running in their states, whether the routes were profitable or not. In fact, by 1977, the number of miles in the Amtrak system had grown to 27,000. Finally, under restructuring in 1979, several routes were dropped as the basic network was cut to 24,000 miles.

1980s—Amtrak's Second Decade

During the 1980s, Amtrak continued to move from supervising to operating the nation's passenger rail system. Early in the decade, Amtrak installed its new Arrow reservation system, with faster computers, and acquired the last non-Amtrak intercity passenger train, the Rio Grande Zephyr, from the Denver and Rio Grande Western.

In 1983, Amtrak, for the first time, directly employed engineers, conductors, and their assistants, beginning on Northeast Corridor trains. The takeover of the operating crews continued for the next several years, until, by 1987, Amtrak employed most of the crews operating passenger trains around the country. After 1982, under Amtrak's bargaining agreements, crews were paid based on a 40-hour work week, not on mileage and other factors as had been the case with the freight lines.

The company also expanded its position in the commuter train business, taking over the commuter trains in the northeast previously operated by Conrail. The company set up a wholly owned subsidiary, Amtrak Commuter Services Corporation, to oversee its commuter operations.

Amtrak's partnerships with various states improved passenger service in their jurisdictions. Under Section 403(b) of the legislation that established the NRPC, Amtrak could operate intercity trains or routes funded by states. California, for example, paid for more trains between Los Angeles and San Diego, in the San Joaquin Valley, and, eventually, between San Jose and Sacramento. New York was one of the first to take advantage of Section 403(b), improving passenger service for the New York-Albany-Buffalo corridor.

But the core route and services faced financial cuts as the Reagan Administration convinced Congress to significantly reduce both the operating and capital grants each year. As President Reagan told an audience, "On the New York to Chicago train, it would cost the taxpayer less for the government to pass out free plane tickets."

Most historians agree that things would have been even worse for Amtrak except for Graham Claytor, a lawyer and railroad executive and the new president and CEO of Amtrak. According to Stephen Goddard, "The grandfatherly attorney left his comfortable office . . . to give Amtrak what it needed—credibility before Congress, in whose hands the troubled railroad would rise or fall." Yet even as the cuts were being made, when Reagan fired the striking federal air traffic controllers, people turned to intercity trains.

In 1981, Congress told Amtrak to make better use of all its resources to minimize federal support. In addition to revenues from the commuter and 403(b) trains, by 1981, Amtrak's real estate revenues were generating about $9 million a year. In 1984 the company acquired the remaining one-half interest in Chicago Union Station.

To help increase its assets, the company established a corporate development department. One of its ventures was to lease the NEC right-of-way to telecommunication companies for installing fiber optics communications systems. MCI Communications was the first company to enter into such a lease, with MCI providing Amtrak with specific fibers and communication circuits as well as with cash. Amtrak used those high capacity circuits for their own network and marketed and leased them to large telecommunication users. Amtrak also turned to mail and express freight service for additional income.

In 1985, Amtrak's supporters argued that shutting down Amtrak completely would result in costly drops in productivity due to traffic jams and crowded airports in the major corridors, especially in the northeast. The prospect of more cars and planes (and the resulting pollution) effectively dampened enthusiasm for eliminating all support for Amtrak, at least for a while.

In 1986, Amtrak became the dominant carrier between New York and Washington, with 38 percent of the total air-rail market. In 1989, the company began another period of capital investment, as Amtrak purchased 104 short-distance passenger cars to alleviate crowding on routes in the Midwest and in California's San Joaquin Valley.

By the end of the decade, Amtrak operations were bringing in more than $1.2 billion in revenues. But with operating expenses in fiscal 1989 of nearly $2 billion, it continued to have an operating loss larger than the $554 million operating grant it received from the federal government. The general capital grant fell from $221 million in fiscal year 1981 to $2 million in fiscal 1986 then averaged $34 million for the rest of the decade.

1990s—Moving Toward Self-Sufficiency

In 1994, Congress and the Clinton Administration demanded that Amtrak operations become self-sufficient by 2002. To accomplish this, the company, under new CEO Thomas Downs, adopted a strategic and business plan for the period 1995 to 2000. As part of the plan, Amtrak decentralized itself into three business units to increase accountability and responsiveness: Northeast Corridor, covering services from Virginia to New England; Amtrak West, which operated state-supported corridor trains and the long-distance Coast Starlight on the West Coast; and Amtrak Intercity, responsible for most of the long-distance routes as well as corridor trains in the Midwest. The company also began raising fares, cutting routes and service, and implementing cost reduction programs for its operations.

But Amtrak needed new rolling stock to replace old equipment, to achieve better travel times, and to meet the requests from states for new intrastate rail services. Through 1990, Amtrak had spent $1.6 billion for cars and locomotives and the capital investment continued during the decade with the delivery of new diesel locomotives, 195 bi-level Superliners, and, in 1996, 50 Viewliners, the first single-level sleeping cars made in the United States in 40 years. In California, 14 new dual-level dining cars were introduced on the state-supported routes, and in Washington, three pendular "tilt" Talgo trains were ordered by Amtrak and the Washington Department of Transportation for delivery in 1998. Trains able to travel 150 miles an hour were for service on the Northeast Corridor beginning in 1999.

Although revenues increased to $1.6 billion in fiscal year 1996, debt and capital lease obligations were almost $1 billion. By 1997, Amtrak was in danger of going bankrupt (in December of that year Downs resigned as CEO and a search was underway for his successor). Congress debated the company's request to designate one-half cent of the Interstate Highway Trust for capital expenditures, but instead passed a tax rebate package of $2.3 billion for Amtrak capital spending over two years and adopted a package of reforms changing various labor requirements, allowing Amtrak to alter the basic system of routes inherited in 1971, setting a cap on liability costs, and establishing a new Reform Board. Funding for the Department of Transportation for fiscal year 1998 included $344 million for Amtrak operations and $250 million for Northeast Corridor capital. It also included $23 billion for highways, $9 billion for aviation, and $4 billion for transit.

On the issue of federal subsidies, there appeared to be agreement that Amtrak should receive support for its equipment and facilities. But Congress still did not establish an ongoing, dedicated source for that payment.

Whether Amtrak would achieve operating self-sufficiency by 2002 was not certain, and several voices were involved in the debate as to what intercity rail passenger service should be. Amtrak's own strategic business plan shifted resources to routes having the greatest growth potential and increased support for key state-funded routes and mail and express freight contracts. Rail advocates believed there were alternatives to eliminating routes or cutting back on service. A special Working Group on Intercity Rail established by Congress recommended that 1) there be passenger rail service in all densely populated corridors with traffic congestion and poor air quality and 2) public/private development of periodic overnight passenger service in historic, scenic, or cultural regions. Others have suggested separating the Northeast Corridor completely from Amtrak. Despite many changes and improvements since its birth in 1971, Amtrak continued to generate as much controversy as it did passenger miles.

Further Reading

"25 Years of AMTRAK—A Look Behind the Smoke and Mirrors," *Mobility Dallas,* http://www.altinet.net/'mobdaldm/md092896.htm.

"Amtrak Legislative Update," Friends of Amtrak, November 18, 1997 http://www.trainweb.com/crocon/amtrak.html.

"Amtrak's Future," http://www.trainweb.com/travel/future.htm.

"Amtrak Source Book," Washington, D.C.: National Railroad Passenger Corporation, 1991.

Bradley, Rodger, *Amtrak: The U.S. National Railroad Passenger Corporation*, Dorset, England: Blandford Press, 1985.

"Congress Acts to Preserve America's National Passenger Railroad System," Amtrak Press Release, November 13, 1997, http://www.amtrak.com/bulletin.html.

"Different Tracks,"(broadcast transcript) http://www.pbs.org/newshour/bb/transportation/march97/rails_3.31.html.

Goddard, Stephen B., *Getting There: The Epic Struggle Between Road and Rail in the American Century*, New York: Basic Books, 1994.

Hosansky, David, "Struggling Amtrak Seeks Share of Federal Highway Money," *Congressional Quarterly Weekly Report,* March 29, 1997, p. 737.

Johnson, Bob, "States Show Amtrak the Way," *Trains Magazine*, July 1997, p. 36.

"Losing Steam," (broadcast transcript) http://www.pbs.org/newshour/bb/transportation/july-dec97/amtrak_11-12.html.

Mitchell, Matthew, "About Amtrak," Delaware Valley Association of Railroad Passengers, http://www.libertynet.org/ dvarp/dvarp.html.

"A New Vision for America's Passenger Rail," Committee on Transportation and Infrastructure Working Group on Intercity Passenger Rail, June 1997, http://www.house.gov/transportation/rail/railrpt.htm.

"Perspective—Derailing Amtrak," *Investors Business Daily,* November 6, 1997.

Vantuono, William C., "Blue-Ribbon Panel Spells the Blues for Passenger Rail," *Railway Age*, August 1997, p. 161.

Wilner, Frank N., "Amtrak at 25: The Railroad That Just Won't Quit," *Railway Age*, May 1996, p. 39.

—Ellen D. Wernick

NEW HOLLAND

New Holland N.V.

World Trade Center, Amsterdam Airport
Schiphol Boulevard 217
1118 BH Schiphol Airport
The Netherlands
(44-181) 479-8800
Fax: (44-181) 479-8825
Web site: http://www.newholland.com

Public Company
Incorporated: 1991 as N.H. Geotech
Employees: 18,619
Sales: US$5.55 billion (1996)
Stock Exchanges: New York
SICs: 3523 Farm Machinery & Equipment; 3524 Lawn & Garden Tractors; 3531 Construction Machinery & Equipment

New Holland N.V. is one of the world's leading manufacturers and distributors of agricultural equipment and a major producer of construction equipment. The company is the market leader in Europe and many parts of Latin America and Asia and ranks third in the North American tractor market. New Holland was formed through the 1991 merger of Fiat Geotech S.p.A. and Ford New Holland, Inc., both of which had grown into industry giants over nearly a century of product and sales expansion and timely acquisitions. Fiat Geotech S.p.A. continues to hold a 69 percent ownership interest in New Holland, having sold the other 31 percent in a 1996 initial public offering. New Holland currently operates 18 production sites in 24 countries, as well as 13 engineering centers around the world. More than 1.5 million New Holland machines are now engaged in agricultural and industrial work somewhere on Earth.

Company Origins

New Holland's roots can be traced back to 1895, when handyman Abe Zimmerman made his first feed mill at his New Holland, Pennsylvania repair shop. Zimmerman soon began making other agricultural products as well. He called his operation the New Holland Machine Company and incorporated it in 1903, the same year Henry Ford incorporated the automobile company he had started up in Detroit. Ford came out with the prototype for the world's first mass produced agricultural tractor in 1907, and ten years later the tractor, known as the Fordson Model F, went into actual production. Decades later, these two fledgling operations would become linked.

Meanwhile, across the Atlantic, Italian auto maker Fiat was developing a tractor of its own. That company's efforts resulted in the development of the 702, Fiat's first mass produced tractor, which hit the market in 1919. In Belgium, another company, Claeys, was entering the picture. Founded in 1906, Claeys began manufacturing harvesting equipment in 1910. Back in the United States, Zimmerman's New Holland company was also thriving. It continued to do well until about 1930, when the Great Depression began to hit rural America hard. As farm income plummeted, so did New Holland's revenue.

Sperry Takes Over in 1947

After about a decade of struggle, New Holland was purchased by a group of four investors. The new owners were able to turn the company around quickly by introducing a new product, the world's first successful automatic pick-up, self-tying hay baler. The baler, invented by local thresherman Ed Nolt, was an instant hit among farmers. It almost single-handedly put New Holland back on solid footing. In fact, the company has continued to manufacture updated models of the baler ever since.

In 1947 New Holland Machine Company was acquired by electronics specialist Sperry Corporation, creating a subsidiary dubbed Sperry New Holland. In the years that followed, Sperry New Holland developed and manufactured a large number of agricultural machines. In particular, the company carved out a niche as a producer of high-quality harvesting equipment. Things were also developing quickly in the European agricultural equipment industry during this period. In 1952 Claeys unveiled the first European self-propelled combine harvester. By the early 1960s, Claeys was one of the biggest combine manufacturers in

Company Perspectives:

The mission: To be a customer-driven organization, flexible, agile and innovative, with our people, dealers, suppliers and partners working together with pride to be the best globally positioned company in the agricultural and industrial equipment business. This is New Holland's mission—the mission of a truly global company, present around the world through its production plants, research and development centers, industrial and commercial joint ventures, and worldwide dealer network. New Holland offers one of the widest, most flexible ranges of agricultural machinery and industrial equipment. This outstanding commitment stems directly from its worldwide industrial and design skills, and a market approach which begins and ends with the customers.

Europe. Sperry New Holland bought a major interest in Claeys in 1964. The same year, Sperry New Holland made a major breakthrough in hay harvesting technology with the introduction of the haybine mower-conditioner, model 460. This machine was capable of performing tasks that previously required two or three separate pieces of equipment. New Holland would go on to revolutionize harvesting equipment in 1974, with the introduction of the world's first twin rotor combine.

As the 1960s continued, Fiat became increasingly active in the manufacture of equipment for agriculture and construction. Late in the decade, that company created a Tractor and Earthmoving Machinery Division. Fiat's earthmoving segment was moved into its own subsidiary, Fiat Macchine Movimento Terra S.p.A., in 1970. Fiat continued to move further into heavy equipment through the 1970s. In 1974 Fiat Macchine Movimento Terra launched a joint venture with American manufacturer Allis Chalmers Corporation, called Fiat-Allis. That year also marked the creation of the company's Fiat Trattori S.p.A. subsidiary. Fiat finally gained entry into the North American market in 1977, with the acquisition of Hesston, a Kansas-based manufacturer of hay and forage machinery. Fiat also purchased Agrifull, a small-sized tractor manufacturer, that year. In 1984 Fiat consolidated all of its agricultural machinery manufacturing under the umbrella of Fiatagri, the new name for Fiat Trattori.

The 1980s Belong to Ford

All the while, Ford was also becoming a global force in agricultural equipment. Its Ford Tractor division had been responsible for a number of industry breakthroughs, including the use of rubber pneumatic tires, power hydraulics, diesel engines, and the three-point hitch. Ford's inexpensive tractors had been largely responsible for the replacement of horses and mules by machines on United States farms over the first several decades of the 20th century. By 1985 Ford Tractor had 9,000 employees, about one third of them located in North America, and 5,000 dealers worldwide, again about a third of them in the United States.

In 1986 Ford purchased Sperry New Holland and merged it with its Ford Tractor Operations to create a new company, Ford New Holland, Inc. By this time New Holland had grown to become one of the best performing companies in the farm equipment business, with 2,500 dealers and more than 9,000 employees of its own, working in 100 different countries. The merger was part of an overall consolidation taking place in the farm equipment industry at the time, a period that saw Tenneco, the parent company of the J.I. Case tractor and farm implement operation, take over the farm implement business of International Harvester. With combined annual sales of $2 billion, the new company made Ford the third largest farm equipment manufacturer in the world. Most of Ford Tractor's executives and managers were moved over to New Holland's Pennsylvania offices, which became Ford New Holland's corporate headquarters.

Within months of this merger, Ford New Holland added on the agricultural division of Versatile Farm and Equipment Co., an agricultural equipment manufacturer that had been founded in Canada in 1947. The combination of Ford's tractors, New Holland's harvesters, and Versatile's large four-wheel-drive machines created a company that produced a wide spectrum of agricultural equipment, and, best of all, there was almost no overlap in what the three entities manufactured and, therefore, little pruning to be done once they were united. One of the few major changes at New Holland was the gradual elimination of its company-store system. Between 1987 and 1989, New Holland's 53 company-owned outlets were sold off or closed, in favor of a dealer development program that provided training and assistance for independent dealers.

Back in Europe, changes were also taking place at Fiat. In 1988 the activities of Fiat-Allis and Fiatagri were merged to form a new company, FiatGeotech S.p.A., which now encompassed Fiat's entire farm and earthmoving equipment sector. By the end of the 1980s, Fiat was Europe's leading manufacturer of tractors and hay and forage equipment. FiatGeotech's revenue for 1989 was $2.3 billion.

1990s: The Fiat Era

By 1990 Ford New Holland had 17,000 employees, revenue of $2.8 billion, and plants in the United States, Canada, Belgium, England, and Brazil, plus joint ventures in India, Pakistan, Japan, Mexico, and Venezuela. In 1991 Fiat purchased 80 percent interest in Ford New Holland. Ford New Holland was merged with FiatGeotech to create a huge new industrial equipment entity dubbed N.H. Geotech—though its North American operation kept the name Ford New Holland for the time being. The purchase surprised nobody in the industry, since Ford had been looking for a buyer for its tractor operation for the better part of a decade. The new international behemoth, headquartered in London, instantly became the world's largest producer of tractors and haying equipment, the second largest producer of combines, and one of the largest producers of diesel engines.

Between 1991 and 1993, the company undertook a number of measures designed to better integrate its many pieces into a coherent whole. Among the goals of this group of projects were a reduction in the time needed to bring new products to market and to focus manufacturing operations on core components. The company's supply chain was also streamlined. N.H. Geotech changed its name to New Holland N.V. in January 1993, although the company's North American operation stuck with the Ford New Holland moniker for two more years. The year 1993 also brought the introduction of the company's Genesis line of 140- to 210-horsepower tractors. The Genesis line proved so popular that it took only a little more than two years to sell 10,000 of them.

New Holland made the completion of its integration process official at its 1994 worldwide convention, at which the company unveiled its new corporate identity and logo. For that year, the company reported net income of $355 million on sales of $4.7 billion. Fiat eventually acquired the other 20 percent of New Holland previously owned by Ford, and in 1995, the 100th anniversary of the New Holland brand name, Ford New Holland was rechristened New Holland North America.

Operating as a wholly owned subsidiary of Fiat, New Holland brought in just more than $5 billion in sales in 1995. By this time, the company controlled 21 percent of the world market for agricultural tractors, 17 percent of the world market for combines, 42 percent of the market for forage harvesters, and significant shares of the world markets for just about every other category of agricultural or construction equipment one could name.

An IPO in 1996

By 1996 New Holland was selling about 280 different products in 130 countries around the world. Globally, 5,600 dealers were selling the company's agricultural equipment and 250 were peddling its construction machinery. During the last quarter of that year, Fiat sold 31 percent of New Holland's stock, 46.5 million common shares, to the public at $21.50 per share, to raise capital to bolster its sagging core automobile business. On November 1, the first day New Holland stock was traded on the New York Stock Exchange, it was the most heavily traded stock on the market.

In addition to the stock offering, 1996 also brought a number of technological innovations and new product unveilings as well. New Holland's new E-Series backhoe-loaders were chosen by *Construction Equipment* magazine as one of the construction industry's 100 most significant products. The company also introduced several new tractor lines, four Roll-Best round balers, and two large self-propelled forage harvesters. New Holland was also active in conducting research on futuristic, driverless machines. Working with NASA and Carnegie Mellon University as part of the NASA Robotics Engineering Consortium, New Holland created a prototype of a self-propelled windrower that cuts, conditions, and puts alfalfa into windrows without requiring a human operator. One further 1996 development at New Holland was the appointment of former U.S. Treasury Secretary and Vice-Presidential candidate Lloyd Bentsen as its chairman of the board.

In July 1997, the 25,000th New Holland Twin Rotor combine rolled off the company's Grand Island, Nebraska assembly line. As the year continued, the company announced the creation of a new Boomer line of light diesel tractors, including four brand new models. Building on its longstanding philosophy of manufacturing products close to where they are sold, the company moved production of the light tractors from Japan to a new facility in Dublin, Georgia. The launch of the Boomer line reflected New Holland's commitment to the production of the kind of compact but powerful machines sought by customers for a variety of off-highway uses. The company is determined to continue developing new products designed to meet the ever-changing needs expressed by its dealers and customers.

Principal Subsidiaries

FiatAllis Latino Americana Ltda (Brazil); FiatAllis North America, Inc.; Fiat Finance U.A.A., Inc.; New Holland Australia Pty Ltd.; New Holland Belgium N.V.; New Holland Deutschland GmbH (Germany); New Holland France S.A.; New Holland Braud S.A. (France); New Holland Canada Ltd.; New Holland Credit Company LLC; New Holland Danmark A/S; New Holland España S.A. (Spain); New Holland Factoring S.p.A. (Italy); New Holland Finance (France); New Holland Italia S.p.A.; New Holland Holding Ltd. (U.K.); New Holland Latino Americana Ltda (Brazil); New Holland Ltd. (U.K.); New Holland Mauritius Ltd.; New Holland North America, Inc. (USA); Holland Tractors (India) Private Ltd.; New Holland Tractor Ltd. (U.K. and Belgium); New Holland Trade N.V. (Netherlands); New Holland UK Ltd.; New Holland Logistics S.p.A. (Italy; 80%); Fiat-Hitachi Excavators S.p.A. (Italy; 57%); Fiat-Hitachi Excavators Belgium S.A. (57%); Fiat-Hitachi Excavators France S.A. (57%).

Further Reading

Bas, Ed, "Ford New Holland's Goal: The Blue Tractor Pulling a Red Harvester," *Ward's Auto World,* June 1987, p. 72.

Fogarty, Bill, "Ford New Holland: Out of the Company Store Business," *Implement & Tractor,* July 1989, p. 15.

"Ford New Holland Here to Stay," *Construction Equipment,* March 1994, p. 14.

"The Impact of Ford New Holland's Buyout," *Agri Marketing,* September 1990, p. 18.

Krebs, Michelle, "New Holland Called a 'Natural' for Ford," *Automotive News,* October 21, 1985, p. 53.

Nesbitt, Scott, "Ford, Fiat Merger Brings Speculation," *Implement & Tractor,* September 1990, p. 1.

"New Holland Grows As Global Leader," *Lancaster (PA) Sunday News,* March 23, 1997, p. 32.

"New Holland Marks 100th Anniversary," *Implement & Tractor,* May–June 1995, p. 26.

Osenga, Mike, "A Look at New Holland's New Tractors," *Diesel Progress,* July 1997, p. 10.

Sturani, Maria, "Fiat's Offering of New Holland Shares Expected to Swell Coffers by $1 Billion," *Wall Street Journal,* November 4, 1996, p. B11.

—Robert R. Jacobson

NordicTrack

104 Peavey Road
Chaska, Minnesota
U.S.A.
(612) 368-2500
Fax: (612) 368-5590
Web site: http://www.nordictrack.com

Wholly Owned Subsidiary of CML Group, Inc.
Incorporated: 1975 as PSI NordicTrack, Inc.
Employees: 3,500
Sales: $267.74 million (1997)
SICs: 3949 Sporting & Athletic Goods, Not Elsewhere Classified

A wholly owned subsidiary of CML Group, NordicTrack is one of the world's leading fitness equipment manufacturers. NordicTrack is best known for its cross-country ski simulator which dominated the home fitness market in the late 1980s. Since that time the company has introduced a range of new fitness related products including leg machines, treadmills, strength trainers, a rider, an abdominal exerciser, and a line of elliptical motion machines. NordicTrack ski machines garnered their first major sales boom through direct response television and magazine advertisements but since 1990 the company has sold its workout equipment through its NordicTrack Fitness at Home retail outlets, the largest fitness specialty retail chain in the United States.

Company Origins in the 1970s

NordicTrack was founded as PSI NordicTrack, Inc. in 1975 by Edward Pauls in Chaska, Minnesota. Pauls, who had studied mechanical engineering at the University of Wisconsin at Madison, was a designer of ski boots and bindings for the Minnesota based Rosemount, Inc. When that firm was sold in 1969, Pauls began to focus on his own inventions, patenting a design for ''outrigger'' skis for use by handicapped skiers. According to *Forbes,* the idea for the NordicTrack ski machine came to Pauls, an avid cross-country skier, during a particularly wet and cold training session on the streets of Chaska. Pauls reasoned that if he could invent an indoor exerciser that duplicated the motions of cross-country skiing, competitive skiers, including his daughter Terri who was a national collegiate cross-country skiing champion, could train year-round and gain a competitive edge. The key to such a device was the recreation of the unique properties of wooden ski against snow, a subtle resistance which Pauls was able to capture through the use of a patented flywheel and one-way clutch mechanism. In response to requests for the ski simulator from cross-country skiing friends, Pauls began to manufacture the machines in his garage, investing $10,000 of his own savings.

As word of mouth in the cross-country skiing community began to spread news of the indoor trainer, and orders started to pile up in the Paulses' garage, manufacturing was moved to a small warehouse in Chaska and workers were hired to manufacture the machines and take telephone orders. Pauls's wife, Florence, a former elementary school teacher, became the business manager of the new venture, organizing the books and the telephone sales force. The Paulses initially placed direct response ads for their machine in ski magazines but as it became apparent that the device was attractive to non-skiers looking for an excellent aerobic workout the advertising campaign was extended to such high-end general interest publications as *Smithsonian* and *Scientific American,* accompanied by the tagline ''The World's Best Aerobic Exerciser.'' With Florence Pauls overseeing telephone sales, the effectiveness of each ad was gauged and the carefully planned campaign adjusted as necessary. According to an account in *Minneapolis/St. Paul City Business,* much of the company's success could be attributed to Florence Pauls's prudent management and Ed Pauls's ability to obtain cheap manufacturing and office equipment. A longtime family friend and former co-worker, Paul Petersen, said of Pauls's approach to problem-solving: ''When I look back at working with Ed, I remember one thing: Anything he did was pig-tight, bull-strong and functionally simple.''

Acquisition by CML Group in 1986

The Paulses' frugal management and well-executed direct response ads, combined with the fitness craze that swept across

Company Perspectives:

One of the world's leading fitness equipment manufacturers and a strong advocate of healthy lifestyles through exercise, NordicTrack is committed to helping people get in shape and stay in shape. Each of the company's high-quality aerobic and anaerobic fitness products is specifically designed for busy people to enjoy at home.

the nation in the late 1970s and early 80s, propelled the small family-run firm into a major competitor in the growing fitness equipment industry. By the mid-1980s the company's Chaska manufacturing and sales operations were employing 200 people and annual sales had risen to about $15 million. Although the business was solidly profitable, Pauls realized that further growth would require the deep pockets of a larger corporation and when CML Group, Inc., a publicly owned company run by entrepreneur Charles M. Leighton, offered Pauls $24 million for NordicTrack he agreed to sell. According to the deal, the Paulses would get seven million shares of CML stock plus a five-year employment contract that would allow Ed Pauls to continue as chairman of the company and Florence Pauls to assume the position of senior vice-president. In addition the Paulses were to receive large sales-contingent bonus payments which were to total more than $26 million by the time the deal expired in 1990.

When CML bought NordicTrack it was a one-product company. The company's $600 cross-country ski machines sold well but CML was looking to grow the company through diversification and expanded distribution. CML CEO Leighton brought in James Bostic, a former auto industry executive, to head up the new subsidiary. During the late 1980s Bostic oversaw the introduction of an array of new NordicTrack products including NordicPower, a strength trainer, and the Executive Power Chair, a $1,200 black leather chair whose arms folded out to allow the busy executive to do some upper body training between meetings. These new products were designed to attract the 52 percent of Americans whom surveys by the College of Sports Medicine had identified as being ''fitness aware'' but who did not follow a regular exercise routine. In an interview with *Advertising Age*'s Monte Williams, Bostic reported that NordicTrack designers sought to create exercise machines that would fit easily into a home environment by resembling furniture, ''not medieval torture instruments.''

In addition to broadening NordicTrack's product line, Bostic expanded NordicTrack's direct response advertising both by increasing the number of magazine ads and by adding network and cable TV spots and infomercials. ''The margin is good in direct response,'' Bostic told *Advertising Age.* ''In addition, it gives us direct contact with our customers and better control and management of selling.'' In spite of Bostic's enthusiasm for the factory direct distribution which had worked so well for NordicTrack in the past, in 1990 the new company president decided to open the first NordicTrack retail outlet in a mall outside of Washington, D.C. ''Some people just need to get in there and kick the tires,'' explained NordicTrack's marketing manager, Henry Barksdale, in an article in *Forbes.*

Boom in the Early 1990s

CML's investment in new advertising and product development for NordicTrack had paid off handsomely by 1991. Compound annual sales growth at the subsidiary for the five years since its acquisition in 1986 was an impressive 53 percent. Sales during the same period rose by more than 500 percent to $135 million, providing about 40 percent of CML's sales. With a 42 percent operating margin, however, earnings on these sales accounted for a stunning 86 percent of CML's operating income.

NordicTrack management continued to introduce new products through the early 1990s in an attempt to increase the company's penetration into the growing home fitness market. By 1992, it was estimated that up to 55 million households were willing to spend $300 or more on in-home exercise equipment and NordicTrack sales represented only three percent of this potential market. New NordicTrack products included the NordicFlex, a muscle builder, and the Aerobic Cross Trainer, which featured a treadmill and stairclimber as well as a NordicTrack skier and upper body exercises. While in 1992 only eight percent of NordicTrack's sales were generated by products other than cross-country ski machines, by the following year this figure had risen to 25 percent.

As the growth in direct order sales began to taper off, NordicTrack looked to its retail outlets to provide a higher percentage of sales. By the end of 1992, the company had opened 18 ''NordicTrack Fitness At Home'' retail outlets through Nordic Advantage, a new retail subsidiary. Nordic Advantage also sought to capitalize on the company's reputation among health-conscious Americans by opening two ''Healthy Kitchen'' retail stores that would sell small kitchen appliances, such as bread ovens and stainless steel cookware, marketed as promoting a healthy lifestyle and two ''Healthy Express'' health food outlets positioned as alternatives to the fast-food vendors of mall food courts. By 1994, in addition to 60 ''NordicTrack Fitness at Home'' outlets the company was operating 12 high-end stores called ''Nordic Sport,'' two family- and youth-oriented locations dubbed ''Fitness for Fun,'' and a larger format ''Factory Direct'' showroom which featured all NordicTrack lines as well as discounted equipment.

NordicTrack's impressive performance continued into the early 90s. Sales almost doubled to $265 million in 1992 only to climb to $378 million the following year. Largely on the basis of NordicTrack's success, CML stock became a darling of Wall Street, soaring to a high of $41 per share in June 1993 and spurring the Boston Globe to name CML ''company of the year'' for 1993. Even as new products and retail outlets kept sales rising, however, the costs involved in these new ventures caused operating margins to shrink alarmingly from a high of 42 percent in 1990 to only 26 percent in 1993.

Concerns about the performance of NordicTrack began to surface in mid-1993 when management imposed a one-week layoff on all office and manufacturing employees. In a memo explaining the decision to employees, Bostic wrote: ''Widespread consumer concern about our nation's lack of leadership, the absence of any plan to build our country's economy, as well as worry about personal financial outlooks and even job security, have kept many, many prospective fitness equipment buyers from responding to our ads and TV commercials as they normally would.'' When copies of the memo circulated on Wall Street CML stock sunk to $26 a share. Although the stock rebounded on the announcement of 1994 income of $84 million on sales of $455 million for the company's NordicTrack subsidiary, analysts remained cautious about the fitness industry in the wake of surveys that indicated an overall decline in the number of frequent fitness participants in the United States. NordicTrack was particularly vulnerable to a downturn in the number of people actively participating in fitness activities because, unlike such products as running shoes, the company's exercise machines did not require frequent replacement.

Collapse in the Mid-1990s

By the second half of 1995, it became clear that CML was in trouble. Throughout the early 90s, NordicTrack had been providing the bulk of CML's sales and an even greater percentage of earnings, reaching almost 70 and 96 percent, respectively by 1994. NordicTrack's phenomenal growth, however, could not be sustained. NordicTrack sales were up for the year overall, thanks to the opening of 26 new retail stores, but comparable store sales and sales generated through the company's direct-response ads decreased significantly. Even more alarming was an abrupt drop in operating income which, at $46 million, had been cut almost in half from the previous year. CML stock fell 60 percent over the course of the fiscal year as management was forced to continually downgrade earnings estimates.

If 1995 was a poor year for NordicTrack, 1996 was a disaster. Riders, a combination stationary bike and upper-body exerciser, had replaced the skier as the new exercise equipment fad, and NordicTrack missed the chance to enter this market while it was at its peak. In addition, a new and expensive direct sales advertising campaign fell flat, failing to deliver during the company's peak winter selling season. Sales for the year fell for the first time since NordicTrack's acquisition by CML, dropping by 27 percent to only $368 million. Most of this decrease was caused by a 50 percent decline in direct response sales. The cost of ineffective advertising as well as a high fixed cost structure, meant that the company was unable to reduce operating expenses quickly in response to the drop in sales, resulting in a net loss of $73 million for the year.

CML responded to this crisis by replacing key management personnel. G. Robert (Bob) Tod, president of CML, took over management of NordicTrack on a day-to-day basis. Under his aegis the company slashed fixed costs by switching to contract manufacturing and closing several manufacturing facilities. NordicTrack also sought to replace skier sales with new products geared specifically to the aging population of baby boomers looking for low impact exercise equipment. An entirely new line of aerobic exercisers called the Ellipse, introduced in the fall of 1997, was designed specifically for this demographic group by promising to provide a stress-free total-body workout. In response to a growing trend towards exercises designed for specific muscle groups, the company also marketed a number of body-toning machines, including AbWorks for the abdomen and LegShaper Plus for the thighs and hips. NordicTrack management also looked to new distribution channels to increase market penetration by reaching an agreement with giant retailer Sears to carry NordicTrack products in 850 stores in the United States and Canada. Sears was the largest retailer of exercise equipment in the country and NordicTrack surveys had indicated that up to 80 percent of their potential market was purchasing equipment in such large retail environments.

In spite of these efforts, NordicTrack sales continued to decline through 1997, dropping to only $268 million for the fiscal year. Cost-cutting measures did little to reduce operating losses which dropped only slightly to $59 million. The NordicTrack cross-country skiers that had been responsible for building the company had lost their appeal to the fad-driven fitness market and the company had so far failed to deliver a product with a similar novelty edge. The NordicTrack Ellipse and eMotion lines of aerobic exercise machines, which came on the market in fiscal 1998, might prove to be the fitness trend of the late 90s. If so, NordicTrack, with its excellent brand identity and strong customer base, should be able to rebuild successfully.

Further Reading

Bailey, Steve, and Steven Syre, ''CML's Chief's Problem: Loving Companies to Debt,'' *Boston Globe,* May 30, 1997, p. 1C.

Cohen, Laurie P., ''Heard on the Street: Exercise Decline Takes Pep Out of Some Stock,'' *Wall Street Journal,* July 15, 1993, p. 1C.

Hyten, Todd, ''NordicTrack Parent on Crash Course to Shape Up,'' *Boston Business Journal,* July 12, 1996, p. 1.

Marcotty, Josephine, ''NordicTrack Sales Goals Are Met; A Boss Pays a Visit to Celebrate,'' *Minneapolis Star Tribune,* August 4, 1993.

McEvoy, Christopher, ''NordicTrack Rolls Out New Store Concepts,'' *Sporting Goods Business,* July 1994, p. 24.

Nissen, Todd, ''NordicTrack Duo Take Path Less Traveled,'' *Minneapolis/St. Paul City Business,* March 12, 1990, p. 1.

Patterson, Cecily, ''Eclectic Chair,'' *Forbes,* December 24, 1990, p. 112.

Pereira, Joseph, ''CML Corp. Net and Sales Show Large Increases,'' *Wall Street Journal,* August 10, 1992, p. 5A.

Pulliam, Susan, ''Heard on the Street: Price of CML, a Maker of Exercise Machines, Appears to Be Too Fat, Some Investors Say,'' *Wall Street Journal,* January 3, 1994, p. 14.

Purpura, Linda, ''Nordic Enters 'Wellness' Field,'' *HFD-The Weekly Home Furnishings Newspaper,* December 7, 1992, p. 53.

Serwer, Andrew E., ''Turning Trends into Retailing Friends,'' *Fortune,* July 25, 1994, p. 246.

Williams, Monte, ''People to Watch (NordicTrack President-CEO Jim Bostic),'' *Advertising Age,* December 3, 1990, p. 36.

—Hilary Gopnik

Nutrition for Life International Inc.

9101 Jameel
Houston, Texas 77040
U.S.A.
(713) 460-1976
Fax: (713) 895-8927
Web site: http://www.nutritionforlife.com

Public Company
Incorporated: 1993
Employees: 200
Sales: $97.40 million (1996)
Stock Exchanges: NASDAQ
SICs: 5122 Drugs, Proprietaries & Sundries

Based in Houston, Texas, Nutrition for Life International Inc. is one of the larger U.S. distributors of nutritional supplements and health-related products. The company offers 320 products, including vitamins, minerals, and antioxidants; personal care items; food and weight management programs; herbal formulas; homeopathic and special formulas; cleaning concentrates; filtration systems; and self-development programs. Most products are packaged as private label items under the trade names of Nutique, Master Key Plus, Oraflow Plus, Lean-Life, Nutri-Cookie, Requin 3, Grand Master, Phytonol, BioWater, E-Lemonator, Phytogreen, BioGlow, BioRub, MasterPiece, and PowerPlay.

Nutrition for Life purchases its nutritional supplements and other products directly from third-party manufacturers. The company then sells these products—made to its specifications—to distributors throughout the world, specifically in the United States, including territories such as the District of Columbia, Puerto Rico, and Guam; Canada; Korea; the Philippines; and the United Kingdom. Nutrition for Life markets its products through a network of thousands of such distributors, independent contractors who own their own businesses. Distributors purchase items from Nutrition for Life for resale to their own clients. Distributors may work on a full- or part-time basis. Nutrition for Life provides them with product development, marketing aids, customer service operations, and record keeping. The company also offers distributors support programs such as international teleconferencing, seminars, a proprietary magazine, business training, and a web site.

Distributors enlist new recruits to form their sales networks. Original distributors earn commissions on their sales as well as those of their new recruits. The larger a distributor's network, the more earning potential he or she enjoys. Nutrition for Life International offers incentives to distributors for building their networks and advertises for new distributors on the company's web site, through teleconferencing, and at regional sales meetings. Its products are endorsed by Brandi Carrier, Miss Fitness Galaxy 1996. Nutrition for Life sponsors two professional cycling teams—Volvo/Cannondale Mountain Bike Racing Team and Saturn Cycling Team—and supports the National Wheelchair Sports Foundation.

Born Through a Merger

In September 1993, David P. Bertrand and Jana Mitchum organized the current company through the merger of Nutrition Express Corporation of Colorado Inc. with Nutrition Express Corporation of Utah Inc. The merger took effect in June 1994.

Bertrand served as president and chairman of the board of the predecessor companies since 1984; he retained these titles in the new corporation. Likewise, Mitchum—Bertrand's sister-in-law—held positions as executive vice-president, secretary, and director of the predecessor companies since 1984. She, too, continued in these positions when the new company formed.

The predecessor companies had been active in the United States since 1984 and in Korea since 1991, although distributors in Korea did not participate in the company's network marketing system. Nutrition for Life's operations extended to Canada and the Philippines beginning in 1993. As in Korea, distributors in the Philippines were not part of the company's network marketing system.

Company Perspectives:

For more than a decade, Nutrition for Life International Inc. has provided thousands of individuals with the opportunity to achieve financial freedom and the means to a healthier and happier life by offering a superior range of health and nutritional products. Today Nutrition for Life International is a recognized leader in the health and nutrition industry. With increasing consumer awareness of nutrition and health, Nutrition for Life International is on the cutting-edge of the industry and well positioned for further growth and expansion.

The Network Marketing System

The new company's distributors purchased products for their own use and for resale to retail clients through a specialized system. Nutrition for Life encouraged its distributors to recruit new distributors to create a network—the recruiting distributor's ''downline.'' The recruiting distributor would receive a commission from all the sales of all the distributors in his or her downline. The company created this marketing program so that existing distributors might maximize their earnings by building sales networks. Nutrition for Life explained in its U.S. Securities and Exchange Commission Form 10-KSB that the company's ''management believes that its network marketing system is well suited to marketing its nutritional supplements and other products because sales of such products are strengthened by ongoing personal contact between retail consumers and distributors, many of whom use the company's products themselves.''

The company depended on adding and retaining distributors to increase its sales, so its recruiting programs offered financial incentives, training and support, nominal fees for starter kits, no inventory requirements, and limited monthly purchase requirements as enticements. Programs to increase distributor sales and recruiting potential included car bonuses, an order assurance program, and personnel recruiting and sales campaigns. For example, prior to mid-1996, Nutrition for Life sponsored an Instant Executive program through which distributors could qualify for the executive distributor level by generating at least $1,000 in product volume on the day of enrollment rather than over time.

Kevin Trudeau's Contributions

Nutrition for Life also produced product literature for distributors to use, as well as established a toll-free number for ordering, customer service operations, and faxing services. In addition, the company sponsored a subscription service for distributors, monthly offering self-development materials—many created by Kevin Trudeau, a noted motivational speaker and marketer. (Trudeau also founded the American Memory Institute, produced a memory training home-study course, and wrote a memory training book published by William Morrow in 1995.) Trudeau sold his sales aids, memory tapes, and other items to Nutrition for Life distributors through his own companies. He became important to Nutrition for Life as an executive-level distributor who demonstrated great success recruiting new distributors who readily achieved executive-level status.

Growth in Distributors and Products

In 1994, Nutrition for Life launched a 24-hour teleconferencing service with announcements, product information, and other recorded messages for distributors. The company also first published its multilingual recruiting publication, *Freedom Magazine,* in 1994 to answer the most common questions of those considering becoming distributors. In addition, Nutrition for Life extended its operations to Puerto Rico in 1994. By September, the company's distributors numbered 37,800.

More development followed the next year: Bertrand and Mitchum issued the company's initial public offering in July 1995, and 25 new products were introduced by Nutrition for Life in the fiscal year ending in September 1995.

Then company sales grew remarkably between September 1995 and September 1996. Nutrition for Life launched 70 new products and increased its 57,300 distributors by more than 30,000 during the fiscal year. The increase in distributors—as well as their monthly sales averages—was attributed in large part to the efforts of Trudeau. Trudeau purchased ads on radio and television and utilized infomercials—in particular his ''A Closer Look'' and ''Vantage Point'' infomercial series—to recruit new distributors.

The Litigation Begins

But by January 1996, the company's marketing program to recruit new distributors became a source of contention. The *Wall Street Journal,* the Bloomberg news wire service, and CNBC issued disparaging reports regarding Trudeau, his marketing practices, and Nutrition for Life's Instant Executive program. A major shareholder of a predecessor company also complained to regulatory agencies and issued unfavorable statements through the Internet regarding Trudeau and Nutrition for Life. Both the company and Trudeau initiated and won legal proceedings against this individual for defamation. Trudeau, for example, was awarded $10 million in damages. Yet, in April 1996, the Attorney General of the State of Illinois brought litigation against Trudeau and his company, the Trudeau Marketing Group, Inc., among others.

Although Nutrition for Life was not named in the lawsuit, the company nevertheless entered into an Assurance of Voluntary Compliance with the Attorney General of Illinois, as well as similar agreements in nine other states: Florida, Hawaii, Idaho, Kansas, Kentucky, Michigan, Missouri, New Jersey, and Pennsylvania. Nutrition for Life agreed to stop calling its program ''Instant Executive,'' though the qualifications to achieve executive distributor status immediately upon enrollment remained unchanged. Nutrition for Life also decided to clarify its marketing and compensation plans, prohibiting distributors from creating their own versions, and to explain clearly that mandatory product purchases were not required in order to become a distributor. The company also encouraged distributor compliance with corporate policies and created an Internet web site with information about Nutrition for Life's products and programs. Nutrition for Life agreed to disclose distributor earnings and clarified parameters under which executive-level distributors could collect commissions on sales within their downlines.

With lawsuits settled in at least eight states, Trudeau changed his commission method in July 1996. Now he based commissions on product sales instead of new member signings. But the past still haunted him.

Nutrition for Life's Involvement in Litigation

In August 1996, Instant Executive distributors and stock and warrant buyers filed suit in U.S. District Court in the Southern District of Texas, Houston Division, against Trudeau; Nutrition for Life and some of its officers; Bernard Sherman, the largest beneficial owner of Nutrition for Life common stock; and Cohig and Associates, Inc., and Neidiger/Tucker/Bruner, Inc., the investment bankers that underwrote Nutrition for Life's July 1995 initial public offering. The distributors and stock buyers charged that Nutrition for Life ran an illegal pyramid scheme, sold unregistered securities, and failed to disclose alleged illegalities, not to mention Trudeau's criminal history. (A state court in Massachusetts issued a three-year suspended sentence after Trudeau pled guilty to larceny in 1990. He served 21 days. Trudeau also filed for bankruptcy in Texas in 1990, although he took no further action on the claim. The following year, Trudeau plead guilty to credit card fraud in Massachusetts. At that time, the court sentenced him to a two-year prison term and 24 months supervised release.)

Then on August 23, 1996, common stock purchasers filed another class action suit in the District Court of Harris County, Texas, against Nutrition for Life, claiming the company and its agents—in particular Kevin Trudeau and the Trudeau Marketing Group—misrepresented or omitted data regarding the company, its marketing, sales, and earnings from July 1995 through July 1996. "Among other things," *Business Wire* reported in August 1996, "this investor lawsuit alleges that NFLI's [Nutrition for Life International] reported revenues and growth were materially overstated during the Class Period and that NFLI was engaging in improper and illegal marketing practices which had the effect of fraudulently inflating NFLI's financial results. In addition, the complaint alleges that NFLI's 'Instant Executive Program' was an illegal pyramid scheme. The complaint also alleges that defendants failed to fully or accurately disclose Trudeau's history of unlawful and criminal conduct, including credit card fraud and larceny."

By September 1996, the Securities and Exchange Commission (SEC) of the United States began investigating Nutrition for Life for violations of the federal securities laws. Throughout these legal battles, Nutrition for Life strongly denied any allegations and accusations, vigorously defending itself against all charges and working to reduce negative media coverage.

Moving Forward Undeterred

Despite its legal battles, Nutrition for Life continued to grow. In September 1996, the company authorized the buyback of 200,000 common shares of stock. Nutrition for Life launched programs in the United Kingdom, expanding its ranks to 87,400 distributors. Its net sales in fiscal 1996 were more than $97 million.

The SEC ended its inquiry in December 1996, taking no action against the company. Though expenses related to settlement of lawsuits totaled $6.4 million, the company's focus shifted from litigation to building its business again. Meanwhile, Trudeau alerted Nutrition for Life to objections of the Federal Trade Commission (FTC) of the United States to his infomercials, including those used to market the Mega Memory tapes sold as self-development aids to Nutrition for Life distributors. With the threat of action by the FTC, the possibilities of Trudeau remaining a distributor of the company or of the continued use by the company of the Mega Memory tapes remained uncertain.

Nevertheless, by March 1997, Nutrition for Life successfully negotiated a recruiting campaign for new distributors. In one month, 8,400 distributors qualified for new executive distributorships. The company even achieved a new daily sales record: $1.5 million.

Nutrition for Life's sales rose in the third quarter of 1997, indicating renewed confidence among consumers and distributors. The company started its network marketing program in the Philippines, its first such activity in the Pacific Rim. Independent distributors totaled 102,000 at the end of the month, far surpassing 100,000—the number of independent distributors commonly held as necessary for a company to sustain long-term growth.

In September 1997, Nutrition for Life installed computer information systems for administrative efficiency, high-quality customer service, and warehouse and shipping management. The company also offered a long-distance calling program through its worldwide network of distributors. Life*dial* 1 Plus, co-sponsored by UniDial Communications, provided a low interstate rate, a calling card with no per-call surcharge, a free toll-free number, special features such as four-way conference calling and voice mail, and opportunities for Nutrition for Life distributors to earn bonus volume. As Steven M. Riddell, director of product sales, explained in a company press release: "The Life*dial* 1 Plus program represents a whole new breadth of service for our distributors and their customers. We are pleased to present this exciting growth opportunity in cooperation with UniDial Communications. The calls are carried on one of the nation's premier fiber-optic networks, and UniDial's state-of-the-art control center constantly monitors the quality of the entire network."

Final judgments on 1996 lawsuits were issued on September 18, 1997. The courts approved settlement agreements for Instant Executives and stock buyers from July 1995 through July 1996 who lost money. In a press release at the time, Nutrition for Life was quick to point out that "the settlements are not an admission of wrongdoing by the company, nor are the judgments a finding of the validity of any claims in the lawsuits or of any wrongdoing by the company. The company has strongly denied and continues to deny all charges of wrongdoing or liability.''

In the Future

Nutrition for Life's business strategy for the future involved increasing the company's sales and profitability. As always, the company intended to work to attract new distributors and to increase product sales to them. It also planned to expand in its existing markets worldwide, as well as into new international markets. In addition, if the opportunity presented itself, Nutrition for Life expected to acquire a complementary business.

Principal Subsidiaries

Nutrition for Life International Ltd. (U.K.).

Further Reading

''Mergers and Acquisitions: Nutrition for Life International Inc.,'' *The Food Institute Report,* September 30, 1996.

Nutrition for Life International Inc., ''Making a Difference in People's Lives'' (brochure), Houston, Tex.: Nutrition for Life International Inc., March 31, 1997.

''Nutrition for Life Lawsuit Settled,'' *Food Labeling News,* July 18, 1996.

—Charity Anne Dorgan

OAK TECHNOLOGY®

Oak Technology, Inc.

139 Kifer Court
Sunnyvale, California 94086
U.S.A.
(408) 737-0888
Fax: (408) 737-3838
Web site: http://www.oaktech.com

Public Company
Incorporated: 1987
Sales: $248 million (1996)
Employees: 380
Stock Exchanges: NASDAQ
SICs: 3674 Semiconductors, Computer Logic Modules, & Related Devices; 8731 Engineering Laboratories & Computer Hardware Research and Development

Born in Xian, China, at the height of World War II, Oak Technology, Inc. founder David Tsang moved with his family to Japan in his teens where he attended Tokyo's Chiba University for a year before relocating permanently to the United States at age 19. After completing his college career at Brigham Young University he moved to California in 1968 and took an entry-level engineering job at Hewlett-Packard (HP). After earning his master's degree in electrical engineering at the University of Santa Clara, Tsang grew disenchanted with HP's corporate politics and in 1974 founded Microcomputer Systems with other disaffected HP colleagues. In 1979 he left Microcomputer Systems to found another technology startup, Data Technology Corporation (DTC), which made high-density floppy disks and controllers for hard disk drives for the burgeoning U.S. computer industry. (The controller is the set of semiconductors or ''chips'' that issues the basic instructions that control a computer's hard drive, where all the user's data is stored. In early microcomputers, the hard disk drive controller was a separate ''card'' or plug-in component that was attached to the computer's main system board.)

After Tsang's departure, Microcomputer Systems sued him and another former employee, Lloyd Ebisu, for allegedly taking Microcomputer's trade secrets with them to DTC. In 1982 a California superior court agreed with Microcomputer, awarding it $1.5 million for the damage Tsang and Ebisu had caused it. In the meantime, in 1981, Tsang's new outfit, DTC, in collaboration with Shugart Associates (which eventually became Seagate Technology) invented the SASI interface—the forerunner of the interconnectivity standard SCSI (Small Computer Systems Interface, or ''scuzzy''). SASI and SCSI made it possible for manufacturers to install the controllers for computer peripherals like printers and CD-ROM drives inside the peripherals themselves rather than on a separate board or card, greatly reducing the complexity of adding new peripherals to a PC. In the SCSI world, computer users could connect a new printer directly to their computer and know that the two devices were preconfigured in the factory to communicate with each other.

Building a Reputation: 1987–89

After DTC went public in 1987, Tsang and his DTC colleagues struggled over the company's future direction. Unable to make his vision prevail, Tsang again decided to strike out on his own. His newest venture, Oak Technology, would manufacture logic chips and graphics controllers (which process raw graphics data for display as images on computer terminals) for the rapidly maturing personal computer industry. With Tsang's Pacific Rim background, Oak focused initially on Taiwan's rapidly growing peripheral add-in or expansion board industry, opening a branch office and subsidiary in Taipei and eventually launching a Japanese subsidiary, Oak Technologies KK. Tsang's intent, however, was for Oak to design, develop, and market but not manufacture its components. Instead, ''fabless'' Oak would form flexible relationships with independent silicon foundries in Taiwan, Japan, and Korea who would supply it with the silicon wafers it would then fashion into semiconductor chips.

By 1988, Oak had unveiled a successful graphics controller for the ''super VGA'' enhanced computer video graphics market as well as a line of low-power integrated circuits for the IBM PS/2 personal computer. Tsang also spied a market in the growing laptop computer market and by 1989 had introduced a space-saving five-chip chip set christened ''OakHorizon'' that included the core system-control logic, clocking circuitry, peripheral con-

Company Perspectives:

Oak Technology, Inc. designs, develops, and markets high-performance multimedia semiconductors and related software to original equipment manufacturers worldwide who serve the multimedia PC, digital video consumer electronics, and digital office equipment markets. Our technological expertise spans five core multimedia-enabling technologies: Optical Storage, MPEG Imaging, Video/Graphics, Audio/ Communications, and Digital Imaging.

Oak's solutions typically consist of hardware, firmware, and software to provide a complete, integrated solution for our customers. Whenever possible, we seek to integrate complementary multimedia technologies to create high-performance, low-cost products that address the target market needs.

trollers, and power management for laptop computers. Oak also unveiled a ready-to-run computer chip design package for PC peripheral board makers that included all the chips and supporting software peripheral manufacturers needed to reach volume production levels for printers, scanners, and other peripheral devices. Tsang's Pacific Rim focus was soon winning Oak major customers like Mitsumi Electric, Hitachi, Creative Technology, and NEC, virtually all based in Asian countries. As one industry analyst would later note, "This is a relationship game, and Tsang has good relationships in the Far East."

A slew of products followed in the ensuing years that established Oak as a premier if low-profile producer of the largely invisible parts that made home computers compute. In 1989, Oak entered the video data compression market by buying up the manufacturing and marketing rights to the video compression and expansion processor business of integrated-circuit maker Advanced Micro Devices (AMD). As the PC grew in processing power, it became possible to display memory-hungry full-motion video images on the PC's terminal, a boon for the graphics industry as well as the home user with a video camera. Video compression/decompression technology enabled PCS to process video images without having to store gigabytes of raw video data in the limited storage space that even the largest PCS contained. As Tsang moved Oak into more diverse and profitable computer components, Oak's first and only video compression product until 1995 would remain the OTI-95C71 Video Compression/Expansion Processor, which it sold as the image-processing engine to manufacturers of fax machines, copiers, and printers.

Swimming Upstream: 1990–93

By the early 1990s Oak had established itself as a successful if little noticed vendor of the video controller and accelerator products and "core logic" circuits that controlled personal computers' display performance and basic internal functioning. Tsang meanwhile continued to search out new component niches and ensure that Oak's engineers were always developing the products that the next stage of computer performance would demand. In 1990, Oak introduced the OTI-067, a new chip set/graphics controller that improved the resolution (or image sharpness) of VGA PC monitors to 1,024 by 768 pixels without requiring more memory. In April 1991, it announced an agreement with micro-controller-maker Zilog Inc. to jointly develop and cross-license a set of controllers for the small disk drives used in laptop computers. By September Oak had introduced its "OakNote" hard disk controller, a three-chip integrated circuit that improved power conservation, video control, and system logic for laptop computers in as small a package as was then technically possible. And by November 1991 Oak's partnership with Zilog had spawned the Z86C99, an integrated disk drive controller on a single chip and Oak's sales had grown to $51 million.

In an industry now crowded with competitors and awash in cheaply priced chip sets, Oak had to struggle to maintain its margins but in July 1991 finally surrendered to the distressed market conditions by announcing layoffs. To ensure its continued growth and avoid an overdependence on specific product groups, in 1991 Tsang led Oak into the CD-ROM controllers market—the basic chip sets that told CD-ROM drives how to interact with a PC's system board. Though Oak's entree into CD-ROM controllers was not initially as large as its earlier commitment to hard disk drive controllers, within five years CD-ROM controllers would grow to account for more than 90 percent of Oak's total revenues.

In early 1992 Oak's OTI-087 new graphics controller was cited by *Electronic Design* magazine for "outperforming" its competitors' VGA video chips, and Oak began shipping the first chip sets for PCS using AMD's new 33-Megahertz 386-generation microprocessor and Cyrix's new 486 microprocessor. In the fall of 1992 Oak and Japan's biggest computer maker, NEC, announced a licensing agreement that allowed NEC to make and market Oak's OTI-018 "Spitfire" video/graphics accelerator as part of its own product offerings. Then in June 1993, Oak unveiled the OTI-107, a video chip that greatly simplified the process of configuring video add-on cards to play videos on PCS. Oak's bread and butter, the graphics controller market, however, was beginning to evaporate as competitors chewed away at Oak's market share. In 1992 Oak's sales fell to $45 million and then dropped again to only $30 million in 1993.

Enter the CD-ROM Controller: 1994

Tsang's decision to steer Oak into the CD-ROM controller business came to Oak's rescue in 1994. In late 1993, it introduced its first major CD-ROM controller product, the OTI-011, which was designed to move the PC peripherals industry a step toward the new PC connectivity ideal: "plug-and-play" (PnP). The goal of PnP, which was spearheaded by Microsoft's development of a PnP operating system to be named Windows95, was a computer that would enable the user to simply plug in a new printer or video card and allow the computer's operating system to automatically identify it and load the appropriate drivers. With PnP, computer users would no longer have to worry about configuring jumper settings or other installation nightmares. Although PnP would remain more an ideal than a reality for several years, Oak ensured that its controllers and chips were compatible with the PnP standards established by the computer industry. For example, by the mid-1990s the ISA standard, the onetime standard for PC's peripheral expansion slots had been all but replaced by a newer, faster standard,

''PCI'' (Peripheral Component Interconnect). In 1995 Oak consequently revamped its ''Spitfire'' graphics accelerator to support the new PCI format.

Similarly, the emergence of the IDE (Integrated Drive Electronics) interface standard had eliminated the need for separate controller cards for each device installed on a computer because IDE allowed all the necessary electronic control circuitry to be located on the drive itself. Here, too, Oak stayed ahead of the curve by releasing the ''MOZART'' OTI-601, the first PC audio controller to incorporate the IDE interface.

Oak's entrance into the CD-ROM controller business was a huge success. By July 1994 it had sold over two million controllers for two- and four-speed CD-ROM drives, and 1.2 million in Japan alone. Now a major supplier of CD-ROM controller products (with close to 60 percent of the market) as well as compression/imaging chips, video/graphics controllers, and PC audio chips, Oak's sales climbed back to $42.6 million in 1994 before vaulting to $111 million in 1995. With the IDE interface established and ''plug-and-play'' CD-ROM drives on the horizon, Oak anticipated an explosion in CD-ROM sales and added a new semiconductor foundry partner in Korea to help it absorb the expected leap in controller orders.

In October 1994, Oak released the OTI-201, a new sound and video compression/decompression controller based on the new multimedia MPEG (Motion Pictures Expert Group) standard. MPEG-based videos were most commonly used for public PC-based information kiosks and corporate training videos. The OTI-201 was the industry's first MPEG decoder designed specifically for multimedia PCS and enabled peripheral manufacturers to offer high-performance MPEG-format graphics and video on a single add-on expansion board. With CD-ROM controllers expected to eventually become a cheap commodity product, Tsang viewed the OTI-201 as another way for Oak to expand its customer base and maintain its heady growth. With Oak's experience producing graphics chips and computer connectivity products, Tsang planned even newer generations of PC video display controllers as well as chips for 3D graphics, recordable CD-ROMs, TV set-top boxes, CD video players, and PC-based video production and teleconferencing.

Riding the Multimedia Wave: 1995

By January 1995 the company that *Investor's Business Daily* had once described as a ''behind the scenes supplier of minor computer parts'' had evolved itself into the world's leading producer of CD-ROM controller chips, which now generated the lion's share of its annual revenues. CD-ROM sales in 1995 were three times what they had been in 1993, spurred by the rapid evolution in CD-ROM drive speeds. Two-speed drives that were considered cutting edge a year or so before had quickly been superseded by quad-speed and then six-speed drives—with each generation rendering the preceding generation obsolete almost overnight. In early 1995, Oak formed a 3-D graphics business unit, and to raise the capital Tsang needed to sustain Oak's growth, he took the company public in February, raising $48 million and then another $81 million in a secondary stock offering in May. ''When we can't keep up with demand,'' Tsang told *Fortune* magazine, ''that is when we will start losing customers.''

By the end of the fiscal year in June, Oak had announced sixfold profit growth to $21 million, purchased new silicon wafer capacity from its Pacific Rim suppliers, and unveiled a new MPEG board product named ProMOTION to help peripheral manufacturers develop full-motion video playback systems for the PC market. Throughout 1995, Oak's stock continued to climb in price. On the heels of its glowing earnings reports and estimates, Tsang and his executive staff issued upbeat reports on the company's prospects to the media and investment community. ''Exceptional demand for our CD-ROM controller chips fueled our record results,'' COO Don Bryson announced in July. ''We continue to benefit as the PC industry shifts from double speed to quad speed [CD-ROM] drives.''

In August Oak announced that it would introduce a new controller, the OTI-910, in 1996 for a new generation of high-density multimedia CD-ROMs that would use eight-speed or faster drives capable of playing traditional CD-ROM games, music CDS, or full-length movie videos. A month later Tsang announced that demand for Oak's CD-Rom controllers would be ''very strong'' and that he planned to double Oak's capacity within a year. At the same time Bryson was optimistically predicting that Oak's new line of MPEG video and graphics controllers would soon reduce Oak's dependence on CD-ROM controllers from 80 to 50 percent of total sales.

In October Oak announced an agreement with United Microelectronics Corp. to form United Integrated Circuits Corp, a semiconductor manufacturing facility in Taiwan to support Oak's anticipated need for greater capacity. More importantly, it announced its first acquisition, the $10.5 million purchase of Massachusetts-based Pixel Magic, a privately held producer of compression and image-processing technology. ''PixelMagic's products and technology are an excellent complement to Oak's existing imaging products,'' Tsang told reporters. ''This acquisition will allow Oak to accelerate its penetration of the emerging digital office equipment market and significantly broaden the set of solutions we can offer to office equipment vendors.''

Bursting the Bubble: 1996

As 1996 began, Oak's good news showed no signs of waning. In January it won a new customer when Taiwan's biggest computer maker, Acer, adopted Oak's video controller for its line of karaoke CD players. Then PC video camera maker Logitech agreed to work with Oak to develop inexpensive video conferencing products for the desktop PC market. And a week later, 12 Asian electronics firms formally adopted Oak's new VideoCD Design System for their CD-based karaoke and video playback machines. In February Oak's year-old stock reached $30 a share, and in March Oak announced that its new graphics controllers would support Microsoft's ''Direct3D'' and ''ActiveMovie'' game and video playback formats.

During a conference call with securities analysts in April, however, Tsang and Bryson unexpectedly announced that Oak's fourth quarter revenues would only be $55 to $60 million rather than the $94 originally expected. In May, the hint of bad news became the real thing when Oak announced that its actual fourth quarter revenues would be only $20 million—not even half the lowered estimate it had given a month before.

Within a day, investors sold off 9.6 million shares of Oak stock, slashing its share price by 25 percent to $12 before the market closed. Tsang blamed the earnings surprise on poor CD-ROM controller sales caused by ''the overall slowdown in the PC industry.'' Oak's customers—the world's CD-ROM drive makers—had overestimated the number of controllers they would need and thus were left with a huge backlog that current CD-ROM drive orders would not absorb any time soon.

Tsang's explanations did not mollify all of Oak's investors, however, and in June an insider-trading class-action lawsuit was filed against Oak and its officers for willfully inflating Oak's prospects in order to drive up the company's stock price. The suit claimed that beginning in mid-1995, Tsang, Bryson, and eight other Oak executives had deliberately begun issuing optimistic statements about Oak's products and financial estimates in order to cash in their shares at a premium when the company's stock rose on the good news. Between July 1995 and May 1996, these Oak insiders had allegedly sold more than four million shares for a net gain of $104 million before the stock's price collapse in May. The suit specifically charged that, contrary to Oak's rosy press releases, Tsang and his colleagues had known that Oak's CD-ROM controllers could not handle the six- and eight-speed drives consumers now wanted; that its next-generation multimedia CD-ROM controller, the OTI-910, was obsolete within months of its release because it could only support six-speed drives; that its new graphics controller, the OTI-64107, was overpriced and technically flawed; that Oak had encouraged its customers to overbuy by offering lenient payment terms; and that Oak's customers were returning products, buying from competitors, or taking over manufacture of controllers themselves. Oak denied the charges and prepared for a long legal siege, which was only compounded in the summer when four more insider-trading suits were filed in federal court.

Recovering: 1996

As its stock and Wall Street profile hit rock bottom in the summer of 1996, Oak tried to weather the storm, opening a software design center in Boca Raton, Florida, to develop mini-applications, firmware, and device drivers for its product lines. It also announced the launch of a ''mixed signal'' design center in Austin, Texas, to develop technologies for integrating analog and digital formats in mixed-signal applications, such as DVD content displayed through a television. It also unleashed a torrent of new products to demonstrate that, investors' allegations to the contrary, its technological edge was very much intact. It unveiled a decoder chip for the latest MPEG format, MPEG-1; a digital audio accelerator supporting the latest PC audio performance specifications (including support for ''digital simultaneous voice over data'' modems); and a graphics accelerator that supported Intel's new multimedia (MMX) processor.

In July Oak also announced a licensing deal with PC audio software maker InVision to package that company's multimedia sound-creation software with Oak's audio controllers, giving PC peripheral manufacturers a complete ''single-chip'' audio product. A month later it partnered with Krypton Isolation, a California-based manufacturer of integrated circuits for the telecommunications industry, to develop a state-of-the-art digital signal coder/decoder (or ''codec'') for the computer modem market. In October it unveiled its ''fifth-generation'' CD-ROM controller, which was capable of supporting 20-speed CD-ROM drives, as well as a new controller for recordable/rewritable CD-ROM drives.

It also reached an agreement with modem maker PCtel to package its modem with Oak's latest digital audio accelerator, the OTI-611 TelAudia3D. Subsidiary Pixel Magic released the first fully programmable Imaging Digital Signal Processor (IDSP) for manufacturers of ink jet and laser printers, fax machines, digital copiers, and scanners, and in November Oak unveiled a graphics accelerator for the new stripped-down network PCS being marketed by Microsoft and Intel. Finally, at the fall COMDEX computer show, Tsang introduced Oak's Interactive DVD Browser, an open-architecture software program for handling the decoding and playback of audio data on the new DVD media—a kind of super CD-ROM capable of storing seven times the data of a standard CD.

Guarded Optimism: 1997

Although Oak's stock continued to languish throughout 1997, it appeared to have demonstrated that its engineers were quite capable of obeying Tsang's mandate to diversify Oak's product line into new niches with promising demand. Where sales of CD-ROM controllers had comprised an unsettling 93 percent of Oak's total revenues in early 1996, by the end of March 1997 that figure had fallen to 86 percent. In January, Don Bryson, one of the three principle Oak executives alleged to have misled investors with rosy forecasts, resigned as Oak's COO and was reassigned to ''special projects.'' In March, Oak announced what it claimed was the fastest CD-ROM controller yet—the OTI-912—a chip capable of supporting the 16-speed CD-ROM drives now entering the mainstream.

By the end of the March 1997 fiscal quarter, however, Oak was still reporting disappointing results—a 43 percent drop in revenues from 1996 and ''substantially fewer'' orders for its CD-ROM controllers. Tsang again attributed this to the ''inventory correction'' that stemmed from drive manufacturers' overbuying in 1996, and at least one industry analyst suggested that despite the report the question of whether Oak would survive its insider-trading scandal was now moot. Between the spring and fall of 1997, Oak continued to announce new product releases. In April, it began market-sampling a new audio chip that supported Intel Corporation's new all-digital PC audio guidelines. In June it launched a single-chip DVD-ROM decoder controller, christened ''Troika,'' for video and audio data compression in PCS and DVD players and a week later unveiled the ''WARP5,'' a 3-D graphics accelerator chip for the consumer electronics industry. Oak was positioning itself to exploit the shift from CD-ROMs to DVDs, whenever it occurred. In October 1997 it released a new copy-protection version of the Troika DVD decoder chip that promised to allay media industry concerns that DVD technology would make it too easy for high-tech pirates to copy movies and music. Oak's 1998 first-quarter earnings report at last seemed to confirm that it had rebounded from its stock scandal. Net sales had increased 129 percent over the first quarter of 1997, and sales of its recordable/rewritable CD-ROM decoders were growing. Nevertheless, the effect of the still pending insider-trading lawsuits on Oak's future remained unclear.

Principal Subsidiaries

Pixel Magic, Inc.; Oak Technology K.K. (Japan); Oak Technology, Taiwan.

Further Reading

''California Superior Court Judge Barton Phelps Awards at Least $1.5 Million,'' *New York Times,* April 30, 1982.

Cataldo, Anthony, ''Oak Technology Backs MMCD Format,'' *Electronic News,* August 28, 1995, p. 60.

MacLellan, Andrew, ''Oak Offers Feature Rich PCI Graphics Controller,'' *Electronic News,* November 6, 1995, p. 84.

——, ''Oak Offers $10.5M for Pixel Magic,'' *Electronic News,* November 13, 1995, p. 72.

——, ''Oak Unveils 3D Controller; Leverages Intel Architecture,'' *Electronic News,* July 15, 1996, p. 104.

''The New America,'' *Investor's Business Daily,* October 6, 1995, p. A5.

''Oak and Philips Have MPEG Devices,'' *Electronic News,* November 7, 1994.

''Oak Opens Mixed Signal Design Center,'' *Electronic News,* July 15, 1996, p. 116.

''Oak Spins MPEG Board Developer Kit,'' *Electronic News,* June 26, 1995, p. 22.

''Oak Tech Sees 4Q Letdown,'' *Electronic News,* May 27, 1996, p. 17.

Schonfeld, Erick, ''A Chip Off the Old CD-ROM,'' *Fortune,* September 18, 1995, p. 245.

Scouras, Ismini, ''Several Report Rough Sledding,'' *EBN,* April 28, 1997.

''Shareholder Suit Filed Against Oak over Trading,'' *Electronic News,* June 24, 1996, p. 54.

Wong, Gerrye, ''Silicon Valley Pioneer'' (profile of David Tsang), *AsianWeek,* March 8, 1996, p. 9.

—Paul S. Bodine

Omnicom

Omnicom Group Inc.

437 Madison Avenue
New York, New York 10022
U.S.A.
(212) 415-3600
Fax: (212) 415-3530

Public Company
Incorporated: 1986
Employees: 22,700
Gross Billings: $2.64 billion (1996)
Stock Exchanges: New York
SICs: 7311 Advertising Agencies; 6719 Holding Companies, Not Elsewhere Classified

The second-largest advertising group in the world, Omnicom Group Inc. operates as the parent company for three separate, independent advertising networks: the BBDO Worldwide Network, the DDB Needham Worldwide Network, and the TBWA International Network. During the late 1990s, Omnicom also operated two independent agencies—Cline, Davis & Mann, and Goodby, Silverstein & Partners—and various marketing service and specialty advertising companies through its Diversified Agency services division. Omnicom was created in 1986 as a holding company, but its history stretched much further back, back to the influential role each of its three subsidiary agencies played in the growth and development of the U.S. advertising industry.

Origins of Batten, Barton, Durstine & Osborn

BBDO was itself the product of a merger. In 1919 Bruce Barton, Roy Durstine, and Alex Osborn opened an advertising agency on West 45th Street in New York City. A few years later, as its business grew, Barton, Durstine & Osborn moved to the seventh floor of a building on 383 Madison Avenue. Three floors above BDO was another advertising agency, the George Batten Company. It seemed odd having competing firms sharing the same address, so a merger was proposed. On May 16, 1928 the George Batten Company joined with BDO to form Batten, Barton, Durstine & Osborn.

The most important man at the Batten agency was William Johns. Johns was more experienced and considerably older than Barton, Durstine, or Osborn. He was therefore made president of BBDO while the job of chairman went to Bruce Barton. Durstine was vice-president and general manager, and Osborn ran a separate BBDO office in his hometown of Buffalo, New York.

Bruce Barton was not a typical advertising man. In fact, he admitted on numerous occasions that he and the profession were not well suited. Barton was trained in theology and philosophy, attracted to politics, and committed to his personal writing projects. He wrote two extremely popular books, *The Man Nobody Knew* (a reappraisal of the life of Jesus Christ) and *The Book Nobody Knew* (a similar reappraisal of the Bible). Then, in the mid-1930s, Barton ran for Congress. He was elected and held office for two consecutive terms. In 1940 he ran for senator but lost by 400,000 votes. Barton was involved only in the creative aspects of BBDO's enterprises.

Durstine was the opposite of Barton. He was in love with the advertising business and what it could obtain for him. Like a number of other agency heads trying to make money during the Depression, Durstine's workaholism became self-destructive. He began drinking heavily, lost his wife and Long Island estate, and was forced to retire from BBDO in 1939.

The vacancy left by Durstine's departure caused some reshuffling of BBDO's management. William Johns by now was too old to handle the day to day operations of the agency. He was "promoted" to chairman, but relieved of all administrative duties. Osborn and Barton were then required to run the agency themselves.

The readjustment proved beneficial to the agency, for BBDO was in need of a new approach to its advertising. Osborn in particular was instrumental in reorganizing the agency and directing it toward the packaged goods advertising business. From the very beginning BBDO had primarily handled accounts for "institutional" clients such as Du Pont Chemical,

Company Perspectives:

Omnicom is a truly global company. We have offices in 85 countries. Nearly half of our revenue is from outside North America. And we're also diversified in other ways. In 1996 our advertising revenues from BBDO Worldwide, DDB Needham Worldwide, TBWA International and Goodby, Silverstein & Partners represented approximately 60 percent of our revenue. Revenue from our specialty advertising and marketing service companies accounted for the remaining 40 percent. Both advertising and marketing services activities are geographically balanced with one-half of revenues coming from North America and one-half from the rest of the world. The diversification of our services and our geographic balance means our revenues are far less dependent on the business cycles of any one country or line of business.

Consolidated Edison, and Liberty Mutual. Although they were consistent customers, these companies neither needed nor wanted extensive advertising. If BBDO was going to grow rapidly enough to compete with large and established agencies, it would have to do advertising for packaged goods. Not only are new packaged goods constantly introduced to the market, but also those already on the shelves are always being improved to keep up with competing brands. In this environment advertising flourishes—that was Osborn's important insight.

Between 1939 and 1945 BBDO gained a number of important non-institutional accounts: Lever Brothers, B.F. Goodrich, Chrysler (Dodge Division), MJB Coffee, and the 3M Company. Not even the upheaval of World War II kept BBDO from growing. Billings increased from $20 million at the height of the Depression to $50 million at the end of the war.

In 1946 management changes again took place at BBDO. Ben Duffy, a veteran account man with the agency for over 15 years, was elected president; and Charlie Brower, who was to lead BBDO in the 1950s and 1960s, became executive vice-president in charge of copywriting. Duffy was an excellent salesman who could close a deal quickly. When Foote, Cone & Belding resigned the $11 million American Tobacco Company account in 1948, Duffy went directly to see American Tobacco's George Hill and secured the account after one meeting. In Duffy's 10 years at the helm of BBDO the agency increased its billings from $50 million to over $200 million.

Unfortunately for BBDO, Duffy was prone to ill health. In 1956 he suffered a stroke in Minneapolis while visiting the chairman of General Foods. He could not continue as the head of the agency, and Charlie Brower subsequently replaced him as president. Brower was the obvious choice. He had been in charge of the creative side of BBDO's advertising for over 20 years and was responsible for much of the agency's success.

Brower had a ''no-nonsense'' approach to advertising. He felt that as president of BBDO he had to do four things: 1) add one million dollars to the payroll; 2) hire talent from the outside; 3) fire many of his best friends; and 4) do away with company time clocks, which he thought made the agency a factory instead of a creative enterprise.

When Duffy retired there was confusion at BBDO, and a number of important clients quit the firm. In fact, until Charlie Brower established himself as president of the company no one was actually in charge. Revlon, a $6 million customer, canceled its account as soon as it heard of Duffy's retirement. Other clients followed Revlon's example. Brower did not allow this situation to continue for long. BBDO appeared headed toward disaster when Brower won for it the most lucrative account in its history—Pepsi Cola. Within a matter of weeks BBDO was financially healthy once again.

For BBDO the 1950s and early 1960s was a period marked by more than management readjustments and client shuffling. It was also a period in which BBDO became intimately and extensively involved in political advertising. Many agencies try to avoid producing campaigns for political movements and parties so that copywriters are not forced to sell opinions they themselves may not hold or to which they may be vehemently opposed. BBDO is one of the few firms that has accepted political advertising as a normal part of its business.

In 1948 BBDO ran its first ad campaign for a political candidate, Republican Thomas Dewey. Both candidate and agency lost this close election but, though Dewey left the political foreground, BBDO simply waited for the next election and a more marketable candidate. It found one in Dwight D. Eisenhower. In 1952 BBDO signed the Republican National Committee as a regular account, and did the advertising in Eisenhower's successful bid for the presidency. The firm was hired again four years later to handle Eisenhower's re-election campaign. Unfortunately for the Republican Party, and Richard Nixon in particular, BBDO's success ended with Eisenhower. A BBDO makeup man was responsible for the ''grey shave'' look of Nixon's face in his 1960 televised presidential debate with John F. Kennedy.

Outside the political realm BBDO continued to expand and sign new clients. Not only did it increase the number of its institutional customers such as CBS Broadcasting (1959) and the SCM Corporation (1961), but also it won product-oriented accounts such as Tupperware (1959), Autolite (1961), McGregor Sporting Goods (1964), and Pepperidge Farm (1964). To match this domestic growth BBDO began to expand internationally for the first time in 1959, opening up offices in London, Paris, Milan, Frankfurt, and Vienna. In 1964 BBDO acquired the Atlanta-based firm of Burke Dowling Adams and with it the accounts of Delta Air Lines and the various governmental agencies of the state of Georgia. The Clyne Maxon firm of New York, with its $60 million in billings, was also merged with BBDO in 1966.

By the time of the worldwide recession during the 1970s, Charlie Brower had retired as president of BBDO. His successor was Tom Dillon, who had been the agency's treasurer since the late 1950s. Like most ad agencies BBDO suffered considerable losses in domestic billings during these years of economic stagnation. However, because of the way the company was structured, BBDO was able to endure this period without undue strain. By opening up offices in new places around the world, the agency entered advertising markets which had previously been closed to it. This international expansion served to offset losses incurred in the domestic market. In addition, BBDO began selling shares to the public in an effort to diffuse operating costs.

In 1976 Bruce Crawford was named president of BBDO. He had been head of the agency's foreign operations. During his eight-year tenure billings at BBDO tripled to $2.3 billion, and his cost management measures kept the company from misusing the benefits of this growth. As one analyst said of BBDO in 1981, ''I've never seen a company so conscious of cost controls.''

Crawford retired on March 31, 1985, and was succeeded by another able manager, Allen Rosenshine. Under his tutelage BBDO continued to expand by acquiring subsidiaries, creating for the agency a genuine worldwide network. It had traditionally been BBDO policy to allow local entrepreneurs the freedom to run their own offices, to encourage individuality and creativity. This practice came to an end under Rosenshine. A number of foreign and international clients expressed concern over these ''local'' shops. They thought there was too little direction coming from top management, and became wary of giving business to BBDO subsidiaries. To remedy the problem Rosenshine attempted to tighten the connections within the BBDO network and provide more centralized leadership.

That same year, BBDO and its various sub-agencies won a total of 530 awards for creativity. Most notable of these was the Grand Prix Gold Lion at the Cannes Film Festival. The trophy is presented to the agency which produces the year's best television commercial. The ad that won this coveted award was the ''Archeology'' commercial made for Pepsi Cola.

With BBDO such a large and vital member of the advertising industry, there was some question as to why it needed or wanted to join in a merger, particularly when the other two potential partners were currently experiencing financial difficulty. What did BBDO have to gain?

The answer was not hard to find. BBDO was one of the last major agencies to expand internationally, waiting until 1959. This late start proved to be a handicap and made BBDO's overseas growth uneven. For instance, BBDO was then the number one firm in Germany and the number two firm in Australia; but ranked 17th in Canada, 26th in France, and 29th in Britain (the most important European market.) The situation was complicated in 1985 by BBDO's being forced to sell its interest in a major South African subsidiary at a considerable loss. This divestiture led to a decrease in BBDO's international revenues of 94 percent and removed BBDO from the South African market where it had been the top agency. The merger with Needham and Doyle Dane Bernbach would provide BBDO with greater international presence, particularly in France, Canada, and Great Britain. According to the policy planning heads at BBDO, this improvement of the agency's foreign business was necessary for BBDO to maintain itself as a formidable worldwide advertising competitor.

Origins of Doyle Dane Bernbach

When those within the advertising industry are asked which agency most exemplifies innovation and creativity, one firm above all others is mentioned—Doyle Dane Bernbach. In the world of advertising, where imitation is the rule, the Doyle Dane Bernbach agency has made itself an exception. Most ad firms follow familiar schools of thought, but not Doyle Dane Bernbach. In the words of David Ogilvy, ''They just sort of created an original school out of air.''

In 1949 Ned Doyle and William Bernbach joined Maxwell Dane in the formation of a new advertising agency. Bernbach and Doyle had been trained at Grey Advertising, and Dane had owned his small ad company for a number of years. Doyle Dane Bernbach's first year billings came to just $500,000, but something about its advertising style suggested it would soon be a major force in the industry. It hired the most creative people it could find, no matter where they came from.

Among Max Dane, Ned Doyle, and Bill Bernbach there existed a well-defined division of labor. Doyle was the account executive in charge of winning and retaining clients; Dane took care of administration and financial matters; and Bernbach handled the creative concerns. Rarely did they cross into each other's designated spheres.

What made the firm unique in the ad industry was Bill Bernbach and his preoccupation with the ''road not taken.'' Born in Brooklyn and educated in English and philosophy at New York University, Bernbach was the ad man's intellectual. His ideas were fresh, striking, and more often than not, couched in subtle humor. He sympathized with the public at large, which found most advertisements boring. His quest was to make ad campaigns exciting and fun while still focusing on the product's attributes. He had little reverence for research. He felt it substituted statistics for ideas and emotions. For him advertising was an art, and as an artist he was primarily concerned with imagery, impression, and point of view.

Bernbach was also a good teacher. He was patient, precise but gentle in his criticisms, and had the ability to nurture natural ability. His ''students'' formed the firm's Creative Team: a small group of copy writers, artists, art directors, and photographers that produced the agency's campaigns. Bernbach led the group but not in an authoritarian manner. It was what he called a ''horizontal hierarchy.'' ''We are all peers here,'' he said.

In the 1950s Doyle Dane Bernbach displayed its style of advertising in four notable campaigns for four near-unknown companies: Polaroid Cameras, Levy Bakery Goods, Ohrbach's Department Store, and El Al Israel Air Lines. These companies, like Doyle Dane Bernbach, were attempting to establish themselves in their respective markets. Polaroid was overshadowed by Kodak, Ohrbach's by Macy's, and few people had ever heard of Levy's Bread or El Al Air. To compensate for this lack of public recognition, the agency created strikingly different ads featuring everything from a cat dressed in a woman's hat to an American Indian claiming that ''you don't have to be Jewish to enjoy Levy's real Jewish rye.'' Not only did the campaigns sell large quantities of cameras, clothes, bread, and airline tickets, they sold Doyle Dane Bernbach advertising as well. In 1954 the

Agency's billings were $8 million; by 1959 that figure had increased to $27.5 million.

In the early 1960s the agency won two new accounts that were to further enhance its reputation: Avis Car Rental Service and Volkswagen. In the rent-a-car business Hertz held the dominant market share. Far behind in second place, Avis wanted to increase its own market share. Most advertising is meant to portray the client in as favorable and strong a position as possible. Doyle Dane Bernbach, however, disregarded this tradition; its campaign stressed Avis's weak position vis-à-vis Hertz. ''We're number two,'' said the ads, ''We try harder. We have to.'' This strategy worked. In two years Avis increased its market share by over 25 percent.

The Volkswagen advertising campaign was a similar story. These small German cars were not what the American consumer wanted, or so it appeared. Again, Doyle Dane Bernbach converted a liability into a saleable asset. Hoping people had tired of the large and overly-embellished American-made cars of the 1950s, Doyle Dane Bernbach said simply: ''Think small.'' The art of the ads was minimalist, usually showing a small picture of the car against a blank white backdrop. The text was equally odd. The short, simple copy was blocked in paragraphs that looked, in the words of copywriter Helmut Krone, ''Gertrude Steiny.'' Not only did Americans purchase these ''ugly'' Volkswagens by the thousands, but the car became a symbol for an entire ''non-conformist'' generation.

Following these successes the agency won accounts from American Air Lines, Seagrams, International Silver, Heinz Ketchup, Sony, Uniroyal, Gillette, Bristol-Myers, and Mobil Oil. The 1960s were the golden age of advertising's ''creative revolution,'' and Doyle Dane Bernbach was at the forefront of this movement.

As the 1960s gave way to the 1970s, the industry witnessed a return to conventional advertising techniques. This trend and the recession which plagued the beginning of the decade spelled trouble for the company. In 1970 Doyle Dane Bernbach lost the $20 million Alka-Seltzer account, even though the ''that's a spicy meat-ball'' commercial was extremely popular and a favorite of the critics. Other agency clients quickly followed Alka-Seltzer's lead. Lever Brothers, Whirlpool, Sara Lee, Quaker Oats, Cracker Jack, Uniroyal, and Life Cereal also canceled their accounts.

Fortunately for the agency, its growth during the 1960s provided it with enough revenue to absorb these losses, at least in the short run. Nonetheless, a company reorganization and reorientation was in order. In 1974 Neil A. Austrian joined the company as executive vice-president. He had expertise in the business aspects of advertising, something that had been missing at the agency. Gradually he transformed the company into a more orderly advertising network. Subsidiaries were acquired to strengthen Doyle Dane Bernbach's worldwide presence and offer more comprehensive client services. In 1975 the agency's billings rose for the first time in the new decade, and this trend continued for seven years.

On October 2, 1982, William Bernbach died of leukemia. His absence left a void at the agency. This raised a difficult question: Could Doyle Dane Bernbach continue without Bill Bernbach?

The question haunted the firm. In 1982 earnings fell 30 percent. This loss was compounded in the next two years by the resignation of important accounts. American Air Lines canceled its account in 1983. Its spot was filled by Pan Am which subsequently left the agency a few months later. Then, in 1984, Polaroid announced it would be taking its business elsewhere. The agency was particularly shocked by this resignation. Its commercials had helped make Polaroid the world's best-selling camera.

In the first half of 1986 Doyle Dane Bernbach was forced to lay off 24 staff members; it had lost almost $113 million in net earnings. The merger with BBDO and Needham Harper Worldwide represented a necessary business decision. It was doubtful that Doyle Dane Bernbach could continue if its fiscal situation were not improved. The security afforded by the Omnicom umbrella promised to relieve the agency of its financial difficulties, and allow it to concentrate on what it did best, namely, innovative advertising.

Origins of Needham Harper Worldwide

In 1924 Maurice Needham opened up his own advertising agency in Illinois. It was named The Maurice H. Needham Company. This title was changed in 1929 to Needham, Louis & Brorby, Inc. The firm then merged with Doherty, Clifford, Steers & Shenfield, Inc. in 1964 to become Needham, Harper & Steers. In 1984 the company name was again changed, this time to Needham Harper Worldwide.

As a Chicago-based agency, it traditionally avoided Madison Avenue type of advertising, and was generally considered to have stronger advertising presence in the Midwest than in the East. Until becoming part of Omnicom, Needham & Harper had not ranked among the largest worldwide agencies. However, this provincialism contributed to its success. Smaller companies, feeling neglected and disrespected by large advertising agencies, often turned to Needham & Harper. This type of client was the foundation of the firm's business.

In addition to that of Maurice Needham, the other name associated with the agency was that of Paul Harper. He came to the company in 1945 when it was Needham, Louis & Brorby. Harper had been educated at Yale and had spent four years in the Marine Corps fighting in the Pacific campaign. After his discharge, he walked into Needham's Chicago office looking for employment. He had no résumé, no writing experience, and no civilian clothes. Despite his scant qualifications Needham gave him a job as a copywriter, and soon Harper was making a name for himself in advertising. He worked primarily in broadcast advertising. Most notably, he produced commercials for Johnson's Wax on the ''Fibber McGee and Molly'' radio show.

As Harper became a man of greater importance at the agency he gradually moved from copywriter to manager. In 1964 he became president of the company and supervised the acquisition by Needham of Doherty, Clifford, Steers and Shenfield in 1965. At this time the name of the agency was changed to Needham, Harper & Steers. In 1967 he became chairman and chief executive officer of the agency, and retained this position until his retirement in 1984.

During the late 1950s and 1960s when companies were substantially increasing their expenditure on advertising, Needham, Harper & Steers, though still only a mid-size agency, grew along with the industry. It concentrated on smaller accounts but also retained a number of large Midwest clients, such as the Household Finance Corporation and the Oklahoma Oil Company. For the former it created the "Never borrow money needlessly" slogan; and for the latter it coined "Put a tiger in your tank."

In 1972 the firm followed the industry trend of publicly trading its shares. This move did not prove to be lucrative. Investors do not generally consider advertising to be a perennially stable business. More so than other industries, it is affected by the fluctuations of the economy. Smaller advertising firms are especially vulnerable and therefore pose higher risks to potential investors. Unlike the larger agencies such as Ogilvy & Mather and Interpublic, Needham, Harper & Steers was unsuccessful in drawing a strong investment interest. Four years after going public Needham & Harper "went private" again.

Although it serviced many small and mid-size accounts, Needham & Harper was primarily known for its "blue chip" clients. It won Xerox in 1968, McDonald's in 1970, Honda in 1977, and Sears in 1982. The agency produced the famous "Brother Dominic" commercials for Xerox, and the "you deserve a break today" slogan for McDonald's. Unfortunately for the agency, in 1984 McDonald's took its domestic business away from Needham and turned it over to Leo Burnett. The bad news continued in 1986, when Needham lost the $40 million Xerox account.

The merger with BBDO and Doyle Dane Bernbach would likely alter the "personality" of Needham Harper. Even though the three agencies intended to operate as separate divisions of Omnicom, there was more to the merger than a simple name change. Already clients expressed displeasure with the prospect of sharing the agency with competitors. The old conflict of interest problem became particularly pronounced when Campbell's Soup, a Needham and Harper client, would not stay with Omnicom if Heinz, a Doyle Dane Bernbach client, remained. Similar difficulties arose between Stroh's and Busch beer, and Honda and Volkswagen automobiles.

The most important question among Needham and Harper customers was whether they would continue to receive the same advertising attention to which they had been accustomed. "Fortunately," says one such client, "Keith Reinhard will still be around." Reinhard joined the firm in 1964, became president of NH&S/Chicago in 1980, chairman and CEO of NH&S/USA in 1982, and chairman and CEO of Needham Harper Worldwide in 1984. He impressed staffers, colleagues, and customers alike with his integrity and hard work. He maintained that the merger with Omnicom would help Needham attract and retain large clients, but claimed that the agency would not treat its smaller customers any differently than it had in the past. Reinhard also hoped Omnicom would restore to Needham a presence in the New York advertising market, something it had lacked since Xerox withdrew its account in 1986.

1986 Formation of Omnicom

When the final documents were signed and Omnicom was formally created, the task of making sense and profits out of the amalgamation fell to BBDO head Allen Rosenshine. As some had anticipated, the process of combining three competing agencies under one umbrella corporation was a tiresome and fitful chore, sparking further speculation about the prudence of the merger in the first place. Omnicom limped from the starting block. More than $40 million was spent on merger and restructuring-related costs, leaving the company essentially profitless for its first year. Several clients were wholly opposed to the merger, and expressed their displeasure by taking their business elsewhere, such as the immediate exit of RJR Nabisco. "As a client," RJR Nabisco's chairman icily remarked, "I see disruption, but little value. With very few exceptions, the wave of mergers has benefitted the shareholders and managers of the agencies." By the time the dust had settled after the merger, the three Omnicom agencies lost $184 million in billings that were directly attributable to the act of the merger itself.

The assimilation process did not get any easier after the end of 1986. When Omnicom's 1987 financial totals were announced, they were depressingly low. For the year, the company earned only $32 million from commissions and fees of $785 million, or 4.1 percent in what traditionally was a double-digit margin business. The year did have its highlights, however, including the gain of several large accounts. Omnicom agencies landed a U.S. Navy account, a large portion of new Pepsi business, including Slice soft drinks and Pizza Hut, and the account for NEC Home Electronics. In all, Omnicom registered $280 million in new business during 1987, but this was not enough to offset other difficulties. The merger was not delivering its desired and expected results, and this failure was beginning to wear on Rosenshine. In the spring of 1988, Rosenshine's dissatisfaction was readily discernible. "Right now, this is the most necessary job I can do," he told reporters. "But if I'm still doing it in two or three years, I don't think I'll be particularly thrilled."

Rosenshine was spared from having to endure a two- or three-year tenure by the return of Bruce Crawford, whose departure from BBDO in 1985 led him to the Metropolitan Opera Company. Crawford served as the Metropolitan Opera's general manager for three years, and then made his return to advertising as Omnicom's chief executive officer. Charged with directing and expediting the restructuring of Omnicom, Crawford took the helm in early 1989 and immediately began paring away superfluous managerial layers and divesting businesses. "With every merger," Crawford announced upon his return, "everybody talks about all these wonderful economies of scale, but it usually amounts to small potatoes. I believe the idea is to build businesses, not worry about the economies of scale to be realized by the joint buying of erasers. My belief is that the management structure is a little too complicated. I believe it is necessary to keep it simple, fast, and that corporate structure and overhead need to be minimized."

Omnicom in the 1990s

Crawford made good on his words, and divested a number of Omnicom businesses, while shuttering others. Concurrently, he developed a more concentrated presence in Britain and Europe, where Omnicom lagged behind other U.S.-based, international advertising agencies. By the beginning of the 1990s, Crawford's strategy was beginning to work wonders, and Omnicom, after a torpid start, was now demonstrating the vitality its creators had envisioned prior to the merger. Despite the effects of a stifling economic recession during the early 1990s, Omnicom registered robust financial gains. In 1991, revenues increased to $1.2 billion and profits grew consistently. This growth trend continued after the recession, when the company recorded an 18 percent increase in revenues to $2.3 billion in 1995 and a 26 percent gain in net income, to $140 million.

By the end of the mid-1990s, any lingering doubt about the prudence of the 1986 merger had been thoroughly washed away. Omnicom held sway as a powerful and creative force as the late 1990s began, with its three agency networks earning numerous prestigious awards and gaining much coveted, new clientele. BBDO, selected by *Advertising Age International* as "The Most Creative Agency Network" in the world in 1996, was awarded multinational accounts for Sara Lee, Mars, Visa, Pepsi, and Bayer. At the Cannes International Advertising Festival in 1996, DDB Needham won more awards than any other agency in the world, the fifth year during the previous six years that the agency had reigned supreme. New clients added to DDB Needham's roster during the year included L'eggs, CompuServe, Wells Fargo Bank, Clorox, Wilson Sporting Goods, Hamilton Beach, and Lockheed Martin. TBWA International's progress during 1996 bolstered Omnicom's global reach. New offices were opened in Latin America (Brazil, Chile, and Argentina), Asia (Singapore, Hong Kong, China), Europe (Warsaw, Munich, Berlin, and Cyprus), and in Durban, South Africa, the agency's third South African office. TBWA also followed the pattern of success established by its sister agencies by winning an enviable list of new clients and earning recognition for its creativity. The agency's Nissan commercial was named the "Best of 1996" by *Time, USA Today, Entertainment Weekly,* and *Rolling Stone*; new clients included Novartis and Canon in Europe, and Gramercy Picture and Sara Lee's Champion Sportswear in the United States.

On top of these three vibrant agencies stood Omnicom, selected in 1997 as *Fortune* magazine's most respected advertising group and ranked by the *Wall Street Journal* as number one in the advertising industry in terms of total return to shareholders. Amid the accolades and applause directed at its three subsidiary agency companies, Omnicom posted strong financial totals, registering a 26 percent gain in net income in 1996 to $176.3 million and an increase in revenues from $2.26 billion to $2.64 billion. Much of the credit for Omnicom's robust growth went to Crawford, who had made the concept of Omnicom work as a viable corporate entity. Crawford stepped down as chief executive officer in January 1997, naming John D. Wren as his successor, but continued to serve as chairman. To Wren fell the task of continuing Crawford's legacy of success and nurturing growth and creativity during Omnicom's second decade of business.

Principal Subsidiaries

BBDO Worldwide Inc.; DDB Needham Worldwide Inc.; Diversified Agency Services; Communicade.

Further Reading

Alden, Robert, "Bernbach's Advertising: A Formula Or Delicate Art?," *New York Times*, May 7, 1961.

Gleason, Mark, "Big Bang of '86 Is Still Shaping the Ad World," *Advertising Age,* April 22, 1996, p. 3.

Kindel, Stephen, "It Looked Good on Paper," *Financial World,* March 8, 1988, p. 36.

MacDougall, A. Kent, "Doyle Dane Bernbach: Ad Alley Upstart," *Wall Street Journal*, August 1965.

McCormack, Kevin, "Crawford Managing Omnicom Like the Met: Playing a Leaner Tune," *ADWEEK Eastern Edition,* January 15, 1990, p. 1.

Rich, Laura, "Omnicom Grows Organically," *ADWEEK Eastern Edition,* February 10, 1997, p. 6.

——, "The Omnicom Shopping Spree: How Wren and Co. Picked Their Targets," *ADWEEK Eastern Edition,* October 14, 1996, p. 32.

Sharkey, Betsy, "Omnicom's Operatics," *ADWEEK Eastern Edition,* April 20, 1992, p. 20.

Wood, James P., *The Story of Advertising,* New York: Ronald Press, 1958.

—updated by Jeffrey L. Covell

Orbital Sciences Corporation

21700 Atlantic Boulevard
Dulles, Virginia 20166
U.S.A.
(703) 406-5000
Fax: (703) 406-3502
Web site: http://www.orbital.com

Public Company
Incorporated: 1990
Employees: 3,100
Sales: $461 million (1996)
Stock Exchanges: NASDAQ
SICs: 3761 Guided Missiles & Space Vehicles; 3829 Measuring & Controlling Devices, Not Elsewhere Classified; 4899 Communications Services, Not Elsewhere Classified; 3812 Search, Detection, Navigation, Guidance, Aeronautical & Nautical Systems & Instruments; 3663 Radio & Television Broadcasting & Communications Equipment; 3764 Guided Missile & Space Vehicle Propulsion Units & Propulsion Unit Parts

Orbital Sciences Corporation, together with its subsidiaries, is an unrivaled, leading-edge space technology company that designs, manufactures, operates, and markets a broad range of space products and develops and provides services grouped into three categories: Launch Systems, Space Systems, and Communications and Information Systems. Launch Systems develops and markets space transportation systems, which include space and suborbital launch vehicles and orbit transfer vehicles. Space Systems includes spacecraft systems and payloads, which include satellites, spacecraft platforms, and space payloads and experiments. Communications and Information Systems are space support products, which include satellite tracking systems and atmospheric environmental monitoring products; and satellite services, which include satellite-based data communications services and remote sensing services for monitoring the Earth. The company's primary customers are the U.S. Government and other commercial, educational, and international markets.

The Early Years, 1980–89

The foundation for Orbital Sciences Corporation was laid in 1980, when David Thompson, Bruce Ferguson, and Scott Webster met at Harvard Business School and worked together on a NASA-sponsored study of commercial space applications. They submitted their study to NASA in 1981 and subsequently won the Space Foundation Prize for Space Business Research.

On April 2, 1982, Space Systems Corporation (SSC) was incorporated in Delaware to develop, manufacture, test, and market commercial space transportation systems. On September 30, 1983, a year after the initial start-up, Orbital Research Corporation (ORC) was incorporated as a wholly owned subsidiary of SSC to be the Managing General Partner of Orbital Research Partners L.P., which was formed on October 20, 1983 for the purpose of designing, developing and commercially marketing an orbit transfer vehicle, to become known as the Transfer Orbit Stage (TOS) Vehicle. The company signed an agreement with NASA for the company's first space product, the TOS Vehicle, and reached a production agreement with Martin Marietta Corporation. That same year, the company secured $2 million in venture capital and opened its first office in Vienna, Virginia, near Washington, D.C., with 12 employees and had opening year revenues of $100,000.

The next year the company's board of directors grew to include prominent figures in the space industry, academia, and finance. The company also raised $50 million from outside investors to finance development of the TOS Vehicle. The number of employees rose to 20 and revenues hit $2 million.

The year 1985 saw the company's design, development, and marketing efforts for the TOS Vehicle move into high gear, with 25 employees and $3 million in revenues. January saw the company entering into the Minuteman CFE Contract with the U.S. Air Force for the production of 20 Minuteman Rocket Consolidated Front End (or attitude control, telemetry, and flight termination) modules, for approximately $33.2 million. In June, the company's Space Data Division entered into the Phase I Starbird Contract with the U.S. Air Force to develop and launch the Starbird launch vehicle and related products and services for approximately $17.8 million.

Company Perspectives:

Orbital Sciences Corporation's fundamental goal is to make space more accessible and useful through highly affordable small space systems that incorporate innovative designs and advanced technologies to reduce the cost of using space.

In 1986, the company moved to a new headquarters in Fairfax, Virginia, and NASA signed a $35 million contract for the first TOS Vehicle and an option for a second. The company had 40 employees and $6 million in revenues.

In 1987, Antonio Elias conceived of a revolutionary, air-launched rocket, later named Pegasus in an employee contest, designed to place small satellites into low-Earth orbit. The company also began investigating a system for collecting data from remote locations using satellites in low-Earth orbit, which evolved into the company's Orbital Communications Corporation (ORBCOMM) commercial communications subsidiary. Additionally, in March, the company signed the NASA TOS Vehicle Contract for the Mars Observer and the Advanced Communications Technology Satellite (ACTS) mission for approximately $78.6 million and signed a Mars Observer and ACTS production subcontract with Martin Marietta. A TOS Vehicle flight activation contract was also signed with Martin Marietta for approximately $6.3 million. Continuing to grow, the company had 50 employees and revenues jumped to $25 million.

In 1988, the Defense Advanced Research Project Agency (DARPA) signed the DARPA Pegasus Contract, the first Pegasus contract for the purchase of one Pegasus launch vehicle with an option for an additional five launches for approximately $36.3 million. The company and Hercules Inc. agreed to jointly develop and produce Pegasus, with Hercules, the subcontractor, investing $32 million in Orbital Sciences. The company also broadened its rocket business and manufacturing capabilities in November by acquiring the stock of Arizona-based Space Data Corporation, one of the world's leading suppliers of suborbital rockets. The $17.5 million deal was achieved through a merger of Space Data into a wholly owned subsidiary of Orbital organized for that purpose. The company's revenues grew to $35 million as 300 new employees were added to the company with the acquisition, jumping the number up to 400 employees total.

The company began construction of a new facility in Chandler, Arizona, in 1989 in order to house the company's expanding rocket production line and support staff. In July, the company entered into a contract with DARPA to supply a ground-launched Taurus rocket and launch services for approximately $10 million, with an option for an additional four launches for another $58.4 million. That same month, the ERINT Contract was signed with the U.S. Army Strategic Defense Command, which provided for the design, development, fabrication, analysis, testing, and delivery of launch systems and services required for five launches of the ERINT target system for approximately $15.6 million, with an option for three additional launches for a total of approximately $5.4 million. In July, the company's Space Data Division entered into the Phase II Starbird Contract with the U.S. Air Force to develop and launch the Starbird launch vehicle and related products and services for approximately $12.6 million. The employee count that year was up to 475 and revenues reached $80 million. In addition, the company won numerous awards in 1989, including the DARPA Outstanding Technical Performance Award, the American Astronautical Society Space Commerce Award, and the Space Foundation Commercial Space Award.

Going Public, 1990–Date

In 1990, Orbital Sciences Corporation faced some of its largest and most significant challenges since the company was founded. That year, the company had a number of impressive space "firsts." In April, the company became the first commercial space company to open its financial future to public participation through the successful completion of an initial public offering of $32.5 million of its common stock, becoming a publicly traded company on the NASDAQ exchange.

Also in April, the company celebrated the initial launch of its Pegasus rocket. The highly successful maiden flight made the air-launched space booster the world's first privately developed Earth-to-space vehicle. Initial launches were conducted of several other of the company's major suborbital rocket systems, including the Minuteman Missile Consolidated Front End, Starbird suborbital vehicle, and High Performance Booster. In addition, three important space experiments were conducted by the company, including the Ultra-Violet Bow Shock flight, the Excede III scientific probe, and the Two-Axis Pointing System mission, the first two on suborbital vehicles and the latter on the Space Shuttle, for a total of eight successfully completed space missions for the year.

Also in 1990, the company filed the world's first license application with the Federal Communications Commission (FCC) for the operation of a network of small low-Earth orbit spacecraft to provide global satellite services of commercial messaging and data communications services via the company's ORBCOMM subsidiary.

The company also signed a contract with the Strategic Defense Initiative Organization (SDIO) in January to provide suborbital launch vehicles and related services in connection with the SDIO Flight Test Services Program (the FTSP Contract) for approximately $34.8 million, with options totaling another $14.9 million.

The Chandler, Arizona facility opened and the number of employees jumped to 725; Orbital achieved significant improvements in its financial position, with recorded revenues of $100 million, a 25 percent increase over 1989 sales; and awards received in 1990 included the National Air and Space Museum Trophy, the National Space Society Space Pioneer Award, the Space Business Roundtable Commercial Space Industry Award, and the *Washington Technology* and *Popular Science* New Product of the Year Awards.

In 1991, the company was established as the preeminent supplier of small launch vehicles by winning an $80 million NASA contract for Pegasus launches and another launch contract from the U.S. Air Force that included up to 40 Pegasus launches. The company was also selected by NASA to build SeaStar, the world's first privately owned environmental monitoring satellite with a commitment for $44 million in image purchases over five years.

The company's ORBCOMM mobile data communications network proposal achieved critical technical and regulatory progress with the FCC and the World Administrative Radio Conference's agreement to allocate the global radio spectrum necessary. ORBCOMM signed agreements with 12 potential user equipment suppliers and international service licensees.

Top management was strengthened with the addition of former NASA Deputy Administrator James R. Thompson and former McDonnell Douglas executive Donald W. Tutwiler. Orbital turned in its best-ever financial performance in 1991, with revenues of $135 million, exceeding by five percent the company's 30 percent target of increase over 1990 revenues. The company raised $65 million in a secondary public offering of stock. In addition, awards received in 1991 included the Virginia Outstanding Industrialist of the Year Award, the *Via Satellite* Executive of the Year Award, and the National Medal of Technology Citation, the last presented by President George Bush and U.S. Commerce Secretary Robert Mosbacher.

Orbital continued its rapid growth in 1992, with revenues of $175 million, representing a 29 percent increase over 1991 revenues. In September, the company's first TOS Vehicle successfully completed its first launch, boosting NASA's Mars Observer spacecraft into Mars intercept trajectory. The Observer would reach Mars in August 1993 and begin providing a wealth of scientific information on Earth's nearest planetary neighbor in order to assist the 1997 launches of several more Mars missions.

Of the company's ten space missions in 1992 (bringing the number of successfully completed missions to 27 in three years of launch operations), five involved new vehicles, a very high proportion for the industry.

Progress continued on the company's ORBCOMM low-Earth orbit mobile satellite communications project, with the signing of 17 companies in 19 countries prepared to offer ORBCOMM services upon receipt of regulatory approvals and deployment of the satellites in 1993 and 1994. The Capabilities Demonstration Satellite was successfully launched in February and began providing valuable information on the planned design and operation of ORBCOMM satellites.

The company also created two new subsidiaries in 1992. The first was Orbital Imaging Corporation (ORBIMAGE), to consolidate the company's Earth-viewing satellite remote sensing initiatives, including the SeaStar ocean color monitoring service, which began service in 1993. The second was Orbital Environmental Systems Group, to focus on meteorological products and satellite tracking systems.

An L-1011 carrier aircraft was purchased by the company to be used with its Pegasus launch vehicle program, the total contract for backlog exceeded $1 billion for the first time in the company's history and the number of employees climbed to 1,150.

In 1993, Orbital carried out 16 space missions, all successfully, including two flights of the Pegasus space vehicle, 11 flights of suborbital rockets, one mission of the TOS orbit transfer vehicle, and two missions of communications satellites and research payloads.

February saw the launch of the first prototype satellite in the ORBCOMM two-way messaging and mobile data communications system, beginning the final phase of space and ground technology development for the revolutionary global PCS network. The network operations simulation was run through end-to-end successfully. In June, Orbital created an equal partnership called ORBCOMM Development Partners L.P. with Teleglobe Mobile Partners, an affiliate of Teleglobe Inc., one of the world's largest intercontinental telecommunications carriers, for the design and development of the low-Earth orbit satellite system. Teleglobe Mobile invested $85 million in the project and provided not only financing, but international service distribution. Orbital agreed to construct and launch satellites for the ORBCOMM System and to construct the satellite control center, the network control center and four U.S. gateway Earth stations.

The ORBIMAGE subsidiary made more progress on the SeaStar project, as well as beginning new projects ranging from satellite-based atmospheric lightning detection to high-resolution imaging for mapping the land surfaces of the Earth.

In September, the company acquired the Pomona, California-based Applied Science Operation (ASO) business unit of The Perkin-Elmer Corporation for approximately $5.8 million in order to produce and market sophisticated space sensors and ground-based analytical instruments primarily for agencies of the U.S. Government and commercial aerospace companies. The 200 new employees based in Pomona brought the number of employees to 1,350.

The company achieved substantial financial improvements in 1993 as revenues climbed to $195 million, a nine percent increase over 1992. The company also moved its corporate headquarters to Dulles, Virginia.

Of the nine successful space missions conducted in 1994, one was the inaugural launch of the company's Taurus space launch vehicle, which took place from Vandenburg Air Force Base in California and another was the maiden voyage of the PegaStar small satellite platform. The APEX satellite, built for the U.S. Air Force by the company's satellite group, was successfully launched aboard a Pegasus rocket and operated flawlessly while in orbit. The only failure for the year was the first use of the new Pegasus XL enhanced-performance rocket, but the total number of successful missions jumped to 40 in 1994.

The ORBCOMM system also made progress that year, receiving a full construction and operating license from the FCC, the first ever granted to a commercial low-orbit satellite network, in October, culminating a four-year crusade the company led to ''rezone'' the desired radio frequencies needed, both in the United States and around the world. ORBCOMM received the only VHF/UHF license for a global satellite network, providing over 600 KHz of primary spectrum in the United States and extended its network of domestic resellers of ORBCOMM services for markets such as trucking, marine and energy facilities, and expanded its international distribution of services to nearly seventy countries.

In August, the company acquired Fairchild Space and Defense Corporation from Matra Aerospace Inc., part of the Matra Hachette Group for approximately $71 million. As a result, Orbital substantially expanded its spacecraft design and production capability and added advanced electronics and satellite-aided vehicle management networks to the product lines. The acquisition also brought 800 new employees to the company.

December saw the acquisition of Magellan Corporation in a merger, bringing personal satellite navigation and communications technologies to the company. The world's leader in the manufacture of consumer-level Global Positioning System (GPS) products, Magellan also produced $40 million per year of inexpensive, hand-held satellite navigators, with the potential to expand into ORBCOMM messaging devices and automotive positioning equipment. Orbital also gained over 150 employees with the acquisition, boosting the number to 2,100. Revenues climbed to $225 million, a 17 percent increase over 1993.

Major Goal Achieved in 1995

For Orbital, 1995 was the year the company achieved its longstanding goal of developing or acquiring all the core technologies and product lines necessary to position the company as the industry's only complete provider of space systems infrastructure.

Orbital became an international company with the acquisition of Vancouver-based MacDonald, Dettwiler and Associates Ltd. (MDA), the world leader in the design and integration of ground stations for remote sensing satellites. The addition of MDA's products enabled the company to offer full end-to-end space mission capabilities. Nearly 800 additional employees were added to the company's ranks with the acquisition. Magellan introduced the world's first hand-held personal GPS navigator to retail for under $200.

Orbital successfully completed 11 major rocket launches, including a Pegasus launch carrying the first two ORBCOMM satellites, the first ORBIMAGE satellite, called MicroLab, and the first successful launch of the Pegasus XL in March. The entire ORBCOMM global mobile data communications network was tested and Teleglobe Mobile invested an additional $75 million in the project. The company employee base grew to 2,700 and revenues were at $364 million, a jump of 21 percent over 1994.

In 1996, following a 1995 failure, the Pegasus program returned to flight with four consecutive, near-perfect Pegasus XL launches, including NASA's Total Ozone Mapping Sensor (TOMS) mission, for which Orbital's Pomona facility supplied the space sensor payload.

Orbital was selected by NASA for a $60 million contract to build the X-34 hypersonic vehicle. The project would test key technologies leading to reusable launch vehicles, the industry's next step to making space less costly and more easily accessible. Magellan sold a record 300,000 GPS navigation units through over 10,000 U.S. retail outlets and in 80 countries worldwide.

In February, ORBCOMM initiated the world's first commercial service for global mobile data communications provided by low-Earth orbit satellites. ORBCOMM also raised an additional $170 million. The satellite mobile telephones the company marketed quickly became one of the top-selling products used with the existing INMARSAT geosynchronous satellite system.

In 1996, the company completed 82 space missions spanning some seven years of operations. The management was strengthened with the addition of former U.S. Air President and COO Frank Salizzoni and Janice Obuchowski, a former Administrator of the National Telecommunications and Information Agency. For the first time, Orbital's total backlog of contract orders and options exceeded $2 billion and overall revenue increased to $461 million, a 27 percent increase from 1995.

As the company looked to the future, it planned to continue to strive for a 100 percent launch success rate on its Pegasus and Taurus missions, stay on schedule for the planned deployment of more ORBCOMM satellites and future ORBIMAGE spacecraft, broaden Magellan's market presence with new products, and continue to grow at 20–25 percent in revenues per year. As the world's only start-to-finish commercial space mission company, Orbital remained securely positioned to continue to dominate the market and experience incredible growth.

Principal Subsidiaries

Orbital Communications Corporation; ORBCOMM Development Partners L.P. (50%); Orbital Imaging Corporation.

Further Reading

Abrams, Doug, "Orbital Seeks O.K. to Send up 20 Small Satellites," *Washington Business Journal,* March 26, 1990, p. 14.
——, "Star Wars Showers Contracts on 2 Area Firms," *Washington Business Journal,* August 10, 1992, p. 3.
Anselmo, Joseph C., "NASA Gives Orbital Second Shot at X-34," *Aviation Week & Space Technology,* June 17, 1996, p. 31.
——, "Ocean-Monitoring Satellite Generates First Images," *Aviation Week & Space Technology,* October 20, 1997, p. 83.
——, "Pegasus XL Launches from the Canary Islands," *Aviation Week & Space Technology,* April 28, 1997, p. 67.
Asker, James R., "ORBCOMM Satellites to Use Unique Disk Shape," *Aviation Week & Space Technology,* September 27, 1993, p. 49.
——, "Orbital Sciences Becomes First Commercial Space Firm to Go Public," *Aviation Week & Space Technology,* April 30, 1990, p. 27.
"Boon for Baby Birds," *U.S. News & World Report,* June 13, 1988, p. 10.
Brokaw, Leslie, "Rocket Man," *Inc.,* March 1990, p. 25.
Carey, John, "A Small Step for Man—A Tiny One for Industry," *Business Week,* August 12, 1991, p. 46.
Greer, Jim, "Rocket Man: Space Booster Going into Orbit," *Houston Business Journal,* March 25, 1991, p. 1.
Kulman, Linda, "The Final Frontier," *U.S. News & World Report,* May 5, 1997, p. 16.
"Lagardere to Sell Fairchild to Orbital for Cash and Stock," *Wall Street Journal, Europe,* June 2, 1994, p. 4.
Mack, Toni, "Pies in the Sky: How Three Recent B-School Graduates Plan to Push $50 Million of Investors' Cash into Heavenly Orbit," *Forbes,* March 26, 1984, p. 41.
Marcial, Gene G., "Orbital Isn't Lost in Space," *Business Week,* November 7, 1994, p. 130.
Olgeirson, Ian, "Space Race Heats Up in the Suburbs," *Denver Business Journal,* July 18, 1997, p. 3A.
"Orbital Sciences Corp.," *Wall Street Journal,* August 6, 1997, p. B4(W)/C15(E).
"Spacecraft Sports 'Out-of-This-World' Composite," *Design News,* September 8, 1997, p.48.

—Daryl F. Mallett

PaineWebber Group Inc.

The PaineWebber Building
1285 Avenue of the Americas
New York, New York 10019-6028
U.S.A.
(212) 713-2000
Fax: (212) 713-4889
Web site: http://www.painewebber.com

Public Company
Incorporated: 1970 as Paine, Webber, Jackson & Curtis Inc.
Employees: 16,000
Total Assets: $52.51 billion (1996)
Stock Exchanges: New York Pacific
SICs: 6159 Miscellaneous Business Credit Institutions; 6211 Security Brokers, Dealers & Flotation Companies; 6282 Investment Advice; 6311 Life Insurance; 6719 Offices of Holding Companies, Not Elsewhere Classified; 6722 Management Investment Companies, Open-End; 6726 Unit Investment Trusts, Face-Amount Certificate Offices, Closed-End Management Investment Offices; 6799 Investors, Not Elsewhere Classified

PaineWebber Group Inc. is one of the largest full-service securities and commodities companies in the industry, offering asset management, investment banking, brokerage activities, and other related services to both institutional and individual investors. PaineWebber runs the country's fourth largest brokerage, although it lags far behind the top three industry giants, Merrill Lynch & Co., Solomon Smith Barney Inc., and Morgan Stanley, Dean Witter, Discover & Co. Nevertheless, from a tiny partnership founded more than 115 years ago, PaineWebber has grown into a major international presence.

Early History

Paine & Webber was founded in 1880 by William A. Paine and Wallace Webber, formerly clerks at Boston's Blackstone National Bank, who set up shop on Congress Street in Boston. The next year, Webber acquired a seat on the Boston Stock Exchange. The firm admitted Charles Paine as a partner in 1881 and changed its name to PaineWebber & Company.

From there, PaineWebber embarked on a steady course of expansion that would last well into the next century. In 1890 the firm joined the New York Stock Exchange. It purchased seats on the Chicago Board of Trade in 1909 and the Chicago Stock Exchange in 1916. PaineWebber opened its first branch office in 1899 in the copper mining town of Houghton, Michigan. Nine branches sprang into existence during World War I, including PaineWebber's first in New York City in 1916. Before this office opened, business in New York had been conducted by wire and through New York brokerage houses. During the feverish years of the late 1920s, five more offices opened and six moved to larger quarters. By its 50th anniversary, in 1930, the firm could boast of 25 branch offices in 22 cities spread throughout the northeast and upper midwest and a position as one of the largest firms on Wall Street.

But the bull market that had fueled this growth came to a shattering end in October 1929, and the Great Depression that followed brought lean times to the brokerage industry. PaineWebber maintained its standing as a leading Wall Street firm, but did not emerge from the Depression unscathed. By the late 1930s, its presence had shrunk to 19 cities. Not only did the Depression mark the end of PaineWebber's steady growth, but it had to face this period of crisis without the guidance of its founders. Wallace Webber had retired in 1894, and William A. Paine, who had continued to head the firm, died in September 1929.

Paine's son Stephen was a partner in the firm by this time, but it was through him that PaineWebber found itself embroiled in one of the major securities fraud cases of the decade. In the Continental Securities Corporation scandal of 1938–1939, a group of American and Canadian financiers gained control of six different investment trusts, sold off their portfolios, and filled them up again with unmarketable securities of dubious value, including shares in dummy companies owned by the conspirators themselves. Creditors of these trusts found themselves defrauded of more than $6 million. PaineWebber, through Stephen Paine, loaned the money used in four of the

Company Perspectives:

PaineWebber is an independent, full-service national securities firm with a leadership position in individual and institutional businesses and a reputation for outstanding research and quality client service.

The firm serves the investment needs of more than two million clients worldwide, including individuals, institutions, corporations, state and local governments, and public agencies with a broad array of products and services.

Leveraging diverse capabilities to create new opportunities for the firm and its clients in today's dynamic investment environment, PaineWebber is a powerful force in financial markets domestically and abroad. With distribution strength and sufficient capital to compete, a strong management team and 16,000 dedicated employees, the firm's strategic focus is to continue to build upon our position as a recognized leader in financial services.

takeovers and sold off the portfolios for the conspirators. The firm itself was ultimately cleared of all wrongdoing and ended its role in the case with damage payments to some of the creditors. But the New York Stock Exchange suspended Stephen Paine and Frank Hope, a fellow partner and former governor of the New York Stock Exchange, for ignoring evidence of the fraudulent nature of these transactions. Paine was also convicted in federal court of mail fraud and served four months in prison.

World War II finally ended America's economic slump, and in 1942 PaineWebber merged with Jackson & Curtis, a fellow old-line Boston house. The resulting conglomeration of Paine, Webber, Jackson & Curtis listed 23 branch offices. For two decades after the merger, PaineWebber remained essentially the same kind of establishment it had been for the first 60 years of its existence: a privately-owned brokerage house that made most of its money in the retail trade, buying and selling securities for private customers. Although it had long been one of the largest firms on Wall Street, it was still tiny by the standards of the late 20th century.

James W. Davant Era, 1964–80

In the late 1960s and the 1970s, lower stock market volume combined with two important legislative changes to radically alter the brokerage industry. The first of these, the Employee Retirement Income Security Act of 1974, increased the importance of institutional investors as a revenue source. The second, the abolition of the brokers' fixed-rate commission structure in May 1975, slashed profit margins by allowing fierce price competition among houses. Together, these factors forced brokerage houses to merge and expand to increase their working capital and compensate for reduced profit margins. Conservative companies whose mainstay had always been the retail trade were forced to enter new markets. PaineWebber, although it was often slow to innovate and continued to rely heavily on retail sales, was caught up just like its competitors in the changes in the brokerage industry during these years.

Much of this change broke upon the firm during the watch of a single CEO, James W. Davant. When Davant assumed the post in 1964, PaineWebber had fewer than 40 branch offices, annual revenues of $30 million, and $1 million in capital. When he retired in 1980, PaineWebber's 229 branches earned revenues of $900 million and capital had reached $240 million.

As if to usher in this new era of change and expansion, PaineWebber moved its headquarters in 1963 from genteel Boston to New York City. In 1967 it made the first acquisition in its history. An industrywide trend had developed in which large, New York-based houses were acquiring regional securities firms to increase their presence nationwide, and PaineWebber joined it by buying the brokerage house of Barret Fitch North, based in Kansas City, Missouri. The acquisition also marked a break from the northeast/upper midwest area of operation to which PaineWebber had confined itself since the turn of the century.

In 1970 PaineWebber moved into the mid-Atlantic region by acquiring the principal offices of the securities firm Abbott, Proctor & Paine, based in Richmond, Virginia. It also conducted unsuccessful merger talks with Dean Witter & Company, the first of several efforts on its part to merge with another major house to form a brokerage juggernaut.

The firm underwent a major reorganization that year, incorporating and changing its name to Paine, Webber, Jackson & Curtis Inc. This decision was taken for the sake of tax benefits and greater operating flexibility. Once again, PaineWebber was joining a trend rather than starting one. In breaking the news of the pending incorporation, the *New York Times* described the company as "one of the last major brokerage-house partnerships." The transformation of the old New York houses from private partnerships to publicly held corporations began as a result of the financial setbacks suffered by the securities industry during 1969 and 1970, when lower stock market volume showed up the fragility of the retail trade and forced companies to search for more dependable sources of capital. PaineWebber finally went public in 1972 when it absorbed Abacus Fund, Inc., an investment company, and paid Abacus stockholders with PaineWebber shares.

The firm took a great leap in 1973 when it opened its first overseas offices, in London and Tokyo. But the other significant events of the remainder of Davant's stewardship have a more familiar ring to them. In 1973 PaineWebber acquired two more firms: F.S. Smithers and Mitchum, Jones & Templeton. The firm underwent another reorganization in 1974, forming a holding company for PaineWebber called PaineWebber Incorporated. Two more proposed mergers with major houses fell through: the first, with Shearson Hammill & Company in 1972, drew a Justice Department antitrust inquiry and would have formed the nation's second largest brokerage house behind Merrill Lynch Pierce Fenner & Smith; the second, with Oppenheimer & Company, fell through in 1976. The company also completed more acquisitions, buying four offices from duPont Walston in 1974 to bolster its retail capacity; acquiring the securities research firm of Mitchell Hutchins, Inc. in 1977; and merging with Blyth Eastman Dillon & Company in 1979.

The merger with Blyth Eastman Dillon nearly proved ruinous, however. PaineWebber, caught up in the intricacies of assimilating the investment banking firm, was blind-sided by the explosion in stock market volume that presaged the bull market of the 1980s. The company's operating systems were overloaded and many customer orders were left unprocessed or even lost. These orders then had to be tracked down manually, at great expense of time and money, and created further order backlogs. Eventually PaineWebber was forced to suspend some of its businesses, including bond and over-the-counter stock trading. For fiscal year 1980, the firm reported a $6.9 million loss on revenues of $896 million in what should have been an exceptional money-making year.

Davant waited until the Blyth Eastman Dillon crisis had simmered down before passing the baton to Donald Marron in May 1980. The two men offered something of a contrast with each other. Davant, described by the *Wall Street Journal* as "courtly" and "low-key," spent virtually all of his adult life with PaineWebber, rising through the ranks to CEO. When asked at the press conference announcing his retirement if he would consider returning to the securities industry, he quoted Oscar Wilde in reply: "To win back my youth . . . there is nothing I wouldn't do—except take exercise, get up early or be a useful member of the community."

Donald Marron Era Began in 1980

Marron, on the other hand, charted a more aggressive and entrepreneurial career on Wall Street. He came to PaineWebber through Mitchell Hutchins, an acquisition he had brought about as president of the smaller firm. He had a reputation as a prodigy and a forceful self-promoter—at the age of 25, he was running D.B. Marron & Company, his own investment banking firm, which merged with Mitchell Hutchins in 1965.

Under Marron, PaineWebber continued to diversify. In 1983 it acquired two strong regional securities companies: Rotan Mosle Financial Corporation, based in the southwest, and First Mid America, headquartered in Nebraska. In 1984 the firm acquired Becker Paribas Futures, a commodity-futures trading firm, to expand its presence in that market and moved into mortgage banking with the purchase of Rouse Real Estate Finance. Also in 1984, a reorganization of the company combined the three subsidiaries, Paine, Webber, Jackson & Curtis; Blyth Eastman Paine Webber; and PaineWebber Mitchell Hutchins, under one name, PaineWebber Incorporated. PaineWebber Group Inc. was established as the parent holding company. In 1985 the company moved its headquarters to 1285 Avenue of the Americas, renamed "The PaineWebber Building." That same year, Marron declared in *Fortune* that he intended to make PaineWebber one of Wall Street's top five investment bankers within four years (it was generally ranked ninth at the time). Pursuing its new goals in investment banking, PaineWebber participated in the leveraged buyouts of National Car Rental in 1986 and Greyhound in 1987 and brokered the purchase of Braniff in 1988 by a group of East Coast investors.

In the wake of the October 1987 stock market crash, most major brokerage houses reported tiny profits or even losses for the fourth quarter of the year. PaineWebber was no exception, citing pretax earnings of $35,000, versus figures in the tens of millions for the previous three quarters. The firm streamlined by selling its commercial paper operations to Citicorp in November 1987 and its venture capital unit to the unit's managers in January 1988. Also in 1987, the company began to move some of its operations to a new, multimillion technology complex in Lincoln Harbor, New Jersey. PaineWebber also moved to bolster its capital, selling an 18 percent equity interest to the Japanese insurance giant Yasuda Mutual Life Insurance Company in November 1987 (the proceeds were earmarked for its merchant banking unit, which had been somewhat belatedly launched in 1986) and acquiring Manufacturers Hanover Investment Corporation in early 1988.

The October 1987 collapse in stock prices frightened away many small investors and few of them returned to the market over the next year. This lack of interest proved damaging to PaineWebber, reliant as it is on its retail operation, which posted a huge loss in 1988. By the following year, however, retail returned to profitability—posting a $100 million turnaround—thanks in large part to an emphasis on noncommission financial instruments, such as certificates of deposit. On the negative side, the funds from Yasuda failed to save the nascent merchant banking operation, which was particularly hurt by one major mistake—its $500 million bridge loan to fund Robert Campeau's buyout of financially troubled Federated Stores. As a result, PaineWebber posted a fourth-quarter 1990 after-tax charge of $71.1 million to increase reserves for merchant banking investments, and Marron decided to pull the plug on merchant banking altogether.

Behind the long bull run of the 1990s, PaineWebber enjoyed relatively steady and healthy growth in the early to mid-1990s, with only the occasional glitch. In 1994 the worst bond market performance since 1932 led to numerous problems industry-wide, including a major negative impact on the derivatives market. Derivatives-related losses in one of PaineWebber's bond mutual funds were so large that the company felt obliged to step in and rescue the fund with a $34 million infusion.

Meanwhile, PaineWebber made its first major acquisition in a decade with the late 1994 purchase of the struggling Kidder, Peabody & Co. from General Electric Co. (GE) for $603 million in common and preferred stock, giving GE a stake in PaineWebber of about 25 percent. The deal increased the number of brokers the firm employed to 6,600 from 5,450 and made PaineWebber the nation's fourth largest brokerage, behind Merrill Lynch & Co., Smith Barney Inc. (which had recently bolstered itself through the acquisition of Shearson), and Dean Witter, Discover & Co. Although the addition of Kidder also increased PaineWebber's strength in the investment banking area, this sector remained a poor cousin to the retail operation. In fact, Joseph J. Grano, Jr., the head of the retail unit since early 1988, became heir apparent to Marron in 1994 when he was named president of PaineWebber Group.

In 1995 and 1996 litigation was resolved that accused PaineWebber of underrepresenting the risk of investments in public proprietary limited partnerships, which were sold by the company in the 1980s and early 1990s. PaineWebber took after-tax charges totaling $292 million in 1995 and 1996 to cover the cost of paying fines and restitution.

With mergers in the financial sector becoming increasingly common in the mid-1990s, PaineWebber was often the object of rumored takeovers. The rumors stemmed in part from the company's perceived weakness in comparison with the big three brokerage firms, which were growing even larger from such mergers as that of Dean Witter and Morgan Stanley Group Inc., which formed Morgan Stanley, Dean Witter, Discover & Co. Also fueling the rumor mill were regulatory changes in the United States, which led to speculation that a commercial bank would find PaineWebber an attractive entrée into the securities industry. This speculation was dampened somewhat by the August 1997 announcement that PaineWebber would buy back six million shares of stock from GE for $219 million, reducing GE's stake to about 23 percent (Yasuda's stake, meanwhile, had fallen to about eight percent by this time). This slightly reduced the power that GE would wield in any takeover battle. In any case, PaineWebber was itself looking for takeover targets; Marron hired an investment bank in summer 1997 to search for an asset management firm, a brokerage, or a small investment bank to acquire. Marron was not worried about the company's size. He told *Business Week* in September 1997: "Size is not the issue. It's momentum—are you growing?" PaineWebber certainly had been growing through most of the 1990s, but it was uncertain whether the company could sustain its momentum since the lengthy bull market itself appeared to be running out of steam.

Principal Subsidiaries

PaineWebber International Inc.; PaineWebber Inc.; PaineWebber International Bank Ltd. (U.K.); PaineWebber International (U.K.) Ltd.; Mitchell Hutchins Asset Management Inc.; Mitchell Hutchins Institutional Investors Inc.; PaineWebber Capital Inc.; Paine Webber Development Corporation; Paine Webber Properties Incorporated; PW Trust Company; Correspondent Services Corporation; PaineWebber Specialists Incorporated; PaineWebber Life Insurance Company.

Further Reading

"Boring, But Making Money," *Economist,* March 17, 1990, p. 78.

Browning, E. S., "PaineWebber May Be Likely Merger Prospect in Wake of Morgan Stanley-Dean Witter Deal," *Wall Street Journal,* February 10, 1997, p. C2.

Carey, Donald, "PaineWebber: Thank You, Yasuda!," *Financial World,* December 27, 1988, p. 12.

Friedman, Jon, "Joe Grano: PaineWebber's Point Man," *Business Week,* May 28, 1990, p. 94.

Jereski, Laura, and Zweig, Jason, "Positioned for the Nineties," *Forbes,* May 13, 1991, pp. 58, 60.

Kerr, Ian, "The Fall of the House of Kidder," *Euromoney,* January 1995, p. 30.

Newport, John Paul, Jr., "Why PaineWebber Is on a Hiring Binge," *Fortune,* September 30, 1985, p. 105.

Paine, Webber & Company: A National Institution, Boston: Paine, Webber & Company, 1930.

Peers, Alexandra, "PaineWebber Plans Streamlining Move, Slates Stock Split," *Wall Street Journal,* February 4, 1994, p. A5B.

Siconolfi, Michael, "PaineWebber Plans Reorganization to Trim Costs by $100 Million a Year," *Wall Street Journal,* September 25, 1995, p. A4.

——, "PaineWebber to Repay Losses in Bond Fund," *Wall Street Journal,* June 8, 1994, pp. A3, A9.

Siconolfi, Michael, and Raghavan, Anita, "PaineWebber's Main Challenge Is Making Kidder Acquisition Work," *Wall Street Journal,* October 18, 1994, pp. C1, C18.

Spiro, Leah Nathans, "PaineWebber: Eat or Be Eaten," *Business Week,* September 8, 1997, p. 122.

——, "Why PaineWebber Got Out of the Kitchen," *Business Week,* March 29, 1993, pp. 76–77.

Spiro, Leah Nathans, and Lesly, Elizabeth, "Joe Grano Could Use a Little Financial Advice," *Business Week,* December 18, 1995, pp. 74–75.

Willis, Gerri, "Tarnished Star's Big Deal: Can Kidder Buy Bolster Slipping PaineWebber?," *Crain's New York Business,* October 24, 1994, pp. 1, 29.

—Douglas Sun
—updated by David E. Salamie

Palomar Medical Technologies, Inc.

60 Cherry Hill Drive
Beverly, Massachusetts 01915
U.S.A.
(508) 921-9300
Fax: (508) 921-5801
Web site: http://www.palmed.com

Public Company
Incorporated: 1991
Employees: 550
Sales: $70.09 million (1996)
Stock Exchanges: NASDAQ
SICs: 3672 Printed Circuit Boards; 3845 Electromedical Apparatus; 6719 Holding Companies, Not Elsewhere Classified

Palomar Medical Technologies, Inc., an international cosmetic laser company, is one of the most promising firms in the United States. The company is one of the leading providers of proprietary laser systems for cosmetic and dermatological laser treatments such as hair removal, age spots, scars, tattoos, leg veins, and skin resurfacing and wrinkle treatment. The company sells its Ruby laser for hair removal, Diode laser for leg vein removal and pediatric tonsillectomy, CO2 laser for wrinkle treatment, and copper vapor laser for tattoo removal. With the aging of the baby boomer generation, Palomar Medical expects to take advantage of an estimated $2.5 billion annual market at the turn of the next century. In fact, the company is already well on its way. Revenues for 1996 totaled $70 million, a phenomenal increase of 220 percent over the previous year's figure of $21 million. Much of the company's success is due to management's ability to arrange strategic partnerships to develop new technologies. One of the most successful of these partnerships is with Massachusetts General Hospital, which has licensed its innovative hair-removal system to Palomar. As the company's revenues continue to increase, management is implementing a strategic plan that includes the acquisition of complementary firms and the expansion of its marketing network into Europe.

Early History

Palomar Medical Technologies, Inc. is a relatively recently formed company that has taken advantage of the burgeoning cosmetic and medical laser system technology. Initially incorporated in 1987 as Dymed Corporation, the firm was established by a group of investors interested in the growing market for high-technology laser applications. At first, the strategy was to arrange partnerships with medical centers or research facilities that worked at the forefront of developing laser systems for medical applications in the fields of cardiology and dermatology. The investment group correctly predicted that all the demographic data, market trends, and forecasts pointed toward the fact that people were willing to pay for services that enabled an individual to improve his or her physical appearance and that cosmetic laser surgery was a more acceptable alternative to the older, more traditional and invasive cosmetic procedures.

Within a few years, the projected market growth was borne out by numerous statistical surveys, one of the most important being a 1992 survey conducted by the American Society of Plastic and Reconstructive Surgeons (ASPRS). The ASPRS survey indicated that most of the cosmetic laser surgery procedures during that year were performed on patients in the 35–50 age range. Patients in the 19–34 age range came in second, and those patients in the 51–64 age range ranked third. Since the largest percentage of the American population was the baby boomers, ranging in age from 27 to 46, the conclusion drawn from the survey was that the baby boomer segment of the population was the age group most inclined to have cosmetic laser surgery. A further demographic breakdown of the survey revealed that approximately 80 percent of the patients undergoing cosmetic laser surgery were women and that those individuals were concerned for the most part with maintaining a youthful appearance; consequently, the removal of facial hair, age spots, and eye and neck wrinkles were high on the list of desired makeovers.

Even though everything seemed to be in place and the market was growing faster than ever, management at the company did not respond quickly enough to consumer demand. Slowly, albeit methodically, the company invested large sums of money into research and development. Unfortunately, the cosmetic laser surgery market was highly competitive, and Dymed Corporation could not find its own niche. As a result, revenues began to decrease as debts mounted, and management was forced to borrow large sums of money to keep the operation afloat.

The Early 1990s

In spite of its potential for growth, the company remained a rather small operation during the early 1990s. Although revenues increased at a steady but slow rate, debt remained high. Realizing the need for a comprehensive change in the way the company conducted its business, management decided to change its name in 1991 to Palomar Medical Technologies, Inc. to portray a more sophisticated and medically-oriented operation. The name change and remaking of the company's image undoubtedly attracted a larger customer base to the services provided by Palomar Medical Technologies.

Yet management at the company was still not able to take advantage of the demographic statistics indicating a billion dollar industry on the horizon. Debt remained high and revenues were sluggish. To compensate for its slow growth, management decided to diversify into the electronics industry. It was thought that manufacturing and marketing electronic products would complement the company's attempt to design and market high-technology laser systems for cosmetic, dermatological, and cardiology purposes. Its first acquisition in this new field was Dynaco Corporation, located in Tempe, Arizona. Dynaco Corporation fabricated flexible circuitry and also assembled flex circuits, cable harnesses, and printed circuit boards. With this purchase, Palomar Medical found itself an electronic contract manufacturer of interconnect packaging products.

Shortly after the acquisition of Dynaco Corporation, management decided to form Dynamem Corporation as a subsidiary to Dynaco. Dynamem was established to manufacture and distribute a patented high-density memory packaging technology for either the network server, workstation, or high-memory motherboard segments of the industry. At approximately the same time, management at Palomar Medical Technologies also decided to form Nexar Technologies, Inc., to develop, manufacture, market, and sell high performance personal computers with rather unique circuit board designs that enabled end-users to upgrade and replace the microprocessor, memory, and hard drive components quickly and easily, without professional assistance. Marketing its system worldwide through resellers, distributors, original equipment manufacturers, independent dealers, and computer superstores, the company targeted those consumers, commercial clients, and government agencies that benefited most from eliminating computer obsolescence. Along with Dynamem and Nexar, management added CD Titles, Inc., a CD ROM publishing company that distributed a wide variety of material and information on CD ROM through personal computer wholesale channels across the United States.

Having made the commitment to enter the electronics industry, management at Palomar Medical Technologies formed Comtel Electronics, Inc. to complement the products and services provided by Dynaco and Dynamem. Comtel Electronics, a manufacturer of surface mounts and through-hole assembly printed circuit boards, flexible circuitry, and thin-core boards, provided the final ingredient to an interconnected group of firms that supplied its products and services to a diversified customer base of original equipment manufacturers in the computer, communications, automotive, industrial, medical instrumentation, and military portions of the electronics industry.

As the electronics subsidiaries of Palomar Medical Technologies grew and provided a stable source of income, management did not ignore its core business, the development of innovative techniques in the field of cosmetic laser treatments. In collaboration with Massachusetts General Hospital, the company was awarded an exclusive licensing arrangement for a highly innovative hair-removal technology. A four-year research agreement was concluded with Wellman Laboratories, the world's largest and most prestigious biomedical laser research facility, to develop and continue investigation on laser-based hair removal methods, providing Palomar Medical Technologies with ready access to the most recent and sophisticated developments in the field. And an agreement was also reached with the New England Medical School, an affiliate of Tufts' School of Medicine, to initiate and conduct clinical trials for a laser-based procedure to remove tonsils painlessly from children.

The Mid-1990s and Beyond

In 1995 Palomar Medical Technologies implemented a far-reaching and comprehensive reorganization strategy to carry them into the next century. One of the first decisions made by management was to form Palomar Electronics Corporation to separate the company's electronics and computer operations from its medical laser segments. After having successfully completed this part of the reorganization by the end of 1996, management then reached the decision to spin off all of the company's electronic and computer operations before the year 2000 and concentrate on the development of its cosmetic laser technology.

In 1995, along with the reorganization of its electronics and computer holdings, management consolidated and expanded its medical laser products and services. During 1995 and 1996, the company acquired Spectrum Medical Technologies, Inc., a firm based in Lexington, Massachusetts that was soon manufacturing Palomar Medical laser systems for hair removal and the RD-1200 ruby laser system for the removal of tattoos and age spots; Tissue Technologies, Inc., the privately held Albuquerque, New Mexico company that developed the Tru-Pulse laser system for skin resurfacing and for the treatment of scars, burns, and wrinkles; and Star Medical Technologies, Inc., a California-based company specializing in the development and manufacture of custom diode laser systems for the treatment of leg veins and unwanted hair and other innovative laser systems for use in the treatment of psoriasis, burn diagnosis, and tonsillectomies.

To offer its cosmetic laser technology directly to the public, one of management's most important moves during this time was to establish a subsidiary known as Cosmetic Technology International, Inc. (CTI). The sole purpose of this new subsidiary was to develop various cosmetic and dermatological centers around the world through partnerships with medical service providers. Within a few months of its founding, in early 1997 CTI signed a letter of intent with the Ambulatory Surgery Division of Columbia/HCA Healthcare Corporation, one of the largest healthcare services providers in the United States. A $20 billion firm that owns and operates more than 350 hospitals, 150 patient surgery centers, and 550 home health care locations in 37 states, Columbia/HCA Healthcare had also established a network of operations in Switzerland and the United Kingdom. Under terms of the agreement, the two companies will develop cosmetic ''Centers of Operational Excellence'' to offer a full-line laser technology and medical devices and services. CTI will provide the equipment, operational support, service, education, and training, and Columbia/HCA will provide the facility space, clinical personnel, and administrative services at those ambulatory surgery centers where Palomar Medical's cosmetic laser surgery procedures are most appropriate. The first three centers of this collaboration opened during the summer of 1997 in Denver, Colorado.

In March 1997, Palomar Medical Technologies received the stamp of approval from the U.S. Food and Drug Administration to market and sell its Epilaser system for removing body hair. Only the second such laser system cleared for cosmetic hair removal in the United States, Palomar's product will compete with the laser system developed by Thermolase Corporation, located in San Diego, California. Both laser systems were seen by industry analysts as a welcome alternative to the painful process of electrolysis that many women undergo to remove facial and bikini-line hair. Palomar immediately began manufacturing approximately 50 Epilaser systems per month and sold them for $120,000 apiece. Management at Palomar Medical estimated the new laser system would bring in $50 million worth of revenues in less than one year and enable the company to take advantage of the growing cosmetic hair-removal market.

In fact, revenues at Palomar Medical Technologies skyrocketed during the mid-1990s, from a mere $470,000 in fiscal 1993, to $21 million in fiscal 1995 and more than $70 million in fiscal 1996. Much of this increase in revenues can be attributed to a management team that is more focused on the development of its core business, namely, cosmetic laser technology, and the ability of the company to take advantage of the burgeoning consumer demand for cosmetic laser services and treatments. Palomar Medical has also benefited from the experience of Louis P. Valente, the company's president and chief executive hired in May 1997. Valente, the former senior vice-president at EG&G, a Fortune 500 company, provides Palomar Medical with the managerial stability and financial expertise needed for the company to develop into one of the premier firms in the cosmetic laser services and treatment industry.

Principal Subsidiaries

Spectrum Medical Technologies, Inc.; Spectrum Financial Services LLC; Dermascan, Inc.; Tissue Technologies, Inc.; Star Medical Technologies, Inc.; Cosmetic Technology International, Inc.; Palomar Electronics Corporation; Nexar Technologies, Inc.; Dynaco Inc.; Palomar Technologies, Ltd. (England); Dynamen, Inc.; Comtel Electronics, Inc.

Further Reading

''Breach of Contract Case Is Settled for $1.9 Million,'' *Wall Street Journal,* August 19, 1997, p. B8(E).

Bulkeley, William, M., ''Palomar Laser Hair-Removal System Cleared,'' *Wall Street Journal,* March 11, 1997, p. B10(E).

Marcial, Gene G., ''More Zip from Zapping Hair,'' *Business Week,* March 4, 1996, p. 94.

''The 100 Fastest Growing Small Public Companies,'' *Inc.,* May 1996, pp. 60–61.

''Palomar Medical Names Valente CEO, President,'' *Dow Jones News Service, Reprint,* May 16, 1997.

''Palomar Medical Technologies, Inc.,'' *Boston Herald,* January 30, 1997, p. 16.

Rosenberg, Ronald, ''FDA Allows Use of Palomar Laser for Hair Removal,'' *The Boston Globe,* March 12, 1997, p. 26.

—Thomas Derdak

Paris Corporation

122 Kissel Road
Burlington, New Jersey 08016
U.S.A.
(609) 387-7300
Fax: (609) 387-2114
Web site: http://www.pariscorp.com

Public Company
Incorporated: 1964 as Paris Business Forms, Inc.
Employees: 190
Sales: $57.4 million (1996)
Stock Exchanges: NASDAQ
SICs: 2678 Stationery, Tablets & Related Products; 2761 Manifold Business Forms; 2771 Greeting Cards; 5044 Office Equipment; 5045 Computers & Computer Peripheral Equipment & Software; 6719 Offices of Holding Companies, Not Elsewhere Classified

Paris Corporation is a holding company with, in 1997, two operating companies of its main subsidiary manufacturing business forms, including computer paper and cut-sheet products. Another line, including business cards, greeting cards, and stationery, is targeted to the small-office and home-office user. Paris markets these products, plus software and other document-management solutions, to a variety of wholesalers and retailers. Formed in 1992, a joint venture with Xerox Corp. was distributing office supplies under the Xerox name to food and drugstore retailers and wholesalers. Paris did very well during the 1980s but has found the 1990s to be a much more difficult business environment as its core products have lost demand because of changes in printing technology.

Paris Business Forms in the 1980s

The company was incorporated as Paris Business Forms in 1964. Dominic P. Toscani, a lawyer, became its president in 1972. Under Toscani, Paris Business Forms became very much a family enterprise. In 1982 his wife, Nancy, was the company's secretary, Dominic P. Toscani, Jr., was operations manager, and another son, Gerard, was sales and marketing manager. The company had net income of $34,000 that fiscal year (the year ended September 30, 1982) on net sales of $10.5 million and had a long-term debt of $4 million. As the nation emerged from the severe recession of the early 1980s, the company's fortunes began to rise. Paris Business Forms had net income of $1.4 million on net sales of $22.5 million in fiscal 1985 and net income of $2.4 million on net sales of $26.9 million in fiscal 1986. The long-term debt had fallen to $657,000 in 1985 and was only $695,000 in fiscal 1986.

In 1986 Paris Business Forms was producing continuous sheets of forms of standard size and uniform format, continuous computer forms customized to meet the specific needs of the end user, and customized (individual) forms. The continuous sheets and forms accounted for 72 percent of the company's sales that year. Typically, these were used for computer-generated reports and documents, including checks, invoices, purchase orders, and airline tickets.

Paris Business Forms bought the paper and produced the forms at a company-owned plant in Burlington, New Jersey, where it also maintained its headquarters. It was marketing its products through about 800 independent distributors, mainly on the East Coast, and to agencies of the federal government, which accounted for 13 percent of sales that year. Other end users included brokers, banks, insurance companies, and hospitals. The firm had three salesmen to call on distributors and four trucks and a delivery van to deliver its products in New York and Pennsylvania.

Paris Business Forms was leasing a sales office and distribution center in Orlando, Florida, in 1986, and it sold a warehouse in Croydon, Pennsylvania that year. In March 1986 the company went public, securing net proceeds of $4 million by selling nearly one-fifth of the outstanding shares of common stock at $7.50 a share. Following the public offering, Toscani—president, chairman, and treasurer—and Frank A. Mattei, a Philadelphia orthopedic surgeon who became a director the following year, each owned about one-third of the stock. Another seven percent was owned by the Caritas Foundation, a nonprofit institution founded by Toscani and administered by his brother, a priest.

Paris Business Forms continued to grow rapidly in the ensuing years, serving about 1,100 distributors in 1987 and about 1,500 in 1988. A warehouse was added to the Burlington property in 1988. By the end of fiscal 1989 Paris was selling to about 1,700 distributors. Net sales that year reached $48.7 million, even though the federal government no longer was a significant customer. Net income came to $2.9 million, and the long-term debt also was $2.9 million. The company began distributing cash dividends to its stockholders in 1988. It was listed on *Forbes'* annual list of the 100 top small businesses in 1989.

In 1987 Paris Business Forms opened a division to sell turnkey, nonfranchised units of a quick-print and desktop-publishing operation known as Fast Forms Plus. At the end of fiscal 1988 there were 13 of these outlets, of which the company owned three—in Burlington; Marlton, New Jersey; and Clearwater, Florida. There were 19 by the end of the following year, of which the company owned units in Burlington and Tampa, Florida. By 1991, however, the firm no longer was engaged in this line of business.

Changes and Challenges of the 1990s

By the end of fiscal 1991 Paris Business Forms was a $60-million-a-year business, serving some 2,300 distributors, some of which were in the south, southwest, and midwest, as well as along the eastern seaboard. The Burlington facility had been expanded and was now divided into separate plants for stock and customized forms. A custom forms plant was leased in Fort Worth, Texas in 1990, and the company also acquired a separate Fort Worth building the same year to produce stock computer paper for sale to customers in the Midwest, Southwest, and Mexico. The firm also had added self-mailers to its product line and was beginning to sell directly to retailers, such as Office Depot, Inc., which took about one-third of its stock computer paper in 1993.

Despite its added volume, the net income of Paris Business Forms slipped to $460,000 in fiscal 1991, compared with $2.4 million the previous year, and the company discontinued its dividend. In fiscal 1992 profit improved only slightly, to $712,000, on sales of $61.8 million. Paris was beginning to experience severe competition from printing companies selling forms directly to retailers and also from a general loss of business as many firms began producing their own business forms. In addition, the company was slow to switch to forms accommodated by the laser and ink-jet printers that were replacing dot-matrix and high-speed impact ones. In fiscal 1993 sales volume dipped to $50.2 million, and the firm lost $998,000. Company stock traded for as low as $1.62 a share that year.

Paris Business Forms made some important changes in the early 1990s. It bought a Jacksonville, Florida plant in 1992 for $1.3 million (counting improvements made) to print stock computer paper. The company sold this plant, however, in 1995 for only $1.05 million. It closed the Fort Worth plant it owned in 1993 and sold it in 1994, replacing it with a leased facility, also in Fort Worth. (The Fort Worth plant it leased had been vacated in 1993.) In December 1992 Paris invested $333,000 in a development-stage joint venture with Xerox Corp. to produce and market office products under the Xerox name.

In fiscal 1994 Paris Business Forms returned to the black but earned only $429,000 on sales of $57.9 million. The following year was much better, however; the company had net income of $3.5 million on net sales of $64.9 million. Rising prices for its products accounted for the hike in revenues, despite a 30 percent drop in volume for computer-paper forms, in part because of paper shortages. Fiscal 1996, however, was the company's worst year yet. Net sales dropped to $57.4 million, and the company incurred a net loss of $3.4 million. In its annual report, Toscani said paper prices had started to decline while the company was caught with a large amount of high-priced inventory. He also cited an ongoing decline in demand for continuous-forms paper products.

Paris Business Forms continued to make major changes in its operations during this period. In fiscal 1995 it became a holding company, transferring substantially all of its operating assets and liabilities to Paris Business Products, Inc., a newly formed subsidiary. The holding company, which became Paris Corporation in January 1996, retained the Burlington plant and cash and near-cash investments. The new subsidiary had a Texas operating corporation, Paris Business Forms, Inc., and a newly formed Florida corporation, Paris Business Products, Inc., as its own subsidiaries. PBF Corp., a Delaware corporation, was a subsidiary that owned the parent company's trademarks.

Signature Corporation, the joint venture with Xerox to distribute office products to the food and drugstore markets, began shipping products in July 1993 and quickly proved a success. Sales doubled in both 1995 and 1996, with the number of stores served increasing from 550 to 6,800—about 13 percent of the total number of food and drugstore outlets in the United States. Paris Corporation held a 44 percent share in this corporation. The Xerox product line consisted of consumables such as binders, indexes, file folders, fax paper, and writing pads; organizers, made from a see-through material, that were designed for document storage; and a ten-item line of papers for desktop laser and ink-jet printer use.

By 1996 Paris Corporation also had introduced Burlington, a retail line specifically targeted to the small-office and home-office markets. Paris's retail line of products was designed to capitalize on ink-jet and laser printer capabilities with offerings such as business cards, greeting cards, and stationery for these small-office and home-office needs. Also a new line was Documents Now, a software package distributors could use to produce short-run custom checks for end users. The distributors also could choose to sell the software, toner, and check stock to customers. Paris was helping distributors lease laser printers as part of the package. Other software modules were being added for production of software-compatible forms, gift certificates, and other documents. The company's on-demand software was being tested by major quick printers, a new market for Paris.

During 1995–96 Paris also introduced a sheet-fed document scanner sold primarily through wholesale clubs, national retailers, and computer stores. "Imaging is becoming a bigger part of [forms management]," Tom Baglio, vice-president of sales and management, told *Form,* a trade magazine. "Our product allows smaller businesses and the people within bigger corporate businesses such as secretaries and administrative assistants to scan in and file [documents] on their PC.'' The company was expanding its product line to include other models. In recent years, said Baglio, senior managers had been brought in to build a new network of suppliers, including overseas manufacturers of its scanners. The firm also contracted with major computer companies to buy old circuit boards, which were recycled into the office products sold through Signature.

Paris Corporation in 1996–97

During fiscal 1996 Paris Corporation's Burlington and Fort Worth plants still produced continuous forms designed to run on dot-matrix and high-speed impact printers, but it was changing its focus to the development and sale of value-added and custom-cut sheet products used on laser and ink-jet printers. Prefed, punched, lined cut sheets, high-quality printing cuts, collated sets, colored cuts, and novelty-cut products had recently been introduced. By 1997 all production was to be allocated to cut-sheet products, as compared with 40 percent in fiscal 1996.

Paris Corporation was marketing not only these products of its own manufacture but also paper-handling products for small offices and home offices, computer-based printers and scanners, office products, and on-demand software through retail superstores and about 2,500 independent dealers in the United States and Canada. Office Depot, Inc. accounted for more than 24 percent of the company's stock computer-paper shipments in fiscal 1996.

Paris had entered into a distribution agreement with Seiko Instruments, Inc. to sell a label printer product through selected markets in the United States. It contracted with Microtek, Inc. to private-label manufacture a scanner product with optical-recognition software capability, and with another Taiwanese company, Asco Products, Inc., to provide a variety of products, such as a private-label paper folder. Paris also was working closely with Touch-It Corp., a producer of heat-sensitive envelopes, folders, and note pads that change color when touched, and Compu-Notes, Inc., a producer of clipboards, binders, and address books made from recycled circuit boards. The company maintained more than 20 warehouse shipping points throughout the United States.

Through midyear, Paris Corporation was faring poorly in 1997. After nine months of the fiscal year, net sales had fallen nine percent from the same period in 1996, to $40.2 million. The loss in revenue was attributed to decreased average selling prices for continuous stock forms. The company's net loss, however, had decreased 27 percent, to $1.6 million. The lower loss reflected improved gross margins due to greater labor efficiencies and capacity utilization and also to a reduced need for investment in new-product marketing and research and development.

In November 1996 Mattei owned or controlled 34 percent of the company's stock. Toscani and his wife owned or controlled 27.9 percent; the Caritas Foundation, 9.7 percent; and FMR Corp., 6.4 percent. The company had no long-term debt.

Principal Subsidiaries

Paris Business Forms, Inc.; Paris Business Products, Inc.; PBF Corporation.

Further Reading

''Companies of the '90s,'' *Focus,* January 3, 1990, p. 70.
''New Directions,'' *Form,* January 1997, p. 48.

—Robert Halasz

Park Corp.

6200 Riverside Drive
Cleveland, Ohio 44135
U.S.A.
(216) 267-4870
Fax: (216) 267-7876

Private Company
Incorporated: 1948
Employees: 11,000
Sales: $2.6 billion (1997 est.)
SICs: 7011 Hotels & Motels; 3312 Blast Furnaces & Steel Mills; 6531 Real Estate Agents & Managers; 6552 Subdividers & Developers, Not Elsewhere Classified; 5051 Metals Service Centers & Offices

Founded by Raymond P. Park, Park Corp. represents a multibillion-dollar collection of a wide range of businesses; Park built his corporate empire by acquiring assets other companies no longer wanted. Sometimes referred to as a recycler of industrial junk, Park Corp. has been involved in a diverse spectrum of business ventures, including copper mining in Arizona, road-building in Costa Rica, steel production in Pennsylvania, and real estate development in Ohio and elsewhere. The length of stay in these businesses was sometimes fleeting, while other business forays were long-term, depending on the irrefutable sagacity of the company's director, Ray Park. Park spent his lifetime buying what others no longer wanted and either liquidated the assets or renovated the entire acquisition. With spectacular frequency, Park realized handsome profits from his myriad deals, enough to create a $2.6 billion business whose foundation rested on the companies, plants, and equipment that dulled the interest of nearly everyone else.

Founder's Background

When he was a teenager, Ray Park learned how to determine the difference between quality lumber and low-grade lumber. The instruction came from his father, who undoubtedly intended for his son to develop an eye for choice lumber in order to steer clear of inferior grades. The teenage Park, however, used the lesson for its opposite purpose. He became adept at selecting what no one else wanted, a master at purchasing whatever had been abandoned, discarded, and forsaken. With this twisted perspective that ran counter to his father's simple lesson, Park built a massive corporate empire whose size and might testified to the potency of Park's philosophy.

Park was raised next to the Columbia River in a small town called White Salmon, 50 miles up the river from Portland, Oregon, and across the border into neighboring Washington State. His father, James Park, taught at a teacher's college and graded wood for lumber companies on weekends and during the summer. After high school, Ray Park began attending Northwestern School of Business in Portland, where he took classes in foundry and machine-tooling, but quit after his freshman year to play the trumpet in local swing bands. His dreams of developing into a professional musician never turned into reality, however. After the outbreak of World War II, Park put his trumpet in a closet and put on an Army Air Corps uniform, the clothes he would wear during a brief stateside tour. At the end of the war, Park returned to the Pacific Northwest, arriving in 1945. It was time to use the knowledge about grading lumber that he learned from his father and to begin his unique entrepreneurial career.

Park Sets Out with $1,000 in 1945

When he returned to the Pacific Northwest, Park had only $1,000 in his pockets, not enough to fund any great business undertaking. He was forced to do what he could with his meager resources, and chose to do something that smacked of deceit. Park bought as much low-grade lumber as he could afford, then set aside the worst of the worst, and sold the balance as high-grade lumber. Park's approach was probably not what his father had in mind when he was teaching him how to tell good lumber from bad, but the practice of finding the best out of the worst was an inexpensive way to raise capital, and a strategy, with a little variation, that Park would use to become a billionaire.

By 1951, Park had sold enough lumber to start his own lumber remanufacturing plant in Eureka, California. With this business, Park recorded sufficient success to accumulate the cash he would need to complete a pivotal, career-defining transaction seven years later. In 1958, a run-down mill owned by Georgia-Pacific Corp. was up for sale, and there were no immediate takers. No one wanted the decrepit mill, but Park paid $50,000 for the facility and learned a valuable lesson that could be repeated again and again in the business world. Park renovated the mill, leased it out, and made a quick profit on his investment. With this deal, Park became aware of the profits that could be made by buying what no one else wanted and either liquidating the physical assets for piecemeal sale or sprucing up the entire acquisition for resale at a higher price than the original investment. This was the strategy that underpinned Park's business moves in the decades to come, enabling him to earn hundreds of millions of dollars by collecting what he referred to as a ''variety of junk.''

Park set out on this course in earnest in 1965. He exited the lumber business and began searching for companies and facilities that others would describe as ''tired'' and ''worn down.'' He planned to either rejuvenate or liquidate whatever acquisitions he selected, and he found that a majority of the candidates that met his criteria were located in the Rust Belt. Consequently, Park moved his family to Charleston, West Virginia, in 1969 to get closer to his homely objects of desire. For a brief time, the Park family lived in a five-bedroom apartment above an old battleship gun plant Park had purchased. The Park family's proximity to one of Park's ''tired and worn down'' acquisitions was symbolic of the relationship between Park's children and Park's business. Park Corp., at an early stage, was a family-run business, an enterprise in which all members of the Park family joined in and helped build. Park's oldest son, Daniel, and later his sons Patrick and Kelly, joined Park in his search to find acquisition candidates. They traveled along with Park in his twin-engine Beechcraft and flew from one Midwestern city to another, appraising old steel mills, stamping plants, machine shops, and virtually anything else that was for sale. Said Patrick Park, ''Growing up, we swept out plants, drove lift trucks, put up siding, and poured concrete floors. If you didn't get your hands dirty, you couldn't know what was going on.''

Key Acquisitions in the 1970s and 1980s

The number of acquisitions completed by Park during his first few years after moving to Charleston were numerous and, according to Park, profitable without exception. The Charleston Ordnance Center he purchased from FMC Corp. in 1971 was obtained for $4.5 million. After this initial investment, Park renovated the massive facility, which sprawled over the equivalent of 34 city blocks, and leased it out to various new tenants. He bought another Georgia Pacific plant and converted it into a shopping center. He acquired an obsolete plant owned by the Ohio Steel Company, renovated it, and sold it three years later for a 100 percent gain on his investment. In 1972 alone, Park acquired eight plants from companies such as Gulf & Western and Wean United and either liquidated the assets piecemeal or renovated the entire plant for sale to another party. By 1973, Park had built his company into a $12 million business, and the intensity of his acquisitive activities did not slacken in the years ahead. Park was an empire builder. In the coming decades Park's business would develop into an enterprise that flirted with the $3 billion-in-sales mark.

As Park continued to acquire properties and either renovate or liquidate them, he occasionally strayed from his approach and assumed the traditional role of an acquirer by running the business as it had been by the seller. Such was the case with Park's 1983 acquisition of the bankrupt Mesta Machine Co. in Homestead, Pennsylvania. Park paid $9 million for the company, which at one time had built enormous presses and rolls for steel mills worldwide. As was usual, Park took a stroll through his newly acquired facility to determine which pieces of equipment he could sell. During his tour he was approached by a Mesta bookkeeper who asked Park what he wanted to do with several purchase orders. Park looked at the equipment and decided to turn everything on and fulfill the purchase orders. After those orders were completed, Park kept the machines running and continued to operate Mesta. This was the first building block in an arm of the Park enterprise that grew robustly in the coming years. During the next decade-and-a-half, Park acquired seven additional divisions from steelmakers around the Midwest and grouped them together with the former Mesta company to form West Homestead Engineering and Machine Co., or Whemco as it more commonly became known.

Other deals were done in a manner more typical of Park's business approach. One of the biggest transactions during the 1980s was Park's foray into the mining business. In 1986, the price of copper fell to 60 cents a pound, dropping to a point that prompted more than a few mining concerns to reevaluate the profitability of copper mining. One such company was Anaconda Minerals, which decided to get rid of its copper mines in Missoula, Montana, and Green Valley, Arizona. Park moved in and acquired the 12,000-acre Arizona mine for $12 million. Six months after Park had acquired the mine, the price of copper more than doubled, reaching $1.40 a pound, and Park quickly leased it to another mining company, Cyprus Minerals, for a 15-year lease. Within six months, Park recouped his original investment and everything after that was profit.

Deal-Making in the 1990s

Heading into the 1990s, Park was in his mid-60s and still continuing to mastermind acquisitions that a short time later would pay big dividends. In 1990, Park acquired the assets of Teledyne Ohio Steel, a Lima, Ohio-based mill roll maker. The deal included real estate and building and all other physical assets situated on the 71-acre facility, including machinery and support equipment used in the production of iron, forged, and spin-cast rolls for the steel industry. Teledyne subsequently became one of the components composing Whemco.

Three years after the Teledyne deal was completed, Park entered into a business deal whose financial magnitude eclipsed all the Park-orchestrated deals before it. Again, the deal was an example of Park obtaining what another company no longer wanted. In 1994, General Motors decided to divest some of the plants it used to manufacture components for its vehicles. General Motors had decided to get rid of the plants because they were in need of repair and the company did not want to pay for any major capital improvements. It was a classic situation for Park to step into and he did, acquiring axle plants for roughly $100 million. The resulting venture was named American Axle & Manufacturing, which, after two experts in efficiency were brought in, developed into a $2.2 billion-in-sales business.

By 1997, American Axle & Manufacturing was the largest privately-owned supplier of auto parts in North America, producing all of General Motors' axles for its line of pickups, Chevy Tahoe, Yukon, and Suburban sport utility vehicles. At this point Park decided to cash in on his investment of $100 million. In 1997 he sold his 86 percent stake in the axle manufacturer to the New York-based Blackstone Group, realizing an estimated $600 million on the deal.

There were two major developments occupying Park Corp.'s attention at the time Park was finalizing his deal with Blackstone Group. The smaller of the two projects was the company's construction of a $25 million hotel at the International Exposition and Trade Center at Cleveland's Hopkin's Airport. The convention center, known as the I-X, measured 2.5 million square feet and ranked as the largest privately-owned convention center in the United States. Its owner, not surprisingly, was Ray Park, whose offices were secreted away in the massive sprawl of the I-X. Park, through a subsidiary of Park Corp. called I-X Corp., was building an all-suites hotel as an addition to the I-X, complete with a ballroom, two restaurants, and a fitness center. Scheduled to open in late 1998, the luxury hotel was supposed to increase business at the I-X and give Park one more powerful revenue-generating asset.

The other development project was decidedly more ambitious, a $215 million undertaking headed by Park's youngest child, Kelly Park. The roots of the development project stretched back to 1988, when Park acquired 300 acres near the company's Whemco headquarters in Homestead, Pennsylvania. On the plot purchased by Park stood the shuttered Homestead works where Andrew Carnegie and Henry Frick consolidated their power in the steel industry during the 1880s. The site contained an enormous amount of old, dilapidated equipment, so much so that it took Park eight years to cart away 900,000 tons of scrap and more than one million tons of concrete from the 10 million square feet of building space. By 1996, the site was ready for development, and under Kelly Park's supervision, a 300-acre mixed-use development was underway. Expected to house residential dwellings, retail space, office space, a movie theater, parks, restaurants, and health care facilities, the first stage of the project was scheduled to open in the spring of 1998. Expectations ran high for the success of the project once it was completed because the site was eight minutes from downtown Pittsburgh, whereas all other shopping malls and multiplex cinemas were in suburban Pittsburgh, 25 minutes away from the downtown area.

As the I-X hotel and the Homestead projects were underway, Park Corp. was planning for the future. The next generation of the Park family was firmly in place as Park Corp. executives. The oldest son, Daniel, and the youngest son, Kelly, worked in Pittsburgh, while Patrick Park worked in Cleveland and his sister, Piper Park, limited her Park Corp. activities to attending board meetings. As the company entered the late 1990s, however, Ray Park, by then in his early 70s, was still in charge and showed no signs of changing the acquisitive behavior that had described him for the previous 40 years. When Ray Park sold his stake in American Axle & Manufacturing and took in the $600 million realized from the deal, he declared he was ready to get back into the "fun" of recycling industrial junk. Given this statement, more acquisitions and the unique profitmaking style of Ray Park were expected to be witnessed in the future.

Principal Subsidiaries

Whemco; I-X Corp.

Further Reading

Balcerek, Tom, "Teledyne Ohio Buy Complete; Firm Will Become Part of Park Corp.'s Whemco Unit," *American Metal Market,* December 7, 1990, p. 16.

Bullard, Stan, "$25M I-X Hotel in Works; Developer Hired by Exhibition Hall Owner, Fall '98 Opening Planned," *Crain's Cleveland Business,* September 2, 1996, p. 1.

Fitzpatrick, Dan, "Park Corp. Plans $215 Million Rebirth at West Homestead Mill," *Pittsburgh Business Times,* August 26, p. 1.

"Ohio Foundry Changes Hands," *American Metal Market,* July 15, 1997, p. 4.

Scolieri, Peter, "Park Signs Deal to Buy Teledyne Ohio," *American Metal Market,* September 14, 1990, p. 8.

Upbin, Bruce, "Recycling Assets," *Forbes,* October 13, 1997, p. 62.

"White Elephant Hunt," *Forbes,* June 1, 1973, p. 65.

—Jeffrey L. Covell

Perkins Family Restaurants, L.P.

6075 Poplar Avenue, Suite 800
Memphis, Tennessee 38119
U.S.A.
(901) 766-6400
Fax: (901) 766-6400
Web site: http://www.perkinsrestaurants.com

Public Limited Partnership
Founded: 1957
Employees: 2,874
Sales: $253 million (1996)
Stock Exchanges: New York
SICs: 5812 Eating Places; 6794 Patent Owners & Lessors

With over 450 restaurants throughout the United States and Canada, Perkins Family Restaurants, L.P. is a full-service, family-oriented chain of mid-priced eateries. In the early 1990s, it ranked among the top five chains in the family-dining segment of the restaurant industry. Originally conceived in the 1950s as a pancake house, the Perkins menu has grown to include more than 100 breakfast, lunch, and dinner items. By the mid-1990s, most locations also featured muffins, cakes, pies, cookies, and pastries prepared at in-store bakeries. The chain is comprised of 134 company-owned units and 331 franchised restaurants. Chainwide sales totaled $678 million in 1996, $235 million of which was retained by the Perkins organization.

Operated as a master limited partnership since 1986, Perkins was on the verge of becoming a wholly owned subsidiary of The Restaurant Company (TRC) in the fall of 1997. Founded as Tennessee Restaurant Company in 1986, TRC had owned a significant stake in Perkins since acquiring the Memphis-based chain that same year. Donald Smith served as chairman and CEO of both TRC and Perkins. In 1997 TRC, which already owned 48 percent of the limited partnership through its Perkins Management Company subsidiary, offered to buy the remaining publicly held shares of the company for $14 each. The deal was subject to a vote by shareholders and was expected to be completed by the end of 1997.

Post-World War II Origins

The Perkins chain was founded by William Smith, but it takes its name from Ohioans Mat and Ivan Perkins. Smith launched his first Smitty's pancake house in Seattle, Washington, in 1957, featuring his own special pancake recipe. The Perkins brothers adopted Smith's recipes and took them to Silverton, Ohio, a suburb of Cincinnati, in 1958, where they opened the first Perkins Pancake House. While similar in all but name, the two restaurant concepts were separately owned and operated throughout the 1950s, 1960s, and most of the 1970s. Franchises under both the Smitty's and Perkins names were sold throughout the Midwest during the ensuing decade.

Though Perkins's food was low-priced—checks averaged $1 per person in the early 1960s—it was not a run-of-the-mill pancake house. The menu included more than two dozen kinds of pancakes and waffles prepared by white-hatted chefs. Pancake choices included the standard buttermilk cakes, as well as potato, banana, curried tuna, "toad-in-the-hole," and Swedish varieties. Waffles were made with strawberries, coconut, butter pecan, and many other nontraditional ingredients. The Perkins brothers added sandwiches to their menu in the early 1960s. Restaurants were decorated in a colonial theme, featuring lantern-style light fixtures and Early American furnishings.

In 1967 Wyman Nelson, a major franchisee headquartered in Minneapolis, Minnesota, began to emerge as a leader of the rather loose-knit organization. That year he expanded service to 24-hours, seven-days-a-week, and changed the name of all his restaurants throughout the state to Perkins "Cake & Stake" to reflect the addition of a dinner menu to the restaurant's offerings. Nelson also mounted an advertising campaign to publicize the changes. Over the course of the ensuing decade, Nelson gradually took over the Smitty's and Perkins chains. In 1969, he purchased the right to develop the dining concept throughout Minnesota. Seven years later, he acquired a nationwide license

Company Perspectives:

Perkins is a mid-scale *family restaurant company serving* abundant *portions of* good food *featuring signature items for breakfast, lunch and dinner while guaranteeing* great service *in a* comfortable, *friendly atmosphere.*

With our employees and franchisees, we will deliver the ''Perkins Promise'' and provide a competitive *return to our investors.*

to the Perkins concept. He completed his consolidation effort in 1978 with the outright purchase of the Perkins trademark and flour distribution rights.

Acquisition by Holiday Inns

Less than a year after Nelson's consolidation, Perkins ''Cake & Steak,'' Inc. was itself acquired by Holiday Corp., parent company of Holiday Inns, Inc. The purchase was part of Holiday's late 1970s/early 1980s diversification into both restaurants and casinos. By 1981, Perkins had 258 restaurants in 29 states. In 1983, the hotel chain moved Perkins' headquarters to its Memphis, Tennessee hometown, where Perkins main office remained through the mid-1990s. Though it remained marginally profitable, Perkins did not fare particularly well under its new ownership structure. James Scarpa of *Restaurant Business* described the chain as ''dated and disorganized'' in a 1990 article, particularly noting its ''downscale coffee shop look.''

Perkins' ownership transferred again in the mid-1980s, when restaurateur Donald N. Smith, a member of Holiday's board of directors, took the 312-unit chain private. At the time, Perkins' balance sheet was a reflection of its decor; it was netting only $3 million on revenues of $103 million. But Smith (no relation to the founder) believed the restaurant chain had excellent potential for growth and profitability. Smith's resumé included executive positions with several well-known restaurant chains. He was credited with developing Pizza Hut's Pan Pizza and Personal Pan Pizza and launching McDonald's breakfast menu. As CEO of Burger King in the late 1970s, he doubled profits on a 50 percent increase in chainwide sales.

With the cooperation of Holiday Corp., Smith formed an investment group dubbed Tennessee Restaurant Company and purchased the chain for about $70 million in 1985. In 1986, he transformed the company into a limited partnership, selling a minority stake to the public. A portion of the funds raised were invested in remodeling and an almost complete overhaul of the menu. New and renewed units featured ceramic tile, green neon, and a solarium. One important and lasting addition to the menu was the Perkins in-store bakery, launched in 1986. The restaurant made omelets, not pancakes, the new featured breakfast item, and put a stronger emphasis on the lunch menu, adding cheese melt sandwiches and specialty salads. The changes boosted check averages, same-store sales, overall revenues, and corporate profitability. By the end of the decade, Smith had tripled Perkins' net to $9.7 million on a 50 percent increase in sales to $150 million.

Growth Targeted in 1990s

Having stabilized the chain, Smith focused on expansion in the early 1990s, hoping to double the number of restaurants by 1995. Perkins' growth plan, dubbed the ''I-95 Strategy,'' concentrated new units in the vicinity of this major East Coast thoroughfare. The chain also opened its first international restaurant in Ontario, Canada—which not coincidentally was Smith's native province—in 1988. Though it had dozens of company-owned units, Perkins continued to emphasize franchising as its key growth vehicle during this period. Corporate restaurants were used as testing grounds for new menu, decor, and marketing ideas.

Driven in large part by expansion, Perkins' sales increased by more than 40 percent from $180.5 million in 1990 to $252.8 million in 1996. But the company's bottom-line performance did not match that top-line growth rate. In fact, net income declined from a high of $15.4 million in 1992 to less than $10 million in 1995 before recovering somewhat to $13.5 million in 1996. Perkins' erratic profitability was matched by an unstable stock price. Shares in the limited partnership, which started trading publicly in 1989 at around $13, grew to over $15 late in 1993 before plunging to less than $8 in late 1994. Steady dividend payouts helped boost the stock back over the $13 mark early in 1997, but that was before stakeholders learned that the partnership would become subject to corporate taxation beginning in 1998. In June 1997, the company announced that tax payments would likely reduce or even eliminate partnership dividends, news that sent Perkins' already battered shares into a mid-year slide to about $10. TRC's late 1997 offer of $14 per share to take the company private helped rebound shares to $13.81 by that September. The agreement had yet to win approval by public shareholders and TRC's lenders in the fall of 1997, but appeared headed for ratification by both groups.

The Mid-1990s and Beyond

Perkins' 1996 annual report outlined a multifaceted program for future growth. All the initiatives were tested in company programs and slated to be adopted in franchises in the late 1990s. A new round of remodelings continued the chain's upscale trend. Company-owned sites refurbished during 1995 and 1996 featured garden rooms, ''libraries'' with bookcase wallpaper, sport-themed rooms, and sunrooms. Perkins arranged financing to assist its franchisees in the renovation process. New market research and customer satisfaction surveys were adopted as well. Perkins even tackled the difficult task of improving productivity in a service business. It combined backroom efficiencies, manager incentives, and a new scheduling system to increase the number of customers served per hour of labor. A closely related program sought to reduce turnover and thereby trim hiring and training costs.

Still led by David Smith in 1997, Perkins' management hoped to parlay its bakeries into increased traffic, increased sales, and even new dining concepts. The company started testing stand-alone bakeries and cafes in 1995. Both formats were designed to adapt Perkins to food courts in a wide variety of settings, from malls to colleges to military bases.

Perkins' family orientation has sharpened its focus on serving children—after all, kids have been called "the status symbols of the 1990s." In 1996 the company began testing KidPerks, a program that incorporated a menu expansion and new entertainment options. In place of the coloring page and crayons typically offered to placate children while they waited for dinner to be prepared and served, KidPerks offered hand-held computer games, comic books, Etch a Sketch toys, and sonic books, as well as free popcorn to quiet growling stomachs. With successful KidPerks programs in place at company-owned restaurants throughout Minnesota, Nebraska, North Dakota, Oklahoma, Tennessee, and Wisconsin, Perkins hoped to bring the concept chainwide by the end of 1997.

As it prepared to return to private ownership, Perkins Family Restaurants appeared poised to pull out of its earnings slump and return to profitable growth. Of course, it will be under no obligation to report financial data as a privately held corporation.

Further Reading

Abelson, Reed, "Perkins Family Restaurants LP," *Fortune,* July 3, 1989, p. 112.

Anreder, Steven S., "Color Me Green," *Barron's,* December 21, 1981, pp. 29–30.

Bonham, Roger D., "Perkins Pancake House," *Restaurant Management,* December 1960, pp. 33–35.

Carlino, Bill, "Perkins Deploys Dinner Program, Unit Redesign," *Nation's Restaurant News,* June 20, 1994, p. 7.

Keegan, Peter O., "Upscale Dinner Rollout Fuels Perkins' Profit Leap," *Nation's Restaurant News,* November 15, 1993, p. 14.

"Perkins Winds Up 1996 with Profits of $13.52M," *Nation's Restaurant News,* February 24, 1997, p. 12.

Prewitt, Milford, "Perkins Turnaround Leads to Expansion Drive," *Nation's Restaurant News,* November 6, 1989, pp. F14–F17.

Riell, Howard, "Smith, Investors to Acquire 80% of Perkins," *Nation's Restaurant News,* April 29, 1985, p. 1.

Scarpa, James, "Perkins Gears for Growth," *Restaurant Business,* January 1, 1990, pp. 60–62.

Strauss, Karen, "Family-Dining Chains Scramble," *Restaurants & Institutions,* July 15, 1993, pp. 90–92.

Townsend, Rob, "The Midscale Advantage: Menu, Service and Value," *Restaurants & Institutions,* August 21, 1991, pp. 26–30.

—April Dougal Gasbarre

Pete's Brewing Company

514 High Street
Palo Alto, California 94301
U.S.A.
(415) 328-7383
Fax: (415) 327-3675
Web site: http://www.peteswicked.com

Public Company
Incorporated: 1986 as Pete's Brewing Company
Employees: 85
Sales: $71 million (1996)
Stock Exchanges: NASDAQ
SICs: 5181 Beer & Ale

The second largest microbrewer in the United States, Pete's Brewing Company sells a line of full-bodied, specialty beers—all bearing the "Pete's Wicked" name—throughout much of the United States and in the United Kingdom. During the mid-1990s, Pete's Brewing sold its microbrews in 47 states. The company sold its beer to more than 300 independent beverage alcohol wholesalers, who, in turn, sold Pete's Wicked beers to more than 200,000 licensed retail accounts.

Origins

Pete's Brewing's signature product, Pete's Wicked Ale, was the result of experimentations that began in a kitchen in Belmont, California, in 1979. Inside the kitchen were a five gallon container, a big kettle, and a garbage can. It was the realization that the same equipment could be used to make beer and wine that prompted Peter Slosberg, in whose kitchen Pete's Wicked Ale was born, to begin brewing beer. Originally, Slosberg had his heart set on creating his own wine, but the fermentation process was too slow for his liking, so he converted his homespun equipment to another cause and tried his hand at brewing beer. It was a fateful decision for the multibillion-dollar U.S. beer industry. Slosberg's impatience proved to be the spark that created one of the largest, most-recognized, most-praised microbrewing companies in the country. Craft brewers, whose ranks grew exponentially during their assault on major brands such as Budweiser, Miller, and Coors, recorded explosive growth during the late 1980s and the 1990s, and Pete's Brewing led the charge, holding sway as a pivotal force that helped change the face of the U.S. beer industry.

Slosberg's aspirations in 1979 were far less ambitious. His hours spent in the kitchen with kettles and garbage cans were those of a hobbyist; time spent away from a professional career that provided for his full financial support. Slosberg started brewing beer to fulfill a passion, not to start a brewing company. He started his professional career with an academic background in engineering, then worked as a cab driver in New York City before making a name for himself as a marketer for high-technology companies.

Slosberg worked as marketing executive during the day and toiled in his Belmont kitchen at night, experimenting with various recipes for brewing beer that harkened back to an era when German purity standards were followed strictly. Although he had forsaken a hobby as a vintner because the fermentation process took too long, Slosberg demonstrated considerable patience with brewing beer. He tinkered with one recipe after another, giving samples to friends and soliciting their suggestions. For seven years Slosberg searched to find what he considered the perfect brew, and once he had, Pete's Wicked Ale and Pete's Brewing were born.

1986 Birth of Wicked Ale

When Slosberg settled on his recipe in 1986 that would become famous as Pete's Wicked Ale, he was working as a marketing manager at Santa Clara-based Rolm Corporation. By this point, after seven years of laboring over various recipes, Slosberg was ready to turn brewing beer into more than a hobby. He took a sabbatical from Rolm and struck a deal with Palo Alto Brewing Co. in January 1986 to brew beer according to his specifications. Next, Slosberg completed the difficult task of raising the money to finance the production and distribution of his first batch of Pete's Wicked Ale by convincing a group of corporate investors to shell out $50,000 and make Pete's Brewing a going concern. By the fall of 1986, Slosberg was ready to

Company Perspectives:

The "Pete's wicked" formula for brand building is a simple one based on six award-winning "Pete's Wicked" brews, the Wicked trade name, and homebrewer and founder Pete. Wicked is an original trade name that attracts beer drinkers to the brand. The quality and uniqueness of the products keep them coming back. Pete's franchise-building objective is to hold in the highest regard every person who drinks "Pete's Wicked" brews. A new generation of American beer drinkers is interested in identifying with brands that their parents didn't have—brands with flavor and variety that they can call their own. These people are the driving force behind the specialty beer market.

put Pete's Wicked Ale to the test and wriggle into the entrenched $40 billion-a-year beer market.

Slosberg convened a meeting in November 1986 at the Jew and Gentile Deli in Mountain View, California, to discuss strategy. In attendance were Slosberg, Mark Bronder, an executive at Institutional Venture Partners, two executives from Rolm, and six other businessmen. At the time, the objective was modest in scope; the individuals gathered around a table in a deli were not discussing how they were going to challenge Anheuser-Busch head on. Instead, they were hoping Pete's Wicked Ale would become a local favorite, perhaps a regional fixture in liquor stores and grocery stores. Large, national brewing companies maintained an intractable hold on the U.S. beer market, and those gathered at the deli did not dream of trying to wrest appreciable market share away from the industry stalwarts. Instead, their focus was on bringing a quality product to market and turning back the pages of history.

Beer, in pre-Prohibition America, contained four ingredients: malted barley, hops, yeast, and water; to add any other ingredients was to violate the tightly embraced German purity standards. The scores of small, regional breweries that composed the industry before Prohibition observed such standards, but following Prohibition, when large, mass-market brewers took control of the industry, rising barley malt prices forced brewers to use cheaper alternatives, such as rice and corn. Further transgressions of German purity standards followed, as behemoth brewing companies added head-stabilizers and preservatives to ensure consistent quality. Microbrewers, who numbered less than three dozen when Slosberg and his cohorts were discussing strategy at the Jew and Gentile Deli, were attempting to woo customers by brewing beer the way it historically had been brewed, by earning sales and cultivating loyalty through a quality product that tasted superior to what they believed were adulterated versions of traditional brewing standards.

By December 1986, the first 200 cases of Pete's Wicked Ale had hit the market, retailing at between $5 and $6 per six-pack. They quickly disappeared from store shelves. The following month, 400 more cases of Pete's Wicked Ale replenished store shelves, and they were quickly shuttled home by customers as well. Bottles of Pete's Wicked Ale, with Slosberg's English bull terrier, Millie, on the label, grabbed customers' attention; the quality of the beer induced them to buy more. Slosberg was happy, but he remained cautious. "We are waiting to prove the concept, then we will build a brewery," he remarked to a reporter from a local newspaper. "We think we have a hit." As Slosberg and his investors bridled their confidence and suppressed the desire to celebrate the success of their fledgling enterprise, disaster struck, checking any grand plans Slosberg had imagined.

Pete's Brewing's brewery, Palo Alto Brewing, filed for bankruptcy in January 1987, squelching the opportunity for Pete's Brewing to increase production totals to meet demand. Panic set in as all those gathered together at the deli in Mountain View were now forced to scurry about, enlist help, and do what they could before the sheriff came to lock the doors of Palo Alto Brewing. "We had to scrounge for people and work the weekend before the door was padlocked," Slosberg remembered. "We had to scour the West Coast for our particular bottle, then we had to go in and bottle, filter, and pasteurize. It was fun for about two hours."

So began a six-month transition period for Pete's Brewing just as the company was sprinting from the starting block. They were difficult months, to be sure, but Slosberg used the time wisely and began rebuilding. Intent on avoiding the prospect of a contract brewer going belly up again, Slosberg selected a veteran in the brewing business when he contracted with the 130-year-old, New Ulm, Minnesota-based August Schell's Brewing Co. to produce the next batch of Pete's Wicked Ale. Slosberg also went after new financial help and raised $400,000 from new supporters. By May 1987, when 1,400 cases of Pete's Wicked Ale were scheduled for delivery to Silicon Valley, Pete's Brewing was back in business and its flagship product was making a name for itself among beer connoisseurs. Pete's Wicked Ale was voted the top ale in the "1987 Great American Beer Festival" in Colorado and ranked as one of the top five beers in the United States. In 1988, Pete's Wicked Ale repeated its achievements, quickly earning a reputation as a premium microbrew.

Vigorous Growth Begins in 1989

Award-winning prestige spurred expansion for Pete's Brewing after the Palo Alto Brewing debacle. Production in New Ulm increased monthly as the demand for Pete's Wicked ale grew. By mid-1989, Pete's Wicked Ale was sold in eight states and distributed by 50 major-brand beer distributors, with its territory of availability expected to reach 12 states by the end of the year. Despite the burgeoning growth recorded by his company, Slosberg continued to work as a marketing executive, serving stints at IBM and Network Equipment Technology as the 1980s drew to a close. Soon, however, the financial prospects for a microbrewer would become much greater, as the microbrew industry embarked on the most prolific growth spurt in its history. Between 1989 and 1993, the number of microbreweries in the United States increased more than tenfold, exploding from fewer than 40 to more than 400. Annual revenues for these small craft breweries skyrocketed as well, leaping from $135 million generated in 1989 to the more than $1 billion racked up in 1993.

The early 1990s were years when microbreweries blossomed, forcing such industry heavyweights as Anheuser-Busch and Miller Brewing to take notice of the growing appetite for gourmet beers. Pete's Brewing, during this definitive period for craft brewers, took full advantage of the halcyon times. Production of Pete's Wicked Ale was switched to a larger brewery called the Minnesota Brewing Company in 1992, the same year five new beers were added to the company's flagship ale: Pete's Wicked Lager, Pete's Wicked Red, Pete's Wicked Honey Wheat, Pete's Wicked Winter Brew, and Pete's Summer Brew. New product introductions, increased production capacity, and the animated growth of the microbrew industry as a whole combined to push Pete's Brewing's sales upward. The company's sales increased at an average annual growth rate of more than 150 percent during the early 1990s, making it the 33rd fastest-growing, private company in the United States. Of the more than 400 microbrewers in the country by 1993, Pete's Brewing ranked as the fifth largest, collecting $12.2 million in sales for the year. As the microbrew industry continued to expand exponentially into the mid-1990s, Pete's Brewing not only kept pace with its competitors but gained ground, and it did so by doing something unprecedented in the craft brewing industry.

As a general rule of thumb, microbrewers spent as little as possible on advertising. They generated awareness of their beers chiefly by word of mouth and by designing attractive, unconventional labels for their bottles. Although some of the larger brewers paid for print and radio advertisements, most did not, and no microbrewer had ever bought television advertising. That distinction ended in 1994, when Pete's Brewing launched its first TV ad. The commercial, which poked fun at the anonymity of Slosberg, set a precedent that other craft brewers would follow and provided a tremendous boost to Pete's Brewing's financial totals and its stature within the microbrew industry. The company's distribution territory expanded as recognition of the Pete's Wicked name increased. After ringing up $12 million in sales in 1993, Pete's Brewing generated $31 million in sales in 1994, making it the second largest microbrewer in the country, second only to Boston Beer Company, maker of Samuel Adams.

Mid-1990s: Brewery and Expansion

Flush with success, Pete's Brewing executives mapped out big plans for 1995. In mid-1995, the company began shipping small quantities of its ale to Great Britain, while executives discussed plans of extending Pete's Brewing's geographic reach into Canada, Australia, and Europe. Production was switched to another, larger brewery, the Stroh Brewing Co. in St. Paul, Minnesota, in late 1995, guaranteeing a long-term supply of the company's six award-winning beers. By far the biggest event in 1995, however, was the company's initial public offering in November, when one-third of Pete's Brewing was sold to public investors. With the proceeds gained from the sale of stock, Pete's Brewing planned to retire some of its debt and build a new $30 million headquarters, retail, and production complex in Napa Valley. After nearly 10 years of relying on contract brewers to produce its beers, Pete's Brewing was ready at last to build its own brewery.

Between 1991 and 1995, Pete's Brewing's sales mushroomed, soaring 2,270 percent. Its market share increased as well, even as the number of microbrewers increased exponentially. The market that was considered too crowded by some when there were 40 craft beer companies, was populated by an estimated 800 companies by the mid-1990s. During these years of staggering growth, Pete's Brewing shouldered competitors aside to rank as the second largest microbrewer in the country.

Production at its new, 250,000-barrel brewery was slated to begin at the end of 1997, giving Pete's Brewing officials one more reason to celebrate the conclusion of a remarkably successful first decade of business. During the company's 10th anniversary year, sales leaped upward again to eclipse $70 million, piquing optimism for the future. As company officials charted Pete's Brewing's course for its second decade of business, plans called for a greater push into international markets and the extension of the Pete's Wicked name to wherever discerning beer drinkers resided.

Further Reading

Atkinson, Bill, "Has Spuds Met His Match?," *Business Journal, San Jose, May* 11, 1987, p. 2.

Burstiner, Marcy, "Beers Without Peers: Anchor, Pete's Find International Thirst for Crafted Brews," *San Francisco Business Times,* June 16, 1995, p. 3.

Dwyer, Steve, "Hail to the Ale," *Prepared Foods,* October 1996, p. 28.

Goldman, James S., "Pete Loves Beer—It's His Business to Love It," *Business Journal—San Jose,* August 14, 1989, p. 1.

Kahn, Aron, "Maker of Pete's Wicked Ale Moves Contract from Minnesota Brewing to Stroh," *Saint Paul Pioneer Press,* August 6, 1995, p. 8.

Khermouch, Gerry, " 'Pete' Comes to Television: As Pete's Brewing Hits TV Airwave, It's a Milestone for Beer Microbrewers," *ADWEEK Eastern Edition, August* 8, 1994, p. 9.

Levine, Daniel S., "New HQ on Tap at Pete's Brewing Co.," *San Francisco Business Times,* June 7, 1996, p. 1.

Liedtke, Michael, "Palo-Alto-Based Pete's Brewing Hopes to Brew Success on Wall Street," *Knight-Ridder/Tribune Business News,* September 24, 1995, p. 9.

Schmitz, Tom, "California Entrepreneur Leaves High-Tech Career to Start a Microbrewery," *Knight-Ridder/Tribune Business News,* November 7, 1993, p. 1.

Thurm, Scott, "Investors Hop Aboard IPO for Pete's Brewing of Palo Alto, Calif.," *Knight-Ridder/Tribune Business News,* November 7, 1995, p. 11.

—Jeffrey L. Covell

PHP Healthcare Corporation

11440 Commerce Park Drive
Reston, Virginia 20191
U.S.A.
(703) 758-3600
Fax: (703) 758-3650

Public Company
Incorporated: 1975
Employees: 3,328
Sales: $232 million (1997)
Stock Exchanges: New York
SICs: 8011 Offices of Physicians; 7363 Help Supply Services; 8063 Psychiatric Hospitals; 8051 Skilled Nursing Care Facilities

PHP Healthcare Corporation and its subsidiaries develop, consolidate, and manage the delivery of healthcare and related support services on a contractual basis to a wide variety of customers, including numerous commercial groups, corporations, and entities, and the entire spectrum of federal, state, and local government agencies. Comprised of two operating divisions, the Commercial Managed Care Division and the Government Managed Care Division, the former provides integrated healthcare delivery services through the company's HMOs in the District of Columbia and the state of Virginia, primarily to government-assisted Medicaid recipients, its statewide Integrated System of Care in the state of New Jersey that contracts services with local HMOs and insurance companies, and family healthcare centers or facilities that are contracted for large corporate employers, while the latter provides healthcare services to a diverse scope of government agencies, including medical staffing, ambulatory care, mental health services, long-term care, and total managed care. Prior to 1993, over 98 percent of the company's total revenues were derived from government-related contracts. However, by the end of fiscal 1996, approximately 60 percent of the firm's total revenues came from the Commercial Managed Care Division. Operating primarily in the Northeast, Eastern, and Southeastern sections of the United States, in 1997 PHP Healthcare Corporation concluded a strategic alliance with HIP Health Plan of New Jersey that overnight more than doubled PHP's annual revenues.

Early History

The founder and driving force behind PHP Health Corporation from the time of its inception until 1995 was a man named Charles H. Robbins. Robbins, growing up in the state of Maryland within the modest means of American middle-class family life, knew from the time of his early manhood that he wanted to own and operate his own business. Yet Robbins, having spent his entire life on the East Coast of the United States, and most of that in the rural areas of the state of Maryland, was not able to decide on the exact type of business he wanted to pursue. Hence, after holding a variety of management positions in companies operating within the Middle Atlantic States, Robbins decided to establish his own consulting firm.

With another person working as a secretary, and Robbins himself providing management consulting services to a wide variety of businesses, the little firm established in the back of a beauty shop in Rockville, Maryland, suddenly began to grow. Robbins had become an expert in accounting methods and innovative management procedures during his journeyman days, and his new consulting firm started receiving requests for assistance from government sources within the state of Maryland to help sort out the difficulties involved in establishing medical care for Medicare and Medicaid recipients. However, this request soon blossomed into a source of work and profit that became one of the cornerstones of Robbins's business.

Growth and Development During the 1980s

No longer a two-person operation, and no longer working out of the back of a beauty shop, Robbins decided to concentrate on, and take advantage of, the need for comprehensive healthcare delivery systems needed by the various levels of local, state, and federal governments. By the early 1980s, revenues of the once small consulting firm had grown to over $25 million, and with a staff of over 300 the company began to expand even more rapidly than anticipated. In order to reflect the exclusive focus on providing integrated healthcare delivery systems, Robbins decided upon PHP Healthcare Corporation as the most appropriate and descriptive title for his burgeoning organization.

As PHP Healthcare Corporation grew, it garnered almost all of its contracts from government sources. Contracts with the federal government included such important agreements as the development of healthcare provisions for long-term care nursing home programs where injured or elderly former American serviceman were located, and numerous ambulatory care projects made in agreement with the United States Navy. At the local and state levels of government, the ever-expanding inmate population of the states of Maryland and Virginia provided PHP Health with long-term contracts for total managed care correctional facilities projects.

With government contracts continuing to increase throughout the decade of the 1980s, PHP Healthcare Corporation expanded dramatically. Revenues seemed to double nearly every two years, and the amount of work required hundreds of new employees. Under the direction of Charles H. Robbins, the company incorporated and managed these vast and overwhelming developments with a professionalism not seen very often in the corporate sector. Robbins gathered a top-notch management team to help him administer the growing business of the company, as well as financial experts in the healthcare industry to help devise a strategy for continued success in the highly competitive and confusing American system of health providers and customers. It was not until the early 1990s, however, that PHP Healthcare Corporation matured into a fully integrated healthcare system provider, and took its place alongside the most successful of the companies within the industry.

The Early 1990s

During the early 1990s, Robbins conferred with his management and strategy team, and created what was termed an "Integrated System of Care" (ISOC), the company's own highly innovative version of vertically integrated healthcare. This strategic approach includes four primary components, Practice Management Services, Network Management Services, Traditional Insurance Functionality, and Change Agent Services. Practice Management Services included the development of and improvement upon such activities as billing support, accounts receivable management, personnel recruitment, facilities management, information services, and additional practice-oriented skills which were designed and implemented to assist physicians in maximizing both the clinical and the economical value of their practice (in whatever area that might be) within the healthcare setting.

The second important component within the company's Integrated System of Care included the development of systems that would provide assistance to those who provided healthcare services so that they could efficiently manage the financial and clinical responsibilities designated to them by HMOs and other payers such as Medicare and Medicaid. The ability to engage in contracting and reimbursement services, utilization management, quality assurance, and credentialing were the kinds of network-based skills which PHP Healthcare Corporation helped healthcare providers develop in order to become more adept and successful at patient care management.

Healthcare providers or delivery systems, whether a small physicians group or large hospital, have to be efficient in the areas of claims payments, subrogation, member services, customer support, and the coordination of benefits if an HMO delegates these types of services to the providers or delivery systems. As a result, within its ISOC Robbins and his team developed a set of skills termed Traditional Insurance Functionality, an integrated system that assists provider-based delivery systems to become more efficient in these areas. The final component within the Integrated System of Care was designated Change Agent Services, where PHP Healthcare Corporation would assist a provider-based delivery system in its strategic planning, managed care education, training in integrated delivery system functionality, and all the necessary procedures for a delivery system to make the difficult transition from a traditional healthcare provider that operated on a fragmented, fee-for-service basis to an Integrated System of Care.

This Integrated System of Care approach to working with healthcare delivery systems, and the strategy for its implementation, led to increased levels of activity and dramatically skyrocketing revenues for the company. In 1993, PHP Healthcare Corporation purchased D.C., Chartered Health Plan, the first HMO that offered managed care to Medicaid recipients in the Washington, D.C. area. In what was one of the last major acquisitions of his tenure at the company, Robbins supervised the expansion of Chartered Health Plan into additional geographic areas and, more importantly, the improvement of its services. Home visits and an extensive phone-calling system were expanded without losing the personal touch—an element of its business that Chartered Health Plan had developed over the years—as well as transportation arrangement for its members, a wellness van that expanded its activities to include free health screenings and patient education, and a comprehensive health education program for teenagers and young adults arranged through the public school system.

Growth During the Mid-1990s

By any measure, 1995 and 1996 were banner years for the company. The expectations that first arose when Chartered Health Plan was purchased in 1993 quickly came to fruition. One of Chartered Health Plan's affiliates, Virginia Chartered Health Plan (VACHP), was incorporated in 1995 as a full partnership between PHP Healthcare Corporation and the Medical College of Virginia, which held a 30 percent interest in VACHP. Operating as an individual practice association (IPA), Virginia Chartered Health Plan included more than 1,000 physicians in and around Richmond, and working at two major hospital systems within the state. With PHP Healthcare Corporation's assistance to rely upon, VACHP grew and expanded rapidly into the second-largest provider of Medicaid managed care in the entire state, with an enrollment surpassing 14,500 people. As a result, total revenues for Virginia Chartered Health Plan increased by $13.9 million from the end of fiscal 1995 to 1996. Chartered Health Plan itself grew rapidly when it was awarded a contract to be the default plan for Medicaid managed care in the District of Columbia. More than doubling its enrollment in the District, it is estimated that more than 80,000 recipients of Medicaid services will ultimately be registered with one of the managed care programs operated by Chartered Health Plan.

Although Charles H. Robbins, the founder and chairman of PHP Healthcare Corporation, resigned in 1995, the company did not lose a step. Jack M. Mazur, an employee of the firm for over 20 years, replaced Robbins and continued his predecessor's strategy and managerial approach which had proved such a success. In May 1996, the Maryland Department of Public Safety and Correctional Services reached a $50 million contract with PHP Healthcare to provide comprehensive healthcare services to inmates in correctional facilities located around Baltimore, Maryland. During the same month, the company was also awarded a large contract to provide psychiatric services to members of the military, both active and retired, at the William Beaumont Army Medical Center located at Fort Bliss, Texas. One month later, the Army extended the company's contract to provide primary care services at military health units throughout northern Virginia.

In July 1996, PHP Healthcare Corporation reported an astounding 800 percent increase in profit over the previous year. Surprisingly, this dramatic upswing in profitability was no fluke, as lucrative contracts continued to pour into the company's coffers. PHP Healthcare Corporation's reputation was growing nationally, and the state government of Arkansas awarded the firm an extension of a contract to provide healthcare services for prisoners within its statewide correctional facilities. By August 1996, the company's total number of government contracts reached a backlog of over $400 million. In September of the same year, the company was contracted once again by the U.S. Army to establish patient care services at both Fort Bennings, Georgia, and Fort Knox, Kentucky. Later in the fall, PHP Healthcare was contracted by the Federal government's Health and Human Services Department to design, develop, and implement multi-state, community-based, fully integrated healthcare provider systems.

In spite of its success with government contracts, management decided to lessen its reliance on such agreements and focus more on the commercial managed care market. This reorientation was immediate as the company completed a major agreement with New Jersey Blue Cross and Blue Shield to acquire numerous centers and physician services in the state for a cost of approximately $30 million. In 1997, this reorientation strategy continued as PHP Healthcare added Stamford Hospital and the Connecticut Health Enterprises Network as a partner, and also agreed to purchase a majority of the assets of HIP Health Plan of New Jersey for $73 million. Under a 20-year contract, PHP Healthcare will acquire 18 of HIP's health centers, including its pharmacy and optical services. The acquisition doubled PHP Healthcare's annual revenues by the end of fiscal 1997.

PHP Healthcare Corporation, with more than 90 healthcare projects in 28 markets, and with locations spreading throughout the United States, is clearly one of the most successful healthcare companies in the United States. With savvy management, a thorough understanding of the marketplace, and an astute sense of timing, the company is looking forward to the opportunities that will present themselves in the next century.

Principal Subsidiaries

Connecticut Health Enterprises, L.L.C.; Georgia Health Enterprise, L.L.C.; Virginia Chartered Health Plan, Inc.; D.C. Chartered Health Plan, Inc.

Further Reading

Greeme, Jay, "Contracts Are Catching On," *Modern Healthcare,* January 31, 1994, pp. 29–37.

Kenkel, Paul J., "Delivering Corporate Healthcare Services," *Modern Healthcare,* June 7, 1993, pp. 24–27.

Kertesz, Sandy Lutz, and Sloane, Todd, "Sorting Out the Stories That Mattered," *Modern Healthcare,* August 26, 1996, p. 44.

Pallarito, Karen, "New Network a First for Connecticut," *Modern Healthcare,* February 12, 1996, pp. 20–22.

"PHP Healthcare Plans Purchase," *Wall Street Journal,* December 20, 1996, p. A4(E).

"PHP Healthcare to Buy Assets from HIP Health Plan," *New York Times,* July 25, 1997, p. C3(N).

Super, Kari E., "Wellness Plans Trying Incentives to Reduce Company Healthcare Costs," *Modern Healthcare,* January 2, 1987, pp. 84–86.

Weissenstein, Eric, and Gardner, Jonathan, "Medicare Managed Care Weighed As Federal Budget-Balancing Tool," *Modern Healthcare,* February 13, 1995, pp. 52–56.

—Thomas Derdak

Piper Jaffray Companies Inc.

Piper Jaffray Tower
222 South Ninth Street
Minneapolis, Minnesota 55402-3804
U.S.A.
(612) 342-6000
Fax: (612) 342-6996
Web site: http://www.piperjaffray.com

Public Company
Incorporated: 1969
Employees: 3,085
Total Assets: $923.74 million (1996)
Stock Exchanges: NASDAQ
SICs: 6211, Security Brokers & Dealers

Through three wholly owned subsidiaries, Minneapolis-based Piper Jaffray Companies Inc. offers general securities brokerage, investment management, corporate and public finance, and trust services to both individual and institutional investors. The company operates 79 branch offices in 17 states. In fiscal 1996, ended September 30, the company posted revenue of $553.9 million and net income of $7.29 million.

Origins

In 1892 a former cashier named George Bishop Lane arrived in the thriving northern prairie town of Minneapolis to start a commercial paper business. Over the preceding century, commercial paper had become a means by which needy merchants could more easily get loans for short-term operating capital in exchange for their signature on a six- to eight-month promissory note. These notes were then turned over to a note dealer, who typically sold them to financial institutions like banks, who in turn used this ''commercial paper'' as a short-term investment.

To George Lane, it seemed clear that the promissory notes generated by Minneapolis's growing grain elevator and milling industry represented a sizable potential market. Therefore, he began participating in commercial paper transactions with major Minneapolis merchants such as Cargill Elevator Company (the forerunner of agricultural giant Cargill Inc.). In 1899 he enlisted George Lang to help him manage his growing volume, and within eight years he already had handled more than $16 million in commercial paper transactions.

Enter C. Palmer Jaffray and Harry Piper: 1913–29

In 1913, as Lane's business continued to thrive, C. Palmer Jaffray and Harry Piper, the sons of a prominent Minneapolis banker and a leading entrepreneur, respectively, decided to leave their steady but dull jobs at the First National Bank of Minneapolis and strike out on their own. Only a year out of Yale University—where their shared Minnesota backgrounds had sparked a close friendship—Jaffray and Piper soon formed Piper, Jaffray and Company, a commercial paper house whose first clients included growing enterprises like Archer Daniels Midland and Pillsbury. Harry Piper quickly emerged as the young firm's salesman and deal maker—the risk taker and entrepreneur who drummed up new business—and Palmer Jaffray became the numbers man, the financial wizard who understood the banking industry and the ins and outs of running a business.

As World War I raged in Europe, George Lane began to take admiring note of his new competitors. Already in his fifties, he needed new blood to keep his business competitive, and in 1917 he convinced Piper and Jaffray to merge their firm with his to form Lane, Piper, and Jaffray, Inc. Despite the Great War's devastation, it spurred a mighty economic boom in the United States, where between 1915 and 1920 alone GNP doubled to $80 billion. A brief recession in 1920–21, however, made it difficult for midwestern grain companies to secure loans from banks, and Lane, Piper, and Jaffray stepped into the breach by persuading small town banks throughout Minnesota and the Dakotas to loan these firms the needed capital.

The economic boom resumed stronger than ever in 1922 and, seeing the growing profits to be made on Wall Street, Lane, Piper, and Jaffray expanded from commercial paper to investment banking. Between 1922 and 1929 they underwrote the stocks and bonds issued for the public stock market by such

Company Perspectives:

Our Mission: We, the people of Piper Jaffray Companies, believe serving our clients is our basic purpose. By placing the interests of our clients first, we serve the best interests of our employees, our shareholders, and our communities. We believe service is the chief contributor to our growth and profitability.

As we serve, we commit to: Work in partnership with our clients to understand their objectives and earn their confidence and respect; provide sound advice, creative financial strategies and suitable investments to meet our clients' objectives; communicate effectively and frequently with our clients; maintain the confidentiality of all client communications; cooperate with each other, promote the personal growth of each employee, and preserve a high-quality work environment; and contribute to the communities in which we live and work.

emerging companies as Minneapolis-Honeywell, Cream of Wheat, Minnesota Mining and Manufacturing (3M), Munsingwear, and Greyhound. Since new companies were not yet required to disclose their financial operations, Lane, Piper, and Jaffray had to determine their client's financial stability through diligent spadework. This scrupulous concern for the facts led them to establish one of the first statistics and research departments in the U.S. investment banking industry.

Showing a willingness to embrace new technologies, Piper and Jaffray also joined with two competitors to participate in a national wire service system for stock transactions. The system enabled them to boast in ads that they could complete a transaction with New York ''in less than 10 minutes.'' While many Americans were allowing the giddy growth of the Roaring Twenties to color their investing judgment, Lane, Piper, and Jaffray kept an even keel, and in one year alone they declined the stock underwriting applications of 692 new firms. In part as a result of such caution, by mid-decade Lane, Piper had offices in four Minnesota cities and Fargo, North Dakota and had purchased an interest in the Chicago firm, Rickards, Roloson & Company. It also expanded its investment products portfolio, adding municipal and construction bonds, debenture, and notes for public utilities to its stable.

The Great Crash and After: 1929–40

In late October 1929, the irrational exuberance that had seen the volume of shares traded on Wall Street rise 500 percent in only seven years was dealt a fatal blow when stocks on the New York Stock Exchange began a precipitous and protracted swoon that liquidated $30 billion in investor's wealth in a matter of a few weeks. Investors who had bought their stocks on margins of only ten to 25 percent cash were ruined when their brokers demanded they make good on their outstanding balances. Many stockholders had no savings outside of their investments, and roughly 25 million of them were ruined almost overnight. Banks across the country failed, businesses were wiped out, and unemployment reached crisis proportions.

Despite its conservative underwriting practices, Lane, Piper was also hit hard and was soon posting a negative net worth. Although the First National Bank of Minneapolis loaned Lane, Piper the money to stay in business and the firm's focus on commercial paper and underwriting rather than speculative trading softened the blow, the Great Depression began to hammer farm commodity prices and Lane, Piper's commercial paper business revenues plummeted from $45.2 million in 1929 to $8.6 million in 1932. Convinced that it had survived the brunt of the Crash's clout, in 1931 Lane, Piper presciently purchased the nearly bankrupt Minneapolis brokerage house, Hopwood & Company (founded in 1914). Hopwood's selling point was its seat on the New York Stock Exchange, which offered the newly christened Piper, Jaffray & Hopwood a way to enter the broader securities market in expectation of the day—if it ever returned—when Wall Street would no longer be a dirty word.

In 1933 Congress took a step toward ensuring that day's arrival by passing the Securities Act of 1933, which required companies offering public stock to submit their books to the public scrutiny of certified accountants and by forming the Securities and Exchange Commission to regulate exchanges and brokers. Fueled by federal funds for public works projects, the municipal bond industry began to turn around in the mid-1930s, and Piper Jaffray aggressively pursued the ''muni'' market with cities, counties, and school districts across the country. It also began to make money hedging the sale of commodities, that is, offsetting the sale of one commodity against a future sale as a way of countering fluctuations in prices. By 1935 it was posting modest, if temporary, profits, and by 1937 assets totaled $2.8 million.

World War II and the 1950s: 1941–60

During World War II, Piper Jaffray benefited from America's economic resurgence by financing the Minnesota-based firms that supplied the U.S. military. It also contributed to the war effort by selling war bonds, and although U.S. sales of commercial paper fell dramatically during the war, in Minnesota they grew. By 1944 Piper Jaffray's commercial paper revenues had climbed to $18.2 million. Moreover, by 1945 its net profits, which had been a meager $1,000 in 1940, rose to $177,000. With the war's end in sight, Piper Jaffray opened a new office in Great Falls, Montana, reflecting its long-standing presence in that region's brokerage and municipal bond markets.

As Minnesota corporations ramped up for the postwar economy, Piper Jaffray teamed with Wall Street investment powerhouse Goldman Sachs to handle their multimillion-dollar stock offerings. In 1946 Harry Piper's son, Harry ''Bob'' Piper, Jr., joined the firm as a runner in the cashier's ''cage.'' He worked his way up the ladder by winning investment accounts for the firm and by the early 1950s had been named a partner. In 1949, as the great 16-year postwar bull market began, Piper Jaffray opened a new office in Billings, Montana.

With the U.S. economy booming, the stock market underwent a major transformation. More and more major companies offered stock (more than 9,000 separate public offerings took place during the decade), the modern mutual fund was born, and institutional investors' share of the stock market rose to an unprecedented 25 percent. Despite these changes, Piper Jaffray remained a traditional firm dominated by informal decision making and training methods, a close-knit family spirit, and a hard-working culture. Nevertheless, in 1954 it set a precedent that few other firms in the industry could match when it appointed Ruth Cranston as its first female partner.

It also improved the speed with which it placed customers' orders on Wall Street by replacing its New York telegraph connection with a teletype, cutting transaction delays from 15 minutes to one minute. By the late 1950s Piper Jaffray's traditional handwritten ledger system for recording transactions had also been replaced by a mechanical keypunch accounting system and it had invested in its first mainframe computer, setting the stage for its rapid adoption of computing innovations in the coming years.

The "Go-Go" 1960s: 1960–70

In 1963, with revenues well more than $3 million, the *Minneapolis Tribune* celebrated the half-century-old partnership of founders Harry Piper, Sr., and Palmer Jaffray, now in their seventies, by touting their firm as "the largest locally owned entity in the Upper Midwest." In 1964 Piper Jaffray installed its first Stockmaster, an electronic stock monitoring system that replaced the now antiquated magnetic tape stock ticker system, Quotron. More important, Piper Jaffray acted on expansion plans set in motion in the 1950s by acquiring Minneapolis-based Jamieson & Co. (founded in 1939). The purchase doubled Piper Jaffray's revenues and size and extended its territory to Duluth, to Eau Claire, Wisconsin, and to unpenetrated regions of the Dakotas. These new branches added to the recent opening in Rapid City, South Dakota (1962) and were followed in 1967 by four- or five-broker offices in Omaha, Nebraska and Bismarck, North Dakota. In 1968 Piper Jaffray acquired the Wausau, Wisconsin-based over-the-counter (OTC) securities firm Altenburg & Gooding and a year later—as Harry Piper, Jr., became Jaffray's chairman and CEO—the company opened an OTC trading office in New York.

Piper Jaffray's formation of a formal Corporate Finance department in the late 1960s also signaled its intent to take on the complicated paperwork it had traditionally farmed out to Goldman Sachs. In 1969 Piper also took a step toward becoming a public stock itself when it incorporated, giving its principals the limited financial liability they would need to remain independent as they grew the business.

Growth: 1971–79

The technology, military, and aerospace boom of the 1960s had fueled a growing market that enriched many U.S. investment firms, who increasingly sought to expand through acquisition. Piper Jaffray found itself among this fast-growing lot, and throughout the 1970s it absorbed smaller, middle- and small-market investment firms. To fund this expansion, it first had to raise capital. In 1971, therefore, it held its first public stock offering, raising some $5.7 million, which during the next decade helped it acquire the faltering securities giant Goodbody & Company as well as firms in Minnesota, Iowa, and the Pacific Northwest. It also opened new territories by launching offices in Lincoln, Nebraska, and in Appleton, Madison, and Milwaukee, Wisconsin.

In 1972 Harry Piper, Jr., told the *Wall Street Journal* that by 1977 "20 to 25 percent of our business may be in things we now do modestly or not at all." In the early 1970s most of Piper Jaffray's business still revolved around buying and selling stock, trading municipal and corporate bonds, and underwriting stock offerings, but Harry Piper declared that the company would attempt to increase its business with institutional investors (then only eight percent of sales) and establish a corporate finance department that would rival the biggest Wall Street operations. In July 1972 Piper Jaffray endured much unwelcome publicity when Harry Piper's wife, Virginia, was kidnapped by an unknown group demanding $1 million in ransom. Harry Piper provided the money, and three days later Virginia was found tied to a tree near Duluth, Minnesota, dazed but alive. (Neither the ransom nor the kidnappers ever surfaced.)

Although the recession of 1973–74 pummeled Piper Jaffray's bottom line and stock, its newly enlarged Corporate Finance department began to establish a profitable new business for the firm—mergers and acquisitions (M&A). By the end of the decade Piper's M&A activity exceeded $760 million. Corporate Finance also entered the private placement market (in which firms raised capital by selling financial instruments to private investors) and the new venture capital market, underwriting the initial public offerings (IPOs) of new-breed companies like supercomputer maker Cray Research.

In 1974 Piper Jaffray reorganized itself into a public holding company, Piper Jaffray Inc., which became the parent company of the operational broker/dealer business, Piper, Jaffray & Hopwood. A year later it established an employee stock ownership trust (ESOT) to encourage its employees to identify more closely with the company's fortunes. When it attempted to raise capital for the ESOT through six public stock offerings, however, some of its shareholders claimed Piper Jaffray's offer price was too low and sued (a jury ruled in their favor in 1981).

In 1978 Piper Jaffray continued its tradition of technological innovation by installing the $4 million "Piper Pipeline," an electronic information and stock monitoring system that gave its customers the same real-time access to Wall Street data as the most sophisticated Manhattan brokerage. The same year, to help keep the Minnesota Vikings football team from leaving town, Piper Jaffray stage-managed a last-minute agreement to construct a new domed stadium for the Twin Cities, for which it oversaw the bond sale.

The Third Generation: 1980–89

By 1981 Piper Jaffray boasted more than 55,000 clients, 37 offices in 11 states, and annual revenues of $50.4 million, a more than threefold increase over 1971. In 1983 Harry Piper, Jr.'s son, Addison ("Tad"), who like his father had started his career in the firm's cashier's "cage," was named CEO. When the Hartford Insurance Group paid $29.3 million for 309,000 Piper Jaffray shares (25 percent of the firm's total shares) the same year, Piper Jaffray suddenly found itself with a new income stream—insurance products. Between 1980 and 1985 Piper Jaffray opened new offices in Denver, Kansas City, and Green Bay, Wisconsin, positioning itself to ride the bull market that began in 1982. Piper Jaffray's Fixed Income department, which handled public and private bond issues for state and local public institutions, was enjoying the success, meanwhile, that the Corporate Finance department had begun enjoying in the 1970s; by 1985 Piper Jaffray was managing or comanaging almost 250 bond issues a year with a total value of some $3.2 billion.

The firm moved into the new 42-story Piper Jaffray Tower in 1985 and in October of the same year opened a new ''Piper Capital Management'' operation to offer mutual funds and manage the money of pension funds, public asset funds, and large individual accounts. Within eight months Capital Management's portfolio had grown to more than $125 million in assets and by mid-1988 to almost $1.5 billion. In 1986 Piper Jaffray moved its stock listing from the Midwest and Chicago exchanges to NASDAQ and in 1987 introduced its first mutual funds. Early the same year it also unveiled a comprehensive five-year corporate plan, christened ''Vision 1992,'' that set ambitious goals for growing retail sales, expanding Piper Capital Management and its fixed-income/public finance markets, and gaining leadership in equity capital markets (the new umbrella term for Corporate Finance, equity trading, and institutional equity sales). Many of the firm's departments were reorganized and unified to streamline the company's operations and emphasize its customer-driven philosophy.

On Black Monday, October 22, 1987, the Dow Jones index dropped a stomach-churning 508 points, wiping out an estimated $500 billion in market value in the span of seven hours. Just as the Great Crash had left Piper with fewer scars than many of its competitors in 1929, however, so again in 1987 Piper Jaffray emerged intact. Its computerized data and reporting systems had handled the surge in trading volume smoothly, its employees had pulled the extra hours needed to calm frantic customers and process mountains of paperwork, and its banking allies had extended the financial resources needed to cover the transaction costs that some its customers were unable to ante up. Moreover, Piper Jaffray had refused to join the general panic, seeing the sell-off as an opportunity to market some of its favorite stocks at bargain-basement prices. As the ''me decade'' closed, Piper Jaffray could boast annual revenues of almost $200 million, a new institutional sales office in London, and a new fiduciary trust services subsidiary, Piper Trust Company. Best of all, *Forbes* magazine named Piper Jaffray first among all U.S. investment bankers for its post-IPO performance during the decade.

Centennial Triumph and Tribulation: 1990–97

By the 1990s Piper Jaffray had established itself as one of the largest regionally based brokers in the United States, with a reputation for expertise in food, agricultural, and medical technology industry stocks. In August 1990, Harry Piper, Jr., died, symbolically completing the passing of the baton of leadership to his son Tad that had begun in the 1980s. With one dramatic exception, Tad Piper's stewardship of the firm in the 1990s seemed to quicken the company's financial and geographic growth and range of investment products. In 1990 Piper Jaffray opened offices in Denver and Los Angeles, expanded its line of mutual funds to 17, and began installing the latest generation of computerized real-time investment data systems. Known as Stockmate, the $3.5 million system used a satellite data feed and a mainframe computer to give its far-flung offices the capability to make ever faster and more accurate trades. Its 1991 year-end revenues stood at $267.8 million—a threefold increase in less than a decade.

In 1992 Piper Jaffray ranked as the fifth largest security underwriter in the nation and before the year was out it had added securities firms in Kansas City and San Francisco to its roster of strategic acquisitions. It also opened offices in Tucson and Phoenix, Arizona and reorganized itself into three new core businesses: Individual Investor Services, Capital Markets (including equity and fixed income investment products), and Investment Management Services (encompassing Piper Capital Management and Piper Trust). In a reflection of its new identity it also dropped ''Hopwood'' from its corporate name, officially closing a six-decade-old chapter in its history.

By 1993 Piper Jaffray had 78 retail offices in 17 states and five straight years of record-setting growth. Moreover, with its tradition of multimillion-dollar annual charity giving and its reputation for conservative, ethical, customer-loyal investing (it had refused to participate in the hostile takeover craze of the 1980s), the firm's stature as it approached its centennial year celebration seemed secure.

In 1994, however, a little understood investment vehicle known as derivatives dealt a serious blow to Piper Jaffray's fortunes. Worth Bruntjen, one of the architects of Piper's Capital Management operation and the manager of its successful Institutional Government Income Portfolio (a short-term bond mutual fund) had attempted to boost his funds' returns by using derivatives, a financial instrument in which the return is tied to—or ''derived'' from—the performance of another instrument such as currencies, commodities, or bonds. Because the link between these interwoven instruments can be so substantial and so complex, the unexpected collapse of a derivative's underlying assets can quickly balloon into an enormous, snowballing loss.

Bruntjen had invested as much as 90 percent of his funds' $3.5 billion assets into such derivatives (in his case, derivatives based on residential mortgages grouped together as securities) and exacerbated his risk by borrowing to fund his purchases. Bruntjen's derivatives were based on his expectation that interest rates would decline, as they had in 1990 and 1991. When they began to rise in 1994, however, Bruntjen's funds rapidly accumulated a roughly $700 million paper loss, an embarrassment that one industry insider called ''one of the most incredible debacles in the financial services industry.'' To add to its injury, Piper had marketed Bruntjen's funds as conservative investments for the risk-averse. When the funds' investors learned of the catastrophe they filed suit against Piper for misleading shareholders and making ''monumental purchases of highly speculative securities.'' Amidst front-page coverage in the *Wall Street Journal,* Piper's carefully built reputation as the ''little old lady of brokerage firms'' seemed about to vanish. Tad Piper told the press, ''We do not believe we have done anything wrong,'' but later admitted, ''We got caught in a market that we thought we understood.'' Piper Jaffray then closed the funds to new investors and added an additional $10 million to ''show faith in the fund.''

The lawsuits wound their way through the courts—Piper Jaffray claiming all the while that it had fully disclosed all the funds' risks and investment tactics in its prospectuses and investors maintaining they had been defrauded. Beginning in 1995 it began paying out more than $100 million in settlements, and in 1996 the National Association of Securities Dealers levied a $1.125 million fine against it for its marketing practices in connection with the funds. In October 1997 the last class action lawsuit was settled for $24 million. Piper Jaffray could begin rebuilding its reputation anew.

Principal Subsidiaries

Piper Capital Management Incorporated; Piper Jaffray Inc.; Piper Trust Company.

Further Reading

Barshay, Jill J., ''Piper Jaffray Settles Last Derivatives Class-Action Suit,'' *Minneapolis Star-Tribune,* October 16, 1997.

''ITT Insurance Unit Agrees to Buy 25% of Piper Jaffray Inc.,'' *Wall Street Journal.*

Johnson, Robert, ''Piper Jaffray Sees Slightly Higher Profit for Year, Citing Small-Investor Activity,'' *Wall Street Journal,* June 8, 1990.

Knecht, G. Bruce, ''Minneapolis Investors Are Hurt by Local Firm They Knew As Cautious,'' *Wall Street Journal,* August 26, 1994, pp. A1, A5.

——, ''Piper Manager's Losses May Total $700 Million,'' *Wall Street Journal,* August 25, 1994, pp. C1, C19.

——, ''Piper Jaffray's Foiled Manager Is Used to Risk,'' *Wall Street Journal,* September 1, 1981, pp. C1, C17.

McGough, Robert, ''Piper Jaffray Acts to Boost Battered Fund,'' *Wall Street Journal,* May 23, 1994, pp. C1, C17.

Nelson, Rick, ''Less Proves More in Piper Suit,'' *Corporate Report Minnesota,* October 1995.

''Piper Jaffray Actions Manipulated Prices of Stock, Jury Finds,'' *Wall Street Journal,* May 8, 1981.

Piper Jaffray Companies, *Celebrating a Century of Service, 1895–1995,* Minneapolis: Piper Jaffray Companies, 1994.

''Piper Jaffray Pushes Diversification Plans,'' *Wall Street Journal,* September 19, 1972.

—Paul S. Bodine

Players International, Inc.

Players International, Inc.

1300 Atlantic Avenue, Suite 800
Atlantic City, New Jersey 08401
U.S.A.
(609) 449-7777
Fax: (609) 340-8165

Public Company
Founded: 1984
Employees: 4,642
Sales: $291.2 million (1997)
Stock Exchanges: NASDAQ
SICs: 7999 Amusement & Recreation, Not Elsewhere Classified; 5810 Eating & Drinking Places; 7011 Hotels & Motels; 7948 Racing, Including Track Operation

Players International, Inc. owns and operates gambling (gaming) operations in Illinois, Louisiana, Missouri, and Kentucky. Three of its entertainment and gaming facilities center around riverboat casinos: on the Ohio River in Metropolis, Illinois; in Lake Charles, Louisiana; and in Maryland Heights, Missouri. The company also owns Players Bluegrass Downs, a thoroughbred racetrack in Paducah, Kentucky.

Early History, 1984–92

Brothers Edward and David Fishman founded Players International in 1984 as an entertainment company and took it public. Their interest in the entertainment industry began some 10 years earlier when, in the mid-1970s, they created a TV game show, "Dealer's Choice," in Las Vegas.

In 1985, the Calabasas, California-based company introduced Player's Club, a discount travel service for middle-income recreational gamblers. For a fee of $125 a year, a member received discounts on rooms, food, beverages, and entertainment at participating casino hotels and cruise ships. Membership renewals, which ran at over 57 percent, were Players' largest source of income. The company also made money by organizing gaming tournaments for casinos in Las Vegas, Atlantic City, and Monte Carlo, and arranging travel for them, and by acting as a marketing agent for an electronic cash advance system for casinos. For the fiscal year ending in March 1990, the company's revenues reached $16.5 million, up from $12 million the year before, and profits increased from half a million dollars to $4 million.

Even though Players Club boasted 100,000 members, the Fishmans felt it was time to diversify their business. In the middle of 1990, they moved into telephone call-in games. Having met Merv Griffin at a blackjack tournament a few years earlier, they went to Merv Griffin Enterprises to negotiate a lease agreement to produce telephone call-in games based on the popular "Jeopardy!" and "Wheel of Fortune" TV shows.

The company also began exploring other entertainment and gaming options, and within a year was part of a joint venture to operate casinos aboard two cruise ships and had applied for a license to operate a riverboat casino in Illinois. The broadened diversification efforts proved wise. Leisure travel slumped due to the recession and the war in the Persian Gulf, and the call-in games never produced as expected. Although the games were successful enough to pay for development costs, and despite promotions by Telly Savalas, Players' celebrity spokesman, by the end of the fiscal year in March 1992, Players was in the red.

From Games to Gaming, 1993–95

The brothers revised their strategy to take advantage of the spread of casino gambling. Whereas in 1988, only two states, Nevada and New Jersey, had legalized gambling in casinos, during the beginning of the 1990s several other states began allowing casinos, in hopes of improving local economies as well as increasing state revenues. According to Janet Purdy Levaux in an *Investors Business Daily* article, by 1993 gamblers were betting $326 billion at casinos and American Indian reservations and wagers at riverboat casinos totaled $27 billion.

For their business this time, however, the Fishmans were not interested in providing discount travel services to casinos. They wanted to get in on the action themselves. Players International decided to concentrate completely on developing riverboat casinos and got out of the call-in games and Players Club activities completely.

Illinois was one of the states that had made casino gambling legal, and that was where the company focused its initial efforts. The Fishmans believed there was a big new market for riverboat casinos in the Midwest, attracting people who would not travel to the gambling operations on the East and West Coasts. As David Fishman explained in a 1991 article in *Barron's*, the company was going after the "big army of novices who are won over by the first pull on a slot machine."

With backing from Merv Griffin, Players opened its first riverboat gambling casino in February 1993, at Metropolis, Illinois, the only riverboat casino operating in southern Illinois. An historical replica of a 19th-century paddlewheeler, the riverboat casino could accommodate 1,200 passengers as it cruised on the Ohio River.

In December, Players expanded its operations south, into southwestern Louisiana, with the opening of a riverboat casino at Lake Charles, Louisiana. The casino in this replica of a paddlewheel riverboat was larger than that in Metropolis, with approximately 27,500 square feet of gaming space. Lake Charles was located about 200 miles west of New Orleans, near the border with Texas. Attracting people from the Houston, Texas, area as well as from western Louisiana, the Players Lake Charles Riverboat soon became one of the highest-grossing riverboat casinos in the country.

But riverboats were not all the company bought that year. It also acquired a thoroughbred racetrack in Paducah, Kentucky, which it named Players Bluegrass Downs. The track hosted live races each fall. During the rest of the year, patrons could watch simulcasts of thoroughbred horse racing events; the track facilities were also leased for special events and activities. The company bought the racetrack for its potential should the Kentucky legislature allow electronic gaming devices at licensed racetracks.

On the management side of the company, David Fishman retired from the company, having served as secretary since 1985. Edward continued to serve as chairman of the board and chief executive officer, and Howard Goldberg, a lawyer who specialized in representing casinos in New Jersey, was named president and chief operating officer.

Expanding and Enhancing Operations, 1994–95

With the improving economy came greater competition for the American leisure dollar. Gaming proliferated as additional states legalized casino gambling and more Native American tribes opened casinos on tribal land. By 1995, some two dozen states had casinos. In addition to such direct gaming competition were the many vacation and tourist options—amusement and theme parks, cruises, resorts—vying for customers, who were demanding more entertainment for their buck. To attract customers, casino operators had to offer more than gaming tables and slot machines. They had to make their properties tourist attractions in and of themselves. Players, with a healthy balance sheet and strong earnings, was in a good position to move in that direction, beginning in Metropolis.

In 1994, a joint venture, in which Players was a partner, built and opened a 120-room hotel adjacent to the Metropolis facility. The company also leased the Merv Griffin Theatre, a cabaret-style theater, which was located beside the hotel and was used for special events and promotions. The company's docking facilities, known as Merv Griffin's Landing, consisted of three permanently moored barges. One barge housed Merv Griffin's Bar and Grill, the Celebrity Buffet restaurant, and meeting rooms. Another barge contained the ticketing area, a gift shop, restrooms, waiting rooms, and a VIP lounge. The third barge was used as a queuing area for people waiting to board the riverboat. Under an agreement with The Griffin Group, Players had the right to use Merv Griffin's name in connection with these properties through December 1996. Mr. Griffin, a major shareholder in the company, acted as the public representative for all of Players' riverboat and dockside casinos and provided promotional services, with the Griffin Group receiving a fee and warrants to buy company shares.

During the fiscal year that ended in March 1995, the company's two riverboat casino facilities brought in $224 million in revenues, and Players had net income of $46 million.

During 1995, the company turned its attention to Lake Charles, beginning a $150 million expansion with the addition of a second riverboat casino. In January, Players acquired all the interests in a partnership that owned the Star Riverboat, which had operated on Lake Pontchartrain near New Orleans, and relocated it to Lake Charles, reopening it in April. The smallest of its three riverboat casinos, the three-deck Star Riverboat, offered approximately 21,730 square feet of air-conditioned gaming space, including 733 slot machines and 47 game tables. The two Lake Charles riverboats shared the same docking facilities.

Under Louisiana law no gambling was allowed while a riverboat was docked, except for 45 minutes between cruises, and a cruise had to be at least three hours long. With two boats, the company was able to stagger those three-hour cruise schedules so that each boat was operating up to 24 hours a day, and a boat was almost continually available for boarding (and gaming).

In October that year, the company replaced the original Lake Charles riverboat, Players II, with the Players III, a larger, more spacious riverboat, with 29,200 square feet of gaming space, 896 slot machines, and 62 tables on its three decks. The new boat could handle over 1300 passengers. The company also acquired the Downtowner, a 134-room hotel, renaming it the Players Hotel, built a 540-space parking garage, and began plans for a 60,000-square-foot entertainment island at the Lake Charles docking area.

The Lake Charles riverboat was moved to Metropolis, where it replaced the company's first riverboat casino. The more spacious riverboat casino, with 862 slot machines and 51 table games, helped accommodate the larger numbers of passengers coming to Metropolis on the weekends and holidays.

But Players was not satisfied with expanding its riverboat casino operations. In June, the company moved on-shore, opening its only land-based entertainment facility, the Players Island Resort, in Mesquite, Nevada. Located about an hour's drive northeast of Las Vegas, the property was marketed as a destination resort with gaming. Visitors had the option of staying at the 500-room hotel, in one of four three-room villas, or making use of the 50-unit recreational vehicle facility. While at the resort, they could take advantage of the world class health spa, a lagoon swimming pool complete with waterfall, an 18-hole golf course, tennis courts, a children's arcade, four restaurants, as well as a 40,000-square-foot casino.

By the middle of 1995, the company was doing so well its stock price had nearly doubled and there was speculation that Players might be a takeover target. *BusinessWeek* cited "its growth prospects, healthy balance sheet, strong earnings, and robust cash flow" as the reasons for the price jump.

In November 1995, Players moved its corporate offices from Las Vegas to Atlantic City, New Jersey. In December, Howard Goldberg was named chief executive officer, replacing Edward Fishman, who remained chairman of the board.

1996 to the Present

Players continued to expand and improve its facilities during 1996. In February the company opened The Island at its Lake Charles facility. This 60,000-square-foot floating entertainment area was designed with a tropical theme, complete with lush vegetation, waterfalls, and rockscapes. Passengers heading for the riverboat casinos walked through it to board, and could visit one of three new restaurants, a sports bar, and a large gift shop. They could also watch an animatronics show with a pirate theme.

March saw the opening of a brand new entertainment and gaming facility in Maryland Heights, Missouri, a suburb of St. Louis. A joint venture with Harrah's, the $300 million Riverport Casino Center consisted of four permanently docked riverboat casinos, totaling some 120,000 square feet. Players was responsible for the licensing, operation, and marketing of two of the four casinos, but shared equally in the development and marketing of the hotel, entertainment, and parking properties. Called Players Island, the company's two riverboat casinos, with a total of 60,000 square feet of gaming space, offered 1,230 slot machines and 75 table games. Carrying the tropical theme established at the Lake Charles Island right into the Maryland Heights casinos, passengers could play the machines and tables amid waterfalls, rockscapes, and palm trees. A massive salt water aquarium served as a partition wall between the two casinos.

All four casinos were on barges moored to an entertainment facility that resembled a turn-of-the-century Missouri riverboat town, containing retail shops, two restaurants, a 600-seat buffet, a child care facility, a 125-seat entertainment lounge, a 10,000-square-foot convention center, and parking for over 5,000 vehicles. A hotel with 291 rooms completed the facility.

Meanwhile, the company added more parking in Metropolis, increasing the total number of spaces to 1,300. In October, Players bought a restaurant barge with plans to renovate it with upgraded buffet facilities, a larger dining room, and a more spacious gift shop. The company hoped to have the new facilities ready by the fall of 1997.

Despite these additions and improvements, the increasing competition in the gaming industry led to a drop in revenues and a net loss for the company in the year ending March 1997. In response, Players decided to eliminate its development activities and to concentrate on operating its existing properties. It closed its development department, sold off a corporate airplane and the original Metropolis riverboat, saw the retirement or termination of 21 senior management staff, and began reviewing the growth opportunities of each of its properties. One conclusion was that the Mesquite resort was not generating sufficient income, so the company sold it in 1997 to RBG, LLC for $30.5 million, using the proceeds to pay down some of its debt. Players also determined that, since the Kentucky legislature still had not taken any action on allowing gaming machines at racetracks, Players Bluegrass Downs was impaired and wrote down the facility to a value of $475,000.

The company moved back into the black again. The Maryland Heights complex more than doubled the revenues from the sold Mesquite property and compensated for the continued drop in revenues from the Lake Charles facility due to increased competition. Despite the difficulties at Lake Charles, the company believed the property still had great potential and, in November 1997, bought the Lake Charles Holiday Inn for $18.5 million. Located right beside Players' existing facility, the hotel had 269 rooms, five restaurants, and over 4,000 square feet of meeting space. Players also undertook a cooperative marketing campaign with its major competitor there, the Isle of Capri Casino. As was becoming more common among vying tourist attractions, the two competitors worked together to sell more people on the idea of Lake Charles as a destination.

The company's belt tightening and shift from developer to operator strengthened its position. However, despite the popularity of Maryland Heights, a cloud hung over it as 1997 ended. In November, the Missouri Supreme Court overturned a ruling by a lower court that it was legal under the state's gaming act for floating casinos to be located in artificial basins fed by either the Mississippi or Missouri Rivers. The court ruled that such casinos must be contiguous to the rivers and sent the case back to the trial court for a hearing. Since the riverboat casinos at Maryland Heights are not on the Missouri River, the ruling threatened their existence.

Principal Subsidiaries

Metropolis, IL 1292 Limited Partnership; PCI, Inc.; Players Bluegrass Downs, Inc.; Players Development, Inc.; Players Entertainment, Inc.; Players Holding, Inc.; Players Lake Charles, LLC; Players Lake Charles Riverboat, Inc.; Players LC, Inc.; Players Maryland Heights, Inc.; Players MH, L.P.; Players Maryland Heights Nevada, Inc.; Players Mesquite Golf Club, Inc.; Players Mesquite Land, Inc.; Players Nevada, Inc.; Players Resources, Inc.; Players Riverboat, LLC; Players Riverboat, Inc.; Players Riverboat Management, Inc.; Players Services, Inc.; Riverfront Realty Corporation; Riverside Joint Venture; Showboat Star Partnership; Southern Illinois Riverboat/Casino Cruises, Inc.; WCBJ Enterprises, Inc.

Further Reading

Byrne, Harlan S., "Players International: It Places Big Chips on 900-Number TV Tie-ins," *Barron's*, April 29, 1991, p. 40.

Horowitz, Carl, "Gambling: Boon or Social Ill," *Investor's Business Daily*, October 18, 1995.

Levaux, Janet Purdy, "Some Are Rolling Snake Eyes in Louisiana," *Investor's Business Daily*, June 20, 1995.

Marcial, Gene G., "... And Casinos on the River," *BusinessWeek*, June 19, 1995.

"Missouri Gaming Rules Could Cost Locals Money," *Reuters*, November 26, 1997.

"The New America: On a Roll—Players International," *Investor's Business Daily*, July 7, 1995.

—Ellen D. Wernick

PPG Industries, Inc.

One PPG Place
Pittsburgh, Pennsylvania 15272
U.S.A.
(412) 434-3131
Fax: (412) 434-2448
Web site: http://www.ppg.com

Public Company
Incorporated: 1883 as Pittsburgh Plate Glass Company
Employees: 31,300
Sales: $7.22 billion (1996)
Stock Exchanges: New York Pacific Philadelphia
SICs: 2812 Alkalied & Chlorine; 2816 Inorganic Pigments; 2821 Plastics Materials, Nonvulcanizable Elastomers & Synthetic Resins; 2851 Paints, Varnishes, Lacquers, Enamels & Allied Products; 2869 Industrial Organic Chemicals, Not Elsewhere Classified; 3211 Flat Glass; 3229 Pressed & Blown Glass & Glassware, Not Elsewhere Classified

PPG Industries, Inc. is a global producer of flat glass, fiber glass, fabricated glass products, coatings and resins, and industrial and specialty chemicals. It is a world leader in the manufacture of flat glass, is the second-largest maker of continuous-strand fiber glass, and is the world's largest producer of automotive and industrial coatings and of optical resins. PPG is a leading supplier of products for manufacturing, building, automotive, chemical processing, and numerous other industries. The company operates about 75 production facilities in Australia, Canada, China, France, Germany, Ireland, Italy, Mexico, the Netherlands, Portugal, Spain, Taiwan, the United Kingdom, and the United States; and supports nine research-and-development facilities worldwide. PPG has grown from the dream of two men into a global corporation that derives more than one-third of its revenues from outside the United States.

Founded in 1883 As a Plate Glass Manufacturer

Captain John B. Ford and John Pitcairn created the Pittsburgh Plate Glass Company (PPG) in 1883. The first financially successful U.S. plate glass manufacturer, the company was located in Creighton, Pennsylvania, northeast of Pittsburgh. It moved its headquarters to Pittsburgh in 1895. Prior to the 1880s over a dozen plate glass makers had tried unsuccessfully to compete with their European counterparts. Despite American technical ability, plate glass for America's growing cities continued to be imported from Belgium, England, France, and Germany.

Manufacturing profits on glass were inconsistent partly due to the independents who controlled glass distribution. In 1896 Pitcairn established a commercial department and PPG became its own warehouser and distributor. Due to disagreements with Pitcairn regarding distribution, John Ford's sons sold their PPG interests and formed the Edward Ford Plate Glass Company. During the Great Depression, Ford merged with Libbey-Owens Sheet Glass to form Libbey-Owens-Ford Glass Company, now owned by Pilkington plc of the United Kingdom.

Pitcairn became president of PPG, and in 1899 he built the Columbia Chemical Company at Barbeton, Ohio. This independent company produced soda ash, a major raw material used in making glass. This plant was a forerunner of PPG's chemical group. By the following year PPG was selling 13 million square feet of plate glass a year and had become the nation's most successful plate glass maker.

Expanded into Paints by Early 20th Century

Pitcairn continued to expand PPG's product line. Because paints and brushes were distributed through the same channels as glass, they were a logical addition to the company. By the end of 1900 PPG had acquired a major interest in Milwaukee, Wisconsin based Patton Paint Company, the precursor to PPG's current coatings and resins group.

In the early years PPG had manufactured only plate glass. It marketed but did not produce window glass, or sheet glass. In 1907, however, the first window-glass factory was added to com-

Company Perspectives:

PPG Industries' mission is to serve customers through effective use of our resources, to provide a fulfilling workplace for our employees, to be recognized as an outstanding corporate citizen, and to generate superior returns to our shareholders. In achieving this mission, our enterprise will be publicly owned, diversified, and global in operation.

pany operations, in Mount Vernon, Ohio. In 1915 a second plant was opened in Clarksburg, West Virginia. Pitcairn's strong interest in innovation and diversification led to the opening of the company's first research-and-development facility in 1910.

The first stage of PPG's development came to an end in 1916 with Pitcairn's death. In 33 years he had led the company through economic panics, foreign competition, and restrictive distribution channels to become the nation's largest plate glass manufacturer. He was also the force behind diversification of the company's product line as well as the development of raw material sources and expansion of marketing outlets for its many products.

In 1919 subsidiaries yielded more than 50 percent of net return for the year. In November 1920 PPG stockholders voted unanimously to fold the company's subsidiaries into the parent company, making them divisions.

Became Automotive Supplier During the 1920s

The 1920s were prosperous for PPG. As steel-cage and concrete-reinforced construction became the standard for building, architects were able to design structures with larger window units, and glass consumption reached record levels in the United States. During this decade, the automobile industry also began using more glass. The switch from the open touring car to the sedan caused an expanded need for glass, and PPG met the demand.

PPG also made several technological innovations during the 1920s. In 1924 the company switched from the batch method of making plate glass to the ribbon method. With this technique, molten glass from a constantly replenished melting furnace flowed through water-cooled shaping rollers. The glass was then cooled and cut into large plates.

In 1928 PPG first mass-produced sheet glass, using the Pittsburgh Process, which improved quality and sped up production. For the first time PPG became a major supplier of window glass. The Pittsburgh Process, invented by PPG, involves drawing a continuous sheet of molten glass from a tank vertically up a four-story forming-and-cooling line. In 1928 the Creighton Process was developed. An economical process for laminating glass for automobile windshields, PPG introduced Duplate laminated safety glass through a glass-plastic unit.

In 1924 PPG produced its first auto lacquer which the company marketed in only a limited number of conservative colors. By 1929 PPG supplied "no less than 500 harmonious hues" to 40 automakers. The company had also begun using a long-lasting, fast-drying finish developed by the Ditzler Color Company, a subsidiary acquired in 1928.

Always seeking to diversify, in 1923 PPG began to use limestone screening, a waste product of soda ash, to manufacture Portland cement. During the Great Depression, PPG developed new paint and glass products. In the 1930s the company developed titanium dioxide pigments, which greatly increased the opacity of light colors. It also created fast-drying Wall-hide flat paint, which made it possible to apply two coats of paint in one day. In 1934 PPG introduced Solex heat-absorbing glass. Also in 1934, it perfected a glass-bending technique that made the production of car windshields easier. In 1938 PPG introduced Herculite tempered glass. Herculite glass was several times stronger and more shatter resistant than ordinary plate glass.

Diversification paid off again for PPG during World War II. In 1940, the year before Japan attacked Pearl Harbor, the glass division had developed Flexseal laminated aircraft glass. During the war, when production of automobiles was temporarily halted and building was curtailed, PPG converted much of its production into materials for military use. Due to the shortage of raw materials during the war, PPG worked hard to develop synthetic resins, which inspired the development of plastics and high-performance paints and industrial coatings.

Explosive Postwar Growth

During the 1950s car production and construction of new homes and glass-and-steel buildings exploded. PPG stepped up production to meet demand, and continued to diversify. Fiber glass had been a laboratory novelty until the 1930s. By 1950, however, it was being used in decorative fabrics and for insulation. In 1952 PPG opened its fiber glass business, making both textiles and reinforcements.

Also during the 1950s, PPG developed lead-free house paints. In 1951, the company created the first latex-based interior paint and three years later brought a latex exterior house paint to the market. PPG was also one of the first companies to produce a no-wax car finish, and its chemical division introduced several new products, including a swimming pool purifier.

In 1955 PPG's sales topped $500 million. The company employed 33,000 people in seven glass plants, three glass-fabricating plants, two specialty plants, two fiber glass plants, 17 coating and resins plants, and five chemical plants. In the early 1960s PPG produced materials for the building, transportation, appliance, container, boating, textile, paper, television, and chemicals industries. In 1963 it became the first U.S. company to manufacture float glass, used in place of plate glass by architects. In the same year, PPG introduced Herculite K, glass three to five times more shatter resistant than ordinary window glass. Herculite K became popular for residential storm- and sliding-door units because of its low cost.

During the early part of the 1960s a heavy capital-investment program moved the company toward $1 billion in sales, a goal it reached in 1968. In the same year, the company changed its name to PPG Industries, Inc., to reflect its size, diversification, and global presence.

During the mid-1960s the company developed a coating process called electrodeposition. Electrodeposition involves submerging positively charged metal parts in a tank containing negatively charged paint particles suspended in water. The opposite charges attract each other, and the metal is coated more uniformly than if it had been sprayed or dipped. In 1969 the chemicals group won the Kirkpatrick Chemical Engineering Achievement Award for developing a process for the simultaneous production of perchloroethylene, widely used in drycleaning, and trichloroethylene, a degreaser.

The oil embargo, the increased price of oil, natural gas, and electricity, and the dwindling production of fuels in the United States revived interest in solar energy in the 1970s. PPG was the first major corporation to develop a flat-plate solar collector, a unit first marketed in 1975. PPG also continued to work on high-luster, long-life automotive finishes. It improved its acrylic lacquers and developed acrylic dispersion topcoat finishes with lower solvent emissions during baking, which are less harmful to the environment. In the early 1970s more Americans began to repair and refinish automobiles in order to extend their cars' life span. PPG's Ditzler unit developed easy-to-apply primers and topcoats that matched factory-applied coatings in performance and appearance.

During the 1970s tinted, insulated, and reflective plate and float glasses came to be known as "performance" glass, or "environmental" glass, as the energy efficient and attractive glass became the preferred material for curtain walls. In 1973 the last plate glass production line was phased out and was replaced by the float glass production method. Also in 1973, Wallhide Microflo consumer paints were introduced. The Microflo process created air pockets in paint films that helped reflect light more efficiently as well as producing easy-to-apply paint with a smooth, washable surface. In 1975 PPG continued to broaden its color line by introducing a new custom-tinting system for consumer paints called the DesignaColor System.

In 1975 PPG established a fifth division, plastic fabricating, and closed several outmoded plants. The corporation also restructured its marketing organization, disbanding the merchandising division established by John Pitcairn in 1896, and continued to develop high-performance glasses, coatings, and fiber glass products. In 1976 PPG reached $2 billion dollars in sales.

The year 1985 was the end of a chapter in PPG's history as the heirs of John Pitcairn sold their remaining stake in PPG back to the company for $530 million. PPG's biomedical systems division was established in 1986 and 1987 with the acquisition of medical-electronics operations from Honeywell, Litton Industries, and Allegheny International. The group produced computer-assisted cardiac recording equipment, patient-monitoring systems, electrocardiogram instruments, defibrillators, and related products for the health-care industry. In 1989 PPG significantly expanded its standing as a leading producer of architectural finishes with the acquisition of Olympic stains and paints and Lucite paints from the Clorox Company for $134 million.

The drop in the U.S. auto and construction markets during the late 1980s hurt PPG's sales. Automakers were PPG's largest customers, and fluctuations in that market reduced the company's profits. In 1989 the company's earnings dropped one percent, interrupting a six-year upward trend. Nevertheless, Vincent A. Sarni, who became chairman in 1984 and CEO in 1983, felt PPG was making progress toward goals set for the ten year period from 1985 to 1994. On February 26, 1990, *Barron's* reported that "The company has stayed consistently ahead of a goal to show an average annual return on equity of 18%." Sarni believed that by 1994 PPG would reach targeted annual sales of $8 billion even without acquisitions.

Difficult Early 1990s Gave Way to Mid-1990s Recovery

PPG fell far short of Sarni's ambitious sales goal as growth was derailed by the recession of the early 1990s, which hit the construction and automotive sector particularly hard. Following the 1990 peak of $6.02 billion in 1990, revenues actually declined to $5.75 billion by 1993. Nevertheless, PPG did manage to stay profitable throughout the recession, despite the difficult environment.

Sarni was more successful with his aim of expanding PPG globally. About one-quarter of the company's revenues came from outside the United States in 1986, but by the early 1990s the figure had grown to more than one-third. Much of this growth was accomplished through acquisitions. In 1990 the company acquired its partners' interests (the two-thirds not already owned by PPG) in Silenka B.V., a Dutch fiber glass producer, bolstering its already strong position in the European fiber glass market. That same year, PPG also bought Finland's Tamglass Automotive OY, which gave PPG a significant presence in the European replacement glass business, and Etablissements Robert Ouvrie S.A. of France, a maker of surfactants and paper specialty chemicals. In June 1991 PPG acquired the automotive coatings business of ICI Canada.

In September 1993 PPG's board surprised many when, for the first time in company history, it appointed an outsider, Jerry E. Dempsey, as chairman and CEO, to replace the retiring Sarni. The board evidently felt that none of the in-house candidates were quite ready to assume the leadership mantle. Dempsey, an engineer by training, had been president and COO of auto parts maker Borg-Warner Corp. from 1979 to 1984 before heading Chemical Waste Management. Meanwhile, the company decided in 1993 to sell off its Biomedical Systems Division. This noncore operation was completely divested by January 1995. The move left PPG with its three core segments: coatings and resins, glass, and chemicals.

Under Dempsey's leadership, PPG enjoyed sales growth of 10 and 11.5 percent in 1994 and 1995, respectively. Profits grew even faster, highlighted by a 50 percent increase in 1995. Fueling this revival was Dempsey's emphasis on heightened marketing efforts, with a particular stress on seeking out new niches for PPG that required skillful marketing. For example, by 1995 Dempsey had transformed Transitions, a troubled unit that made color-changing sunglasses, into a $100 million business growing at a rate of 40 percent per year. Dempsey also sought out new ways to leverage PPG's existing expertise, as for example in the coatings unit's running of entire paint operations in auto plants. During this period, growth was also achieved through acquisitions, including the 1995 purchases of the American Finishes refinish coatings business of Lilly Industries and of Matthews Paint Co., a leading manufacturer of paints for outdoor metal signs.

Dempsey retired in late 1997, with PPG on the upswing and his having overseen an orderly leadership succession. In December 1995 Executive Vice-President Raymond W. LeBoeuf, who had joined the company in 1980 as treasurer, became president and chief operating officer. LeBoeuf subsequently succeeded Dempsey as CEO in July 1997 and as chairman in November 1997.

LeBoeuf immediately set lofty goals for PPG for the remainder of the decade, aiming for $10 billion in sales (compared to $7.22 billion in 1996) and a doubling of net earnings from the $744 million of 1996. To achieve these goals, the company was likely to continue Dempsey's emphasis on marketing, to seek out profitable acquisitions, and to continue to expand geographically, with emphasis on the Latin American and Asia-Pacific regions.

Principal Subsidiaries

LYNX Services from PPG, L.L.C.; Market View, Inc.; Matthews Paint Company; PPG Architectural Finishes, Inc.; PPG Industries International, Inc.; PPG Industries Securities, Inc.; Transitions Optical, Inc. (51%); PPG Canada Inc.; PPG Iberica, S.A. (Spain; 60%); PPG Industries, (Deutschland) GmbH (Germany); PPG Industries Fiber Glass B.V. (The Netherlands); PPG Industries France; PPG Industries Glass S.A. (France); PPG Industries Italia S.r.l. (Italy); PPG Industries (U.K.) Limited; PPG Industries Chemicals B.V. (The Netherlands); Transitions Optical Limited (Ireland; 51%); PPG Holdings (U.K.) Limited; PPG Holdings B.V. (The Netherlands); PPG Industries Holdings GmbH (Germany); PPG Coatings (Hong Kong) Co. Ltd. (60%); PPG-Feng Tai, Ltd. (Hong Kong; 55%); PPG Industries Asia/Pacific Ltd. (Japan); PPG Industries Argentina S.A.; PPG Industries de Mexico, S.A. de C.V.; PPG Industries Export Sales Corporation (U.S. Virgin Islands); PPG C.I. Co. Ltd. (Japan; 51%); PPG Industries Taiwan Ltd. (55%); Taiwan Chlorine Industries Ltd. (60%)

Further Reading

Baker, Stephen, "A New Paint Job at PPG," *Business Week,* November 13, 1995, pp. 74, 78.

Berss, Marcia, "Leveraged for Takeoff," *Forbes,* November 22, 1993, pp. 86, 88.

Byrne, Harlan S., "PPG Industries Inc.: It Tops the Goals Set in Its Ambitious 'Blueprint,' " *Barron's,* February 26, 1990, pp. 48–49.

A Concern for the Future: A History of PPG Industries, Inc., Pittsburgh: PPG Industries, 1976.

Curtis, Carol E., "Patience Money in Pittsburgh," *Forbes,* March 11, 1985, p. 40.

Hunter, David, "Specialities Surge for PPG's Chemicals Group: A Big Push for International Growth," *Chemical Week,* March 2, 1994, p. 26.

Lappen, Alyssa A., "Buying Back the Family Jewels," *Forbes,* September 17, 1990, pp. 101, 104, 108.

Norton, Erle, "PPG Industries Selects Two Contenders for CEO's Post to Newly Created Office," *Wall Street Journal,* April 6, 1994, p. B9.

——, "PPG Names LeBoeuf, President, Chief of Operations, Positions Heir Apparent," *Wall Street Journal,* December 15, 1995, p. B11.

Paull, Barbara I., "Signature: Vincent A. Sarni," *Managing,* July 1985, p. 19.

Saporito, Bill, "PPG: Shiny, Not Dull," *Fortune,* July 17, 1989, p. 107.

Sheeline, William E., "Managing a Clan Worth $1 Billion," *Fortune,* June 4, 1990, pp. 239, 242, 246.

Storck, William J., "PPG's New Chairman Looks to Continue Company's Winning Ways," *Chemical & Engineering News,* January 10, 1994, pp. 10–12.

—Virginia L. Smiley
—updated by David E. Salamie

PRESIDENT CASINO ON THE
ADMIRAL
St. Louis, Missouri

President Casinos, Inc.

800 North First Street
St. Louis, Missouri 63102
U.S.A.
(314) 622-3000
Fax: (314) 622-3049
Web site: http://www.presidentcasino.com

Public Company
Incorporated: 1992
Employees: 2,800
Sales: $183.6 million (1997)
Stock Exchanges: NASDAQ
SICs: 7993 Coin-Operated Amusement Devices; 7999 Amusement & Recreation; 6719 Holding Companies

President Casinos, Inc. develops, owns, and operates riverboat and/or dockside gaming casinos and related operations through its subsidiaries in Davenport, Iowa; Biloxi, Mississippi; and St. Louis, Missouri. Additionally, the company owns and manages hotel and ancillary facilities associated with its riverboat operations in Davenport, and operates two non-gaming dinner cruise, excursion, and sightseeing vessels on the Mississippi River in St. Louis, Missouri. Other of its vessels are chartered to unrelated third parties. President Casinos is the successor to businesses begun in St. Louis, Missouri, since 1985, Davenport, Iowa, since October 1990, and Biloxi, Mississippi, since August 1992. The company targets middle-income recreational gamblers.

President Casinos' venture *The President* riverboat in Davenport, Iowa, opened in April 1991, becoming one of the first gaming vessels in the country. During that period the company also opened *The President Casino Mississippi* in Biloxi, Mississippi, while President Casino's founder, Pittsburgh-based-entrepreneur John Connelly, rallied for gambling legalization in Missouri. Connelly had purchased *The Admiral,* a St. Louis-based entertainment vessel from Streckfus Steamers in 1981, then sold it to a group of investors in 1982. By 1988 Connelly was managing *The Admiral* as a dockside entertainment facility, and eventually repurchased the vessel in 1990.

Connelly, formerly one of the country's 400 richest people—and President Casino's founder, CEO, chairman, and director—has owned the Gateway Clipper fleet in Pittsburgh since 1958 and the Sheraton Hotel at Station Square in Pittsburgh since 1981. He also founded World Yacht Enterprises, a fleet of dinner cruise, sightseeing, and excursion boats in New York City in 1984, and heads J. Edward Connelly Associates, Inc., a marketing and premiums firm based in Pittsburgh. The *New York Times* and *Fortune* magazine have referred to Connelly as the "father" of incentive bank marketing.

Gambling on New Markets in the Early 1990s

In June 1992, the newly formed corporation President Casinos, Inc. prepared to make a public offering with an estimated $70 million worth of shares. The proceeds were needed to pay off debts and to prepare for expansion into gaming operations in St. Louis, Missouri—assuming that gambling would be legalized there—and to further expansion along Mississippi's Gold Coast, since gambling had been approved there the previous year, subject to a county by county popular vote. An SEC filing stated that at least $3 million raised in the stock offering would be paid directly to Connelly to reimburse him for his personal costs in launching the Mississippi corporation.

Connelly's Mississippi-expansion efforts were complicated by a lawsuit filed against him by Dallas, Texas hotelier and competitor Jack Pratt, whose Pratt Hotel Corporation operates hotels and casinos in the United States, Mexico, and the Caribbean. Both Pratt and Connelly, among others, had applied for gambling licenses in Harrison County, where gaming had been approved. The suit claimed that Connelly and his subsidiaries interfered with the Pratt group's lease for the Broadwater Beach Hotel, Casino, and Resort Club in Biloxi, Mississippi, a strategically located property. The Pratt group had successfully campaigned for passage of a local gambling referendum and had already signed a lease for the property, based on unresolved contingencies. According to Paton Huntley of the *Pittsburgh Business Times,* "Mr. Pratt claims Mr. Connelly subsequently persuaded the resort's owner to violate the lease so he could purchase the property for himself and establish gambling operations there—a move the suit calls an 'unlawful activity and conspiracy.' The suit asks that Mr. Pratt's lease be upheld and

Company Perspectives:

In a competitive industry dependent upon unit expansion for significant growth, growing the Company means increasing the number of sites. The Company continually and selectively explores gaming developments in current and emerging markets, including riverboat, land-based and Indian gaming opportunities.

seeks unspecified damages from Mr. Connelly's interests and the resort's former owner, the Joe W. and Dorothy Dorsett Brown Foundation.'' A temporary restraining order was filed, prohibiting the transfer of the resort to anyone refusing to honor Mr. Pratt's lease. The Pratt Hotel Corporation was engaged in a similar ongoing legal battle in New Jersey, involving an Atlantic City casino property, against real estate developer Donald Trump and *Penthouse* publisher Bob Guccione, as reported by Paton Huntley. Eventually, all claims in the ''Pratt Litigation'' were dismissed ''with prejudice.'' The Pratt settlement agreement initially cost the company a hefty $1 million first installment, financed by a loan made to the Company by BH Acquisition Corporation, a company controlled by Connelly. The note funded the first of four payments to Pratt's group.

Connelly claimed in the Securities and Exchange Filing Notes that new market expansion was required to offset threatened company revenues in Davenport, Iowa. Ebbing revenues were anticipated as a consequence of the legalization of gambling on the other side of the Mississippi River, in the state of Illinois. Connelly then sold his President Riverboat Casino-Mississippi company to the Davenport firm for 177,867 shares of stock, where Connelly already held a 72.5 percent interest. From its dockside and riverboat operations in Iowa and Mississippi, President Riverboat Casinos reported fiscal 1993 revenues of $61.3 million, showing a net profit of $3 million.

The company entered into a partnership to manage a land-based gaming casino to be owned by the St. Regis Mohawk Indian Tribe, but by 1995, due to an upheld management agreement with the Tribe, President Casinos wrote off its $4.1 million investment in the project. Elsewhere, a Gary, Indiana riverboat join-venture project was reconsidered and the company again backed out, writing off another $1.1 million. An option agreement in Philadelphia, Pennsylvania, followed suit with an investment write-off of $11 million due to the uncertainty of riverboat gaming legalization within that state. In Mississippi, the company sold its floating casino in Tunica (which had opened in 1993 and closed in 1995 as a result of competition and poor location), for approximately $15 million, freeing needed cash.

In an effort to improve its Biloxi market position, the company chartered the *Gold Coast* barge from American Gaming and Entertainment Ltd., with the hope of establishing a casino large enough to compete with the dozen others then operating along the Mississippi Gulf Coast. Revenues from the *Gold Coast* barge were at a break-even level due to competitive pressures, the strain of paying considerable rental fees on the vessel, fees to lease the mooring site, and fees for parking facilities.

In September 1993, the company had applied to the Missouri Gaming Commission for two gaming licenses, one for the $37.8 million riverboat casino, *The Admiral*, a five-deck, 400-foot long, 90-foot wide vessel, which had served as the largest passenger vessel on the Mississippi for 40 years. Originally christened the *S.S. Albatross*, the vessel operated as a dining and entertainment cruise ship since 1940. After an extensive renovation, President Casinos planned to dock it at the base of the famous Gateway Arch in St. Louis, within walking distance of Busch Stadium, the Cervantes Convention Center, the Trans World Dome, and linked to hotels, restaurants, and offices by a Metro Link light-rail system. The second license request was for a barge that would moor next to it.

The company had already canceled a second stock offering the previous June, after losing its bid for a Louisiana gaming license. The stock revenues were to finance the costs of moving into the Louisiana and Missouri markets, in addition to providing working capital. Due to the limited licensing of prime, dockside locations along designated St. Louis river fronts, and given that permanently-docked boats are less expensive to operate than cruising ones, competition for dockside positions was intense.

Fortunately for the company, in May 1994, Connelly's efforts were rewarded and a gaming license was granted. The vessel, sporting 64 blackjack tables, 10 craps tables, 22 poker tables, and approximately 400 video poker machines commenced operations. Later in the year, Missouri voters approved a constitutional amendment permitting ''games of chance,'' including slot machines, which *The Admiral* soon added to its repertoire. The company pays leasing fees for the site, payable to the City of St. Louis. Missouri regulations do not require that dockside vessels actually cruise, but simulated cruising requirements are imposed, which allow entry on a vessel for only a 45-minute period every two hours.

Fleeting Fears Concern Local Officials: 1995

In 1995 President Casinos submitted a bid to open a casino complex in downtown St. Louis near Laclede's Landing, the site of an existing gaming complex. Parking at the company's existing site was inadequate, and Company Management considered moving *The Admiral* downtown. Three competing companies had also applied for licensing. According to Rob Staggenborg of the *St. Louis Business Journal*, at least one person on the board of aldermen feared that should the city grant a second gaming license to President Casinos, the company ''would in effect have a monopoly on the downtown river front.'' By this time *The Admiral*'s performance had proven disappointing compared to revenues of competitors in the suburbs, and financial analysts speculated that the financing of such a major project, involving infrastructure development costs, would be difficult for President Casinos to procure. The company determined that while having a second riverboat casino would allow for virtually continuous boarding for guests upon one of the two vessels, the capital outlay could not be justified. *The Admiral* remained positioned at the base of the Arch, and although five St. Louis-area mooring licenses have been granted President Casinos, gaming operations are limited to its original gaming vessel, and the remaining licenses permit the operation of the company's dinner cruise, excursion, and sightseeing riverboats.

The company was soon finding it difficult to remain financially afloat. President Casinos had reported a fiscal 1994 loss of $20.2 million, largely reflecting expenses incurred in pursuing possible new business in Iowa, Louisiana, Massachusetts, Pennsylvania, and Virginia. The company announced in early 1995 that it would be more selective in pursuing opportunities in the future, and that they would be disposing under-utilized assets. President Casinos had more than competition to contend with. Floods caused the periodic closing of the Davenport operations, where *The President*, a 70-year-old vessel, was required to undergo an extensive five-month Coast Guard hull inspection. It was temporarily replaced by a smaller, three-deck vessel, offering one-third less gambling space. In the meantime, *Lady Luck Bettendorf*, a competing vessel across the river, was luring more and more of the market.

The time had come for an executive shift. Coinciding with rumors of Connelly's ill health, in March 1995 John S. Aylesworth came on board as executive vice-president and chief operating officer of President Casinos. He had worked as a managing executive officer for Beverly Hills' billionaire Marvin Davis's operations, as chief financial officer of Spectra-Vision, and was previously with the Sports Club Company, an operator of premier health and fitness facilities. Connelly told Rob Staggenborg of the *St. Louis Business Journal* that ''The realignment of responsibilities of our senior management and the addition of John Aylesworth to our management team greatly enhances our operational strength.''

By the mid-1990s the entire industry had experienced insufficient returns on investments, and President Casinos was floundering. In three years time the company amassed more than $100 million in debt. After shares had fallen more than 80 percent since January of 1995, Aylesworth reported that deep-pocketed gaming concerns had out-competed them. A stockholder proxy statement revealed that Connelly and Connelly-controlled businesses had received nearly $4.7 million from President Casinos during the 1995 fiscal year, as reported by Len Boselovic in *Knight-Ridder/Tribune Business News*. Annual lease payments of $3.2 million for the Biloxi casino property were paid to a Connelly company, in addition to $883,000 ''for the use of a plane owned by a Connelly affiliate, purchasing $140,000 of promotional items from a Connelly affiliate, and $45,000 to Connelly's Drury Inn Hotel, where President Casinos executives stayed and ate while they were in St. Louis on business,'' according to Boselovic. In the summer of 1997 President Casinos agreed to pay Connelly, who owned 31.8 percent of the company, approximately $40 million for the Biloxi site gaming operation, rather than to continue renting the property. President Casinos reported that the sale allowed them to concentrate on operations in St. Louis and Davenport. The company stated that ''the payments were arms-length transactions at fair market prices.''

Recovery Plan for the Late 1990s

The company's retrenchment strategy included the selling of assets—and cost cutting. In a July, 1997 interview with Frank Legato of *Casino Journal*, CFO Aylesworth said, ''When I was approached for this job, I knew exactly what had happened here, without even being in that [this] industry. We knew what we had to do. First, President had invested a lot of money and had realized no return on it. If that happens too long, the interest you're paying is going to eat you alive—that's Business 101. We had to monetize as many of our assets as we could, and we had a lot of excess,'' he continued. Within a year of Aylesworth's leadership the company sold approximately $20 million worth of non-revenue-producing assets which were needed to fund interest payments and requisite capital expenditure programs. In Iowa, the company made efficient use of time and money toward refurbishing *The President* by adding more slots and other amenities to the vessel while it underwent the extensive close-down for the hull inspection, along with making improvements to its adjoining entry barge. Corporate overhead costs were slashed by $5 million in fiscal 1997. Virtually all of its capital expenditure program was funded through the sale of assets, and the company showed a net cash increase from investments. The original Biloxi vessel, *President Casino Mississippi,* and another non-revenue-producing cruising vessel, worth a combined estimated value of $45 million, remained to be sold.

In the meantime, market analysts noted the competitive challenges ahead: In St. Louis, an enormous joint venture project between Harrah's and Player's International at Riverport Center threatened to overshadow the smaller casinos, although the company had expressed confidence that the metropolitan area would be impacted more than the company itself. The historical significance of *The Admiral* set it apart from the newer casinos, some said. In Biloxi, a growing resort area, President Casinos sought a joint-venture partner to further develop a 260-acre site, which included two hotels, a 138-slip marina, a dockside casino, and an adjacent 18-hole golf course. In addition, if gambling were to be legalized in Pennsylvania, the company held a prime site on the Philadelphia waterfront, as a gamble on future casino prospects.

Principal Subsidiaries

The Connelly Group, L.P.; The President Riverboat Casino-Mississippi, Inc.; President Riverboat Casino-Missouri, Inc.

Further Reading

Boselovic, Len, ''President Casinos Inc. Abandons Biloxi, Mississippi Gaming Operation,'' *Knight-Ridder/Tribune Business News,* July 25, 1996, p. 7250193.

Derks, Sarah A., ''President Riverboat Casinos Inc.,'' *St. Louis Business Journal,* January 25, 1993, p. 21.

''Floating Casino Is Sold,'' *New York Times,* August 16, 1995, p. D7.

Gotthelf, Josh, ''Connelly Benefits, President Casinos Deeper in Debt,'' *St. Louis Business Journal,* June 23, 1997, p. 42A.

Huntley, Paton, ''Connelly Eyes IPO, But Lawsuit Rattles Gold Coast Casino Effort,'' *Pittsburgh Business Times,* June 22, 1992, pp. 1–2.

Kerks, Sarah A., ''Connelly Raising $100 Million; Bonds to Pay for Second Gambling Boat Here,'' *St. Louis Business Journal,* September 27, 1993, p. 1.

Legato, Frank, ''President Casinos,'' *Casino Journal,* July 1997, pp. 1–4.

''President Casinos Inc. Reports Loss Widened in Fiscal 4th Quarter,'' *Wall Street Journal,* May 1, 1995, p. 13.

Ramirez, Anthony, ''Stocks Surge on Positive Inflation News,'' *New York Times,* April 13, 1993, p. D8.

Staggenborg, Rob, ''Aylesworth Steps into Key Role at President Casinos,'' *St. Louis Business Journal,* April 17, 1995, p. 1A.

——, ''2 Aldermen Express Concern Over President Casinos Bid,'' *St. Louis Business Journal,* April 17, 1995, p. 8A.

—Terri Mozzone

Primedia Inc.

745 Fifth Avenue
New York, New York 10151
U.S.A.
(212) 745-0100
Fax: (212) 745-0121
Web site: http://www.k-iii.com

Public Company
Incorporated: 1989 as K-III Holdings Inc.
Employees: 7,200
Sales: $1.37 billion (1996)
Stock Exchanges: New York
SICs: 2711 Newspapers: Publishing, or Publishing & Printing; 2721 Periodicals: Publishing, or Publishing & Printing; 2731 Books: Publishing, or Publishing & Printing; 2741 Miscellaneous Publishing; 4899 Communications Services, Not Elsewhere Classified; 7375 Information Retrieval Services; 7812 Motion Picture & Video Tape Production; 8244 Business & Secretarial Schools

Primedia Inc. is a newspaper, periodical, and book publisher whose publications include consumer and trade magazines, reference books, and educational materials and services. The company also owns Channel One News, a television news program that reaches millions of students each day. In addition, Primedia owns specialized databases and database products, produces educational films, and runs a secretarial school chain. The company changed its name from K-III Communications Corporation in November 1997.

Acquisition-Fueled Growth, 1989–94

Primedia got its start in 1989 as K-III Holdings, a new venture financed by the investment group Kohlberg, Kravis, Roberts and Co. (KKR). KKR, a leveraged-buyout specialist that had managed the $25 billion buyout of RJR Nabisco Inc. in 1989, had very deep pockets and was ambitious to become a major player in publishing. It also had a willing collaborator in William F. Reilly, president of Macmillan Inc. KKR teamed with Reilly to make a bid for the publishing giant in 1988, but it was sold instead to publishing tycoon Robert Maxwell.

Under Maxwell, Macmillan began to be sold off in pieces. Reilly, while still president of Macmillan, became a partner in K-III Holdings Inc., which was organized to seek some of these properties. The "K" in "K-III" stood for KKR, and the "III" represented Reilly and two other partners, Charles G. McCurdy, Macmillan's chief financial officer, and Beverly C. Chell, its general counsel. The three received about 13 percent of K-III Holdings' stock between them.

In 1989 K-III purchased Macmillan's Direct Marketing Group, which included Macmillan Book Clubs—renamed Newbridge Book Clubs—and Gryphon Editions, for $143 million. It also bought Intertec Publishing Corp., a producer of technical magazines, for $167 million. Reilly left Macmillan to become chairman and chief executive officer of K-III in February 1990. In May 1990 K-III purchased Ward's Communications, publisher of auto industry publications, from Thomson Corp. Three months later K-III acquired Reader's Garden Inc., a company operating special-interest book clubs, and in December 1990 it bought Field Limited Partnership and Funk & Wagnalls for about $200 million.

These acquisitions raised K-III's sales volume to about $500 million a year. Its holdings included 25 trade magazines, numerous specialized directories for various industries, Field Publications' *Weekly Reader* for schoolchildren, and Funk & Wagnalls' encyclopedia and other educational materials. In 1991 the company, which had been renamed K-III Communications, purchased eight magazines, including *New York, Seventeen, Premiere, Soap Opera Digest,* and *New Woman,* and the *Daily Racing Form* from Rupert Murdoch's News Corp. for $650 million. The following year was chiefly devoted to digesting its acquisitions, but the company purchased Krames Communications Co., a publisher of medical pamphlets that doctors distribute to patients, from Hachette S.A. It also purchased Musical America Publishing, Inc. and Films for the Humanities, Inc.

Company Perspectives:

Primedia is an information company in an information age. As people are increasingly overwhelmed by a barrage of information, Primedia has recognized the value of being the primary source of pertinent information.

Primedia's specialty media, education and information properties all share a distinction that reflects the Primedia mission—to be the authoritative source of specialized information for highly targeted audiences.

In 1993 K-III purchased United Media's Pharos Books division, publisher of *The World Almanac.* This acquisition included World Almanac Education, a direct marketer of educational and reference works to libraries. K-III also purchased Nelson Publications, a line of child development products and directories serving the electronics market. In addition, the company bought three trade journals from Wiesner, Inc., a publisher of directories for corporate pilots and corporate flight departments, nine regional directories used by corporate purchasing agents, and the publication *Soybean Digest.*

K-III's 1993 revenues came to $844.7 million, of which education accounted for 46 percent, magazine publishing for 38 percent, and information for 16 percent. Reilly's goal, it was reported, was to raise K-III's annual revenues to $1.5 billion to $2 billion within five years, to be followed by a public offering of stock. This objective carried a heavy price tag, however. Despite its large sales volume, K-III lost $86.5 million in 1993 (on top of $145.3 million in 1992) because of the high cost of financing its acquisitions. The company's debt was $661.3 million at the end of the year. Investors had pumped $461 million into the company since July 1989.

Undaunted, K-III raised its stake in education in March 1994 by acquiring Katharine Gibbs Schools Inc., a chain of seven secretarial schools in the northeast, from Phillips Colleges, which had purchased it from Macmillan in 1989. Also during 1994, the company acquired Haas Publishing Companies, Inc.; a leading line of child development products from Gruner + Jahn USA Publishing; *Stagebill;* and the premier source of information on heavy mobile equipment serving the construction industry.

K-III's biggest acquisition of 1994, however, was the purchase of Channel One Communications Corp. from Whittle Communications L.P. for about $250 million. Its flagship property, Channel One News, was a controversial, advertiser-supported 12-minute daily news show telecast to almost 12,000 secondary schools and nearly eight million secondary school students in 47 states. Revenues had exceeded $70 million in its most recent fiscal year, and operating profit was believed to be about $20 million. Although Channel One News won a Peabody Award for its coverage of AIDS, many educators were critical of the program. One study reported that 42 percent of air time was devoted to advertisements, a pop quiz, contests, music, and banter between the young anchors and correspondents. K-III had net sales of $964.8 million in 1994 and a net loss of $41.4 million, following an income-tax credit of $42.1 million.

More Acquisition, More Debt in 1995 and 1996

Between December 1993 and March 1995 K-III added more than 50 magazines at a cost of nearly $650 million. In January 1995 it acquired PJS Publications, publisher of such specialty magazines as *McCall's Needlework, Sew News, Shooting Times,* and *Crafts.* A month later it sold *Premiere* to Hachette and New World Communications Group for about $20 million but acquired Maclean Hunter Ltd.'s U.S. publishing properties, including *American Printer* and *Coal,* for about $55 million to $60 million.

K-III's yen for new properties continued unabated through the rest of 1995. In June it acquired McMullen & Yee Publishing, owners of such titles as *Truckin'* and *All Chevy,* for about $55 million. *Chicago,* a city magazine, was purchased from Landmark Communications. The company also bought Bacon's Information, a provider of comprehensive media information services to the public relations industry, and the newsletter *Craftrends Magazine.*

The K-III acquisition process was to appoint a ''deal man'' for each of its three divisions—publishing, education, and information—to identify targets. Each acquisition had to meet five criteria: cover a niche market, hold a dominant position in this niche, face little competition, possess management expertise, and generate high cash flow. Once acquired, a property was expected to maintain high cash flow or be sold or shut down. Magazine editors and publishers were allowed considerable leeway as long as the numbers remained favorable. In a review held every three months, they were asked for detailed budgets for circulation and sales for one year and looser projections for the next four years.

In 1995 K-III's net sales rose to $1.05 billion, but it lost $75.4 million despite an income-tax credit of $59.6 million—chiefly because of interest expenses that came to $105.4 million on its debt of $1.1 billion. Notwithstanding its shaky numbers, K-III sold 15 million shares (one-ninth of the outstanding shares of common stock) to the public at $10 a share in November 1995. (Investors in funds put together by KKR earlier had paid an average of about $6 a share.)

The $141 million in net proceeds from the initial public offering was earmarked to reduce debt, but K-III warned in its prospectus that it did not expect to earn a net profit soon, in part because it was willing to borrow more money to finance future deals. Shortly after the stock sale the company agreed to buy 14 magazines from Cahners Consumers Magazines, including *Power & Motoryacht, American Baby, Modern Bride,* and *Sail.* And in April 1996 it acquired Westcott Communications Inc., a producer of educational and career training programs via satellite and videotapes, for $422 million. Westcott was the nation's largest producer of national training courses broadcast by satellite.

K-III also made a number of lesser acquisitions in 1996. These included Tri-State Publishing & Communications, Inc.; the trade magazines *Lighting Dimensions, Millimeter,* and *Theatre Crafts International;* and the news services division of

Facts on File Inc. It also purchased *Horticulture* magazine and certain net assets of ADC of Greater Kansas City, Inc. and VSD Communications, Inc.

The most high-profile of K-III's publications continued to be *New York.* According to a *New York Times* story published in 1996, Henry R. Kravis, a KKR partner, had killed or tried to kill articles in the weekly that were critical of Wall Street investment bankers. When its editor was fired in 1996, he and many of his colleagues blamed Kravis. K-III executives replied that circulation figures, although rising, had been disappointing. (*New York*'s circulation was some 425,000, compared with about 2.1 million for *Seventeen,* which had the highest circulation of any K-III magazine.)

K-III posted revenues of $1.37 billion in 1996, of which education accounted for 45 percent, media for 35 percent, and information for 20 percent. Operating income came to $85.9 million, but the company spent $125.5 million on interest payments. The deficit before considering income tax was $45.3 million, but since K-III accumulated $53.3 million in tax credits on future profits, it ended the year with net income of $8 million. The long-term debt at year's end was $1.57 billion. KKR owned 83 percent of the outstanding shares of common stock in March 1997.

K-III/Primedia in 1997

Reilly announced in March 1997 that K-III would sell some of the 52 businesses that it had acquired in its eight-year history and issue 12.5 million new shares of common stock. The new issue was canceled in April, however, because of a fall in the price of existing shares. The properties Reilly put on the block accounted for $260 million in revenue in 1996 and $25 million in earnings before considering debt service and taxes. On the other hand, Reilly said he expected to spend $200 million to $250 million each year for the foreseeable future to acquire businesses, focusing on "niche markets, publications that have more than a 50-percent market share and have authoritative content."

The most valuable property up for sale was the *Daily Racing Form.* Although the standard source for horse racing bettors and virtually the only publication in its field, it had lost readers as the public shifted its gambling interest to the new casinos cropping up throughout the nation. By industry estimates circulation was off as much as half since its 1991 acquisition. The other properties on the block included Newbridge Book Clubs, Krames Communications, and *New Woman.* During the following months Times Mirror bought Krames and Rodale Press bought *New Woman.*

K-III was renamed Primedia in November 1997. At this time the business consisted of three units: education, information, and media. The education unit consisted of educational programming (Channel One News, The Classroom Channel, and Films for the Humanities and Sciences), periodicals/supplementary materials (periodicals and skill books for students from kindergarten through 12th grade, including *Weekly Reader*), professional book services (consisting of 20 scientific and professional book services), supplementary educational programs (12 continuity programs), and professional training (the Katharine Gibbs Schools). The information segment consisted of directories (69 specialized databases), apartment guides (in 50 markets, plus a publication distribution network), the *Daily Racing Form* database, and reference materials (Funk & Wagnalls and *The World Almanac*). The media segment consisted of consumer magazines (13 magazines), special interest magazines (35), and trade and technical magazines and database products (74 of these magazines and an unspecified number of database products).

Principal Subsidiaries

Channel One Communications Corporation; Daily Racing Form, Inc.; Intertec Publishing Corporation; K-III Holdings Corporation III; K-III HPC, Inc.; K-III Magazine Corporation; K-III Reference Corporation; Lifetime Learning Systems, Inc.; McMullen Argus Publishing, Inc.; Nelson Information, Inc.; Newbridge Communications, Inc.; PJS Publications, Inc.; The Katharine Gibbs Schools, Inc.; Weekly Reader Corporation; Westcott Communications, Inc.

Further Reading

Browning, E.S., "Impatient Investors in KKR's Media Empire Begin to Wonder: Isn't It Time Firm Sold Out?" *Wall Street Journal,* September 15, 1997, p. C2.

Carmody, Deirdre, "A Quiet K-III Is Gaining Attention," *New York Times,* November 29, 1993, p. D6.

Furman, Phyllis, "K-III Finally Lands Its IPO, Despite Market Adversity," *Crain's New York Business,* November 6, 1995, p. 51.

Helyar, John, "Racing Form Is in Stretch Run," *Wall Street Journal,* May 16, 1997, p. B7.

Jereski, Laura, "KKR Hopes K-III Communications' Offering Brings Hefty Margin Above Rival Media Firms," *Wall Street Journal,* October 13, 1995, p. C2.

"KKR to Buy Macmillan Book Clubs and Intertec for $310 Million," *Publishers Weekly,* June 16, 1989, p. 16.

Knecht, G. Bruce, "K-III to Issue Stock and Sell Businesses, Such as Daily Racing Form, to Cut Debt," *Wall Street Journal,* March 12, 1997, p. B6.

Manly, Lorne, "Progress Through Process," *Folio,* March 15, 1995, pp. 60–61, 74.

Mathews, Jay, "Channel One News Content Gets Poor Marks," *Washington Post,* January 23, 1997, p. E3.

Mirabella, Alan, "Emerging Media Giant Chases Cash, Not Flash," *Crain's New York Business,* March 14, 1994, pp. 1, 43.

Pogebrin, Robin, "When a Magazine Is Too Brash for the Bottom Line," *New York Times,* September 29, 1996, Sec. 3, pp. 1, 11.

Reilly, Patrick M., "A KKR Vehicle Finds Profit and Education a Rich But Uneasy Mix," *Wall Street Journal,* October 12, 1994, pp. A1, A11.

——, "Whittle's Sale of Channel One Completed by K-III," *Wall Street Journal,* October 3, 1994, p. B10.

Rothman, Andrea, "Will Bill Reilly Become a Magazine Mogul?" *Business Week,* May 6, 1991, p. 78.

Smith, Randall, "KKR's K-III Investment Format Draws Mixed Reviews," *Wall Street Journal,* July 7, 1994, pp. C1, C13.

—Robert Halasz

PRINCESS CRUISES®
It's more than a cruise, it's the Love Boat

Princess Cruise Lines

10100 Santa Monica Boulevard
Los Angeles, California 90067
U.S.A.
(310) 553-1770
Fax: (310) 284-2857
Web site: http://www.princesscruises.com

Wholly Owned Subsidiary of Pacific and Oriental Steam Navigation Co.
Founded: 1965
Employees: 8,500
Sales: $1 billion (1996 est.)
SICs: 4480 Water Transportation of Passengers

From its stronghold on the Pacific, Princess Cruise Lines is the world's third largest cruise line behind Carnival Corp. and Royal Caribbean Cruise Lines. At more than 30 years old, Princess is one of the U.S. market's oldest continuously operating passenger ship lines. Its roster of 65 cruises, including a worldwide tour scheduled to set sail in March 1998, docks at more than 225 ports on six continents.

Popularized by the television series "The Love Boat," Princess Cruise Lines is so closely identified with the late 1970s, early 1980s show that it continued to use the tagline "It's more than a cruise, it's the Love Boat" through the late 1990s. Over the course of its more than three decades in business, the Princess fleet has expanded dramatically. In 1965, it operated one converted ferryboat with a 318-passenger capacity, plying the West Coast of Mexico. In 1997 it owned a coterie of eight "floating resorts" that shuttled nearly 500,000 passengers to 230 ports around the globe each year. With the addition of three more "Grand Class" ships, the line expected to have annual capacity for 750,000 passengers by the turn of the 20th century.

Founded in 1965

The Princess line was founded in the fall of 1965 by Stanley MacDonald, a Seattle entrepreneur. It was named for its first ship, the 6,000-ton Princess Patricia, a ferryboat chartered from the Canadian National Railways' fleet. Princess Pat had a 318-passenger capacity. Princess was among the first lines to popularize cruises to the west coast of Mexico—dubbed the "Mexican Riviera." Come summer 1966, the ship returned to its tasks for the railroad in Alaska and Canada. Following a second successful season shepherding snowbirds seaward, MacDonald chartered an Italian-made ship and dubbed it, quite logically, the Princess Italia. Continued high demand for berths led to the charter of the Princess Carla for the 1968 season. In 1971 MacDonald leased the Norwegian vessel Island Venture and renamed it the Island Princess.

But MacDonald did not stay in the cruise business for long. In 1974 he sold Princess to Great Britain's Peninsular and Oriental Steam Navigation Company (P&O), one of the world's oldest and largest diversified shipping firms. With the financial backing of this industry giant, the California-based cruise line purchased the Island Princess as well as its sister ship, the Sea Venture. A retrofit transformed the Sea Venture into the Pacific Princess, a 20,000-ton vessel with room for 640 passengers. P&O also transferred its Spirit of London to Princess, which renamed it the Sun Princess. The line canceled its leases on the Italia and Carla. Within a year of its adoption into the P&O family, Princess had become one of the world's largest passenger cruise lines.

The Love Boat Years

Still, a fiscally fit parent company, nicely appointed ships, and top-notch service might never have brought Princess the fame and growth it earned by becoming affiliated with a television series. Airing for nearly a decade from 1977 to 1986, "The Love Boat" was produced by Aaron Spelling and became one of his longest running projects. Set on the Island Princess and the Pacific Princess, the show featured a core cast consisting of the ship's crew and a revolving cast of well-known celebrities embroiled in a variety of lighthearted plots. The sitcom placed a strong emphasis on romance and exotic destinations.

In addition to putting Princess's "seawitch" logo in front of millions of viewers worldwide each week, the prime time show

Company Perspectives:

The Caribbean, Alaska, Europe and the Panama Canal, these are just a taste of the world that awaits you on ships as legendary as the places they visit. You can journey as far north as Norway's North Cape and as far south as Tierra del Fuego's Cape Horn. You can circle the continents of South America and Africa and traverse the Indian Ocean and the North China Sea. Dropping anchor in over 200 ports on six continents, Princess goes to the ends of the earth to bring you an unforgettable cruise.

has been credited with introducing cruising to a younger clientele, thereby broadening the industry's appeal from a core group of wealthy retirees to middle-income people in their 30s and 40s. No longer merely a means of transportation, cruising became a vacation end unto itself. Christopher Boyd of *Florida Trend* asserted, " 'The Love Boat' television series, featuring a Princess ship, helped change the image of cruising. Suddenly, cruising meant romance, intrigue and beautiful people." From 1979 through 1993, the industry grew at a compound annual rate of 9.4 percent. Princess cultivated the "Love Boat" image long after the show was canceled, even using the "Captain Stubing" character, played by actor Gavin MacLeod, in promotions and television ads.

1980s Expansion Culminates in Merger

Princess was one of three cruise lines operating in the United States to seize the growth initiative in the mid-1980s. Princess took delivery of its first custom-built passenger ship, the Royal Princess, in 1984. This vessel, which could transport nearly three times as many guests as the line's first ferryboat, moved all guest cabins to the outside of the ship, thereby giving all its passengers the luxury of an ocean view. The line's fleet grew to five ships with the 1986 adoption of P&O's Sea Princess. It was not long before the tide of cruisegoers rose to meet this capacity; from 1983 to 1994, the passenger count exploded from about a half million to 4.5 million.

Adding vessels to the fleet enabled Princess to expand its roster of destinations, giving its passengers a wider choice of vacation spots. Princess was one of the first to popularize cruises to Alaska, a destination that became an industry hot spot in the late 1980s and early 1990s. And though it concentrated for many years on European, Alaskan, and Mediterranean routes, the line was by the mid-1990s offering cruises to Asia, India, the Holy Land, South America, Hawaii, and the all-important Caribbean.

Princess emerged as one of America's largest passenger fleets in 1988, when P&O acquired Sitmar Cruises, a line headquartered about 300 yards from Princess, for about $210 million and merged it with the existing U.S. operation. James Nolan of the *Journal of Commerce and Commercial* characterized Sitmar as the "Cadillac of the industry." *Travel Weekly's* Jerry Brown called the marriage "one of the biggest events in the cruise industry in many years." The union added the Star, Sky, Dawn, and Fair Princesses to the fleet, which by this time totaled nine ships. It also expanded Princess's cruise routes to include New England and South America. At about the same time, P&O consolidated its U.S. cruise, hotel, motorcoach, and rail operations under the Princess name and logo. These included the Denali Princess Lodge, Kenai Princess Lodge, and the Fairbanks Princess Hotel, all in Alaska.

Nonstop Growth in the 1990s

Anticipating the continued expansion of the cruise industry at a rate of ten percent annually through the 1990s, the "Big Three"—Carnival, Royal Caribbean, and Princess—became embroiled in a race to build ever-larger ships with greater capacity for people and amenities. Aside from the obvious ability to carry more passengers, there were several advantages to building larger ships. They generated more than three times the cash flow of their 1,000-passenger predecessors and provided economies of scale in overhead and purchasing by spreading out the cost of running a single vessel among this larger client base. Victoria Hallstrom of Lehman Brothers told *Travel Weekly's* Ernest Blum that the new "superships" and "megaships" had the potential to "pay for themselves in five years."

Their massive size also made room for an array of activities and amenities that put these ships on a par with vacation destinations like Las Vegas and Walt Disney World. Families were a particular target of these behemoths; on-board distractions included play areas for kids, media rooms and dance floors geared toward teens, and more traditional casinos, bars, health clubs, and Broadway-style shows for adults.

Decommissionings in 1990 and 1991 made room for Princess's $1.5 billion-plus investment in gargantuan new "superships" dubbed the "Grand Class." These massive cruise ships had passenger capacities of more than 1,500 each, yet offered roomier staterooms and more private balconies than their predecessors as well as spacious public areas. The Crown Princess, launched in 1990, and the Regal Princess, introduced in 1991, weighed in at 70,000 tons and had room for 1,590 vacationers. The 1995 launch of the 77,000-ton Sun Princess added room for nearly 2,000 passengers. Its sister ship, the Dawn Princess, was launched in 1997 and dispatched to the waters of Alaska and the Caribbean. In addition to two more 77,000-ton vessels, Princess planned to christen the "grandest of the grand" (to date), the 109,000-ton Grand Princess, by the end of the decade. With a capacity for 2,600 passengers, the ship was too wide to navigate the Panama Canal.

Though the cruise line retired three other ships during this period, it kept the two original "Love Boats," the Island Princess and the Pacific Princess, in operation. The Island Princess, in fact, was scheduled to offer Princess's first-ever world cruise, a 64-day trip from Rome to San Francisco beginning in March 1998.

Princess was not the only leading line building mammoth cruisers in the 1990s. Industry leaders Carnival and Royal Caribbean were also busy ordering 100,000-ton-plus vessels, continually upping the stakes in the battle to build the biggest boats. These across-the-board capacity increases kept the Big Three's market shares fairly constant throughout the 1990s, maintaining a high level of competition among the top rivals. In fact, while Princess doubled its berths in the last decade of the 20th century, Carnival Corp. increased its capacity by more than 450 percent and Royal Caribbean boosted its volume by nearly 370 percent.

Princess distinguished itself among its competitors with technological and marketing innovations during this period. The company developed sophisticated in-house booking, reservation, and management information systems and cooperated in the creation of tourist agency networks like Apollo, Sabre, and Worldspan. In 1997 Princess won praise for its introduction of a unique financing package dubbed the ''Love Boat Loan.'' Though it charged anywhere from 14.9 percent to 26.9 percent interest, the program allowed vacationers to finance the cost of a cruise for up to 48 months.

The cruise line suffered a black eye in 1991, when two passengers videotaped a Princess employee dumping bags of garbage into the ocean off the Florida Keys. Worse than the $500,000 fine was the public relations scandal that followed. Princess was able to redeem itself by inaugurating a comprehensive waste management program dubbed ''Planet Princess.'' Within just a few years, the line had won praise from some of the cruise industry's biggest environmental critics, including the Center for Marine Conservation.

By the mid-1990s only seven percent of Americans had taken a cruise, leading many in the industry—including executives at Princess—to conclude that there remained a large untapped market of potential cruisers. In March 1997 a spokesman for Princess told *Travel Weekly,* ''We [in the cruise industry] are about to enter an era of dramatic prosperity—a great boom and upswing in the economy.'' Princess appeared amply prepared to accommodate that boom.

Further Reading

Blum, Ernest, '' 'Big 3' Lines Gobbling Market Share; The Watchword, Capacity,'' *Travel Weekly,* December 16, 1996, p. 75.

——, ''Harris: Cruise Concentration Is a Good Thing,'' *Travel Weekly,* March 14, 1994, p. 5.

——, ''Once Ecologically Tainted, Princess Cruises Cleans Up Its Act,'' *Travel Weekly,* March 10, 1994, pp. 1–2.

——, ''Princess Exec Sees Potential for Smooth Sailing Ahead,'' *Travel Weekly,* April 4, 1996, p. C6.

Boyd, Christopher, ''The Big Squeeze,'' *Florida Trend,* September 1994, pp. 54–57.

Brown, Jerry, ''Princess Celebrates Silver Anniversary; Line Comes a Long Way in 25 Years,'' *Travel Weekly,* February 5, 1990, p. C14.

——, ''Princess Cruise's Chief Weighs Thorny Issue Facing Shiplines,'' *Travel Weekly,* December 5, 1985, pp. 1–3.

——, ''Princess Cruises Orders 4th Vessel As Part of $1.3 Billion Expansion,'' *Travel Weekly,* April 22, 1996, pp. 1–2.

——, ''Princess Cruises Plans New Marketing Strategies, Fleet Expansion,'' *Travel Weekly,* February 20, 1986, p. 53.

——, ''Princess Cruises Unveils Innovative Design of Sleek New Vessel,'' *Travel Weekly,* June 5, 1989, p. 81.

——, ''Princess Expands to Meet Demand,'' *Travel Weekly,* February 6, 1995, p. 54.

——, ''Princess Official Still Sees Room in Crowded Cruise Market,'' *Travel Weekly,* January 17, 1994, p. 90.

——, ''Princess Orders 77,000-Ton Ship, Largest in Line's 10-Vessel Fleet,'' *Travel Weekly,* January 25, 1993, pp. 1–2.

——, ''Princess Shows No Sign of Slowing Down After Launching Regal,'' *Travel Weekly,* August 5, 1991, pp. C4–C5.

——, ''Princess-Sitmar: 'Sensible' Match,'' *Travel Weekly,* September 15, 1988, pp. 1–3.

''Buoyed by Profits, Princess OKs Fifth 'Grand' Vessel,'' *Travel Weekly,* March 31, 1997, p. 63.

Cioffi, Lori, ''Princess Brings Far-Flung Empire Under One Name,'' *Travel Weekly,* October 3, 1988, pp. 1–2.

''Court Divides Princess Fine,'' *Travel Weekly,* July 19, 1993, p. 31.

''Cruise Official Looks Ahead,'' *Travel Weekly,* March 7, 1994, p. 45.

Davies, John, '' 'Love Boat' Moving to Alaskan Cruises,'' *Journal of Commerce and Commercial,* January 16, 1986, pp. 1A–2A.

Deady, Tim, ''Piloting the 'Love Boat,' '' *Los Angeles Business Journal,* December 20, 1993, pp. 12–13.

Del Rosso, Laura, ''Princess Executive: Lines Building Fleets for 'Bright Future,' '' *Travel Weekly,* March 17, 1997, p. 41.

DuPont, Dale K., ''Princess Cruise Lines Agrees to Change Advertising in Florida Suit,'' *Miami Herald,* April 9, 1997, n.p.

Gonzales, Monica, ''Let's Cruise,'' *American Demographics,* February 1988, p. 21.

Lincoln, Lori, ''Cruise Bookings Up—But Why?,'' *Travel Weekly,* October 5, 1995, pp. 1–3.

'' 'Love Boat Loans,' '' *Travel Weekly,* March 13, 1997, p. 12.

Nolan, James, 'Love Boat Owners Buy 'Cadillac' of Industry,'' *Journal of Commerce and Commercial,* August 1, 1988, 3B.

''Princess Launches Internal Reservations System,'' *Travel Weekly,* October 10, 1994, p. 32.

''Princess Schedules Its First World Sailing for Spring 1998,'' *Travel Weekly,* March 6, 1997, p. C22.

Reed, Ted, ''Princess Plans Entrance into Caribbean Market,'' *Journal of Commerce and Commercial,* March 2, 1994, p. 7B.

''The Rise and Rise of the Princess Empire,'' *Sea View Communications,* http://www.seaview.co.uk/princess—cruises—history.html.

—April Dougal Gasbarre

Reeds Jewelers, Inc.

2525 South 17th Street
Wilmington, North Carolina 28401
U.S.A.
(910) 350-3100
Fax: (910) 350-3353
Web site: http://www.reedsusa.com

Public Company
Founded: 1946
Employees: 791
Sales: $99 million (1997)
Stock Exchanges: NASDAQ
SICs: 5944 Retail—Jewelry Stores

Reeds Jewelers, Inc. is the 11th largest retail jewelry chain in the United States. As of November 1997, the company had 101 stores in 13 southeastern and midwestern states. The company's stores are located primarily in regional malls and operate under the names Reeds Jewelers, Melart Jewelers, and Mills Jewelers. More than half of their sales are from diamonds and precious gems, with the remainder from gold jewelry, semi-precious gems, and brand name watches. The Zimmer family owns the controlling share of Reeds stock.

Building a Family Business, 1946–81

The jewelry business was in the blood of the Zimmer family. Bill Zimmer learned about gold, diamonds, and precious gems from his parents while working in their store in upstate New York. After serving in Europe during World War II, he was stationed in the South before being discharged, and, after getting married, decided he wanted to stay in the region.

In 1946, Bill and his wife, Roberta, bought a small jewelry store in downtown Wilmington, North Carolina, and named it Reeds, the family trade name. During the next 14 years the company expanded as the Zimmers opened stores throughout North and South Carolina and in Florida. At the same time, the Zimmer family was growing. Herbert was born in 1946, Arlene in 1949, Jeffrey in 1957, and Alan in 1959. All four children worked in the business before going to college.

Zimmer was a terrific salesman, and he provided personal service, friendship, and good deals to his customers. He gave his store managers considerable freedom, since that was how he liked to operate. By 1979, the Zimmers controlled two dozen retail outlets, mainly in North and South Carolina. Bill and Roberta ran the original store in Wilmington, and managers or minority partners operated the other 23. The stores offered fine merchandise including diamond rings and jewelry, gold jewelry and chains, watches, and rings containing rubies, sapphires, and emeralds or gemstones such as opals and garnets. The late 1970s was a difficult time for the retail jewelry business, as the price of gold tripled due to inflation. Like most jewelry retailers, Reeds borrowed to buy its merchandise. With interest rates close to 20 percent, about 10 percent of what the company was bringing in was going to pay the carrying costs for their inventory.

Then, in 1979, the Wilmington store was robbed. "They took over $690,000 of numbered inventory, plus about $300,000 worth of merchandise that we had on consignment and were storing for all the stores. We lost over $1.25 million," Bill Zimmer told *Business/North Carolina.* And Zimmer did not have any insurance on the stolen merchandise. "I sold an insurance policy, put a mortgage on our home. I had a tough going for about two years, but we survived," he explained to *Business/North Carolina.*

Modernization and Acquisitions During the 1980s

Alan Zimmer, the youngest son, came home from college to join the family business in December 1981. He had earned an undergraduate degree in business from the University of Georgia in three years and was working on his M.B.A. at Tulane University. Joining the company as executive vice-president, Alan took charge of merchandising. He completed his master's through independent study.

Although Alan did not officially become president and CEO for several years, he convinced his father to begin making major operational changes immediately. One of the first things he addressed was the company's decentralization. Reeds was essen-

Company Perspectives:

The company specializes in the sale of fine jewelry, and emphasizes "Quality, Value, and Service."

tially a collection of 24 independent operators. The store managers did their own buying and merchandising, hired their own staff, set their own credit policies, and made their own deals with customers. Alan Zimmer changed that. He hired professional managers, from other jewelry chains such as Kay Jewelers and Zales, developed a merchandizing staff, and divided the company into five regions, hiring regional managers for each. He centralized the company's diamond and jewelry buying as well as its advertising printing, saving money from the resulting economies of scale. He also hired James Rouse to be the company's first full-time financial officer, installed a computer system for inventory control, and began opening new stores. At the time, the jewelry industry was a $13 billion market, with some 32,000 individually-owned stores in the United States.

On February 28, 1982, the end of the company's fiscal year, Reeds had revenues of $9.3 million and losses of $177,000. The next year, the company was out of the red, making a profit of $15,000 on revenues of $11.2 million. And a year after that, in 1984, profits were up to $418,000 on sales of $12.6 million, as Alan's changes began to have an effect. That same year, Reeds Jewelry was incorporated in North Carolina, making a number of affiliated corporations into subsidiaries of a single organization. In 1985, Bill became chairman of the Reeds board and Alan was named president and CEO.

By the end of fiscal 1986, sales had more than doubled, to nearly $26 million, with net profit of $1.6 million. During 1986, Alan convinced his father and the other members of the family to take the company public. He stressed the need to avoid problems faced by families when some members are interested in the business and others are not. He also thought he would be able to more easily attract professional management if the company were held publicly. In December, the family sold 17 percent of the company, 600,000 shares, on the NASDAQ market, trading as REED.

Alan took the company's share of the proceeds, $3.7 million, and began acquiring other jewelry chains. In 1987, Reeds bought Dreyfus Jewelry Company of Memphis for about $6.2 million. That family-owned chain had 19 stores in the Southeast and Midwest, and the acquisition increased Reeds size to a 57-store chain. In 1988, Reeds purchased Gray's Jewelers, Inc., a five-store chain based in Tulsa, Oklahoma, for approximately $2.1 million.

In 1988, Zimmer and Rouse implemented two other changes, addressing the company's marketing and credit policies. In both cases, the changes meant altering longtime ways of operating.

As was true for the retail jewelry industry as a whole, Reeds offered its customers easy credit. With the typical customer spending an average of $320 every time he or she visited Reeds, readily available credit generated strong sales. But when bad debt expenses doubled to $2.3 million between fiscal years 1987 and 1988, it was obvious that the policy had to be tightened. Hiring a credit specialist, Reeds established credit standards for the entire company and centralized the credit check process. As a result, where at one time nearly 85 percent of Reeds' customers bought on credit, by 1989, the figure was just over half, close to the industry average. The company's wholly owned subsidiary, Reeds Financial Services, Inc., administered all credit extension, collection, and related activities for the company.

And while credit was being tightened, the company ended its practice of offering half-price sales. Such promotions were how the industry historically operated. A store owner would mark an item up 200 percent and then sell it at 50 or 75 percent off. According to *Business/North Carolina*, "The goal was to get a big enough down payment to cover the cost of the goods and then let monthly payments—fattened with interest at 18 to 21 percent annually—provide the gravy."

But Zimmer wanted to move the company into a more upscale market, and instead of promoting price "deals," began concentrating on quality, value, and service. The changes in credit and marketing took a toll on the company's financial picture in fiscal 1989. While net sales rose six percent to $49.5 million, same-store sales were down over 10 percent, and net earnings were flat. One bright spot was that bad debt expenses fell to $1.9 million. But Zimmer and Rouse saw the change in image as a long-term strategy. While acknowledging that they had to improve their marketing, they stuck with their new direction for the company.

Overcoming Economic Challenges, 1990–95

The recession of the early 1990s was a difficult period for retailers in the jewelry industry, including Reeds. While the company remained profitable, net earnings dropped in fiscal 1990 and 1991. But in 1992, the worst seemed to be over, as company sales grew by nearly six percent to over $53 million and profits by 13 percent.

Even during these leaner times, Zimmer kept expanding the company, opening a few stores each year. The cities he chose for new locations were mid-size and small markets such as Raleigh-Durham, North Carolina, and Huntsville, Alabama, or upscale resort areas like Hilton Head, South Carolina. The selling space in Reeds shops ranged in size from 500 to 2,100 square feet, and averaged about 11,000 square feet. Except for the original Wilmington shop, which it owned, Reeds leased all its stores, with the vast majority being located in enclosed regional malls.

By 1993, as the economy improved, so did the jewelry industry. A record 9.7 million carats of diamonds were imported into the United States that year, worth $4.5 billion. This was an increase in weight of 26 percent from the year before. Some 248 tons of gold was made into gold jewelry, eight percent more than in 1992. Reeds, with 71 stores, was also doing much better, with net sales of $67.3 million for the year ending in February 1994, and earnings up to $3.2 million.

At about this time, analysts noted that a crack was apparently developing in a long-term seasonal pattern in the jewelry industry. Traditionally, the fourth quarter of the year is the period for the highest sales and earnings, with the Christmas holidays accounting for 41 percent of the industry's annual sales. Kenneth Gassman, a specialty retailing analyst at Davenport & Co. of Richmond, Virginia, noted in a 1994 *Wall Street Journal* article that at Reeds, sales in January and February 1994 rose nine percent, after the holidays. In fiscal 1993, 93 percent of Reeds' earnings had come during the fourth quarter. In fiscal 1994 that had dropped to 71 percent even though the percentage of sales for the quarter remained almost stable. By the end of fiscal 1996, earnings for the first two quarters had increased significantly, and the fourth quarter accounted for only 67 percent of annual earnings. The economy and improved advertising may have contributed to people buying more jewelry throughout the year rather than just at Christmas.

Reeds continued to do well. In fiscal 1995, sales increased 15 percent, to $77.5 million, and earnings passed the $4 million mark. In September 1995, the company moved into the Washington, D.C./Baltimore market with the acquisition of Melart Jewelers, Inc., for $2.2 million.

1996 to the Present

With a strong U.S. dollar and low inflation, the price of gold declined, and in 1996, the demand for gold jewelry set a new record. Yet as that record was being set, Reeds' sales mix was changing.

The majority of the merchandise sold by the company fell into three categories: diamonds and precious gems, gold jewelry and semi-precious gems, and watches. The gold jewelry was primarily 14 carat, and in fiscal 1993, the gold jewelry and semiprecious gems such as opals, amethysts, and garnets, represented over a quarter (25.9 percent) of Reeds' sales. By the end of fiscal 1996, that percentage had dropped to just over one-fifth (20.9 percent) of all sales. Watches were also less popular sales items, dropping from 17.6 percent of all sales in fiscal 1993 to 11.9 percent in fiscal 1996. What had become more popular was jewelry with diamonds and precious gems such as rubies, sapphires, and emeralds. Whereas those gems represented 42.6 percent of items sold in Reeds stores in fiscal 1993, by fiscal 1996, they made up more than half the merchandise sold (56.9 percent).

In fiscal years 1996 and 1997, the company's revenues continued to climb, but for the year ended February 1997, sales in stores that had been open for 12 months were flat and average sales per store decreased by four percent. To correct the situation, Reeds undertook an initiative, the goal of which, according to Alan Zimmer in a company press release, was "to increase the number of career-minded professionals in our sales force and to improve the focus and skills of our sales and management associates."

In the highly competitive and fragmented retail jewelry business, Alan Zimmer built a sizable regional chain through acquisitions, expansion, and quality service. At the same time he improved the company's operations, applying more modern business principles. As a result, in 1997, Reeds was the only publicly held retail jewelry chain with stores located entirely in the United States to be profitable for 15 straight years. Looking to the future, Zimmer expected to extend that record.

Principal Subsidiaries

Reeds Corporate Services, Inc.; Reeds Insurance Services, Ltd.; Reeds Financial Services, Inc.; Reeds Jewelers of North Carolina, Inc.; The Melart Jewelers, Inc.

Further Reading

Donsky, Martin, "The Family Jewels," *Business/North Carolina*, 1989.

Marcial, Gene, "The Glitter at Reeds," *BusinessWeek*, January 10, 1994, p. 57.

Moukheiber, Zina, "There's Going to Be One Boss," *Forbes*, September 12, 1994, p. 82.

Peers, Alexandra, "Jewelry Market Begins to Recapture Sparkle, Renewing Burnish of Some Stocks in Industry," *Wall Street Journal*, April 22, 1994, p. C2.

—Ellen D. Wernick

Reuters Holdings PLC

85 Fleet Street
London EC4P 4AJ
England
+44 171 250 1122
Fax: +44 171 510 5896
Web site: http://www.reuters.com

Public Company
Incorporated: 1865 as Reuter's Telegram Company Limited
Employees: 15,500
Sales:£2.9 billion (US$4.2 billion) (1995)
Stock Exchanges: London NASDAQ
SICs: 7383 News Syndicates; 7375 Information Retrieval Services; 4899 Communications Services, Not Elsewhere Classified

As the premier news organization and supplier of computerized financial information services, Reuters Holdings PLC serves financial and business communities in all of the world's major markets and the news media in more than 160 countries. Though it is widely recognized as a news agency, news services generate a mere five percent of annual revenues. However, news remains a significant contributor to the Reuters package, for these stories influence the sale and transmission of financial data, which constitutes the remaining 95 percent of the company's sales. Reuters' network of dedicated computers boasts more screens than its top three competitors combined, transmitting over two-thirds of the world's foreign exchange data and one-third of the market for equity information. Reuters products include real-time financial information and transaction services, numerical and textual historical databases, as well as news, news pictures, and news video. Financial data are drawn from exchanges and over-the-counter markets, while currency exchange rates and other market information are contributed directly by subscribers. Reuters journalists, photographers, and cameramen make up a worldwide news reporting network.

Reuters has from its inception employed any and all means at its disposal to achieve timely dissemination of news and information. From the founder's mid-19th-century use of carrier pigeons to scoop the competition to the late 20th-century exploitation of satellites and global computer networks to provide round-the-clock data, this company has remained at the forefront of its industry.

Mid-19th-Century Origins

Reuters is named for its founder, Julius Reuter. A native of Germany, Reuter was born Israel Beer Josaphat in 1816. He converted from Judaism to Christianity and adopted his new name while on a brief trip to London in the 1840s. After working as a publisher in Berlin, he fled the city during the revolution of 1848 and arrived in Paris. Here he is said to have worked for Charles Havas, the French news agency pioneer, before setting up in business himself. In 1849 Reuter started his own newssheet, translating information taken from French newspapers into German and sending this data to provincial papers in his homeland. The business failed after a few months. Reuter left for Germany to establish a service in Aachen, supplying financial and general news from the financial centers of Paris, Brussels, and Berlin to the merchants and bankers in Cologne and elsewhere. The enterprising Reuter used carrier pigeons to bridge the gap in the telegraph line then existing between Aachen and Brussels, thereby achieving a seven-hour jump on the local mail train.

By the end of 1850 the gap in the telegraph line was closed and Reuter moved to London. In response to the laying of a cable across the English Channel, linking the stock exchanges of London and Paris, he opened an office near the London Stock Exchange in October 1851. In addition to being the financial center of the Victorian world, London was becoming the communications center for the growing world telegraph network. Free trade and a free press added to the atmosphere Reuter needed to succeed in his new venture. He had long been impressed by the potential of telegraphic communication and the profits to be derived from the sale of news and information via this medium. Twice a day, for a fixed-term payment, his Sub-

Company Perspectives:

The Reuter Trust Principles: that Reuters shall at no time pass into the hands of any interest, group or faction; that the integrity, independence and freedom from bias of Reuters shall at all times be fully preserved; that Reuters shall supply unbiased and reliable news services to newspapers, news agencies, broadcasters and other media subscribers and to businesses, governments, institutions, individuals and others with whom Reuters has or may have contracts; that Reuters shall pay due regard to the many interests which it serves in addition to those of the media; and that no effort shall be spared to expand, develop and adapt the news and other services and products of Reuters so as to maintain its leading position in the international news and information business.

marine Telegraph office provided London and Paris brokers and merchants with opening and closing prices in both capitals. He gradually widened his geographic range and in 1857 made a contract with the recently established telegraphic news agency in Russia.

The repeal of the newspaper stamp duty—a tax on the sale of newspapers—in 1855 was to transform the British press, making way for the penny daily papers and the rise of popular journalism. Newspapers had more space for news, and their readership extended rapidly. The *London Times* already had its own network of correspondents in Europe, the Near East, India, China, and the United States, and refused to make any contract with Reuter. In 1858, despairing of the *Times,* Reuter approached several other London daily papers and persuaded them to subscribe to his news service. This was a breakthrough. The *Times* eventually softened its attitude and made a contract for telegrams.

Reuter was by this time offering general and political news, received by telegraph from all over Europe, as well as financial information. Reuter pioneered the information embargo and foreshadowed real-time transmission of information in 1859, when he persuaded Napoleon III to give him an advance copy of a speech. Reuter held the address until the French leader began speaking, then transmitted it to the newspapers via telegraph. The speech heralded the war of Italian liberation.

After several unsuccessful attempts to lay a cable across the Atlantic, a transatlantic line was finally laid in 1866. By this date Reuter was already receiving news from agents in many parts of the world beyond Europe. His correspondent in the United States reported the Civil War and was two hours ahead of rivals in announcing the news of the assassination of President Abraham Lincoln in 1865.

Julius Reuter was a businessman, collecting and selling news, rather than a journalist. The first editor was Sigismund Engländer, a Viennese revolutionary, who had fled to Paris at the same time as Reuter in 1848. Engländer was one of several emigrés employed in the early years of the business. His great knowledge of the politics and culture of Europe opened many doors. When the Russo-Turkish War broke out in 1877, he went to Constantinople as chief correspondent.

Incorporation in 1865

In 1865 Julius Reuter's private business became Reuter's Telegram Company Limited. The new company was incorporated with a nominal capital of £250,000. Reuter was appointed managing director. One reason for the restructuring was to raise capital to pay for a cable from England to Norderney on the north German coast. This cable became the link in the first telegraph to India in 1866. In pursuing his grand design of creating a world news agency, Reuter was ready to become a cable owner as well as a cable user. In 1869 he and Baron Émile d'Erlanger, a Paris banker, financed a French cable across the Atlantic. This company was absorbed by its rival, the Anglo-American Telegraph Company, in 1873. After this, Reuters became less exposed to the charge of seeking to monopolize news supply.

In the 1860s Reuters faced two main news agency rivals, Charles Havas in Paris and Bernard Wolff in Berlin. From this period until the 1930s Reuters, Havas, and Wolff divided most of the news of the world outside North America between themselves. The leading member of the "ring combination" was Reuters. The company's exclusive territories were the most extensive, and its network of offices and agencies, correspondents and stringers made it the largest news contributor to the pool. This activity, and Britain's predominance within the world telegraph system, made the Reuter office—by now in Old Jewry, London—the international clearing center for news. Reuters had established an enviable reputation for speed, accuracy, and impartiality in news collection and distribution.

In 1865 Reuters opened an office in Alexandria, its first office outside Europe. Offices were established in Bombay and other Indian cities from 1866. India became an important territory for Reuters. As the world's communications network spread to India and the East, the company followed the cable to China and Japan in 1871 and on to Australia in 1872. The prestige of Reuters—and also its profitability—came to depend heavily upon the growing British Empire. Reuters was to report the many wars which accompanied imperial expansion. From the 1870s the transmission of private telegrams for both businesses and individuals within the empire became a major Reuters activity. This was especially successful in the East where the substitution of code words for common phrases saved words and thus money. The revenue from this enterprise helped to pay for the news services, which increasingly lost money.

In 1878 Reuter retired as managing director. He had been granted a barony in 1871 by the Duke of Saxe-Coburg-Gotha, a title recognized by Queen Victoria in 1891. His son Herbert succeeded him as managing director. Baron Herbert de Reuter did not possess the same business acumen as his father, but he raised the standard of journalism within Reuters, meeting the public demand for more popular news in the 1890s. He introduced the latest technology to Reuters, but he also led the company down some dangerous paths. Forays into advertising and banking very nearly led to financial ruin. The setting up of a

Reuters bank was his final mistake. Business worries and the death of his wife contributed toward his suicide in 1915.

Reuters Taken Private in 1916

The Boer War of 1899–1902 had been a great drain on the company's resources, but it had been well reported and enhanced the reputation of Reuters for impartiality. It had placed correspondents on the Boer side as well as the British. From this scene of operations came the new head of Reuters. Soon after Herbert's death, Roderick Jones, manager in South Africa, became the first non-family managing director. To escape a hostile takeover bid, the company returned to private ownership in 1916. Jones and Mark Napier, the company's chairman, formed a group to buy the entire shareholding. Reuter's Telegram Company now became Reuters Limited. Napier died in 1919, leaving Roderick Jones as the principal proprietor and executive head, a post which he held until 1941.

World War I was a difficult time for the company. The cost of reporting was high both in terms of profits and of the independence that Reuters strove to achieve in all its business and news transactions. The private telegram business was no longer so profitable, since the censors would not allow the use of codes. Reuters was accused of being in the pay of the British government, and this was a difficult charge to deny. Roderick Jones was also head of the Department of Propaganda at the Ministry of Information, work for which he was knighted.

As head of Reuters between the two world wars, Roderick Jones ran the business as an autocracy. Reuters found it hard to keep its lead over the other international news agencies, especially the Associated Press and the United Press, both U.S. agencies. Jones thought that Reuters could seek to work *with* the British government, so long as it was not seen to be working *for* it. Reuters badly needed government subscriptions. Jones was careful not to ask for subsidies.

In 1920 Reuters set up a trade department to expand the distribution of business news. This was followed three years later by a service of price quotations and exchange rates sent in Morse code by long-wave radio to Europe. This became the company's chief commercial service in Europe, later reaching other parts of the world via more powerful radio transmitters. In 1927 Reuters started using teleprinters to distribute news to London newspapers. In 1934 the company began news transmission to Europe by Hellschreiber, a forerunner of the radio teleprinter.

Takeover by Newspaper Cartel in 1925

In 1925 the Press Association (PA) had taken a majority shareholding in Reuters. It followed this in 1930 by purchasing the remainder of the Reuter shares, except for 1,000 retained by Roderick Jones. In 1941 the PA directors forced Jones to resign. It felt that he had compromised the agency in his dealings with the British government. The government itself helped to ease Jones out. The Reuter Trust was now established to ensure the independence of the agency. From 1941 the company was jointly owned by the PA and the Newspaper Proprietors' Association (NPA). A commonwealth dimension was added when the Australian Associated Press (AAP) and the New Zealand Press Association (NZPA) joined the partnership in 1947. The Press Trust of India joined in 1949, only to leave four years later.

Christopher Chancellor was general manager during the 1940s and 1950s. Under his leadership Reuters did not crumble along with the British Empire, despite the growing ascendancy of the U.S. news agencies. The range of economic services expanded, and Reuters assisted in the establishment of news agencies in postwar Europe, and later in the Third World. In Chancellor's day, the newspaper owners of Reuters were not adventurous. They were aiming at little more than balancing the books. They expected to pay the minimum annual contribution towards the running of Reuters and to get their news cheap.

Computerized Information Brings Rapid Expansion in Late 20th Century

Walton Cole, who succeeded Chancellor in 1959, had strengthened the news file during the later stages of World War II as managing editor. Cole died in 1963. His successor, Gerald Long, sought to make Reuters an aggressive and profitable international news organization. Notably, he persuaded a reluctant Reuters board to enter the market for computerized information. This initiative was eventually to transform the company's character and to earn it huge profits. Long encouraged Michael Nelson, the manager of Reuters Economic Services, to lead Reuters into price reporting via computer terminals. In partnership with Ultronic Systems Corporation of the United States, Reuters started a desktop market-quotation system called Stockmaster in 1964. It served Reuters clients throughout the world outside North America. In just 10 years the profits from Stockmaster and its successor Videomaster amounted to £4 million.

In 1971 the collapse of the Brenon Woods Agreement, which had regulated rates of exchange, encouraged Reuters to undertake another daring yet calculated initiative. This was the introduction of the Reuter Monitor Money Rates service in 1973. Catering to the needs of the decentralized money markets, Monitor was the first of a number of contributed data products designed to serve the international business community. The Reuter Monitor Dealing service followed in 1981. This enabled dealers in foreign currencies to conclude trades over video terminals. These innovations gradually made Reuters more profitable than ever before. In 1963 the company had made a profit of £51,000; in 1973 profits reached more than £709,000; and in 1981 profits were more than £16 million.

On the news front, there were similar technological advances. In 1968 an Automatic Data Exchange (ADX)—a computerized message-switching system for faster handling and distribution of news throughout the world—went into operation in the London editorial offices. This was the first of its kind to be used by an international news organization. In 1973 Reuters formed a U.S. subsidiary, Information, Dissemination and Retrieval Inc. (IDR), to develop and manufacture systems and equipment for the company's use in cable television news and retrieval services. For the first time in 1973 Reuter journalists in New York began to use video display units for writing and sending news.

1984 IPO Presages Rapid Growth

Glen Renfrew, a 32-year veteran of Reuters, became managing director in 1981. Charged with the development of Reuters' computer services since their inception in 1964, Renfrew has been hailed as the architect of the media firm's spectacular growth throughout the 1980s. A key to his strategy was the 1984 flotation of Reuters Limited as a public company, Reuters Holdings PLC. As part of the restructuring, the composition of the board was broadened to make it more international, and the number of directors was increased to include the first representatives from outside the newspaper world. A separate company, Reuters Founders Share Company, was formed to maintain the Reuter Trust principles. Through this company the trustees and their chairman retained a single share with the power to outvote all other shares to prevent a takeover bid. Sir Christopher Hogg, chief executive of Courtaulds plc, became chairman of Reuters in 1985.

The flotation raised about £52 million of new capital which was available for investment in new products and new technology. Reuters Monitor quickly expanded to become the agency's largest operation. The company went into the international news picture business in 1985 when it purchased the United Press International picture service, and launched a news picture terminal in 1987. In 1985 Reuters acquired control of Visnews Ltd., the international television news agency in which it had held a stake since 1959. Revenues more than doubled from less than US$1 billion in 1986 to over US$2.7 billion by the time Renfrew retired in 1991. Net income nearly quadrupled from US$119 million to US$430 million during that same period, while earnings per share tripled. In line with this remarkable financial performance, Reuters' stock price shot from US$8.25 at issue to nearly US$29 at the close of 1991. Worldwide staff numbers more than tripled from less than 3,000 in 1980 to more than 10,000 by 1991.

A 1989 reorganization categorized Reuters' services under five areas—real-time information, transaction products, trading room systems, historical information, and media products. The related products were named with a view to the 21st century—Equities 2000, Money 2000, Dealing 2000, and Triarch 2000. That same year, Reuters' geographical divisions were organized according to three time zones—Reuters Asia; Reuters America; and Reuters Europe, Middle East, and Africa.

The 1990s and Beyond

Former foreign correspondent Peter Job was selected to succeed Renfrew as managing director in March 1991. Though Reuters made a number of significant acquisitions in the early 1990s, Job emphasized the internal development of new products to serve emerging information needs over the purchase of market share in existing segments. Key to this strategy was Reuters New Media Inc., a division created in 1993 to foster fresh markets. Andrew Nibley, executive vice-president of the new operation, told *Editor & Publisher's* Jodi Cohen that New Media's chief objective was "to be the number one news application in cyberspace." In doing so, the company placed a strong emphasis on the Reuters brand, transforming it from a behind-the-scenes role to a distinct image as the leader in "the business of information."

Reuters launched the next-generation versions of its core product lines—Markets 3000, Treasury 3000, Securities 3000, and Money 3000—in 1996. The company continued to grow vigorously in the early 1990s, increasing revenues from US$2.7 billion in 1991 to US$4.2 billion by 1995. Though net income grew more slowly, from US$430 million to US$642 million, the company boasted a US$1.4 billion stockpile by the end of 1996.

Principal Subsidiaries

Reuter Nederland BV (Netherlands); Reuter Services SARL (France); Reuters AG (West Germany); Reuters Australia Pty Ltd.; Reuters Hong Kong Ltd.; Reuters Information Services Inc. (U.S.A.); Reuters Italia S.p.A. (Italy); Reuters Japan K.K.; Reuters Ltd. (99.7%); Reuters Middle East Ltd. (Bahrain); Reuters SA (Switzerland); Reuters Singapore Pte Ltd.; Reuters Svenska Aktiebolag (Sweden); Rich Inc. (U.S.A.); L.H.W. Wyatt Brothers Ltd.; Instinet Corporation (U.S.A.); I.P. Sharp Associates Ltd. (Canada); Visnews Ltd. (51%).

Further Reading

Boyd Barrett, Oliver, *The International News Agencies,* London: Constable, 1980.
Chen, Jodi B., "Invasion of the Body Snatchers," *Editor & Publisher,* May 25, 1996, pp. 28–30.
Collins, Henry M., *From Pigeon Post to Wireless,* London: Hodder and Stoughton, 1925.
Desmond, R. W., *The Information Process: World News Reporting to the Twentieth Century,* Iowa City: University of Iowa Press, 1978.
Fenby, Jonathan, *The International News Services (A Twentieth Century Fund Report),* New York: Schocken Books, 1986.
Hayes, John R., "Acquisition Is Fine, But Organic Growth Is Better," *Forbes,* December 30, 1996, pp. 52–55.
Jones, Roderick, *A Life in Reuters,* London: Hodder and Stoughton, 1951.
Lawrenson, John, and Lionel Barber, *The Price of Truth: The Story of the Reuters Millions,* London: Sphere, 1986.
Read, Donald, *The Power of News: The History of Reuters,* Oxford: Oxford University Press, 1994.
Six Drown Saving Chicken: And Other True Stories from the Reuters "Oddly Enough" File, New York: Carroll & Graf Publishers, 1996.
Storey, Graham, *Reuters Century,* London: Max Parrish, 1951.

—Justine Taylor
—updated by April Dougal Gasbarre

Revere Ware Corporation

1000 S. Chermain Street
Clinton, Illinois 61727
U.S.A.
(217) 935-7200
Fax: (217) 935-7398

Wholly Owned Subsidiary of Corning Consumer Products Company
Incorporated: 1928 as Revere Copper & Brass
Employees: 500
Sales: $125 million (1995 est.)
SICs: 3469 Metal Stampings, Not Elsewhere Classified; 3262 Vitreous China Table & Kitchen Articles; 3263 Fine Earthenware (Whiteware) Table & Kitchen Articles

Revere Ware Corporation manufactures one of America's best-known brands of cookware. Its copper-bottomed pots, first brought out in the 1930s, are classic kitchen staples. The Revere Ware brand is estimated to have 25 percent of the U.S. market share for cookware. The brand sells at both department stores and at mass merchants. Revere Ware is owned by Corning Consumer Products, Inc., which also manufactures a variety of well-known cookware lines.

Early History

Revere Ware Corporation began as a division of Revere Copper & Brass, a metal company based in New York. Revere Copper & Brass was formed in 1928 from a merger of six small copper and brass companies. One of the six firms in the 1928 merger traced its roots back to the famed American revolutionary and silversmith Paul Revere. This company, Taunton-New Bedford Copper Company, had bought the assets of Paul Revere and Son in 1801. Another company in the 1928 merger, the Rome Manufacturing Company, also had a lengthy history. It had manufactured tea kettles and other housewares since 1892. But the principal products of Revere Copper & Brass were industrial, not housewares. The company manufactured copper pipes, bars, tubes, and sheets. Soon after its inception it was one of the largest copper manufacturers in the United States.

Revere Copper & Brass invented its famous cookware line in the 1930s, seeking to diversify away from strictly industrial products. At a time when most cooking was done in heavy cast-iron pots, researchers at the company attempted to make a lighter weight, easier to clean pot out of copper. The first Revere pots were copper with a chrome-plated inner lining. But this metal combination did not work well. Though copper was an excellent heat conductor and light weight, the chrome lining was easily scarred by acidic foods. Concentrated research at Revere Copper & Brass led to a new combination. The new pots were made of stainless steel, a light, durable, smooth, stain- and scratch-resistant metal. The company electro-plated copper to the bottom of the pot, to give great heat conductivity. The pot handle was made of plastic, an industry first. The design of the handle was based on a silversmith's hammer, and its curved knob was echoed in the rounded inner surface of the pot. Revere Ware, in development since 1932, debuted in 1939 at the Chicago Housewares Show. It was an instant hit, and this brand of cookware soon became the most profitable division of Revere Copper & Brass.

When the United States entered World War II, Revere turned its production over to war materials. The company had made copper and brass articles such as water pipes for plumbing, but in 1942 began making cartridge and rocket cases and smoke bombs. Production of housewares halted completely until the end of the war. Revere bought a new plant in Riverside, California, in 1948, and another in Clinton, Illinois, in 1950. These plants began to manufacture Revere Ware cooking pots, as metal quotas permitted. The company's other plants converted back to prewar production for a short time, but again made war materials when the United States entered the Korean War. Revere continued to make weapons during the Vietnam War. By the mid-1960s, Revere had dozens of plants, and was making sales of around $350 million annually.

Expansion in the 1960s and 1970s

In 1966 Revere Copper & Brass decided to diversify by investing in another metal, aluminum. The copper and brass fabricating industries had their ups and downs, with many cost factors the company could not control or predict. Aluminum seemed altogether a more profitable venture. Revere owned a 33 percent interest in Ormet Corp., a primary aluminum producer, so it already had some experience in the aluminum industry. Revere decided to make massive investments in aluminum through two projects. The company built an alumina refinery (alumina is the middle product between bauxite, a mined raw material, and aluminum) in Maggotty, Jamaica. And it also built an aluminum smelter and rolling mill in Scottsboro, Alabama. The aluminum industry was dominated by three large companies: Aluminum Co. of America, Reynolds Metal Co., and Kaiser Aluminum & Chemical Corp. In comparison to these large producers' plants, both Maggotty and Scottsboro were small, but Revere planned to increase capacity later. For example the energy contract the Scottsboro plant negotiated with the Tennessee Valley Authority allowed for the plant to triple in size. But both facilities were plagued with problems from the beginning. The Maggotty plant was poorly designed, small and inefficient, and the same was said of the Scottsboro plant. And the Scottsboro plant depended in part on delivery of alumina from Maggotty. Between 1966 and 1976 the company funneled about $240 million into its aluminum projects, and during this time, profits sank. Profits in 1966 were $22 million on sales of just over $350 million; 10 years later sales reached almost $500 million, but profits were a miniscule $2.2 million.

Not all the problems were due to the aluminum investments. Net income fell sharply in 1971, when copper prices tumbled and coal and copper strikes hurt the company. Revere posted a loss in 1972, in part because the company wrote off huge debts due to its Maggotty plant. The company was forced to cut back its production of copper in 1973 because it had difficulty securing low-priced copper scrap. Scrap prices were controlled in the United States, but American dealers were allowed to export copper scrap and sell it at much higher prices abroad. In 1973 copper scrap was selling for between 60 and 68 cents a pound in the United States, and for more than 95 cents a pound on the London Metal Exchange. Because of this sizable price differential, domestic dealers sold abroad, and companies like Revere Copper & Brass could barely secure enough scrap to keep going, even though demand for copper products was high.

To add to the company's difficulties, in 1974 the Jamaican government raised its levy on bauxite ore mined in its country, hiking the cost of Revere's Maggotty alumina plant considerably. Jamaica had been plagued by inflation, and badly needed cash. Six companies—Revere, Alcan, Reynolds Metals, Aluminum Co. of America, Kaiser Aluminum & Chemical, and Anaconda—had negotiated with the government for weeks in secret, trying to find a new tax formula that all could agree to, when Jamaica suddenly announced its own plan as final. The production levy increased from about 26 cents a ton to 50 cents a ton, plus a tax figured as a percentage of the U.S. price for aluminum ingot. This made Revere's Maggotty plant, already inefficient and costly to run, a complete money drain. Revere had worked out a deal with a consortium of six Japanese companies to invest in Maggotty, aiming to double the plant's production. The increase in size was supposed to finally make the plant cost-effective. But the Japanese consortium pulled out of the deal in the wake of the bauxite levy increase, and Revere was unable to finance the $160 million expansion alone. The company paid the bauxite levy "under protest," while continuing to hope for concessions from Jamaica. By August 1975, Maggotty had become too expensive to run, and the plant shut down. But as part of its contract with the Jamaican government, Revere needed to get permission for a shut-down, and it was still liable for taxes pegged at earlier production rates. The company offered to sell the Maggotty plant to the Jamaican government for $65 million, but the offer was declined. In 1976 Revere stopped paying its bauxite tax, and filed a court claim asking to be freed of further dues. The company also filed a claim with the Overseas Private Insurance Corp. (OPIC), an entity that insured American businesses from failure abroad due to government actions such as nationalization. Revere claimed the Jamaican levy amounted to expropriation of its plant. But Revere lost its cases both in the Jamaican court and with OPIC.

The other aluminum companies had larger facilities in Jamaica, and continued to function despite the higher tax. But Revere could not make Maggotty profitable. As it seemed unable to unload Maggotty, Revere put its Scottsboro aluminum smelting plant up for sale. Briefly, it seemed as if the whole company would be sold, and then a deal materialized with Alcan to buy the Scottsboro plant for $205 million. But the sale to Alcan, which was accepted in July 1977, was blocked in federal court for anti-trust reasons, and by December, the sale was off. Revere was left with facilities it could not afford to operate. Housewares was its only profitable division.

Reorganization in the 1980s

From here it was a quick slide to bankruptcy. Revere sold a portion of its aluminum building products unit in 1980, getting $10 million for it from Norandex, a Cleveland company. But it was still unable to sell Scottsboro, which it eventually shut down in 1982. The company sought Chapter 11 in November 1982, claiming "massive and continuing losses" from its aluminum operations. Revere had a loss of $21.3 million in the first half of 1981, on sales of close to $320 million. Under Chapter 11 of the federal bankruptcy laws, the company was allowed to continue operating while it tried to pay its debts. In 1983 Asarco, the huge metals conglomerate which had owned 33 percent of Revere, sold its share to Bear, Stearns & Co., a New York investment firm, for $17 million.

The only profitable portion of Revere continued to be its Revere Ware brand housewares. The division's sales were estimated at about $54 million in 1977, and were up to $80 million by 1984. In 1985 Revere Copper & Brass announced that it would sell its housewares division, and asked $100 million for it. Considering that a third of the entire company had gone to Bear, Stearns for only $17 million a few years earlier, the price seemed extraordinarily high. After a few months, Revere announced that, though there were several interested parties, it no longer wished to make the sale. The company decided to make some improvements in the housewares business and its organization, and to hold on to it. In 1986 Revere consolidated its housewares unit with two related units, Revere Foil & Containers, Inc. and Revere Ware Courtesy Stores, Inc., into one subsidiary company, called Revere Ware, Inc. The new subsidiary was based in Clinton, Illinois, the location of the main Revere Ware manufacturing plant. The other plant that had made Revere Ware, in Rome, New York, was shut down. At almost the same time the new subsidiary was formed, Revere Copper & Brass submitted to a takeover by a Florida venture capital firm, Oxford Financial Group. Oxford had already bought up over 40 percent of Revere's stock. Its takeover preempted a leveraged buyout by a New York-based investment group that included Revere's chief executive officer.

Under new ownership, Revere Ware embarked on an ambitious program of brand expansion. The Revere Ware brand was extended to cutlery and small appliances. Revere Ware marketed a gourmet line of pots and pans, retailing for around $200, in an effort to capture the high end of the market. There was even a Revere Ware microwave oven. The company invested in updated packaging, and tried to give the overall brand a more innovative, high-tech image. The aggressive product development and exploration of new markets brought Revere Ware record sales and profits. With this success, Revere Ware's parent again put the division up for sale. While $100 million had seemed too much two years earlier, in 1988 Revere Copper & Brass was able to divest its housewares unit for an even better price. The well-known glass cookware manufacturer Corning Glass was happy to pay an estimated $120 million for Revere Ware. The sale to Corning was finalized in April 1988.

New Life as a Subsidiary in the 1990s

Revere Ware came under the umbrella of Corning's Consumer Products division, which already made some of the best-known American cookware brands, including Pyrex, Corning Ware, and Visions. These were all glass products. Revere Ware complemented Corning's line nicely by being its only metal cookware brand. Corning had researched Revere Ware well before buying the unit. Consumer surveys had told the company that the Revere brand was extremely well-known, despite little advertising. Consumers considered the brand old-fashioned, though they also identified Revere Ware with quality and durability. Corning worked to expand the new image Revere Ware had been promulgating before it was bought. Under Corning's management, Revere Ware developed its Pro-Line, a high-priced stainless and copper line for the upscale market, as well as a lower-priced classic line for the mass market. Both the upscale and lower-priced lines were immediately successful. Corning also backed Revere's new products with print advertising, something that had not been done much previously. In its first year under new ownership, Revere Ware saw big jumps in sales of some items, such as a 52 percent increase in tea kettles, and an increase of almost 60 percent in sales of its aluminum-disc cookware.

By 1994, Revere Ware had about equal penetration in upscale department stores and in mass markets. The brand dominated the stainless steel cookware market, and was a presence as well in aluminum cookware. Revere offered over a hundred different items, mostly in cookware. In 1994 Revere licensed its name to a line of non-stick bakeware manufactured by G & S metal products, in an effort to gain exposure in that category as well. The company continued to spend money on print advertising, and to bring out new cookware sets aimed at specific consumer groups. For example in 1995 Revere brought out a set of stainless steel cookware that was relatively low-priced—under $100—but designed for sale in department stores. Updated safety features as well as plainer packaging were designed to capture the tastes of 25- to 39-year-olds. Print advertising for this new line alone was estimated at over $5 million in 1996, and the line was also supported with in-store demonstrations, literature, and training programs. The company also paid "selling specialists"—sales people subsidized by Revere to focus on Revere products during key sales periods. Under Corning, Revere seemed to be improving on the marketing inroads the company had started in the mid-1980s, as the old-fashioned brand continued to innovate and expand.

Further Reading

"Alcan Unit to Drop Bid for Revere Facility," *Wall Street Journal,* December 20, 1977, p. 31.

"Asarco Completes Sale of Revere Copper Stake," *Wall Street Journal,* January 13, 1983, p. 46.

Casey, Lisa Ann, "Corning Hones Department Store Strategy," *HFD,* May 29, 1989, pp. 82–85.

"Chapter 11 for Revere," *Business Week,* November 8, 1982, p. 50.

Cook, James, "Staying on Top," *Forbes,* July 1, 1977, pp. 54–56.

Ellis, Beth R., "Corning Buy Boosts Lines, Distribution," *HFD,* May 9, 1988, pp. 1–2.

Gupta, Udayan, "Revere Copper Accepts Lower Bid Due to Tax Law," *Wall Street Journal,* November 19, 1986, p. 12.

Harris, Roy J., Jr., "Jamaica Proposed Bauxite Legislation to Produce $200 Million Over 13 Months," *Wall Street Journal,* May 17, 1974, p. 3.

Jordan, Carol L., "Revere Copper Decides to Keep Ware Div.," *American Metal Market,* October 29, 1985, pp. 1–2.

——, "Revere Copper Mulls Sale of Ware Div. in Ill., N.Y.," *American Metal Market,* August 29, 1985, pp. 1–2.

"National Steel Is Negotiating to Buy Revere," *Wall Street Journal,* January 31, 1977, p. 11.

Perry, Brian, "Cameron Joins Revere Ware; Sets 'Aggressive' Product Development Course," *HFD,* September 21, 1987, pp. 57–58.

——, "Revere Entering Kitchen Appliances: Cookware Firm Forms New Unit," *HFD,* November 2, 1987, pp. 1–4.

Rappleyea, Warren, "Corning Glass' Acquisition of Revere Ware Tagged at $120M," *American Metal Market,* May 3, 1988, p. 2.

"Revere, American Smelting Report '71 Profit Skidded," *Wall Street Journal,* January 2, 1972, p. 13.

"Revere Copper & Brass to Write Off $8,350,000 in Alumina Plant Costs," *Wall Street Journal,* January 2, 1973, p. 4.

"Revere Copper Is Withholding Payment of Jamaican Tax on Bauxite Production," *Wall Street Journal,* April 21, 1976, p. 11.

"Revere Copper Reports a Loss for 4th Period," *Wall Street Journal,* February 13, 1976, p. 10.

"Revere Forced to Cut Copper Production Due to Scrap Difficulties," *Wall Street Journal,* August 16, 1973, p. 20.

"Revere's Sale Blocked," *Business Week,* December 26, 1977, p. 44.

"Revere Sells Portion of Unit to Norandex," *Wall Street Journal,* August 11, 1980, p. 22.

"Revere's Woes Blamed on Market, Government," *Iron Age,* November 10, 1982, p. 69.

Schwartz, Judith D., "How Corning Inc. Prevented Revere Ware from Going to Pot," *Adweek's Marketing Week,* October 23, 1989, pp. 76–77.

Stankevich, Debby Garbato, "Revere Name Due on G&S Bakeware," *HFD,* April 18, 1994, p. 149.

——, "Revere's Solutions: $99 Cookware for Department Stores," *HFD,* November 20, 1995, pp. 27–28.

"Upscale Cookware, Cutlery Goods from Revere to Bow," *HFD,* September 21, 1987, pp. 73–74.

—A. Woodward

Riddell Sports Inc.

900 Third Avenue
New York, New York 10022
U.S.A.
(212) 826-4300
Fax: (212) 826-5006

Public Company
Incorporated: 1927
Employees: 613
Sales: $72.1 million (1996)
Stock Exchanges: NASDAQ
SICs: 3949 Sporting & Athletic Goods, Not Elsewhere Classified; 5091 Sporting & Recreational Goods & Supplies; 6794 Patent Owners & Lessors; 7999 Amusement & Recreation Services, Not Elsewhere Classified

Riddell Sports Inc. is the world's leading manufacturer of football helmets and the world's leading reconditioner of football helmets, shoulder pads, and other sports protective equipment. It also markets collectible products, mainly helmets, and licenses its Riddell and MacGregor trademarks to other companies, primarily for use on athletic footwear and apparel. In 1997 it purchased a company supplying uniforms and operating facilities for cheerleaders and dance teams.

Making Helmets and Shoes, 1927–79

The company was founded in 1927 by John T. Riddell, coach of the Evanston, Illinois high school football team. Riddell designed the first screw on removable cleat in 1922 so that his players' footgear would not have to be refitted each time field conditions called for a change in the length of the cleats. He then found a company that would make football shoes with this cleat, but in 1927 he quit teaching and coaching to open his own company. Based in Chicago, Riddell, Inc. also developed and manufactured the first soft-spike baseball shoe. In 1939 Riddell perfected the first molded basketball but had to discontinue making them during World War II because of difficulty in getting the right materials; it never resumed making this product.

John Riddell's most lasting development may have been the plastic-shell football helmet, which he devised in 1939. This was a welcome replacement for the time-honored leather ones with cloth or felt liners that were stiff, sweat-fouled, hot in autumn, and cold in winter. Riddell then invented the web sling suspension that provides a pocket of air between the player's head and the hard outer shell of the helmet. This was adopted by the military during World War II and remained in use. Gerry Morgan, who later became the firm's chairman, told the *Chicago Tribune* in 1976, ''Every GI who went through training wore one, and we gave it [the patent] to the government for what I regret was a ridiculously low fee.'' Riddell also was responsible for the chin strap and the first low-cut football shoe, both in 1940.

Riddell died in 1945. By 1950 his company had perfected the one-piece helmet. ''We finally got the right material, a compound of rubber and plastic that would take all the stress,'' Morgan said. It also ''was tough enough to withstand temperature changes.'' Morgan went on to call the human head ''the damnedest thing to fit. It comes in all shapes and sizes—egg heads, square heads, flat heads, and lopsided heads. The head isn't round, it's elongated, especially larger heads.''

Riddell began selling helmets to professional football teams shortly after World War II and by 1949 had the largest share of the pro market. Morgan traveled with the pro teams for several seasons, designing, improvising, and adjusting new equipment ideas. One of these was a bar attached to the helmet of Cleveland Browns quarterback Otto Graham to protect his face. This eventually led to the double bar, the face mask, and other protective devices. Another idea was less successful: a two-way radio so that Browns coach Paul Brown could communicate with Graham while the quarterback was on the field. Riddell installed a citizen's-band radio into a helmet, but when the Browns tried to use it, two women were talking on the frequency. Eventually the club realized that if the coach could send in a play on the radio, the opponent could get a receiver and listen in, too.

By 1975 Riddell was unique among sporting equipment manufacturers in making only two products: helmets and shoes. It earned close to $1 million that year on revenues of about $9.9 million. By the mid-1970s the company was furnishing all National Football League teams except the New England Patriots with helmets. The company's 200 employees produced

250,000 helmets in 1975, at prices ranging from $20 to $40. This was double the previous year's output because of recent federal legislation setting standards for helmet durability and reliability. Riddell also was making baseball helmets and all-leather shoes for both football and baseball.

Riddell was sold to Wynn's International Inc., a California-based conglomerate, in 1975. The following year a number of new products were introduced, including several models of casual and training shoes for jogging and general recreation, an expanded line of popular-priced football shoes, special-purpose footwear for softball and soccer, a new vinyl-cleat football shoe for the youth market, and lighter weight football face masks. Net sales reached $15.1 million in 1979, when Riddell was also selling warmup suits and T-shirts to retailers. The company was having trouble finding skilled shoemakers and meeting competition in the shoe business, however, so it dropped all footwear manufacturing in 1979. The following year Wynn's sold Riddell and another subsidiary, Bell Helmets Inc., to an undisclosed party for $10.5 million in cash and notes and the assumption of $443,000 in debt.

Aside from the unprofitable expansion of its shoe business, Riddell's chief problem in the late 1970s was the product liability suits that had caused its insurance premiums to rise tenfold in 1976, following a $5.3 million judgment against the company in the case of a youth paralyzed by a broken neck. Morgan blamed high school coaches who taught their players to use the helmet to block or tackle an opponent, thereby risking trauma to the neck. In 1977 sources for the sporting goods industry estimated a total of $150 million in lawsuits pending against the seven remaining U.S. helmet manufacturers.

Frank Gordon, the company's president, told the *Chicago Tribune* in 1977 that Riddell had stopped reconditioning helmets because of the liability issue. ''It used to be a big part of our business,'' he said, ''but we have found that it's hard to tell when a plastic shell has been weakened, particularly if it's over four years old.'' Gordon, a lawyer, went to on say that the company was protecting itself by assembling a stable of experts—physicists, doctors, and people in biomechanics—ready to testify in court in support of the company's contentions in defense of its helmets. Although dropping out of the reconditioning business itself, Riddell sold patented parts necessary for reconditioning and refurbishing its helmets to other reconditioning firms.

Broadened Line of Products, 1985–97

Riddell still was the nation's largest manufacturer of football helmets at the beginning of 1985, when the privately held company was sold to MacGregor Sporting Goods Inc. for $5.5 million and the assumption of about $700,000 in liabilities. This transaction infuriated Michael Blumenfeld, founder and chief executive of Dallas-based BSN Corp., who had sought the company himself. MacGregor broadened Riddell's football product lines in such areas as shoulder pads, small protective pads, and hand and arm pads. Virtually all of its products were being manufactured at the Chicago facility.

MacGregor retained Riddell for only three years. In 1988 it sold the company and Equilink Licensing Group (which was licensing the MacGregor trademark) for $38.2 million in cash and notes to a group led by the Nederlander family, which renamed the company Riddell Sports and moved its executive offices to New York City. Robert Nederlander became chief executive officer. MacGregor received a 25.5 percent stake in this group and retained the right to license the Riddell name for protective products other than those used for football. Riddell had annual sales of about $14 million at this time.

Riddell now held 60 percent of the National Football League helmet market, and one of its assets was the right to market helmets with the names of the league's teams on them. In 1989 Riddell signed an agreement (renewed in 1994) with the NFL's licensing arm, promising to make helmets, shoulder pads, and other gear available to the league's teams for free if 90 percent of a team's players used its helmets. Players who wore helmets made by other companies were required to conceal the logos of those companies. In 1991 it entered into a five-year exclusive licensing pact providing that the Riddell trademark would appear on the front center and chin strap of each company helmet worn by an NFL player.

The liability issue continued to drive up Riddell's costs and, consequently, its helmet prices during the 1980s. The company, which had reentered the reconditioning business late in the decade, announced in December 1989 that it would no longer recondition or recertify helmets once they were ten years old because it said recent studies showed the helmet shell was no longer effective after this period. The change in policy worked hardship for the many high schools that could ill afford to resupply their players with new helmets at $90 apiece.

Riddell lost $1.2 million on net revenues of $21.3 million in 1989. The company had a net profit of $1.9 million the following year on net revenues of $30.4 million and $2.2 million in 1991 on net revenues of $35.5 million, of which football helmet sales accounted for 47 percent. It became a public company in 1991, when one third of the shares of common stock were sold at $8 a share in an offering that netted the company about $14.9 million. Three months later, as part of a transaction valued at $19 million, Riddell transferred to BSN about 27 percent of its stock to acquire BSN's Protective Equipment Division, whose All American Sports Co. was the nation's leading reconditioner of used football helmets. This division also included Maxpro Sports Inc., manufacturer of helmets and shoulder pads.

Riddell introduced ice hockey shoulder pads to its product line in 1992. It signed Chicago Black Hawk player Jocelyn Lemieux to redesign and promote these pads, which Lemieux redesigned to fit his specifications. ''I've had them add a bubble-like foam all over rather than flat padding,'' he told a *Chicago Tribune* sportswriter in 1993. ''Their pads were too big and bulky at first,'' Lemieux added, ''like football pads. I have tried to make it more comfortable while still keeping the protection.'' Lemieux indicated that vanity was also a consideration. ''The first thing a hockey player does when he puts on new equipment is run to the bathroom and look in the mirror to see how he looks. No one wants to see himself real wide and bulky with pads.''

Riddell's profits fell in 1992, and the following year it lost $5.7 million on revenue volume that dropped to $48.8 million from $56.4 million the previous year. Blumenfeld, as chief of BSN's successor, Sport Supply Group Inc., continued his long-standing pursuit of the company, offering to buy it for Sport

Supply stock valued at $14.5 million and the assumption of Riddell's $23 million in revolving bank debt. A harsh critic of the company's management, Blumenfeld earlier had proposed a management takeover, citing Riddell's poor earnings, declining stock price, and alleged lack of strategic direction and poor execution of its operating plan. Riddell common stock was trading at $2.50 a share in 1993, compared with a high of $16 in September 1991. His bid was rejected, however, by Nederlander and his partners, who continued to hold the largest block of the company's stock.

Riddell lost almost as much money—$4.9 million—in 1994 as in 1993, even though its revenues rose to $55.4 million. The following year it earned a modest $470,534 after taxes on net revenues of $67 million. In 1996 the company had net income of $2.8 million on net revenues of $72.4 million.

Riddell Sports in 1996–97

In 1996 Riddell Sports' Riddell, Inc. subsidiary was manufacturing helmets at its Chicago plant and was purchasing shoulder pads from other sources for sale to institutional and retail customers. Helmets accounted for 21 percent and shoulder pads for nine percent of the parent company's revenues in 1996. Riddell was also selling accessory pads, including thigh, hip, rib, and knee pads. In addition, this subsidiary began selling baseballs and softballs, protective baseball equipment, and certain other baseball and softball equipment for high school and college players in 1996. Later in the year it added practicewear such as T-shirts, shorts, fleece warmups, and other basic athletic clothing to its product line.

All American Sports was selling reconditioning services and new athletic products to schools and other institutions. It was the leading reconditioner of football helmets, shoulder pads, and related equipment. This subsidiary also was reconditioning equipment for other sports, including baseball and lacrosse helmets, catchers' masks, and gloves. Reconditioning accounted for 30 percent of the parent company's revenues in 1996.

Riddell Sports' fastest growing line in 1996 consisted of sports collectible products, primarily authentic and replica football helmets of professional and college teams, offered in miniature and full-size models. The company also had license agreements for other collectible products with organizations such as the National Hockey League, Major League Baseball, and Lucasfilm, Ltd. With respect to the latter, it was planning to sell half-scale Star Wars miniature collectibles based on Darth Vader and other characters. Sales of sports collectibles accounted for 29 percent of the parent company's revenues in 1996.

Through its licensing subsidiaries, Riddell Sports had granted certain third parties the right to use the Riddell and MacGregor trademarks in connection with the sale of athletic shoes, clothing, and other products. The company owned half the stock of MacMark Corp., which owned the MacGregor trademark. License income came to three percent of the parent company's revenues in 1996.

Riddell got a boost in 1997, when San Francisco 49ers quarterback Steve Young switched to a Riddell helmet after suffering his third brain concussion in ten months. Eight out of ten NFL players already were wearing the heavily padded Riddell headgear. The debate over whether the league was doing enough to prevent serious head injuries in a game dominated by bigger and faster players than in the past had resulted in many rules changes in the past two years and also in a league committee on mild traumatic injuries.

Riddell extended its scope in May 1997 by agreeing to acquire Varsity Spirit Corp., a supplier of uniforms for cheerleaders, dance teams, and booster clubs. The company also operated cheerleader and dance team camps, clinics, and competitions. Riddell paid about $91 million for Varsity, which had net income of $5.2 million in 1996 on revenues of $88.4 million. Also in 1997, Riddell began marketing miniature baseball helmets bearing the logos of major league baseball teams.

In addition to its Chicago plant, the company had ten facilities for the reconditioning of athletic equipment, of which one was in Canada. It also maintained a screen-printing operation in Elk Grove, Illinois, that could customize its practicewear to bear almost any logo, team name, or other design that the customer requested. Except for the company-owned Chicago factory, all these facilities and its New York City executive offices were being leased. In May 1997 Nederlander owned 44 percent of Riddell's stock personally and 10 percent as general partner of M.L.C. Partners Limited Partnership. Leonard Toboroff, a vice-president and director of the firm, held 17 percent. The company's long-term debt was $31.1 million at the end of 1996.

Principal Subsidiaries

All American Sports Corporation; Equilink Licensing Corp.; Proacq Corp.; Raleigh Athletic Equipment Corporation; RHC Licensing Corp.; Ridmark Corporation; Riddell, Inc.; SharCo Corporation.

Principal Operating Units

Consumer Products Group; Institutional Products Group.

Further Reading

Ciccone, F. Richard, "At This Firm, 11 Heads Are Better Than 1," *Chicago Tribune,* October 7, 1976, pp. 1, 4.
Edgerton, Michael, "Riddell Tackles Product Liability," *Chicago Tribune,* March 8, 1978, Sec. 4, p. 6.
Husar, John, "Liability Suits Threaten Helmet Makers," *Chicago Tribune,* June 5, 1977, Sec. 3, p. 3.
Johnson, Roy S., "How Many Fingers Is He Holding Up?," *Fortune,* October 13, 1997, p. 29.
Kiley, Mike, "Lemieux Designs New Career," *Chicago Tribune,* January 21, 1993, Sec. 4, p. 4.
Mateja, James, "Firm Scores with Sales of Helmets," *Chicago Tribune,* March 27, 1975, p. 4.
Okeson, Sarah, "Court Is Stadium As Illinois Helmet Makers Do Battle," *Chicago Tribune,* November 16, 1989, Sec. 2, p. 5.
"Sport Supply Offers to Acquire Riddell in $14.5 Million Deal," *Wall Street Journal,* December 29, 1992, p. B3.
Storch, Charles, "MacGregor Has Buyer for 2 Units," *Chicago Tribune,* March 24, 1988, Sec. 3, p. 3.
——, "Rival Helmet Company Joins Riddell's Team," *Chicago Tribune,* September 24, 1991, Sec. 3, p. 3.
Temkin, Barry, "Helmet Rule Sure to Sack Budgets," *Chicago Tribune,* May 13, 1990, Sec. 3, p. 20.

—Robert Halasz

Ride, Inc.

8160 304th Avenue Southwest
Preston, Washington 98050
U.S.A.
(206) 222-6015
Fax: (206) 222-6499
Web site: http://www.rideinc.com

Public Company
Incorporated: 1992 as Ride Snowboard Co.
Employees: 286
Sales: $75.7 million (1996)
Stock Exchanges: NASDAQ
SICs: 3949 Sporting & Athletic Goods, Not Elsewhere Classified

One of the largest snowboard companies in the United States, Ride, Inc. is a leading designer, manufacturer, and marketer of snowboards, clothing, and related accessories. Ride's merchandise was marketed under the brand names Ride, Liquid, 5150, Preston, Cappel, and SMP Clothing. Manufacturing operations were based in Preston, Washington.

1992 Debut

As the 1992–93 winter ski season in the state of Washington neared, there were three individuals who awaited the arrival of snowstorms with distinct, anxious interest. In September 1992, Roger Madison, James Salter, and Tim Pogue had joined forces to found Ride Snowboards, a start-up venture expected—the three founders hoped—to cash in on the burgeoning growth recorded by the snowboarding industry during the early 1990s. The idea for the company was Madison's. A former top executive at AEI Music Network and a graduate of Harvard's business school, Madison had gone on to establish SonnenBraune, a manufacturer of indoor tanning equipment based in Redmond, Washington, a suburb of Seattle not far from the foothills of the Cascade Mountains. Just entering his 30s at the time, Madison was in search of an alternate-season business to complement SonnenBraune and he approached Salter, who ran a sporting-goods marketing and excess-inventory business named C.A.S. Sports Agency Inc. Madison was looking to establish a snowboard company, and Salter appeared to be someone with the expertise to get the venture up and running. Before running C.A.S. Sports, Salter had headed a leading snowboard company named Kemper Snowboards, serving as president from 1987 until the company's sale in 1990. When Madison approached Salter about starting a snowboard company, Salter suggested including Tim Pogue, operations manager for Kemper Snowboards at the time. Madison agreed and his consent set the stage for the initial cast of characters that would build Ride into an industry stalwart.

Pogue, whom Madison would later describe as a ''marketing genius,'' brought his own special talents to the undertaking, as did his two other colleagues. Madison, given his educational background, agreed to provide legal and business advice. In addition to these services, he provided the company with free office space and $250,000 in start-up money. Salter was an adept salesman and well-known throughout the industry, where he could boast of a wealth of distribution and manufacturing contacts. Pogue, of all the founders, was the iconoclast. A rabid snowboarding enthusiast, Pogue had at one time managed the professional riding team at Burton Snowboards Inc., a Vermont-based snowboard manufacturer that had pioneered the industry and stood as the unrivaled champion of the snowboard market at the time Madison, Salter, and Pogue plotted their course with their entrepreneurial venture. Pogue knew the snowboard market first-hand, as did Salter; and with Madison lending his business acumen and capital to the venture, Ride started off as a promising newcomer to the snowboarding scene in September 1992.

To make Ride's debut known to the world, Pogue recruited a team of well-known professional snowboard riders to help market the company's products. Each member of the Ride team was asked to help in the creation of the first line of snowboards, offering design and marketing ideas that helped refine the company's conceptual approach to the market. From the start, Ride targeted the fastest-growing niche of the snowboard market: young, trick-oriented riders known as ''freestylers.'' Many of these teenage converts to the sport of snowboarding had

Company Perspectives:

Our primary competitive advantage on the retail sales floor and on the mountain is our earned reputation for technologically innovative, performance-oriented products that give riders the strongest, lightest and most reliable snowboard equipment in the industry. As our reputation grows, so too do the expectations of our riders. Exceeding their high expectations is what drives our commitment to continuous improvement in our design, engineering and manufacturing processes. Most snowboard companies rely on third-party design technicians, engineers and manufacturing facilities to create new products. At Ride, our in-house development staff—made up of highly experienced engineers and riders—collaborates with customers, retailers and our team of some of the world's premier snowboard riders to help us attain our goal of being the first to market with products that redefine industry standards.

adopted the ideals, attitudes, and fashion styles typical of skateboarders and surfers. On the snow and at ski resorts, they were treading on unfamiliar ground, unlectured in the dictates of behavior at ski areas. Their emergence on the ski slopes, which began with a trickle and quickly developed into an irrepressible rush, was not well-received by skiers, touching off a derisive and divisive feud between the two factions. Accordingly, many of the younger, freestyle snowboarders viewed skiers as the Establishment and reveled in describing themselves as anti-Establishment, a perspective articulated by Pogue. Freestyle riders found a welcome voice in Pogue, who presented himself as a counterculture symbol of their mores. For Ride, this connection with the fastest-growing, most lucrative segment of the market went a long way toward establishing the company as a thriving concern.

Pogue wasted no time in allying Ride with the trendy freestyle movement. At the ski industry's biggest trade show in 1993, Pogue grabbed the attention of attending retailers by setting up a massive purple skateboard ramp as a display and serving beer from a keg. Retailers were rapt and flooded Ride with orders for the company's merchandise. The reaction was so overwhelming Ride did not have enough money to meet the demand and, consequently, some orders were left unfilled.

Although regrettable, the company's inability to meet demand during its first abbreviated season did fit in with part of the operating strategy devised by Madison, Salter, and Pogue. The founders had resolved to distribute their products to selected dealers, rather than flooding the market with as many snowboards as they could produce. ''Honda may be the world's top seller of motorcycles,'' Salter remarked, ''but we prefer to be the Harley-Davidson of snowboards.'' They were striving to give the Ride brand name an elite image within the snowboarding world, and in future seasons purposefully pulled in the reins on distribution. The founders had ambitious dreams, to be sure, such as usurping the number one seat occupied by Burton Snowboards, but in their assault against competitors the trio had chosen a more methodical approach, one that could enable them to realize higher profit margins.

By the end of the company's first year, a partial year consisting of the final three months, Ride had generated $208,000 in sales. It was an encouraging start, particularly the reaction ignited by Pogue at the 1993 ski industry trade show. As 1993 got underway, the Ride executives, with Madison serving as chairman, Salter as chief executive officer, and Pogue as president, scrambled to secure the capital they would need to expand the company's operations. Friends and family members were coaxed out of cash to keep the enterprise going and the money was promptly used to strengthen Ride's operations. Money was needed to manufacture the company's snowboards, which were produced under contract in Austria by Pale Ski & Sports GmbH, and with the introduction of Ride's clothing line, marketed under the name Cappel, additional financial resources were required. As the 1993–94 winter season approached, finding sufficient capital to keep the company going was becoming a strain, but the year concluded with robust financial results. For the year—the company's first full year—sales leaped to $5.9 million and net income totalled $414,000, the first profit recorded by Ride (in 1992, the company lost $209,000 on its revenues of $208,000).

By the end of 1993, the vigorous growth of the snowboard industry was beginning to attract attention from outside the winter recreation industry. Tens of millions of dollars were being spent each year on snowboard equipment and clothing, and the annual total was rising meteorically. When Ride first opened its doors, there were an estimated 1.2 million snowboarders in the United States. One year later, that figure had soared to nearly three million, and projections for future growth suggested even greater growth. Despite the energetic growth of the snowboard industry and despite Ride's remarkable initial success, the company was in dire need of capital. By the beginning of 1994, the founders had tapped their family and friends for $2.5 million, but their persuasive pleas for cash had reached an end. Financial institutions, according to Madison, were not interested in lending any money, so that left the trio with two choices: private placement or conversion to public ownership. The Ride executives chose to go public, and in so doing became the first pure snowboard stock on the market.

Ride Goes Public in 1994

Plans for Ride's initial public offering (IPO) crystallized in the spring of 1994. The founders hired a small underwriter, Barron Chase Securities of Boca Raton, Florida, and in May the company made its debut on the NASDAQ Exchange, raising nearly $6 million from the IPO. Each of the founders became a millionaire overnight, as Wall Street embraced the first offering from out of the snowboard ranks. Pogue, in a familiar move, brought out kegs of beer and served cups to investors, as well as Ride-branded condoms, titillating Wall Street with his unique spin on representing a decidedly ''anti-corporate'' company basking in the limelight of the corporate mecca of the world. Pogue was ebullient and somewhat naive, confiding later, ''I had no idea what going public meant. I figured it was just the prize for having made it.'' Pogue would soon be enlightened to the ramifications of public ownership, but in the wake of the

May 1994 IPO the celebrations were in full swing as Ride's future became brighter with each passing day.

After two years of hustling for cash, the founders suddenly found themselves flush with cash after the IPO and immediately put their money to work. Ride went on an acquisition binge that carried into 1995, purchasing clothing and snowboard brands and a manufacturing plant. In August 1994 they picked up C.A.S. Sports, Salter's original equipment and close-out business. Additionally, a new brand of snowboards, marketed under the name "Liquid," was introduced in 1994. Liquid snowboards, retailed at prices lower than the company's Ride snowboards, were distributed to regional and large-format sporting goods retailers, rather than the specialty snowboard and ski shops where Ride-branded merchandise was sold.

Against this backdrop, Ride's stock value surged ahead, leaping in an 18-month period from $2 per share to $35 per share. The company and its stock value were growing by leaps and bounds, and Salter promised more of the same, projecting 30 percent annual market growth. Investors listened and believed, fueling the company's eye-catching rise in the highly fragmented snowboard industry. Financial totals for 1994 provided tangible evidence of Ride's resplendent success, underscoring the soaring optimism at the company's headquarters. From the $5.9 million recorded in 1993, sales exploded to $25.3 million; net income, which had totalled $414,000 in 1993, hit $1.8 million.

On the heels of 1994's remarkable financial totals, the founders continued to acquire companies and assimilate them into the Ride fold, still infused with confidence by the company's achievement on the stock market and on the slopes. The company changed its name from Ride Snowboard Co. to Ride, Inc. in June 1995, in order to reflect the diversified scope of the company's activities. A second public offering of stock in August 1995 yielded Ride net proceeds of more than $23 million, and from there Madison, Salter, and Pogue moved to purchase several acquisition targets. In September 1995, Ride acquired Thermal Snowboards, Inc., gaining manufacturing operations that were organized into a subsidiary named Ride Manufacturing, Inc., and 5150 Snowboards, Inc., a brand of snowboards that later was merged into Ride Snowboard Co. The following month, Ride acquired SMP Clothing, Inc., a surfing and skateboard apparel manufacturer that was organized as a subsidiary. When the deal-making in 1995 was concluded and the financial results were tallied for the year, the figures were as encouraging as ever. Sales jumped from $25.3 million to $74.8 million and net income soared from $1.8 million to just under $6 million. Externally, Ride appeared to occupy an enviable position in the $200 million U.S. snowboard industry. The company was making a concerted push overseas, hoping to rake in millions from the Japanese market. Domestically, Ride ranked as the second largest company of its kind in the country, trailing only industry stalwart Burton Snowboards, and its revenue growth was record-setting, ballooning from $5.8 million to $75 million in a scant two years. Internally, however, there were problems everywhere. Pogue and his fellow founders were about to be introduced to the attendant problems of too-rapid growth and the power of investors over a publicly traded concern.

Problems Surface in Mid-1990s

On the whole, the acquisition campaign sparked by the company's May 1994 IPO had proven deleterious. There were exceptions, such as the addition of a company-owned manufacturing facility through the purchase of Thermal Snowboards, which reduced Ride's reliance on third-party contractors and, consequently, increased profit margins, but many of the company's problems in the mid-1990s stemmed from acquisitions made in 1994 and 1995. No acquisition had a more negative impact on Ride than the purchase of C.A.S. Sports. The addition of C.A.S. Sports ran contrary to the company's strategy of limited distribution and angered specialty retailers, creating a maelstrom of animosity between Ride and its most important customers. Owners of specialty snowboard and ski stores, once the exclusive retailers of Ride-branded merchandise, were incensed to find their larger competitors offering the same merchandise from C.A.S. at significantly reduced prices.

There were other problems as well, problems that arose from the way in which the acquisitions were organized into the company. As the company expanded, the founders chose to operate the acquisitions independently, which led to superfluous managerial layers. At one time Ride had four chief financial officers—too many for a company of Ride's size. One analyst noted as much, remarking, "A $60 million company running four independent units is clearly inefficient," but perhaps more damaging to the company's health was the lack of long-range planning. Market research at Ride consisted of calling a handful of retailers and friends, and, reportedly, numerous decisions were based solely on suggestions made by employees and team riders. The approach simply did not work effectively and may have led to a costly misstep in Japan, where projections fell far short of reality. Salter was convinced the Japanese market could deliver big growth and consequently he directed his distributor in Japan to sign a large contract. Shortly thereafter, the Japanese snowboard market became saturated with merchandise and the distributor was forced to cancel orders, leaving Ride saddled with inventory and unable to meet its growth projections.

As 1995 wore on, Ride's predicament worsened. An industry survey suggested that the snowboard market was growing at about half the rate Salter had promised, which caused the financial community to reevaluate its assessment of Ride. Investors took a wary backstep, distancing themselves from the troubled snowboard company. Subsequently, their anxiety was heightened by the inexperience of Ride executives in the integral art of investor relations. Some analysts claimed Salter refused to take their calls, a charge Salter flatly denied, but whichever side was right was immaterial. Ride's stock value plunged 50 percent in one month. The time for wholesale changes had arrived. The darling of Wall Street was reeling from poor management and too-rapid growth. Madison, Salter, and Pogue had been introduced to the ramifications of public ownership.

After the value of Ride's stock dropped dramatically, investors demanded management changes. Salter resigned as chief executive officer in May 1996, and after his departure Pogue agreed to support the board of directors' decision to recruit a more experienced leader. Pogue's ebullience had turned to disenchantment, and the prospect of stewarding Ride's fortunes was no longer as attractive as it once had been. Said Pogue, "The numbers everybody wanted and the reality of what Ride could do were two different things. It wasn't about snowboarding anymore. It was about pleasing Wall Street."

New Management for the Late 1990s

The individual selected to effect the turnaround was Robert Hall, a former ski-industry executive who arrived in August 1996 and took over as chief executive officer in October. Pogue was pleased with the selection, but after being relegated to a lesser role by Hall he decided it was time to leave the company he had helped found. Pogue resigned the same month Hall took command, leaving Madison and Hall to lead the charge toward recovery. Hall restructured the company along functional lines, making its organizational structure more streamlined and efficient, and he sold the troublesome C.A.S. Sports business back to Salter. Hall also implemented long-range planning at Ride for the first time, but the changes made in late 1996 were not enough to cure Ride of its ills immediately. The company recorded a negligible sales gain in 1996 of less than $1 million and posted a $5.5 million loss, which was primarily the result of the costly mistake made in Japan.

As Ride headed into the late 1990s, its future fate was in the hands of Hall, who was working to reshape the company into a vibrant snowboard competitor once again. Although the company experienced financial difficulties in 1996, its position in the snowboard industry was formidable. In the years ahead, the highly fragmented snowboard industry was expected to enter into a consolidation phase, which, according to analysts, would make the big companies bigger. As one of the leading companies in the industry, Ride was expected to benefit from industry consolidation and, its executives hoped, hold sway as an industry giant in the 21st century.

Principal Subsidiaries

Ride Snowboard Company; Ride Manufacturing, Inc.; Ride Canada, Inc.; SMP Clothing, Inc.

Principal Divisions

Winter Sports; Apparel; International; Manufacturing; Finance; Administration.

Further Reading

Epstein, Joseph, "Ride: As in Wild," *Financial World,* January 2, 1996, p. 24.

Grinbaum, Rami, "Redmond's Ride Snowboard Looks to IPO for Lift," *Puget Sound Business Journal,* March 11, 1994, p. 13.

Markels, Alex, "A Snowboard Start-Up Hits Big Bumps," *Wall Street Journal,* November 27, 1996, p. B1.

Park, Clayton, "Ride Snowboard Attracts 'Shredders' and Investors," *Puget Sound Business Journal,* February 3, 1995, p. 1.

"Ride, Inc. Announces Third Quarter Sales," *PR Newswire,* October 3, 1997, p. 1.

—Jeffrey L. Covell

Roadhouse Grill, Inc.

Suite 160
6600 North Andrews Avenue
Fort Lauderdale, Florida 33309
U.S.A.
(954) 489-9699
Fax: (954) 489-1485
Web site: http://www.roadhousegrill.com

Public Company
Incorporated: 1996
Employees: 4,100
Sales: $62.4 million (1996)
Stock Exchanges: NASDAQ
SICs: 5812 Eating Places; 6794 Patent Owners & Lessors

Roadhouse Grill, Inc. operates a series of more than 40 casual dining, family-oriented restaurants throughout the southeastern United States under the name "Roadhouse Grill." The restaurant chain is known for its honky-tonk atmosphere and its grilled steak, chicken, and fish entrees. Although primarily located in Florida, Roadhouse Grill also owns restaurants in Georgia, South Carolina, Mississippi, Louisiana, Ohio, and New York. Another eight locations—in California, Oregon, and Malaysia—are either franchised or licensed to others.

The Early Years

The initial concept for the Roadhouse Grill restaurant chain was developed through the partnership of J. David Toole III and John Y. Brown. Toole brought many years of experience to the project, having served previously as a regional supervisor for Ryan's Family Steak House and having already been involved in the development of Logan's Roadhouse, a midwest-based chain with a concept very similar to that of Roadhouse Grill. His partner, John Y. Brown, was also a veteran of the restaurant industry. A former chairman of Kentucky Fried Chicken, Brown had most recently founded Kenny Rogers' Roasters, another chicken-based restaurant chain. Toole joined Brown in 1992 after leaving the Logan's project, and the two men began developing Roadhouse Grill.

The first Roadhouse Grill opened in Pembrooke Pines, Florida, in March 1993. Along with bringing restaurant industry experience to the company, Brown was also able to provide the financial support to get the company off the ground. The three investment groups that backed the Roadhouse concept were all financially connected to Brown's Kenny Rogers' Roasters. These investors were Horn Venture Partners of Cupertino, California; the Malaysia-based Berjaya Group; and Sabi International Ltd., which is based in Cyprus. In the first calendar year of operation, Toole, Brown, and their investors were able to open six restaurants, all located in the Dade, Broward, and Palm Beach counties of southeast Florida.

Despite the fact that there was ever-increasing competition developing in the steakhouse market, Roadhouse Grill took on a very aggressive expansion campaign in its second year. With money supplied by the three initial investors, Toole and Brown opened another 10 restaurants, bringing the total number of units in operation to 16. This expansion moved the company into northern Florida and into Georgia.

It was during this growth spurt that the company opened its first ground-up prototype unit, in Deerfield Beach, Florida, occupying 7,500 square feet and seating nearly 230. Prior to that point in time, the company had merely been renovating existing buildings and turning them into Roadhouse Grill units. The new Roadhouse Grill unit cost the company about $1.1 million to build. Construction of the building accounted for most of the cost, but the elaborate interior cost roughly $291,000.

Unfortunately, the rapid pace of expansion initially forced Toole to put some inexperienced managers in charge of fully operational facilities. The company was young and did not have a large enough base of employees to ensure that experienced people ran each restaurant. Luckily for Toole, however, the quick growth of the company and its rising sales worked to hide this problem. Later, as word spread of Roadhouse Grill's success, they had no problem finding more qualified managers for the restaurants. These employees played a big role in the success of the company, which placed great pride in its customer service. As Toole pointed out in the March 27, 1995 issue of the *Bradenton Herald,* "Regardless of the concept, if you are not consistent with your services, you will fail. The customer must receive the same service every time they come in." This

Company Perspectives:

The Roadhouse Grill concept offers a fun, value-oriented dining experience that features premium quality grilled entrees and friendly service consistent with the Company's motto, "Good Food and a Smile . . . That's Roadhouse Style!"

attention to customer service was just one of the factors that led to the early success of Roadhouse Grill.

Inside a Roadhouse Grill

The atmosphere found inside each Roadhouse Grill created a very unique dining experience for its customers. From the brick and cedar walls, to the loud music that greeted customers when they entered, the restaurant was designed with a honky-tonk feel. Adding to this laid-back feeling were the barrels of peanuts found throughout the restaurant; customers were encouraged to eat the peanuts as they waited for their meal and to toss the shells on the floor. The restaurant's interior was designed around multilevel seating that allowed patrons to view the grill and the kitchen. Customers could watch the steaks being prepared on a mesquite grill, alongside crocks of homemade soup and containers of hand-cranked ice cream. There was even an in-house bakery where customers could watch biscuits being made before being brought to their table.

In the evenings, the restaurant chain targeted families who desired quality dining at an affordable price. The menu at each Roadhouse Grill featured steaks, ribs, chicken, and seafood—all grilled to order. All appetizers were priced at less than $5, with the most popular being the "Roadhouse Cheese Wrap," which was an eggroll stuffed with Monterey jack and cheddar cheeses and jalapeno peppers. Entrees were priced between $2.99 for a house salad and $15.99 for the 16-oz. ribeye. The restaurant also featured the "Messy Sundae"—a parfait glass coated entirely with hot fudge and filled with homemade ice cream, chopped peanuts, whipped cream, and a cherry. Furthermore, all children's menu items were priced at $2.99, every Roadhouse Grill was equipped with video games in the lobby, and each child received his or her own balloon.

The restaurant also attempted to appeal to business people during their lunch hour by featuring a special menu section called "Lunch in a Rush." It contained 13 extra-quick menu items, ranging from a grilled chicken sandwich to soup and salad specials. This part of the menu, which the company guaranteed to be served in less than 10 minutes, accounted for around 25 percent of a typical restaurant unit's daily sales.

Continued Growth in the Mid-1990s

By 1994 the restaurant chain was holding its own against the bigger competition supplied by the Outback, Lone Star, and Longhorn Steak Houses. Individual Roadhouse Grill restaurants were averaging between $50,000 and $75,000 per week, leading to an average of $3 million in revenue per unit per year.

The company continued to expand throughout the remainder of 1994 and into 1995. Meanwhile, management began to question whether to look for further funding from private sources or to go public to fund the company's future. In February 1995, the Berjaya Group became the majority backer of the company by providing $22.5 million in funds, giving it a 52 percent stake in the company. Berjaya also became a licensee of the company and began plans to develop Roadhouse Grill units in Malaysia.

Also in 1995, Toole began to negotiate franchise deals for Roadhouse Grill. A San Diego-based company, HomeTown Buffet, became one of the first to franchise the restaurants and thus bring Roadhouse Grill to the west coast. The group's first Roadhouse Grill franchise, located in Gresham, Oregon, performed extremely well, prompting HomeTown to open a second unit in the San Diego area. One year later, HomeTown Buffet was purchased by Buffets, Inc., the owner and operator of the Old Country Buffet chain. Therefore, plans were developed to transform some HomeTown Buffets into Roadhouse Grills in locations where HomeTown and Old Country Buffets were located in close proximity.

Roadhouse Grill Goes Public in 1996

By the time Roadhouse Grill was ready for its initial public offering (IPO), the company had grown to include 30 company-owned restaurants and six franchised or licensed units. The target for the stock was placed at $9–$11 per share by Piper Jaffray, Inc. and Robertson, Stephens & Co., the underwriters for the offering. Things were beginning to look good for the company as it returned its first profit, an operating income of $144,693, in June 1996.

Many people were very impressed with the growth of Roadhouse Grill and even more impressed with Toole. As one Wall Street banker remarked in the August 1995 issue of *Restaurant Hospitality,* "He is a very basic guy who works the fundamentals. He knows the numbers, what customers want, and how to make employees happy. That's a plus." But despite the initial enthusiasm, clouds of doubt began to swirl around the restaurant sector and Roadhouse Grill as the date for the IPO drew closer. Concerns about rising food and labor costs, combined with increasing competition in the steakhouse segment, became a sore point with potential investors. Roadhouse's management made assurances that the company would do everything possible to continue identifying and responding to the changing conditions in the restaurant business.

Roadhouse's assurances were not enough to keep the stock price from falling, however. When trading finally began in November 1996, the stock price was marked down to $6 from the initial level of $9–$11. The company, which still managed to raise $15 million from the sale of 2.5 million shares, used the proceeds from the public offering to pay back debts to a former chairman, with the remainder of the money being used to fund the company's continued expansion.

The End of the Decade and Beyond

On August 5, 1997, Toole officially resigned as president and CEO of Roadhouse Grill, Inc. He stated in a company press release, "The company has reached a size where it makes sense to bring in a seasoned industry veteran to take the Company to the next level.'' His departure left the vice-president of operation, Brad Haber, and chief financial officer, Dennis Jones, to head up the management team. Meanwhile, the search for Toole's replacement was put in the hands of an executive search firm.

After having built Roadhouse Grill from the ground up, Toole had paved the way for someone to step in and lead the company into its next round of expansion. Roadhouse opened its 40th restaurant on September 9, 1997 in Marreo, Louisiana and made plans to open an additional four units during the remainder of the year. Also included in the company's plans was a decision to begin restructuring its building procedures and use multiple contractors in the construction of the new Roadhouse Grill units.

In just four years of existence, Roadhouse Grill had grown to include more than 40 company-owned restaurants and was expecting to add another 20 units in 1998. Furthermore, even without Toole's leadership at the company's helm, Roadhouse Grill was reporting increased earnings for 1997. It was clear that Roadhouse Grill had the necessary strengths for continued success in a competitive steakhouse marketplace.

Further Reading

Carlino, Bill, ''Buffets Inc. Purchases Rival HomeTown Buffet,'' *Nation's Restaurant News,* June 17, 1996, pp. 1, 57.

Farkas, David, ''Space Available: Power Toole,'' *Restaurant Hospitality,* August 1995, pp. 66–70.

Gustke, Constance, ''A Steak in the Future,'' *Restaurant Business,* September 1, 1996, p. 54.

Hayes, Jack, ''Brown's Roadhouse Shifts into Overdrive,'' *Nation's Restaurant News,* May 23, 1994, pp. 3–4.

''HomeTown Posts 6-Month Profits, Tests Rollout for Roadhouse Grill,'' *Nation's Restaurant News,* September 18, 1995.

Porretto, John, ''Roadhouse Grill Planned in Biloxi, Miss.,'' *Sun Herald, Biloxi, Miss.,* January 7, 1997.

''Restaurant Grills Up for an IPO,'' *Private Equity Week,* November 25, 1996, p. 11.

Shillington, Patty, ''Fort Lauderdale, Fla.-Based Roadhouse Grill Raises $15 Million in IPO,'' *Miami Herald,* November 29, 1996.

Stiff, Ashby, ''Roadhouse Steaks Arrive Tender, Cooked As Ordered,'' *Tallahassee Democrat,* December 29, 1995.

Williams, Tedra T., ''Roadhouse Grill Opens in Bradenton, Florida: Above-Average Market Cited,'' *Bradenton Herald,* March 27, 1995.

Woitas, Nanette, ''New Steak House Hoofs It to Tampa,'' *Tampa Tribune,* March 15, 1995.

—Robert A. Passage

ROHN

ROHN Industries, Inc.

6718 West Plank Road
Box 2000
Peoria, Illinois 61656
U.S.A.
(309) 697-4400
Fax: (309) 697-5612

Public Company
Incorporated: 1918 as UNR Industries, Inc.
Employees: 700
Sales: $154 million (1996)
Stock Exchanges: NASDAQ
SICs: 3441 Tower Sections; 1623 Transmitting Towers

ROHN Industries, Inc. is one of the leading manufacturers of towers, poles, mounts, and other items for the telecommunications and wireless communications industries, including support structures for antennae, private microwave, cellular telephone, personal communications systems, commercial and amateur broadcasting, and home television. The company is also one of the leading suppliers of shelters and cabinets to house sensitive electronic telecommunications equipment. ROHN Industries has undergone a complete transformation during the 1980s and 1990s, having declared bankruptcy in 1982, sold off its core businesses in steel manufacturing and materials handling during the mid-1990s, and finally changing its name from UNR Industries to ROHN Industries to reflect the reorientation of its operations toward the telecommunications and wireless communications industries. The dramatic changes seem to have helped—after a lengthy period of time the company is once again profitable, and has started an expansion strategy that management hopes will propel it into the next century.

Early History

The history of ROHN Industries, Inc. can be traced through UNR Industries, Inc., which opened for business in 1918. Incorporated during the same year, UNR Industries was created in order to take advantage of the burgeoning demand for high-quality mechanical and structural steel tubing. With its headquarters located in Chicago, Illinois, the company provided its products to plumbing firms, construction companies, building contractors, and a host of other customers in the Midwest. UNR Industries was fortunate to have started its operations in Chicago, since the city was growing rapidly and construction was occurring every other block within the metropolis. Hence, the demand for steel tubing appeared to be unlimited, and throughout the remainder of the 1920s UNR Industries grew as steadily as the city of Chicago.

After the stock market crash of 1929, and the advent of the Great Depression which swept across the American landscape and affected every business great or small, UNR Industries reduced its workforce, but nonetheless managed to remain solvent and conduct business. During this decade, the company continued providing high-quality mechanical and structural steel tubing, but at lower costs and decreasing volumes. Although there were almost no construction projects underwritten by independent contractors the United States Federal government, under the Public Works Administration (PWA) and the Works Progress Administration (WPA), provided funding for public improvement projects. Working closely with the federal government and its PWA and WPA programs, the city of Chicago was able to hire contractors for specific public improvement projects. The contractors, in turn, signed agreements with UNR Industries for the manufacture and delivery of different kinds of steel tubing.

After the Japanese bombed the U.S. Naval Base at Pearl Harbor, Hawaii, and the U.S.'s Declaration of War on Japan and Germany, heavy industry and manufacturing within the United States improved dramatically. With the U.S. armed forces demanding large volumes of equipment and material, the economy quickly recovered from the devastating effects of the Depression, and companies such as UNR Industries were contracted to provide products for the ever-expanding U.S. war effort. By the end of the war in 1945, UNR Industries was well-positioned to capitalize on the growing economy within the United States, which the global conflict had helped to put in high gear.

The Postwar Period

During the immediate postwar years, UNR Industries continued its emphasis on manufacturing mechanical and structural steel tubing. However, the company also began to expand its manufacturing operations to take advantage of new trends in the marketplace. Consequently, the company focused on products that would provide a steady and reliable profit. Besides the manufacture of steel tubing, management decided to enter into the production of stainless steel and composite sinks. The construction boom during the postwar period saw housing starts at an all-time high, and management at UNR Industries regarded it as a lucrative venture to provide sinks for new homes built across the Midwest.

During the remainder of the 1950s, and throughout the 1960s, UNR Industries cautiously expanded its product line. The two core businesses of the company included the manufacture of steel tubing, and the production of high-quality stainless steel and composite sinks. In addition, however, UNR Industries began to manufacture steel and, later on, plastic shopping carts. As the small-town grocery store and the corner meat market began to disappear with the drastic change in American demographics and lifestyle, people shifted to the nearest supermarket. Supermarkets were large warehouses of food, so to speak, and located on plots of land with large adjacent parking lots. People needed shopping carts in order to load their groceries while in the store, and then take them to the car after all the necessary food was purchased. Producing shopping carts was not only profitable for the company, but was to bring a reliable source of income into the firm's coffers for over 20 years.

Expansion and Transition

In the early 1970s, UNR Industries took a major step in acquiring Rohn, Inc. Dwight Rohn, whose family owned Rohn, Inc., manufactured his first tower for home television reception in 1948. Rohn and the management team at the company, which primarily consisted of family members, correctly predicted the future growth of the communications industry. Soon the company was making not only towers, but poles, masts, and mounts used by companies to support antennae. Although Rohn, Inc. began to design and produce a wide variety of towers and poles for the communications industry, during the late 1940s and early 1950s demand for such support structures remained relatively small. The annual sales figures for Rohn, Inc. averaged approximately $2 million throughout the entire decade of the 1950s.

It was not until the 1960s and 1970s that demand for Rohn, Inc.'s products in this market began to skyrocket. Self-supporting towers, fiberglass equipment shelters, concrete equipment shelters, cabinets to house electronic communications equipment, steel poles, antenna masts and tubing, and satellite antenna mounts were manufactured by the company and provided to firms working in the telecommunications and wireless communications industries. As Rohn's profile began to increase, as well as its sales figures, the company soon became an attractive acquisition candidate for those firms looking to diversify their product line. UNR Industries, aware of the growth of the telecommunications and wireless communications industries, bought family-owned Rohn, Inc. at a bargain price, and quickly incorporated the new acquisition's product line into its own. Along with the acquisition of Rohn came support structure manufacturing facilities located in Alabama, Indiana, and Illinois.

At about the same time of the Rohn purchase, UNR Industries began to manufacture a line of livestock handling products, which was marketed to farmers, ranchers, fairs, expositions, and equestrian facilities, and also such items as privacy fencing materials to the military, and custom fabrication and hot-dip galvanizing services. By the end of the 1970s, management at the company decided to form a holding company, called UNR Industries, Inc., in order to organize and coordinate the manufacturing operations of its wide-ranging product line.

The decade of the 1970s seemed to indicate that the company's prospects were bright and limitless. Unfortunately, this was not the case. During the 1980s, UNR Industries employed environmentally hazardous materials in its manufacturing process and operations, including oils and solvents. Similarly, the company also used asbestos at some of its manufacturing sites, and in the housings for electric equipment used in the operation of various communications sites. By 1982, management at UNR Industries was overwhelmed with the number of state, federal and personal lawsuits filed against the company as a "responsible party" for using hazardous materials detrimental to the health of individuals. As a consequence, the company was compelled to file for reorganization under Chapter 11 of the United States Bankruptcy Code. For the remainder of the decade, UNR Industries battled for its survival under the constraints of bankruptcy law.

The 1990s and Beyond

It was not until the early 1990s that UNR Industries began to recover from its almost decade-long struggle to survive. The shining light of the company's operations throughout the 1970s and 1980s had been subsidiary Rohn, Inc., and now management decided to focus on Rohn's product line and implement a radical reorganization strategy to bring UNR Industries back to profitability. Through a concerted capital expenditure campaign to upgrade and improve Rohn's manufacturing facilities in Alabama, Indiana, and Illinois, management at UNR began to concentrate on meeting the market's demands for support structure products, such as guyed towers, self-supporting towers, fiberglass equipment shelters, concrete equipment shelters, cabinets, steel poles, fiberglass poles, concrete poles, satellite antenna mounts, antenna masts and tubing, receiver mounts, and television tripods. As a result of this reorganization strategy, UNR Industries' sales jumped from $73 million in 1993, to $107 million in 1994, over a 25 percent increase. In 1995, sales dramatically increased by 33 percent, to $142 million.

With such an impressive increase in sales due to management's strategy of concentrating on the manufacture of products for the telecommunications and wireless communications industries, the next step for the company was a natural one. In 1995, the board of directors at UNR Industries decided to sell off the majority of the company's operating divisions and subsidiaries that did not manufacture products for major telecommunications markets. UNR Industries' Leavitt Division, which represented the company's core business of manufacturing structural and mechanical steel tubing since its inception in 1918, was sold in August 1996. Unarco Commercial Products

Division, a manufacturer of steel and plastic shopping carts purchased in 1992 to augment the company's product line in this market, was also sold during the summer of 1996. UNR Home Products Division, a manufacturer of stainless steel and composite sinks, was sold in September 1996. And the assets of Real Time Solutions, Inc., a growing subsidiary that provided computerized warehouse management and control systems, was sold in December of the same year. Although the company still sold livestock handling products to farmers and ranchers, and provided custom fabrication and hot-dip galvanizing services to a small list of clients, in just one year UNR Industries had reduced its non-telecommunications product line to less than 10 percent of its total sales volume.

Having successfully completed its reorganization strategy, UNR Industries began to focus on building the infrastructure for the telecommunications systems of the future, and providing high-quality products for major markets, including personal communications systems, enhanced specialized mobile radio systems, paging services, radio television broadcast, wireless cable, private microwave, and direct broadcast satellite systems. The growth of the cellular telephone market in the United States alone, from five million subscribers in 1990 to over 40 million in 1996, exemplified the increasing demand for the company's products. Cellular telephones require cell sites located across the United States in order to operate. With only 6,000 cell cites in 1990, the number had grown to over 20,000 by the end of 1996, and each cell site required a tower and shelter valued at approximately $100,000 for its telecommunications equipment. UNR Industries took advantage of this explosive growth and became an industry leader in the manufacture of towers, poles, and shelters for the cellular phone market.

By the beginning of 1997, as the company's expertise and market share grew, UNR Industries was manufacturing every possible configuration of tower for the telecommunications industry, from its self-support tower of 900 feet to small antenna mounts. In fact, the firm's towers had become so popular that they were used in all the telecommunications markets, including television broadcast, AM/FM radio broadcast, microwave, cellular telephone, personal communications systems, radar, surveillance camera mounts, solar power stations, and weather stations. Because of the increasing demands for the company's towers, UNR Industries expanded its presence overseas and, by the summer of 1997, was marketing and selling its towers in more than 55 countries, including almost all the European nations, and many developing countries around the world.

In January 1997, the company significantly increased its manufacturing capacity with the completion of a new 180,000-square-foot facility located in Frankfort, Indiana. This facility was designed for the exclusive production of tower components, masts, and mounts. In March 1997, UNR Industries moved its corporate headquarters from Chicago to Peoria, Illinois, and in May 1997, the company formally changed its name from UNR Industries, Inc. to ROHN Industries, Inc. in order to reflect the company's reorientation from a holding company to a highly specialized firm.

With sales amounting to $154 million for fiscal 1996, and gross profits recorded at $47 million, ROHN Industries has successfully carved out a niche market for itself. As the telecommunications industry continues to expand, with such developments as the introduction of high definition television which will require new antenna support systems, ROHN appears to be well-positioned to take advantage of growing market demands.

Further Reading

Bellis, Matt, "Vector Signal Analysis Aids Test of DSP-Based Wireless Designs," *Electronic Design,* February 17, 1997, pp. 116–20.

"Pact Reached to Sell Assets of Home Products Unit," *Wall Street Journal,* August 28, 1996, p. B4(W).

Reina, Laura, "Helping Hands," *Supermarket News,* May 26, 1997, pp. 9–12.

"UNR Industries," *Wall Street Journal,* September 6, 1996, p. C22(W).

"UNR Industries," *Wall Street Journal,* December 20, 1996, p. B5(W).

"UNR Industries," *Wall Street Journal,* March 18, 1997, p. B17(W).

—Thomas Derdak

Like no vacation on earth.™

Royal Caribbean Cruises Ltd.

1050 Caribbean Way
Miami, Florida 33132
U.S.A.
(305) 539-6000
Fax: (305) 539-6168
Web site: http://www.rccl.com

Public Company
Founded: 1969
Employees: 12,500
Sales: $1.4 billion (1996)
Stock Exchanges: New York
SICs: 4481 Deep Sea Passenger Transportation, Except By Ferries

Royal Caribbean Cruises Ltd. is the world's second largest cruise company (behind top-ranking Carnival Corp.) with 17 cruise ships and a total of 29,100 passenger berths as of September 1997. Founded in 1969, the company has been instrumental in changing the cruise industry from a trans-ocean carrier service into a vacation option in and of itself. Royal Caribbean offers over 80 different itineraries and its ships call at more than 140 destinations in the Caribbean, Bahamas, Mexico, Alaska, Europe, Bermuda, Panama Canal, Hawaii, New England, China, and Southeast Asia. The company, a Liberian corporation, operates under two separate brands, Royal Caribbean International (12 ships) and Celebrity Cruises (five ships). While the company operates globally in terms of its itineraries and destinations, the majority of its passengers are from North America. Selling its cruises almost exclusively through some 30,000 independent travel agencies worldwide, the company targets the upper end of the volume market and the lower end of the premium market. The company also operates two private destinations, one in Haiti and one in the Bahamas, and two on-shore Crown and Anchor Clubs. Members of the Wilhelmsen family of Norway and of the Pritzker and Ober families in the U.S. control a majority of the stock.

Early History

Royal Caribbean Cruises Ltd. can trace its history to the beginning of today's passenger cruise industry. When three major Norwegian shipping companies founded Royal Caribbean Cruise Line in 1969, a cruise was an around-the-world or trans-ocean voyage on a large passenger liner, and was something only the wealthy could afford.

According to Cruise Lines International Association, an industry trade group, an estimated half a million passengers took cruises of three nights or more in 1970, the year Royal Caribbean began offering cruises.

The company built and operated three ships during the 1970s, offering cruises throughout the Caribbean. In fact, Royal Caribbean was the first line to design ships specifically for warm water year-round cruising. Prior to this, a cruise line company would use its passenger liners for cruises in the Caribbean in the months they were not transporting people across the Atlantic or Pacific.

Royal Caribbean's first vessel, the 700-passenger *Song of Norway*, began service in November 1970, and introduced glass-walled dining rooms, expansive sun decks located in the middle of the ship, and the company's signature Viking Crown Lounge projecting out from the ship's funnel, high above the sea. Edwin Stephan, one of the company's founders and Royal Caribbean's president at the time, got the idea for the lounge from the revolving restaurant atop the Space Needle at the 1962 World's Fair in Seattle. He anticipated that not only would passengers have a terrific view from this cocktail and observation lounge, but its design would set the vessel apart from other ships and make Royal Caribbean vessels instantly recognizable.

In 1971, the *Nordic Prince* entered service in the Caribbean and the company began offering passengers air/sea vacations, with the air fare to Miami included in the price of the cruise. The following year, with the introduction of the *Sun Viking*, Royal Caribbean became the biggest cruise line in the Caribbean with weekly departures from Miami on 7- and 14-day vacations.

For the remainder of the decade, Royal Caribbean focused on establishing its name brand. To do this, it concentrated on ensuring a consistent high quality for all its cruises and on generating and meeting demand. In 1973 it opened a marketing office in London and, in 1978, took the unprecedented step of cutting the *Song of Norway* in two and adding an 85-foot

Company Perspectives:

Presenting a consistent high-quality product regardless of ship size, cruise length or destination.

midsection, increasing the passenger capacity to 1,000. This was the first cruise ship to be lengthened in this way. In 1980, the same thing was done to the *Nordic Prince*. As Royal Caribbean entered the 1980s, the three ships in its fleet ranged in size from 18,445 to 23,149 tons, with berths for 714 to 1,012 passengers.

The 1980s—Resort-Style Cruising on Megaships

The *Song of America* debuted in 1982. Weighing 37,584 tons and with 1,402 berths, it was the largest cruise ship built in 20 years. The new ship enabled Royal Caribbean to expand its itineraries and in 1985, it moved outside the Caribbean for the first time, offering summer cruises to Bermuda from New York City.

The cruise industry grew as the target population—middle- and upper-income people—grew older and richer, quadrupling in the 15 years Royal Caribbean had been on the seas. In 1985, over 2 million passengers took cruises marketed in North America, according to a *Forbes* article, with nearly two-thirds of them heading for the Caribbean. And projections were that the demand would only increase.

Cruise companies began a building spree in anticipation of the demand, taking advantage of low interest rates and shipyards eager for the business. Royal Caribbean initiated its first major capital expansion program, expanding *Viking Serenade* by 536 berths and building four new ships in four years. The new ships developed the ''megaship'' concept and introduced resort-style cruising. The first of the new vessels, the 874-foot *Sovereign of the Seas*, entered service in 1988. It weighed over 73,000 tons, had berths for 2,276 passengers, and featured two indoor/outdoor cafes, two glass elevators, a five-story atrium, and nearly three football fields of open deck on which passengers could stroll.

In April 1988, Richard Fain was named chairman and CEO of the company. Two months later, Royal Caribbean and Admiral Cruises, a passenger cruise service that had operated for almost 100 years, combined their operations although each kept their separate brand identity. Later that year the company underwent a fundamental ownership change. First, one of the original founding companies, Anders Wilhelmsen & Co., became the sole owner by buying out the other two partner companies. Then Wilhelmsen entered into a joint agreement with the Pritzker family (owners of Hyatt Hotels Corp. and other holdings) and the Ofer family, owners of a large shipping company. The result, once the process was completed in 1992, was that A. Wilhelmsen A.S., a Norwegian corporation, and Cruise Associates, a Bahamian general partnership, became the principal owners of Royal Caribbean. Members of the Wilhelmsen family of Norway controlled A. Wilhelmsen A.S. and members of the Pritzker family of Chicago and of the Ofer family controlled Cruise Associates.

1990–94—Passengers Grow Younger

In 1990, while the ownership restructuring was going on, Royal Caribbean opened its new headquarters at the Port of Miami and consolidated all functions in one location. The *Nordic Empress* entered service, the first ship built specifically for short cruises such as the company's 3- and 4-night cruises in the Bahamas. With the addition of *Viking Serenade*, the company also added seasonal cruises to Alaska as well as in Europe.

Travel agents played a critical part in the company's operations, with some 30,000 independent agencies making essentially all the bookings for the cruises. To simplify that process, Royal Caribbean introduced CruiseMatch 2000, the world's first automated cruise booking system for travel agents. The new computer system allowed travel agents direct access to the company's computer reservation system, making it easy to book cruises. The year ended unhappily, however, when a shipyard fire damaged *Monarch of the Seas*, delaying its launch.

Monarch did enter service in 1991. Royal Caribbean's largest vessel to date, weighing nearly 74,000 tons, with berths for over 2,300 passengers, the new ship was based in San Juan. *Viking Serenade* was rebuilt for short cruises, adding berth capacity, a new dining room and cafe, and a Viking Crown Lounge. This enabled the company to enter the year-round Mexico market with 3- and 4-night cruises from Los Angeles. The company also established an international sales and marketing department to increase the number and percentage of its passengers from outside North America. That department oversaw operations of the company's sales offices in London, Oslo, and Frankfurt.

Royal Caribbean's strategy in the very competitive cruise/vacation market was to target the upper portion of the ''mass'' market, promising a quality product for slightly more money than other volume competitors such as Carnival Cruise Lines. But to fill its ships during a recession (and a war in the Gulf which affected cruises in the Mediterranean), the company had to offer discount prices. That factor, combined with the costs of servicing the debt from its shipbuilding activities, led to a sharp drop in profits in 1991.

With the entry of the final megaship in its expansion program, the *Majesty of the Seas*, in 1992, Royal Caribbean became the first cruise line to offer year-round megaship cruises in the major Caribbean markets. The building program begun in 1987 had more than tripled the company's number of berths to 14,228, and brought the fleet's number to nine ships. That year also saw the end of Admiral Cruises, when Royal Caribbean sold its two-ship fleet and discontinued service.

During 1992 the company introduced Enterprise 2000, the company's new computer information system, which was used for reservations, passenger ticketing, sales tools used by the company's sales force, and tools for travel agents.

Royal Caribbean also initiated its ''Save the Waves'' program to preserve the environment by not dumping things overboard. In addition, each ship recycled about 20,000 aluminum cans each week and the company purchased more than 1 million pounds of recycled products each year.

With its fleet in order, the company took action to reduce its debt, beginning with its first public debt offering of $126 million subordinated notes in 1992. The following year Royal Caribbean went public, offering 11.5 million shares of common stock on the New York Stock Exchange. During 1994, the company was able to lower its borrowing rates by refinancing its banking arrangements with a $750 million revolving credit facility. It then issued $125 million in senior notes. By the end of the year, the company had reduced its debt-to-capital ratio to 47 percent from a high of 75 percent in 1992. The company also built a second office facility in Miami to accommodate the Passenger Services Department.

Royal Caribbean celebrated 1994 with a five percent increase in revenues and a 28 percent rise in net income, without adding to its fleet capacity. Part of that success may have come from the company's advertisements on cable television. Over the years, the cruise industry's audience had expanded to include younger adults, not just those nearing or in retirement. Royal Caribbean aimed at people 25 to 54 who made $40,000 or more. Rather than focusing on opportunities to socialize or nonstop activities, it positioned itself as "a vacation during which people can relax completely in their own way: with a trip to the spa, a jog around the deck, or a day on the white sands of an island beach," as described in a 1995 article in *MediaWeek.* And, recognizing the reality of that younger market, the company offered activities to entertain children.

"Two Great Brands . . . One Great Vacation Company," 1995 to the Present

The battle for consumers' leisure dollars continued to intensify, with cruise lines, resorts, and timeshare developers concentrating on offering all-inclusive vacations. Between 1995 and 1998, Royal Caribbean undertook its second major capital expansion program, building six Vision-class ships at a cost of approximately $1.5 billion. Each new ship used more than two acres of glass in the design and featured a seven-deck atrium with glass elevators, skylights and glass walls, a pool and entertainment complex covered by a moveable glass roof, a two-deck main dining room, a state-of-the-art show theater, a glass-encased indoor/outdoor cafe, and a shopping mall.

The largest of these new ships carried 2,000 passengers and weighed 75,000 tons. The smallest had 1,804 berths and weighed 70,000 tons, twice the number of people and three times the weight of the original *Song of Norway.* The expansion anticipated increasing company's berth capacity by approximately 74 percent, from 14,228 to over 24,700 berths.

The first of the new vessels, the *Legend of the Seas,* entered service in 1995, bringing the Viking Lounge silhouette to Hawaii and expanding Royal Caribbean's cruises in Alaska. The ship's amenities included an 18-hole miniature golf course with all the features, water hazards, and proportions of an average golf course; not surprising, perhaps, with Royal Caribbean the official cruise line of the Professional Golfers' Association.

Designed to be faster than most cruise ships, the new vessels permitted more flexibility in itinerary planning. The company entered the Far East market and was the first to offer year-round cruises there and in Southeast Asia. Two more new ships began cruises in 1996, the 1,800-berth *Splendor of the Seas* and the 1,950-berth *Grandeur of the Seas.* Also in 1995, the company sold the *Nordic Prince,* one of its original three ships, for approximately $55 million, recognizing a gain of some $19.2 million.

Royal Caribbean's offerings in the Caribbean also included stops at two private company-operated destinations: CocoCay, an island in the Bahamas owned by the company, and Labadee, a peninsula on the north coast of Haiti leased by the company. Passengers could shop at artisan markets, eat picnics along the beach, and windsurf, snorkel, and sail. In 1995 the company added to these the industry's first on-shore club, the Crown & Anchor, at St. Thomas in the U.S. Virgin Islands.

In December 1995, a series of class-action suits were filed alleging that the company misrepresented to its passengers the amount of its port charge expenses. These were followed in 1996 with class-action suits alleging that seven cruise lines, including Royal Caribbean, should have paid commissions to travel agents on port charges included in the price of cruise fares. In February 1997, Royal Caribbean and other companies agreed that all components of the cruise ticket price, other than governmental taxes and fees, would be included in the advertised price.

During 1996, some 973,000 passengers went on Royal Caribbean cruises, over 100,000 more than sailed in 1995. That year saw the sale of another of the company's original ships, the *Song of Norway,* for $40 million (a gain of $10.3 million), and the establishment of the $1 million Royal Caribbean Ocean Fund.

In July, Royal Caribbean bought Celebrity Cruise Line Inc. for $515 million. Celebrity became a wholly-owned subsidiary and continued to operate under its own brand name. Celebrity served the premium cruise vacation market, owned five ships with approximately 8,200 berths, and offered 40 different itineraries ranging from six to 18 nights, and stopping in over 50 ports in Alaska, Bermuda, the Caribbean, and through the Panama Canal. The addition of Celebrity Cruises greatly enhanced the company's presence in the premium, destination market of one- and two-week cruises, and its acquisition increased Royal Caribbean's total market share in 1996 to approximately 27 percent of the 4.7 million North Americans who went on cruises that year.

Royal Caribbean continued its capital expansion program by contracting for two Eagle-class ships to be delivered in the fall of 1999 and 2000. These were to be the largest passenger cruise ships built to date, each weighing 130,000 tons and accommodating 3,100 passengers, and were being designed to attract families and those seeking active sports and entertainment activities. Among the planned amenities: rock climbing facilities, conference centers, and a wedding chapel.

During January 1997 a new television advertising campaign debuted, introducing a new brand identity—Royal Caribbean International—and presenting Royal Caribbean as a global vacation brand with a focus on worldwide cruise vacations. That same month, the company and two of Hyatt Hotels' Puerto

Rican properties began jointly marketing what was a first in the Caribbean, a week-long vacation package that included both a cruise and a stay at a hotel. To attract new passengers, Royal Caribbean also marketed its vessels as conference sites for groups ranging from romance writers to dental anesthesiologists, and combined cruising and golf with Golf Ahoy!, a shore excursion program for people who would rather play golf than shop, sunbathe, or sightsee. And to help passengers finance their cruise, the company announced ''CruiseLoans,'' allowing people to charge all the expenses, including upgrades, excursions, and on-board spending. The program was administered by Citicorp's Citibank NA.

In the fall of 1997, the company sold $9 million of stock to repay some of its debt and announced it would sell the *Sun Viking*, its smallest ship and the last of its original three vessels, to Star Cruises for $30 million. At the same time, Celebrity Cruises took delivery of the 1,850 berth *Mercury*, the last of a five-ship expansion program begun in 1990, bringing its total fleet capacity to some 8,200 berths.

With its two brands, Royal Caribbean Cruises, Ltd. had strong name recognition in both the popular, warm-weather vacation market and the seasonal cruise market. Its new ships received press attention because of their size and facilities. Between 1996 and 2000, the company expected to increase its berth capacity by 102 percent, to 38,000. And other cruise lines were doing the same, as industry capacity was expected to grow 12.4 percent in 1998 and 11.7 percent in 1999, according to the Cruise Line Industry Association. With the number of passengers growing only at an average 7.6 percent a year since 1981, Royal Caribbean Cruises would need to use all its creativity and traditional service quality to attract new passengers to cruising in order to fill their ships.

Principal Subsidiaries

Celebrity Cruise Line Inc.

Further Reading

Behar, Richard, ''Floating Resorts,'' *Forbes*, January 26, 1987, p. 62.

''Can I Play Golf on My Vacation?'' http://www.reply.net/clients/cruise/revelk.html.

DeGeorge, Gail, ''Royal Caribbean May Be Taking on Water,'' *Business Week*, May 25, 1992, p. 34.

Keates, Nancy, ''Danielle and Joey Urban Can't Believe Mickey Mouse Let Them Down,'' *Wall Street Journal*, http://wsj.com., October 24, 1997.

''Our History: Viking Crown Lounge,'' http://www.rccl.com/1.3/1.3.2/1.3.2.2/1.3.2.2.html.

''RCCL Reaffirms Its Commitment to the Ocean Environment,'' *Travel Weekly*, November 4, 1996, p. C19.

''RCCL to Debut 'Legend of the Links,' '' *Travel Weekly*, November 7, 1994, p. C22.

Rice, Faye, ''What to Do on Your Summer Vacation,'' *Fortune*, June 12, 1995, p. 20.

''Royal Caribbean Cruises Ltd. History,'' Royal Caribbean Cruises Ltd., March 1997.

''Save the Waves,'' http://www.rccl.com/1.1/1.1html.

''Sea Change,'' *Travel Weekly*, January 9, 1997, p. 20.

''Royal Caribbean and Citicorp Unveil CruiseLoan,'' Dow Jones, October 3, 1997.

''Trolling for Cruisers Among Upscale Viewers,'' *MediaWeek*, May 27, 1995, p. S22.

—Ellen D. Wernick

The Scotts Company

14111 Scottslawn Road
Marysville, Ohio 43041
U.S.A.
(937) 644-0011
Fax: (937) 644-7183
Web site: http://www.scottscompany.com

Public Company
Founded: 1868
Employees: 2,394
Sales: $751.9 million (1996)
Stock Exchanges: New York
SICs: 2873 Nitrogenous Fertilizers; 2874 Phosphatic Fertilizers; 3524 Lawn & Garden Tractors & Home Lawn & Garden Equipment; 6719 Holding Companies, Not Elsewhere Classified

With just over half of the do-it-yourself lawn care market, The Scotts Company is America's leading producer and marketer of grass seed, fertilizers, herbicides, and pesticides. In addition to its consumer lawn care business, Scotts holds over 10 percent of the commercial lawn care market. Professional clients include three-fourths of America's top 100 golf courses as well as such Major League Baseball venues as Fenway Park, Yankee Stadium, and Wrigley Field. The Scotts family of brands includes organic soils and mulches under the Hyponex label, which boasts a 45 percent stake in its market, as well as Miracle-Gro plant foods, with a dominant 59 percent share of their segment. By the end of 1997, operations in Europe, Asia, Africa, Australia, and Latin America generated about 10 percent of Scotts' annual sales.

Scotts' sales increased from $413.6 million in 1992, when the company went public, to over $750 million in 1996. Some of this growth came from acquisitions, including the 1995 purchase of Stern's (now Scott's) Miracle-Gro Products, Inc. A restructuring of the merged companies moved several Miracle-Gro executives into key positions at Scotts. Theodore Host, president since 1991 and CEO for scarcely one year, tendered his resignation in 1996. Charles M. Berger, a former member of Miracle-Gro's board of directors, was hired as president, CEO, and chairman of the board that same year.

19th-Century Origins of O.M. Scott & Sons

The company was created by Civil War veteran Orlando McLean Scott, who moved to the small central Ohio town of Marysville in 1866. Scott worked at a seed elevator for four years before purchasing his own business, a hardware store, in 1870. The founder's "white-hot hatred of weeds" led him to start a seed-processing sideline, sorting weed seeds from crop seeds for local farmers. While his 99.91 percent weed-free farm seed cost more, Scott assured his customers that it would save them time and money by reducing weeding chores and increasing yields. Although he had added grass seed to the product offering by 1870, this segment did not become an important part of the business until the early 20th century.

Scott's sons Dwight and Hubert joined the company in the first decade of the twentieth century. Dwight has been credited with the launch of Scott's mail-order grass seed business in 1906. This new distribution outlet spread the family's reputation throughout the region to Pennsylvania, Virginia, Kentucky, and West Virginia. The company made its first commercial sale to Long Island, New York's Brentwood golf course in 1916. By 1921, Scotts seeded one-fifth of America's golf courses.

In 1928, O.M. Scott & Sons launched Turf Builder, the first fertilizer formulated specifically for grass. The growth agent combined soybean and cotton seed meals to provide the extra nitrogen needed for a greener, healthier lawn. The company launched its own promotional magazine, *Lawn Care*, in 1928 as well. According to Scotts, the publication soon became "the most widely read turf bulletin in print," with millions of subscribers by the post-World War II era.

Research Drives Mid-Century Growth

Americans made a mass migration from the cities after World War II, and lush, green lawns became a hallmark of suburbia. Not coincidentally, chemical fertilizers, herbicides,

Company Perspectives:

This new company has the two strongest national brands—Scotts and Miracle-Gro—plus many others, in an industry where many of our competitors are regional producers of undifferentiated products. Combining the strengths of The Scotts Company—its brands, manufacturing and research capabilities, and distribution network—with the Miracle-Gro organization's proven advertising and marketing expertise, its entrepreneurial culture, and the power of the Miracle-Gro brand—should create significantly increased value for the company's shareholders.

and pesticides came into their own during this period. Named for second-generation leader Dwight Scott, Scotts' Marysville research complex emerged as a harbinger of growth at this time. The company placed particular emphasis on weed killers in the immediate postwar years, launching 4-XD broadleaf herbicide in 1945, followed by Scutl, Clout, and Halts for crabgrass in the 1950s. In 1956, the company used new chemical products and processes to create a new Turf Builder formulation that weighed less than the original, smelled better, and was gentler to grasses. Scotts also developed the first lawn spreader and the first patented Kentucky bluegrass, as well as other innovations for home and commercial lawns. The research campus itself grew to include four greenhouses, 13 laboratories, a library, and over 100 acres of experimental grasses.

The Scotts ownership structure evolved from full family control to a closely held company in the postwar era. Then, in 1971, O.M. Scott & Sons was acquired by ITT Corp.'s Harold Geneen, who reportedly snapped up the profitable firm after a 15-minute analysis of its balance sheet. Although the lawn company remained profitable throughout its 15-year membership in the conglomerate, it became clear that Scotts was not very compatible with ITT. Tadd C. Seitz, who had joined Scotts in 1972 and advanced to president and CEO in 1983, realized that his small segment of the huge conglomerate was getting lost in a labyrinthine bureaucracy. In 1989 he told *Business First-Columbus* that Scotts "continued to get less and less attention at a time when we needed some ways to improve business."

Seitz led a highly leveraged buyout of the company in 1986. Scotts' managers borrowed $190 million (about 90 percent) of the $211 million price tag from the investment banking firm of Clayton Dubilier Inc. O.M. Scott & Sons became the primary subsidiary of CDS Holding Corp., a private company 61 percent owned by Clayton Dubilier. Many of Scotts' senior executives took out second mortgages and personal loans in order to buy into the deal.

Scotts was rejuvenated under Seitz, who was able to quadruple the company's sales during his tenure. Given the slow, two percent to three percent annual growth rate of the fertilizer industry, Seitz sought expansion through a combination of new product introductions and strategic acquisitions. Burgeoning environmentalism in the early 1990s spurred Scotts' interest in the development of new organic fertilizers like Iron Bull, iron-fortified steer manure. In 1990, Scotts formed a partnership with Sandoz Crop Protection Corp. to research and develop biological pesticides using insect viruses, bacteria, protozoa, and plant extracts. The aim was to create narrowly targeted products that would have a strictly limited effect on the environment.

Scotts debt was reduced to $125 million by the fall of 1988, when a restructuring allowed the $111 million acquisition of Hyponex Corp. The lawn care company went public in 1992 as The Scotts Company, selling 12.5 million shares at $19 each, using the proceeds to cut debt to just $32 million. That year, the company acquired Republic Tool and Manufacturing, a manufacturer of fertilizer spreaders and other lawn and garden equipment. The public offering also helped Scotts sever its ties to investment bank Clayton Dubilier through a 1993 stock repurchase. With sales of over $466 million that fiscal year, Scotts negotiated the purchase of Grace-Sierra Horticultural Products Co. in 1994.

Merger of Scotts and Miracle-Gro in 1995

Scotts most important acquisition came in 1995, when it announced the purchase of Stern's Miracle-Gro Products through an exchange of $195 million worth of equity. With about $115 million in annual sales, Miracle-Gro was much smaller and younger than Scotts. The gardening company had evolved out of the business relationship between nurseryman Otto Stern and advertising executive Horace Hagedorn. Hagedorn helped Stern build a small but profitable mail order plant business in the late 1940s. Around this time, Stern began including a tiny sample of water-soluble fertilizer with each plant he sent out. This extra boost helped get the "starts" well established, thereby assuring customers' gardening success. It was not long before Stern's clients were clamoring to order more of the growth agent. In 1950, Stern and Hagedorn launched a partnership to market the fertilizer, which adman Hagedorn dubbed Stern's Miracle-Gro. Despite the name, it was Hagedorn and his family who eventually controlled the business. Over the years, they developed water-soluble foods for roses and tomatoes as well as tools designed to make application of fertilizer easier and more convenient. Sales grew from $165,000 in 1960 to $55 million in 1980 and $115 million by 1995.

Though Miracle-Gro had less than half the sales of Scotts, the Hagedorns emerged from the 1995 transaction as Scotts' leading shareholders, with over one-third of the stock. The Hagedorn influence became increasingly evident in the months and years to come. Early in 1996, Horace Hagedorn and the Scotts board of directors ousted CEO Theodore Host barely 11 months after he had taken office. At that time, Scotts recruited former Miracle-Gro director Charles M. Berger from H.J. Heinz Co. to serve as president, CEO, and chairman of the board. A restructuring that same year found former Miracle-Gro director Jim Rogula in charge of Scott's largest business segment, Consumer Lawns. Former Miracle-Gro president John Kenlon led the Consumer Gardens Group and, perhaps most significantly, Horace Hagedorn's son, Jim, was promoted to the head of all U.S. business. Tadd Seitz, who had served as CEO from 1983 to 1995, ended more than a quarter-century at Scotts with his September 1997 retirement.

With new management came a new marketing strategy. Under Host, Scotts had pursued the "push" method of marketing, using dealer promotions to get more product on store shelves. Spurred by stockholder unrest over weak profitability—net income had averaged just 2.6 percent of sales in the four fiscal years from 1991 through 1994—Host launched a major promotional campaign in 1995 in an effort to augment sales and market share. The program offered financial incentives to retailers who bought product in the fall of 1995 that would be delivered to stores in the spring of 1996. The strategy was successful on one level; it increased sales from $733 million in fiscal 1995 to $752 million in fiscal 1996. But instead of boosting profits, the deep discounts to retailers resulted in a $2.5 million loss on fiscal 1996. Host forfeited his job, and Scotts' stock price slid to a low of $16.75.

Given the fact that it was cofounded by an advertising executive, Miracle-Gro had a long-established strategy of "pulling" customers in with print, radio, and television ads. By devoting millions to its ad budget each year, Miracle-Gro created high demand for its product, thereby enabling it to command a high profit margin from retailers. CEO Berger sought to shift Scotts to pull marketing by increasing its advertising budget and building on its highly recognized, but heretofore under-exploited, brand. The new strategy focused on creating what Horace Hagedorn called "the Procter and Gamble of lawn and garden."

The Miracle-Gro cofounder stayed with Scotts long enough to see it return to profitability during the first half of fiscal 1997, then retired that spring. With a refocused marketing strategy in place, the new Scotts team turned to boosting the operational side of the business in 1997, scheduling $40 million in capital investments for the years leading up to the turn of the 21st century. This combination was expected to boost annual sales past the $1 billion mark by the year 2000.

Principal Subsidiaries

Scotts Grass Co.; Scotts Sod Co.; Scotts Energy Co.; Scotts Pesticide Co.; Scotts Green Lawns Co.; Scotts Plant Co.; Scotts Tree Co.; Scotts Service Co.; Scotts Products Co.; Scotts Fertilizer Co.; Scotts Park Co.; Scotts ProTurf Co.; Scotts Control Co.; Scotts Professional Products Co.; Scotts Turf Co.; Scotts Best Lawns Co.; Scotts Weed Control Co.; Scotts Golf Co.; Scotts Garden Co.; Scotts Design Co.; Scotts Tech Rep Co.; Scotts Broad Leaf Co.; Scotts Insecticide Co.; Scotts Spreader Co.; Scotts Improvement Co.; Hyponex Corp.; Old Fort Financial Corp.; O.M. Scott & Sons, Ltd. (U.K.); Republic Tool & Manufacturing Corp.; Scotts-Sierra Horticultural Products Co; Scott's Miracle-Gro Products; O.M. Scott International Investments Limited (U.K.).

Further Reading

Baker, Stephen, "False Spring for Scotts," *Business Week,* March 11, 1996, p. 38.

Bambarger, Brad, "O.M. Scott & Sons," *Lawn & Garden Marketing,* October 1987, p. 24.

Cigard, Jane Forman, "The Scotts Co.," *Lawn & Garden Marketing,* September 1990, p. 53.

Edmondson, Brad, "Green Lawns and Rebates from Scott," *American Demographics,* October 1986, p. 22.

"Fertilizer Hits Fan: Vendors Compete Over New Product," *Discount Store News,* September 5, 1994, pp. 48–49.

Leibowitz, David S., "A Pair of Highfliers Laid Low," *Financial World,* July 21, 1992, p. 75.

Lilly, Stephen, "Scott Execs Went into Hock to Buy Equity Stake," *Business First-Columbus,* February 20, 1989, p. 7.

Mills, Charles B. *First in Lawns: O.M. Scott & Sons,* New York: Newcomen Society of England, 1961.

Murray, Matt, "Turning the Tables: Miracle-Gro Family Seeds Ranks of Firm That Bought It Out," *Wall Street Journal,* July 23, 1996, pp. A1, A10.

"O.M. Scott and Sons Co.," *Ohio Business,* July 1990, p. 81.

Proctor, Gordon, "Scott Goes Organic with Pesticides," *Business First-Columbus,* June 4, 1990, pp. 1–2.

Sabatini, Patricia, "Sowing New Seeds: Longtime Heinz Exec to Run Scotts Co.," *Pittsburgh Post-Gazette,* August 8, 1996.

Sains, Ariane, "They're All 'Just Folks' at Stern's Miracle-Gro," *Adweek's Marketing Week,* November 14, 1988, p. 36.

"Scotts Co.," *Business First-Columbus,* July 26, 1993, p. 56A.

Underwood, Elaine, "The Glow from Miracle-Gro," *Adweek's Marketing Week,* May 27, 1991, p. 17.

"Why I Bought the Company," *Journal of Business Strategy,* January–February 1989, pp. 4–8.

Williams, Brian, "A Blooming Success," *Columbus Dispatch,* July 27, 1997, pp. 1H, 2H.

—April Dougal Gasbarre

Scotty's, Inc.

5300 N. Recker Highway
Winter Haven, Florida 33882
U.S.A.
(941) 299-1111
Fax: (941) 294-6840

Wholly Owned Subsidiary of GIB Group
Incorporated: 1925 as Home Builders Supply, Inc.
Employees: 7,000
Sales: $650 million (1996 est.)
SICs: 5251 Hardware Stores

Scotty's, Inc. is a large hardware store chain, operating almost exclusively in Florida. It is one of the largest building supplies retailers in the country, and in Florida it is second only to the massive Home Depot chain. Scotty's operates over 100 stores. A few are so-called "superstores" of 40,000 to 50,000 square feet, while most are much smaller. The stores are found both in rural areas and in metropolitan neighborhoods. Scotty's has long specialized in the do-it-yourself home improvement market, selling to homeowners who prefer to do their own construction work rather than hire expensive contractors. This market segment grew enormously during the 1970s, when Scotty's was a publicly owned company on the New York Stock Exchange. About a third of Scotty's' sales currently come from professional builders, with the remainder coming from do-it-yourselfers and non-professional customers. Scotty's is now privately owned by a Belgian conglomerate, GIB.

Early History

Scotty's was founded in 1925 as Home Builders Supply, Inc. In 1968 the name was changed to Scotty's Home Builders Supply, Inc. Scotty's was a modest chain of hardware stores at that time, with less than 30 stores. Scotty's stores sold building materials and supplies, household fixtures, carpets, hand tools, and other typical hardware merchandise. Scotty's began to expand rapidly in the mid-1960s, with sales increasing twelvefold over a decade. Scotty's grew both by building new stores and by acquiring other building supply businesses. In 1970 Scotty's bought up both a lumber company in Punta Gorda, Florida, and a small chain of building supply stores in Ocala and Lake City. The next year Scotty's acquired Gator Lumber Company, and then bought a modular home manufacturer called Modu-Tech Structures, Inc., in Pembroke, Florida. Modu-Tech manufactured two models of prefabricated houses, a two-bedroom and a three-bedroom model. Modu-Tech was renamed Scotty's Instant Buildings, Inc., and operated as a subsidiary of Scotty's. The company bought more lumber yards and building supply retailers, including the $100,000 purchase of Truitt Building Supplies in Wauchula, Florida, in 1972. In 1973 the company changed its name from Scotty's Home Builders Supply to simply Scotty's, Inc., and the next year the company was listed on the New York Stock Exchange. Sales in 1974 were $80 million, and the firm now operated over 50 stores.

Scotty's had its eye on expansion, and suffered only one bad year in the 1970s. Fiscal 1975 brought a sharp downturn to the U.S. economy, and builders were particularly hard hit, as new home sales came to a standstill. Scotty's, which had traditionally catered to people who improved or rebuilt their existing homes, was also surprisingly affected by the recession. Even the do-it-yourselfers apparently put off building projects, and sales at Scotty's took an unexpected 25 percent dip. The company was building six to eight new stores a year, and in 1975 already had bought land for 12 new Scotty's. But the recession stalled these plans. Nevertheless, the company went ahead with a huge new computerized warehouse at its headquarters in Winter Haven, Florida. The warehouse and distribution center, which opened in January 1975, was a vast 160,000 square feet, able to store 65 percent of the inventory of the whole Scotty's chain. Inventory was handled by a central computer, which simplified ordering and made it easier to keep all the chain's stores well stocked. Perhaps the biggest advantage of the new warehouse was that it put less of a space burden on Scotty's individual stores. They did not need space to store their inventory, since it was being held for them centrally at Winter Haven, and thus new stores could be built smaller. This was to cut Scotty's construction costs by as much as 60 percent, and also reduce operating overhead.

Scotty's was one of a group of hardware chains that catered to the do-it-yourself builder, and it was followed lovingly on Wall Street because of high profits and enthusiastic projections. Scotty's benefited from several building trends in the late 1970s. By that time, more than half of U.S. housing was over 20 years old—the age when most houses start needing significant repairs and improvements. Scotty's customers were part of this growing group of homeowners with aging shelters, and so its customer base naturally increased. About 65 percent of Scotty's customers were people doing their own repair work, and the stores tried to make it easier for amateurs, with salespeople who could not only sell them the materials but provide basic instruction as well. Rising mortgage rates were also to some extent good for Scotty's. As mortgage rates climbed, more people were tempted to add on to their existing homes rather than buy new ones, and these people, too, became Scotty's customers.

Scotty's also benefited from a building boom localized in Florida, which gave the hardware chain an expanding pool of new home builder customers. Thousands of workers flocked to central Florida to work on the expansion of Disney World and other large construction projects there, and these people then needed housing. Scotty's was able to sell lumber to contractors making new houses, as well as to weekend refurbishers.

Aging housing, rising mortgage rates, and the influx of workers all contributed to profits at Scotty's that at times took astonishing leaps. For example, in fiscal 1978 Scotty's earnings increased 90 percent. Total sales were $156 million, almost double what they had been when the company was listed on the stock exchange four years earlier. The chain had grown to almost 70 stores, and plans were in place to grow to 100 over the next five years.

Challenges in the 1980s

Scotty's continued to rack up impressive increases in both sales and profits into the early 1980s, despite a more difficult business climate. Scotty's was dependent on home builders, and building rates were tied in large part to interest rates. As interest rates topped 12 percent in the early 1980s, building slowed. But because a significant percentage of Scotty's business came from the do-it-yourself market, its sales were not deeply hurt. Sales topped $200 million in 1979, and came to almost $250 million the next year. This was in spite of Scotty's management's complaints about a slackening home building market and troubling interest rates. A little less than 40 percent of the company's sales and profits came from building products, just over a quarter came from lumber and plywood, and miscellaneous other categories, such as plumbing supplies and lawn and garden goods, accounted for the rest.

Scotty's was increasing the number of its stores by about 10 percent a year, and one reason for its sales success was its profitable store opening galas. The company heavily promoted grand openings, and made them into three-day events. These galas were apparently well attended, and sales figures during openings sometimes ballooned extraordinarily. In 1981 the Scotty's chain had 81 stores, and single-day sales chainwide had never broken $2 million. But one grand opening weekend, the chainwide sales came in at $5.6 million, breaking the previous record rather impressively.

Though sales continued to increase as the chain grew, profits could not always keep pace. And beginning in 1982, Scotty's faced competition from national chains, which built up rapidly in Florida. The two chief competitors were Mr. HOW Warehouse and Home Depot. These national chains operated huge, brightly lit, fully air-conditioned stores that had tons of shelf space and stocked many more items than Scotty's. Between 1982 and 1985, Home Depot and other Scotty's competitors opened more than 2.5 million square feet of hardware and home center stores in Florida. By the mid-1980s it was not unusual to find four different building supply stores at a single intersection in some urban areas. These new stores tended to make Scotty's look old-fashioned, and Scotty's had to invest heavily in a redesign program. The typical Scotty's store before the influx of competitors had a split floor plan, with an air-conditioned selling space and then a much larger, nonair-conditioned warehouse. Scotty's began to build its new stores larger, with more air-conditioned space, larger displays, brighter graphics, and more items for sale. Scotty's also remodeled or rebuilt existing stores to conform with the new design.

By 1985, the Scotty's chain had grown to 113 stores, still almost entirely in Florida. Sales were at $425 million, though heavy investment in new stores and in redesigning old ones ate into profits. The company built a new data center for $2.5 million at its Winter Haven headquarters. The data center linked with the individual stores' point-of-sale terminals, so the chain could keep better track of daily sales and inventory needs. Scotty's also opened a new manufacturing plant in Winter Haven in 1985. This factory made trusses, vanities, and prehung doors that were then sold under Scotty's private label. Scotty's also extended its private label to a variety of items, from measuring tapes to cow manure. Many of these private label items were imports. The imports were mostly inexpensive, but because they did not have familiar brand names, they were put under the Scotty's label.

New Scotty's stores increased the total number of s.k.u.'s (shelf-keeping units) they stocked, typically from about 10,000 units to 13,000. This still lagged far behind Home Depot, which often stocked as many as 40,000 items. Scotty's also changed by expanding into some new product categories such as housewares, pet products, and auto parts. These improvements were made under pressure from Scotty's competitors. But one way in which Scotty's remained distinct from Home Depot and the other home center chains was in the size of stores. Scotty's did open some large warehouse stores, but most of its new buildings were 49,000 square feet and under. Scotty's management decided it was wiser to have a lot of smaller stores, especially in densely populated urban areas, than to build big stores that depended on customers driving long distances.

Transition into the 1990s

Scotty's had been on the New York Stock Exchange since 1974. Since 1979, some of its stock had been owned by a Belgian conglomerate, GIB Group. GIB was a retailer, with investments in a variety of U.S. hardware firms. In 1988, GIB bought up a large chunk of Scotty's stock which had been owned by former Scotty's president James Sweet. The purchase of Sweet's shares brought GIB's ownership to 43 percent. A year later, GIB bid $15 a share for all the remaining Scotty's stock. Scotty's became a private subsidiary, fully owned by the Belgian company. GIB also owned all or part of several Midwestern hardware chains such as Handy Andy and Central Hardware. At the time of the sale to GIB, Scotty's had grown to 162 stores. The chain was about even with Home Depot, each with roughly a 35 percent share of the home building supply retail market in Florida. However, the company was not performing strongly. It did not have the breadth of products Home Depot and the other national chains had. Scotty's stores also closed on Sundays, cutting weekend sales badly. Under new ownership, Scotty's received a new chief executive, Daryl Lansdale. Lansdale had been head of home center retail operations for W.R. Grace & Co, and he set out to correct some of Scotty's problems. Lansdale ordered a remodeling campaign, making some stores bigger, and closing down poorly performing stores. Lansdale doubled the variety of items sold in the chain's biggest stores, and increased the amount of air-conditioning. Some stores added a drive-through lumberyard, so customers could shop without leaving their cars. By 1994, Scotty's rebuilt 35 stores and increased the amount of merchandise in 50 others. Following Home Depot's lead, Scotty's began to emphasize the interior design aspect of home improvement by offering a bigger variety of fashion-conscious products. Scotty's also began putting out pamphlets with advice and instructions for do-it-yourself projects. Though it had long courted the do-it-yourself customer, the pamphlets were something learned from Home Depot. Scotty's also sponsored a Scotty's Contractor School offering a course in contracting that met state licensing requirements. The school was also a valuable marketing tool.

In spite of these changes, the profit picture at Scotty's was far from its double-digit heyday in the 1970s. By 1996, Home Depot passed up Scotty's in the Florida home building supply market. Scotty's was still one of the largest chains in the nation, ranked 13th overall. But Scotty's had dominated the Florida market for decades, and it did not seem a good sign that the chain now had to settle for being number two. In reaction, Scotty's Belgian owner fired CEO Daryl Lansdale and brought in Thomas Morris, a former executive at Sears, Roebuck. GIB's sudden action was tied to slipping sales at Scotty's—they dropped 1.2 percent in 1996—and to pressure in Europe to cut costs. When Morris took over, one of his first initiatives was to weed out excess expenses and simplify store operations. He abandoned Scotty's radio advertising and closed the corporate customer service department. Morris also hired a consulting firm to come up with a simplified store operating plan that could be consistent across the Scotty's chain. Scotty's bought new software to handle distribution from its central warehouse, and used a computer program to decide on the most effective way to schedule employees. Besides reducing expenses, Morris planned to increase Scotty's sales to professional contractors. The chain started running a special "pro yard" in each of its market areas. And to improve sales to do-it-yourself builders, Scotty's began stocking more products in new categories such as unfinished furniture. Scotty's also actively courted women customers, adding or improving departments dedicated to linens, floor coverings, and housewares. Brighter lighting and white paint jobs were also added into the Scotty's redesign plan, specifically to create an atmosphere more hospitable to women shoppers.

And Scotty's did not abandon its basic, smaller hardware stores. Morris's plan called for Scotty's to run a portfolio of stores of different sizes, depending on market needs. Store sizes ran from small hardware stores, contractor yards, and super-hardware stores to large scale home centers. But the small stores were what contrasted most with the national chain home centers, and Morris hoped to attract customers who did not want to fight crowds at the bigger stores. Also with small stores, Scotty's could build in towns considered too insignificant for the national chain stores. With this in mind, CEO Morris planned to add as many as 50 new stores to the Scotty's chain by 1999.

In little over a year since taking over from Lansdale, CEO Morris had overseen the remodeling or re-merchandising of 33 stores. Sixteen poorly performing stores were closed. Scotty's contractor business increased, in part through the success of its contractor school. In its first two years, the contractor school had 5,000 students, and Scotty's direct-mailed to 90,000 contractors across the state. Per store sales increased about eight percent under the new management plan. New stores were opened with gala celebrations, with gimmicks such as coupons dropped on customers from a helicopter. These galas had worked well for Scotty's in the past, and they promoted a positive and celebratory atmosphere, even though the chain was in many ways struggling. GIB sold Handy Andy, the second largest hardware chain it owned, in 1996, and Handy Andy then liquidated. There was some speculation that Scotty's parent might unload it as well. But this remained only a rumor, and Scotty's management insisted that GIB was totally committed to Scotty's success. Though Home Depot had passed it up in market share in Florida, Scotty's was nevertheless a strong second, with stores of all sizes in rural and urban areas alike. And management seemed fueled by the fierce competition with Home Depot to implement fresh ideas, including the contractor school and pro yards, that encouraged customer loyalty. Thus, despite the company's decline in prominence with the entrance into Florida of the national chains, Scotty's appeared more vigorous than ever.

Further Reading

Albright, Mark, "CEO Ousted at Scotty's Home Improvement Centers of Florida," *Knight-Ridder/Tribune Business News,* February 21, 1996, p. 2210171.

Brent, Elizabeth, "Scotty's Centralized Yards Focus on Serving Larger Builder Accounts," *National Home Center News,* August 5, 1996, p. D27.

Coletti, Richard J., "Turf Wars: Scotty's Defends Its Native Soil Against Invading Home Depot," *Florida Trend,* July 1994, pp. 66–69.

Cory, James M., "Scotty's New Strategy," *Chilton's Hardware Age,* March 1985, pp. 86–89.

"Florida Home Improvement Chain Scotty's to Air Drop Coupons from Copters," *Knight-Ridder/Tribune Business News,* September 5, 1997, p. 905B1131.

"GIB Buys Central Hardware, Bids for Rest of Scotty's," *Chilton's Hardware Age,* June 1989, pp. 15–16.

Hye, Jeanette, "Scotty's Rocks with New Mission Under CEO Morris," *National Home Center News,* July 15, 1996, p. 1.

Kelly, Joseph M., "Scotty's Aims at Women with Leased Categories," *Home Improvement Market,* November 1996, p. 15.

''Scotty's Changes Its Name, Picks Cooney As President,'' *Wall Street Journal,* October 29, 1973, p. 16.

''Scotty's Home Improvement Chain of Florida Broadens Product Selection,'' *Knight-Ridder/Tribune Business News,* March 7, 1997, p. 307B0962.

''Scotty's Inc. Says Net for Fiscal First Half Increased Nearly 28%,'' *Wall Street Journal,* January 12, 1979, p. 17.

''Scotty's: Ready to Stand Against All Comers,'' *Chain Store Age Executive,* April 1986, pp. 52–54.

''Scotty's Sees 25% Drop in Fiscal '75 Earnings,'' *Wall Street Journal,* February 10, 1975, p. 13.

Shakin, Bernard, ''Building Supply Chains: They Profit from Persistent Do-It-Yourselfers,'' *Barron's,* October 27, 1975, pp. 11, 68–69.

Shuster, Laurie, ''Scotty's Boosts Contractor Sales, Raids Competition for Sales Staff,'' *Home Improvement Market,* August 1996, p. 32.

——, ''Scotty's Looks to Stay Out of Home Depot's Way,'' *Home Improvement Market,* August 1996, p. 201.

——, ''Scotty's Takes Pro Sales Seriously,'' *Home Improvement Market,* August 1996, pp. 32–33.

Troxell, Thomas N., Jr., ''Knock on Wood,'' *Barron's,* April 6, 1981, pp. 32–33.

—A. Woodward

Shakespeare Company

6111 Shakespeare Road
Columbia, South Carolina 29223
U.S.A.
(803) 754-7011
Fax: (803) 754-7991

Wholly Owned Subsidiary of K2 Inc.
Incorporated: 1897
Employees: 950
Sales: $200 million (1997 est.)
SICs: 3229 Pressed & Blown Glass, Not Elsewhere Classified; 3648 Lighting Equipment, Not Elsewhere Classified; 5091 Sporting & Recreational Goods

An integral subsidiary of K2 Inc., Shakespeare Company manufactures fishing tackle equipment, marine antennas, fiberglass utility poles, and monofilament. For nearly 90 years Shakespeare operated as an independent company, developing a diversified presence in sporting goods and industrial products through its expertise in using fiberglass. Anthony Industries acquired the company in 1980. In 1996, Anthony Industries changed its name to K2 Inc. Shakespeare, with operations in Europe, Asia, and Australia, accounted for a considerable percentage of K2 Inc.'s annual sales and profits during the late 1990s.

19th-Century Origins

The Shakespeare Company was born out of frustration. Its formation celebrated the patented invention of William Shakespeare, Jr., and the elimination of one of the most burdensome chores plaguing fishing enthusiasts during the 19th century. Anglers throughout the world were overly familiar with the problem: If a thumb did not carefully guide a fishing line as it wound up on the reel spool, it would jam against the framework of the reel and become hopelessly tangled. A relaxing morning of leisurely fishing could quickly turn into a maddening exercise of frustration, as the task of unraveling a mess of fishing line presented itself to the inattentive angler. Many who loved fishing hated this peculiarity of the multiplier reel for obvious reasons, but the problem had been around for nearly a century and no one had found a solution. No one until a patent medicine salesman from Kalamazoo, Michigan, set himself to the task of developing a better reel. His creation revolutionized the sport of fishing and gave birth to a diversified enterprise that would thrive for the ensuing century under the corporate banner of Shakespeare.

Although William Shakespeare, Jr., had some training in mechanics and craftsmanship, he spent his days peddling patent medicines in and around Kalamazoo. When not hawking elixirs, Shakespeare often grabbed his fishing rod and reel and bait-casted on the banks of the Kalamazoo River or at one of his home state's myriad lakes. Like his angler friends, Shakespeare was frustrated by the inherent inadequacy of multiplier reels, and in 1895 he fell back on his mechanical background and attempted to come up with a solution. Using a small jeweler's lathe, Shakespeare carved precise, curving grooves along the lengths of two round brass rods and created a device that wound back fishing line evenly on the reel spool. He named it the ''level-wind,'' and took his creation on his next fishing trip. The level-wind worked well, drawing the line in evenly without the aid of a thumb. Those fishing alongside Shakespeare gawked at his homespun reel and asked to use it. Shakespeare made several more level-winds and handed them out. The level-winds were an immediate hit, and that was all the market testing Shakespeare needed. He filed for a patent and quickly prepared himself for his new entrepreneurial career.

Shakespeare was granted a patent in 1896. The following year he formed the William Shakespeare Jr. Company, the predecessor to the handful of Shakespeare businesses in operation during the 1990s. Shortly after starting his company, Shakespeare began working on other reel models and fishing-related equipment, developing a full line of fishing tackle equipment, including split bamboo rods and artificial lures, that could add to the sales generated by his innovative level-wind. From its start, however, the company was best known for its reels, the signature product of the William Shakespeare Jr. Company during its early years. Sold under various brandnames through the company's first half-century of business, the family of high-quality Shakespeare reels were known to generations of fishing enthusiasts as ''Marhoff,''

''Ideal,'' ''Superior,'' ''Criterion,'' ''Balcli,'' ''President,'' and ''Wondereel.'' By all measures, Shakespeare's venture was a success; business was brisk and the company was etching a lasting presence in the fishing tackle market. Shakespeare proved to be an astute businessman, however, by not letting the parade of one successful reel after another lull him into complacency. Shakespeare realized that no matter how successfully his reels sold, his company would still be fettered to the wide-ranging cyclicality of a seasonal business and vulnerable to the same market capriciousness that affected all leisure-oriented businesses. Shakespeare's response was to diversify, to develop other businesses outside the sporting goods industry and thereby reduce his company's dependence on the vagaries of the nation's economy and the changing seasons.

Shakespeare's first major diversification was into the automotive products industry, a business area that, like all facets of the automotive industry, was growing robustly during the early decades of the 20th century. He formed a subsidiary named Shakespeare Products Company in 1921, which, from its inaugural year forward, figured as a mainstay business for the Shakespeare enterprise. Through Shakespeare Products Company, later to become the company's Automotive Products Division, Shakespeare Company produced flexible control components used in engine components, making a name for itself as a manufacturer of parts that featured twisted wire cables encased in coiled flexible wire tubing.

The foray into automotive products occurred at a propitious juncture in the nation's history, giving Shakespeare nearly a decade to build his automotive products venture into an established business before the Great Depression descended on the country and made survival in business a laudatory achievement. The company's automotive products business helped compensate for the loss of business produced by its fishing tackle business during the 1930s, and, consequently, helped it withstand the devastating blows delivered by a moribund economy. Shakespeare Company persevered through the Great Depression as a result, and after the end of World War II, when restrictions on the use of raw materials for civilian use were removed, Shakespeare Company was able to grow aggressively. The postwar years witnessed the ascension of the second generation of Shakespeares, led by Henry Shakespeare, William Shakespeare, Jr.'s son. Under Henry Shakespeare's tutelage, Shakespeare Company would proliferate, developing into the multifaceted enterprise in operation during the 1990s.

Post-World War II Diversification

Expansion, diversification, and growth were the dominant themes describing Shakespeare Company during the postwar years, and the push to become bigger and broader got off to a rousing start one year after the end of World War II. During the war, experiments with heat-hardenable polyester resin reinforced with high-strength glass fibers in structural aircraft parts gave birth to fiberglass and the manifold applications of its use. Dr. Arthur M. Howald, technical director of the Plaskon Company, was one of the legions of individuals who experimented with fiberglass's strength and flexibility to create improved quality in existing products. Dr. Howald's area of interest was in manufacturing a fishing rod constructed with fiberglass. After conducting experiments with fiberglass fishing rods, Dr. Howald turned over his results to Shakespeare Company. The company took it from there, experimenting first with fiberglass casting rods and then with fiberglass fly rods, eventually investing $1 million in the project before introducing the first fiberglass fishing rod on the market in 1946, the revolutionary Wonderod.

The Wonderod quickly changed the face of the fishing tackle industry, making bamboo and steel rods virtually obsolescent. It also cemented the company's reputation as a maker of high-quality fishing rods and, equally important, it demonstrated the immeasurable potential of fiberglass. Having scored its first success with fiberglass, the company looked for other applications for fiberglass rod technology and made its move by entering the golf business. In 1946, Shakespeare began manufacturing golf clubs with fiberglass shafts, which led to the introduction of the WonderShaft and marked the beginning of the company's involvement in manufacturing golfing equipment.

As the company's designers and engineers celebrated their successes with the Wonderod and their entry into the golf business, strategic decisions at the executive level presaged the energetic diversification that would occur during the 1950s, 1960s, and 1970s. In 1946—a busy year for the company—the fishing rod manufacturing operations were moved to Columbia, South Carolina, and incorporated as a subsidiary named Columbia Products Company. Another subsidiary made its debut in 1946 when the company's fishing line production operations were moved to Esterville, Iowa, and organized as a subsidiary named Soo Valley Company, Inc. (A decade later, Soo Valley relocated to Columbia, South Carolina.) In the wake of the major developments of 1946, Shakespeare pursued an aggressive expansion and diversification program, using its founder's initial diversification into the automotive market as a blueprint for future growth.

In 1959, the company widened the scope of its operations by acquiring Waverly, Ohio-based Parallel Products Company, a maker of archery equipment that was organized into Shakespeare's Columbia Products subsidiary. Next, the company made its first move into a foreign market, forming a subsidiary in Canada named Shakespeare Company (Canada) Limited in 1960. Located in a suburb of Toronto, Shakespeare's Canadian subsidiary marketed sporting goods to Canadian markets. By the mid-1960s, diversification into the production of automotive parts, golf equipment, and archery, coupled with steady geographic and physical expansion, had created a formidably-sized Shakespeare enterprise. Multifaceted and poised for expansion on three fronts, the company was collecting nearly $50 million in annual sales midway through the 1960s and showed no signs of slowing its growth. In the years ahead, the company not only increased its involvement in its established businesses, but also entered new markets, intent on extending the Shakespeare name into a grab bag of businesses.

After using fiberglass to manufacture fishing rods and golf club shafts, Shakespeare began looking for other applications for the strong yet flexible material, having realized the benefits of using fiberglass as a replacement for steel. Through Columbia Products, the company began manufacturing commercial fiberglass antennas, which developed into a thriving business. Success with antennas bred further diversification, bringing the company into the business of manufacturing utility pole line hardware and other utility-related products that depended on strong and durable construction. This burgeoning arm of the company's manufacturing operations was allotted expanded production space in 1965, when Columbia Products opened a $1.5 million manufacturing facility in Newbury, South Carolina, that housed Shakespeare's antenna and utility pole manufacturing activities. The construction of this facility occurred in the same year Shakespeare opened a new production plant in Fayetteville, Arkansas, for its line of fishing reels and golf clubs. Operated by a subsidiary named Shakespeare of Arkansas, Inc., the facility also served as a warehouse and distribution center for the company's activities in the southern and western United States.

Following the establishment of its two new manufacturing facilities, Shakespeare concentrated on building its existing businesses through acquisitions, taking a temporary reprieve—with one exception—from entering new business areas. In 1966, the company acquired Pflueger Corporation, an Akron, Ohio-based fishing tackle manufacturer whose experience in the fishing industry was as lengthy as Shakespeare's. Having bolstered its original business, the company next moved to expand its other business areas. In 1968, Shakespeare incorporated steel and aluminum golf shafts into its golf line and purchased Plymouth Meeting, Pennsylvania-based Plymouth Golf Ball Company, a maker of golf balls founded in 1916. The following year, Shakespeare built up its archery business, acquiring Big Rapids, Michigan-based Root Archery Company. In 1970, the company acquired the manufacturing and sales rights to Golden Eagle Bow, and subsequently consolidated both archery acquisitions into Columbia Products Company. The one exception to the company's strategy of strengthening established businesses during this period was the creation of a ski division in 1970, facilitated by a distribution and sales arrangement with Yugoslavia-based Elan Ski Company. Operated through the Shakespeare Sporting Goods Division, the ski segment manufactured skis, bindings, poles, and a line of ski apparel.

After consolidating Columbia Products Company and Soo Valley Company in 1971 to form the Shakespeare Industrial Products Division, the company comprised five business segments: Shakespeare Sporting Goods Division, Shakespeare Industrial Products Division, Pflueger Division, Shakespeare Automotive Products Division, and Shakespeare Company (Canada) Limited. Combined, these business segments operated plants in six states and held interests in operations located in a dozen foreign countries stretching from Europe to Asia to Australia. Together, the sprawling Shakespeare enterprise was generating $60 million in sales a year by the early 1970s, having achieved much of its growth by developing expertise in fiberglass manufacturing processes. The company was most widely known for its fishing tackle equipment, but when the company went public in 1972 it was supported by much more than rod, reel, and line production. Fiberglass had opened new doors for the company, creating a much more diversified enterprise than its founder had ever envisioned. When Shakespeare debuted on the New York Stock Exchange during its 75th anniversary year, fiberglass was used in a broad assortment of products, including archery equipment, skis, fishing equipment, and in the company's WonderThread, which had developed from the company's fishing-line technology and steered it into the monofilament business. Much had changed at the company since the advent of fiberglass, and certainly wholesale changes had swept through the company and reshaped it since William Shakespeare, Jr.'s days. The company was the product of decades of change, and further definitive developments were in the offing as Shakespeare moved forward as a publicly traded company.

Among the highlights during the remainder of the 1970s were two expansions at the company's Newbury production facility—one in 1972 and another in 1975—which made the Newbury plant the largest fiberglass pole production facility in the world. Toward the end of the decade, another important development occurred when Shakespeare introduced the ''Ugly Stik,'' the company's new fishing rod. Ugly Stiks eventually developed into the bestselling fishing rods in the United States, holding sway as the market leader for nearly two decades, but the chief benefactor of their popularity was not Shakespeare but the company's future owners. Waiting in the wings at the end of the 1970s was a Los Angeles-based company determined to develop a stronger presence in recreational products and industrial products through acquisitions. Shakespeare represented an opportunity the Los Angeles company could not pass up.

New Ownership in the 1980s

Anthony Industries Inc., founded in 1946, operated exclusively as a pool contractor during its first three decades of existence, but beginning in the mid-1970s the company began to diversify aggressively. The company acquired Hilton Athletic Apparel, a maker of bowling shirts and jackets, in 1974, and by 1978 had acquired Simplex Industries, Inc., a manufacturer of laminated, coated, and reinforced paperboard products. These two acquisitions, and the original in-ground swimming pool business, represented the foundation of Anthony Industries' recreational and industrial products segments. Under the management of Bernard I. ''Bif'' Forester, who assumed control over the company in 1973, Anthony Industries was searching to build on the foundation in each business segment, and Shakespeare met the company's criteria exactly, enabling it to become significantly stronger in both segments with one acquisition. The transaction was completed in 1980, bringing Shakespeare Fishing Tackle, Shakespeare Electronics & Fiberglass, Shakespeare Monofilament, and Shakespeare Flexible Controls into Anthony Industries' fold. Anthony Industries sold Shakespeare Flexible Controls, the successor to the foray into the automotive market in 1921, the year after the acquisition, but the remaining Shakespeare businesses were embraced wholeheartedly, adding considerably to its parent company's stature.

Anthony Industries continued with its acquisition campaign after purchasing Shakespeare, adding both recreational and industrial businesses to its operations. The most important of the acquisitions to follow was the company's acquisition of ski manufacturer K2 Corporation in 1985, precipitating the name change of Anthony Industries to K2 Inc. a decade later. In the years leading up to the name change, company executives paid a great deal of attention to the development of the K2 brand and to targeting other acquisitions that increased Anthony Industries' presence in recreational and industrial markets. Although much of the company's strategic focus was aimed at K2, Shakespeare benefited directly from some of the acquisitions completed by Anthony Industries. In 1990, Britain-based Nymofil,

Ltd. was acquired and merged into Shakespeare Monofilament and in 1991 the decorative light pole business belonging to Stanhope Inc. was acquired to strengthen Shakespeare Electronic & Fiberglass's business.

Despite the attention directed at K2, Shakespeare's contributions to its parent company's financial health were considerable. Shakespeare's industrial products businesses, comprising Shakespeare utility poles and its monofilament operations, constituted the bulk of its parent company's industrial products segment, which accounted for nearly 70 percent of total annual profits during the 1990s. On the recreational products side, Shakespeare's fishing equipment and marine antennas were also important contributors to Anthony Industries' bottom line. Shakespeare's fishing rod business, led by the company's signature Ugly Stik, continued to reign as a market leader in the years leading up to the name change.

During the 1990s, the success of Shakespeare businesses helped Anthony Industries and its successor, K2 Inc., more than double annual sales from less than $300 million to the $638 million generated in 1997. Shakespeare Fishing Tackle accounted for roughly $85 million in annual sales and the industrial products division, led by Shakespeare Monofilament and Shakespeare Electronic & Fiberglass, contributed approximately $200 million to the parent company's annual sales total. Without Shakespeare, K2 Inc. would lose a considerable percentage of its financial might and much of what made it a diversified company. For these reasons, Shakespeare's role as a K2 Inc. subsidiary appeared secure as Shakespeare celebrated its 100th anniversary and looked toward its second century of business, having traveled a long way from the banks of the Kalamazoo River.

Principal Subsidiaries

Shakespeare (Hong Kong) Ltd.; Pacific Rim Metallic Products Ltd.; Shakespeare International Ltd. (U.K.); Shakespeare Company (UK) Ltd.; Shakespeare Monofilament U.K. Ltd.; Shakespeare Hengelsport, B.V. (Netherlands); Shakespeare (Australia) Pty. Ltd.; Shakespeare International GmbH (Germany).

Further Reading

Beaty, Wayne, ''Composite Poles Now Include Transmission Class,'' *Electric Light & Power,* November 1995, p. 42.
Shakespeare Company, ''Brief History of the Shakespeare Company,'' Columbus, S.C.: Shakespeare Company, 1975.
''Shakespeare on Stage,'' *Monsanto Magazine,* 1972.
''Wildly Still Alive, Says K2; Restructures Outdoor Group,'' *Sporting Goods Business,* February 24, 1997, p. 14.

—Jeffrey L. Covell

Shiseido Company, Limited

7-5-5, Ginza, Chuo-ku
Tokyo 104-10
Japan
(03) 3572-5111
Fax: (03) 3574-8380
Web site: http://www.shiseido.co.jp/e

Public Company
Incorporated: 1927
Employees: 22,045
Sales: ¥588.57 billion (US$5.12 billion) (1997)
Stock Exchanges: Tokyo Luxembourg
SICs: 2844 Perfumes, Cosmetics & Other Toilet Preparations; 5812 Eating Places; 5999 Miscellaneous Retail Stores, Not Elsewhere Classified; 7231 Beauty Shops; 7991 Physical Fitness Facilities

Shiseido Company, Limited is the leading cosmetics company in Japan and one of the largest in the world. At home and in more than 50 countries abroad, Shiseido offers a variety of makeup, skin-care, and hair-care products. In Japan, the company markets additional products, including toiletries, foodstuffs, pharmaceuticals, and fine chemicals. Shiseido franchises about 25,000 cosmetics retail outlets in Japan, both stand-alone and within department stores and supermarkets. It also runs various salons, upscale boutiques, health clubs, and restaurants. Of the company's sales, about 74 percent come from its cosmetics division; about 16 percent from its toiletries division, which comprises hair-care products, facial cleansers, soaps, bath additives, and fine toiletries; and the remaining 10 percent from a catch-all ''others'' division which covers pharmaceuticals, salon skin-care and hair-care products, fashion goods, fine chemicals, and salons, boutiques, health clubs, and restaurants. Increasingly global in its emphasis—although not traditionally successful overseas—Shiseido now derives about 13.5 percent of its sales from outside of Japan. The company's various products are manufactured at nine plants in Japan and ten abroad.

Beginnings as Western-Style Pharmacy in 1870s

In 1872 Yushin Fukuhara, former head pharmacist for the Japanese Admiralty, opened the Shiseido Pharmacy on the Ginza in Tokyo—a bold stroke that created Japan's first Western-style pharmacy. The characters in the store's name and the store's philosophy were derived from classic Asian philosophy. Shiseido's name implies ''richness of life,'' which, according to Confucian thought, can be reached only through harmony of mind, body, and soul. The small store, in a populous shopping area, attracted purchasers of traditional remedies as well as curiosity-seekers interested in the novelty of Western imports; personalized service and high-quality products won their loyalty. In the 1880s Shiseido began to manufacture medicines, and in 1888 the company introduced a new product to Japan: toothpaste. Shiseido began selling cosmetic products that were processed by the standards used for medicines in 1897. The first such product was Eudermine skin lotion.

During the late 19th century, Japan was transformed by changes that had swept the country since the lowering of the two-centuries-old international trade barriers in the mid-1850s: some women still wore traditional white rice powder, hair lacquer, and stylized brows; others wore the lip salve, rouge, and skin-tone powder worn by Western women.

Traditional Japanese cosmetics and medicinal remedies came from herbs, other plants, and minerals that were ground and processed according to recipes that had been part of the Japanese culture since being introduced from China in the sixth and seventh centuries. Similar ingredients and processes were used to produce both lip balm and lipstick. The pharmacist was the purveyor of both.

In Japan, cosmetics for men had their heyday in the courtly and elegant latter part of the first millennium A.D. During the 19th century men still wore theatrical makeup—only males were permitted stage careers—but during the period, many Kabuki performers were poisoned by the lead in their makeup. In order to prevent future tragedies, the Japanese government established strict product and marketing regulations which were so elaborate, frustrating, and time-consuming that few foreign companies tackled the Japanese market. The regulations also

Company Perspectives:

We aim to identify new, richer sources of value and use them to create beauty in the lives and culture of those we serve. Our Criteria for Corporate Activity are: We seek to bring joy to our customers; we are concerned with results, not procedures; we share frankly with each other our real priorities; we give free rein to our thoughts and boldly challenge conventional wisdom; we act in the spirit of thankfulness.

hurt domestic companies, however. In the two years it took to license a product, many products lost their timeliness, and thus their appeal.

Emphasis on Cosmetics in the Early 20th Century

Japanese shipping was impeded just before and after the turn of the century, due first to the Sino-Japanese War of 1894 to 1895, then to the Russo-Japanese War of 1904 to 1905. Because of the difficulty in obtaining imports, by 1915 Shiseido's cosmetics replaced foreign products in popularity, to the point that the company began to shift its emphasis away from pharmaceuticals and to concentrate almost exclusively on the manufacture of cosmetics. In addition, in 1902 the company opened Japan's first soda fountain. The sale of foods remained a modest but profitable venture.

Shinzo Fukuhara, the son of Yushin Fukuhara, led Shiseido during this period and became Shiseido's first president in 1927. Shinzo Fukuhara had spent five years studying pharmacology at Columbia University in New York City, and had visited France for one year. In France, he made important ties with artists whose ideas influenced the development of Shiseido's marketing, advertising, and packaging. Shiseido's marketing director, Noboru Matsumoto, had also studied in the United States, at New York University.

Tokyo's growth helped the family business grow and prosper, even through World War I, when production and delivery of the company's products were adversely affected by wartime restrictions. It was after the war, in 1923—remembered in Japan as the year of the great Kanto Earthquake—that Shiseido took a daring step that would eventually expand its business far beyond the city and make it a national concern. At Matsumoto's urging, the company opened a series of retail outlets for Shiseido products in a franchise operation, in principle not unlike the franchise concept Ray Kroc of McDonald's introduced in the United States some 30 years later.

Shiseido had built its business as a family-run operation, paying special attention to the needs of its customers in Tokyo and the surrounding area. Repeat business resulted both from product excellence and personalized service. Special needs were recorded along with transactional details so that reminders could be tailored to each customer and timed to catch orders for replenishment. The franchised shops were to replicate the Tokyo store, with stock variations responding to local tastes and needs. The idea caught on because most franchisees, like the founding family, were willing to work long hours to earn customer loyalty.

In addition to over-the-counter retail sales, franchise owner-operators began conducting a mail-order business in 1937. They called it the Camellia Club, referring to the art nouveau-inspired flower logo designed by Matsumoto that Shiseido began using in 1915. The 25,000 franchise stores continued to do a steady large-volume business, with club members reaching about 9.6 million by the late 1980s. By then, the stores issued credit cards to members and kept in touch through a monthly magazine featuring fashion and beauty pointers.

The company's size ballooned quickly, outgrowing its status as a limited partnership. Reorganized as a corporation in 1927, Shiseido was listed on the Tokyo Stock Exchange. Neither the depression nor the following years of Japanese military buildup and war did much to flatten the company's growth curve.

By the 1940s Shiseido had become a trendsetter in the cosmetics industry. Even the bombing and devastation of many manufacturing sites during World War II did not result in the company's destruction. With the economic policies introduced by General Douglas MacArthur during the postwar years, Shiseido reorganized, and in 1949 the company was again listed on the Tokyo Stock Exchange.

Regaining its position as the country's cosmetics leader in the early 1950s—a position not seriously tested until the 1970s when foreign companies began to challenge Shiseido in earnest—Shiseido opened thousands of additional outlets, prospering with the franchisees as the economy's upsurge produced newly affluent customers. In 1952 the company set up a wholesale network for sales of soap, toothpaste, and sundries. The following year the Shiseido Institute of Beauty Technology was opened.

Overseas Expansion Begins in 1957

In 1957 Shiseido began international operations when it initiated manufacturing and sales operations in Southeast Asia. In 1960 the company began marketing in Hawaii. International operations boomed in the 1960s, as subsidiaries were established in Hawaii, New York, and Milan. Others opened during the following two decades in Singapore, New Zealand, Bangkok, Australia, France, West Germany, and the United Kingdom. In 1965 Shiseido began marketing products that were formulated especially for export markets.

During the early 1970s Shiseido introduced its broad product line in the United States, but the expected sales volume failed to materialize. About ten years later, Yoshio Ohno—at that time director of overseas operations—took a different, more successful approach: Shiseido offered an exclusive product line to each of several top-flight fashion retailers, including Bloomingdale's in New York and Bullock's in Los Angeles. By the mid-1980s these lines were earning $75 million annually and growing by 40 percent each year. This strategy succeeded not only in the United States, but in other countries as well.

Product Lines Revamped in the 1970s and 1980s

During the 1970s interest in the company's broad product line as a whole began to wane, and Shiseido began to consider new organizational and marketing directions. Many owner-operators who had worked diligently for decades to maintain a loyal customer following were nearing retirement and seemed out of touch with the interests and tastes of the new generation of consumers. To young consumers, the stores lacked the freshness and excitement that earlier generations had found in them. Shiseido refurbished the stores, and new marketing analysis and techniques were applied.

Serge Lutens, a French "international image creator," joined Shiseido in 1980. The following year, the company began marketing cosmetics in China. Segmentation of the broad product line into five age groups for marketing purposes was instituted in 1982, with encouraging results. Other ideas that succeeded as part of this new approach were product diversification and retail diversification among the company's stores. Rather than making each store an outlet for all product lines, stores were organized into sub-specialties targeted at specific markets. Some became convenience stores, carrying household products as well as cosmetics. Others carried youth-oriented fashions. High-end beauty consultation services and exclusive product lines, similar to those in the high-fashion centers overseas, were other specialties. Still other stores carried cosmetics and fitness aids for men and women. In spite of this diversification, Shiseido had no intention of departing from its major role in the cosmetics industry; Shiseido stores carried other products primarily to attract customers for the company's beauty aids.

Despite Shiseido's size, the company did not abandon its founder's practice of associating beauty aids with health. For example, products in the Elixir skin-care product line contained an ingredient to protect sunbathers from ultraviolet rays. The company carefully researched all market segments, targeting them with certain products. For the rapidly growing older group, Shiseido introduced Medicated Flowline Active, used to prevent hair loss, promote its regeneration, and aid in circulation of the blood. Cle de Peau Program Care was designed to prevent skin from aging and to help it recover a youthful look. A chain of sports clubs and restaurants and a line of health foods also promoted physical fitness. In 1986 Shiseido acquired Carita S.A., a French beauty salon and beautician school chain, and in 1987 Shiseido opened another beauty salon, Alexandre Zouari, in Paris. The company acquired Zotos International Inc., the leading U.S. supplier of professional hair and salon products in 1988, and Davlyn Industries, Inc., a U.S. maker of cosmetics, the following year.

Some product lines were discarded despite brisk sales. Environmental concerns caused Shiseido to phase out products such as aerosol spray cans and nonbiodegradable diapers. New products and product lines continued to spur additional business. Research and development had been important to Shiseido's operations since its earliest days, and during the 1980s pharmaceuticals, as well as cosmetics, were being developed and tested in the company's domestic and overseas research centers. In 1988 pharmaceuticals reentered the Shiseido product family with the introduction of a line of over-the-counter drugs. Shiseido introduced its first prescription drug in 1993 with Opelead, used in cataract surgery and cornea transplants.

During the late 1980s Shiseido entered a three-year reorganization under the direction of president and CEO Yoshiharu Fukuhara, a grandson of Shiseido's founder and nephew of Shinzo Fukuhara. This restructuring strengthened the company's sales network and reaffirmed its long-held leadership position in the field. At the same time, Shiseido also bolstered its research and development operations by opening new research facilities in France in 1988, and in the United States in 1989.

Global Expansion in the 1990s

During the early and mid-1990s, Shiseido stepped up its efforts to become a global power in cosmetics. In part this was a response to price deregulation in Japan which began in 1991. With the company losing its traditional control over the pricing of its products at the retail level, revenues and profits inevitably began to fall. The effect of deregulation was compounded by the simultaneous rise in Japan of the type of discount chains that were prevalent in the United States. As the decade continued, Japanese trade barriers to imported cosmetics began to fall, and Shiseido faced serious competition at home for the first time in its history.

In response to these threats to its home market, Shiseido, which had traditionally targeted the high end of the cosmetics market, made a conscious effort to develop more lower-priced products. The company also divided its domestic cosmetics business into two units: cosmetics, which handled consultation-oriented products, and "cosmenity," which handled self-selected products. The two sectors were differentiated further in April 1996 when the marketing operations of the two units were completely separated.

It was in the overseas market, however, that Shiseido was making serious waves; building and acquiring factories, expanding into new markets, and growing through joint ventures and acquisitions. In 1990 the company established Beauté Prestige International S.A. in Paris to develop and market fragrances. The following year, production of perfumes and skin-care products began at the company's first European factory, located in Gien, France. After some tentative moves in China in the early 1980s, Shiseido became more serious about this rapidly growing market in the 1990s. In 1991 a joint venture called Shiseido Liyuan Cosmetics was set up with Beijing Liyuan Co. to develop, produce, and market premium cosmetics. Two years later production began at a new factory in Beijing, which led in 1994 to the debut of the highly successful, high-end, Aupres line of cosmetics, developed exclusively for the Chinese market. By mid-1997, Shiseido products were available in 130 stores in 32 Chinese cities. By the same time, company products were marketed in more than 50 countries worldwide, with the addition of Lebanon in 1995; Brazil, Cyprus, Israel, and Turkey in 1996; and the Czech Republic, Hungary, Croatia, and Vietnam in 1997. With sales in Asia and Europe increasing, Shiseido moved to increase its capacity by starting construction on a second plant in Taiwan in May 1997, and by reaching an agreement in June 1997 to develop a new production site in France's Loire region, scheduled to begin operations in January 1999.

On the other side of the Pacific Ocean, meanwhile, Shiseido was just as busy. In November 1996 the company bought the North American Hair Salon Division of Helene Curtis Inc. from Unilever United States, Inc., thereby adding the Helene Curtis professional salon hair-care lines to those of Zotos. Helene Curtis

Japan Inc. was added in early 1997. Manufacturing capacity in North America was a concern, and in March 1997 Shiseido bought its fourth U.S. factory, planning to convert the New Jersey facility into one of the largest cosmetic plants in the world.

This heightened activity outside of Japan was intended to help the company reach the ambitious goals set by management in 1996. As part of a ''Global No. 1'' five-year plan, Shiseido aimed by 2001 to increase net sales from foreign operations to ¥120 billion, from ¥64.5 billion in fiscal 1997. The company also wanted overseas sales, which had grown from only eight percent of total revenues in fiscal 1997 to 13.4 percent in fiscal 1998, to double to 25 percent by 2001.

A year filled with noteworthy events, 1997 was also Shiseido's 125th anniversary, and the company marked the occasion by introducing Eudermine, its original product, to markets outside of Japan (1997 happened to also be the centenary of Eudermine's debut). In June 1997 Yoshiharu Fukuhara took over as chairman, while Akira Gemma succeeded Fukuhara as president and CEO. As they worked to attain their self-imposed goals, this new management team was likely to seek out additional overseas acquisitions. It appeared that Shiseido had finally gotten serious about its longtime global ambitions, and that success was beginning to follow in the wake of the company's new ventures.

Principal Subsidiaries

Osaka Shiseido Co., Ltd.; Shiseido Kako Co., Ltd.; Shiseido Beautech Co., Ltd.; Mieux Products Co., Ltd.; IPSA Co., Ltd.; Haramachi Paper Co., Ltd.; ETWAS Co., Ltd.; Shiseido Fine Toiletry Co., Ltd.; Shiseido Sales Co., Ltd.; Shiseido Pharmaceutical Co., Ltd.; Shiseido Logistics Company Ltd.; SFC Co., Ltd.; The Ginza Co., Ltd.; Shiseido Parlour Co., Ltd.; Shiseido Beauty Salon Co., Ltd.; Shiseido Real Estate Development Co., Ltd.; Shiseido Wellness Co., Ltd.; Mikawaya Co., Ltd.; Shiseido Lease Co., Ltd.; D'ici là Co., Ltd.; Ettusais Co., Ltd.; Shiseido Cosmenity Co., Ltd.; Qi Salon Cosmetics Co., Ltd.; Shiseido International Corporation (U.S.A.); Zotos International, Inc. (U.S.A.); Davlyn Industries, Inc. (U.S.A.); Shiseido Cosmetics (America) Ltd. (U.S.A.); Shiseido America Inc. (U.S.A.); Shiseido of Hawaii, Inc. (U.S.A.); Shiseido Cosmetici (Italia) S.p.A.; Shiseido Deutschland GmbH. (Germany); Shiseido United Kingdom Co., Ltd.; Carita S.A. (France); Alma Coiffure S.A. (France); Shiseido International Europe B.V. (The Netherlands); Shiseido Singapore Co., (Pte.) Ltd.; Shiseido (Australia) Pty., Ltd.; Shiseido (N.Z.) Ltd. (New Zealand); Shiseido International France S.A.; Beauté Prestige International S.A. (France); Shiseido Philippines, Inc.; Shiseido Thailand Co., Ltd.; Shiseido France S.A.; Taiwan Shiseido Co., Ltd.; Shiseido Liyuan Cosmetics Co., Ltd. (China); Les Salons du Palais Royal Shiseido S.A. (France); Shiseido Canada Inc.; Piidea Canada, Ltd.

Further Reading

Born, Pete, ''Shiseido Celebrates 125th with Eudermine,'' *WWD,* July 11, 1997, p. 13.

——, ''Shiseido's Vision for Global Expansion,'' *WWD,* April 26, 1996, p. 6.

Cody, Jennifer, ''Shiseido Strives for a Whole New Look,'' *Wall Street Journal,* May 27, 1994, p. A5.

do Rosario, Louise, ''Cleaned and Preened,'' *Far Eastern Economic Review,* April 1, 1993, pp. 68–69.

——, ''Make Up and Mend,'' *Far Eastern Economic Review,* December 19, 1991, pp. 70–71.

''Fragrance Helps You Live Longer,'' *Economist,* October 23, 1993, p. 86.

Hutton, Bethan, ''Acquisitions Behind Surge at Shiseido,'' *Financial Times,* November 12, 1997, p. 17.

''Japan's Shiseido Plans New Cosmetics Line for the U.S. Market,'' *Wall Street Journal,* May 23, 1997, p. A11.

Kilburn, David, ''Shiseido Blooms Anew: Fukuhara Expands the Vision of Japanese Giant,'' *Advertising Age,* October 3, 1988, p. 12.

Ono, Yumiko, ''Japan's Shiseido Studies Moves in U.S. Market,'' *Wall Street Journal,* April 19, 1996, p. B7.

Shirouzu, Norihiko, ''Deregulation Jolts Shiseido's Foundation: Cosmetics Firm Looks to U.S. As Home Rivalries Grow,'' *Wall Street Journal,* June 14, 1996, p. A10.

''Shiseido Aims to Become Global No. 1 in Worldwide Cosmetics,'' *Cosmetics International,* November 25, 1996, p. 10.

''Shiseido Is Seeking to Acquire Its Fourth Factory in the U.S.,'' *Wall Street Journal,* December 2, 1996, p. B12.

Slavin, Barbara, ''Saving Face,'' *Forbes,* December 31, 1984, p. 138.

Tanner, Andrew, ''Is Beauty More Than Skin-Deep?'' *Forbes,* December 16, 1985, p. 148.

''Wrinkled,'' *Economist,* November 4, 1995, p. 69.

—Betty T. Moore
—updated by David E. Salamie

Sierra Pacific Industries

P.O. Box 496028
Redding, California 96049
U.S.A.
(216) 267-4870
Fax: (216) 267-7876

Private Company
Incorporated: 1951
Employees: 3,200
Sales: $1 billion (1997 est.)
SICs: 2411 Logging; 2421 Sawmills & Planing Mills—General; 2436 Softwood Veneer & Plywood; 2611 Pulp Mills; 2653 Corrugated & Solid Fiber Boxes; 2431 Millwork; 2621 Paper Mills

The largest timber company in California, Sierra Pacific Industries harvests and mills timber in northern California. During the late 1990s, Sierra Pacific produced an estimated 1.3 billion board feet annually, ranking as the third-largest producer of lumber in the country behind Weyerhaeuser and Georgia-Pacific. The timber to produce the lumber was logged from 1,332,000 acres of land controlled by the company and its owners, the Emmerson family. At the head of the family was ''Red'' Emmerson, who began the business with his father. By virtue of the vast tracts of prime timberland owned by Sierra Pacific, Emmerson ranked as the largest private landowner in the country, a distinction he attained by eclipsing media mogul Ted Turner in 1997.

Founder's Origins

Archie Aldis ''Red'' Emmerson began learning the forest products business as a young child, when he watched his father build crude, temporary sawmills in the family backyard. Red Emmerson was a toddler at the time, living in Newburg, Oregon, with his mother, Emily, and his father, Raleigh Humes ''Curly'' Emmerson. Newburg was in forest country, part of the timber-rich Pacific Northwest, where nearly every occupation during the early decades of the 20th century had something to do with timber and its derivatives. Curly Emmerson was no exception, but his years in Newburg as a sawmill operator were not successful. His business failed, and by the time Red was five years old, he and his wife had decided to go their separate ways. Curly Emmerson eventually left Newburg and headed south to northern California. Emily Emmerson remained in Newburg, in charge of raising Red.

Emily Emmerson did not assume the sole responsibility of raising Red for long; she left that duty to others, namely Seventh Day Adventists. After his parents were divorced, Red Emmerson was sent to a small town in eastern Washington State named Spangle. There, the young Emmerson attended a Seventh Day Adventist boarding school called the Upper Columbia Academy. Emmerson proved to an industrious worker at a young age. He put himself through school by attending to the school farm and by driving a truck, for which he earned 35 cents an hour. Emmerson also spent one summer working on a cattle ranch. His penchant for extracurricular labor aside, Emmerson did not fair well at the Upper Columbia Academy, at least in the minds of those in charge of the boarding school. The Seventh Day Adventists failed to produce their desired results with Emmerson, and expelled him for hanging a condom on a classroom chalkboard. It was time for Emmerson to move on once again.

With his days at Upper Columbia Academy at an end, Emmerson moved to northeastern Washington State to finish his education at a public high school in Omak, in the heart of the state's cattle country. By the time Emmerson had finished high school, he had been exposed to three localities dominated by their natural environment: Newburg by vast tracts of timber, Spangle by endless fields of agricultural crops, and Omak by multitudinous herds of cattle. For his future, Emmerson did not select any of these communities, but he returned to his roots in a sense by reuniting with his father in northern California, where towering forests were as plentiful as in Newburg. From the end of his high school years forward, the theretofore itinerant Red Emmerson remained in northern California, becoming by the century's end the largest private landowner in the United States.

Emmerson did not raise to such lofty heights on his own. Initially, he had the help of his father, and together they built the foundation for the Sierra Pacific Industries of the 1990s. When

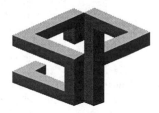

Company Perspectives:

Sierra Pacific's confidence in the future is solidly rooted in some of the finest timberland in the world. Stretching from near the Oregon border on the Pacific Coast to the Lake Tahoe area of central California, Sierra Pacific lands grow Ponderosa Pine, Sugar Pine, White Fir, Douglas Fir and Cedar. The land includes one of the first official tree farms in California, which has produced three timber harvests since 1944. Sierra Pacific lands represent the largest private industrial forest ownership in California.

Emmerson joined his father in northern California, his father was working in the lumber business. Red followed Curly's lead, and finished up his teenage years as a greenchain puller piling lumber as it exited the sawmill. The industriousness that had demonstrated itself at a young age continued to be displayed as Emmerson entered adulthood: By the time he was 20 years old Emmerson and his father had leased a sawmill; two years later, the father and son team had built a mill of their own, and Red Emmerson was managing the entire business.

Post-1950s Development

Together, the two Emmersons fared better in the forest products business than Curly Emmerson had done 20 years earlier with little Red Emmerson watching nearby. With Red Emmerson taking on nearly all of the managerial duties associated with running the company at an early age, much of the credit for Sierra Pacific's survival went to him. And survival was not an easy accomplishment during the era when Red Emmerson took command. The wave of prosperity created after World War II rejuvenated many industries, including the construction industry, which was the largest single market for lumber companies such as Sierra Pacific. The demand for new housing, which had remained stifled during the country's decade-long Depression and inhibited to a large extent during the war, sharply increased during the postwar years, making the harvesting and manufacture of timber a lucrative business to enter. As a result, the number of lumber mills in operation soared, but as more and more new lumber companies entered the business and satisfied the demand for construction lumber, competition within the industry became increasingly severe. Such was the case during the 1960s when Emmerson was directing the fortunes of Sierra Pacific.

Small, under-capitalized lumber companies were forced to exit the business, engendering a precipitous drop in the number of mills in operation throughout the country. From 1950 to 1970, the number of lumber mills in the United States plunged from more than 50,000 to less than 35,000, as the lumber industry underwent two decades of significant change. In the new business environment created during this span, the logging and manufacture of timber became an industry in which only those companies able to make efficient use of raw materials could effectively compete. Integrated plants that used as much of a log as possible became crucial to success in logging's new era, a period in which the manufacture of plywood, particleboard, and paper became integral contributors to a lumber company's profitability. Well-financed companies able to change with the times and incorporate new logging and manufacturing techniques into their operations were able to flourish, while others dropped by the wayside.

Not far north of Sierra Pacific's operations in northern California, market conditions were particularly harsh, and their severity did not recognize state borders. In Oregon, the number of lumber mills plummeted between 1950 and 1970, falling from 1,455 to a mere 450. As elsewhere, the necessity for efficiency and diversification had weeded out those companies unable to change with the times. Under Emmerson's stewardship, Sierra Pacific not only changed with the times but it sometimes took the lead as an innovator. For instance, well before paving mill yards became a common practice, Emmerson paved his, an innovation that reduced man-hours in the loading yard and prevented his saws from getting jammed by gravel and mud clinging to uncut timber. Less damage to the saws meant less time spent changing dull saws, saving further money for the company.

After two decades of disruptive change dramatically altered the face of the timber industry, those companies that had survived did not settle into a more peaceful period of existence. The decade between the mid-1970s and the mid-1980s was framed by two painful economic recessions, forcing timber companies such as Sierra Pacific to either adapt to the economic environment or beat a hasty retreat. Chiefly to blame were rising interest rates, which crippled the construction market, and cheap timber from Canada and the southern United States. Many timber companies failed to adapt to new economic conditions and another instance of corporate Darwinism swept through the industry, weeding out those companies that could not measure up to the times. Sierra Pacific took full advantage of the situation and managed to record enviable growth as other companies struggled to survive. Between 1976 and 1986, the company spent roughly $60 million acquiring the assets of its financially strapped competitors. Sierra Pacific's remarkable progress did not go unnoticed, as one timber leader, Louisiana Pacific Corp.'s chairman Harry Merlo, testified, "As people got out of sawmilling, what did they do? They sold their assets to Red. He was the last man standing."

Having withstood the test of times and endured—even prospered—during anemic economic conditions, Sierra Pacific exited the mid-1980s in good stead. Ahead, however, loomed disastrous trouble. The potential problem for the company stemmed from a series of amendments to the 1964 Wilderness Act that began in 1976. These amendments and other legislation were increasingly reducing the amount of land available for timber harvests on public land, causing great concern among those forest products companies that lacked their own timber acreage. Sierra Pacific was one of those anxiety-ridden forest products companies.

The crescendo of debate over the use of publicly owned timberland for logging reached its peak in 1987, when a storm of controversy was touched off over concern for the Northern Spotted Owl. For Sierra Pacific, the situation quickly became grave. All its mills were in northern California, where large factions of environmentalists were struggling mightily to curtail logging on great stretches of public forestland—and succeeding. Emmerson was forced into a choice. ''It was either buy land,'' he concluded, ''or go broke.'' In his mind, there was not much debate over the two choices. ''This business is the only thing I knew how to do,'' he later related. ''This was my home. Where else was I going to go?''

1987: Timber Holdings Begin to Accumulate

His mind resolved on pushing ahead and gaining a sizeable amount of private timberland to feed his mills, Emmerson made his decision at a fortuitous time. In 1987, the giant railroad company Santa Fe Southern Pacific Corp. was implementing a strategic plan to concentrate on its core business. An integral facet of this plan required that the company shed interests outside the scope of its score business, which included 522,000 acres of California timberland it owned. The land was put up for sale and Emmerson grabbed it, risking nearly everything he owned to do so.

To complete the transaction, Emmerson offered all 10 of Sierra Pacific's mills as collateral and convinced a syndicate of a dozen banks to lend him the $460 million needed to buy Santa Fe's timberland. ''I hocked my heart and soul,'' Emmerson remembered, and received criticism for his risky move. Some industry pundits believed the $880-per-acre purchase price was too high, and further skepticism erupted when the stock market crashed in October 1987. When the sale was closed, however, all those who muttered that Red Emmerson had made the mistake of his life were quickly silenced. Shortly after the deal was completed, the U.S. Forestry Service began restricting timber harvests on public lands in response to numerous court orders. The value of privately-owned timberland quickly skyrocketed, nearly doubling overnight. ''We were lucky,'' Emmerson noted. ''I bought that land because it was available, not because it was strategic.''

Once convinced of the soundness in purchasing timberland, Emmerson became an irrepressible advocate of buying as much land as possible. ''You can never own too much land,'' he declared, ''because you never know what other restrictions will be coming down the pipe.'' After recording phenomenal success with the Santa Fe deal, Emmerson spent the next eight years buying land, laying out more than $600 million to acquire 400,000 acres.

Emmerson's penchant for acquiring tracts of timberland continued to demonstrate itself during the late 1990s. In May 1997, Sierra Pacific paid $50 million to Louisiana-Pacific for a 38,000-acre plot of white fir and pine in northern California. Although the acreage gained in the deal was relatively small compared to the more than one million acres under Emmerson's control, the deal had a symbolic importance. With the 38,000 acres gained, Emmerson became the largest private landowner in the United States, slipping past Ted Turner. It was a feat essentially achieved in one decade's time, and as Emmerson scanned the horizon into future decades additional land acquisitions seemed more than likely. Nearing his seventies as the 1990s drew to a close, Emmerson had developed a voracious appetite for land late in life. The intensity of his desire for land was perhaps the single most important factor in Sierra Pacific's existence. With the next generation of Emmersons working beneath him at Sierra Pacific, Red Emmerson likely was imparting the importance of land ownership to his children: the inheritors of his business and the probable leaders of Sierra Pacific's future.

Principal Subsidiaries

Sierra Pacific Windows; Sierra Pacific Foundation.

Further Reading

DeLacy, Ron, ''California's Sierra Pacific Wants Fibreboard's Wood Products Division,'' *Knight-Ridder/Tribune Business News,* June 20, 1995, p. 6.

Denne, Lorianne, '' 'War' on Clearcutting May Be Headed This Way,'' *Puget Sound Business Journal,* April 1, 1991, p. 11.

Glover, Mark, ''Sierra Pacific Industries Halts Negotiations to Buy California Sawmill,'' *Knight-Ridder/Tribune Business News,* January 5, 1994, p. 1.

Graebner, Lynn, ''Camino Mill Sale Collapses; Future Is Unclear,'' *Business Journal Serving Greater Sacramento,* January 10, 1994, p. 10.

Hawn, Carleen, ''What the Spotted Owl Did for Red Emmerson,'' *Forbes,* October 13, 1997, p. 82.

''L-P to Sell California Coastal Timberland,'' *Pulp & Paper,* July 1997, p. 29.

Schnitt, Paul, ''Lumber Mill in California's Amador County Shuts Down,'' *Knight-Ridder/Tribune Business News,* January 31, 1997, p. 13.

Swett, Clint, ''California Lumber Mill's Workers Uneasy After Buyout,'' *Knight-Ridder/Tribune Business News,* December 27, 1996, p. 12.

——, ''Sale Rescues Camino, Calif., Lumber Mill's 280 Jobs,'' *Knight-Ridder/Tribune Business News,* May 8, 1994, p. 5.

''Two Buyers Found for Bohemia Assets,'' *Forest Industries,* September 1991, p. 6.

—Jeffrey L. Covell

The St. Paul Companies, Inc.

385 Washington Street
Saint Paul, Minnesota 55102
U.S.A.
(612) 310-7911
Fax: (612) 310-8294
Web site: http://www.stpaul.com

Public Company
Incorporated: 1853 as St. Paul Fire and Marine Insurance Company
Employees: 12,200
Total Assets: $20.68 billion (1996)
Stock Exchanges: New York
SICs: 6211 Security Brokers, Dealers & Flotation Companies; 6282 Investment Advice; 6331 Fire, Marine & Casualty Insurance; 6351 Surety Insurance; 6411 Insurance Agents, Brokers & Services; 6719 Offices of Holding Companies, Not Elsewhere Classified; 6722 Management Investment Companies, Open-End; 6726 Unit Investment Trusts, Face-Amount Certificate Offices, Closed-End Management Investment Offices

The St. Paul Companies, Inc. is Minnesota's oldest business corporation and one of the oldest insurance companies in the United States. The St. Paul is a worldwide insurance organization with three main units: St. Paul Fire and Marine Insurance Company, which is the fourteenth largest property-liability underwriter in the United States and the country's largest medical liability insurance underwriter; St. Paul Re, a New York-based reinsurer for nonlife insurance companies worldwide; and St. Paul International Underwriting, which provides property-liability insurance outside the United States from its base in London, England. The St. Paul also holds a 78 percent stake in The John Nuveen Company, which specializes in asset management and investment banking.

Early History

In the years preceding the founding of The St. Paul people living in the Minnesota Territory were insured primarily by agents representing eastern insurance companies. Most wintertime claims and claim payments had to wait for spring, when travel and communication resumed.

In 1853 Alexander Wilkin, the secretary of the territory, and The St. Paul's first and youngest president, approached his neighbors, George and John Farrington, with the idea of starting a Saint Paul, Minnesota-based insurance company. The need for local fire insurance was particularly great, and George Farrington, a local banker, saw the opportunity to stem the flow of cash out of the territory. Farrington introduced a bill of incorporation in the territorial legislature that same year, and Saint Paul Fire and Marine Insurance Company was incorporated.

The St. Paul was to operate as a mutual company, but it also sold traditional, or stock, policies. Mutual policyholders were to share in both the profits and losses of the company; stock policyholders would not. The company's charter permitted it "to make insurance on all descriptions of property against loss or damage by fire," and "to make insurance on all descriptions of boats and vessels, the cargoes and freights thereof. . . ."

The company needed to sell $100,000 of insurance to raise the capital to begin business. To accomplish this end, the company's ten founders each applied for $10,000 policies on their own property. Shortly thereafter it was discovered that none of the founders possessed property worth $10,000. The members of the board rejected their own applications and rewrote them for $5,000 each. In February 1854 the company issued its first policy, a mutual policy for $800. It insured the home and furnishings of Robert A. Smith, the territory's librarian and private secretary to Governor Willis A. Gorman, who in turn purchased the company's first stock policy.

The St. Paul sustained its first fire loss in April 1855 when a row of offices and a bakery burned to the ground, resulting in $3,000 in claims. This loss was followed by a much greater problem, the panic of 1857, in which many New York companies folded. In Saint Paul all but three of the local banks were forced to close. The St. Paul and other insurance companies were forced to accept "notes of indebtedness" as premium payments. These notes could not be converted into cash to cover day-to-day operating expenses and, as a result, 47 fledgling insurance companies closed. The St. Paul, faced with severe

Company Perspectives:

The St. Paul Companies will be a premier worldwide provider of property-liability insurance products and services in strategically selected markets. We will be known by our customers as one of the leading global providers of value-added insurance products and services; by our employees as an exceptional place to work; and by our shareholders as a superior long-term investment.

cash flow problems, elected not to issue any new policies for a time and was forced to sell its office furniture to maintain operations.

A period of stagnation occurred starting in 1861, during the Civil War. The St. Paul's president, Alexander Wilkin, died on a Mississippi battlefield. He was succeeded by James C. Burbank, the company's first full-time president, in April 1865. Also in 1865, The St. Paul reorganized as a stock company. One of Burbank's first duties was to oversee The St. Paul's expansion into the Canadian market. By 1866 the company was writing business in Manitoba. A shareholder-elected board voted to pay semiannual dividends, and in July 1867 the company issued its first stock dividend, of $1.50 per share. Following the Civil War, The St. Paul grew. It constructed a new corporate headquarters. A model for fire-resistant structures of the future, the building was built of metal and stone.

Reputation Grew Out of the Great Chicago Fire of 1871 and the San Francisco Earthquake of 1906

In 1871 the Great Chicago Fire strained the company's resources. The fire left 275 people dead and 100,000 people homeless and destroyed more than 17,000 buildings. More than 200 insurance companies experienced fire-related losses and many were financially ruined; about one-quarter of the 200 companies went out of business and most that survived paid as little as 4¢ on the dollar to settle their claims. At a meeting of The St. Paul's board, it was agreed that all claims would be paid in full. President Burbank predicted that this decision ultimately would bring a return as word got out that the company was covering its losses. In that year claims submitted by policyholders exceeded by 165 percent the amount the company collected in premiums. The St. Paul paid a total of $140,000 to cover losses. The St. Paul's assets were greatly reduced, and it paid no dividends that year. The company's sales did improve as a result of the decision to pay all claims, however, and The St. Paul recouped its losses.

Burbank died in 1876, and the company's secretary, Charles H. Bigelow, was elected president. Shortly thereafter The St. Paul was faced with the insurance price war of 1877. The insurance market was becoming more competitive as the country grew and prospered. The result was too many insurance companies offering lower prices to compete. Under Bigelow's leadership the company dropped unprofitable agencies, introduced new products such as cyclone insurance and crop hail coverage, and instituted more stringent guidelines in accepting new customers. The St. Paul rode out the price war intact, without lowering its rates. Insurance buyers were not only affected by the price; product and service diversity were also important to a successful business plan.

During the late 19th century, the company expanded into new types of insurance coverage. The San Francisco Earthquake and Fire of 1906 took a heavy toll on The St. Paul's new product development plans, however. Claims in excess of $1.2 million were paid, in full, and the company's reputation grew. In 1911 Charles Bigelow died, and his son, Frederic Bigelow, succeeded him as president. In the years following Frederic Bigelow's appointment, the United States prepared for World War I. The St. Paul adjusted its charter to include losses incurred resulting from acts of war. In 1917 The St. Paul covered the loss of 260 vessels, totaling more than $4 million, most of which was repaid by Germany over 50 years. During the war The St. Paul began overseas expansion in a modest fashion, when it began to issue policies in Great Britain to cover losses incurred as a result of bomb damage, but in a relatively short period of time the British government cut the rates charged by U.S. companies by about 50 percent. The St. Paul, however, continued to insure against bomb damage in England for the duration of the war. The St. Paul also added automobile insurance to its product line during this period.

As a result of massive losses incurred during World War I, most European insurance companies were all but paralyzed. The St. Paul became a charter member of the American Foreign Insurance Association (AFIA), a group of companies that pooled its resources, and with combined capital of $135 million, began to market insurance abroad. The company was soon doing business in 25 foreign markets, and another period of diversification and new product development began.

Throughout the 1920s The St. Paul introduced all-risk coverage for the jewelry trade and for other ''priceless objects'' of artistic and historical significance. The policy insured items in transit from almost every known risk, except theft, because fire and marine insurance companies were prohibited from writing liability coverage. The St. Paul's leadership decided, therefore, that a liability company was needed, and in 1926 a subsidiary, St. Paul Mercury Indemnity Company, was formed. The St. Paul also added aircraft insurance and surety bonds to its product line in 1929.

After serving as The St. Paul's president for 27 years, Frederic Bigelow became chairman in 1938, and Charles F. Codere became The St. Paul's fifth president. Shortly thereafter, the United States entered into World War II. At the onset of the war, U.S. insurance companies wrote marine insurance through a specially formed syndicate, but as losses grew, the U.S. government assumed the burden of covering the staggering war losses. The War Damage Corporation, a company financed by the federal government and run by private insurance companies, wrote more than nine million policies and collected close to $250 million in premiums by the war's end.

Continued to Diversify in Postwar Period

In 1948 Charles Codere became chairman, and A. B. Jackson was elected The St. Paul's new president. Codere and Jackson worked well together, and the company greatly expanded its product lines and services. Liability insurance was offered to real estate brokers, insurance agents, and hospitals. The St. Paul refined its package policy program, allowing its agents to offer more and diverse coverage in one policy. Package policies had been introduced during World War II to provide the military with an insurance package to cover liability, shipping, and fire insurance. This method of issuing coverage continued after the war, with The St. Paul offering packages for a variety of commercial risks. Jackson also was instrumental in the organization of two new associations to insure nuclear reactors.

In 1957, with the acquisition of the Western Life Insurance Company of Helena, Montana, The St. Paul broke into the life insurance market. By 1964 Western Life sales had more than doubled. The St. Paul's agents were now able to sell all forms of insurance, sales volume continued to increase, and The St. Paul acquired several general agencies—which sold the insurance products of many different companies—to work with its independent agents more effectively. Management training programs were also initiated in 1958, computers were installed in 1956 to speed up the handling and processing of information, and in 1961 The St. Paul rebuilt and enlarged its offices.

When Charles Codere retired in 1963, A. B. Jackson succeeded him and Ronald M. Hubbs became The St. Paul's next president. During the 1960s the emphasis was on customer service. Hubbs was instrumental in the development of more than 40 property and liability service centers nationwide. Each center was self-contained; it had its own underwriters, risk management staff, marketing, claims and policy services, and office support personnel. The company believed decentralization would bring it closer to its customers.

In 1968 The St. Paul reorganized. Saint Paul Fire and Marine Insurance Company became The St. Paul Companies, Inc. The name St. Paul Fire and Marine Insurance Company was retained for the property-liability insurance subsidiary. In the years following the reorganization, The St. Paul Companies diversified its insurance-related business and branched into other areas of consumer and business services.

In 1970 St. Paul Guardian Insurance Company was formed to market personal lines of insurance. Two years later St. Paul Investment Management Company, an investment management firm, was started, and in 1973 St. Paul Life Insurance Company, whose purpose was to market life insurance through independent agents representing St. Paul Fire and Marine, was formed.

In 1973 A. B. Jackson retired as chairman. He was succeeded by Ronald Hubbs, and Carl B. Drake became the eighth president of The St. Paul Companies. Less than one year later, The St. Paul acquired John Nuveen & Co., a trader, marketer, underwriter, and distributor of securities. Nuveen was founded in Chicago in 1898 and had been a pioneer in tax-exempt bonds for individual investors, which it introduced in 1961. The St. Paul also added St. Paul Risk Services Inc., which provided consulting services to self-insure institutions and firms, and St. Paul Surplus Lines, which again broadened the coverage offered by St. Paul Fire and Marine.

In the midst of this growth the public was becoming more concerned about the quality of the products and services it was receiving. This concern, combined with changes in the medical field—in particular, new drugs, transplants, the growth of large group medical practices and group medical plans, and less personal doctor-patient relationships—contributed to an increased number of medical liability claims. Insurance companies selling malpractice coverage began to suffer massive losses. Medical cases often take years to settle, and court awards continued to grow.

The St. Paul, the largest carrier of medical liability insurance, stopped accepting new policies for a short time. When the company began to write new business again, it based premiums on the practitioners' past record. This ''claims made'' standard had been used in other types of liability for many years. It led to more accurate pricing and seemed to stabilize the market. The company also raised its malpractice premiums. The company later created a medical services division, which brought together The St. Paul's underwriting, marketing, and administrative expertise in health care-related fields. The company introduced simplified-language policies, starting with its personal liability catastrophe coverage, with the hope that it would reduce claims.

1980s and 1990s: Period of Retrenchment

In 1980 Chairman Drake refocused mainly on insurance-related businesses. The company began to divest most non-insurance subsidiaries (with the exception of the John Nuveen asset management and investment banking unit) and resumed expansion of its insurance-related interests. Under a new president, Robert J. Haugh, these divestitures were completed by 1984, when The St. Paul's net loss was $210 million. The company then undertook a new series of acquisitions. Among these purchases were Seaboard Surety Company, a provider of fidelity and surety bonds, and Swett & Crawford Group, a Los Angeles-based wholesale broker in excess and surplus lines. Atwater McMillian (renamed St. Paul Specialty Underwriting in 1988), a company that handles specialty risk accounts and surplus lines, was formed in 1981.

During the 1980s more demanding consumers, an evolving marketplace, and government deregulation resulted in another price war that hurt The St. Paul's liability business. During the same years The St. Paul also expanded its involvement in European markets. The company acquired the London-based Minet Holdings PLC in 1988, making The St. Paul the seventh largest insurance brokerage firm in the world. Shortly after the Minet acquisition, The St. Paul established St. Paul (U.K.) Limited.

On May 1, 1990, Robert J. Haugh retired and was replaced by The St. Paul's new chairman, president, and CEO, Douglas W. Leatherdale, who continued the company's strategy for an increasing presence in the European market. The St. Paul also formed Minet Europe Holdings Limited, as part of the Minet Group, to manage the expansion of The St. Paul's European market.

After two and a half bitter years of litigation and regulatory oversight, The St. Paul in mid-1990 successfully ended an attempted hostile takeover by Alleghany Corp. In May 1992 The St. Paul completed an initial public offering for the highly successful—and newly renamed—The John Nuveen Company, selling eight million shares at $18 per share and leaving The St. Paul with a 74 percent stake (which increased to 77 percent by mid-1997). For the year, John Nuveen enjoyed record revenues of $221 million, 23 percent higher than the previous year, but The St. Paul as a whole did not fare as well. Record catastrophic storms that year, including Hurricanes Andrew and Iniki and Typhoon Omar, led to a record $305 million in catastrophe losses, which when coupled with a $365 million write-down on the goodwill associated with the continuously troubled Minet Group subsidiary, resulted in the worst operating loss in company history: $333.8 million.

In May 1993 The St. Paul launched a restructuring of its U.S. underwriting businesses (known collectively as St. Paul Fire and Marine Insurance), partly in response to the losses of the previous year. Nearly two dozen departments were streamlined into three new entities: St. Paul Specialty, which housed such niche underwriting operations as medical services; St. Paul Personal & Business, responsible for underwriting personal insurance for individuals and commercial insurance for small business owners; and St. Paul Commercial, responsible for midsized commercial customers. In August 1993 the St. Paul Personal & Business unit was bolstered through the $420 million purchase of Economy Fire & Casualty from Kemper Corporation. With no repeat of the spate of catastrophic 1992 storms, The St. Paul return to profitability in 1993, posting record operating earnings of $386.6 million, with records following for 1994 ($413.9 million) and 1995 ($464.9 million) as well.

Results for 1996 were not nearly so rosy, as the company suffered its second worst catastrophe losses in history—$207 million—stemming in large part from an east coast blizzard, flooding in the west and southwest, and Hurricane Fran. In July of that year, St. Paul Fire and Marine strengthened its position in the small to midsized commercial underwriting market with the purchase of Northbrook Holdings, Inc. from Allstate Insurance Company for $190 million. Then in December The St. Paul decided to sell its loss-making Minet Group, finally unloading it in May 1997 to the insurance brokerage firm Aon, based in Chicago. Meanwhile, John Nuveen added $13.6 billion to its assets under management through the acquisitions of Flagship Resources in January 1997 and of Rittenhouse Financial Services in July 1997. St. Paul International Underwriting, the underwriter of non-U.S. property and liability insurance, was active as well, opening new offices in France, Germany, Canada, Mexico, and South Africa and acquiring the Botswana General Insurance Company of South Africa in October 1997.

In the rapidly consolidating insurance industry of the 1990s, The St. Paul Companies continued to be on the side of the acquirers. With the company's strong balance sheet backing him, Leatherdale planned to make additional acquisitions similar to that of Economy and Northbrook Holdings to stay as competitive as possible. He was also likely to continue to expand St. Paul International as potential for growth in Europe, Latin America, and Africa seemed more sure than that of the mature insurance market of the United States.

Principal Subsidiaries

St. Paul Fire and Marine Insurance Company; St. Paul Re; St. Paul International Underwriting (U.K.); The John Nuveen Company (78%).

Further Reading

Dorfman, John R., "Laughing in the Storm," *Forbes,* November 7, 1983, p. 270.

Dykewicz, Paul, "St. Paul Restructures Comp, Reinsurance," *Journal of Commerce & Commercial,* May 6, 1993, p. 10A.

Fletcher, Meg, "St. Paul, Alleghany Truce Could Curtail Hostile Insurer Bids," *Business Insurance,* June 4, 1990, pp. 3, 45.

"A History of the St. Paul," St. Paul: The St. Paul Companies, 1988.

Kunz, Virginia Brainard, "Fires, Hurricanes, Diamonds, Elephants: St. Paul Companies' Colorful History," *Ramsey County History,* Fall 1996, pp. 3–32.

Moylan, Martin J., "St. Paul Cos.' Restructuring Puzzles Analysts, Worries Staff," *Journal of Commerce & Commercial,* November 24, 1993, p. 8A.

Mullins, Ronald Gift, "Aon Acquires Minet Group from St. Paul," *Journal of Commerce & Commercial,* April 14, 1997, p. 10A.

——, "St. Paul Says '92 Big Storms Cost Company $305 Million," *Journal of Commerce & Commercial,* January 21, 1993, p. 11A.

Schifrin, Matthew, "The Artful Contrarian," *Forbes,* February 17, 1992, p. 184.

Stavro, Barry, "Risk Is Relative," *Forbes,* March 10, 1986, p. 63.

—William R. Grossman
—updated by David E. Salamie

Sylvan, Inc.

333 Main Street
P.O. Box 249
Saxonburg, Pennsylvania 16056-0249
U.S.A.
(412) 352-7520
Fax: (412) 352-7550

Public Company
Incorporated: 1989
Employees: 900
Sales: $79.1 million (1996)
Stock Exchanges: NASDAQ
SICs: 0182 Food Crops Grown Under Cover

Sylvan, Inc. is a global player in the mushroom industry, with operations devoted both to growing fresh mushrooms and to supplying mushroom spawn (the equivalent of seed) to other mushroom growers. Starting with two mushroom farms and one domestic spawn laboratory in 1989, Sylvan has sought to lessen its dependence on the highly competitive business of growing fresh mushrooms by becoming an international supplier of spawn to other mushroom growers. It has also developed complementary biotechnology products related to growing mushrooms. By 1996 approximately 30 percent of the company's operating income was derived from international spawn operations. Along the way, the company closed the largest mushroom-growing facility in the United States and acquired spawn production facilities abroad, first in France and England, then in Mexico, South America, and other international markets.

First Incorporated in 1989

The company was first incorporated in Delaware as Sylvan Foods Holdings, Inc. (SFHI) on March 27, 1989, for the purpose of acquiring all of the outstanding capital stock of Myco-Sci, Inc. The acquisition was made through SFHI's wholly owned subsidiary, Sylvan Foods, Inc., which was merged with Myco-Sci, Inc. effective April 4, 1989, and the name of Myco-Sci, Inc., the surviving corporation, was changed to Sylvan Foods, Inc. SFHI directly held all of the stock of Sylvan Foods and at this time had no other material assets or operations. Its principal offices were located in Worthington, Pennsylvania, about 50 miles northeast of Pittsburgh.

The acquisition of Myco-Sci, Inc. cost $33.4 million. The purchase price and acquisition costs were financed by a $22 million bank term loan, $5 million contributed by The Prospect Group, and the remainder with cash. This leveraged buyout resulted in a heavy debt burden for Sylvan. The Prospect Group, an investment firm, became the majority owner by virtue of its $5 million equity investment.

Myco-Sci, Sylvan's Predecessor

Myco-Sci, the predecessor of Sylvan Foods, was originally established as Butler County Mushroom Farms, Inc., in West Winfield, Pennsylvania, in 1937, where it used an abandoned limestone mine to grow mushrooms. By 1963, Butler had acquired a larger limestone mine in Worthington, Pennsylvania, and began to produce mushrooms there in 1966. By the early 1970s, Butler was the dominant producer of fresh mushrooms in the United States. Pennsylvania was the mushroom-growing center of the nation, in part because it was conveniently located near the largest U.S. market for mushrooms on the East Coast.

With increased competition, though, Butler found itself losing fresh mushroom market share to its major domestic competitors in the 1970s. The company began to implement alternative production and marketing strategies, one of which was to take advantage of a largely untapped market in the southeastern United States. In 1981 Butler participated in the creation of a modern above-ground mushroom-growing operation in northern Florida called Quincy Corporation.

At the same time Butler also patented its recently developed spawn production technology and constructed a facility near Kittanning, Pennsylvania, to produce spawn for the U.S. mushroom industry as well as to produce other types of fungi. In a 1984 corporate reorganization, the spawn production unit became an independent subsidiary and was named Sylvan Spawn

Company Perspectives:

Sylvan, Inc. is a key global supplier of products for mushroom growers. The company is the world's leading producer and distributor of spawn, the mushroom equivalent of seed. Sylvan has differentiated its spawn products through research, proprietary production technology and dedicated service. Its products include spawn for the Agaricus *mushroom and for other species, in particular* Pleurotus *and Shiitake. Sylvan also sells a variety of related products to mushroom growers. The company is an important U.S. producer of fresh mushrooms at Quincy Farms, its modern facility near Tallahassee, Florida.*

Sylvan distributes its spawn products primarily in North America, Europe, Australia and South America. It is expanding to markets in Asia. The company operates U.S. spawn production facilities in Pennsylvania and Nevada. It has international spawn plants in France, England, the Netherlands and Australia. In addition, Sylvan is constructing a new spawn plant in Hungary.

Laboratory, Inc., and Butler became a wholly owned subsidiary of Myco-Sci. In 1987 Butler changed its name to Moonlight Mushrooms, Inc. By that time it had closed its West Winfield underground mushroom farm and expanded the capacity of its more efficient underground farm at Worthington.

During the 1980s Quincy was able to take advantage of certain technological innovations to improve crop yields and quality. By having more pounds of fresh mushrooms available, it increased its market share and became a major producer in the Southeast. By the end of the decade it was producing about 18 million pounds annually, compared to some 50 million pounds produced at the underground farm in Worthington. In 1991 Sylvan Foods expanded capacity at the Quincy facility by 25 percent and installed technologically advanced equipment to improve productivity there.

At the end of the 1980s Sylvan Spawn Laboratory was the second largest producer of spawn in the United States. It established a modern mushroom research and development facility in West Winfield, Pennsylvania.

When Sylvan Foods acquired Myco-Sci in 1989, the company's two mushroom farms in Pennsylvania and Florida were producing 67 million pounds of mushrooms, of which approximately 61 million pounds were of fresh quality. Sylvan Spawn Laboratory had increased its net sales by an average of more than 30 percent per year for three years prior to the acquisition.

Sylvan Foods Goes Public

In February 1990, The Prospect Group, which was a majority owner of Sylvan Foods, approved a plan of liquidation to sell or distribute its assets. On August 20, 1990, Sylvan Foods became a public company as a result of the liquidation of The Prospect Group, which involved distributing shares of Sylvan Foods to Prospect's shareholders. Sylvan's financial success had made it an excellent candidate to be a publicly held company.

At the time of its liquidation, The Prospect Group held a 53.1 percent ownership interest in Sylvan Foods and distributed some 2.7 million shares of Sylvan to Prospect shareholders. Several individuals who were principals in The Prospect Group also controlled another investment firm, The Noel Group. When The Prospect Group was liquidated, it delivered shares of Sylvan Foods to individuals at Noel, so that Noel and/or its principals started off with a 5.3 percent stake in Sylvan Foods at the time it went public.

When it became a public company in 1990, Sylvan Foods had three wholly owned operating subsidiaries: Moonlight Mushrooms, Inc., Quincy Corporation, and Sylvan Spawn Laboratory, Inc. Sylvan Foods' capital structure was highly leveraged. As a result of the loan agreement in connection with the acquisition of Myco-Sci, Sylvan was required to prepay the loans in an amount equal to 75 percent of Sylvan's free cash flow after taxes, debt service, operating expenses, and capital expenditures. The payments were to be made annually from 1990 through 1995. As collateral for the loan, Sylvan granted the bank a security interest in all of its assets and a pledge of all of the capital stock of its subsidiaries.

Early 1990s Acquisitions

On October 31, 1991, Sylvan Foods acquired Somycel S.A. (France) and Darlington Mushrooms Laboratories Ltd. (England) for approximately $18 million. Somycel was the former French unit of H.J. Heinz Co. Ltd. that made mushroom spawn. The French company was Europe's leading spawn producer and was well established in the mushroom spawn market in Europe, which was twice as large as the American market. One attractive characteristic of Somycel was its strong research tradition of producing disease-resistant strains of mushroom spawn.

The purchase of Somycel made Sylvan Foods the leading provider of spawn worldwide. The deal was financed through more than $10 million in bank loans and subordinated debt. An additional $7.3 million came from the sale of one million shares of Sylvan Foods common stock to The Noel Group. Sylvan executives also sold 250,000 shares they held to Noel, giving Noel control of 25.2 percent, or 1.53 million shares, of Sylvan. The Noel Group was a closely held investment banking firm that was founded in 1969. It invested in equity securities in small-to-medium sized companies in various fields. At this time Sylvan expanded its board of directors from five to six members. The new seat was filled by Noel managing director Donald Pascal, giving Noel three seats on Sylvan's board. The other two Noel seats were held by Samuel Pryor and Gilbert Lamphere, who was formerly chairman, president, and CEO of The Prospect Group.

Sylvan Foods continued its expansion into the European spawn market in 1992 with the acquisition of Hauser Champignonkulturen AG for approximately $3.8 million. During the year Sylvan Foods reorganized its growing spawn operations, decentralizing them into specific geographic markets.

New spawn products were introduced into Central and South America and into Southeast Asia. The company also completed a 49,000-square-foot state-of-the art spawn plant in Dayton, Nevada, which began commercial production in January 1993.

Labor Troubles Spell End for Moonlight Mushrooms

Labor disputes at Moonlight Mushrooms led to a shutdown of the Worthington underground mushroom farm in 1993. It was the largest in the United States, producing about 50 million tons of mushrooms a year. It employed about 1,000 people and also provided income to farmers who grew hay and straw used in the farm. The mushrooms were grown in some 120 miles of underground tunnels.

In October 1993, workers represented by the United Steelworkers overwhelmingly rejected the wage and benefit concessions requested by Moonlight. The contract proposal was made to workers after Moonlight filed a 60-day plant closing notice that called for a shutdown by January 31, 1994. The rejected proposal called for wage cuts of 50 cents an hour, with pickers' wages—the single largest group of employees—falling to $7.48 an hour. It also limited Moonlight's company contribution for health care, meaning that employees who were paying $78 a month for family coverage would have seen their bills increase to $208 per month.

Steps to halt operations were taken immediately following the union vote and included halting deliveries of raw materials for making compost. The closing of the subsidiary removed 45 to 50 million pounds of mushrooms a year from the market. Total U.S. production of mushrooms was estimated to be about 750 million pounds. In dollar volume, mushrooms were the largest vegetable crop in Pennsylvania, and the state was the largest U.S. producer of common and cultivable exotic mushrooms. In May 1994 Sylvan Foods sold substantially all of the assets of its Moonlight Mushrooms, Inc., subsidiary to an investment group based in western Pennsylvania for an undisclosed amount. The farm eventually reopened as a non-union farm.

Name Changed to Sylvan, Inc., 1994

In his 1994 letter to shareholders, Chairman, President, and CEO Dennis C. Zensen explained, "On July 1, 1994, we changed the name of our company from Sylvan Foods Holdings, Inc., to Sylvan, Inc., because our research and production activities now focus on spawn and other technologically oriented fungal products." At the same time the company changed its state of incorporation from Delaware to Nevada.

In 1994 Sylvan set record levels of earnings and return on sales. It reported net income of $6.4 million on net sales of $69.8 million. Net sales for 1993 were $105.3 million, but that included results from the discontinued Moonlight Mushrooms subsidiary. Pro forma net sales for 1993, restated to exclude Moonlight's contribution, were $62.8 million. That meant 1994's net sales showed an 11 percent increase over 1993's adjusted net sales.

Sylvan attributed its improved profitability to its recent investments in research, people, and facilities. The company increased market share in most of its spawn markets, and for the last half of 1994 was sold out of its spawn due to strong demand. Sylvan claimed to be the spawn price leader in both North America and Europe. The company's mushroom-growing operation, Quincy Farms, also had a good year in 1994.

For 1995 Sylvan reported slightly higher net income of $6.5 million on record net sales of $75.8 million. While spawn sales rose to record levels in the United States, the company noted that its European spawn operations were constrained by limited production capacity. The company was taking several steps to increase European capacity. Its first international start-up facility, located in Horst, the Netherlands, was gradually being brought up to full production levels. It completed the modernization and expansion of its Yaxley, England, spawn facility. A new spawn production plant was under construction near Budapest, Hungary, to serve established markets in Hungary as well as emerging markets in Turkey, Yugoslavia, and Eastern European countries. The Budapest plant would record its first sales in the third quarter of 1997.

Sales of nutritional supplements for mushrooms were down in 1995, reflecting changing grower preferences. Sylvan quickly introduced a competitive product for that market and began exploring other improved nutritional supplements. The company's Casing Inoculum (CI), a product that accelerates mushroom growth, continued to show strong sales in 1995.

While Quincy Farms established new records in productivity, crop yields, and product quality in 1995, it failed to exceed its 1994 record level of profitability. Sylvan noted that soft demand for fresh mushrooms at the retail level resulted in a lower average price per pound for Quincy mushrooms. The company planned to expand Quincy's geographical distribution to shift more of its product to the fresh market.

Sylvan's operating results continued along the same lines in 1996, with strong international and domestic spawn sales offset somewhat by a soft market for fresh mushrooms. The company noted that spawn again accounted for a growing portion of Sylvan's total revenues, with net sales of spawn products increasing by 14 percent over 1995 levels. By expanding its spawn operations internationally—a new spawn production plant in Australia went onstream in mid-1996—Sylvan had truly become a global corporation. Sales outside North America had grown from $22.6 million in 1992 to $31.6 million in 1996, a 40 percent increase.

Sylvan's aggressive investment in new and expanded facilities resulted in a new spawn inoculum facility being completed in Kittanning, Pennsylvania, in the second half of 1996. The inoculum produced there would supply other Sylvan spawn production plants around the world. A second inoculum facility was planned for Langeias in central France. Inoculum is the genetic material in the mushroom spore that gets propagated and scaled up multiple times to form a mushroom. Through research and development of inoculum, Sylvan is able to maintain the genetic stability of its mushroom strains to withstand bacterial, fungal, and viral contamination that can wipe out a grower's crop.

Future Growth: International Spawn Markets

Since 1994 and earlier, Sylvan has supported its strategy of becoming a leading supplier of spawn products by investing heavily in new and expanded facilities as well as in research and development. It has engineered a shift from being primarily a mushroom grower to becoming a leading spawn supplier. In 1990, mushroom sales were about $65 million and spawn sales were only about $5 million. In 1996, mushroom sales accounted for 37 percent of total revenues, or approximately $29.3 million, the lowest in the company's history. Sylvan claimed to hold leading market share in spawn in the United States, Canada, the Netherlands, the United Kingdom, Germany, Hungary, Scandinavia, and Australia. It looked for growth to come from such markets as Ireland, Italy, France, Eastern Europe, South America, and Asia.

Internationally, Sylvan's long-term strategy recognized that Asia would eventually be the world's largest spawn market. China, the world's largest mushroom producer, was expected to become a major market for spawn products, once its method of mushroom growing evolved from a cottage industry to one that used more advanced techniques. It was Sylvan's goal to be there first, once China's mushroom growers adopted more up-to-date methods of growing.

Principal Subsidiaries

Quincy Corporation; Sylvan Spawn Laboratories, Inc.; Sylvan Foods S.A. (France); Sylvan Foods (U.K.) Ltd.; Sylvan Foods Netherlands B.V.; Sylvan Spawn Laboratory (Nevada), Inc.

Further Reading

McKay, Jim, ''Mushroom Workers Reject Offer,'' *Pittsburgh Post-Gazette,* October 16, 1993, p. C7.

——, ''New Vote Can't Save Mushroom Farm,'' *Pittsburgh Post-Gazette,* December 4, 1993, p. D7.

——, ''Sylvan, Inc. Positions to Be World's Largest Mushroom Product Distributor,'' *Pittsburgh Post-Gazette,* June 2, 1997.

Mooney, Bill, ''Shutdown of Operations Scheduled for Sylvan Foods Holdings, Inc.'s Moonlight Mushrooms Subsidiary,'' *PR Newswire,* October 18, 1993, p. 931018.

Olson, Thomas, ''Investment Group Keeps Coming Back for Sylvan's Equity,'' *Pittsburgh Business Times and Journal,* January 6, 1992.

Redd, Adrienne, ''Eastern Pa.'s Largest Vegetable Crop Mushrooming,'' *Eastern Pennsylvania Business,* June 20, 1994.

''Sylvan Foods Unit to Shut Mushroom Farm,'' Iain *Reuter Business Report,* November 4, 1993.

—David Bianco

Teva Pharmaceutical Industries Ltd.

5 Basel St.
P.O. Box 3190
Petach Tikva 49131
Israel
+972 3-926-7267
Fax: +972 3-923-4050

Public Company
Incorporated: 1944
Employees: 2850
Sales: US$954 million (1995)
Stock Exchanges: Tel Aviv NASDAQ
SICs: 2834 Pharmaceutical Preparations; 2833 Medicinals & Botanicals; 3842 Surgical Appliances & Supplies; 2099 Food Preparations, Not Elsewhere Classified; 2860 Industrial Organic Chemicals

With over one-third of the nation's drug sales, Teva Pharmaceutical Industries Ltd. is Israel's largest pharmaceutical company. Notwithstanding its domestic dominance, the majority—over two-thirds—of Teva's sales are generated outside its home market, with more than half of its annual revenues coming from North America. A series of drug developments and strategic acquisitions made Teva America's largest generic drug manufacturer by 1996. Europe was another key growth market for the Israeli company, accounting for over 17 percent of sales in 1996. Teva emphasized the development of patented drugs in the early 1990s as well, launching ethical pharmaceuticals for the treatment of multiple sclerosis and Wilson's disease. In addition to its generic and proprietary drug businesses, the company also manufactures, wholesales, and markets hospital supplies, bulk pharmaceuticals, and veterinary drugs and vaccines.

Teva's many growth strategies multiplied sales from $295 million in 1990 to $954 million in 1996. A publicly traded company since 1951, Teva saw its market value mushroom from $17 million in 1985 to $3.3 billion by January 1997, making it Israel's most valuable public firm.

Company Predates Israeli State

Teva (Hebrew for "nature") was founded in 1935 by Elsa Kuver and Dr. Gunter Friedlander in Jerusalem. The company's early history was strongly influenced by global politics. During the 1930s, three forces converged to encourage Jewish immigration into the British-controlled area then known as Palestine. Underlying this population shift was the Zionist movement, which strove to create a modern Jewish nation in the ancient Hebrew homeland. During the years between the two world wars, the British mandated partition of the region into separate Israeli and Arabic states and sanctioned Jewish immigration to certain areas of Palestine in order to create a Jewish majority. At the same time, Nazi persecution of German Jews drove hundreds of thousands to emigrate from that country. Due in part to the intervention of World War II, the establishment of an Israeli state by the United Nations did not come until 1948, but in the meantime the Jewish population of Palestine increased to over 600,000.

Prior to World War II, Germany was the center of the global pharmaceutical industry. Many immigrants from that country brought with them pharmaceutical expertise that provided a firm foundation upon which the Israeli drug industry—including Teva—was built. Notwithstanding the ongoing violence of the Middle East, Teva enjoyed some advantages over its competitors around the world. For one, there is Israel's high concentration of scientists—the nation boasts more scientists per capita than any nation in the world. Furthermore, the Israeli government granted Teva tax subsidies to encourage the development and production of new drugs. It was in this environment that Teva grew, going public in 1951 on the Tel Aviv Stock Exchange (TASE).

Industry Consolidation Begins in 1960s

Eli Hurvitz, the man who would engineer Teva's emergence on the global drug scene first became involved with Teva in 1968, when he was appointed to Teva's board of directors. Trained as an economist, Hurvitz had started his career in 1953 at Assia Chemical Laboratories. His promotion into management at Assia in 1963 coincided with the beginning of a period of consolidation within Israel's pharmaceutical industry. This

Company Perspectives:

Teva is committed to uncompromising quality standards. The Company is constantly striving to improve the efficiency of the systems that nourish research, development, production and marketing—the components needed to maintain Teva's position as a leading company in the generic global market. By investing a sizable portion of income in innovative research, supported by the firm base of Israeli science, Teva will continue to develop innovative products. Adherence to this formula will guide Teva into the next millennium stronger and bigger than ever before.

trend peaked with the 1976 union of Teva, Assia, and Zri to create the nation's largest drugmaker, Teva Pharmaceutical Industries. Hurvitz was appointed general manager (CEO) of the merged companies.

In a bid to boost its production capacity, Teva acquired its number-two competitor, Ikapharm, in 1980. The deal struck with Ikapharm parent Koor Industries—Israel's largest manufacturing concern—included an exchange of 20 percent of Teva's equity for the state-of-the-art drug plant. This element of the agreement would prove troublesome in the years to come. Having accumulated a 42 percent stake in Teva, Koor launched a bid for control in 1984. Teva's Founders Group, comprised of the stockholding heirs to Teva's originators, thwarted the takeover attempt. Though the two groups called a truce by the end of the year, Teva's ownership issues would not end there, for the company often used its equity to broker deals.

Overseas Expansion Begins in 1980s

Having consolidated its domestic position, Teva began to expand geographically in the early 1980s. The company perceived an opportunity to penetrate the U.S. market when the federal Waxman-Hatch Act passed Congress in 1984. This legislation concerned generic drugs, treatments that have lost their patent protection. Also known as multi-source or off-patent medicines, generics are chemically identical to branded prescription drugs, but are priced at 30 percent to 70 percent less than patented versions. Waxman-Hatch reduced the regulatory hurdles for generics, thereby cutting the time and money required to bring generic drugs to market. Thus, while generics were far less expensive to develop than new drugs, they also commanded far lower profit margins.

Teva used the generics segment as its entree into the American pharmaceutical market. In 1985, the company forged an agreement with chemical conglomerate W.R. Grace to create TAG Pharmaceuticals, a 50/50 joint venture. A relative newcomer to the pharmaceutical industry, Grace contributed over 90 percent of TAG's $23 million starting capital base, while Teva threw in $1.5 million and its decades of experience and expertise. In 1985, TAG acquired Lemmon Co., a Pennsylvania-based company with a tarnished history. Infamous for marketing Quaaludes in the 1970s, Lemmon had had four corporate owners in its scant 15 years in business. Under its newest parents, Lemmon became the sales and distribution arm for generics manufactured by Teva in Israel. Though CEO Hurvitz later reflected that "an Israeli who's coming to the States has a David and Goliath syndrome," he reminded himself that little David prevailed in that Biblical battle. The potential Teva saw in Lemmon soon turned to profits; the U.S. venture's sales more than doubled from $17 million at the time of its acquisition to about $40 million in 1987, by which time it was marketing seven generic versions of branded drugs.

That year, Teva raised $18.4 million through the sale of American Depositary Receipts on the NASDAQ exchange. Around the same time Koor Industries, which by this point was flirting with bankruptcy, sold $14.8 million worth of its Teva holding on the open market, thereby reducing its stake in Teva to about 22 percent. Teva used the proceeds of its equity offering to acquire Abic Ltd., Israel's second-ranking drug marketer, for $26.6 million in 1988. The deal included a provision whereby Canadian investor Charles Bronfman took an equity position in Teva. That same year, Teva acquired two Israeli companies from U.S.-based Baxter International Inc.: Travenol Laboratories (Israel) Ltd., a manufacturer of health care products and equipment, and Travenol Trading Company Ltd., an importer of Baxter products, for a total of $8.2 million.

Meanwhile, as part of a $1 billion debt restructuring, Koor transferred its stake in Teva to two creditors, Israeli banks Hapoalim and Leumi. The banks, in turn, sold about 17 percent of Teva to British publishing magnate Robert Maxwell for $30.2 million. The Maxwell connection was cut in 1993, when his estate divested the holding for $166 million, a significant appreciation. Teva severed its ties to W.R. Grace in 1991, when it purchased Grace's 50 percent share of TAG Pharmaceuticals for $35 million. Grace, in turn, divested its stake in Teva to the public for $36.4 million.

Teva's sales more than doubled from less than $100 million in 1987 to $268.5 million in 1989, and net increased from about $7 million to over $16 million during the same period. While this growth rate must have been a source of pride for CEO Hurvitz and his executive team, it would pale in comparison to the increases chalked up in the 1990s.

Acquisitions and New Drugs Play Vital Roles in 1990s Growth

In the early 1990s, Teva invested aggressively in acquisitions, research and development, and increased production capacity. From 1992 through 1996, Teva spent a total of over $420 million on a rash of acquisitions that extended its reach into France, Italy, Great Britain, and Hungary. Teva's U.S. sales surpassed its domestic revenues in 1993, and overseas employment exceeded native workers three years later. In 1996 alone, Teva acquired Approved Prescription Services/Berk, the U.K.'s second-largest generic drug marketer and Hungary's Biogal. That same year, Teva catapulted to the top of the U.S. generics segment via a $290 million stock swap with America's Biocraft Laboratories, Inc. Since the merger was structured as a pooling of interests, Teva restated its financial information as if the two companies had always been one. [Editor's note: This corporate history quotes actual financial figures.]

During this same time, Teva plowed hundreds of millions into research and development and capital improvements. The company's new drug developments concentrated on so-called ''orphan'' drugs in the therapeutic areas of neurological disorders and autoimmune diseases. The term is most often used to describe compounds that are discovered by major drug companies, but whose patents have been allowed to lapse because the disease or condition targeted by the drug has too few patients to justify the development expenditures required to bring it to market. Smaller companies like Teva who ''adopted'' an orphan drug could apply for a new seven-year, exclusive patent on the compound, thereby allowing it time to make a profitable return on its investment.

Generics continued to form the core of Teva's sales. From January 1996 through July 1997, in fact, Teva garnered more generic drug approvals from the U.S. Food and Drug Administration than any other company in the world. However, proprietary drugs emerged as a high-profit growth vehicle in the early 1990s. The company's first major new drug, known as Copaxone, was originated more than two decades earlier in the laboratories of Israel's Weizmann Institute, where doctoral student Dvora Teitelbaum was studying the use of synthetic proteins to quell multiple sclerosis (MS) attacks in animals. Together with Professors Michael Sela and Ruth Arnon, Teitelbaum spent 15 years isolating and researching the polymer COP-1 (later branded Copaxone), passing preliminary clinical trials in 1986. The treatment reduced the relapse rate for people in the early stages of relapsing-remitting MS by anywhere from 25 percent to 30 percent in clinical trials. At that time, the Weizmann Institute teamed up with Teva to bring the drug to market. Since Copaxone's patent had expired during the long development process, Teva requested and received orphan drug status from the U.S. Food and Drug Administration (FDA). About one-third of America's 350,000 MS sufferers stood to benefit from the treatment.

Initially launched in Israel, Copaxone earned FDA approval in 1997 and was expected to be approved for sale in Canada and Europe by the end of that year. The rollout achieved several milestones, both for Teva and for MS sufferers. Copaxone was the first drug developed in Israel to achieve FDA approval for distribution in America. Unlike its interferon-based competitors, it was also the first drug developed specifically to treat MS.

Since Teva had little experience marketing branded drugs on the world stage, it enlisted the help of global pharmaceutical powerhouse Hoechst Marion Roussel. This ''David and Goliath'' team formed a joint venture, Teva Marion Partners (TMP), to coordinate distribution. Initial sales reports on the drug were promising. Within one month of its launch, TMP recorded 10,000 inquiries from doctors and patients about Copaxone. Within six weeks, the company had 4,000 patients on the daily injection program and reported adding over 1,000 more each month. Analysts forecast that Copaxone alone would add at least $50 million to Teva's sales total in 1997 and increase from there.

The story of Teva's transformation from a tiny Israeli drug company into an international pharmaceutical innovator garnered a great deal of attention from investment houses around the world in the mid-1990s. Even before the Copaxone launch, Teva's sales had tripled from $295 million in 1990 to $954 million in 1996 as net income increased from $18.7 million to $73.2 million. But while leading brokerage houses like Merrill Lynch, Standard & Poor's, and AG Edwards had rated the stock a ''buy,'' it remained a highly volatile equity, surging from less than $50 per share in April 1997 to $67 in June, then backsliding to $57 in September.

This roller-coaster performance could be attributed to any number of black marks on Teva's record. In March 1996, CEO Hurvitz was indicted on charges that he had evaded $18 million in corporate taxes as head of Teva's Promedico subsidiary (since divested) from 1980 to 1986. Nonetheless, Teva's board signed him to a five-year contract in January 1997. That August, Teva was subjected to an FDA recall on a batch of antibiotics. The problem (which rendered the drugs ''less effective, but not harmful,'' Teva officials emphasized) was traced to a supplier. That same year found the company in a dispute over Copaxone royalties with its development partner, the Weizmann Institute. And Teva U.S. subsidiary GATE pharmaceuticals was named among the nine defendants in a class action suit over the diet drug fen-phen.

Still, most of the investment firms following Teva stood by the company. In July 1997, U.S. brokerage Gruntal & Co. asserted that ''Teva should be seen as a rising star in the dynamic world medical drug market.'' Israeli business newspaper *Globes* has called the company ''This century's Israeli success story.'' With several new drugs in the pipeline and ongoing development of generic drugs, Teva appeared poised to carry through its saga of success into the 21st century.

Principal Subsidiaries

Teva Pharmaceuticals USA, Inc.; Abic Ltd. (99.3%); Salomon, Levin and Elstein Ltd.; Asia Chemical Industries Ltd; Plantex Ltd.; West-European; Biogal Pharmaceutical Works Ltd. (Hungary; 97%); Approved Prescription Services Ltd. (U.K.); Prosintex-Industrie Chimiche Italiane S.r.l. (Italy); Teva Medical Ltd.; Teva medical Trading Ltd.; Gry-Pharma GmbH (Germany; 93.3%); Biological Laboratories Teva Ltd.; Paca Industries Ltd.; Teva Holdings Ltd.; Prographarm Laboratories (France; 34%); Portman Pharmaceuticals Inc. (U.S.A.; 30%).

Further Reading

Beck, Galit Lipkis, ''Teva to Raise More Than $100M in US Bond Issue,'' *Jerusalem Post,* February 25, 1997, p. 8.

''Blimey: Koor,'' *Economist,* April 3, 1993, pp. 66–67.

Burton, Jonathan, ''Eli Hurvitz,'' *Chief Executive,* July/August 1995, p. 24.

Byrne, Harlan S., ''Teva Pharmaceutical,'' *Barron's,* February 7, 1994, pp. 53–54.

''Copaxone Maintains Teva Optimism,'' *Israel Business Today,* July 15, 1997, p. 16.

Dichek, Bernard, ''Teva Pharmaceuticals Industries,'' *Israel Business Today,* August 27, 1993, p. 35.

Friedlin, Jennifer, ''Playing with the Big Boys,'' *Jerusalem Post,* October 16, 1996, p. 6.

Goldgaber, Arthur, ''Teva Pharmaceutical: Slammer Dunk,'' *Financial World,* April 15, 1997, pp. 26–27.

Mann, David, and Cynthia Miller, ''Israeli Company Develops Breakthrough MS Treatment,'' *Northern California Jewish Bulletin,* October 14, 1994.

''Medical Success Story: With Copolymer-1, Weizmann Scientists Offer M.S. Patients the Gift of Hope,'' *Jewish Exponent,* January 23, 1997.

Olster, Marjorie, ''In the Land of the Profit$: A Guide to Personal Investing in Israel,'' *MOMENT,* August 31, 1995.

Reichert, Kent, ''After Rocky History, Fletcher Pins Hopes on Lemmon Partners,'' *Philadelphia Business Journal,* October 12, 1987, pp. 1–3.

Sandler, Neal, ''Grace Ups Its Stake in Teva,'' *Chemical Week,* August 5, 1987, p. 12.

Sivy, Michael, ''Soaring to Lofty Profits on the Wings of Peace,'' *Money,* November 1993, pp. 54–56.

''Teva Pharmaceutical Industries Ltd.,'' http://www.macom.co.il/Government/MIT/economy/Done-vol1/teva.html.

Timor, Emanuel, and Ronen Kotlowsky, ''Teva: This Century's Israeli Success Story,'' *Globes,* http//www.globes.co.il/cgi-bin/Serve_Arena/level/English/1.4.4/19970123/1.

—April Dougal Gasbarre

THIOKOL

AEROSPACE & INDUSTRIAL TECHNOLOGIES

Thiokol Corporation

2475 Washington Blvd.
Ogden, Utah 84401-2398
U.S.A.
(801) 629-2270
Fax: (801) 629-2251
Web site: http://www.thiokol.com

Public Company
Incorporated: 1929 as Thiokol Chemical Corporation
Employees: 5,300
Sales: $890.1 million (1997)
Stock Exchanges: New York Pacific Boston Midwest Philadelphia
SICs: 3053 Gaskets, Packing & Sealing Devices; 3324 Steel Investment Foundries; 3369 Nonferrous Foundries, Except Aluminum & Copper; 3452 Bolts, Nuts, Screws, Rivets & Washers; 3483 Ammunition, Except Small Arms, Not Elsewhere Classified; 3546 Power-Driven Hand Tools; 3764 Guided Missile & Space Vehicle Propulsion Units & Propulsion Unit Parts

Thiokol Corporation is the world's largest producer of solid rocket motors and other parts for the aerospace and defense industries. Its Huck International, Inc. subsidiary manufactures precision fastening systems for international aerospace and industrial markets, while Howmet Corporation—a company Thiokol holds a majority stake in—is a leader in precision cast superalloy and titanium components for turbine engines used in jet aircraft and in utility power generation. Thiokol regained its independence from the salt and chemicals conglomerate Morton International in 1989, when Thiokol's rocket boosters were cited as the cause of the 1986 *Challenger* space shuttle explosion. Thiokol had been acquired by Morton in 1982 as part of that company's attempt to protect itself from unwelcome takeover attempts and diversify into markets unrelated to its core salt and chemical operations. Since regaining its independence, Thiokol itself has rapidly diversified its mix of operations.

Origins in 1926 Invention of Synthetic Rubber

Thiokol owes its origins to two chemists, Joseph C. Patrick and Nathan Mnookin, who were trying to invent an inexpensive antifreeze. In 1926, in the course of an experiment involving ethylene dichloride and sodium polysulfide, they created a gum whose outstanding characteristic was a terrible odor. The substance clogged a sink in the laboratory, and none of the solvents used to remove it were successful. Then the frustrated chemists realized that the resistance of the material to any kind of solvent was a useful property. They had invented synthetic rubber, which they christened "Thiokol," from the Greek words for sulfur (*theion*) and glue (*kolla*). Thiokol Chemical Corporation was subsequently founded on December 5, 1929.

Mnookin and Patrick initially negotiated with Standard Oil to develop the product, but they could not reach an agreement. Finally, a salt merchant named Bevis Longstreth provided the financial support for the construction of a plant in Kansas City, Missouri. The plant, however, produced an odor so obnoxious that local residents asked the mayor to remove the company from the area. As a result, Thiokol was forced to move to Trenton, New Jersey, in 1935.

At the onset of World War II the company hoped that the rubber shortage would increase demand for Thiokol, but organic rubber was recycled instead. Thiokol Inc. was thus relegated to making hoses for specialized uses during the wartime period. Dow Chemical Co. purchased 30 percent of Thiokol in 1948, and later sold its share of the company on the open market in 1953, when, according to Wall Street analysts, Thiokol was not a promising takeover candidate. In 1944, when Bevis Longstreth died, no one on the board of directors was willing to replace him; Joseph W. Crosby, a department head, ended up in Longstreth's position as vice-president and general manager.

Moved into Defense Contracting in the Mid-1940s

When it was brought to Crosby's attention that the Jet Propulsion Laboratory at the California Institute of Technology was buying large quantities of the company's solvent resistant polymer, he decided to talk to some of the institute's scientists.

Company Perspectives:

We are a company of high integrity and excellence. We continually enhance our commitment to safety and quality. We have highly competent, dedicated employees. We have management, technical, and manufacturing expertise that puts us in an industry leadership position. We have the desire to achieve, excel, and win.

We engineer and manufacture solid propulsion motors, fastening systems, and, through our Howmet affiliate, high-performance castings. Our customers are leading global manufacturers in aerospace, transportation, and industrial markets and the United States government. We strive to maintain leadership through technical excellence and new product development using optimum designs, processes, and facilities. We have a strong, established business base in our current markets, and we are aggressively expanding into additional new markets where there is potential for growth and above-average financial returns.

There he learned that the polymer was the best rocket fuel the scientists had ever used.

In the 1950s, the first rockets were powered by liquid fuel. This required heavy tanks to hold not only the fuel and the oxidizer but also the binding agent that held them together. Rocket fuel was so dangerous that one part fuel was mixed with four parts oxidizer to reduce flammability. Thiokol's polymer began attracting attention because it was fuel and binding agent in one.

Management at Thiokol decided to go straight to the military with its product, and the U.S. Army agreed to finance a laboratory. Research began even before the building was finished. The company's research director recalled mixing propellant late at night in a room illuminated by his car's headlights before any electric lights had been installed.

The Korean War benefited Thiokol considerably. Solid rocket fuel began to displace liquid, and the company's solvent resistant sealants were selling very well. During this time Thiokol began to design and manufacture rocket engines, and with a 70 percent share of the solid rocket fuel market the company achieved a significant measure of success.

During the 1960s the company worked on the propulsion systems for the Minuteman 3 rocket, the Poseidon submarine, and the Sam-D missile. It also provided flares and other pyrotechnic devices for the war in Vietnam. Almost two-thirds of the company's business came from the government; in fact, Crosby spent as much time in Washington as he did at the company's headquarters in Trenton, New Jersey.

Although Thiokol conducted most of its business with the government at this time, during the 1960s it also became involved in several humanitarian projects. Thiokol's educational division operated training programs for the unemployed, including Native Americans. Housing programs for low-income residents of Gulfport, Mississippi, and Raleigh, North Carolina, were also administered by Thiokol. The company's extensive contact with the military gave it an edge in the competition for these educational and housing programs, which were government-funded.

While government contracts were lucrative, they were also undependable, since programs were funded according to the policies of the political party in power. To ensure its continued success, Thiokol used its income from aerospace contracts to diversify into specialty chemicals, fibers, off-road vehicles, and household products such as Spray-n-Wash. While the market for these products was somewhat cyclical, demand was not linked in any direct way to the political climate, which influenced the size and number of the government programs that Thiokol depended on. The need to partially disassociate itself from the U.S. government became clear in 1970 when fewer government contracts caused sales to drop from $245 million to $205 million. After the market for synthetic fibers declined in 1975, Thiokol again reappraised its situation and decided to rely on specialty chemicals as the division that would provide the company with financial stability in case aerospace contracts were discontinued. The fiber and off-road operations were sold.

Takeover by Morton Industries in 1982

In the 1970s Thiokol experienced a 20 percent annual growth rate. The specialty chemicals and the Texize household products divisions were performing well, while the military contracts remained lucrative. Towards the end of the decade Thiokol became a prime candidate for merger with Morton Industries, which had embarked on a diversification program and was attracted to Thiokol's control of 40 percent of the solid rocket fuels market, as well as its lucrative Texize household products division. Morton's interest in Thiokol came out of necessity—it needed debt on its balance sheet to repel takeover bids. In addition, the company's previous attempts at diversification showed only mixed results. In Thiokol, Morton also saw a company concentrated in the rapidly growing defense industry. Propelled by feverish expansion under the Reagan administration, Thiokol stood to benefit greatly from its established role as a special-purpose rocket builder. Morton considered it possible to invest the vast profits from its salt and chemical businesses into highly lucrative new Thiokol rocket systems. Indeed, Thiokol's place as the supplier of rockets to America's ambitious space shuttle program positioned it well for work in Reagan's strategic defense initiative.

Morton completed its takeover of Thiokol in 1982. One year later a severe disagreement arose between the upper management of each company. As a result, the top management at Thiokol walked out. Among the defectors was Robert Davies, president of Thiokol, considered one of the brightest executives in the aerospace and chemical industries. Four other high-level executives with experience in aerospace either retired or quit when Davies left. Consequently, Morton's Charles S. Locke was given complete control of both companies.

Despite these defections, few industry analysts questioned the wisdom of the Thiokol-Morton merger. In the first year after the merger the company posted record earnings. Two years later earnings per share increased 26 percent. Morton's and Thiokol's specialty chemicals divisions worked well together, and the new company offered chemical purification products, electronics and metal recovery chemicals, coatings, polymers, and chemicals for the electronics industry.

The household products division saw many of its items, including Glass Plus, Yes Detergent, and Spray & Wash, achieve a 10 to 20 percent market growth in a crowded and highly competitive field. To further strengthen its position in the household products market, Morton Thiokol began to manufacture its own packaging materials, becoming one of the first companies in the industry to do so. In 1985 the household products division was sold to Dow Chemical in order to prevent an attempted takeover by that chemical firm.

1986 Challenger *Disaster Led to 1989 Demerger of Morton and Thiokol*

In the mid-1980s, Morton Thiokol's staff of engineers won a contract to produce rocket boosters for NASA's space shuttle *Challenger.* On January 28, 1986, NASA reportedly asked Morton Thiokol for its approval to go ahead with the launch of the shuttle *Challenger,* despite temperatures that had dipped below freezing. Company engineers, who knew that the shuttle's boosters were not rated for operation below 40 degrees, were ignored in the executive-level decision process. Just over a minute after launch, a flare of fire from one of the boosters ignited the shuttle's external fuel tank, destroying the orbiter and killing its seven astronauts.

While Locke ordered an investigation of the accident, he failed to handle the public relations crisis that followed. At one point after the blast he told the *Wall Street Journal* that "the shuttle thing will cost us ten cents a share." While quoted out of context, Locke nonetheless came across as callous and tactless. In a demonstration of good faith, Locke conducted more than $400 million of redesign work on the boosters, working at cost.

The company suffered further damage in December 1987 when an explosion at its MX missile plant killed five employees. Furthermore, work on the boosters revealed new design flaws that had to be corrected. In 1989, despite extensive redesign work and the resumption of shuttle flights, Morton Thiokol lost a bid for a new booster design to Lockheed Corporation. At this point, Locke decided to spin off the Thiokol division.

Before dividing the companies, Locke transferred Thiokol's chemical businesses to the Morton side of the company. Morton also retained Thiokol's promising automotive airbag business. The companies were officially split on July 1, 1989, when Locke offered stockholders shares in Morton International, with options to trade them for Thiokol shares. Morton International, with $1.4 billion in sales and 8,000 employees, remained concentrated mostly in chemicals and salt, while investing nearly $100 million in its airbag business.

Independent Thiokol Diversified in the 1990s

Utah-based Thiokol Corporation emerged as a $1.1 billion company with 12,000 employees. Nevertheless, its profitable chemicals and airbag businesses had been carved away by Morton—all that remained was rockets. With greatly relaxed tensions between the United States and the Soviet Union, defense spending began to fall. Thiokol's new management team—retired U.S. Air Force general Robert T. Marsh as chairman and Edwin Garrison as president and CEO—found itself in charge of a company with a declining market and the prospect of losing the shuttle booster business to Lockheed.

During this time, however, NASA was strapped for funds, and, unwilling to carry the development costs of Lockheed's trouble-plagued booster, the agency expressed interest in extending its contract with Thiokol and its proven boosters. Thiokol subsequently signed a contract in 1991 to supply NASA with 142 solid rocket motors for the space shuttle program through 1997. Thiokol also began looking for commercial markets, finding a new customer in Motorola, whose 77-satellite Iridium system would provide seamless, worldwide cellular telephone service. Motorola hoped to use Thiokol's Castor rockets to get its system into orbit.

Despite these positive developments, the overall market for propulsion systems continued to decline as the 1990s continued. While Thiokol derived more than $1 billion in net sales from its propulsion operations in the early 1990s, by fiscal 1997 this figure had been reduced to $606.1 million. Given this obvious trend, Thiokol moved decisively to make itself less dependent on its propulsion operations.

In 1991 Marsh retired and Garrison added the chairmanship of Thiokol to his duties, remaining president and CEO. Late that same year, Thiokol purchased Huck Manufacturing Company for $150 million as part of its diversification effort. Huck, based in Irvine, California, made high grade rivets, lock bolts, and other fasteners for industrial and commercial transportation systems—notably nondefense markets. Huck was soon renamed Huck International, Inc. and operated as a subsidiary of Thiokol. Thiokol subsequently bolstered Huck through the 1992 acquisition of a majority interest in the German-based Kamax-Aerobolt GmbH & Co. KG, a maker of fasteners for the European market; the early 1994 acquisition of the Deutsch Fastener Company, an aerospace fastener maker based in California; and the February 1995 purchase of Automatic Fastener Corporation, a Branford, Connecticut-based producer of rivets for the automotive and light truck markets. Meanwhile, in June 1993 Garrison retired as president and CEO (remaining chairman), with John R. Myers replacing him. But after Myers resigned only four months later, James R. Wilson was named president and CEO of Thiokol. In October 1995 Garrison retired as chairman, and Wilson assumed that role as well.

In December 1995 Thiokol and the Carlyle Group, a Washington D.C.-based private merchant bank, joined forces to acquire Howmet Corporation, with Thiokol holding an initial 49 percent of Howmet and Carlyle 51 percent. The Greenwich, Connecticut-based Howmet, with annual revenues of about $900 million, was a world leader in the manufacture of precision castings of superalloys and titanium, utilized primarily for jet aircraft and industrial gas turbine engine components. Thiokol had an option to purchase all of Carlyle's interest in Howmet after three years. In late 1997, however, Thiokol and Carlyle reached an agreement whereby Thiokol would purchase an additional 11 percent of Howmet, while at the same time Carlyle would sell common stock of Howmet through an initial public offering. Following the IPO, Thiokol would have a majority stake in Howmet. Beginning two years after the IPO, Thiokol would have the option of purchasing Carlyle's remaining shares in Howmet at market price.

Through its acquisition of Huck and its majority stake in Howmet, Thiokol had succeeded in rapidly diversifying itself. In 1991 all of the company's profits derived from propulsion systems, while by 1997 Huck and Howmet accounted for 16 percent and 39 percent, respectively, of Thiokol profits. Meanwhile, during this period, the company was restructuring its propulsion operations both to reflect an increasing emphasis on commercial markets over those of defense and to make them more efficient. During fiscal 1997, Thiokol created a single Thiokol Propulsion Group under which were consolidated three divisions—space, defense and launch vehicles, and science and engineering. The company named Robert Crippen, former astronaut and former director of NASA's Kennedy Space Center, to head the new group as its first president.

Approaching a new century, Thiokol was counting on its new Propulsion Group to increasingly seek out commercial customers for its boosters, as the defense market continued to look weak. The company, which had virtually erased its debt by 1997, was at the same time in a very strong position to increase its stake in Howmet and to seek out acquisitions that would further beef up Huck.

Principal Subsidiaries

Huck International, Inc.; Howmet Corporation (60%).

Further Reading

''After an Aerospace Spin-off, Morton Is Ready for an Upswing,'' *Chemical Week,* May 23, 1990, pp. 14–19.

Bancroft, Thomas, ''Morton Thiokol: New Beginnings?,'' *Financial World,* April 4, 1989, p. 22.

Dorfman, John R., ''Thiokol Is Now Less Dependent on Aerospace, But It Still Can't Get Investors to Take a Flier,'' *Wall Street Journal,* August 30 1996, p. C2.

''Morton Thiokol Completes Spinoff,'' *Journal of Commerce,* July 6, 1989.

''Morton Thiokol Is to Spin Off Chemical Line, *Wall Street Journal,* February 28, 1988, p. A3.

''Morton Thiokol: Reflections on the Shuttle Disaster,'' *Business Week,* March 14, 1988, pp. 82–91.

Siler, Charles, ''Life Beyond Challenger,'' *Forbes,* September 21, 1987, p. 44.

Smith, Bruce A., and Anthony L. Velocci, Jr., ''Howmet Purchase Helps Thiokol Diversify,'' *Aviation Week & Space Technology,* October 23, 1995, pp. 68, 72.

—John Simley
—updated by David E. Salamie

Thorn Apple Valley, Inc.

26999 Central Park, Suite 300
Southfield, Michigan 48076
U.S.A.
(248) 213-1000
Fax: (248) 213-1104
Web site: http://www.tavi.com

Public Company
Incorporated: 1959 as Frederick Packing Company
Employees: 4,274
Sales: $955.8 million (1997)
Stock Exchanges: NASDAQ
SICs: 2011 Meat Packing Plants; 2013 Sausages & Other Prepared Meats

Thorn Apple Valley, Inc. is a major producer of consumer packaged meat and poultry products in the United States. The company manufactures bacon, hot dogs, luncheon meats, hams, smoked sausages, and turkey products as well as numerous other products, marketing them under premium and other proprietary brand labels. The products are sold nationally to wholesalers, supermarkets, and food service operators. Thorn Apple also is one of the nation's largest slaughterers of hogs and sells fresh pork to other manufacturers of meat and poultry products throughout the United States.

Early History

The founder of Thorn Apple, Henry Dorfman, emigrated to the United States from Poland after World War II. He and his father escaped the Treblinka concentration camp that held many of his family members and other Polish Jews by jumping from a train. For the next three years, the two men hid in tunnels in central Poland. A master butcher by trade, Dorfman found work after the war selling meat to the U.S. government for officials living in Germany.

In 1949 Dorfman emigrated to the United States, settled in Detroit, and opened a butcher shop. Ten years later he and a partner bought Frederick Packing Company, a small hog slaughtering facility in Detroit. Dorfman was the primary owner of the company and the operation's driving force. The company purchased, butchered, and sold pork to consumers and wholesalers.

In less than two years, Dorfman had repaid his purchase loan for Frederick Packing. He then began to expand the operation by acquiring other small slaughterhouses and meat processing plants located in the East and Midwest. Following additional acquisitions—including the purchase of Herrud and Company of Grand Rapids, Michigan, in 1969—Dorfman changed the company's name to Frederick and Herrud to better reflect the diversification of its operations into manufacturing and processing, in addition to packing. The former Herrud later became Thorn Apple's Grand Rapids Division, which manufactured smoked sausages, hot dogs, and luncheon meats. In the early 1970s, Dorfman acquired meat businesses in North Carolina that produced deli products, smoked meat products, and bacon; these companies eventually became a part of Thorn Apple's Carolina Division in Holly Ridge, North Carolina.

Went Public in 1971

In 1971 the company reincorporated in Delaware to take advantage of the tax and business benefits offered by that state's incorporation laws. Also that year, Dorfman took his company public and began trading stocks on the NASDAQ. In the initial public offering, his family retained 70 percent of the shares. With some of the capital proceeds from the $16 per share purchase price, Dorfman bought two meat processing companies in Michigan and one in North Carolina. His expansion strategy involved acquiring small regional competitors that had achieved strong brand identities and consumer awareness and improving operating efficiencies by consolidating production into his existing plants. One of the company's next purchases was the Colonial hot dog brand in Massachusetts. Colonial's Boston plant was closed, and production was moved to plants in Michigan and North Carolina. In 1977 the company reincorporated again in Michigan because of changes in the state's business laws and to reflect the location of the corporate headquarters in the Detroit suburb of Southfield.

Company Perspectives:

Thorn Apple Valley has become a leading meat producer with a broad range of both private label and branded products in all of the major product categories. Our product portfolio includes several #1-selling national branded products. We have substantially increased our market coverage, and we are poised to experience the benefits of our aggressive facility expansion and renovation program. We are well positioned for significant growth, and we plan to leverage our reputation as a provider of premium quality products and service to return to profitability and grow the Company in the years ahead.

In the early 1980s many large food conglomerates were taking over independent meatpackers to increase their market shares. Dorfman, by contrast, believed that future success depended on producing meats more cheaply than the conglomerates and giving consumers a better product. Despite a soft economy and a stagnant meatpacking industry, he increased capital expenditures for plant modernization and improvements and devoted resources to product development and production. While this strategy resulted in several lean years for the company, Dorfman accepted the limited financial return as the cost of building a strong corporate infrastructure.

Repositioned As Supplier of Premium Products in the Mid-1980s

Also during this period, the company changed its image to a producer of high quality and premium brand products. To reflect this change, in 1984 Dorfman renamed the company Thorn Apple Valley, which was one of its marketing names for premium products. Later that same year, the company expanded to become vertically integrated and began operation of National Food Express, Inc., a transportation subsidiary intended to ensure prompt delivery of perishable products from its Grand Rapids Division to its customers.

Despite the company's expanded market penetration, Thorn Apple's stock performed poorly, due in large part to the company's significant reliance on the unstable hog market. In 1987 the stock had declined to three dollars per share, a reduction of approximately three quarters of the original offering price three years earlier. Dorfman's son Joel wanted to take over the business and implement some new business practices to which he believed the market would react positively, but Dorfman was reluctant to step aside. However, when one of the nation's largest meat processing companies, Smithfield Foods, initiated a stock purchase for Thorn Apple at $10 a share in 1987, both Dorfmans agreed that something needed to be done. They declined Smithfield's purchase offer and set out to change the company's organizational structure and strategic posture.

Under the leadership of Joel Dorfman as president, the company operated according to a motto that was engraved on a plaque in the corporate conference room: "We are through just surviving." Because the company's decentralized structure resulted in duplicated efforts among the various Thorn Apple divisions, Joel reorganized the divisions into a centralized structure. He also made fundamental changes in plant utilization, production, marketing, and advertising.

Acquisitions continued, and in 1988 Thorn Apple began to expand into the western part of the United States with the purchase of the Tri-Miller Packing Company, a regional meat processing company in Hyrum, Utah. Tri-Miller was a successful full-line pork processor with slaughtering and production activities at its plant. Shortly thereafter Thorn Apple acquired another transportation company, Miller's Transport, Inc., to handle distribution and delivery service in the western United States.

Marketing was changed to emphasize premium products with a higher profit margin and newer items, such as turkey products, that reflected consumer preferences for leaner meats. By 1991 Thorn Apple's sales of premium products accounted for 40 percent of the company's manufactured products, up significantly from 28 percent in 1990.

The company's stock began to improve. Further changes included a tightening of the management structure, continued alterations to the marketing plan, and the establishment of a central distribution warehouse in Detroit. Plant operations were revised to eliminate plant managers, and renovations to the plants were designed to give each employee more room and time to work. Significant gains were made in the production yields of fresh pork. Yields, or the amount of meat from the hog that is able to be sold, improved three percent per hog to 59 percent between 1989 and 1991. This improved efficiency directly affected the company's bottom line; for every one percent of additional meat salvaged, revenues increased $6 million.

Improved Financial Performance in Early 1990s

By December 1991 Thorn Apple completed a public offering of 300,000 shares of common stock. The net proceeds of approximately $9 million were used to reduce short-term debt, finance working capital needs, and make acquisitions. In July 1992 the company spent $3.8 million to acquire the assets of Suzannah Farms, a meat processor in Pennsauken, New Jersey, that had net sales in 1991 of $38 million. Production of the Suzannah line of products was moved to Thorn Apple's Deli and Smoked Meats Division plant in Detroit. At the same time, the company contracted with Atlanta Corporation of Elizabeth, New Jersey, the license holder for Suzannah Farms' brand name, to make hams and related meat products under the trademark Krakus. This acquisition and licensing agreement helped position Thorn Apple to improve the company's penetration in the deli market and food service.

Financially, Thorn Apple performed well in the early 1990s. It was among the top U.S. food and beverage companies despite posted losses in 1990. In 1991 the company had the highest percentage of return on invested capital at 38.4 percent and the fourth best percentage sales gains, bettering such companies as Coca-Cola, Kellogg, and General Mills. Thorn Apple ranked 17th in sales among U.S. meatpackers in 1991. The company achieved average annual rates of 6.7 percent growth in sales, 89.8 percent growth in earnings per share, and an improvement of 1.2 percent in net income to net sales from 1988 to 1992.

Management attributed the increases to improved marketing efforts, streamlined operations, and a reduction in the volatility of fresh meat margins, which was in large part due to advances in purchasing strategies and the company's overall reduction of fresh meat in its total production mix.

In 1992 Thorn Apple enhanced profitability by maintaining its position as a low-cost producer of consumer packaged meat and poultry products and high-quality fresh pork. The company improved its manufactured product mix of consumer packaged higher-margin products such as turkey and smoked sausage and increased its capacity and sales of higher-margin value-added items such as boneless products and shelf-ready products. Sales of high-quality products were enhanced late in 1991 with the acquisition of Cavanaugh Lakeview Farms in Chelsea, Michigan, a seller of gourmet meat products under the Cavanaugh name. Thorn Apple's other premium brand products were marketed under the following labels: Thorn Apple Valley, Colonial, Triple M, Herrud, Bar H, Royal Crown, and Ole Virginie.

The majority of earnings in the early 1990s came from the company's manufactured products division, where strong earnings growth is dependent upon manufacturing efficiencies and increased sales volume of premium product lines. Generally, manufactured meat and poultry products have a profit margin that is three times higher than fresh pork and related byproducts, which are heavily influenced by market conditions. Specifically, hog prices are cyclical and determined by supply and demand; these in turn directly affect the cost and profit margin of fresh pork and related products.

Improved operating efficiencies in manufactured products were achieved through increasing capacity and reducing ineffective production processes. Sausage and related products production at the Grand Rapids Division increased from 150,000 pounds per week to approximately 2.5 million pounds weekly in the 1990s. The Deli and Smoked Meats Division in Detroit increased from 200,000 pounds weekly to over three million pounds weekly, and bacon production was increased to over two million pounds weekly from 300,000 pounds per week at the Carolina Division. Annual hog slaughtering averaged 5,000 at the Tri-Miller Packing Company subsidiary. Production of various processed meats increased to 700,000 pounds weekly since Thorn Apple's purchase of the Utah company in 1988.

In the early 1990s, Thorn Apple sold its fresh pork and manufacturing products to more than 900 customers in the United States, Canada, and several Pacific Rim countries. No single customer was responsible for more than 10 percent of the company's sales, and the 10 largest customers represented less than 30 percent of total sales. International sales for fiscal year 1992 were 1.5 percent of the company's total sales. Management expected additional opportunities for increased sales of fresh pork and processed meat in Korea, Japan, and Mexico in the mid to late 1990s to increase that total percentage.

Thorn Apple paid its first quarterly cash dividend to shareholders in 1992, which reflected a slight decline in the company's perceived need for capital. Marketing enhancements focused on customer-oriented satisfaction through the introduction of value-added products such as vacuum packaged boneless pork, which is distributed to retail outlets and exported to Japan. The company also continued to develop strong wholesaler and retailer loyalty through dependable service and delivery of consistently high quality products.

Restructuring Efforts Highlighted Mid-1990s

Thorn Apple's performance in the mid-1990s lagged behind that of the early 1990s, as net sales stagnated from fiscal 1992 through fiscal 1995 and net income fell each year, from the high of $21.1 million in 1992 to just $5.3 million in 1995. Although net sales increased dramatically in fiscal 1996, the increase was largely attributable to a major acquisition and meanwhile the company posted a net loss of $21.7 million. These financial travails were not, however, a harbinger of a long-term decline but rather reflected a company in transition, restructuring and repositioning itself for future growth.

Among the main aims of Thorn Apple's restructuring were the modernizing of its plants, the lowering of costs as a byproduct of this modernization, and the shifting and adding to production and distribution facilities to make them more strategically located. In an early move in the restructuring, Thorn Apple in early 1995 recorded a $7.9 million restructuring charge to close Tri-Miller Packing, whose facilities were considered redundant after the expansion of the company's Grand Rapids, Michigan, plant, and to move and consolidate the corporate headquarters.

Shortly thereafter, in May 1995, Thorn Apple paid $64.6 million to acquire the Wilson Foods Retail Division from Foodbrands America, Inc. In the process, the company gained three production facilities—in Forrest City, Arkansas; Shreveport, Louisiana; and Concordia, Missouri (the last two of these were shut down within a year of the acquisition to further consolidate production)—and two premium brands, Wilson and Corn King, used for hot dogs, luncheon meats, ham products, and specialty sausage items. The addition of Wilson certified boneless hams gave Thorn Apple Valley five number-one selling national branded products, building on the company's top-selling bun-sized skinless smoked sausage and its three top-selling premium sliced luncheon meats: ham, turkey breast, and turkey ham. The Wilson Foods acquisition was also of strategic importance geographically because it provided Thorn Apple with a larger presence in the Midwest, where its hot dog brands were weak while Wilson and Corn King hot dogs were top sellers. Nevertheless, the size of Wilson Foods, which had annual sales of about $220 million, made the integration of the new brands, products, and facilities difficult to manage, leading to the fiscal 1996 net loss of $21.7 million. Joel Dorfman told *Crain's Detroit Business:* "The Wilson and Corn King acquisition may have been at the wrong time. All combined, it has been a management problem for us."

Meanwhile, Thorn Apple Valley was also making significant capital investments in its existing plants as well as building a plant from the ground up for the first time. The company's fresh-pork slaughterhouse in Detroit was renovated, although problems with a sophisticated hydraulic system that powered 500 conveyors took a year to resolve. At its peak, the upgraded plant was expected to be able to slaughter and process 1,800 hogs an hour, which was more than double the capacity of any competitor's plant. In October 1995, Thorn Apple opened its $40-million state-of-the-art pork and turkey processing plant in

Ponca City, Oklahoma. The new plant was slated to eventually have capacity to produce 75 to 125 million pounds of meat products a year. In April of the following year, the company opened a new distribution center in Edwardsville, Kansas, and closed a small distribution facility in Clearfield, Utah.

In March 1997 Smithfield Foods once again attempted to take over Thorn Apple Valley but was again rebuffed. About Smithfield's proposal for an "alliance" between the two companies, Joel Dorfman told the *Wall Street Journal:* "We have not positioned this company strategically for it to be acquired in the near-term." By this time, the Dorfmans were confident that the company's restructuring efforts were beginning to pay off. Financial results for the fiscal year ending May 30, 1997, backed up this confidence as Thorn Apple posted a net loss of just $3.2 million, which even took into account a $5 million restructuring charge for costs associated with suspending a joint production agreement at a production facility located in Council Bluffs, Iowa. Although net sales fell slightly to $955.8 million, full-year cash flow amounted to $24.3 million, a vast improvement over the negative $10.7 million of fiscal 1996.

After suffering through a painful period of restructuring, Thorn Apple Valley seemed to have placed itself in a more competitive position than ever. Joel Dorfman summarized in a July 1997 press release: "As a result of our three-year strategic repositioning program, we now have a product lineup that includes five number-one selling items produced at some of the most modern, strategically located, low-cost facilities in the industry." Dorfman intended to continue to increase the portion of company revenues that derived from processed meats (relative to that of fresh pork). And, he also aimed to more aggressively target overseas sales opportunities, with the opening of a sales office in Moscow in mid-1997, and through sales in Mexico, the Caribbean, and Korea, where the top hot dog brand was Corn King.

Principal Subsidiaries

Coast Refrigerated Trucking Company Inc.; Miller's Transport, Inc.; National Food Express, Inc.

Principal Divisions

Carolina Division; Deli & Smoked Meats Division; Dixie Foods Division; Fresh Pork Division; Grand Rapids Division; Ponca City Division; Transportation Division.

Further Reading

Eberwein, Cheryl, "Thorn Apple Harvest," *Corporate Detroit,* January 1992.

Gibson, Richard, and Douglas A. Blackmon, "Smithfield Foods Proposes an 'Alliance' But Thorn Apple Valley Rejects Offer," *Wall Street Journal,* March 21, 1997, p. B9C.

Gutner, Toddi, "Father Doesn't Know Best," *Forbes,* August 17, 1992.

Roush, Matt, "Meat-Packer Living High on the Hogs," *Crain's Detroit Business,* July 25, 1994, p. 12.

"Selling Out," *Inc.,* November 1990.

Smith, Rod, "Thorn Apple Valley Makes Transition to 'Premier' Status," *Feedstuffs,* November 4, 1996, p. 6.

——, "Thorn Apple Valley Positions as National, Premium Supplier," *Feedstuffs,* October 23, 1995, p. 8.

Stopa, Marsha, "Lean Times in Meat Biz: Thorn Apple Struggles But Expects Turnaround," *Crain's Detroit Business,* September 2, 1996, p. 2.

——, "A Short Falloff in the Valley," *Crain's Detroit Business,* October 23, 1995, pp. 1, 24.

——, "Thorn Apple Beefs Up," *Crain's Detroit Business,* March 31, 1997, p. 2.

—Allyson S. Farquhar-Boyle
—updated by David E. Salamie

TLC Beatrice International Holdings, Inc.

9 West 57th Street, Suite 3910
New York, New York 10019
U.S.A.
(212) 756-8900
Fax: (212) 888-3093

Private Company
Incorporated: 1983 as TLC Group, Inc.
Employees: 4,700
Sales: $2.23 billion (1996 est.)
SICs: 2024 Ice Cream & Frozen Desserts; 2086 Bottled & Canned Soft Drinks & Carbonated Waters; 2099 Food Preparations, Not Elsewhere Classified; 5084 Industrial Machinery & Equipment; 5142 Packaged Frozen Foods; 5143 Dairy Products, Except Dried or Canned; 5145 Confectionery; 6719 Offices of Holding Companies, Not Elsewhere Classified

TLC Beatrice International Holdings, Inc. is invariably linked with its late African American founder, Reginald F. Lewis, a Harvard-educated lawyer turned entrepreneur. Known as a hard-nosed dealmaker, Lewis successfully played the 1980s leveraged buyout game; TLC (which stands for "The Lewis Company") is the resulting legacy of Lewis's shrewd maneuvers. The company was founded in 1983 as TLC Group, Inc., a holding company for Lewis's purchase of McCall Pattern Company; he invested $1 million to buy the sewing-pattern firm and sold it in mid-1987 for a 90-to-1 gain. Lewis then parlayed those impressive earnings through the late 1987 $985 million leveraged buyout of the international foods division of Beatrice Company. Over the next 10 years, TLC Beatrice was widely known as the nation's largest black-owned business (as determined by *Black Enterprise* magazine). The company retained the distinction even following Lewis's untimely death in early 1993, after which the Lewis family—headed by Lewis's widow, Philippine-born Loida Lewis—held a majority stake. In late 1997, however, the company sold its food distribution business, which had accounted for 85 percent of 1996 revenues. The sale left TLC Beatrice with a snack-food company in Ireland, ice cream manufacturers in Spain and the Canary Islands, and soft drink bottling operations in the Netherlands, Belgium, France, and Thailand—as a group these businesses generated about $358 million in sales during 1996.

Entrepreneur from Age 10

Reginald Francis Lewis was born on December 7, 1942, in East Baltimore. Growing up in a working-class neighborhood, described by him as "semi-tough," Lewis early on displayed an entrepreneurial spirit. He got his first job at the age of 10 selling the twice-weekly *Baltimore Afro-American,* the local black newspaper, and quickly increased his route from 10 to more than 100 customers. When he went away for a summer camp, his mother took over the route with Lewis paying her a salary and pocketing the profits. Soon thereafter, he took on a more profitable route delivering the daily *Baltimore News American,* and sold his *Baltimore Afro-American* route to a friend for $30.

During high school, Lewis had several jobs and was a star on the baseball diamond and the football gridiron. Following graduation in 1961, he attended Virginia State University, a traditionally black college, on a football scholarship. During his freshman year, however, a nagging shoulder injury led Lewis to concentrate on academics, forfeiting his scholarship in the process. After graduation in 1965, his attendance at a Harvard University summer law program was impressive enough to lead to his being admitted to Harvard Law School despite less than stellar grades at college and his not having taken the LSAT.

Graduated from law school in 1968, Lewis then joined the prestigious Manhattan law firm Paul, Weiss, Rifkind, Wharton & Garrison and was assigned to the corporate law department, where he gained invaluable experience handling a variety of tasks: setting up corporations, handling securities law filings, preparing joint venture agreements, and working on various transactions involving venture capital deals, mergers, and initial public offerings. But wishing to be on his own, Lewis stayed at Paul, Weiss only until 1970 when he launched his own law firm, which specialized in the venture capital area, primarily in the emerging market for Minority Enterprise Small Business Investment Companies. Known as MESBICs, and operated under the auspices of the U.S. Small Business Administration (SBA), these were venture capital firms formed by corporations or foundations; they invested money—including matching funds from the SBA—into minority-owned businesses. Lewis became one of the leading lawyers specializing in MESBICs; in the process, he gained a great deal of experience in the art of structuring acquisitions through debt financing, experience on which he would draw heavily for his 1980s LBOs.

Lewis continued to do MESBIC work through the early 1980s. Meanwhile—longing to take over and run companies himself, rather than simply helping others to do the same—Lewis began to seek out acquisition targets. In 1975 he attempted and failed to acquire Parks Sausage, a black-owned firm based in Baltimore. Two years later, Lewis began another unsuccessful takeover effort, this time of a Vernon, California-based manufacturer of leisure furniture called Almet. After 18 months of negotiations, the deal fell apart at the last minute. In 1982 Lewis purchased a radio station in the U.S. Virgin Islands, intending to make it the base for a regional Caribbean Basin Broadcasting network. These grandiose plans never materialized, however, as the station was continually in the red, leading Lewis to sell it in July 1986.

TLC Group Formed in 1983 to Acquire McCall Pattern

Just as the peak period for corporate takeovers and leveraged buyouts was beginning, Lewis was finally able to join the fray himself. In 1983 the conglomerate Esmark, Inc. took over Norton Simon Industries, another conglomerate, in a hostile takeover. Lewis learned from a *Fortune* magazine article that one of the Norton Simon companies that Esmark planned to divest was McCall Pattern Company, a maker of home sewing patterns founded in 1870. With fewer and fewer people sewing at home, McCall was seemingly on the decline—though it had posted profits of $6 million in 1983 on sales of $51.9 million. At the time, McCall was number two in its industry, holding 29.7 percent of the market, compared to industry leader Simplicity Patterns with 39.4 percent.

In mid-1983 Lewis established a holding company, TLC Group, Inc., for his bid to take over McCall. After securing $24 million in financing from investment banking firm First Boston Corp. and putting up $1 million in cash—part of which was secured via personal loans—TLC Group acquired McCall in January 1984. Lewis had finally completed his first LBO.

From the beginning Lewis's plan was to turn McCall around quickly and then sell it at a profit—thus generating funds for more ambitious takeovers. He did just that. By containing costs, improving quality, beginning to export to China, emphasizing new product introductions—even moving into the production of greeting cards—and focusing on cash flow, Lewis led McCall to its two most profitable years ever in 1985 and 1986, when the company posted income of $12 million and $14 million, respectively. Shortly after an aborted attempt at an initial public offering, Lewis in December 1986 began to cash out his investment in McCall through a recapitalization that generated $19 million for Lewis and other shareholders. Then, an auction resulted in the June 1987 sale of McCall to the John Crowther Group, a U.K. textile manufacturer, with Crowther paying $65 million in cash and assuming $32 million in McCall debt. With the addition of McCall real estate worth an estimated $6 million that they retained ownership of, TLC Group shareholders cleared a total of $90 million from their three-and-a-half year investment of $1 million. Lewis's share was 81.7 percent of the $90 million.

On December 9, 1988, McCall filed for Chapter 11 bankruptcy protection. Two lawsuits were subsequently filed against Lewis alleging that he had misrepresented McCall's financial well-being prior to the sale. Lewis won both cases, and also gained a small settlement from a libel countersuit he had filed against his accusers.

Late 1987 LBO Created TLC Beatrice

In April 1986 Beatrice Company, one of the best-known food companies in the country, with a history dating back to the 1895-founded Beatrice Creamery Company, was taken private through a $6.2 billion highly leveraged buyout led by Kohlberg Kravis Roberts & Co. (KKR). Over the next 18 months, Beatrice was stripped of much of its assets to pay down debt. (The final remnants of Beatrice were sold to ConAgra in 1990.) In June 1987—the same month that he completed the sale of McCall—Lewis learned about an auction of Beatrice's international food operations, which consisted of 64 operating units scattered around 31 countries in South America, Asia, Canada, and Europe, with the units a variety of food distribution and food manufacturing operations. Searching for an internationally active company with a diverse mix of businesses—including some that could be sold following an IPO to pay down debt—as his next takeover target, Lewis quickly determined that the $2.5-billion Beatrice international division fit his criteria almost perfectly and soon pulled together a takeover plan.

Lewis and his associates at the TLC Group quickly put together an initial bid—$950 million—and submitted it to Beatrice in July 1987. They next worked to secure the financing for the takeover, with the help of Drexel Burnham Lambert and its LBO guru Michael Milken, who had been impressed with Lewis's McCall wheeling and dealing. In order to reduce the amount needed to finance the LBO, Lewis came up with a plan to sell off some of the division's assets simultaneous with the takeover.

In November, the deal was consummated—with a final price of $985 million, and with the TLC Group becoming TLC Beatrice International Holdings, Inc. upon its completion. Almost immediately thereafter, previously negotiated asset sales were completed which together brought in $430 million: Beatrice's Canada division was sold for $235 million to Onex Corp., a Toronto-based buyout firm; the Australian operating unit was sold to Cadbury Schweppes Australia for $105 million; and a Spanish meatpacking facility was sold to the Ballve family of Spain for $90 million. Milken and Drexel pulled together $450 million in junk bond financing in return for a 35 percent stake in TLC Beatrice. Lewis, who himself contributed only $16 million in cash, held a majority, 51 percent stake in the company, making TLC Beatrice—whose revenues were now approximately $2 billion following the asset sales—the largest black-owned company in the United States, as calculated by *Black Enterprise* magazine. Although Lewis disliked the media's emphasis on his ethnicity, he told *Black Enterprise* in 1988 that African American entrepreneurs could now aim higher: "I think the sky is the limit. When it comes to African Americans, I think our experience in this country puts us in a position to know that you achieve through very, very hard work, and that's very much in vogue these days. . . . I'm often disturbed by the notion of the so-called glass ceiling, but you know, glass can be broken."

Lewis's Short, Troubled Leadership of TLC Beatrice

By late 1989 Lewis had sold an additional $438 million in TLC Beatrice assets—including all of its Latin American units and all of its Asian units except for its Bireley's bottling operation in Thailand—paring the company's debt down to $100 million and its revenues to $1.1 billion a year. With 15 operating units and 7,000 employees, TLC Beatrice was now primarily a Western European firm. Its biggest operation was that of Franprix, the largest wholesale supermarket distributor in the Paris metropolitan area; others included various European ice cream manufacturers, a snack food maker in Ireland, and soft drink bottling operations in Europe, in addition to the one in Thailand.

In November 1989 Lewis filed a prospectus with the Securities and Exchange Commission to sell 35 percent of TLC Beatrice's common shares to the public. But a depressed market for IPOs and investor concerns about the enormous sum of money Lewis would gain from the offering—more than a quarter of a billion dollars according to *Fortune,* and perhaps at the expense of common shareholders—scuttled the IPO. Lewis seriously considered attempting another IPO in 1991, but decided against it, concerned about another failure.

TLC Beatrice's peak year under Lewis's leadership came in 1990, when the company posted a sales increase of 31 percent to $1.49 billion and tripled the previous year's net income to $45.6 million. Despite this success, Lewis—who was often accused of being more interested in making deals than running companies—made several attempts to acquire other businesses in the late 1980s and early 1990s. Most of these were nonfood companies and based in the United States—one of Lewis's aims was to have a hedge against fluctuations in European economies and currencies. None of the deals came off, however. Among the targets that Lewis made bids for were AmBase, a diversified financial services firm; the remaining domestic operations of Beatrice; and Scovill Apparel Fasteners Group, a maker of zippers (Lewis also seriously considered but never pursued bids for Capital Markets Assurance Corp., a financial guaranty company; the Baltimore Orioles baseball team; Paramount; and Chrysler). According to Lewis's posthumously published autobiography, *"Why Should White Guys Have All the Fun?",* KKR rejected Lewis's bid for the stripped-down Beatrice even though Lewis submitted a higher offer than the $1.3 billion paid by ConAgra; KKR never even acknowledged Lewis's bid.

In early December 1992, Lewis was diagnosed with brain cancer and told he had six to eight weeks to live. In mid-January 1993, Lewis announced his retirement from day-to-day operations and created an office of the chairman to assume his duties, appointing his long-time associate and half-brother, Jean S. Fugett, Jr., to the new post. Lewis died on January 19 at the age of 50.

Post-Reginald Lewis Era, 1993–Present

Fugett, a lawyer and former tight end for the Washington Redskins and the Dallas Cowboys of the National Football League, remained as chairman of TLC Beatrice for just one year. Following a year's bereavement (customary in her native Filipino culture), Lewis's widow, Loida Nicolas Lewis—an immigration lawyer who had been an informal adviser to her husband throughout his career—took over as chairman on February 1, 1994, at a now-floundering company.

With Europe in recession, TLC Beatrice had posted a net loss of $17 million in 1992 and was barely profitable in 1993, while the company's resurgent debt of $271 million (as of December 1993) was partially responsible for sharply lower working capital. In response to the company's problems, Fugett had revived one of Reginald Lewis's odd diversification ideas—that of acquiring the Baltimore Orioles. This went nowhere, in part because of a revolt by the company's minority shareholders, particularly the partners who held the Drexel interest in the company—which stood at 26 percent—an entity known as Carlton Investments L.P. Carlton threatened to take their shares public through a partial offering, which they had the right to do beginning May 1993. Loida Lewis's stepping in to take over as chairman was apparently enough for Carlton to withdraw its threat.

In May 1994, however, Carlton filed suit against the Lewis family for the return of a $22.1 million bonus that was paid to Reginald Lewis in 1992; the bonus had been approved by the TLC Beatrice board as supplementary pay for the previous five years. (Following Reginald Lewis's death, his 51 percent stake in the company had passed to Loida Lewis and the Lewises' two daughters, one of whom joined the TLC Beatrice board of directors.) After a long and bitter battle during which Carlton accused the late Lewis of plundering the company's assets, Carlton and the Lewis family in July 1997 reached a settlement in which the Lewis family agreed to return $15 million to TLC Beatrice coffers.

The ongoing litigation hampered but did not derail Loida Lewis's efforts to turn the company's fortunes around. By mid-1994 she had already made several moves aimed at reining in company expenses, including selling the company jet, trimming 250 jobs from headquarters, and reducing general expenses by $25 million. Lewis also sold three underperforming units: in June 1994 TLC Beatrice sold Choky, its powdered drinks operation in France; the following month it sold Premier Is A/S, an ice cream maker in Norway; and in September 1994 it sold its majority interest in Gelati Sanson S.p.A., an Italian ice cream unit. In November 1994 Lewis refinanced a $170 million bank loan, in the process cutting the company's debt load to about $159 million, with its debt to equity ratio being reduced from 4.9 to 1 to 2.8 to 1. At the same time, Lewis speeded up the expansion of TLC's Leader Price discount, entirely private-label, supermarkets, which had debuted in France in 1991 and had proven to be extremely successful. In mid-1994 there were 135 Leader Price stores across France; this figure would nearly double over the next three years.

By early 1997, Lewis had earned glowing reviews in the press for her management of TLC Beatrice. She had successfully increased profits and cut debt substantially. It appeared that she was positioning the company for another IPO attempt. In the spring of that year, however, Lewis placed the company's food distribution business in France—250 Leader Price and 400 Franprix stores—up for sale. Among the reported reasons for the sale were the growing consolidation of the food industry in France, and a new French law restricting the size of future stores, which increased the value of existing stores. In September 1997 TLC Beatrice sold its French stores to Saint-Etienne, France-based food retailer Casino S.A. for $459 million (FFr2.8 billion) plus repayment of an intercompany loan of about $114 million (FFr700 million). That the price paid was a premium was evident in that the French food stores sold for 25 times operating earnings, as compared to the average figure of 14 for American food companies of similar size at that time.

The food operations sold comprised 85 percent of TLC Beatrice's 1996 revenues, leaving the company with a group of operations that generated only $358 million in 1996 sales. These operations included Tayto Ltd., a snack food company in Ireland; ice cream makers in Spain, Helados La Menorquina S.A., and in the Canary Islands, Interglas S.A.; and four soft drink bottling operations: Sunco N.V. in Belgium, Frisdranken Industries Winters B.V. in the Netherlands, St. Alban Boissons S.A. in France, and Bireley's in Thailand. Lewis used some of the proceeds from the sale to further reduce company debt. As of early 1998 it was unclear what Lewis's next moves might add to the short yet fascinating history of TLC Beatrice.

Principal Subsidiaries

Sunco N.V. (Belgium); Interglas S.A. (Canary Islands); St. Alban Boissons S.A. (France); Tayto Ltd. (Ireland); Frisdranken Industries Winters B.V. (Netherlands); Helados La Menorquina S.A. (Spain); Bireley's (Thailand).

Further Reading

Barrett, Paul M., ''The Last Word: Ex-Drexel Officials Battle Reginald Lewis Even After His Death,'' *Wall Street Journal,* April 15, 1997, pp. A1, A6.

Benson, Barbara, ''Beatrice Needs TLC, CEO to Recover,'' *Crain's New York Business,* July 25, 1994, pp. 17, 19.

Berman, Phyllis, ''Payoff Time?,'' *Forbes,* November 22, 1993, pp. 100, 104.

''A Businessman, a Thinker, and a Succeeder,'' *Philadelphia Tribune,* February 11, 1997.

Calonius, Erik, ''For Reg Lewis: Mean Streets Still,'' *Fortune,* January 15, 1990, pp. 123–24.

Chapelle, Tony, ''Time to Take the Spotlight at TLC,'' *New York Times,* November 27, 1994, pp. F1, F6.

Dingle, Derek T., ''TLC Beatrice Sells Off Major Food Division,'' *Black Enterprise,* December 1997, p. 19.

Edmond, Alfred, Jr., ''Business History Deferred: The TLC Beatrice IPO,'' *Black Enterprise,* February 1990, pp. 23–24.

——, ''Dealing at the Speed of Light,'' *Black Enterprise,* June 1988, pp. 151–52, 154, 156–58, 160, 162.

——, ''Reginald Lewis Cuts the Big Deal,'' *Black Enterprise,* November 1997, pp. 42–46.

''Family in an Accord to Return $15 Million to TLC Beatrice,'' *New York Times,* March 6, 1997, p. D10.

Finch, Peter, ''TLC Beatrice Is Almost Paid For. What's the Next Course?,'' *Business Week,* November 20, 1989, pp. 33–34.

''The Glass Ceiling,'' *Economist,* August 26, 1995, p. 59.

Holloway, Nigel, ''The Missionary Widow,'' *Far Eastern Economic Review,* August 31, 1995, p. 70.

Horowitz, Janice M., ''Buying into the Big Time: A Tycoon Reaches the Top,'' *Time,* August 24, 1987, p. 42.

Kupfer, Andrew, ''The Newest Member of the LBO Club,'' *Fortune,* January 4, 1988, p. 32.

Lavin, Douglas, and Lisa Shuchman, ''Casino to Buy Beatrice Line, Spurning Rival,'' *Wall Street Journal,* September 4, 1997, p. B6.

Lewis, Reginald F., and Blair S. Walker, *''Why Should White Guys Have All the Fun?'': How Reginald Lewis Created a Billion-Dollar Business Empire,* New York: Wiley, 1995, 318 p.

Lim, Gerard, ''Loida Lewis Grabs the Reins at TLC Beatrice,'' *AsianWeek,* January 21, 1994.

McCarroll, Thomas, ''A Woman's Touch,'' *Time,* October 28, 1996, pp. 60–62.

Perry, Nancy J., ''Reg to Riches,'' *Fortune,* September 14, 1987, pp. 122–23.

Ringer, Richard, ''Shareholders Hail Changes at Beatrice: Shifts at the Top Come After Fall in Revenues,'' *New York Times,* January 7, 1994, p. D3.

Scott, Matthew S., ''Black Business Loses a Star: Lewis Dies of Cancer at 50,'' *Black Enterprise,* March 1993, p. 17.

Silverman, Edward R., and Dena Bunis, ''Tycoon Reginald Lewis Dies,'' *Newsday,* January 20, 1993, p. 8.

Solomon, Jolie, ''Operation Rescue,'' *Working Woman,* May 1996, pp. 54–59.

Stodghill, Ron, II, ''TLC Beatrice Could Use More Than TLC,'' *Business Week,* January 24, 1994, p. 35.

Temes, Judy, ''Debt Eased, TLC Plots Moves,'' *Crain's New York Business,* April 15, 1991, pp. 1, 41.

''TLC Beatrice Is to Settle 3 Related Legal Disputes,'' *Wall Street Journal,* July 25, 1997, p. B2.

Wiley, Elliott, ed., *RFL, Reginald F. Lewis: A Tribute,* New York: Bookmark Publishing, 1994, 210 p.

—David E. Salamie

Trend-lines®

Trend-Lines, Inc.

135 American Legion Highway
Revere, Massachusetts 02151
U.S.A.
(617) 853-0900
Fax: (617) 853-0631
Web site: http://www.trend-lines.net

Public Company
Founded: 1981
Employees: 1,225
Sales: $208.6 million (1996)
Stock Exchanges: NASDAQ
SICs: 5251 Hardware Stores; 5941 Sporting Goods & Bicycle Stores; 5961 Catalog & Mail-Order Houses

Trend-Lines, Inc. sells woodworking tools and accessories and golf equipment, operating two chains of specialty stores and distributing two national catalogs. The company is the largest specialty retailer of woodworking tools in the United States, with 168 stores located in the Northeastern, Mid-Atlantic, and Western states, as of September 1997. The 98 Woodworkers Warehouse and 23 Post Tool stores, along with the Trend-Line catalog, offer hand tools, power tools and accessories, and how-to books for the woodworking enthusiast. The 47 Golf Day stores, located in New England and the Northeast, and the Golf Day catalog offer brand name and private label golf merchandise. Sixty-seven percent of Trend-Lines' sales come from its retail stores and the remaining 23 percent from its mail-order catalogs.

From Upholstery to Woodworking

Stanley D. Black, the founder, CEO, and chairman of Trend-Lines, began his career as a salesman after he dropped out of high school, selling items as varied as office supplies and toothpaste. Gradually, he built up two businesses, one manufacturing metal fasteners and one selling clamps and other upholstery tools to the furniture industry. By 1981, Black noticed there was a strong demand for the company's merchandise from shops serving woodworking hobbyists and professionals who needed tools and accessories for projects ranging from home remodeling to cabinet and furniture making. Within two years the company had switched its focus to the consumer woodworking market. In 1983, Black launched the Trend-Lines catalog, using rented mailing lists, and opened a Woodworkers Warehouse outlet store at the company's distribution center in Massachusetts. This was followed, in 1986, by the first Woodworkers Warehouse retail store, which advertised everyday low prices for hard-to-find items and high quality name brands.

Expanding into Retail, 1987–93

While the company recognized the role its retail store could play, Trend-Lines was primarily a catalog operation. The company published its catalog four times a year, sending it out around the United States to people on the Trend-Lines mailing list, people who had made inquiries, and people on lists Trend-Lines rented or exchanged with other companies. Customers could call a toll-free number to place their order, which was then shipped within 48 hours.

Trend-Lines sold merchandise ranging from power and hand tools to wood finishes, glue, blades, and books, and its lines were much broader than those of such growing home improvement superstores as Lowe's and Home Depot. Someone looking for a power drill, for example, could choose from 70 different kinds in the Trend-Lines catalog compared to 30 at Home Depot. The selections included name brands such as Black & Decker, Emglo, Stanley Bostitch, and Delta, as well as Trend-Lines' own private label products sold under its Reliant, Carb-Tech, and Vulcan trademarks.

The retail approach proved popular, and the company opened more stores in Massachusetts and other states in New England, staffing them with associates and managers who were woodworkers themselves, and promoting low prices for top quality merchandise. Most of the Woodworkers Warehouse stores were located in strip malls to take advantage of the foot traffic and parking, and were between 4,500 and 5,500 square feet in size. But the catalog was the big revenue producer, accounting for over 70 percent of the $33 million in sales in fiscal 1989.

Black had found a niche market he could serve successfully through his combined catalog/retail approach, but woodworkers generally did most of their buying during the fall and winter, when it was too cold to be outside and they turned to their tool benches and workshops. To offset that seasonality, Black decided to go after another group of avid hobbyists, but one that bought expensive merchandise during the spring and summer—golfers. According to a 1995 *Forbes* article, he wanted to buy Golf Day, a moneylosing cataloger, in 1988, but the $600,000 asking price was too high. So he waited a year and in 1989 purchased the Golf Day name and mailing list for $100,000. The following year Trend-Lines mailed its first Golf Day catalog and opened a Golf Day outlet store at its distribution center.

During the early 1990s, the company continued to grow, expanding the mailing lists for its catalogs and opening a few new retail stores each year. The Golf Day stores were slightly smaller than the Woodworkers, between 4,000 and 5,000 square feet. In addition to merchandise, each store had a practice-hitting area where shoppers could try out the equipment. In the stores or through the Golf Day catalog, customers could buy some 5,000 items, ranging from clubs, bags, and hand carts to shoes and apparel to balls, videos, and golf cart seat covers made of sheepskin. Golf Day also sold private label golf merchandise under its Honors trademark. By March 1994 (the end of fiscal 1993), there were 30 Woodworkers Warehouse stores and five Golf Day stores, primarily in New England, but also in New York, New Jersey, and Pennsylvania. That year sales reached $99.9 million, with the woodworking operations accounting for over two-thirds of the revenue, and the Trend-Lines catalog bringing in over half of the total.

Rapid Growth, 1994–95

In 1994, the company began two years of rapid expansion. To pay down its debt and raise money for its growth plans, Trend-Lines went public in June, issuing 2,550,000 shares of Class A common stock and earning some $19.7 million. In July, it issued another 337,000 shares, for approximately $2.7 million. The total shares sold represented 33 percent of the company, with Black and his wife keeping 65 percent.

The company used the $22 million to pick up the pace of its store openings, adding 52 Woodworkers Warehouse and five more Golf Day locations during the year. A typical tool store cost $350,000 to open, including $290,000 of inventory, while the typical golf store cost $395,000, including $270,000 of inventory. In deciding where to open a new store, Trend-Lines went to their catalog customers, usually selecting sites where there was strong name recognition and an existing customer base. Both chains had similar real estate requirements, and with many serving the same customers, they were often located in the same mall or at least close to each other. That strategy helped keep costs down because the company could use the same trucks, distribution centers, and general managers for both the tool and golf stores.

Because its tool selection was so much larger than that of its competitors, Trend-Lines often opened Woodworkers Warehouse stores only a few blocks from a Home Depot or other hardware giant; some opened right next door. Black found the superstores actually generated traffic for the woodworking stores when shoppers could not find what they wanted elsewhere. In some instances, staff at competitors called a Woodworkers Warehouse to see if it had what a customer was asking for. As Black told John Hechinger of *Wall Street Journal*, ''Trend-Lines caters to the enthusiast, Home Depot, the generalist.''

Black also used some of the stock proceeds in November to move into new facilities in Revere, Massachusetts. The 286,000-square-foot quarters housed the company's executive offices and its distribution and centralized telemarketing operations.

In January 1995, Trend-Lines moved beyond its Northeastern/Mid-Atlantic territory when it bought California-based Post Tool from West Union Corporation. The new wholly owned subsidiary had 17 Post Tool stores in California and Nevada and a distribution center. In addition to merchandise for the woodworker, Post Tool stores carried power and hand tools and accessories for general mechanical and automotive work. Trend-Lines quickly integrated Post Tool into its information management system and began opening new Post Tool locations in California.

Throughout the year, the company continued to launch new stores in the East, so that by the end of fiscal 1995, it was operating 141 retail stores. For the first time in the company's history, retail sales were greater than those from the catalogs.

But the shift from catalog to retail proved costly, and fiscal 1995 saw another first—a decline in profits. Analysts put the blame on the rapid expansion and poor site selection, combined with a weak holiday season and blizzards throughout New England and the Northeast, the company's major market.

1996 to the Present

Watching the price of his company's stock drop to $5 a share was a rough experience for Stanley Black, a man who saved money by buying overruns and misprinted boxes for shipping his merchandise. To correct the situation, Black made some major management changes, bringing in people with experience in large retail chains. In October 1996, the company hired Richard Griner, from Family Dollar Stores, to become president, and a few months later lured Walter Spokowski from Home Depot to be executive vice-president in charge of merchandising. Within an 8-month period, the company also added senior staff experienced in the areas of information management, distribution and transportation, and real estate management. The new team closed several underperforming Woodworkers Warehouse stores and one Golf Day shop, cut the number of openings almost in half, and consolidated distribution facilities. They also changed the company's marketing approach, replacing the ''everyday low prices,'' with sales on targeted items to bring people into the stores for a specific purpose. Stores reported the promotional change worked, with more store traffic and higher sales of both the promoted items and regular-priced merchandise.

By the end of fiscal 1996, Trend-Lines was back on solid footing, as total sales increased nearly 20 percent, to $208.6 million. In line with a more focused approach to expansion, the company closed three stores and opened 26 new ones: 10 Woodworkers Warehouses, five Post Tools, and 11 Golf Days. This brought the total number of locations to 159. The retail side of the business continued to account for a growing percentage of the business, reaching 67 percent of the company's total sales. For the first time since Golf Day was bought in 1989, the golf chain stores outsold the catalog, by approximately $200,000.

During 1997, the stores themselves got a lot of attention. The company unveiled a new prototype for each chain at the Revere headquarters. The model used brighter colors, displayed brand name logos along every wall, organized better product displays, and improved lighting. The new design was expected to add only a few thousand dollars to the cost of a new store and was to be used in all new Woodworking and Golf Day stores. The existing stores would be redesigned over time.

The new team also reorganized the company's structure, combining the two chains into a single field operation and centralizing merchandising responsibility at the district manager level.

The company's financial picture continued to improve. In the first half of the fiscal year, net income was 104 percent above that of 1996, and both of Trend-Lines' markets were growing. The 1995 "Woodworking in America" survey, sponsored by the *American Woodworker Magazine,* found that an estimated 18.6 million people, approximately 10 percent of the adult population, were involved in woodworking activities and spent more than $6.3 billion a year on the tools and accessories they needed for their projects. Furthermore, the study found that they tended to pursue their woodworking hobby for an average of 15 years.

On the golf side of the business, the National Golf Foundation's 1996 report on the sport in the U.S. found participation had increased by three percent in a year, with some 25 million Americans playing 490 million rounds of golf. The popularity of Tiger Woods helped interest more young people in the game, and women represented the fastest-growing segment of the sport. Trend-Lines responded to these figures with special marketing programs and discrete sections in the new store model.

Stanley Black carved out two markets targeted at upscale baby boomer enthusiasts. After discovering that it took more than salesmanship and entrepreneurial sense to successfully expand his chains, he quickly hired people with the retail management skills a larger operation needed. With 168 stores, located primarily in the Northeast, Trend-Lines had most of the country available for new locations, and could continue to use its catalogs to identify areas where mail-order customers lived and where their name recognition was greatest. Both the woodworking and golf markets were highly fragmented, with no single chain dominating either business. Taking these factors together, several analysts were predicting good things for Trend-Lines into the new century.

Principal Subsidiaries

Post Tool, Inc.

Further Reading

Hechinger, John, "Trend-Lines Is Chipping Away Bad Memories with Solid Results," *Wall Street Journal*, September 1997.

Hood, Wayne, and Diane L. Roberts, "Trend-Lines, Inc.," Prudential Securities, June 26, 1997.

Paglucia, Gina M., "Trend-Lines, Inc.," Fechtor, Detwiler & Co., Inc., September 25, 1997.

Richter, Steven, and Paige Brown, "Trend-Lines, Inc.," Tucker Anthony Equity Research, July 21, 1997.

Schifrin, Matthew, "What Do Woodworkers Do in the Summer?" *Forbes*, May 22, 1995, p. 116.

"$10 Store: Trend-Lines a Retail Turnaround," http://www.thestreet.com, May 16, 1997.

—Ellen D. Wernick

Tribune Company

435 North Michigan Avenue
Chicago, Illinois 60611
U.S.A.
(312) 222-9100
Fax: (312) 222-1573
Web site: http://www.tribune.com

Public Company
Incorporated: 1861
Employees: 10,700
Sales: $2.41 billion (1996)
Stock Exchanges: New York Midwest Pacific
SICs: 2711 Newspapers: Publishing, or Publishing & Printing; 2721 Periodicals: Publishing, or Publishing & Printing; 2731 Books: Publishing, or Publishing & Printing; 4832 Radio Broadcasting Stations; 4833 Television Broadcasting Stations; 4899 Communication Services, Not Elsewhere Classified; 7383 News Syndicates; 7822 Motion Picture & Video Tape Distribution; 7941 Professional Sports Clubs & Promoters

Tribune Company is one of the largest media companies in the United States. Its diversified businesses are arranged within three main operating units: Tribune Broadcasting, Tribune Publishing, and Tribune Education. Tribune Broadcasting owns and operates 16 television and four radio stations; develops and syndicates television shows, including the ''The Geraldo Rivera Show'' and ''Soul Train,'' through Tribune Entertainment; owns the Chicago Cubs major league baseball team; runs CLTV News, the only 24-hour local cable news channel in Chicago; and holds a 21.9 percent stake in The Warner Bros. Television Network (The WB). Tribune Publishing publishes the *Chicago Tribune* and three other market-leading newspapers: the *Sun-Sentinel* (Fort Lauderdale, Florida), *The Orlando Sentinel,* and the *Daily Press* (Hampton Roads, Virginia); produces Internet versions of these four papers; runs the Tribune Media Services syndication service; and owns various niche magazines and journals. Tribune Education is the nation's leader in supplemental education publishing, through such publishers as Educational Publishing Corporation, Everyday Learning Corporation, NTC/Contemporary Publishing Company, and The Wright Group. In the mid-1990s, Tribune Company has also become very active in the area of interactive services and Internet businesses, through investments made by Tribune Ventures, which have included four percent of America Online, Inc., seven percent of Excite, Inc., and 13 percent of Mercury Mail, Inc.

Started with Chicago Daily Tribune *in 1847*

The company originated with the first publication of the *Chicago Daily Tribune* on June 10, 1847. The newspaper's founders were James Kelly, who also owned a weekly literary newspaper, and two other journalists, John E. Wheeler and Joseph K. C. Forrest. At the time, the paper was one of three major dailies published in Chicago.

The founders soon parted company, however, and the *Chicago Daily Tribune* had gone through several changes in ownership and editorial policy by 1855, when it was sold to a man who would be influential in its history, former Cleveland, Ohio newspaperman Joseph Medill. His associates in the purchase were Charles Ray, a physician, journalist, and political activist in Springfield and Galena, Illinois, and John Vaughan, a coproprietor of Medill's Cleveland paper. Under Medill's leadership, the *Tribune* maintained a strong antislavery stand but abandoned the antiforeign, anti-Catholic, and antisaloon campaigns that the paper had led previously. It also reorganized its presentation of news, establishing separate departments for local, national, and international stories.

Coming out of the economic panic of 1857, the *Tribune* was having financial problems, but so was a competitor, the *Democratic Press.* The two papers merged in 1858, resulting in the *Chicago Daily Press and Tribune.* Active in the partisan journalism common in its day, the paper was allied with the recently formed Republican Party. It supported Abraham Lincoln in his unsuccessful campaign to unseat U.S. Senator Stephen Douglas in 1858 and in his successful campaign for the presidency in 1860.

Company Perspectives:

We build businesses that inform, educate, and entertain our customers in the ways, places, and at the times they want. By doing so, we create value for our customers, our employees, and our shareholders.

In 1860 the paper's name was returned to the *Chicago Daily Tribune.* The following year the Tribune Company was incorporated and the paper became the *Chicago Tribune.* That year, 1861, also brought the start of the Civil War, during which the *Tribune* gained national fame for its excellent wartime news coverage and its support of the Union cause. The paper's Sunday edition appeared during the war, disappeared for a while, and was resumed after the war, to the chagrin of local ministers. In October 1871 came a disaster against which the *Tribune* had warned—the Great Chicago Fire—which devastated the city, filled as it was with wooden buildings and suffering a lack of firefighting equipment and regulations. As the city rebuilt, Joseph Medill was elected mayor on the Union-Fireproof ticket. Medill declined to run for a second term in 1873; in 1874 he emerged victorious in a struggle with managing editor Horace White for editorial control of the *Tribune.*

The *Tribune* grew and prospered, as did Chicago itself, in the years after the fire. As it entered the last decade of the 19th century, the paper was attractive, vocal, and profitable, reporting annual income of $1.5 million a year. In 1895 the *Tribune* lowered newsstand prices and increased circulation. Joseph Medill's son-in-law, Robert Patterson, became increasingly important to the *Tribune;* he was named general manager in 1890, after having been managing editor for seven years. At Medill's death at age 76 in 1899, Patterson assumed the titles of editor-in-chief of the newspaper and president of Tribune Company. Medill's last words reportedly were, ''What is the news this morning?''

In 1900 a formidable competitor came to Chicago, as William Randolph Hearst began publishing the *Chicago American,* a paper with a Democratic political alliance and a sensational reporting style. It was an evening paper but later added a morning edition as a direct competitor to the *Tribune.* The *Tribune* and the Hearst papers engaged in a circulation war that lasted 20 years, marked at times by physical violence among newspaper vendors.

The early part of the century also was marked by the rise to power by two of Joseph Medill's grandsons, Robert R. McCormick and Joseph Patterson. Their mothers, Katherine Medill McCormick and Elinor Medill Patterson, battled frequently over *Tribune* affairs after Medill's death. Katherine McCormick's eldest son, Medill McCormick, made a mark on the *Tribune* as a reporter and later business executive, but left the paper in 1910; he had been plagued by psychiatric illness and, upon recovery, opted for a career in politics. Meanwhile, Robert Patterson, Joseph Patterson's father, had died in 1910. In 1911 Joseph Patterson was elected chairman of Tribune Company and Robert McCormick was named president. Their immediate accomplishments were Patterson's upgrading of the Sunday paper and McCormick's initiation of a paper mill to produce newsprint for the *Tribune.*

According to their biographers, Patterson and McCormick had many differences, including political ones—McCormick was a staunchly conservative Republican, while Patterson was far more liberal. Still, under their leadership Tribune Company expanded and diversified, and both became well-known public figures, retaining titles from their World War I military service—Colonel McCormick and Captain Patterson. During the war, the *Tribune* had more correspondents at the front than any other Chicago morning daily, and McCormick and Patterson themselves were among these correspondents. After the war, the *Tribune* pulled off a major publishing coup with early publication of the Treaty of Versailles. By 1920 the *Tribune* had the largest circulation of any Chicago newspaper.

Diversified in Early 20th Century

By then, the parent company also had expanded beyond Chicago, with Patterson's opening of the *New York News*—formally the *Illustrated Daily News* and later known as the *Daily News*—in 1919. Eventually, the New York paper, a lively tabloid, became the largest circulation newspaper in the United States. In 1924 Tribune Company formed a subsidiary to publish a weekly national magazine, *Liberty,* designed to compete with the *Saturday Evening Post* and *Collier's.* It passed *Collier's* in circulation, but did not attract adequate advertising, so was sold in 1931.

Also in 1924, Tribune Company launched a more enduring venture, with the leasing of Chicago radio station WDAP, whose call letters it changed to WGN—standing for World's Greatest Newspaper, a nickname the Tribune had given itself. Two years later, Tribune Company bought the entire station. The station's early programming included coverage of the Scopes trial and a comedy show called ''Sam 'n' Henry,'' which eventually went network as ''Amos 'n' Andy.''

The year 1925 was marked by the Tribune Company's opening of its new headquarters, Tribune Tower, a Gothic tower that is still a Chicago landmark, and the company's decision to provide funds to a journalism school at Northwestern University in Evanston, Illinois, just north of Chicago. The school became known as the Joseph Medill School of Journalism, one of the most prestigious in the United States.

The 1920s provided many political and crime stories that made the decade a lively one for newspapers, but the 1920s ended with the worst stock market crash in history, ushering in the Great Depression. Tribune Company weathered the economic downturn by cutting unprofitable and marginal ventures, such as *Liberty* and the Tribune's European edition, which had begun during World War I. Editorially, McCormick's *Tribune* was vociferously opposed to President Franklin Roosevelt's New Deal programs, while Patterson's *Daily News* generally was sympathetic to them. Later, however, the cousins joined in opposition to Roosevelt over U.S. entry into World War II. After the bombing of Pearl Harbor, though, the papers supported the war effort.

Joseph Patterson died in 1946. Briefly, McCormick took over the oversight of the *Daily News,* but concluded it was in good hands with Patterson's widow, Mary King Patterson, and other top executives. In 1948 came the death of Joe Patterson's sister, Eleanor (Cissy) Patterson, who had owned the *Washington Times-Herald.* Tribune Company took over the paper and operated it until 1954, when it was absorbed by the *Washington Post.*

Entered TV Broadcasting in 1948

In 1948 the *Tribune* made one of the most famous mistakes in journalistic history: going to press early because of a printers' strike, the paper published the headline "Dewey Defeats Truman" in the 1948 presidential election. The strike ended the following year with no other comparable disasters. The year 1948 also brought a happier milestone in the company's history, the commencement of broadcasting by WGN-TV, which by the late 1980s was one of the most successful independent television stations in the United States.

Robert McCormick died in 1955 and Chesser Campbell succeeded him as president of Tribune Company. The following year, the company bought Hearst's *Chicago American.* In 1963 Tribune Company acquired Gore Newspapers Company of Fort Lauderdale, Florida, publisher of the *Fort Lauderdale News* and the *Pompano Sun-Sentinel.* Later that year, the *New York Daily News* acquired certain assets of the *New York Mirror,* which had folded. In 1965 Tribune Company bought the Sentinel-Star Company, a publisher in Orlando, Florida.

In 1967 the *Chicago Tribune* responded to suburban growth by beginning to publish a tabloid aimed at suburban readers. The *Suburban Trib* continued until 1983, when the *Tribune* opted for zoned editions of the main paper to handle suburban coverage and appeal.

In 1968 there came a major corporate reorganization, with Tribune Company dropping its Illinois incorporation and reincorporating in Delaware, which provided a better climate for companies planning expansion and diversification. The company also split its privately held stock by a ratio of four for one and set up a separate subsidiary to publish the *Chicago Tribune.* The Chicago newspaper opened 1969 by abandoning the policy of partisan slanting of news, while it remained conservative on the editorial page. Also in 1969, the *American* was revamped as the tabloid *Chicago Today. Today,* however, operated at a deficit and ceased publication in 1974, with the *Tribune* going to all-day editions to replace the afternoon tabloid.

In 1974 Tribune Company shareholders approved changes in bylaws that were widely perceived to be paving the way for taking the company public. Two dissident shareholders, Josephine Albright—Joseph Patterson's daughter—and her son, Joseph Albright, challenged the bylaw changes in a lawsuit that was dismissed in 1979. In 1975 company officials denied any immediate plans to go public, which, indeed, the company did not do until 1983.

In the 1970s the company continued its acquisitive ways, buying a Los Angeles shopper in 1973 and changing it into the *Los Angeles Daily News* and purchasing the *Times-Advocate* in Escondido, California, in 1977. The New York *Daily News* was beset with strikes by pressmen, deliverers, and editorial personnel in 1978, but the parent company still had a record profitable year. Photoengravers also struck the paper briefly in 1979. An afternoon edition of the *Daily News* began publishing in 1980 to go up against the *New York Post;* however, the edition did not succeed in terms of circulation or profits, so it closed the following year. Also in 1980, the company launched a longer-lived venture, the Independent Network News, an alternative to the three major television networks' news programs, originating in the studios of Tribune Company's New York television station, WPIX. The venture was discontinued in 1990.

Bought Chicago Cubs in 1981

In 1981 Tribune Company acquired the Chicago Cubs baseball team from William Wrigley for $20.5 million. The Cubs turned in some good seasons for their new owners, winning the National League Eastern Division title in 1984 and 1989. In 1988, once a city ban was lifted, the company installed lights in Wrigley Field and began Cubs night games; the park had been the last in the major leagues with day baseball only.

Also in 1981, Tribune Company began seeking buyers for the New York *Daily News,* which had experienced declines in circulation and advertising and rises in costs and competition. When a proposed sale to Texas financier Joe Allbritton fell through, the company opted to revitalize the *Daily News,* taking a charge of $75 million in the second quarter of 1982 to do so. The paper won concessions from its unions that were expected to result in savings of $50 million a year.

Bought Additional TV Stations in Mid-1980s

The year 1983 brought the Tribune Company's purchase of WGNO-TV in New Orleans, as well as the public stock offering that had been the subject of speculation for so long. In October, seven million shares of Tribune Company stock went up for sale to the public at $26.75 each.

Tribune Company acquired two key employees from the *Chicago Sun-Times* in 1984 after the *Sun-Times* was sold to Rupert Murdoch, the controversial publisher of the *New York Post.* James Hoge, who had been publisher of the *Sun-Times,* moved into that post at the *Daily News,* and popular columnist Mike Royko switched to the *Chicago Tribune* from the *Sun-Times.*

The company also continued acquiring broadcast operations, buying Atlanta independent WGNX-TV in 1984 for $32 million and, the following year, buying Los Angeles station KTLA-TV for $510 million, the largest price ever paid for a TV station. The move also made Tribune Company the fourth largest broadcaster in the United States, just behind the three major networks. Because of the KTLA purchase, Tribune Company had to divest itself of the *Los Angeles Daily News* to comply with Federal Communications Commission rules; Jack Kent Cooke, whose other business interests included cable television, real estate, and professional sports, was the buyer. The price was $176 million; Tribune Company had paid $24 million for the paper.

In 1985 three production unions went on strike against the *Chicago Tribune,* a labor conflict that ended in the company's favor. With the strike, the *Tribune* discontinued its afternoon edition, a move it had planned anyway, with newspaper circulations slumping around the United States.

Production of television programs became a major business for Tribune Company in the 1980s; the company had formed Tribune Entertainment Company for this purpose in 1981. It also continued acquiring print properties, buying Daily Press Inc., a Newport News, Virginia publisher, in 1986 and reselling Daily Press's cable TV operations; in 1988 Tribune Company bought five weekly newspapers in Santa Clara County, California.

Mindful of the rash of unfriendly corporate takeovers in the 1980s, Tribune Company enacted shareholder-rights plans as defenses against such possibilities; a 1987 plan gave shareholders a right to acquire a new series of preferred shares in the event of a potential buyer obtaining ten percent of the company's common shares or making a tender offer for the company. In 1987 shareholders ratified a two-for-one stock split.

In 1988 the *Chicago Tribune* replaced its system of independent distributors with a more centralized system. The change resulted in legal challenges by the distributors, with one awarded $1.9 million by an arbitrator.

In August 1990 company veteran Charles Brumback became Tribune president and CEO. That year, the company encountered more labor relations problems. Nine of the ten unions at the *Daily News* went on strike in October; the newspaper struggled to publish with replacement workers and eventually, as the strike dragged into 1991, Tribune Company announced the paper would close unless it was sold. British publisher Robert Maxwell came to the newspaper's rescue, reaching agreements with the unions that allowed him to take over. The company paid Maxwell $60 million to assume the *Daily News'* liabilities. Tribune Company had been forced to take a *Daily News*-related charge of $255 million in 1990, leading to a net loss for the year of $63.5 million.

Added Interactive Media and Education Publishing in the 1990s

The early and mid-1990s were a time of enormous change across all media-related industries. Cable television continued to grow, the consolidation and diversification of media companies became commonplace, and the Internet emerged as a new format with which to contend and within which to compete. Tribune Company placed itself at the center of all of these changes. The company, which traditionally had been managed fairly conservatively, grew bolder as the decade progressed under Brumback's leadership and that of his successor, John Madigan, who became president in 1994, added the CEO slot in 1995, and then tacked on the chairmanship as well in early 1996.

The company's newspaper publishing unit, known as Tribune Publishing, was scaled back some during this period to focus on its most profitable papers, with several weeklies and smaller dailies being divested. By 1997, only four daily newspapers remained in the fold—*Chicago Tribune,* the Fort Lauderdale *Sun-Sentinel, The Orlando Sentinel,* and the Newport News, Virginia-based *Daily Press.* Starting in 1995, online versions of each of these papers began to be developed, with the Internet edition of the *Chicago Tribune* debuting on the World Wide Web the following year. Also in 1996, a joint venture with America Online (AOL) called Digital City, Inc.—80 percent owned by AOL and 20 percent owned by Tribune—led to the creation of a series of Digital City web sites, which provided local, interactive news and information. Tribune Company also formed a unit called Tribune Ventures to invest in various emerging media businesses. By mid-1997, $100 million had been spent to purchase stakes in various interactive services and cyberspace businesses, including AOL (four percent), electronic payment specialist CheckFree Corporation (five percent), Internet search company Excite, Inc. (seven percent), e-mail service Mercury Mail, Inc. (13 percent), transaction software company Open Market, Inc. (six percent), and online grocery shopper Peapod LP (13 percent).

Meanwhile, the company's broadcasting and entertainment sector, known as Tribune Broadcasting, entered cable programming for the first time in 1993 with the launch of CLTV News, Chicago's first 24-hour, local news cable channel; a similar channel was launched in 1997 in Central Florida through a joint venture of the *Orlando Sentinel* and Time Warner Cable. Tribune Company also purchased a 31 percent stake in TV Food Network, a 24-hour basic cable channel covering food, nutrition, and fitness, which by the end of 1996 could be seen in more than 19 million cable households.

With federal regulations on radio and television ownership being loosened, Tribune's group of television broadcast stations grew dramatically in the 1990s. The company began the decade with just six stations but added ten more by 1997. WPHL in Philadelphia was purchased in 1992, WLVI in Boston in 1994, KHTV in Houston in 1996 for $102 million, and KTTY in San Diego also in 1996 for $71 million. In March 1997 Tribune Company became the number two television group in the United States by acquiring Renaissance Communications Corp. for $1.1 billion in cash. The deal brought six more stations to the Tribune fold—KDAF in Dallas, WDZL in Miami, KTXL in Sacramento, WXIN in Indianapolis, WTIC in Hartford, and WPMT in Harrisburg—bringing the total to 16. Ten of the stations were affiliated with the relatively new Warner Bros. Television Network, better known as The WB. This fit in well with Tribune Company's 21.9 percent equity stake in The WB; the company had acquired an original 12.5 percent interest in August 1995, then invested an additional $21 million in the fifth U.S. television network in March 1997.

Already possessing strong positions in two business sectors, Tribune Company quickly added a substantial third leg to its operations with the beginnings of Tribune Education in 1993. From that year through 1996, the company spent more than $400 million to acquire several prominent publishers of supplemental education materials, including Contemporary Books, The Wright Group, Everyday Learning Company, Jamestown Publishers, Educational Publishing Corporation, NTC Publishing Group, and Janson Publications. In just three years, Tribune Education was the number one publisher of supplemental education materials, a publishing sector growing rapidly because of increasing school enrollment while also providing high profit margins. In 1997 Tribune Education spent $80 million for an 80.5 percent stake in Landoll, Inc., a leading publisher of children's books for the mass market, thus providing entrée into the consumer market.

Through the highly competitive and rapidly consolidating 1990s media world, Tribune Company had emerged in the late 1990s as a major player in several sectors, some of which it had entered only earlier in the decade. The company's strategy of investing in various emerging technologies seemed particularly adroit considering the quick rise and often quicker fall of so many high-tech ventures. The newly aggressive Tribune Company seemed certain to be one of the major media companies well into the 21st century.

Principal Subsidiaries

Tribune Publishing Company; Chicago Tribune Company; Tribune Media Services, Inc.; Sun-Sentinel Company; Sentinel Communications Company; Tribune Interactive; The Daily Press, Inc.; Tribune National Marketing Company; Tribune Broadcasting Co.; Tribune Broadcasting News Network, Inc.; ChicagoLand Television News, Inc.; Oak Brook Productions, Inc.; ChicagoLand Microwave Licensee, Inc.; Tribune Regional Programming, Inc.; Tribune New York Radio, Inc.; Tribune Denver Radio, Inc.; WGN Continental Broadcasting Company; Tribune Entertainment Company; Tribune (FN) Cable Ventures, Inc.; KWGN Inc.; WGNO Inc.; WGNX Inc.; KTLA Inc.; WPHL-TV, Inc.; WPIX Inc.; WLVI Inc.; Tribune Network Holdings Company; KSWB Inc.; KHTV Inc.; Renaissance Communications Corporation; Tribune California Properties, Inc.; Chicago National League Ball Club, Inc.; Diana-Quentin, Inc.; Tribune Education Company; NTC/Contemporary Publishing Company; Wright Group Publishing, Inc.; NewMedia Source, Inc.; Jamestown Publishers, Inc.; Everyday Learning Corporation; Educational Publishing Corporation; Tribune Education Sales, Inc.; Tribune Properties, Inc.; Tribune New York Properties, Inc.; Riverwalk Center I Joint Venture; Tower Acquisition Company, Inc.

Principal Operating Units

Tribune Broadcasting; Tribune Publishing; Tribune Education.

Further Reading

Alkin, Michael, "The Tribune Company: Batter Up," *Financial World*, March 18, 1997, pp. 24, 26.

Borden, Jeff, "Merger Heat for Trib Co.: Big Media Combines Make It Also-Also Ran," *Crain's Chicago Business*, August 7, 1995, pp. 3, 34.

——, "Trib's Blessing and Curse: Cash," *Crain's Chicago Business*, May 6, 1996, pp. 1, 78.

——, "Tribune Rewrites Corporate Future," *Crain's Chicago Business*, January 20, 1992, pp. 1, 45.

——, "With *News* an Old Story, Trib Is in a Mood to Shop," *Crain's Chicago Business*, May 20, 1991, p. 3.

Fawcett, Adrienne, "Tribune's Vision Goes Well Beyond Online Newspapers," *Advertising Age*, June 2, 1997, pp. S-8, S-10.

Fitzgerald, Mark, "Broadcasting Dominant," *Editor & Publisher*, July 13, 1996, p. 17.

Littleton, Cynthia, "Renaissance Buy Should Boost Tribune Entertainment," *Broadcasting & Cable*, July 8, 1996, p. 9.

Milliot, Jim, "Tribune Spends $97 Million on Publishing Acquisitions," *Publishers Weekly*, July 12, 1993, p. 12.

Milliot, Jim, and Kinsella, Bridget, "Tribune Acquires EPC, NTC for Total of $282 Million," *Publishers Weekly*, February 12, 1996, p. 10.

Rathbun, Elizabeth A., "Tribune's Renaissance," *Broadcasting & Cable*, July 8, 1996, pp. 4, 8–9.

Smith, Richard Norton, *The Colonel: The Life and Legend of Robert R. McCormick, 1880–1955*, Boston: Houghton Mifflin, 1997.

Squires, James D., *Read All About It!: The Corporate Takeover of America's Newspapers*, New York: Times Books, 1993.

Teinowitz, Ira, "Taking Charge at Tribune Co.: New President Madigan Sees Growth Ahead," *Advertising Age*, June 6, 1994, p. 11.

——, "Tribune Looks Forward with Latest Acquisitions," *Advertising Age*, August 2, 1993, p. 20.

Wendt, Lloyd, *Chicago Tribune: The Rise of a Great American Newspaper*, Chicago: Rand McNally, 1979.

—Trudy Ring
—updated by David E. Salamie

Ugly Duckling Corporation

2525 East Camelback Road, Suite 1150
Phoenix, Arizona 85016
U.S.A.
(602) 852-6600
Fax: (602) 852-6696
Web site: http://www.uglyduckling.com

Public Company
Incorporated: 1977 as Ugly Duckling Rent-A-Car System, Inc.
Employees: 1,776
Sales: $75.6 million (1996)
Stock Exchanges: NASDAQ
SICs: 5611 New & Used Car Dealers; 6141 Personal Credit Institutions; 6719 Holding Companies, Not Elsewhere Classified

Ugly Duckling Corporation is a vertically integrated firm in the used car sales and financing industry. In the firm's 1996 annual report, Chairman and CEO Ernest C. Garcia II stated, "We are the only major company that serves virtually all segments of the sub-prime auto finance market." Ugly Duckling dealerships sell used cars to those with modest incomes and little or no credit. Those dealerships are part of one of the nation's largest "buy-here pay-here" chains, for they finance almost all cars they sell. Ugly Duckling's second source of income is through Champion Financial Services, which has a network of branch offices to buy sub-prime installment contracts from third-party used car dealers. Third, Ugly Duckling's Cygnet Finance subsidiary offers independent used car dealers a line of credit which allows them to expand their operations. Although most of Ugly Duckling's business occurs in its home state of Arizona, it is quickly expanding into other states in an attempt to consolidate a very fragmented industry.

Origins

The Ugly Duckling story began in 1977 when Ugly Duckling Rent-A-Car System, Inc. was formed in Tucson by 63-year-old Thomas S. Duck, Sr., a retired insurance salesman. Just to keep busy, he started his company by using $10,000 of his savings to buy a few used cars to sell. Soon his franchise business expanded into other states.

Ugly Duckling Rent-A-Car entered a growing industry dominated by the Big Three: Avis and Hertz, both started in 1947, and National. In the 1970s all rental car firms struggled with the energy shortage. In the 1980s price wars engulfed the industry, encouraged by the success of low-cost rental companies like Budget Rent-A-Car and of course Ugly Duckling. By 1985 Ugly Duckling was the nation's fifth largest car rental company. Its sales reached $65 million from 550 franchises at the end of 1985, but in 1989 the company declared bankruptcy, thus ending phase one of this story.

A transition period began in 1990 with the involvement of Ernest C. Garcia II. Born in Gallup, New Mexico, in 1957, Garcia studied business at the University of Arizona in Tucson before working in real estate, banking, and securities. In 1990 he formed a company called Duck Ventures, Inc., which purchased the assets of Ugly Duckling Rent-A-Car. Meanwhile, Garcia had to work through some major financial and legal difficulties before moving on.

In October 1990 Garcia pled guilty to felony bank fraud related to the savings-and-loan crisis of the 1980s. In 1987 Garcia had obtained a $20 million loan from Charles Keating's Lincoln Savings & Loan. That gave Garcia's real estate development company the funds it needed to buy back some stock from an investor. However, Garcia also agreed at the time of the loan to buy land from a Lincoln subsidiary. The Resolution Trust Company found the two transactions were improperly linked, without directly blaming Garcia. In December 1993 the U. S. District Court for the Central District of California sentenced Garcia with a $50 fine and a three-year probation, a light penalty due to Garcia's full cooperation with the authorities. Meanwhile, his real estate company had declared Chapter 11 bankruptcy and he had filed personally for Chapter 7 bankruptcy.

Garcia in 1992, while his case was still in the district court, incorporated Ugly Duckling Holdings, Inc., an Arizona firm which purchased Duck Ventures, Inc. and made it a subsidiary.

Company Perspectives:

Ugly Duckling Corporation aspires to be the leader in the sub-prime used car sales and finance industry. To accomplish this, we must provide superior value and service to our customers, hire and retain the best employees by offering them a challenging, enjoyable, and rewarding work environment, and deliver an excellent return on investment to our stockholders.

He started out by buying a small used-car dealership in Phoenix and later in 1992 purchased a second dealership in Tucson.

Garcia could have changed the company's name, but he stuck with Ugly Duckling. "We have enormous fun with the duck and we go with the name tongue in cheek," said Garcia in the August 25, 1996 *Arizona Tribune.* "We're just using it to have fun. We're not saying our cars are ugly or anything else, because if you look at our facilities, if you look at the automobiles . . . we're clearly selling a very competitive and clean product."

Ups and Downs from 1993 to 1995

In 1993 Garcia acquired three Ugly Duckling dealerships. The next year the company built four brand new dealerships with an improved upscale look. Although the firm still catered to those with lower incomes, it wanted to do so in a more positive atmosphere compared to the dirty and dusty lots of some sub-prime dealerships.

Ugly Duckling closed one dealership in 1994 because it did not measure up to the firm's high standards. In addition, in late 1995 it closed its dealership in Gilbert, Arizona, because the firm's experiment to sell later model used cars there failed. The Gilbert dealership tried in 1995 to sell cars two to seven years newer and often twice the cost of those at other Ugly Duckling dealerships, but the company's infrastructure and financing programs could not accommodate those kinds of vehicles. So Ugly Duckling sold the land and dealership building for $1.7 million.

By the mid-1990s Ugly Duckling was gaining popularity in its Arizona home base. "You go to Tucson or Phoenix and people know The Duck," said William Gibson, Cruttenden Roth's senior investment analyst in the October 14, 1996 *Investor's Business Daily.* "It's an icon in those cities."

To help its customers buy a used car and establish a positive credit rating, Ugly Duckling offered several innovations. From January through March, it offered to help customers prepare their income tax returns and even pay preparation fees. In return, a customer could use his or her forthcoming tax refund for credit toward a car down payment, instead of waiting extra weeks for the government to send a refund check.

Another program was established as an incentive to make installment payments on time. If customers paid all or almost all of their payments when due, they were refunded their down payment when the contract was completed. Down payments accounted for 10 to 15 percent of the purchase price, so this was a substantial refund.

Third, Ugly Duckling offered qualified customers the chance to gain a Visa credit card. The company actually secured those cards by paying a $250 deposit to the credit card firm. This demonstrated a great deal of confidence in Ugly Duckling customers and gave them an opportunity to rebuild positive credit histories.

Fourth, the company dealerships had onsite repair facilities to service the used cars it sold. Broken-down cars were a major reason for customers no longer making their car payments, so Ugly Duckling offered repair contracts to their used car customers. Not surprisingly, these optional contracts were financed.

Since many Ugly Duckling customers did not have credit cards, the company allowed them to pay cash for their monthly installments at their dealerships. Most car dealers did not give customers that option.

In 1994 Ugly Duckling acquired Champion Financial Services from Steve Darak. Champion became a subsidiary and Darak became Ugly Duckling's chief financial officer. Acquired mainly because of its management's skills and its contract servicing software, Champion Financial became Ugly Duckling's second source of making money. When it was purchased in 1994, Champion had sub-prime contracts worth $1.9 million.

Through a network of branch offices, the first one opening in April 1995, Champion Financial Services purchased sub-prime car installment contracts from third-party used car dealers. Those contracts generally were with customers with more resources than those who purchased a used car from an Ugly Duckling dealership.

At the end of 1995, after four years in business, Ugly Duckling's financial picture was quite mixed. The good news was that total revenues, the bulk of which were comprised by used car sales, had consistently increased, reaching $58.2 million revenues ($47.8 million from car sales alone) at the end of 1995. However, in three of those four years the company lost money, including losses of $2 million and $4 million in 1994 and 1995, respectively.

Growth and Competition in 1996 and 1997

In April 1996 the Arizona firm of Ugly Duckling Holdings, Inc. reincorporated in Delaware under the new name of Ugly Duckling Corporation.

As Ugly Duckling expanded its used car sales, it simultaneously reduced its rental car business. By August 1996 it had closed more than 100 rental franchises, leaving about 40 still in operation. The firm planned to completely end that type of business when its last franchise contracts expire within 10 years.

In June 1996 Ugly Duckling became a public corporation. On the NASDAQ exchange under the symbol Ugly, its IPO consisted of 2.3 million shares of common stock sold at $6.75 per share. It was underwritten by Cruttenden Roth Inc. of Irvine, California. Later in the month more stock was sold for a total of 3.1 million shares. That month's offerings raised $17.8 million in additional equity, including $14.8 million in cash and the conversion of $3 million in subordinated debt to common stock. The firm raised $65 million in its secondary stock offering at $15 per share in November 1996, underwritten by Cruttenden

Roth and also Friedman, Billings, Ramsey & Company of Arlington, Virginia. Ugly Duckling used funds from these stock offerings to open a new Arizona dealership but mainly to reduce its total debt from $49.8 million in 1995 to $26.9 million at the end of 1996.

In 1997 Ugly Duckling continued to raise money through stock sales and other means. In February 1997 it announced it had sold to institutional investors five million shares of common stock at $18.625 per share. The investors included Boston's Wellington Management Company and Fort Lee, New Jersey's Kramer Spellman L.P., the owner of five percent of Ugly Duckling's shares. Some stock analysts were surprised by the success of this offering, since many stocks in the subprime auto sales and financing industry had declined recently by about 30 percent. In the February 12, 1997 *Wall Street Journal,* one of Kramer Spellman's managers stated, "There are good companies and bad companies and I think we're seeing some of the shakeout."

That same article described how Ugly Duckling was taking advantage of the problems in other car financing companies. In early 1997 Mercury Finance admitted to "accounting irregularities." Chairman Garcia said that 30 of his 35 managers formerly worked for Mercury and that "Up until last week it [Mercury Finance] was a great thing. Whatever their problems . . . , for 12 years they were the leader in the industry and we consider their people to be the best trained."

In May 1997 GE Capital increased its line of credit available to Ugly Duckling Corporation from $50 million to $100 million. Under the terms of that Revolving Credit Facility, GE Capital had the power to limit Ugly Duckling's decisions such as incurring more debt, making loans or cash advances to company leaders, paying dividends, and merging with another firm.

Ugly Duckling announced in July 1997 that it had signed an agreement with First Merchants Acceptance Corporation to provide it up to $10 million in "debtor in possession" financing. Earlier First Merchants had filed a Chapter 11 bankruptcy petition, so the Bankruptcy Court had to approve any financing provided by Ugly Duckling to First Merchants.

Ugly Duckling aggressively opened several used car dealerships in 1997. It started in January by purchasing five subprime car dealerships and $35 million in finance contracts from Seminole Finance Corporation in the Tampa/St. Petersburg, Florida, area.

In April 1997 it completed its acquisition of some of the assets of E-Z Plan, Inc., a sub-prime sales and finance firm based in San Antonio, Texas. For $26.3 million, Ugly Duckling purchased seven "Red McCombs EZ Motors" used car dealerships, including vehicle inventory and finance contracts. The same week it also opened its first dealership in Las Vegas. Later in the year it added two other dealerships in New Mexico.

By August 1, 1997, Ugly Duckling operated a total of 24 dealerships in Arizona, New Mexico, Florida, Texas, and Nevada, which made it the largest public "buy here, pay here" chain in the nation. Most dealerships included 100 to 300 used vehicles of all kinds, ranging in age from five to 10 years old with an average price of about $7,100.

In addition, Ugly Duckling by August 1, 1997, operated a total of 64 branch offices in 17 states. These offices had purchased finance contracts from about 2,710 third-party dealers through Champion Financial Services, Inc.

The finance contracts purchased by Ugly Duckling from third-party dealers usually required customers to buy casualty insurance within 30 days of purchasing a vehicle. Most bought insurance on their own, but Ugly Duckling was able to purchase a policy for them and then charge them the premiums. The firm through its Drake Insurance Agency subsidiary contracted with American Bankers Insurance Group to force customers to get their car insurance. By the end of December 1996 Ugly Duckling had signed up through this process about 1,200 customers. Although not a major part of Ugly Duckling operations, the firm was considering expanding its services to cover life, disability, and unemployment insurance.

In September 1996 Ugly Duckling announced that it was adding a third revenue generator to its portfolio, to supplement its used car sales and Champion Finance income. It formed Cygnet Finance, Inc. as a subsidiary to offer a source of alternative credit to buy-here pay-here independent used car dealers. Ugly Duckling's leaders felt that many of the nation's independent dealers were undercapitalized and had trouble gaining access to more traditional sources of financing, so Cygnet could bridge that gap. By the end of 1996 Cygnet had hired a former GE Capital employee to be Cygnet's vice-president, tested its proprietary software used to closely monitor participating dealers, and enrolled its first independent dealer in its finance program.

To promote these various services, in November 1996 Ugly Duckling hired two new advertising firms. First, it replaced Moses & Anshell of Phoenix with the Riester Corporation of Phoenix to conduct its general marketing. Second, it hired the Dallas firm Dieste & Partners to start Ugly Duckling advertising in Spanish. With the number of Spanish speakers rapidly growing in the Southwest, that last move was indeed timely.

Since loan defaults were an obvious problem in Ugly Duckling's industry, the firm used its Champion Acceptance Corporation to verify loan application data and use collection techniques for both owned and serviced loans.

Ugly Duckling's overall financial performance showed definite improvement in 1996 and appeared to be continuing in 1997. Total 1996 revenues increased almost 30 percent to $75.6 million. Instead of losing money as it had in 1992, 1994, and 1995, Ugly Duckling in 1996 had net earnings of $5.9 million. The company's first quarter 1997 report showed revenues of $30.6 million, up 58 percent from first quarter 1996, and net earnings reached $3.3 million, compared to $1.1 million in first quarter 1996.

This 1997 expansion was reflected in the number of company employees. From 652 employees on December 31, 1996, the firm had increased to 1,776 employees by early September 1997.

Although Ugly Duckling had made major strides in just a few years, it faced some tough competitors in the late 1990s. The used car business really boomed in the 1990s, with many players entering this volatile industry. The basic incentive was that used cars earned about a 10 percent profit per car, compared to just two percent for each new car sold. Many new car dealers and also rental car agencies began selling their good used cars. In addition, several large companies entered the used car market. For example, Circuit City started CarMax, a huge chain of used car dealerships. Another player was AutoNation, USA, which purchased Alamo-Rent-a-Car to have a ready source of over 100,000 used cars every year. Of course, many of these operations sold newer cars to more affluent customers than those targeted by Ugly Duckling.

Although Ugly Duckling gained most of its revenue from used car sales, that percentage dropped significantly from 82 percent in 1995 to 71 percent in 1996. The firm in 1996 saw major increases in its revenues from interest income, gain on sale of loans, and servicing and other income. And since the company finances almost all the cars it sells, one analyst in the November 11, 1996 *Washington Post* said Ugly Duckling was "a bank masquerading as a used-car lot." That was a good way of describing what seemed to be Ugly Duckling's strategy in 1997: to continue to sell used cars but also strive to be a major player in the financial and credit aspects of the sub-prime used car retail industry.

Principal Subsidiaries

Duck Ventures, Inc.; Ugly Duckling Car Sales, Inc.; Champion Acceptance Corporation; Champion Financial Services, Inc.; UDRAC, Inc.; Champion Receivables Corporation; Drake Insurance Services, Inc.

Further Reading

Byrne, John A., "Keeping Out of Mischief Now," *Forbes,* October 8, 1984, p. 238.

Croft, Nancy L., "It's Never Too Late," *Nation's Business,* September 1986, p. 18.

Dunaj, Diana, "Ugly: Tucson Car Rental Firm Turns Beautiful Profits," *Arizona Business Gazette,* December 30, 1985, p. A1.

Elliott, Alan R., "Swan-To-Be," *Investor's Business Daily,* October 14, 1996.

Giblin, Paul, "Ugly Duckling Looks to Turn into a Swan with Expansion," *Arizona Tribune,* August 25, 1996.

Knight, Jerry, "Dealing in Stock Cars, Both New and Used," *Washington Post,* November 11, 1996, p. WB27.

Pulliam, Susan, "Ugly Duckling, Subprime Auto Lender Run by Convicted Felon, Manages to Raise Money," *Wall Street Journal,* February 12, 1997, p. C2.

—David M. Walden

Uncle Ben's Inc.

5721 Harvey Wilson Dr.
Houston, Texas 77251
U.S.A.
(713) 674-9484
Fax: (713) 670-2227
Web site: http://www.unclebens.com

Wholly Owned Subsidiary of Mars, Inc.
Incorporated: 1942 as Converted Rice, Inc.
Employees: 750
Sales: $1 billion (1997 est.)
SICs: 2044 Rice Milling

A subsidiary of Mars, Inc., Uncle Ben's Inc. is one of the world's leading marketers of rice. It boasts an estimated one-fourth of the United States market for dry rice and ranks number one in Great Britain and France. The company produces a broad variety of rice products, including boil-in-bag, instant, microwaveable, and wild rices as well as cooking sauces, couscous, and fried rice mixes. Uncle Ben's products can be found in over 100 countries worldwide, and the company has production facilities in Australia, Germany, Great Britain, the Netherlands, and Belgium, as well as its Texas headquarters plant. In addition to its namesake brand, Uncle Ben's sells foods under the Country Inn, Suzi Wan, and Kan Tong labels.

Created as a private partnership, Uncle Ben's was acquired from its founders by Forrest Mars' Food Manufacturers, Inc. during its first few years in business. It became a subsidiary of privately held Mars, Inc. in 1964, when Forrest Mars merged his company with his father's confectionery. Uncle Ben's rice is without a doubt Mars' most healthful product intended for human consumption. With estimated sales of over $13 million, the candy giant's other products include Combos snacks; M&Ms, Snickers, Skittles, and other candies; Dove premium ice cream; and Pedigree and Whiskas pet foods. Though the company does not release financial information, author Jan Pottker singled out Uncle Ben's as Mars' best-performing subsidiary in the 1990s.

Under Forrest and his progeny, Mars and its subsidiaries have operated under a cloak of secrecy. For example, while Uncle Ben's has a World Wide Web presence, the site is closed to the public.

Mid-20th-Century Origins

The origins of Uncle Ben's can be traced to the 1930s, when British food chemist Eric Huzenlaub embarked on the development of a process to increase the nutritional value of white rice. At that time, modern milling methods removed rice kernels' nutrient-bearing husk and outer skins, resulting in a pleasingly pearly white, but nutritionally empty carbohydrate. After a decade of research, Huzenlaub came up with a way to seal in rice's naturally occurring vitamins and minerals. Dubbed ''conversion'' or ''parboiling,'' the technique employed vacuum pressure to pull air from raw rice, then ''pushed'' the water-soluble nutrients back into each grain using high-pressure steam heating. Once the rice had dried, it could continue through the usual milling process. Not only did the technique—for which Huzenlaub obtained international patents—seal in nutrients, it also extended shelf life to years, made the grain impervious to weevils, and reduced cooking time.

Huzenlaub knew he had developed a food manufacturing process that had the potential to positively revolutionize the diets of millions of people around the world. He intended to establish mills in India (then a colony of Great Britain) and other nations where rice was a dietary staple, but was prevented from doing so by the advent of World War II. Hoping to establish some kind of foothold in the rice industry, Huzenlaub turned to the United States. Though per capita rice consumption was comparatively puny—Americans ate 98 percent less rice per year than Indians—the U.S. was the world's biggest consumer market, and offered immense potential for growth. In 1942, Huzenlaub pitched his process to several major millers, but to no avail. Only one person showed any interest in rice conversion, Houston food broker Gordon Harwell.

Having made his own attempts at converting rice, Harwell was certain of the process's efficacy. He convinced a reluctant Huzenlaub to join him in a partnership known as Converted

Company Perspectives:

Rice is now right up there with pasta as America's favorite dish. It's so versatile, you can eat it every night and never get bored.

Rice, Inc. Exhausting his personal savings, Harwell salvaged a boiler and a pressure tank from a junkyard, rented space in a warehouse, and started producing rice to feed the U.S. Armed Forces. By the end of 1944, the company had two mills and was processing about 200 tons of rice each day. One high-ranking Army officer considered the new rice one of the war's most important breakthroughs.

Acquisition by Forrest Mars

Around this same time Forrest Mars, son of candy maker Frank C. Mars, was looking for a new business interest. Forrest was at that time operating his own company, London-based Food Manufacturers, Ltd. Starting out in the early 1930s with $50,000 and the overseas rights to his father's Milky Way candy bar, Forrest had proven highly successful. He acquired a pet food business mid-decade and built it into the industry leader. Forrest returned to the U.S. in 1940, founding M&M Limited to produce and market the bite-sized chocolates with the colorful candy shell. Seeking further diversification, he bought into Converted Rice not long after its founding. Mars' investment and a timely government loan provided much-needed capital for the fledgling firm.

The company took its current name and brand identity from the tale of a Texan who was renowned for his award-winning rice. The story goes that ''Uncle Ben,'' a black farmer, grew rice so good that other farmers used it as a standard of excellence. Since the ''real'' Uncle Ben had long since died, Harwell asked Frank Brown, maitre d' of a Chicago restaurant, to pose as the character. Brown's beaming, bow-tied, visage became the company logo. This little-known event has been designated a milestone in the history of advertising, constituting the first time a raw commodity was given a brand name. Harwell registered not only the name but also the term ''converted'' as corporate trademarks.

The launch of Uncle Ben's rice was well-timed. The product was a staple of many soldiers' wartime diet. Government price controls helped support America's relatively young rice-growing industry. At the war's end, Uncle Ben's Converted Rice earned a place among a growing category of convenience foods. Not only did this new product cook up faster than unconverted rice, it was also easier to prepare; so simple, in fact, that Uncle Ben's advertisers boasted that it ''cooks up perfect every time.'' Having achieved the top spot in the U.S. rice market by 1952, Uncle Ben's was launched in the United Kingdom and later France and Austria.

Uncle Ben's started out as a partnership, but it was not long before the infamously imperious Forrest Mars gained full control and made it a subsidiary of Food Manufacturers. By 1960, Uncle Ben's was contributing about $30 million to Food Manufacturers' estimated annual sales of $200 million. Following the death of his stepmother, Forrest Mars wrested control of Mars, Inc. from his step-family in 1964 and merged it with his own firm, making Uncle Ben's a subsidiary of Mars.

Growth Encouraged by Advertising

American rice consumption grew steadily throughout the intervening years, increasing from about six pounds per capita per year in the 1940s to about 10 pounds by the end of the 1970s. As he had with his candies and pet foods, Forrest Mars captured much of this growth by backing Uncle Ben's with hefty advertising outlays. By the early 1990s, LNA/Arbitron estimated Uncle Ben's annual ad budget at $18 million, or well over 10 percent of sales.

This strong ad support would become something of a stumbling block in later years, when many consumers rejected the use of stereotypical images of African Americans in advertising. Such advertising icons as Aunt Jemima, Cream of Wheat's Rastus, and Uncle Ben came under fire, and some were even revised to accommodate modern tastes. While his portrait remained unchanged, Uncle Ben shrunk down over the years from a full-sized image that took up the entire box front to a small oval at the top. In fact, the portrait disappeared from the box in the 1980s. Some observers cast this move as a reaction to consumer protests, but the company asserted that it was merely a marketing maneuver in preparation for a brand extension. The image was eventually reinstated, and remained a brand logo into the late 1990s.

When Forrest retired in 1973, his eldest son, Forrest, Jr., became chairman, CEO, and copresident in charge of the candy division. Younger son Frank was copresident with responsibility for Mars' other products, including Uncle Ben's. Though the Uncle Ben's subsidiary had its own president as well, it was clear that the Mars brothers were the ultimate authority.

Strong Growth Predicted in 1990s and Beyond

In a rare interview with *Food Processing* magazine, Uncle Ben's executive Tony DeLio noted three food trends that were expected to impact his company in a positive way in the 1990s. As it had since the end of World War II, convenience continued to be an important consideration. Uncle Ben's strove to develop side dishes and ''meal helpers'' that were easy and quick to prepare. DeLio also emphasized the growing ''entertainment'' value of foods, particularly those of the ethnic or exotic variety. He also cited responsible eating—encompassing both environmentally and nutritionally sound foods—as an important consumer consideration in the 1990s. Uncle Ben's got a little help in this area from the U.S. Department of Agriculture, whose ''Food Pyramid'' guidelines recommended rice among the carbohydrates that should form the foundation of a healthy diet. Furthermore, the company has benefited and should continue to benefit from ever-increasing rice consumption in its key markets, the United States and the United Kingdom. Per capita rice consumption in the U.S. doubled to over 20 pounds per year from 1979 to 1992.

Uncle Ben's introduced products that met some or all of these factors. Microwaveable rice, rice-in-an-instant, fast-cooking brown rice, and boil-in-bag rice were promoted for their convenience. Country Inn flavored rices, Kan Ton fried rice mix and Eastern Traditions rices, as well as couscous and rice pilafs added variety to the equation. Meal Makers brand cooking sauce and add-meat mix brought Uncle Ben's into the main dish arena. The company entered the "neutraceutical" or "functional food" segment in 1997 with the introduction of rice fortified with calcium, vitamins, and other minerals. Uncle Ben's even signed on Nigerian-born NBA star Hakeem "the Dream" Olajuwon to promote a new brand of rice. Dubbed Hakeem's Dream Rice, the new product was targeted at consumers in the Middle East and Africa.

Uncle Ben's emerged as Mars' most promising growth vehicle in the 1990s, when the parent company lost its U.S. candy supremacy to longtime rival Hershey and its pet food interests struggled to compete in that hotly contested market.

Further Reading

Criswell, Ann, "Meet a Very Rice Family," *Houston Chronicle,* November 4, 1992, p. 1.

Desloge, Rick, "D'Arcy Snags Uncle Ben's Rice Account," *St. Louis Business Journal,* March 6, 1995, p. 1.

Engleberg, Adrian, "The Rice Race," *New Orleans Magazine,* January 1988, p. 14.

Fisher, Christy, and Judann Dagnoli, "Battle in the Rice Field; General Foods, Uncle Ben's Blast Comparative Ads," *Advertising Age,* February 6, 1989, pp. 3–4.

Fisher, Christy, "Rice Is Nice, But . . . Uncle Ben's Tests Add-Meat Vegetable Sauces," *Advertising Age,* May 27, 1991, p. 32.

Katayama, Frederick H., "Uncovering Mars' Unknown Empire," *Fortune,* September 26, 1988.

Kent, George, "Two Practical Men Revolutionize the Processing of Rice," *Washington Post,* January 16, 1944, p. 6B.

Kevin, Kitty, "Uncle Ben's Mooves Rice: Calcium Plus Rice Brings Functional Food to the Rice Aisle," *Food Processing,* April 1997, pp. 34–35.

Martin, Justin, "Mars Has a New Center," *Fortune,* February 5, 1996, p. 38.

McCarthy, Michael, "Uncle Ben to Cook with One Agency?" *ADWEEK Eastern Edition,* March 1, 1993, p. 3.

Meyer, Ann, "Mission from Mars," *Prepared Foods,* March 1992, p. 49.

Meyers, Harold B., "The Sweet, Secret World of Forrest Mars," *Fortune,* May 1967, pp. 154–57, 208–10.

Morgan, Dan, "The Rice Connection," *Washington Post,* August 7, 1977, p. B1.

Pottker, Jan, *Crisis in Candyland: Melting the Chocolate Shell of the Mars Family Empire,* New York: National Press Books, Inc., 1995.

——, "Sweet Secrets," *Washingtonian,* January 1996, pp. 59–62.

Siragusa, Gail, "Microwave-Specific Rice Carving a Market Niche," *Supermarket News,* October 15, 1990, p. 20.

"The Story of Uncle Ben," Houston, Tex.: Uncle Ben's, Inc., 1988.

Toops, Diane, "Trend Tracking: Uncle Ben's Tony DeLio Speculates on Convenience, Entertainment and Responsibility," *Food Processing,* August 1997, pp. 46–47.

Turcsik, Richard, "Stirring the Sauces," *Supermarket News,* October 10, 1994, pp. 31–32.

—April Dougal Gasbarre

U.S. Delivery Systems, Inc.

11 Greenway Plaza, Suite 250
Houston, Texas 77046
U.S.A.
(713) 867-5070
Fax: (713) 867-5050

Wholly Owned Subsidiary of Corporate Express, Inc.
Incorporated: 1993
Employees: 9,000
Sales: $346 million (1995)
SICs: 4215 Courier Services Except By Air; 4212 Local Trucking Without Storage; 7381 Detective & Armored Car Services

An integral part of the fastest-growing office-supplies company in the United States, U.S. Delivery Systems, Inc. serves as the delivery backbone for its parent Corporate Express, Inc., operating a fleet of 7,500 delivery vehicles throughout the country. U.S. Delivery was founded in 1993 as a combination of six same-day, local delivery service companies. A spate of acquisitions followed—all same-day local delivery service companies—as the company rapidly developed into the largest national company capable of providing local delivery service. In 1996, the company merged with Corporate Express, which operated in more than 190 locations in the United States, Canada, the United Kingdom, and Australia.

Origins

U.S. Delivery made its debut in the business world in 1993, and shortly thereafter drew the attention of industry observers. Their interest was piqued for several reasons. The company was recording explosive financial growth, its geographic reach was rapidly enveloping the country, and, perhaps most intriguing, it was attempting to do what no other company in the courier industry had ever accomplished. At the time, the courier industry was a $15 billion-a-year-business and highly fragmented, comprising roughly 10,000 small companies who provided same-day, local delivery services. U.S. Delivery, in its push to become an industry pioneer, was intent on entirely changing the face of its industry. U.S. Delivery was attempting to take all the best-run companies of the industry's 10,000 competitors, merge them together, and create the first national company to provide same-day, local delivery service. It was a lofty ambition, one that required a careful study of key acquisition candidates, the financial wherewithal to wage an extensive acquisition campaign, and the savvy to meld the disparate collection of individual courier companies into one coherent and efficient whole. It was a concept envisioned by the individual behind U.S. Delivery, Clayton K. Trier, who proved to be aptly suited to the task before him.

Trier's greatest skill was in the corporate art of identifying, negotiating, and completing acquisitions. His professional career before he took the helm at U.S. Delivery had demonstrated such. An accountant by training and a former Arthur Andersen partner, Trier earned his reputation during the late 1980s while serving as the chief financial officer of Allwaste, Inc., an industrial waste cleaning company operating in a highly fragmented industry. Trier was one of the chief reasons Allwaste recorded phenomenal growth between 1987 and 1990. The waste cleanup industry was going through a major consolidation phase, and during a three-year period Trier orchestrated the purchase of at least 49 waste service firms. ''He [Trier] helped identify many of the opportunities we took advantage of,'' remembered an Allwaste senior executive, ''and he was instrumental in negotiating and finalizing the acquisitions we were involved in.'' Despite Trier's decisive contributions to Allwaste's growth, the company's meteoric rise was followed by an equally demonstrative downward spiral. By 1990, after the hazards of asbestos removal were publicized, Allwaste's stock value (which was used to finance the numerous acquisitions spearheaded by Trier) dropped significantly and the company never fully recovered. Trier resigned in 1990, vacating his post as president to start his own company, Trier & Partners Inc., a consulting firm for a wide range of environmental companies.

Trier would use the same acquisitive skill honed at Allwaste to build U.S. Delivery into a national mainstay. But before the mammoth chore of shaping myriad separate pieces into a seamless whole could begin, the intervention of one of Trier's longtime business associates was required, because the idea of creating U.S. Delivery was not Trier's. Credit for that inspiration fell to Trier's friend, Mike Baker, a former associate counsel for Browning-Ferris Industries who called Trier in 1993 and discussed the possibility of uniting six local delivery companies in Texas, California, and New York. According to Trier, his first reaction was, "You mean those spiky-haired guys on bicycles," but as he thought further the idea sounded right for the times and suited to his talents. By 1993, economically recessive conditions had prompted corporate America to make wholesale changes, and two of those changes, as Trier saw it 1993, provided lucrative opportunities for something the American business world had yet to see: a national company able to deliver same-day, local delivery service. Companies throughout the country were reducing the financial burdens stemming from carrying large inventories by switching to "just-in-time" delivery of materials and components: a boon for delivery companies. Further, the emphasis on reducing costs wherever possible had led businesses to eliminate many in-house departments, including courier service, creating a pressing need for a company able to compensate for all the delivery activities formerly done by company employees. Add to the equation that the courier industry was highly fragmented and would require someone well versed in the procedures of acquiring one small company after another, and Trier was hooked. Before the end of the year in 1993, U.S. Delivery was formed, with Trier holding sway as the company's president, chief executive officer, and chairman.

When Baker called Trier about the possibility of joining six local delivery companies together, his suggestion was not a hollow thought, barren of any financial might. Baker, since his days at Browning-Ferris Industries, had gone on to found his own venture capital firm, Utah-based Notre Capital Ventures, which staked Trier $300,000 and promised to cover $2 million in start-up expenses to get the fledgling U.S. Delivery up and running. Neither Baker nor Trier were aspiring entrepreneurs plotting their actions in the corner of a household kitchen. Their plan was big business, requiring vast sums of cash. With no time to waste, the particulars of creating a national, yet locally-oriented delivery company were brought together. A group of investors were brought into the fold, including the owners of two local delivery companies that Trier and Baker had targeted as U.S. Delivery's initial acquisition candidates. First on the acquisition list were two delivery companies based in Houston, where U.S. Delivery established its headquarters. They were Eastway Delivery Services of Houston Inc., which had operations in eastern Texas and Louisiana, and ViaNet Inc., which served Texas, Louisiana, and Tennessee. The other four companies of the six original companies were two Northeast firms, First National Courier Systems Inc. and Grace Courier Service Inc., and two West and Midwest companies, U.S. Courier Corporation of San Francisco and U.S. Service Corporation of America. In addition to these six delivery companies, Trier was also in pursuit of Maryland-based CallCenter Services Inc. to provide inbound telemarketing services for retail distribution. These were the initial building blocks of a company that was expected to cover as much of the nation as possible.

With the six delivery companies supported by the national telemarketing company, Trier hoped to serve at least 22 markets at first, including eight of the 10 largest metropolitan areas in the country. As 1993 turned to 1994, however, all Trier had was hope. Until the spring of 1994, U.S. Delivery had few existing assets, no operations, and, except on paper and in the minds of a handful of individuals, did not exist. The magical force that would bring life to the company was an initial public offering (IPO) of stock, the completion of which was a prerequisite for the consummation of the contracts to purchase the seven companies that would compose the core of U.S. Delivery. Everything hinged on the IPO, and as the spring of 1994 drew to a close Trier and cohorts pinned their hopes on the appealing concept of a nationally-operated local delivery service to the investing public.

1994 Public Offering Ignites Expansion

In March 1994, Trier filed with the Securities and Exchange Commission for permission to sell 40 percent of the company to the public, hoping to garner between $36 million and $48 million from the IPO. When U.S. Delivery's stock debuted on the New York Stock Exchange in May, the company raised $30 million, slightly less than Trier's publicly revealed estimates but enough to make U.S. Delivery a reality. Once this major hurdle was cleared, the push was on to weave the fabric of a locally-oriented delivery company that could blanket the country. There were still 9,994 small courier companies available for the taking.

Once out from the starting block, Trier never looked back and never seemed to stop and gloat over what he had. U.S. Delivery went on a buying spree, purchasing the best companies in their respective cities across the nation. Sales by the end of 1994 hit $156 million, profits registered $6.5 million, providing a yardstick for future growth. By early 1995, the company maintained offices in 34 U.S. markets, and Trier was ready to make the impact of U.S. Delivery on the courier industry more profound.

In February 1995, Trier acquired Michigan-based American Distribution System Inc., a company involved in logistics management—the coordination of transportation, distribution, and warehousing of products—for industrial, commercial, and retail clients on a national basis. The acquisition was regarded as a significant step toward U.S. Delivery's pursuit of developing into a national local-delivery staple, giving it a thread of administrative support to connect its growing legions of local delivery companies. American Distribution also had contracts with a network of 250 same-day, local delivery companies, providing Trier with a ready-made list of potential acquisition candidates. Trier was ecstatic about the acquisition, saying, "I've never seen anything that fits as well together as U.S. Delivery's local delivery business and the contract logistics management business." Trier continued, "We're going to be able to increase our local revenues by taking advantage of the additional volumes of freight that American Distribution controls for its customers. And U.S. Delivery will increase American Distribution's revenue base by introducing them to our national account customers."

The acquisition spree did not slow before the purchase of American Distribution, nor did it slacken afterwards. During the month preceding the addition of American Distribution, U.S. Delivery had acquired five more local delivery companies, and in the months following the acquisition Trier continued to bolster the company's prowess, selecting what he determined were the best companies in each city he pinpointed. By the end of the summer in 1995, U.S. Delivery had acquired 33 small delivery companies since its IPO, with nine more purchases pending. All told, U.S. Delivery served 85 cities by the fall of 1995. ''We're blanketing the map,'' Trier noted with confidence, as he announced plans to add 30 more markets to U.S. Delivery's fold by 1997. As Trier had anticipated, U.S. Delivery was generating the bulk of its business from corporations that were outsourcing their distribution and delivery services. As a result, U.S. Delivery was winning the national accounts of massive conglomerates such as Exxon, which preferred to deal with one delivery operator rather than a swarm of small, local companies.

As U.S. Delivery was competing in the mid-1990s, it was the first and the largest public company in the same-day local delivery business, and was taking every measure to retain its distinction as the latter. Six more local delivery companies were purchased in September and October 1995, extending the geographic scope of the company's fleet of vans and trucks. The consistent influx of new businesses had been pushing sales upward since the IPO, and as 1995 drew to a close, sales for the year exceeded $340 million. Not surprisingly, Trier was pushing for further growth, vowing to add between $100 million and $150 million to the company's revenue volume by the end of 1996. Before that target date arrived, however, U.S. Delivery would be in a dramatically different position. By the end of 1995, Trier was involved in negotiations that would alter significantly U.S. Delivery's future.

1995 Merger with Corporate Express

The deal that made 1996 a year of great change for U.S. Delivery began next to a swimming pool in Palm Springs, California. Gathered together in Palm Springs were the nation's leading entrepreneurs, each a candidate for *Inc.* magazine's annual award bestowed to the nation's top entrepreneur. Trier was there and so was Jirka Rysavy, founder and chief executive of Corporate Express, Inc. The two businessmen had several things in common: Both were respected and successful entrepreneurs, Trier was 43 years old, Rysavy was 41, and both had attained stardom in the entrepreneurial field in much the same way. Rysavy had founded Corporate Express in 1986 by purchasing an unprofitable office-supply store in downtown Boulder, Colorado. He spent the ensuing decade acquiring as many small office-supply stores as possible, quickly securing a sizeable presence in a highly fragmented industry. The similarities were there, and each man recognized them. Further, their businesses had an obvious synergistic relationship—one was a delivery service and the other sold office-supply merchandise, which needed to be delivered. Given these shared characteristics, it was not surprising that as the two entrepreneurs lounged by the pool in Palm Springs their conversation turned to the topic of merging their companies.

Two months later, the deal was announced. The two companies jointly revealed they had executed a definitive agreement to merge that would create a corporate office-supply enterprise with a fleet of 7,500 vans and trucks and more than $1.6 billion in revenues. Trier was excited about the deal and what it meant for the future of U.S. Delivery. ''Our management team is highly enthusiastic about this strategic alliance,'' he told reporters. ''We believe that the pairing of Corporate Express' information technology systems and marketing experience with U.S. Delivery's understanding of the transportation and distribution needs of large commercial enterprises will create an organization capable of providing a unique mix of services both domestically and internationally. We believe joining forces with Corporate Express will allow us to grow at an accelerated pace, both internally and through acquisitions.''

In March 1996 the merger agreement was ratified by the shareholders of both companies, wedding together the nation's fastest-growing retailer of office supplies with the fastest-growing provider of same-day local delivery service. Under the terms of the agreement, Trier was given the responsibility of running U.S. Delivery as a subsidiary of Corporate Express. With both companies working together toward a common goal, Trier and Rysavy charted their course for the late 1990s, intent on creating a national force without rival.

Further Reading

''Corporate Express Agrees to Buy U.S. Delivery,'' *Wall Street Journal,* January 8, 1996, p. 3.

Ketelsen, James, ''Learning the Hard Way,'' *Forbes,* December 18, 1995, p. 130.

Lewis, Jerry W., ''Corporate Express: From $100 to $3 Billion Market Value,'' *Boulder County Business Report,* June 1996, p. 1.

Pybus, Kenneth, ''Allwaste Ex-President Goes Public with Nationwide Delivery Network: U.S. Delivery Seeking $48 Million to Buy 7 Businesses,'' *Houston Business Journal,* April 11, 1994, p. 1.

——, ''U.S. Delivery Breaks New Ground in Purchasing Michigan Company,'' *Houston Business Journal,* February 24, 1995, p. 2.

Schonfeld, Erick, ''Delivering Growth,'' *Fortune,* September 4, 1995, p. 137.

—Jeffrey L. Covell

ValueVision International, Inc.

6740 Shady Oak Road
Minneapolis, Minnesota 55344-3433
U.S.A.
(612) 947-5200
Fax: (612) 947-0188
Web site: http://www.vvtv.com

Public Company
Incorporated: 1990
Employees: 1,200
Sales: $159.5 million (1996)
Stock Exchanges: NASDAQ
SICs: 4833 Television Broadcasting Stations; 5961 Catalog & Mail-Order Houses

ValueVision International, Inc. is the third-largest home-shopping television network in the United States. An integrated direct marketing company which markets its products to consumers through electronics and print media, ValueVision International was founded in 1990 and incorporated in Minnesota in June of that year. Two of the company's corporate officers, Chairman and CEO Robert L. Johander, formerly president of Telethon Marketing Company, and President and COO Nicholas M. Jaksich, formerly vice-president of distribution and operations for Lillian Vernon Corporation, began at the same time and remained as of 1997. The company has rapidly grown to establish a solid market position as the third-largest home-shopping television network in the United States, after Home Shopping Network, Inc. and QVC Network, Inc.

Home Shopping and Direct Marketing, Apparatus and Products

The company's principal electronic media activity is its television home-shopping network, which uses recognized on-air television home-shopping personalities to market brand-name merchandise and proprietary and private-label consumer products at competitive or discount prices to millions of homes across the country. The company's live, 24-hour-per-day television home-shopping programming is distributed primarily through long-term cable affiliation agreements and the purchase of month-to-month full- and part-time block lease agreements of cable and broadcast television time. In addition, the company distributes its programming through company-owned or company-affiliated Ultra-High Frequency (UHF) broadcast television stations, low-power television (LPTV) stations, and to satellite dish owners via a leased communications satellite transponder.

The company, through its wholly owned subsidiary ValueVision Direct Marketing Company, Inc. (VVDM), is also a direct-mail marketer of a broad range of general merchandise which is sold to consumers through direct-mail catalogs and other direct-marketing solicitations. Products offered include domestics, housewares, seasonal items, home accessories, electronics, apparel, giftware, collectibles, and related merchandise. Through VVDM's wholly owned subsidiary Catalog Ventures, Inc., the company sells a variety of fashion jewelry, health and beauty aids, books, audio and video cassettes, and other related consumer merchandise through the publication of five consumer specialty catalogs. The company also manufactures and markets, via direct mail, women's foundation undergarments through VVDM's subsidiary Beautiful Images, Inc.

Developments During the 1990s

In 1991, one year after start-up of televised operations, the company introduced its Video Shopping Cart service, in which customers could order as many items as they wished in a 24-hour period and pay a single shipping and handling charge for the entire order. The following year the company began leasing blocks of cable television time from certain cable operators for its programming, posting a net loss of $1.8 million. In 1993 sales surpassed $14 million, despite a similar net loss.

At the end of January 1994, the company's programming was available to approximately 10.7 million cable homes, 2.6 million of which were full-time equivalent (FTE) cable homes, or homes which received the company's home-shopping program for any period less than 24 hours per day.

That same month, in an attempt to quickly put its TV order-processing and program production infrastructure to much wider use, the company proposed the acquisition of National Media Corporation. A month later, the company made a tender offer for a majority of the outstanding shares of National Media and March saw the two companies enter into a merger agreement. A month later, however, the company terminated the deal with National Media, citing inaccurate representations and breach of warranties by, as well as adverse regulatory developments concerning, the latter company. National Media filed four purported class-action lawsuits against the company, alleging deception and manipulative practices by ValueVision. In 1996, both companies agreed to dismiss all claims and enter into joint operating agreements involving telemarketing and post-production capabilities and to enter into an international joint venture agreement. The company was also granted the right, over three years, to purchase a half-million shares of National Media's stock. Also in 1996, the company sold its investment in National Media for $8.5 million.

In December, the company completed the acquisitions of WHAI-TV 43, an independent full-power television broadcast station serving the New York City market, for $7.3 million. Net income for 1994 reached $37.6 million, with a net loss of $1.9 million.

January 1995 was a busy month for the company. The first benchmark was the signing of an affiliation agreement with Time Warner Cable Direct, the nation's second-largest cable operator, adding nearly two million additional homes to the company's reach. A week later, the company hit its first single day of over $1 million in orders. Two days after that, the company added "The Brand Name Channel" to its program logo. By the end of the first month of 1995, the company's programming was available to approximately 12.2 million cable homes, 3.5 million of which were FTE cable homes, a 38.5 percent increase, the remaining homes being full-time cable and accounting for a 14 percent increase over the previous year.

As part of the same deal in which it acquired WHAI, the company also purchased and acquired three additional full-power television broadcast stations in various parts of the United States. Joining the company were WVVI-TV 66, serving the Washington, D.C. market; KVVV-TV, serving the Houston, Texas market; and WAKC-TV 23, an ABC affiliate serving Cleveland and Akron, Ohio. The total purchase price for all four stations was approximately $22.4 million. In July, the company changed its NASDAQ stock symbol from VVTVA to VVTV, reflecting the fact that the company no longer would offer multiple classes of common stock.

As the promise of government-mandated ease of access to cable channels by noncable-owned networks like ValueVision had become mired in governmental bureaucracy, the company sought supplemental opportunities to deploy its television production, systems, telemarketing, fulfillment, and customer service operating capacity. In pursuit of this, in August, the company entered into a strategic alliance with Montgomery Ward & Co., Incorporated, the nation's largest privately held retailer. As part of the deal, Montgomery Ward purchased nearly 1.3 million shares of the company's stock for $8 million and also purchased advertising spot time on cable systems affiliated with the company pursuant to cable affiliation agreements. Additionally, in an attempt to establish itself as a direct-marketing company, ValueVision began leveraging its television home-shopping infrastructure and expertise to acquire and integrate the Montgomery Ward Direct (MWD) catalog and print merchandising business to build its direct marketing operations. Some of the MWD assets the company intended to acquire included a three million name customer list developed since 1991, $8 million in inventory, $4 million in operating capital, and a sales stream that, even when pared back to reach acceptably profitable levels, the company expected would add approximately $70 million to its annualized revenues.

The company also introduced in 1995 an installment payment program called ValuePay, which allowed customers to purchase and pay for merchandise in two-to-four equal monthly installments. The program was introduced to increase sales while, at the same time, reduce return rates on merchandise with above-normal selling prices. Net income for 1995 was $53.9 million, a 43.4 percent increase over the previous year, attributable primarily to the growing number of homes receiving the company's programming, with a net loss of $6.1 million.

At the end of January 1996, the company's programming was available to approximately 13.6 million cable homes, 7.2 million of which were FTE cable homes, leaving 3.7 million full-time cable homes, a 106 percent increase over the previous year. The following month the company completed the sale of the WHAI and WAKC television stations to West Palm Beach, Florida-based Paxson Communications Corporation, the largest owner and operator of broadcast television stations in the United States, for $40 million. In May, the company completed the acquisition of independent television station KBGE-TV 33, the nation's 13th largest area of dominant influence (ADI), serving the Seattle-Tacoma, Washington market, for approximately $4.6 million.

By the end of June, the company's programming was available through affiliation and time-block purchase agreements with approximately 250 cable systems in addition to its wholly owned, full-power UHF television broadcast stations. Additionally, the company's programming was broadcast full-time over nine owned or affiliated low-power television stations in major markets and was available unscrambled to homes equipped with satellite dishes. In mid-August, the company signed a cable affiliation agreement with Tele-Communications, Inc. (TCI), the nation's largest cable operator, under which TCI would provide the company with access to nearly four million additional homes.

Throughout the year, the company continued to broaden its merchandise mix by expanding the range and quantity of non-jewelry items. September saw the company purchase all the assets of Montgomery Ward Direct L.P., the retailer's four-year-old catalog business, marketing its home decor and furnishings. The following month, the company acquired a direct mail operation called Beautiful Images, Inc., a Phoenix, Arizona-based leading direct marketer of women's undergarments. William Fitzgerald, the owner of Beautiful Images and former president and CEO of Hanover House, a direct marketing company, was named CEO of the MWD catalog operations.

In November, ValueVision Direct Marketing, Inc., a wholly owned subsidiary of the company, acquired two direct marketing companies, Catalog Ventures, Inc., specializing in the acquisition and launch of consumer catalogs, and Mitchell & Webb, Inc., a full-service direct marketing and creative agency specializing in catalog design, marketing services and circulation for Catalog Ventures as well as other clients. The sister companies, both located in Boston, Massachusetts, published five catalogs: Nature's Jewelry, The Pyramid Collection, Serengeti, NorthStyle, and The Mind's Eye. Revenues for the company in 1996 hit $88.9 million, a 65 percent increase over the previous year, with net income of $11 million, a huge jump over the previous year's loss. Revenues were higher due primarily to increased sales volume and higher gross margin percentages in most product categories, excepting electronics.

1997: Setting the Stage for the Future

In January 1997, the company relocated its Montgomery Ward Direct fulfillment facility from Minneapolis, Minnesota, to Bowling Green, Kentucky. By the end of January, the company's programming was reaching 19.8 million homes. March saw the company announce an agreement to acquire 15 percent of NetRadio Network, a subsidiary of Navarre Corporation, a leading national distributor of music, computer software, and interactive CD-ROM products. As part of the agreement, the company's shopping program audio feed would be carried by NetRadio.

In mid-April, the company initiated an Internet web site which allowed computer users to see and hear the same program the company broadcasted on cable television systems. The following month the company announced an agreement in which Ivana Trump Mazzucchelli would sell her "House of Ivana" line of products, including jewelry, clothing, fragrances, and skin care items, during regular on-air appearances on the company's televised programming. At the beginning of July, the company acquired 5.1 percent of CML Group, Inc. and at the end of that same month, the company sold its WVVI television station to Paxson for $30 million.

In October, the company and Montgomery Ward restructured the operating agreement between the two companies governing the use of the Montgomery Ward name. Under the new agreement terms, ValueVision would cede exclusive use of the name for catalog, mail order, catalog "syndications," and television shopping programming back to Montgomery Ward by March 1998. The company also agreed to repurchase the nearly 1.3 million shares of stock Montgomery Ward bought as part of the original deal. By the end of the year, revenues surpassed $159 million, a nearly 80 percent increase over the previous year.

Principal Subsidiaries

ValueVision Direct Marketing, Inc.; Beautiful Images, Inc.; Catalog Ventures, Inc.

Further Reading

Beatty, Sally Goll, "Broadcasting," *Wall Street Journal*, November 18, 1997, p. B10(W)/B6(E).

Brown, Rich, "Home Shopping Catalogue," *Broadcasting & Cable*, December 2, 1996, p. 58.

——, "ValueVision Builds War Chest: Home Shopper Has Money to Spend and Is Buoyed by Climbing Sales," *Broadcasting & Cable*, September 11, 1995, p. 44.

Burgi, Michael, "Home Shopping Network ValueVision International," *MEDIAWEEK*, December 12, 1994, p. 8.

"Changing Channels," *WWD*, May 16, 1997, p. 8.

Edelson, Sharon, "National Media, ValueVision in $150 Million Merger Pact," *WWD*, March 8, 1994, p. 2.

——, "Value Vision's National Ambitions," *WWD*, February 1, 1994, p. 16.

"Financing with a Twist," *Broadcasting & Cable*, March 21, 1994, p. 56.

Foisie, Geoffrey, "ValueVision Sees Value in Merger; But National Media May Try to Fight Takeover by Home Shopping Network," *Broadcasting & Cable*, February 14, 1994, p. 42.

"Home Shopping Deal," *WWD*, December 7, 1994, p. 4.

"Home Shopping Network," *Television Digest*, March 14, 1994, p. 8.

Kahn, Aron, "ValueVision to Buy Montgomery Ward Mail-Order Unit," *Knight-Ridder/Tribune Business News*, June 11, 1996, p. 6110125.

"Montgomery Ward," *Television Digest*, December 12, 1994, p. 5.

"Montgomery Ward & Co.," *Advertising Age*, August 1, 1994, p. 42.

"Montgomery Ward Buys Stake in Home Shopper," *ADWEEK Eastern Edition*, December 12, 1994, p. 18.

"National Media," *MEDIAWEEK*, March 14, 1994, p. 28.

"National Media Corp. Unanimously Rejected the Unsolicited Tender Offer for NMC by Home Shopping Concern ValueVision," *Broadcasting & Cable*, February 21, 1994, p. 80.

"Navarre, ValueVision Buy into NetRadio," *Broadcasting & Cable*, March 31, 1997, p. 40.

"Paxson Communications," *Television Digest*, November 26, 1996, p. 6.

Rathbun, Elizabeth A., "Paxson Buys 2 TVs, Drops Infomercial Cable Plan," *Broadcasting & Cable*, August 28, 1995, p. 6.

"Retail Forecasters at New York Convention Predict Boom in Home Shopping," *Knight-Ridder/Tribune Business News*, January 30, 1994, p. 01300306.

"Selling Electronics Electronically," *Television Digest*, August 1, 1994, p. 14.

"Service Merchandise, ValueVision Sign Deal for TV Home Shopping," *WWD*, March 16, 1994, p. 25.

"TV Station Sales," *Television Digest*, August 28, 1995, p. 6.

"2 Top Executives Leaving ValueVision," *New York Times*, August 29, 1997, p. C5(N)/D5(L).

"U.S. Appeals Court, D.C.," *Television Digest*, November 13, 1995, p. 6.

"ValueVision," *Television Digest*, March 14, 1994, p. 7.

"ValueVision," *Television Digest*, August 29, 1994, p. 4.

"ValueVision Buys Catalog Firms," *Wall Street Journal*, November 26, 1996, p. B10(W).

"ValueVision in Deal to Purchase Ward's Direct Catalog Business," *WWD*, June 11, 1996, p. 11.

"ValueVision Loses $3.8M in Quarter," *WWD*, May 27, 1994, p. 11.

"ValueVision On Board with Time Warner, Montgomery Ward," *Broadcasting & Cable*, December 12, 1994, p. 72.

"ValueVision Pounces," *WWD*, February 8, 1994, p. 12.

"ValueVision Said It Will Restructure Management," *Television Digest*, September 1, 1997, p. 6.

White, Todd, "ValueVision Buys Media," *Variety*, March 14, 1994, p. 65.

Wieffering, Eric J., "Poor Reception," *Corporate Report-Minnesota*, May 1994, p. 40.

—Daryl F. Mallett

Vistana, Inc.

Vistana, Inc.

8801 Vistana Centre Drive
Orlando, Florida 32821
U.S.A.
(407) 239-3100
Fax: (407) 239-3566

Public Company
Founded: 1980
Employees: 1,287
Sales: $96.9 million (1996)
Stock Exchanges: NASDAQ
SICs: 6531 Real Estate Agents & Managers; 6552 Land Subdividers & Developers; 6159 Miscellaneous Business Credit Institutions

Vistana, Inc. is a leading developer and operator of vacation ownership (''timeshare'') resorts in the United States. In September 1997, the company had more than 1,500 units in its six resorts and approximately 68,000 vacation ownership interests sold. Its resort properties were located in Florida (Vistana Resort, Vistana's Beach Club, and Hampton Vacation Resort-Oak Plantation), Colorado (Eagle Point Resort and Falcon Point Resort), and Arizona (the Villas of Cave Creek). In addition to its own operations, Vistana develops timeshare resorts under joint ventures with Promus Hotel Corporation and the Professional Golf Association of America. Through its resorts, the company also markets and sells timeshares, finances the purchase of vacation ownership interests, and provides management and telecommunications services. Co-CEOs Raymond Gellein, Jr., and Jeffrey Adler control some 70 percent of the company stock.

Background

The real estate timeshare concept began in the 1960s in the French Alps, as escalating costs led developers of resort condominiums to come up with a new way to sell their units. Their solution: subdivide the ownership of the units on a weekly basis, making them more affordable. Using this new type of ownership, someone could buy the exclusive right to use a furnished apartment unit at a resort, usually one week a year, for several decades. In the United States, buyers generally purchased a fee simple deed, gaining ownership to a fraction of the unit, which was treated as any other real estate interest. In Europe, developers sold a buyer a right to use (lease) the unit, but without an ownership interest.

Although the concept began with ski resorts, it quickly spread to resorts at beaches and golf courses and eventually to nearly any vacation venue, including houseboats, cruise ships, and campgrounds. For the price of the timeshare ($5,000 to $15,000) plus an annual maintenance fee ($125 to $400), the purchaser had a fixed-price vacation for decades. In 1974, Resort Condominiums International, Inc. added value to the purchase of a timeshare by organizing an international exchange network which enabled an owner, for a fee, to swap his or her ''vacation interval'' for a similar period at another timeshare resort. In 1978, timeshare ownership in the United States was a $3 million business.

For a while, the hardsell tactics of developers and difficulties owners had reselling their timeshares caused problems for the industry. During the 1980s, many states tightened regulations covering the marketing and promotion of timeshare units, requiring that promoters provide a prospectus and allowing a cooling-off period after sales.

The 1980s—Focus on Florida

At the start of the decade, worldwide sales of vacation ownerships stood at approximately $490 million. Vistana began operating in 1980, with the development of Vistana Resort, the first timeshare resort in Orlando, Florida. Orlando, in the central part of the state, was home to Walt Disney World, Sea World, and Cypress Gardens, and about an hour's drive to Atlantic and Gulf beaches. The first phase of the development, the Courts, offered 98 luxury villas, along with a large swimming pool and a championship tennis complex.

Raymond Gellein, Jr., became chief executive officer in 1981, and in 1983, Jeffrey Adler was named executive vice-president. Both men had been officers at Continental Illinois National Bank and Trust Co. of Chicago.

When selling its one-week fee simple Vacation Ownership Interests (VOIs), Vistana offered buyers the option of either an

Company Perspectives:

Vistana's Vision is to become the highest quality timeshare operation in the world, whose commitment to exceeding guest expectations drives the planning and delivery of all decisions.

annual or an alternate-year interest. With one week a year reserved for maintenance, the company could sell 51 annual VOIs or 102 alternative-year VOIs per villa.

As the Central Florida area added new attractions, Vistana Resort grew to accommodate more people. The second phase, the Falls, was completed in 1982, adding more villas, a club house, two swimming pools, and a children's playground.

A typical villa at Vistana Resort had two bedrooms and two baths (some with whirlpool bathtubs), a dining area and living room, and a terrace or balcony, with sleeping space for six to eight people. The fully equipped kitchen included a dishwasher and microwave oven, laundry facilities, and plates, utensils, and glassware for eight people. The resort provided daily housekeeping service, including washing the dishes. The units were fully furnished and carpeted.

Vistana continued to develop the 135-acre Orlando complex, building three restaurants, more tennis courts, an 18-hole miniature golf course, recreation centers with saunas, exercise rooms, and other amenities, and facilities for volleyball, shuffleboard, and jogging.

The timeshare vacation was becoming more popular as the leisure industry grew and earlier abuses were stopped. In 1985, sales exceeded $1.5 billion. One big reason for their popularity was the convenience of having a pre-arranged, fixed-price vacation at a location the owner liked. A major sales pitch was to compare the cost of a weekly timeshare vacation over five to 10 years with the cost of paying for hotel rooms for week-long vacations over the same period.

Major hotel chains such as Marriott and Hilton were not slow in responding to the competition, and began operating their own vacation ownership properties. Since marketing was the most expensive component in timeshare resorts once they were built, hotel chains, with their familiar brand names, had a decided advantage in that area.

At the end of 1986, Vistana was sold to a corporate acquirer. Gellein and Adler continued to head the company, and in 1989, they purchased and opened Vistana's Beach Club on Hutchinson Island, near West Palm Beach, about two hours south of Orlando. The Beach Club consisted of a nine-story building with 48 two-bedroom condominium apartments right on the beach, and various recreational facilities.

Expansion, 1990–95

In 1991, Gellein and Adler, with a third partner, repurchased Vistana and, in 1995, bought out the partner. By the mid-90s, the Orlando area was home to six timeshare resorts and the second largest concentration of timeshare ownerships in the world, accounting for more than a quarter of all timeshare interests in the United States. Worldwide, the timeshare industry had sales of $4.76 billion. Vistana continued to expand its properties, adding a second apartment building (for a total of 76 units) at Vistana's Beach Club and developing more villas at Vistana Resort. In 1995, Vistana sold 5,190 VIOs at an average price of $9,664, and had revenues of $81.1 million. In 1995 (and again in 1996) *Condé Nast Traveler* magazine selected Vistana Resort as a ''Gold List'' resort, the only timeshare resort on its list of the top 500 resorts in the world.

The owners of Vistana's interests lived in more than 100 countries, with about 30 percent of the sales to foreign purchasers. Florida was a popular vacation destination for the foreign market and Vistana took advantage of that, focusing on the South and Central American market, particularly Argentina, Guatemala, and Chile. The company maintained a direct foreign sales office in Santiago, Chile.

Vistana used three approaches to market the majority of its VOIs. In one program, a Vistana Preview Coordinator, located in the lobby of a hotel, vacation condominium, or other attraction near a Vistana resort, provided visitor information as well as information about Vistana to interested potential buyers. Between 1980 and 1996, the VPC program attracted some 400,000 people to tours of Vistana properties.

The second approach, the VIP/In-House Program, also used one-on-one contact. The difference here was that this program concentrated on people already staying at a Vistana property—owners, renters, or those on a timeshare exchange.

The third marketing strategy was to use a network of independent brokers to sell its VOIs abroad. The company also made use of other approaches, including direct mail, telemarketing, and vacation sampler programs, in which a potential buyer could experience timeshare ownership as a guest before deciding to purchase.

1996 to the Present

During the second half of the decade, Vistana took several steps to broaden its offerings and gain access to new markets. In June 1996, the company acquired the 16-acre Oak Plantation Villas in Kissimmee, just south of Orlando. Oak Plantation had been a rental apartment complex, and Vistana began converting the 242 one- and two-bedroom units and the property to a timeshare resort.

That year Vistana signed a five-year agreement with Promus Hotel Corporation. Promus was one of the world's largest hotel companies and owned and/or franchised more than 800 hotels, under the Embassy Suites, Hampton Inn, and Homewood Suites brand names. Under the agreement, the two companies would jointly acquire, develop, manage, and market vacation resorts in North America under the Embassy Vacation Resort, Hampton Vacation Resort, and Homewood Vacation Resort brands. Vistana would also have the option to operate the vacation resorts on a franchise basis.

While not the first timeshare developer to have a joint venture with a hotel chain (HFS licensed its Ramada hotel brand name to timeshare operator Mego Financial Corporation, and Promus also licensed it Embassy Vacation Resort brand to Signature Resorts) Vistana was the first to use one hotel company's different market concepts to reach various groups of potential buyers. The first activity under the agreement was to rename the Oak Plantation Villas in Kissimmee as the first mid-market Hampton Vacation Resort, which Vistana operated as a franchise. Prices for VOIs at that resort ranged from $7,250 to $10,950.

In December, Vistana bought 14 acres of land in Myrtle Beach, South Carolina, another popular timeshare area, moving out of Florida for the first time. The Myrtle Beach resort, with 48 units in its first phase, would be operated on a franchise agreement as an Embassy Vacation Resort when it opened in 1998.

Vistana also went after another market segment in 1996: golfers. In the fall the company began building the first phase of a 408-unit vacation resort at World Golf Village near St. Augustine, Florida. World Golf Village was the centerpiece of a major planned community that would eventually include the World Golf Hall of Fame, a championship golf course, a hotel and conference center, a golf academy, plus restaurants and stores. To help its marketing activities, Vistana also reached an agreement with the Professional Golfers Association (PGA) Tour Golf Course Properties, Inc. to have access to the PGA Tour databases.

Expanding further into the golf market, Vistana and PGA of America entered a joint venture to develop PGA Vacation Resorts by Vistana. The first of these was planned for Port St. Lucie, Florida, beside an existing 36-hole championship golf facility, with construction to begin in 1997.

In December, Gellein and Adler incorporated the various partnerships and corporations that operated and owned the company's various businesses. During 1996, the company sold 5,794 VOIs at an average price of $10,366, and had total revenues of $96.9 million. This was an increase of more than 19 percent over 1995 sales, which the company attributed to higher sales prices and more interests sold. Vistana's marketing efforts outside the United States resulted in sales of $9.9 million, more than double the company's foreign sales in 1995. Sales and marketing expenses rose to over 46 percent of timeshare sales, partly due to greater international costs and the expenses associated with beginning to sell interests at Hampton Vacation Resort—Oak Plantation.

In February 1997, Gallein and Adler took Vistana public, selling 4.6 million shares and raising $49.5 million. They used the proceeds to pay down the debt caused by the repurchase of the company and the redeeming of options to purchase interests in the partnerships which operated Vistana Resort and Vistana's Beach Club and to help capitalize its expansion. The two men became co-CEO's of the new entity, with Gellein serving as chairman and Adler as president, and together controlled 70.5 percent of the stock.

The company did well following its initial public offering, with sales better each quarter than they had been in 1996, and revenue for the first half of the year up 33 percent. In September, Vistana bought The Success Companies and Points of Colorado, a privately-owned group of timeshare companies. The acquisition, which cost approximately $35.6 million in cash and stock, netted Vistana two undeveloped properties and three established resorts in a new geographic market for the company. The resorts, the Villas of Cave Creek, near Scottsdale, Arizona; Eagle Point Reserve in Vail, Colorado; and Falcon Point Resort in Avon, Colorado, had more than 130 units at the time of the purchase.

The timeshare industry continued to grow. By 1997, there were over 4,000 timeshare resorts around the world, with 37 percent in the United States. Most of these were in Florida (25 percent), with California (eight percent), Colorado (six percent), and Hawaii (five percent) other favorite locations. According to Smith Barney, "the typical timeshare owner is about 50 years old, earns $65,000 a year, is well-educated, married and has one child living at home." The majority of timeshare owners (60 percent) lived in the United States. But more resorts were being built in Europe, with Spain and the Canary islands offering the largest concentration of timeshare ownerships in the world. Marriott became the first U.S. hospitality company to take its timeshare brand, Marriott Vacation Club International, to Europe, and new markets included urban destinations, such as New York City and Asia. At the Berjaya Vacation Club in Malaysia, for example, a timeshare week cost US$6,500 for 38 years.

Vistana's relationships with Promus Hotels and PGA of America expanded its already extensive development and management experience and improved its marketing operations. With only three percent of U.S. households owning a timeshare interest, the vacation ownership market looked to continue to grow. As Michael Muller, an analyst at Montgomery Securities, told *Investor's Business Daily*, "Vistana's three-prong growth strategy—expanding Vistana branded properties, opening resorts with Promus, and developing golf resorts—should continue to fuel the company's earnings and sales well into the future."

Principal Subsidiaries

Vistana Management, Ltd.; Vistana Development, Ltd.

Further Reading

Anthony, Deborah S. et al, "Timesharing: Enviable Growth Lures Major Hospitality Companies into Industry," Arthur Anderson 1996, http://www.hotel-online.com/Neo/Trends/Andersen/Timesharing-EnviableGrowth.html.

"Fact for Consumers from the Federal Trade Commission. Timeshare Tips—October 1992," http://www.webcom.com/ lewrose/brochures/timetips.html.

Parets, Robyn Taylor, "Building Resorts As Timeshares Rebound," *Investor's Business Daily*, August 14, 1997.

Razzi, Elizabeth, "Timeshares Grow Up," Kiplinger OnLine, October 1995, http://www.kiplinger.com/magazine/archives/1995/October/timeshar.html.

Rice, Faye, "What to Do on Your Summer Vacation," *Fortune*, June 12, 1995.

"Time Sharing Investment," Asia Business News 1996, http://www.abn-online.com/moneytalk/articles/3.html.

"Vacation Timesharing," Better Business Bureau, Inc. 1995, http://www.bosbbb.org/lit/0027.htm.

"Vistana, Inc. Completes Acquisitions of Vacation Ownership Resort Companies in Western U.S.," Vistana, Inc., September 17, 1997.

"Vistana, Inc. Reports Second Quarter EPS of 18 Cents," Vistana, Inc., August 12, 1997.

—Ellen D. Wernick

Waddell & Reed, Inc.

6300 Lamar Avenue
Shawnee Mission, Kansas 66202-4247
U.S.A.
(913) 236-2000
Fax: (913) 236-1543
Web site: http://www.waddell.com

Wholly Owned Subsidiary of Torchmark Corporation
Incorporated: 1937
Employees: 2,130
Total Assets: $5.93 billion (1996)
Stock Exchanges: New York (pending)
SICs: 6311 Life Insurance; 6331 Fire, Marine & Casualty Insurance; 6719 Holding Companies, Not Elsewhere Classified

Waddell & Reed, Inc. is one of the nation's leading financial services organizations, managing mutual fund portfolios and institutional investment funds, including the investment assets of parent company Torchmark Corporation, primarily a marketer of insurance products, and its subsidiaries. The company manages more than one million mutual fund accounts, valued at more than $20 billion. Through Waddell & Reed's affiliate, United Investors Life, a variety of life insurance and variable annuity products are offered. According to Bob Hechler, president of Waddell & Reed, "There are now over 2,700 equity mutual funds, but only one in four have been around long enough to have a five-year track record." The year 1997 marked the 60th anniversary of the company.

Getting in on the Investment Company Act of 1940

Waddell & Reed was founded on September 3, 1937 by two World War I Air Force pilots, Chauncey Waddell and Cameron Reed, who decided to take the plunge into the financial business after their return from military service. Chauncey Waddell joined a New York securities firm that became Herrick, Waddell & Co., while Cameron Reed began his financial career through the establishment of Consolidated Trust Inc., a forerunner of United Funds. Before long their merger formed Herrick, Waddell & Reed and was based in Kansas City. Soon after the United States Congress approved the Investment Company Act of 1940, the company became one of the first to register under the new law. The partners recognized that mutual funds could offer an enormous investment opportunity for people and, consequently, began two of the country's first mutual funds, United Income Fund and United Accumulative Fund. By 1943, Waddell & Reed became the principal underwriter of United Funds, Inc. Herrick was dropped from the company name in 1949. By 1950 Waddell & Reed managed assets reaching $700 million, making it one of the top five mutual fund sales organizations in the country.

As the first company to open a mutual fund sales outlet in a department store, Waddell & Reed made news with its 1958 opening in Buffalo, New York. It was a novelty for department store shoppers to have the option of buying fund shares along with the everyday tangible items they purchased. Other early company innovations included the policy of hiring a substantial force of part-time sales agents, as opposed to the customary hiring of all full-time personnel, a policy that engendered considerable and far-reaching criticism from the industry. In 1961 Waddell & Reed had a staff of 4,500 managers and representatives, of whom nearly half were part-time employees, including accountants and school teachers who concentrated selling efforts in smaller cities and towns. Critics, including those on the board of the New York Stock Exchange, argued that the part-time employees were underqualified salesmen [persons] selling a prepackaged product and not adequately trained. Leery of the relatively new mutual fund sales industry, critics feared that sales of general securities might be jeopardized, which would antagonize brokerage houses, and voiced concerns that unscrupulous or undertrained salesmen could do harm to public confidence. In response, company officials explained that their employees were carefully selected, trained, and supervised. The part-time sales personnel were not responsible for selecting individual securities, but could do a respectable job of explaining the preselected program, how mutual funds worked, what

Company Perspectives:

In 1964, Cameron Reed said what was to become the guiding principal for the firm: "Long experience has dictated that, as a general approach to financial planning, everyone needs three things: 1) cash for emergencies and current living; 2) insurance for protection; and 3) a plan for investing surplus funds accumulated over a long period for possible profit and growth." Waddell & Reed still follows that philosophy. Since the time of the company's founding, the company mission has been: Helping people make the most of their financial future. The company offers its financial planning services and products through financial advisors and believes that personal, face-to-face service is the best way to serve its clients.

services they provided, and so on. More than 90 percent of Waddell sales were made through its own representatives. The company continued its rapid expansion, with United Funds assets reaching $1 billion by 1961.

1970s Plan for the Pacific Stock Exchange

"Differences over matters of sales policy," was the explanation given by Dudley F. Cates, as he resigned from his position of president of Waddell & Reed in 1963. He had served as president of the Continental Research Corporation and as investment manager of the United Funds before taking the executive post with Waddell & Reed. He was succeeded by Cameron Reed, former president and company co-founder. The company applied for membership to the Pacific Coast Stock Exchange, which would enable the new brokerage subsidiary of Waddell & Reed (called the Kansas City Securities Corporation) to provide investment management of the four United Funds. At that time, a seat on the exchange cost approximately $10,000. The move was touted as a plan to pass along savings to the 330,000 shareholders of United Funds by cutting management fees—a move that aroused wide interest in the entire securities world, according to Vartan, writing for the *New York Times.* Waddell told Vartan that if the subsidiary gained admission to the Pacific Exchange, "Waddell & Reed will propose to its client, United Funds, that its investment advisory and management fee be reduced in each year by an amount equal to some agreed percentage of the brokerage commissions or the profits earned by its subsidiary." He added that transactions of United Funds, which included the United Accumulative Fund, the United Income Fund, the United Science Fund, and the United Bond Fund, had generated about $4.2 million in brokerage commissions in each of the two prior years. Company executives predicted that the Pacific Exchange's approval of the subsidiary would eventually mean greater competition among the nation's stock exchanges. Those who favored Waddell's seat argued that membership was the potential source of much new business and that when orders could not be filled regionally, brokers were forced to go to the New York Stock Exchange, where commissions had to be shared. Waddell's application was approved in 1965, still arousing fears that a membership parade would ensue, whereby some of the biggest institutional customers in the business would become brokers themselves.

During this period, Cameron Reed resigned as president and director, selling his stockholdings to members of the du Pont family and their associates. The sale involved almost 49,000 shares, giving the du Pont group about 24 percent of the voting stock. The company began having problems with internal relations, resulting in the resignations of several key research executives. William Armstrong, vice-president of Waddell & Reed's investment management division, was the first to go. He was also serving as director and as vice-president of United Funds, Inc. Several others followed suit, mainly among the research analysts. *New York Times* reporter Terry Robards communicated that the bear market of 1966, which followed a period of record highs, led several key men at Waddell & Reed to believe that the decline in share prices was temporary. The company went ahead with a decision to move heavily into cash and out of equities, within two months of the time when the market hit bottom. "The decision to re-invest was not made until the market had rebounded substantially from its low," he reported, which resulted in a relatively poor increase in net assets.

In 1969 the Continental Investment Corporation of Boston bought Waddell & Reed for $82.5 million. Adverse operating results were disclosed in 1975. The company lost $16.2 million that year, following earnings of $4.3 million the year before and $8 million in 1972.

An Old School Management Style for the 1980s

In 1979 Russell Thompson, a University of Missouri M.B.A., began serving as Waddell & Reed's United Income Fund portfolio manager. The small town Kansas native wore the reputation of conservative manager and soon established one of the best ten-year equity records in the business. Oliver wrote in *Forbes,* "In the 1980s Thompson clung steadfastly to the school of investing that emphasizes what a company would be worth if its business operations and other assets were auctioned off." During the 1980s, when many of his portfolio holdings were taken over in leveraged buyouts, his type of management worked very well.

Liberty National Insurance Holding Company, later renamed Torchmark Corporation, a Birmington, Alabama-based health and life insurer, bought Waddell & Reed for $160 million in 1981. In the 1980–1981 period, the company's managers decided that two things were important. First, that interest rates were going to fall. They responded by purchasing a lot of interest-sensitive investments, mostly in the financial services sector. Second, they trusted that assets were undervalued, so they bought companies that were asset-rich. They bought a million shares of RCA, for example, at $22 per share. RCA was later bought out by General Electric for $68 per share. By 1991, Thompson outpaced the Standard and Poor's 500 index by almost 300 basis points and ranked number one in Lipper Analytical Service's ranking of equity income funds of more than $1 billion.

Thompson held the view that the critical variable in forecasting the markets was inflation, which characteristically controls interest rates. He and other senior managers developed a process for investing that they termed "top-down rotational." Their method first involved a clear determination of where they stood in the economic cycle, from the early stages through the inflationary stages. Then as the economic cycle progressed, they would structure the portfolio to do well in that particular part of the cycle and then choose stocks that should do well in the segments they had stressed. In addition, they would search for companies in the process of change—companies that had not necessarily done well, but that they expected to do well, within the industries they had selected. They also sought out companies that grew dividends.

In the summer of 1991 when company analysts believed the economy was weakening and that the Federal Reserve Board would soon ease interest rates, the company continued to keep a significant number of financial stocks, which included Wells Fargo, Bank of America, and Household Financial. Then Saddam Hussein attacked Kuwait and the fund suffered dramatically. Bank examiners became much more restrictive, because of political and economic uncertainties, and the real estate market plummeted—the financial stocks halved. Thompson and others decided that despite the war the U.S. economy was not going to go away and that the financial assets would soon improve once the Federal Reserve began to ease. They added to the company's financial portfolio, and those stocks soon doubled. When interest rates were low the company invested in a large number of cyclicals. It also focused on the infrastructure stocks, such as Foster Wheeler and Morrison-Knudsen. The company bought Deere, Caterpiller, Ingersoll-Rand and, in electronics, Motorola, AMP, and Intel. The company is seldom fully invested and normally reserves 15–20 percent in cash, which facilitates getting in and out of industries.

Waddell & Reed and its affiliates always relied heavily on internal research. The company's analysts/portfolio managers cover their industries and provide needed information. They also make buy and sell recommendations based on information from company sources, Wall Street, and various literature sources. Thompson told Sharon Harvey of *Institutional Investor,* "In some cases, we think we have better analysts than the Street does." For larger holdings, Thompson would talk to the companies himself. He added that the company "would like to be characterized as a fund that anticipates change."

Catering to middle-class America (people with incomes from $40,000 to $100,000 a year in 1996) the company continued in its "homey" marketing tradition. It refused to market on the Internet, through brokerage firms like Merrill Lynch & Co., or through PaineWebber Group, Inc., in the belief that an exclusive product gave Waddell & Reed sales representatives an advantage with customers. Typically, the sales representatives become acquainted with future customers in a coffee shop; those customers have been attracted by the idea of a conservative stance in fund management. Representatives meet face to face with clients at least once or twice a year. The approach tends to attract loyal customers. As a sales philosophy, the company emphasizes multiple sales over time, rather than a one-time sale of a particular product.

Catching Up with the 1990s

Groundwork for new changes had been laid in the early 1990s. Poor producers were culled from the sales personnel; 40 percent of the sales force was cut. Company analysts had determined that baby boomers were amassing assets and were willing to pay for professional financial advice. In an attempt to adjust to changes such as the growing market, Waddell officials decided to rebuild their sales force, with the goal of hiring 3,500 representatives by the year 2001. The company also needed to rethink its policy concerning sales load, since personal finance magazines and books about investing consistently discouraged investors from paying a sales commission. Even so, load funds continued to constitute bigger business than their no-load rivals. The United Funds carry a sales load of 4.25–5.75 percent commissions to invest. Waddell & Reed Funds do not charge a sales load when customers invest, but they may pay one when they sell. Studies indicated that investors were increasingly willing to pay for help to pick among the thousands of mutual funds available in the market.

Responding to the need for a larger, better trained sales force, additional changes implemented by the company included the replacement of its 1970s financial planning software, making graphics, estate planning, and other planning features available as a sales tool to help representatives. New levels of support were set up for the newly hired sales personnel. The pay increased to $2,000 a month, contingent upon a determined amount of commissions, for up to six months after the representative's first 90 days (replacing an old program that paid only $750 a month for three months, at which time commissions were expected to provide a comfortable living). Managers were given incentives for spending more time with new representatives. Titles were upgraded, and after meeting state licensing requirements sales representatives became financial advisors, as a further inducement to baby boomers looking for expert advice. The sales force decreased by 280 during 1996, according to company reports, which may reflect a 1993 cut in sales commissions on its funds to 5.75 percent from eight percent; the company is considering further cuts.

Although financial advisors can sell other funds to customers, incentives are geared toward selling United and Waddell & Reed Funds. Critics argue that investors do not merely want help in choosing a fund, but that they want to choose between many fund choices. They charge that the exclusive-product appeal is not in touch with the contemporary supermarket trend. The performance of Waddell and Reed's Funds showed great profits, but lagged, nevertheless, behind the industry boom.

In November 1997, Torchmark Corporation announced that its asset management subsidiary, Waddell & Reed, planned to make an initial public offering of common stock early in 1998. Torchmark had plans for a tax-free spinoff of its remaining shares, subject to regulatory approval. The parent company claimed that the action provided an opportunity to enhance shareholder value and that the spinoff would split the asset management business from the insurance businesses, which would allow a more accurate determination of the value of each company. R. K. Richey, chairman and CEO of Torchmark would become chairman of the executive committee of the board of directors of both companies. Keith A. Tucker, Torchmark vice-chairman and board member, would become chairman and CEO of Waddell & Reed.

Further Reading

Gustke, Constance, "A Country Contrarian's Picks," *Fortune,* August 29, 1988, pp. 32–34.

Hansen, Bruce, "Waddell Capitalizes on Trends in Investment to Double Firm's Size," *Memphis Business Journal,* October 28, 1991, p. 34.

Harvey, Sharon, "Portfolio Strategy: Top Down, Top Notch," *Institutional Investor,* April 19, 1991, p. 181.

"Mutual Fund's Shares Sold in Buffalo Store," *New York Times,* September 11, 1958, p. 52.

Oliver, Suzanne, "Two Ways to Beat the Market," *Forbes,* December 23, 1991, pp. 178–79.

"Post at Waddell & Reed Is Resigned by Cates," *New York Times,* October 3, 1963, p. 54.

Robards, Terry, "Waddell & Reed Is Shifting Aides," *New York Times,* September 19, 1967, pp. 61, 69.

Romano, Mary, "Kansas Firm, Avoiding Glitz, Earns Solid Returns," *Wall Street Journal,* April 4, 1996.

"$16-Million Loss Set By Waddell & Reed," *New York Times,* April 10, 1975, p. 61.

Smith, Gene, "Mutual Funds: Part-Time Salesmen Strongly Defended," *New York Times,* December 11, 1961, p. 52.

Vartan, Vartanig G., "Mutuals Found [Fund] Cool on Waddell," *New York Times,* December 22, 1964, p. 38.

——, "Waddell & Reed to Pass Saving of Broker Plan to United Funds," *New York Times,* January 12, 1965, pp. 47, 52.

"Waddell & Reed, Inc. Fills a Major Position," *New York Times,* January 12, 1962, p. 56.

"Waddell Seeking a Role in Trading," *New York Times,* December 19, 1964, p. 37.

"Wide Impact Seen in Waddell Listing," *New York Times,* February 19, 1965, pp. 47, 49.

—Terri Mozzone

Walter Industries, Inc.

1500 North Dale Mabry Highway
Tampa, Florida 33607
U.S.A.
(813) 871-4811
Fax: (813) 871-4430

Public Company
Incorporated: 1955 as Jim Walter Corporation
Employees: 7,584
Sales: $1.51 billion (1997)
Stock Exchanges: NASDAQ
SICs: 1222 Underground Mining-Bituminous Coal; 1521 General Contractors-Single Family Homes; 2999 Products of Petroleum & Coal, Not Elsewhere Classified; 3321 Gray & Ductile Iron Foundries; 5169 Chemicals & Allied Products, Not Elsewhere Classified; 6719 Offices of Holding Companies, Not Elsewhere Classified

Walter Industries, Inc. is a holding company with diversified operations through its subsidiaries, in home building, natural resources development, and various industrial businesses. Jim Walter Homes, Inc. builds and sells detached, single-family residential homes, mainly in the southern United States; other company subsidiaries offer home mortgages and homeowner's insurance and manufacture window components. Jim Walter Resources, Inc. is involved in coal mining in Alabama and in extracting methane gas from coal seams. The company's primary industrial operations include Applied Industrial Materials Corporation, the world's largest marketer and distributor of petroleum coke; Sloss Industries Corporation, which manufactures foundry coke, furnace coke, slag wool, and specialty chemicals; United States Pipe and Foundry Company, the leading maker of ductile iron pressure pipe in the nation; and JW Aluminum Company, a supplier of specialty aluminum products. Walter Industries is the successor company to Jim Walter Corporation and was created when Kohlberg Kravis Roberts & Company (KKR) took Jim Walter private in a 1987 highly leveraged buyout. Walter Industries and its then-parent company, Hillsborough Holdings Corporation (HHC), soon ran into severe difficulties stemming from litigation over asbestos liabilities, leading to a five-year-plus period, starting in December 1989, in which the company operated under Chapter 11 bankruptcy protection. Walter Industries emerged from bankruptcy in March 1995, going public once again in January 1996. KKR still holds about 26 percent of company stock.

Origins as Marketer of Shell Homes in 1940s

In 1946 James W. Walter borrowed $400 from his father, a citrus grower, and purchased a "shell," or unfinished home, for $895 from Tampa, Florida, builder, O. L. Davenport. When just three days later, the 23-year-old, newly married Walter sold the home to a passerby for a profit, he saw a way out of his $50-a-week truck-driving job and $50-a-month apartment. Walter convinced Davenport, also in his 20s, to take him on as a partner. As Walter remembered in *Nation's Business* in 1970, "we made out all right, but I thought we could move faster." Walter encouraged Davenport to run bigger advertisements featuring photographs of the homes; they sold more houses. Walter was enthusiastic about building the business even faster. Davenport was reluctant, and after two years, they dissolved the partnership of Davenport & Walter. The men decided to divide the business: one of them would take the assets of about $50,000, the other the business. Since Davenport was the founder, he first opted to take the business. A day after he made his decision, he told his partner he had changed his mind and chose the assets instead. Davenport took his share and bought a motel and small construction firm in Troy, Alabama. Jim Walter continued the business, now called the Walter Construction Company.

In the post-World War II era, housing was scarce. Jim Walter sold unfinished, traditionally constructed homes as affordable, alternative housing. The wood homes were built on concrete foundations or wood pilings. Each home was completely finished on the outside with an unfinished interior. Buyers installed plumbing, electrical systems, insulation, walls, and doors themselves. Homes were sold directly to owners prior to construction, through one of Jim Walter Homes Division sales offices.

In 1955 Jim Walter incorporated the Walter Construction Company as the Jim Walter Corporation. Three men who would be pivotal to the company's success through the coming decades had already joined the firm. James O. Alston came to the company in 1947 and was instrumental in its early growth. Alston was president of the corporation from 1963 to 1970, chairman of the homebuilding operation, and vice-chairman of the corporation by 1970. Arnold F. Saraw, a partner in Walter Construction, was secretary-treasurer of the corporation from 1955 to 1970. In 1970 he was promoted to senior vice-president, heading the corporate mortgage division. The third man, Joe B. Cordell, an accountant who joined the company in 1958 was vice-president and chief financial officer, becoming president in 1974 and chief executive officer in 1983.

Expansion into Mortgages in the 1950s

During the 1950s the company expanded and entered the mortgage business. Initially, financing was difficult. The turning point for the fledgling company came in 1956 when Chicago creditors Walter E. Heller & Company approved a $1 million line of credit. Jim Walter's mortgages, like his homes, were attractive to buyers who found more conventional sources too costly. Jim Walter Corporation's innovative financing plan was outlined in the May 19, 1987 edition of *Financial World*: "most of the houses . . . are financed on the basis of ten percent fixed mortgages or installment notes maturing in up to 20 years. Unlike a conventional mortgage, . . . Jim Walter's buyers spread the interest and principal payments evenly across the term to lessen its risk of defaults." Such mortgages were possible because the company required the purchaser to own the land on which the house was to be built. The equity in the land substituted for the traditional cash down payment. The company's mortgage portfolio was traditionally one of its strongest assets. The mortgage finance division maintained more than $1 billion in installment notes in the 1970s. By 1987 Jim Walter's $1.6 billion mortgage portfolio was larger than those of most Florida savings and loans. An evaluation performed in 1988 by Financial Security Assurance, in a maneuver designed to help KKR and Walter Industries refinance $1.2 billion in bank debt, put the value of Walter's mortgage portfolio at $1.75 billion.

Sales of Walter homes historically ran counter to other builders' sales due to the availability of low-cost financing. Low, fixed interest rates, combined with an affordable product, ensured that when housing starts were generally down and money was tight, buyers looked for alternatives such as those offered by Jim Walter. During 1982 Jim Walter built 10,000 of the 300,000 homes constructed that year. In 1986 Walter homes accounted for just 6,500 of the 500,000 homes built. The company tallied some of its best years during recessions in the housing industry.

From 1955 to 1962, Jim Walter Corporation was primarily involved in the building industry. Walter's only notable acquisition during the 1950s was the First National Bank in St. Petersburg, Florida, later sold. This foray was the start of a policy of diversification.

Diversification in the 1960s and 1970s

During the 1960s and 1970s, the company made a large number of acquisitions and mergers. Walter acquired no less than 15 different subsidiaries in the 1960s, ranging from building-materials and industrial-products manufacturers to a California savings and loan. The Celotex Corporation merger was initiated in 1962 and completed in 1964. A pioneer in sound insulation and a leading manufacturer of building products, Celotex also made a spray-on asbestos insulation. The company also acquired a sugar firm and an oil exploration company. Two paper companies acquired in 1968, Marquette Paper Corporation and Knight Paper Company, rounded out Jim Walter's early acquisitions.

On March 9, 1964, Jim Walter Corporation was first listed on the New York Stock Exchange. Shares initially sold for $.50. From 1969 until 1979, stockholders enjoyed positive results: dividends increased from $.40 to $1.80 per share; book value increased from $6.46 to $34 per share. By 1970, the shares had twice split three ways.

Over the course of the 1960s, over 200 competitors tried to emulate the company's success in the production of shell homes. By the end of the 1970s, Jim Walter, the originator of the concept, was the only one left and his "rags-to-riches" saga had become a part of Florida folklore. A Tampa cab driver, who did not recognize his passenger, regaled Jim Walter with the story of Jim's life. In 1968, on the 20th anniversary of the founding of the company, Jim Walter commemorated his beginnings by buying back the original shell house he had first owned for just three days in 1946.

In 1969 the company bought United States Pipe and Foundry Company of Birmingham, Alabama, for $135 million in stock and cash. By 1979, U.S. Pipe had increased profits five times over. In the July 13, 1979, issue of *Forbes,* Walter called the purchase "the quickest deal I ever made."

At the time of the acquisition, U.S. Pipe's modest coke operation and unmined coal reserves attracted little attention. By 1973, however, the Arab oil embargo made coal mining a potential bonanza. In 1976 the company created a subsidiary, Jim Walter Resources, Inc., to direct the company's mine-development program. Since Jim Walter knew home building but not mining, he hired experienced people to guide the mining division. The magnitude of the task, faced by a company with no experience in the difficult longwall mining that was required due to the depth of the coal, was daunting. The company's robust cash flow was able to absorb the crush of capital expenditures during the nearly ten years it took to make the mines operational.

During the 1970s Jim Walter continued to diversify the company, adding another dozen subsidiaries. By the end of the decade Jim Walter was involved in coal mining; marble, limestone, and granite quarrying; oil and gas production; gypsum and asbestos mining; a savings and loan association; an insurance company; a paper-marketing firm; water and waste-water pipe manufacturing; and retail jewelry. While the various mergers and acquisitions broadened Jim Walter's base of operations, the bulk of its revenues remained in the building industry, with more than 200,000 shell homes completed by 1979. Sales in 1979 exceeded $2 billion a year.

Asbestos Litigation and KKR Takeover in the 1980s

In 1972 Panacon Corporation, the third-largest Canadian producer of asbestos, was merged into Celotex Corporation. As the link between asbestos and cancer became clear, lawsuits from workers began to accumulate. Jim Walter's 1986 10-K form reported that two subsidiaries, Celotex and Carey Canada Inc., were codefendants with a number of other miners, manufacturers, and distributors of asbestos products in a "substantial number" of lawsuits alleging work-related injuries. Many of the suits requested punitive as well as compensatory damages. According to the company, "the aggregate damages sought in these cases is substantial." What followed was a series of convoluted suits, and counter suits, on behalf of both defendants and plaintiffs, with mixed results. The company thought its insurance carriers would handle the claims, but coverage after 1977 disallowed asbestos-related claims. In 1985 the subsidiaries and codefendants entered into an agreement to resolve the claims. All claims filed after June 19, 1985, were to be referred to the Asbestos Claim Facility, set up by the agreement, with the cost of litigation or mediation to be shared by all the defendants according to a formula based on their asbestos litigation experiences.

Jim Walter's home-building division continued to produce strong results through the 1980s. In 1986 the company maintained 103 sales offices scattered through 29 states, most of them in the South. The homes were constructed by local construction firms who were subcontracted to do the work. Shell homes now accounted for only 28 percent of units sold while sales of 90 percent-completed homes totaled nearly 60 percent. In the same year, homebuilding and related financing accounted for 14 percent of total revenues for the company, contributing $108.4 million.

By the mid-1980s Celotex found itself staggering under an ever mounting litigation load. In 1984 approximately 21,100 lawsuits representing 25,600 persons were pending against one or more of the subscribers of the Asbestos Claim Facility, including Celotex. By the following year this figure had climbed to 28,800 lawsuits representing 34,900 persons, and a year later there were approximately 43,900 bodily injury claims pending. By the time Kohlberg Kravis Roberts moved to acquire the company in 1987, pending lawsuits exceeded 50,000, only to climb again, to 58,000, in the following year. The actions taken by the subsidiaries, however, allowed KKR to proclaim the company's litigation risk "manageable." Under corporate law, the parent company could not be held liable for claims against its subsidiaries.

Kohlberg Kravis Roberts proceeded with its purchase of Jim Walter Corporation for $2.4 billion—including $1.1 billion in junk bonds—in August 1987. The company was a perfect takeover target; it had healthy profits, strong cash flow, and a raft of subsidiaries that could be sold to reduce debt. Share price for the takeover jumped to $60, with bidding at one point reaching the heady level of $67 per share. At KKR's request, Jim Walter joined the group of investors who bought the company. He became a chairman of Hillsborough Holdings Corporation and Walter Industries, Inc.—two companies organized to acquire Jim Walter Corporation—and retained his existing management team.

The company was split into two holding companies following the sale. Jim Walter Corporation retained ownership of Celotex, and Hillsborough Holdings Corporation became the parent of the other subsidiaries. Jim Walter Corporation was sold to Jasper Corporation in April 1988. The other subsidiaries merged into HHC, all under the name of Walter Industries, Inc., which was the main subsidiary of HHC. Several of the company's businesses, including the marble quarrying and paper operations, were quickly sold to pay down debt.

Chapter 11 Protection, 1989–95

In 1989 Houston attorney Stephen D. Sussman, of Sussman Godfrey, filed a suit on behalf of asbestos victims in Beaumont, Texas, an industrial area where many of the plaintiffs lived. The new lawsuit named KKR, Hillsborough Holdings, and Walter Industries as principal defendants. The suit put an end to KKR's plan to restructure the debt assumed by Hillsborough Holdings Corporation. Further asset sales were blocked, and the price of HHC's junk bonds plummeted. HHC was unable to meet the obligations imposed by the sale of the junk bonds that funded the buyout. On December 27, 1989, Hillsborough Holdings Corporation and 31 of its subsidiaries each filed for Chapter 11 bankruptcy in Tampa. Only two subsidiaries, Cardem Insurance Co. and Jefferson Warrior Railroad Company, did not file petitions for court-protected reorganization.

In April 1990 Judge Alexander L. Paskay, chief bankruptcy judge for the U.S. Bankruptcy Court in the Middle District of Florida, recommended that the asbestos suit filed in Texas be heard in his court. In July the U.S. District Court for the same district adopted his recommendation, and the case was moved to the Tampa federal bankruptcy court.

While the legal wrangling continued, in early 1991 the CEO of Walter Industries, Joe Cordell, announced his retirement because of his battle with cancer. Lacking solid leadership from within the company, Walter Industries conducted an executive search that led to the hiring of G. Robert (Bull) Durham, who had retired two years earlier after turning around Phelps Dodge Corp. When asked by *Financial World* in 1991 why he would come out of retirement to take over such a troubled company, Durham replied, "There is not a whole lot of fun to running a company that is doing well." Jim Walter continued as chairman of Walter Industries.

Despite the new leadership, the company would be unable to reorganize until the asbestos litigation was resolved. Judge Paskay finally issued a ruling in April 1994, stating that Walter Industries could not be held liable for the Celotex asbestos claims. Appeals ensued, with the company initially proposing a reorganization plan that set aside no funds to settle the continuing claims. Under pressure from its creditors, however, on March 17, 1995, Walter Industries emerged from Chapter 11 through a plan that settled the more than $2.6 billion in claims by having the company contribute $375 million to the Celotex Settlement Fund, which had been set up by Celotex and included the asbestos claimants. Part of the payment was in the form of Walter Industries stock; by early 1997 the fund claimed a 10.9 percent stake in the company.

Immediate Postbankruptcy Years

Upon the company's emergence from bankruptcy, KKR held just 12 percent of Walter Industries. KKR remained committed to its investment, however, and by January 1997 had increased its stake to 26 percent. In January 1996 Walter Industries became a public company listed with NASDAQ. Jim Walter, meanwhile, retired in October 1995 and was succeeded as chairman by Durham, with Kenneth E. Hyatt, who had been president of Celotex, taking over as president. The company's troubles seemingly over, Durham himself then retired in June 1996, with Hyatt becoming chairman, CEO, and president. At the same time, Richard E. Almy was named executive vice-president and chief operating officer, having previously served as president and COO of JW Aluminum and JW Window Components.

Walter Industries recovered quickly from its dark days of bankruptcy, surging in the strong market for new homes of the mid-1990s. The financial picture was strong enough by December 1995 for the company to be able to retire the $490 million in junk bonds that it had used to finance the reorganization plan just nine months earlier. More evidence of a recovery came in the form of a return to acquisitions. In June 1997 Walter Industries acquired Neatherlin Homes Inc., a builder of low-priced homes based in Texas. In September of that same year, the company announced that it would pay about $400 million for Applied Industrial Materials Corporation (AIMCOR), a private company based in Stamford, Connecticut, with about $450 million in revenues and $50 million in operating income annually. AIMCOR, through its Carbon Products Group, was the world leader in the production of petroleum coke, which is used in numerous industrial processes, including the manufacture of steel and cement. Its Metals Group manufactured and sold a variety of ferroalloys, metals, and specialty materials used in the steelmaking and metal-casting industries. AIMCOR fit in nicely with Walter Industries' other industrial subsidiaries, such as U.S. Pipe, Sloss Industries, and JW Aluminum.

After posting a heavy loss in fiscal 1995, a net loss of just $84.7 million was posted for 1996, and the company was back in the black in 1997 with net income of $37.1 million. Well on the road to recovery, Walter Industries had the same solid core of businesses that had made it an attractive takeover target in the mid-1980s. By aggressively building on this core through acquisitions, Walter Industries seemed capable of exceeding the glory days of the original Jim Walter Corporation.

Principal Subsidiaries

Applied Industrial Materials Corporation; JW Aluminum Company; Homes Holdings Corporation; Jim Walter Homes, Inc.; Jim Walter Homes of Louisiana, Inc.; Walter Home Improvement, Inc.; Neatherlin Homes, Inc.; Jim Walter Homes of Georgia, Inc.; JW Window Components, Inc.; Jim Walter Window Components, Inc.; Vestal Manufacturing Company; Sloss Industries Corporation; Southern Precision Corporation; Mid-State Holdings Corporation; Mid-State Homes, Inc.; United States Pipe and Foundry Company, Inc.; Railroad Holdings Corporation; Jefferson Warrior Railroad Company, Inc.; Computer Holdings Corporation; Jim Walter Computer Services, Inc.; Land Holdings Corporation; Walter Land Company; J.W.I. Holdings Corporation; J.W. Walter, Inc.; Hamer Holdings Corporation; Hamer Properties, Inc.; Best Insurors, Inc.; Best Insurors of Mississippi, Inc.; Jim Walter Insurance Services, Inc.; Cardem Insurance Co., Ltd. (Bermuda); Coast to Coast Advertising, Inc.; United Land Corporation; Dixie Building Supplies, Inc.; Jim Walter Resources, Inc.; Walter International Sales, Inc. (Barbados); Black Warrior Transmission Corp. (50%); Black Warrior Methane Corp. (50%).

Further Reading

Barrett, Amy, ''Bad-Time Bull,'' *Financial World,* July 23, 1991, pp. 28–29.

de Lisser, Eleena, ''Walter Industries Ends Proceedings Under Chapter 11,'' *Wall Street Journal,* March 20, 1995, p. B4.

Heller, Emily, ''Walter Inds. Faces Legal Crossroads,'' *Tampa Bay Business Journal,* October 9, 1992, p. 1.

Lambert, Wade, and Greg Steinmetz, ''Walter Industries Is Found Not Liable for Asbestos Claims at a Former Unit,'' *Wall Street Journal,* April 19, 1994, p. A4.

Lesly, Elizabeth, and Gail DeGeorge, ''Another Embarrassment for KKR?'' *Business Week,* August 1, 1994, pp. 56–57.

Marcial, Gene G., ''Walter's Firm New Foundation,'' *Business Week,* January 13, 1997, p. 55.

Moscow, Alvin, *Building a Business: The Jim Walter Story,* Sarasota, Fla.: Pineapple Press, 1995.

Regan, Bob, ''Durham Gets Back into Driver's Seat: Ex-PD Chief Steers Walter Industries,'' *American Metal Market,* June 13, 1991, p. 4.

Sachar, Laura, ''Building the Blue-Collar Dreams,'' *Financial World,* May 19, 1987.

—Lynn M. Kalanik
—updated by David E. Salamie

Western Beef, Inc.

47-05 Metropolitan Avenue
Ridgewood, New York 11385
U.S.A.
(718) 417-3370
Fax: (718) 628-2359

Public Company
Incorporated: 1963 as Ranchers Packing Corp.
Employees: 2,000
Sales: $340.87 million (1996)
Stock Exchanges: NASDAQ
SICs: 5144 Poultry & Poultry Products; 5147 Meats & Meat Products; 5411 Grocery Stores

Western Beef, Inc. operates a wholesale food business consisting mainly of meat and poultry products and a network of warehouse-type retail food stores known for rock-bottom prices and tailored to the preferences of the various ethnic groups represented in each store's market area. The wholesale business operates in New York, New Jersey, and eastern Pennsylvania, while the retail stores (19 at the end of 1996) are all located in the New York City metropolitan area.

Ranchers Packing, 1963–83

Western Beef was formed in part from the operations of Ranchers Packing Corp., which was founded in 1963 by Martin Rochman to process, package, and sell flaked, chopped, and ground meat that had been frozen. A processing and packing plant was constructed the following year in New Hyde Park, Long Island. Production began in 1965. Net sales reached nearly $1.2 million in 1968, when net income was $143,249. Ranchers Packing went public in 1969, offering about one quarter of its outstanding common stock at $5 a share. By 1972, however, the company was in the red. In that year it lost $49,000 on net sales of $1.05 million and had a long-term debt of $339,000. After making a small profit in 1973, the company lost $139,000 in 1974 and $201,000 in 1975.

In 1975 Ranchers Packing opened what was essentially a new business when it converted the New Hyde Park plant to a retail discount store offering a variety of meat, cheese, and other food products at low prices to "volume purchasers." But in February 1976 Ranbar Packing, Inc., took over Ranchers Packing in an exchange of stock and closed the store.

Founded in 1973, Ranbar, with a plant in Flushing—a community in New York City's borough of Queens—was a distributor of meat and poultry products and other provisions, largely in New York City and nearby parts of New York, New Jersey, and Connecticut. It was owned by Peter Castellana, who was convicted in the early 1950s of selling adulterated meat and in 1964 of taking part in looting a company of $1.3 million. When Castellana and five others were indicted in 1963, U.S. Attorney Robert Morgenthau described it as the "biggest" and "most audacious" bankruptcy fraud case ever to come before the courts in the Southern District of New York. Castellana served four years of a five-year sentence.

Following Ranbar's acquisition of Ranchers Packing, its management became Ranchers Packing's management, acting as trustee for the Castellana family, which held nearly half the common stock. Castellana assumed the position of director-secretary of Ranchers Packing in 1977 and controlled most of the business functions of the company and Ranbar, its subsidiary.

During 1977 Ranchers Packing's net sales fell to $11.4 million from $26.8 million the previous year, and its net loss widened from $789,000 to $3.4 million. Ranbar filed for reorganization under Chapter 11 of the federal bankruptcy laws and began shifting the company's operations to retail trade in order to continue in business with less capital needs. Also that year, a Securities and Exchange Commission lawsuit charged Ranchers Packing and Castellana with a number of business irregularities, leading to a consent agreement barring them from further violations of federal securities laws. In 1978 Ranbar and its secretary-treasurer were indicted on 52 counts of defrauding the federal government in a scheme involving stolen food stamps. The company pleaded guilty and was fined $520,000.

Shortly before the end of 1978 two of Castellana's sons formed F & J Meat Packers, Inc. to service Ranbar's wholesale

Company Perspectives:

Western Beef, Inc. operates 19 high-volume supermarkets, and is the largest and most visible warehouse supermarket chain in the New York metropolitan area. The company takes great pride in knowing the neighborhoods where its stores are located. Not only does the Company provide a full range of value-priced perishable and grocery products for its many ethnic customers, it also employs many neighborhood people. The Company is also one of New York's largest wholesale meat and poultry distributors.

customers. By the end of the year Ranbar had discontinued almost 90 percent of its wholesale operations. That year the company, through its parent, Ranchers Packing, had a net profit of $282,337 on net sales of $31.6 million. Ranbar emerged from bankruptcy in 1979 by agreeing to pay its unsecured creditors 25 cents on the dollar over a seven-year period. Ranchers Packing continued to be profitable in 1979 and 1980.

In August 1980 Ranbar closed its remaining packing operations as the result of legal action by the U.S. Department of Agriculture that demanded a modification of the Flushing plant. This facility now became solely a retail store doing business under the trade name ''Western Beef.'' Ranchers Packing continued to be profitable and in 1982 had net income of $316,198 on net sales of $77.9 million. Shortly before the end of the year, F & J Meat Packers was acquired by Ranchers Packing. Frank Castellana, a son of Peter and previously president of F & J, became president of Ranchers Packing. The senior Castellana was listed as sales manager.

Quarex Industries, 1983–93

Ranchers Packing was renamed Quarex Industries, Inc. in 1983. During the year the company acquired a store in Spring Valley, New York, that was similar to its store in Flushing. The company opened stores in Union and East Orange, New Jersey, in 1985 under the Western Beef name but sold the Union and Spring Valley stores in 1986. The company acquired Western Beef Supermarkets, Inc. in 1985 to operate as a wholesale grocery distributor.

In 1986 a report by the President's Commission on Organized Crime described Quarex as a ''significant force in the meat business'' that had ''close ties'' to the Mafia group known as the Gambino crime family. Peter Castellana was alleged to be a member of this family and a cousin of the family's recently murdered ''boss,'' Paul Castellana, Sr. The commission also reported that poultry producer Frank Perdue had given a deposition saying that because of the involvement of the senior Castellana in several bankruptcies, Quarex had a bad credit reputation in the meat industry. Perdue added that ''the only way we would sell him, we had to have the money up front.''

Quarex's wholesale meat business was, in 1987, purchasing products from slaughterhouses, meat-and-poultry processors, and other suppliers and selling them to about 700 customers: supermarket chains, retailers, institutions, and other distributors. A fleet of mostly refrigerated tractors, trailers, trucks, and vans carried more than 2.5 million pounds of product a week in a 125-mile radius from a centrally located warehouse in Ridgewood, the Queens community where the company also kept its offices. The two Western Beef stores, plus a third that opened in Elmont that year, sold grocery items but emphasized meat, poultry, dairy, produce, delicatessen, and other perishable foods in warehouse-type facilities of about 30,000 square feet each, mostly refrigerated. During 1987 Quarex had net income of $1.4 million on net sales of $151 million.

During 1988 Quarex transferred the operation of its tractors and trailers to a new subsidiary, Awesome Transportation, Inc.. By then the company was serving about 1,100 wholesale customers. In 1992 it acquired P.S.L. Food Market, Inc., which owned seven Western Beef supermarkets and was also controlled by the Castellana family. P.S.L. opened its first store in Ridgewood in 1985. The other six also were in New York City. At the same time Quarex acquired Southern Blvd. Supermarkets, Inc., another Castellana-controlled company, with a New England wholesale produce business that was later sold.

Western Beef, 1993–97

Quarex was renamed Western Beef in 1993. By then its business, which had been about two-thirds wholesale, was more than half retail. There were 14 retail stores by the end of 1994. All were in New York City, except for ones in Elmont, East Orange, and Mineola. The stores, whose goods were tailored to ethnic communities, were open seven days a week. Two had on-site bakeries. Western Beef had net income of $4.4 million on net sales of $274.1 million in 1993.

Sales and profits continued to advance in 1994 and 1995, and by the end of 1995 there were 17 Western Beef supermarkets. However, the company's stock was selling for about half the price that comparable operations commanded. The president, now Peter Castellana, Jr., complained that investment-banking firms had closed their doors to Western Beef because of its alleged Mafia links. To put these allegations to rest, he asked his father to stop coming in to work and hired a company investigating corporate wrongdoing to clear his firm. This company did clear Western Beef later in the year, but recommended that to avoid further stigma, Western Beef should end its wholesale operations. The wholesale division was accounting for nearly a third of Western Beef's sales but less than 10 percent of its profits.

The younger Castellana was hoping that the clearing of wrongdoing by Western Beef would enable him to forge ties with investment banks so that the company could raise money, through a secondary public offering, for expansion of its supermarket chain without taking on more debt. Before the year was out, however, Western Beef had become a target of an organizing drive by the United Food and Commercial Workers. In an April 1997 appearance in front of one of the company's two Manhattan supermarkets, AFL-CIO President John Sweeney alleged that Western Beef had harassed and fired two pro-union workers. He also accused the company of ''stealing overtime'' from workers, subjecting them to random drug testing, and paying ''indecent wages.''

Western Beef in 1996

At the end of 1996 there were 19 Western Beef supermarkets, all of them high-volume, low-price operations with a warehouse-store format. Nonperishable items were displayed in an area maintained at normal room temperatures, while in most of the stores meat was displayed in large refrigerated rooms. Western Beef sold both bulk meat, custom cut by its store butchers, and a full variety of prepackaged meats. Dairy and deli products were sold in separate refrigerated areas. The company's stores also sold frozen foods in stand-alone freezers, a complete line of dry groceries, and nonfood products such as paper products and household utensils. Thirteen of the stories had full-service delicatessen departments and four had brick-oven bakeries. The stores ranged in size from 9,000 to 83,000 square feet, with an average of 30,000 square feet.

The wholesale business purchased beef, pork, poultry, and provisions directly from major slaughterhouses, meat and poultry processors, and other suppliers on a daily basis. Additionally, the company distributed food products to its own retail stores from its warehouse in Ridgewood, where it also maintained its offices. These facilities were leased. The company owned 4 and leased the other 15 of its supermarkets. A fleet of mostly refrigerated tractors, trailers, trucks, and vans carried more than 150 million pounds of product annually to more than 1,000 customers in a radius of 250 miles.

Western Beef had revenues of $340.9 million in 1996, of which retail accounted for 69 percent and wholesale for 31 percent. Net income came to nearly $6 million. Western Beef's profit margin was well above the average in its industry. The company's long-term debt was $9.8 million in September 1996. Officers and directors held 64 percent of the shares of common stock.

Principal Subsidiaries

Awesome Transportation, Inc.; Quarex Operating Co., Inc.

Further Reading

Crowe, Kenneth C., ''AFL-CIO's Sweeney Opens National Organizing Effort,'' *Newsday,* April 30, 1997, pp. 47A–48A.

Grutzner, Charles, ''Six Jailed in Plot to Loot Company,'' *New York Times,* February 16, 1965, p. 24.

Hosenball, Mark, ''Quarex Tied to Mafia, President's Commission Says,'' *Supermarket News,* March 17, 1986, p. 10.

''Meat Concern in Queens Indicted in Case Involving Stolen U.S. Food Stamps,'' *New York Times,* April 11, 1978, p. 33.

Ranzal, Edward, ''Bankruptcy Laid to Gangster Plot,'' *New York Times,* May 28, 1963, pp. 1, 22.

Temes, Judy, ''Sins of the Father,'' *Crain's New York Business,* April 1, 1996, pp. 1, 33.

——, ''Western Beef Stock No Longer Branded,'' *Crain's New York Business,* December 9, 1996, p. 18.

—Robert Halasz

Young & Rubicam Inc.

285 Madison Ave
New York, New York 10017
U.S.A.
(212) 210-3000
Fax: (212) 370-3796

Private Company
Incorporated: 1923 as Young & Rubicam Advertising
Employees: 11,749
Gross Billings: $1.35 billion (1996)
SICs: 7311 Advertising Agencies

The fourth-largest advertising company in the world, Young & Rubicam Inc. specializes in advertising, public relations, direct marketing, corporate and product identity consulting, and health-care communications. Young & Rubicam operated more than 300 agency offices in 64 countries, and counted American Express, Colgate-Palmolive, Miller Brewing, the U.S. Postal Service, and Viacom among its largest clients.

The history of 20th-century advertising is populated by a handful of men. Stanley Resor, Claude Hopkins, Albert Lasker, Marion Harper, Bill Bernbach, Leo Burnett, and David Ogilvy are the names that come quickly to mind. Also included within this group would be Raymond Rubicam, the man cited by David Ogilvy as the single most important influence in his advertising career. Said Ogilvy, ''He taught me that advertising can sell without being dishonest.'' He was only the second living person ever elected to the American Advertising Federation Hall of Fame.

Born in Philadelphia in 1882 to a family that had prospered in the import-export business, Rubicam seemed destined to lead an easy and comfortable life. However, when young Raymond's grandfather died the estate fell to his wife's side of the family instead of to Rubicam's father, who was a writer for a trade journal. The situation worsened when Raymond's father died of tuberculosis. The young boy was then shuttled from relative to relative because his widowed mother could not care for him. Due in large part to his unconventional and lonely childhood, Rubicam was a poor and unruly student. He left school in his early teens to work as a grocery clerk in Denver and never attended school again. Later, he returned to his native Philadelphia hoping to become a short story writer, but he became an advertising man instead.

His first position was as a copywriter for the Armstrong Advertising Company in Philadelphia. The owner, F. Wallis Armstrong, was generally regarded as an autocratic tyrant who harassed his employees on a regular basis, and Rubicam more regularly than most. When offered a more lucrative position at the larger and more renowned N.W. Ayer Company, Rubicam accepted with gratitude. While at Ayer he wrote two advertisements which made him a reputation within the industry. The first was for Steinway pianos. Steinway had traditionally been averse to advertising. The owners of the company did not regard it as an estimable craft and consequently did as little of it as possible. To satisfy this particularly skeptical client Rubicam produced the famous ''Instrument of the Immortals'' ad. It not only caused a stir in the 1920s when it first appeared (Steinway sales rose by 70 percent), but has stood the test of time. It is still considered one of the most effective advertisements ever written. The other Rubicam creation of note was the ''Priceless Ingredient'' slogan developed for Squibb over-the-counter drugs.

Rubicam would have stayed indefinitely at the Ayer agency had the elder Ayer not died and left the business to his son-in-law. Rubicam was hoping to be made copy chief but was passed over in favor of an older man. Because of this unpromising situation, Rubicam decided to quit Ayer in 1923. Along with another dissatisfied Ayer employee, account executive John Orr Young, he started his own advertising agency in New York. The new Young & Rubicam firm had nothing but enthusiasm to offer prospective clients, but that proved enough to persuade General Foods to give it the struggling Postum beverage account. Postum was then followed by other General Foods accounts. Young & Rubicam did the advertising for products such as Grape-Nuts, Sanka Coffee, Jell-O, and Calumet baking powder.

The office atmosphere at the Young & Rubicam agency was different from that at any other ad firm. It was markedly loose, lively, and informal; it had the imprint of its founder Raymond Rubicam. Nearly all agency directors, both in the past and in the present, have emerged from the accounting rather than from the creative department. Rubicam was different. He was the creative man *par excellence*, and he ran his agency accordingly. What the office lacked in structure and standard operating procedure (no one made it to work before 9:30 in the morning) it more than made up for in talent and vitality. An example would be what were called "gang ups" at the agency. When work on a new campaign was initiated, all copywriters, artists, photographers, and copy chiefs involved in the project would lock themselves in a room to labor over the details. These "gang ups" usually lasted well into the night and were very exhausting. Only a rare breed of person could produce effectively in that kind of environment—but Rubicam always found such people. He hired his staff on the basis of their writing and artistic skill, and their willingness to work long and odd hours. He cared little about the typical qualifications of educational background and work experience. He wanted people with innovative ideas rather than impressive résumés.

The agency grew steadily throughout the 1920s and 1930s. Even the Depression did not hinder its ability to gain new clients and increase revenues. It may have been a loosely organized advertising company, but more often than not the ad campaigns were of exceptional quality. Billings went from $6 million in 1927 to $12 million in 1935, and then jumped to $22 million in 1937. During this period Young & Rubicam gained such lucrative accounts as Travelers Insurance, Bristol-Myers, Gulf Oil, and Packard automobiles. However, it also voluntarily resigned the extremely large Pall Mall account from the American Tobacco Company. The owner of American Tobacco, George Washington Hill, was notorious for badgering those who were unfortunate enough to do his advertising. The relationship between George Hill and Young & Rubicam grew so strained that Rubicam decided it would be in the best interest of the agency to forfeit the $3 million account. Rarely has the news of a large business loss met with such a sigh of relief at an advertising firm. The $3 million loss was well worth the boost in morale.

In 1934 John Orr Young retired. He had lost interest in the business and was allowing others to slowly take over his duties. Despite the great amount of money he was making, he wanted an early retirement. His position as head of new business was filled by Sigurd Larmon, who was to become an important influence at the agency for decades. Rubicam, who had been progressively exerting more and more influence at the firm, now had majority interest in the business. In the next 10 years Rubicam led an ascending firm through the advertising industry's first "creative revolution." The agency was successful because Rubicam, while always encouraging his creative department to be original and take chances, was nonetheless careful with the gifted but fragile personalities who surrounded him. Although it is a cliché to say a business is its people, the maxim holds particularly true in advertising; an ad agency has no other form of inventory. The agency's staff was pushed but also nurtured, and resignations were rare. In the words of former copy supervisor George Gribbin, "One of the great assets of this agency is that a man here feels he can express himself as a writer."

Post-World War II Global Expansion

When Raymond Rubicam retired to Arizona in 1944, Young & Rubicam was the second largest advertising company in the world. Only the J. Walter Thompson agency did more business. The void left by a man such as Raymond Rubicam could have caused confusion at the agency and left it without direction, but that scenario did not happen. Rubicam had trained his successors well, especially George Gribben. Gribben had long been one of the most influential men at the firm and, upon Rubicam's retirement, was named creative director in charge of all advertising production. He was instrumental in bringing Young & Rubicam into the second advertising "revolution" which took place in the late 1950s and 1960s. In 1951 the agency reached the $100 million mark in total billings and by 1960 that figure had more than doubled to $212 million.

In the 1960s advertising grew as an industry. Firms such as Ogilvy and Mather, Doyle Dane Bernbach, and Leo Burnett initiated a period of innovation that broke all previous advertising rules and conventions. They helped re-establish advertising as an artistic craft. Though overshadowed by these smaller, more "visible" ad agencies, the larger companies like Young & Rubicam and J. Walter Thompson also benefited from the renaissance.

More money than ever was being spent by companies on advertising. The growth in business was paralleled by staff increases and subsidiary acquisitions within particular agencies. This internal growth, however, proved to be problematic. In 1971 the worldwide economic recession brought the rapid rise in advertising expenditures by manufacturers to a quick halt. Nearly all advertising companies suffered billings losses, and many of the smaller "creative" shops were forced out of business altogether. Young & Rubicam itself was in trouble. Its payroll and other expenses were too high, and the agency was not growing. A "changing of the guard" took place among the company's management. Ed Ney became chairman and chief executive officer, Alex Kroll became creative director, and Alexander Brody was placed in charge of international operations. These men were to lead the agency into a period of unprecedented growth.

Ney's first action was to reduce the staff at the New York office by one-third and relinquish some of the losing accounts that were draining the agency. One of those to go was the Bristol-Myers account; they had been a client for over 25 years. Then he set out to reorganize and increase the company's financial resources in order to renew its ability to purchase subsidiaries and broaden its range of services. Rather than sell shares to the public to raise capital, Ney instead manipulated retirement benefits and agency-held stock to generate the funds he needed. These maneuvers allowed him greater flexibility and privacy when it came time to decide when and where to use the money. For instance, in 1973 Ney supervised the acquisition of Sudler & Hennessey (a health care ad firm) and Wunderman, Ricotta & Kline (a direct marketing company). These two agencies added $62 million to the firm's balance sheet and pushed it past J. Walter Thompson to become number one in domestic billings. In a little over five years Ney had taken Young & Rubicam from third to first in the industry. Ney, however, was not yet satisfied. In addition to purchasing a number of small Midwestern and Southwestern ad shops, he also arranged in 1979 for Young & Rubicam to merge with the Marsteller agency, which had long been among the leaders in the public relations business. Not only did Marsteller's $306 million in billings help Young & Rubicam stay ahead of J. Walter Thompson, it also gave the agency the strong public relations department it needed.

While Ed Ney was building Young & Rubicam on the domestic front, Alexander Brody was increasing the company's presence abroad. The firm successfully broke through cultural and political barriers by linking up with Hungary's leading advertising agency (Mahir), illustrating that the Eastern Bloc countries should no longer be considered "non-markets." More importantly, Brody was instrumental in orchestrating the agency's most important joint venture to date, the 1981 merger of Young & Rubicam's Tokyo office with Dentsu's Tokyo office. Never before had the number one and number two advertising companies in the world joined together on a business venture such as this one. The new subsidiary, called DYR, gave Dentsu a firmer foothold outside Japan and strengthened Young & Rubicam's position in Tokyo.

In 1985 Ed Ney announced that he was resigning as chairman and chief executive officer of Young & Rubicam. He named as his successor Alex Kroll, the former head of Young & Rubicam U.S.A. and the man responsible for resurrecting the agency from its creative doldrums. Under his leadership the firm reasserted itself as an "idea" shop. During a seven-month period in 1977 the agency procured $77 million in new business. Accounts included Pabst beer, Oil of Olay skin cream, and Kentucky Fried Chicken. When Young & Rubicam lost the Chrysler account in 1979, Kroll's persistence helped to win the very prestigious Lincoln-Mercury account, worth $65 million. Kroll was also the man who hired comedian and television personality Bill Cosby to do Jell-O Pudding commercials.

Following in the footsteps of Ney, one of the most effective administrators in the advertising industry, was no easy task. Kroll insisted he would try to emulate Ney's methods and patterns of success. Remaining the number one world agency required a commitment to growth and diversification. Kroll was prepared to take the necessary steps to secure Young & Rubicam's position at the top of the advertising industry, but not at the expense of the company's reputation for creativity.

Changes During the 1990s

As chairman and chief executive officer, Kroll enjoyed considerable success during his first half-decade at the helm of Young & Rubicam. The agency reigned as an industry power during the latter half of the 1980s, as it had during the first half of the decade. Young & Rubicam was praised by industry observers for its global might and the quality of its advertising, demonstrating a rare ability to be both creative and large, but by the end of the 1980s conditions in the U.S. advertising industry began to change swiftly. An industry-wide slump in 1990 called a quick end to the expansion years of the 1980s, when the prevailing trend among the larger advertising companies was to open agency after agency in a global race for domination. Further, an era of corporate cutbacks began, as a nationwide economic recession settled in during the early 1990s, which forced advertising companies not only to develop creative advertising ideas, but to convince cost-conscious clients that advertising spending should be spared from budget cuts.

At Young & Rubicam, the momentum built up during the 1980s was quickly lost. As economic conditions soured, the agency lost its edge, and those who once applauded the company's ability to meld creativity and worldwide clout were describing the early 1990s version of Young & Rubicam as "stodgy and musclebound." By 1993, the company's situation had become dire. Employee layoffs were imminent and several large clients such as Johnson & Johnson, Warner-Lambert, and AT&T took their business elsewhere, underscoring the need for dramatic changes.

Young & Rubicam's turning point occurred in late 1993, when a new generation of management took control and began to reshape the company. Kroll relinquished his command in December 1993 and passed the baton to Peter Georgescu, the Romanian-born son of an executive of Standard Oil of New Jersey. In describing Young & Rubicam's state before he took command, Georgescu said, "We were big, intellectual, conservative, and introspective," qualities that had led to uninspired advertising presentations and bred apathy among the company's employees. Georgescu was determined to change this. A strategy he conceived in 1990 was being implemented as he took charge in late 1993, one that was supposed to transform Young & Rubicam from a company with a geographical orientation to a company focused on client services. The years of establishing fiefdom after fiefdom throughout the world by opening new agency offices were over. As this was underway, Georgescu recruited a new team of senior executives who had made their mark in the advertising business at smaller, flexible, and innovative agencies. The addition of these new executives was intended to breathe new life into Young & Rubicam and spark a new era of advertising creativity.

New life was shown shortly after Georgescu began making wholesale changes, particularly in 1995 when Young & Rubicam picked up $500 million in new business in the United States alone. Young & Rubicam won Viacom's Showtime Networks account, prevailed in presentations for 7Up, Dimetapp, and Keycorp, and in early 1996 the company gained the $100 million Blockbuster Video account. Young & Rubicam increased its Sears business and reestablished its relationship with AT&T by developing a new corporate image campaign for the telecommunications giant. After several years of being described as stodgy and musclebound, "confused and staid," Young & Rubicam entered the mid-1990s with a refurbished corporate personality. Under Georgescu, the company's leadership was described as "warm," its creativity "passionate," and its presentations "fun." The turnaround had worked, and Young & Rubicam was once again recognized as a powerful, creative force in the advertising industry.

By 1997, Georgescu's influence on Young & Rubicam's financial stature was readily discernible. Between 1994 and 1997, advertising billings nearly doubled, reaching $7.3 billion, making Young & Rubicam the fourth-largest advertising agency in the world. As the company plotted its course for the 21st century, it promised to be a worldwide leader in the advertising industry, having learned a valuable lesson from the past to create widespread optimism for the future.

Principal Subsidiaries

Burson-Marsteller; Black, Kelly, Scruggs; Healy; Bravo Group.

Further Reading

Cummings, Bart, "An Interview with Ed Ney," *Advertising Age*, January 3, 1983.

Daniels, Draper, *Giants, Pigmies, and Other Advertising People*, Chicago: Crain Communications, 1974.

Eleftheria, Parpis, "Young & Rubicam, New York," *ADWEEK Eastern Edition*, April 15, 1996, p. 38.

Farrell, Greg, "With a New Reel in Hand, Y&R's 'Ted & Ed Show' Sends Ratings Soaring," *ADWEEK Eastern Edition*, November 13, 1995, p. 26.

Fox, Stephen, *The Mirror Makers*, New York: Morrow, 1984.

Hume, Scott, "JWT, Y&R Will Face Off for Kraft," *ADWEEK Eastern Edition*, July 7, 1997, p. 3.

Miles, Laureen, "Stalking the CEO: Campaign Spending, $1–$10 Million," *MEDIAWEEK*, May 20, 1996, p. 50.

Nokes, Roger, "Saved by the Bell," *ADWEEK Eastern Edition*, May 9, 1994, p. 26.

Richmond, Susannah, "How to Resolve Y&R's Troubles," *Campaign*, January 14, 1994, p. 20.

Rubicam, Raymond, "Memoirs," *Advertising Age*, February 9, 1970.

Taylor, Cathy, "Changing of the Guard at Y&R," *ADWEEK Eastern Edition*, December 20, 1993, p. 2.

Wascoe, Dan, Jr., "Young & Rubicam's 1,000-Mile Corridor," *Back Stage*, May 25, 1990, p. 24B.

—updated by Jeffrey L. Covell

INDEX TO COMPANIES

Index to Companies

Listings in this index are arranged in alphabetical order under the company name. Company names beginning with a letter or proper name such as Eli Lilly & Co. will be found under the first letter of the company name. Definite articles (The, Le, La) are ignored for alphabetical purposes as are forms of incorporation that precede the company name (AB, NV). Company names printed in bold type have full, historical essays on the page numbers appearing in bold. Updates to entries that appeared in earlier volumes are signified by the notation **(upd.)**. Company names in light type are references within an essay to that company, not full historical essays. This index is cumulative with volume numbers printed in bold type.

INDEX TO INDUSTRIES

Index to Industries

BEVERAGES

BIOTECHNOLOGY

CHEMICALS

CONGLOMERATES

CONSTRUCTION

CONTAINERS

DRUGS

ELECTRICAL & ELECTRONICS

ENGINEERING & MANAGEMENT SERVICES

ENTERTAINMENT & LEISURE

FINANCIAL SERVICES: BANKS

FINANCIAL SERVICES: NON-BANKS

FOOD PRODUCTS

FOOD SERVICES & RETAILERS

HEALTH & PERSONAL CARE PRODUCTS

HEALTH CARE SERVICES

HOTELS

INFORMATION TECHNOLOGY

INSURANCE

LEGAL SERVICES

MANUFACTURING

MATERIALS

MINING & METALS

PAPER & FORESTRY

PERSONAL SERVICES

PETROLEUM

PUBLISHING & PRINTING

REAL ESTATE

RETAIL & WHOLESALE

RUBBER & TIRE

TELECOMMUNICATIONS

TEXTILES & APPAREL

TOBACCO

TRANSPORT SERVICES

UTILITIES

WASTE SERVICES

NOTES ON CONTRIBUTORS

Notes on Contributors

AZZATA, Gerry. Freelance writer.

BIANCO, David. Freelance writer, editor, and publishing consultant.

BODINE, Paul S. Freelance writer, editor, and researcher in Milwaukee, specializing in business subjects; contributor to the *Encyclopedia of American Industries, Encyclopedia of Global Industries, DISCovering Authors, Contemporary Popular Writers,* the *Milwaukee Journal Sentinel,* and the *Baltimore Sun.*

COHEN, M. L. Novelist and freelance writer living in Paris.

COVELL, Jeffrey L. Freelance writer and corporate history contractor.

DERDAK, Thomas. Freelance writer and adjunct professor of philosophy at Loyola University of Chicago.

DORGAN, Charity Anne. Detroit-based freelance writer.

GASBARRE, April Dougal. Archivist and freelance writer specializing in business and social history in Cleveland, Ohio.

GOPNIK, Hilary. Ann Arbor-based freelance writer.

HALASZ, Robert. Former editor in chief of *World Progress* and *Funk & Wagnalls New Encyclopedia Yearbook*; author, *The U.S. Marines* (Millbrook Press, 1993).

INGRAM, Frederick C. South Carolina-based business writer who has contributed to *GSA Business, Appalachian Trailway News,* the *Encyclopedia of Business,* the *Encyclopedia of Global Industries,* the *Encyclopedia of Consumer Brands,* and other regional and trade publications.

JACOBSON, Robert R. Freelance writer and musician.

KNIGHT, Judson. Freelance writer.

MALLETT, Daryl F. Freelance writer and editor; actor; contributing editor and series editor at The Borgo Press; series editor of SFRA Press's *Studies in Science Fiction, Fantasy and Horror*; associate editor of Gryphon Publications and for *Other Worlds Magazine*; founder and owner of Angel Enterprises, Jacob's Ladder Books, and Dustbunny Productions.

MOZZONE, Terri. Iowa-based freelance writer specializing in corporate profiles.

PASSAGE, Robert A. Freelance writer based in Kalamazoo, Michigan.

PEIPPO, Kathleen. Minneapolis-based freelance writer.

SALAMIE, David E. Part-owner of InfoWorks Development Group, a reference publication development and editorial services company.

WALDEN, David M. Freelance writer and historian in Salt Lake City; adjunct history instructor at Salt Lake Community College.

WERNICK, Ellen D. Freelance writer and editor.

WEST, Melissa. Freelance writer.

WHITELEY, Laura E. Freelance writer based in Kalamazoo, Michigan.

WOODWARD, A. Freelance writer.